New And Complete English-German And German-English Pocket Dictionary Part 2

J. F. Leonhard Tafel

In the interest of creating a more extensive selection of rare historical book reprints, we have chosen to reproduce this title even though it may possibly have occasional imperfections such as missing and blurred pages, missing text, poor pictures, markings, dark backgrounds and other reproduction issues beyond our control. Because this work is culturally important, we have made it available as a part of our commitment to protecting, preserving and promoting the world's literature. Thank you for your understanding.

NEW AND COMPLETE
ENGLISH-GERMAN AND GERMAN-ENGLISH
POCKET DICTIONARY,

WITH THE

PRONUNCIATION OF BOTH LANGUAGES,

ENRICHED WITH THE TECHNICAL TERMS

OF THE

Arts and Sciences.

FOR THE USE OF BUSINESS MEN AND SCHOOLS.

BY

Dr. J. F. Leonhard Tafel and Louis H. Tafel, A.B.

PART II.—GERMAN AND ENGLISH.

PHILADELPHIA:
PUBLISHED BY I. KOHLER,
911 ARCH STREET.
1881.

Entered, according to Act of Congress, in the year 1870, by

L. KOHLER,

in the Clerk's Office of the District Court of the United States for the Eastern District of Pennsylvania.

STEREOTYPED BY
MACKELLAR, SMITHS & JORDAN,
PHILADELPHIA.

A, **a**, *s.* A; wer A sagt muß auch B sagen, he who begins a thing must go on with it.

Aal, Äl, *m. pl.* -e, eel; kleiner -, grig; -fasten, -kasten, *m. pl.* -kästen, eel-trunk; -reuse, -rüsse, *f.* eel-pot; -teich, -teich, *m. pl.* -e, eel-pond.

Aap, Äp, *m.* mizzen-stay-sail.

Aar, är, *m. pl.* -e, eagle.

Aas, äs, *n. pl.* Äser, carrion, carcase.

Aasen, äsen, *vt.* to feed; to scrape (a hide).

Ab, ap, *pr.* and *av.* off, from, of, down; ab und zu, to and fro; auf und ab, up and down.

Abändern, ap'endörn, *vt.* to alter, modify, change. **Abänderlich**, -lich, *a.* changeable, *av.* changeably, alterably. **Ab'änderung**, -ung, *f.* change, alteration, modification.

Abängstigen, ap'engstigen, *vt.* to torment.

Abarbeiten, ap'arbäten, *vt.* to work off; to wear out: to get afloat.

Abärgern, ap'ergörn, *vt. r.* to vex.

Abart, ap'ärt, *f.* variety; degenerate breed. **Abarten** (fein), *a.* to degenerate. **Ab'artung**, -ung, *f.* degeneration.

Abästen, ap'ästen, *vt.* to lop off the branches.

Abätzen, ap'ätsen, *vt.* to remove by caustics.

Abbacken, ap'backen, *vt. i.* to finish baking.

Abbaken, ap'bäken, *vt.* to mark with buoys; to stake off.

Abbalgen, ap'balgen, *vt.* to skin, flay; *vr.* to fatigue one's self by wrestling or boxing.

Abbeeren, ap'bä-ren, *vt.* to strip of berries. [mand.

Abbefehlen, ap'befälen, *vt.* to counter-

Abbeißen, ap'bäisen, *vt.* to bite off.

Abbeizen, ap'bäetsen, *vt.* to macerate, steep.

Abbersten, ap'bersten (*Prt.* abbarst, ab-borst, *Pp.* abgeborsten sein,), to burst off; fly off.

Abberufen, ap'berufen, *vt.* to recall. **Abberufung**, -ung, *f.* recall.

Abbeten, ap'bäten, *vt.* to beg off; to read off carelessly.

Abbetteln, ap'betteln, *vt.* to obtain by begging.

Abbeugen, ap'böügen, *f.* **Abbiegen**.

Abbezahlen, ap'betsälen, *vt.* to pay off.

Abbiegen, ap'bigen, *vt. i.* to bend off, to turn away.

Abbild, ap'bilt, *n. pl.* -er, effigy, image, portrait. **Abbilden**, ap'bilden, *vt.* to portray, paint, picture. **Ab'bildung**, -ung, *f.* representation, picture, copy; portraiture.

Abbimsen, ap'bimsen, *vt.* to smooth with pumice.

Abbinden, ap'binnden, *vt.* to unbind, untie; to hoop; to wean.

Abbitte, ap'bitte, *f.* apology, deprecation. **Ab'bitten**, *vt.* to ask pardon for: to obtain by begging.

Abblasen, ap'bläsen, *vt.* to blow off, away.

Abblatten, ap'blatten, **Abblättern**, ap'-blettörn, *vt.* to strip of leaves. **Abblättern**, *vi.* to exfoliate.

Abblitzen, ap'blitsen, *vi.* to miss fire.

Abblühen, ap'blüh-en, *vi.* to cease blooming: to wither.

Abbohrer, ap'börör, *m.* jumper (for drilling).

Abborgen, ap'borgen, *vt.* to borrow from.

Abbrand, ap'brant, *m. pl.* **Abbrände**, waste, loss (Min.).

Abbrassen, ap'brassen, *vt.* to brace.

Abbrauchen, ap'bröüchen, *vt.* to wear off.

Abbrechen, ap'brechen, *vt.* to break off; to pull down; demolish; kurz -, to cut short; Zelte -, to strike tents; das Lager -, to decamp.

Abbrennen, ap'brennen, *vt.* to burn down, set on fire; to discharge, fire off; to harden, temper (steel); *vi.* (*Prt.* abbrannte, *Pp.* abgebrannt) to burn down, to be consumed.

Abbreviatur, apbreviatyr', *f.* abbrevia-

7

tion. **Abbreviren,** -fi'ren, vt. to abbreviate.

Abbringen, ap'bring-en, vt. to divert, dissuade.

Abbröckeln, ap'bröckeln, vt. to break off in small pieces, to crumble off; vi. to crumble, break off.

Abbruch, ap'bruch, m. pl. **Abbrüche,** breaking off; damage, injury, harm; - thun, to damage, injure. **Abbrüchig,** ap'brüchig, a. brittle.

Abbrühen, ap'brüh-en, vt. to scald.

Abbürsten, ap'bürzhten, vt. to brush off.

Abbüßen, ap'büßen, vt. to expiate, atone for. **Abbüßung,** ap'büßung, f. expiation.

Abc, abetsa', n. abece, alphabet; **-schüler,** -shühler; **Abcschütze,** -shütse, m. abecedarian.

Abdachen, ap'dachen, vt. to unroof; vi. to slope. **Ab'dachung,** -ung, f. slope, declivity.

Abdämmen, ap'demmen, vt. to dam up. **Abdämmung,** ap'demmyng, f. damming up.

Abdampfen, ap'dampfen, vi. to evaporate. **Ab'dampfung,** -yng, f. evaporation. **Abdämpfen,** ap'dempfen, vt. to evaporate.

Abdanken, ap'danken, vt. to discharge, dismiss, disband; vi. to resign. **Ab'dankung,** f. resignation; dismission.

Abdarben, ap'darben, vt. to pinch or stint one's self in order to save.

Abdecken, ap'decken, vt. to uncover, unroof; to flay, skin; den Tisch –, to clear the table. **Ab'decker,** m. flayer. **Abdeckerei,** apdeckerěi', f. dwelling or trade of a flayer.

Abdienen, ap'dīnen, vt. to pay off by personal service.

Abdisputiren, ap'dispytīren, vt. r. to dispute away, to wrangle.

Abdorren, ap'dorren, vi. to dry up, to wither away.

Abdrechseln, ap'drecsělu, vt. to turn off. **Abdrehen,** ap'drā-en, vt. to twist off.

Abdreschen, ap'dreshen (Prt. abdrosch, Pp. abgedroschen), vt. to thrash off; to cudgel.

Abdringen, ap'dringen (Prt. abbrang, Pp. abgebrungen), vt. to extort, exact, to wring from.

Abdrohen, ap'drō-en, vt. to extort by threatening.

Abdruck, op'dryck, m. pl. -brücke, impression, copy, mark. **Abdrucken,** ap'drycken, vt. to print off, copy, impress, stamp. **Abdrücken,** ap'drücken, vt. to separate by pressing; to fire off; to extort; to break (the heart).

Abdunsten, ap'dynzhten, vi. to evaporate. **Abdünsten,** ap'dünzhten, vi. to evaporate. **Abdünstung,** f. evaporation.

Abend, ā'bent, m. pl. -e, evening, eve; west, occident; am –, in the evening; heute –, this evening, to-night; gestern –, last evening; zu – essen, to sup; -brod, -brōt, n. supper; -dämmerung, -demmĕrung, f. evening twilight; -glocke, f. evening bell; evening chime; -land, -lant, n. pl. -länder, occident; -lich, a. vesper, of evening; western; occidental; av. in the evening; -mahl, -mäl, n. the Lord's supper; -musik, -mysik', f. serenade, music in the evening; -roth, rōt, n. sunset sky, evening sky; -sonne, -sonne, f. setting sun; -stern, -stern, m. evening star, Hesperus, Venus; -wind, -vint, m. pl. -winde, west wind.

Abenteurer, ā'běntöürer, n. adventure, -lich, a. adventurous, av. -ly; -lichkeit, -lichkāit, f. eccentricity. **Abenteurer,** ā'běntöürěr, m. adventurer.

Aber, ā'ber, cj. but, however.

Aberglaube, ā'bergläübe, m. -ens, superstition. **Abergläubiger,** ā'Lergläubiger, s. superstitious, bigoted person. **Abergläubisch,** a. superstitious, av. -ly. **Aberglaubigkeit (-käet),** f. superstitiousness.

Abermals, ā'bermäls, av. again, once more, anew. **Abermalig,** -mälig, a. repeated, reiterated.

Aberwitz, ā'bervits, m. craziness, folly. **A'berwitzig,** a. crazy, foolish.

Abeschern, ap'eshern, vr. to harass one's self; auch **Abäschern.**

Abessen, ap'essen, vt. to eat up or off; vi. to finish eating.

Abfahren, ap'fāren, vt. to take off by driving over, upon, to any thing, to break; vi. (Prt. abfuhr, Pp. abgefahren) to depart, setout; to set sail. **Abfahrt,** ap'fart, f. departure, setting out; offing.

Abfall, ap'fall, m. pl. **Abfälle,** falling off; waste, loss, parings; apostasy.

Abfallen, ap'fallen, vi. to fall off;

to desert, apostatize; to lose flesh. **Abfällig**, ap'fellig, a. sloping; disapproving.
Abfangen, ap'fang-en, to intercept, catch: to stab (a deer, etc.).
Abfärben, ap'färben, vt. to color, stain; vi. to lose color.
Abfassen, ap'fassen, to compose, pen, draw up; to arrest. **Ab'fassung**, -ung, f. composing, drawing up; arrest.
Abfaulen, ap'foulen, vi. to rot off.
Abfedern, ap'federn, vt. to pick off feathers: vi. to lose feathers.
Abfegen, ap'fegen, vt. to scour, sweep off.
Abfeilen, ap'feilen, vt. to file off.
Abfertigen, ap'fertigen, vt. to dispatch; kurz -, to be short with, to rebuff. **Ab'fertigung**, -ung, f. dispatching, finishing, sending off.
Abfesseln, ap'fesseln, vt. to unfetter, unchain. [discharge.
Abfeuern, ap'feuern, vt. to fire off, to
Abfinden, ap'finnden, vt. to content, to satisfy the claims of; to portion, endow. **Ab'findung**, ap'findung, f. satisfying, contentment; **Summe**, -summe, f. money of acquittance or of indemnity.
Abfleischen, ap'fleischen, vt. to scrape off the flesh.
Abfliegen, ap'fliegen, vi. to fly off.
Abfliessen, ap'fliessen, vi. to flow off, to run off. **Abflössen**, ap'flössen, vi. to raft or float away. **Abfluss**, ap'fluss, m. g. -flusses, flowing off; discharge; gutter, waste-pipe, drain.
Abfordern, ap'fordern, vt. to demand, request; call off. **Ab'forderung**, -ung, f. demand, request, recall.
Abfragen, ap'fragen, vt. to question, examine, ask.
Abfressen, ap'fressen, vt. to eat off.
Abfrieren, ap'frieren, vt. to freeze off; to lose by being frostbitten.
Abfuhr, ap'fur, f. removal. **Abführen**, ap'führen, vt. to carry off, lead off; to drain; to purge, cleanse; mislead. **Ab'führend**, a. excretory; purgative; -es **Mittel**, purge. **Abführung**, -ung, f. removal, purgation.
Abfüttern, ap'füttern, vt. to feed.
Abgabe, ap'gäbe, f. delivery; tax, tribute.
Abgang, ap'gang, m. pl. **Abgänge**, departure; waste; scrapings, filings, shavings; decease; - einer **Waare**,

sale. **Abgängig**, ap'geng-ig, a. waste salable.
Abgärben, ap'gärben, vt. to tan, dress; to beat.
Abgäten, ap'gäten, vt. to weed.
Abgeben, ap'geben, vt. to deliver, to give up; sich - mit, to trouble one's self with.
Abgedroschen, ap'gedroschen, a. trite.
Abgefeimt, ap'gefeimt, **Abgefeimt**, -heit, a. cunning, crafty, arrant.
Abgehen, ap'ga-en, vi. to go off, set out, depart; to sell; mit **Tod** -, to decease.
Abgelebt, ap'gelebt, a. decrepit, decayed; -heit, -heit, f. decrepitude.
Abgelegen, ap'gelegen, a. distant, remote; settled; -heit, -heit, f. remoteness.
Abgeleitet, ap'geleitet, a. drawn off; derivative, derived.
Abgemessen, ap'gemessen, a. measured; -heit, -heit, f. exactness.
Abgeneigt, ap'geneigt, a. disinclined, averse, unfavorable, unfriendly, disaffected; -heit, -heit, f. disaffection, averseness.
Abgenutzt, ap'genutzt, a. worn out.
Abgeordneter, ap'geordneter, s. delegate, deputy.
Abgerben, f. **Abgärben**.
Abgesandte, ap'gesante, der -, pl. -n, ambassador.
Abgeschieden, ap'geschieden, a. secluded, solitary; deceased; -heit, -heit, f. retiredness, seclusion, solitude.
Abgeschliffen, ap'geschliffen, a. polished; polite, refined; -heit, -heit, f. refinement.
Abgeschmackt, ap'geschmackt, a. insipid, tasteless, flat, absurd; -heit, -heit, f. insipidity, absurdity.
Abgesondert, ap'gesondert, a. separated, separate.
Abgespannt, ap'gespannt, a. slackened, relaxed, enervated; -heit, -heit, f. relaxation, atony, exhaustion.
Abgestanden, ap'gestanden, a. stale, dead.
Abgestorben, ap'gestorben, a. dead; insensible to.
Abgestumpft, ap'gestumpft, a. blunted, dull, obtuse; -heit, -heit, f. obtuseness, dullness.
Abgewinnen, ap'gewinnen (Prt. gewann ab, Pp. abgewonnen), to win, gain, get from; - den **Wind**, die **Sun**,

tc gain the wind, the weatherage of a ship.
Abgewöhnen, ap'gevöhnen, *vt.* to wean from, disaccustom.
Abgezogen, ap'getsōgen, *a.* drawn off; deducted; retired; *-heit, -hāet, f.* retirement, seclusion.
Abgieren, ap'gīren, *vi.* to sheer off.
Abgießen, ap'gīsen, *vt.* to pour off, decant; *n. s.* decantation.
Abglanz, ap'glants, *m.* reflected splendor; image.
Abgleichen, ap'glēlchen, *vt.* to equalize; adjust. **Ab'gleicher**, *m.* adjuster. **Ab'gleichstange**, -stange, *f.* adjusting-tool. **Abgleichung**, ap'glēlchyng, *f.* adjustment; *-wage, -svāge, f.* adjusting-balance.
Abgleiten, ap'glāeten, **Ab'glitschen**, -glitshen, *vi.* to slip, glide off.
Abglühen, ap'glüh-en, *vt.* to make red-hot; to cease glowing.
Abgott, ap'gott, *m. pl.* -götter, idol. **Abgötterei**, apgötterēī', *f.* idolatry. **Abgötterer**, ap'götterēr, *m.* idolater. **Abgöttisch**, ap'göttish, *a.* idolatrous.
Abgraben, ap'grāben, *vt.* to dig off; to turn off the course.
Abgrasen, ap'grāsen, *vt.* to graze; to mow.
Abgrenzen, ap'grentsen, *vt.* to limit, bound.
Abgrund, ab'grunt, *m. pl.* Abgründe, abyss, precipice, deep, depth.
Abgunst, ap'gunst, *f.* disaffection, illwill. **Abgünstig**, ap'günstig, *a.* disaffected, averse.
Abgürten, ap'gürten, *vt.* to ungird, unbuckle.
Abguß, ap'gus, *m.* pouring off; cast, copy.
Abhaben, ap'hāben, *vt.* to have (the hat) off.
Abhacken, ap'hacken, *vt.* to chop off, cut off.
Abhägen, ap'hāgen, *vt.* to hedge in, fence in.
Abhaken, ap'hāken, *vt.* to unhook.
Abhalten, ap'halten, *vt.* to keep off, hold off. **Ab'haltung**, -yng, *f.* holding off, hinderance.
Abhandeln, ap'handeln, *vt.* to cheapen; to buy; to discuss.
Abhanden, ap'handen, *av.* not at hand; — kommen, to be lost.
Abhang, ap'hang, *m. pl.* -hänge, slope, declivity; jäher —, precipice. **Ab's**

hangen, *vi.* to hang down; to slope to depend on; *vt.* to take down
Abhängig, ap'hengig, *a.* sloping; dependent on; *-keit, -kāet, f.* dependence.
Abhärmen, ap'hermen, *vr.* to pine away, languish.
Abhärten, ap'herten, *vt.* to harden; to make hardy. **Abhärtung**, -yng, *f.* hardening, strengthening.
Abhaspeln, ap'haspeln, *vt.* to reel off, unwind.
Abhauen, ap'hāū-en, *vt.* to hew down, cut down, to chop off.
Abhäuten, ap'hōūten, *vt.* to flay, skin.
Abheben, ap'hāben, *vt.* to lift off, take off: Karten —, to cut cards.
Abhelfen, ap'helfen, *vt.* to help down; to remedy, redress, remove.
Abherzen, ap'hertsen, *vt.* to kiss (or hug) heartily.
Abhilfe, ap'hilfe, **Abhülfe**, *f.* redress, remedy.
Abhobeln, ap'hōbeln, *vt.* to smooth, to plane off.
Abhold, ap'holt, *a.* averse, disinclined, unfavorable; — sein, to bear illwill to.
Abholen, ap'hōlen, *vt.* to fetch; to come for, to go for; to call away.
Abhorchen, ap'horchen, *vt.* to overhear, to learn by listening.
Abhören, ap'hören, *vt.* to examine, try, hear; to learn by hearing.
Abhülfe, *s.* Abhilfe.
Abhülsen, ap'hülsen, *vt.* to shell, husk.
Abhüten, ap'hüten, *vt.* to graze off, feed.
Abhütten, ap'hütten, *vt.* to spoil a mine by neglect.
Abirren, ap'īrren, *vi.* to deviate, stray, swerve. **Abirrung**, -yng, *f.* deviation, aberration.
Abjagen, ap'yāgen, *vt.* to rescue, recover from.
Abjochen, ap'yochen, *vt.* to unyoke.
Abkommen, ap'kommen, *vt.* to comb out.
Abkappen, ap'kappen, *vt.* to rebuke; to hew off.
Abkargen, ap'kargen, *vt.* to stint.
Abkarten, ap'karten, *vt.* to concert.
Abkaufen, ap'kāūfen, *vt.* to buy from, purchase from. **Abkäufer**, ap'kāūfēr, *m.* buyer, purchaser.
Abkehren, ap'kēren, *vt.* to brush off sweep off.

Abketten, ap'ketten, vt. to unchain.
Abklären, ap'klären, vt. to clear, clarify, decant.
Abklatschen, ap'klatshen, vt. to clap out; to stereotype, to impress copies.
Abkleiden, ap'klēden, vt. to partition off.
Abklopfen, ap'klopfen, vt. to cleanse by beating; to knock off; to drub soundly.
Abknellen, Abkneipen, ap'knellen, ap'kneipen. vt. to nip off, to pinch off.
Abknicken, ap'knicken, vt. to break off, snap off. [button.
Abknöpfen, ap'knöpfen, vt. to un-
Abkochen, ap'kochen, vt. to decoct, boil; gelinde —, to parboil, coddle. **Ab'kochung,** -ung, f. decoction.
Abkommen, ap'kommen, vi. to come off, get off, deviate; to grow out of use; to decay; s. n. agreement, settlement; -schaft, -shaft, f. descendants, posterity. **Abkömmling,** -kömmling, m. descendant, offspring.
Abkoppeln, ap'koppeln, vt. to uncouple.
Abkratzen, ap'kratsen, vt. to scratch off, scrape off.
Abkriegen, ap'krigen, vt. to obtain from, to carry off.
Abkriegen, ap'krigen, vt. to obtain by warring.
Abkühlen, ap'kühlen, vt. to cool off, to refresh; fein Müthchen —, to vent one's spleen. **Ab'kühlfaß,** -faß, n. pl. -fässer, cooling-vat, cooler. **Ab'kühlofen,** -öfen, m. pl. -öfen, annealing-furnace. **Ab'kühlrinne,** -rinne, f. cooling-channel. **Ab'kühltrog,** -trög. m. cooler.
Abkündigen, ap'kündigen, vt. to resign; to publish the banns. **Ab'kündigung,** -igung, f. resignation; proclamation.
Abkunft, ap'kunft, f. descent, origin; von niedriger —, of low descent.
Abküpfen, ap'küpfen, **Ab'küppen,** vt. to top.
Abkürzen, ap'kürtsen, vt. to shorten, abridge, abbreviate, curtail. **Ab'kürzung,** -ung, f. abbreviation; curtailing.
Abladen, ap'läden, vt. to unload. **Ab'lader,** -ēr, m. unloader.
Ablaß, ap'lass. m. pl. **Abläffe,** drain; watergate; indulgence. **Ablaffen,** ap'lassen, vt. to let off; to drain;

to temper; to cease, desist; to abate; to sell.
Ablativ, ap'latīf, m. ablative (case).
Ablauern, ap'louern, vt. to lurk for; to obtain by watching.
Ablauf, ap'lāuf, m. pl. **Abläufe,** drain; result; expiration, elapse. **Ablaufen,** ap'laufen, vt. i. to run off, down; to fall due; to wear off by running; to cease running; to elapse; den Rang —, to outdo; die Uhr ist abgelaufen, the watch is down.
Abläugnen, ap'läugnen, vt. to deny, abnegate, disown. **Ab'läugnung,** -ung, f. denial, abnegation.
Ablauschen, ap'loushen, vt. to learn by listening.
Abläutern, ap'lōutern, vt. to clarify, clear.
Ableben, ap'lēben, n. demise, decease.
Ablecken, ap'lecken, vt. to lick off.
Ableeren, ap'lēren, vt. to empty, clear.
Ablegen, ap'lēgen, vt. to lay aside, put down; Lettern —, to distribute; Gewehr —, to cast; Rechenschaft —, to account for; Rechnung —, to give account of; e. Eid —, to take an oath; Zeugniß —, to bear witness, depose. **Ableger,** ap'lāger. m. layer, sprig, scion. **Ab'legung,** -ung, f. laying down; — eines Gelübdes, profession.
Ablehnen, ap'lānen, vt. to decline, shift off, keep off; **Ab'lehnung,** -ung, f. refusal, declining.
Ableiten, ap'lēten, vt. to turn away, lead off; to derive. **Ab'leiter,** ap'lēter, m. conductor. **Ab'leitung,** -ung, f. leading away; derivation.
Ablenken, ap'lenken, vt. to avert, turn off, divert; vi. to take another direction.
Ablernen, ap'lērnen, vt. to learn from, imitate.
Ablesen, ap'lēsen, vt. to pick off, gather; to read aloud; to call over.
Ableugnen, s. Abläugnen.
Abliefern, ap'līfern, vt. to deliver **Ab'lieferung,** -ung. f. delivery.
Abliegen, ap'līgen (Prt. lag ab, Pp. abgelegen, vi. to lie at a distance; weit —, to be far away; abgelegner Wein, settled wine.
Ablisten, ap'lizhten, to trick out of, to get by cunning.
Ablocken, ap'locken, vt. to entice away; to get by coaxing or flattery.

Ablockern, ap'lockern, *vt.* to loosen.
Ablohnen, ap'lōnen, *vt.* to pay off.
Ablörschen, ap'lörshen, *vt.* to sink a pit to a small depth.
Ablöschen, ap'löshen, *vt.* to extinguish, quench; to slake (lime); to cool.
Ablösen, ap'lösen, *vt.* to loosen, untie, unbind; to amputate, cut off, sever; to relieve (a guard); to redeem (a pawn); *vr.* to grow loose: to drop. **Ab'lösung**, -ŭng, *f.* loosening; amputation: relief.
Ablugsen, ap'luksen, *vt.* to learn by watching stealthily.
Abmachen, ap'machen, *vt.* to adjust, settle.
Abmagern, ap'māgērn, *vi.* to grow lean.
Abmähen, ap'mā-en, *vt.* to mow off, cut down.
Abmahlen, ap'mālen, *vt.* to grind, finish grinding.
Abmahnen, ap'mānen, *vt.* to warn from, dissuade.
Abmalen, ap'mālen, *vt.* to paint, copy, portray, depict.
Abmärgeln, ap'mergeln, *vt.* u. *vr.* to emaciate, macerate.
Abmarsch, ap'marsh, *m. pl.* -märsche, march, marching off, departure. **Abmarschiren**, -marshī'ren, *vi.* to march off.
Abmartern, ap'martērn, *vt.* to torment, torture, worry.
Abmatten, ap'matten, *vt.* to exhaust, fatigue, tire: **Metalle** —, to dull, to dim. **Ab'mattung**, -ŭng, *f.* harassing, weariness, fatigue.
Abmeißeln, ap'mēisseln, *vt.* to chisel off.
Abmerken, ap'merken, *vt.* to learn by observing.
Abmessen, ap'messen, *vt.* to measure, measure out. **Ab'messung**, -ŭng, *f.* measuring, mensuration.
Abmiethen, ap'mīten, *vt.* to hire, rent from. **Ab'miether**, *m.* tenant.
Abmüden, ap'mūden, *vt.* to weary, fatigue.
Abmühen, ap'mūh-en, *vr.* to trouble, exert one's self.
Abmüßigen, ap'mūsigen, *vt.* to find leisure, time.
Abnagen, ap'nāgen, *vt.* to gnaw off, pick.
Abnähen, ap'nā-en, *vt.* to quilt; to tuck.
Abnahme, ap'nāme, *f.* taking off; sale; diminution, decrease, decline; amputation; — e. Eides. receiving an oath. **Abnehmen**, ap'nāmen, *vt.* to take away; to receive; to buy, to amputate; to perceive; to lessen (meshes); *t.* **Eib** —, to receive one's oath; *t.* **Rechnung** —, to credit an account. **Abnehmer**, ap'nāmer, *m.* buyer, purchaser.
Abneigen, ap'nāgen, *vt.* to turn away, avert. **Ab'neigung**, -ŭng, *f.* aversion, disinclination.
Abnorm, apnorm', *a.* abnormal, irregular.
Abnöthigen, ap'nötigen, *vt.* to extort, to force from.
Abnutzen, ap'nutsen, *vt.* to wear out, use, waste. **Ab'nutzer**, -nutser, *m.* usufructuary, user.
Abonnement, abon'neman̄g, *n.* subscription. **Abonnent**, abonnent', *m.* -en, *pl.* -en, subscriber. **Abonniren**, abonnī'ren, *vt.* to subscribe.
Abordnen, ap'ordnen, *vt.* to delegate. **Ab'ordnung**, -ŭng, *f.* delegation.
Abpachten, ap'pachten, *vt.* to rent, to farm, to take in lease.
Abpacken, ap'packen, *vt.* to unpack, unload. [wait for.
Abpassen, ap'passen, *vt.* to watch,
Abpflocken, ap'pflöcken, *vt.* to mark off with pegs.
Abpflücken, ap'pflücken, *vt.* to pluck off.
Abplacken, ap'placken, *vt.* to plague, tire: sich —, to toil, drudge.
Abplätten, ap'pletten, *vt.* to smooth.
Abpochen, ap'pochen, *vt.* to knock off; to bully out of. [coin.
Abprägen, ap'prägen, *vt.* to stamp,
Abprallen, ap'prallen, *vi.* to rebound, recoil.
Abpressen, ap'pressen, *vt.* to press out; to extort, exact.
Abpretzen, ap'pretsen, *vt.* to dismount.
Abprügeln, ap'prügeln, *vt.* to beat, cudgel soundly.
Abputzen, ap'putsen, *vt.* to clean, cleanse, wipe off.
Abquälen, ap'qwälen, *vt.* to torment: sich —, to worry over.
Abquerlen, ap'qwērlen, *vt.* to twirl, mill.
Abquetschen, ap'qwetshen, *vt.* to crush off.
Abrahmen, ap'rāmen, *vt.* to skim, take off the cream.
Abrasen, ab'rāsen, *vt.* to graze, browse.
Abrasiren, ap'rasīren, *vt.* to shave; to raze, demolish.

Abr 13 **Abs**

Abraspeln, ap'raspeln, *vt.* to rasp off.
Abrathen, ap'räten, *vt.* to dissuade.
Abrauchen, ap'räuchen, *vt. i.* to evaporate.
Abraufen, ap'räufen, *vt.* to pull off; — fich, to scuffle.
Abräumen, ap'reumen, *vt.* to take away, clear off.
Abrechen, ap'rechen, *vt.* to rake off.
Abrechnen, ap'rechnen, *vt.* to subtract, deduct; to settle accounts. **Ab'rechnung,** -ung, *f.* account; settling of accounts; settlement; discount.
Abrede, ap'rāde, *f.* agreement, appointment; eine — nehmen, to concert together; in — stellen, to deny.
Abreden, ap'räden, *vt.* to agree, concert; to dissuade; fich —, to tire one's self with talking.
Abreiben, ap'reiben, *vt.* to rub off.
Ab'reibebret, -bret, *n.* rubber.
Abreichen, ap'räichen, *vt.* to hand, to reach.
Abreise, ap'räise, *f.* departure. **Abreisen,** ap'räisen, *vt.* to depart.
Abreißen, ap'räissen, *vt.* to tear off, pull off, break off; to demolish.
Abreiten, ap'reiten, *vt.* to ride away, *vt.* to break (a horse).
Abrennen, ap'rennen, *vi.* to run away; *vt.* to run off.
Abrichten, ap'richten, *vt.* to train, break in, dress, adjust; **Ab'richtung,** -ung *f.* adjustment, training.
Abringen, ap'ring-en, *vi.* to get by wrestling.
Abrinnen, ap'rinnen, *vi.* to run off.
Abriß, ap'ris, *m. pl.* -e, sketch, draught, design.
Abrollen, ap'rollen, *vt.* to roll away, off, down.
Abrücken, ap'rücken, *vt. i.* to remove, move off; edge off.
Abruf, ap'ruf, *m.* recall; proclamation. **Abrufen,** ap'rufen, *vt.* to call off, recall; to proclaim; — lassen, to send for, to recall.
Abrunden, ap'runden, *vt.* to round off.
Abrupfen, ap'rupfen, *vt.* to pluck off.
Abrutschen, ap'rutshen, *vi.* to glide down.
Abrütteln, ap'rütteln, *vt.* to shake off.
Absäbeln, ap'säbeln, *vt.* to cut off (with a sword); to chop off.
Absagen, ap'sägen, *vt.* to counterorder; to decline; abgesagter Feind, a sworn enemy.

Absatteln, ap'satteln, *vt.* to unsaddle; to unhorse.
Absatz, ap'sats, *m. pl.* Absätze, stop, pause; paragraph; sale, market; heel; offset (of a wall); landing (of a staircase).
Absäugen, ap'säugen, **Absäugeln,** ap'säugeln, *vt.* to suckle sufficiently; to wean; to propagate by layers.
Abschaben, ap'shāben, *vt.* to scrape off. **Ab'geschabt,** *pp.* worn out. **Abschabsel,** ap shabsel, *n.* shavings, parings.
Abschachern, ap'shachern, *vt.* to get by chaffering; to higgle.
Abschaffen, ap'shaffen, *vt.* to abolish; to part with; to remove. **Ab'schaffung,** -ung, *f.* abolition; abrogation.
Abschäfen, ap'shäken, *vt.* to fleet (a tackle).
Abschalen, ap'shālen, *vt.* to chisel off (the crust of a stone). **Abschälen,** ap'shälen, *vt.* to peel, pare. [off.
Abscharren, ap'sharren, *vt.* to scrape
Abschätzen, ap'shetsen, *vt.* to estimate, value, tax. **Ab'schätzung,** -ung, *f.* valuation.
Abschaum, ap'shaum, *m.* scum, dross. **Abschäumen,** ap'shäumen, *vt.* to skim, scum.
Abscheiden, ap'shäiden, *vt.* to separate, draw off; to seclude one's self; to depart this life.
Abscheu, ap'sheu, *m.* horror, abhorrence, disgust. **Abscheulich,** ap sheu'lich, *a.* abominable, detestable, horrible; -feit, -käet, *f.* abominableness, atrocity.
Abscheuchen, ap'shküchen, *vt.* to scare off, to frighten away.
Abschicken, ap'shicken, *vt.* to send off; to forward, dispatch; to delegate. **Ab'schickung,** ap'shickung, *f.* sending off; delegation.
Abschieben, ap'shīben, *vt.* to shove off.
Abschied, ap'shīt, *m. pl.* -e, separation, departure; farewell, leave; dismission, discharge; — nehmen, to take leave, to bid farewell; **-besuch,** -besuch, *m. pl.* -e, farewell visit; **-gruß,** -kuss, *m. pl.* -grüße, parting kiss; **-predigt,** -prädigt, *f.* valedictory sermon; **-rede,** -räde, *f.* farewell address; **-schmaus,** -shmous, *m.* parting dinner; **-trunk,** -trunk, *m.* parting cup.
Abschiefern, ap'shīfern, *vt.* to exfoliate; to scale off.

2

Abschi 14 **Absi**

Abschießen, ap'shīsen, *vt.* to shoot off, fire off, discharge.
Abschiffen, ap'shiffen, *vi.* to ship, to set sail; *vt.* to ship.
Abschildern, ap'shildērn, *vt.* to delineate, depict.
Abschinden, ap'shinnden, *vt.* to skin, flay. [ness.
Abschirren, ap'shirren, *vt.* to unharness.
Abschlachten, ap'shlachten, *vt.* to slaughter, butcher.
Abschlag, ap'shläg, *m. pl.* -schläge, decrease, diminution; deduction; draining off; auf —, in part payment, on account. **Abschlagen**, ap'shlägen, *vt.* to beat off, knock off, strike off; to repel, repulse; to refuse, decline (a petition); to fall (in price); das Wasser —, to make water. **Abschlägig**, ap'shlägig, *a.* refusing, denying; — Antwort, refusal. **Abschläglich**, ap'shläglich, *a.* paid on account.
Abschleifen, ap'shlēifen (*Prt.* schliff ab; *Pp.* abgeschliffen), *vt.* to grind off; to smooth, polish.
Abschleifen, ap'shlēifen, *vt.* to drag away; to wear out.
Abschleifern, ap'shlēnkērn, *vt.* to fling away.
Abschleppen, ap'shleppen, *vr.* to weary one's self by dragging; *vt.* to drag away.
Abschleudern, ap'shlēudērn, *vt.* to sling away.
Abschließen, ap'shlīsen, *vt.* to lock, close; to conclude; to balance, settle. **Abschließung**, ap'shlīsung, *f.* locking, balancing. **Abschluß**, ap'shlūss, *m. pl.* Abschlüsse, closing, conclusion.
Abschmeicheln, ap'shmēichēln, *vt.* to obtain by flattery.
Abschmelzen, ap'shmeltsen, *vt.* to molt off.
Abschmieren, ap'shmīren, *vt.* to copy negligently.
Abschnallen, ap'shnallen, *vt.* to unbuckle.
Abschnappen, ap'shnappen, *vt. i.* to snap off.
Abschneiden, ap'shnēiden (*Prt.* schnitt ab, *Pp.* ab'geschnitten), *vt.* to cut off; to clip, pare.
Abschnellen, ap'shnellen, *vt.* to jerk off; *vi.* to fly off.
Abschnitt, ap'shnitt, *m. pl.* -e, cut;

segment, section; paragraph. **Abschnitzel**, ap'shnitsel, *m.* chip, clipping, paring.
Abschnüren, ap'shnūbren, *vt.* to unlace; to measure out.
Abschöpfen, ap'shöpfen, *vt.* to skim, scum, to scoop off.
Abschrauben, ap'shrōyben, *vt.* to unscrew.
Abschrecken, ap'shrecken, *vt.* to deter; to scare off, discourage.
Abschreiben, ap'shrēiben, *vt.* to copy, transcribe. **Abschreiber**, ap'shrēiber, *m.* copyist, transcriber.
Abschreiten, ap'shrēiten, *vt.* to pace, to measure by steps.
Abschrift, ap'shrift, *f.* copy, transcript, duplicate; — nehmen, to double.
Abschroten, ap'shröten, *vt.* to cut off transversely; to grind coarsely.
Abschürfen, ap'shürfen, *vt.* to scrape off.
Abschüssig, ap'shūssig, *a.* steep, sloping, declivitous; -keit, -kēet, declivity, steepness. [off.
Abschütteln, ap'shüttēln, *vt.* to shake
Abschütten, ab'shütten, *vt.* to pour off.
Abschwächen, ap'shvechen, *vt.* to weaken, enfeeble; to attenuate. [off.
Abschwären, ap'shvären, *vi.* to slough
Abschwärzen, ap'shvertsen, *vt.* to blacken; *vi.* to lose the black color.
Abschwatzen, ap'shvatsen, *vt.* to coax out of.
Abschwefeln, ap'shwāfēln, *vt.* to free from sulphur; to smoke with sulphur.
Abschweifen, ap'shvēifen, *vi.* to digress, deviate. **Abschweifung**, *f.* digression.
Abschwemmen, ap'shvemmen, *vt.* to wash away, off.
Abschwenken, ap'shvenken, *vi.* to wheel off, turn aside; *vt.* to rinse.
Abschwitzen, ap'shvitsen, *vt.* to remove by sweating.
Abschwören, ap'shvöhren, *vt.* to abjure; to deny by oath.
Abscisse, ap-tsis'se, *f.* abscissa.
Absegeln, ap'sāgēln, *vi.* to sail away.
Absehen, ap'sā-en, *vt.* to look away; to abstract; to design, intend; to comprehend; *s. n.* (gun) sight.
Abseigern, ap'sēigern, *vt.* to separate silver from copper.
Abseihen, ap'sēl-en, *vt.* to strain, filter.
Absein, ap'sēēn, *vi.* to be distant, absent, null; to be empty.

Abſeits, ap'sīts', *av.* aside.
Abſenden, ap'senden, *vt.* to send away, dispatch. **Ab'ſendung, -ung,** *f.* shipping, dispatching; deputation.
Abſengen, ap'sengen, *vt.* to singe off.
Abſenken, ap'senken, *vt.* to sink (a shaft); to propagate by layers; *vi.* to slope.
Abſetzen, ap'setsen, *vt.* to set down, deposit; to throw off; to remove, depose; to cashier; to wean; to sell. **Ab'ſetz-ciſterne, -tsisterne,** *f.* settling-cistern. **Ab'ſetzung,** ap'setsung, *f.* deposition.
Abſicht, ap'sikht, *f.* design, view, intention, aim, purpose; ſeine — erreichen, to obtain one's end. **Ab'ſichtlich,** ap'-sikhtlich, *a.* intentional, premeditated, designed. **Ab'ſichtlos, -lōs,** *a.* unintentional, undesigned.
Abſickern, ap'sickěrn, *vi.* to percolate, ooze.
Abſieben, ap'sīben, *vt.* to sift off.
Abſieden, ap'sīden, *vt.* to seethe, boil.
Abſingen, ap'sing-en, *vt.* to sing off, chant.
Abſitzen, ap'sitsen, *vi.* to alight; dismount; to sit apart.
Abſolut, apsolut', *a.* absolute; *av.* -ly. **Abſolution,** apsolutsiōn', *f.* absolution. **Abſolviren,** apsolfī'ren, *vt.* to absolve.
Abſonderlich, apson'děrlich, *a.* peculiar, singular; *av.* especially. **Ab'ſondern,** ap'sondĕrn, *vt.* to separate, sever; to seclude. **Ab'ſonderung,** ap'sonderung, *f.* separation.
Abſpannen, ap'zhpaunen, *vt.* to unharness, unyoke; to unbend. **Ab'ſpänſtig (Abſpenſtig),** ap'zhpenstig, *a.* averse; — machen, to alienate.
Abſpeiſen, ap'zhpeïsen, *vt.* to feed, treat; to content; furz —, to cut short, snub.
Abſperren, ap'zhperren, *vt.* to shut off, debar, confine, seclude, separate.
Abſpiegeln, ap'zhpīgěln, *vt.* to reflect, mirror.
Abſpinnen, ap'zhpinnen, *vt.* to spin off.
Abſplittern, ap'zhplittĕrn, *vt.* i. to splinter; to exfoliate.
Abſprechen, ap'zhprechen, *vt.* to adjudicate, arbitrate; to be dogmatical. **Ab'ſprechend,** ap'zhprechent, *a.* positive, authoritative, peremptory.
Abſprengen, ap'zhpreng-en, *vt.* to blast off, break off; *vi.* to gallop away.

Abſpringen, ap'zhpring-en, *vi.* to fly off, burst off; to leap off; to rebound.
Abſpulen, ap'zhpuhlen, *vt.* to unwind (from a spool).
Abſpülen, ap'zhpühlen, *vt.* to wash away; to rinse.
Abſtammen, ap'zhtammen, *v.* to descend, come from. **Ab'ſtammung, -ung,** *f.* descent, parentage.
Abſtand, ap'zhtant, *m. pl.* **Abſtände,** distance; interval; difference.
Abſtatten, ap'zhtatten, *vt.* to pay, discharge, give, render. **Ab'ſtattung, -ung,** *f.* rendering, giving.
Abſtäuben, ap'zhtäuben, *vt.* to dust.
Abſtechen, ap'zhtechen, *vt.* to stab, pierce; to kill; to dig off; to drain; to tap; to rack; to engrave; to contrast; — den Wind, to gain the wind. **Ab'ſtecher,** ap'zhtecher, *m.* excursion, trip.
Abſtecken, ap'zhtecken, *vt.* to unpin; to mark out. **Ab'ſteckpfahl, -pfāl,** *m. pl.* -pfähle, picket, stake.
Abſtehen, ap'zhtā-en, *vi.* to stand off; to desist; to decay, fade; to get stale; to abstain, recede from; to yield up, resign.
Abſtehlen, ap'zhtālen, *vt.* to steal from.
Abſteigen, ap'zhtīgen, *vi.* to alight, dismount, descend. **Ab'ſteige-quartier,** -quartīr, *n.* lodging.
Abſtellen, ap'zhtellen, *vt.* to remove, abolish.
Abſtemmen, *vt.* to chisel off.
Abſterben, ap'zhterben, *vi.* to die, fade away, decay; *s. n.* death, decease.
Abſtich, ap'zhtich, *m. pl.* -e, contrast; tapping.
Abſtimmen, ap'zhtimmen, *vi.* to vote; to tune.
Abſtoßen, ap'zhtōssen (*Prt.* ſtieß ab, *Pp.* abgeſtoßen), *vt.* to thrust off, knock off, repel; to push off; to wean; to chisel off. **Ab'ſtoßend,** *a.* repulsive. **Ab'ſtoßung, -ung,** *f.* repulsion.
Abſtrafen, ap'zhtrāfen, *vt.* to chastise, punish.
Abſtrahiren, apzhtrahī'ren, *vi.* to abstract, to comprehend; *vi.* to resign. **Abſtrakt,** apzhtrakt', *a.* abstract. **Abſtraktion,** apzhtraktsiōn', *f.* abstraction.
Abſtreichen, ap'zhtrīchen, *vt.* to wipe off; to strike level, to strap (a razor).

Abſtreifen, ap'zhtrāsſen, vt. to strip off.
Abſtreiten, ap'zhtrāiten (*Prt.* ſtritt ab *Pp.* abgeſtritten), vt. to dispute, to deny.
Abſtricken, ap'zhtricken, vt. to knit off.
Abſtrömen, ap'zhtrŏhmen, vi. to flow off rapidly; to crowd away; vt. to float off; to wash away.
Abſtufen, ap'zhtuſen, vi. to graduate, to form into steps. **Abſtufung,** -ung, f. gradation, graduation.
Abſtumpfen, ap'zhtumpfen, vt. to blunt, dull; to truncate (a cone).
Abſturz, ap'zhturts, m. pl. **Abſtürze,** precipice, steep. **Abſtürzen,** ap'zhtürtsen, vt. i. to precipitate.
Abſtutzen, ap'zhtutsen, vt. to clip, curtail.
Abſud, ap'sud, m. decoction.
Abſurd, apsurd', a. absurd. **Abſurdität,** -itāt', f. absurdity.
Abt, apt, m. pl. **Aeb'te,** abbot.
Abtakeln, ap'tākěln, vt. to unrig. **Ab'takelung,** -ung, f. unrigging.
Abtanzen, ap'tantsen, vt. to dance off.
Abteilich, aptēi'lich, a. abbatial.
Abteufen, ap'tŏiſen, vt. to sink (a shaft).
Abtheilen, ap'tāĕlen, vt. to divide. **Ab'theilung,** -ung, f. division.
Abthun, ap'tun, vt. to take off, put off.
Aebtiſſin, ĕptis'sin, f. abbess.
Abtraben, ap'trăben, vi. to trot off.
Abtragen, ap'trăgen, vt. to carry away; to pull down, level, dismantle, raze; to wear out; to pay, discharge (a debt). **Abtrag,** ap'trăg, m. payment; detriment; — **thun,** to injure.
Abtrauſen, ap'trăuſen, **Abtrăuſeln,** ap'trăuſeln, vt. to trickle down, drop down.
Abtreibemittel, ap'trĕibemittel, n. abortive draught. **Abtreiben,** ap'trēiben, vt. to drive off; expel; to overdrive; to cause abortion; to fell.
Abtrennen, ap'trennen, vt. to separate, dismember.
Abtreten, ap'trĕten, vt. to tread down, wear off; to resign, give up; vi. to withdraw, retire, retreat. **Abtretung,** ap'trētung, f. cession; resignation, abdication.
Abtriefen, ap'trīfen, vi. to trickle down.
Abtrinken, ap'trinken, vt. to sip off.
Abtritt, ap'tritt, m. pl. -e. going off; privy, water-closet; lee-way.

Abtrocknen, ap'trocknen, vt. to wipe off, to dry.
Abträpfeln, ap'trŏpfĕln, vi. to trickle down, drop off.
Abtrotzen, ap'trotsen, vt. to bully out.
Abtrumpfen, ap'trumpfen, to trump; to answer sharply.
Abtrünnig, ap'trŭnnig. a. apostate, rebellious, disloyal, faithless; **treit,** -kēét, f. desertion, defection.
Abtummeln, ap'tummeln, vr. to fatigue one's self.
Aburtheilen, ap'urtŝělen, vt. to decide, judge.
Abverdienen, ap'fĕrdīnen, vt. — eine Schuld, to work off by service.
Abwägen, ap'văgen, vt. to weigh; to compare.
Abwalken, ap'valken, vt. to full, mill; to drub soundly.
Abwälzen, ap'vĕltsen, vt. to roll down, off.
Abwarten, ap'varten, vt. to wait for; to attend to. **Ab'wartung,** -ung, f. attendance, nursing.
Abwärts, ap'vĕrts, av. downwards, aside.
Abwaſchen, ap'vashen, vt. to wash off; to cleanse.
Abwäſſern, ap'vĕssĕrn, vt. to drain, water.
Abwechſeln, ap'vĕksĕln, vt. to alternate, change; vi. to alternate. **Ab'wechſelnd,** a. av. alternating, by turns; changing. **Ab'wechſelung,** -ung, f. alternation, variety, change.
Abweg, ap'văg, m. by-way, by-path; wrong way.
Abwehren, ap vă-ren, vt. to keep off, to parry, avert.
Abweichen, ap'vĕĕchen, vt. to soften; to soak.
Abweichen, ap'vĕichen, vi. to deviate, decline; differ, vary; depart; z. x. diarrhœa. **Ab'weichung,** -ung, f. deviation; anomaly; declination, variation (of the magnetic needle).
Abweiden, ap'vĕĕden, vt. to feed, graze.
Abweiſen, ap'vĕisen, vt. to dismiss; to refuse. **Ab'weiſung,** -ung, f. refusal.
Abwelken, ap'vĕlken. vt. i. to wither; to pine away.
Abwenden, ap'venden, vt. to turn away, to avert. **Abwendig,** ap'vendig. a. averse, estranged; — **machen,** to alienate, estrange.

Abw 17 **Ach**

Abwerfen, ap'verfen, *vt.* to throw off; to cast off; to yield, bring in; to shake off (the yoke).
Abwesend, ap'väsent, *a.* absent. **Ab'wesenheit,** -häet, *f.* absence.
Abwickeln, ap'vickeln, *vt.* to unwind, wind off.
Abwinden, ap'vinden (ab'wand, ab'gewunden), *vt.* to unwind, untwist.
Abwischen, ap'vishen, *vt.* to wipe off; to dust, clean.
Abwurf, ap'vurf, *m.* offal.
Abwürgen, ap'vürgen, *vt.* to strangle, slay, butcher.
Abzahlen, ap'tsälen, *vt.* to pay off; discharge. **Ab'zahlung,** -ung, *f.* payment.
Abzählen, ap'tsälen, *vt.* to number, count, reckon.
Abzahnen, ap'tsänen, *vt.* to shed the teeth; to take off with the toothplane. [off.
Abzapfen, ap'tsapfen, *vt.* to tap, draw
Abzäumen, ap'tsäumen, *vt.* to unbridle.
Abzehren, ap'tsä-ren, *vt. i.* to exhaust, waste, consume, pine away. **Ab'zehrung,** ap'tsärung, *f.* consumption.
Abzeichen, ap'tsichen, *n.* sign, mark.
Abzeichnen, ap'tsichnen, *vt.* to mark out, draw; to sketch, delineate; — mit Kreide, to chalk. **Ab'zeichnung,** -ung, *f.* drawing, d.-sign, sketch.
Abzerren, ap'tserren, *vt.* to tear off, wrest off. [still.
Abziehblase, ap'tsiblāse, *f.* alembic.
Abziehen, ap'tsi-en, *vt.* to draw off, pull off; to take off; subtract, deduct; to distill; to take an impression (print); to set (a razor); *vi.* to march off. **Ab'ziehseife,** -seife, *f.* smoothing-file. **Ab'ziehfeder,** -feder, *n.* razor-strap. **Ab'ziehmuskel,** -mus'kel, *f.* abductor. **Ab'ziehpflug,** -pflug, *m. pl.* -pflüge, drainingplough. **Ab'ziehstein,** -stein, *m. pl.* -e, hone. **Ab'ziehzahl,** -tsäl, *f.* subtrahend. **Ab'ziehzeug,** -tsoig, *m. pl.* -e, utensils for distilling.
Abzielen, ap'tsilen, *vt.* to aim at; to aim towards; to have in view, to intend.
Abzug, ap'tsug, *m. pl.* -züge, retreat, departure; draining; impression, proof-sheet; subtraction, deduction.
Abzugsbogen, -bögen, *m. pl.* -bögen, proof-sheet. **Ab'zugsgraben,** -grä-

ben, *m. pl.* -gräben, drain. **Ab'zugsröhre,** -röre, *f.* waste-pipe.
Abzwacken, ap'tsvacken, **Ab'zwicken,** ap'tsvicken, *vt.* to pinch off, nip off.
Abzwecken, ap'tsvecken, *vt.* to intend.
Abzwingen, ap'tzving-en, *vt.* to extort wring from.
Acazie, akä'tsi-e, *f.* acacia; locust-tree.
Accent, aktsent'. *m. pl.* -e, accent. **Accentuiren,** aktsentyi'ren, *vt.* to accentuate.
Accepisse, aktseppis'se, *f.* **Accept,** aktsept', *m.* acceptance. **Acceptiren,** aktseptī'ren, *vt.* to accept, honor, to promise to pay.
Accribens, aktsidents', *n. pl.* -ten, perquisite.
Accisbar, aktsis'bär, *a.* exciseable. **Accise,** aktsi'se, *f.* excise. **Acciseinnehmer,** aktsi'se-ennämer, *m.* exciseman.
Acclamation, akklamatsiōn', *f.* acclamation.
Accord (Akkord), akkord'. *m. pl.* -e, chord, accord, harmony; agreement, compact. **Accordiren,** akkordī'ren, *vt.* to harmonize; to agree; to compromise.
Accusativ, ak'kysatīf, *m. pl.* -e, accusative.
Aceton, atseton', *n.* pyro-acetic spirit. **Acetyl,** atsetīl', *n.* acetyle.
Ach, *ij.* alas! ah!
Achat, achāt', *m. pl.* -e, agate. **Achatartig,** achāt'ärtig, *a.* agaty. **Achatonyx,** -önix, *m.* agate-onyx. **Achatsiegel,** -sīgel, *n.* agate-seal.
Achromatisch, achromat'ish, *a.* achromatic; -es Fernrohr, — Teleskop', achromatic telescope.
Achse, axe, *f.* axle, axletree; axis, pivot, spindle; centre of motion.
Achsel, ax'el, *f.* shoulder; die — zucken, to shrug the shoulders. **Ach'selband,** -bant, *n. pl.* -bänder, shoulder-strap. **Ach'selgrube,** -grube, *f.* armpit. **Ach'selträger,** -träger, *m.* double-dealer.
Ach'selzucken, -tsucken, *n.* shrugging.
Achsenband, ax'enbant, *n. pl.* -bänder, axletree hoop. **Ach'senblech,** -blech, *n. pl.* -e, clout. **Ach'senbüchse,** -büxe, *f.* axletree-box. **Ach'senfutter,** -futter, *n.* **Ach'senlager,** -läger, *n.* axletree-bed. **Ach'sennagel,** -nägel, *m. pl.* -nägel, linch-pin. **Ach'senriegel,** -rīgel, *m.* transom of the gun-carriage. **Ach'senschmiere,** -shmīre, *f.*

2*

axle-grease. **Achsenschraube**, -schröpfe, f. axle-nut. **Achsenstag**, -stes, m. pl. -stöße, axle-washer. **Achsenstrich**, -strich, m. pl. -e, axis (Arch.).
Acht, f. eht.
(I.) **Acht**, acht, a. eight.
(II.) **Acht**, acht, f. attention, care; in — nehmen, to take care of: — geben auf, to attend to: sich in — nehmen, to guard one's self.
(III.) **Acht**, acht, f. ban, proscription, outlawry.
Achtbar, acht'bär, a. respectable; -keit, -keit, f. respectability.
Achteck, acht'eck, n. pl. -e, octagon. **Achteckig**, -eckig, a. octagonal.
Achten, ach'ten, vt. to mind, to attend to, esteem, regard.
Achten, äch'ten, vt. to proscribe, outlaw.
Achtel, ach'tel, n. the eighth part. **Achter**, achte, achtes, a. eighth. **Achtens**, ach'tens, av. eighthly, in the eighth place. **Achterlei**, ach'terläe, a. of eight different kinds. **Achtfach**, acht'fach, a. eightfold, octuple. **Achthalb**, -halp. a. seven and a half. **Achtjährig**, acht'yärig, a. eight years old.
Achtlos, acht'lōs, a. careless, unmindful, inattentive. **Achtlosigkeit**, -ich-keit, f. inattention, carelessness.
Achtmal, acht'mäl, av. eight times. **Achtmalig**, -mälig, a. eight times repeated.
Achtsam, acht'sam, a. attentive, mindful, heedful, careful, av. -ly. **Achtsamkeit**, -keit, f. attentiveness, heedfulness, carefulness.
Achtserklärung, achts'erklärung, f. proscription, outlawry.
Achtspännig, acht'zhpennig, a. with eight horses, drawn by eight horses. **Achtstündig**, acht'zhtündig, lasting eight hours. **Achtstündlich**, acht'zhtündlich, a. av. happening every eighth hour. **Achttägig**, acht'tägig, of eight days. **Achttäglich**, acht'täg-lich, a. every week.
Achtung, ach'tung, f. attention, regard, esteem.
Achtzehn, acht'tsān, a. eighteen. **Acht-zehnter**, a. eighteenth. **Achtzig**, acht'tsig, a. eighty. **Achtziger**, n. octogenarian. **Achtzigjährig**, acht'-tsig-yärig, a. eighty years old. **Acht-zigster**, a. eightieth.
Ächzen, äch' sen, vi. to groan.

Acker, ak'ker, m. field. **Ackerbau**, -böy, m. agriculture, husbandry. **Ackerfeld**, -felt, n. pl. -er, **Ackerland**, -lant, n. pl. -länder, arable land. **Ackergaul**, -göyl, m. pl. -gäule, farm-horse. **Ackergeräthe**, -gyrāte, n. agricultural implements. **Ackergesetz**, -gesets, n. pl. -e, agrarian law. **Ackern**, ack'ern, vt. to plough, till. **Ackersmann**, **Ackermann**, m. pl. **Ackersleute**, -löute, m. husbandman, farmer, plougher. **Ackerzeit**, -tsält, f. ploughing-season. **Ackerzeug**, -tsöig, n. ploughing-tools.
Act, akt, m. pl. -e, action; act. **Acte**, ak'te, f. acts, judiciary acts, parliamentary acts. **Actie**, ak'tsi-e, f. share, stock. **Actiengesellschaft**, ak'tsi-en-gesellshaft, f. joint-stock company. **Actieninhaber**, -in'hāber, **Actionär**, ak'tsionär, m. stockholder, shareholder. **Activ**, ak'tīf, a. active, actual. **Actuar**, aktuār', m. pl. -e, clerk, actuary.
Acupunctur, aküpünctyr', f. acupuncture.
Addiren, addī'ren, vt. to add. **Addition**, additsiōn', f. addition.
Adel, ä'del, m. nobility, nobleness. **Adelig**, a. noble. **Adeln**, ä'deln, vt. to ennoble. **Adelsbrief**, -brīf, m. pl. -e, patent of nobility. **Adelsrank**, -stand, m. nobility. **Adelsstolz**, -stolts, m. pride of nobility, aristocratic pride; a. proud of nobility.
Ader, ä'der, f. vein; artery: goldene —, hemorrhoidal vein; — zur — lassen, to bleed, to let blood. **Äderchen**, ä'derchen, n. little vein. **Aderhaut**, -höyt, f. pl. -häute, choroid, membrane. **Aderig**, ä'derig, a. veiny, veined. **Aderlaß**, -lass, m. pl. -lässe, bloodletting, bleeding. **Aderschlag**, -shlāg, m. pl. -schläge, pulse, pulsation.
Adjunkt, adyünkt', m. pl. -e, assistant.
Adjustiren, adyushtī'ren, vt. to adjust. **Adjutant**, adyutant', m. pl. -en, adjutant, aid-de-camp.
Adler, äd'lēr, m. eagle. **Adlerstein**, -stēn, m. pl. -e, eagle-stone. **Adlernase**, -nāse, f. aquiline nose.
Administration, administratsiōn', f. administration. **Administriren**, administrī'ren, vt. to administer.
Admiral, admirāl', m. admiral. **Admiralität**, -ralitāt', f. admiralty

Ad   19   **Al**

Admiralsſchiff, -shiff, n. pl. -e, ad'miralship.
Adoptiren, adoptī'ren, vt. to adopt. **Adoptirt**, adoptī'rt, a. adopted.
Adreſſe, adrĕs'ṣe, f. direction, address. **Adreßbuch**, -buch, n. pl. -bücher, directory. **Adreſſiren**, adreſſī'ren, vt. to address.
Advent, advĕnt', m. advent.
Adverb, advĕrb', n. pl. -ien, adverb.
Advokat, advokät', m. pl. -en, lawyer, advocate.
Affe, affe, m. -n. pl. -n, ape, monkey. **Affen**, ĕf'fen, vt. to ape, mock. **Afferei**, ŏfferĕī', f. apishness. **Äffin**, ĕf'fīn, f. she-monkey, **Äffisch**, ĕf'fīsh, a. apish.
Affekt, affĕkt', m. affection. **Affektiren**, affektī'ren, vt. to affect. **Affiziren**, affīzī'ren, vt. to affect.
Affinität, affinität', f. affinity.
After, af'tĕr, m. buttocks, anus; backside. **Afterbürge**, -bürge, m. -n, pl. -n, second bail. **Afterpacht**, -pacht, m. under-tenure. **Afterrede**, -rĕde, f. slander, calumny.
Agende, agĕn'de, f. prayer-book, agenda, liturgy.
Agent, agent', m pl. -en, agent. **Agentſchaft**, -shaft, f. **Agentur**, -tyr, f. agency.
Agio, ä'shio, n. agio, premium.
Agiren, agī'ren, vt. to act, play, mimic.
Agrikultur, agrikyltyr', f. agriculture.
Ah, ä, ij. Ah.
Ahle, ä'le, f. awl.
Ahn, än, m. pl. -en, ancestor, forefather.
Ahnden, än'den, vt. to resent, punish. **Ahndung**, -yng, f. resentment, punishment.
Ähneln, ä'neln, vi. to resemble somewhat.
Ahnen, än'en, vt. to have a presentiment of, to anticipate.
Ahnfrau, än'frau, f. ancestress, grandmother, grandam. **Ahnherr**, än'hĕrr, m. -n, pl. -n, ancestor, grandsire.
Ähnlich, än'lich, a. similar, like, resembling. **Ähnlichkeit**, -käet, f. similarity, similitude, resemblance, likeness.
Ahnung, än'yng, f. presentiment, foreboding.

Ahorn, ä'horn, m. pl. -e, maple, maple-tree.
Ähre, ä're, f. ear; **Ähren leſen**, to glean; -leſe, -läṣe, f. gleaning; -leſer, -läsĕr, m. gleaner.
Akademie, akademī', f. academy. **Akademiker**, -dä'miker, m. academician, academist. **Akademiſch**, -däm'ish, a. academic.
Akonit, akonitt'. m. aconite.
Akuſtiſch, akyzh'tish, a. acoustic. **Akuſtik**, f. acoustics.
Alabaſter, alabas'tĕr, m. alabaster. **Alabaſterbruch**, -bruch, m. pl. -brüche, alabaster-quarry.
Alarm, alarm', m. alarm; -glocke, f. alarm-bell. **Alarmiren**, alarmī'ren, vt. to alarm.
Alaun, alaün', m. alum; -artig, -ärtig, a. resembling alum; -bergwerk, -bĕrgvĕrk, n. pl. -e, **Alaunbruch**, -bruch, m. pl. -brüche, **Alaungrube**, -grybe, f. alum-quarry or pit. **Alaunblumen**, -blymen, s. pl. alum-flowers. **Alauner**, -ärts, n. pl. -e, alum-ore. **Alauniſch**, a. aluminous. **Alaunkeſſel**, -keṣel, m. **Alaunpfanne**, -pfanne, f. alum-boiler. **Alaunkies**, -kīs, m. pl. -e, aluminous pyrites. **Alaunleder**, -lädĕr, m. alum-leather, white leather. **Alaunſchiefer**, -shī'fĕr, m. alum-slate. **Alaunzucker**, -tsucker, m. alum-sugar.
Albern, al'bĕrn, a. silly, foolish. **Albernheit**, al'bĕrnhäet, f. silliness, foolishness.
Album, al'bym, n. album.
Alchemie, **Alchimie**, **Alchymie**, alchimī', f. alchemy.
Alcoran, al'korän, f. Koran.
Alfanzerei, alfantsĕrĕī', f. foolery, nonsense.
Algebra, al'gebrä, f. algebra.
Alkaheſt, al'kahest, n. alkahest.
Alkali, al'kali, n. alkali.
Alkohol, al'kohŏl, m. alcohol.
Alkoven, al'kŏfen, m. alcove, bedchamber.
All, all, n. universe; all. **Aller**, **alle**, **alles**, a. all, every, whole. **All**, av. all, entirely, wholly. **Allbekannt**, -bekannt, a. notorious; av. -ly. **Allbereits**, all'bĕräets, av. already. **Allda**, alldä', av. there, in that place. **Alldieweil**, all'dīvĕīl, cj. since, because.
Allee, allā', f. avenue, walk, alley.

Allegorie, allegori', f. allegory. **Allegorisch**, allegō'rish. a. allegoric, -al, av. -ally. **Allegorisiren**, allegorisi'ren, vt. to allegorize.
Allein, allān', a. av. alone; cj. but. **Allein'besitz**, -besitz, m. exclusive possession. **Allein'handel**, -handel, m. monopoly. **Allein'herrscher**, -hérrshēr, m. monarch. **Allein'herrschaft**, -shaft, f. monarchy. **Alleinig**, allīn'ig, a. only, exclusive, sole.
Allemal, al'lęmāl, av. always, every time. **Al'lenfalls**, -falls, av. at all events; perhaps. **Al'lenfallsig**, -fallsig, a. casual, eventual. **Al'lenthalben**, -halben, av. everywhere. **Al'lerbeste**, -beste, n. u. a. best of all. **Allerdings**, al'lērdings, av. undoubtedly, sure enough, to be sure, indeed. **Al'lererst**, -erst, a. av. first of all. **Allergnädigst**, -gnā'dikst, a. most gracious, av. -ly. **Al'lerhand**, -hant, a. of all kinds. **Allerheiligen**, -hāē'ligen, a. all-saints. **Allerheiligstes**, -ikstēs, n. holy of holies. **Al'lerhöchst**, -hökst', a. highest of all. **Al'lerlei**, -lāē, a. of all kinds. **Al'lerletzt**, -letzt, av. a. last of all. **Al'lerliebst**, -līlst, a. most lovely, loveliest, dearest, most beloved. **Al'lermeist**, -māēst, av. a. most of all; particularly. **Allerschönst**, -shönst', a. most beautiful. **Allerseelentag**, -sā'lentag, m. all-souls' day. **Al'lerseits**, -seits, av. on all sides. **Allerwege**, al'lērvāge, av. everywhere. **Allerwenigstens**, -vā'nikstens, av. least of all. **Allesammt**, al'lesammt, av. all, all together. **Allgegenwart**, -gā'genvart, f. omnipresence, ubiquity. **Allgegenwärtig**, -vertig. a. omnipresent, ubiquitous. **Allgemach**, all'gemach, av. gradually. **Allgewalt**, all'gevalt, f. omnipotence: -ig, a. omnipotent. **Allgütig**, allgü'tig, a. all-bounteous, infinitely bountiful. **Allhier**, allhīr', av. here.
Allianz, alliants', f. alliance; **Alliirt**, alli-īrt', a. allied: s. ally.
Alliteration, alliteratsiōn', f. alliteration.
Allmacht, all'macht, f. omnipotence. **Allmächtig**, -mecht'ig, a. omnipotent. **Allmälig**, allmäl'ich, a. gradual, av. gradually, by degrees. **Allmende**, all'mende, f. commons.

Allopath, allopāt', m. -en, pl. -en, allopath. **Allopathie**, f. allopathy.
Alltägig, all'tägig, a. daily. **Alltäglich**, a. daily, common: -es **Fieber**, quotidian fever. **Alltäglichkeit**, -hākēt, f. commonness. **Alltags**, all'tāgs, av. a. of every day, common, commonplace; **erfahrung**, -ērfār-ung, f. every day's experience; **mensch**, -mensh, m. -en, pl. -en, commonplace fellow.
Alluvion, alluvion', n. alluvium.
Allweis, allvēis', a. all-wise; **heit**, -hāēt', f. supreme, infinite wisdom. **Allwissend**, allvis'sent, a. omniscient. **Allwissenheit**, -vis'senhāēt, f. omniscience. **Allwo**, allvō', av. where. **Allzu**, all tsū, av. too, too much. **Allzumal**, all'tsumāl, av. altogether.
Almanach, al'manach, m. almanac.
Almandin, al'mandin, m. almandine.
Almosen, al'mōsen, n. alms, charity; **amt**, n. pl. -ämter, almonry. **Almosenbüchse**, -büksę, f. **Almosenkasten**, -kasten, m. alms-box. **Almosenpfleger**, -pflēgēr, m. almoner.
Aloe, ā'loę, f. aloe; **holz**, -holts, n. agallochum.
Alp, m. nightmare, incubus.
Alphabet, alfabāt', n. pl. -e, alphabet **Alphabetisch**, -bāt'ish, a. alphabetic, -al, av. -ally.
Alraun, alraūn', m. mandrake (Bot.).
Als, als, cj. as, but, than, when. **Alsbald**, alsbalt', **Alsobald**, av. forthwith, immediately.
Alsdann, alsdann', av. then.
Also, all'sō, cj. thus, so; therefore, then.
Alt, allt, m. alto; high tenor; tenor.
Alt, allt, a. old, aged; stale; ancient, antique; second hand. **Alter**, older; elder; **Älteste**, el'tęsst, oldest; eldest. [platform.
Altan, alltān', m. pl. -e, balcony.
Altar, alltār', m. pl. **Altär'e**, altar; **tuch**, -tuch, n. pl. -tücher, altar cloth.
Altbacken, allt'backen, a. stale. **Altein**, el'tēln, vi. to grow elderly.
Alter, all'tęr, n. age; old age; vor **Alters**, in ancient times, anciently, of old; formerly. **Älterlich**, el'tęrlich, a. parental, av. -ly. **Ältern**, el'tērn. s. pl. parents **Alternativ**,

Alt   21   **Ana**

-lös, *a.* „bereft of parents, „orphaned. **Elternmord,** -mert, *m.* **Elternmörder,** -mörder, *m.* parricide. **Eltern,** al'tern, *vi.* to grow old. **Alternative,** alternati'fe, *f.* alternative. **Alterthum,** al'tertum, *n.* antiquity. **Alterthümler,** -tümler, *m.* **Alterthumsforscher,** -forsher. *m.* antiquary, antiquarian. **Alterthümlich,** -tümlich, *a.* antiquarian. **Alterthumskunde,** -kunde, *f.* archæology. **Altersfolge,** -folge, *f.* seniority. **Altersschwäche,** -shveche, *f.* weakness of old age. **Altfränkisch,** -frenkish, **Altmodisch,** -modish, **Altväterisch,** -täterish *a.* old-fashioned, old, antique. **Altgesell,** -gysell, *m.* -en, *pl.* -en, foreman, head-journeyman. **Altgläubig,** -gleübig, *a.* orthodox. **Altklug,** alt'klug, *a.* precocious, forward. **Ältlich,** elt'lich, *a.* elderly. **Altmutter,** -mutter, *f. pl.* -mütter, grandmother. **Altermutter,** el'termutter, *f. pl.* -mütter, great-grandmother. **Altvater,** alt'fäter, *m.* grandfather: ancestor. **Altervater,** el'terfäter, *m. pl.* -väter, great-grandfather.
Altstimme, alt'shtimme, *f.* alto (voice).
Am, amm, = an tem, at the.
Amalgam, amalgäm', *n.* amalgam. **Amalgamiren,** amalgami'ren, *vt.* to amalgamate.
Amazone, amatsō'ne, *f.* amazon.
Ambition, ambitsiōn', *f.* ambition.
Amboß, am'bōs, *m. pl.* -e, anvil.
Ambra, am'bra, *n.* ambergris; **Duft,** duft, *m. pl.* -düfte, perfume, fragrance. **Ambrasäure,** -seürg, *f.* ambreic acid.
Ambrosia, ambrō'sia, *f.* ambrosia.
Ameise, ame'ize, *f.* ant, emmet. **Ameisenbär,** -bär, *m.* -*n.* *pl.* -en, ant-bear, ant-eater. **Ameiseni,** ei, *n. pl.* -eier, ant-egg. **Ameisenfresser,** -nēst. *n. pl.* -er, **Ameisenhaufen,** -heüfe, *m.* ant-hill. **Ameisensäure,** -seürg, *f.* formic acid.
Amen, ām'en. *G.* amen.
Amethyst, ametist', *m.* amethyst.
Amiant, amiant', *m.* amianthus.
Amtmann, am'mann, *m. pl.* -männer, bailiff, chief magistrate.
Amme, am'me, *f.* wet-nurse, nurse.
Ammoniak, ammon'iak, *m.* ammonia,

spirits of hart's-horn. **Ammonium,** ammō'nium, *n.* ammonium.
Amnestie, amnēstī', *f.* amnesty.
Amor, ām'or, *m.* Cupid, Love.
Ampel, am'pel, *f.* lamp.
Amphibie, amfī'bi-e. *f.* amphibious animal. **Amphibisch,** amfī'bish, *a.* amphibious.
Amphitheater, am'fitēāter, *n.* amphithe'atre. [putate.
Amputiren, ampytī'ren, *vt.* to am-
Amsel, am'sel, *f.* ousel, blackbird.
Amt, amt, *n. pl.* **Ämter,** office; employment, post, commission; magistracy. **Amtfrei,** -frēī, *a.* without office. **Amthaus,** -hoūs. *n.* bailiff's house, office; court. **Amtlich,** *a.* official. **Amtlos,** -lōs, *a.* out of office. **Amtmann,** *m. pl.* -leute, bailiff. **Amtsalter,** -alter, *n.* seniority. **Amtsbezirk,** -betsirk, *m. pl.* -e, jurisdiction. **Amtsbruder,** -bryder, *m. pl.* -brüder, colleague. **Amtseifer,** -eifer, *m.* official zeal. **Amtsfolge,** -folge, *f.* succession in office. **Amtsdiener,** -dīner, *m.* beadle. **Amtsführung,** -füryng, *f.* conducting of an office. **Amtsgebühr,** -gebühr, *f.* perquisites of an office. **Amtsmiene,** -mīng, *f.* official air, professional gravity. **Amtspflicht,** -pflicht, *f.* official duty. **Amtsschreiber,** -shrēiber, *m.* public clerk, recorder. **Amtsverwalter,** -fervalter, *m.* bailiff's deputy. **Amtsverweser,** -fervāser, *m.* administrator of an office. **Amtswürde,** -vürde, *f.* professional dignity.
Amulet, amylēt', *n. pl.* -te, amulet.
Amüsant, amüsant', *a.* amusing, funny.
An, an, än, *pr.* on, at, near, by, in.
Anachronismus, anachronīs'myss, *m.* anach'ronism.
Analogie, analōgī', *f.* analogy.
Analyse, analī'se, *f.* analysis, resolution. **Analysiren,** analisī'ren, *vt.* to analyze. **Analytik,** analīt'ic, *f.* analytics. **Analytisch,** analīt'ish, *a.* analytic, -al, *av.* -ally.
Ananas, än'anas, *f.* pine-apple.
Anarchie, anachī', *f.* anarchy. **Anarchisch,** anarch'ish, *a.* anarchic, -al, *av.* -ally.
Anatomie, anatomī', *f.* anatomy. **Anatomisch,** anatō'mish, *a.* anatomic, -al, *av.* -ally.

Anä 22 **And**

Anäugeln, an'äugeln, *vt.* to look tenderly at.
Anbacken, ån'backen, *vi.* to cling, cleave, stick to.
Anbau, ån'båu, *m.* cultivation; addition (to a building). **An'bauen,** *vt.* to cultivate; to add.
Anbefehlen, ån'befůlen, *vt.* to command.
Anbeginn, ån'beginn, *m.* beginning.
Anbei, anbeï, *a.* inclosed, annexed.
Anbeißen, ån'beißen, *vt.* to bite, to swallow the bait.
Anbelangen, ån'belang-en, *vt.* to concern, to relate to. [yelp at.
Anbellen, ån'bellen, *vt.* to bark at,
Anbequemen, ån'bequämen, *vt.* to accommodate to.
Anberaumen, ån'beråumen, *vt.* to appoint, fix.
Anberg, ån'berk, *m.* slope.
Anbeten, ån'beten, *vt.* to worship, adore. **An'beter,** worshipper, adorer.
Anbetteln, ån'betteln, *vt.* to beg from.
Anbetung, ån'betung, *f.* adoration, worship; **-swürdig,** -würdig, *a.* adorable.
Anbieten, ån'bïten, *vt.* to offer, proffer; *vi.* to start; to bid first (*Prt.* bot an, *Pp.* angeboten).
Anbinden, ån'binden (*Prt.* band an, angebunden), *vt.* to tie, bind, to fasten: kurz angebunden sein, to be quick, to speak short; *vi.* mit einem —, to quarrel with.
Anbiß, ån'biss, *m. pl.* -bisse, bite; breakfast.
Anblasen, ån'blåsen (*Prt.* blies an, *Pp.* angeblasen), *vt.* to blow upon.
Anblick, ån'blick, *m.* aspect, view, sight: beim ersten —, at first sight.
Anblicken, ån'blicken, *vt.* to look at, to glance at, to view; zornig —, to frown at
Anblinzen, ån'blintsen, **An'blinzeln,** *vt.* to wink at.
Anblöken, ån'blöcken, *vt.* to bleat, to low at.
Anbohren, ån'bören, *vt.* to bore, pierce; to tap, broach.
Anbrechen, ån'brechen, *vt. i.* to break, begin; to open.
Anbrennen, ån'brennen, *vi.* to catch fire; to burn; *vt.* to kindle, to set on fire.
Anbringen, ån'bring-en, *v.* to bring in: to apply; to sell

Anbruch, ån'bruch, *m. pl.* **-brüche** break, beginning, dawn. **Anbrüchig,** ån'brüchig, *a.* rotten, unsound, decayed.
Anbrüllen, ån'brüllen, *vt.* to bellow at, low at, roar at.
Anbrummen, ån'brummen, *vt.* to growl at, grumble at.
Andacht, ån'dacht, *f.* devotion. **Andächtelei,** ån'dechteleï, *f.* hypocritical devotion. **Andächteln,** ån'dechteln, *vi.* to affect devotion. **Andächtig,** ån'dechtig. *a.* devout, devotional; *av.* -ly. **An'dächtler,** *m.* canting hypocrite.
Andachtsbuch, ån'dachtsbuch, *n. pl.* **-bücher,** book of devotion. **Andachtsübung,** -übung, *f.* act of devotion; devotion. **Andachtsvoll,** ån'dachtsfoll, *a.* devout.
Andenken, ån'denken, *n.* remembrance, recollection, memory; memorial.
Ander, an'der, *a.* other, different; second; nichts anderes, nothing else. Eins ums Andere, in turns; alternately; andern Falles, otherwise, else. **Ändern,** en'dern, *vt.* to alter, change, reform, vary. **Anders,** an'ders, *av.* otherwise, differently, in another way. **Anderthalb,** an'dert-halp, *a.* one and a half. **Anderswo,** an'dersvö, **An'derswärts,** -verts, *av.* elsewhere. **Änderung,** en'derung, *f.* alteration, change, variation. **Anderweit, Anderweitig,** an'derweïtig, *a.* in another way, different, *av.* -ly.
Andeuten, ån'deüten, *vt.* to hint, intimate, suggest, signify, foreshadow; to indicate. **An'deutung,** -ung, *f.* hint, intimation; indication.
Andichten, ån'dichten, *vt.* to impute falsely. **An'dichtung,** -ung, *f.* imputation.
Andonnern, ån'donnern, *vt.* to thunder at.
Andrang, an'drang, *m.* throng, press, crowd; congestion. **Andrängen,** an'drengen, *vt.* to press, to crowd towards, to throng; sich —, to obtrude one's self.
Andrehen, ån'drä-en, *vt.* to screw on; to turn on, to start. Einem eine Nase —, to impose upon
Andrerseits, an'drersäits, *av.* on the other side.

Andringen, ån'dring-en, *vt.* to push forward, to press against, to rush upon. **Andringlich**, ån'dringlich, *a.* pressing, urging, urgent, importunate, *av.* -ly, indiscreetly.

Androhen, ån'drö-en, *vt.* to threaten (with), menace. **Androhung**, ån'drö-ung, *f.* threat, menace.

Andruck, ån'druck, *m.* what is joined in printing.

Andrucken, ån'drücken, *vt.* to join, add by printing. **Andrücken**, ån'drücken, *vt.* to press against, squeeze against.

Anduften, ån'duften, *vt.* to exhale fragrance towards.

Andurch, an'durch, *av.* thereby.

Aneifern, ån'eifern, *vt.* to incite, stimulate, spur on.

Aneignen, ån'eignen, *vt.* to appropriate. **Aneignung**, ån'eignung, *f.* appropriation.

Anekdote, anèkdö'te, *f.* anecdote.

Anekeln, ån'eckeln, *vt.* to disgust, to be loathsome to.

Anempfehlen, ån'empfëlen, *vt.* to recommend. **Anempfehlung**, -ung, *f.* recommendation.

Anerben, ån'erben, *vt.* to inherit.

Anerbieten, ån'erbîten (*Prt.* anerbot, *Pp.* anerboten), to offer; *s. n.* offer.

Anerkennen, ån'erkennen (*Prt.* anerkannte, *Pp.* anerkannt), to own, acknowledge, allow, avow, recognize. **Anerkennung**, -ung, *f.* acknowledgment, recognition.

Anerschaffen, ån'erschaffen, *a.* innate, imparted by creation.

Anfacheln, ån'fecheln, *vt.* to fan. **Anfachen**, ån'fachen, *vt.* to blow into a flame, kindle, inflame.

Anfahren, ån'fåren (*Prt.* anfuhr, *Pp.* angefahren), to drive up to, to arrive at, stop at; to put in (*Mar.*): *vt.* to convey, transport; to snub, to speak short to. **Anfahrtschacht**, -shacht. *m. pl. -e*, entrance-shaft.

Anfall, ån'fall, *m. pl. -fälle*, assault; fit, paroxysm. **Anfallen**, ån'fallen, *vt.* to assail, assault, attack.

Anfang, ån'fang, *m. pl. -fänge*, beginning. **Anfangen** (*Prt.* anfing, *Pp.* angefangen), *vt.* to begin. **Anfänger**, ån'feng-ĕr, *m.* beginner: springer (Arch.) **Anfänglich**, ån'fenglich, *a. av.* original, -ly; in the beginning. **Anfangs**, *av.* at first; -buchstabe, -bychståbe, *m. -n ê pl. -n*, initial letter. **Anfangsgründe**, -gründe, *pl.* rudiments, first elements.

Anfassen, ån'fassen, *vt.* to seize, lay hold of.

Anfechten, ån'fechton (*Prt.* anfocht, *Pp.* angefochten), to attack, combat; to trouble; to entice, tempt. **Anfechtung**, -ung, *f.* temptation, trial.

Anfeinden, ån'feinden, *vt.* to insult, to make one's enemy. **Anfeindung**, -ung, *f.* making enemies.

Anfesseln, ån'fesseln, *vt.* to fetter, enchain.

Anfeuchten, ån'feuchten, *vt.* to moisten. **Anfeuchtung**, -ung, *f.* moistening.

Anfeuern, ån'feuern, *vt.* to light a fire, to heat; to inflame, animate. **Anfeuerung**, -ung, *f.* incitement, animation.

Anfirnissen, ån'firnissen, *vt.* to varnish.

Anflechten, ån'flechten, *vt.* to join by plaiting.

Anflehen, ån'flê-en, *vt.* to implore, supplicate.

Anfletschen, ån'fletshen, *vt.* to show the teeth to.

Anflicken, ån'flicken, *vt.* to join to by patching.

Anflößen, ån'flöhsen, *vt.* to float to.

Anflug, ån'flyg, *m.* slight smattering, tincture; efflorescence.

Anforderung, ån'forderung, *f.* claim, demand.

Anfrage, ån'fråge, *f.* inquiry, application. **Anfragen**, *vt.* to ask, inquire.

Anfressen, ån'fressen (*Prt.* anfraß, *Pp.* angefressen), *vt.* to gnaw, nibble, corrode.

Anfrieren, ån'friren (*Prt.* anfror, *Pp.* angefroren), *vi.* to freeze to.

Anfrischen, ån'frishen, *vt.* to refresh; to revive, arouse; to reduce (metals). **Anfrischofen**, -öfen, *m. pl. -öfen*, refining-furnace. **Anfrischung**, ån'frishyng, *f.* encouragement; reduction (of metals).

Anfügen, ån'fühg-en, *vt.* to join to, to subjoin.

Anfühlen, ån'fühlen, *vt.* to feel, touch, handle.

Anführen, ån'führen, *vt.* to lead; to cite, allege; to guide, to mislead, cheat. **Anführer**, *m.* leader, conductor; -in, *f.* conductress. **An-**

führung, -ung, *f.* conduct, lead; command; quotation.
Anfüllen, än'füllen, *vt.* to fill up, to cram. **Anfüllung**, -ung, *f.* filling.
Anfurth, än'furt, *f.* landing-place, wharf.
Angabe, än'gäbe, *f.* statement, declaration, averment.
Angaffen, än'gaffen, *vt.* to gape at.
Angähnen, än'gänen, *vt.* to yawn at.
Angeben, än'gäben (*Prt.* angab, än'gäb, *Pp.* angegeben), to state, denounce, inform against, specify.
Angeber, än'gäber, *m.* informer.
Angeberei, än'gäberei, *f.* denunciation, informing, tale-bearing.
Angebinde, än'gebinde, *n.* gift, present.
Angeblich, än'gäb'lich, *a.* professed, pretended.
Angeboren, än'gebören, *a.* innate, inborn.
Angebot, än'gebot, *n. pl. -e*, first bidding.
Angedeihen, än'gedei-en, — lassen, *vt.* to bestow, confer upon, to impart.
Angedenken, än'gedenken, *f.* Andenken.
Angehänge, än'geheng-e, *n.* amulet.
Angehen, än'gä-en (*Prt.* anging, *Pp.* angegangen), to approach, advance toward; to come in sight; to apply, solicit; *vi.* to begin; to suffice; to be tolerable; to concern, to relate to; to burn, take fire. **Angehend**, än'gä-ent, *pr.* concerning.
Angehören, än'gehör-en, to belong. **Angehörig**, -hörig, *a.* related to; belonging to. **Angehörige**, *s. pl.* kinsmen, relations.
Angel, ang'el, *f.* hinge, hook; fish-hook.
Angeld, an'gelt, *n.* earnest-money.
Angelegen, än'gelegen (*Pp. v.* anliegen), *a.* adjacent; important; sich — sein lassen, to make a point of, to make it one's business. **Angelegenheit**, -häet, *f.* affair, business, matter, concern. **Angelegentlich**, än'gelägentlich, *a.* concerned, pressing, anxious, particular, *av.* -ly.
Angelhaken, ang'-elhäken, *m.* fishing-hook. **Angeln**, ang'eln, *vi.* to angle.
Angeloben, än'gelöben, *vt.* to vow. **Angelöbniß**, än'gelöbniss, *n.* vow, solemn promise.

Angelpunkt, ang'elpunkt, *m. pl. -e*, centre, pole. **Angelruthe**, -ruhe, *f.* fishing-rod.
Angemessen, än'gemessen, *a.* appropriate, fit, suitable, conformable; -heit, -häet, *f.* conformity, fitness, suitableness.
Angenehm, än'genäm, *a.* agreeable, pleasing, *av.* -ly.
Anger, ang'er, *m.* grassy place, green.
Angesehen, än'gesä-en, *a.* respected, prominent, respectable; *cj.* considering. [settled.
Angesessen, än'gesessen, *a.* resident,
Angesicht, än'gesicht, *n.* face, countenance, visage; presence. **Angesichts**, *av.* in the presence of.
Angewöhnen, än'gewöhnen, *vt.* to accustom, inure. **Angewohnheit**, -wöhnhäet, *f.* habit, custom, practice. **Angewöhnung**, -wöhnung, *f.* accustoming; custom.
Angießen, än'gisen, *vt.* to pour to, to pour upon; to join by casting.
Anglimmen, än'glimmen, *vi.* (*Prt.* anglomm, *Pp.* angeglommen), *vi.* to take fire.
Anglisiren, anglisi'ren, *vt.* to anglicize; to dock the tail of a horse.
Anglotzen, än'glotsen, *vt.* to stare at.
Angreifen, än'greifen (*Prt.* angriff, *Pp.* angegriffen), *vt.* to take hold of, to seize, touch; to undertake; to attack, charge; sich —, to strain one's self. **Angreifend**, än'greifent, *a.* aggressive, offensive. **Angreifer**, än'greifer, *m.* aggressor. **Angriff**, än'griff, *m. pl. -e*, attack, charge, assault.
Angrenzen, än'grentsen, *vi.* to border on.
Angrinsen, än'grinsen, *vt.* to grin at.
Angrunzen, än'grunsen, *vt.* to grunt at.
Angst, angst, *f.* (*pl.* Ängste), anguish, anxiety, alarm.
Ängsten, eng'sten, **Ängstigen**, engstigen, *vt.* to fill with anguish, to alarm, distress. **Angstgeschrei**, *n.* cry of distress, shriek, scream. **Ängstlich**, engsht'lich, **Angstvoll**, angsht'fell, *a.* anxious, nervous, timorous. **Ängstlichkeit**, -käet, *f.* anxiety, solicitude. **Angstschweiß**, angsht'shwäes, *m.* cold sweat.
Angürten, än'gürten, *vt.* to gird on.

Anh   25   **Anf**

Anhaben, ăn'hāben, *vt.* to have on, wear. Einem etwas —, to injure, to get the better of one, to get hold of.
Anhaften, ăn'haften, *vi.* to adhere, stick to.
Anhäkeln, ăn'häkĕln, *vt.* to fasten with a little hook, to clasp.
Anhaken, ăn'häken, *vt.* to hook on.
Anhalten, ăn'halten, *vt.* to hold to, to press towards; to stop, to check; *vi.* to persevere; to cling to; to apply for, sue for; to woo, court. **An'haltend**, *a.* uninterrupted.
Anhang, ăn'hang, *m. pl.* **Anhänge**, appendage, appendix, supplement; codicil. **Anhängen**, ăn'hang-en, *vi.* to hang to, to adhere. **Anhängen**, ăn'heng-en, to append, to hang to, to attach to; to add, affix; to infect with; sich —, to stick. **Anhänger**, ăn'heng-ĕr, *m. -in, f.* adherent, follower, partisan. **Anhängig**, ăn'hengich, *a.* adherent; — sein, to be pendent; einen Prozeß — machen, to bring an action against. **Anhänglich**, ăn'henglich, *a.* attached to, clinging, affectionate; -keit, -kăet, *f.* affectionateness; attachment.
Anhängsel, ăn'hengsel, *n.* appendage. [upon.
Anhauchen, ăn'houchen, *vt.* to breathe
Anhauen, ăn'hau-en, *vt.* to begin chopping, cutting.
Anhäufen, ăn'hoüfen, *vt.* to heap up.
Anhäufung, -ung, *f.* accumulation, accretion, aggregate.
Anheben, ăn'hāben, *vt.* to lift up; to begin, commence.
Anheften, ăn'heften, *vt.* to fasten to, fix to; to stitch, to sew to.
Anheilen, ăn'hăelen, *vt. i.* to join by (in) healing.
Anheim, anhäëm', *av.* home; — fallen, to fall back, to devolve; — stellen, -stellen, — geben, to leave to, to refer, submit to.
Anheimeln, ăn'hăemeln, *vt.* to remind of home.
Anheischig, ăn'hăeshig, *a.* sich — machen, to pledge one's self to; to promise.
Anhetzen, ăn'hetsen, *vt.* to start (game); to set on (a dog); to incite, instigate. **Anhetzer**, ăn'hetsĕr, *m. -in, f.* setter-on, inciter. **An'hetzung**, -ung, *f.* setting on; instigation.
Anhöhe, ăn'hō-e, *f.* height, eminence, rising ground.

Anholen, ăn'hōlen, *vt.* to haul, ta tighten (ropes).
Anis, ăn'is, anīs', *m.* anise. **An'issamen**, -sāmen, *m.* anise-seed. **An'iszucker**, -tsuckĕr, *m.* sugared anise.
Anjagen, ăn'yagen. *vt.* to start (game); *vi.* angejagt kommen, to come rushing.
Anjochen, ăn'yochen, *vt.* to yoke to.
Ankämpfen, ăn'kempfen, *vi.* to struggle against, to fight with.
Ankauf, ăn'kăuf, *m. pl.* **Ankäufe**, purchase, bargain.
Ankaufen, ăn'kăufen, *vt.* to buy, purchase; *vr.* to settle.
Ankeilen, ăn'kĕilen, *vt.* to fasten with wedges, to wedge.
Anker, an'ker, *m.* anchor; kleiner —, grapnel. **Anker werfen**, to cast anchor; vor — geben, to moor, anchor; vor — liegen, to ride at anchor; die lichten, to weigh anchor; vor — treiben, to drag the anchor. **An'ferarm**, -arm, *m. pl. -e*, arm of an anchor. **An'kerboje**, bō-ye, *f.* **An'ferzeichen**, -tsăechen, *n.* buoy. **An'kerflügel**, -flü-gel, *m.* fluke of an anchor. **An'fergeld**, -gĕlt, *n.* anchorage (duty).
An'kergrund, -grunt, *m.* anchorground, anchorage. **Ankern**, an'kĕrn, *vi.* to anchor. **An'kerschuh**, -shu, *m. pl. -e*, shoe of an anchor.
An'kertalje, -talye, *f.* fish-tackle.
An'kertau, -tau, *n. pl. -e*, cable.
An'kerwinde, -vinde, *f.* capstan, windlass.
Anketten, ăn'ketten, *vt.* to chain.
Ankitten, ăn'kitten, *vt.* to cement.
Ankläffen, ăn'kleffen, *vt.* to yelp at.
Anklage, ăn'klăge, *f.* accusation; impeachment.
Anklagen, ăn'klāgen, *vt.* to accuse, impeach, charge with. **Ankläger**, ăn'klāgĕr, *m. -in, f.* accuser.
Anklammern, ăn'klammĕrn, *vt.* to fasten with clamps; sich —, to cling to.
Anklang, ăn'klang, *m. pl.* **Anklänge**, sound; sympathy, approval.
Ankleben, ăn'klāben, *vt.* to paste on; to post up; *vi.* to stick; to cleave to.
Ankleiden, ăn'klĕiden, *vt. n. r.* to dress. **An'kleidezimmer**, -tsimmĕr, *n.* dressing-room.
Ankleistern, ăn'klĕizhtĕrn, *vt.* to paste on.

Anklingen, ǎn'kling-en, *vi.* to resound, to make to ring.
Anklopfen, ǎn'klŏpfen, *vi.* to knock, to rap.
Anknüpfen, ǎn'kenüpfen, *vt.* to tie to, to join.
Anködern, ǎn'kŏhdĕrn, *vt.* to allure, bait.
Ankommen, ǎn'kŏmmen, *vi.* to come, to arrive; schlecht — bei, to have ill success; es darauf-lassen, to run the risk; es kommt auf ihn an, it depends on him. **Ankömmling,** ǎn'kömmling, *m.* new-comer.
Ankörnen, ǎn'körnen, *vt.* to allure, bait.
Ankündigen, ǎn'kündigen, *vt.* to announce. **Ankündigung,** -ung, *f.* announcement, proclamation.
Ankunft, ǎn'kunft, *f.* arrival.
Ankuppeln, ǎn'kuppeln, *vt.* to couple.
Anlächeln, ǎn'lĕcheln, *vt.* to smile on.
Anlachen, ǎn'lachen, *vt.* to look at laughing, to smile upon.
Anlage, ǎn'lāge, *f.* plan, sketch, first beginning: disposition, talent; pleasure-ground; eine — machen, to lay out.
Anlanden, ǎn'landen, *vi.* to land.
Anlangen, ǎn'lang-en, *vi.* to come to, to arrive; to concern, relate to; was mich anlangt, as for me. **An's langend,** with respect to, concerning.
Anlass, ǎn'lass, *m.* occasion, cause, subject, matter; inducement; — geben, to give rise to: to occasion, induce. **Anlassen,** ǎn'lassen, *vt.* to keep on (a coat, &c.); to let water into a pond; to set a-going (a mill); to anneal (metals); hart —, to rebuke, snub, rattle; es lässt sich an zu, it has the appearance of.
Anlauf, ǎn'lauf, *m.* run, onset, assault; einen — nehmen, to take a running start. **Anlaufen,** *vi.* to run up, to swell, rise; to increase; to tarnish; to become dim, hazy; er ist schön angelaufen, he met with a fine reception.
Anlegen, ǎn'lēgen, *vt.* to lay or put upon; to take aim; to put on (clothes); to invest; die Hand —, to take in hand; die letzte Hand —, to put the finishing stroke to; Colonien —, to found colonies.
Anlehen, ǎn'lā-en, *n.* loan.

Anlehnen, ǎn'lānen, *vt.* to lean against.
Anleihe, ǎn'leï-e, *f.* loan. **Anleihen,** *vt.* to lend.
Anleimen, ǎn'līmen, *vt.* to glue to.
Anleiten, ǎn'lāeten, *vt.* to guide or lead to; to train; to instruct. **An's leitung,** *f.* leading, direction; instruction.
Anlernen, ǎn'lĕrnen, *vi.* to acquire by study.
Anliegen, ǎn'līgen (-lag, -gelegen), *vi.* to lie close to; to fit;to be adjacent; einem —, to solicit, to press any one. **An'liegen,** *n.* concern, solicitude, desire, petition, request.
Anlocken, ǎn'locken, *vt.* to allure, entice, decoy. **Anlockung,** ǎn'lockung, *f.* allurement, enticement.
Anlöthen, ǎn'löhten, *vt.* to solder to.
Anlügen, ǎn'lūhgen, *vt.* to belie, deceive.
Anluven, ǎn'lŭfen, *vi.* to luff.
Anmachen, ǎn'machen, *vt.* to fix, fasten; das Feuer —, to kindle, make a fire; to temper.
Anmalen, ǎn'mālen, *vt.* to paint or color.
Anmahnen, ǎn'mānen, *vt.* to exhort, incite. **Anmahnung,** ǎn'mānung, *f.* exhortation.
Anmarsch, ǎn'marsh, *m.* advance. **Anmarschiren,** ǎn'marrshīren, *vi.* to march on, advance on.
Anmassen, ǎn'māsen, *vt.* to assume, arrogate, presume, claim. **Anmassend, Anmasslich,** *a.* assuming, arrogant. **Anmassung,** *f.* arrogance, assumption, arrogation, presumption.
Anmelden, ǎn'mĕlden, *vt.* to announce; sich —, to present one's self; sich — lassen, to send in one's name.
Anmerken, ǎn'mĕrken, *vt.* to mark, note, put down, remark; perceive, observe. **Anmerkung,** ǎn'mĕrkung, *f.* remark, note, comment, illustration.
Anmessen, ǎn'mĕssen, *vt.* to measure, to take the measure of; to adapt, fit, suit, apportion.
Anmuth, ǎn'mŭt, *f.* grace, charm, sweetness. **Anmuthig,** *a.* graceful, charming, delightful, pleasant; -ly, *av.* **Anmuthen** = Zumuthen.
Annageln, ǎn'nāgeln, *vt.* to nail to.
Annagen, ǎn'nāgen, *vt.* to begin to gnaw; to gnaw, nibble at.

Annähen, än'nä-en, *vt.* to sew to; — einen Block, to fix a block (Mar.).
Annahen, än'nä-en, *vi.* sich annähern, än'nä-ern, to approach. **Annäherung**, än'nä-erung, *f.* approach.
Annahme, än'näme, *f.* acceptation, reception, acceptance; admission; adoption, engagement.
Annalen, annä'len, *s. pl.* annals.
Annehmen, än'nämen, *vt.* to receive, accept; to assume; admit, engage; to embrace; to receive into service; an Kindes Statt —, to adopt; den Schein —, to pretend; sich Jemandes —, to assist or protect any one; sich einer Sache —, to espouse a cause.
Annehmlich, Annehmbar, än'nämbär, *a.* pleasant, acceptable, *av.* -ly; -keit, -käet, *f.* pleasantness, acceptableness, agreeableness.
Annieten, än'nętsen, *vt.* to moisten, damp.
Annieten, än'nīten, *vt.* to rivet to.
Anomalie, anomalī', *f.* anomaly.
Anonym, änonīm', *a.* anonymous, *av.* -ly.
Anordnen, än'ordnen, *vt.* to arrange; order. **Anordnung**, än'ordnung, *f.* arrangement, ordering, regulation, disposition.
Anpacken, än'packen, *vt.* to collar, lay hold of, grasp, seize, attack.
Anpassen, än'pässen, *vt.* to fit, accommodate, suit, adapt; *vi.* to fit, suit, to be suitable.
Anpfählen, än'pfälen, *vt.* to supply with stakes, to pale up, prop.
Anpflanzen, än'pflantsen, *vt.* to cultivate, raise. **Anpflanzer**, än'pflantser, *m.* planter, settler. **Anpflanzung**, -ung, *f.* planting, cultivation; plantation.
Anpflöcken, än'pflöcken, *vt.* to peg to.
Anpichen, än'pichen, *vt.* to pitch.
Anpissen, än'pissen, *vt.* to piss against or upon.
Anpochen, än'pochen, *vi.* to knock, rap.
Anprall, än'prall, *m.* bounce. **Anprallen**, än'prallen, *vi.* to bound against.
Anpreisen, än'preisen, *vt.* to praise, extol, puff. **Anpreisung**, -ung, *f.* praising, puffing.
Anprellen, än'prellen, *vt.* to bound, throw against.
Anprobiren, än'probīren, *vt.* to try on.

Anquaken, än'quäken, *vt.* to croak at.
Anqualmen, än'qualmen, *vt.* to blow the fume into any one's face.
Anrasten, än'räken, *vi.* to run aground.
Anrathen, än'räten, *vt.* to advise.
Anrauchen, än'räuchen, *vt.* to smoke at; ein Pfeifchen —, to light a pipe.
Anrechnen, än'rechnen, *vt.* to reckon, to charge to account, to rate, account, impute, ascribe.
Anrecht, än'recht, *n.* claim, demand.
Anrede, än'räde, *f.* address, harangue, speech. **Anreden**, än'räden, *vt.* to address, accost, harangue.
Anregen, än'rägen, *vt.* to move, stir up, animate, incite. **Anregung**, *f.* impulsion, suggestion, reminding.
Anreiben, än'reiben, *vt.* to rub on.
Anreihen, än'räe-en, *vt.* to string, file.
Anreiten, än'reiten, *vt.* to ride near, charge.
Anreiz, än'reits, *m.* impulse, incentive. **Anreizen**, än'reitsen, *vt.* to incite, entice, abet. **Anreizung**, -ung, *f.* incitement.
Anrennen, än'rennen, *vi.* to run, rush against.
Anrichten, än'richten, *vt.* to prepare, dish up, dress; Unheil —, to make mischief; etwas Schönes —, to make a precious work of it.
Anriechen, än'riechen, *vt.* to smell at; to perceive by smelling, to scent, sniff.
Anrollen, än'rollen, *vi.* to come rolling, to drive up.
Anrosten, än'roshten, *vi.* to begin to rust.
Anrüchig, Anrüchtig, än'rüchtich, *a.* notorious, ill-famed, infamous. **Anrüchigkeit**, -käet, *f.* notoriousness, disreputation.
Anrücken, än'rücken, *vi.* to approach, draw near.
Anruf, än'ruf, *m.* appeal. **Anrufen**, än'rufen, *vt.* to call to, invoke, to appeal to, to challenge.
Anrühmen, än'rühmen, *vt.* to praise.
Anrühren, än'rühren, *vt.* to touch, feel, handle, hurt; to mix, temper. **Anrührung**, -ung, *f.* touch; mixing.
Ansäen, än'sä-en, *vt.* to sow (a field).
Ansagen, än'sägen, *vt.* to announce, to notify of.
Ansägen, än'sägen, *vt.* to begin to saw

Anſäſſig, än'säsĭG, a. domiciled, settled, resident; **-ſeit, -käѣt,** f. domiciliation, residence.

Anſat, än'sats, m. disposition, inclination, propensity; rate; deposit, crust; manner of blowing (a flute); epiphysis (Anat.); apophysis (Bot.); **-feile, -fēī-le,** f. flat file; **-größe, -grö̈hse,** f. differential; **-ſtück, -zhtück,** n. mouthpiece of an instrument.

Anſaugen, än'sǒŋgen, vt. to begin to suck; ſich —, to suck fast.

Anſchaffen, än'shaffen, vt. to procure, provide, furnish, create. **Anſchaffung, -ŭng,** f. providing, procuring, furnishing.

Anſchäften, än'shěften, vt. to provide with a shaft; to stock (a gun); to nail the joists to the sleepers (Carp.).

Anſchauen, än'shäŭen, vt. to look at, gaze at. **Anſchaulich,** a. clear, perspicuous; **— machen,** to give a clear idea of. **Anſchauung,** än'shäŭyng, f. intuition, contemplation.

Anſchein, än'shǟn, m. appearance, show, likelihood. **Anſcheinen,** vt. i. to shine upon, appear, have the appearance of. **Anſcheinend, Anſcheinlich,** a. apparent, seeming, av. -ly, in appearance.

Anſchicken, än'shicken, ſich —, to begin, prepare, set about; ſich gut dazu —, to go the right way to work.

Anſchielen, än'shīlen, vt. to squint at, ogle.

Anſchießen, än'shīsen **(-ſchoß, -geſchoſſen),** vt. to print in addition; to wound by shooting; to try (a gun); das neue Jahr —, to usher in by shooting; vi. to shoot forth, to rush against, to crystallize, to begin shooting; s. n. crystallization. **Anſchießkeſſel, -keſſel,** m. filler. **Anſchießpinſel, -pinsel,** m. gilding-brush.

Anſchirren, än'shĭrren, vt. to harness.

Anſchlag, än'shläg, m. striking against; affixing, posting; poster, bill, placard; estimate, calculation, design, plan, project; plot; touch (Mus.); butt (of a gun); in **— bringen,** to allow for, to take into account. **Anſchlagen,** än'shlägen, vt. to strike against; to post; to nail; to chime; to estimate, rate, tax, value; to take effect; to ar-wer, succeed; to strike; to aim. **Anſchlag- gewinkel,** m. back-square. **Anſchlag- zettel, -tsěttel,** m. poster, handbill, placard.

Anſchließen, än'shlīsen, vt. to chain to; to add; vi. to fit close, to join. **Anſchluß,** än'shlŭss, m. joining, accession, annexation; thing annexed.

Anſchmeicheln, än'shmīchěln, vr. ſich, **—,** to insinuate one's self by flattery.

Anſchmieden, än'shmīden, vt. to weld.

Anſchmiegen, än'shmīgen, vr. ſich **—,** to cling to, to nestle, to insinuate one's self.

Anſchnallen, än'shnallen, vt. to buckle on. [at.

Anſchnarchen, än'shnarchen, vt. to snarl

Anſchnauben, än'shnŏyben, vt. to snarl at, to snub.

Anſchneiden, än'shnēĭden, vt to cut or carve. **Anſchnitt,** m. first cut; notch.

Anſchnüffeln, än'shnüffeln, vt. to snuff at, smell at.

Anſchnüren, än'shnühren, vt. to lace to, to tie up.

Anſchrauben, än'shrŏyben, vt. to screw on.

Anſchreiben, än'shrēĭben, vt. to write down, to put to account, to charge; gut angeſchrieben ſein bei, to be in favor with.

Anſchreien, än'shrēĭen, vt. to cry at, to hail.

Anſchub, än'shyb, m. first batch.

Anſchuhen, än'shy-en, vt. to shoe; — e. Paar Stiefel, to foot.

Anſchuldigen, än'shyldigen, vt. to accuse, charge.

Anſchüren, än'shühren, vt. to poke, kindle, stir.

Anſchuß, än'shyss, m. crystallization; first shot; **— des Waſſers,** rush.

Anſchwängern, än'shveng-ern, vt. to impregnate (Chem.).

Anſchwärzen, än'shvertsen, vt. to blacken, slander. **Anſchwärzung,** f. slandering, calumniation.

Anſchwatzen, än'shvatsen, vt. **— Zuſchwatzen.**

Anſchweißen, än'shvǟssen, vt. to weld; to braze; to wound by shooting.

Anſchwellen, än'shvellen, vt. to swell; vi. änshvěllen, to swell.

Anſchwemmen, än'shvemmen, vt. to float, deposit. **Anſchwemmt,** al-

luvial. **Anschwimmen**, ăn'shvim-men, vi. to swim to.
Ansegeln, ăn'sägeln, vt. to sail near; to strike in sailing.
Ansehen, ăn'säen, vt. to look at, to eye, behold; über die Achsel —, to slight; n. s. the looking at, regard, look, view, appearance, external show; aspect, consideration, respect, authority, consequence; sich — geben, to assume, put on airs. **Ansehnlich**, ăn'sän-lich, a. considerable, respectable; portly; *keit, f. considerableness. **Ansehung**, ăn'sä-ung, f. looking at, regard; in —, in consideration of, with respect to, as for, concerning.
Ansetzen, ăn'setsen, vt. to set or put near to: to estimate; put down; tax, rate; to fix, appoint, settle; vi. to attempt; assault; to thrive, grow fat; to continue (of veins, Min.).
Ansicht, ăn'sicht, f. sight, prospect; view, opinion. **Ansichtig**, ăn'sichtich, a. — werden, to behold, discover, descry, to have or get a sight of.
Ansiedeln, ăn'sīdeln, vr. sich —, to settle, colonize. **Ansiedelei**, ănsīdelā', f. settlement, colony. **Ansiedler**, m. settler, colonist. **Ansiedlung**, f. settlement, colonization, colony.
Ansinnen, ăn'sinnen, vt. to desire, demand, require; s. n. request, demand.
Anspannen, ăn'zhpannen, vt. to stretch; to harness; to yoke.
Anspeien, ăn'zhpīen, vt. to spit at, upon.
Anspielen, ăn'zhpīlen, vi. to begin to play; to allude. **Anspielung**, -ung, f. allusion.
Anspissen, ăn'zhpīsen, vt. to spit, to pierce with a spit; to impale.
Anspinnen, ăn'zhpinnen (-spann, -gesponnen), vt. to begin to spin; to spin together; to contrive, plot, plan.
Anspließen, ăn'zhplīsen, vt. to splice.
Anspornen, ăn'zhpornen, vt. to spur, incite on, to.
Ansprache, ăn'zhpräche, f. a speaking to, address: **Ansprechen**, ăn'zhpre-chen, vt. to address, speak to; to accost; to claim, demand, request; to interest; to sound (easily) (Mus.).
Ansprengen, ăn'zhpreng-en, vt. to make a spring; to springle; vi. to

come galloping, to charge. **Anspringen**, ăn'zhpring-en (-sprang, -gesprungen), vi. to leap, jump against.
Anspritzen, ăn'zhpritsen, vt. to squirt at, sprinkle.
Anspruch, ăn'zhpruch, m. claim, pretension; naming (Hunt.); *sies, -los, a. unpretending, unassuming, modest; *slosigkeit, -lösichkāet, f. modesty. **Anspruchsvoll**, ăn'zhpruchsfoll, a. assuming, presumptuous, a. -ly, av.
Ansprung, ăn'zhprung, m. leap; scab.
Anspucken, ăn'zhpucken, vt. to spit at.
Anspülen, ăn'zhpūhlen, vt. to wash, deposit (earth). **Anspülung**, -ung, (angespültes Land), alluvium.
Anstacheln, ăn'zhtacheln, vt. to spur, prick, incite.
Anstalt, ăn'zhtalt, f. arrangement, preparation; establishment, institution.
Anstammen, ăn'zhtammen, vt. to inherit. **Angestammt**, hereditary, ancestral; innate, inborn.
Anstand, ăn'zhtant (from anstehen), m. stand, post; grace, fine deportment; delay; hesitation, objection. **Anständig**, ăn'zhtendich, a. decent, proper, becoming, av. -ly; *keit, f. decency, decorum, propriety.
Anstarren, ăn'zhtarren, vt. to stare at.
Anstatt, anzhtatt', pr. instead, in lieu, in place of.
Anstaunen, ăn'zhtaunen, vt. to gaze at, stare at, wonder at.
Anstechen, ăn'zhtechen, vt. to prick, tap, broach; die Pumpe —, to fetch a pump. **Anstechbohrer**, -börer, m. piercer, borer, boring-bit.
Anstecken, ăn'zhtecken, vt. to stick on, put on; to infect; ein Licht —, to light a candle. **Ansteckend**, a. contagious, infectious. **Ansteckung**, ăn'zhteckung, f. contagion, infection.
Anstehen, ăn'zhtä-en, vi. to stand close to; to sit close; to participate in; to fit, to be suitable, becoming; to stand or stop undecided, to hesitate; es — lassen, to delay, defer, put off.
Ansteigen, ăn'zhtēigen (-stieg, -gestiegen), vi. to ascend; to slope upward.

Anſtellen, ån'zhtęllen, *vt.* to place close to; to appoint; to put to work; to arrange, prepare; Klage —, to institute a suit; e. Vergleichung —, to draw a parallel; etwas —, to do some mischief; ſich auf Wild —, to take a stand for game; ſich —, to pretend, feign; ſich freundlich —, to feign kindness. **Anſtellig,** ån'zhtęllich, *a.* able, handy, skillful. **Anſtellung,** ån'zhtęllung, *f.* place, appointment.

Anſtiften, ån'zhtiften, *vt.* to contrive, instigate; *s. n.* instigation, contriving. **Anſtifter,** *m.* instigator, author.

Anſtimmen, ån'zhtimmen, *vt.* to tune; ein Lied —, to begin a song; ein Inſtrument —, to sound. **Anſtimmung,** ån'zhtimmung, *f.* tuning, intonation, sounding.

Anſtoß, ån'zhtōs, *m.* striking, stumbling; shock, impulsion, impulse; stammering; offence; Stein des Anſtoßes, stumbling-block. **Anſtoßen,** ån'zhtōsen (-ſtieß, -geſtoßen), to strike, push against; to land; to border, confine; to offend, shock, give offence, to hesitate; mit der Zunge —, to lisp, stammer. **Anſtoßend,** *a.* adjacent, contiguous. **Anſtößig,** ån'zhtōshich, *a.* offensive, objectionable, scandalous, *av.* -ly; -igkeit, -ichkået, *f.* offensiveness.

Anſtreben, ån'zhtrāben, *vi.* to strive against.

Anſtreichen, ånzhtrēichen (-ſtrich, -geſtrichen), *vt.* to mark, point; to note.

Anſtreifen, ån'zhtrāēfen, *vi.* to graze, touch.

Anſtrengen, ån'zhtręng-en, *vt.* to stretch, strain, exert; *vr.* to stretch, exert one's self. **Anſtrengung,** *f.* straining, effort, exertion.

Anſtrich, ån'zhtrich, *m.* coating, painting, color, varnish, tincture, smack, smattering; touch, dash; trace (of a deer).

Anſtricken, ån'zhtricken, *vt.* to join by knitting; Strümpfe —, to foot stockings.

Anſtücken, ån'zhtücken, *vt.* to piece, patch.

Anſtürmen, ån'zhtürmen, *vi.* to storm, rush against.

Anſtützen, ån'zhtütsen, *vt.* to rest against, prop.

Anſuchen, ån'sųchen, *vi.* to apply, petition, solicit; *n.* petition; auf Anſuchen, at the request.

Antaſten, ån'tazhten, *vt.* to touch; to encroach upon.

Antheil, ån'tåel, *m.* portion, part, share; — nehmen, to participate in; to sympathize with.

Anthun, ån'tųn (-that, -gethan), *vt.* to put on; to hurt, to inflict, *v.* do; ſich den Tod —, to kill one's self; Hand —, to make for, to touch at.

Antichriſt, an'tikrizht, *m.* antichrist.

Antilope, an'tiloppę, *f.* antelope.

Antimon, antimōn', *n.* antimony. **Antimon'glanz,** -glants, *m.* ore of antimony. **Antimon'ige Säure,** *f.* antimonious acid. **Antimonium,** antimō'nium, *n.* antimony. **Antimon'ſaures Salz,** *n.* antimoniate. **Antimon'ſilber,** *n.* antimonial silver.

Antik, an'tīk, *a.* ancient, antique, old. **Antiquar,** antiquår', *m.* antiquary, antiquarian. **Antiquitäten,** -tä'ten, *s. pl.* antiquities.

Antlitz, ån'tlits, *n.* face, countenance.

Antrag, ån'trāg, *m.* offer, proposal, proposition. **Antragen,** ån'trāgen, *vt.* to propose, offer, motion, to move.

Antrauen, ån'trou-en, *vt.* to marry, join in marriage.

Antreffen, ån'treffen (-traf, -getroffen), *vt.* to find, meet with.

Antreiben, ån'trēiben, *vt.* to drive, impel, incite; e. Reif —, to drive a hoop; die Planken —, to wring the planks (Mar.); to begin to refine (Min.); *vi.* to approach in driving, to drive against.

Antreten, ån'trēten (-trat, -getreten), to tread on; to enter on.

Antrieb, ån'trīb, *m.* impulse, instigation; natürlicher —, instinct.

Antritt, ån'tritt, *m.* entrance, entering; -predigt, *f.* inaugural sermon.

Antwort, ant'vort, *f.* answer, reply. **Antworten,** *vt.* to answer.

Anvertrauen, ån'fertrou-en, *vt.* to intrust, to confide to.

Anverwandt, ån'fervant, *a.* related to; -er, *m.* -e, *f.* relation, kinsman, kinswoman; -ſchaft, *f.* relationship; relatives, kindred.

Anwachs, ån'vax, *m.* increase, increment. **Anwachſen,** ån'vaxen (-wuchs, -gewachſen), *n.* to grow to;

to grow up, rise, swell, increase. Ḁn'gewachſen, a. adnate.
Anwalt, ån'valt, m. attorney. advocate, agent; -ſchaft, f. attorneyship. agency.
Anwandeln, ån'vandeln, vt. to befall, come over; to be the matter with. Anwandelung, ån'vandelung, f. fit, paroxysm.
Anwartſchaft, ån'vartshaft, f. expectancy, reversion.
Anwehen, ån'vā-en, vt. to blow upon, to seize, to fall on.
Anweiſen, ån'vēlsen (-wieſ, -gewieſen), vt. to assign, appoint, advise; refer. Anweiſung, f. order, assignment; check, draft, bill of exchange; direction, advice.
Anweißen, ån'vēlssen, vt. to whitewash.
Anwendbar, ån'ventbår, a. applicable; -keit, f. applicability. Anwenden, ån'venden, vt. to apply, accommodate, to turn, employ, use. Anwendung, f. application.
Anwerben, ån'vērben, vt. to raise, engage, enlist, levy, enroll. Anwerbung, f. levy, enlisting.
Anweſend, ån'vāsent, a. present. Anweſenheit, f. presence.
Anwidern, ån'vīdern, vt. to disgust.
Anwohnen, ån'vōnen, vi. to dwell near, live near; to be present at. Anwohner, m. confinee, one living near.
Anwuchs, ån'vux, m. increase, growth.
Anwünſchen, ån'vūnshen, vt. Böſes —, to imprecate. Anwünſchung, -ung, f. imprecation.
Anwurf, ån'vurf, m. rough-casting; deposit; first throw at dice or ninepins; the lead.
Anwurzeln, ån'vurtseln, vi. to take root.
Anzahl, f. ån'tsāl, f. number.
Anzapfen, ån'tsapfen, vt. to tap, broach.
Anzeichen, ån'tsēichen, n. sign, presage, omen. Anzeichnen, vt. to mark, note. Anzeichnung, f. marking.
Anzeige, ån'tsēige, f. information, advertisement. Anzeigen, vt. to advertise, announce, notify; anzeigendes Fürwort, demonstrative pronoun. Anzeiger, ån'tsēiger, m. advertiser, intelligencer.
Anzetteln, ån'tsetteln, vt. to warp;

— eine Verſchwörung, to plot, conspire. Anzettelung, f. plotting. Anzettelter, ån'tsettler, m. author, contriver (of a plot).
Anziehen, ån'tsī-en (-zog, -gezogen), vt. to draw on, put on; to attract; to stretch, strain; vi. to draw; to take; to attract. Anziehend, a. attracting, interesting. Anziehung, ån'tsīung, f. attraction; -kraft, f. attraction, attractive power. Anzug, ån'tsūk, m. approach; dress. Anzüglich, ån'tsūhglich, a. personal, offensive, insulting; -keit, -kået, f. offensiveness.
Anzünden, ån'tsünden, vt. to set on fire; to light, kindle.
Aeolsharfe, ā'olsharfe, f. Æolian harp.
Apfel, ap'fel, m. apple; -baum, -baūm, m. apple-tree; -kuchen, -kychen, m. apple-pie; -muß, mŭs, n. apple-butter; -ſäure, -sŏŭre, f. malic acid; -ſchale, -shāle, f. apple-peeling; -ſine, -sīne, f. China orange; -wein, -vēin, m. cider.
Apologie, apologī', f. defence, apology.
Apoſtel, apozh'tel, m. apostle; -amt, n. apostleship; -geſchichte, f. Acts (of the apostles). Apoſtoliſch, apozhtō'lish, a. apostolic.
Apotheke, apotā'ke, f. apothecary's shop. Apotheker, m. apothecary; -gewicht, n. apothecaries'-weight; -kunſt, f. pharmacy; -waaren, -vāren, s. pl. drugs.
Apparat, apparāt', m. apparatus.
Appellation, appellatsiōn', f. appeal; -gericht, n. court of appeals. Appelliren, appelli'ren, vi. to appeal.
Appetit, appetīt', m. appetite; hunger; -lich, a. appetizing, inviting, tempting; neat.
Apriſose, ap'rĭcōse, f. apricot.
April, aprīl', m. April; -narr, m. April fool.
Aequator, äquā'tor, m. equator.
Aequivalent, äquiſalent', n. equivalent.
Arabeſke, arabés'ke, f. arabesque.
Aragonſpath, ar'agonzhpåt, m. needlespar, aragonite.
Arbeit, ar'bået, f. labor, toil, work, task. Arbeiten, vi. to work, labor, toil. Arbeiter, ar'bæter, m. workman, worker, laborer; -in, f. work-

woman. **Arbeit**, ar'bāetlōs, a. unemployed. **Ar'beitsam**, a. diligent, industrious, av. -ly, busy, ar. -ily; -keit, f. diligence, industry. **Arbeits-haus**, -hous, n. workhouse. **Ar'beits-loch**, n. man-hole, working-hole. **Ar'beitslohn**, m. wages, hire. **Ar'beitstube**, -zhtybe, f. workshop; study. **Ar'beitstisch**, m. work-table.

Arche, ar'che, f. ark.

Architekt, architēkt', m. architect.

Archiv, archīf', n. archives. **Archivar**, archivär', m. recorder; keeper of the archives.

Arg, ark, a. bad, wicked, mischievous. **Aerger**, er'ger, m. anger, chagrin, vexation; -lich, a. vexatious: irritable; angry; -lichkeit, -lichkāet, f. voxatiousness. **Aergern**, er'gern, vt. to vex, fret, irritate, make angry: to give offence. **Aergerniss**, er'gērniss, n. offence, anger; scandal. **Arglist**, ark'lizht, f. craft, cunning, maliciousness; -ig, a. crafty, cunning; -igkeit, -ichkāet, f. craftiness. **Arglos**, ark'lōs, a. harmless, innocent. **Arg'losigkeit**, f. harmlessness, innocence. **Argwohn**, ark'vōn, m. suspicion. **Argwöhnen**, ark'-vöhnen, vt. to suspect, distrust. **Arg'-wöhnisch**, a. suspicious, distrustful; av. -ly.

Arie, ä'ri-e, f. aria, air, tune, song.

Aristokrat, arizhtokrät', m. aristocrat; -ie, arizhtokratī', f. aristocracy. **Aristokratisch**, a. aristocratic.

Arithmetik, arithmet'ik, f. arithmetic.

Arkade, arkä'de, f. arcade.

Arm, arm. a. poor.

Arm, arm, m. pl. **Aerme**, arm; branch; -band, -bant, n. bracelet; -binde, f. sling; -bruch, m. fracture of the arm; -brust, -bryzht, m. crossbow. **Aermchen**, ěrm'chen, n. little

Armee, armā', f. army. [arm.

Aermel, er'měl, m. sleeve.

Armenanstalt, ar'menänzhtalt, f. institution for the relief of the poor. **Ar'menhaus**, -hous, n. poor-house. **Ar'menpfleger**, -pflāger, m. almoner, overseer of the poor.

Armfeile, arm'fēile, f. rubber, coarse file.

Armiren, armī'ren, vt. to arm, equip.

Armleuchter, arm'lēuchter, m. chandelier.

Armlich, ěrm'lich, a. poor, av. -ly,

scauty, needy, av. -ily; -keit, f. poverty; meanness; littleness. **Armselig**, arm'sālich, a. poor, needy, beggarly; -keit, f. poorness, wretchedness.

Armsessel, arm'sēssel, m. arm-chair.

Armspange, -zhpang-e, f. bracelet.

Aroma, arō'mā, n. aroma. **Aromatisch**, aromat'ish, a. aromatic, -al.

Arrack, ar'rak, m. arrack.

Arrest, arrēzht', m. arrest, seizure, imprisonment. **Arretiren**, arretī'ren, vt. to arrest.

Arsch, ärsh, m. arse, buttocks, posteriors.

Arsenal, arsenäl', n. arsenal.

Arsenik, arsen'ik, m. arsenic; -kies, -kīs, m. arsenical pyrites.

Art, ärt, f. species, sort, kind, breed, stock, race; nature, way; manner; form, frame, cast, cut.

Artesisch, artā'sish, a. artesian.

Artig, är'tich, a. neat, pretty, nice, av. -ly; agreeable, pleasant, pleasing; well-bred, genteel, civil, polite; av. -ly; -keit, f. neatness, agreeableness; genteelness, civility, politeness.

Artikel, artik'el, m. article. **Artikulation**, artikulatsiōn', f. articulation. **Artikuliren**, artikulī'ren, vt. to articulate.

Artillerie, artillěrī', f. artillery. **Artilleriest**, artillērizht', m. artillerist; gunner.

Artischoke, artishok'e, f. artichoke.

Arzenei, artsenāī', f. medicine; -kunde, kynde, f. pharmacology; -kunst, f. physic, medicine. medical science. **Arzenei'lich**, a. medicinal. **Arzenei'mittel**, n. remedy, medicine. **Arzenei'lehre**, -lāre, s. -kunde, kynde, f. medical science. **Arzt**, artst, m. physician, doctor. **Aerztlich**, ärtst'lich, a. medical.

Asbest, asbēzht', m. asbestus, asbestos.

Asche, ash'e, f. ashes. **Asch'biei**, -blāī, n. bismuth. **Aschermittwoch**, m. Ash-Wednesday. **Asch'grau**, -grāu, a. ashy, ash-colored. **Aschig**, ash'ich a. ashy, full of ashes. **Asch'laug**, -lāūch, m. shallot, scallion. **Asch'-salz**, -salts, n. alkali.

Aspe = **Espe**.

Ass, ass, pl. **Asse**, n. ace.

Assecuranz, assekyrants', f. insurance.

Assecurator, assekyrā'tor, m. insurer

Affe   33   **Auf**

Afsecuriren, assekurī'ren, vt. to insure.
Assigniren, assignī'ren, vt. to assign.
Assistent, assizhtert', m. assistant.
Ast, azht, m. (pl. Äste), bough, branch; knot. Ästchen, ezht'ch'en, n. twig, sprig.
Aster, azh'ter, f. aster, starwort.
Aesthetik, estet'ik, f. æsthetics.
Ästig, ezht'ich, a. branchy; knotty.
Astrolog, azhtrolōg', m. astrologer.
Astrologie, azhtrologī', f. astrology.
Astronom, azhtronōm', m. astronomer. Astronomie, -nomī', f. astronomy. Astronomisch, astronomical.
Asyl, asīl', n. asylum.
Atheismus, ate-is'muss, m. atheism.
Atheist, atāizht', m. atheist; infidel.
Athem, ā'tem, m. breath. A'themlos, -lōs, a. breathless. Athemzug, ā'temtsyk, m. breathing, respiration.
Aether, ā'ter, m. ether. Ae'therjäure, -säūre, f. lampic acid. Ae'therjaures Salz, n. lampiate. Aetherisch, ātā'rish, a. ethereal.
Athlet, atlāt', m. pl. -en, athlete; -isch, a. athletic.
Athmen, āt'men, vi. to breathe.
Atlas, at'lass, pl. -e, m. atlas.
Atlas, at'lass, m. satin.
Atmosphäre, atmosfā-re, f. atmosphere.
Atom, atōm', n. atom; -isch, a. atomic.
Attich, at'tich, m. dane-wort, dwarf elder.
Attribut, attribyt', n. attribute.
Atzel, at'sel, f. [. Elster.
Atzen (ätzen), ät'sen, vt. to feed, bait; to corrode, etch, macerate. Aetzung, äts'ung, f. baiting; etching.
Auch, ūch, av. also; wenn —, even if.
Auction, ōuktsiōn', f. auction.
Audienz, ōudi-ens', f. audience.
Aue, āu'-e, f. green, meadow, pasture.
Auerhahn, ōu'erhān, m. woodcock; mountain-cock. Au'erhenne, -henne, f. mountain-hen. Auerochs, ōu'er-ox. m. pl. -en, ure-ox, aurochs.
Auf, ōuf, prep. up, upon, on, in, into.
Aufackern, ōuf'ackern, vt. to plough up.
Aufarbeiten, ōuf'arbāeten, vt. to finish.
Aufbauen, ōuf'bōy-en, vt. to build up.
Aufbäumen, ōuf'bēumen, n. beaming (Mar.).   [to be up.
Aufbefinden, ōuf'befinden, sich —, rr.
Aufbehalten, ōuf'behalten (-hielt, -halten), vt. to keep on; to keep up.

Aufbeißen, ōuf'bāsßen (-biß, -gebissen) vt. to open by biting.
Aufbersten, ōuf'bērzhten (-borst, -geborsten), vi. to burst, crack.
Aufbewahren, ōuf'bevāren, vt. to keep, save, preserve.
Aufbiegen, ōuf'bīgen (-bog, -gebogen), vt. to bend upwards.
Aufbieten, ōuf'bīten (-bot, -geboten), vt. to call up, raise, summon; to proclaim; Alles —, to make every effort, to strain every nerve.
Aufbinden, ōuf'binden (-band, -gebunden), vt. to tie up; to unbind; einem etwas —, to hoax, to impose upon.
Aufblähen, ōuf'blā-en, vt. to puff up, inflate; to swell.
Aufblasen, ōuf'blāsen (-blies, -geblasen), vt. to blow up, inflate.
Aufblättern, ōuf'blettern, vt. to open the leaves.
Aufbleiben, ōuf'blāiben (-blieb, -geblieben), vi. to stay up, sit up; to remain open.
Aufblicken, ōuf'blicken, vi. to look up.
Aufblitzen, ōuf'blitsen, vi. to flash up.
Aufblühen, ōuf'blüh-en, vi. to blossom, bloom, flourish, rise.
Aufbrauchen, ōuf'brōychen, vt. to consume, spend, use up.
Aufbrausen, ōuf'brōysen, vi. to bubble, effervesce; to get into a passion; -d, a. fretful, passionate.
Aufbrechen, ōuf'brechen (-brach, -gebrochen), vt. to break open, to break up; to bud open; to rise, depart.
Aufbrennen, ōuf'brennen (-brannte, -gebrannt), vt. to burn in; to brand, mark; to strike.
Aufbringen, ōuf'bringen, (-brachte, -gebracht), vt. to bring up, to raise; to irritate; ein Schiff —, to bring in a prize.
Aufbruch, ōuf'bruch, m. breaking up; departure, setting out; decampment; opening, evisceration.
Aufbucht, ōuf'bucht, f. rounding-up.
Aufbürden, ōuf'bürden, v.. to burden, impose, charge; n. the charge.
Aufdämmen, ōuf'demmen, vt. to dam up, shut in.
Aufdämmern, ōuf'demmern, vi. to dawn.
Aufdecken, ōuf'decken, vt. to uncover; spread; to discover.

Auf 34 **Auf**

Aufbinden, ŏŭf'ding-en, *vt.* to bind (to a master).

Aufdrängen, ŏŭf'dreng-en, *vr.* sich —, to intrude.

Aufdrehen, ŏŭf'drā-en, *vt.* to screw; to unscrew; untwist.

Aufdringen, ŏŭf'dring-en, *vt.* to press, force upon. **Aufdringlich,** *a.* importunate; -keit, -kāet, *f.* importunity.

Aufdrucken, ŏŭf'drŭcken, *vt.* to impress, imprint.

Aufdrücken, ŏŭf'drücken, *vt.* to crack open, press open.

Aufdunsen, ŏŭf'dŭnsen, *vt.* to swell, bloat. **Aufgedunsen,** ŏŭf'gedŭnsen, *a.* bloated, turgid.

Aufenthalt, ŏŭf'ent-halt, *m.* abode, residence, stay; delay, hindrance; demurrage (Mar.). **Aufenthaltsort,** ŏŭf'ent-haltsort, *m.* (place of) abode, residence.

Auferlegen, ŏŭf'ĕrlāgen, *vt.* to impose.

Auferstehen, ŏŭf'ĕrshtā-en, *pp.* arisen. **Auferstehen,** ŏŭf'ĕrshtā-en (-stand, -standen), to rise up; to rise from the dead. **Auferstehung,** ŏŭf'ĕrshtā-ŭng, *f.* resurrection.

Auferwecken, ŏŭf'ĕrvecken, *vt.* to raise from the dead, to resuscitate. **Auferweckung,** -ŭng, *f.* resuscitation.

Auferziehen, ŏŭf'ĕrtsī-en (-zog, -zogen), *vt.* to bring up.

Aufessen, ŏŭf'essen (-aß, -gegessen), *vt.* to eat up.

Auffahren, ŏŭf'fāren (-fuhr, -gefahren), to start, spring up; to fly into a passion; to run upon (Mar.); to mount (from a pit); *vt.* to cut up (roads); to fill up, raise; -b, *a.* irritable, passionate. **Auffahrt,** ŏŭf'fart, *f.* ascent; driving upwards, ascension.

Auffallen, ŏŭf'fallen (-fiel, -gefallen), *vt.* to fall upon, to strike open (by falling), to wound; to strike. **Auffallend,** striking, conspicuous.

Auffangen, ŏŭf'fang-en (-fieng, -gefangen), *vt.* to catch; to intercept.

Auffassen, ŏŭf'fassen, *vt.* to take up, receive, conceive, comprehend. **Auffassung,** -ŭng, *f.* comprehension.

Auffinden, ŏŭf'finden (-fand, -gefunden), *vt.* to find out.

Aufflammen, ŏŭf'flammen, *vi.* to flame, blaze.

Aufflechten, ŏŭf'flechten (-flocht, -geflochten), *vt.* to untwine.

Aufflicken, ŏŭf'flicken, *vt.* to patch on.

Auffliegen, ŏŭf'flīgen (-flog, -geflogen), *vt.* to fly up, soar; to fly open. **Aufflug,** ŏŭf'flūg, *m.* soaring, flight.

Auffordern, ŏŭf'fordern, *vt.* to summon. **Aufforderung,** -ŭng, *f.* summons, challenge; invitation.

Auffressen, ŏŭf'fressen (-fraß, -gefressen), *vt.* to eat up.

Auffrischen, ŏŭf'frishen, *vt.* to refresh, rub up; encourage; animate. **Auffrischung,** -ŭng, *f.* refreshment.

Aufführen, ŏŭf'führen, *vt.* to raise, erect, build; to exhibit, to show, to perform; to post (a sentry); sich —, to behave. **Aufführung,** -ŭng, *f.* building; performance; posting (a sentry); mounting (a gun); conduct, behavior.

Auffüllen, ŏŭf'füllen, *vt.* to fill up.

Aufgabe, ŏŭf'gābe, *f.* delivering; putting; advice; task, theme; lesson; problem.

Aufgabeln, ŏŭf'gābeln, *vt.* to fork up; to pick up; to find.

Aufgang, ŏŭf'gang, *m.* rising, ascending; ascent: — der Sonne, sunrise, east. **Aufgangspunkt,** ŏŭf'gangspŭnkt, *m.* rising-point, orient.

Aufgeben, ŏŭf'gāben (-gab, -gegeben), *vt.* to hand up, deliver; to give up, drop; to lay on, impose, set; den Geist —, to expire, die; einem Räthsel —, to put forth, propose.

Aufgeblasen, ŏŭf'gebläsen, *a.* inflated, puffed up, haughty; -heit, -hāet, *f.* inflation; haughtiness.

Aufgebot, ŏŭf'gebōt, *n.* levy, ban, bans.

Aufgebracht, ŏŭf'gebracht, *a.* incensed, angry.

Aufgehen, ŏŭf'gā-en (-ging, -gegangen), *vt.* to go up, rise; open, dissolve; expand; to be spent; to go on, fit.

Aufgeklärt, ŏŭf'geklärt, *a.* enlightened; -heit, -hāet, *f.* enlightenment.

Aufgeld, ŏŭf'gĕlt, *n.* agio, exchange; hand-money.

Aufgelegt, ŏŭf'gelĕkt, *a.* disposed to.

Aufgeräumt, ŏŭf'gerăumt, *a.* put in order; good-humored; cheerful, merry; -heit, -hāet, *f.* good humor; cheerfulness.

Aufgeweckt, ŏŭf'gevĕckt, *a.* brisk, lively, sprightly, gay, jovial; -heit, -hāet, *f.* sprightliness.

Auf   35   **Auf**

Aufgießen, ŏŭf'gēsen (-goß, -gegossen), *vt.* to affuse, infuse, pour upon.
Aufgraben, ŏŭf'grāben (-grub, -gegraben), *vt.* to dig up.
Aufgreifen, ŏŭf'greĭfen (-griff, -gegriffen), *vt.* to seize, pick up.
Aufgürten, ŏŭf'gürten, *vt.* to gird up; to ungird.
Aufguß, ŏŭf'guss, *m.* affusion, pouring upon.
Aufhaben, ŏŭf'hāben, *vt.* to have on.
Aufhacken, ŏŭf'hacken, *vt.* to hoe.
Aufhäkeln, ŏŭf'hākĕln, *vt.* to unclasp.
Aufhaken, ŏŭf'haken, *vt.* to unhook, hang up.
Aufhalten, ŏŭf'halten (-hielt, -gehalten), *vt.* to hold up; to stop; restrain, delay, detain; to hold open; fich —, to live, dwell, remain; über etwas —, to find fault with. **Auf'halter,** *m.* breeching (of horses); relieving tackle (Mar.). **Aufhaltfette, -kette,** *f.* breeching-chain. **Auf'haltring, -ring,** *m.* breechingring. **Aufhaltung, -ung,** *f.* detention.
Aufhängen, ŏŭf'hĕng-en, *vt.* to hang up, suspend.
Aufhaspeln, ŏŭf'haxhpeln, *vt.* to reel; fich wieder —, to recover slowly.
Aufhauen, ŏŭf'haü-en, *vt.* to hew, cut, knock open.
Aufhäufen, ŏŭf'höüfen, *vt.* to heap up, pile up, accumulate. **Aufhäufung,** ŏŭf'höüfung, *f.* accumulation.
Aufheben, ŏŭf'hāben (-hob, -gehoben), *vt.* to raise, lift, take up; to keep, reserve, reposit; break up; abolish; *s. n.* lifting up; making much ado. **Aufhebung, -ung,** *f.* raising up, abolition.
Aufheften, ŏŭf'heften, *vt.* to pin up; to fix.
Aufheitern, ŏŭf'hĕĭtern, *vt.* to clear up; to cheer. **Aufheiterung, -ung,** *f.* clearing, cheering.
Aufhelfen, ŏŭf'helfen (-half, -geholfen), *vt.* to help, succor.
Aufhellen, ŏŭf'hèllen, *vt.* to clear up, to develop.
Aufhenken, ŏŭf'henken, *vt.* to hang up.
Aufhetzen, ŏŭf'hetzen, *vt.* to hunt up, to start, rouse; to instigate, incite. **Auf'hetzer,** *m.* instigator.
Aufholen, ŏŭf'hōlen, *vt.* to draw in, to pull up; to hoist up: ein Schiff —, to bring a ship to the wind. **Auf'holer,** *m.* relieving-tackle.

Aufhorchen, ŏŭf'horchen, *vi.* to listen.
Aufhören, ŏŭf'bŏhren, *vi.* to cease, leave off; to listen.
Aufjagen, ŏŭf'yāgen, *vt.* to hunt up, to rouse.
Aufjauchzen, ŏŭf'yŏŭchzen, *vi.* to shout, to exult.
Aufkaufen, ŏŭf'kaüfen, *vt.* to buy up, engross. **Auf'kauf,** *m.* buying up, engrossing. **Aufkäufer,** ŏŭf'käüfer, *m.* engrosser, forestaller.
Aufkeimen, ŏŭf'kĕĭmen, *vi.* to sprout, germinate; to spring or come up.
Aufketzern, ŏŭf'ketsern, *vt.* to cleave with wedges.
Aufkippen, ŏŭf'kippen, *vt.* to tilt.
Aufklaffen, ŏŭf'klaffen, *vi.* to gape, to get a rent.
Aufklaftern, ŏŭf'klaftern, *vt.* to pile up.
Aufklappen, ŏŭf'klappen, *vt.* to cock (the hat).
Aufklären, ŏŭf'klāren, *vt.* to clear up, explain, illuminate, enlighten; fich —, to clear up. **Aufklärer,** ŏŭf'klārĕr, *m.* enlightener. **Aufklärung, -ung,** *f.* enlightening, illumination.
Aufklauben, ŏŭf'klŏŭben, *vt.* to pick up, grub up.
Aufkleben, ŏŭf'klāben, *vt.* to stick to; to paste on.
Aufkleistern, ŏŭf'klĕĭxhtern, *vt.* to paste on.
Aufklettern, ŏŭf'klĕttern, **Aufklimmen,** ŏŭf'klimmen, *vi.* to climb up.
Aufklinken, ŏŭf'klinken, *vt.* to unlatch.
Aufklopfen, ŏŭf'klopfen, *vt.* to knock open; to beat against.
Aufklotzen, ŏŭf'klotsen (*n.*) der Weizen, pudding-style. [open.
Aufknacken, ŏŭf'knacken, *vt.* to crack
Aufknöpfen, ŏŭf'knöpfen, *vt.* to unbutton.
Aufknüpfen, ŏŭf'knüpfen, *vt.* to tie up; to hang; to untie, unknot.
Aufkochen, ŏŭf'kochen, *vt.* to boil up.
Aufkommen, ŏŭf'kommen (-kam, -gekommen), *vi.* to get up, rise; to thrive; recover; to gain ground, spring up. **Aufkömmling,** ŏŭf'kömling, *m.* upstart, parvenu.
Aufköpfen, ŏŭf'köpfen, *vt.* to head (needles).
Aufkrämpen, ŏŭf'krempen, *vt.* to cock (a hat).
Aufkratzen, ŏŭf'kratsen, *vt.* to scratch open.

Auf 36 **Auf**

Auffriegen, auf'krīgen, *vt.* to get open; to get (as a task).
Auffündigen, auf'kündiģen, *vt.* to warn, renounce, break. **Auffündigung,** -ung, *f.* warning, dismission.
Auflachen, auf'lachen, *vt.* to laugh out.
Auflachen, auf'lachen, *vt.* to tap; to make an incision.
Aufladen, auf'laden (-lub, -geladen), *vt.* to load, burden, charge. **Auflader,** *m.* lader, packer.
Auflage, auf'lāge, *f.* edition, impression; tax, duty, impost.
Auflanger, auf'lang-er, *m.* futtock (Mar.).
Auflassen, auf'lassen (-ließ, -gelassen), *vt.* to leave on; to leave open.
Auflauern, auf'lou-ern, *vi.* to watch for, to lie in ambush, waylay. **Auflauerer,** *m.* waylayer, lurker, spy.
Auflauf, auf'lāuf, *m.* uproar, riot; puff-paste. **Auflaufen** (-lief, -gelaufen), *vi.* to run upwards; to swell, increase; to run on; to make sore by running. **Aufläufer,** auf'läufer, *m.* smelter; sailor-boy.
Aufleben, auf'lāben, *vi.* to revive; *vt.* to refresh (a painting).
Auflecken, auf'lecken, *vt.* to lick up.
Auflegen, auf'lägen, *vt.* to lay upon, put on; impose; apply; to reprint; lay up, store up; dismantle a ship; aufgelegt sein, to be disposed.
Auflehnen, auf'lānen, *vt.* to lean on; to rear; *vt.* to rebel, mutiny.
Aufleimen, auf'lāmen, *vt.* to glue upon.
Auflesen, auf'lāsen (-las, -gelesen), *vt.* to pick up, glean, gather.
Aufliegen, auf'līgen (-lag, -gelegen), *vi.* to lie, rest upon; to be incumbent on; *vr.* sich —, to lie one's self sore.
Auflockern, auf'lockern, *vt.* to loosen.
Auflodern, auf'lodern, *vi.* to blaze up.
Auflösbar, auf'löhsbār, *a.* dissolvable, dissoluble; -keit, käet, *f.* dissolvability. **Auflösen,** auf'löhsen, *vt.* to loose, loosen, untie, unfix; to dissolve, resolve, decompose. **Auflösung,** auf'löhsung, *f.* solution, dissolution.
Aufmachen, auf'machen, *vt.* to open; uncork; crack, unseal; undo (a knot); sich —, to set out.

Aufmarschiren, auf'marshīren, *vi.* to march up.
Aufmerken, auf'merken, *vt.* to attend; note down. **Aufmerksam,** auf'merksam, *a.* attentive; -keit, käet, *f.* attention.
Aufmuntern, auf'muntern, *vt.* to rouse, cheer, stir up, encourage, incite. **Aufmunterung,** -ung, *f.* encouragement.
Aufmutzen, auf'mutzen, *vt.* to upbraid; throw up to.
Aufnageln, auf'nāgeln, *vt.* to nail on.
Aufnähen, auf'nā-en, *vt.* to sew on.
Aufnahme, auf'nāme, *f.* reception, admission, admittance; — an Kindes statt, adoption. **Aufnehmen,** auf'nāmen (-nahm, -genommen), *vt.* to take up, receive, admit; absorb; sketch; wieder —, to resume; übel — to take ill; es — mit, to cope with.
Aufnieten, auf'nīten, *vt.* to rivet on.
Aufnöthigen, auf'nöhtigen, *vt.* to press, force upon.
Aufnotiren, auf'notīren, *vt.* to note down, put down.
Aufopfern, auf'opfern, *vt.* to sacrifice. **Aufopferung,** -ung, *f.* sacrifice, devotion.
Aufpacken, auf'packen, *vt.* to pack upon; to pick up; to make off with; to unpack.
Aufpassen, auf'passen, *vt.* to fit on; to attend, watch. **Aufpasser,** auf'passer, *m.* spy.
Aufpflanzen, auf'pflanzen, *vt.* to plant, set up; place, mount. (up.
Aufpflügen, auf'pflūgen, *vt.* to plow
Aufpicken, auf'picken, *vt.* to pick up.
Aufplatzen, auf'platzen, *vt.* to burst open, to fly open.
Aufprägen, auf'prägen, *vt.* to stamp on.
Aufprallen, auf'prallen, *vt.* to bounce, rebound against.
Aufprobiren, auf'probīren, *vt.* to try on.
Aufprotzen, auf'protzen, to limber up.
Aufputzen, auf'putzen, *vt.* to trim, adorn.
Aufquellen, auf'quellen (-quoll, -gequollen), *vi.* to spring up, to well.
Aufraffen, auf'raffen, *vt.* to snatch up; sich —, to get up, rise, recover.
Aufräumen, auf'räumen, *vt.* to clear up, put away; to set in order; to empty, plunder; to thin out.
Aufrechnen, auf'rechnen, *vt.* to cast up, count up.

Aufrecht, óyf'rĕcht, a. upright, erect; — halten, to maintain, keep up, sustain; -haltung, -hàltung, f. support.

Aufregen, óyf'rägen, vt. to rouse, excite, stir up. **Aufregung**, -ung, f. excitement.

Aufreiben, óyf'rīben (-rieb, -gerieben), vt. to rub on; to destroy, to carry off, to kill.

Aufreihen, óyf'rīh-en, vt. to string.

Aufreißen, óyf'rīsen (-riß, -gerissen), vt. to rend, to tear open; throw open; to draw, sketch; to tear (cloth); sich —, to rouse one's self.

Aufreizen, óyf'rītsen, vt. to rouse, irritate, excite.

Aufrennen, óyf'rennen (-rannte, -gerannt), vt. to run against.

Aufrichten, óyf'richten, vt. to raise, erect, to set upright. **Aufrichtig**, óyf'richtig, a. candid, sincere; -keit, -kkàt, f. sincerity.

Aufriegeln, óyf'rīgeln, vt. to unbolt.

Aufritzen, óyf'ritsen, vt. to slit, scratch open.

Aufrollen, óyf'rollen, vt. to roll up.

Aufrücken, óyf'rücken, vt. to march up, move up; to upbraid for.

Aufruf, óyf'ruf, m. appeal, proclamation. **Aufrufen**, óyf'rufen, vt. to call up, appeal, summon.

Aufruhr, óyf'rur, m. uproar, riot. **Aufrühren**, óyf'rühren, vt. to stir up, raise up; wieder —, to revive. **Aufrührer**, m. rioter, insurgent, rebel; -isch, -ish, a. rebellious, riotous, mutinous. [up.

Aufrütteln, óyf'rütteln, vt. to shake

Aufsagen, óyf'sägen, vt. to recite; to renounce; to give warning, notice.

Aufsammeln, óyf'sammeln, vt. to gather, pick up.

Aufsatteln, óyf'satteln, vt. to saddle.

Aufsatz, óyf'sats, m. set, mess, course; essay, treatise, composition, memoir.

Aufsässig, óyf'sĕtsich, a. adverse, hostile, inimical.

Aufsaugen, óyf'sŏygen, vt. to suck up.

Aufscharren, óyf'sharren, vt. to scrape up.

Aufschauen, óyf'skāū-en, vi. to look up.

Aufschäumen, óyf'shŏymen, vi. to effervesce, foam.

Aufscheuchen, óyf'shŏycħen, vt. to scare up.

Aufscheuern, óyf'shŏyern, vt. to scour.

Aufschichten, óyf'shichten, vt. to pile up.

Aufschieben, óyf'shīben (-schob, -geschoben), vt. to shove open; to defer, delay, put off, procrastinate, suspend, adjourn; aufgeschoben ist nicht aufgehoben, omittance is no quittance.

Aufschießen, óyf'shīssen (-schoß, -geschossen), vt. to shoot up; das Ankertau —, to coil the cable.

Aufschlag, óyf'shläg, m. striking upon, turning up; facing, cuff; increase (of price); young growth; arsis (Mus.). **Aufschlagen**, óyf'shlägen (-schlug, -geschlagen), vt. to strike upwards; to turn up; to set up, pitch; to put up (a booth); to knock up (the balls in Print.); to break open; to open; to rise, advance (in price); to untwist (a rope). **Aufschlagebrett**, óyf'shlägebrett, n. sleeve-board; -schaufel, shŏyfel, f. float-board, ladle-board, ladle; -tisch, m. folding-table.

Aufschließen, óyf'shlīssen (-schloß, -geschlossen), vt. to unlock.

Aufschlitzen, óyf'shlītsen, vt. to rip, rip up, slit.

Aufschluß, óyf'shluss, m. opening, explanation.

Aufschmieren, óyf'shmīren, vt. to smear upon.

Aufschnallen, óyf'shnallen, vt. to unbuckle; to buckle on.

Aufschnappen, óyf'shnappen, vt. to snap up, catch.

Aufschneiden, óyf'shnīden (-schnitt, -geschnitten), vt. to cut up, cut open; to stretch, exaggerate; to brag, boast. **Aufschneider**, m. braggart, boaster; exaggerator; -ei, f. exaggeration, boasting, rodomontade.

Aufschnitt, óyf'shnitt, m. slit, opening, cutting open.

Aufschnüren, óyf'shnühren, vt. to unlace; to tie on.

Aufschobern, óyf'shōbern, vt. to stack up, pile up.

Aufschöpfen, óyf'shöpfen, vt. to scoop up, dip up.

Aufschößling, óyf'shössling, m. sprig; stripling.

Aufschrauben, óyf'shrŏyben, vt. to unscrew; screw on.

Aufschrecken, óyf'shrecken, vt. to frighten up, to startle.

Aufschreiben, ŏŭf'shrīben (-fchrieb, -gefchrieben), *vt.* to write down, note, enter, register.
Aufschreien, ŏŭf'shrēī-en (-fchrie, -gefchrieen), *vi.* to scream, shriek, cry out.
Aufschrift, ŏŭf'shrift, *f.* address, direction, inscription.
Aufschub, ŏŭf'shŭb, *m.* delay, respite.
Aufschüren, ŏŭf'shühren, *vt.* to stir up, poke.
Aufschürzen, ŏŭf'shürtsen, *vt.* to gird up; ein Segel —, to furl; fich —, to tuck up one's clothes. [up.
Aufschütteln, ŏŭf'shütteln, *vt.* to shake
Aufschütten, ŏŭf'shütten, *vt.* to heap up, hoard up, store up.
Aufschwatzen, ŏŭf'shwatsen, *vt.* to talk any one into buying *or* taking.
Aufschwellen, ŏŭf'shvellen (-fchwoll, -gefchwollen), *vi.* to swell, rise, expand; to belly out; *vt.* to swell.
Aufschwingen, ŏŭf'shving-en (-fchwang, -gefchwungen), *vr.* fich —, to soar, mount. **Aufschwung**, ŏŭf'shvŭng, *m.* flight; elevation.
Aufsehen, ŏŭf'sä-en (-fah, -gefehen), *vi.* to look up, to gaze up; *n. s.* das —, sensation, surprise. **Auf'seher**, *m.* overseer, superintendent.
Aufsein, ŏŭf'sēn (-war, -gewefen), *vi.* to be up; to be open.
Aufsetzen, ŏŭf'setsen, *vt.* to put up, set up, stack up; to raise; to put on; to serve up; to write down, compose; den Anker —, to fish the anchor; die Stangen —, to hoist the yards; einem Hörner —, to cuckold any one; eine Rechnung —, to cast up an account; fich —, to sit upright; *vi.* (vom Pferde), to bite the crib; (vom Hirfch), to recover the antlers. **Auf'setzfiunde**, -zhtŭnde, *f.* hour of rest (Min.).
Aufficht, ŏŭf'sicht, *f.* supervision, superintendence; control, care.
Aufsieden, ŏŭf'sīden (-fott, -gefotten), *vt.* to boil up.
Aufsitzen, ŏŭf'sitsen (-faß, -gefeffen), *vi.* to sit up; to perch; to mount, to get on horseback; Einem —, to bear ill-will; fich —, to get sore by sitting. **Auf'fitzftange**, -zhtang-e, *f.* perch.
Aufspalten, ŏŭf'zhpalten, *vt.* to split open, to cleave.
Aufspannen, ŏŭf'zhpannen, *vt.* to stretch, strain, string, bend, extend; to pitch (nets); to set, unfurl (sails); to cock (a gun).
Aufsparen, ŏŭf'zhpären, *vt.* to spare, save, reserve. [store up.
Aufspeichern, ŏŭf'zhpäichern, *vt.* to
Aufsperren, ŏŭf'zhperren, *vt.* to gape, yawn. [perform.
Aufspielen, ŏŭf'zhpīlen, *vt.* to play,
Aufspießen, ŏŭf'zhpīsen, *vt.* to spit, pierce.
Aufsprengen, ŏŭf'zhpreng-en, *vt.* to burst *or* break open; to blow up; to sprinkle; to start (game). **Auf'springen** (-fprang, -gefprungen), *vi.* to fly open, spring open; to cleave, crack; to chap; to start up.
Aufsprossen, ŏŭf'zhprossen, *vi.* to sprout. **Auf'sprößling**, ŏŭf'zhprössling, *m.* sprout, upstart.
Aufsprudeln, ŏŭf'zhprŭdeln, *vi.* to bubble up, boil up; to fly into a passion.
Aufspüren, ŏŭf'zhpühren, *vt.* to track.
Aufstacheln, ŏŭf'zhtacheln, *vt.* to stimulate, goad.
Aufstand, ŏŭf'zhtant, *m.* insurrection, rebellion.
Aufstapeln, ŏŭf'zhtapeln, *vt.* to pile up.
Aufstäuben, ŏŭf'zhtäuben, *vt.* to rouse up, to start.
Aufstechen, ŏŭf'zhtöchen (-ftach, -geftochen), *vt.* to prick *or* cut open; dicht bei dem Winde —, to haul the wind.
Aufstecken, ŏŭf'zhtecken, *vt.* to stick (upon); to pin, truss, put up; to fix; to set, plant.
Aufstehen, ŏŭf'zhtä-en, *vi.* (-ftand, -geftanden), to stand up; rise; to stand open; to rise against.
Aufsteifen, ŏŭf'zhtēīfen, *vt.* to stiffen.
Aufsteigen, ŏŭf'zhtēīgen (-ftieg, -geftiegen), *vi.* to mount, arise, ascend; to spring up; to begin to blow (Mar.).
Aufstellen, ŏŭf'zhtellen, *vt.* to set *or* put up; to lay down.
Aufstören, ŏŭf'zhtören, *vt.* to arouse; to start up; fich —, to form, draw up.
Aufstoßen, ŏŭf'zhtösen (-ftieß, -geftoßen), *vt.* to push op n; to push *or* thrust upward; to stamp, to start up; *vi.* to rise (from the stomach); to melt with; to ground (Mar.).
Aufstreben, ŏŭf'zht.äben, *vi.* to strive upward, soar up; to rise aloft; to aspire (to).

Aufstreifen, ŏŭf'zhtrāifen, *vt.* to turn back *or* up; to fold back; to tuck up; to unstring; to fret, graze; to trail.

Aufstreuen, ŏŭf'zhtröü-en, *vt.* to strew upon.

Aufstutzen, ŏŭf'zhtŭtsen, *vt.* to turn up; to trim. [upon.

Aufstützen, ŏŭf'zhtŭtsen, *vt.* to lean

Aufsuchen, ŏŭf'sŏŏchen, *vt.* to seek or search for.

Auftakeln, ŏŭf'tăkeln, *vt.* to rig.

Aufthauen, ŏŭf'tŏu-en, *vi.* to thaw.

Aufthürmen, ŏŭf'thürmen, *vt.* to tower, pile up.

Auftischen, ŏŭf'tishen, *vt.* to serve up.

Auftrag, ŏŭf'träg, *m.* charge, commission. **Auftragen,** ŏŭf'trägen (-trug, -getragen), *vt.* to carry up; to serve up; to spread; to charge with; Farben —, to apply, to lay on; einen Riß —, to draw. **Auftragewalze,** -valze, *f.* roller.

Auftreiben, ŏŭf'trēīben (-trieb, -getrieben), *vt.* to drive up, rouse; to raise, find; *vi.* to run aground.

Auftrennen, ŏŭf'trennen, *vt.* to unsew, unstitch, rip up.

Auftreten, ŏŭf'trēten (-trat, -getreten), *vi.* to tread upon; to rise, appear. **Auftritt,** ŏŭf'tritt, *m.* appearance, scene.

Auftrocknen, ŏŭf'trocknen, *vt.* to dry up.

Aufwachen, ŏŭf'vachen, *vi.* to wake up, awake.

Aufwachsen, ŏŭf'vachsen (-wuchs, -gewachsen), *vi.* to grow up.

Aufwägen, ŏŭf'vägen, *vt.* to weigh up.

Aufwallen, ŏŭf'vallen, *vi.* to boil up, bubble up. **Aufwallung,** -ŭng, *f.* emotion, effervescence.

Aufwand, ŏŭf'vant, *m.* expense, expenditure, display. [up.

Aufwärmen, ŏŭf'vermen, *vt.* to warm

Aufwarten, ŏŭf'varten, *vi.* to wait on, to serve up. **Aufwärter,** ŏŭf'vẽrter, *m.* waiter, servant.

Aufwärts, ŏŭf'vẽrts, *av.* upward('s).

Aufwartung, ŏŭf'vartŭng, *f.* attendance.

Aufwaschen, ŏŭf'vashen (-wusch, -gewaschen), *vt.* to wash up.

Aufwechsel, ŏŭf'vēksel, *m. f.* Aufgeld.

Aufwecken, ŏŭf'vecken, *vt.* to awaken.

Aufweichen, ŏŭf'vāichen, *vt.* to soften, mollify.

Aufweisen, ŏŭf'vēīsen (-wies, -gewiesen), *vt.* to show, exhibit.

Aufwenden, ŏŭf'venden, *vt.* to expend, lay out.

Aufwerfen, ŏŭf'verfen (-warf, -geworfen), *vt.* to throw *or* cast upward; to throw open, to fling open; to raise (a doubt): to start, propose (a question); sich — wider, to rise, rebel against; sich — zum, to set up for.

Aufwichsen, ŏŭf'vik-sen, *vt.* to wax (a mustache); to treat.

Aufwickeln, ŏŭf'vickeln, *vt.* to wind up; to unwind, unfold.

Aufwiegeln, ŏŭf'vīgeln, *vt.* to stir or raise up.

Aufwiegen, ŏŭf'vīgen (-wog, -gewogen), *vt.* to outweigh, overbalance.

Aufwiegler, ŏŭf'vīgler, *m.* mutineer, instigator, agitator. **Aufwiegelung,** -ŭng, *f.* stirring up, instigation.

Aufwinden, ŏŭf'vinden (-wand, -gewunden), *vt.* to wind up; to unwind.

Aufwühlen, ŏŭf'vühlen, *vt.* to root up; to stir up.

Aufzählen, ŏŭf'tsälen, *vt.* to count, enumerate, detail. **Aufzählung,** ŏŭf'tsälŭng, *f.* enumeration.

Aufzäumen, ŏŭf'tsŏumen, *vt.* to bridle.

Aufzehren, ŏŭf'tsären, *vt.* to consume.

Aufzeichnen, ŏŭf'tsāīchnen, *vt.* to note; to sketch.

Aufzerren, ŏŭf'tserren, *vt.* to pull up.

Aufziehen, ŏŭf'tsī-en (-zog, -gezogen), *vt.* to draw up; to raise, to bring up; to ask to dance; to banter, jeer, rally; to set (sail); to string (an instrument); to wind up (a watch); *vi.* to draw up, to parade; to collect, rise, draw near; to mount (guard). **Aufzug,** ŏŭf'tsŭk, *m.* drawing up, procession; pomp, parade; act.

Aufzwingen, ŏŭf'tsving-en (-zwang, -gezwungen), *vt.* to force upon, press upon.

Augapfel, ŏug'apfel, *m.* apple of the eye, pupil. **Augbolzen,** -boltsen, *m.* eye-bolt. **Auge,** ŏu'ge, *n.* (*pl.* -n), eye; point, spot (of dice); bud, germ (of plants); pip, point (of cards); face (of a letter in Print.); treadle (of an egg); ins — fassen, *vt.* to watch; ein Dorn im — sein, to be a thorn in one's side; in's — fallen, to strike the eye; aus den — verlieren, to lose sight of; große —n machen, to be all astonishment. Augen, Äu'gen, vt. to bud. Äeugeln, Äu'geln, vi. to ogle; to inoculate. Au'genarzt, -ärtst, m. oculist. Au'genblick, -blick, m. moment, twinkling, instant; -lich, a. instantaneous, immediate, av. -ly; momentary. Au'genbraune, Au'genbrane, -bräu-e, f. eyebrow. Au'genbutter, -butter, m. gum of the eye. Au'genentzündung, -entsündung, f. inflammation of the eyes, ophthalmy. Au'genfell, -fell, film, albugo. Au'genglas, -gläs, n. eye-glass. Au'genhaut, -hout, f. coat of the eye. Augenhäutchen, äu'genhäutchen, n. choroid membrance. Au'genhöhle, -höhle, f. orbit, socket of the eye; -kitzel, -kitsel, m. gratification of the eye; -knorpel, -k(e)norpel, m. tarsus, cartilage of the eye; -lied, -līd, n. eyelid; -lust, -lŭzht, f. delight of the eye; -maß, -mäs, n. ein gutes —, a just eye, faculty of measuring with the eye; -merk, -merk, n. aim; -schein, -shēn, m. appearance, view; -scheinlich, -shēnlich, a. evident; -scheinlichkeit, -shēnlichkāet, f. evidence; -sprosse, -shprosse, f. browantler; -star, -zhtär, m. cataract; -weide, -vāede, f. delight of the eye; -wimper, -vimper, f. eyelash; -winkel, -vinkel, m. canthus; -zahn, -tsän, m. eye-tooth, canine tooth; -zeuge, -tsēūge, m. eye-witness; -zeugniß, -tsēūgniss. n. ocular testi-Augit, ōugitt', m. augite. [mony. August, äuguzht', m. August. Aurikel, ōurik'el, f. auricula. Aurora, ōurō'rä, f. Aurora, dawn. Aus, ōus, pr. an. out, out of, from; finished. Ausarbeiten, ōus'arbāeten, vt. to elaborate, compose; vi. to cease working. Aus'arbeitung, -ung, f. elaboration, composition. Ausarten, ōus'ärten, vi. to degenerate. Ausartung, ōus'ärtung, f. degeneracy, deterioration, degeneration. Ausathmen, ōus'ätmen, vt. to breathe out. Ausbaden, ōus'bāden, vt. to atone for. Ausbauen, ōus'bōuen, vt. to finish. Ausbedingen, ōus'bēding-en, vt. to reserve. Aus'bedingung, -ung, f. reservation. Ausbessern, ōus'bessern, vt. to mend,

repair. Ausbesserung, ōus'besserung, f. repair, mending.
Ausbeugen, ōus'bēugen, f. Ausbiegen.
Ausbeute, ōus'bēute, f. booty, gain, yield; spoil.
Ausbeuteln, ōus'bēuteln, vt. to belt to fleece.
Ausbeuten, ōus'bēuten, vt. to work; to exhaust.
Ausbiegen, ōus'bīgen (-bog, -gebogen), vt. to turn aside; to bend.
Ausbieten, ōus'bīten (-bot, -geboten), vt. to expose for sale; to outbid.
Ausbilden, ōus'bilden, vt. to cultivate, improve. Aus'bildung, -ung, f. cultivation, improvement, refinement.
Ausbitten, ōus'bitten (-bat, -gebeten), vt. to beg, request.
Ausblasen, ōus'blāsen (-blies, -geblasen), vt. to blow out.
Ausbleiben, ōus'blēiben (-blieb, -geblieben), vi. to stay out; to delay; to fail; s. n. non-appearance.
Ausbluten, ōus'blūten, vi. to cease bleeding.
Ausbohren, ōus'bōren, vt. to bore, drill; to chamfer.
Ausbraten, ōus'brāten (-briet, -gebraten), vt. to fry out.
Ausbrauchen, ōus'brōuchen, vt. to cease using, to use up.
Ausbrechen, ōus'brechen (-brach, -gebrochen), vt. to break out, take out; to draw (a tooth); to top; vi. to break out. burst out, come out; to break forth (into); to vomit.
Ausbreiten, ōus'brāiten, vt. to spread, extend, stretch; to display, divulge, publish, propagate, circulate; to enlarge, expatiate. Aus'breitung, -ung, f. extension; propagation.
Ausbrennen, ōus'brennen (-brannte, -gebrannt), vt. to burn out; to cauterize, sear, scorch; eine Kanone —, to scale, to dry out.
Ausbringen, ōus'bring-en (-brachte, -gebracht), vt. to bring out, to hatch; to get off, circulate, spread, divulge; eine Gesundheit —, to toast, to give a toast; to drive out, keep out (Print.).
Ausbruch, ōus'bruch. m. breaking out; eruption, explosion; burst, flash, gush, fit (of passion); sally; zum — kommen, to break out.
Ausbrüten, ōus'brüten, vt. to hatch, to plot.

Ausband, ŏŭs'bȳnt, *m.* paragon; best, worst; — aller Schelme, arch-rogue.
Ausbürsten, ŏŭs'bürzhten, *vt.* to brush (out).
Ausdampfen, ŏŭs'dampfen, *vi.* to evaporate. **Ausdämpfen**, ŏŭs'dempfen, *vt.* to evaporate; to extinguish; to unkennel.
Ausdauer, ŏŭs'dŏu-er, *f.* perseverance, constancy, endurance. **Ausdauern**, ŏŭs'dŏuern, *vi.* to persevere, endure, persist, hold out; —de Pflanze, perennial plant.
Ausdehnbar, ŏŭs'dānbär, *a.* malleable, ductile; expansible; -keit, -käet, *f.* expansibility; malleability, ductility. **Ausdehnung**, -ung, *f.* stretching, extension, expansion.
Ausdenken, ŏŭs'denken (-dachte, -gedacht), *vt.* to contrive, devise, invent, find out; to imagine.
Ausdeuten, ŏŭs'dŏiten, *vt.* to interpret, expound, explain.
Ausdienen, ŏŭs'dīnen, *vt.* to serve out; to become unfit.
Ausdörren, ŏŭs'dörren, *vt.* to dry up, parch. **Ausdorren**, ŏŭs'dorren, *vi.* to dry, scorch.
Ausdrehen, ŏŭs'drā-en, *vt.* to turn off, turn down.
Ausdreschen, ŏŭs'dreshen (-brosch, -gedroschen), *vt.* to thrash out.
Ausdruck, ŏŭs'druck, *m.* expression; term, word. **Ausdrucken**, ŏŭs'drucken, *vt.* to impress clearly; to finish printing. **Ausdrücken**, ŏŭs'drücken, *vt.* to press out, squeeze out; to express, utter. **Ausdrücklich**, -lich, *a.* express, explicit, *av.* -ly. **Ausdruckslos**, ŏŭs'druckslös, *a.* unmeaning, expressionless. **Ausdrucksvoll**, -foll, *a.* expressive, meaning: eloquent.
Ausduften, ŏŭs'duften, *vt.* to exhale.
Ausdulden, ŏŭs'dulden, *vi.* to suffer to the end; to suffer no more.
Ausdunsten, ŏŭs'dunzhten, **Ausdünsten**, ŏŭs'dünzhten, *vt.* to evaporate; to perspire. **Ausdünstung**, -ung, *f.* evaporation.
Auseinander, ŏŭs-ĕnan'der, *av.* asunder.
Auserkoren, ŏŭs'erkören, *pp.* chosen, elected.
Auserlesen, ŏŭs'erlāsen (-las, -lesen), *vt.* to choose, select; *a.* choice, exquisite, select.

Aussersehen, ŏŭs'ersā-en (-sah, -sehen), *vt.* to choose, select; to single out; to destine, doom.
Auserwählen, ŏŭs'ervälen, *vt.* = Auserlesen.
Ausfahren, ŏŭs'fāren (-fuhr, -gefahren), *vi.* to take a drive, to take a ride, to take an airing; t fly out; to slip; to ascend the shaft (Min.); im Gesicht ausgefahren sein, to have pustules, pimples in the face. **Ausfahrt**, ŏŭs'färt, *f.* ride, drive; doorway; gate-way; getting out of the pit (Min.).
Ausfall, ŏŭs'fall, *m.* falling out, shedding; falling; sally; sallyport; deficit. **Ausfallen** (-fiel, -gefallen), *vi.* to fall out; come out; to shed; to sally out; günstig —, to succeed; nicht gut —, to go against; ein Glied —, to dislocate by falling.
Ausfasen, ŏŭs'fäsen, *vt.* u. *r.* to ravel, unravel.
Ausfechten, ŏŭs'fechten (-focht, -gefochten), *vt.* to fight out; to cease fighting.
Ausfegen, ŏŭs'fägen, *vt.* to sweep out.
Ausfeilen, ŏŭs'feilen, *vt.* to file out.
Ausfertigen, ŏŭs'fertigen, *vt.* to expedite; to draw up, make out, execute; ein Kind —, to portion. **Ausfertigung**, -ung, *f.* equipment; execution; dispatch; portioning.
Ausfinden, ŏŭs'finden (-fand, -gefunden), *vt.* to find out. **Ausfindig machen**, to find out, discover.
Ausfischen, ŏŭs'fishen, *vt.* to fish up, find.
Ausflammen, ŏŭs'flammen, *vt.* to scale (a gun).
Ausflicken, ŏŭs'flicken, *vt.* to mend; botch, patch.
Ausfliegen, ŏŭs'flīgen (-flog, -geflogen), *vi.* to fly out.
Ausfliessen, ŏŭs'flīssen (-floss, -geflossen), *vi.* to flow out.
Ausflucht, ŏŭs'flucht, *f.* flight, escape, evasion, excuse, shift, subterfuge, shuffle. Ausflüchte machen, to shuffle, prevaricate.
Ausflug, ŏŭs'flūg, *m.* flying out, flight; trip, ramble, excursion.
Ausfluss, ŏŭs'fluss, *m.* flowing out, efflux, effluence, issue; outlet, mouth, effluvium; discharge, exhalation; emanation.
Ausflut, ŏŭs'flȳt, *f.* waste-weir.

Ausfordern, ŏys'fordern, *vt.* to challenge, call out. **Ausforderung,** -ung, *f.* challenge.
Ausforschen, ŏys'forshen, *vt.* search out; sift out, feel out; to pump, spy, trace out. **Ausforschung,** -ung, *f.* searching.
Ausfragen, ŏys'frägen, *vt.* to ask after; to search out.
Ausfuhr, ŏys'fuhr, *f.* exportation. **Ausführbar,** ŏys'führbär, practicable, achievable; -feit, -kāet, *f.* practicability, practicableness. **Ausführen,** ŏys'führen, *vt.* to lead out, export; to perform, execute, accomplish, effect, realize, prosecute; to finish, amplify. **Ausfuhrhandel,** ŏys'fųrhandel, *m.* export-trade. **Ausführlich,** ŏys'führlich, *a.* full, detailed, complete, ample, large, *av.* -ly; -feit, -kāet, *f.* fullness, completeness, prolixity. **Ausführung,** ŏys'führung, *f.* exporting, evacuation, excretion; execution, realization; performance, amplification; -gang, -gang, *m.* excretory duct, emunctory.
Ausfüllen, ŏys'füllen, *vt.* to fill out; amplify. **Ausfüllung,** -ung, *f.* filling; -wort, -vort, *n.* expletive (word).
Ausfuttern, ŏys'fųttern, *vt.* to line (a coat).
Ausfüttern, ŏys'füttern, *vt.* to feed.
Ausgabe, ŏys'gäbe, *f.* expense, expenditure; disbursement; distribution; edition.
Ausgang, ŏys'gang, *m.* issue, egress, exportation; end, termination, outlet, vent.
Ausgäten, ŏys'gäten, *vt.* to weed out.
Ausgeben, ŏys'gäben (-gab, -gegeben), *vt.* to give out, to deliver, deal, expend, spend; to publish; to produce; to yield; to sound; fich — für, to pass one's self as. **Ausgeber,** ŏys'gäber, *m.* distributer, dispenser, steward; -in, *f.* housekeeper; stewardess.
Ausgebot, ŏys'gebōt, *n.* sale, auction; first bid.
Ausgeburt, ŏys'gebŭrt, *f.* production; embodiment, incarnation; abortion.
Ausgedient, ŏys'gedīnt, *pp.* unfit for service; veteran, invalid.
Ausgedorrt, ŏys'gedo-rt, *a.* dried up, withered.

Ausgehen, ŏys'gä-en (-gieng, -gegangen), *vi.* to go out, start out, set out, issue; to emanate, originate with; to end, terminate; to fade; to fail; — auf, to go in pursuit, quest, search of; to aim at, to have in view; einem —, to be out of; to come to an end; to be extinguished.
Ausgelassen, ŏys'gelassen, *a.* extravagant, wanton, unruly, licentious; *av.* -ly; -heit, -hāet, *f.* extravagance, wantonness.
Ausgenommen, ŏys'genommen, *pr.* except.
Ausgezeichnet, ŏys'getskēchnet, *pp.* distinguished.
Ausgießen, ŏys'gīssen (-goß, -gegossen), *vt.* to pour out, effuse.
Ausgleichen, ŏys'glēchen (-glich, -geglichen), *vt.* to compensate, equalize, adjust. **Ausgleichung,** -ung, *f.* equalization, balance, compensation, adjustment. **Ausgleichwage,** -wāge, *f.* adjusting scales.
Ausgleiten, ŏys'glāeten (-glitt, -geglitten), *vi.* to slide, slip.
Ausglühen, ŏys'glüh-en, *vt.* to anneal, temper metals, etc., *vi.* to cease glowing.
Ausgraben, ŏys'gräben (-grub, -gegraben), *vt.* to dig out, untomb, disinter; to unearth (a fox, etc.).
Ausgrübeln, ŏys'grübeln, *vt.* to find out by meditating.
Ausguß, ŏys'guss, *m.* effusion, outlet, conduit, sink; -stelle, -kelle, *f.* ladle (Min.).
Aushacken, ŏys'hacken, *vt.* to hoe out.
Aushaken, ŏys'häken, *vt.* to hook out.
Aushalten, ŏys'halten (-hielt, -gehalten), *vt.* to endure, bear; to hold out; to sustain (Mus.); to stand, to weather out, serve out; *vi.* to last, hold out.
Aushängen, ŏys'heng-en, *vt. i.* to hang out.
Ausharren, ŏys'harren, *vi.* to persevere.
Aushauchen, ŏys'hŏychen, *vt.* to breathe out, to exhale.
Aushauen, ŏys'hŏu-en (-hieb, -gehauen), *vt.* to hew or cut out; to prune; to thin; to flog, whip. **Aushau-stempel,** -zhtempel, *m.* stamp.
Ausheben, ŏys'häben (-hob, -gehoben), to lift out, heave out; to unhinge; to select, levy; to draw (wine).

Aus 43 **Aus**

Ausheden, ŏys'hĕcken, vt. to hatch out.
Ausheimisch, ŏys'haemish, a. foreign.
Aushelfen, ŏys'hĕlfen (-half, -geholfen), vi. to help, aid.
Aushöhlen, ŏys'höhlen, vt. to hollow out, excavate. **Aushöhlung,** -ung, f. excavation.
Aushöfern, Aushötern, ŏys'höhkern, vt. to hawk.
Aushölen, ŏys'hōlen, vi. to lift the arm for striking; to sound, pump, sift any one.
Aushorchen, ŏys'horchen, vt. to learn by listening.
Aushören, ŏys'böhren, vt. to hear to the end.
Aushülfe, ŏys'hülfe, f. help, aid, assistance.
Aushülsen, ŏys'hülsen, vt. to husk, peel.
Aushungern, ŏys'hung-ern, vt. to famish, starve, to subdue by hunger.
Aushusten, ŏys'hŭzhten, vt. to cough up, expectorate.
Ausjäten, ŏys'yāten, vt. to weed out.
Ausjochen, ŏys'yochen, vt. to unyoke.
Auskammen, ŏys'kommen, vi. to comb (out).
Auskarde, ŏys'karde, f. finishing-card, finisher.
Auskaufen, ŏys'käufen, vt. to buy out; to outbid; to use well.
Auskehren, ŏys'kären, vt. to sweep out. **Auskehricht,** ŏys'kārĭcht, n. sweepings.
Auskeifen, ŏys'kĕifen, vt. to chide.
Auskeilen, ŏys'kĕilen, vt. to provide with wedges; to drub; to run to a point.
Auskeltern, ŏys'kĕltern, vt. to press out.
Ausklatschen, ŏys'klatshen, vt. to hiss out; to blab.
Ausklauben, ŏys'klŏyben, vt. to pick out.
Auskleben, ŏys'klāben, vt. to paper, to line.
Auskleiden, ŏys'klāeden, vt. to undress, to strip.
Auskleistern, ŏys'klŏizhtern, vt. to paper, line.
Ausklopfen, ŏys'klopfen, vt. to knock out, to beat.
Ausklügeln, ŏys'klühg-eln, vt. to hatch out, find out.
Auskochen, ŏys'kochen, vt. to boil (out).

Auskommen, ŏys'kommen (-kam, -gekommen), vi. to come out; to peep out; to break out; to get out, leak out; — mit, to do, to serve one's purpose; to get on with any one; — mit, to live on, subsist on; s. n. competency, subsistence; sein — haben, to make one's living, to have a competence; sein gutes — haben, to have a good livelihood; to be well off.
Auskramen, ŏys'krämen, vt. to display.
Auskratzen, ŏys'kratsen, vt. to scratch out.
Auskriechen, ŏys'krīchen (-kroch, -gekrochen), vi. to creep out.
Auskriegen, ŏys'krīgen, vt. to get off.
Auskundschaften, ŏys'kuntshaften, vt. to spy out, espy.
Auskunft, ŏys'kunft, f. information, resource, issue; — geben, to inform; -mittel, -mittel, n. means, expedient.
Auskünsteln, ŏys'künzhteln, vt. to contrive, devise.
Auslachen, ŏys'lachen, vt. to laugh at.
Ausladen, ŏys'läden (-lud, -geladen), vt. to unload, discharge, take out. **Ausladung,** -ung, f. discharge, unloading.
Auslage, ŏys'läge, f. expense; advance, disbursement.
Ausland, ŏys'lant, n. foreign countries; im, ins —, abroad. **Ausländer,** ŏys'lender, m. -in, f. foreigner. **Ausländisch,** ŏys'lendish, a. outlandish, foreign.
Auslassen, ŏys'lassen (-liess, -gelassen), vt. to let out; to leave out, omit; to melt; den Zorn —, to wreak one's anger on: sich —, to express one's self. **Auslassung,** -ung, f. omission.
Auslaufen, ŏys'läufen (-lief, -gelaufen), vi. to run out, sail out; to put to sea; to leak out.
Auslaugen, ŏys'läugen, vt. to lixiviate, to wash with lye.
Ausläuten, ŏys'lĕuten, vt. to toll out, make known by tolling; to ring the last bell.
Auslecken, ŏys'lĕcken, vt. to lick out.
Ausleeren, ŏys'lāren, vt. to empty, clear, evacuate. **Ausleerung,** ŏys'lārung, f. evacuation.
Auslegen, ŏys'lägen, vt. to lay out; inlay; expose; put up; explain,

expound, interpret. **Ausleger,** ǒys'-lāger, *m.* interpreter; boom (Mar.).
Auslegung, -ŭng, *f.* exposition, interpretation, exegesis.
Ausleiden, ǒys'lēiden (-litt, -gelitten), *vi.* to suffer to the end.
Ausleiern, ǒys'lēī-ern, *vt.* to wear out.
Ausleihen, ǒys'lēī-en (-lieh, -geliehen), *vt.* to lend out.
Auslenken, ǒys'lenken, *vt.* to turn out.
Auslernen, ǒys'lērnen, *vt.* to serve one's time.
Auslesen, ǒys'lāsen (-las, -gelesen), *vt.* to choose, select; to read through.
Ausliefern, ǒys'līfern, *vt.* to deliver.
Auslieferung, -ŭng, *f.* delivery.
Auslöschen, ǒys'löshen, *vt.* to extinguish, put out; to efface, blot out; *vi.* to go out, to be extinguished.
Auslosen, ǒys'lōsen, *vt.* to raffle.
Auslösen, ǒys'löhsen, *vt.* to redeem, ransom, release; to loosen. **Auslösung,** -ŭng, *f.* ransom.
Ausmachen, ǒys'machen, *vt.* to make out; to settle, fix, decide; to shell.
Ausmalen, ǒys'mālen, *vt.* to picture, paint.
Ausmarschiren, ǒys'marshīren, *vi.* to march out.
Ausmauern, ǒys'móyěrn, *vt.* to wall up.
Ausmeißeln, ǒys'mǟseln, *vt.* to chisel out.
Ausmergeln, ǒys'mērgeln, *vt.* to emaciate.
Ausmerzen, ǒys'mērtsen, *vt.* to reject, to weed out.
Ausmessen, ǒys'messen (-maß, -gemessen), *vt.* to measure out.
Ausmöbliren, ǒys'möbilīren, *vt.* to furnish.
Ausmiethen, ǒys'mīten, *vt.* to let, to rent.
Ausmisten, ǒys'mizhten, *vt.* to clean out a stable; to purify.
Ausmitteln, ǒys'mitteln, *vt.* to find out, discover.
Ausmustern, ǒys'myzhtern, *vt.* to muster out.
Ausnahme, ǒys'nāme, *f.* exception; -weise, -vēīse, *av.* exceptionally.
Ausnehmen, ǒys'nāmen (-nahm, -genommen), *vt.* to take out; to except, exclude: sich —, to appear; sich gut —, to look well, to have a good effect. **Ausnehmend,** ǒys'nāment, *av.* exceedingly.

Ausösen, ǒys'ōhsen, *vt.* to bail out (a boat).
Auspacken, ǒys'packen, *vt.* to unpack.
Auspeitschen, ǒys'pēītshen, *vt.* to whip, scourge.
Auspfänden, ǒys'pfenden, *vt.* to pawn.
Auspfändung, -ŭng, *f.* distraining.
Auspfeifen, ǒys'pfēīfen (-pfiff, -gepfiffen), *vt.* to hiss.
Auspflücken, ǒys'pflücken, *vt.* to pluck out, to untwist.
Auspichen, ǒys'pichen, *vt.* to pitch.
Ausplappern, ǒys'plappern, *vt.* to blab out, to divulge.
Ausplatzen, ǒys'platsen, *vt.* to burst (into).
Ausplaudern, ǒys'plóydern, *vt.* to blab out.
Ausplündern, ǒys'plündern, *vt.* to plunder.
Auspochen, ǒys'pochen, *vt.* to beat out.
Auspelzen, ǒys'pelzhtern, *vt.* to stuff, quilt.
Ausposaunen, ǒys'posōunen, *vt.* to trumpet forth, to proclaim.
Ausprägen, ǒys'prägen, *vt.* to coin, mint, stamp.
Auspressen, ǒys'pressen, *vt.* to press out, squeeze out; to extort.
Auspumpen, ǒys'pumpen, *vt.* to pump out.
Ausputzen, ǒys'pytsen, *vt.* to clean out; to snuff out.
Ausquetschen, ǒys'quetshen, *vt.* to squeeze out.
Ausradiren, ǒys'radīren, *vt.* to erase.
Ausrasen, ǒys'rāsen, *vi.* to have done raging.
Ausrauchen, ǒys'rǟuchen, *vt.* to finish smoking.
Ausraufen, ǒys'rǟufen, *vt.* to pull out, tear out.
Ausräumen, ǒys'rǟōmen, *vt.* to clean out.
Ausrechnen, ǒys'rechnen, *vt.* to reckon, compute, calculate. **Ausrechnung,** -ŭng, *f.* calculation, computation.
Ausrede, ǒys'rāde, *f.* excuse. **Ausreden,** *vt. u. r.* to dissuade; to finish speaking; to excuse.
Ausregnen, ǒys'rägnen, *vi.* to have done raining.
Ausreiben, ǒys'rēīben (-rieb, -gerieben), *vt.* to rub out.
Ausreichen, ǒys'rēīchen, *vi.* to suffice, to be sufficient.
Ausreißen, ǒys'rēīsen (-riß, -gerissen), *vt.* to tear out, pull out; to draw (a

tooth); *vi.* to run away, desert; to fall **Ausreißer**, ŏys'rēĭsser, *m.* deserter, runaway.

Ausreiten, ŏys'rēĭten (-ritt -geritten), *vi.* to ride out.

Ausrenken, ŏys'renken, *vt.* to wrench out, to sprain, dislocate.

Ausreuten, ŏys'rēuten, *vt.* to root out.

Ausrichten, ŏys'räden, *vt.* to rig out a ship.

Ausrichten, ŏys'richten, *vt.* to effect, perform, do; Richte —, to labor in vain; ein Wild —, to draw a cover.

Ausringen, ŏys'ring-en, *vt.* to wring.

Ausrollen, ŏys'rollen, *vt.* to roll out; to unroll.

Ausrotten, ŏys'rotten, *vt.* to root out, to extirpate. **Aus'rottung**, -ung, *f.* extirpation.

Ausrücken, ŏys'rücken, *vt.* to disengage (Machin.); *vi.* to march out. **Aus'rückzeug**, -tsöuk, *n.* disengaging-gear.

Ausruf, ŏys'ryf. *m.* outcry, exclamation; proclamation. **Ausrufen**, ŏys'ryfen (-rief, -gerufen), *vt.* to call out, exclaim. **Ausrufer**, ŏys'ryfer, *m.* auctioneer. **Ausrufung**, ŏys'ryfung, *f.* exclamation; -zeichen, -tsĕĭchen, *n.* exclamation.

Ausruhen, ŏys'ry-en, *vi.* to rest.

Ausrupfen, ŏys'rypfen, *vt.* to pull out, pluck out.

Ausrüsten, ŏys'rüsten, *vt.* to fit out, equip, arm, man, endow. **Aus'rüstung**, -ung, *f.* equipment, outfit.

Aussaat, ŏys'sät, *f.* seed-corn. **Aussäen**, ŏys'sä-en, *vt.* to sow, to scatter seed.

Aussage, ŏys'sägə, *f.* declaration, predicate. **Aussagen**, *vt.* to declare, predicate, depose.

Aussatz, ŏys'sats, *m.* leprosy. **Aussätzig**, ŏys'setsich, *a.* leprous; -er, *m.* leper.

Aussaufen, ŏys'soufen (-soff, -gesoffen), *vt.* to drink out (of animals).

Aussaugen, ŏys'sougen, *vt.* to suck out, exhaust, fleece.

Ausschaben, ŏys'shäben, *vt.* to scrape out.

Ausschälen, ŏys'shälen, *vt.* to shell, peel.

Ausscharren, ŏys'sharren, *vt.* to scrape out, rake out.

Ausscheiden, ŏys'shäĕden (-shied, -geschieden), *vt.* to separate, sever, part;

to wash (ore); *vi.* to secede, with-draw.

Ausschelten, ŏys'shelten (-schalt, -geschölten), *vt.* to chide, scold.

Ausschenken, ŏys'shenken, *vt.* to pour out; retail (liquors).

Ausscheuern, ŏys'shĕŭern, *vt.* to scour.

Ausschicken, ŏys'shicken, *vt.* to send out.

Ausschieben, ŏys'shīben (-schob, -geschoben), *vt.* to push out.

Ausschießen, ŏys'shīssen (-schoß, -geschossen), *vt.* to shoot out; to exclude, eject.

Ausschiffen, ŏys'shiffen, *vi.* to set sail; *vt.* to disembark, discharge.

Ausschimpfen, ŏys'shimpfen, *vt.* to abuse, revile.

Ausschirren, ŏys'shirren, *vt.* to unharness.

Ausschlafen, ŏys'shläfen (-schlief, -geschlafen), *vt.* to sleep away.

Ausschlag, ŏys'shläk, *m.* first blow or stroke; breaking out, eruption; efflorescence; turn, bias, decision; casting vote; den — geben, to decide, turn the scale: to determine. **Ausschlagen**, ŏys'shlägen (-schlug, -geschlagen), *vt.* to strike out, beat out, dash out; to strike first, attack; to kick, jerk (of horses); to ring out the hour; to leaf, bud, sprout; to become wet (of walls); to break out; *vt.* to hammer out, laminate (metals); to refuse, decline, reject; to line: to paper; to parry.

Ausschleifen, ŏys'shlēĭfen (-schliff, -geschliffen), *vt.* to grind out.

Ausschleifen, ŏys'shlēĭfen, *vt.* to drag out.

Ausschlemmen, ŏys'shlemmen, *vt.* to clear of mud.

Ausschließen, ŏys'shlīssen (-schloß, -geschlossen), *vt.* to shut out, exclude; to justify (Print.). **Ausschließlich**, ŏys'shlīslich, *a.* exclusive, *av.* -ly. **Ausschließung**, -ung, *f.* exclusion; *pl.* justifiers (Print.). **Ausschluß**, ŏys'shluss, *m.* exclusion.

Ausschmälen, ŏys'shmälen, *vt.* to reprove.

Ausschmieren, ŏys'shmīren, *vt.* to besmear.

Ausschmücken, ŏys'shmücken, *vt.* to embellish.

Ausschnäuzen, ŏys'shnŏŭtsen, *vt.* to blow the nose.

Ausschneiden, ŏus'shnīden (-schnitt, -geschnitten), **Ausschnitzen,** ŏus'shnitzen, *vt.* to cut out. **Ausschnitt,** ŏus'shnitt, *m.* cut; retail; **-handel,** *m.* retail (of dry-goods).
Ausschnüren, ŏus'shnühren, *vt.* to unlace, untie.
Ausschöpfen, ŏus'shöpfen, *vt.* to draw out, scoop out, bail out (a boat).
Ausschrauben, ŏus'shrŏuben, *vt.* to unscrew.
Ausschreiben, ŏus'shrīben (-schrieb, -geschrieben), *vt.* to write out, to copy; to pirate; *s. n.* proclamation, order.
Ausschreien, ŏus'shrēīen (-schrie, -geschrien), *vt.* to cry, proclaim.
Ausschreiten, ŏus'shrēīten (-schritt, -geschritten), *vi.* to stride, go too far, exceed; to measure by steps.
Ausschroten, ŏus'shrōten, *vt.* to roll (casks out of a cellar).
Ausschuß, ŏus'shuss, *m.* refuse, offal; choice; committee.
Ausschütteln, ŏus'shütteln, *vt.* to shake out.
Ausschütten, ŏus'shütten, *vt.* to pour out.
Ausschwärmen, ŏus'shvermen, *vi.* to swarm; to stop frolicking.
Ausschwatzen, ŏus'shvatsen, *vt.* to blab (out).
Ausschweifen, ŏus'shvīfen, *vi.* to swerve, slope, deviate, digress; to go to excess; *b, a.* excessive, extravagant, dissolute. **Ausschweifung,** ŏus'shvīfung, *f.* sloping, digression; extravagance, debauch, excess.
Ausschwenken, ŏus'shvenken, *vt.* to rinse.
Ausschwitzen, ŏus'shvitsen, *vt.* to exude; to cease perspiring; to forget.
Aussehen, ŏus'sā-en (-sah, -gesehen), *vi.* to look out; to look, appear; to see to the end; *s. n.* appearance, look, air.
Außen, ŏus'sen, *av.* out, without, out of doors, abroad; on the outside.
Aussenden, ŏus'senden (-sandte, -gesandt), *vt.* to send out.
Außenseite, ŏus'sensēīte, *f.* outside.
Außenstehen, ŏus'senzhtīfen, *s. pl.* back of the stern-post. **Au'ßenwelt, -velt,** *f.* outer world. **Au'ßenwerf, -vērk,** *n.* outwork. **Au'ßenwinkel, -vinkel,** *m.* external angle.

Außer, ŏus'ser, *pr.* out of, beside except, without; **-dem, -dām,** *conj.* moreover, besides. **Aeußerer, äus'-serer,** *a.* outer, outward, exterior; external, outside. **Außerhalb,** ŏus'serhalp, *pr.* out of, without; *av.* outwardly, on the outside. **Aeußern, äus'sern,** *vt.* to utter, express, vent, speak, manifest; **sich —,** to appear, break out. **Außerordentlich,** ŏus'ser-or'dentlich, *a.* extraordinary. **Aeußerst, äus'serzht,** *av. a.* utmost, utter, external, outermost, uttermost. **Aeußerung, äus'serung,** *f.* uttering, utterance, expression. **Außerwesentlich,** ŏus'servāsentlich, *a.* not essential, accidental, contingent.
Aussetzen, ŏus'setsen, *vt.* to set out, expose; to disembark; to appoint, designate; to suspend, stop, intermit, discontinue; to find fault with; to appoint, settle; to lead (at billiards); to dispossess.
Aussicht, ŏus'sicht, *f.* prospect, view.
Aussieben, ŏus'sīben, *vt.* to sift.
Aussieden, ŏus'sīden, *vt.* to boil out.
Aussingen, ŏus'sing-en, *vt.* to finish singing.
Aussinnen, ŏus'sinnen (-sann, -gesonnen), *vt.* to devise, contrive.
Aussöhnen, ŏus'söhnen, *vt.* to reconcile. **Aussöhnung, -ung,** *f.* reconciliation.
Aussondern, ŏus'sondern, *vt.* to separate, single out. **Aussonderung, -ung,** *f.* separation.
Ausspähen, ŏus'zhpä-en, *vt.* to spy out.
Ausspann, ŏus'zhpann, *m.* relay, stage. **Ausspannen,** *vt.* to stretch, extend; set; unharness; to unyoke.
Ausspazieren, ŏus'zhpatsīren, *vi.* to walk out.
Ausspeien, ŏus'zhpēīen (-spie, -gespieen), *vt.* to spit out.
Ausspenden, ŏus'zhpenden, *vt.* to dispense, distribute.
Aussperren, ŏus'zhpęrren, *vt.* to spread; to shut out.
Ausspicken, ŏus'zhpicken, *vt.* to interlard; to ornament.
Ausspielen, ŏus'zhpīlen, *vi.* to play out; to lead.
Ausspioniren, ŏus'zhpionīren, *vt.* to spy out. [deride.
Ausspotten, ŏus'zhpotten, *vt.* to mock, **Aussprache,** ŏus'zhpräche, *f.* pronunciation; elocution. **Aussprechen,**

ŏŭs′zhprĕchen (-ſprach, -geſprochen), vt. to pronounce, utter, speak. **Aus̓sprechlich**, ŏŭs′zhprĕchlich, a. expressible, utterable.

Ausſprengen, ŏŭs′zhpreng-en, vt. to sprinkle, spread, divulge, circulate; to put into gallop. **Ausſpringen**, ŏŭs′zhpring-en (-ſprang, -geſprungen), vt. to burst off; to jut out.

Ausſpritzen, ŏŭs′zhpritsen, vt. to squirt, sprinkle.

Ausſpruch, ŏŭs′zhpruch, m. sentence, judgment.

Ausſprühen, ŏŭs′zhprüh-en, vt. i. to sparkle, scintillate, to vomit forth.

Ausſpucken, ŏŭs′zhpŭcken, vt. to spit out.

Ausſpülen, ŏŭs′zhpühlen, vt. to rinse, cleanse.

Ausſpüren, ŏŭs′zhpühren, vt. to trace out: to track, hunt.

Ausſtaffiren, ŏŭs′zhtaffīren. vt. to dress up, trim up, trick off. **Aus̓staffirung**, -ŭng, f. equipment, garnishing.

Ausſtand, ŏŭs′zhtant, m. arrears, outstanding money.

Ausſtatten, ŏŭs′zhtatten, vt. to furnish, endow, portion. **Aus̓stattung**, -ŭng, f. portion, dowry, endowment.

Ausſtechen, ŏŭs′zhtĕchen (-ſtach, -geſtochen), vt. to dig out, prick out: to cut; ein Tau —, to veer away; to pay out (a cable); to supplant, get the better of; to hew out, carve. **Ausſtecher**, ŏŭs′zhtĕcher, m. boom.

Ausſtecken, ŏŭs′zhtĕcken, vt. to put up, out: to hang out, hoist: to set out.

Ausſtehen, ŏŭs′zhtä-en (-ſtand, -geſtanden), vi. to stand out, undergo, bear; to have owing.

Ausſteigen, ŏŭs′zhtēigen (-ſtieg, -geſtiegen), vt. to descend, alight; to get down, disembark.

Ausſtellen, ŏŭs′zhtellen, vt. to offer, present to view; to exhibit, expose; to lay out: to find fault with; to draw (a bill of exchange). **Aus̓stellung**, -ŭng, f. exhibition; drawing on.

Ausſterben, ŏŭs′zhtĕrben (-ſtarb, -geſtorben), vi. to die out, away.

Ausſteuer, ŏŭs′zhtŏŭ-er, f. portion, endowment. **Aus̓steuern**, vt. to portion, endow.

Ausſtöbern, ŏŭs′zhtöhbern, vt. to track out; trace out.

Ausſtopfen, ŏŭs′zhtopfen, vt. to stuff.

Ausſtoß, ŏŭs′zhtōs, m. push, thrust, pass, allonge. **Ausſtoßen**, ŏŭs′zhtōsen (-ſtieß, -geſtoßen), vt. to push, thrust; to make a pass (Fenc.); to set out (top-sail)s; den Boden —, to stave; to heave (a sigh); to set up (a cry); to cut off, glide (a syllable).

Ausſtrahlen, ŏŭs′zhträlen, vt. to radiate.

Ausſtrecken, ŏŭs′zhtreckcn, vt. to stretch out, extend.

Ausſtreichen, ŏŭs′zhtrēichen (-ſtrich, -geſtrichen), vt. to strike out, blot out; to unplait; to stretch (hides); to beat (the field for).

Ausſtreuen, ŏŭs′zhtröü-en, vt. to strew, scatter, spread.

Ausſtrömen, ŏŭs′zhtröhmen, vi. to stream forth, gush out.

Ausſtudiren, ŏŭs′zhtudīren, vt. to study out, to devise; to finish studying.

Ausſuchen, ŏŭs′sŭchen, vt. to select, pick out.

Ausſtapezieren, ŏŭs′tapetsīren, vt. to paper.

Austauſch, ŏŭs′tŏŭsh, m. exchange, barter. **Austauſchen**, ŏŭs′tŏŭshen, vt. to exchange, to barter.

Auſter, ŏŭzh′ter, f. cyster.

Austheilen, ŏŭs′tāēlen, vt. to distribute, divide; to deal out. **Aus̓theilung**, -ŭng, f. distribution, division, administration.

Austhun, ŏŭs′tŭn (-that, -gethan), vt. to put off or out.

Austilgen, ŏŭs′tilgen, vt. to extirpate. **Aus̓tilgung**, -ŭng, f. extirpation, extermination.

Austoben, ŏŭs′tōben, vi. to give vent to; to be spent.

Austrag, ŏŭs′träk, m. decision; pl. umpire. **Aus̓tragen** (-trug, -getragen), vt. to carry out; to defame; vi. to amount to.

Austreiben, ŏŭs′trēiben (-trieb, -getrieben), vt. to drive out, expel, cast out. **Aus̓treibung**, -ŭng, f. expulsion.

Austreten, ŏŭs′träten (-trat, -getreten), vt. i. to tread out, step out; to come forth; to overflow; to wear cut; to sprain, dislocate (by stepping); to leave, withdraw, secede from.

Austrinken, ŏŭs′trinken (-trank, -getrunken), vt. to drink out, empty.

Austritt, ŏus'tritt, *m.* stepping out, egress; running away; withdrawal, secession: balcony: recess (Min.).
Austrocknen, ŏus'trocknen, *vt.* to dry out.
Austrommeln, ŏus'trommeln, *vt.* to drum out; to explode.
Austunken, ŏus'tunken, *vt.* to sop out.
Ausüben, ŏus'ühben, *vt.* to practise, exercise. **Ausübung**, ŏus'ühbung, *f.* practice, exercise; in — bringen, to bring into practice.
Auswachsen, ŏus'vaxen (-wuchs, -gewachsen), *vi.* to grow up; to sprout.
Auswägen, ŏus'vägen (-wog, -gewogen), *vt.* to weigh out; to retail.
Auswahl, ŏus'väl. *f.* choice, selection; assortment. **Auswählen**, ŏus'välen, *vt.* to choose, select, cull, single out.
Auswandern, ŏus'vandern, *vi.* to emigrate. **Auswanderer**, *m.* emigrant. **Auswanderung**, -ung, *f.* emigration.
Auswärtig, ŏus'vertich, *a.* external, foreign. **Auswärts**, ŏus'verts, *av.* outward, outwards, abroad.
Auswaschen, ŏus'vashen (-wusch, -gewaschen), *vt.* to wash out.
Auswechsel, ŏus'vexel, *m.* exchange. **Auswechseln**, ŏus'vexeln, *vt.* to exchange.
Ausweg, ŏus'väk, *m.* way (out), escape; shift, expedient.
Ausweichen, ŏus'vēlchen (-wich, -gewichen), *vi.* to yield, give way; avoid, shun; elude, evade. **Ausweichschiene**, -shīne, *f.* swift, slide-rail. **Ausweichung**, -ung, *f.* evasion; giving way, elongation, transition.
Ausweiden, ŏus'väiden, *vt.* to eviscerate, gut. [weep out.
Ausweinen, ŏus'vānen, *sich* —, to
Ausweis, ŏus'vēls, *m.* evidence; permit. **Ausweisen**, ŏus'vēlsen.(-wies, -gewiesen), *vt.* to turn out, expel, banish, exile; to show, prove, determine. [wash.
Ausweißen, ŏus'vēlssen, *vt.* to white-
Ausweiten, ŏus'vēlten, *vt.* to widen.
Auswendig, ŏus'vendich, *a.* outward, external, outside, by heart; — wissen, to know by heart;—lernen, to learn by heart, — by rote, commit to memory.
Auswerfen, ŏus'verfen (-warf, -geworfen), *vt.* to cast, fling, throw out; to throw first; to cast, drop (anchor); to heave (the lead); to expectorate,

eject; to exclude, expel; to appoint, settle (an annuity, etc.); to geld (a horse).
Auswetzen, ŏus'vetsen, *vt.* to whet out, wipe out; to repair, make amends for; to avenge.
Auswickeln, ŏus'vickeln, *vt.* to unwrap; to untangle.
Auswinden, ŏus'vinden (-wand, -gewunden), *vt.* to unwind.
Auswirken, ŏus'virken, *vt.* to scrape off; to effect, procure.
Auswischen, ŏus'vishen, *vt.* to wipe out.
Auswittern, ŏus'vittern, *vt. i.* to scent out, ferret out; to decompose; *vi.* to decompose; to cease thundering.
Auswuchs, ŏus'vux, *m.* excrescence.
Auswurf, ŏus'vurf, *m.* first throw; outcast, refuse; spittle, expectoration.
Auswüthen, ŏus'vühten, *vi.* to spend one's fury.
Auszacken, ŏus'tsacken, *vt.* to notch.
Auszahlen, ŏus'tsälen. *vt.* to pay (out).
Auszahlung, -ung, *f.* payment.
Auszählen, ŏus'tsälen, *vt.* to count to the end.
Auszanken, ŏus'tsanken, *vt.* to scold.
Auszehren, ŏus'teä-ren, *vi.* to pine away, waste away. **Auszehrung**, -ung, *f.* consumption.
Auszeichnen, ŏus'tsäechnen, *vt.* to distinguish. **Auszeichnung**, -ung, *f.* distinction.
Ausziehen, ŏus'tsī-en (-zog, -gezogen), *vt.* to draw out, extract, get off; pull off, put off; to undress, strip off; to stretch (cloth); to rifle (guns); *vi.* to move, remove, march out, set out; to take the field; to run; to make the first move. **Ausziehtisch**, ŏus'tsītish, *m.* extension-table. **Ausziehung**, ŏus'tsī-ung, *f.* extraction.
Auszieren, ŏus'tsīren, *vt.* to adorn, deck, decorate. **Auszierung**, -ung, *f.* decoration.
Auszischen, ŏus'tsishen, *vt.* to hiss.
Auszug, ŏus'tsuk, *m.* removal, march, exodus; extract, epitome.
Auszupfen, ŏus'tsupfen, *vt.* to pull out, pluck out.
Autokrat, ŏutokrät', *m.* autocrat.
Automat, ŏutomät', *n.* automaton.
Autor, ŏutŏr', *m.* author. **Autorisiren**, ŏutorisī'ren, to authorise, empower.

Aut 49 **Bal**

Autorität, òutorītät', *f.* authority.
Autorschaft, òu'torshaft, *f.* authorship.
Avarie, avarī', = Haverie.
Avertissement, avèrtissͤ/ment, *n.* advertisement.
Avers, avèrs', *m.* obverse.
Avis, avī', *m.* advice, announcement.
Axe, axe, *f.* = Achse.
Axt, axt, *f.* ax, axe.
Azen, ā'tsen, *vt.* to corrode, etch; to feed; bait. **Azung**, ā'tsȳng, *f.* etching; baiting.
Azimuth, ā'tsimyt, *m.* azimuth.
Azur, ā'tsyr, *m.* azure, ultramarine.

Baar, bär, *a.* bare, naked; destitute, void; cash, ready money; **-fuß, -fus**, *a.* barefooted; **-schaft, -shaft**, *f.* cash, ready money.
Babbeln, bab'beln, *vi.* to prattle, blab.
Bach, bach, *m.* brook, creek, rivulet.
Bache, bach'e, *f.* wild sow.
Bachstelze, bachzhtèl'tse, *f.* wagtail.
Backbord, bak'bört, *n.* larboard.
Backe, back'e, *f.* **Backen**, *m.* cheek; side.
Backen, back'en (buk, gebacken), *vt.* to bake; to fry.
Backenbart, back'enbärt, *m.* whiskers. **Backenknochen**, -k(e)nochen. *m.* cheek-bone. **Backenstreich**, -zhtrāch. *m.* box, slap in the face. **Backenzahn**, -tsän, *m.* cheek-tooth, molar.
Bäcker, beck'er, *m.* baker; **-junge, -yȳnge**, *m. -n, pl. -n*, baker's boy. **Bäckerei**, beckërāī', *f.* bakery. **Bäckergesell**, -gesell, *m. -en, pl. -en*, journeyman baker. **Backhaus**, -hoys, *n.* bakery. **Backofen**, -öfen, *m.* oven. **Backstein**, -zhtāēn, *m.* brick. **Backtrog**, -tròk, *m.* brake, kneading-trough. **Backwerk**, -vërk, *n.* pastry.
Bad, bäd, *n.* bath; watering-place; **das — brauchen**, to take the waters. **Badecur**, bä'dekyr, *f.* use of mineral waters. **Badegast**, -gazht, *m.* visitor of a watering-place. **Badehemd**, -hemt, *n. -es, pl. -en*, bathingshirt. **Baden**, bä'den, *vi.* to bathe; to steep. **Badeplatz**, -plats, *m.* bathing-place.
Bader, bäd'er, *m.* barber, surgeon.
Badeschiff, bäd'eshiff, *n.* floating-bath. **Badestube**, -zhtybe, *f.* bathing-

room, bagnio. **Badewanne**, -vanne, *f.* bathing-tub.
Baggage, bagā'zhe, *f.* baggage, luggage; **-wagen**, -vägen, *m.* baggage-wagon.
Bagienraa, bäg'yenrä, *f.* cross-jack-yard.
Bähen, bä'en, *vt.* to foment; bathe, stupe (a wound); to toast (bread).
Bahn, bän, *f.* path, way; road, course, orbit; **die — brechen**, to beat the path, to break the ice; **auf die — bringen**, to start, show the way; — **der Sonne**, ecliptic; face (of a hammer, anvil, etc.); **-blatt**, *n. pl.* **-blätter**, swing-bed-plate. **Bahnen**, bän'en, *vt.* to beat, smooth, to clear (the way); to make level, to pave.
Bahre, bär'e, *f.* barrow; bier.
Bai, bāē, *f.* bay.
Bajazzo, bayat'so, *m.* clown, buffoon.
Bajonnet, bajonnèt', *n.* bayonet.
Bake, bä'ke, *f.* beacon, buoy.
Balance, balän'se, *f.* equipoise; balance. **Balancier**, balän'sī-ā, *m.* working-beam (Mint). **Balanciren**, bal insī'ren, *vt.* to balance.
Balcon, balkön', *m.* balcony.
Bald, balt, *av.* soon, early, speedily, ere long; almost, nearly; easily; **bald—bald**, now—now, sometimes— sometimes. [dais.
Baldachin, baldachīn', *m.* canopy.
Balde, bęl'de, *f.* in —, shortly, soon.
Baldig, bal'dik, *a.* speedy.
Balg, balk, *m.* skin, slough; urchin. **Balgen**, *vr.* to wrestle, fight. **Balgerei**, balgerāī', *f.* row, fight.
Balje, bal'ye, *f.* tub, half-tub; washing-tub.
Balken, bal'ken, *m.* beam, rafter, joist; — **der Kuhbrücke**, orlop-beams. **Balkplanken**, *s. pl.* sides of a ship.
Ball, bal, *m.* ball, dancing-party.
Ball, bal, *m.* ball; globe.
Ballade, ballä'de, *f.* ballad.
Ballast, ballazht', *m.* ballast.
Ballen, bal'len, *vt.* to bale, pack, bag; to conglomerate; **-binder**, -binder, *m.* packer; **-weise**, -vāīse, *av.* in bales, by the bale.
Ballet, ballèt', *m.* ballet.
Ballon, ballōn', *m.* balloon; football.
Ballschuhe, bail'shy-e, *s. pl.* pumps. dress-shoes.

Ballſpiel, bal'zhpīl, n. game of ball.
Balſam, bal'sam, m. balm, balsam.
Balſamiren, balsamī'ren, vt. to balm, embalm; perfume. **Balſamiſch**, balsä'mish, a. balmy, balsamic.
Bambus, bam'bus, m. bamboo.
Band, bant, n. pl. **Bänder**, band, ribbon, bandage, fillet; ligament; m. pl. **Bände**, volume; pl. **Bande**, fetters. **Bandachat**, -achāt', m. striped agate.
Bande, ban'de, f. band, set, gang; cushion (of a billiard-table).
Bandelier, bandelīr', n. shoulder-belt.
Bänderreich, ben'derēich, a. voluminous.
Bändigen, ben'digen, vt. to break, master, tame, subdue.
Bandit, bandit', m. -ten, pl. -ten, bandit, robber, outlaw. [worm.
Bandwurm, bant'vurm, m. tape-
Bange, bang'e, a. anxious, av. -ly, uneasy, apprehensive; — machen, to alarm, frighten. **Bangen**, bang'en, vi. to be afraid. **Bangigkeit**, bang'ichkāt, f. anxiety, apprehension.
Bänglich, beng'lich, a. anxious.
Bank, bank, f. pl. **Bänke**, bench; form; shelf; bed (of oysters); pl. **Banken**, bank; — halten, to keep bank; durch die —, in the lump, in the gross; auf die lange — ſchieben, to lay on the table, to delay, put off. **Bank's actie**, -aktsī-e, f. bank-stock, bank-bill. **Bankagent**, -agent, m. -en, pl. -en, broker. **Bankbruch**, -bruch, **Bankerott**, bankrott', m. bankruptcy; **Bankerott**, a. s. bankrupt; — machen, to fail, turn bankrupt. **Bankzuste**, -nōte, f. bank-bill.
Bann, bann, m. ban, excommunication; in den — thun, to excommunicate. **Bannen**, vt. to lay, exorcise, charm, to root to the spot, to charm, enchant. **Bannfluch**, -fluch, m. anathema.
Banner, ban'nēr, n. banner.
Banquier, ban'ki-ā, m. banker.
Banſe, ban'se, f. bay (in a barn).
Banſen, ban'sen, m. paunch.
Bär, bār, m. -en, pl. -en, bear.
Barbar, barbār', m. en, pl. -en, barbarian. **Barbarei**, barbarēī', f. barbarity, savageness, wilderness. **Barbariſch**, barbär'ish, a. barbarous, av. -ly.
Barbier, barbīr', m. barber. **Barbie-** ren, barbī'ren, vt. to shave. **Barbiergeſell**, -geſell, m. -en, pl. -en, journeyman barber. **Barbiermeſſer**, -mēsser, n. razor. **Barbierſtube**, -zhtube, f. barber's shop, shaving-saloon.
Barchent, bar'chent, m. fustian; feiner —, dimity.
Barde, bar'de, m. -n, pl. -n, bard.
Bärenhäuter, bä'renhŏiter, m. sluggard. **Bärenjagd**, -yacht, f. bear-hunt.
Barfuß, bar'fus, a. barefooted.
Bärin, bā'rin, f. pl. -nen, she-bear.
Barke, bar'ke, f. bark; kleine —, lighter.
Barmherzig, barmhērts'ich, a. merciful, compassionate; **Barmherzigkeit**, -kāt, f. mercifulness, compassionateness.
Bärmutter, bär'mutter, f. womb.
Barsch, barsck', a. ridiculous, odd, queer.
Barometer, barromā'ter, m. barometer.
Barracke, barrack'e, f. hut, barrack.
Barre, bar're, f. **Barren**, m. bar (of gold); bar (in a river). [nast.).
Barren, bar'ren, m. double bars (Gym-
Bars, bars, (**Barſch**), m. perch.
Barſch, barsh, a. rough, harsh, av. -ly.
Bart, bārt, m. beard, barb; wattle (of a cock). **Bärtig**, bārt'ich, a. bearded. **Bartlos**, bārt'lōs, a. beardless. **Bartſeife**, -sāefe, f. shaving-soap.
Baryt, baritt', m. baryta; kohlenſaurer —, carbonate of baryta.
Baſalt, basalt', m. basalt.
Baſe, bāse, f. aunt; cousin; base (Chem.).
Baſilisk, basilisk', m. basilisk.
Basrelief, barelīf', m. bas-relief.
Baß, bass, m. bass, base. **Baßgeige**, -gēige, f. base-viol. **Baſſiſt**, bassīzst', m. -en, pl. -en, base (singer), basso. **Baßſchlüſſel**, -shlüssel, m. base-clef **Baßſtimme**, -zhtimme, f. base (voice).
Baſt, bazht, m. bast. **Baſten**, bezh'ten, a. made of bast. **Baſtſtrick**, -zhtrick, m. bast rope.
Baſtard, bazh'tart, m. bastard.
Baſtei, baztēī', f. bastion.
Bataillon, batalyon', n. battalion.
Batiſt, batizht', m. cambric, lawn.
Batterie, batterī', f. battery; galvaniſche —, galvanic battery.

Baten, bat'sen, *m.* piece of money (nearly 3 cts.).
Bau, bŏu, *m.* building; cultivating; erection; mechanism (of a watch); structure, build; hole, cover (of a fox, etc.); burrow (of a rabbit). **Bauanschlag,** bŏu'änshläk, *m.* estimate. **Bauart, Bŏu'ärt,** *f.* style of architecture.
Bauch, bŏuch, *m.* belly, abdomen, paunch; bunt (of sails); einen — haben oder machen, to bulge out; **sdiener, -diner,** *m.* glutton; **sgrimmen, -grimmen,** *n.* gripes; **sgurt, -gurt,** *m.* belly-band, girdle, truss; **srednner, -rädner,** *m.* ventriloquist; **süsse, -zhtücke,** *s. pl.* futtock riders (Mar.); **swasserjucht, -vassersucht,** *f.* ascites; **sweh, -vä,** *n.* pain in the bowels, belly-ache.
Bauen, bŏu'en, *vt.* to build, construct, erect; to cultivate, till; to work (mines).
Bauer, bŏuer, *m.* -*e*, *pl.* -*n*, builder; cultivator, peasant, husbandman; **sfrau (Bäuerin,** bäü'erin). *f.* countrywoman; **sgut, -gut,** *pl.* **squter, shof, -höf,** *m.* farm. **Bauerisch,** bäü'erish, *a.* boorish; rustic. **Bauernhaus,** bŏu'ernhŏus, *n.* farm-house. **Bau- ermädchen, -mëtchen,** *n.* **Bau'er- birne, -dirne,** *f.* country-girl. **Bau- ernstand, -zhtant,** *m.* peasantry.
Baufällig, bŏu'fellich, *a.* ruinous, decaying; **skeit, -käët,** *f.* decay.
Bauherr, bŏu'herr, *m.* -*n*, *pl.* -*n*, builder. **Bau'holz, -holts,** *n.* timber.
Baukunst, bŏu'kunzht, *f.* architecture. **Baulich,** bŏu'lich, *a.* habitable, in good repair. **Baulustig, -luzhtich,** *a.* fond of building.
Baum, bŏum, *m.* tree; beam (weaver's) boom. **Bäumchen,** bŏüm'- chen, *n.* little tree, sapling. [tect.
Baumeister, bŏu'mäëzhter, *m.* archi-
Baumeln, bŏu'meln, *vi.* to dangle.
Baumen, bŏum'en, *vi.* to ascend a tree. **Bäumen, bŏü'men,** *vi.* to rear, prance.
Baumfrucht, bŏum'frucht, *f.* fruit. **Baum'hacker, -hacker,** *m.* woodpecker. **Baum'öl, -öhl,** *n.* olive oil, sweet-oil. **Baum'rinde, -rinde,** *f.* bark. **Baumschlag, -shläk,** *m.* foliage. **Baum'schule, -shule,** *f.* nursery. **Baum'stark, -zhtark,** *a.* very strong, sturdy, robust. **Baum'wolle, -volle,**
f. cotton. **Baum'wollen,** *a.* cotton. **Baum'zucht, -tsucht,** *f.* nursery (of trees).
Bausbak, bŏus'back, *m.* or *f.* chubfaced person; **sig,** *a.* chubby, chubfaced, blowzy.
Bausch, bŏush, *m.* pad, bolster; in — und Bogen, in the lump, in the gross. **Bäuschen,** bŏush'en, *vi.* to swell, bunch. **Bauschig,** bŏush'ich, *a.* bunchy.
Baustelle, bŏu'zhtelle, *f.* buildingground. site. **Bauwerk,** bŏu'vërk, *n.* building.
Bazar, bats'ar, *m.* bazaar.
Beabsichtigen, beap'sichtigen, *vt.* to intend, aim at.
Beachten, beach'ten, *vt.* to attend to. **Beach'tenswerth, -värt,** *a.* worthy of notice. **Beach'tung, -ung,** *f.* notice.
Beamter, beam'ter, *m.* officer, functionary.
Beängstigen, beeng'zhtigen, *vt.* to frighten. **Beäng'stigung, -ung,** *f.* anxiety, uneasiness, torment.
Beantworten, beant'vorten, *vt.* to answer. **Beant'wortung, -ung,** *f.* answer, reply.
Bearbeiten, bear'bäëten, *vt.* to cultivate, treat, elaborate. **Bear'bei- tung, -ung,** *f.* treating, elaboration.
Beaufsichtigen, beŏuf'sichtigen, *vt.* to oversee, supervise, control.
Beauftragen, beŏuf'trägen, *vt.* to commission, charge.
Bebauen, bebŏu'en, *vt.* to cultivate, build upon.
Beben, bä'ben, *vi.* to tremble, shake. **Bebung,** bäb'ung, *f.* quivering.
Becher, bech'er, *m.* cup, goblet. **Bech'ern,** *vi.* to tipple, tope.
Becken, beck'en, *n.* basin.
Bedacht, bedacht', *m.* consideration. **Bedächtig,** bedëch'tig, *a.* considerate, cautious; **skeit, -käët,** *f.* prudence, caution. **Bedachtsam,** bedacht'sam, *a.* thoughtful, cautious; **skeit, -käët,** *f.* thoughtfulness; caution.
Bedanken, bedank'en, *rr.* to thank.
Bedarf, bedarf'. *m.* want, need.
Bedauern, bedŏu'ern, *vt.* to pity, regret; **swürdig, -würdich,** *a.* deplorable, pitiable.
Bedecken, bedeck'en, *vt.* to cover. **Bedeck'ung, -ung,** *f.* covering, escort.
Bedenken, bedenk'en (bedachte, bedacht), *vt.* to consider, ponder; *s. m.*

consideration, doubt, hesitation, scruple; advice. **Bedenklich**, bedenk'lich, a. nice delicate; full of risk, suspicious, critical, scrupulous; **-keit**, -kāēt, f. irresolution; scruple; critical condition, hazard. **Bedenk'zeit**, -tsāīt, f. time for consideration.

Bedeuten, bedöü'ten, vt. to inform, to enjoin; to signify, indicate, augur, presage; vi. to be important, of consequence, to signify; **-d, Bedeutsam**, bedöüt'sam, a. significant, important, considerable. **Bedeut'ung**, -ung, f. signification, meaning; consequence, importance; **-voll**, -foll, a. significant, meaning.

Bedienen, bedin'en, vt. to serve, wait on; sich —, to use, make use of, employ; to help one's self. **Bedien'ter**, m. servant, officer. **Bedien'tenstube**, -zhtube, f. servants' room. **Bedien'ung**, f. service, attendance.

Bedingen, beding'en (bedung, bedungen), vt. to condition, stipulate. **Bedingt'**, a. conditional. **Beding'ung**, -ung, f. condition; **-sweise**, -vēīse, av. conditionally, on condition.

Bedrängen, bedreng'en, vt. to press hard, harass, oppress. **Bedräng'niß**, n. distress, oppression, pressure, embarrassment. **Bedrängung**, bedreng'ung, f. pressure, embarrassment.

Bedrohen, bedrō'en, vt. to threaten, menace.

Bedrücken, bedrück'en, vt. to press, oppress. **Bedrücker**, bedrück'er, m. oppressor. **Bedrück'ung**, -ung, f. oppression.

Bedünken, bedünk'en, vr. imp. to seem; appear; s. n. opinion.

Bedürfen, bedürf'en, vt. to want, need, lack. **Bedürf'niß**, n. want, need, necessity, lack. **Bedürftig**, bedürft'ich, a. needy, poor; **-keit**, -kāēt, f. neediness, poverty.

Beehren, beēr'en, vt. to honour; accept.

Beeidigen, beēīd'ichen, vt. to swear; to declare upon oath.

Beeifern, beēīf'ern, vr. to exert one's self; to strive.

Beeinträchtigen, beāēn'trechtigen, vt. to injure, wrong, harm, hurt, prejudice. **Beein'trächtigung**, -ung, f. injury, prejudice.

Beendigen, beēnd'ichen, vt. to finish, conclude. **Beend'igung**, -ung, f. conclusion, termination.

Beengen, beeng'en, vt. to narrow, straiten, contract, cramp.

Beerben, beerb'en, vt. to be heir to.

Beerdigen, beērd'ichen, vt. to bury, inter.

Beere, bā're, f. berry.

Beet, bāt, n. bed, flower-bed.

Befähigen, befā'ichen, vt. to enable, fit, authorize. **Befähigung**, befā'ichung, f. qualification, authorization.

Befahren, befār'en (befuhr, befahren), vt. to ride on; to navigate; to enter (a mine).

Befallen, befal'len (-fiel, -fallen), vt. to befall, seize.

Befangen, befang'en, a. embarrassed, disconcerted; biased, prejudiced, prepossessed; **-heit**, -hāēt, f. embarrassment.

Befassen, befas'sen, vr. to meddle with.

Befehl, befāl', m. command, order. **Befehlen**, befāl'en (befahl, befohlen), vt. to command, order, bid, charge. **Befehlerisch**, befāl'ērish, a. imperious, domineering. **Befehligen**, befāl'ichen, vt. to command. **Befehlshaber**, befāls'hāber, m. commander.

Befestigen, befezh'tichen, vt. to fasten, fix, attach. **Befestigung**, -ung, f. fortification; **-swerk**, -verk, n. defence.

Befeuchten, befäüch'ten, vt. to wet, moisten.

Befeuern, befäü'ern, vt. to fire, heat, animate.

Befiedert, befī'dert, a. winged.

Befinden, befin'den (befand, befunden), vr. to do, to be; to find, esteem, think. **Befindlich**, befind'lich, a. being, contained.

Beflecken, befleck'en, vt. to stain, soil, pollute. **Befleck'ung**, f. soiling, pollution.

Befleißen, **Befleißigen**, befläīs'ichen, vr. to bestow pains upon, to apply one's self. **Befleiß'igung**, -ung, f. application, close study. **Befliß'en**, beflis'sen, a. studious, assiduous; **-heit**, -hāēt, f. assiduity.

Beflören, beflör'en, vt. to cover with crape; to cloud.

Beflügeln, beflüh'geln, vt. to wing, feather; to add wings; to hasten, animate; to cut lanes (through a forest).

Befolgen, befol'gen, *vt.* to follow, obey, practise.
Befördern, beför'dern, *vt.* to forward, expedite, assist, promote, advance. **Beförderung**, -ung, *f.* furtherance, advancement; forwarding.
Befrachten, befrach'ten, *vt.* to freight. **Befrachtung**, -ung, *f.* freighting.
Befragen, befrä'gen, *vt.* to ask, interrogate. **Befragung**, -ung, *f.* questioning, interrogation.
Befreien, befrei'en, *vt.* to free, deliver. **Befreier**, *m.* deliverer. **Befreiung**, befrei'ung, *f.* deliverance.
Befremden, befrem'den, *vt.* to surprise. **Befremdlich**, *a.* strange, odd, surprising. **Befremdung**, *f.* surprise, astonishment.
Befreunden, befroın'den, *vt.* to befriend; *vr.* to make friends with; to reconcile one's self with, to acquaint one's self with.
Befriedigen, befrīd'ichen, *vt.* to satisfy, content. **Befriedigung**, -ung, *f.* fence; satisfaction.
Befruchten, befruch'ten, *vt.* to fertilize, fecundate, fructify, impregnate. **Befruchtung**, -ung, *f.* fecundation.
Befugen, befū'gen, *vt.* to authorize, legitimate, entitle. **Befugt**, befukt', *a.* competent, authorized, justified. **Befugniß**, befuk'niss, *n.* authority, competence, right.
Befühlen, befühl'en, *vt.* to feel, touch, handle.
Befürchten, befürch'ten, *vt.* to fear. **Befürchtniß**, *n.* **Befürchtung**, -ung, *f.* apprehension, fear.
Begaben, begā'ben, *vt.* to gift, endow. **Begabung**, -ung, *f.* endowment.
Begaffen, begaf'fen, *vt.* to gape, stare at.
Begatten, begat'ten, *vr.* to couple, copulate. **Begattung**, -ung, *f.* copulation.
Begeben, begäb'en (begab, begeben), *vr.* to betake one's self, to go, repair, resort to; to set out; to give up, renounce; to happen, occur; **-heit**, -hket, *f.* occurrence.
Begegnen, begäg'nen, *vi.* to meet; to happen. **Begegniß**, begäg'niss, *n.* occurrence.
Begehen, begä'en (beging, begangen), *vt.* to visit; to measure out; to keep, celebrate; to commit.
Begehr, begär', *n.* desire, demand.

Begehren, begär'en, *vt.* to desire, long for; to ask, require, want.
Begehung, begā'ung, *f.* celebration; commission.
Begeifern, begäif'ern, *vt.* to slabber; attack, asperse.
Begeistern, begäisz'tern, *vt.* to inspirit, animate, inspire. **Begeist'erung**, -ung, *f.* inspiration, transport, excitement, enthusiasm.
Begier, **Begierde**, begīr'de, *f.* desire, lust. **Begierig**, begīr'ig, *a.* desirous.
Begießen, begīs'sen (begoß, begossen), *vt.* to moisten, water, wet; to fix with lead.
Beginn, beginn', *m.* beginning. **Beginnen** (begann, begonnen), *vt.* to begin, commence.
Beglaubigen, beglāu'bichen, *vt.* to attest, certify, authenticate, accredit. **Beglaub'igung**, -ung, *f.* credentials; **-schreiben**, -shrēiben, *n.* certificate.
Begleiten, beglāit'en, *vt.* to accompany. **Begleiter**, *m.* companion, concomitant. **Begleitung**, beglāit'ung, *f.* accompaniment, suit(e), retinue, train.
Beglücken, beglück'en, *vt.* to make happy, to bless. **Beglückt**, *a.* happy, blessed. **Beglück'ung**, -ung, *f.* rendering happy. **Beglückwünschen**, -vünshen, *vt.* to congratulate.
Begnadigen, begnä'dichen, *vt.* to pardon. **Begna'digung**, -ung, *f.* pardoning, pardon.
Begnügen, begnüh'gen, *vt.* to content one's self, to be contented, satisfied.
Begraben, begrä'ben (begrub, begraben), *vt.* to bury, inter. **Begräbniß**, begräp'niss, *n.* burial, funeral; **-platz**, -plats, *m.* burying-place.
Begreifen, begrāif'en (begriff, begriffen), *vt.* to touch, handle, feel; include; comprehend, understand. **Begreiflich**, begrāif'lich, *a.* comprehensible, conceivable.
Begrenzen, begrents'en, *vt.* to confine, limit, border, bound. **Begrenz'ung**, -ung, *f.* bounding; boundary.
Begriff, begriff', *m.* conception, notion, idea; im — sein, to be about to, to be on the point of.
Begründen, begrün'den, *vt.* to found, establish. **Begründ'ung**, -ung, *f.* foundation.

Begrüßen, begrühsen, *vt.* to salute, greet.
Begünstigen, begün'zhtichen, *vt.* to favor, support. **Begün'stigung**, -ŭng, *f.* favor, support.
Begütert, begüh'tert, *a.* wealthy, opulent, rich.
Behacken, beha:k'en, *vt.* to hoe, clear.
Behaftet, behcf'tet, *a.* affected, afflicted.
Behagen, behä'gen, *vi.* to please, delight; to take pleasure; *s. n.* delight, comfort, pleasure. **Behaglich**, be hāk'lich, *a.* pleasing, comfortable; *keit*, -käet, *f.* comfortableness.
Behalten, behal'ten (behielt, behalten), *vt.* to keep, retain. **Behälter**, behel'ter, *m.* **Behält'niß**, *n.* reservoir, conservatory; case, room.
Behandeln, behan'deln, *vt.* to handle, treat, discuss. **Behand'lung**, -ŭng, *f.* management, handling, dealing.
Behängen, beheng'en, *vt.* to hang with, to deck.
Beharren, beharr'en, *vi.* to continue, remain, persevere. **Beharrlich**, beharr'lich, *a.* persevering, constant; *keit*, -käet, *f.* perseverance, constancy. **Beharr'ung**, -ŭng, *f.* perseverance; *vermögen*, -fermöhgen, *n.* inertia.
Behauen, behäu'en, *vt.* to hew, cut off.
Behaupten, behäup'ten, *vt.* to assert, affirm, maintain, support, hold, defend; sich —, to keep one's ground. **Behaupt'ung**, -ŭng, *f.* assertion, holding out.
Behausung, behōus'ŭng, *f.* abode, residence.
Behelf, behělf', *m.* resource, shift. **Behel'fen** (behalf, beholfen), *vr.* to resort to; to make do.
Behelligen, behěll'ichen, *vt.* to trouble, importune. **Behelligung**, behěll'ichŭng, *f.* trouble.
Behend, behent', *a.* quick, nimble, handy; *igkeit*, -ichkäet, *f.* dexterity, nimbleness.
Beherbergen, behär'bergen, *vt.* to harbor, lodge.
Beherrschen, behěrr'shen, *vt.* to rule, sway. **Beherr'scher**, *m.* ruler, sovereign. **Beherr'schung**, -ŭng, *f.* sway, rule.
Beherzigen, behěrts'ichen, *vt.* to take to heart. **Beher'zigung**, -ŭng, *f.* consideration, reception. **Beherzt**, behěrtst', *a.* courageous, manful; *heit*, -häet, *f.* courage, intrepidity.
Behexen, behěx'en, *vt.* to bewitch, charm.
Behindern, behin'děrn, *vt.* to hinder.
Behorchen, behǒrch'en, *vt.* to listen to, to overhear.
Behörde, behör'de, *f.* magistracy, office, authority.
Behuf, behuf', *m.* behoof, behalf. **Behufs'**, for the sake of.
Behülflich, behülf'lich, *a.* expedient, useful.
Behüten, behüh'ten, *vt.* to guard, watch, keep. **Behutsam**, behŭt'sam, *a.* cautious; *keit*, -käet, *f.* caution, heedfulness.
Bei, bī, *pr.* by, at, with, in, near, close to, at the house of.
Beianker, bī'anker, *m.* ketch-anchor.
Beibehalten, bī'behalten (-behielt, -behalten), *vt.* to keep, retain.
Beibiegen, bī'bīgen (-bog, -gebogen), *vt.* to enclose. **Beigebogen**, bīgebōgen, *a.* enclosed.
Beiblatt, bī'blatt, *n. pl.* -blätter, supplement, extra.
Beibringen, bī'bring-en (-brachte, -gebracht), *vt.* to bring in, adduce (proofs); to give, deal (a blow); administer (poison); to affect, inspire with, impart; to teach; to suggest, hint, insinuate; to break (bad news).
Beichte, bīch'te, *f.* confession; zur — gehen, to confess; eine — hören, to confess, to hear confession. **Beichten**, bīcht'en, *vi.* to confess. **Beichtkind**, bīcht'kinnt, *n. pl.* -er, confessor, penitent. **Beicht'stuhl**, -zhtul, *m.* confessional, confession-chair. **Beicht'vater**, -fäter, *m.* confessor. **Beicht'zettel**, -tsettel, *m.* certificate of confession.
Beide, bīe'de, *pron.* both. **Beiderlei**, bīe'derlīe, of both sorts, both. **Beiderseits**, bīe'dersēits, *av.* on both sides. **Beiderseitig**, -sēitich, *a.* mutual, reciprocal.
Beidrucken, bī'drŭcken, *vt.* to print with.
Beifall, bī'fal, *m.* applause, approbation. **Beifal'len** (beifiel, beigefallen), *vi.* to occur, to come to one's remembrance, to recur; to recall; to hit at, to side with; to assent, applaud. **Beifällig**, bī'fellich, *a.* as

senting, favorable, gracious; *av.* -ly.
Beifolgen, bĕī'folgen, *vt.* to follow. **Beifolgend,** *a.* enclosed.
Beifügen, bĕī'fűhgen, *vt.* to add, subjoin, annex. **Beigefügt,** bĕī'gefügt. *a.* annexed. **Beifügung,** -ŭng, *f.* addition.
Beifuß, bĕī'fŭs, *m.* parrel-truss (Mar.).
Beigeben, bĕī'gāben (-gab, -gegeben), *vt.* to add, to join to.
Beigehen, bĕī'gā-en (-gieng, -gegangen), *vi.* to go with, accompany; sich — lassen, to presume, dare; to fancy.
Beigeschmack, bĕī'geshmack, *m.* tang, taste.
Beigesellen, bĕī'gesellen, *vt.* to associate.
Beihülfe, bĕī'hülfe, *f.* succor, supply.
Beikommen, bĕī'kommen (-kam, -gekommen), *vi.* to accompany; Einem —, to reach, to get at; to equal, match; seinem Schaden —, to repair; nicht —, to fall short of.
Beil, bĕīl, *n.* hatchet, axe.
Beilage, bĕī'lāge, *f.* enclosure; extra.
Beilager, bĕī'lāger, *n.* nuptials.
Beiläufig, bĕī'läufich, *a.* approximate; incidental; about, near, by the way.
Beilegen, bĕī'lägen, *vt.* to join, enclose; to attribute, ascribe; to settle, compose; to lay up, deposit; einen Namen —, to surname; to lie to (Mar.).
Beileid, bĕī'lăed. *n.* condolence; — bezeigen, to condole.
Beiliegen, bĕī'līgen (-lag, -gelegen), *vi.* to lie with. **Beiliegend,** *a.* enclosed.
Beimessen, bĕī'messen (-maß, -gemessen), *vt.* to attribute, impute.
Beimischen, bĕī'mishen, *vt.* to admix, mix with. **Beimischung,** -ŭng, *f.* admixture.
Bein, bĕēn. *n.* bone; leg.
Beinahe, bĕī'nă-e, *av.* almost, nearly.
Beiname, bĕī'nāme, *m.* nickname.
Beinbruch, bĕēn'brŭch, *m.* fracture. **Beinchen,** bĕēn'chen, **Beinlein,** lăēn, *n.* ossicle. **Beindrechsler,** -drĕkslēr, *m.* turner in bone. **Beinern,** bĕēn'ern, *a.* bone, bony. **Beinfraß,** -fräs, *m.* caries. **Beinharnisch,** -harnish, *m.* greaves. **Beinhaus,** -hŏŭs, *n.* charnel-house.

Beinhaut, -hŏŭt, *n.* periosteum. **Beinicht,** -icht, *a.* hard as bone. **Beinig,** bĕēn'ich, *a.* bony. **Beinkleider,** -klăēder, *s. pl.* pants, trowsers, pantaloons. **Beinschwarz,** -shvarts, *n.* bone-black, bone-ashes. **Beinspath,** -zhpät, *m.* bone-spavin.
Beiordnen, bĕī'ordnen, *vt.* to coordinate, adjoin. **Beiordnung,** -ŭng, *f.* coordination.
Beipflichten, bĕī'pflichten, *vi.* to assent, consent. **Beipflichtung,** -ŭng, *f.* approbation.
Beisammen, bĕīsam'men, *av.* together.
Beisatz, bĕī'sats, *m.* apposition.
Beischießen, bĕī'shīssen (-schoß, -geschossen), *vt.* to contribute.
Beischlaf, bĕī'shlāf, *m.* cohabitation. **Beischläferin,** bĕī'shläferin, *f.* concubine.
Beischließen, bĕī'shlīssen (-schloß, -geschlossen), *vt.* to enclose. **Beischluß,** bĕī'shlŭss, *m.* enclosure, something enclosed.
Beischuß, bĕī'shŭss, *m.* contribution.
Beisein, bĕī'săen, *n.* presence.
Beiseit, bĕīsĕīt', *av.* part, beside, aside.
Beisetzen, bĕī'setsen, *vt.* to put to, set on; to deposit, entomb; ein Segel —, to unfurl; alle Segel —, to crowd the sails, all the canvas.
Beisitzer, bĕī'sitser, *m.* assessor.
Beispiel, bĕī'zhpīl, *n.* example, instance; zum —, for example, such as, viz. e. g.; ein — geben, to set an example; sich zum — nehmen, to take as model; durch —e belegen, to exemplify; -los, -lös, *a.* unexampled, unprecedented, unparalleled.
Beispringen, bĕī'zhpring-en (-sprang, -gesprungen), *vi.* to succor.
Beißen, bĕīs'sen (biß, gebissen), *vt.* to bite. **Beißig,** bĕīs'sich, *a.* biting. **Beißkorb,** -korp, *m.* muzzle. **Beißzange,** -tsang-e, *f.* pincers, nippers.
Beistand, bĕī'zhtant, *m.* assistance.
Beistecken, bĕī'zhtecken, *vt.* to give; to shut up (in prison).
Beistehen, bĕī'zhtā-en (-stand, -gestanden), *vi.* to assist.
Beisteuer, bĕī'zhtŏĭ-er, *f.* contribution. **Beisteuern,** *vt.* to contribute.
Beistimmen, bĕī'zhtimmen, *vi.* to as-

sent. Beistim'mung, -ung, f. assent, consent.
Beitrag, bēī'trāk, m. contribution.
Beitragen, bēī'trägen (-trug, -getragen), vt. to contribute.
Beitreiben, bēī'trēīben (-trieb, -getrieben), vt. to collect.
Beitreten, bēī'trāten (-trat, -getreten), vi. to accede, agree. Beitritt, bēī'tritt, m. accession; agreement.
Beiwagen, bēī'vägen, m. extra-carriage.
Beiweg, bēī'vāk, m. by-way, by-road.
Beiwohnen, bēī'rōnen, vi. to attend; to cohabit. Beiwohnung, -ung, f. presence; cohabitation.
Beiwort, bēī'wort, n. adjective.
Beizählen, bēī'tsālen, vt. to add, number among.
Beize, bāē'tse, f. hawking; lye; ooze (Min.). Beizen, bāēt'sen. vt. to hawk; to macerate; to soak; to tan (a hide); to tinge (wood); to dress (fur).
Beizeichen, bēī'tsāēchen, n. accidental (Mus.); countermark.
Beizeiten, bēītsēīt'en, av. betimes.
Bejahen, beyā'en, vt. to affirm; to answer in the affirmative. Bejahung, beyā'ung, f. affirmation; -weise, -vēīse, av. affirmatively.
Bejammern, beyam'mern, vt. to lament, bewail, bemoan; -swerth, -vārt, a. deplorable, lamentable.
Bekämpfen, bekem'pfen, vt. to combat, to fight with.
Bekannt, bekannt', a. known; — machen, to notify, publish; sich — machen mit, to get acquainted with. Bekann'te, m. or f. acquaintance. Bekanntlich, bekannt'lich, av. notoriously. Bekanntmachung, bekannt'machung, f. publication. Bekanntschaft, -shaft, f. acquaintance.
Bekehrbar, bekār'bär, a. convertible.
Bekehren, bekār'en, vt. to convert.
Bekehrer, bekār'er, m. converter.
Bekehrung, -ung, f. conversion; -sucht, -sucht, f. proselytism.
Bekennen, beken'nen (bekannte, bekannt), vt. to confess, avow, acknowledge, own, profess. Beken'ner, m. confessor, professor, believer in, receiver, follower. Bekenntniß, n. confession, creed.
Beklagen, beklāg'en, vt. to lament, bewail, bemoan; sich —, to complain; -swerth, -vārt, a. pitiable, lamentable. Beklag'te, m. or f. defendant.
Beklatschen, beklat'shen, vt. to clap; to applaud; to tell tales on; to defame, scandalize.
Bekleben, beklā'ben, vt. to paste upon.
Beklecken, Beklecksen, beklēck'sen, vt. to blot, blur, spot, stain.
Bekleiden, beklāē'den. vt. to clothe, dress, cover; — den Unter, to dress; — ein Tau, to serve; — ein Zimmer, to paper; — einen Schacht, to line; ein Amt —, to fill an office. Bekleidung, -ung, f. clothing, dress; lining, covering.
Bekleistern, beklāē'zhtern, vt. to paste; to gloss.
Beklemmen, beklem'men, vt. to press, pinch, oppress. Beklem'mung, -ung, f. oppression, anxiety. Beklommen, beklom'men, a. oppressed, anxious.
Beklopfen, beklopf'en, vt. to knock, beat, belabor.
Bekommen, bekom'men, vt. (bekam, bekommen), to get, receive, obtain; nicht gut —, not to agree with.
Beköstigen, bekōzh'tichen, vt. to feed, board, diet. Beköstigung, -ichung, f. boarding, board, diet.
Bekräftigen, bekref'tichen, vt. to confirm. Bekräftigung, -ung, f. confirmation.
Bekränzen, bekrent'sen, vt. to wreathe, garland.
Bekreuzen, bekröūt'sen, vt. to cross.
Bekriegen, bekrī'gen, vt. to war, make war upon.
Bekritteln, bekrit'teln, vt. to carp at.
Bekümmern, beküm'mern, vt. to afflict, grieve; sich um etwas —, to care for, interest one's self. Beküm'merniß, n. affliction. Beküm'mert, a. afflicted, grieved, anxious for.
Bekunden, bekun'den, vt. to depose, aver.
Belachen, belach'en, vt. to laugh at.
Beladen, belā'den, vt. to load, freight.
Belagern, belā'gern, vt. to besiege. Bela'gerer, m. besieger Bela'gerung, -ung, f. siege.
Belang, belang', m. consequence, amount. Belangen, belang'en, vt. to concern, regard: to go to law with, to sue, accuse. Belang'ung, -ung, f. persecution, accusation.

Bel 57 **Ben**

Belaften, bęlazh'ten, *vt.* to charge, burden, load down; to debit. **Beläftigen**, bęlęzh'tiģen, *vt.* to molest, trouble, importune. **Beläftigung**, bęlęzh'tiģung, *f.* molestation, trouble.

Belauben, bęläū'ben, *vt.* to leaf. **Belaubt'**, *a.* leafy. [watch.

Belauern, bęlou'ern, *vt.* to lurk, spy,

Belauf, bęlkuf', *m.* amount. **Belaufen**, bęläuf'en, — fiḋ, to amount.

Belaufḋen, bęlou'shen, *vt.* to listen to, to overhear.

Beleben, belā'ben, *vt.* to enliven, animate. **Belebt**, bęlēpt', *a.* lively, sprightly. **Belebung**, bęlāb'ung, *f.* animation. vivification.

Belecken, bęlęck'en, *vt.* to lick at.

Beleg, bęlāk'. *m.* proof, document.

Belegen, bęlā'gen, *vt.* to lay over, cover with; to pave; to hoop (a cask), to shoe (a wheel); to belay (a rope); to preoccupy, secure (a place); to face (with marble); to line; to cover (a mare); to seize.

Belehnen, bęlān'en. *vt.* to feoff, enfeoff, invest. **Belehnung**, -ung, *f.* feoffment, investiture.

Belehren, bęlār'en, *vt.* to inform, instruct.

Beleibt, bęlēipt', *a.* corpulent; **-heit**, *f.* fatness, obesity, corpulence.

Beleidigen, bęlī'diģen, *vt.* to offend, affront, insult. **Beleidiger**, *m.* offender. **Beleidigung**, bęlī'digung, *f.* offence, insult, affront.

Belesen, bęlā'sen. *a.* well read; **-heit**, *-hkęt*, *f.* extensive reading.

Beleuḋten, bęlōiḋ'ten, *vt.* to enlighten, illuminate, light up: to elucidate, illustrate, to throw light upon; to illumine (a painting). **Beleuḋtung**, -ung, *f.* illumination, lights.

Bellern, bęl'fern, *vi.* to bark, yelp; senid.

Belieben, bęlīb'en, *vt.* to like; to choose; *s. n.* will, liking. **Beliebt**, bęlīpt', *a.* beloved, popular. **Beliebig**, bęlīb'iḋ. *a.* arbitrary, chosen, preferred, to one's liking.

Bellen, bęll'en, *vi.* to bark, yelp.

Belletriftiḋ, bęlletrizh'tish, *a.* pertaining to belles-lettres.

Beloben, bęlōb'en. *vt.* to commend, praise. **Belobung**, bęlōb'ung, *f.* commendation, praise.

Belohnen, bęlōn'en, *vt.* to reward, requite. **Belohnung**, -ung, *f.* reward, recompense.

Belügen, bęlüh'gen, *vt.* to lie to, to belie.

Belustigen, bęlụk'sen, *vt.* to cozen, cheat.

Beluftigen, bęlụzh'tigen, *vt.* to amuse, divert. **Beluftigung**, -ung, *f.* diversion, amusement.

Bemäḋtigen, bęmęḋ'tiģen, *vr.* (with gen.), to take possession of; to seize.

Bemalen, bęmā'len, *vt.* to paint; soil; mark.

Bemannen, bęman'nen, *vt.* to man.

Bemänteln, bęmęn'teln, *vt.* to cloak.

Bemasten, bęmazh'ten, *vt.* to mast.

Bemausen, bęmōus'en, *vt.* to pilfer.

Bemeistern, bęmīzh'tern, *vt.* to master, overcome.

Bemelden, bęmēl'den, *vt.* to mention. **Bemeldet**, *a.* aforesaid.

Bemerkbar, bęmęrk'bār, *a.* perceivable. **Bemerken**, *vt.* to remark, notice, perceive; **-swerth**, -vārt, *a.* remarkable. **Bemerkung**, -ung, *f.* remark, observation, note.

Bemitleiden, bęmit'līden, *vt.* to pity.

Bemittelt, bęmit'telt, *a.* opulent, wealthy.

Bemoost, bęmōst', *a.* mossy.

Bemühen, bęmüh'en, *vt.* to trouble; fiḋ —, to take pains; to endeavor. **Bemühung**, -ung, *f.* trouble, endeavor, pains.

Benaḋbart, bęnaḋ'bart, *a.* neighboring.

Benaḋriḋtigen, bęnāḋ'riḋtiḋen, *vt.* to inform, send word to, to acquaint with, advertise. **Benaḋriḋtigung**, -iḋung, *f* advertisement, information.

Benaḋtheiligen, bęnāḋ'tōiliḋen, *vt.* to injure, prejudice, harm, hurt.

Benagen, bęnā'gen, *vt.* to gnaw, nibble.

Benannt, bęnannt', *a.* denominate; named.

Benarbt, bęnarpt', *a.* scarred.

Benebeln, bęnā'beln. *vt.* to cover with mist; to dim, cloud; intoxicate. **Benebelt**, *a.* tipsey, intoxicated.

Benefiz, bęnęfits'. *n.* benefit.

Benehmen, bęnā'men (benabm, benommen), *vt.* to take away, deprive of; fiḋ —, to behave; *s. n.* behavior, conduct.

Beneiden, benēī'den. *vt.* to envy; *swerth*, -värt, *a.* enviable.
Benennen, benen'nen (benannte, benannt), *vt.* to name. **Benennung**, benen'nung, *f.* appellation.
Benetzen, benet'sen, *vt.* to moisten, wet.
Bengel, beng'el, *m.* club; rude, coarse fellow, clown; *haft*, -haft, *a.* clownish.
Benöthigt, benöh'tiḡt, *a.* in need, in want of.
Benutzen, benut'sen, *vt.* to make use of.
Beobachten, beōb'ächten, *vt.* to observe, perform, keep. **Beobachter**, *m.* observer. **Beobachtung**, beōb'ächtung, *f.* observation, observance.
Beordern, beŏr'dĕrn, *vt.* to order.
Bepacken, bepack'en, *vt.* to pack, load.
Bepanzern, bepan'tsern, *vt.* to harness, dress in armor.
Beperlen, bepĕrl'en, *vt.* to pearl, impearl.
Bepflanzen, bepflan'tsen, *vt.* to plant.
Bepissen, bepis'sen, *vt.* to piss upon.
Bequem, bequām', *a.* convenient, fit, suitable, comfortable, commodious; *av.* -ly. **Bequemen**, bequām'en, *vt.* to accommodate, adapt; *sich* —, to submit to. **Bequemlichkeit**, bequām'lichkāt, *f.* convenience, leisure, comfort; *pl.* accommodations.
Berappen, berap'pen, *vt.* to roughcast, plaster.
Berasen, berā'sen, *vt.* to turf.
Beraspeln, berazh'peln. *vt.* to rasp.
Berathen, berāt'en (berieth, berathen), *vt.* to advise; *sich* —, consult, confer with. **Berather**, berāt'er, *m.* counselor, adviser. **Berathschlagen**, berāt'shlägen, *vt.* to consult, deliberate, confer. **Berathschlagung**, berāt'shlägung, *f.* consultation, deliberation.
Berauben, berāub'en, *vt.* to rob, deprive of. **Beraubung**, -ung, *f.* deprivation.
Beräuchern, beräuch'ĕrn, *vt.* to smoke, fumigate.
Berauschen, beroush'en, *vt.* to intoxicate.
Berechnen, berech'nen. *vt.* to calculate, compute. **Berechnung**, -ung, *f.* calculation, computation.
Berechtigen, berech'tichen, *vt.* to authorize, empower, entitle. **Berechtigung**, -ung, *f.* title, right.

Bereden, berād'en, *vt.* to persuade, prevail on, induce; to talk over, speak of; *sich* — mit, to consult, confer, concert. **Beredsam**, berēd'sam, *a.* eloquent, *av.* -ly; *keit*, -kāst, *f.* eloquence. **Beredt**, berēt', *a.* eloquent, fluent, expressive.
Bereich, berāich', *m.* reach, stretch, compass.
Bereichern, berāich'ern, *vt.* to enrich.
Bereifen, berāif'en, *vt.* to cover with hoar-frost.
Bereifen, berāif'en, *vt.* to hoop (a barrel).
Bereisen, berāis'en, *vt.* to travel over, frequent, visit.
Bereit, berāit', *a.* ready, *av.* readily; — sein, to be in readiness. **Bereiten**, berāit'en, *vt.* to prepare.
Bereiten, berāit'en (beritt, beritten), *vt.* to ride over; — ein Pferd, to break. **Bereiter**, *m.* horse-breaker.
Bereits, berāits', *av.* already. **Bereitschaft**, berāit'shaft, *f.* readiness. **Bereitwillig**, berāit'villich, *a.* ready, willing, *av.* -ly; *keit*, -kāst, *f.* readiness, willingness, zeal, promptitude.
Berennen, beren'nen (berannte, berannt), *vt.* to inclose, block up, invest; to storm, assault.
Bereuen, beröu'en, *vt.* to repent.
Berg, bĕrk, *m.* mountain, mount; Berg ab, down hill; Berg auf, up hill; zu Berge stehen, to stand on end (of hair); hinter dem — halten, to be reserved; da stehen die Ochsen am —, here we are brought to a stand. **Bergamt**, bĕrk'amt, *n. pl.* -ämter, mining-office.
Bergamotte, berkamot'te, *f.* bergamot; *öl*, -öhl, *n.* oil of bergamot.
Bergart, bĕrk'ärt, *f.* mineral, ore. **Bergbewohner**, -bevöner, *m.* mountaineer. **Bergblau**, -blāu, *n.* ultramarine, mountain-blue. **Bergbraun**, -brāun, *a.* umber.
Bergen, bĕrk'en (barg, geborgen), *vt.* to hide, conceal, to save; to take in (the sails). **Berggeld**, -gelt *n.* salvage. **Berggegend**, -gägent, *f.* mountain-region, highland. **Berghütter**, -hüttser, *s. pl.* wates. **Bergicht**, berkicht, *a.* mountain-like. **Bergig**, berk'ich, *a.* mountainous, hilly. **Bergskette**, -kette, *f.* mountain-chain.

Berg'knappe, -k(e)nappe, m. -n, pl. -n. **Berg'mann,** -mau, pl. Bergleute, miner. **Berg'kuppe,** -kuppe, f. mountain-top. **Berg'leder,** -lader, n. miner's apron. **Berg'männisch,** bĕrk'mennish, a. mining. **Berg'öl,** -öhl, n. petroleum. **Berg'predigt,** -prädicht, f. sermon on the mount. **Berg'rath,** -rät, m. pl. -räthe, board of mines; counsellor of mines. **Berg'rücken,** -rücken, m. ridge. **Berg'salz,** -salts, n. rock-salt. **Berg'schloß,** -shloss, n. pl. -schlösser, castle on a mountain. **Bergschlucht,** bĕrk'-shlycht, f. defile, mountain gorge. **Berg'spitze,** -zhpitse, f. peak, mountain-top.

Bergung, bĕrk'ung, f. salvage.

Bergwand, bĕrk'vant, f. pl. -wände, crag, precipice. **Berg'werk,** -verk, n. mine, working of mines; -**wissenschaft,** -vissenshaft, f. science of mining. **Berg'wetter,** -vĕtter, s. pl. damp (in mines).

Bericht, bericht', m. report, account, (official) return, advice, information. **Berichten,** vt. to report, inform. **Bericht'erstattung,** -ĕrzhtattyng, f. report. **Berichtigen,** bericht'ichen, vt. to correct, adjust, set to rights; to settle, balance, clear; to prick the sheets (Print.). **Berichtigung,** correction, adjustment, payment.

Beriechen, berīch'en (beroch, berochen), vt. to smell at.

Beritten, beritt'en, a. mounted.

Bernstein, bĕrn'zhtăen, m. amber, -en, a. made of amber; -**koralle,** f. amber-beads; -**öl,** -öhl, n. amber-oil.

Bersten, bĕrzht'en (borst, geborsten), vi. to burst.

Berüchtigt, berücht'icht, a. notorious, ill-famed.

Berücken, berück'en, vt. to catch, insnare.

Berücksichtigen, berück'sichtichen, vt. to consider, attend to. **Berücksichtigung,** -yng, f. regard, consideration.

Beruf, beryf', m. call, duty, business, profession. **Berufen** (berief, berufen), vt. to call, appoint; sich — auf, to appeal to, refer to; **Berufung,** beryf'yng, f. appeal.

Beruhen, bery'en, vi. to rest, depend on; — lassen, to abandon, desist from. **Beruhigen,** bery'ichen, vt. to quiet, appease, assuage, console, ease to set at ease or rest; sich — bei, to acquiesce in, to reconcile one's self to **Beruhigung,** bery'ichyng, f. appeasement, acquiescence in, ease, consolation.

Berühmt, berühmt', a. renowned, celebrated; -**heit,** -häet, f. celebrity, renown.

Berühren, berüh'ren, to touch, handle; to relate to; to hint at. **Berührung,** berüh'rung, f. contact, touch.

Berupfen, beryp'fen, to pluck, pick.

Berußen, bery'ssen, vt. to blacken with soot.

Besäen, besä'en, vt. to sow (a field); to stud.

Besagen, besäg'en, vt. to say, signify. **Besagt,** besacht', a. aforesaid.

Besän, besän', f. mizzen; den — losmachen, to set the mizzen.

Besanden, besan'den, vt. to strew with sand.

Besänftigen, besenft'ichen, vt. to soften. **Besänftigung,** -yng, f. appeasement; -**mittel,** -mittel, n. palliative.

Besanmast, besän'macht, m. mizzenmast. **Besansegel,** -sägel, n. mizzensail. **Besanstag,** -shtäk, n. mizzen-stay. **Besanwand,** -vant, f. pl. -wände, mizzen-shroud.

Besatzung, besatz'yng, f. garrison; ward (of a lock).

Besaufen, besoy'fen (besoff, besoffen), vt. to get drunk.

Beschaben, beshă'ben, vt. to scrape, shave, rub.

Beschädigen, beshä'dichen, vt. to hurt, damage. **Beschädigung,** -yng, f. damage, (particular) average (Mar.).

Beschaffen, beshaf'fen, a. constituted, qualified; -**heit,** -häet, f. quality, condition, state, nature; -**heitswert,** -häetsvert, n. pl. -wörter, adjective.

Beschäftigen, beshäf'tichen, vt. to occupy, employ, engage. **Beschäftigung,** -yng, f. business, occupation.

Beschälen, beshä'len, vt. to cover (a mare). **Beschäler,** m. stallion.

Beschämen, beshä'men, vt. to make ashamed, to confound, abash, shame. **Beschämung,** -yng, f. confounding, abashing, confusion, shame.

Beschatten, beshat'ten, vt. to shade shadow.

Beschaken, beshat'sen, vt. to assess.
Beschatzung, -ung, f. assessment.
Beschauen, beshau'en, vt. to behold, view, look, contemplate, look on. **Beschaulich**, a. contemplative. **Beschauung**, -ung, f. contemplation.
Bescheid, beshide', m. answer, decision, order, pledge (in drinking); — geben über, to give information. **Bescheiden** (beschied, beschieden), vt. to apportion, allot, assign, order; to summon, send for; to inform; sich — lassen, to be open to conviction; sich —, to acquiesce in, to concede. **Bescheiden**, a. modest, unassuming; av. -ly, -heit, -häit, f. modesty.
Bescheinigen, beshein'ichen, vt. to certify, attest. **Bescheinigung**, -ung, f. certificate.
Bescheißen, beshais'sen (beschiß, beschießen), vt. to beshit; to cheat (vulgar).
Beschenken, beshenk'en, vt. to present, gift.
Bescheren, beshä'ren (beschor, beschoren), vt. to shear; to shave.
Bescheren, beshä'ren, vt. to impart, bestow, give, confer. **Bescherung**, -ung, f. present, gift.
Beschicken, beshick'en, vt. to send to; to put in order, to melt (ore); to alloy (gold, etc.); to manure, till, cultivate; to tend, nurse (a child); to take care of; to cover (of stags). **Beschickung**, -ung, f. alloying (of metals); taking care of.
Beschießen, beshis'sen (beschoß, beschossen), vt. to fire, batter, cannonade, bombard, shell (a town, etc.). **Beschießung**, -ung, f. bombardment.
Beschiffbar, beshiff'bar, a. navigable. **Beschiffen**, beshiff'en, vt. to navigate. **Beschiffung**, -ung, f. navigation.
Beschimpfen, beshim'pfen, vt. to insult, affront, abuse, disgrace. **Beschimpfung**, -ung, f. insult, affront, outrage, injury.
Beschirmen, beshirm'en, vt. to shelter, screen, protect, shield. **Beschirmung**, -ung, f. protection, defence.
Beschlafen, beshlaf'en (beschlief, beschlafen), vt. to consider for a night, to take counsel of one's pillow; to lie with.
Beschlag, beshläk', m. sheathing, hoeing, cover, iron-binding, mounting, clasp, hold, hoop; mould; efflorescence; seizure, sequestration;

mit — belegen, to sequester. **Beschlagen**, beshlä'gen (beschlug, beschlagen), vt. to beat, hammer round; to shoe (a horse); to furl (a sail); to stock (a farm); to line (a hind); to seize, sequester, confiscate, lay an embargo on; gut — sein, to be well versed in; vi. to tarnish; to grow mouldy. **Beschläge**, beshlä'ge, s. pl. mountings, iron-work, clout (of a wheel); clasp (of a book). **Beschlagnahme**, -name, f. seizure, confiscation.
Beschleichen, beshlei'chen (beschlich, beschlichen), vt. to come stealthily upon, creep upon, surprise.
Beschleunigen, beshläun'ichen, vt. to hasten, accelerate. **Beschleunigung**, -ichung, f. acceleration.
Beschließen, beshliss'en (beschloß, beschlossen), vt. to lock, shut up; to conclude, close; inclose; to resolve, decree. **Beschluß**, beshluss', m. conclusion, decision, resolution.
Beschmieren, beshmi'ren, vt. to besmear, soil.
Beschmitzen, beshmit'sen, vt. to soil, to mark.
Beschmutzen, beshmut'sen, vt. to smut, soil, stain.
Beschneiden, beshnei'den (beschnitt, beschnitten), vt. to cut, prune, clip; to circumcise. **Beschneidung**, f. circumcision.
Beschneien, beshnei'en, vt. to snow upon.
Beschnüffeln, beshnüff'eln, vt. to sniff at, smell at.
Beschönigen, beshöh'nichen, vt. to color, palliate. **Beschönigung**, -ichung, f. palliation.
Beschränken, beshreng'ken, vt. to bound, limit, confine, circumscribe, cramp. **Beschränkt**, beshrenkt', a. limited: narrow-minded. **Beschränkung**, -ung, f. limitation.
Beschreiben, beshrei'ben (beschrieb, beschrieben), vt. to describe; to write upon; sh, a. descriptive. **Beschreibung**, beshreib'ung, f. description.
Beschreien, beshrei'en (beschrie, beschrien), vt. to cry at, charm.
Beschreiten, beshrei'ten (beschritt, beschritten), vt. to stride, bestride, cross.
Beschuhen, beshu'en, vt. to shoe.
Beschuldigen, beshul'dichen, vt. to ac-

e··se, to charge with. **Beschul'digung**, -ichung, *f.* accusation.
Beschützen, beshüt'sen, *vt.* to defend, protect. **Beschützer**, *m.* defender, protector. **Beschützung**, -ung, *f.* protection.
Beschwatzen, beshvat'sen, *vt.* to talk over.
Beschwerde, beshvēr'de, *f.* trouble, complaint. **Beschweren**, beshvā'ren, *vt.* to load, charge; sich —, to complain. **Beschwerlich**, beshvār'lich. *a.* troublesome; -keit, -kāet, *f.* inconvenience, trouble, toil. **Beschwerung**, beshvār'ung, *f.* load, trouble; incumbrance, mortgage.
Beschwichtigen, beshvich'tichen, *vt.* to still, appease.
Beschwingen, beshving'en, *vt.* to wing, accelerate.
Beschwören, beshvöh'ren, *vt.* to conjure, to swear to. **Beschwörer**, *m.* conjurer, exorciser. **Beschwörung**, beshvöhr'ung, *f.* conjuring, exorcising.
Beseelen, besā'len, *vt.* to animate, inspirit.
Besegeln, besā'geln, *vt.* to sail over.
Besehen, bezā'en (besah, besehen), *vt.* to look at, view. **Besehenswerth**, -vārt, *a.* worth seeing.
Beseitigen, besēit'ichen, *vt.* to put aside, remove. **Beseitigung**, -ichung, *f.* removal.
Beseligen, besāl'ichen, *vt.* to bless. **Beseligung**, besāl'ichung, *f.* salvation.
Besen, bā'sen, *m.* besom, broom; -binder, -binder, *m.* broommaker; -reis, -rēis, *n. pl.* -er, birch-twig; -stiel, -zhtīl, *m.* broom-stick, broomstaff.
Besessen, besēs'sen, *a.* possessed.
Besetzen, besets'en, *vt.* to occupy, garrison; trim. **Besetzung**, -ung, *f.* trimming; occupation.
Beseufzen, besēūf'tsen, *vt.* to sigh over.
Besichtigen, besich'tichen, *vt.* to view, survey. **Besichtigung**, -ichung, *f.* inspection, view.
Besiegeln, besēl'geln, *vt.* to seal.
Besiegen, besē'gen, *vt.* to conquer, overcome.
Besingen, besing'en, *vt.* to sing of.
Besinnen, besin'nen (besann, besonnen), *vr.* to recollect; sich eines Andern —,

to change one's mind. **Besinnung**, -ung, *f.* consciousness; die — verlieren, to lose one's senses.
Besitz, besits', *m.* possession. **Besitzen**, (besaß, besessen), to possess. **Besitzer**, besits'er, *m.* possessor. **Besitznahme**, -nāme, *f.* seizure, occupancy. **Besitzung**, -ung, possession.
Besoffen, besof'fen, *a.* drunken; -heit, -hāet, *f.* drunkenness.
Besohlen, besō'len, *vt.* to sole.
Besolden, besol'den, *vt.* to hire, pay. **Besoldung**, -ung, *f.* salary, pay.
Besonder, beson'der, *a.* singular, peculiar, particular; -heit, -hāet, *f.* peculiarity, individuality. **Besonders**, beson'ders, *av.* separately, apart; especially.
Besonnen, beson'nen, *a.* sober, thoughtful, considerate; -heit, -hāet, *f.* soberness, presence of mind.
Besorgen, besor'gen, *vt.* to take care of, to direct, conduct, manage, carry on; to do, to acquit one's self of. **Besorger**, *m.* manager, commissioner. **Besorglich**, besork'lich, *a.* apprehensive; -keit, -kāet, *f.* apprehensiveness, solicitude. **Besorgniß**, besork'niss, *f.* apprehension, fear. **Besorgt**, besorkt', *a.* anxious, apprehensive, uneasy. **Besorgung**, besork'ung, *f.* management, execution.
Bespicken, beshpick'en, *vt.* to interlard.
Bespiegeln, bezhpīg'eln, *vr.* to view one's self in a mirror.
Besprechen, bezhprēch'en (besprach, besprochen), *vt.* to bespeak, speak of; sich —, to confer, consult, deliberate. **Besprechung**, *f.* conference, consultation.
Besprengen, bezhpreng'en, *vt.* to sprinkle over, besprinkle.
Bespringen, bezhpring'en (besprang, besprungen), *vt.* to cover.
Bespritzen, bezhprit'sen, *vt.* to squirt over.
Bespucken, bezhpuck'en, *vt.* to bespit, spit upon.
Besser, bes'ser, *a. av.* better. **Bessern**, bes'sern, *vt.* to better, ameliorate, improve. **Besserung**, bes'serung, *f.* improvement, amelioration, convalescence, recovery, reformation; -mittel, *n.* corrective.
Bestallen, bezhtal'len, *vt.* to appoint, invest. **Bestallung**, -ung, *f.* appointment; inauguration.

Beſtand, bəzhtant', *m.* duration, continuance; clear amount, balance; remainder; in — nehmen, to farm, rent. **Beſtändig,** bəzhtən'dĭċh, *a.* constant. *av.* -ly; **-keit, -käet,** *f.* constancy, firmness. **Beſtandtheil, -täel,** *m.* constituent part, ingredient, element.
Beſtärken, bəzhtər'ken, *vt.* to confirm, strengthen, fortify. **Beſtärkung, -ung,** *f.* confirmation.
Beſtätigen, bəzhtāt'ĭċhen, *vt.* to confirm, ratify, sanction. **Beſtät'igung, -ung,** *f.* ratification, sanction.
Beſtatten, bəzhtat'ten, *vt.* to bury, inter. **Beſtat'tung, -ung,** *f.* burial, interment.
Beſtauben, bəzhtāu'ben, *vt.* to become dusty, gather dust. **Beſtäuben,** bəzhtäu'ben, *vt.* to cover with dust.
Beſte, bəzh'te, *a.* best; der erſte Beſte, anybody; *s. n.* the good, benefit; zum Beſten geben, to spend; Einen zum — haben, to make sport of; nach meinem — Wiſſen, to the best of my knowledge.
Beſtechen, bəzhtēċh'en (beſtach, beſtochen), *vt.* to bribe, corrupt. **Beſtech'lich,** *a.* venal, corruptible; **-keit, -käet.** *f.* venality. **Beſtechung,** bəzhtēċh'ung, *f.* corruption. bribery.
Beſteck, bəzhtĕck', *n.* case; day's work; knives and forks. **Beſteck'en,** *vt.* to stick, to plant; to pole (beans).
Beſtehen, bəzhtā'en (beſtand, beſtanden), *vi.* to stand, undergo; to last, endure; to be, exist, subsist; persist; *s. n.* existence, subsistence.
Beſtehlen, bəzhtā'len (beſtahl, beſtohlen), *vt.* to steal from; to rob.
Beſteigen, bəzhtēĭg'en (beſtieg, beſtiegen), *vt.* to mount, ascend; to go on board; to climb; to cover.
Beſtellen, bəzhtĕl'len, *vt.* to appoint, order, deliver, cultivate. **Beſtellung,** bəzhtĕll'ung, *f.* order, commission, assignation.
Beſtens, bəzh'tens, *av.* best, in the best manner.
Beſternt, bəzhtērnt', **Beſtirnt,** bəzhtĭrnt', *a.* starry, studded with stars.
Beſteuern, bəzhtēŭ'ern, *vt.* to tax. **Beſteu'erung, -ung,** *f.* taxation.
Beſtie, bəzh'tĭ-e, *f.* beast.
Beſtimmen, bəzhtim'men, *vt.* to define, fix, designate; appoint; induce; ſich — für, to decide, resolve, pitch upon. **Beſtimmt,** bəzhtimmt' *a.* fixed, positive, certain; **-heit, -häet,** *f.* precision, certainty; mit —, positively. **Beſtim'mung, -ung,** *f.* designation; destiny, destination; determination; fate, lot; **-grund, -grunt,** *m.* motive.
Beſtmöglich, bəzhtmöhk'lĭċh, *a. av.* as well as possible.
Beſtoßen, bəzhtō'sen (beſtieß, beſtoßen), *vt.* to work; to knock.
Beſtrafen, bəzhträ'fen, *vt.* to punish, chastise. **Beſtraf'ung, -ung,** *f.* chastisement, punishment.
Beſtreben, bəzhträ'ben, *vt.* to endeavor, strive; to exert one's self, to make efforts. **Beſtreb'ung, -ung,** *f.* effort, endeavor, exertion.
Beſtreichen, bəzhtrēĭ'ċhen (beſtrich, beſtrichen), *vt.* to besmear, overspread.
Beſtreiten, bəzhtrēĭ'ten (beſtritt, beſtritten), *vt.* to contest, combat, oppose, dispute; bear, defray, pay.
Beſtreuen, bəzhträŭ'en, *vt.* to strew.
Beſtricken, bəzhtrick'en, *vt.* to insnare, entangle.
Beſtürmen, bəzhtĭrm'en, *vt.* to assault, assail, importune.
Beſtürzt, bəzhtĭrtst', *a.* consternated, dumfounded. **Beſtürz'ung, -ung,** *f.* consternation, confusion.
Beſuch, bəsuċh', *m.* visit, call; e. — machen, to pay a visit. **Beſuchen,** bəsu'ċhen, *vt.* to visit, to call on; to come and see; to frequent, attend.
Beſudeln, bəsud'eln, *vt.* to soil, defile, taint, pollute. **Beſud'elung, -ung** *f.* defilement, pollution.
Betagt, bətäkt', *a.* aged, stricken in years.
Betakeln, bətä'keln, *vt.* to rig; to warp (the end of a rope).
Betaſten, bətash'ten, *vt.* to couch, feel, handle, finger. **Betaſt'ung, -ung,** *f.* feeling, handling, touch.
Betäuben, bətäu'ben *vt.* to stun, din, deafen; benumb, stupefy, overcome; to silence. **Betäub'ung, -ung,** *f.* stunning, stupor; **-mittel,** *n.* narcotic.
Betbruder, bāt'bruder, *m.* hypocrite.
Beten, bā'ten, *vi.* to pray, say prayers; beseech.
Bethätigen, bətä'tĭċhen, *vt.* to prove, manifest (by actions).
Bethauen, bətäu'en, *vt.* to bedew.

Bethaus, bĕt'hŏys, n. pl. -häuſer, meeting-house.
Betheiligen, bĕtkŏl'ĭchen, vt. to give a share; ſich —, to interest one's self, to participate; betheiligt ſein, to be interested, concerned. **Betheil'i̱gung**, -ŭng, f. participation.
Betheuern, bĕtŏü'ern, vt. to protest. **Betheu'erung**, -ŭng, f. protestation, asseveration.
Betitelt, bĕtĭt'elt, a. titled.
Bethören, bĕtŏh'ren, vt. to fool, infatuate. **Bethör'ung**, -ŭng, f. infatuation, delusion.
Betonen, bĕtōn'en, vt. to accent, emphasize.
Betracht, bĕtracht', m. consideration, regard; in — nehmen, to take into consideration. **Betrachten**, bĕtracht'en, vt. to consider, view, contemplate. **Beträchtlich**, bĕtrĕcht'lich, a. considerable; -keit, -käet, f. considerableness. **Betrachtung**, bĕtracht'ŭng, f. consideration; contemplation.
Betrag, bĕträk', m. amount. **Betragen**, bĕträ'gen (betrug, betragen), vi. to amount; ſich —, to behave; s. n. behavior, conduct.
Betrauern, bĕtrŏü'ern, vt. to mourn, bewail.
Betreff, bĕtrĕff', m. respect, regard; in —, with respect to, touching. **Betreffen**, bĕtrĕf'fen (betraf, betroffen), vt. to concern; to befall; to catch; was mich betrifft, as for me.
Betreiben, bĕtreī'ben (betrieb, betrieben), vt. to drive upon; conduct, carry on.
Betreten, bĕtrā'ten (betrat, betreten), vt. to tread, step upon; to catch, surprise; pp. embarrassed, perplexed.
Betrieb, bĕtrĭb', m. management; auf —, by the impulse of; in vollem —, in full activity; -ſam, -sam, a. industrious, active; -ſamkeit, -samkäet, f. industry, activity.
Betroffen, bĕtrŏf'fen, a. struck, perplexed, shocked, confounded, dumfounded; -heit, -häet, f. perplexity.
Betrüben, bĕtrüh'ben, vt. to trouble, grieve, afflict. **Betrübniß**, bĕtrühp'nĭss, affliction, grief.
Betrug, bĕtrŭk', m. fraud, deceit. **Betrügen**, bĕtrüh'gen, vt. to cheat, deceive. **Betrüger**, bĕtrüh'ger, m. -in, f. cheat, deceiver, imposter. **Betrügerei**, bĕtrühgĕrī', f. cheat, deceit, imposition. **Betrügeriſch**, bĕtrühg'erish, a. fraudulent, deceitful.
Betſchweſter, bĕt'shvĕzhter, f. devotee; hypocrite. **Bet'ſtuhl**, -zhtyl, m. footstool, folding stool; pew.
Bett, bĕtt, n. pl. -en, bed; -decke, -decke, f. coverlet, bedcover, blanket.
Bettel, bĕt'tel, m. begging, mendicity, mendicancy; trash, trumpery, trifle; -arm, a. beggarly; -brief, -brīf, m. begging-letter; -brod, -brōt, n. beggar's livelihood; -ei, -ēī', f. begging, mendicity; importunate petition; -frau, -frŭū, f. beggar (woman); -haft, a. beggarly; -mann, m. pl. -leute, beggar. **Betteln**, bĕt'teln. vi. to beg, ask alms. **Bettelpfaffe**, -pfaf'fe, m. hedge-priest. **Bet'telſtab**, -zhtāp, m. beggary; an den — bringen, to reduce to mendicity. **Bet'telſtolz**, -zhtŏlts, a. beggarly pride. **Bet'telvogt**, -fokt, m. beadle.
Betten, bĕt'ten, vt. to bed, make one's bed. **Bett'flaſche**, -flashe, f. warming-pan. **Bett'genoß**, -genōss, m. -en, pl. -en, bed-fellow, bed-mate. **Bett'himmel**, -himmel, m. canopy, tester. **Bettlägerig**, bĕtt'lāgerich, a. bedrid; — ſein, to be sick-a-bed.
Bettler, bĕtt'lĕr, m. beggar; -iſch, a. beggarly.
Bettſtelle, bĕtt'zhtelle, f. bedstead. **Bett'überzug**, -ühbertsŭk, m. bedlinen. **Bett'vorhang**, -forhang, m. bed-curtain. **Bett'wäſche**, -veshe, f. **Bett'zeug**, -tsĕŭk, n. bed-linen.
Beugen, bĕū'gen, biegen, bī'gen, vt. to bend, bow. **Beugſam**, bĕūk'sam, a. flexible, pliable. **Beugung**, bĕūg'ŭng, f. bending, bend, flexure.
Beule, bĕū'le, f. boil, tumor; bump, swelling.
Beunruhigen, be-ŭn'ryĭchen, vt. to alarm, infest, disquiet, disturb. **Beunruhigung**, be-ŭn'ryĭchŭng, f. trouble, disturbance, infestation.
Beurkunden, be-ŭr'kŭnden, vt. to authenticate, verify, prove. **Beur'kundung**, -ŭng, f. authentication, verification.
Beurlauben, be-ŭr'lāŭben, vt. to furlough (besser furlow), to give leave

of absence; ſich —, to take leave, withdraw. **Beur'laubt**, -lŏybt, *pp.* on furlough.

Beurtheilen, be-yr'tāėlen, *vt.* to judge, criticise. **Beur'theilung**, -yng, *f.* judging, critical examination, criticism; -ſtraft, -kraft, *f.* power of judging.

Beute, bŏü'te, *f.* booty, spoil, prey, plunder.

Beutel, bŏü'tel, *m.* bag, purse. **Beu'teln**, *vt.* to bolt; to shake. **Beu'telratte**, -ratte, *f.* opossum. **Beu'telſchneider**, -shnēĭder, *m.* pick-purse, cheat. **Beu'teltuch**, -tych, *n. pl.* -tücher, bolting-cloth. **Beutler**, bŏüt'ler, *m.* glover, pursemaker.

Bevölkern, beföl'kern, *vt.* to people, populate. **Bevöl'kerung**, -yng, *f.* population.

Bevollmächtigen, befoll'mŏchtichen, *vt.* to empower, authorize. **Bevoll'mächtigter**, *m.* plenipotentiary, attorney. **Bevoll'mächtigung**, -yng, *f.* authorization.

Bevor, befōr', *av. & conj.* before.

Bevormunden befōr'mynden, *vt.* to keep in tutelage.

Bevorstehen, befōr'zhtā-en, *vi.* to impend, to be near, to approach.

Bevortheilen, befōr'tāėlen, *vt.* to take the advantage of.

Bewachen, bevach'en, *vt.* to watch, guard.

Bewaffnen, bevaff'nen, *vt.* to arm. **Bewaff'nung**, -yng, *f.* arming.

Bewahren, bevār'en, *vt.* to save, protect.

Bewähren, bevā'ren, *vt.* to prove, try, test. **Bewährt**, bevārt', *a.* proved, tried, approved. **Bewähr'ung**, -yng, *f.* proving, approbation.

Bewältigen, bevėl'tichen, *vt.* to overpower, master.

Bewandern, bevan'dern, *vt.* to travel through. **Bewan'dert**, bevan'dert, *a.* versed.

Bewandt, bevant', *a.* (turned), existing; -niß, *n.* case; state; nach — der Umſtände, according to circumstances.

Bewäſſern, bevės'sern, *vt.* to water.

Bewegbar, bevāk'bår, *a.* movable.

Bewegen, bevā'gen, *vt.* to move, induce. **Beweglich**, bevāk'lich, *a.* movable, voluble, glib, lively; -feit, -kāėt, *f.* mobility, volubility. **Be-**

weg'ung, -yng, *f.* motion; -ſgrund, -grynt, *m.* motive.

Bewehren, bevā'ren, *vt.* to arm.

Beweiden, bevāė'den, *vt.* to feed on, to graze.

Beweinen, bevāėn'en, *vt.* to lament, bewail.

Beweis, bevāės', *m.* proof, evidence, token, argument; demonstration; -bar, -bår, *a.* demonstrable, provable. **Beweiſen**, bevāė'sen (bewies, bewieſen), *vt.* to prove. evince. show, demonstrate. **Beweis'grund**, -grynt, *m.* argument.

Bewenden, beven'den (bewandte, bewandt), *vi.* to rest; es dabei — laſſen, to rest satisfied with; *s. m.* rest; dabei hat es ſein —, there the matter rests.

Bewerben, bevėr'ben (bewarb, beworben), *vi.* to woo, court; to canvass for, apply for. **Bewerb'ung**, -yng, *f.* courting; application.

Bewerfen, bevėr'fen (bewarf, beworfen), *vt.* to pelt, strike dumb, cover with; to plaster, rough-cast.

Bewerkstelligen, bevėrk'zhtėllichen, *vt.* to effect, bring about, accomplish.

Bewilligen, bevill'ichen, *vt.* to grant, yield, allow; to agree to. **Bewill'igung**, -yng, *f.* allowance; appropriation.

Bewillkommen, bevill'kommen, *vt.* to welcome. **Bewill'kommung**, -yng, *f.* welcoming, greeting.

Bewirken, bevìr'ken, *vt.* to effect.

Bewirthen, bevìrr'ten, *vt.* to entertain, treat. **Bewirth'ung**, -yng, *f.* entertainment.

Bewohnbar, bevōn'bår, *a.* habitable; -keit, -kāėt. *f.* habitableness. **Bewohnen**, bevōn'en, *vt.* to inhabit. **Bewohner**, bevōn'er, *m.* -sin, *f.* inhabitant.

Bewölken, bevöl'ken, *vt.* to cloud.

Bewunderer, bevyn'dėrėr, *m.* admirer. **Bewundern**, bevyn'dern, *vt.* to admire; -ſwerth, -svårt, *a.* admirable, wonderful. **Bewun'derung**, -yng, *f.* admiration.

Bewußt, bevysst', *a.* conscious, known; -ſein, -sāėn, *n.* consciousness.

Bezahlen, betsāl'en, *vt.* to pay, discharge, clear. **Bezahl'ung**, -yng, *f.* pay, payment.

Bezähmen, betsā'men, *vt.* to tame, re-

strain, govern, bridle, moderate; ſich —, to control one's self.
Bezaubern, bet͡säu'bern, *vt.* to charm, enchant, fascinate, bewitch, ravish. **Bezau'berung**, -ung, *f.* enchantment, fascination.
Bezeichnen, bet͡säich'nen, *vt.* to mark, designate, signify, express. **Bezeichnung**, bet͡säich'nyng, *f.* designation, description.
Bezeigen, bet͡säi'gen, *vt.* to show, express, testify.
Bezeugen, bet͡säu'gen, *vt.* to attest, testify, depose, declare.
Bezichtigen, bet͡sich'tichen, *vt.* to charge, accuse, impute.
Beziehen, bet͡sī'en (bet͡sog, bet͡sogen), *vt.* to string (an instrument); to draw, get; to refer, relate to.
Beziffern, bet͡sif'fern, *vt.* to mark with ciphers.
Bezirk, bet͡sirk', *m.* district, circuit.
Bezug, bet͡suk', *m.* relation, reference; set of strings. **Bezüglich**, bet͡sük'lich, *a.* relative, *av.* -ly.
Bezwecken, bet͡sveck'en, *vt.* to peg; to aim at, intend.
Bezweifeln, bet͡svāi'feln, *vt.* to doubt.
Bezwingen, bet͡sving'en (bet͡swang, bet͡swungen), *vt.* to overcome, subdue, conquer. **Bezwinglich**, bet͡sving'lich, *a.* conquerable.
Bibel, bī'bel, *f.* bible, sacred scriptures; -feſt, -fezht, *a.* scriptureproof; -lehre, -lāre, *f.* scriptural doctrine; -stelle, -zhtelle, *f.* passage of the bible.
Biber, bī'ber, *m.* beaver; -hut, -hyt, beaver.
Bibliothek, bibliotäk', *f.* library. **Bibliothekar**, bibliotäkār', *m.* librarian.
Biblisch, bīb'lish, *a.* biblical.
Bieder, bī'der, *a.* upright, honest, fair, just, *av.* -ly; -keit, -kāet, *f.* uprightness, honesty. **Biedermann**, bī'dermann, *m.* upright, honest man. **Bie'derſinn**, -ſinn, *m.* uprightness, probity.
Biegen, bī'gen (bog, gebogen), *vt.* to bend, bow, inflect, turn, curve, crook; ſich —, to bend. **Biegsam**, bīk'sam, *a.* flexible, pliant, supple; -keit, -kāet, *f.* suppleness, flexibility, pliancy. **Bieg'ung**, -yng, *f.* flexion.
Biene, bī'ne, *f.* bee; -brod, -brōt, *n.* bee-bread; -haus, -hōus, *n.* bee-house, apiary; -königin, -könichin, *f.* queen-bee; -korb, *m.* bee-hive; -meister, -māehter -vater, -fāter, *m.* bee-master, hiver; -schwarm, -shvarm, *m.* swarm of bees; -ſtock, -zhtock, *m.* bee-hive; -zucht, -t͡sucht, *f.* rearing, keeping of bees.
Bier, bīr, *n.* beer; -brauer, -brōyer, *m.* brewer; -brauerei, -brōyerāi', *f.* brewery; -eſſig, -essich, *m.* alegar; -faß, -fass, *n. pl.* -fässer, beer-barrel, beer-cask; -flasche, -flashe, *f.* beer-bottle; -glas, -glās, *n. pl.* -gläser, beer-glass, tumbler; -haus, -hōus, *n. pl.* -häuser, beer-house; -hefe, *f.* yeast (of beer), barm; -schank, -schank, *m.* right of retailing beer; -schenke, -shenke, *f.* beer-house; -suppe, -suppe, *f.* beer-soup; -wirth, -vīrt, *m.* beer-house keeper.
Bieten, bī'ten (bot, geboten), *vt.* to bid, offer, command.
Bieſt, bīts, *f.* nipple, teat, woman's breast.
Bigott, bigott', *a.* bigoted. **Bigotterie**, bigotterī', *f.* bigotry.
Bild, bilt, *n, pl.* -er, picture, painting, portrait, image, effigy, figure, statue; -chen, -chen, *n.* small picture, **Bilden**, bīld'en, *vt.* to form, shape, fashion, model, mould, compose; polish, cultivate, school, train, discipline; -d, *av.* plastic. **Bild'eranbeter**, -anbāter, *m.* iconolater, worshipper of images. **Bild'erausstellung**, -ōyszhtellyng, *f.* exhibition of pictures. **Bil'derbibel**, -bībel, *f.* illustrated bible. **Bild'erbuch**, -buch, *n. pl.* -bücher, picture-book. **Bil'dergallerie**, -gallerī, *f.* picture-gallery. **Bil'derhandel**, -handel, *m.* trade in paintings and pictures. **Bil'derhändler**; -hendler, *n.* picture-dealer. **Bil'derrahmen**, -rämen, *m.* pictureframe. **Bil'derschrift**, -shrift, *f.* hieroglyphics. **Bildhauer**, bilt'hōyer, *m.* sculptor, statuary; -arbeit, -arbāet, *f.* -ei, -āi, *f.* sculpture, carving, statuary. **Bildlich**, bilt'lich, *a.* figurative, metaphorical, tropical, typical, *av.* -ly. **Bildner**, bilt'ner, *m.* modeler, moulder, sculptor, former; -ei, -āi, *f.* sculpture. **Bildniß** = **Bild**. **Bildsam**, bilt'sam,

a. ductile, flexible, pliant, *av.* -ly; **-feit**, -kȅet, *f.* plasticity, flexibility, pliancy. **Bild'ſäule**, -seüle, *f.* statue. **Bild'ſchniger**, -shnitser, *m.* carver, sculptor; **-ei**, -ēī, *f.* carving, sculpture. **Bild'ſchön**, -shöhn, *a.* very beautiful. **Bil'bung**, -ung, *f.* forming, framing, composing, formation; cultivation, refinement. **Bild'weberei**, -väberȫ, *f.* fancy weaving. **Bild'werk**, -vèrk, *n.* sculpture, carving, imagery.

Billard, bill'yart, *n.* billiards. — **ſpielen**, to play at billiards; **-ball**, -ball, *m.* **-kugel**, -kugel, *f.* billiard-ball; **-ſtod**, -zhtock, *m.* billiard-stick, cue; **-ſpiel**, -zhpïl, *n.* billiards.

Billen, bil'len, *s. pl.* buttocks (of a ship).

Billet, bilyet', *n.* ticket; note, billet.

Billig, bil'lich, *a.* equitable, fair, moderate, reasonable, cheap, low. **Billigen**, bil'lichen, *vt.* to approve, find fair; to give one's consent to. **Billigkeit**, bil'lichkȅet, *f.* equitableness, fairness, equity, reasonableness, cheapness, moderation. **Bil'ligung**, -ung, *f.* approbation, consent.

Billion, billiōn', *f.* billion.

Bilſe, bil'se, *f.* **Bil'ſenkraut**, -krout, *n.* henbane, hyoscyamus.

Bimſen bim'sen, *vt.* to polish, pumicate. **Bims'ſtein**, -zhtȅen, *m.* pumice-stone.

Binde, bïnn'de, *f.* band, fillet; fascia (Archit.); sling. **Binden**, bïn'den (band, gebunden), *vt.* to bind, tie, fasten; to pack; to hoop (a cask); to oblige, restrain; ſich —, to bind one's self, to make one's self dependent upon. **Binder**, bïn'der, *m.* binder. **Bin'dewort**, -vort, *n. pl.* **-wörter**, conjunction. **Bindfaden**, bïnt'fäden, *m.* pack-thread, twine. **Bind'mittel**, -mittel, *n.* cement.

Binnen, bin'nen, *prp.* within; **-land**, -lant, *pl.* **-länder**, inland region.

Binſe, bin'se, *f.* rush.

Biograph, bi'ogrȁf, -en, *pl.* -en, biographer. **Bi'agraphie**, grafī, *f.* biography. **Biographiſch**, -ish, *a.* biographical.

Birke, bïr'ke, *f.* birch, birch-tree. **Birken**, bïr'ken, *a.* birchen; **-ſaft**, **-ſaft**, *n.* birch-juice; **-wald**, -valt,

pl. **-wälder**, *m.* birch-wood. **Birk'hahn**, -hän, *m.* heath-cock.

Birnapfel, bīrrn'apfel, *m.* pear-mast. **Birn'baum**, -baūm, *m.* pear-tree. **Birne**, bïrr'ne, *f.* pear; **-moſt**, -mozht, **-wein**, -vȁen, *m.* perry. **Birn'quitte**, -quitte, *f.* pear-quince.

Bis, biss, *av.* till, until; as far as. **Biſam**, bī'sam, *m.* musk; **-artig**, -ärtich, *a.* musky; **-kake**, -katse, *f.* musk-cat, civet-cat; **-ſchwein**, -shväen, *n.* peccary.

Biſchof, bish'of, *m.* bishop; bishop (drink). **Biſchöflich**, bish'öflich, *a.* episcopal.

Bisher, biss'hȁr, *av.* hitherto, till now; **-ig**, *a.* existing till now.

Bismuth, biss'mųt, *m.* bismuth, *s.* Wismuth.

Biß, biss, **Biſſen**, *m.* bite, bit, morsel; **Bis'chen**, *n.* a (little) bit; **-enweiſe**, -vȅlse, *av.* by bits.

Bisweilen, bisvȅll'en, *av.* sometimes.

Bitte, bitte, *f.* request, entreaty, prayer. **Bitten**, bit'ten (bat, gebeten), *vt.* to ask, pray, beg, entreat. request, crave, solicit.

Bitter, bit'ter, *a.* bitter, *av.* -ly; **-böſe**, -böhse, *a.* very wicked; very angry; **-feit**, -kȅet, *f.* bitterness, sharpness, pungency, acrimony. **Bit'terlich**, *av.* bitterish, somewhat bitter.

Bittſchreiben, bitt'shrȅlben, *n.* **Bitt'ſchrift**, *f.* petition, address. **Bitt'ſteller**, -zhteller, *m.* petitioner, suitor; **-in**, *f.* suitress. **Bitt'weiſe**, -vȅlse, *av.* by way of petition, entreatingly.

Blach, blach, *a.* plain; **-feld**, -fȅld, *n. pl.* **-er**, plain, level field.

Bläten, blä'-en, *vt.* to puff up, blow up, inflate; to cause flatulency, ſich —, to be puffed up, inflated. **Blähſucht**, blä'sucht, *f.* flatulence. **Blähung**, blä'ung, *f.* flatulence, wind.

Blamiren, blamī'ren, *vt.* to defame, disgrace.

Blank, blank, *a.* blank, white, bright, glittering, unsheathed.

Blankett, blan'kett, *n.* carte-blanche. **Blankſchett**, blank'shȅtt, *n.* busk. **Blank'ſtoßbank**, -zhtōsbank, *m.* horse (tanners).

Blasbente, biäs'dëulte, *f.* tuyere, tweer. **Blaſe**, blȁ'se, *f.* bubble, blister, bladder, pimple; **-balg,** -balk, *m.* bellows. **Blaseinstrument,** bläs'ze-inzhtrument, *n.* wind-instrument. **Blasen,** blä'sen (blies, geblasen), *vt.* to blow, sound. **Bläser,** blä'ser, *m.* blower; short (M'u.). **Bla'seröhre,** -röhre, *f.* blow-pipe, pea-shooter.

Blaß, blass, *a.* pale. **Blässe, bles'se,** *f.* paleness. **Blaßgelb, blass'gelp,** *a.* pale-yellow.

Blatt, -blatt, *n. pl.* **Blätter,** leaf, blade, board; paper; reed (Weav.); vom — **spielen,** to play at sight; das — hat sich gewendet, the tables are turned. **Blättchen,** blett'chen, *n.* leaflet.

Blatter, blat'ter, *f.* blister, pustule; *pl.* **Blattern,** small-pox. **Blätterig,** blet'terich, *a.* leafy, foliated. **Blätterlos, -lös,** *a.* leafless. **Blättern,** blet'tern, *vi.* to turn over the leaves, to run over, skim a book; sich —, to shed the leaves; to exfoliate; to scale off. **Blat'tertig, -teek,** *m.* puff-paste. **Blatt'gold, -golt,** *n.* leaf-gold. **Blatt'laus, -lous,** *n.* plant-louse. **Blatt'seite, -seite,** *f.* page. **Blatt'zinn, -tsinn,** *n.* tin-foil, leaf-tin.

Blau, blåu, *a.* blue; **-äugig, -äugich,** *a.* blue-eyed; **-bart, -bärt,** *m.* blue-beard. **Bläue, blä're,** *f.* blue, azure, blue starch. **Bläuel, blä'el,** *m.* beetle; **-stange,** *f.* axle-tree. **Bläuen, blå'en,** *vt.* to dye blue; to drub, beat. **Blaufärber,** -förber, *m.* dyer in blue. **Blau'holz, -holts,** *n.* log-wood. **Blau'meise, -mäese,** *f.* tit-mouse. **Blau'säure, -seüre,** *f.* Prussic acid. **Blau'spath, -zhpät,** *m.* blue spar. **Blau'strumpf, -zhtrumf,** *m.* spy, informer.

Blech, blech, *n.* plate, tin. **Blechen, blech'en** (vulg.), to pay, to fork over; to come down. **Blech'en, Blech'ern,** *a.* made of tin *or* iron-plate. **Blech'waare,** -väre, *f.* tin-ware.

Blecken, bleck'en, *vt.* to show, bare (the teeth).

Blei, blei, *n.* lead.

Bleiben, blei'ben (blieb, geblieben), *vi.* to remain, stay, rest; stehen —, to stand still.

Bleich, blaich, *a.* (bleak) pale, pallid, wan, faint, faded. **Bleiche, blaiche,** *f.* paleness, pallor, wanness, bleach-field, bleachery. **Bleichen,** bleich'en, *vt.* to bleach, whiten, blanch. **Bleichsucht, blaich'sucht,** *f.* green-sickness, chlorosis. **Bleichsüchtig, -süchtich,** *a.* chlorotic.

Bleiern, blei'ern, *a.* leaden, lead. **Blei'erz, -ärts,** *n.* lead-ore. **Blei'gelb, -gelp,** *n.* chrome-yellow. **Blei'gießer, -gieser,** *m.* plumber. **Blei'glätte, -gletta,** *f.* litharge. **Blei'hütte, -hütte,** *f.* lead-works. **Blei'kugel, -kugel,** *f.* ball (of lead), bullet. **Blei'loth, -löt,** *n.* plummet, lead, plumb-line. **Blei'recht, -recht,** *a.* plumb, perpendicular. **Blei'stift, -zhtift,** *m.* lead-pencil. **Blei'weiß, -veis,** *a.* white-lead, ceruse.

Blende, blen'de, *f.* blind, screen, cover, blinker. **Blenden,** blen'den, *vt.* to blind, dazzle. **Blend'laterne,** laterne, *f.* dark lantern. **Blend'leder, -läder,** *n.* blind, blinker. **Blend'ling, -ling,** *m.* bastard, mongrel. **Blend'werk, -värk,** *n.* deception, delusion.

Blind, blint, *a.* blind; mock, false; dull (mirror); -er Bogen, monksheet; -e Patrone, blank cartridge; -es Schußloch, *n.* sham port; -es Raa, sprit-sail-yard; -e Klippen, sunken rocks, reefs; die Boje steht —, the buoy is not floating. **Blind'darm, -darm,** *m.* blind-gut. **Blin'de,** *m. or f.* blind man *or* woman. **Blindekuh, blindeku',** *f.* blind-man's buff. **Blind'heit, -häet,** *f.* blindness. **Blind'lings, -links,** *av.* blindly, rashly, at random. **Blindgeboren, blint'gebören,** *a.* born blind. **Blind'schleiche, -shleiche,** *f.* blindworm, slow-worm.

Blink, blink, *a.* gleaming, *s. n.* clear spot (in a cloudy sky). **Blink'en, Blinkern,** *vi.* to sparkle, gleam, glisten.

Blinzeln, blin'tseln, *vi.* to blink, wink, twinkle. **Blinzer,** blin'tser, *m.* blinkard.

Blitz, blits (blinken), *m.* lightning, flash of lightning, glimpse; **-ableiter, -apläeter,** *m.* lightning-rod. **Blitzen,** blits'en, *vi.* to lighten. **Blitz'schnell, -shnell,** *a.* quick as lightning; -e, *f.* rapidity of lightning. **Blitz'strahl, -zhträl,** *m.* flash of lightning.

Block, block, *m.* block, log; pig; sheave; ein laufender —, a running block. **Blockade**, blockā'de, f. blockade, blocking up. **Blockhaus**, -höus, n. pl. -häuser, blockhouse. **Blockiren**, blocki'ren, vt. to blockade, block up. **Blocksäge**, -säge, f. pit-saw.

Blöde, blöh'de, a. weak, feeble; dimsighted, weak-eyed; bashful, timid; silly, imbecile. **Blödigkeit**, blöh'dĭchkäet f. weakness of sight; timidity, bashfulness; silliness, imbecility. **Blödsinn**, blöhd'sinn, m. imbecility, silliness; **-ig**, a. weak, silly, imbecile.

Blöken, blö'ker, vi. to bleat, low, bellow.

Blond, blont, a. blonde, fair, light-haired.

Bloss, blös. a. bare, naked, nude, mere, uncovered: av. barely, merely, only. **Blösse**, blöh'se, f. bareness, nakedness. **Blössen**, blöh'sen, vt. to bare. **Blossstellung**, -zhtellung, f. exposure.

Blühen, blüh'en, vi. to bloom. flower, blossom, blow, flourish. **Blümchen**, blühm'chen, n. floweret.

Blume, blu'me, f. flower, blossom; **-beet**, -bāt, n. flower-bed; **-blatt**, n. pl. -blätter, petal; **-flor**, -flōr, m. blowth, flowering-time; **-garten**, -gärten, m. flower-garden; **-gärtner**, -gärtner, m. florist, flowergardener; **-kelch**, -kelch, m. calyx; flower; **-kohl**, -kōl, m. cauliflower; **-kranz**, -krants, m. chaplet, garland, wreath of flowers; **-lese**, -läse, f. anthology; **-staub**, -zhtäub, m. pollen; **-strauss**, -zhtrous, m. bouquet, bunch of flowers; **-topf**, -tepf, m. flower-pot; **-zwiebel**, -tsvībel, m. bulb.

Blut, blut, n. blood; **-ader**, -äder, f. vein; **-arm**, -arm, a. extremely poor; **-bad**, -bäd, n. slaughter, bloodshed, massacre, carnage; **-durst**, -durzht, n. bloodthirstiness; **-dürstig**, -dürzhtich, a. bloodthirsty, sanguinary; **-egel**, -igel, -Igel, m. leech: bloodsucker. **Bluten**, blut'en, vi. to bleed. **Blutfluss**, blut'fluss, m. hemorrhage. **Blutgefäss**, -gefes, n. bloodvessel. **Blutgeld**, -gelt, n. price of blood. **Blutgericht**, -gericht, n. criminal court. **Blutgier**, -gīr, f. bloodiness: **-ig**, a. murderous, sanguinary, bloody.

Blüthe, **Blüte**, blüh'te, f. blossom, bloom, flower, prime; **-knospen**, -k(e)nospen, f. flower-bud; **-stand**, -zhtant, m. inflorescence; **-staub**, -zhtäub, m. pollen; **-zeit**, -tsēīt, f. flowering-time, youth.

Bluthund, blut'hunt, m. blood-hound. **Blutig**, blut'ich, a. bloody. **Blutjung**, -yung, a. very young. **Blutlauf**, -läuf, m. circulation of the blood. **Blutlos**, -lōs, a. bloodless. **Blutrache**, -räche, f. revenge (for murder). **Blutroth**, -rōt, a. bloodred. **Blutrünstig**, -rünzhtich, a. bleeding, bloody. **Blutschande**, -shande, f. incest. **Blutschänder**, -shender, m. incestuous person; **-isch**, a. incestuous. **Blutschwäre**, -shväre, f. furuncle. **Blutsfreund**, -fraūnt, m. kinsman, kinswoman; **-schaft**, -shaft. f. consanguinity, relation by blood. **Blutstropfen**, -tropfen, m. drop of blood. **Bluttriefend**, -trīfent, a. bleeding. **Blutumlauf**, -läuf, m. circulation of the blood. **Blutvergiessen**, -fergīsen, n. bloodshed. **Bluturtheil**, -ŭrtāēl, n. sentence of death. **Blutverlust**, -ferlust, m. loss of blood. **Blutwasser**, -vasser, n. lymph, ichor, serum. **Blutwenig**, -vänich, a. extremely little. **Blutwurst**, -vŭrzht, f. bloodpudding. **Blutzeuge**, -tsöūge, m. martyr.

Bock, bock, m. buck, ram, he-goat; block, jack, thristle; coach-box; fault, blunder; einen — schiessen, to commit a blunder; den — zum Gärtner machen, to set the fox to keep the geese; ins Bockshorn jagen, to bully, frighten. **Böckchen**, böck'chen, n. kid. **Bockssprung**, -zhprung, m. caper; Bockssprünge machen, to caper, prance, gambol, romp. **Bocken**, bock'en, vi. to lust, to rub; to pitch, heave up and down.

Bocksen, bock'sen, vt. to bowse (a gun, etc.).

Boden, bō'den, m. bottom, ground, soil; floor; head (of a cask); loft garret; **-bohrer**, -bōrer, m. second bit, widening-bit; **-fliese**, -flēsen, n. calking iron; **-los**, -lōs, a. bottomless, unfounded; **-satz**, -sats, m. sediment, dregs, lees; **-thür**, -tühr, f. loft-door.

Bodmerei, bōdmerāī', f. bottomry.

Bog 69 **Bra**

Bogen, bō'gen, m. bow; arch, arc, curve; bend; sheet (of paper); in **Baufch und —,** in the lump; **-fenfter, -leuchter,** n. bay-window, bow-window; **-gang, -gang,** m. arcade; **-laube, -läube,** f. arbor, bower; **-fchüße, -chütze,** m. archer, bow-man; **-weife, -veīse,** av. in sheets, by the sheet.
Bogig, bōg'ich, a. bent, curved, sinuous.
Bohle, bō'le, f. plank, board. **Bohlen,** bō'len, vt. to plank.
Bohne, bō'ne, f. bean; **-ftrah, -zhtrō,** n. bean-straw; **grob wie —,** uncouth, very coarse.
Bohrbank, bōr'bank, f. boring-bench. **Bohreifen, -eīsen,** n. boring-bar. **Bohren,** bōr'en, vt. to bore, drill, perforate, **in den Grund —,** to sink. **Bohrer,** bō'rer, m. gimlet. **großer —,** auger. **Bohrloch,** n. pl. **-löcher,** bore-hole, auger-hole. **Bohrmafchine, -mashīne,** f. boring-machine. **Bohrmehl,** bōr'māl, n. bore-dust. **Bohrzeug, -tsöük,** n. boring-tools.
Boje, bō'ye, f. buoy.
Boll, Bollig, bol'lich, hard, stiff.
Bolle, bol'le, f. bulb, boil. **Bollgewächs, -gevēx,** n. bulbous plant.
Bollwerk, bol'věrk, n. bulwark, rampart.
Bolzen, bolt'sen, m. bolt; arrow; wedge (shoemak.).
Bombardiren, bombardī'ren, vt. to bombard, shell; s. n. bombardment.
Bombaft, bombazht', m. bombast, boasting.
Bombaffin, bom'bassäē(n), m. bombasine.
Bombe, bom'be, f. bomb, shell.
Boot, bōt, n. boat; **-hafen, -anker,** m. grapnel; **-mann,** pl. **-leute,** m. boatman, sailor.
Borax, bō'rax, m. borax; **-fäure, -säure,** f. boracic acid.
Bord, bort, m. board; brim, brink.
Bordell, bordĕll', n. brothel.
Bordiren, bordī'ren, vt. to border. **Bordleifte, -leezhte,** f. wale.
Borg, bork, n. preventer.
Borg, bork, m. credit, trust; **auf —,** on credit. **Borgen,** bor'gen, vt. to borrow, lend.
Borgketten, bork'ketten, s. pl. yard-chains, **Borgwandtau, -vandtóy,** a. swifter.
Borke, bor'ke, f. bark; scab, crust.

Born, born, m. spring, well.
Börfe, bör'se, f. purse; exchange **-halle, -halle,** f. exchange-hall; **-fpiel, -zhpīl,** n. stock-jobbing.
Borfte, bor'zhte, f. bristle. **Borften, -sten,** vi. to bristle. **Borftig,** bor'-zhtich, a. bristly.
Borte, bor'te, f. lace; **-macher, -mwirker,** m. lace-maker.
Bösartig, böhs'ärtich, a. malignant, malicious, **-keit, -kaēt,** f. malignancy. **Böfe,** böh'se, a. bad, ill, evil, wicked; s. m. the devil. **Boshaft,** bōs'haft, a. malicious, mischievous; av. -ly. **Bosheit,** bōs'hāet, f. malice, malignity, wickedness. **Böslich,** bōhs'lich, a. av. malicious, malignantly.
Boffeln, bos'seln, vi. to bowl, play at nine-pins; **-bahn, -bän,** f. nine-pin alley; **-kugel, -kūgel,** f. bowl.
Boffiren, bossī'ren, vt. to emboss.
Boswillig, bōhs'willich, a. malevolent, av. -ly; **-keit, -kaēt,** f. malevolence.
Botanik, botā'nik, f. botany; **-er,** m. botanist. **Botanifch,** botā'nish, a. botanic. -al.
Bote, bō'te, m. **-n,** pl. **-n,** messenger; **-lohn, -lōn,** m. messenger's wages or fee. **Botmäßig,** bōt'māsich, a. obedient, tributary; **-keit, -kaēt,** f. dominion. **Botfchaft,** bot'shaft, f. message, errand, embassy; **-er,** m. messenger; ambassador.
Bottich, bot'tich, m. coop, tub, vat. **Böttcher,** bött'cher, m. cooper; **-arbeit, -arbaēt,** f. cooper's work **-handwerk, -handvěrk,** n. coopery **-lohn, -lōn,** m. cooperage.
Bouillon, buľyon, n. broth, beef-tea, **-tafel, -tafel,** f. portable-soup.
Bouteille, butēl'ye, f. bottle.
Boxen, box'en, vt. to box. **Boxer,** box'er, m. boxer.
Brach, bräch, prt. v. **Brechen.**
Brach, bräch. a. fallow, unplowed **-acker, -acker,** m. fallow, fallow-ground. **Brache, brä'che,** f. fallow, fallowness. **Brachen, brä'chen,** vt. to fallow; to break flax. **Brachmonat, -mōnat,** m. June.
Brachgut, brack'gut, refuse of merchandize.
Bramfegel, bräm'sägel, n. top-gallant sail; **-ftange, -zhtange,** f. top-gallant mast.

Bramarbas, bramar'bass, m. braggart, bully. **Bramarbasiren**, -sī'ren, vi. to brag, bully.

Brand, brant, m. burning, conflagration; fire, combustion; **-blase**, -blā-se, f. blister (from burning); **-brief**, -brīf, m. incendiary letter. **Branden**, bran'den, vi. to surge, rage. **Brand'er**, m. fire-ship. **Brand's flecken**, -flĕcken, m. burn, scald. **Brand'kasse**, -kasse, f. fire insurance office. **Brand'fuchs**, -fux, m. -en, pl. -en, chestnut-horse. **Brandig**, bran'dich, a. blasted, blighted. **Brandigt**, bran'dicht, a. smelling or tasting as if burnt or burning. **Brand'mal**, -māl, n. brand. **Brand'marken**, -marken, vt. to brand. **Brand'mauer**, mŏy-er, f. fire-proof wall. **Brand'opfer**, -opfer, n. burnt-offering. **Brand'schaden**, -shäden, m. loss or damage caused by fire. **Brand'schatzen**, -shatsen, vt. to levy or impose contributions (under threats of conflagration). **Brand'schatzung**, -ung, f. contribution, extortion. **Brand'schiff**, -shiff, n. fireship. **Brand'stifter**, -zhtifter, m. incendiary. **Brandstiftung**, brant'-zhtiftung, f. incendiarism. **Brand'ung**, -ung, f. breakers, surf, surge. **Brand'versicherung**, f. fire-insurance; **-anstalt**, -ānzhtalt, f. fire insurance office. **Brand'zeichen**, -tsäĕchen, n. fire-sign.

Branntwein, brannt'vāĕn, m. brandy; **-blase**, -blāse, f. still; **-brenner**, -brenner, m. brandy-distiller; **-brennerei**, -brennerēī', f. distillery; **-flasche**, -flashe, f. brandy-bottle; **-schenke**, -shenke, f. brandy-shop.

Brasse, bras'se, f. brace; große —, main brace; die — anholen, to haul on the braces; — aufholen, to brace the yards in.

Brassen, bras'sen, vt. to brace.

Bratbock, brät'bock, m. rack, jack-frame. **Braten**, brä'ten (briet, gebraten), vt. to roast, fry, broil; s. roast, roast-meat. den — riechen, to smell a rat; **-wender**, -vender, m. turn-broach, turn-spit. **Brat'pfanne**, -pfanne, f. frying-pan. **Brat'rost**, -rozht, grid-iron, roaster.

Bratsche, brat'she, f. counter-tenor viol. **Bratschist**, brät'sh"st, m. violist.

Bratspieß, brät'zhpīs, m. spit. **Bratwurst**, -vurzht, f. sausage.

Brauch, brōych (f. Gebrauch), m. use, usage, custom; **-bar**, -bär, a. useful, serviceable, fit for use; **-barkeit**, -barkāĕt, f. usefulness, fitness for use. **Brauchen**, brōych'en, vt. to want, need, require; use.

Brauen, brōy'en, vt. to brew. **Brauer**, brōy'er, m. brewer; **-ei**, f. brewery, also **Brau'haus**, **Brau'innung**, f. brewers' company or guild. **Brau'kessel**, -kessel, m., **Brau'pfanne**, -pfanne, f. brewing-pan. **Brau'knecht**, -k(e)nĕcht, m. brewers' man.

Braun, brǎun, a. brown; **-bier**, -bīr, n. brown-beer. **Bräune**, brŏū'ne, f. brownness; (Med.) quinsy; **-entzündliche** —, angina; **häutige** —, croup. **Bräunen**, brǎunen, vt. to brown, make brown; vi. to become brown. **Braun'kohl**, -kōl, m. blue cabbage, red cabbage. **Braun'kohle**, -kōle, f. brown coal. **Braun'roth**, -rōt, a. brownish red. **Braun'stein**, -zhtāĕn, m. peroxide of manganese.

Braus, brōys, m. bustle, tumult; revelry; in Saus und — leben, to revel and riot. **Brause**, brōyse, f. fermentation. **Brausen**, brōysen, vi. to rush, hum, buzz, work, froth, roar, bluster; to be impetuous, turbulent, boisterous. **Braus'kopf**, m. boisterous fellow.

Braut, brōyt, f. pl. **Bräute**, bride, betrothed, affianced; **-bett**, -bett, n. bridal bed; **-führer**, -führer, m. bride's-man; **-in**, -jungfer, -yungfer, f. bride's-maid; **-geschenk**, -geshenk, n. bridal present; **-geschmeide**, -geshmāĕde, n. bridal jewels. **Bräutigam**, brŏū'ticham, m. bridegroom. **Braut'kammer**, -kammer, f. bridal chamber; **-kleid**, brōyt'-klāĕd, n. pl. -er, wedding-dress; **-kranz**, -krants, m. bridal wreath. **Bräutlich**, brŏū't'lich, a. bridal, nuptial. **Braut'nacht**, -nacht, f. wedding-night, nuptial night; **-paar**, -pār, n. couple; **-ring**, -ring, m. wedding-ring; **-schatz**, -shats, m. dower, dowry, portion; **-schmuck**, -shmuck, m. wedding-dress; **-stand**, -zhtant, m. state of being engaged, betrothed; **-werber**, brōyt'verber, m. wooer, suitor.

Brav, bräf, a. brave, good, honest, intrepid, gallant, av. -ly; **-heit**, -hāet, f. bravery, courage.
Brechbank, brĕch'bank, f. baker's bench. **Brechen**, brĕch'en (brach, gebrochen), vt. to break, pluck, bruise, crack; die Ehe —, to commit adultery; vi. to break, burst; to fail, become bankrupt; sich —, to vomit. **Brecherlich**, brĕch'erlich, a. squeamish. **Brechmittel**, -mittel, n. emetic. **Brechnuß**, brĕch'nuss, f. nux vomica. **Brechpulver**, -pylfer, n. emetic. **Brechung**, -ung, f. refraction (of light). **Brechweinstein**, -vāenzhtāen, m. tartar emetic.
Brei, brāī, m. pap. **Breiig**, brāī'ich, a. pappy.
Breit, brāēt, a. broad, wide; weit und —, far and wide. **Breite**, brāē'te, f. breadth, width; latitude. **Breiten**, brāēt'en, vt. to spread, extend, expand. **Breitekreis**, -krāēs, m. parallel of latitude.
Breme, brā'me, f. ox-fly.
Bremse, brem'se, f. gad-fly; brake: barnacles, twitch. **Bremsen**, brem'sen, vt. to squeeze, press; to apply the barnacles (to a horse).
Brennbar, brenn'bär, a. combustible. **Brennen**, bren'nen (brannte, gebrannt),vt. i. to burn, scorch, parch, consume; to distill; cauterize; to brand; to sting; to catch fire; to make (charcoal); to burn, be on fire. **Brenner**, bren'ner, m. burner; -ei, -āī', f. distillery. **Brennglas**, -glās, n. pl. -gläſer, burning-glass, lens. **Brennholz**, -holts, n. firewood, fuel. **Brennmaterial**, -matāriāl, n. fuel. **Brennkolben**, -kolben, m. still, alembic, retort. **Brennessel**, -nessel. f. nettle. **Brennofen**, -ōfen, m. kiln, furnace, oven. **Brennöl**, -ōhl. n. lamp-oil. **Brennpunkt**, -pynkt, m. focus. **Brennspiegel**, -zphīgel, m. burning-mirror. **Brenzeln**, brent'seln, vi. to smell or taste burnt. **Brenzlich**, brents'lich, a. empyreumatic; -e Säure, f. pyro-acid.
Bresche, brēshe, f. breach; e. — schießen, to batter a breach.
Brett, brĕtt, n. pl. -er, board, plank, deal; -chen, -chen, n. little board. **Brettern**, bret'tern. a. board, plank. **Bretterwand**, vant, f. partition of boards. **Brettmühle**, -mühle, f saw-mill. **Brettsäge**, -sāge, f. pit saw. **Brettspiel**, -zphīl, n. backgammon, draughts. **Brettstein**, -zhtāen, m. man.
Bretzel, brĕt'sel, f. bretzel; twist.
Bricke, brick'e, f. a fried lamprey.
Brieke, brick'e, f. a small board.
Brief, brīf, m. letter, epistle; **-bote**, -bōte, m. -n, pl. -n, letter-carrier -geld, -gĕlt, n. postage. **Brieflich**, brīf'lich, a. av. written, epistolary· by letter. **Briefpapier**, -papīr, n. letter-paper; note-paper. **Briefpost**, -pozht, f. mail, letter-post. **Briefschaften**, -shaften, s. pl. letters, papers. **Briefsteller**, -zhteller, m. letter-writer. **Briefstreicher**, -ztrāēcher, m. letter-folder. **Brieftaube**, -tōybe, f. carrier-pigeon. **Brieftasche**, -tashe, f. pocket-book. **Briefträger**, -träger, m. letter-carrier. **Briefumschlag**, -umshlāk, m. envelope, cover. **Briefwechsel**, -vĕxel, m. correspondence.
Brigade, brigā'de, f. brigade. **Brigadier**, brigad'ā, m. brigadier-general.
Brigantine, brigantī'ne, f. brigantine.
Brigg, f. brig.
Brille, bril'le, f. spectacles, eye-glass; **-nfutteral**, -fytterāl, n. spectacle-case. **Brillenmacher**, -macher, m. spectacle-maker.
Bringen, bring'en (brachte, gebracht), vt. to bring. bear, convey, conduct, take; an sich —, to acquire, to get possession of; um etwas —, to deprive of; etwas vor sich —, to prosper, thrive; in Gang —, to set a going; an den Tag —, to bring to light; zu Wege —, zu Stande —, to bring about, effect; zur Verzweiflung —, to drive to despair; ums Leben —, to kill, murder; zu Papier —, to pen, write down; zum Schweigen —, to silence; in Rechnung —, to take into account; an den Mann —, to provide for; aufs Tapet —, to introduce; einen zu Etwas —, to induce.
Bröckeln, bröck'eln, vt. to crum, crumble, break. **Bröcklich**, -lich, a. friable, crumbling. **Brocken**, brock'en, m. crumb, morsel, scrap; **-weise**, -vēīse, a. in crumbs.
Brod, brōt, n. bread; subsistence;

Brø   72   **Bru**

fein — haben, to enjoy a competence; — verdienen, to make a living; -bäcker, -becker, m. baker. Brod'herr, bröt'hĕrr, m. -n, pl. -n, employer. Brod'forb, -korp, m. bread-basket. Brod'frumme, -krumme, f. bread-crumb. Brodlos, bröd'lōs, a. breadless, unemployed. Brod's neib, -neĭd, m. (professional) envy. Brod'ftubien, -zhtudi-en, z. pl. studies to gain a subsistence. Brod'teig, -tāĕk, m. bread-dough.

Brodhahn, broy'hän, m. a sort of white beer.

Brombeere, brom'bāre, f. blackberry; -hecke, -hecke, f. blackberry-patch; Bram'beerftrauch, -zhtrōŭch, m. pl. -ftrāūcher, blackberry-bush, bramble.

Bronze, brŏ(n)se, f. bronze. Bronziren, brōnsī'ren, vt. to bronze.

Brofame, brŏ'same, f. crumb.

Broschen, bröhs'chen, n. sweetbread.

Broschiren, broshī'ren, vt. to stitch, sew; to weave (flowers). Broschüre, broshüh're, f. stitched book.

Bruch, bruch, m. breaking; fraction; breach, rupture, fracture, hernia; -arzt, -ārtst, m. hernia-curer; -band, -bant, n. truss. Brüchig, brüch'ich, a. brittle. Bruchstein, -zhtāĕn, m. quarry-stone. Bruchstück, bruch'zhtück, n. fragment.

Brücke, brück'e, f. bridge; fig. transition; -bau, -bou, m. building of bridges; -bogen, -bōgen, m. arch of a bridge; -ngelb, -gĕlt, n ·ſjoll, -tsoll, m. bridge-toll; -kopf, -kopf, m. tête-de-pont, bridge-head; -pfeiler, -pfēller, m. pillar; -wage, -wăge, f. patent weigh-machine.

Bruder, brŭ'der, m. brother. Brü-derchen, brü'derchen, n. little brother. Bruderfind, -kint, n. pl. -er, nephew; ſie finb — er, they are cousins. Bruderkuß, -kuss, m. fraternal kiss. Brüderlich, brüh'derlich, a. brotherly, fraternal; -feit, -kāĕt, f. fraternity. Bruderliebe, -lĭbe, f. brotherly love. Bruderlos, -lōs, a. brotherless. Brudermord, -mort, m. fratricide. Brudermörder, -mürder, m. fratricide. Brüder-schaft, -shaft, f. brotherhood, fraternity.

Brühe, brüh'e, f. broth, sauce. Brü's hen, -hen, vt. to scald. Brüh'heiß, -hēĕs, Brüh'warm, -varm, a. boiling-hot, scalding-hot.

Brüllen, brül'len, vt. to roar, bellow, brawl, clamor. Brüllochs, -ox, m. -en, pl. -en, brawler.

Brummbär, brumm'bär, m. -en, pl. -en, bear; growler. Brummeifen, -ēĭsen, n. Jew's-harp. Brummen, brum'men, vi. to low, hum; fig. to growl, grumble. Brummer, -mer, m. grumbler, growler. Brumm's fliege, -flĭge, f. dung-fly. Brumm's kreifel, -krēĕsel, m. humming-top.

Brunft, brunft, f. rut. Brunften, vi. to rut.

Brunnen, brun'nen, m. well, spring, fountain; -arzt, -ārtst, m. physician of a watering-place; -kur, -kŭr, f. use of mineral waters; -gaſt, -gazht, m. visitor of a watering-place; -kreſſe, -krĕsse, f. water-cress; -meiſter, -māĕzhter, m. inspector of water-works; -röhre, -rōhre, f. conduit-pipe; -schwengel, -shvĕngel, m. swipe, sweep; -waſſer, -vasser, n. well-water, pump-water; springwater. Brunnquell, -quĕll, m. fountain-head, source.

Brunſt, brunzht, f. conflagration, ardor; rut, lust. Brünſtig, brün'zhtich, a. hot, ardent, fervent; lustful; -feit, -kāĕt, f. ardor, warmth, passion, love.

Bruſt, bruzht, f. pl. Brüſte, breast, chest, bosom; ſich in die — werfen to assume airs of authority; -ader, -āder, f. thoracic vein; -bein, -bāĕn, n. breast-bone, sternum; -beklemmung, -beklĕm'ung, f. oppression of the chest; -beſchwerde, -beshvĕrde, f. affection of the chest; -bild, -bilt, n. pl. -er, bust. Brüſten, brüzh'ten, vt. to strut, boast. Bruſt-entzündung, -bryzhtentsūndung, f. inflammation of the chest; -fell, -fĕll, n. stomacher; -muskel, -muskel, f. pectoral muscle; -ſtück, -zhtück, n. breast-piece; -waſſer-ſucht, -vassersucht, f. pectoral dropsy; -wehr, -vār, f. breast-work, parapet, rampart.

Brut, brut, f. brood, hatch, incubation.

Brutal, brutāl', a. brutal; -ität, brutalität', f. brutality.

Bratbiene, brut'bĭne, f. drone. Brü-

Bru 73 **Buu**

ten, brüh′ten, *vt.* to brood, hatch. **Bruthenne,** brūt′hen ne, *f.* brooding-hen. **Brutzeit,** -tsĕīt, *f.* brooding-time.

b. rutto, brut′tō, *a.* gross (weight).

Büblein, büp′chen, *n.* little boy. **Bube,** bū′be, *m.* -n. *pl.* -en, boy, bad boy, knave, rogue; **austreich,** -ūtrāsch, *m.* -nstück, -zhtück, *n.* knave r, roguery. **Büberei,** bübheraī′, *f.* -raēf. **Bübisch,** bühb′ish, *a.* knavish.

Buch, buch, *n. pl.* Bücher, book; quire (of paper); -**binder,** -binnder, *m.* bookbinder; -**drucker,** -drucker, *m.* printer; -**druckerei,** -druckereī′, *f.* printing, typography; printing-office; -**druckerkunst,** -kunzht, *f.* typography; -**druckerpresse,** -presse, *f.* printing-press; -**druckerschwärze,** -shverze, *f.* printer's ink, printing-ink.

Buche, bū′che, *f.* beech. **Buchen,** bū′chen, *a.* beechen.

Buchen, bū′chen, *vt.* to book, enter, charge.

Buchenholz, bū′chenholts, *n.* beech-wood.

Bücherbrett, büh′cherbrĕtt, *n.* book-shelf. **Büchernarr,** -narr, *m.* -en, *pl.* -en, bibliomaniac. **Büchersaal,** -säl, *m. pl.* -säle, library. **Büchersammlung,** -lung, *f.* library. **Bücherschrank,** -sh ank, *m.* book-case. **Bücherstand,** -zhtant, *m.* book-stall. **Büchersprache,** -shpräche, *f.* refined language. **Bücherwesen,** -väsen, *n.* literature. **Bücherwurm,** -vurm, *m. pl.* würmer, book-worm.

Buchfinke, buch′finke, *m.* chaffinch. **Buchhalter,** buch′halter, *m.* book-keeper; -**ei,** -ēī′, *f.* book-keeper's office. **Buchhaltung,** -ung, *f.* book-keeping; einfache —, by single entry; doppelte —, by double entry. **Buchhandel,** buch′handel, *m.* book-trade. **Buchhändler,** -hentler, *m.* book-seller. **Buchhandlung,** -hantlung, *f.* book-store, book-seller's shop. **Buchladen,** -läden, *m.* bash.

Buchbaum, buх′bahm, *m.* box-tree.

Buchstabe, buch′zhtābe, *m.* -ns, *pl.* -n, letter, type, character; großer —, capital (letter); -**rechnung,** -rechnung, *f.* algebra. **Buchstabiren,** buchzhtabī′ren, *vt.* to spell; fa sch —

to misspell. **Buchstäblich,** -zhtäplich, *a.* literal.

Bucht, bucht, *f.* inlet, bay, cove, creek, -**ig,** *a.* creeky; sinuate.

Buchweizen, buch′vētsen, buckwheat.

Buckel, buck′el (biegen), *m.* back, hump, humpback; bunch; -**eisen,** -ēīsen, *n.* curling-tongs, curling-irons; -**ig,** -ich, *a.* humpbacked, hunchbacked; -**iger,** -icher. *m.* hunchback; sich bucklig lachen, to split one's sides with laughing. **Buckeln,** buck′eln, *vt.* to carry on one's back.

Bücken, bück′en, *vr.* to bend, stoop, bow; humble one's self. **Bückling,** bück′ling, *m.* bow; einen — machen, to make a profound bow.

Bückling, bück′ling, *m.* red herring.

Bude, bū′de, *f.* booth, stall, shop; hut; -**ngeld,** -gĕlt, *n.* stallage.

Büffel, büff′fel, *m.* buffalo.

Bug, buk (biegen), *m.* bow, bend, bent, shoulder, withers; auf einen andern — wenden, to tack or veer. **Bügel,** büh′gel, *m.* bow, hoop; handle; stirrup; -**eisen,** -ēīsen, *n.* smoothing iron, goose. **Bügeln,** büh′geln, *vt.* to iron, smooth. **Buglahm,** buk′läm, *a.* shoulder-shotten; — machen, *vt.* to splay (a horse). **Bugsiren,** -sīren, to tow, warp. **Bugspriet,** -zhprīt, *n.* bow-sprit. **Bugstange,** -zhtang-e, *f.* fore-mast. **Bugsirtau,** buksīr′tau, warping-hawser.

Buhldirne, būl′dīrne, *f.* wanton girl, prostitute. **Buhle,** bū′le, *f.* paramour. **Buhlen,** bū′len, *vi.* to court, woo, to make love; to caress, **Buhler,** bū′ler, *m.* lover, paramour; -**in,** *f.* mistress, lewd woman. **Buhlerei,** bulereī′, *f.* coquetry, gallantry; lewdness, debauchery. **Buhlerisch,** bū′lerish, *a.* coquettish, wanton, lewd. **Buhlschaft,** bul′shaft, *f.* love-affair, intrigue; amorous intercourse; paramour.

Bühne, büh′ne, *f.* stage; scaffold. **Bühnen,** bühn′en, *vt.* to board, line; -**mäßig,** -mäsich, *a.* theatrical.

Bulle, bul′le, *f.* bull, edict.

Bulle, bul′le, *m.* bull. **Bullenbeißer,** -bēīser, *m.* bull-dog.

Bund, bunt, *m.* bunch, bundle, truss, knot; cut, bobbin. band, tie, bandage; union, confederation, confederacy, league, covenant; -**brüchig,**

-brüchik, a. breaking the covenant. **Bündel**, bün'del, m. or n. bundle, parcel, wisp, handful. **Bundesgenoß**, -genoss, m. -en, pl. -en. ally. **Bundeslade**, -lade, f. ark. **Bundestag**, bund'estäk, m. diet. **Bündig**, bün'dich, a. binding, valid, conclusive, concise; **-keit, -kået**, f. conciseness. **Bündniß**, bünt'niss, n. alliance, league.

Bunt, Buntfarbig, bunt'farbich. a. variegated, party-colored, gay-colored, colored, stained, motley, mixed, checkered. **Buntsleckig**, -fleckich, **Buntscheckig**, -sheckich, a. spotted, checkered.

Bunzen, bunt'sen, m. puncheon.

Bürde, bür'de, f. burden, charge, load.

Burg, burk, f. strong-hold, lodge, fortress, castle, citadel. **Bürge**, bür'ge, m. -n, pl. -n, bail, security, surety; einen — stellen, to give security. **Bürgen**, bür'gen, vt. to bail. warrant. **Bürger**, bür'ger, m. citizen, burger, burgess, commoner; **-eid**, -ked, m. citizen's oath. **Bürgersfrau**, -frāu, f. citizen's wife. **Bürgerkrieg**, -krig. m. civil war. **Bürgerlich**, bür'gerlich, a. civil, citizen's. **Bürgermeister**, -mäshter, m. mayor, burgomaster; **-amt**, n. mayoralty. **Bürgerrecht**, -recht, n. citizenship. **Bürgerschaft**, f. the citizens, the body of citizens. **Bürgerschule**, -shule, f. public school. **Bürgersinn**, -sinn, m. patriotism. **Bürgersoldat**, -soldät, m. -en, pl. -en, militia-man, soldier of the national guard. **Bürgerstand**, -shtant, m. the body of citizens. **Bürgerwache**, -vache, f. national guard. **Burgflecken**, burk'flecken, m. borough. **Burggraben**, -graben, m. moat. **Burggraf**, -gräf, m. -en, pl. -en, burggrave, castellan. **Bürgschaft**, bürk'shaft. f. surety, bail. **Burgverließ**, -ferlīs, n. dungeon, keep. **Burgvogt**, burk'fokt, m. castellan. **Burgwarte**, burk'varte, f. watch-tower.

Burrstein, bur'zhtåen, m. burr-stone.

Bursche, bur'she, m. -n, pl. -n, fellow; student; boy, lad, youth, apprentice.

Burschen, bur'shen, vi. to go hunting.

Burschenleben, bur'shenlāben, n. student's life. **Burschenschaft**, -shaft, f. (political) association of German students.

Bürste, bür'zhte, f. brush. **Bürsten**, bur'zhten, vt. to brush; **-binder**, -binnder, m. brush-maker.

Bürzel, bür'tsel, m. rump, croup **-baum**, -bāūm, m. sommerset. **Bürzeln**, bur'tseln, vi. to tumble, fall.

Busch, bush, m. bush, underwood, thicket. **Büschel**, bush'el, m. bunch, tuft. **Buschig**, bush'ich, a. bushy, shrubby. **Buschklepper**, bush'klepper, m. bush-ranger; foot-pad. **Buschwerk**, bush'verk, n. bushes, shrubbery.

Busen, bū'sen, m. bosom, breast; bay, gulf; **-freund**, -freūnt, m. bosomfriend; **-nadel**, -nädel, f. brooch, breast-pin. **Busenstreif**, -zhtråef, m. frill, tucker.

Buße, bus'se, f. penitence, repentance, atonement, punishment. **Büßen**, büh'sen, vt. to mend, repair, atone for. **Büßer**, büs'ser, m. -in, f. penitent. **Bußfertig**, -fertich, a. penitent. **Bußpsalm**, -psalm, m. penitential psalm. **Bußtag**, bus'tāk, m. fast-day. **Büßung**, buhs'sung, f. repentance, atonement.

Büste, büzh'te, f. bust.

Butte, but'te, **Bütte**, büt'te, f. tub, coop.

Büttel, büt'tel, m. beadle, jailor; **-ei**, -ëi', f. jail.

Buttenstreben, but'tenzhtäfen, m. back of the stern post.

Buttenträger, but'tenträger, m. pedler.

Butter, butter, f. butter; **-bämme**, -bemme, **-brod**, -brōt, n. slice of buttered bread; **-blume**, -blūme, f. buttercup; **-faß**, -fass, n. pl. -fässer, churn; **-milch**, -milch, f. buttermilk. **Buttern**, but'tern, vt. to churn, to turn, to butter. **Butterschnitte**, -shnitte, f. = **Butterbämme**. **Buttertopf**, -topf, m. butter-pot, butter jar, butter-crock.

Butzen, but'sen, m. core.

Bux, box, f. box.

Cabale, kabā′lẹ, *f.* intrigue; — ſchmieden, to caiʍl, intrigue; **Cabalemacher**, kabā′lẹmacher, *m.* intriguer.
Cabinet, kabinẹt′, *n.* cabinet, closet; -rath, -rāt, *m.* cabinet-council.
Cacao, ka′kaō, *m.* cacao; -baum, -bạum, *m.* cacao-tree.
Cadet, kadẹt′, *m.* -ten, *pl.* -ten, cadet.
Caffee, *f.* Kaffee.
Calciniren, kalsinī′ren, *vt.* to calcine.
Calcium, kal′sium, *n.* calcium.
Calculation, kal′kulatsiōn′, *f.* calculation. **Calculiren**, kalkulī′ren, *vt.* to calculate.
Caliber, kalī′ber, *n.* caliber.
Camelot, kam′elot, *m.* camlet, camelot.
Camerad, kamerād′, -en, *pl.* -en, comrade; -schaft, shaft, *f.* comrade-ship, fellowship.
Cameralisch, kamerāl′ish, *a.* cameralistic. **Cameralist**, -izht′, *m.* -en, *pl.* -en, financier. **Cameralwesen**, -vāsen, *n.* **Cameralwissenschaft**, -vissenshaft, *f.* cameralistics.
Campecheholz, kampā′shẹholts, *n.* logwood.
Campher, kam′fer, *m.* camphor.
Campiren, kampī′ren, *vi.* to camp, encamp.
Canaille, kanall′yẹ, *f.* mob, rabble.
Canal, kanāl′, *m.* canal, channel.
Canapee, kan′apā, *n.* couch, settee, sofa.
Canarienfect, kanā′ri-ensēkt, *m.* canary. **Canarienvogel**, -fōgel. *m.* canary-bird.
Canaster, kanazh′ter = Knaſter.
Candidat, kandidāt′, *m.* -en, *pl.* -en, candidate. **Candidatur**, -ụr, *f.* candidate-ship.
Candiszucker, kan′distsucker, *m.* sugar-candy.
Canel, kan′el, *m.* (fine) cinnamon.
Cannibal, kannibāl′, *m.* cannibal, savage.
Canon, kā′nōn, *m.* canon; -isch, -ish, *a.* canonical. **Canonisiren**, kanonisī′ren, *vt.* to canonize.
Canton, kantōn′, *m.* canton. **Cantonisiren**, kantonī′ren, *vi.* to cantonize, canton.
Cantor, kan′tor, *m.* cantor, leader of choir, director of church-music.

Cap, kāp, *m.* cape, promontory.
Capellan, kapēlläu′, *m.* chaplain.
Capelle, kapēl′lẹ, *f.* chapel; orchestra. **Capellmeister**, -mäezhter, *m.* director of an orchestra, leader of a band.
Caper, kā′per, *m.* privateer. **Caperei**, kāperēī′, *f.* privateering. **Capern**, kā′pern, *vt.* to seize, capture. **Caperschiff**, -shiff, *n.* privateer.
Capital, kapitāl′, *m.* capital. **Capitalist**, kapitalizht′, *m.* -en, *pl.* -en, capitalist, moneyed man.
Capitän, kapitän′, *m.* captain; -schaft, -shaft, *f.* captaincy.
Capitel, kapit′el, *n.* chapter.
Capitulation, kapitulatsiōn′, *f.* capitulation. **Capituliren**, -tulī′ren, *vi.* to capitulate.
Capriole, kapriō′lẹ, *f.* caper; -n machen, to caper.
Caputze, kaput′sẹ, *f.* capoch, hood. **Caputziner**, kaputsī′ner, *m.* capuchin.
Capwein, kāp′vīen, *m.* Constantia, cape (wine).
Carabiner, karabī′ner, *m.* carbine. **Carabinier**, karabīn′yä, *m.* carbineer.
Carat, karāt′. *n.* carat.
Caravane, karavā′nẹ, *f.* caravan.
Cardamome, kardamō′mẹ, *f.* cardamomum.
Cardinal, kardināl′, *m. pl.* -äle, cardinal; *a.* cardinal: -zahlen, -tsälen. *s. pl.* cardinal numbers.
Caressiren, karessī′ren, *vt.* to caress, fondle.
Carmin, karmin′, *m.* carmine. **Carmoisin**, karmoasīn′ *n.* crimson.
Carneval, kar′nevāl, *m.* carnival.
Caricatur, karikatur′, *f.* caricature.
Cariole, kariō′lẹ, *f.* cariole, gig.
Carosse, karos′sẹ, *f.* coach of state.
Caserne, kasēr′nẹ, *f.* barracks.
Cassabuch, kas′sābuch, *n.* cash-book. **Casse**, kas′sẹ, *f.* cash; -dieb, -dīb, *m.* defaulter, peculator; -diebstahl, -dībzhtäl, *m.* defalcation. **Cassiren**, kassī′ren, *vt.* to cashier, annul. **Cassirer**, *m.* cashier, cash-keeper.
Castell, kazhtēll′, *n.* small castle.
Castorhut, kazh′torhụt, *m.* beaver (hat)

Caſt   76   **Cla**

Caſtrat, kazhträt', *m.* eunuch. **Caſtriren**, kaṣhtrī'ren, *vt.* to castrate, emasculate. geld.
Catalog, ketalōg', *m.* -en, *pl.* -en, catalogue.
Caution, kǫutsiōn', *f.* surety, security, bail; — ſtellen, to give bail.
Cavalier, kavalīr', *m.* cavalier. **Cavallerie**, kavallerī'. *f.* cavalry. **Cavalleriſt**, kavallerizht', *m.* -en, *pl.* -en, horseman, trooper.
Ceder, tsä'der, *f.* cedar. **Cedern**, *a.* cedar.
Cenſiren, tsensī'ren, *vt.* to review, examine. **Cenſur**, tsęnsyr', *f.* censure, criticism, review.
Cent, tsęnt, *m.* cent; pro cent, per cent. **Centner**, tsęnt'ner, *m.* hundredweight, quintal; ſchwer, -shvär, *a.* excessively, heavy.
Central, tsenträl', *a.* central. **Centraliſiren**, tsentralisī'ren, *vt.* to centralize. **Centrum**, tsęn'trųm, *m.* centre; ſbohrer, -bōrer, *m.* buttontool.
Ceremonie, tsęręmō'ni-ę, *f.* ceremony. **Ceremoniell**, tsęręmō'ni-ěll, *a.* ceremonial. **Ceremoniös**, tsęręmō'ni-öhs. *a.* ceremonious, formal, *av.* -ly.
Cervelatwurſt, sěrvęlät'vųrzht, *f.* brain-sausage.
Chaiſe, shä'sę, *f.* carriage.
Chalkolith, kalkolit', *m.* -en, *pl.* -en, copper-uranite.
Chamäleon, ḥamä'leōn, *n.* chameleon.
Champagner, shampan'yěr, *m.* champaign (wine).
Chaos, kä'os, *m.* chaos.
Charade, sharä'dę, *f.* charade.
Charakter, karak'ter, *m.* character; ſiſiren, -isī'ren, *vt.* to characterize. **Charakteriſtiſch**, -izht'ish, *a.* characteristic, *av.* -ally.
Charfreitag, karfrī'täk, *m.* Good Friday.
Charnier, sharnīr', *n.* hinge.
Charpie, sharpī', *n.* lint.
Charwoche, kä.'voḥę, *f.* passion-week.
Chauſſée, shossä', *f.* turnpike-road, high-road.
Chemie, ḥemī', *f.* chemistry. **Chemiker**, ḥī'miker, *m.* chemist. **Chemiſch**, ḥä'mish, *a.* chemical.
Cherub, ḥä'rųb, *m.* cherub.
Chicane, shikä'nę, *f.* trick, shift; sophistry. **Chicaniren**, -nī'ren, *vt.* to vex, trick.

Chimäre, kimä'rę, *f.* chimera.
Chinarinde, kī'näriṇdę, *a.* Peruvian bark.
Chirurg, ḥirųrg', *m.* surgeon; ſie, -ī', *f.* surgery.
Chlor, ḥlōr, *n.* chlorine; ſalf, -kalk, *m.* chloride of lime. **Chloroform**, ḥlō'roform, *m.* chloroform.
Chocolate, shokolä'tę, *f.* chocolate.
Cholera, kō'lęrä, *f.* cholera. **Choleriſch**, kōlä'rish, *a.* choleric.
Chor, kōr, *m.* chorus; *n.* choir. **Choral**, korål', *m.* choral (song); ſbuch, -buḥ, *n. pl.* -bücher, choralbook. **Chorhemd**, -hęmt. *n.* -es, *pl.* -en, surplice, alb. **Choriſt**, korizht', *m.* -en, *pl.* -en, chorist, chorister.
Chriſt, krizht, *m.* Christ; Christian; ſabend, -äbent, *n.* christmas-eve; ſenheit, -enhäet, *f.* Christendom; ſenthum, -entųm, *n.* Christianity. **Chriſtenfind**, -kint, *m.* infant Jesus. **Chriſtlich**, krixht'liḥ, *a.* Christian. **Chriſttag**, -täk, *m. pl.* -tage, Christmas-day. **Chriſtus**, krixht'ųs, *m.* Christ.
Chrom, krōm, *n.* chromium. **Chromatiſch**, krōmat'ish, *a.* chromatic. **Chromgelb**, -gęlp, *n.* chrome-yellow. **Chromgrün**, -grüṇ, *n.* chrome-green.
Chronik, krō'nik, *f.* chronicle. **Chroniſch**, krō'nish, *a.* chronical. **Chronologie**, -logī', *f.* chronology.
Chur, kųr, ſ. Kur.
Cichorie, tsikō'ri-ę, *f.* succory.
Cigarre, tsigar'rę, *f.* cigar.
Circulation, tsirkųlatsiōn', *f.* circulation. **Circuliren**, -lī'ren, *vi.* to circulate.
Cirkel, tsir'kel, ſ. Zirkel.
Ciſterne, tsizhtěr'nę, *f.* cistern.
Citadelle, tsitaděllę, *f.* citadel.
Cither, tsit'ter, *f.* cittern, cithern.
Citiren, tsitī'ren, *vt.* to cite, quote; to summon.
Citronat, tsitronät', *m.* candied lemon peel. **Citrone**, tsitrō'nę, *f.* lemon. **Citrongelb**, -gęlp, *a.* lemon-colored.
Civil, tsifīl', *a.* civil. **Civiliſation**, -satsiōn', *f.* civilization. **Civiliſiren**, -sī'ren, *vt.* to civilize. **Civilrecht**, -rěḥt, *n.* civil law.
Clarinette, klarinět'tę, *f.* clarionet.
Claſſe, klas'sę, *f.* class. **Claſſiſch**, klas'sish, *a.* classic.
Clauſel, klǫu'sel, *f.* clause, condition.

Clabiatur, klafiatŭr', *f.* key-board.
Clavier. klafīr', *n.* piano (forte).
Client, kli-ęnt', *m.* -en, *pl.* -en, client.
Club, klŭb', *m.* ſ. **Klub.**
Clyſtier, klizhtŭr', *n.* clyster, ſ. **Klyſtir.**
Coalition, ko-alītsiōn', *f.* coalition, alliance.
Cocarde, kokar'de, *f.* cockade.
Cochenille, koshęnīl'lę, *f.* cochineal.
Cocosnuß, kok'ossnyss, *f.* cocoa-nut.
Cölibat, tsölībăt', *n.* celibacy.
Colibri, kö'lĭbrī, *m.* humming-bird.
Collecte, kollęk'tę, *f.* collection.
College, kollä'gę, *m.* -n, *pl.* -n, colleague. **Collegium,** kollā'gĭŭm, *n.* college; lecture.
Collision, kollīsiōn', *f.* collision.
Colonial, kolonīăl', *a.* colonial: -waaren, -vāren, *s. pl.* colonial produce. **Colonie,** kolonī', *f.* colony. **Colonisiren,** kolonīsī'ren, *vt.* to colonize.
Colonne, kolon'nę, *f.* column (of an army).
Colophonium, kolofō'nĭŭm, *n.* rosin, colophony.
Coloriren, kolorī'ren, *vt.* to color.
Coloß, coloss'. *m.* colosseus; giant. **Colosseum, Coliseum,** kolisä'ŭm, *n.* Colosseum, Coliseum.
Columne, kolŭm'nę, *f.* column (Print.).
Combination, kombīnatsiōn', *f.* combination. **Combiniren,** kombīnī'ren, *vt.* to combine.
Comet, komāt', *m.* -en, *pl.* -en, comet.
Comite, komitä, *n.* committee.
Commandant, kommandant', *m.* -en, *pl.* -en, commander, governor. **Commandiren,** -dī'ren, *vt.* to command. **Commando,** -man'dō, *n.* command; detachment.
Commis, komˈmī, *m.* clerk.
Commißär, kommissār', *m.* commissioner, commissary. **Commißariat,** -sarĭāt', *n.* commissary department. **Com'misbrod,** -brōt, *n.* soldier's bread; ammunition-bread. **Commißion,** kommīssiōn', *f.* commission. **Commißionär,** -siōnār', *m.* commissioner.
Commode, kommō'dę, *f.* chest of drawers, bureau.
Communicant, kommūnīkant', *m.* -en, *pl.* -en, communicant. **Communication,** -katsiōn', *f.* communication. **-graben,** -grāben. *r.* zigzag trench.

Communiciren, -tsī'ren, *vt.* to communicate; to partake of the Lord's supper. **Communion,** kommŭniōn', *f.* communion. **Communismus,** kommŭnīs'mŭss, *m.* communism, socialism.
Comödiant, komödiant', *m.* ſ. **Komödiant.**
Compagnie, kompanī', *f.* company, partnership.
Compagnon, kompanyōn', *m.* associate, partner.
Comparativ, kom'paratīf, *m.* comparative (degree).
Compaß, kom'pass, *m.* compass.
Competent, kompętęnt', *a.* competent, authorized.
Complement, komplęmęnt', *n.* complement.
Compliment, komplīment', *m.* compliment, bow; -iren, -tī'ren, *vt.* to compliment; to salute.
Complott, komplott', *n.* plot, conspiracy.
Componiren, kompōnī'ren, *vt.* to compose, write. **Componist,** -pōnizht', *m.* composer. **Composition,** kompositsiōn', *f.* composition.
Compost, kompozht', *m.* compost, manure.
Comptoir, kōm'toär, *n.* counting-room, office.
Concav, konkāf', *a.* concave.
Concentration, kontsęntratsiōn', *f.* concentration. **Concentriren,** -trī'ren, *vt.* to concentrate.
Concept, kontsępt', *n.* sketch, minute.
Conceſſion, kontsęssiōn', *f.* concession; license.
Concert, kontsert', *n.* concert.
Concilium, kontsī'lĭŭm, *n.* council.
Condition, kondītsiōn', *f.* condition.
Conditor, kondīt'or, *m.* confectioner; -ei, -ī', *f.* confectioner's shop, confectionery.
Condolenz, kondolęnts', *f.* condolence.
Confect, konfękt', *n.* sweetmeat, confectionary.
Conferenz, konfęręnts', *f.* conference.
Confeſſion, konfęssiōn', *f.* confession.
Confiscation, konfīskatsiōn', *f.* confiscation. **Confisciren,** -tsī'ren, *vt.* to confiscate.
Congreß, kongress', *m.* congress.
Conjunctiv, kon'yŭnktīf, *m.* subjunctive (mood). [script
Conscribirter, konskrībīr'ter, *m.* con-

Consignation, konsignatsiōn', f. consignment.
Consistorialrath, konsizhtoriäl'rät, m. counselor of the consistory. **Consistorium**, konsizhtō'riŭm, n. consistory.
Consonant, konsonant', m. -en, pl. -en, consonant.
Consonanz, konsonants', f. consonance, agreement.
Constabel, kou'zhtäbel, m. gunner; constable.
Constitution, konzhtitŭtsiōn', f. constitution. [struction.
Construction, konzhtrŭktsiōn', f. con-
Consul, kon'sŭl, m. consul; -at, -lät', n. consulship.
Continent, kontinent', m. continent.
Conto, kon'tō, n. account. count.
Contract, kontrakt', m. contract, bargain. **Contrahent**, kontrahent'; m. -en, pl. -en, contractor.
Contrebande, kon'terbande, f. contraband.
Contribution, kontribŭtsiōn', f. contribution.
Convalesciren, konfalēstsī'ren, vt. to recover, get well.
Convenienz, könfeni-ents', f. convenience.
Convent, konfent', n. convent.
Conversation, konfērsatsiōn', f. conversation; -lexikon, -lēxicon, n. encyclopedia.
Convex, konfēx', a. convex.
Copal, kopäl', m. copal.
Copie, kō'pi-e, f. copy. **Copiren**, kopī'ren, vt. to copy. **Copist**, kopizht', m. -en, pl. -en, copyist, transcriber.
Coquet, kokētt', a. f. Kokett.
Corduan, kordŭān', m. cordovan, cordwain; -arbeiter, -arbäeter, m. cordwainer.
Corporal, korporäl', m. corporal.
Correct, korrēkt', a. correct, accurate; -heit, -häet, f. correctness. **Correction**, korrēktsiōn', f. correction. **Correctur**, korrēktŭr', f. proof, correction.
Correspondent, korrezhpondent', m. -en, pl. -en, correspondent. **Correspondenz**, -pondents', f. correspondence. **Correspondiren**, -zhpondī'ren, vi. to correspond.
Corrigiren, korrigī'ren, vt. to correct.
Corsar, korsär', m. -en, pl. -en, corsair, pirate.

Cour, kŭr, f. court; die — machen, to court.
Courage, kŭräzh', f. courage.
Courbette, kŭrbet'te, f. curvet.
Courier, kŭrīr', m. courier.
Cours, kŭrs, m. course, circulation, currency, exchange.
Cousine, kŭsī'ne, f. (female) cousin.
Couvert, kŭvērt', n. cover, envelop.
Creatur, kreatŭr', f. creature.
Credit, krēdit', m. credit; -brief, -brīf, m. letter of credit. **Creditiren**, crēditī'ren, vt. to credit, to sell on credit.
Cretin, krēt'kēn, m. cretin, idiot.
Criminal, f. Kriminal.
Crocus, krō'kŭs, m. crocus.
Crucifix, krŭtsifīx', n. crucifix.
Cubic, kŭbīk', a. cubical; -fuß, -fŭs, m. cubic-foot; -wurzel, -vŭrtsel, f. cube root.
Cultiviren, kŭltifī'ren, vt. to cultivate. **Cultur**, kŭltŭr', f. culture, cultivation. **Cultus**, kŭl'tŭs, m. religious rites.
Cur, kŭr, f. cure.
Curator, kŭrä'tor, m. guardian.
Curiren, kŭrī'ren, vt. to cure.
Current, kŭrrent', a. current; -drucken, -drŭcken, vt. to italicize; -schrift, -shrift, f. current hand; italics.
Cyan, tsiän', n. cyanogen.
Cyclus, tsik'lŭs, m. cycle. **Cycloide**, tsiklō'de, f. cycloid.
Cylinder, tsilin'der, m. cylinder. **Cylinderisch**, tsilin'drish, a. cylindrical.
Cymbel, tsim'bel, f. cymbal.
Cynisch, tsī'nish, a. cynical.
Cyperkatze, tsip'erkatse, f. cyprian cat. **Cypresse**, tsiprēs'se, f. cypress; -baum, -baŭm, m. cypress-tree.
Czar, tsär, m. -en, pl. -en, czar. **Czarin**, tsär'in, f. czarina, empress of Russia.

Da, dä, av. there, then, where, when, since, whereas.
Dabei, dabēī', av. thereat, thereby, near it: — bleiben, to persist in.
Dach, dach, n. pl. Dächer, roof: -decker, -decker, m. thatcher, tiler, shingler; -fahne, -fāne, f. weather-cock; -fenster, -fenzhter, n. garret-window. **Dachkammer**, dach'kammer, f. attic garret. **Dachrinne**, dach'rinne, a gutter.

Dachs, dax, *m.* badger; terrier. **Dachs'bau**, -boŭ, *m.* kennel of a badger; **-beinig**, -bŭnich, *a.* badger-legged; **-hund**, -hunt, *m.* terrier.

Dachstube, dach'zhtūbĕ, *f.* attic, garret. **Dachtraufe**, -troŭfĕ, *f.* eaves. **Dach'ziegel**, -tsīgel, *m.* tile.

Dadurch, dādurch, *av.* thereby, by, through it.

Dafern, dāfĕrn', *conj.* if, in case that.

Dafür, dafür', *av.* for it; — **halten**, *n.* opinion.

Dagegen, dagä'gen, *av.* against that, in exchange, on the contrary.

Daguerrotyp, daghĕrŏtīp', *n.* daguerreotype.

Daheim, dahīm, *av.* at home.

Daher, dā'hĕr, *av.* thence, hence, from that place; for that reason, therefore. **Daherum**, dāhĕrum, *av.* thereabout.

Dahin, dā'hīn, *av.* thither, there, to that place, quarter; that way; along, down. **Dahinten**, dahin'ten, *av.* behind there. **Dahinter**, dahin'ter, *av.* behind that, it; — **kommen**, to find out.

Dahlen, dā'len, *vi.* to dally, trifle, play the fool.

Daktylisch, daktīl'ish, *a.* dactylic.

Damalig, dä'mälich, *a.* of that time; der —e **Präsident**, the then president. **Damals**, dā'mähls, *av.* then, at that time.

Damascener, damastsä'ner, *m.* Damascirte **Klinge**, *f.* damaskin. **Damaseiren**, damastsī'ren, *vt.* to damask. **Damast**, damazht', *m.* damask; **-en**, *a.* damask.

Dame, dā'mĕ, *f.* lady, dame, madam, queen (cards); **-brett**, -brĕtt, *n.* draught-board; **-sattel**, -sattel, *m.* side-saddle, lady's saddle.

Damit, damit', *av.* therewith, with it, by it, thereby; — ist mir nicht gedient, that will not serve my turn; damit (daß), in order that; damit nicht, lest.

Damm, damm, *m.* dam, mole, bank, mound, dike, pier; perinaeum. **Dämmen**, dĕm'men, *vt.* to dam, embank; to curb, restrain.

Dämmerig, dĕm'mĕrich, *a.* twilight, dusky, dim, gray. **Dämmern**, dĕm'nern, *vi.* to dawn, grow twilight, to grow light. **Dämmerung**, -ung, *f.* twilight; day-break; Morgen —, dawn; Abend —, dusk, evening-twilight.

Dämon, dā'mōn, *m.* demon; devil. **Dämonisch**, dämō'nish, *a.* demoniac, demonlike.

Dampf, dampf, *m.* steam, vapor, smoke, fume, reek, damp; **-boot**, -bōt, *n.* steamboat; **-bad**, -bād, *n.* steambath. **Dampfen**, dampf'en, *vi.* to steam, smoke, fume, exhale, evaporate. **Dämpfen**, dĕm'pfen, *vt.* to damp, suffocate, quench, smother, stifle, suppress, extinguish, put out, subdue. **Dampfer**, dam'pfer, *m.* steamer. **Dämpfer**, dĕm'pfer, *m.* damper, moderator; steamer. **Dampfig**, dampf'ich, *a.* asthmatic, broken-winded. **Dampfkessel**, daṃpf'kessel, *m.* steam-boiler. **Dampfkraft**, dampf'kraft, *f.* steam-power. **Dampfmaschine**, -mashīne, *f.* steam-engine. **Dampfmühle**, -mühle, *f.* steam-mill. **Dampfnudeln**, -nŭdeln, *s.pl.* steam-dumplings. **Dampfpresse**, -prĕsse, *f.* steam-press. **Dampfschiff**, -shiff, *n.* steamship, steamer. **Dämpfung**, dĕmpf'ung, *f.* damping, suppression, suffocation. **Dampfventil**, -fentīl, *n.* steam-valve. **Dampfwagen**, -vägen, *m.* locomotive (engine).

Danach, dankā' (Darnach, darnāch'), *av.* thereafter, after that, upon it. **Daneben**, danā'ben, *av.* near it, next to it, close by. **Danieder, Darnieder**, darnī'der, *av.* down, down there.

Dank, dank, *m.* thanks; — **sagen**, to thank, to give thanks; **-bar**, -bār, *a.* thankful, grateful, *av.* -ly; **-barkeit**, -bārkāĕt, *f.* thankfulness, gratefulness, gratitude. **Danken**, dang'ken, *vi.* to thank, return thanks; einem zu — haben, to be indebted to any one. **Dankenswerth**, dang'kensvārt, *a.* thanksworthy. **Dankfest**, -fĕzht, *n.* thanksgiving-day. **Danklied**, -līd, *n. pl.* -er, thanksgiving hymn. **Dankopfer**, -opfer, *n.* thank-offering. **Danksagung**, -sāgung, *f.* thanksgiving.

Darau, därän' (Dran), *av.* thereon, thereat, at that, at it, whereon. **Darauf**, darŏŭf' (Drauf, drŏŭf), *av.* thereon, thereupon, upon that. **Daraus**, darŏŭs' (Draus, drŏŭs), *av.*

thereout, therefrom, thence. out of that. Daraußen, f. Draußen.

Darben, dar'ben, vi. to want, to be indigent.

Darbieten, där'bīten (-bot, -geboten), vt. to offer.

Darbringen, där'bring-en (-bradhte, bargebracht), vt. to offer, present. Dar'bringung, -bringyng, f. offering.

Darein, dar̃sn' (Drein, drẹ̈n), av. thereinto, into that, into it.

Darhalten, där'halten (-hielt, bargehalten), vt. to reach or hold forth.

Darin, darīn', av. therein, in that, in it.

Darlegen, där'lägen, vt. to lay down, expose, show, exhibit, display, submit.

Darleihen, där'lā-en. n. loan. Darleihen, där'lēi-en, vi. to lend. Darleiher, där'lēi'er, m. lender.

Darm, darm, m. gut, intestine, bowels; -bruch, -bruch, m. intestinal rupture; -gicht, -gicht, f. colic. Darm'ſaite, -ṡāete, f. cat-gut, gut-string.

Darnach, darnäch', av. f. Danach. Darob, daröb', av. (thereupon), on that account, for that.

Darre, dar're, f. kiln.

Darreichen, där'rāēchen, vt. to offer, hand.

Darren, dar'ren, vt. to kiln-dry. Darr'ofen, -öfen, m. Darr'kammer, -kammer. f. drying oven, kiln. Darr'jucht, -sycht, f. consumption, atrophy.

Darstellen, där'zhtellen, vt. to present, represent, exhibit. Darstellung, där'zhtellyng. f. exhibition, presentation.

Darthun, där'tyn (-that, -gethan), to show, prove, demonstrate, explain, expose.

Darüber, darüh'ben. f. Drüben. Darüber, darüh'ber, Drüber, drüh'ber, av. over that, over it; thereon, thereof. Darum, där'ym (Drum drym), av. about that, for that, for it; for that reason. Darunten, darṿn'ten (Drunten, drṿn'ten), av. below, beneath. Darunter, darṿn'ter (Drunter, drṿn'ter), av. thereunder, under that, under it, thereby, below it, among it; — ſein, to be of the

number. Darzwiſchen, f. Dazwiſchen.

Darzählen, där'tsälen, vt. tc count or pay down.

Das, däs, neut. article, the.

Daſein, dä'ṡẹn, n. existence, presence.

Daſelbſt, dasölpst', av. there, in that place.

Dasmal, däs'mäl, av. this time.

Daß, dass, conj. that; — nicht. lest.

Daſtehen, dä'zhtā-en (-ſtand, bageſtanden), vi. to stand there.

Data, dä'tä, s. pl. data. Datiren, datī'ren, vt. to date. Dativ, dat'īf, m dative. Dato, dä'tō, av. of the date bis —, till now.

Dattel, dat'tel, f. date; -kern, -kẽrn m. kernel of the date; -palme, -palme, f. date-tree; -walb, -valt, m. date-grove.

Datum, dä'tum, n. date.

Daube, döy'be, f. staff, stave, clapboard.

Däuchten, döücht'en, imper. mir däucht, me thinks, it appears, it seems to me.

Dauer, dö̃u'er, f. duration, continuance; -haft, -haft, a. lasting, durable; -haftigkeit, -haftichkēet, f. durableness, durability. Dauern, döu'ern, vi. to last, endure, continue, remain; es bauert mich, it grieves me, I regret, I am sorry for; I regret, pity, sorrow.

Daumen, döum'en, m. thumb, inch; lift (in mills); einem ben — halten, to keep a tight hand over. Däumling, dẽum'ling, m. thumb-stall; thimble: little man, mannikin. Daum'ſchraube, -shröybe, f. thumb-screw, thumbkin.

Daune, dạü'ne, f. down.

Daus, döys, m. deuce; ace; ber —, the deuce!

Davit, dä'vit, m. davit.

Davon, däfön', av. thereof, therefrom, from that, of that; off, away. Davor, däfōr', av. before that, for that, for it; from that, from it; of that. Dazu, dätsy', av. thereto, to that or it, for that or it. Dazwiſchen, datschvish'en, Darzwiſchen, av. between that or it. Dazumal, da'tṡymal, av. then, at that time.

Debet, dä'bet, n. debit.

Decan, dekän', m. dean.

Decantiren, dekantī'ren, vt. to decant.
Decantirung, -tīr'ŭng, f. decantation.
Decatiren, dekatī'ren, vt. to sponge and gloss (cloth).
December, detsem'ber, m. December.
Decher, dech'er, m. (dicker), ten.
Decimal, detsimäl', a. decimal; -bruch, -bruch, m. decimal fraction.
Deck, deck, n. deck: das — streichen, vt. to lay a deck; -bett, -bett, n. coverlet, upper covering. Decke, deck'e, f. cover; coverlet; ceiling. Deckel, deck'el, m. cover, lid; — einer Druckpresse, tympan; -krug, -krŭk, m. tankard. Decken, deck'en, vt. to cover, deck, overlay. Deckmantel, deck'mantel, m. cloak, cover, mask, pretence, pretext. Deckplatte, deck'-platte, f. junction-plate. Deck's werfen, -verfen, s. pl. deck-transoms.
Declamation, deklamatsiōn', f. declamation. Declamiren, deklamī'ren, vt. to declaim, speak.
Declination, deklinatsiōn', f. declension, declination. Decliniren, -nī'ren, vt. to decline.
Decoct, dekokt', n. decoction.
Decoration, decōratsiōn', f. decoration.
Defekt, defekt', a. defective, imperfect.
Defensive, defensī've, f. defensive.
Deficit, de'fitsit, n. deficit.
Defilee, defilā', n. defile, mountain-pass. Defiliren, -lī'ren, vi. to defile, file off.
Definition, definitsiōn', f. definition. Definitiv, definitīv', a. deciding, decisive, definite.
Degen, dā'gen, m. sword; champion, warrior; -gehenf, -gehenk, n. sword-belt, waist-belt; -geklirr, -geklirr, n. clash of swords; -hieb, -hīb, m. sword-cut; -klinge, -kling-e, f. sword-blade; -knopf, -k(e)nopf, m. pommel of a sword; -quaste, -quaste, f. sword-knot.
Dehnbar, dān'bär, a. ductile, extensible; -keit, -kāet, f. ductility, dilatability, extensibility. Dehnen, dān'en, vt. to stretch, extend, expand. Dehnung, dān'ŭng, f. extension, expansion.
Deich, dēch, m. dike, dam. Deichen,

dēch'en, vt. to build or repair a dike.
Deichsel, dēīk'sel, f. shaft, pole, thill; adz, addice; -nagel, -nāgel, m. thill-pin; -pferd, -pfārt, n. thill-horse.
Dein, dāēn, sig, -ich, a. pron. thy, thine, your. Deinethalben, dāē'nethalben, for (thy) your account, for (thy) your sake, in (thy) your behalf.
Deismus, dēīs'mŭss, m. deism. Deist, dē'īzht, m. -en, pl. -en, deist.
Delicat, delikät', a. delicate, fine, soft, nice. Delikatesse, delikatēs'se, f. delicacy.
Delinquent, delinquent', m. -en, pl. -en, delinquent.
Delphin, dėlfīn', m. dolphin.
Dem, dām, art. to the, to whom.
Demagog, demagōg', m. -en, pl. -en, demagogue.
Demant, dem'ant, m. -en, pl. -en, diamond; -en, a. diamond.
Demnach, däm'näch, cj. then, therefore, accordingly. Demnächst, -next, av thereupon, thereafter. Demnungeachtet = Dessenungeachtet.
Demokrat, demōkrät', m. -en, pl. -en, democrat; -ie, -ī', f. democracy; -isch, -ish, a. democratic; av. -ally.
Demonstration, demonzhtratsiōn', f. demonstration. Demonstriren, -zhtrī'ren, vt. to demonstrate.
Demuth, dāmŭt, f. humility. Demüthig, dā'mūthich, a. humble, av. humbly; -en, vt. to humble, humiliate. Demüthigkeit, -kāet. f. humbleness, meekness. Demüthigung -ichŭng, f. humiliation.
Den, dān, art. the, that one, that.
Dengeln, deng'eln, vt. to hammer out, to sharpen.
Denkart, denk'ärt, f. mind, mode of thinking. Denkbar, denk'bär, a. conceivable, imaginable; -keit, -kāet, f. conceivableness. Denken, denk'en (dachte, gedacht), vt. to think, conceive of; to fancy, imagine. Denker, denk'er, m. thinker. Denklehre, -lār-e, f. logic. Denkmal, -māl, n. pl. -mäler, monument. Denkmünze, -müntse, f. medal. Denkschrift, -shrift, f. memoir, memorial, inscription. Denkspruch, -zhpruch, m. apophthegm, aphorism, sentence, maxim. Denkwürdig, -vürdich, a. memorable; -keit, -kāet,

f. memorableness, memorable event; memoirs. **Denkzeichen,** -tzeichen, *n.* memento, token of remembrance. **Denkzettel,** -tzettel, *m.* memorandum, sensible token of remembrance.

Denn, denn, *cj.* than; for; reicher — er, richer than he; es sei denn daß, unless; denn er kann, for he can.

Dennoch, den'noch, *cj.* yet, nevertheless, however.

Denuntiant, denuntsiant', *m.* -en, *pl.* -en, denouncer, informer. **Denunziren,** -tsī'ren, *vt.* to denounce.

Departement, depart'mang, *m.* department.

Depesche, depä'she, *f.* dispatch.

Deponiren, deponī'ren, *vt.* to depose, lay down. **Depot,** de'pō, *n.* depot.

Deputation, deputatsiōn', *f.* deputation. **Deputiren,** deputī'ren, *vt.* to send a delegation.

Der, där, *m. art.* the; *pron.* that (one); who, which.

Derb, derp, *a.* compact, solid; hardy, sturdy, hard, downright; **-heit,** -hāet, *f.* firmness, roughness.

Dereinst, därēnzht', *av.* one day. **Derenthalben,** -halben, **Derentwegen,** -vägen, *av.* on their account, on whose account. **Dergestalt,** där'gezhtalt, *av.* in such a manner, so. **Dergleichen,** -glēichen, *av.* the like; such, such as. **Dermaleinst,** där'mälzēnzht; *av.* in the future. **Dermalen,** -mälen, *av.* at present, now. **Dermalig,** där'mälich, *a.* actual, present. **Dermaßen,** där'mäsen, *av.* to such a degree, so much. **Dero,** där'ō, *pron.* your. **Derselbe,** därsēl'be, **Derselbige,** -ichy, *pron.* the same.

Deserteur, desertühr', *m.* deserter. **Desertiren,** desertī'ren, *vi.* to desert.

Desfalls, des'fals, *av.* in this case, therefore. **Desgleichen,** desglēich'en, *av.* likewise, of the like kind. **Deshalb,** des'halp, *av.* for this reason, therefore.

Desideratum, desiderā'tum, *n.* desideratum.

Despot, despōt', *m.* -en, *pl.* -en, despot. **Despotisch,** despō'tish, *a.* despotic, -al, *av.* -ally. **Despotismus,** -tis'mus, *m.* **Despotie,** despotī', *f.* despotism.

Dessenthalben, des'sent-halben, **-wegen,** -vägen. **-willen,** -villen, *av.* therefore, for that reason, on that account.

Dessenungeachtet, des'enun geachtet, *cj.* notwithstanding.

Dessert, dessert', *n.* dessert.

Destilliren, dezhtillī'ren, *vt.* to distill **Desto,** dezh'tō, *conj.* the; je — besto, the — the; je größer, besto besser, the greater, the better. **Deswillen, Deßwillen,** des'villen, *av.* for that reason.

Detachiren, detashī'ren, *vt.* to detach. **Detail,** detal'ye (Getheil), *n.* detail, particulars. **Detailiren,** detalyī'ren, *vt.* to detail.

Deuten, dēu'ten, to point to, to hint at; to interpret, expound, explain; refer. **Deutlich,** dēut'lich, *a.* clear, distinct, plain; **-keit,** -kāet, *f.* distinctness, clearness.

Deutsch, dēutsch, *a.* German; *s. n.* German; **-land,** -lant, *n.* Germany.

Deutung, dēut'ung, *f.* interpretation, exposition.

Dezember, detsem'ber, *m.* December.

Diadem, diadām', *n.* diadem.

Diakonus, diak'ōnus, *m.* deacon.

Dialog, dialōg', *m.* -en, *pl.* -en, dialogue.

Diamant, diamant', *m.* -en, *pl.* -en, diamond; **-en,** *a.* diamond.

Diarrhöe, diarrhö', *f.* diarrhœa.

Diät, diät', *f.* diet.

Dicht, dicht, *a.* tight, dense, close, thick; *av.* -ly.

Dichtart, dicht'ärt, *f.* style of poetry. **Dichten,** dicht'en, *vi.* to tighten; to meditate, contrive, invent, to write poetry. **Dichter,** dicht'er, *m.* poet; **-in,** -in, *f.* poetess, female poet; **-isch,** -ish, *a.* poetic, -al, *av.* -ally; **-ling,** -ling, *m.* poetaster.

Dichtheit, dicht'hāet, *f.* density, tightness.

Dichtkunst, dicht'kunzht, *f.* poetry, imaginative composition. **Dichtung,** dicht'yng, *f.* fiction, invention; poetry, poem.

Dick, dick, *a.* thick. **Dicke,** dick'e, **Dickheit,** -hāet, *f.* thickness, bigness, largeness. **Dicht,** dik, *n.* thicket. **Dickkopf,** -kopf, *m.* blockhead. **Dickleibig,** -lēibich, *a.* thick headed. **Dickleibig,** -lēibich, *a.* corpulent; **-keit,** -kāet, *f.* corpulence. **Dicklich,** dick'lich, *a.* thickish.

Dictiren, diktī′ren, *vt.* to dictate.
Dieb, dēb, *m.* thief; -in, -in, *f.* female thief. **Dieberei,** dēberī′, *f.* theft, thievery. **Diebisch,** dē′ish, *a.* thievish, *av.* -ly. **Diebsbande,** -bande, *f.* gang of thieves. **Diebslaterne,** -laterne, *f.* dark lantern. **Diebsschlüssel,** -shüssel, *m.* pick-lock. **Diebstahl,** -shtäl, *m.* theft, larceny; — mit Einbruch, burglary; gelehrter —, plagiarism.
Diele, dī′le, *f.* deal, plank, board. **Dielen,** dī′len, *vt.* to board, floor; -kopf, -kopf, *m.* bracket.
Dienen, dī′nen, *vi.* to serve. **Diener,** dīn′er, *m.* servant-waiter; -in, -in, *f.* waiting-maid. **Dienlich,** dīn′lich, *a.* serviceable, beneficial, subservient. **Dienst,** dīnzht, *m.* service, employment, office.
Dienstag, dī′nzhtäk, *m.* Tuesday.
Dienstbar, dīnzht′bär, *a.* bound to service; -keit, -kāet, *f.* service, bondage. **Dienstbeflissen,** beflissen, *a.* obliging, officious; -heit, -hāet, *f.* kindness, obligingness. **Dienstbote,** -bōte, *m.* -n, *pl.* -n, servant, domestic. **Diensteifer,** -ēifer, *m.* obligingness, officiousness. **Dienstfertig,** -fertig, *a.* officious, obliging; -keit, -kāet, *f.* obligingness, kindness. **Dienstherr,** dīnzht′her, *m.* -n, *pl.* -n, master, employer. **Dienstleistung,** -līsztung, *f.* service. **Dienstlohn,** -lōn, *m.* wages, hire. **Dienstlos,** -lōs, *a.* out of service, unemployed. **Dienstmädchen,** -mētchen, *n.* girl, sewing-maid. **Dienstmagd,** -makt, *f.* servant-maid, menial. **Dienstmann,** *m. pl.* Dienstleute, servingman, bondsman. **Dienstpflicht,** -pflicht, *f.* liableness to service; -ig, *a.* liable to service. **Diensttuend,** -tu-ent *a.* performing active service; -e Leute, effective men. **Diensttüchtig,** -tüchtich, *a.* able to do service. **Diensttauglich,** -gu′tāglich, *a.* unfit for service. **Dienstwillig,** -villich, *a.* ready to oblige, kind, obliging; -keit, -kāet, *f.* obligingness, kindness. **Dienstzeit,** -tsāet, *f.* time of service.
Diesemnach, dī′zemnäch, *av.* according to this. **Diesfalls,** -fals, *av.* in this case. **Diesjährig,** -yärich, *a.* of this year. **Diesmal,** dīs′māl, *(v.* this time. **Diesseits,** dīs′sāits, *w.* on this side of. **Diesseitig,** -sēitich, *a.* situated on this side, our.

Dietrich, dī′rich, *m.* pick-lock.
Dieweil, dīvēil′, *av.* while, because.
Dilettant, dīlettant′, *m.* -en, *pl.* -en, dilettant, amateur.
Dill, dill, *f.* dill.
Ding, ding, *n.* thing. **Ding′elchen, Dingerchen,** ding′erchen, *n.* little thing.
Dingen, ding′en (dung, gedungen), *vt.* to hire, engage, employ.
Dinstag, din′zhtāk, *m.* Tuesday.
Dinte, din′te, *f.* ink, f. Tinte.
Diplom, diplōm′, *n.* diploma. **Diplomat,** diplomāt′, *m.* -en, *pl.* -en, diplomatist. **Diplomatisch,** -ish, *a.* diplomatic.
Director, dirēk′tor, *m.* **Dirigent,** dirigent′, *m.* -en, *pl.* -en, director, leader. **Directorium,** dirēktō′rium, *n.* directory. **Dirigiren,** dirigī′ren, *vt.* to direct, manage, conduct.
Dirne, dir′ne, *f.* maid, girl; wench.
Discant, diskant′, *m.* descant, soprano.
Disciplin, distsiplīn′, *f.* discipline. **Discipliniren,** distsiplinī′ren, *vt.* to discipline.
Dispensiren, dispensī′ren, *vt.* to dispense, free from.
Disponiren, dispon′ren, *vt.* to dispose.
Disputation, disputatsiōn′, *f.* disputation. **Disputiren,** disputī′ren, *vt.* to dispute.
Dissonanz, dissonants′, *f.* dissonance.
Distel, dizh′tel, *f.* thistle.
District, distrīkt′, *m.* district.
Dividende, dīvīden′de, *f.* dividend. **Dividiren,** -dī′ren, *vt.* to divide. **Division,** dīvisiōn′, *f.* division.
Doch, doch, *av.* yet, however, nevertheless; pray.
Docht, decht, *m.* wick.
Docke, deck′e, *f.* rail, balaster; standard; doll; skain; dock, dock-yard; — mit Fluthüren, dry-dock. **Docken,** dock′en, *vt.* to dock, to lay in dock.
Doctern, dock′tern, *vt.* to doctor, quack. **Doctor,** dock′tor, *m.* -s, *pl.* -to′ren, doctor, physician; -enwürde, -vürde, **Doctorat,** dockorät′, *n.* doctorate, doctorship.
Document, deckyment′, *n.* document. **Documentiren,** -tī′ren, *vt.* to prove by documents.

Dogge, dock'e, f. bull-dog.
Dohle, dō'le, f. jackdaw.
Dohne, dō'ne, f. gin, noose, springe.
Dolch, dolch, m. dagger; ſtich, -zhtich, m. stab.
Dolde, dol'de, f. umbel, cluster.
Dolmetſchen, dol'metshen, vt. to interpret. **Dolmetſcher,** dol'metsher, m. interpreter. **Dolmetſchung,** -ung, f. interpretation.
Dom, dōm, m. dome, cupola; cathedral.
Domäne, demā'ne, f. domain, crownlands.
Dom'herr, dōm'hërr, m. -n, pl. -en, canon, prebendary. **Domkirche,** -kirche, f. cathedral. **Dom'pfaff,** -pfaff, m. -en, pl. -en, canon; bullfinch. **Dom'prediger,** -prädiger, m. pastor of a cathedral.
Domino, dom'luō, m. domino (mark); s. n. domino (game).
Donner, don'ner, m. thunder; vom — gerührt, thunder-struck; ſkeil, -kĕll, m. thunderbolt. **Donnern,** don'nern, vi. to thunder. **Don'nerſchlag,** -shlăk, m. thunder-clap. **Don'nerstag,** -tăk, m. Thursday. **Don'nerſtimme,** -zhtimme, f. thundering voice. **Don'nerwetter,** -vĕtter, n. thunder-storm, tempest. **Don'nerwort,** -vort, n. word of terrible import.
Doppeladler, dop'pelădler, m. double eagle, eagle with two heads. **Doppelbier,** dop'pelbīr, n. strong beer. **Dop'peldeutig,** -deūtich, a. ambiguous, av. -ly. **Dop'peldrehbank,** -drābănk, f. duplex lathe. **Dop'pelflinte,** -flinte, f. double-barrelled gun. **Dop'pelgänger,** -gĕng-er, m. wraith, fetch. **Dop'pellauter,** -louter, m. diphthong. **Doppeln,** dop'peln, vt. to double. **Dop'pelſinn,** -sinn, m. equivoque, -ichkāet, f. ambiguity. **Dop'pelſinnig,** -sinnich, a. ambiguous, av. -ly. **Dop'pelpfad,** -shpăt, m. Iceland spar. **Doppelt,** dop'pelt a. double(d). **Doppelzüngig,** dop'peltsüngich, a. double-tongued; -keit, -kāet, f. double-dealing, duplicity. **Dop'pelzüngler,** -tsüngler, m. double-dealer.
Dorf, dorf, n. pl. **Dörfer,** village: -bewohner, -bevŏner, m. villager. **Dörfchen,** dörf'chen, n. little village.
Dorfgemeinde, -gemānde, f. country parish. **Dorfjugend,** -yugend f. young villagers. **Dorfkirche,** -kirche, f. country church. **Dorfner,** dörf'ner, m. villager. **Dorfpfarre,** -pfarre, f. country parsonage. **Dorfpfarrer,** -pfarrer, **Dorfgeiſtlicher,** -gäshtlicher, m. country parson, village parson. **Dorfſchaft,** -shaft, f. village, villagers. **Dorfſchenke,** -shenke, f. village-inn. **Dorfſchule,** -shule, f. country school. **Dorfſchulmeiſter,** -mästzhter, m. village schoolmaster.
Dorn, dorrn, m. pl. -en, thorn; -buſch, -bush, m. thorn-bush, bramble, brake. **Dornen,** dorr'nen, a. thorny; -hecke, -hecke, f. thorn-hedge; -krone, -krōne, f. crown of thorns; -ſtrauch, -zhtrouch, m. brier. **Dornig,** dorn'ich, a. thorny, briery.
Dorren, dorr'en, vi. to dry. **Dörren,** dör'ren, vt. to dry, bake, kiln-dry.
Dort, dort, av. there, yon, yonder; -oben, -ōben, drō'ben, av. there above, up there, above. **Dorther,** dort'hār, av. thence, from there. **Dorthin,** dort'hĭn, av. thither, that way; bis —, till there, till then, that far. **Dortig,** dort'ich, a. of that place, there; meine dortigen Freunde, my friends there of that place.
Dose, dō'se, f. box; dose.
Dohle, dōh'se, f. working-square; guillevat.
Dotter, dot'ter, m. yolk; -blume, -blume, f. buttercup, dandelion; -gelb, -gelp, a. yolk-colored.
Doublette, dublĕt'te, f. duplicate.
Drache, drach'e, m. dragon; (paper) kite.
Drachme, drach'me, f. drachma, dram.
Dragoner, dragōn'er, m. dragoon.
Draht, drăt, m. (thread) wire; -arbeit, -arbāet, f. filigree, filigrane. **Drähtern,** drä'tern, a. wiry, made of wire. **Drahtgitter,** drät'gitter, n. wiregrate, wire-work. **Drahtpuppe,** -puppe, f. puppet. **Drahtſaite,** -säte, f. wire-string. **Drahtſieb,** -sib, n. wire-sieve. **Drahtzange,** -tsange, f. wire-pliers. **Drahtzieher,** -tsī-ĕr, m. wiredrawer. **Drahtzug,** -tsuk, m. wiredrawing.
Drall, drăl, a. tight, compact, sprightly, lively.

Drama, drä'mä, *n.* drama. **Dramatisch,** dramat'ish, *a.* dramatic, **-al,** *av.* -ally.

Dran, drăn, *av.* on that, on it.

Drang, drang, *m.* throng, pressure, urgency, impulse, impetus, stress; hurry. **Drängen,** dreng'en, *vt.* to press, throng, crowd. **Drangsal,** drang'säl, *n.* affliction, hardship.

Draperie, drapeʳī', *f.* drapery.

Drauen, drau'en, *vt.* to threaten, f. Drohen.

Drauf, drouf, *av.* thereupon, on that, on it. **Draus,** drôus, *av.* out of that, out of it. **Draußen,** drôus'sen, *av.* without, out of doors; abroad.

Drechseln, drex'eln, *vt.* to turn, etc. f. Drehen, etc.

Dreck, dreck, *m.* dirt; **-ig,** *a.* dirty.

Drehen, drā'en, *vt. & vi.* to turn. **Drehbank,** -bank, **Drehschiebank,** drex'elbank, *f.* turning-lathe, turner's lathe. **Drehbasse,** -bass, *f.* swivel or pivot-gun. **Drehbaum,** drā'bäum, *m.* turning-pike. **Drehbrücke,** -brüke, *f.* swivel-bridge, swing-bridge. **Dreheisen,** -eisen, *n.* turning tool. **Dreher,** drā'er, **Drechsler,** drex'ler, *m.* turner; winch. **Drehkreuz,** -kreŭts, *n.* turning-cross. **Drehling,** drā'ling, *m.* trundle; lantern-wheel. **Drehmeißel,** -mässel, *m.* turning-chisel. **Drehorgel,** -orgel, *f.* hand-organ. **Drehrad,** -räd, *n. pl.* -räder, turning-wheel. **Drehstuhl,** -shtūl, *m.* turning-tool. **Drehtishel,** -shtishel, *f.* turning-graver.

Drei, drī, *a.* three; **-beinig,** -bäinich, *a.* three-legged; **-blatt,** -blatt, *n.* trefoil; **-decker,** -decker, *m.* three-decker. **Dreieck,** drī'eck, *n.* triangle; **-ig,** *a.* triangular. **Dreieinig,** drī'āinich, *a.* triune; **-keit,** -käit, *f.* trinity. **Dreier,** drī'er, *m.* a penny-fee, -bit, *a.* of three kinds. **Dreifach,** -fach, **Dreifaltig,** faltich, *a.* threefold; **-keit,** -käit, *f.* trinity; **-feitsblume,** -blume, *f.* pansy, heart's-ease. **Dreifarbig,** -farbich, *a.* tri-colored. **Dreifuß,** drī'fūs, *m.* tripod, trevet. **Dreifüßig,** -füssich, *a.* three-footed, three-legged. **Dreigötterei,** -götterāī, *f.* tritheism. **Dreiherrscher,** drī'herrsher, *m.* triumvir; **-schaft,** -shaft, *f.* triumvirate. **Dreihundertstel,** drīhūn'dertstel *n.*

three-hundredth part. **Dreijährig,** drī'yärich, *a.* triennial, three years old. **Dreijährlich,** -yärlich, *a.* triennial, *av.* -ly. **Dreimal,** drī'mäl, *av.* thrice, three times; **-ig,** *a.* repeated three times. **Dreikönigsfest,** -köh'niksfëzht, *n.* epiphany. **Dreimonatlich,** drēīmōnätlich, *a.* quarterly.

Drein, drāen, *av.* into it, into, in.

Dreipfünder, drī'pfünder, *m.* three-pounder. **Dreiruderer,** -rūder(er), -ryder, *n.* trireme. **Dreisüßig,** -shīk, *m.* amble, pace. **Dreischneidig,** -shnaidich, *a.* three-edged. **Dreiseitig,** -säitich, *a.* trilateral. **Dreißig,** drēīs'ich, *a.* thirty; **-jährig,** -yärich, *a.* of thirty years; **-jähriger Krieg,** thirty-years' war. **Dreißiger,** drēīs'iger, *m.* man of thirty years. **Dreißigst,** drēīs'ichzht, *a.* thirtieth.

Dreist, drēīzht, *a.* bold, pert; **-igkeit,** -ichkäit, *f.* boldness.

Dreistöckig, drī'zhtöckich, *a.* three-storied. **Dreitägig,** drī'tägich, *a.* of three days, three days old, lasting three days; **triduan. Dreitägig,** *a.* tertian; **-es Fieber,** tertian fever. **Dreiwinklich,** -vinklich, *a.* triangular. **Dreizack,** drī'tsack, *m.* trident. **Dreizehn,** drī'tsān, *a.* thirteen; **-ter,** -ter, *a.* thirteenth.

Dreibrachen, drī'brachen, *vt.* to trifallow.

Dreschen, dresh'en (brosch, gebroschen), *vt.* to thrash. **Drescher,** dresh'er, *m.* thrasher. **Dreschflegel,** drësh'flägel, *m.* flail. **Dreschtenne,** -tenne, *f.* thrashing-floor. **Dressiren,** drēs-sī'ren, *vt.* to train, break. **Dressur,** drēs'syr, *f.* training, breaking.

Drift, drift, *f.* drift (Mar.).

Drillbohrer, drill'borer, *m.* drill. **Drillen,** *vt.* to drill. bore. **Drillich,** dril'lich. *m.* drilling. boring. **Drilling,** -ling, *m.* pin-wheel, wallower, trundle, lantern.

Drin, drin, *av.* therein.

Dringen, dring'en (brang, gebrungen), *vi.* to throng, urge, penetrate, crowd, press, swarm, break through.

Drinnen, drin'nen, *av.* within.

Dritt, dritt, *a.* third. **Drittel,** drit'tel, *n.* third (part). **Drittens,** drit'tens, *av.* thirdly. **Dritthalb,** -halp, *a.* two and a half. **Drittletzt,** -letst, *a.* antepenult.

Drs 86 **Du**

Drab, drŏb, av. on that account.
Droben, drŏ'ben, av. there, above.
Drogueriehandlung, drogerī'haut-lung, f. drug-store, drug-shop.
Droguerienhändler, -hendler, m. druggist. Droguerienwaaren, -vä-ren, s. pl. drugs.
Drohen, drō'en, vt. i. to threaten, menace. Drohbrief, -brīf, m. threatening letter.
Drohne, drō'ne, f. drone.
Dröhnen, drŏh'nen, vi. to resound, roar.
Drohung, drō'ung, f. threat, menace.
Drollig, drol'lich, a. droll, funny.
Dromedar, drō'medär, n. dromedary.
Droschke, drosh'ke, f. drosky.
Drossel, dros'sel, f. thrush.
Drüben, drüh'ben, av. on the other side. Drüber, Darüber, darüh'ber, av. thereon, about that.
Druck, druck, m. pressure, squeeze, impress, print, printing. Drucken, druck'en, vt. to print, press, impress. Drücken, drück'en, vt. to press, squeeze; to oppress. Druck'end, -ent, a. oppressive. Drucker, druck'er, m. printer. Drücker, drück'er, m. trigger. Druckerei, druckerēī', f. printing-office. Druckerschwärze, -shvertsĕ, f. printing-ink. Druckfehler, druck'fäler, misprint. typographical error. Druckkosten, -kozťsten, s. pl. expenses of printing. Druckpapier, -papīr, n. printing paper. Druckprobe, -probe, f. proof. Druckschrift, -shrift, f. print, book. Druckstempel, -zhtempel, m. piston. Druckstange, -zhtang-e, f. forcer. Drucksen, druk'sen, vi. to hesitate, delay.
Drum, drum, av. therefore.
Drunten, drun'ten, av. (there) below.
Drunter (darunter), av. (there) under, below; among.
Drüse, drüh'se, f. gland. Drüsig, drühsich, a. glandular; glandered.
Du, dū, pron. thou, you.
Dublette, dublětte, f. duplicate.
Ducaten, dukā'ten, m. ducat.
Ducht, ducht, f. yarn.
Ducken, duck'en, ri. to duck, bow; sich —, to stoop, to duck. Duckmäuser, -mě:ser. m. sneak.
Dudeln, dū'deln, vi. to play on the bagpipe, to play or sing badly.

Dudelsack, dū'delsack, m. bagpipe.
Duell, du-ěll', n. duel. Duellieren, du-ěllīr'en, vr. sich —, to duel, fight a duel.
Duett, du-ětt', n. duet.
Duft, duft, m. scent, smell, odor, fragrance. Duften, duft'en, vi. to exhale fragrance. Duftig, duft'ich, a. fragrant.
Dulden, dul'den, vi. to suffer; to bear, endure. Dulder, dul'der, m. sufferer. Duldsam, duld'sam, a. indulgent, tolerant, enduring; -keit, -kāet, f. tolerance. Duldung, dul'dung, f. suffering, toleration.
Dullen, dul'len, s. pl. thole-pins, tholes.
Dumm, dum, a. foolish, stupid; -dreist, -drīzht, a. fool-hardy, impudent. Dummheit, -hāet, f. foolishness, stupidity. Dummkopf, -kopf, m. blockhead.
Dumpf, dumpf. a. hollow, dead (sound); -heit, -hāet, f. hollowness. Dumpfig, dumpf'ich, a. damp, moist.
Düne, düh'ne, f. down, dune.
Düngen, düng'en, vt. to manure, fertilize. Dünger, düng'er, m. manure, fertilizer.
Dünkel, düng'kel, m. conceit, presumption.
Dunkel, dung'kel, a. obscure, dark, dusky; s. n. obscurity, darkness; -farbig, -farrbich, a. dark-colored; -heit, -hāet, f. darkness, obscurity.
Dünkel, düng'kel, m. conceit, conceitedness, presumption; -haft, -haft, a. conceited, presumptuous, arrogant. Dünken, düng'ken, vi. to appear, seem; sich —, to fancy, think, presume.
Dünn, dünn, a. thin, slender, lean, fine, subtle, small. Dünne, Dünnheit, Dünnung, f. thinness; thinning.
Dunsen, dun'sen, vi. to dilate, swell.
Dunst, dunzht, m. vapor, steam; blauen — vormachen, to humbug, mystify, swindle. Dunsten, dun'zhten, vi. to vapor, emit vapor, perspire. Dünsten, dün'zhten, vt. to stew. Dunstig, dun'zhtich, a. vapory, damp. Dunstkreis, dunzht'krāes, m. atmosphere.
Duodez, du-odāts', n. duodecimo, half-sheet; ein Buch in —, a du-lecimo

volume. **Duodecimalsystem**, duo-
detsimāl'sizhtem, *n.* duodecimal
arithmetic. **Duodecimal'maß**, -mäs,
n. duodecimal measure.
Dupfen, dupf'en, *vt.* to dot, to tap.
Durch, dųrch, *prep u. av.* through, by;
-**aus**, -óus; *av.* throughout, thoroughly, absolutely; -**aus nicht**, not
at all, by no means, not in the least;
-**ackern**, -ackern, *vt.* to plough
through; -**arbeiten**, -arbäeten, *vt.*
to work through, thoroughly;
-**ätzen**, -ätsen, *vt.* to corrode, etch;
-**beben**, -bäben, *vt.* to thrill; -**betteln**, -bětteln, *vt.* to beg through;
-**blättern**, -blět'tern, *vt.* to turn
over, run over; -**bläuen**, -bläüen,
vt. to beat soundly; -**blick**, -blick, *m.*
look through, vista; penetration;
oversight; -**blicken**, -blicken, *vt.* to
look through, pierce through; -**bo-
ren**, -bören, *vt.* to bore through, perforate; -**brechen**, -brěch'en (-brach,
-gebrochen), *vt.* to break through;
-**bringen**, -bring-en (-brachte, -ge-
bracht), *vt.* to bring or get through;
Durch den Winter —, to winter; sich
—, to get one's livelihood by; -**bruch**,
-bruch, *m.* breach, rupture, eruption; cutting-press; -**denken**, -deng'-
ken (-dachte, -gedacht), *vt.* to think
on, *or* upon, meditate over, to ponder, to reflect on; -**drängen**, -dreng-
en, *vt.* to force through; sich —, to
crowd through, press through,
squeeze through; to bore through;
-**dringen**, -dring-en (-drang, -ge-
drungen), *vi.* to press through, get
through, pierce through; to penetrate; to bring about, succeed;
-**dringend**, -dring end, *a.* penetrating, sharp, keen, piercing; -**dringlich**, -dringlich, *a.* penetrable;
-**Dringlichkeit**, -dringlichkäet, *f.* pe-
netrability, permeability, pervious-
ness; -**drücken**, -drücken, *vt.* to
press through; -**duften**, -dufften, *vt.*
to perfume, fill with fragrance;
-**düften**, *vt.* to perfume, scent; -**eilen**, -ëllen, *vi.* to haste *or* hurry
through; -**fahren**, -fären, *vi.* to pass
through, drive through, rush
through; -**fahrt**, -fart, *f.* passage,
gateway, thoroughfare; -**fahrtszoll**,
-fartstsoll, *m.* transit duty; -**fall**,
-fall, *m.* diarrhoea, flux, looseness;
failure; -**fallen**, -fallen (-fiel, -ge-
fallen), *vi.* to fall through; to fail
-**fechten**, -fěchten (-focht, -gefochten),
vt. to vindicate, defend, maintain
(by arguments); to beg one's way
through; -**feilen**, -fēilen, *vt.* to file
through; -**fliegen**, -flīgen (-flog, -ge-
flogen), *vt.* to fly through; -**fließen**,
-flīs'sen (-floß, -geflossen), *vt.* to flow
through; -**forschen**, -forshen, *vt.* to
search through, investigate; -**fressen**, -frěssen (-fraß, -gefressen), *vt.* to
eat through, gnaw through; cor-
rode; -**frieren**, -frīren (-fror, -gefro-
ren), *vt.* to freeze through, to chill
through: -**fuhr**, -fųr, *f.* transit, passage; -**führen**, -führen, *vt.* to lead,
carry, convey through; to carry
out, follow out, accomplish; to support, sustain (a character) to the
end; -**gang**, -gang, *m.* passage,
transit, thoroughfare; -**gängig**,
-gěngich, *a.* pervious; general, universal, prevailing; -**gehen**, -gā-en
(-ging, -gegangen), *vt.* to go *or* walk
through; to go off, run away, desert;
to run over, peruse, examine; to
wear out (shoes); -**gehends**, -gā-ents,
av. generally; -**gießen**, -gīsen (-goß,
-gegossen), *vt.* to pour through, filter; -**glühen**, -glüh-en, *vt.* to glow
through, make red-hot; -**graben**,
-gräben (-grub, -gegraben), *vt.* to dig
through, pierce; -**greifen**, -grēifen
(-griff, -gegriffen), *vi.* to act decided-
ly, take energetic measures; to succeed, prevail; -**hauen**, -hou-en (-hieb,
-gehauen), *v.* sich —, to cut one's
way through; -**hecheln**, -hěcheln, *vt.*
to hatchel, criticise, traduce; -**helfen**, -hělfen (-half, -geholfen), *vt.* einem —, to help out; -**irren**, -ĭrren,
vt. to wander through; -**jagen**,
-yägen, *vt.* to chase through, hunt
through, hurry through; *vi.* to run
through; -**kämpfen**, -kempfen, *vt.* to
fight through, to fight to the end;
sich —, to cut one's way out; -**klingen**, -kling'en (-klang, -geklungen),
vt. to sound through; -**kommen**,
-kommen (-kam, -gekommen), *vi.* to
come through, pass, escape; to come
off; -**können**, -können (-konnte, -ge-
konnt), *vt.* to get through; -**kreuzen**,
-krëut'sen, *vt.* to cross, thwart;
-**lassen**, -lassen (-ließ, -gelassen), *vt.*
to let through, transmit; to filter;
-**laucht**, -loucht- *f.* highness; -**lauch**-

tig, -löchtich, a. serene, illustrious; -laufen, -läuf'en (-lief, -gelaufen), vt. to run through; to dip into; to wear through; -läutern, -läu'tern, vt. to strain through, to purify, refine thoroughly; -leben, -lāben, vt. to live through, experience; to pass one's life; -lesen, -läsen (-las, -gelesen), vt. to read through, to read over, peruse; -leuchten, -löüchten, vt. shine through; -liegen, -ligen (-lag, -gelegen), vt. to make sure by lying; -löchern, -löch'ern, vt. to perforate, make full of holes; -lügen, -lühgen (-log, -gelogen), vt. to get out of a scrape by a lie; -machen, -machen, vt. to pass through, experience; -marsch, -marsh, m. passage, march through; -marschiren, -marshi'ren, vt. to march through; -messer, -messer, m. diameter; -mustern, -mushtern, vt. to review all over; to scan, survey, examine thoroughly; -nässen, -nes'sen, vt. to wet through and through; -passiren, passīren, vt. to pass through; -peitschen, -peītshen, vt. to scourge, lash (soundly); -plündern, vt. to plunder, ravage; -pressen, pressen, vt. to press through, squeeze through; -prügeln, -prühgeln, vt. to cudgel soundly; -räuchern, -räüchern, vt. to fumigate; -rauschen, -roūshen, vt. to rush through, rustle through; -rechnen, -rēchnen, vt. to count over; -regnen, -rāgnen, vt. to rain through; -reiben, -rēiben (-rieb, -gerieben), vt. to rub through; -reise, -rāēse, f. travelling through, passage; -reisen, -rāēsen, vt. to pass through, traverse, cross, to travel over; -reisender, -rāēsender, m. passenger; -reissen, -rēissen (-riss, -gerissen), vt. to rend, to tear asunder; vt. to break, rend asunder; -reiten, -rēiten (-ritt, -geritten), vt. to cross on horseback, to ride through; -rennen, -ren'nen (-rannte, -gerannt), vt. i. to run through; run over; to run one through with; -rinnen, -rinnen (-rann, -geronnen), vt. to run through; -rütteln, -rütteln, vt. to shake thoroughly; -säuern, -söü'ern, vt. to leaven thoroughly; -schauen, -shōü'en, vt. to look through; to examine attentively; to see through, to penetrate;

-scheinen, -shāēnen (-schien, -geschienen), vt. to shine through, to illuminate; -scheinend, -shāēnend, translucent, pellucid, transparent; -schiessen, -shīsen (-schoss, -schossen), vt. to shoot through; to riddle, pierce with; to lead, space, interline (Print.); to interleave, interfoliate; -schiffen, -shif'fen, vt. to sail over, to navigate; -schimmern, -shimmern, vt. to shine through, glisten through, to sparkle; -schlafen, -shläfen (-schlief, -schlafen), vt. to pass sleeping; -schlag, -shlak, m. filter, colander, strainer; piercer; -schlagen, -shlägen (-schlug, -geschlagen), vt. to break through, strain, filter; to pierce, penetrate; to blot; to sink; to have effect; to tell upon; sich —, to fight one's way out; -schleichen, -shlēichen (-schlich, -geschlichen), vt. to sneak through; -schlüpfen, -shlüpfen, vt. to slip through, sneak through; noch gut —, to have a narrow escape; -schneiden, -shneīden (-schnitt, -geschnitten), vt. to cut through; -schnitt, -shnitt, m. cutting through, cutting-press; average; -schnittlich, -shnittlich, a. ar. mean average, on an average; -schnittspreis, -preīs, m. average price, -schnittspunkt, -pünkt, m. point of intersection; -summe, -summ, f. medial sum; -zahl, -tsāl, f. mean number; -schuss, -shüss, m. lead (Print.); -schwimmen, -shvim'men (-schwamm, -schwummen), vt. to swim through; -sehen, sāēn (-sah, -gesēhen), vt. to look through, see through; examine, revise; -setzen, -setsen, vt. to pass through, to cross; vt. to carry through; -sicht, -sicht, f. review, revision; -sichtbild, -bilt, n. pl. -er, transparent picture, transparency; -sichtlehre, -lāre, -lāre, f. dioptrics; -sichtig, -sichtich, a. transparent, pellucid; -sichtigkeit, -sichtichkāēt, f. transparency, translucency, pellucidity; -singen, -singen (-sang, -gesungen), vt. to sing to the end, to fill with songs; -sinken, -sinken (-sank, gesunken), vt. to sink through; -sitzen, -sitsen (-sass, -gesessen), vt. to wear out by sitting; to pass sitting; to sit up; -sollen, -sollen, müssen, -müssen, vt. to be obliged to pass through; -sonnen,

-sonnen, *vt.* to insolate, sun, bask; -sorgen, -sorgen, *vt.* to pass in sorrow; -spielen, -shp'llen, *vt.* to play through; to spend in gambling; -stänkern, -zhtenk'ern, -stinken, -zhtink'en,*vt.* to fill with stench; to rummage; -stechen, -zhtěchen (-stach, -gestochen), *vt.* to pierce, to open, to cut through; to run through, drive through, push through; -stich, -zhtich, *m.* cutting, cut; -stöbern, -zhtöhbern, *vt.* to rummage, ferret out, to ransack, search; -stochern, -zhtochern, *vt.* to prick through; -stoß, -zhtōs, cutting-press; -stoßen, -zhtōsen (-stieß, -gestoßen), *vt.* to thrust through, push through; -streichen, -zhtrěich'en(-strich, -strichen), *vt.* to cross out; to ramble over, roam through; -strömen, -zhtröhmen, *vt.* to gush through, penetrate, pervade; -stürmen, -zhtürm'en,*vt.* to rage through, to rush through; -suchen, -suchen, *vt.* to search through, to seek through; -suchung, -such'ung, *f.* search; -tanzen, -tantsen, *vt.* to pass dancing, to spend in dancing; -taumeln, -tghumeln, *vt.* to reel *or* stagger through; -tönen, -töh'nen, *vt.* to fill with sounds, to resound, re-echo; -träumen, -träum'en, *vt.* to dream away, to pass dreaming; -treten, -trāten (-trat, -getreten, *vt.* to step through; -treiben, -trěiben (-trieb, -getrieben, *vt.* to drive through; to strain; to carry through; -trieb, -trīb, *m* passage; -trieben, -trīben, *a.* practiced, skilled, artful, cunning; -triebenheit, -trīben hāet, *f.* cunning, craftiness; -wachen, -vach'en, *vt.* to watch through; to pass waking; -wachung, -vach'ung, *f.* watching, night-watches; -wachsen, -vaxen (-wuchs, -gewachsen), *vi.* to grow through; -wachsenes Fleisch, lean meat streaked with fat; interlarded meat; -wagen, -vāgen, *vi.* to venture through; -walken, -valken, *vt.* to drub, thrash; -wandeln, -vandeln, *vt.* to wander through; walk through; -wandern, -vand'ern, *vi.* to wander through, to roam over; -wärmen, -vermen, *vt.* to warm; -wässern, -vès'sern,*vt.* to water, irrigate; -waten, väten, *vt.* to wade through; -weben, -vāb'en (-wob,

-woben), *vt.* to interweave; -wehen, -vā-en, *vt.* to blow through, ventilate; -weinen, -vēn'en, *vt.* to pass weeping, to pass in tears; -winden, -vinden (-wand, -gewunden), *vt.* to intertwine; to twist with; -wintern, -vin'tern, *vt.* to winter, to keep through winter; sich —, to pass the winter; -wirken, -vĭrken, *vt.* to work *or* knead thoroughly; to interweave; -wühlen, -vüh'len, *vt.* to work *or* dig through; to rummage, ransack; -würzen, -vürt'sen, *vt.* to season, scent; -zählen, -tsälen, *vt.* to count over; -zechen, -tsěch'en, *vt.* to pass carousing; -zeichnen, -tsäechnen, *vt.* to trace; to draw through transparent paper; -zerren, -tserren, *vt.* to drag through, pull through; einen —, to jeer, taunt; to march through; -zucken, -tsuck'en, *vt.* to thrill, to flash through; -zug, -tsug, *m.* passage, marching through; -zwängen, -tsveng-en, *vt.* to force through; to squeeze through.

Dürfen, dürf'en (durfte, geburft), *vt.* to be allowed, permitted: to be able; to need, dare: er darf es thun, he may do it. **Dürftig**, dürf'tich, *a.* needy, indigent, meagre; -keit, -kāet, *f.* neediness, indigence, poverty, poorness, scantiness, insufficiency.

Dürr, dürr, *a.* dry, arid. **Dürre**, dürr're, *f.* dryness, aridity, drought. **Dürrsucht**, Dürr'sucht, -sucht, *f.* atrophy, consumption.

Durst, dvrzht, *m.* thirst. **Dürsten**, dürzh'ten, *vi.* to be dry, thirsty. **Durstig**, dvrzht'ich, *a.* thirsty, athirst, dry.

Düse, düh'se, *f.* tuyere, tweer.

Düster, düzh'ter, *a.* gloomy, dusky, dark, dull; dim, cloudy, sullen; sad, mournful; -keit, -hāet, *f.* gloominess, duskiness, dimness.

Düte, düh'te, *f.* paper-bag, cornet.

Dutzend, dvt'sent, *n.* dozen; -weise, -vēlse, *ar.* by the dozen.

Duzbruder, dvts'bryder, *m.* crony, intimate friend. **Duzen**, dvts'en, *vt* to thou.

Dynamik, dinā'mik, *f.* dynamics **Dynamisch**, -mish, *a.* dynamical. **Dynamometer**, dinamō'meter, *m.* dynamometer.

Ebbe, ĕb'bẹ, *f.* ebb; — und Fluth, ebb and flow, tide. **Ebben,** ĕb'ben, *vi.* to ebb.

Eben, ā'bẹr, *a.* even, plain, flat, level; *av.* just, exactly, accurately, precisely; so —, just now, even now; **=bild,** -bilt, *n. pl.* -er, image, exact likeness; sie ist das — ihrer Mutter, she is the very image of her mother; **=bürtig,** -bürtich, *a.* equal, of equal birth; **=bürtigkeit,** -kāĕt, *f.* equality (in birth, etc.); **=derselbe,** -dĕrsĕlbẹ, *pron.* the very same. **Ebene,** ā'bẹnẹ, *f.* plain. **Ebenen,** ā'bẹnẹn, *vt.* to level, smooth. **Ebenfalls,** ā'benfalls, *av.* likewise, too, also. **Ebenheit,** -hāĕt, *f.* evenness; exactness, accuracy, precision.

Ebenholz, ā'benholtz, *n.* ebony.
Ebenmaß, ā'benmās, *n.* symmetry.
Ebenmäßig, -māsich, *a.* symmetrical, proportionate.

Eber, ā'ber, *m.* boar; **=hirsch,** -hirrsh, *m.* Indian hog.

Echo, ā'chō, *n.* echo; ein — geben, to echo, re-echo.

Echt, ĕcht, *a.* lawfully begotten, legitimate; genuine, true, sterling, natural, durable, lasting; **=heit,** -hāĕt, *f.* lawfulness, legitimacy; genuineness, authenticity, purity.

Eckchen, ĕck'chen, *n.* little corner. **Ecke,** ĕck'ẹ, *f.* corner. **Eckenschrank,** ĕck'enshrank, *m.* corner cupboard. **Eck'haus,** -hōus, *n. pl.* -häuser, corner house. **Eckig,** ĕck'ich, *a.* cornered, angular. **Eckstein,** -zhtāĕn, *m.* corner-stone; quoin. **Eckzahn,** ĕck'tsān, *m.* corner-tooth.

Edel, ā'del, *a.* noble, precious; **=dame,** -dāmẹ, *f.* **=frau,** -frōu, *f.* noble lady; **=denkend,** -denkend, *a.* noble-minded; **=fräulein,** -frāŭlāĕn, *n.* a noble (unmarried) lady; **=hof,** -hōf, *m.* manor-house, baronial hall; **=knabe,** -k(ẹ)nābẹ, page; **=knecht,** -k(ẹ)nĕcht, *m.* esquire, a knight's attendant; **=mann,** -mann, *pl.* -leute, nobleman; **=muth,** -myt, *m.* noble-mindedness; generosity, magnanimity; **=müthig,** -mūhtich, *a.* noble-minded, generous, magnanimous; **=sinn,** -sinn, *m.* noble mind, magnanimity, generosity; **=stein,** -zhtāĕn, *m.* gem, jewel, precious stone.

Edict, ẹdikt', *n.* edict, manifesto.
Effecten, ĕffŏk'ten, *s. pl.* effects, goods, chattels, movables.
Egal, ẹgāl', indifferent.
Egge, ĕgẹ, ĕg'gẹ, *f.* harrow. **Eggen,** ĕg'gen, *vt.* to harrow.
Egoismus, ẹgo-is'nus, *m.* egotism, selfishness. **Egoist,** ẹgo-izht', *m.* -en, *pl.* -en, egotist. **Egoistisch,** ẹgo-izht'ish, *a.* egotistical, selfish.
Ehe, ā'ẹ, *av.* before, ere.
Ehe, ā'ẹ, *f.* matrimony, marriage, wedlock; **=band,** -band, *n.* nuptial bond, marriage-tie; **=bett,** -bĕtt, *n.* marriage-bed; **=brechen,** -brĕchen, *vi.* to commit adultery; **=brecher,** -brĕcher, *m.* adulterer; **=brecherin,** -brĕcherin, *f.* adulteress; **=brecherisch,** -brĕcherish, *a.* adulterous; **=bruch,** -bruch, *m.* adultery.
Ehedem, ā'ẹdām, *av.* in olden times, formerly.
Ehefrau, ā'ẹfrāŭ, *f.* wife, consort.
Ehefreuden, -frāŭden, *s. pl.* connubial joys. **Ehegatte,** -gattẹ, *m.* -n, *pl.* -n, husband, spouse, consort. **Ehegattin,** -gattin, *f.* wife, spouse, consort. **Ehegemahl,** ā'ẹgẹmāl, *m.* **Ehegenoß,** ā'ẹgẹnoss, *m.* **=in,** *f.* spouse, consort.
Ehegestern, ā'ẹgĕzhtern, *av.* the day before yesterday.
Eheleute, ā'ẹlāŭtẹ, *s. pl.* married people. **Ehelich,** ā'ẹlich, *a.* matrimonial, connubial, conjugal, conjugial, nuptial; legitimate.
Ehemalig, ā'ẹmālich, *a.* former, old. **Ehemals,** ā'ẹmāls, *av.* formerly, in former times, in times past.
Ehemann, ā'ẹmann, *m.* husband. **Ehen,** ā'ẹn, *vt.* to marry; sich —, to marry, contract a marriage. **Ehepaar,** -pār, *n.* married couple.
Eher, ā'er, *ar.* sooner, rather; je eher je besser, the sooner the better.
Ehern, ā'ern, *a.* brazen, of brass, bronze, copper.
Eheschänder, ā'ẹshender, *m.* adulterer.
Ehescheidung, -shāĕdung, *f.* divorce.
Ehesegen, -sāgen, *m.* conjugial blessing.
Ehest, ā'ezht, ebesten, *av.* as soon as possible; am ebesten, soonest.
Ehestand, ā'ezhtant, *m.* matrimony, wedlock. **Ehestener,** -zhtĕŭẹr, *f.*

dower, dowry. **Eh'estifter, -zhtifter,** *m.* *sin,* match-maker. **Eh'estiftung,** -ung, *f.* match-making; marriage-articles. **Ehrweib,** ā'ygvēlp, *n.* wife.

Ehrbar, ār'bär, *a.* honorable: -**keit,** -kāet, *f.* honorableness. **Ehrbegier,** ār'begīr, *f.* ambition. **Ehre,** ār'y, *f.* honor; eine — erzeigen, erweisen, to do any one honor. **Ehren,** ār'eu, *vt.* to honor; -**amt,** ār'enamt, *n. pl.* -ämter, post of honor; -**bezeigung,** -**bezeugung,** *f.* expression of honor, respect, homage; -**erklärung,** -ēr-klärung, *f.* apology; -**kränkung,** -krenkung. *f.* insult, defamation, injury; -**mann,** -mann. *m.* man of honor, gentleman; -**mitglied,** -mit-glīd, *n. pl.* -er, honorary member; -**pforte,** -pforte, *f.* triumphal arch: -**platz,** -plats, *m.* place of honor; -**punkt,** -punkt, *m.* point of honor; -**räuber,** -räuber. *m.* slanderer, de-famer, calumniator; -**rettung,** -ret-tung, *f.* vindication; -**rührig,** -r..h-rīḥ, *a.* slanderous, calumnious, de-famatory; -**rührigkeit,** -rührickāet. *f.* defamation, defamatory nature of; -**sache,** -vache, *f.* matter of honor; -**stelle,** -zhtelle, *f.* post of honor, ex-alted position, dignity, honor; -**stufe,** -zhtufe, *f.* degree of honor; -**tag,** -tāg. *m.* day of honor; -**tanz,** -tants. *m.* dance of honor; -**titel,** -tittel, *m.* honorary title; -**voll,** -foll, *a.* hon-orable, glorious; -**wache,** -vache, *f.* guard of honor; -**werth,** -vārt, *a.* honorable, respectable; -**wort,** -vort, *n.* word of honor; -**zeichen,** -tsäechen, *n.* badge of honor, sign of honor, distinction. **Ehrerbietig,** ār'erbītiḥ, *a.* respectful, *av.* -ly. **Ehrerbietung,** -bītung, *f.* respect, reverence, defer-ence. **Ehrfurcht,** ār'furcht, *f.* vener-ation, reverence; -**voll,** -foll, *a.* respectful, reverential, *av.* -ly. **Ehr-gefühl,** ār'gefühl, *n.* sense of honor. **Ehrgeiz,** ār'gīts, *m.* ambition; -**ig,** *a.* ambitious. **Ehrlich,** ār'lich, *a.* honest; -**keit,** -kāet, *f.* honesty, probity. **Ehrliebe,** ār'lībe, *f.* love of honor. **Ehrliebend,** -lībend, *a.* careful of one's honor. **Ehrlos,** ār'-lōs, *a.* honorless, disgraceful. **Ehr-losigkeit,** -lōsiḥkāet, *f.* infamy, dis-honorableness. **Ehrsam,** ār'sam, *a.* honorable, respectable. **Ehrsucht,**

ār'sucht, *f.* ambition. **Ehrsüchtig,** ār'süchtig, *a.* ambitious, *av.* -ly **Ehrvergessen,** ār'fergessen, *a.* un mindful of honor, mean. **Ehrwi-drig,** ār'vīdriḥ, *a.* dishonorable, dis-graceful, *av.* -ly. **Ehrwürde,** ār' vürde, *f.* reverence (title). **Ehr-würdig,** ār'vürdiḥ, *a.* venerable, reverend.

Ei, āi, *Intj.* hey! eh! ah! why! (h! aye!

Ei, āē, *n. pl.* **Eier,** egg.

Eibe, ēi'be, *f.* yew, yew-tree; -**holz,** -holts, yew.

Eichapfel, āeḥ'apfel, *m.* oak-apple. **Eichbaum,** āeḥ'baūm, **Eiche,** āe'ḥe, *f.* oak, oak-tree.

Eiche, āiḥ'e, *f.* gauge, standard.

Eichel, āeḥ'el, *f.* acorn; gland; -**för-mig,** -förmiḥ, *a.* glandiform.

Eichen, āiḥ'en, *vt.* to gauge.

Eichen, āēḥ'en, *a.* oaken, oak; -**es Holz,** oak-wood; -**hain,** -hāēn, *m.* oak-grove; -**zweig,** -tsvēīk. *m.* oak-bough.

Eicher, āiḥ'er, **Eichmeister,** -māezh-ter, *m.* gauger.

Eichhorn, āēḥ'horn. *n. pl.* -börner. **Eichhörnchen,** āēḥ'hörnḥen, *n.* squir-rel.

Eichstab, āīḥ'zhtāb, *m.* gauge, gaug-ing-rod.

Eichwald, āēḥ'valt, *m.* oak-forest.

Eid, āēd, *m.* oath.

Eidam, āē'dam, *m.* son-in-law.

Eidbruch, āēd'bruḥ, *m.* perjury. **Eid-brüchig,** -brüḥiḥ, *a.* perjured, for-sworn, guilty of perjury.

Eidechse, āē'dexe, *f.* lizard.

Eider, **Eidergans,** āē'dergans, *f.* eider-duck. **Eiderdunen,** -dunen, *s. pl.* eider-down.

Eidgenoss, āēt'genoss, *m.* confederate; **Eidgenossenschaft,** āēt'genossenshaft, *f.* Helvetic confederacy. **Eidlich,** āēt'liḥ, *a.* sworn, confirmed by oath. **Eidschwur,** āēt'shvyr, *m.* oath, taking an oath.

Eier, āē'er, *pl.* of **Ei,** eggs; -**kuchen,** -kuḥen, *m.* omelet; -**schale,** -shāle, *f.* egg-shell; -**stock,** -zhtock, *m.* ovary.

Eifer, āīf'er, *m.* zeal. ardor, eagerness fervency, warmth, haste, anger; -**er,** *m.* zealot; -**ig,** (**Eifrig**), zealous, ar-dent, eager, warm, animated, *av.* -ly. **Eifern,** āīf'ern, *vi.* to be zeal-ous, jealous; to declaim; to be an

gry; to rival, emulate. **Eiferſucht,**
-ſucht, f. jealousy, **Eiferſüchtig,**
-ſüchtig, a. jealous, envious.
Eiförmig, ĭ̄'fŏrmiċh, a. egg-shaped, oval, ovate.
Eigen, ī'gen, a. own, proper, peculiar, incident to; odd; particular, singular; -dünkel, -dünkel, m. self-conceit; -händig, -hendiċh, a. autographic, with one's own hand; -heit, -hāet, f. peculiarity, singularity, oddity; -liebe, -lībe, f. self-love; -lob, -lōb, n. self-praise; -mächtig, -mĕċhtiċh, a. arbitrary; -name, -nāme, m. proper name; -nutz, -nuts, m. self-interest, selfishness; -nützig, -nütsiċh, a. selfish. **Eigens,** ĭ̄g'ens, av. particularly, expressly, on purpose. **Eigenſchaft,** ī'genshaft, f. quality, property; -wort, -vort, n. adjective. **Eigenſinn,** -sinn, m. waywardness, wilfulness, caprice; -ig, a. wilful. stubborn, av. -ly. **Eigenthum,** ī'gentum, n. property, ownership. **Eigenthümer,** ī'gentümer, m. owner, proprietor, possessor. **Ei'genthümlich,** -tümliċh, a. proper, peculiar, particular, av. -ly; -keit, -kāet, f. peculiarity. **Ei'genthumsrecht,** -tumsreċht, n. right of possession. **Eigentlich,** ī'gentliċh, a. proper, precise, just, exact, av. -ly. **Ei'genwille,** -ville, m. self-will, wilfulness. **Ei'genwillig,** -villiċh, a. self-willed, wilful, obstinate, av. -ly; a. arbitrary. **Eignen,** ī'gnen, vt. to own; ſich —, to befit for. **Eigner,** ī̄k'ner, m. owner.
Eiland, ī̄'lant, n. island.
Eilbote, ī̄l'bōte, m. -n, pl. -n. courier. **Eile,** ī̄'le, f. haste, hurry, speed. **Eilen,** ī̄l'en, vi. to haste, hurry, speed: -d, eilends, eilig (eilfertig), a. hasty, speedy, av. -ily.
Eilf, ilf, a. eleven: -eck, -ek, n. hendekagon, undecagon.
Eilfertigkeit, ilf'fertiċhkāet, f. haste, speed, dispatch.
Eilfjährig, ilf'yăriċh. a. eleven years old. **Eilfmal,** ilf'māl, av. eleven times. **Eilft,** ilft, a. eleventh. **Eilftens,** ilf'tens, av. in the eleventh place.
Eilpoſt, ī̄l'pozht, f. express mail; lightning stage. **Eilzug,** ī̄l'tsŭk, express train.
Eimer, īm'er, m. bucket, pail.

Ein, ĕn, a. one; article, a, an.
Ein, ĕn, av. into, towards.
Einackern, ĕn'ackern, vt. to plough in.
Einander, ĕnan'der, pron. av one another, each other; an —, together; aus —, apart.
Einärnten, ĕn'ĕrnten, vt. to harvest, reap, earn, gain.
Einäſchern, ĕn'ĕshern, vt. to lay in ashes.
Einathmen, ĕn'ătmen, vt. to inhale, breathe, inspire.
Einäugig, ĕn'ăugiċh, a. one-eyed.
Einätzen, ĕn'ătsen, vt. to etch in.
Einballen, ĕn'ballen, vt. to bale, pack.
Einbalſamiren, ĕn'balsamīren, vt. to embalm.
Einband, ĕn'bant, m. binding.
Einbedingen, ĕn'bĕding-en, vt. to stipulate.
Einbegreifen, ĕn'begreīfen (-begriff, -begriffen), vt. to comprise, include, contain.
Einbehalten, ĕn'behalten, vt. to keep back. to detain, withhold.
Einbeißen, ĕn'beīsen (-biß, -gebiſſen), vt. to bite into.
Einbeizen, ĕn'băŏtsen, vt. to etch in, to stain.
Einberichten, ĕn'beriċhten, vt. to report.
Einbeugen, ĕn'bĕugen, **Einbiegen,** -bīgen, vt. to bend (inward), to indent.
Einbilden, ĕn'bilden, vt. to imagine, conceive, fancy, think, believe, persuade; ſich viel —, to be conceited, to presume upon. **Einbildung,** -ŭng, f. imagination. fancy, conceit; -kraft, -kraft, f. imagination, fancy.
Einbinden, ĕn'binden (-band, -gebunden), vt. to bind; to inculcate, urge upon.
Einblaſen, ĕn'blāsen (-blies, -geblaſen), vt. to breathe into. to blow; to prompt. **Einbläſer,** ĕn'blāser, m. prompter.
Einbläuen, ĕn'blāŭen, vt. to beat into one, to flog into one.
Einbohren, ĕn'bōren, vt. to perforate, bore into; ſich —, to pierce by boring.
Einbrechen, ĕn'breċhen (-brach, -gebrochen), vt. to break into.

Einbrennen, ȧēn'brėnnen (-brannte, -gebrannt), *vt.* impress by burning, to brand; scald; to match (a cask); *vi.* to make a fire.
Einbringen, ȧēn'brĭng-en (-brȧchte, -gebrȧcht), *vt.* to bring in, to yield; to get in; to recover, retrieve; to make good, to repair.
Einbruch, ȧēn'brŭch, *m.* breaking-in, house-breaking, burglary; invasion; — der Nacht, nightfall.
Einbürgern, ȧēn'bürgern, *vt.* to naturalize. **Einbürgerung,** -ung, *f.* naturalization.
Einbuße, ȧēn'bȳsė, *f.* loss. **Einbüßen,** ȧēn'büsen, *vt.* to loose.
Eincassiren, ȧēn'kassīren, *vt.* to collect.
Eindämmen, ȧēn'dėmmen, *vt.* to dam, dike, embank.
Eindingen, ȧēn'dĭng-en (-bung, -gebungen), *vt.* to stipulate, include (in the bargain).
Eindorren, ȧēn'dȯrren, *vi.* to dry up, shrink.
Eindrängen, ȧēn'drėng-en, *vt.* to force into, crowd, intrude.
Eindreschen, ȧēn'drėshen (-brȯsch, -broschen), *vi.* to thrash into.
Eindringen, ȧēn'dringen (-brang, -brungen), *vi.* to invade, force one's way into, to enter, to insinuate one's self; to penetrate. **Eindringlich,** ȧēn'dringlich, *a.* impressive, affecting, *av.* -ly.
Eindruck, ȧēn'drŭck, *m.* impression. **Eindrucken,** -drucken, *vt.* to imprint. **Eindrücken,** ȧēn'drücken, *vt.* to impress, press in, to imprint, crush. **Eindrücklich,** -drücklich, *a.* impressive; -keit, -kāēt, *f.* impressiveness.
Einėggen, ȧēn'ėggen, *vt.* to harrow in.
Einen, ȧēn'en, *vt.* to unite.
Einengen, ȧēn'ėng-en, *vt.* to straiten, confine, limit.
Einer, ȧēn'er, *m.* unit, one; digit; -lei, -lāē, *a.* of one kind; *av.* one and the same; -leiheit, -lāēhāēt, *f.* sameness, identity, congruity.
Einernten, ȧēn'ėrnten, *vt.* to reap, harvest, gain.
Einfach, ȧēn'fach, *a.* simple, single, plain: -e Zahl, unit; -heit, -hāēt, *f.* simplicity.
Einfädeln, ȧēn'fädeln, *vt.* to thread.

Einfahren, ȧēn'fāren (-fuhr, -gefahren), *vi.* to get in, drive in, carry home. **Einfahrt,** ȧēn'fart, *f.* entrance, gateway.
Einfall, ȧēn'fall, *m.* invasion, inroad; incidence (of light); ruin, downfall; fancy, idea, sally, flash of wit; auf den — kommen, to take into one's head. **Einfallen,** ȧēn'fallen (-fiel, -gefallen), *vi.* to enter, fall in, invade; to join; to interrupt: to occur, to come into one's mind; to fall down, to go to ruin; to catch (of a latch); wie es ihm einfällt, at random; sich nicht — lassen, not to dream of. **Ein'fallslinie,** -lini-e, *f.* line of incidence.
Einfalt, ȧēn'falt, *f.* simplicity. **Einfältig,** ȧēn'feltich, *a.* simple, plain, single, silly. **Ein'faltspinsel,** -pinsel, *m.* simpleton.
Einfangen, ȧēn'fang-en (-fing, -gefangen), *vt.* to catch, take up, seize.
Einfarbig, ȧēn'farbich, *a.* one-colored.
Einfassen, ȧēn'fassen, *vt.* to inclose, confine, include; to border, edge; to trim; to bind (a carpet, etc.); to barrel (beer); to sack (corn); to enchase (with gems). **Einfassung,** ȧēn'fassung, *f.* confining, bordering, trimming; edging, enchasing, framing.
Einfeuern, ȧēn'fēüern, *vt.* to heat; to kindle a fire.
Einfinden, ȧēn'finden (-fand, -gefunden), *vt.* sich —, to appear, meet, come.
Einflechten, ȧēn'flėchten (-flocht, -geflochten), *vt.* to plait, braid, intertwine, interweave, interlace.
Einfleischen, ȧēn'flāēshen, *vt.* to embody; eingefleischter Teufel, a fiend incarnate.
Einfließen, ȧēn'flīsen (-floß, geflossen), *vi.* to flow in. **Einflößen,** -flösen, *vt.* to instill, infuse, inspire.
Einfluß, ȧēn'flŭss, *m.* influence, influx.
Einflüstern, ȧēn'flüshtern, *vt.* to suggest, to whisper.
Einfordern, ȧēn'fȯrdern, *vt.* to call in, collect.
Einförmig, ȧēn'förmich, *a.* uniform, monotonous; -keit, -kāēt, *f.* uniformity, monotony.
Einfressen, ȧēn'frėssen (-fraß, -gefressen), *vt.* to corrode.
Einfrieren, ȧēn'frīren (-fror, -gefro-

ren), *vi.* to freeze in, to be frozen up, to be ice-bound.
Einfügen, ṡèn'fü̇hgen, *vt.* to insert.
Einfuhr, ṡèn'fṳ̇r, *f.* getting in; importation. **Einführen,** ṡèn'führen, *vt.* to carry in, convey in, get in; to introduce, inaugurate; to import. **Einführung,** -ṳng, *f.* introduction.
Einfuhrzoll, ṡèn'furtsoll, *m.* import-duty.
Eingabe, ṡèn'gǡbe, *f.* petition.
Eingang, ṡèn'gang, *m.* entrance, entry; importation; introduction; preface, prologue, exordium; adit (in mines); **-zoll,** -tsoll. *m.* import-duty.
Eingeben, ṡèn'gǡben (-gab, -gegeben), *vt.* to give, administer; to prompt, suggest; to present (a petition); to bring on, enter (an action).
Eingebildet, ṡèn'gebildet, *a.* conceited, vain, arrogant.
Eingeboren, ṡèn'gebören, *a.* only-begotten.
Eingeboren, ṡèn'gebören, *a.* native, indigenous; *s.* native.
Eingebung, ṡèn'gǡbung, *f.* inspiration, suggestion.
Eingehen, ṡèn'gǡ-en (-ging, -gegangen) *vi.* to go in, enter; to be imported; to shrink, contract; **auf etwas —,** to humor, to yield, to consent to; **— lassen,** to abrogate, abolish; to make (a bet). **Eingehend,** -gǡhend, *a.* entering; re-entering (angle).
Eingenommen, ṡèn'genommen. *or.* prepossessed, prejudiced, — **sein von,** to be taken with; — **von sich,** self-conceited; **-heit,** -hāèt. *f.* prepossession, predilection, partiality for, inclination to.
Eingeständniß, ṡèn'gezhtentniss, *n.* avowal, confession.
Eingestehen, ṡèn'gezhtā-en (stant -gestanden), *vi.* to confess.
Eingeweide, ṡèn'gevǡède, *s. pl.* bowels, guts, intestines, entrails.
Eingewöhnen, ṡèn'gevönen, *vt.* to get accustomed to a place. **Eingewöhnen,** ṡèn'gevöhnen, *vt.* to accustom to a place.
Eingezogen, ṡèn'getsōgen. *a.* retired, secluded; **-heit,** -hāèt, *f.* seclusion, retirement.
Eingießen, ṡèn'gīssen (-gọss, -gegossen), *vt.* to pass in, infuse, inspire.
Eingraben, ṡèn'grǡben (-grub, -gegra-

ben), *vt.* to earth, to dig in; **inner;** **sich —,** to burrow.
Eingreifen, ṡèn'grèifen (-griff, -gegriffen), *vi.* to seize on, encroach, press upon; to take hold, to lay hold on; to interlock; to bite (of an anchor); to catch (teeth of a wheel). **Ein'griff,** -griff, *m.* encroachment.
Einguß, ṡèn'guss, *m.* infusion, inspiration.
Einhägen, ṡèn'hǡgen, *vt.* to fence in, hedge in.
Einhäkeln, ṡèn'hǡkeln, **Einhaken,** -hāken, *vt.* to hook in.
Einhalt, ṡèn'halt, *m.* check, stop. **Einhalten,** -halten (-hielt, -gehalten), *vi.* to hold in, stop, check.
Einhändigen, ṡèn'hẹndichen, *vt.* to deliver. **Einhändigung,** -ṳng, *f.* delivery.
Einhauchen, ṡèn'höuchen, *vt.* to breathe into, inspire.
Einhauen, ṡèn'hǡu-en (-hieb, -gehauen), *vi.* to hew in, cut in; to cut open, to slash, to charge, to walk into.
Einheben, ṡèn'hǡben (-hob, -gehoben), *vt.* to heave in; to put in.
Einheften, ṡèn'heften, *vt.* to stitch in, insert.
Einheimisch, ṡèn'hāèmish, *a.* homemade, home-bred, home-born, native, domestic, intestine, indigenous.
Einheit, ṡèn'hāèt, *f.* unity.
Einheizen, ṡèn'hāètsen, *vi.* to make a fire in.
Einhelfen, ṡèn'hȧlfen (-half, -geholfen), *vt.* to help in; to prompt.
Einhellig, ṡèn'hellich, *a.* unanimous, concurrent, *av.* -ly, by a common consent; **-keit,** -kāèt, *f.* unanimity, common consent.
Einher, ṡènhǡr', *av.* on, along; **gehen,** -gǡ-en, *vi.* to walk in a stately manner; **-stolzieren,** -zhtotsīèren, **-stroten,** -zhtrotsen, *vi.* to strut along.
Einhetzen, ṡèn'hetsen, *vt.* to break in, to drill, train.
Einholen, ṡèn'hōlen, *vt.* to haul home, to collect; to go to meet; to overtake.
Einhorn, ṡèn'horn, *n. pl.* **-hörner,** unicorn.
Einhufig, ṡèn'hṳfich, *a.* solipedous, whole-hoofed, *s.* soliped.

Einhüllen, șèn'hüllen, *vt.* to wrap in, envelop.

Einig, șèn'ich, *a.* one, only, sole, united; — fein, to agree together; -er Maßen, somewhat; — werden, to come to an agreement: mit sich — werden, to make up one's mind. **Einige**, șèn'ige, *pron.* several, some. **Ein'igen**, *vt.* to unite: sich —, to come to terms. **Einigkeit**, șèn'ichkåt, *f.* unity, oneness, unanimity, concord, agreement.

Einimpfen, șèn'impfen, *vt.* to inoculate, vaccinate; instill.

Einjagen, șèn'yägen, *vt.* to break in (for a chase); Schrecken —, to frighten.

Einjährig, șèn'yärich, *a.* one year old; -lich, *a.* annual.

Einkauf, șèn'käuf, *m.* purchase, bargain, marketing. **Einkaufen**, șèn'käufen, *vt.* to buy, purchase, procure, cater; to get a place by purchase. **Einkäufer**, șèn'käufer, *m. -in, f.* purchaser, buyer. **Einkaufspreis**, șèn'käufsprèïs, *m.* prime-cost, cost.

Einkehr, șèn'kèr, *f.* putting up; inn, tavern, public house; — des Gemüths, abstraction.

Einkerben, șèn'kèrben, *vt.* to notch, indent.

Einkerkern, șèn'kèrkèrn, *vt.* to imprison. **Einkerkerung**, -ung, *f.* imprisonment.

Einklagen, șèn'klägen, *vt.* to sue one for.

Einklammern, șèn'klammern, *vt.* to put in brackets.

Einklang, șèn'klang, *m.* unison; harmony; agreement.

Einkleiden, șèn'klèïden, *vt.* to give the veil (to nuns); to give the cowl (to monks): sich — lassen, to take the hood (veil); to invest with, to install (in office).

Einklemmen, șèn'klemmen, *vt.* to pinch in, to clamp.

Einklinken, șèn'klinken, *vt.* to latch; *vi.* to catch.

Einkneten, șèn'k(e)näten, *vt.* to knead in.

Einknicken, șèn'k(e)nicken, *vi.* to fold in.

Einkochen, șèn'kochen, *vt.* to inspissate by boiling; *vi.* to grow thick by boiling; o evaporate.

Einkommen, șèn'kommen (-kam, -gekommen). *vi.* to come in, apply, petition, sue; *s. n.* income, revenue.

Einkreisen, șèn'kreïsen, *vt.* to encircle.

Einkriechen, șèn'kriechen (-kroch, -gekrochen), *vi.* to creep in.

Einkünfte, șèn'künfte, *s. pl.* revenue, income, rents.

Einladen, șèn'läden (-lud, -geladen), *vt.* to load in, ship; to invite, bid. **Ein'ladung**, -lädung, *f.* loading; invitation; -karte, -kart_e, *f.* -schreiben, -schrèïben, *n.* card or letter of invitation.

Einlage, șèn'läge, *f.* laying in, inclosure, inclosed letter, etc.; stake (at play); capital invested, share, stock.

Einlaß, șèn'lass, *m.* admission, admittance. **Einlassen**, șèn'lassen (-ließ, gelassen), *vt.* to let in, admit; to mortise (timber, etc.); sich —, to engage in, meddle with; in ein Gespräch —, to join in conversation with. **Ein'laßkarte**, -karte, *f.* admission ticket. **Ein'lassung**, -ung, *f.* admission, admittance.

Einlaufen, șèn'läufen (-lief, -gelaufen), *vi.* to come in, arrive; shrink.

Einläuten, șèn'läuten, *vt.* to chime in.

Einlegen, șèn'lägen, *vt.* to lay in, put in, put together; to fold up; to salt, pickle; to preserve; Ehre — mit, to gain credit for; ein Wort — für, to intercede for; -messer, -messer, *n.* clasp-knife.

Einleiten, șèn'läïten, *vt.* to introduce, preface; to contrive, manage. **Ein'leitend**, -leïtend, *a.* introductory. **Einleitung**, șèn'läïtung, *f.* introduction.

Einlenken, șèn'lenken, *vt.* to turn in, turn back; to reform, mend.

Einleuchten, șèn'leüchten, *vi.* to be obvious, clear.

Einliefern, șèn'lifern, *vt.* to deliver in, make over. **Einlieferung**, șèn'lifferung, *f.* delivery.

Einlogiren, șèn'lozhïren, *vt.* to quarter, lodge, house.

Einlösen, șèn'löhsen, *vt.* to redeem, ransom, cash. **Ein'lösung**, -ung, *f.* redemption, ransom.

Einlöthen, șèn'löhten, *vt.* to solder in (uniting metals).

Einlullen, ằn'lullen, *vt.* to lull asleep.
Einmachen, ằn'machen, *vt.* to put in, wrap in, pack up; to preserve, pickle.
Einmal, ằn'mâl. *av.* once, auf —, at once; ·ig, *a.* (done) but once.
Einmarsch, ằn'marsh, *m.* march in, entrance, entry; ·iren, -iren, *vi.* to march in, enter.
Einmauern, ằn'môy-ern, *vt.* to immure, wall up.
Einmengen, ằn'meng-en, *vt.* to mix in; intermix; sich —, to meddle with, interfere.
Einmüthig, ằn'mühtich, *a.* unanimous, *av.* -ly; ·keit, -kăět, *f.* unanimity.
Einnähen, ằn'nä-en, *vt.* to sew in, embale.
Einnahme, ằn'näme, *f.* taking in; receipt, taking, occupation, storming (of a place); revenue. **Ein'nehmen,** -nämen (·nahm, ·genommen), *vt.* to take in, receive, earn; to take, storm; to captivate, charm; to prepossess. **Einnehmer,** ằn'nämer, *m.* receiver, collector; exciseofficer.
Einnetzen, ằn'netsen, *vt.* to wet, sprinkle, sponge.
Einnieten, ằn'nĭten, *vt.* to rivet in.
Einnisten, ằn'nizhten, **Einnistein,** ằn'nizhteln, *vr.* to nestle, to insinuate (one's self.)
Einnöthigen, ằn'nöhtichen, *vt.* to press to take.
Einöde, ằn'öhde, *f.* solitude, wilderness.
Einölen, ằn'öhlen, *vt.* to oil, grease.
Einpacken, ằn'packen, *vt.* to pack up.
Einpassen, ằn'passen, to fit, adjust, to let in (into the wood).
Einpfählen, ằn'pfälen, *vt.* to pale, fence with palings.
Einpfarren, ằn'pfarren, *vt.* to unite with a parish.
Einpferchen, ằn'pferchen, *vt.* to pen in, to coop up.
Einpflanzen, ằn'pflantsen, *vt.* to implant, plant.
Einpfropfen, ằn'pfropfen, *vt.* to ingraft, inoculate.
Einpökeln, ằn'pökeln, *vt.* to pickle, salt.
Einprägen, ằn'prägen, *vt.* to impress, imprint, to inculcate, enjoin, to stamp.
Einpredigen, ằn'prädichen, *vt.* to inculcate by preaching.
Einprügeln, ằn'prühgeln, *vt.* to beat into.
Einpudern, ằn'pŭdern, *vt.* to powder (one's hair, etc.).
Einpumpen, ằn'pumpen, *vt.* to pump in.
Einpuppen, ằn'puppen, *vr.* to change to a chrysalis.
Einquartiren, ằn'quartĭrĕn, *vt.* to quarter, billet.
Einrahmen, ằn'rämen, *vt.* to put into a frame, to frame.
Einrammeln, ằn'rammeln, *vt.* to ram in.
Einräuchern, ằn'räŭchern, *vt.* to smoke, fumigate.
Einräumen, ằn'räumen, *vt.* to give room to, to yield one's place; to admit, allow, permit.
Einrechnen, ằn'rechnen, *vt.* to reckon in, include, comprise.
Einrede, ằn'räde, *f.* contradiction, opposition, remonstrance. **Einreden,** ằn'räden, *vt.* to persuade, interrupt, contradict, to oppose.
Einreiben, ằn'rĕĭben (-rieb, -gerieben), *vt.* to rub in. **Einreibung,** ằn'rĕĭbyng, *f.* embrocation, rubbing.
Einreichen, ằn'räichen, *vt.* to hand in; present.
Einreihen, ằn'räĕ-en, *vt.* to range in, enrol, enlist.
Einreissen, ằn'räissen (-riss, -grissen), *vt.* to tear down, rend, pull down; to prevail, gain.
Einrenken, ằn'renken, *vt.* to set, put in.
Einrennen, ằn'rennen (-rannte, -gerannt), *vt.* to run against, smash.
Einrichten, ằn'richten, *vt.* to set; to put to rights; to set in order. **Ein'richtung,** -ŭng, *f.* regulation, arrangement.
Einrosten, ằn'rozhten, *vt.* to rust in.
Einrücken, ằn'rücken, *vi.* to enter, march into; to encamp, quarter in; *vt.* to insert. **Ein'rückgebühr,** -gebühr, *n.* costs of advertisement.
Einrückung, ằn'rückyng, *f.* insertion.
Einrühren, ằn'rühren, *vt.* to stir into, to beat up; to mix, mingle.

Ein 97 **Ein**

Eins, ȝēns, a. one; f. one; es ist mir Alles eins, it is all one (indifferent) to me; — sein, to agree; nicht — sein, to differ, disagree.

Einsaat, ȝēn'sät, f. seed-corn, corn sown. **Einsäen**, ȝēn'sä-en, vt. to sow (a field).

Einsagen, ȝēn'sägen, vt. to prompt; indite.

Einsalben, ȝēn'salben, vt. to anoint.

Einsalzen, ȝēn'saltsen, vt. to salt, pickle.

Einsam, ȝēn'sam, a. lonely, solitary; -keit, -kīet, f. solitude, loneliness, solitariness.

Einsammeln, ȝēn'sammeln, vt. to collect, gather. **Einsammler**, ȝēn'sammler, m. collector. **Ein'sammlung**, -ųng, f. collection.

Einsatz, ȝēn'sats, m. laying, staking; stakes; pool; set, nest (of boxes, etc.); pile of weights; hold-fast.

Einsaugen, ȝēn'sŏųgen (-sog, -gesogen), vt. to suck in, imbibe, absorb. **Ein'sauųgung**, -ųng, f. absorption.

Einsäumen, ȝēn'sŏųmen, vt. to hem.

Einschalten, ȝēn'shalten, vt. to intercalate, insert. **Ein'schaltung**, -ųng, f. intercalation, insertion.

Einschärfen, ȝēn'sherfen, vt. to enjoin, inculcate. **Ein'schärfung**, -ųng, f. inculcation.

Einscharren, ȝēn'sharren, vt. to scratch in, to bury.

Einschenken, ȝēn'shenken, vt. to pour in, to pour out.

Einschicken, ȝēn'shicken, vt. to send in.

Einschieben, ȝēn'shīben (-shob, -geschoben), vt. to shove in, push in, insert.

Ein'schiebsel, -shīpsel, n. insertion, parenthesis.

Einschießen, ȝēn'shīsen (-shoß, -geschoßen), vt. to shoot down, batter down; to pay in; to insert; to introduce; to put into the oven; sich —, to practice shooting.

Einschiffen, ȝēn'shiffen, vt. to embark, to ship. **Ein'schiffung**, -ųng, f. embarkation.

Einschirren, ȝēn'shirren, vt. to harness.

Einschlachten, ȝēn'shlachten, vt. to butcher, slaughter (for one's own use).

Einschläfen, ȝēn'shläfen (-shlief, -geschlafen), vi. to fall asleep. **Einschlä-**

fern, ȝēn'shläfern, vt. to lull to sleep, to lull into security. **Ein-schläferungsmittel**, -ųngsmittel, n. soporific, narcotic.

Einschlag, ȝēn'shläk, m. cover, envelop; woof, weft; advice. **Ein'schlagen**, -shläken (-schlug, -geschlagen), vt. to stick in; to break open, to stave (a cask); to barrel; envelop, pack up; to take (a road); to adopt; to clasp hands; to break ground; to strike (of lightning); to concern; to turn out, succeed, to thrive well; nicht —, to fail.

Einschleichen, ȝēn'shlīchen (-schlich, -geschlichen), vi. to creep in, steal in.

Einschleppen, ȝēn'shleppen, vt. to drag in, bring in; smuggle in.

Einschließen, ȝēn'shlīsen (-schloß, -geschlossen), vt. to lock in, inclose, include; to block up; to inclose (in brackets). **Ein'schließlich**, -shlīeslich, a. inclusive, av. -ly.

Einschlucken, ȝēn'shlucken, vt. to swallow.

Einschlummern, ȝēn'shlummern, vi. to fall asleep.

Einschlüpfen, ȝēn'shlüpfen, vi. to glide in, slip in.

Einschlürfen, ȝēn'shlürfen, vt. to sip in.

Einschluß, ȝēn'shluss, m. inclusion, inclosure, parenthesis.

Einschmeicheln, ȝēn'shmīcheln, vr. to insinuate one's self.

Einschmelzen, ȝēn'shmeltsen (-schmolz, -geschmolzen), vt. to melt down.

Einschmieren, ȝēn'shmīren, vt. to smear, grease.

Einschneiden, ȝēn'shnīden (-schnitt, -geschnitten) vt. to cut into, to carve, make an incision. **Ein'schneidig**, -shnīdich, a. one-edged.

Einschneien, ȝēn'shnīen (-schnīe, -geschnīen), vt. to cover with snow.

Einschnitt, ȝēn'shnitt, m. incision, cut, notch.

Einschnüren, ȝēn'shnūhren, vt. to lace up; to cord.

Einschöpfen, ȝēn'shöpfen, vt. to fill in, fill up, to draw.

Einschränken, ȝēn'shrenken, vt. to limit, confine, restrain, restrict. **Ein'schränkung**, -ųng, f. limitation, restriction, reduction.

Einschrauben, ȝēn'shrŏųben (also irreg.), vt. to screw in.

Einschrecken, ᵊēn'shrĕcken, *vt.* to frighten.
Einschreiben, ᵊēn'shrīben (-ſchrieb, -geſchrieben), *vt.* to write in, to write down, register, book, enroll. **Ein'ſchreibegebühr,** -gebühr, *f.* entrance-money, fees for registering.
Einschreiten, ᵊēn'shrēiten (-ſchritt, -geſchritten), *vi.* to interfere, interpose. **Ein'ſchreitung,** -ung, *f.* interposition, intervention.
Einschrumpfen, ᵊēn'shrŭmpfen, *vi.* to shrink.
Einschüchtern, ᵊēn'shü̆chtern, *vt.* to intimidate, dismay.
Einschulen, ᵊēn'shŭlen, *vt.* to train, manage.
Einschuß, ᵊēn'shŭss, *m.* capital advanced, stock, share.
Einschütten, ᵊēn'shütten, *vt.* to pour in.
Einschwärzen, ᵊēn'shvertsen, *vt.* to blacken; to smuggle in.
Einschwatzen, ᵊēn'shvatsen, *vt.* to persuade, to make believe.
Einsegnen, ᵊēn'sāknen, *vt.* to bless, consecrate. **Ein'ſegnung,** -ung, *f.* consecration.
Einsehen, ᵊēn'sā-en (-ſah, -geſehen), *vt.* to look into; to see, comprehend, be aware of, to be sensible; to get an insight, to understand.
Einseifen, ᵊēn'sāifen, *vt.* to lather, soap.
Einseitig, ᵊēn'sēitich, *a.* one-sided, crooked, biased, partial; -keit, -käet, *f.* one-sidedness, partiality.
Einsenden, ᵊēn'senden (-ſandte, -geſandt), *vt.* to send in, transmit.
Einsenken, ᵊēn'senken, *vt.* to sink in; to inter.
Einser, ᵊēn'ser, *m.* unit, one.
Einsetzen, ᵊēn'setsen, *vt.* to set in, place in, put in; to pawn; to imprison; to stake (money); to sew on (a patch); wieder —, to restore, reinstate; ſich —, to seat one's self in, to make, appoint one's self. **Ein'ſetzung,** -ung, *f.* installation, appointment.
Einsicht, ᵊēn'sicht, *f.* comprehension; penetration, understanding, knowledge; -ig, -voll, -foll, *a.* intelligent, judicious, sensible.
Einsiedelei, ᵊēnsīdelāi', *f.* hermitage.
Einsiedeln, ᵊēn'sīdeln, *vt.* to live in solitude, in a hermitage.

Einsieden, ᵊēn'sīden (-ſott, -geſotten) *vt.* to boil down.
Einsiedler, ᵊēn'sītler, *m.* hermit, anchorite; -iſch, -ish, *a.* solitary.
Einsilbig, ᵊēn'silbich, *a.* monosyllabic; -es Wort, monosyllable.
Einsinken, ᵊēn'sinken (-ſank, -geſunken), *vi.* to sink (in); to give way.
Einsitzen, ᵊēn'sitsen (-ſaß, -geſeſſen), *vt.* to take a seat in.
Einsitzig, ᵊēn'sitsich, *a.* with one seat.
Einsmals, ᵊēns'māls, *av.* once.
Einspannen, ᵊēn'zhpannen, *vt.* to harness, put to; to yoke; to stretch (in a frame).
Einspänner, ᵊēn'zhpenner, *m.* one-horse carriage. **Einspännig,** ᵊēn'zhpennich, *a.* drawn by one horse.
Einsperren, ᵊēn'zhperren, *vt.* to shut up, confine, imprison, cage; in ein Kloſter —, to cloister. **Ein'ſperrung,** -ung, *f.* imprisonment.
Einspinnen, ᵊēn'zhpinnen (-ſpann, -geſponnen), *vt.* to spin in.
Einsprache, ᵊēn'zhprāche, *f.* objection, exception, protest; — thun, to protest. **Einsprechen,** ᵊēn'zhprechen (-ſprach, -geſprochen), *vt.* to call on, to make a call, pay a visit; to protest; Muth —, to encourage; Troſt —, to comfort.
Einsprengen, ᵊēn'zhpreng-en, *vt.* to sprinkle; to burst open; to gallop in, to ride with full speed into.
Einspritzen, ᵊēn'zhpritsen, *vt.* to inject.
Einspruch, ᵊēn'zhpruch, *m.* objection.
Einst, einstens, ᵊēnzht'ens, *av.* once, at one time, formerly; in the future time.
Einstampfen, ᵊēn'zhtampfen, *vt.* to stamp in, ram in; to break by ramming *or* stamping.
Einstand, ᵊēn'zhtant, *m.* entrance (into an office). **Einstehen,** ᵊēn'zhtā-en (-ſtand, -geſtanden), *vi.* to stand in, enter; to answer for.
Einstecken, ᵊēn'zhtecken, *vt.* to put in, pocket; imprison.
Einsteigen, ᵊēn'zhtāigen (-ſtieg, -geſtiegen), *vi.* to mount into, to get in; to enter; to embark.
Einstellen, ᵊēn'zhtellen, *vt.* to put in, place in; to constitute, appoint; to put off; to discontinue work, to make a strike; to stop (payment); to stable (a horse); ſich —, to appear; set in (of winter, etc.).

Einstimmen, ɛən'zhtimmen, *vt.* to accord, join in ; to agree, consent ; to harmonize; to coincide. **Einstimmig,** ɛən'zhtimmiĥ, *a.* harmonious, unanimous; **-keit,** -kāet, *f.* unanimity, harmony.
Einsmals, ɛənzht'māls, *av.* once upon a time.
Einstödig, ɛən'zhtöckiĥ, *a.* one-storied.
Einstopfen, ɛən'zhtopfen, *vt.* to stuff in, fill in.
Einstoßen, ɛən'zhtōssen (-stieß, -gestoßen), *vt.* to thrust in; to ram down; to break by knocking, to break open ; to stave in (a barrel); to run in (a splinter); to knock out (one's brains).
Einstreichen, ɛən'zhtrēĥen (-strich, -gestrichen), *vt.* to pocket.
Einstreuen, ɛən'zhträüen, *vt.* to strew in *or* over.
Einströmen, ɛən'zhtröhmen, *vi.* to flow in, to rush in.
Einsturz, ɛən'zhturts, *m.* fall, ruin. **Einstürzen,** ɛən'zhtürtsen, *vi.* to fall down.
Eintweilen, ɛənzht'vēllen, *av.* in the mean time. **Einstweilig,** -vēlliĥ, *a.* temporary.
Eintägig, ɛən'tägiĥ, *a.* of one day, ephemeral.
Eintauchen, ɛən'tōyĥen, *vt.* to dip in, immerse.
Eintauschen, ɛən'tōyshen, *vt.* to exchange, barter.
Eintheilen, ɛən'tēelen, *vt.* to divide, distribute, classify. **Eintheilung,** -ung, *f.* distribution, classification.
Eintönig, ɛən'töhniĥ, *a.* monotonous; **-keit,** -kāet, *f.* monotony.
Eintracht, ɛən'tracht, *f.* concord, unanimity. **Einträchtig,** ɛən'trēĥtiĥ, *a.* harmonious, unanimous, *av.* -ly, in unity.
Eintrag, ɛən'trāk, *m.* woof, weft; prejudice, disparagement. **Eintragen,** ɛən'trägen (-trug, -getragen), *vt.* to carry in, bring in, yield; to enter, book, register. **Einträglich,** ɛən'träkliĥ, *a.* lucrative, **-keit,** -kāet, *f.* profitableness.
Einträufeln, ɛən'trüfeln, *vt.* to drip in, drop in.
Eintreffen, ɛən'treffen (-traf, -getroffen), *vi.* to arrive; coincide, happen.

Eintreiben, ɛən'trēiben (-trieb, -getrieben), *vt.* to drive in, to collect.
Eintreten, ɛən'trāten (-trat, -getreten), *vi.* to go in, enter; to come on; to set in; to fall out; to break by treading on; to kick open, to break open. **Eintritt,** ɛən'tritt, *m.* entrance, entry, ingress: beginning admission; **-sgeld,** -gĕlt, *n.* admission-fee; **-skarte,** -kartẹ, *f.* ticket (of admission).
Eintrocknen, ɛən'trocknen, *vt.* to dry up.
Einträpfeln, ɛən'tröpfeln, *vt.* to drop in, drip in.
Eintunken, ɛən'tunken, *vt.* to dip in.
Einüben, ɛən'ühben, *vt.* to exercise, drill, train.
Einung, ɛən'ung, *f.* union.
Einverleiben, ɛən'ferlēiben, *vt.* to incorporate, embody, unite; insert. **Einverleibung,** -ung, *f.* incorporation.
Einverständniß, ɛən'fērzhtentnis, *n.* agreement. **Einverstehen,** ɛən'ferzhtā-en (-verstand, -verstanden), *vi.* to agree with.
Einwand, ɛən'vant, *m.* objection, reply.
Einwanderer, ɛən'vanderer, *m.* immigrant. **Einwandern,** -vandern, *vi.* to immigrate. **Einwanderung,** -ung, *f.* immigration.
Einwärts, ɛən'vērts, *av.* inward(s).
Einweben, ɛən'väben (-wob, -gewoben), *vt.* to weave in.
Einwechseln, ɛən'vexeln, *vt.* to change, exchange.
Einweichen, ɛən'vāeĥen, *vt.* to soak, steep, macerate. **Einweichung,** -ung, *f.* maceration.
Einweihen, ɛən'vēi-en, *vt.* to initiate, instruct, acquaint with; inaugurate, ordain; consecrate. **Einweihung,** -ung, *f.* initiation; consecration.
Einweisen, ɛən'vēisen (-wies, -gewiesen), *vt.* to introduce. **Einweisung,** -ung, *f.* introduction.
Einwenden, ɛən'venden (-wandte, -gewandt), *vt.* to object, reply. **Einwendung,** -ung, *f.* objection.
Einwerfen, ɛən'verfen (-warf, -geworfen), *vt.* to throw in, object.
Einwickeln, ɛən'vickeln, *vt.* to envelop, wrap up, to swaddle.
Einwiegen, ɛən'vīgen, *vt.* to rock asleep.

Einwilligen, ȧēn'villichen, vi. to agree, consent to. **Einwilligung**, -ung, f. consent.
Einwirken, ȧēn'vīrken, vi. to act on, operate upon, to influence, to have effect upon. **Einwirkung**, -ung, f. operation, influence.
Einwohnen, ȧēn'vōnen, vi. to habituate one's self; to make one's self at home; s. inwohnen. **Einwohner**, -voner, m. inhabitant.
Einwühlen, ȧēn'vühlen, vi. to dig into: to bury one's self.
Einwurf, ȧēn'vurf, m. objection.
Einwurzeln, ȧēn'vurtseln, vi. to root, to take root.
Einzahlen, ȧēn'tsālen, vt. to pay in.
Einzäunen, ȧēn'tsäunen, vt. to hedge in, fence in.
Einzeichnen, ȧēn'tsäechnen, vt. to inscribe, subscribe.
Einzelheit, ȧēn'tselhāet, f. detail, particulars. **Einzeln**, ȧēn'tseln, a. single.
Einziehen, ȧēn'tsī-en (-zog, -gezogen), vt. to draw in, to move in; to seize, confiscate: to march in, enter.
Einzig, ȧēn'tsich, a. alone, only, sole.
Einzug, ȧēn'tsūk, m. entry, entrance, removal to.
Einzwängen, ȧēn'tsvēng-en, vt. to force in, between; to squeeze in, to press together; to constrain.
Eirund, āe'rund, a. oval, ovate, egg-shaped.
Eis, ēīs, n. ice. -achat, -achät, m. colorless agate; -bahn, -bän, f. slide; -bär, -bär, m. white bear, polar bear; -berg, -bērk. m. glacier, iceberg; -brecher, -brēcher, m. ice-breaker.
Eisen, ēī'sen, n. iron; -bahn, -bän, f. railroad, railway; -bahnhof, -bänhōf, m. depot, station; -bahnwagen, -bänvāgen, m. railroad-car, car, railway-wagon; -bahnwärter, -bänvēr-ter, m. railroad-guard, line-keeper; -bahnzug, -bäntsūk, m. train, railroad-train; -baum, -baum, m. iron-wood; -beize, -bāetse, f. iron-liquor; -beschläge, -beshlāge, s. pl. iron-work; -blech, -blēch, n. sheet-iron; -draht, -drāt, m. iron-wire; -erz, -ārts, n. iron-ore; -farbe, -farbe, f. iron-gray; -fresser, -frēsser, m. braggart, bully, fire-eater; -gießerei, -gīsserāi, f. iron-foundry; -gitter, -git-ter, n. iron-grate; -gußwaare, -gus-vāre, f. cast-iron ware; -haltend, -haltend, a. ferruginous; -hammer, -hammer, m. -hütte, -hütte, f. forge, iron-works; -handel, -handel, m. iron-trade; -händler, -hentler, m. hardware-merchant, ironmonger; -hart, -hart, a. hard as iron; -holz, -holts, n. iron-wood; -kalk, -kalk, m. calcined iron; -kies, -kīs, m. iron pyrites; -kiesel, -kīsel, m. iron-flint, ferruginous quartz; -oxidhydrat, -oxīdhīdrāt, n. hydratic oxide of iron; -schlacke, -schlacke, f. iron-dross; -schmied, -schmīd. m. blacksmith; -waare, -vāre, f. iron-ware, hardware. **Eisern**, ēī'ern, a. iron, of iron; unfeeling.
Eisfeld, ēīs'felt, n. pl. -er, field of ice. **Eisgang**, -gang, m. breaking up of the ice. **Eisgrau**, -grau, a. hoary with age. **Eisgrube**, -grube, f. ice-pit, ice-house. **Eisig**, ēī'sich, a. icy. **Eiskalt**, -kalt, a. icy cold, cold as ice. **Eiskeller**, -keller, m. ice-cellar. **Eispunkt**, -punkt, m. freezing-point. **Eisscholle**, -sholle, f. floe of ice, lump of ice. **Eisspath**, -shpāt, m. ice-spar. **Eiszapfen**, -tsapfen, m. icicle.
Eitel, āī'tel, a. empty, mere, weak; vain, self-conceited, vain-glorious; -keit, -kāet, f. vanity, self-conceit, nothingness.
Eiter, āīter, m. matter, pus; -beule, -boule, f. bile, abscess; -ig, a. purulent, mattery. **Eitern**, āī'tern, vi. to suppurate. **Eiterung**, -ung, f. suppuration.
Eiweiß, āī'vēīs, n. white of an egg.
Ekel, ēck'el, m. disgust, aversion; a. fastidious, delicate, disgusting; -ig, -haft, -haft, a. fastidious. **Ekelig-keit**, ēck'elichkāet, f. loathsomeness. **Ekeln**, ēck'eln, vt. to excite disgust, to affect with loathing, to feel disgust.
Elasticität, elazhtītsītāt', f. elasticity, buoyancy. **Elastisch**, elazht'ish, a. elastic.
Ellbogen, el'bōgen, m. elbow; -mus-kel, -muskel, m. cubital muscle; -nerv, -nērf. m. -en, ulnar nerve.
Elegant, elegant', a. elegant, stylish, av. -ly. **Eleganz**, elegants, f. elegance.

Elektricität, elĕcktritsitāt', *f.* electricity. **Elektrisch,** elĕck'trish, *a.* electrical. **Elektrisiren,** -sī'ren, *vt.* to electrify.
Element, element', *n.* element: constituent. **Elementarisch,** -tăr'ish, *a.* elementary, primary. **Elementarschule,** -shūle, *f.* primary school.
Elend, ā'lent, *n.* misery; *a.* miserable, wretched, *av.* -ly.
Elenthier, el'entīr, *n.* elk.
Elephant, elefant', *m.* -en, *pl.* -en, elephant.
Elf, ĕlf, *a.* eleven; *f.* Eilf.
Elfe, ĕlfe, *f.* elf, fairy.
Elfenbein, ĕl'fenbaēn, *n.* ivory; **-ern,** -ērn, *a.* made of ivory.
Elle, el'le, *f.* ell; **sehen,** *f.* Ellbogen.
Ellenwaaren, el'lenvāren, *s. pl.* dry goods.
Eller, el'ler, **Erle,** er'le, *f.* alder. **Ellern,** el'lern, *a.* of alder.
Elster, el'zhter, *f.* magpie.
Eltern, el'tern, *s. pl.* parents; *f.* Aeltern.
Email, emal'ye, *f.* enamel; **-farbe,** -farbe, *f.* vitrifiable pigment.
Emailliren, emalyī'ren, *vt.* to enamel.
Emigrant, em'igrant, *m.* -en, *pl.* -en, emigrant.
Empfang, empfang', *m.* reception, receipt. **Empfangen,** empfang'en (-fing. empfangen), *vt.* to receive, take; welcome; to conceive. **Empfänger,** empfeng'er, *m.* receiver. **Empfänglich,** empfeng'lich, *a.* susceptible; **-keit,** -kāet, *f.* susceptibility. **Empfängniß,** -niss, *n.* conception. **Empfangschein,** -shaēn, *m.* receipt.
Empfehlbar, empfāl'bār, **Empfehlenswerth,** -vārt, *a.* recommendable. **Empfehlen,** empfā'len (-fahl, empfohlen), *vt.* to recommend, commend. **Empfehlung,** -yng, *f.* recommendation, respects; **-brief,** -brīf, *m.* letter of recommendation.
Empfindbar, empfint'bār, *a.* sensitive; perceptible, sensible; **-keit,** -kāet, *f.* sensibleness; sensibility. **Empfindelei,** empfindelā', *f.* sentimentality. **Empfinden,** empfin'deln, *vi.* to affect sensibility, to be sentimental. **Empfünden,** empfin'den (empfand, empfunden), *vt.* to feel, perceive, be sensible of, penetrated with. **Empfindlich,** empfint'lich, *a.* sensible, sensitive, irritable, susceptible; touchy. **Empfindlichkeit,** -kāet, *f.* sensibility, sensitiveness, irritability, susceptibility. **Empfindsam,** empfint'sam, *a.* feeling, sentimental; **-keit,** -kāet, *f.* sentimentality; nice sensibility. **Empfindung,** empfind'yng, *f.* feeling, sensation, sentiment; **-los,** -lōs, *a.* unfeeling, senseless; **-vermögen,** -fermōhgen, *n.* sensitive faculty, perception.
Empor, empōr', *av.* up, upwards, on high; **-arbeiten,** -arbāeten, *vt.* sich —, to work up one's self. **Empören,** empöh'ren, *vt.* to stir up, shock, revolt; to be indignant of; sich —, to revolt, rebel, rise upon. mutiny against. **Empörer,** empöh'rer, *m.* mutineer, revolter, insurgent. **Emporfahren,** empōr'fāren (-fuhr, -gefahren), *vi.* to start up. **Emporheben,** empōr'hāben (-hob, -gehoben), *vt.* to lift up. **Emporkirche,** -kirche, *f.* gallery, aisle. **Emporkömmling,** -kömmling, *m.* upstart. **Emporschauen,** -shāū-en, *vi.* to gaze up. **Emporschwingen,** empōr'shving-en (-schwang, -geschwungen). *vr.* to soar up. **Empörung,** empöh'ryng, *f.* revolt, rebellion, mutiny.
Emsig, ēn'sich, *a.* assiduous, active; **-keit,** -kāet, *f.* assiduity, assiduousness; activity, industry.
Endabsicht, ent'apsicht, *f.* final design. **Ende,** en'de, *n.* end, conclusion. **Enden,** en'den, **Endigen,** en'digen, *vt.* to end, finish, complete, conclude, accomplish; *vi.* to cease, end. **Endlich,** ent'lich, *a.* finite; final ultimate; *av.* at last, at length, finally. **Endsilbe,** -silbe, *f.* final syllable. **Endung,** end'yng, *f.* ending, termination, conclusion. **Endursache,** end'yrsache, *f.* final cause. **Endurtheil,** end'yrtāel, *n.* final judgment. **Endziel,** ent'tsīl, *n.* (final) aim. **Endzweck,** -tsveck, *n.* purpose, intent, end, aim.
Energie, enērgī', *f.* energy. **Energisch,** enērg'ish, *a.* energetic, *av.* -ally.
Engagiren, engazhī'ren, *vt.* to engage.
Engbrüstig, eng'brüshtich, *a.* asthma-

tic; -feit, -keet, f. asthma. Eng,
enge, eng'e, a. narrow, close, tight,
small, strait; f. narrowness, close-
ness, tightness.

Engel, eng'ol, m. angel; -schaar,
-schär, f. angelic host.

Engen, eng'en, vt. to narrow, straiten,
confine; vi. to contract, shrink.

Engherzig, eng'hērtsiġ, a. narrow-
minded, illiberal; -keit, -keet, f.
illiberality. Eng'paß, -pass, m. defile, strait, narrow pass.

Enkel, eng'kel, m. grandson, grandchild ; -in, f. granddaughter.

Entadeln, entä'deln, vt. to degrade.

Entarten, entär'ten, vi. to degenerate.
Entar'tung, -ŭng, f. degeneracy, degeneration.

Entäußern, entöüs'ern, vt. to free, rid,
to part with.

Entbehren, entbär'en, vt. to want, to
be destitute of, to do without; to
spare, dispense with. Entbehrlich,
entbär'liġ, a. dispensable, unnecessary. Entbehrung, entbär'ŭng, f.
deprivation.

Entbieten, entbī'ten (-bot, entboten),
vt. to send for, to order; to send
word.

Entbinden, entbin'den (-band, entbun-
den), vt. to unbind, release, disengage, set free; to deliver (a woman
in labor). Entbind'ung, -ŭng, f.
releasing, disengagement; delivery,
childbirth; -kunst, -kŭnzht, f. midwifery, obstetrics.

Entblöden, entblöh'den, vi. to dare,
venture, to be so bold as to, to di-
vest one's self of bashfulness.

Entblößen, entblöh'sen, vt. to bare,
strip. Entblöß'ung, -ŭng, f. deprivation.

Entblühen, entblüh'en, vi. to blow
out, blossom forth.

Entbrennen, entbren'nen (-brannte,
entbrannt), vi. to inflame, to fly into
a passion.

Entdecken, entdeck'en, vt. to discover,
detect, find out, descry. Entdeck'er,
-decker, m. discoverer. Entdeck'ung,
-ŭng, f. discovery, detection.

Ente, en'te, f. duck: -nbunst, -dŭnzht,
m. duck-shot; -nfang, -fang, m. de-
coying of ducks; -nheerd, -hård, m.
decoy-pond; -njagd, -yakt, f. duck-
shooting.

Entehren, entä'ren, vt. to dishonor,

deflour; -ich, a. disgraceful. Ent-
ehr'ung, -ŭng, f. degradation, defamation.

Enteilen, entäl'en, vi. to hasten
away.

Enterben, enterb'en, vt. to disinherit.
Enterbung, enterb'ŭng, f. disinheri-
tance.

Enterich, Enteriġ, ent'eriġ, m. drake.

Entern, en'tern, vt. to board (a vessel).

Entfahren, entfä'ren (-fuhr, entfahren), vi. to escape.

Entfallen, entfal'len (-fiel, entfallen),
vi. to drop, escape, fail.

Entfalten, entfal'ten, vt. to unfold,
display.

Entfärben, entfer'ben, vt. to discolor,
make pale; siċh —, to grow pale.

Entfernen, entfern'en, vt. to remove;
siċh —, to withdraw, retire. Entfernt, entfernt', a. distant, far off,
remote. Entfern'ung, -ŭng, f. removal; departure; distance.

Entfesseln, entfes'seln, vt. to unfetter,
unchain.

Entflammen, entflam'men, vt. to inflame.

Entfliegen, entflī'gen (-flog, entflogen),
vi. to fly away.

Entfliehen, entflī'en (-floh, entflohen),
vi. to flee, run away, escape.

Entfließen, entflīs'sen (-floß, entflossen),
vi. to flow from.

Entfremden, entfrem'den, vt. to alienate, estrange. Entfremd'ung, -ŭng,
f. alienation, estrangement.

Entführen, entführ'en, vt. to carry
away; to elope with. Entführer,
entführ'er, m. ravisher. Entfüh'-
rung, -ŭng, f. abduction, ravishment.

Entgegen, entgä'gen, av. against;
-arbeiten, -arbäeten, vi. to work
against, counteract; -gehen, -gä'en
(-ging, gegangen), vi. to go to meet;
-gesetzt, -gesetst, a. opposite; -hal-
ten, -halten (-hielt, -gehalten), vt. to
present; -handeln, -handeln, vi. to
act in opposition, counteract, contravene; -kommen, -kommen (-kam,
-gekommen), vi. to come to meet;
-sehen, -sä-en (-sah, -gesehen), vt. to
look towards, expect; -setzen, -set-
sen, vt. to oppose; -setzung, -set-
sŭng, f. opposition; -treten, -träten
(-trat, getreten), vi. to meet. Ent-
gegnen, entgäg'nen, vt. to reply.

Entgehen, ent'gā'-en (-ging, entgangen), vi. to escape.
Entgelt, entgėlt, n. compensation; ohne —, gratis. **Entgelten**, entgėl'ten (-galt, entgolten), vt. to compensate, atone for.
Entgleiten, entglāē'ten (-glitt, -glitten), vi. to glide from, escape.
Enthaaren, ent-hār'en, vt. to unhair.
Enthalten, ent-hält'en (enthielt, enthalten), vt. to contain, abstain from. **Enthaltsam**, -sam, a. abstemious, abstinent; -keit, -kęət, f. abstemiousness, abstinence. **Enthaltung**, ent-halt'yng, f. abstinence, forbearance.
Enthaupten, ent-hāūp'ten, to behead, decapitate. **Enthauptung**, -yng f. beheading, decapitation.
Entheben, ent-hā'ben (-bob, entboben), vt. to free from, relieve from.
Entheiligen, ent-hāēl'ichen, vt. to profane. **Entheiligung**, -yng, f. profanation.
Enthüllen, ent-hül'len, vt. to unveil, disclose, reveal.
Enthusiasmus, entyuṣiās'mus, m. enthusiasm. **Enthusiasmiren**, -mī'ren, vt. to fill with enthusiasm, to inspire. **Enthusiast**, -siazht', m. -en, pl. -en, euthusiast.
Entjungfern, entyyng'fern, vt. to deflour.
Entkleiden, entklāē'den, vt. to undress, unclothe.
Entkommen, entkom'men (-kam, entkommen), vi. to get off, escape.
Entkörpern, entkör'pern, vt. to disembody.
Entkräften, entkref'ten, vt. to enfeeble, debilitate. **Entkräftung**, -yng, f. enervation.
Entladen, entlā'den (-lub, entlaben), vt. to unload, unburden; discharge.
Entlang, entlang', av. along.
Entlarven, entlar'fen, vt. to unmask.
Entlassen, entlas'sen (-ließ, entlassen), vt. to dismiss, discharge. **Entlassung**, -yng, f. dismissal, discharge.
Entlasten, entlazh'ten, vt. to unload, unburden, ease.
Entlaufen, entläū'fen (-lief, entlaufen), vi. to run away, escape.
Entledigen, entlā'dichen, vt. to set free, deliver, release, discharge, exempt, disencumber, ease; ſich —, to get rid of, to rid one's self of; to perform, execute. **Entledigung**, -lā'dichyng, f. delivery, discharge.
Entlegen, entlā'gen, a. remote, distant; -heit, -hāēt, f. distance, remoteness.
Entlehnen, ent'lā'nen, vt. to borrow, quote.
Entleiben, entlēī'ben, vt. to kill, murder; ſich —, to commit suicide.
Entleiden, ent'lāēd'en, vt. to disgust, dissatisfy with.
Entleihen, entlēī'en (-lieh, entliehen), vt. to borrow.
Entlocken, entlock'en, vt. to elicit.
Entmannen, entman'nen, vt. to emasculate, unman; castrate, effeminate. **Entmannung**, entmann'yng, f. castration.
Entmasten, entmazh'ten, vt. to unmast.
Entmenschen, entmen'shen, vt. to unman, brutalize. **Entmenscht**, entmensht', av. barbarous, unfeeling.
Entmuthigen, entmyt'ichen, vt. to discourage. dishearten.
Entnehmen, entnā'men (-nahm, -nommen), vt. to take away, gather, conclude, infer; draw upon.
Entnerven, entnėr'fen, vt. to enervate, unnerve. **Entnerbung**, -nėr'fyng, f. enervation.
Entquellen, entquėl'len (-quoll, -quollen), vi. to flow forth, issue.
Enträthseln, entrėt'seln, vt. to unriddle.
Entreißen, entrēī'sen (-riß, entrißen), vt. to tear from.
Entrichten, entricht'en, vt. to pay, discharge.
Entrinnen, entrin'nen (-rann, -rannte), to run away, escape.
Entrollen, entroll'en, vt. to unroll, display, unfold.
Entrücken, entrück'en, vt. to snatch away.
Entrüsten, entrüzh'ten, vr. ſich —, to become indignant. **Entrüstung**, -yng, f. indignation.
Entsagen, entsā'gen, vt. to renounce. **Entsagung**, entsāg'yng, f. renunciation.
Entsatz, entsats', m. relief, succor.
Entschädigen, entshā'dichen, vt. to indemnify. **Entschädigung**, -yng, f. indemnification.

Ent 104 **Ent**

Entscheiden, entshīd'en (entschieb, entschieben), *vt.* to decide; ‑s, *a.* decisive. **Entscheid'ung**, ‑ung, *f.* decision.

Entschieden, entshīd'en, *a.* decided.

Entschlafen, entshlä'fen (‑schlief entschlafen), *vi.* to fall asleep: die.

Entschlagen, entshlä'gen (‑schlug, ent‑schlagen), *vi.* to get out, to part with, to cast, put away.

Entschleiern, entshlāe'ern, *vt.* to unveil.

Entschliessen, ent'shlīs'sen (‑schloß, entschlossen), *vr.* to resolve. **Entschliess'ung**, ‑ung, *f.* resolution.

Entschlossen, entshlos'sen, *a.* resolute, determined; ‑heit, ‑hāet, *f.* resoluteness.

Entschlummern, entshlum'mern, *vi.* to fall asleep, to expire gently.

Entschlüpfen, entshlüp'fen, *vi.* to slip from, escape.

Entschluß, entshluss', *m.* resolution.

Entschuldigen, entshul'dichen, *vt.* to excuse, exculpate; sich —, to apologize. **Entschul'digung**, ‑ung, *f.* excuse, apology.

Entschweben, entshväb'en, *vi.* to float away.

Entschwinden, entshvin'den (‑schwand, entschwunden), *vi.* to disappear, vanish, pass away.

Entseelt, entsält', *a.* lifeless, dead.

Entsetzen, entsets'en, *vt.* to dismiss. relieve; sich —, to be shocked. **Entsetzlich**, entsets'lich, *a.* shocking, horrible; ‑keit, ‑kāet, *f.* horribleness. **Entsetz'ung**, ‑ung, *f.* dismissal, removal, dismission.

Entsiegeln, entsī'geln, *vt.* to unseal.

Entsinken, entsīn'ken (‑sank, entsunken), *vi.* to drop, sink, fail.

Entsinnen, entsīn'nen (‑sann, entsonnen), *vr.* to recollect.

Entsittlichen, entsitt'lichen, *vt.* to demoralize. **Entsitt'lichung**, ‑ung, *f.* demoralization.

Entspinnen, entshpin'nen (‑spann, entsponnen), *vr.* to arise; begin.

Entsprechen, entshpröch'en (‑sprach, entsprochen), *vi.* to answer, correspond, to fall out according to.

Entspringen, entshpring'‑en (‑sprang, entsprungen), *vi.* to escape; to arise, take rise, spring up.

Entstehen, entshtā‑en (‑stand, entstan‑

ben), *vi.* to arise, exist, originate, to take rise; fail, want.

Entsteigen, entshtēig'en (‑stieg, entstiegen), *vi.* to come from, arise from.

Entstellen, entshtel'len, *vt.* to disfigure, garble, misrepresent. **Entstellung**, ‑ung, *f.* misrepresentation.

Entströmen, entshtröh'men, *vi.* to gush from, flow from.

Entstürzen, entshtürts'en, *vi.* to rush from, gush from.

Entsündigen, entsün'dichen, *vt.* to purify.

Enttäuschen, enttöüsh'en, *vt.* to undeceive.

Entthronen, entthrōn'en, *vt.* to dethrone. **Entthron'ung**, ‑ung, *f.* dethronement.

Entvölkern, entfölk'ern, *vt.* to depopulate. **Entvöl'kerung**, ‑ung, *f.* depopulation.

Entwachsen, entvax'en (‑wuchs, entwachsen), to grow out of; to outgrow.

Entwaffnen, entvaff'nen, *vt.* to disarm.

Entweder, entvā'der, *conj.* either.

Entweichen, entvēich'en (‑wich, entwichen), *vi.* to give way, withdraw, retire, disappear, run away. **Entweichung**, entvēich'ung, *f.* escape, disappearance.

Entweihen, entvēi'en, *vt.* to profane. **Entweih'ung**, ‑ung, *f.* profanation, desecration.

Entwenden, entven'den, *vt.* to pilfer, purloin, to make away with, steal.

Entwerfen, entvēr'fen (‑warf, entworfen), *vt.* to plan, design, trace, sketch, draw up; to project; to lay down.

Entwickeln, entvick'eln, *vt.* to develop, explain. **Entwick'elung**, ‑ung, *f.* development.

Entwinden, entvin'den (‑wand, entwunden), *vt.* to wrest from, take from.

Entwirren, entvir'ren, *vt.* to unravel.

Entwischen, entvish'en, *vi.* to slip away, escape.

Entwöhnen, entvöh'nen, *vt.* to wean; disuse. **Entwohnt**, entvönt', *a.* unaccustomed.

Entwölken, entvölk'en, *vt.* to uncloud.

Entwürdigen, entvür'dichen, *vt.* to disgrace, degrade. **Entwür'digung**, ‑ung, *f.* degradation.

Entwurf, entwurf', m. sketch, plan, scheme, project.
Entwurzeln, entwur'tseln, vt. to unroot, eradicate.
Entzaubern, enttsau'bern, vt. to disenchant.
Entziehen, enttsî'en (-zog, entzogen), vt. to draw away, take away, bereave, deprive, withdraw; sich —, to withdraw from.
Entziffern, enttsiff'ern, vt. to decipher, explain.
Entzücken, enttsück'en, vt. to transport, enrapture. **Entzück'ung,** -ung, f. trance, transport, rapture.
Entzündbar, enttsünt'bär, a. inflammable; -keit, -kaet, f. inflammability. **Entzünden,** entts'n'den, vt. to kindle, inflame. **Entzünd'ung,** -ung, f. inflammation.
Entzwei, enttsvae', ar. asunder, in two: -en, vt. to disunite, divide; vr. to quarrel, fall out.
Enzian, en'tsiän, m. gentian.
Epaulette, epolett'e, f. epaulet, shoulder-strap.
Ephen, ef'fäu, m. ivy.
Epidemie, epidemî', f. epidemy. **Epidemisch,** epidäm'ish, a. epidemic, -al.
Epilepsie, epiläpsî', f. epilepsy. **Epileptisch,** epiläp'tish, a. epileptic.
Epilog, epilôg', m. epilogue.
Episode, episô'de, f. episode.
Epistel, epizh'tel, f. epistle.
Epoche, epoch'e, f. epoch.
Equipage, equipä'zhe, f. equipage.
Equipiren, equipî'ren, vt. to equip, man.
Er, är, pron. he.
Erachten, eräch'ten, vt. to consider, think; s. n. opinion, consideration.
Erbarmen, erbarm'en, vr. to feel pity, to pity, commiserate; s. n. compassion, pity, mercy; -swerth, -värt, a. pitiable. **Erbärmlich,** erbärm'lich, a. pitiable, pitiful, miserable, wretched, adv. -ly, paltry; -keit, -kaet, f. miserableness.
Erbauen, erboy'en, vt. to build, erect, raise, edify. **Erbaulich,** erboy'lich, a. edifying. **Erbau'ung,** -ung, f. foundation, erection; edification.
Erbe, er'be, m. -en, pl. -n, heir, inheritor; n. inheritance.
Erbeben, erbä'ben, vi. to shake, tremble.

Erben, erb'en, vt. to inherit, to be the heir of; to descend upon.
Erbeten, erbä'ten, vt. to obtain by prayer.
Erbetteln, erbät'teln, vt. to beg, to obtain by begging.
Erbeuten, erböi'ten, vt. to capture.
Erbfeind, erp'faent, m. hereditary enemy, sworn enemy. **Erbfolge,** erp'folge, f. hereditary succession, entail. **Erbgut,** erp'gut, n. inherited property, inheritance, heir-loom.
Erbieten, erbî'ten (-bot, -boten), vt. to offer.
Erbin, erb'in, f. heiress.
Erbitten, erbit'ten (-bat, erbeten), vt. to ask, request; to obtain by supplication.
Erbittern, erbit'tern, vt. to embitter, exasperate, exacerbate, madden. **Erbitterung,** erbit'terung, f. exasperation.
Erblasser, erp'lasser, m. testator; -in, f. testatrix.
Erbleichen, erbläech'en (-blich, erblichen), vi. to grow pale, to die.
Erblich, erp'lich, a. hereditary.
Erblicken, erblick'en, vt. to descry, behold, catch sight of.
Erblinden, erblin'den, vi. to grow blind.
Erblühen, erblüh'en, vi. to bloom, blossom.
Erborgen, erborg'en, vt. to borrow.
Erbosen, erbös'en, vt. to make angry; vr. to fret. **Erbost,** erböst', a. angry, enraged.
Erbötig, erböht'ich, a. ready.
Erbpacht, erp'pacht, m. fee-farm. **Erbprinz,** erp'prints, m. -en, pl. -en, hereditary prince.
Erbrechen, erbrech'en (-brach, erbrochen), vt. to break open, to force (a lock); to open, unseal; sich —, to vomit.
Erbrecht, erp'recht, n. heirship, hereditary right. **Erbschaft,** -shaft, f. inheritance.
Erbse, erp'se, f. pea; -suppe, -suppe, f. pea-soup.
Erbstück, erp'zhtück, n. heir-loom. **Erbsünde,** -sünde, f. original sin, hereditary sin. **Erbtheil,** -täel, m. portion. **Erbzins,** erp'tsins, m. hereditary rent, quit-rent, ground-rent; -mann, -mann, m. pl. -leute, lease-holder.

Erdachse, ert'axe, *f.* axis of the earth.
Erdbahn, ert'bān, *f.* orbit of the earth.
Erdball, ert'ball, *m.* globe, world.
Erdbeben, -bāben, *n.* earthquake.
Erdbeere, -bāre, *f.* strawberry.
Erdbeerbaum, -bǎūm, *m.* arbutus.
Erdbeschreiber, -beshrēīber, *m.* geographer.
Erdbeschreibung, -shrēībụng, *f.* geography.
Erdbirne, -bīrne, *f.* potato.
Erdbohrer, -bōrer. *m.* ground-auger, scooping-iron.
Erde, ēr'de, *f.* earth, ground, soil; auf —n, on earth.
Erden, ēr'den, *a.* earthen.
Erdenge, ert'ẹnge, *f.* isthmus.
Erdenken, ērdẹnk'en (-dachte, erdacht), *vt.* to devise, invent, imagine; contrive.
Erdenklich, ērdẹnk'lich, *a.* imaginable.
Erderschütterung ert'ērshütterụng, *f.* earthquake.
Erdfahl, ērd'fāl, *a.* earth-colored.
Erdfall, -fal, *m.* landslide, land-slip.
Erdfarbig, -farbich, *a.* earth-colored.
Erdferne, -ferne, *f.* apogee.
Erdfläche, ērt'flęche, *f.* surface of the earth.
Erdgeschoß, -geshōs, *n.* ground-floor.
Erdharz, -härts, *n.* bitumen.
Erdicht, ērd'icht, *a.* earthy.
Erdichten, ērdicht'en, *vt.* to invent, devise, fabricate, forge; to acquire by poetical compositions.
Erdichtet, ērdicht'et, *a.* false, feigned, fictitious, imaginary.
Erdichtung, -ụng, *f.* fiction, invention.
Erdig, ērd'ich, *a.* earthy, earthen.
Erdkloß, ērd'klōs, *m.* clod.
Erdkobalt, -kobalt, *m.* cobalt-bloom.
Erdkohle, -kōle, *f.* earthy brown-coal.
Erdkreis, -krēīs, *m.* **Erdkugel,** -kụgel, *f.* globe.
Erdkunde, -kụnde, *f.* geology.
Erdmesser, -messer, *m.* geometer, geometrician.
Erdmessung, -kụnzht, *f.* geometry.
Erdnähe, -nā-e, *f.* perigee.
Erdolchen, ērdolch'en, *vt.* to poniard, stab.
Erdpech, ērt'pech, *n.* asphaltum.
Erdreich, -rēīch, *n.* ground, land, soil.
Erdreisten, ērdrēīzh'ten, *vr.* to dare, to venture, presume.
Erdrosseln, ērdrȯs'seln. *vt.* to strangle, throttle.
Erdrücken, ērdrück'en, *vt.* to oppress, crush.
Erdscholle, ērt'sholle, *f.* clod.
Erdschüttung, -shüttụng, *f.* earth-work.

Erdschwamm, ērt'shvamm, *m.* mushroom.
Erdstoß, -zhtōs, *m.* earthquake, shock.
Erdstrich, -zhtrich, *m.* zone, climate.
Erdzunge, -zhtụje, *f.* terrace.
Erdulden, ērdụl'den, *vt.* to suffer, endure.
Erdumschiffung, ert'ụmshiffụng, *f.* circumnavigation of the earth.
Erdumsegler, -sākler, *m.* circumnavigator.
Erdwachs, -vax, *n.* ozocerite.
Erdzunge, -tsụng-e, *f.* neck of land.
Ereifern, ērēī'fern, *vr.* sich —, to become angry, to get into a passion.
Ereignen, ērāēk'nen, *vr.* sich — to come to pass.
Ereilen, ērēī'len, *vt.* to come up with, to overtake.
Eremit, ẹrẹmit', *m.* -en, hermit.
Ererben, ērẹrb'en, *vt.* to inherit.
Erfahren, ērfä'ren (-fuhr, erfahren), *vt.* to prove, try, learn, know; *a.* experienced, skilful, expert; **-keit, -häst,** *f.* expertness, skilfulness.
Erfahrung, ērfär'ụng, *f.* experience, practice; **-smäßig,** -māsich, *a.* empiric, -al, *av.* -ally.
Erfassen, ērfas'sen, *vt.* to seize, take hold of.
Erfechten, ērfecht'en (-focht, erfochten), *vt.* to gain (the victory), to win.
Erfinden, ērfīnd'en (-fand, erfunden), *vt.* to invent, devise.
Erfinder, ērfīnd'er, *m.* inventor; **-in,** *f.* inventress: **-isch,** -ish, *a.* inventive.
Erfindung, ērfīnd'ụng, *f.* invention, discovery, contrivance; **-sgeist, -gäězht,** *m.* inventive faculty.
Erflehen, ērflā'en, *vt.* to entreat, implore.
Erfolg, ērfolk', *m.* result, success, consequence, issue.
Erfolgen, ērfolk'-en, *vi.* to follow, ensue, result, succeed.
Erfordern, ērfor'dern, *vt.* to require.
Erforderlich, erfor'derlich, *a.* requisite.
Erfordernis, ērfor'derniss, *n.* requisite.
Erforschen, ē-forsh'en, *vt.* to search into, inquire, examine, investigate, scrutinize.
Erforscher, ērforsh'er, *m.* investigator.
Erforschung, -ụng, *f.* search, investigation.
Erfragen, ērfrā'gen, *vt.* to find out by asking.
Erfrechen, ērfrẹch'en, *vr.* sich —, to dare, presume.
Erfreuen, ērfrēū'en, *vt.* to rejoice

Erf   107   Eri

cheer, gladden: fich —, to rejoice. Erfreulich, ĕrfrŏĭ..'lich, a. pleasing, cheering, delightful.
Erfrieren, ĕrfrī'ren (-fror, erfroren), vi. to freeze (to death).
Erfrischen, ĕrfrĭsh'en, vt. to refresh. Erfrischung, ĕrfrĭsh'ŭng, f. refreshment.
Erfüllen, ĕrfül'len, vt. to fulfil, to fill up, to satisfy. Erfüll'ung, -ŭng, f. accomplishment, fulfilment; in — geben, to be fulfilled.
Ergänzen, ĕrgĕnt'sen, vt. to make up, complete. Ergänz'ung, -ŭng, f. completion, supplement; -band, -bant, m. supplementary volume.
Ergeben, ĕrgāben (-gab, ergeben), vt. to give up, surrender, submit, devote, prove, show; a. devoted, obedient: -heit, -hāĕt, f. devotion. Ergebniß, ĕrgăp'niss, n. result, product. Ergebung, ĕrgāb'ŭng, f. surrender, submission, resignation.
Ergehen, ĕrgā'en (erging, ergangen), vi. fich —, to walk; to indulge in; to befall; -lassen, to issue, publish; über fich — lassen, to submit to.
Ergetzen, ĕrgĕt'sen, vt. to delight, amuse; fich —, to delight in, amuse one's self with. Ergetzlich, ĕrgĕts'lich, a. delightful: -keit, -kāĕt, f. delightfulness. Ergetz'ung, -ŭng, f. delight, enjoyment.
Ergiebig, ĕrgī'bich, a. yielding, productive, fertile: -keit, -kāĕt, f. fertility, productiveness.
Ergießen, ĕrgīs'sen (-goß, -gossen), vt. to pour out; fich —, to overflow, disembogue; to issue forth.
Erglänzen, ĕrglĕnt'sen, vi. to glow, radiate, to shine forth.
Ergötzen, ĕrgĕts'en, f. Ergetzen.
Ergreifen, ĕrgrīf'en, vt. to seize, take hold of; to take up, affect.
Ergrimmen, ĕrgrĭm'men, vi. to grow angry.
Ergrübeln, ĕrgrŭh'beln, vt. to find out by meditation.
Ergründbar, ĕrgrŭnt'băr, a. fathomable. Ergründen, ĕrgrŭn'den, vt. to fathom, sound, dive into, penetrate into.
Erguß, ĕrguss, m. pouring forth.
Erhaben, ĕrhāb'en, a. sublime, elevated: -heit -hāĕt, f. sublimity, elevation.

Erhalten, ĕrhalt'en (erhielt, erhalten), vt. to keep, preserve, save; to receive, get, obtain. Erhalter, ĕrhalt'er, m. preserver. Erhalt'ung, -ŭng, f. preservation, maintenance, support.
Erhangen, ĕrheng'en, vt. to hang.
Erhärten, ĕrhĕrt'en, vt. to harden; to confirm.
Erhaschen, ĕrhash'en, vt. to catch, snatch.
Erheben, ĕrhā'ben (erhob, erhoben), vt to raise, lift up, elevate; praise, extol; fich —, to rise, arise, start, Erheblich, ĕrhāp'lich, a. considerable: -keit, -kāĕt, f. considerableness, consequence, importance. Erheb'ung, -ŭng, f. elevation.
Erheirathen, ĕrhēi'rāten, vt. to obtain, acquire by marriage.
Erheischen, ĕrhāe'shen, vt. to require.
Erheitern, ĕrhāe'tern, vt. to brighten, gladden, clear up. Erheit'erung, -ŭng, f. exhilaration.
Erhellen, ĕrhĕl'len, vt. to clear up, illuminate; vi. to appear, to be evident.
Erhenken, ĕrhenk'en, vt. to hang.
Erheucheln, ĕrhĕūch'eln, vt. to obtain by hypocrisy; to feign, to put on.
Erhitzen, ĕrhĭt'sen, vt. to heat; fich —, to grow warm or hot. to overheat one's self; to grow angry, to inflame. Erhitzt, ĕrhĭtst', a. heated, angry. Erhitz'ung, -ŭng, f. overheating; anger.
Erhöhen, ĕrhŏh'en, vt. to heighten, elevate, raise, lift up. Erhöh'ung, -ŭng, f. elevation; eminence.
Erholen, ĕrhōl'en, vr. fich —, to recover: to recreate, amuse one's self; fich Raths — bei, to ask the advice of. Erhol'ung, -ŭng, f. recovery, recreation; -ftunde, -zhtŭnde, f. leisure hour, hour of recreation.
Erhören, ĕrhŏh'ren, vt. to hear; to learn: to grant.
Erinnern, ĕrĭn'nern, vt. to remind; fich —, to remember. Erinnerlich, -lich, a. fo viel mir — ift, as far as I can remember. Erin'nerung, -ŭng, f. remembrance, recollection; -vermögen, -fĕrmŏhgen, n. faculty of remembering; -kunst, -kŭnzht, f. mnemonics.
Erjagen, ĕryā'gen, vt. to overtake, to get by hunting.

Erkalten, erkält'en, *vi.* to cool, abate.
Erkälten, erkęlt'en *vr.* fich —, to catch cold. **Erkältung,** erkęlt'yng, *f.* cold.
Erkämpfen, erkęmpf'en, *vt.* to obtain by fighting; einen Sieg —, to gain a victory.
Erkaufen, erkäuf'en, *vt.* to purchase, buy, redeem; to hire, bribe, corrupt. **Erkäuflich,** erkäuf'lich, *a.* venal, corruptible, bribable.
Erkennen, erkęn'nen (erkannte, erkannt), *vt.* to know, perceive, discern; to recognize; to acknowledge, own; to admit; to be sensible of; to judge, take cognizance of; to pass judgment on. **Erkenntlich,** erkęnt'lich, *a.* grateful; discernible, distinguishable; -keit, -käet, *f.* acknowledgment, thankfulness. **Erkenntniß,** erkęnt'nis, *n.* perception, knowledge; cognizance; judgment, sentence, verdict. **Erkennung,** erkęn'nung, *f.* knowledge, recognition; -wort, -vort, *n.* watchword; -zeichen, -tsäechen, *n.* countersign.
Erker, ęrk'er, *m.* balcony, jetty, jutty; -fenster, *n.* bay-window, bow-window.
Erkiesen, erkī'sen, *vt.* to choose, select.
Erklärbar, erklär'bär, *a.* explicable. **Erklären,** erklä'ren, *vt.* to explain, explicate, interpret, expound; declare. **Erklärung,** erklär'yng, *f.* explanation, interpretation; declaration.
Erklecklich, erkleck'lich, *a.* considerable.
Erklettern, erklęt'tern, **Erklimmen,** erklim'men, *vt.* to climb (up).
Erklingen, erkling'en (erklang, erklungen), *vi.* to sound, resound, ring.
Erklügeln, erklüh'geln, *vt.* to find out by meditating, to hatch out.
Erkoren, erkō'ren, *pp.* chosen.
Erkranken, erkrank'en, *vi.* to fall sick.
Erkühnen, erkühn'en, *vr.* to dare, be bold enough, to venture.
Erkundigen, erkun'dichen, *vr.* to inquire. **Erkundigung,** -yng, *f.* inquiry, investigation.
Erkünsteln, erkün'zhteln, *vt.* to affect. **Erkünstelt,** erkün'zhtelt, *a.* affected, artificial. **Erkünstelung,** -yng, *f.* affectation.

Erlaben, erläb'en, *vt.* to refresh.
Erlahmen, erläm'en, *vi.* to grow lame.
Erlangen, erlang'en, *vt.* to reach, obtain.
Erlaß, erlass', *m.* remission; order, decree, edict. **Erlassen,** erlass'en (erließ, erlassen), *vt.* to remit; to publish. **Erläßlich,** erlęss'lich, *a.* pardonable, venial. **Erlassung,** -yng, *f.* remission, absolution.
Erlauben, erläu'ben, *vt.* to permit. **Erlaubniß,** erläup'nis, *f.* permission, allowance. **Erlaubt,** erläupt', *pp.* allowed, lawful.
Erlaucht, erlōcht', *a.* illustrious, noble.
Erlauern, erlōy'ern, *vt.* to watch for.
Erläutern, erlöü'tern, *vt.* to clear, elucidate. **Erläuterung,** erlöü'terung, *f.* explanation, elucidation.
Erle, ęr'le, *f.* alder.
Erleben, erläb'en, *vt.* to reach, to live to see, to experience, to witness; den Tag nicht —, to die before the day.
Erledigen, erlä'dichen, *vt.* to ease, get rid of; to disengage, release; to settle, decide; Erz —, to wash ore; der Saft —, to liberate, set free. **Erledigt,** erlä'dicht, *pp.* vacant. **Erledigung,** -yng, *f.* release; vacancy.
Erlegen, erlä'gen, to lay down, pay; kill, slay.
Erleichtern, erleich'tern, *vt.* to ease, facilitate. **Erleichterung,** -yng, *f.* relief, ease.
Erleiden, erleī'den (erlitt, erlitten), *vt.* to suffer, endure, undergo, sustain.
Erlernen, erlęr'nen, *vt.* to learn. **Erlernung,** -yng, *f.* learning.
Erleuchten, erlöüch'ten, *vt.* to illuminate, light, enlighten. **Erleuchtung,** -yng, *f.* illumination, enlightening.
Erliegen, erlī'gen (erlag, erlegen), *vi.* to sink under, succumb.
Erlenkönig, er'lenkönich, *m.* erlking.
Erlogen, erlō'gen, *pp.* false, untrue.
Erlöschen, erlösh'en (erlosch, erloschen), *vi.* to go out; to decline, to die away; *vt.* to extinguish.
Erlösen, erlöh'sen, *vt.* to redeem, ransom, rescue, deliver. **Erlöser,** erlöh'ser, *m.* saviour, redeemer, deliverer. **Erlösung,** -yng, *f.* redemption, delivery.

Erlügen, ĕrlüh'gen, vt. to invent a lie.
Erlustigen, ĕrlŭzh'tichen. vr. to amuse one's self; über etwas —, to make sport of.
Ermächtigen, ĕrmĕch'tichen, vt. to empower, authorize; sich —, to usurp. **Ermäch'tigung,** -ŭng, f. authorization; usurpation.
Ermahnen, ĕrmä'nen, vt. to admonish, exhort. **Ermah'nung,** -ŭng, f. exhortation, admonition.
Ermangeln, ĕrmang'eln, vi. to fail, to be wanting. **Ermang'elung,** -ŭng, f. want, default, fault.
Ermannen, ĕrman'nen, vr. to rouse one's self.
Ermäßigen, ĕrmäs'ichen, vt. to moderate, abate.
Ermatten, ĕrmat'ten, vi. to fail, flag, decline; vt. to enfeeble, weaken. **Ermat'tung,** -ŭng, f. lassitude, weariness.
Ermel, ĕrm'el, m. f. Ärmel.
Ermessen, ĕrmĕs'sen (ermaß, ermessen), vt. to measure, estimate, judge, weigh, ponder, infer; conceive; n. s. judgment, estimation.
Ermorden, ĕrmŏr'den, vt. to murder, slay. **Ermord'ung,** -ŭng, f. murder.
Ermüden, ĕrmüh'den, vt. to tire, fatigue, weary; vi. to tire, to be fatigued. **Ermüd'ung,** -ŭng, f. fatigue, weariness.
Ermuntern, ĕrmŭn'tern, vt. to rouse, waken, enlive, excite, animate, stimulate. **Ermun'terung,** -ŭng, f. incitement, encouragement.
Ermuthigen, ĕrmŭt'ichen, vt. to encourage, animate, inspirit. **Ermuth'igung,** -ŭng, f. encouragement.
Ernähren, ĕrnä'ren, vt. to nourish, feed, support. **Ernährer,** ĕrnä'rer, m. nourisher, supporter; -in, f. nurse, foster-mother. **Ernäh'rung,** -ŭng, f. nourishment, support, maintenance.
Ernennen, ĕrnĕn'nen (ernannte, ernannt). vt. to nominate, appoint, create. **Ernen'nung,** ŭng, f. nomination, appointment, creation, collation.
Erneuern, ĕrnŏi'ern, vt. to renew, renovate. **Erneu'erung,** -ŭng, f. renewal, renovation.

Erniedrigen, ĕrnīd'richen, vt. to lower, humble, humiliate. **Ernie'drigung,** -ŭng, f. humiliation.
Ernst, ĕrnzht, m. earnest, ardor, zeal, eagerness; seriousness; a serious, grave, severe, austere, stern, xv. -ly; -haft, -haft, a. serious, grave; **Ernsthaftigkeit,** -haftichkĕĕt, f. gravity, seriousness. **Ernstlich,** ĕrnzht'lich, a. serious, earnest, express, forcible, av. in earnest, intently, strenuously.
Ernte, ĕrn'te (Ärnte). a. harvest; -fest, -fezht, n. harvest-home; -frau, -krantz, m. harvest garland; -monat, -mōnat, m. harvest, -month; August. **Ernten,** ĕrn'ten, vt. to harvest, reap; to make (hay).
Erobern, ĕrō'bern, vt. to conquer; get, win, save, spare. **Eroberer,** ĕrōb'erer, m. conqueror. **Erob'erung,** -ŭng, f. conquest.
Eröffnen, ĕrŏff'nen, vt. to open, unclose; to notify; to discover, disclose. **Eröff'nung,** -ŭng, f. opening, disclosure, notification.
Erörtern, ĕrŏr'tern, vt. to discuss. **Erörterung,** ĕrŏrtĕr'ŭng, f. discussion.
Erpicht, ĕrpicht', a. eager, mad after.
Erpressen, ĕrprĕs'sen, vt. to extort, exact. **Erpres'sung,** -ŭng, f. exaction, extortion.
Erquicken, ĕrquick'en, vt. to refresh, recreate, revive, reanimate, quicken; -d, **Erquicklich,** ĕrquick'lich, a. refreshing, quickening. **Erquick'ung,** -ŭng, f. refreshment, recreation.
Errathen, ĕrrät'en (errieth, errathen), vt. to guess, divine, conjecture, find out, solve, explain, unriddle.
Erregbar, ĕrräk'bär, a. excitable, irritable; -keit, -kĕĕt, f. excitability, irritability. **Erregen,** ĕrräg'en, vt. to stir up, to excite, move. **Erre'gung,** -ŭng, f. agitation, excitation, emotion.
Erreichen, ĕrräch'en, vt. to reach, attain, extend to, to gain, arrive at, overtake; to come to.
Erretten, ĕrret'ten, vt. to save, rescue, deliver. **Erretter,** ĕrret'ter. m. deliverer, preserver, saver; saviour. **Erret'tung,** -ŭng, f. salvation.
Errichten, ĕrrich'ten, vt. to raise, set up, erect, institute, found; to make, establish.

Erringen, ĕrring'en (errang, errungen), *vt.* to get by wrestling; einen Vortheil —, to obtain an advantage; to gain (a victory).
Erröthen, ĕrröht'en, *vi.* to blush.
Ersättigen, ĕrsĕt'tigen, *vt.* to satiate, satisfy.
Ersatz, ĕrsats', *m.* amends, compensation; surrogate, substitute.
Ersaufen, ĕrsŏuf'en, *vi.* **Ersäufen,** ĕrsŏŭf'en, *vt.* to drown.
Erschaffen, ĕrshaf'fen (erschuf, erschaffen), *vt.* to create. **Erschaffung,** -ung, *f.* creation.
Erschallen, ĕrshel'len (*reg. u.* erscholl, erschollen), *vi.* to resound.
Erscheinen, ĕrshaēn'en (erschien, erschienen), *vi.* to appear. **Erscheinung,** ĕrshaēn'ung, *f.* appearance, apparition.
Erschießen, ĕrshīs'sen (erschoß, erschossen), *vt.* to shoot (to death).
Erschlaffen, ĕrshlaf'fen, *vt.* to slack, slacken; *vi.* to fail, slack. **Erschlaffung,** -ung, *f.* relaxation.
Erschlagen, ĕrshlä'gen (erschlug, erschlagen), *vt.* to slay, strike dead, to kill.
Erschleichen, ĕrshleīch'en (erschlich, erschlichen), *vt.* to get surreptitiously. **Erschleichung,** ĕrshleīch'ung, *f.* surreption.
Erschließen, ĕrshlīs'sen (erschloß, erschlossen), *vt.* to unlock, to open.
Erschmeicheln, ĕrshmīĕch'eln, *vt.* to obtain by flattery.
Erschnappen, ĕrshnap'pen, *vt.* to snap, snatch, catch.
Erschöpfen, ĕrshöpf'en, *vt.* to exhaust, empty, scoop out; to drain off, to spend.
Erschrecken, ĕrshreck'en (erschrack, erschrocken), *vt.* to frighten, terrify; to be frightened, to be struck with fear, to be startled. **Erschrecklich,** ĕrshreck'lich, *a.* dreadful, terrible.
Erschüttern, ĕrshüt'tern, *vt.* to shake, stagger, strike; sich —, to tremble. **Erschütterung,** -ung, *f.* shock, concussion, commotion.
Erschweren, ĕrshvār'en, *vt.* to aggravate, render more difficult.
Erschwingen, ĕrshving'en (erschwang, erschwungen), *vt.* to reach, gain, win. **Erschwinglich,** ĕrshving'lich, *a.* attainab'e.

Ersehen, ĕrsā'en (ersah, ersehen), *vt.* to see, learn.
Ersetzen, ĕrsets'en, *vt.* to replace, make up, compensate, reimburse. **Ersetz'bar,** -bār, **Ersetz'lich,** -lich, *a.* reparable.
Erseufzen, ĕrsĕŭf'tsen, *vi.* to sigh deeply.
Ersichtlich, ĕrsicht'lich, *a.* evident.
Ersinnen, ĕrsin'nen (ersann, ersonnen), *vt.* to devise, contrive, invent, imagine. **Ersinn'lich,** -lich, *a.* imaginable.
Erspähen, ĕrzhpā'en, *vt.* to espy.
Ersparen, ĕrzhpā'ren, *vt.* to spare, save. **Ersparniß,** ĕrzhpär'niss, *n.* saving.
Ersprießen, ĕrzhprīs'sen (ersproß, ersprossen), *vi.* to shoot up; to be of use, to do good to. **Ersprieß'lich,** -lich, *a.* useful, beneficial.
Erst, ärzht, *a. av.* first, previous, *av.* -ly, only, at first, before, but; jetzt —, but now, just now.
Erstarren, ĕrzhtar'ren, *vi.* to be benumbed, to be chilled, grow numb. **Erstar'rung,** -ung, *f.* stiffness, numbness, torpor.
Erstatten, ĕrzhtat'ten, *vt.* to compensate, restore, reimburse, repay; to make restitution; to render account; to return. **Erstat'tung,** -ung, *f.* restitution, compensation.
Erstaunen, ĕrzhtŏŭn'en, *vi.* to be astonished, amazed, surprised; *s. n.* astonishment, amazement; sichwerth, -värt, **Erstaun'lich,** -lich, *a.* astonishing, surprising, stupendous, *av.* -ly.
Erst, er, st, stes, ärzht'er, *a.* first.
Erstechen, ĕrzhtech'en (erstach, erstochen), *vt.* to stab, lance, perforate, pierce, run through.
Erstehen, ĕrzhtā'en (erstand, erstanden), *vi.* to get up, rise, spring up, revive; *vt.* to buy at an auction; to serve out; to suffer.
Ersteigen, ĕrzhteīg'en (erstieg, erstiegen), *vt.* to mount, ascend.
Erstens, ĕrzh'tens, *av.* firstly, in the first place.
Ersterben, ĕrzhtĕr'ben (erstarb, erstorben), *vi.* to die away, expire, become extinct.
Erstgeboren, ärzht'geboren, *a.* firstborn. **Erst'geburt,** -geburt, *f.* primogeniture; the first born.
Ersticken, ĕrzhtick'en, *vt. i.* to suffocate

choke; smother, be suffocated, stifle; **ung**, -ung, f. suffocation.
Erstlich, ärzht'lich, av. first, firstly.
Erstling, ärzht'ling, m. firstling.
Ersterben, erzhtǒrb'en, a. dead.
Erstrecken, erzhtreck'en, vt. to extend, stretch; sich —, to extend to, to reach.
Erstürmen, erzhtürm'en, vt. to take by storm, by assault.
Ersuchen, ersuch'en, vt. to ask, request.
Ertappen, ertap'pen, vt. to seize, catch, to take in the very act, to overtake.
Ertheilen, ertäel'en, vt. to bestow, impart, confer, grant; Unterricht —, to give instruction, lessons.
Ertödten, ertöd'ten, vt. to mortify.
Ertönen, ertön'nen, vi. to sound, resound.
Ertrag, erträk', m. produce, revenue, yield. **Ertragen**, erträ'gen (ertrug, ertragen), vt. to bear, sustain, suffer. **Erträglich**, erträk'lich, a. sufferable, endurable, tolerable.
Ertränken, ertrenk'en, vt. to drown.
Ertrinken, ertrink'en (ertrank, ertrunken), vi. to drown.
Ertrotzen, ertrots'en, vt. to get by defiance.
Erübrigen, erühb'richen, vi. to spare, lay by.
Erwachen, ervach'en, vi. to awake.
Erwachsen, ervax'en (erwuchs, erwachsen), vi. to grow up, spring up; to accrue; pp. adult.
Erwägen, erväg'en (erwog, erwogen), vt. to weigh, ponder, consider. **Erwägung**, erväg'ung, f. consideration.
Erwählen, erväl'en, vt. to choose, elect, make choice of. **Erwähler**, erväl'er, m. elector. **Erwählung**, -ung, f. election.
Erwähnen, ervä'nen, vt. to mention. **Erwähnung**, -ung, f. mention.
Erwärmen, ervärm'en, vt. to warm.
Erwarten, ervar'ten, vt. to expect, await, stay for. **Erwartung**, -ung, f. expectation.
Erwecken, erveck'en, vt. to awake, waken, rouse, excite, revive.
Erwehren, ervä'ren, vr. sich —, to keep off, to get rid of, to forbear, resist.
Erweichen, erväich'en, vt. to soften, mov°, macerate; vi. to soften.

Erweis, ervēīs', m. proof, evidence. **Erweisen**, ervēīs'en (erwies, erwiesen), vt. to prove, evidence, show, bestow. **Erweislich**, ervēīs'lich, a. provable, evincible, demonstrable, av. -ly; -keit, -käet, f. demonstrableness.
Erweitern, ervēīt'tern, v.. to widen, extend. **Erweiterung**, -ung, f. enlargement, expansion, extension.
Erwerb, ervěrp', m. acquisition, earnings, gain. **Erwerben**, ervěrb'en (erwarb, erworben), vt. to acquire, gain, earn. **Erwerbfleiß**, -flēīs, m. industry. **Erwerbung**, -ung, f. acquisition.
Erwidern, ervīd'ern, vi. to reply. **Erwiderung**, -ung, f. answer, reply.
Erwischen, ervish'en, vt. to seize, surprise.
Erwuchern, ervuch'ern, vt. to gain by usury.
Erwünschen, ervünsh'en, to wish for.
Erwürgen, ervürg'en, vt. to strangle, choke.
Erz, ärts, n. ore; **-ader**, -äder, f. (metallic) vein, lode.
Erzählen, ertsäal'en, vt. to tell, narrate, recite, recount. **Erzählung**, -ung, f. tale, narration, story.
Erzart, ärts'ärt, f. species of ore.
Erzauge, ärts'äuge, n. grain of ore.
Erzbild, ärts'bĭlt, n. bronze.
Erzbischof, ärts'bishof, m. archbishop. **Erzbischöflich**, -bishöflich, a. archiepiscopal. **Erzbisthum**, ärts'bisstum, n. archbishopric.
Erzblume, ärtsblyme, f. marcasite.
Erzbösewicht, ärts'böhsevicht, m. archvillain.
Erzbruch, ärts'bruch, m. mine.
Erzeigen, ertsäeg'en, vt. to exhibit, show, do, impart; to render (services).
Erzengel, ärts'eng-el, m. archangel.
Erzeugen, ertsĕīg'en, vt. to produce. **Erzeuger**, ertsĕīg'er, m. genitor, procreator. **Erzeugniß**, ertseūk'niss, n. produce, product, production. **Erzeugung**, ertseūg'ung, f. production.
Erzfeind, ärts'fäent, m. arch-foe.
Erzhaltig, ärts'haltich, a. containing ore.
Erzherzog, ärts'hertsok, m. archduke -**lich**, -lich, a. archducal; **-thum** -tum, n. archduchy, archdukedom.

Erziehen, ertsī'en (erzog, erzogen), *vt.* to bring up, educate. **Erzieher,** ertsī'er, *m.* educator. **Erziehung,** -ung, *f.* education; **‑anstalt, ‑än**zhtalt, *f.* seminary, educational establishment.

Erzielen, ertsīl'en, *vt.* to aim at, attain, obtain.

Erzittern, ertsit'tern, *vi.* to tremble, shiver, quake.

Erzkunde, ārts'kunde, *f.* metallurgy. **Erzofen,** ārts'ōfen, *m.* furnace.

Erzogen, ertsō'gen, *a.* educated, brought up.

Erzschicht, ārts'shicht, *f.* shift.

Erzürnen, ertsürn'en, *vt.* to anger, irritate, exasperate, vex.

Erzvater, ārts'fäter, *m.* patriarch. **Erzväterlich,** -fäterlich, *a.* patriarchal.

Erzwingen, ertsving'en (erzwang, erzwungen), *vt.* to force, enforce.

Es, ās, *pron.* it.

Esche, esh'e, *f.* ash, ash-tree. **Eschen,** esh'en, *a.* ashen.

Esel, ās'el, *m.* ass; **-in,** *f.* she-ass. **Eseltreiber,** -treiber, *m.* ass-driver.

Espe, ezh'pe, *f.* aspen, asp.

Esse, ẽs'se, *f.* forge; chimney.

Essbar, ess'bār, *a.* eatable. **Essen,** ẽs'sen, *n.* meal, repast; meat, food; mess, dishes; (aß, gegessen), *vt.* to eat; **zu Mittag —,** to dine; **zu Abend —,** to sup.

Essenkehrer, es'senkärer, *m.* chimney-sweep. **Essenklappe,** -klappe, *f.* damper, damper-plate.

Essenz, essents', *f.* essence.

Esser, ẽs'ser, *m.* eater, feeder.

Essig, es'sich, *m.* vinegar; **-brauer,** -brouer, *m.* vinegar manufacturer; **-geist,** -gāezht, *m.* pyroacetic spirit; **-gurke,** -gurke, *f.* pickled cucumber, gherkin; **-mutter,** -mutter, *f.* mother of vinegar; **-säure,** -säure, *f.* acetic acid.

Esslust, ẽss'luzht, *f.* appetite. **Ess'saal,** -säl, *m.* dining-room. **Esswaaren,** -vāren, *s. pl.* victuals, eatables. **Esszeit,** -tseït, *f.* meal-time.

Estrich, esh'trich, *m.* pavement, plaster-floor.

Etlich, et'lich, *pron.* some, any, several.

Etwa, et'vä, *av.* perhaps, by chance;

anywhere. **Etwas,** et'vass, *pron.* something, somewhat, some, any.

Euer, öu'er, *a.* your. **Euretwegen,** öu'rētvāgen, **Euretwillen,** -villen, *av.* on your account, for your sake, in your behalf.

Eule, öu'le, *f.* owl.

Eurig, öu'rich, *pron.* your.

Euter, öu'ter, udder, bag.

Evangelisch, efang-gā'lish, *a.* evangelical. **Evangelist,** efang-gelizht', *m.* evangelist. **Evangelium,** efang-gā'lium, *n.* gospel (good tidings).

Ewer, ev'er, *m.* lighter, wherry

Ewig, ā'vich, *a.* eternal, everlasting, perpetual; **-keit,** -käet, *f.* eternity, perpetuity, everlasting; **in —, von — zu —,** in alle —, from everlasting to everlasting, to all eternity, forever and ever. **Ewiglich, ewig,** *av.* eternally, forever,

Examen, exā'men, *n.* examination, trial. **Examiniren,** exāminī'ren, *vi.* to examine, prove, try. **Examinand,** exāminant', *m.* one to be examined. **Examinationscommission,** -natsiōn'commission, *f.* board of examiners.

Excellenz, extsēllents', *f.* excellency.

Excentricität, extsentritsität', *f.* eccentricity. **Excentrisch,** extsen'trish, *a.* eccentric, -al, -ally, &c.

Exempel, exem'pel, *n.* example, instance; sum; **ein — nehmen,** to take example by; **ein — statuiren,** to set an example; **zum —,** for example, for instance. **Exemplar, exemplär',** *m.* copy. **Exemplarisch,** -ish, *a.* exemplary; *av.* exemplarily.

Exerciren, exertsī'ren, *vt.* to drill, train, practice, exercise. **Exercierplatz,** -plats, *m.* drilling-ground. **Exercitium,** exertsi'tsium, *n.* specimen, task, exercise.

Existenz, exizhtents', *f.* existence; living. **Existiren,** exizhtī'ren, *vi.* to exist.

Experiment, experiment', *n.* experiment. **Experimentiren,** -mentī'ren, *vi.* to experiment.

Explodiren, explōdī'ren, *vi.* to explode.

Explosion, explosiōn', *f.* explosion.

Extrakt, extrackt', *m.* extract.

Fabel, fä'təl, f. fable: **Dichter**, -dichter, m. fabulist, fabler; **haft**, -haft, a. fabulous, av. -ly. **Fabeln**, fä'beln, vi. to fable, invent fables; to rave.

Fabriciren, fabritsī'ren, vt. to fabricate. **Fabrik**, fabrick', f. manufactory. **Fabrikant**, fabrikant', m. -en, pl. -en, manufacturer.

Fach, fach, n. pl. **Fächer**. compartment, partition, shelf, drawer, row, case, pannel; line, province, branch, department, business, profession; box (letter); **baum**, -baūm, m. sheeting-pile, pile-plank.

Fächeln, fech'eln, vt. to fan.

Fachen, fach'en, vt. to form into compartments.

Fächer, fech'er, m. fan. **Fächern**, fech'ern, vt. to fan. **Fächerpalme**, -palme, f. fan-palm.

Fächser, fex'er, m. layer, shoot, scion.

Facit, fä'tsit, n. sum, amount, answer.

Fackel, fack'el, f. torch, flambeau. **Fackeln**, fack'eln, vi. to blaze, flash. **Fackelzug**, -tsŭk, m. torch-light procession.

Factor, fak'tor, m. agent, manager, clerk, foreman, workmaster; **ei**, -ēī', f. agency, factory.

Factur, faktūr', f. invoice.

Facultät, fakultät', f. faculty.

Fade, fä'de, a. stale, dull, flat, insipid; unmeaning, lean, lame.

Fädeln, fä'deln, vt. to thread (a needle). **Faden**, fä'den, m. thread, cord; **scheinig**, -shaēnich, a. threadbare.

Fagot, fagot', n. bassoon; **ist**, -izht', m. -en, bassoonist.

Fähig, fä'ich, a. able, fit, capable, clever, susceptible; **keit**, -kǣet, f. ability, capacity, faculty, fitness.

Fahl, fäl, a. fallow, tawny; faded.

Fähnchen, fän'chen, **Fähnlein**, -laēn, n. little flag, pennon; troop of horsemen. **Fähndrich**, fēn'drich, m. ensign, standard-bearer. **Fahne**, fä'ne, f. flag, banner, colors: **schmied**, -shmīt, m. farrier (of cavalry): **scheu**, -shy, m. color-sheath; **stock**, -zhtock, m. color-staff, ensign-staff: **träger**, -träger, m. ensign, standard-bearer; **wacht**,

-wacht, f. color-guard; **weihe**, -vēī'e, f. consecration of the colors.

Fahrbahn, fär'bän, f. track, channel. **Fahrbar**, fär'bär, a. passable. **Fähre**, tä're, f. ferry. **Fahren**, fä'ren, (fuhr, gefahren), vi. to drive, ride, run, sail, row, start; vt. to carry, convey. **Fahrend**, fär'end, a. errant, traveling. **Fahrgeld**, fär'gelt, n. fare. **Fahrlässig**, fär'lässich, a. careless, negligent, inattentive; **keit**, -kǣet, f. inattention, carelessness. **Fährmann**, fär'mann, m. pl. **leute**, ferry-man. **Fahrniss**, fär'niss, m. chattel. **Fahrstrahl**, fär'zhträl, m. radiusvector. **Fahrstraße**, fär'zhträsse, f. road, highroad. **Fahrt**, fart, f. passage, course. **Fährte**, fär'te, f. track. ball, print, pricking (of a hare); **von der — abkommen**, to be at fault. **Fahrwasser**, -vasser, n. channel. **Fahrweg**, -vak, m. road. **Fahrzeug**, -tsoǖk, n. boat, ship, vessel.

Falb, falp, a. fallow, pale. **Falbe**, fal'be, m. fallow, cream-colored horse. **Falbel**, fal'bel, f. flounce, fringe, furbelow. **Falbeln**, fal'beln, vt. to flounce.

Falke, fal'ke, m. falcon, hawk; **beize**, -baētse, **jagd**, -yakt, f. hawking. **Falkener**, fal kener. **Falkenier**, -nīr', **Falk'ner**, **Falk'enjäger**, -yäger, m. falconer, hawk.

Fall, fall, m. fall: case, incident, accident; **gesetzten**, suppose. **Falle**, fal'le, f. trap; valve, gate (of a mill). **Fallbrücke**, fall'brücke, f. draw-bridge. **Fallen**, fal'len (fiel, gefallen), vi. to fall, tumble, drop, hit; to light on; to descend: **zur Last —**, to inconvenience; **in Ohnmacht —**, to swoon, faint. **Fällen**, fell'en, vt. to fell, cut. **Fällig**, fell'lich. a. due, payable. **Fallisement**, fallisment', n. bankruptcy. **Falliren**, fallī'ren, vi. to fail, break. **Fallreep**, fall'rǣp, n. ladder-rope. **Falls**, falls, av. in case that. **Fallschirm**, fall'shirm, m. parachute. **Fallstrick**, fall'zhtrick, m snare. **Fallsucht**, -sucht, f. epilepsy, falling-sickness. **Fallsüchtig**, -süchtich, a. epileptic.

10*

Falſch, falsh, *a.* false, counterfeit, wrong, erroneous, mistaken, treacherous, faithless, perfidious; angry, *av.* -ly.

Fälſchen, fĕl'shen, *vt.* to falsify, adulterate, counterfeit, forge. **Fälſcher,** fĕl'sher, *m.* falsifier, forger, counterfeiter. **Falſchheit,** falsh'hăĕt, *f.* falseness, falsehood, falsity, untruth, double-dealing. **Fälſchlich,** felsh'lĭch, *av.* falsely, deceitfully. **Fälſchung,** felsh'ŭng, *f.* falsification, forgery, adulteration, counterfeiting.

Falte, fal'te, *f.* fold, plait; wrinkle. **Falten,** fal'ten, *vt.* to fold, plait; **-los, -los,** *a.* unwrinkled. **Faltig,** falt'ĭch, *a.* folded, plaited, having folds.

Falz, falts, *f.* fold; groove; **-bein,** -băen, *n.* paper-folder. **Falzen,** falt'sen, *vt.* to fold.

Familie, famī'li-e, *f.* family; **-nkrankheit,** -krankhăĕt, *f.* hereditary disease; **-nkreis,** -krăĕs, *m.* family-circle, domestic circle.

Famos, famōs', *a.* glorious, fine.

Fanatiker, fanat'iker, *m.* fanatic. **Fanatiſch,** fanat'ish, *a.* fanatical. **Fanatiſiren,** fanatisī'ren, *vt.* to fanaticize. **Fanatismus,** fanatis'mus, *m.* fanaticism.

Fang, fang, *m.* catch, capture; **-eiſen,** -ĕisen, *n.* iron-trap. **Fangen,** fang'en (fing, gefangen), *vt.* to catch, take.

Fant, fant, *m.* -es, *pl.* -en, youngster. **Fantaſie,** fantasī', *f.* fancy, imagination. **Fantaſiren,** -sī'ren, *vi.* tɩ rave, dote. **Fantaſt,** fantazht', *m.* -en, *pl.* -en, fancy-monger, coxcomb.

Farbe, far'be, *f.* color, hue, dye, paint. **Färbeginzter,** -ginzhter, *m.* dyer's broom. **Färbeholz,** fĕr'behŏlts, *n.* dye-wood. **Färbekunſt,** fĕr'bekŭnzht, *f.* dyeing. **Färben,** fĕr'ben, *vt.* to color, dye, paint. **Farbenkaſten,** far'benkazhten, *n.* box of paints or colors. **Far'benſtein,** -zhtăĕn, *m.* grinding-stone; ink-block. **Färber,** fĕr'ber, *m.* dyer; **-ei,** -ăī', *f.* dye-house; dyeing; **-ſatte,** -flotte, *f.* dyer's bath. **Färbeſtoff,** fĕr'bezhtŏff, *m.* dye-stuff. **Farbig,** far'bĭch, *a.* colored.

Farinzucker, farīn'tsŭcker, *m.* brown sugar, granulated sɩɡar.

Farn, farn, *n.* **-kraut,** -kröyt. *n.* fern.

Farre, far're, *m.* bull, bullock. **Färſe,** fĕr'se, *f.* heifer; young cow.

Faſan, fasăn', *m.* pheasant; **-enhaus,** -hŏus, *n. pl.* -häuſer, pheasant-coop; **-erie, -erī',** *f.* pheasantry.

Faſching, fash'ĭng, *m.* carnival.

Faſcikel, fastsick'el, *n.* bundle or file of writings, acts, public documents.

Faſelei, fäſelăī', *f.* giddiness, silliness, dotage. **Faſelhans,** fä'selhans, *m.* dotard. **Faſeln,** fä'seln, *vi.* to talk foolishly, to trifle. **Faſein,** fä'seln, *vt.* to unravel. **Faſen,** fä'sen, *m.* thread fibre; *vt. i.* to unravel; **-nackt,** *a.* stark naked.

Faſer, fä'ser, *f.* fibre; **-ig,** *a.* fibrous. **Faſern,** fä'sern, *vt.* to feaze, **Faſicht,** fas'ĭcht, *a.* fibrous, thready.

Faß, fass, *n. pl.* Fäſſer, cask, vat, barrel, vessel, tub; **-band,** -bant, *m.* hoop; **-binder,** -bĭnder, *m.* cooper; **-bohrer,** -bōrer, *m.* bung-borer. **Fäßchen,** fĕss'chen, *n.* little barrel. **Faßdaube,** fass'dŏube, *f.* stave.

Faſſen, fas'sen, *vt.* to seize, grasp, to take hold of; to tan; to conceive, understand, comprehend; to hold, contain; *vi.* to bite (of an anchor). **Faßlich,** fass'lich, *a.* intelligible, conceivable; **-keit,** -kăĕt, *f.* conceivableness. **Faſſung,** fass'ŭng, *f.* seizing; lining; tunning; setting; composure, countenance; außer **-** bringen, to disconcert; **-kraft,** -kraft, *f.* capacity, comprehension.

Faſt, fazht, *av.* almost, nearly, well nigh.

Faſten, fazh'ten, *vi.* to fast; *s. n.* fast, fasting; **-ſpeiſe,** -zhpăīse, *f.* Lent-food; **-zeit,** -tsăĕt, *f.* Lent. **Faſtnacht,** fazht'nacht, *f.* Shrove Tuesday. **Faſttag,** fazht'tak, *m.* fast-day.

Fatal, fatăl', *a.* fatal, shocking, odious, calamitous; **-ität, -ität',** *f.* ill-luck, misfortune.

Faul, fŏul, *a.* foul, putrid, rotten; idle, lazy, sluggish; faule **Auſ**-shifts, subterfuge. **Faulbett,** fŏyl'bett, *n.* conch. **Fäule,** fŏy'le, *f.* rottenness. **Faulen,** fŏy'len, *vi.* to rot, putrefy. **Faulenzen,** fŏyl'entsen, *vi.* to be idle, lazy. **Faulenzer,** fŏyl'entser, *m.* lazy fellow, idler, sluggard; **-ei, -ăī',** *f.* laziness, slothfulness, idleness. **Faulheit,** fŏyl'hăĕt, *f.* rottenness, putridity, *an*

Fau   115   **Fei**

neß, idleness, sloth, indolence. **Fäulniß**, föul'nies, *f.* rottenness, putrefaction. **Faulthier**, föul'tīr, *n.* sloth.

Faust, föuzht, *f.* fist; auf eigene —, on one's own account; ins **Fäustchen** lachen, to laugh in one's sleeve; **-dick**, -dick, *a.* as big as a fist; **-handschuh**, -handshų, *m.* mitten; **-kampf**, -kampf, *m.* boxing; **-recht**, -recht, *n.* club-law, sword-law, right of might.

Favorit, favorīt', *m.* -en, favorite.

Februar, februār', *m.* February.

Fechtboden, fecht'bōden, *m.* fencing-school. **Fechten**, fecht'en (focht, gefochten), *vi.* to fight, fence. **Fechter**, fecht'er, *m.* fencer. **Fechtkunst**, fecht'-kųnzht, *f.* fencing. **Fechtmeister**, -maezhter. *m.* fencer, fencing-master. **Fechtplatz**, fecht'plats, *m.* **Fecht's-schule**, -shųle, *f.* fencing-school. **Fechtübung**, -ühbųng, *f.* fencing-exercise.

Feder, fā'der, *f.* feather, plume, quill; pen; spring; **-ball**, -bal, *m.* shuttle-cock; **-bett**, -bett, *n.* feather-bed; **-büchse**, -büxe, *f.* pencase; **-busch**, -bųsh, *m.* plume, tuft of feathers; crest; **-erz**, -ärts, *n.* zinkenite; **-hart**, -hart, **-kräftig**, -kreftich, *a.* elastic; **-harz**, -härts, *n.* elastic gum, gum elastic, India-rubber; **-hut**, -hųt, *m.* hat with plumes, cocked hat; **-kiel**, -kīl, *m.* quill; **-kissen**, -kissen, *n.* feather-cushion; **-leicht**, -leicht, *a.* light as a feather, feathery; **-lesen**, -lāsen, *n.* picking of feathers; nicht viel — machen, to handle roughly; **-los**, -lōs, *a.* featherless, plumeless, unfeathered; **-strich**, -zhtrich, *m.* stroke of the pen; **-schutz**, -zhtųts, *m.* plume; **-vieh**, -fī, *n* poultry.

Fee, fā, *f.* fairy. **Feenhaft**, fān'haft, *a.* fairy-like. **Feerei**, fāerā', *f.* fairy world.

Fegfeuer, fā'gefoier, *n.* purgatory. **Fegen**, fā'gen, *vt.* to sweep, cleanse, clean. **Feger**, fā'ger, *m.* sweeper.

Fehde, fā'de, *f.* feud, quarrel; — bieten, to challenge; **-brief**, -brīf, *m.* challenge, cartel; **-handschuh**, -hantshų, *m.* gauntlet, glove.

Fehl, **Fehler**, fāl'er, *m.* fault, blemish, defect. **Fehlbar**, fāl'bär, *a.* fallible; **-keit**, -kaet, *f.* fallibility. **Fehlbitte**,

fāl'bitte, *f.* useless request; eine — thun, to meet with a refusal. **Fehlen**, fāl'en, *vi.* to fail, miss, err, mistake, misspell, mispronounce; to be absent. **Fehler** = **Fehl**; **-frei**, -frī, *a.* faultless; **-haft**, -haft, *a.* faulty, defective, imperfect, incorrect. **Fehlgeburt**, fal'gebųrt, *f.* abortion. **Fehlgehen**, fāl'gā-en (-ging, -gegangen), *vi.* to miss the way. **Fehlgreifen**, fāl'greifen, *vi.* to mistake. **Fehlgriff**, fal'griff, *m.* mistake. **Fehllos**, fāl'lōs, *a.* faultless. **Fehlreiten**, -reiten (-ritt, -geritten), *vi.* to ride the wrong way. **Fehlschießen**, -shīsen (-shōß, -geschossen), *vi.* to miss one's mark in shooting. **Fehlschlagen**, -shlägen (-shlųg, -geschlagen), *vi.* to miss in striking; to fail, prove a failure; to be disappointed. **Fehlschluß**, fāl'shlųss, *m.* false conclusion, paralogism. **Fehltreten**, -träten (-trat, -getreten), *vi.* to make a false step. **Fehltritt**, -tritt, *m.* false step; fault.

Fehm, fām, *f.* secret criminal court; **-gericht**, -gericht, *n.* vehmic court *or* tribunal; **-richter**, -richter, *m.* judge of a vehmic court; **-schöppen**, -shöppen, *m.* assessor of a vehmic court.

Feier, fēī'er, *f.* cessation of business, vacation, celebration; **-abend**, -äbent, *m.* time of rest, leaving work; — machen, to leave off working; **-kleid**, -klāed, *n. pl.* -er, holiday-garment; **-lich**, -lich, *a.* solemn, *av.* -ly; **-lichkeit**, -lichkāet, *f.* solemnity. **Feiern**, fēī'ern, *vi.* to cease from working; to celebrate. **Feiertag**, -täk, *m.* holiday.

Feifel, fēī'fel, *f.* fives, vives.

Feig, fāek, *a.* soft, weak, cowardly, timid.

Feige, fēī'ge, *f.* fig; box, blow; **-baum**, -baum, *m.* fig-tree; **-blatt**, -blatt, *n. pl.* -blätter, fig-leaf.

Feigheit, fāek'hāet, *f.* cowardice, cowardliness. **Feigherzig**, -hērtsich, *a.* fainthearted, cowardly; **-keit**, -kāet, *f.* faintheartedness. **Feigling**, -ling, *m.* coward.

Feil, fāel, *a.* venal, for sale; **-e Dirne**, prostitute. **Feilbieten**, fēīl'bīeten (-bot, -geboten), *vt.* to offer for sale.

Feile, fēī'le, *f.* file. **Feilen**, fēīl'en, *vi.* to file, finish off; **-hauer**, -hāu-er,

Fei 116 **Fer**

m. file-cutter. **Feil'icht,** -icht, *n.* filings.

Feilschen, fīel'shen, *vt.* to offer *or* expose for sale; to bargain, haggle, beat down.

Feilspäne, fēll'zhpäne, *s. pl.* filings, file-dust.

Fein, fīen, *a.* fine, delicate, refined, polite, elegant; artful; genteel; *av.* -ly.

Feind, fīent, *a.* hostile, inimical; *m.* enemy, foe; opponent, adversary; der böse —, fiend, arch-fiend, devil; *in, f.* (female) enemy. **Feindlich,** fīent'lich, *a.* hostile, inimical; *s*keit, -kāet, *f.* hostility, ill-will. **Feind's schaft,** -shaft, *f.* enmity, hatred, ill-will; *slich,* -lich, *a.* inimical, hostile. **Feindselig,** -sälich, *a.* hostile; *s*keit, -kāet, *f.* hostility.

Feinheit, fīen'hāet, *f.* fineness, delicacy, niceness, tenderness, nicety, finesse.

Feist, fāezht, *a.* fat, fleshy. **Feiste, Feistigkeit,** fāezht'ichkāet, *f.* fatness. **Feisten,** fāezht'en, *vt.* to fatten.

Feld, fēlt, *n. pl.* -er, field, plain; pannel, square, ground; dominion, province, department; in weitem —, far from being settled; zu — ziehen, to take the field; *sarbeit,* -arbāet, *f.* field-labor, field-work; *sarzt,* -ārtst, *m.* army physician; *sbau,* -bōu, *m.* agriculture; *sbett,* -bett, *n.* folding-bed; *sbinde,* -binde, *f.* sash, scarf; *schirurg,* -kirurk, *m.* army surgeon; *sflasche,* -flashe, *f.* canteen; *sfrucht,* -frucht, *f.* produce of the fields; *sgeschrei,* -geshrāe, *n.* war-cry, watchword; *shauptmann,* -hāuptmann, *sherr,* -herr, *m.* *s*en, commander-in-chief, general, captain; *sjäger,* -yāger, *m.* gamekeeper; sharpshooter; *skessel,* -kessel, *m.* camp-kettle; *skoch,* -kōch, *m.* army-cook; *skümmel,* -kümmel, *m.* caraway; *slager,* -lāger, *n.* camp; *smarschall,* -marshal, *m.* field-marshal; *smesser,* -messer, *m.* surveyor, land-surveyor; *smessung,* -ung, *smessungskunst,* -kunzht, *f.* surveying; *smusik,* -musick, *f.* military music; *sposten,* -pozhten, *m.* outpost of an army; *sprediger,* prādicher, *m.* chaplain (to a regiment); *sschaden,* -shāden, *m.* damage done to fields; *sschütze,* -shütze,

m. field-guard; *spath,* -zhpät, *m.* feldspar; *sstück,* -zht.ck, *n.* field-piece; landscape; *sstuhl,* -zhtyl, *m.* camp-stool, folding-stool; *swache,* -vache, *f.* outpost, picket; *swacht meister,* -vachtmāezhter, *m.* major of cavalry; *swirtschaft,* -virtshaft, *f.* husbandry, agriculture; *szeichen,* -tsāechen, *n.* military sign; *szug,* -tsyk, *m.* campaign.

Felge, fēll'ge, *f.* felly; jaunt; *shauer,* -hāuer, *m.* wheel-wright. **Felgen,** fēll'gen, *vt.* to provide with fellies. **Felgen,** fēll'gen, *vt.* to break up, fallow.

Fell, fēll, *n.* skin, hide, fur; *seisen,* -āisen, *n.* knapsack, portmanteau, wallet; *shändler,* -hendler, *m.* furrier, fell-monger, skinner.

Fels, Felsen, fēl'sen, *m.* rock. **Fels abhang,** fels'aphang, *m.* precipice, rocky steep. **Felsenfest,** fēl'senfezht, *a.* firm as a rock, unshaken. **Fels'engrund,** -grunt, *m.* foundation of rocks. **Fels'enklippe,** -klippe, *f.* rocky cliff. **Fels'enkluft,** -kluft, *f.* cleft in a rock. **Fels'enschlucht,** -shlycht, *f.* rocky gorge. **Felsenspitze,** -zhpitze, *f.* peak, top of a rock. **Fels'enstück,** -zhtück, *n.* fragment of rock. **Fels'enwand,** -vant, *f.* precipitous rock; precipice. **Felsig,** fel'sich. **Felsicht,** fel'sicht, *a.* rocky.

Fenchel, fen'chel, *m.* fennel.

Fenster, fenzh'tor, *n.* window; opening; *sblei,* -blāi, *n.* glazier's lead; *sbogen,* -bōgen, *m.* bow-window; *sflügel,* -flügel, *m.* sash; *sgitter,* -gitter, *n.* lattice, window-grate; *sgardine,* -gardī'ne, *f.* window-curtain; *sglas,* -glās, *n.* window-glass, table-glass; *skissen,* -kissen, *n.* window-cushion; *skitt,* -kitt, *m.* putty; *sladen,* -lāden. *m.* window-shutter; *srahmen,* -rāmen, *m.* window-frame; *sscheibe,* -shāibe, *f.* window-pane; *sschirm,* -shirm, *m.* window-shade, blind.

Ferien, fā'ri-en, *s. pl.* vacation, holidays.

Ferkel, fēr'kel, *n.* pig, shote. **Ferkeln,** fēr'keln, *vi.* to farrow, to pig.

Fernambuk, fērn'ambyk, *n.* log-wood.

Fern, fērn, **ferne,** *av. a.* far, distant, remote; von —, afar, from afar, at a distance: das sei —, far be it; — bleiben, sich — halten, to keep out of reach; — **von ſich halten**, to keep at a distance; — **ſtehen einer Sache**, to be a stranger to.

Fernh, fērnt, *av.* last year; **-ig**, *a.* of last year.

Ferne, fērn'e, *f.* remoteness, farness, distance. **Ferner**, fērn'er, *av.* farther; moreover; further, ulterior; **-hin**, -hīn, *av.* for the future, henceforward. **Fernglas**, fērn'glās, **Fernrohr**, fērn'rōr, *n.* spy-glass, spying-glass, telescope. **Fernſcheinig**, -shēnich *a.* perspective. **Fernſicht**, fērn'sicht, *f.* perspective; **-ig**, *a.* far-sighted.

Ferſe, fär'se, *f.* heel; **-ngeld**, -gēlt, *n.* — **geben**, to take to one's heels, to skedaddle

Fertig, fer'tich, *a.* ready, dexterous, prepared; — **werden mit**, to finish, to get the better of. **Fertigen**, fer'tichen, *vt.* to make, fabricate, manufacture: to dispatch, expedite. **Fertigkeit**, fer'tichkāet, *f.* readiness, promptness, facility, dexterity, practice. **Fertigung**, -ung, *f.* making, forming, performing.

Feſſel, fes'sel, *f.* fetter, chain, shackle. **Feſſeln**, fes'seln, *vt.* to fetter, chain, shackle.

Feſt, fezht. *a.* fast, strong, solid, firm; stout, steady: tight, sure; — **machen**, to fix, fasten, fortify.

Feſt, fēzht, *a.* feast, festival; **-abend**, -ābent, *m.* evening before a feast.

Feſte, fezht'te, *f.* stronghold, fortress, firmament. **Feſtigkeit**, -kāet, *f.* fastness, firmness, solidity, compactness.

Feſtkleid, fēzht'klāet, *n. pl.* **-er**, festive robe, holiday-dress. **Feſtlich**, fezht'lich, *a.* festive, solemn, *av.* -ly.

Feſtland, fezht'lant, *n.* continent. **Feſtſetzen**, -setsen, *vt.* to appoint, settle, fix.

Feſttag, fēzht'tāk, *m.* feast-day, holiday, festival.

Feſtung, fezht'ung, *f.* fortress; **-bau**, -bŏu, *m.* fortification; **-ſtrafe**, -zhtrāſe, *f.* confinement in a fortress.

Fett, fett, *a.* fat, greasy; rich, fertile; *s. n.* fat, grease: **-fleck**, -flēck, *m.* grease-spot. **Fettich**, **Fettig**, fet'tich *a.* fat, greasy: **-keit**, -kāet, *f.* fatness, greasiness; richness.

Fetchen, fets'chen, *n.* bit. **Fetzen**, fets'-en. *m.* piece, cut, scrap; *vt.* to shred, slash, scratch, tatter.

Feucht, fēücht, *a.* moist, damp, humid. **Feuchten**, fēücht'en, *vt.* to wet, moisten, damp(en). **Feuchtigkeit**, -kāet, *f.* moistness, moisture, humidity, dampness.

Feuer, fēü'er, *n.* fire, flame; ardor, spirit, sprightliness, liveliness, mettle, heat; **-ball**, -bal, *m.* fire-ball; **-bock**, -bock, *m.* andiron, dog; **-bohne**, -bōne, *f.* scarlet-bean; **-brand**, -brant, *m.* fire-brand; **-eifer**, -ēifer, *m.* ardor, fervor, ardent zeal; **-eimer**, -ēmer, *m.* fire-bucket; **-eſſe**, -esse, *f.* chimney forge; **-fangend**, -fangent, *a.* inflammable, apt to take fire; **-farben**, -farben, *a.* fire or flame-colored; **-feſt**, -fezht, *a.* fire-proof; **-flamme**, -flamme, *f.* fiery flame; **-funken**, -fynken, *m.* spark of fire; **-gitter**, -gitter, *n.* fender; **-geiſt**, -gāezht, *m.* aspiring genius; **-geſchrei**, -geshrāē, *n.* alarm of fire, cry of fire: **-gewehr**, -gevār, *n.* musket; *pl.* fire-arms: **-glocke**, -glocke, *f.* alarm-bell, fire-bell; **-haken**, -hāken, *m.* fire-hook, poker; **-herb**, -hārt, *m.* hearth, fire-place; **-ig**, (**feurig**,) fēü'rich, *a.* fiery, burning, ardent, fervent. hot, brisk, generous, passionate: flashing, glowing, sparkling; **-kugel**, -kūgel, *f.* red-hot shot; bomb; **-kunſt**, -kynzht, *f.* pyrotechnics; **-lärm**, -lērm, *m.* alarm of fire; **-leiter**, -lāeter, *f.* fire-ladder; **-mal**, māl, *n.* burn, mole; **-mann**, -mann, *pl.* **-leute**, fireman; **-mauer**, -mŏu-er, *f.* chimney, shaft of a chimney; fire-proof wall; **-meſſer**, -mēsser, *m.* pyrometer: **-n**, (**feuern**,) fēü'ern, *vt.* to fire, burn; *vi.* to burn, sparkle, shine: **-ofen**, -ōfen, *m.* stove, oven; **-pfanne**, -pfanne, *f.* fire-pan, brazier; **-probe**, -prōbe, *f.* fire-ordeal; **-rad**, -rād, *n. pl.* **-räter**, fire-wheel; **-rohr**, -rōr, *n.* gun; *pl.* fire-arms; **-roth**, -rōt, *a.* red as fire, flame-colored: **-ſäule**, -sēü'le, *f.* fiery pillar; **-brunſt**, -brynzht, *f.* fire, conflagration: **-ſchaufel**, -shŏufel, *f.* fire-shovel: **-ſchirm**, -shirm, *m.* fire-screen; **-ſchwaden**, -shvāden. *m.* fire-damp, (Min.); **-ſchwamm**, -shvamm. *m.* tinder; **-ſetzen**, -setsen, *n.* working mines by fire; **-sgefahr**, -gefār, *f.* danger of fire; **-snoth**,

-**nôt,** *f.* distress from fire; conflagration; **-zeicen,** -zhpēi-ent. *a.* volcanic; **-spritze,** -zhpritse, *f.* fire-engine; **-stahl,** -zhtāl, *n.* steel (for striking fire); **-stätte,** -zhtette, *f.* burned-out place; fireplace, hearth; house; **-stein,** -zhtaen, *m.* flint; **-versicherung,** -fērsicherung, *f.* fire insurance; **-versicherungsanstalt,** -anzhtalt, *f.* insurance office; **-ung,** (**Feuerung**), feü'erung, *f.* firing, fuel, fire-wood; **-wache,** -vache, *f.* firewatch; **-wand,** -vant, *f.* back of a hearth; **-warte,** -varte, *f.* beacon; **-werk,** -vērk, *n.* fire-works; **-werfer,** -vērker, *m.* pyrotechnic; **-werferei,** -vērkārēī, *f.* pyrotechnics; **-zange,** -tsang-e, *f.* fire-tongs; **-zeichen,** -tsīechen, *n* fire-signal; **-zeug,** -tseūk, *n.* tinder-box. **Feurig,** feü'-rich, *f.* **Feuerig.**

Fiaker, fī'acker, *m.* hack, hackney-coach; cabman.

Fibel, fī'bel, *f.* horn-book, primer, spelling-book.

Fiber, fī'ber, *f.* fibre.

Fichte, fich'te, *f.* pine, pine-tree; **-napfel,** -apfel, *m.* pine-cone; **-harz,** -härts, *n.* resin, turpentine; **-holz,** -holts, *n.* pine-wood; white-deal; **-wald,** -valt, *m. pl.* -wälter, pine-forest; **-wäldchen,** -veltchen, *n.* pine-grove.

Ficke, fick'e, *f.* pocket, fob.

Ficken, fick'en, *vi.* to rub backwards and forwards; to whip, flog. **Fickfacken,** fick'facken, *vi.* to bustle about, flirt, intrigue. **Fickfacker,** *m.* intriguer.

Fideicommiß, fīde-ikommiss', *n.* entail.
Fidel, fīdāl', *a.* jolly, merry.
Fidibus, fī'dibus, *m.* lighter.
Fieber, fī'ber, *n.* fever; **-iziges —,** inflammatory fever; **kaltes —,** ague; **-anfall,** -än'fall, *m.* fit, paroxysm of fever; **-angst,** -ankzht, paroxysm of fear; **-artig,** -ärtich, *a.* **-haft,** -haft. **-isch,** -ish, *a.* feverish, aguish, feverous; **-frost,** -frozht, *m.* chill; **-hitze,** -hitse, *f.* fever-heat; **-krank,** -krank, *a.* sick of a fever; *s. m.* fever-patient; **-rinde,** -rinde, *f.* bark, Peruvian bark; **-schauer,** -shöy'er, *m.* ague-fit, chill; **-tag,** -tāk, *m.* day on which a fever comes on.

Fiedel, fī'del, *f.* fiddle; **-bogen,** -bō-gen, *n.* fiddle-stick. **Fiedeler,** fī'-

deler, *m.* fiddler. **Fiedeln,** fī'deln, *vi.* to fiddle.

Figur, figur', *f.* figure. **Figürlich** figühr'lich, *a.* figurative, *av.* -ly.

Filialgeschäft, fīliāl'geshelt. *n.* branch establishment. **Filial kirche,** -kirche. *f.* out-parish.

Filtriren, filtrī'ren, *vi.* to filter, strain **Filtrirpapier,** -papīr, *n.* filtering paper. **Filtrirsack,** -sack, *m.* filtering-bag. **Filtrirstein,** -zhtaēn, *m.* filtering-stone, strainer. **Filtrirtrichter,** -trichter, *m.* filtering-funnel.

Filz, filts, *m.* felt; miser, niggard; **-en,** fil'tsen, *vt.* to felt; **-hut,** -hut, *m.* felt-hat, felt; **-ig,** fil'tsich, **-icht,** -icht, *a.* of felt, like felt, downy; sordid, stingy, niggardly; **-keit,** -kāet, *f.* niggardliness, stinginess. **Filzschuh,** filts'shu, *m.* felt-shoe. **Filzsohle,** -sōle, *f.* felt *or* hair-sole.

Finanzcollegium, finants'kollāgium, *n.* exchequer, treasury-office. **Finanzen,** finan'tsen. *s. pl.* finances. **Finanzmann,** -mann, *m.* financier. **Finanzrath,** -rāt, *m.* counselor of the exchequer. **Finanzwesen,** -vāsen, *n.* finances.

Findelhaus, fin'delhōus, *n. pl.* **-häuser,** foundling hospital **Findelkind,** -kint, **Findling,** fint'ling. *m.* foundling. **Finden,** fin'den (fand, gefunden), *vt.* to find; to come to, to light on, meet with: **Statt —,** to take place; **sich —,** *ie.* to submit to, to bear, yield. **Finder,** fin'der, *m.* finder.

Finger, fing'er, *m.* finger; **-glied,** -glīt, *n. pl.* -er, joint of the finger; **-hut,** -hut, *m.* thimble; **-probe,** -prō-be, *f.* rule of the thumb; **-ring,** -ring, *m.* ring; **-sing,** -ling, *m.* stall; brace, gudgeon. **Fingern,** fing'ern, *vt.* to finger. handle. touch. **Fingersprache,** -ats, *m.* fingering. **Fingerzeig,** -tsāēk, *m.* hint.

Fingiren, fingī'ren, *vt.* to feign. simulate. **Fingirt,** fingī't', *a.* feigned, simulated, fictitious.

Fink, fink, *m.* finch.

Finne, fin'ne, *f.* pointed extremity, summit, hill; fin; pin, peg; pimple, pustule; measle (of hogs). **Finnig,** finn'ich. *a.* pimpled; measled (of hogs).

Finster, fĭn′zhter, *a.* dark, obscure, gloomy, sour; **-ling,** -lĭng, *m.* obscurant; **-niß,** -nĭss, *f.* darkness, obscurity.
Finte, fĭn′tẹ, *f.* feint, fib, diversion.
Fips, fĭps, *m.* fillip.
Firlefanz, fĭr′lẹfants, *m.* foolery, nonsense; **-er,** *m.* trifler, buffoon.
Firma, fĭr′mä, *f.* firm.
Firmament, fĭrmäment′, *n.* firmament.
Firmeln, fĭr′meln, *vt.* to confirm.
Firmelung, fĭr′melụng, *f.* confirmation.
Firniß, fĭr′nĭss, *m.* varnish. **Firnissen,** fĭr′nĭssen, *vt.* to varnish.
First, fĭr′zhtẹ, *f.* top; roof (Min.); **-bau,** -bŏụ, *m.* working of ore in ascending shafts.
Fis, fĭss. *n.* F sharp.
Fiscal, fĭskäl′, *m.* attorney, solicitor, treasurer.
Fisch, fĭsh, *m.* fish: **-aar,** -är, **-adler,** -ätler, *m.* osprey, sea-eagle; **-angel,** -ang-el, *f.* fishing-hook; **-artig,** -ärtĭch, *a.* **-ähnlich,** -änlĭch. *a.* fish-like; **-band,** -bänt, *n.* butt, butt-hinge; **-bein,** -bẹ̈n, *n.* whale-bone; **-brut,** -brụt, *f.* fry. **Fischen,** fĭsh′en, *vi.* to catch fish, to fish. **Fischer,** *m.* fisher, fisherman; **-in,** *f.* a fisher's wife; **-garn,** -gärn, **-netz,** -nets, *n.* fishing-net; **-stechen,** -zhtĕchen. *n.* mock sea-fight (of fishermen). **Fischfang,** -fang. *m.* fishing, catching fish; **-gräte,** fĭsh′-grätẹ, *f.* fish-bone; **-hälter,** -helter, *m.* fish-pond; **-handel,** -handel. *m.* fish-trade; **-haut,** -hŏụt, *f.* fish-skin: **-kasten,** -kazhten. cauf. well; **-kelle,** -kellẹ. *f.* trowel; **-kieme,** -kĭ′mẹ, *f.* gill. **fisch-ear; -laich,** -lĭẹ̈ch, *m.* spawn; **-ohr,** **-öhr,** *n.* **-es,** *pl.* **-en,** gill; **-otter,** -ötter, otter; **-reich,** -rẹ̈ch, *a.* abounding in fish; **-schuppe,** -shụppẹ. *f.* scale; **-stachel,** -zhtächel, *f.* fish-gig; **-tag,** -täk, *m.* fish-day, fast-day; **-teich,** -tẹ̈ch, *m.* fish-pond; **-thran,** -trän, *m.* fish-oil, train-oil; **-weib,** -vẹ̈p. *n.* fish-woman; **-zug,** fĭsh′-tsụk, *m.* draught .f fishes.
Fiscus, fĭss′kụs, *m.* exchequer, fisc; treasury.
Fispern, fĭzh′pern. *vi.* to whisper.
Fistel, fĭzh′tel, *f.* falsetto, false voice; fistula.
Fittich, fĭt′tĭch, *m.* wing.

Fitzen, fĭt′sen, *vt.* to bind *or* tie into skeins; to entangle.
Fix, fĭx, *a.* fixed, firm, stated; **-er Gehalt,** fixed salary. **Fixiren,** fĭksĭ′ren, *vt.* to fix, settle, appoint. **Fixstern,** fĭx′zhtèrn, *m.* fixed star.
Flach, flăch, *a.* flat, level, shallow, plane. **Fläche,** flĕch′ẹ, *f.* plain, plane, flat, surface, area; **-nfuß,** -fụss, *m.* square foot; **-ninhalt,** -nĭnhalt, *m.* square content; **-nmaß,** -mäss, *n.* square measure; **-nmeßkunst,** **-nmeßkunzht,** *f.* planimetry. **Flachheit,** flăch′hẹ̈t, *f.* flatness, shallowness, superficiality.
Flachs, flax, *m.* flax; **-bau,** -bŏụ, *m.* cultivation of flax: **-breche,** -brĕchẹ, *f.* (flax) brake. **Flächsen,** flĕx′en, *a.* flaxen, linen. **Flachshaar,** -här, *n.* flaxen hair; **-riffel,** -rĭffel, *f.* ripple: **-samen,** -sämen, *m.* flaxseed, linseed.
Flackern, flăck′ern, *vi.* flicker, flare.
Fladen, flä′den, *m.* pancake, flatcake.
Flagge, flag′gẹ. *f.* flag, colors. **Flaggen,** *vi.* to unfold a flag, signal with a flag.
Flamingo, flaming′gō, *m.* flamingo.
Flamme, flam′mẹ, *f.* flame, blaze. **Flammen,** flam′men, *vi.* to flame, blaze; *vt.* to singe. **Flammicht,** **Flammig,** flam′mĭch, *a.* flaming, blazing.
Flanell, flanĕll′, *m.* flannel.
Flanke, flang′kẹ. *f.* flank, side.
Fläschchen, flĕsh′chen, *n.* small bottle, vial. **Flasche,** flash′ẹ. *f.* bottle, flagon, flask; **-nbier,** -bĭr, *n.* bottled beer; **-nfutter,** -fụtter, *n.* bottle-case; **-nkorb,** -korp, *m.* bottle-basket; **-nzug,** -tsụk, *m.* pulley, tackle. **Flaschner,** flash′ner, *m.* tinman, tinner.
Flatterhaft, flat′terhaft. *a.* fickle, changeable, flighty; **-igkeit,** -kẹ̈t, *f.* fickleness, inconstancy. **Flattern,** flat′tern, *vi.* to flutter, flit, flirt, flare.
Flau, flŏụ. *a.* weak, dull, dead, flat; **-heit,** -hẹ̈t, *f.* weakness, latness, dullness.
Flaum, flŏụm, *m.* down; **-feder,** -fäder, *f.* down. **Flaumig, Flaumicht** *a.* downy.
Flause, flŏụ′sẹ, *f.* humbug, shift, fib.

Flechse, flĕx'e, *f.* sinew, tendon. **Flechsig**, flĕx'ich, *a.* tendinous.
Flechte, flĕch'te, *f.* plait, braid, tress; lichen (bot.), tetters; herpes (med.).
Flechten, flĕch'en (flocht, geflochten), *vt.* to plait, braid, twist. **Flechtwerk**, flĕcht'verk, *n.* wicker-work, plaiting.
Fleck, flĕck, *m.* spot; patch; piece; stain; tripe. **Flecken**, flĕck'en, *m.* village; stain, spot: *vt.* to spot, stain: *vi.* to be stained, soiled. **Fleckfieber**, flĕck'fiber, *n.* petechial fever. **Fleckig**, flĕck'ich, *a.* spotted, stained. **Fleckkugel**, -kŭgel, **Fleck'sseife**, -säife, *f.* scouring-ball.
Fledermaus, flä'dermŏys, *f.* bat. **Flederwisch**, -vish, *m.* duster.
Flegel, flä'gel. *m.* flail; clown, boor; -ei, -ēī', *f.* rudeness; -haft, -haft, *a.* clownish, rude.
Flehen, flä'en, *vi.* to implore, entreat, beseech: *s. n.* entreaty, supplication. **Flehentlich**, -lich, *a.* imploring, *av.* -ly.
Fleisch, flăesh, *n.* flesh; meat; living being; pulp (of fruit): **-bank**, -bank, *f.* shamble, butcher's stall; **-brühe**, -brü-e, *f.* broth, beef-tea; **-er**, -er, *m.* butcher; **-farbe**, -farbe, *f.* fleshcolor, carnation; **-farbig**, -farbich, *a.* flesh-colored; **-faser**, -fäser, *f.* (muscular) fibre; **-fressend**, -fressent, *a.* carnivorous; **-hacker**, -hacker, *m.* butcher; **-ig**, flăesh'ich, *a.* fleshy; pulpous; **-kammer**, -kammer, *f.* larder; **-kloß**, -klōs, *m.* meat-ball; **-lich**, -lich, *a.* fleshy; carnal, *av.* -ly; **-keit**, -kăet, *f.* fleshiness, carnal-mindedness; **-los**, -lōs, *a.* fleshless; **-markt**, -markt, *m.* meat-market; **-messer**, -messer, *n.* butcher's knife; **-pastete**, -pazhtäte, *f.* meat-pie; **-schnitte**, -shnitte, *f.* steak, cutlet; **-speise**, -shpĕī-e, *f.* animal food, meat; **-suppe**, -suppe, *f.* broth; **-wunde**, -vunde, *f.* flesh-wound.
Fleiß, flĕīss, *m.* industry, diligence, application: mit —, on purpose; diligently. **Fleißig**, flĕī-s'ich, *a.* diligent, industrious, careful, *av.* -ly.
Flennen, flĕn'nen, *vi.* to cry, weep.
Fletschen, flĕt'shen. *vt.* to flatten; die Zähne —, to show one's teeth.
Flickarbeit, flick'arbăet, *f.* patchwork. **Flicken**, flick'en, *vt.* to patch, mend, repair; darn. **Flicker**, flick'er, *m.* repairer, patcher, mender; **-ei**, -ĕī', **Flickwerk**, -vĕrk, *n.* patchwork, botchery.
Flieder, flī'der. *m.* **-strauch**, -zhtrŏych, *m. pl.* -sträucher, elder (bot.).
Fliege, flī'ge, *f.* fly; spanische —, cantharides. **Fliegen**, flī'gen (flog, geflogen), *vi.* to fly, flit, flutter; **-bred**, -dreck, *m.* fly-speck; **-klappe**, -klappe, *f.* fly-flap; **-schrank**, -shrank, *m.* safe, pantry; **-wedel**, -vădel. *m.* flybrush.
Fliehen, flī'en (floh, geflohen), *vi.* to flee, fly, hasten; to pass away; *vt.* to flee, shun, avoid; **-der**, -der, *m.* fugitive.
Flies, flīs, *n.* fleece.
Fließen, flī'sen (floß, geflossen), *vi.* to flow, run, pass away; to blot; **-d**, flīs'ent, *a.* flowing, fluent, **Fließpapier**, -papīr, *n.* blotting-paper.
Fliete, flī'te, *f.* lancet.
Flimmer, flim'mer, *m.* glimmer, glitter. **Flimmern**, flim'mern, *vi.* to glimmer, glisten.
Flink, flink, *a.* brisk, quick. lively, nimble; **-heit**, -hăet, *f.* briskness, activity.
Flinkern, flink'ern, *vi.* to glitter.
Flinte, flin'te, *f.* gun, musket; **-nkolben**, -kolben, *m.* butt of a gun; **-nkugel**, -kŭgel, *f.* musket-ball; **-nlauf**, -lăuf, *m.* gun-barrel; **-nschaft**, -shaft, *m.* gun-stock; **-nschuß**, -shyss, *m.* gun-shot.
Flistern, flizht'ern, *vi.* to whisper, buzz.
Flitter, flit'ter, *m.* spangle, glitter, gewgaw; **-nglanz**, -glants, *m.* (empl.) glitter; **-ngold**, -golt. *n.* tinsel; **-njahr**, -yăr, *n.* first year after marriage; **-nkram**, -kram, *m.* bawble; **-nmonat**, -mōnat, *m.* **-nwochen**, -vŏchen, *f. pl.* honey-moon. **Flittern**, flit'tern, *vi.* to glitter; **-werk**, -vĕrk, *n.* finery, bawbles.
Flocke, flock'e, *f.* lock, flake. **Flockicht**, **Flockig**, flock'ich, *a.* flaky. **Flockseide**, flock'sĕīde, *f.* flock-silk. **Flockwolle**, flock'volle, *f.* flockwool.
Floh, flō, *m.* flea; **-biß**, -biss, *m.* fleabite.
Flor, flōr, *m.* crape, gauze, veil.
Flor, flōr, *m.* bloom, flower, prosperity.
Florbinde, flōr'binde, *f.* crape-band

-tuch, -tuch, n. gauze; -weber, -väber, m. gauze-weaver.

Floskel, flos'kel, f. oratorical ornament.

Floß, flos, m. raft, float. Flöße, flöh'-se, f. raft. Flosse, flos'se, f. fin. Flößen, flöh'sen, vt. to float (wood); to rinse; to pour in, inspire. Floßfeder, -fäder, f. fin.

Flöte, flöh'te, f. flute. Flöten, flöh'ten, vi. to play on the flute; -bläser, -spieler, -zpfler, flute-player; -register, -register, n. -zug, -tsuk, m. flute-stop (in organs).

Flötzen, flöh'ten, vi. to flow, float or drive away; — gehen, to be lost.

Flott, flott, a. floating, afloat; merry, glorious, jolly. Flotte, flot'te, f. fleet, navy.

Flöß, flöhts, n. horizontal layer; bed, stratum.

Fluch, fluch, m. curse, malediction, oath. Fluchen, fluch'en, vt. i. to curse, swear. Flucher, fluch'er, m. curser, swearer.

Flucht, flucht, f. flight, escape; bee-line. Flüchten, flüch'ten, vt. to save, secure; to flee. Flüchtig, flüch'tich, a. fugitive, fleeing, retreating; volatile; flighty; fleeting; -keit, -kaet, f. quickness; fleetingness. Flüchtling, flücht'ling, m. fugitive, refugee.

Flug, fluk, m. flight; swarm, flock. Flügel, flüh'gel, m. wing; grand-piano; leaf (of a door); -mann, -mann, m. pl. -männer, file-leader; -en, flüh'gein, vt. to wing; hasten; -schlag, -shlak, m. clap, stroke (of the wings); -thor, -tör, n. folding gate; -thür, f. -tühr, folding-door. Flügge, flüg'ge, a. fledged.

Flugs, fluks, av. immediately, straightway, quickly. Flugschrift, fluk'-shrift, f. pamphlet.

Flunkern, flunk'kern, vi. to glitter; to boast.

Flur, flur, f. field, grounds, plain; porch, entry; -schütz, -shüts, m. field-guard.

Fluß, fluss, m. flow, run; river, stream; fusion; rheumatism; -artig, -ärtig, a. rheumatic; like a river; -bad, -bäd, n. river-bath; -bett, -bett, n. bed of a river; -gebiet, -gebīt, n. basin (of a river). Flüssig, flüs'sich, a. fluid, liquid; infusion, melted; -keit, -kāēt, f. fluidity; fluid, liquid. Flußkalk, -kalk, m. -mittel, -mittel, n. flux; -pferd, -pfārt, m. hippopotamus; -schiffahrt, -shiffart, f. river-navigation; -spath, -zhpāt, m. fluoride of calcium; -spathsäure, -eēūre, f. fluoric acid; -wasser, -vasser, n. river-water.

Flüstern, flüsh'tern, vi. to whisper.

Fluth, flyt, f. flood, sea, wave; tide; flow, gush. Fluten, flyt'en, vi. to flow, swell; to stream.

Focke, fock'e, f. fore-sail (on the fore-yard). Fockrahe, fock'rä-e, f. fore-yard.

Föderal, föderäl', a. federal.

Fodern, fō'dern, vt. to demand, f. Fordern.

Fohlen, fō'len, n. foal; vi. to foal.

Föhn, fühn, m. (furious) south-wind.

Föhre, föh're, f. fire, pine.

Folge, fol'ge, f. succession, sequence, series; sequel; consequence; aftertime; conclusion; -leisten, -lāězhten, vi. to obey. Folgen, folg'en, vi. to follow, ensue, succeed; to obey; to pursue; -d, a. following. Folgerichtig, fol'gerichtich, a. consistent, consequent. Folgern, fol'gern, vt. to deduce, conclude. Folgerung, -ung, f. conclusion, deduction, inference. Folgesatz, -sats, m. conclusion, consequent; -widrig, -vīdrich, a. inconsistent; -widrigkeit, -kāēt, f. inconsistency; -zeit, -tsāīt, f. future time. Folglich, folk'lich, conj. consequently, then. Folgsam, folk'sam, a. obedient, docile; -keit, -kāēt, f, docility, obedience.

Foliant, foliant', n. -en, folio (volume).

Folter, fol'ter, f. torture, rack; -bank, -bank, f. rack; -kammer, -kammer, f. torture-chamber. Folterer, fol'terer, m. torturer. Foltern, fol'tern, vt. to torture, rack, torment.

Fond, fōn(g), m. fund, capital; public funds.

Fontaine, fontä'ne, f. fountain.

Foppen, fop'pen, vt. to fool, jeer, mystify. Fopper, fop'per, m. railer, jeerer.

Förderer, för'derer, m. furtherer, patron. Förderlich, för'derlich, a. conducible, serviceable.

Fordern, for'dern, vt. to summon,

challenge; demand, ask; — **laffen**, to send for.
Förbern, för'dern, *vt.* to forward, bring forth; to hasten, advance; to promote, dispatch; **zu Tage —**, to bring to light. **Förberung**, för'der‑ung, *f.* promotion, furtherance.
Forberung, fer'derung, *f.* demand, claim, summons, challenge.
Forelle, forel'le, *f.* trout.
Form, form, *f.* form, shape, figure; mould; block; model. **Formalien**, formä'li‑en, *s. pl.* **Formalität**, for‑malität', *f.* formality. **Format**, for‑mät', *n.* size. **Formel**, form'el, *f.* formula. **Form'en**, ‑en, *vt.* to form, shape, mould. **Formiren**, formi'‑ren, *vt. r.* to form. **Formlich**, förm'lich, *a.* formal, ceremonious; real; **‑feit**, ‑käet, *f.* formality. **Form'los**, ‑lös, *a.* formless, shapeless. **Formu‑lar**, formulär', *n.* formulary, blank, form.
Forschbegier de), forsh'begir, *f.* spirit of inquiry, inquisitiveness. **Forsch'‑begierig**, ‑ich, *a.* inquisitive. **For‑schen**, for'shen, *vi.* to inquire, search, seek. **Forsch'er**, ‑er, *m.* searcher, inquirer. **Forsch'ung**, ‑ung, *f.* search, inquiry, investigation.
Forst, forzht, *m.* forest. **Förster**, förzh'ter, *m.* forester; **‑ei**, ‑ei', *f.* house *or* office of a forester.
Fort, fort. *av.* away, on; forth, for‑ward, off; — **und —**, continually; **‑an**, ‑än, *av.* henceforth; **‑arbeiten**, ‑arbäeten, *vi.* to work on; **‑bauen**, ‑böу‑en, *vt.* to build on; **‑begeben**, ‑begäben (‑gab, ‑begeben), *vr.* to go off, leave; **‑bewegen**, ‑bevä'gen, *vt. r.* to move on; **‑bringen**, ‑bring‑en (‑brachte, ‑gebracht), *vt.* to bring off; advance; *vr.* to get one's livelihood; **‑bauern**, ‑dóуern, *f.* continuance; **‑bau‑ern**, ‑dóуern, *vi.* to continue, last, endure; **‑eilen**, ‑ëilen, *vi.* to hurry away; **‑erben**, ‑erben, *vr.* to descend (by inheritance); **‑fahren**, ‑fären (‑fuhr, ‑gefahren), *vi.* to continue; to drive off, depart; *vt.* to carry away; **‑fliegen**, ‑flïgen (‑flog, ‑geflo‑gen), *vi.* to fly away: to continue flying; **‑fließen**, ‑flïssen (‑floß, ‑ge‑flossen), *vi.* to flow on: to continue flowing; **‑führen**, ‑tühren, *vt.* to carry away, tear away; to carry on, continue; **‑gang**, ‑gang, *m.* continu‑ation; progress, advance; depar‑ture; **‑gehen**, ‑gä'en (‑ging, ‑gegan‑gen), *vi.* to go away, depart; to pro‑ceed, go on; **‑helfen**, ‑hèlfen (‑half, ‑geholfen), *vt.* to help on, assist; **sich —**, to get along; **‑hin**, fort'hïn *av.* henceforth; **‑jagen**, ‑yägen, *vt.* to chase away, drive away, turn off; to gallop off; **‑klingen**, ‑klingen (‑flang, ‑geflungen), *vi.* to continue sounding; **‑kommen**, ‑kommen (‑fam, ‑gekommen), *vi.* to get away; to thrive, prosper; **‑können**, ‑kón‑nen (‑konnte, ‑gekonnt), *vi.* to be able to get off; **‑laßen**, ‑lassen (‑ließ, ‑ge‑lassen), *vt.* to let off; **‑laufen**, ‑läu‑fen (‑lief, ‑gelaufen), *vi.* to run away; to extend along; to continue; **‑le‑ben**, ‑läben, *vi.* to live on, continue living; **‑leiten**, ‑läeten, *vt.* to lead off; to lead on; **‑lesen**, ‑läsen (‑las, ‑gelesen), *vi.* to read on; **‑machen**, ‑machen, *vi.* to continue; **sich —**, to depart; **‑müssen**, ‑müssen (‑mußte, ‑gemußt), *vi.* to be obliged to leave; **‑nehmen**, ‑nämen (‑nahm, ‑genom‑men), *vt.* to take away; **‑packen**, ‑packen, *vr.* to pack off, leave; **‑pflanzen**, ‑pflantsen *vt.* to propa‑gate; **‑pflanzung**, ‑pflantsung, *f.* propagation; **‑reisen**, ‑räesen, *vi.* to depart, leave; **‑reißen**, ‑räis'en (‑riß, ‑gerissen), *vt.* to tear away; **‑reiten**, ‑reiten (‑ritt, ‑geritten), *vi.* to ride off; **‑rücken**, ‑rücken, *vi.* to move on; **‑schaffen**, ‑shaffen, *vt.* to remove, get off; **‑schicken**, ‑shicken, *vt.* to send off; **‑schieben**, ‑shīben (‑schob, ‑ge‑schoben), *vt.* to push forward; **sich —**, to make off; **‑schießen**, ‑shīsen (‑schoß, ‑geschossen), *vi.* to shoot on; **‑schiffen**, ‑shiffen, *vi.* to sail off; **‑schlafen**, ‑shläfen (‑schlief, fortgeschlafen), *vi.* to sleep on; **‑schleichen**, ‑shlëichen (‑schlich, ‑geschlichen), *vi.* to sneak off; **‑schleppen**, ‑shleppen, *vt.* to drag off; **‑schleudern**, ‑shlëudern. *vt.* to hurl away; **‑schreiten**, ‑shrëiten (‑schritt, ‑geschritten), *vi.* to progress, proceed, go on; **‑schritt**, ‑shritt, *m.* progress. advance, improvement; **‑segeln**, ‑sä‑geln, *vi.* to sail off; **‑sein**, ‑sëїn (‑war, ‑gewesen), *vi.* to be absent; **‑setzen**, ‑setsen, *vt.* to continue, pur‑sue; **‑setzung**, ‑setsung, *f.* continua‑tion, pursuit; **‑springen**, ‑zhpring‑en (‑sprang, ‑gesprungen), *vi.* to run

away, jump away; **stoßen, -stoßen** (-stieß, -gestoßen), *vt.* to push away, spurn; **stürmen, -stürmen, stürzen,** -stürzen, *vi.* to rush away; **tragen, -tragen** (-trug, -getragen), *vt.* to bear away, carry off; **treiben, -treiben** (-trieb, -getrieben), *vt.* to drive away; **währen, -waren, *vi.* to continue; während, -warend, *a.* continual. perpetual; **weisen, -weisen** (-wies, -gewiesen), *vt.* to turn off, send away; **wollen, -wollen,** *vi.* to wish to depart; **zeugen, -zeügen,** *vt.* to propagate; **ziehen, -ziehen** (-zog, -gezogen), *vt.* to draw away; *vi.* to move off, depart. migrate.

Fossil, fossil', *n. -s, pl.* -ien, fossil, mineral.

Fourage, furäzh'e, *f.* forage. **Fouragiren, -zhī'ren,** *vt.* to forage. **Fourier, furī'r,** *m.* quartermaster.

Fournir, furnīr', *n.* veneer.

Fracht, fracht, *f.* freight, load, cargo; carriage; **brief, -brif,** *m.* bill of lading; **führer, -führer. fuhrmann, -fūrmann,** *m. pl.* -fuhrleute; **gut, -gut,** *n. pl.* -güter, goods to be forwarded; cargo, lading; **schiff, -shiff,** *n.* merchant-ship; **schiffer, -shiffer,** *m.* shipper; **wagen, -vägen,** *m.* waggon, wagon.

Frack, frack, *m.* (dress) coat.

Frage, frä'ge, *f.* question, interrogation, query; a hand (of cards); eine — thun. — stellen, to ask a question. **Fragen,** frä'gen (frug, gefragt), *vt.* to ask, question, interrogate; — nach, to ask for; to care for.

Frager, fräg'er, *m.* questioner, inquirer. **Frageweise,** frä'gevēise, *av.* as a question, interrogatively; **wort, -vort,** *n.* interrogative; **zeichen, -tsäechen,** *n.* interrogation-point.

Fraglich, fräk'lich, *a.* questionable, doubtful.

Fragment, frakment', *n.* fragment; **arisch, -är'ish,** *a.* fragmentary.

Fragselig, fräk'sälich, *a.* inquisitive.

Franco, frang'kō, *a.* post-paid. **Frank, frank,** *a.* frank, free, open. **Frankiren,** frankī'ren, *vt.* to frank.

Franse, Franze, fran'tse, *f.* fringe. **Fransig,** fran'sich, *a.* fringed.

Franz, frants. French; **band, -bant,** *m.* calf binding; **baum, -baüm.** *m.* dwarf fruit tree; **branntwein, -brantvæn,** *m.* French brandy.

Fraß, fräs, *m.* eating, provender food.

Fratze, frat'se, *f.* grimace; odd person; **bild, -bilt,** *n. pl.* -er, carricature; grimace; **haft, -haft,** *a.* ridiculous, farcical, grotesque.

Frau, frau, *f.* mistress, lady, wife, woman, female. **Frauenbild, -bilt,** *n.* image of the Virgin Mary; woman; **hemd, -hemd,** *n.* -es, *pl.* -en, chemise, shift; **hut, -hut,** *m.* bonnet; **kleid, -klæt,** *n. pl.* -er, dress, gown; *pl.* clothes; **liebe, -lībe,** *f.* love of woman; love for women; **put, -puts,** *m.* finery; **raub, -raüp,** *m.* ravishment, rape; **schuster, -shyzhter,** *m.* ladies' shoemaker; **person, -pērsōn,** *f.* woman; **stimme, -zhtimme,** *f.* female voice; **zimmer, -tsimmer,** *m.* ladies' room; lady, woman. **Fräulein, fräö'læn,** *n.* young lady.

Frech, freck, *a.* bold, impudent, insolent, saucy; **heit, -hæt,** *f.* boldness, impudence, insolence.

Fregatte, fregat'te, *f.* frigate.

Frei, frœ, *a.* free, independent, frank, open; leisure; unconfined; easy; loose; **en Künste,** liberal arts, fine arts; **beuter, -bæter,** *m.* freebooter, robber; **billet, -bilyet,** *n.* free-ticket; **brief, -brīf,** *m.* charter, privilege, patent; passport; **corps, -kōr,** *n.* corps of volunteers; **denker, -denker,** *m.* free-thinker; **e,** frœ'e, *n.* open air.

Freien, frœ'en, *vt.* to court, woo. **Freier,** frœ'er, *m.* wooer, suitor.

Freifrau, frœ'fraü, *f.* baroness. **Freigeben,** frœ'gäben (-gab, -gegeben), *vt.* to free, emancipate, set free, release, to give a holiday; **gebig, -gäbig,** *a.* liberal, free, generous; **gebigkeit, -kæt,** *f.* liberality; **geboren, -gebōren,** *a.* freeborn; **gebung, -gäbung,** *f.* release, emancipation; **geist, -gæzht,** *m.* freethinker; **gut, -gut,** *n. pl.* -güter, freehold; goods duty-free; **hafen, -häfen,** *m.* free-port; **halten, -hälten,** *vt.* to treat; **heit, -hæt,** *f.* freedom, liberty; privilege, immunity; **heitsgeist, -gæzht,** *m.* spirit of liberty; **heitskrieg, -krīk,** *re.* war of independence; **herr, -herr,** *m. -n, pl. -n,* baronet, baron; **herrin, -herrin,** *f. pl.* -nen, baroness; **herzig, -hērtsich,** *a.* open-hearted; **herzigkeit**, -kāet, *f.* ingenuousness; **lassung**, -lassung, *f.* release, emancipation; **lich**, -lich, *av.* of course, certainly, indeed, to be sure; **machen**, -machen, *vt.* to set free; to frank; **maurer**, -möurer, *m.* free-mason; **muth**, -mŋt, *m.* **muthigkeit**, -mühtichkäet, *f.* candor, ingenuousness; **pass**, -sass. *m.* freeholder; **schar**, -shār, *f.* volunteer-corps; **schärler**, -shärler, *m.* volunteer; **schein**, -shāen, *m.* license; **schule**, -shule, *f.* free-school; **schütze**, -shütse, *m.* marksman (at a shooting-match); **sinnig**, -sinnich. *a.* liberal; **sinnigkeit**, -kāet, *f.* liberality; **sprechen**, -zhprèchen (-sprach, -gesprochen), *vt.* to acquit, absolve; *s. n. und* **sprechung**, -zhprèchung, *f.* acquittal: **staat**, -zhtāt, *m.* republic; **statt**, -zhtatt, **stätte**, -zhtette, *f.* asylum, refuge; **stunde**, -zhtȳnde, *f.* leisure hour.

Freitag, frēy'tāk, *m.* Friday.

Freiwerber, frēy'vèrber, *m.* matchmaker, wooer for another; **willig**, -villich, *a.* voluntary free will, spontaneous; **williger**, *m.* volunteer; **willigkeit**, -kāet, *f.* spontaneity, voluntariness; **zettel**, -tsèttel, *m.* license, permit.

Fremd, frȩmt, *a.* strange, unknown, foreign; **st**, *m. f.* stranger, foreigner; **se**, foreign country; **artig**, -ārtich, *a.* foreign, strange; **ling**, -ling, *m.* stranger, foreigner.

Freskomalerei, frèskōmāleréy', *f.* fresco-painting.

Freßbegierde, frèss'begïrde, *f.* greediness, gluttony, voracity. **Freßen**, frès'sen, *vt.* to eat, devour; consume; corrode; um sich —, to devour; rankle; zu — geben, to feed; *s. n.* food, meat, provender. **Freßer**, frès'ser, *m.* glutton; (big) feeder; **ei**, -ēï', *f.* gluttony; banquet (ironic).

Freude, frȫi'de, *f.* joy, gladness, pleasure, delight. satisfaction: **los**, -lōs, *a.* joyless. **Freuden**, frȫu'den, **becher**, -bècher. *m.* cup of joy; **fest**, -fĕsht, *n.* festivity, rejoicing; **haus**, -hōȳs, *n.* house of joy; brothel; **leer**, -lār, **los**, -lōs, *a.* joyless; **mädchen**, -mētchen, *n.* prostitute; **reich**, -rēich, *a.* rich in joys; **störer**, **zhtörer**, *m.* disturber of joys, vexer.

Freutrunken, -trŋnken, *a* intoxicated with joy, entranced. **Frensig**, fräüd'ich, *a.* joyous, joyful, glad. **keit**, -kāet, *f.* joyfulness, gladness. **Freuen**, frȫu'en, *vt. u. r.* to rejoice, delight, gladden; sich —, to be glad, rejoice.

Freund, frȫȳnt, *m.* sin, -in, *f.* friend; **lich**, -lich, *a.* friendly, kind; joyful, pleasant; **lichkeit**, -kāet, *f.* friendliness, kindness; **los**, -lōs, *a.* friendless. **Freundschaft**, -shaft. *f.* friendship, kindness, favor; **lich**, -lich, *a.* friendly, kind; **lichkeit**, -kāet, *f.* friendliness; **dienst**, -dinzht, *m.* friendly service, favor, good office.

Frevel, fră'fel, *m.* crime, outrage, sin, wickedness; trespass; **haft**, -haft, *a.* outrageous. criminal; **that**, -tāt, *f.* atrocity. **Freveln**, frăf'eln, *vi.* to commit a crime, outrage. **Frevler**, frăf'ler, *m.* criminal, malefactor, transgressor.

Friede(n), frī'de(n), *m.* peace. **Friedensbote**, frī'densbōte, *m.* -n, *pl.* -n, messenger of peace: **bruch**, -brŋch, *m.* breach of peace. **Friedensrichter**, frī'densrichter, umpire; justice of the peace; **schluss**, -shlȳss, *m.* conclusion of peace; **stifter**, -zhtifter, *m.* peace-maker. **Friedfertig**, frīt'fertich, *a.* peaceable, peaceful, inoffensive; **keit**, -kāet, *f.* peacefulness. **Friedhof**, -hōf, *m.* cemetery. **Friedlich**, -lich, *a.* peaceable, peaceful; *av.* peaceably. **Friedliebend**, -lībent, *a.* peaceable. **Friedsam**, -sam, **Friedselig**, -sālich, *a.* peaceful.

Frieren, frī'ren (fror, gefroren), *vi.* to freeze: to be cold, feel cold.

Fries, frīs, *m.* frieze; **rod**, -rock, *m.* dreadnaught.

Friesel, frīs'el, *m. or n.* miliary fever.

Frisch, frish, *a.* fresh, new, recent; vigorous, bold; — auf, cheer up; — zu, on: von —em, anew, afresh; auf — er That, in the very act. **Frische**, frish'e, *f.* freshness, vigor. **Frischen**, frish'en, *vt.* to refresh; refine. **Frischofen**, -ōfen. *m.* refining furnace, refinery.

Friseur, friseūr', *m.* hairdresser. **Frisiren**, frisī'ren, *vt.* to dress the hair of.

Frist, frīzht, *f.* term, delay, time, days

Fri 125 **Fuh**

of grace. **Fristen,** frĭzh'ten, *vt.* to delay, respite; to spare. **Frist'ung,** -ŭng, *f.* delay, prolongation.
Frivol, frĭfōl', *a.* frivolous.
Froh, frō, *a.* merry, joyful, glad, happy, cheerful. **Fröhlich,** fröh'lĭch, *a.* merry, cheerful, glad, jolly; **-keit,** -kāet, *f.* gladness, gaiety. **Froh-locken,** -lock'en, *vi.* to exult, shout, rejoice.
Frohn, frōn, **-bote,** -bōte, *m.* **-n,** *pl.* **-n,** beadle; **-dienst,** -dĭnzht, *m.* **-e,** frō'ne, *f.* base service, feudal service. **Frohnen,** frōn'en, *vi.* to do feudal service. **Fröhnen,** fröh'nen, *vi.* to serve, indulge. **Frohnleichnamsfest,** frōnlīch'nāmsfezht, Corpus Christi day. **Frohnpflichtig,** -pflĭchtĭch, *a.* owing feudal service.
Frohsinn, frō'sĭnn, *m.* cheerfulness, mirth; **-ig, -ich,** *a.* cheerful.
Fromm, fromm, *a.* pious, religious; good, gentle. **Frömmelei,** frömme-lēī', *f.* affected piety. **Frommen,** fromm'en, *vi.* to be of use, to profit. **Frömmigkeit,** frömm'ĭchkāet, *f.* piousness, piety. **Frömmler,** frömm'-ler, *m.* devotee.
Fronte, fron'te, *f.* front.
Frosch, frosh, *m.* frog; **-laich,** -lāēch, *m.* spawn of frogs.
Frost, frozht, *m.* frost, cold, coldness; **-beule,** -bēūle, *f.* chilblain. **Frösteln,** frözht'eln, *vi.* to shiver, be cold. **Frostig,** frosht'ĭch, *a.* frosty, cold; **-keit,** -kāet, *f.* frostiness. **Frostpunkt,** -pŭnkt, *m.* freezing-point.
Frucht, frŭcht, *f. pl.* **Früchte,** fruit, grain, corn; product, result, effect; **-auge,** flower-bud; **-bar, -bär,** *a.* fruitful; **-keit,** -kāet, *f.* fruitfulness, fertility; **-baum,** -bāum, *m.* fruit-tree. **Fruchten,** frŭcht'en, *vi.* to bring forth fruit; to be useful, to profit. **Fruchtfeld,** -felt, *n. pl.* **-er,** wheat-field; **-haut,** -hōut, *f.* **-hülle,** -hülle, *f.* seed-vessel; **-los,** -lōs, *a.* fruitless, vain; **-losigkeit,** -losĭchkāet, *f.* fruitlessness; **-reich,** -rāich, *a.* fruitful. **Frugal,** frŭgāl', *a.* frugal, simple.
Früh, früh, *a. av.* early, in the morning, soon; — **morgens,** early in the morning; **heute** —, this morning; **-apfel,** -apfel, *m.* early apple. **June-apple; -e,** früh'e, *f.* early time,

morning; **-jahr,** -yǟr, *n.* spring**-ling,** -lĭŋk, precocious, forward; **-ling,** -lĭng, *m.* spring, spring-time; **-lingsmorgen,** -morgen, *m.* spring-morning; **-messe,** früh'messe, *f.* matins; **-obst,** -ōpst, *n.* early fruit; **-reife,** -rāife, *f.* precociousness; **-stück,** -zhtück, breakfast; **-stücken,** -zhtücken, *vi.* to breakfast; **-zeitig,** -tsāēĭtĭch, *a.* early, precocious; — **-zeitigkeit,** -kāet, *f.* earliness, precocity.
Fuchs, fŭx, *m.* fox; red-haired man; ducat; freshman; **-balg,** -balk, *m.* fox-skin; **-bau,** -bōu, *m.* fox-earth, burrow; **-eisen,** -ēīsen, *n.* fox-trap; **-en,** fŭx'en, *vt.* to vex. **Füchsin,** fŭx'ĭch, *a.* foxy. **Füchsin,** fŭx'ĭn, *f.* (she-)fox. **Fuchsjagd,** -yakt, *f.* fox-hunt; **-jäger,** -yǟger, *m.* fox-hunter; **-pelz,** -pelts, *m.* fur of a fox; **-roth,** -rōt. *a.* foxy, fox-colored, sorrel: **-schwanz,** -shvants, *m.* fox-tail; handsaw; **-schwänzen,** -shventsen, *vi.* to flatter, fawn; **-schwänzer,** -shventser, *m.* fawner.
Fuchtel, fŭch'tel, *f.* broad sword; rod. **Fuchteln,** fŭch'teln, *vi.* to strike with the flat sword; to castigate.
Fuder, fŭ'der, *n.* wagon-load.
Fug, fŭk, *m.* authority, right; mit — and Recht, with good reason.
Fuge, fŭ'ge, *f.* joint, seam; fugue (Mus.). **Fügen,** füh'gen, *vt.* to fit, join, unite; to direct, ordain; **sich** — **in,** to submit to, yield; **sich** —, to happen. **Füglich,** fühk'lĭch, *a.* proper, fit; convenient; *av.* -ly; **-keit,** -kāet, *f.* fitness. **Fügsam,** fühk'sam, *a.* pliant, yielding, obedient. **Fügung,** -ŭng, *f.* joining; juncture; dispensation.
Fühlbar, fühl'bär, *a.* perceptible, sensible, palpable; **-keit,** -kāet, *f.* perceptibility. **Fühlen,** füh'len, *vt.* to feel, touch; perceive. **Fühlfaden,** -fāden, *m.* feeler (of insects): auch **Fühlhorn,** *pl.* -hörner. **Fühl'los,** -lōs, *a.* unfeeling, insensibl—. **Fühl'losigkeit,** -lōsĭchkāet, *f.* insensibility.
Fuhre, fŭ're, *f.* carriage, conveyance; load. **Führen,** füh'ren, *vt.* to lead, guide, conduct, bring; command; to fill (an office); to carry on; to carry (arms); to wield: **das Wort** — für, to speak for; to keep (books).
Führer, füh'er, *m.* leader, guide.

11*

Führend, fŭr′hĕmt, n. -ĕ, pl. -en, blouse. **Fuhrlohn**, fŭr′lōn, m. cartage, wagonage, carriage, freight. **Fuhrmann**, fŭr′mann, m. pl. Fuhrleute, waggoner, carrier; driver. **Führung**, führ′ŭng, f. guidance, leadership; dispensation. **Fuhr′werk**, -vĕrk, n. conveyance, carriage, cart, wagon; -wesen, -vāsen, n. means of conveyance.

Fülle, fŭl′le, f. fulness, abundance, plenty; stuffing. **Füllen**, fŭl′len, vt. to fill; to stuff; to bottle (beer, etc.).

Füllen, fŭl′len, n. foal, colt; vi. to foal.

Füllhorn, fŭll′hŏrn, n. pl. -hörner, horn of plenty, cornucopia. **Füllsel**, fŭll′sel, n. stuffing. **Füllung**, -ŭng, f. filling, stuffing, panel.

Fund, fŭnt, m. finding, discovery; what is found; einen — thun, to find.

Fundament, fŭndament′, n. foundation; -al, -āl′, a. fundamental.

Fundgeld, fŭnt′gelt, n. reward. **Fundgrube**, -grŭbe, f. mine.

Fünf, fünf, num. five; -eck, -ĕck, n. pentagon; -erlei, -ĕrlīĕ, av. of five sorts: -fach, -fach, a. fivefold; -fältig, -feltich, a. fivefold, quintuple; -jährig, -yärich, a. five years old; -jährlich, -yärlich, a. quinquennial; -mal, -māl, av. five times; -malig, -mālich, a. done five times; -stündig, fünf′zhtündich, a. of five hours; -tägig, -tāgich, a. of five days. **Fünfte**, fünf′te, a. fifth. **Fünftel**, fünf′tel, n. fifth part, fifth. **Fünftens**, fünf′tens, av. fifthly. **Fünftehalb**, fünft′halp, a. four and a half. **Fünfzehn**, -tsān, num. fifteen; -te, a. fifteenth. **Fünfzig**, fünf′tsich, num. fifty; -er, m. fifty years old; of the year 50; -stel, n. fiftieth.

Fünkchen, fŭnk′chen, n. little spark. **Funke(n)**, fŭng′ke, m. -ns, pl. -n, spark; ray. **Funkeln**, fŭnk′eln, vi. to sparkle, shine. **Funkelnagelneu**, -nāgelnōü, **Funkelneu**, a. quite new; span-new, spick and span new.

Für, für, prep. for, as, about, instead of.

Fürbaß, führ′bass, av. forward, on. **Fürbitte**, -bitte, f. intercession; — einlegen, to intercede.

Furche, fŭr′che, f. furrow, wrinkle.

Furchen, fŭr′chen, vt. to furrow wrinkle.

Furcht, fŭrcht, f. fear, dread, fright, awe; in — setzen, to frighten; -bar, -bār, a. fearful, dreadful, terrible; -barkeit, -kāĕt, f. formidableness. **Fürchten**, fürch′ten, vt. to fear, dread, apprehend; sich —, to be afraid. **Furchterlich**, -ĕrlich, a. frightful, dreadful, terrible. **Furchtlos**, fŭrcht′lōs, a. fearless, undaunted. **Furcht′losigkeit**, -lōsichkĕĕt, f. fearlessness. **Furchtsam**, fŭrcht′sam, a. fearful, timid; -keit, -kāĕt, f. timidity.

Fürder, für′der, av. further.

Furie, fŭ′ri-e, f. fury.

Fürlieb, fürlīb′, av. — nehmen, to be satisfied with, to take pot-luck.

Fürsorge, führ′sorge, f. care, foresight.

Fürsprache, führ′zhprāche, f. intercession, good offices. **Fürsprechen**, -zhprechen (-sprach, -gesprochen), vi. to intercede. **Fürsprecher**, m. advocate, intercessor.

Fürst, fürzht, m. -en, pl. -en, prince, sovereign. **Fürstenkrone**, -krōne, f. crown; -mäßig, -māsich, a. av. princely; -sohn, -sōn, m. prince; -thum, -tŭm, n. pl. -thümer, principality; -würde, -vürde, f. princely dignity. **Fürstin**, -türzh′tin, f. princess. **Fürstlich**, fürzht′lich, a. princely.

Furt, fŭrt, m. ford.

Fürwahr, fŭrvär′, av. truly, surely, indeed, in truth.

Fürwort, führ′vort, n. pl. -wörter, pronoun.

Furz, fŭrts, m. fart; -en, vi. to fart.

Fusel, fŭs′el, m. fusel, (inferior) whisky.

Fuß, fŭss, m. pl. Füße, foot, leg: footing, establishment; -angel, -ang-el, f. man-trap; -bad, -bād, n. pl. -bäder, foot-bath; -ball, -ball, m. ball of the foot; -bank, -bank, m. footstool; -boden, -bōden, m. floor; -breit, -brĕĕt, a. having the breadth of a foot; -chen, fühs′chen, n. little foot; -en, fŭs′en, vi. to set one's foot on; to rely on; -fall, -fall, m prostration; -fällig, -fellich, a. prostrate, kneeling. **Fußgänger**, -genger, m. foot-passenger, walker; -gestell, -gezhtell, n. pedestal; -gicht, -gicht, f. podagra; -pfad, -pfād, m.

foot-path; **-reife**, -räfee, *f.* journey on foot; **-fchemel**, -shämel, *m.* foot-stool; **-fohle**, -sōle, *f.* sole of the foot; **-foldat**, -sŏldāt', *m. -en*, *pl. -en*, foot-soldier; **-fpur**, -zhpŭr, **-ftapfe**, zhtäpfe, *f.* footstep, track; **-ftrig**, -zhtŭek, *m.* footpath; **-ftoß**, -zhtōs, *m.* kick; **-teppich**, -tĕppĭch, *m.* carpet; **-tritt**, -tritt, *m.* kick; step; track, footboard; **-volf**, -fŏlk, *n. pl. -völfer*, foot-soldiers, infantry; **-wafchen**, -vashen, *n.* washing of the feet; **-weg**, -vāk, *m.* footpath; **-wurzel**, -vŭrtsel, *f.* tarsus; **-zehe**, -tsān, *f.* toe.

Futter, fŭt'ter, *n.* feed, provender, food, fodder.

Futter, fŭt'ter. *n.* case, sheath, lining; **-al**, -ăl. *n.* case, box, sheath.

Futter, fŭt'ter. **-bau**, -bŏу, *m.* raising, culture of forage, **-beutel**, -bĕutel, *m.* nosebag; **-faften**, -käzhten, *m.* bin for oats, etc.; **-forn**, -kŏrn, *n.* feed-corn.

Futterleinwand, fŭt'terleānvant, *f.* linen for lining.

Futtern, füt'tern, *vt.* to feed, corn, bait.

Futtern, fŭt'tern, *vt.* to line, case, sheath.

Futterfack, fŭt'tersack, *m.* feed-bag.
Fütterung, füt'terŭng, *f.* feeding, food.

G.

Gabe, gä'be, *f.* gift, present, donation; gift, talent.

Gabel, gä'bel, *f.* fork, tendril (bot.); crotch (mech.): **-deichfel**, -dĕlksel, *f.* shafts; **-förmig**, -fŏrmĭch, *a.* forked, crotched; **-frühftüd**, -frūh'-zhtŭck, *n.* meat-breakfast: **-icht**, **-ig**, *a.* forked, forky; **-n**, gä'beln, *vt. i.* to fork, pitch; **-pferd**, -pfārt, *n.* thiller, thill-horse; **-fafe**, -tsäcke, **-zinfe**, -tsinke, *f.* prong.

Gackern, gack'ern, *vi.* to cackle.
Gaffel, gäf'fel, *f.* fork; prop.
Gaffen, gäf'fen, *vi.* to gape.
Gähnen, gä'nen, *vi.* to gape, yawn; *s. n.* yawning.
Gährbottich, gär'bŏttĭch, *m.* fermenting vat. **Gähre**, gä're, *f.* fermentation.
Gähren, gä'ren (*reg. u. gebr. gegohren*), *vi.* to ferment, work. **Gährung**, gär'ŭng, *f.* fermentation.

Gais, gāes, *f.* goat; **-bof**, -bŏck, *m.* he-goat.

Galan, gälän', *m.* lover. **Galant**, galänt', *a.* showy, gallant, courteous. **Galanterie**, gälänterī', *f.* gallantry, courtesy; **-arbeit**, -ärbāet, *f.* jewelry, fancy goods; **-händler**, -hĕntler, *m.* dealer in fancy goods; jeweler; **-waaren**, -vāren, *s. pl.* fancy goods, jewelry; millinery.

Galeere, gälā're, *f.* galley; **-fflave**, -sklāfe, *m. -n*, *pl. -n*. galley-slave.

Galgen, gäl'gen, *m.* gallows, gibbet; **-dieb**, -dīb, **-fchwengel**, -shvĕng-el, **-ftrick**, -zhtrick, **-vogel**, -fōgel, *m.* jail-bird; **-frift**, -frizht, *f.* reprieve from the gallows; respite.

Galla, gäl'lä, *f.* gala, pomp.
Gallapfel, gäll'apfel, *m.* gall, gallnut; **-fäure**, -sēŭre, *f.* gallic acid; **-falz**, -sälts, *n.* gallate. **Galle**, gäl'le, *f.* gall, spleen, bile. **Gallen**, gäl'len, **-artig**, -ärtĭch, *a.* like gall, bilious, bitter: **-bitter**, -bitter, *a.* bitter as gall; **-blafe**, -blāse, *f.* gall-bladder; **-fieber**, -fīber, *n.* bilious fever; **-fucht**, -sŏcht, *f.* jaundice; **-füchtig**, -sŏchtĭg, *a.* jaundiced; sullen.

Gallerie, gälleri', *f.* gallery.
Gallerte, gäl'lĕrte, *f.* jelly, gelatine.
Gallig, gäl'lĭch, *a.* bilious, bitter.
Galloche, gällŏsh'e, *f.* galoche.
Galmei, gälmē', *m.* calamine.
Galopp, gälŏpp', *m.* gallop; **-iren**, -ī'ren, *vi.* to gallop.

Galvanifch, gälfä'nish, *a.* galvanic. **Galvanifiren**, gälfänĭsī'ren, *vt.* to galvanize. **Galvanismus**, -nĭs'mŭss, *m.* galvanism. **Galvanoplaftik**, -plästĭk, *f.* electrotypy.

Gamafche, gämäsh'e, *f.* gaiter.

Gang, gäng, *m.* going, walk, motion, progress, gait, pace; errand, commission; pass, round; way, alley; passage, corridor; vein; set of millstones; im —e, in motion, at work; on foot, in vogue; **-bar**, -bär, *a.* passable, practicable; frequented, current; in working order. **Gängelband**, gĕng'elbänt, *n. pl. -bänder*, leading-strings. **Gängeln**, gĕng'eln, *vt.* to lead in leading-strings.
Ganghaft, gäng'häft, *a.* worked.
Gans, gans, *f. pl.* **Gänfe**, goose. **Gänfe**, -gĕn'se, **-blume**, -blŭme, *f.* daisy; **-braten**, -brāten, *m.* roast goose; **-gekröfe**, -gekrōhse, *n.* gib

lets; **Haut**, -hôut, f. goose-skin; goose-flesh; **Kiel**, -kïl, m. goose-quill; **Leber**, -lâber, f. goose-liver; **Marsch**, -marsh, m. Indian file; **rich**, -rĭċh, m. gander; **Stall**, -zhtall, m. goosery.

Gant, gant, f. auction, public sale.

Ganz, gants, a. whole, entire; all, total, complete, full; av. -ly, quite, all; — **und gar nicht**, not at all; — **durch**, throughout; — **gut**, right good; — **recht**, quite right. **Ganze**, gant'sẹ, n. whole; im — n, in the whole, after all; by wholesale, in a lump. **Gänzlich**, gents'lich, a. whole, entire, complete, total; av. wholly, entirely, quite, fairly.

Gar, gär, a. ready, finished; (cooked) done; dressed (leather); refined (metals); av. quite, entirely, very, even; — **nicht**, not at all; — **fein**, none at all; — oft, very often; **warum nicht** —, why truly, why indeed.

Garantie, garantī', f. guarantee.
Garantiren, -tī'ren, vt. to guarantee, warrant.

Garbe, gar'bẹ, f. sheaf, bundle.

Gärben, gĕr'ben, vt. to tan, dress. **Gärber**, gĕr'ber, m. tanner; **ei**, -ēï', f. tannery, tan-yard, tanning.

Garde, gar'dẹ, f. guard. **Garderobe**, garderob'ẹ, f. wardrobe, cloak-room.

Gardine, gardī'nẹ, f. curtain; **npredigt**, -prädicht, f. curtain-lecture.

Garkoch, gär'kŏch, m. keeper of a cook-shop. **Garküche**, -küchẹ, f. cook-shop.

Garn, garn, n. yarn; **Baum**, -bäum, m. yarn-beam, yarn-roller, warp-beam; **Gabel**, -gäbel, f. forked stake (hunt.); **Händler**, -hẹntler, m. dealer in yarn; **Presse**, -prẹssẹ, f. bundle-press; **Winde**, -vindẹ, f. reel; **Zug**, -tsŭk, m. fishing with nets.

Garnison, garnisön', f. garrison.

Garstig, kar'zhtich, a. ugly, nasty, dirty; **keit**, -kăĕt, f. ugliness.

Garten, gär'ten, m. garden; **Bau**, -bŏu, m. **Kunst**, -kŭnzht, f. horticulture; **Erde**, -ĕrdẹ, f. garden-mould; **Frucht**, -frŭcht, f. garden-produce; **Haus**, -hŏus, n. pl. -bäuser, summer-house; **Haue**, -häuẹ, f. weeding-hoe; **Laube**, -lăubẹ, f. arbor, bower; **Leiter**, -lăĕter, f. double ladder;

Scheere, -shârẹ, f. garden-shears **Zaun**, -tsăun, m. garden-fence. **Gärtner**, gĕrt'ner, m. gardener; **ei**, -ēï', f. gardening.

Gas, gäs, n. gas; **Anstalt**, -änzhtält f. gas works; **artig**, -ärtich, a. gaseous; **Beleuchtung**, -belĕŭchtŭng, f. **licht**, -licht, n. gas-light, illumination by gas; **Brenner**, -brenner, m. gas-burner.

Gäschen, gĕsh'en, vi. to ferment, froth, lather. **Gäscht**, gĕshṭ, m. yeast, froth, foam; fermentation.

Gasen, gä'sen, m. gassing.

Gas, -gäs, **lampe**, -lampẹ, f. gas-lamp; **messer**, -měsser, m. gasometer, gas-meter; **regulator**, -regulātor, m. gas-governor; **röhre**, -röhrẹ, f. gas-pipe.

Gasse, gas'sẹ, f. alley, street; **Nlied**, -līd, pl. -er, **Hauer**, -hăŭer, m. street-tune; **Rinne**, -rinnẹ, f. gutter; **Schleuse**, -shlĕŭsẹ, f. sewer.

Gast, gazht, m. guest; **zu** — **laben**, to invite to dinner or supper; **Bett**, -bett, n. spare-bed; **erei**, -erēï'. f. entertainment, banquet, feast, treat; **frei**, -frēī, **freundlich**, -frĕuntlich, a. hospitable; **freiheit**, -frēīhăĕt, **freundlichkeit**, -frĕuntlichkăĕt, f. hospitality; **freund**, -frĕunt, m. guest, host; **geber**, -gäber. **wirth**, -vīrt, m. **in**, f. host, landlord; hostess, landlady; **haus**, -hŏus, **hof**, -höf, m. hotel, inn; **herr**, -hĕr, m. - n, pl. -n, entertainer, host; **iren**, gazhtī'ren, vt. to entertain; vi. to be a guest; **lich**, -lich, a. hospitable; **lichkeit**, -lichkăĕt, f. hospitality; **mahl**, -mäl, n. entertainment, banquet, feast, treaty; **recht**, -recht, n. hospitality; **rolle**, -rollẹ. f. part performed by a stranger (a star); **stube**, -zhtŭbẹ, f. spare-room; **wirthschaft**, -vīrtshaft, f. inn, hotel; **zimmer**, -tsimmer, n. spare-room.

Gäten, gä'ten, vt. to weed.

Gatte, gat'tẹ, m. husband, consort, spouse. **Gatten**, gat'ten, vt. to unite, join; **Karten** —, to pack (the cards); **Waaren** —, to sort; **sich** —, to match, couple, pair; copulate; to meet.

Gatter, gat'ter, n. railing, grate.

Gattin, gat'tin, f. wife, spouse. **Gattung**, gat'tŭng, f. kind, species, sort

Gau, gäu, *m. or n.* district, region, country.

Gauch, gäuch, *m.* gawk, fool.

Gaudieb, gäu′dīb, *m.* cunning thief.

Gaukelbild, gäu′kelbilt, *m. pl.* -er, illusion, phantom. **Gaukelei**, -ēī′, *f.* **Gaukelspiel**, -zhpīl, *n.* delusion, juggling, trick. **Gaukeln**, gäu′keln, *vi.* to flutter; to juggle. **Gaukler**, gäuk′ler, *m.* juggler; monkey-flower (bot.); **-isch**, -ish, *a.* juggling, delusive, *av.* -ly.

Gaul, göul, *m.* horse, nag.

Gaumen, göu′men, *m.* palate.

Gauner, gäun′er, *m.* cheat, swindler, rogue: **-ei**, -ēī′, *f.* cheating, imposture. **Gaunern**, gäun′ern, *vi.* cheat; sharp.

Gaze, gät′se, *f.* gauze.

Gazelle, gatsēl′le, *f.* gazelle, antelope.

Geächteter, ge-ēcht′eter, *m.* outlaw.

Geäse, ge-ās′e, *n.* feeding, pasture.

Gebäck, **Gebäck**, gebeck′, *n.* pastry, baking, batch.

Gebaren, gebä′ren, *vr.* to behave. **Gebärde**, f. **Geberde**.

Gebären, gebā′ren, *vt.* to bear, bring forth, to give birth to.

Gebäude, gebēu′de, *n.* building.

Gebe, gā′be, *a.* and *av.* current, usual.

Gebein, gebēn′, *n.* bones.

Gebell, gebēll′, *n.* barking, baying, yelping.

Geben, gā′ben (gab, gegeben), *vt.* to give, bestow, impart; **es gibt**, there is, there are; **Was gibt es**, what is the matter? **von sich —**, to exhibit; to emit, cast off. **Geber**, gā′ber, *m.* giver, author, dispenser.

Geberde, **Gebärde**, gebēr′de, *f.* gesture. **Geberden**, gebēr′den, *vr.* to make gestures; to behave; **-spiel**, -zhpīl, *n.* action, pantomime, mimicry. **Geberdung**, -ung, *f.* gesticulation, demeanor, behavior.

Gebet, gebēt′, *n.* prayer; **-buch**, -buch, *n. pl.* **-bücher**, prayer-book.

Gebiet, gebīt′, *n.* dominion, command, sway, government; jurisdiction, territory, precinct; department, extent, province, sphere; — **eines Bischofs**, bishopric, diocese; **-en**, *vt.* (gebot, geboten), *vt.* to order, command, bid; to restrain, bridle. **Gebieter**, gebī′ter, *m.* commander. ruler, master: **-in**, -in, *f.* mistress, lady; **-isch**, -ish, *a.* commanding, imperious, peremptory, imperative.

Gebild, gebīlt′, *n. pl.* -e, creature, creation, form, image.

Gebinde, gebīn′de, *n.* bundle.

Gebirge, gebīr′ge, *n.* mountains, mountain chain. **Gebirg'ig**, -ich, *a.* mountainous. **Gebirgsbewohner**, -bevō′ner, *m.* mountaineer; **-kamm**, -kamm, *m.* mountain-ridge; **-kette**, -kette, *f.* mountain-chain.

Gebiß, gebiss′, *n.* teeth; — **anlegen**, to bit.

Gebläse, geblā′se, *n.* bellows; **das — anlassen**, to set the bellows agoing **-form**, -form, *f.* tuyere, tweer; **er-biste — luft**, *f.* hot blast.

Geblüt, geblüht, *n.* blood.

Gebogen, gebō′gen, *f.* **Biegen**.

Geboren, gebō′ren, *f.* **Gebären**.

Gebot, gebōt′, *n.* commandment, command, order.

Gebräme, gebräm′e, *n.* border, edging; — **von Pelz**, furred border.

Gebräu, gebrēu, *n.* brewing.

Gebrauch, gebrouch′, *m.* use, employment, usage, custom; **-en**, -en, *vt.* to use, make use of. **Gebräuchlich**, gebrēuch′lich, *a.* usual, customary; **-keit**, -kāēt, *f.* usualness.

Gebrause, gebrou′se, *n.* roaring, rushing.

Gebrechen, gebrēch′en (gebrach, gebrochen), *vi.* to be wanting; to fail, lack, to be in want of; *s. n.* want, deficiency, fault, defect, infirmity. **Gebrechlich**, gebrēch′lich. *a.* frail, weak, feeble, infirm, decrepit; **-keit**, -kāēt, *f.* frailty, infirmity. **Gebrochen**, gebrōch′en, *pp.* broken; ruptured; **es Dach**, curve roof; **-e Zahl**, fraction; **-e Treppe**, stairs with a landing-place; **-es Englisch**, broken English.

Gebrüder, gebrüh′der, *s. pl.* brothers.

Gebrüll, gebrüll′, *n.* roaring, bellowing.

Gebrumme, gebrum′me, *n.* murmuring, grumbling.

Gebühr, gebühr′, *f.* duty, due, fee; propriety, decorum. **Gebühren**, gebüh′ren, *vr.* fich —, to be becoming, proper, fit; **-d**, *a.* due, fit, proper, decent; *av.* -ly.

Gebunden, gebun′den, *pp. v.* **Binden**, bound; metrical, in verse.

Geburt, gebŭrt′, *f.* birth, delivery

extraction, race; **Шelfer**, -hêlfer, *m.* accoucheur; **shilfe**, -hilfe, *f.* midwifery; **sort**, -ort, *n. pl.* -örter, birthplace; native place; **Stadt**, -zhtątt, *f.* native town; **stag**, -täk, *m.* birthday; **weben**, -vâ-en, *s. pl. f.* extractor, forceps.

Gebüsch, gebüsh', *n.* bush, thicket, underwood.

Ged, gěck, *m.* -en, *pl.* -en, fool, fop, coxcomb; **enhaft**, *a.* foppish.

Gedächtniß, gedècht'niss, *n.* memory, remembrance, recollection, reminiscence; **sfeier**, -fēier, *f.* **stag**, -tǎk, *m.* anniversary; **sfunst**, -kǫnzht, *f.* mnemonics.

Gedanke, gedǎnk'e, *m.* thought; **-ngang**, -gang, train of ideas; **-los**, *a.* thoughtless, unthinking; **-keit**, -hǎet, *f.* thoughtlessness; **strich**, -zhtrich, *m.* break, dash; **-voll**, -foll, *a. av.* thoughtful, pensive.

Gedärm, gedêrm', *n.* entrails, bowels, intestines, guts, garbage.

Gedeck, gedęck', *n.* cover; table-cloth with napkins.

Gedeihen, gedeih'-en (gebieh, gebieben), *vi.* to thrive, prosper, succeed; to turn out; *s.* prosperity, success; **-lich**, -lich, *a. av.* prosperous, successful, -ly.

Gedenken, gędenk'en, *vt.* to think of, remember; to mention; to intend; *s.* memory.

Gedicht, ɣedicht', *n.* poem, poetry; fable, fiction.

Gediegen, gedī'gen. *a.* solid, genuine, true, sterling; **-keit**, -hǎet, *f.* solidity, pithiness, genuineness.

Gedränge, gedreng'e, *n.* thronging, throng, pressure, crowd, bustle. **Gedrängt**, gędręngt', *a. av.* compressed, concise, succinct, -ly; **-heit**, -hǎet, *f.* conciseness. **Gedrungen**, gedrung'en, *a.* compact, tight; concise; **-keit**, -hǎet, *f.* compactness, compactedness; conciseness.

Geduld, gedult', *a.* patience; **-ig**, -ich, *a. av.* patient, -ly; —en or sich —, to have patience, to wait patiently, to bear with.

Geeignet, geęěg'net, *a. av.* proper, appropriate, suitable, -ly.

Gefahr, gefǎr', *f.* danger, peril, risk. **Gefährden**, gefǎr'den, *vt.* endanger, imperil, to bring or put into danger, peril; to put to hazard. **Gefährlich**, gefǎr'lich, dangerous, perilous, hazardous, -ly; seriously; **-keit**, -kǎět, *f.* dangerousness, perilousness. **Gefahrlos**, gefǎr'lōs, *a.* dangerless, -ly; without risk or hazard.

Gefährte, gefǎ-r'te, *m.* companion, fellow.

Gefährt(e), gefǎr'te, *n.* vehicle, conveyance; carriage.

Gefäll, gefěll', *n.* fall, descent; revenue, income.

Gefallen, gefal'len, *vi.* to please, like; sich — lassen, to submit to, to put up or agree with; *m.* pleasure, liking; favor, service, obligation; satisfaction. **Gefällig**, gefěll'ich, *a.* pleasing, agreeable, complaisant, kind, -ly; **-keit**, -kǎět, *f.* favor, kindness, pleasantness, pleasure, complaisance. **Gefälligst**, gefěl'lichst, *n.* please, be pleased, if you please. **Gefallsucht**, gefall'suŏht, *f.* coquetry; **-süchtig**, -süchtich, *a.* coquettish.

Gefangen, gefang'en, *a.* captive; — machen, to take prisoner; — halten, to keep a prisoner; — nehmen, to take captive, prisoner; to arrest; to captivate; — setzen, to imprison; **-nahme**, -nǎme, *f.* capture, seizure, captivation; **-schaft**, -shaft, *f.* captivity. **Gefangener**, gefang'ener, *m.* prisoner, captive. **Gefangenwärter**, -verter, **-hüter**, -hüter, *m.* jailer. **Gefänglich**, gefeng'lich, *a.* — einziehen, to imprison. **Gefängniß**, gefeng'niss, *f.* jail, prison; **strafe**, -zhtrǎfe, *f.* punishment by imprisonment. **Gefängnißwärter**, -verter, *m.* jailer.

Gefäss, gefěss', *n.* vessel, vase, tube, canal; handle, haft, hilt; **-chen**, -chen, *n.* small vessel. **Gefasst**, gefasst', *a.* prepared, ready, calm, collected, composed; — halten sich, to keep one's self ready, to be in readiness; — machen sich, to prepare one's self.

Gefecht, gefěcht', *n.* fight, battle, affair.

Gefieder, gefīd'er, *n.* plumage, feathers. **Gefiedert**, gefīd'ert, *a.* feathered.

Gefilde, gefil'de, *n.* field. plain.

Geflammt, g-flamnt', *n.* watered, tabbied, grained.

Gef 131 **Geh**

Geflecht, gefle̱cht', n. texture.
Geflissentlich, geflis'sentlich, av. on purpose, designedly, intentionally.
Geflüster, geflüs'ter, n. whisper, whispering.
Geflügel, gefü̱'gel, n. poultry, fowls.
Geflügelt, a. winged, flying.
Gefolge, gefol'ge, n. suit(e), train, attendance; retinue, followers, attendants.
Gefräß, gefräss', n. food; -ig, -ich, a. voracious, ravenous, gluttonous; -igkeit, -käet. voracity, gluttony.
Gefreiter, gefrei'ter, m. corporal; exempt.
Gefrieren, gefrī'ren (gefror, gefroren), vi. to freeze, congeal; -punkt, -pŭnkt, m. freezing point, zero. **Gefrorenes,** gefror'enes, n. ice, ice-cream.
Gefüge, gefü̱'ge, n. structure, construction, frame, joints. **Gefügig,** -ich, a. pliable, flexible, ductile; docile; complying; -keit, -käet, f. pliancy, facility; complying temper.
Gefühl, gefühl', n. feeling, sense, touch, sensation, sentiment; sensibility; -los, -lōs, a. av. senseless, insensible, unfeeling; -losigkeit, f. insensibility, want of sense, apathy; hardness; -voll, -foll, a. sensible, feeling, tender, full of feeling, affectionate, -ly.
Gegen, gä'gen, pr. toward, towards; to, against; about; near; for, in comparison with; -anklage, -anklä-ge, -beschuldigung, -beshŭldichung, f. recrimination, retortion, countercharge; -anstalt, -anzhtalt, f. counterplot, countermine; -befehl, -befäl', m. counter-order; -besuch, -besych, m. return of a visit; -beweis, -bevēis, m. counter-evidence; -bild, -bilt, n. counterpart; -bürge, -bürge, m. counter-bail, counter-pledge.
Gegend, gä'gent, f. country, region, quarter, part; umliegende —, neighborhood, environs.
Gegendienst, gä'gendīnsst, m. return, service in return. **Gegenforderung,** gä'genforderung, f. counter-claim, offset; -füßler, -fühssler, m. antipode; -gewicht, -gevicht, m. counterweight, counterpoise, counterbalance; — das — halten, to balance, to counterbalance, counterpoise, countervail, to equal; -gift, -gift, n. antidote, counter-poison; -grund, -grunt, m. contrary reason; -klage, -kläge, f. counter charge; -liebe, -lībe, f. return of love, mutual love; -mittel, -mittel, m. antidote, remedy; -part, -part, m. opponent, adversary; -partei, -partēi, f. opposite party, opposition; -pfand, -pfant, n. counter-pledge; -quittung, -kvittung, f. counter-receipt; -rechnung, -recẖnung, f. check account, discount. Rechnung und Gegenrechnung, debit and credit. **Gegenrevolution,** gegenrefolu̱tsiōn', f. counter-revolution; -satz, -sats, m. opposite; antithesis; opposition, contrast, contrary; -schrift, -shrift, m. rejoinder; refutation; -seite, -seite, f. opposite side; reverse; -seitig, -sēitich, a. opposite; reciprocal, -ly, mutual, a. -ly, av.; -seitigkeit, -käet, f. reciprocity; -stand, -zhtant, m. object, subject; -stück, -zhtück, m. counterpart; -theil, -tāil, n. contrary; im —, on the contrary; reverse; -über, -üh'ber, n. over-against, opposite, abreast; -unterschrift, -untershrift, f. counter-signature; mit — versehen, to countersign; -versprechen, -ferzhprechen, n. counter-promise; -vorstellung, -forzhtellung, f. remonstrance; -wart, -vart, f. presence, the present; -wärtig, -vërtich, a. av. present, at present, now, for the present; -wehr, -vār, f. defence; -werth, -vërt, m. equivalent; -wirkung, -virrkung, f. reaction, counter-effect; -zeuge, -tsëûge, m. counter-witness.
Gegner, gäg'ner, m. adversary, opponent.
Gehaben, gehäb'en, vr. sich —, to behave, conduct one's self; to be well, ill. Gehabt euch wohl, good-bye, farewell, adieu.
Gehege, gehä'ge, n. hedge; fence, inclosure, precinct.
Gehalt, gehalt', m. contents; pl. measure (of a vessel): salary, pay, wages; intrinsic value, worth; alloy, standard; -los, -lōs. a. empty, shallow, chimerical; -losigkeit, -käet, f. emptiness, shallowness; -reich, -reich, -voll, -foll, a. pithy, nervous,

of real value. **Gehalten**, gehal'ten, *a.* bound, obliged.
Gehässig, gehäs'sich, *a.* odious, -ly, *av.* hateful, -ly, *av.* malicious, malignant, spiteful, -ly, *av.*; **-keit**, -käet, *f.* ill will, aversion; hatefulness, odiousness, odium.
Gehau, gehäu', *n.* cutting, clearing, felling of trees.
Gehäuse, gehäy'se, *n.* case; box, capsule, shell, cod, ball.
Geheim, gehēm', *a. av.* secret, -ly, *av.* clandestine, privy, private, hidden; **-mittel**, -mittel, *n.* arcanum; **—er Rath**, privy counselor; **-schreibekunst**, -shrēibekunst, *m.* cryptography; **-schreiber**, -shrēiber, *m.* secretary; **-niß**, -niss, *n.* secret, arcanum, mystery; **-reich**, -reich. **-voll**, -foll, *a.* mystic, mysterious, *a.* -ly, *av.*; **-krämer**, -krämer, *a.* mysterious person.
Geheiß, gehēss', *n.* command, order, bidding; **auf —**, by order, command.
Gehen, gā'-en (ging, gegangen), *v.* to go, to walk; to pass; to swell (dough); (mech.) to work; **— zu Grunde**, to go to ruin; **— von Statten**, to succeed; **— sich befinden**, to do well, to be; **er befindet sich wohl**, he is well; **wohl gehen für wohl ergehen**, to prosper; to succeed; **wie geht es Dir, Ihnen?** how do you do? how are you? **Ich bin wohl. mir geht es wohl**, I am well, I am doing well.
Gehener, gehey'er, *fig.* secure, not haunted; **immer mit der Negation: nicht geheuer**, haunted; unclear, doubtful.
Gehilfe, gehilf'e, *m.* assistant.
Geheul, gehēül', *n.* howling; roaring, cries, lamentation.
Gehirn, gehirrn', *n.* brain, brains.
Gehölz, gehölts', *n.* wood; **am Hause**, plantation.
Gehör, gehöhr', *n.* hearing; audience; **gutes —**, a good, a quick, sharp ear; **— geben**, to grant, to give way, to hear.
Gehorchen, gehorch'en, *vi.* to obey, to submit.
Gehören, gehöh'ren, *vi.* to belong to, to be due; to be fit, becoming.
Gehörig, gehöh'rich, *a.* due, duty; *av.* belonging; **Gehör'nerv**, -nerf, *a.* auditory nerve.

Gehörnt, gehörnt', *a.* horned, (bot.) cornuted.
Gehorsam, gehor'sam, *m.* obedient, *a.* -ly, *av.* dutiful, *a.* -ly, *av. s.* obedience; **— leisten**, to yield obedience to obey. **Gehor'samen**, -samen, *vi.* to obey.
Gehre, gä're, *f.* bevel, wedge; oblique direction.
Geier, gei'er, *m.* vulture, hawk.
Geifer, gīē'fer, *m.* slaver, drivel, spittle. **Geifern**, gēēf'ern, *vi.* to slaver, to slabber, to fret and fume.
Geige, gei'ge, *f.* violin, fiddle; *vi.* to fiddle, to play on the violin; **-bogen**, -bögen, *m.* bow, fiddle-bow; **-harz**, -härts, *n.* colophony; **-saite**, -saēte, *m.* fiddle-string; **-sattel**, -sattel, **-steg**, -zhtāg, *m.* bridge of a violin. **Geiger**, gei'ger, **[spieler**, -zpēl-ler, *m.* violinist.
Geil, gaēl. *a.* fat, greasy, fertile; luxuriant, rank; lascivious, lecherous, libidinous, lustful, -ly, voluptuous, -ly, *av.* wanton, -ly, *av.*; obscene, -ly, *a.*; **-heit**, -hāēt, *f.* lasciviousness.
Geiß, gais, *f.* goat; mountain-goat, wild goat; **-bock**, -bock. *m.* he-goat; roe-buck; **-fuß**, -fus, *m.* handspike; socket-chisel; (mech.) horse.
Geißel, geis'sel, *f.* hostage.
Geißel, gais'sel, *f.* scourge, whip, lash, cow-hide. **Geißeln**, -eln, *vi.* to scourge, lash, whip, to cow-hide; **-ung**, -ung, *f.* lashing, flagellation.
Geist, gäēst, *m.* spirit, ghost; soul, life; mind; vivacity, temper, sprightliness; genius. **Geisterbanner**, gäēsterbanner, **-beschwörer**, -beshvöhrer, *m.* exorcist; **-seher**, -sä-er, *m.* visionary. **Gei'sesbildung**, -bildung, *f.* cultivation of mind; **-frucht**, -frucht, *f.* production of the mind; **-gegenwart**, -gegenvart, *f.* presence of mind; **-kraft**, -kraft, *f.* power of mind, energy; **-schwache**, -shvech, *f.* debility of mind; **-schwung**, -shvung, *m.* genius, flight of the genius; **-los**, -lōs, *f.* spiritless, flat, destitute of wit or genius **-losigkeit**, -lōsichkäēt, *f.* insipidity **-reich**, -gäēst'reich, *a.* ingenious sprightly; **-voll**, -foll, *a.* full of spirit; witty. **Geistig**, gais'tich, *a.* intellectual, -ly, *av.* mental; spiritual

spiritous, generous (wine). **Geist'-
lich**, -lich, a. ecclesiastical, clerical,
spiritual, religious, -ly, av. ghostly;
s. clergyman, ecclesiastic, minister,
pastor; -**feit**, -**käet**, f. clergy, clergyman.

Geiz, geits, m. avarice, covetousness.
Geizen, geit'sen, vi. to covet; to be
niggardly. **Geizig**, geit'zich, a.
covetous, -ly, av. avaricious, -ly, av.
Geiz'er, **Geizhals**, geits'hals, m. miser, niggard.

Gekicher, gekich'er, n. tittering.
Geklapper, geklap'per, n. rattling,
clacking.
Geklatsche, geklat'she, n. clapping;
gossiping.
Geklirre, geklirr'e, n. clashing, clank,
clang.
Geknirsch, gek(e)nirsh', n. gnashing,
grinding.
Geknister, gek(e)nis'ter, n. crackling.
Gekrach, gekrach', n. crash, cracking.
Gekreisch, gekraish', n. screaming,
shrieking.
Gekritzel, gekrit'sel, n. scribbling,
scrawl.
Gekröse, gekröh'se, n. pluck, ruff,
tripe.
Gelächter, gelech'ter, n. laughter.
Gelag, geläk', n. banquet, feast, revel;
layer, stratum.
Gelahrtheit, gelärt'häet, f. learning,
erudition.
Geländer, gelen'der, n. balustrade,
railing.
Gelangen, gelang'en, vi. to arrive,
reach, join, got, attain; — **laffen**,
to bring out; to address.
Gelärm, gelerm', n. tumult, noise.
Gelass, gelass', n. room, space.
Gelassen, gelas'sen, a. patient, -ly, av.
calm, cool, a. -ly. a. **Gelassenheit**,
-häet, f. patience, calmness of mind,
moderation.
Gelaufe, gelau'fe, n. running. **Geläu-
fig**, geläufich, a. fluent, easy, current, voluble, familiar, -ly, av.;
-**feit**, -**käet**, f. fluency, easiness,
volubility.
Gelaunt, gelaunt', a. disposed; gut —
fein, to be in spirits, in good humor;
nicht gut — fein, to be out of humor.
Geläute, geläu'te, n. ringing.
Gelb, gelp, a. yellow. **Gelbbeere**,
gelp'bäre, m. French berry. **Gelb'-

erde**, -ärde, n. yellow earth; **-hals**,
-holts, n. yellow wood, fustic; -**sucht**,
-sucht, f. jaundice; -**süchtig**, -süchtich,
a. jaundiced. **Gelb'gießer**, -**ßsser**,
m. brazier, brass-founder. **Gelb'-
lich**, lich, a. yellowish. **Gelb'schnabel**, -shnabel, m. green-horn.

Geld, gelt, n. money; baares —, ready money, cash; **Papiergeld**, currency. **Geld'beutel**, -beütel, n
purse, porte-monnaie. **Geld'buße**,
-busse, fine; **-curs**, -kurss, m. course
of exchange; **-erwerb**, -ärvärp, m.
money-making; **-forderung**, -for-
derung, f. claim of money; -**geiz**,
-geits, -**gier**, -gir, f. avarice, greediness for money; -**mäkler**, -mekler,
m. (money) broker; -**mangel**, -man-
gel, m. scarcity of money; -**noth**,
-nöt, f. distress of money; -**sache**,
-sache, f. money-matter; -**schuld**,
-shuld, f. money-debt; -**sendung**,
-sendung, f. remittance of money;
-**strafe**, -shtrafe, f. fine; -**stück**,
-zhtük, n. piece of money, coin;
-**verlegenheit**, -förlägenhäet, f. pecuniary embarrassment; -**vorschuß**,
-forshuss, m. advance of money;
-**vortheil**, -fortael, m. pecuniary advantage; -**wechsler**, -vexler, m. banker; -**wucher**, -vucher, m. usury,
stock-jobbing.

Gelegen, geläg'en, a. situate, situated;
convenient, opportune, -ly, av.;
-**heit**, -häet, f. occasion, opportunity, convenience; -**heitlich**, -lich, a.
occasional, a. -ly, av. incidental, -ly,
accidentally.

Gelehrig, geläh'rich, a. docile; -**keit**,
-käet, f. docility, tractableness.
Gelehrt, gelärt', a. learned; -**heit**,
-häet, **Gelehrsamkeit**, -samkäet, f.
learning, scholarship; -**er**, s. learned
man, scholar.

Geleise, geläi'se, n. track, rut.
Geleite, geläi'te, n. escort, convoy,
safeguard; attendance, retinue,
train. **Geleiten**, vt. to escort, to
accompany.

Gelenke, gelenk'e, n. joint; link; in-
ternode: knuckle; -**ig**, -ich, a. flexible, pliant, supple, limber, a. -ly,
av.; -**igkeit**, -käet, f. flexibility,
suppleness; -**sam**, -sam, -**keit**, -käet,
f. das.

Gelichter, gelich'ter, n. cast, stamp
make, set.

Gel 134 **Gem**

Geliebter, gelīb'tẹr, **Geliebte**, m. u. f. lover, mistress, sweetheart.
Gelinde, gẹlin'dẹ, a. soft, smooth, gentle, slight, a. -ly, av. **Gelindigkeit**, -kǟet, f. mildness, softness; indulgence.
Gelingen, gẹling'en (gelang, gelungen), vi. to succeed, prosper, to speed; es gelingt mir, I succeed, prosper in.
Gelispel, gẹlis'pel, n. lisping, whispering.
Geloben, gẹlōb'ẹn, vt. to vow, to promise solemnly. **Gelobt**, gelōbt', n. votive, promised;— es Land, land of promise.
Gelöbniß, gẹlöp'niss, s. pl. -sse, **Gelübde**, -lüp'dẹ, solemn promise, vow.
Gelock, gẹlock', s. n. curls, ringlets.
Gelöse, gẹlös', n. dung, fiants.
Gelt, gělt, n. truly! Is it not so?
Gelt, gělt, a. barren.
Gelte, gěl'tẹ, f. pail, bucket, tub.
Gelten, gěl'ten, vt. to geld; to castrate (a female animal).
Gelten (galt, gegolten), vi. to be worth; to be of value; to be current, valid, good; to cost; to prevail; to have authority, influence; to pass for, to stand, count or go for; to be required; — für, to pass for; to be esteemed, to go for; — lassen, not to question; — bei, to have credit with; geltend machen, to make good; to urge, to enforce, to vindicate; es gilt, it concerns; — mir, I'm pointed, aimed at; es gilt nicht, it does not count. **Geltung**, gělt'ụng, f. value, authority, currency; — verschaffen, to enforce.
Gelübde, gelüb'dẹ, n. vow.
Gelüste, gẹlüss'tẹ, n. desire, concupiscence; appetite. **Gelüsten**, gẹlüss'ten, vi. to desire, to covet, to long for, to lust after.
Gemach, gemach', a. av. easy, comfortable, softly, gently; s. n. apartment, room: heimliches —, privy, necessary. **Gemächlich**, gemäch'lich, a. comfortable, easy (av. -ily); -keit, -kǟet, s. f. convenience, ease, easiness, comfortableness.
Gemächt, gemächt', n. genitals, privy parts.
Gemahl, gemǟl', m. -es, pl. -e, consort, spouse, husband. **Gemahlin**, -in, f. wife, spouse, consort.

Gemahnen, gemä'nen, vt. to remind, to put in mind; vi. to seem, appear.
Gemälde, gemǟl'dẹ, pl. gemǟl'de, n. painting, picture; description; -ausstellung, -ǫysztellụng, f. exhibition of pictures; -saal, -sǟl, m. pl. -sǟl-ẹ, picture gallery.
Gemäß, gemǟss', a. av. according, conformable, av. -bly, in conformity with; -heit, -hǟet, f. conformity.
Gemäßigt, gemǟss'icht, a. av. temperate, moderate, av. -ly.
Gemäuer, gemǫy'er, n. walls, building; ruins.
Gemein, gemaen', a. av. common, plentiful, frequent; ordinary, general, current; mean, vulgar; -es Beste, Wohl, public good, welfare; -es Wesen, commonwealth. **Gemein'de**, **Gemeine**, gemaen'ẹ, f. community. **Gemein'geist**, -gǟezht, m. public spirit. **Gemein'gut**, -gụt, n. common property; commons. **Gemein'heit**, -hǟet, f. community; vulgarity, meanness. **Gemein'iglich**, -iglich, a. av. commonly, generally, usually. **Gemein'nützigkeit**, -nütsichkǟet, f. public utility. **Gemein'platz**, -plats, m. commonplace. **Gemein'sam**, -sam, a. av. common, joint. **Gemein'schaft**, -shaft, f. community; intercourse; union, partnership; familiarity; -lich, -lich, a. av. common, joint, in common. **Gemein'sinn**, -sinn, m. public spirit. **Gemein'wesen**, -vǟsen, n. commonwealth.
Gemenge, gemeng'ẹ, n. mixture, medley; alloy; confused mass. **Gemengsel**, gemeng'sẹl, n. medley.
Gemessen, geměs'sen, a. av. precise, strict(ly); sober, sedate; -heit, -hǟet, f. preciaion, strictness.
Gemetzel, gemẹts'el, n. butchery, slaughter, carnage, massacre.
Gemisch, gemish', n. mixture, medley, composition.
Gemme, gem'mẹ, f. gem.
Gemse, gem'sẹ, f. chamois; scraper (Min.).
Gemurmel, n. gemụr'mel, n. murmur, murmuring. **Gemurr(e)**, gemụrr', n. muttering, grumbling.
Gemüse, gemüh'sẹ, n. vegetables, greens.
Gemüth, gemüht', mind; heart; soul. **Gemüthlich**, -lich, a. av. good-hu-

mored, good-natured; easy, comfortable; ‎ſeit, -kāet, f. cosiness; comfort, ease; heartiness; good nature; tenderness of mind. **Ge＝müthś'art**, -art, f. temper; disposition of mind. **Gemüths'bewegung**, -bewägung, f. agitation of mind; emotion; ‎ſtimmung, -zhtimmụng, ‎verfaſſung, ‎-fērfaassụng. ‎zuſtand, tsụzhtạnt, f. state of mind.
Gen, gēn, für gegen, pr. to, toward, towards.
Genas, genạs', pr. v. **Geneſen**.
Genäſchig, genēsh'ịḥ, a. av. fond of dainties, dainty, lickerish.
Genau, genäū', a. av. fitting, close, tight, straight, strict, exact, perfect, accurate, precise, av. -ly. **Genau＝igkeit**, genäụ'iḥkäet, f. accuracy, precision, exactness, strictness; economy.
Genealogie, genealogī', f. genealogy.
Genehm, genäm', a. av. approved of, agreeable to; — ‎ſein, to please; — ‎halten, approve of: agree to, accept; grant. **Genehmigen**, genäm'iḥen, vt. approve of, agree to. **Genehm'i＝gung**, -ụng, f. approval, consent, ratification, acceptation.
Geneigt, genäegt', a. av. inclined, disposed, prone, addicted, apt, ar. -ly; subject; favorable, well disposed, kind, av. -ly. **Geneigtheit**, -häet, f. inclination, propensity, bias, disposition, proneness; good will.
General, generäl', m. general. **Gene＝ralbass**, -bass, m. thorough-bass.
Generallieutenant, generäl'lëutenant, m. lieutenant-general. **Generalma＝jor**, generäl'mayör, m. major-general. **General'marſch**, -marsh, m. general march. **Generalität**, generälität', f. the body of the general officers of an army. **Generalin**, generä'lïn, f. general's lady. **Gene＝raliſſimus**, generälis'simus, m. commander-in-chief.
Geneſen, genā'sen (genaś, geneſen), vi. to recover; to regain health. **Ge＝neſ'ung**, -ụng, f. recovery, convalescence.
Genial, genüäl', **Genial'iſch**, -ish, a. ar. full of genius; genial, jovial.
Genie, shenī', m. genius; ‎ſtreich, -zhtrāeḥ m. eccentric freak.
Genick genick', n. neck, nape.

Genießen, genīs'sen (genoß, genoſſen), vt. to enjoy, to have the use, the benefit of; to taste, to eat. **Genieß'bar**, -bār, a. av. eatable, drinkable.
Geniren, shenīr'en, vt. to trouble, to inconvenience; to constrain, embarass; ‎ſich —, to feel under restraint; ‎ſich nicht —, to make one's self at home.
Geniſt, genist', n. litter, brushwood, twigs; broom, genista.
Genitalien, genïtä'liën, pl. s. genitals.
Genitiv, gen'itif, m. genitive (Gram.).
Genius, gen'iụs, m. genius; pl. **Geni＝en**, genii.
Genommen, genəm'men, pp. v. neh＝men.
Genoß, genoss' (genoß, genoſſen), v. **Genießen**.
Genoß, genöss', m. companion, consort, comrade, fellow, partner, colleague; associate, accomplice; ‎ſin, f. female companion, consort. **Ge＝noſſenſchaft**, genos'senshaft, f. company, society, partnership, association, fellowship.
Genug, genụg', a. av. enough, sufficient, -ly; — thun, to satisfy. **Ge＝nüge**, genü'gə, n. u. f. sufficiency, competency, satisfaction: ‎leiſten, -lǟzhten, to satisfy, content, to please; to give satisfaction. **Genü＝gen**, genü'gen, vi. to suffice, to be enough, to satisfy, answer; ‎ſich — laſſen, to be satisfied. **Genüg'lich**, -liḥ. **Genügſam**, -ſam, a. av. easily satisfied, frugal, reasonable; av. -ly; — ‎ſein, to be content, satisfied with little. **Genugſam**, genuk'sam, a. av. sufficient; ‎ſeit, -käet, f. sufficiency. **Genugthuung**, genụk'tụ＝ụng, f. satisfaction.
Genuß, genụss', m. enjoyment, use, usufruct; pleasure, delight; ‎ſucht, -sụḥt, f. thirst for pleasure; ‎ſüch＝tig, -sịḥtiḥ, a. thirsting for pleasure. pleasure-loving.
Geodäſie, geōdäsī', f. geodesy. **Ge＝odätiſch**, -ish, a. av. geodetic. **Geog＝noſie**, geōgnōsī', f. geognosy. **Ge＝ognoſt**, geōgnost', m. geognost. **Ge＝ograph**, geōgräf', m. geographer. **Geographie**, geōgräfī', f. geography. **Geographiſch**, -ish, a. av. geographic. **Geolog**, geōlōg', m. geologist.

Geologie, gĕōlōgī', *f.* geology. **Geo-logisch,** -ish, *a. av.* geologic. **Geometer,** -mā'ter, *m.* geometrician. **Geometrie,** gĕōmĕtrī', *f.* geometry. **Geometrisch,** -mĕtrish, *a. av.* geometric.
Gepäck, gĕpĕck', *n.* baggage, luggage.
Gepfiffen, gĕpfĭf'fen, *pp. v.* Pfeifen.
Gepflogen, gĕpflō'gen, *pp. v.* Pflegen.
Geplapper, gĕplap'per, *n.* chattering, babbling.
Geplärr, gĕplĕrr', *n.* bawling, howling.
Gepolter, gĕpŏl'ter, *n.* rumbling noise.
Gepräge, gĕprä'gĕ, *n.* impression, stamp.
Geprahl, gĕpräl', *n.* boasting, bragging.
Gepränge, gĕprĕng'ĕ, *n.* pomp, glow, pageantry.
Geprassel, gĕpras'sel, *n.* clattering, crackling noise.
Gerade, gĕrä'dĕ, *a. av.* straight, upright, direct, *av.* -ly; exactly, just; — aus, *n.* straightforward; — hin, -hin, *av.* baŏf.; rashly, inconsiderately. **Gerademachung,** -machung, *f.* rectification. **Geradweg,** -vĕg, *av.* frankly, plainly, freely. **Geradezu,** gĕrä'dĕtsŭ, *av.* straightforward, straight on, directly; upright, openly, frankly; bluntly; cavalierly. **Geradheit,** gĕräd'häĕt, *f.* rectitude, uprightness, integrity. **Geradsinn,** -sinn, *m.* baŏf. **Geradsinnig,** -sinnich, *a. av.* open-hearted, upright. **Geradlinig,** -linich, *a. av.* rectilineal.
Gerassel, gĕras'sel, *n.* rattling, clattering.
Geräth, *n.* **Geräthschaft,** gĕrät'shaft, *f.* tool, vessel, implement, utensil, furniture, chattel.
Gerathen, gĕrä'ten (gerieth, gerathen), *vi.* to light, fall, hit upon; to fall, get into; succeed, prosper; in Brand —, to catch fire.
Gerathen, gĕrä'ten, *pp. v.* Rathen.
Geraum, gĕroŭm', *a. av.* spacious, wide; -e Zeit, long time. **Geräumig,** gĕroŭm'ich, *a. av.* spacious, ample, roomy; -keit, -käĕt, *f.* spaciousness, roominess.
Geräusch, gĕroŭsh', *n.* noise, bustle; -los, -lōs, *a. av.* noiseless, silent; -voll, -foll, *a. av.* noisy, full of noise, bustle.

Geräusch, gĕroŭsh', *n.* pluck (of animals).
Geräusper, gĕroŭsp'er, *n.* continual hawking.
Gerben, siehe Gärben.
Gerecht, gĕrĕcht', *a. av.* just, righteous, *av.* -ly; -igkeit, -ichkäĕt, *f.* justice, righteousness; privilege. **Gerechtsame,** -same, *f.* right, privilege, immunity, prerogative.
Gerede, gĕrä'dĕ, *n.* talk, rumor; albernes —, nonsense.
Gereichen, gĕräi'chen, *vi.* to tend; to prove, to redound, to conduce.
Gereuen, gĕroŭ'en, *vi.* to repent; ich — lassen, to repent; es gereut mich, I repent of it.
Gericht, gĕricht', *n.* dish, mess.
Gericht, gĕricht', *n.* judgment; justice; court, court of justice, tribunal; jurisdiction. **Gerichtlich,** -lich, *a. av.* judicial, *av.* -ly. **Gerichtsbarkeit,** -barkäĕt, *f.* **Gerichtsbezirk,** -bezirk, *m.* jurisdiction. **Gerichtsdiener,** -diner, *m.* beadle, constable. **Gerichtshalter,** -halter, *m.* **Gerichtsbeamter,** -beamter, *m.* justiciary. **Gerichtskosten,** -kosten, **Gerichtsgebühren,** -gebühren, **Gerichtssporteln,** -sporteln, *s. pl.* fees. **Gerichtsstube,** -stube, *f.* court-room. **Gerichtstag,** -tak, *m.* court-day. **Gerichtsverwalter,** -vervalter, *m.* justiciary, deputy-justiciary.
Gering, gering', *a. av.* little; light, small, poor, mean, low; unimportant; -fügig, -fügich, *a. av.* insignificant, trifling. **Geringfügigkeit,** -käĕt, *f.* insignificance, trifle. **Geringhaltig,** -haltich, *a. av.* small in value: of base alloy; weak. **Geringschätzig,** -shĕtsich, *a. av.* disdainful, scornful, contemptuous, *av.* -ly; mean, contemptible, vile, *av.* -ly; -keit, -käĕt, *f.* meanness, contempt. **Geringschätzung,** -ung, *f.* contempt, disregard.
Gerinne, gĕrin'ne, *n.* running; pipe, gutter. **Gerinnen,** gĕrin'nen (gerann, geronnen), *vi.* curdle, clot, coagulate, congeal.
Gerippe, gĕrip'pe, *n.* skeleton, carcass.
Gerippt, gĕrippt', *a. av.* ribbed, groined; fluted.
Gern, gĕrn, *av.* fain, willingly, readily, gladly, freely; usually.
Geröll, gĕrŏll'e, *n.* pebble.

Gerfte, gĕr'ste, *f.* barley. **Gerften,** gĕr'sten, *a.* barley, of barley. **Gerftenfaft,** -saft, *m.* barley-broth, beer. **Gerftenfchleim,** gĕr'stenshläem, *m.* barley-gruel.

Gerte, gĕr'te, switch, whip.

Geruch, gerych', *m.* smell, scent, odor, flavor; **-los,** -lōs, *a. av.* scentless, odorless, savorless; destitute of the faculty of smelling. **Geruchs'nerv,** -nĕrf, *m.* olfactory nerve. **Geruchs'finn,** -sinn, *m.* sense of smelling.

Gerücht, gerücht', *n.* rumor, report; reputation.

Geruhen, gery'en, *vi.* to be pleased, to deign, to condescend.

Gerülle, gerül'le, *n.* loose, rolling rocks, rubbish.

Gerumpel, gerymp'el, *n.* rumbling.

Gerümpel, gerüm'pel, *n.* rubbish, lumber.

Gerüft, gerüst', *n.* scaffold; housing, frame.

Gesammt, gesammt', *a. av.* whole, united, total, *av.* -ly; all; **-betrag,** -beträk, *m.* sum total, total amount.

Gesandter, gesan'ter. *m.* ambassador, minister, envoy; päpstlicher —, nuncio, legate. **Gesandt'schaft, -schaft,** *f.* embassy.

Gesang, gesang', *m.* singing; song; geistlicher —, hymn; — der Nachtigall, warbling; **-buch,** -bych, *n.* hymn-book, psalm-book.

Gesäß, gesäss', *n.* seat, posteriors, fundament.

Gesäuge, gesöyge', *n.* howling, whistling, humming. **Gesäusel,** gesöy'sel, *n.* whispering, rustling.

Geschäft, geshĕft', *n.* business, affairs, employment, occupation. **Geschäftig,** geshĕft'ich, *a. av.* busy, active, bustling; **-keit, -kĕet,** *f.* activity. **Geschäftsführer,** -führer, *m.* manager, factor. **Geschäftsfreund, -fröünt,** *m.* business friend, business connection. **Geschäftskreis,** -krĕĕs, *m.* sphere of business. **Geschäftsmann,** -mann, *m.* business-man, man of business.

Geschehen, geshā'en (geschah, geschehen), *vi.* to happen, chance, befall, occur, take place, come to pass, be done.

Gescheidt, f. Gescheut.

Geschenk, geshenk', *n.* present, gift, donation.

Gescheut, geshëut', *a. av.* clever, prudent, smart, discreet; nicht recht —, out of one's wits, crack-brained; **-heit,** -hĕet, *f.* cleverness, prudence, discretion.

Geschichte, geshichte, *f.* history; story, tale, narrative. **Geschichten,** geshicht'chen, *n.* little tale, anecdote. **Geschichtenbuch,** -buch, *n.* story-book. **Geschichtschreiber,** -shrēber, *m.* historian. **Geschichtlich,** -lich, *a. av.* historical.

Geschick, geshick', *n.* skill, turn, dexterity, address, talent; fitness, aptness; fate, destiny, lot; vein, lode. **Geschicklichkeit,** -kĕet, *f.* dexterity, adroitness, address, skill, talent, art. **Geschickt',** geshickt', *a. av.* dexterous, skillful, clever, ingenious, artful; able; fit, adapted; *av.* -ly, opportune, seasonable; **-keit, -hĕet,** = Geschicklichkeit.

Geschirr, geshirr', *n.* vessel, utensil, tools, harness, plate; **-holz, -helts,** *n.* carriage-timber; **-kammer, -kammer,** *f.* harness-room.

Geschlacht, geshlacht', *a. av.* soft, tender; — machen, to refine, polish, civilize.

Geschlecht, geshlĕcht', *n. pl.* -er, race, genus, sex; kind, species; gender; generation; descent, family, kindred. **Geschlechtlich,** -lich, *a. av.* sexual; generic; **-los,** -lōs, *a. av.* sexless. **Geschlechtskunde, -kynde,** *f.* genealogy. **Geschlechtsname, -name,** *m.* surname, family name. **Geschlechtsregister,** -register, *n.* genealogy, pedigree. **Geschlechtstheile,** -tĕele, *s. pl.* genitals. **Geschlechtstrieb,** -trĭb, *m.* sexual instinct. **Geschlechtswort,** geshlĕchts'vort, *n.* article.

Geschlossen, *pp. v.* Schließen.

Geschmack, geshmack', *m.* taste; savor, flavor; liking, relish. **Geschmacklos, -lōs,** *a. av.* tasteless, savorless, insipid; **-igkeit, -ichkĕet,** *f.* insipidity, tastelessness. **Geschmackvoll, -foll,** *a. av.* tasteful, elegant, tasty, *av.* -ily. **Geschmackwidrig, -vĭdrig,** *a.* tasteless, inelegant; **-keit, -kĕet,** *f.* inelegance; want of good taste, offense against good taste.

Geschmatz, geshmats', *n.* smacking. **Geschmeide,** geshmĕi'de, *n.* trinkets, jewels, jewelry.

Gef 138 **Gefi**

Geſchmeidig, geshmeī'dich, *a. av.* supple, pliant, soft; **-keit, -kāēt,** *f.* suppleness, pliancy; — der Metalle, ductility, malleability.
Geſchmeiß, geshmēēss', *n.* dung of birds of prey; dung *or* eggs of flies; vermin, rabble.
Geſchmetter, gerhmĕt'ter, *n.* crashing, pealing, warbling.
Geſchmier, geshmīr', *n.* greasing; scrawling, scribbling.
Geſchnatter, geshnat'ter, *n.* cackling, chattering.
Geſchniegelt, geshnī'gelt, *a.* spruce, trim.
Geſchöpf, geshöpf', *n.* creature.
Geſchoß, geshōss', *n.* missile, projectile, fire-arms; young branch, shoot; floor, story.
Geſchrei, geshrāē', *n.* cry, clamor, outcry, shriek, scream; discredit, disrepute; noise, bustle.
Geſchütz, geshūts', *n.* ordnance, artillery, cannon; **-kunſt, -kŭnzht,** *f.* gunnery.
Geſchwader, geshvād'er, *n.* squadron; swarm.
Geſchwätz, geshvĕts', *n.* talk, prate, babble. **Geſchwätzig,** geshvĕts'ich, *a. av.* talkative. **Geſchwätzigkeit, -kāēt,** *f.* talkativeness.
Geſchweigen, geshvēīg'en, *vt.* to pass by, not to mention. **Geſchweige,** geshvēīg'e, *vi.* not to mention, except.
Geſchwind, geshvīnt', *a. av.* swift, fast, quick, speedy, *av.* **-ly. Geſchwindigkeit, -kāēt,** *f.* swiftness, velocity, speed, haste; **-e Höhe,** impetus.
Geſchwirr, geshvirr', *n.* whiz, whir; chirping.
Geſchwiſter, geshvizh'ter, *n.* brother, sister; *gew. pl.* brothers and sisters. **Geſchwiſterkind', -kint,** *n.* cousin-german, first-cousin. **Geſchwiſterlich, -lich,** *a. av.* brotherly, sisterly.
Geſchwulſt, geshvŭlst', *f.* swelling, tumor.
Geſchwür, geshvühr', *n.* abscess, ulcer, sore.
Geſell, gesell', *m.* fellow, companion; journeyman; associate. **Geſellen,** gesell'en, *vt.* associate, accompany, join. **Geſellig, -ich,** *a. av.* sociable; social; **-keit, -kāēt,** *f.* sociableness, sociability, sociality, conviviality.

Geſellſchaft, -shaft, *f.* company, society, party; partnership; geſchloſſene —, club. **Geſellſchafter, -shafter,** *m.* **-in, -in,** *f.* companion. **Geſellſchaftlich, -lich,** *a. av.* social, sociable; gregarious. **Geſellſchaftsſpiel, -spīl,** *n.* social game.
Geſenk, gesenk', *n.* boss, print, swage.
Geſetz, gesets', *n.* law, decree, statute, rule; —e machen, legislate. **Geſetzbuch, -buch,** *n.* code. **Geſetzentwurf, -entvurf,** *m.* bill. **Geſetzgebend, -gābent,** *a. av.* legislative. **Geſetzgeber, -gāber,** *m.* law-giver, legislator. **Geſetzgebung, -gābung,** *f.* legislation, legislature. **Geſetzlich, -lich,** *a. av.* lawful, legal, legitimate; **-keit, -kāēt,** *f.* lawfulness, legality, legitimacy. **Geſetzeskraft, -kraft,** *f.* legal sanction. **Geſetzlos, -lōs, *a. av.* lawless, illegal, unlawful, anarchical; **-igkeit, -ichkāēt,** *f.* lawlessness, illegality, anarchy. **Geſetzmäßig, -māssig, *a. av.* legal, lawful, legitimate; **-keit, -kāēt,** *f.* legality, lawfulness, legitimacy. **Geſetzwidrig, -vīdrig, *a. av.* illegal, unlawful; **-keit, -kāēt,** *f.* illegality, unlawfulness.
Geſetzt, gesetst', *a. av.* grave, steady, staid, sober, sedate; fixed; — daß, suppose that; **-heit, -hāēt,** *f.* gravity, steadiness, sedateness.
Geſeufze, gesēūf'tse, *f.* sighing, groaning.
Geſicht, gesicht', *n.* sight, eye-sight, view; face, countenance, look; apparition, vision; *pl.* **Geſichter,** faces; *pl.* **Geſichte,** visions. **Geſichtchen,** gesicht'chen, *n.* little face. **Geſichtsbildung, -bildung,** *f.* physiognomy, features, countenance. **Geſichtsfarbe, -farbe,** *f.* complexion. **Geſichtskreis, -krāēs,** *m.* horizon, sight. **Geſichtspunkt, -pŭnkt,** *m.* point of view. **Geſichtszug, -tsŭk,** *m.* feature.
Geſims, gesims', *n.* shelf, cornice; — eines Kamins, mantelpiece, chimney-piece. **Geſimshobel, -hōbel,** *m.* moulding-plane.
Geſinde, gesinn'de, *n.* domestics, menials. **Geſindel,** gesinn'del, *n.* rabble, mob.
Geſinnt, gesinnt', *a. av.* disposed, minded; *av.* **-ly. Geſinnung, -ŭng,** *f.*

disposition, mind, opinion, feeling, sentiment.

Gesittet, gesit'tet, a. av. mannered, well-bred. **Gesittung**, -ung, f. cultivation, civilization.

Gesonnen, geson'nen, a. disposed, intending; — fein, to intend, to design, to purpose.

Gespan, gespan', m. companion, partner, assistant. **Gespann**, gespann', n. team; -schaft, -shaft, f. company; county, palatinate. **Gespannt**, gespannt', pp. von spannen, a. av. stretched, intent, intense, attentive; — sein mit, to be on ill terms with.

Gespenst, gespenst', n. pl. -er, spectre, ghost, sprite, goblin; apparition, phantom. **Gespensterstunde**, -stunde, midnight hour. **Gespenstig, Gespenstisch**, -ish, a. av. spectral; ghastly.

Gespiele, gespīl'e, m. sin, f. playmate, companion.

Gespinnst, gespinnst', n. web; something spun.

Gespött, gespött', n. mockery, scoffing, derision.

Gespräch, gespräch', n. conversation; dialogue; -ig, -ig, a. av. talkative, affable, loquacious, av. -ly -igkeit, -keet, f. talkativeness, affability. **Gesprächsweise**, -veise, av. in conversation.

Gestade, gestäd'e, n. shore, beach.

Gestalt, gestalt', f. figure, form, shape, appearance; -los, -lōs, a. av. shapeless; -losigkeit, kēet, f. shapelessness. **Gestalten**, gestal'ten, vt. to form, shape, fashion, mould. **Gestaltung**, -ung, f. formation; configuration, form, figure.

Geständig, geshten'dig, a. av. confessing, av. -ly; — sein, to confess, acknowledge, avow, own. **Geständniss**, geshtend'niss, n. confession.

Gestank, geshtank', m. stench, stink.

Gestatten, geshtat'ten, vt. to permit, allow, grant. **Gestattung**, -ung, f. permission, allowance.

Gesteck, f. Besteck.

Gestehen, geshtä'en (gestand, gestanden), vt. to confess, own, allow; vi. to curdle, coagulate, congeal.

Gestein, geshtīn', n. rock, stone.

Gestell, geshtell', n. frame, stand; — eines Raubvogels, feet.

Gestern, gesh'tern, av. yesterday; — Morgen, — früh, yesterday morning; — Abend, last evening, last night; — vor acht Tagen, yesterday sennight; vorgestern, the day before yesterday. **Gestrig**, gest'rich, a. av. yesterday('s).

Gestiefelt, geshtī'felt, a. booted, in boots.

Gestielt, geshtīlt', a. stalked, petiolate.

Gestirn, geshtīrrn', n. constellation, star. **Gestirnt**, geshtīrrnt', a. starred, starry.

Gestöber, geshtöh'ber, n. drift, drizzling of snow.

Gesträuch, geshtröüch', n. thicket, shrubs, bushes, shrubbery.

Gestreng, geshtreng', a. av. severe, strict; (title) your worship.

Gestrichen, geshtrich'en, pp. v. Streichen.

Gestrick, geshtrick', n. knitting, network, netting.

Gestrubel, geshtry'del, n. bubbling up; whirlpool.

Gesträuppe, geshtrüp'pe, n. bushes, thorny thicket, undergrowth.

Gestübe, geshtüb'be, n. coal dust.

Gestunden, geshtyund'en, vt. to respite, delay, put off. **Gestundung**, -ung, f. respite, delay.

Gestüte, geshtü'te, n. stud.

Gesuch, gesych', n. petition, suit, request, prayer.

Gesudel, gesy'del, n. scribble, scrawl; daub, dirty work.

Gesumm', Gesumme, gesymm'se, n. humming, buzzing.

Gesund, gesynt', a. av. healthy, healthful, av. -ly; sen, -en, vi. to recover health. **Gesundheit**, -hēet, f. health, healthiness; wholesomeness, salubrity; soundness; Eine — ausbringen, to toast any one, to drink any one's health.

Gesunken, gesynk'en, pp. von Sinken.

Gethan, getän', pp. von thun, done.

Getön, getöhn', n. sounds; clamor, noise.

Getöse, getöh'se, n. noise, din.

Getrabe, geträ'be, n. trotting.

Getrampel, getram'pel, n. trampling.

Getränk, getrenk', n. drink, beverage, potion; geistiges —, spirituous liquors, spirits.

Getrauen, getröy'en, vr. fich —, to dare, venture, risk.
Getreide, getrǟ́de, n. corn, grain. **Getreideboden**, -bōden, m. corn-land; corn-loft, granary. **Getreidehandel**, -handel, m. corn-trade. **Getreidehändler**, -hēntler, m. corn merchant. **Getreidemarkt**, -markt, m. corn-market.
Getreu, Getreulich, getröü'lich, a. av. faithful, honest, -ly, true, truly.
Getriebe, getrī'be, n. pinion; whirl.
Getroffen, getroffen, pp. v.Treffen.
Getrost, getrōzht', a. av. confident, of good cheer, confidently; cj. cheer up! **Getrösten**, getröhzh'ten, vt. to hope, expect confidently.
Getümmel, getüm'mel, n. tumult, turmoil, bustle.
Geübt, geühbt', a. av. versed, expert, practised; **-heit**, -hāēt, f. expertness, practice.
Gevatter, gefat'ter, m. godfather; **-in**, -in, f. godmother, gossip. **Gevatterschaft**, -shaft, f. sponsorship.
Gevierre, gefī're, n. quadripartition. **Geviert**, gefīrt', a. ar. quadripartite; quaternary; (Schild) quartered; vierfach geviert, counter quartered. **Geviertes**, gefīr'tes, n. square, sequence: ins Gevierte, square. **Geviertschein**, -shęēn, m. quadrature, quartile.
Geflügel, gefüh'gel, n. birds, fowls.
Gewächs, gevèx', n. plant, vegetable, herb; growth; excrescence; **-haus**, -hōus, n. hot-house, conservatory, green-house. **Gewachsen**, gevak'sen, a. one's equal; — fein, to be one's equal, a match.
Gewahr, gevār', a. sensible, aware; — werben, to perceive, discover, become aware.
Gewähr, gevǟr', f. vouch, warrant, warranty, security; — leiften, warrant, guarantee. **Gewährleiftung**, -laēzhtyng, f. warranty, guaranty. **Gewährsmann**, -mann, m. surety, bail.
Gewahrsam, gevār'sam, m. custody, safe-keeping, ward.
Gewährung, gevǟr'yng, f. granting, accomplishment.
Gewalt, gevalt', f. force, power, violence, vehemence; authority, dominion; oberfte —, supremacy; — anthun, to do, offer violence; to wrench, explain in a forced way. Gewalt haben über, to be master of; mit Gewalt, forcible. **Gewalthaber**, -haber, m. potentate. **Gewaltherrscher**, -hērrsher, m. despot. **Gewaltherrschaft**, -shaft, f. despotism. **Gewaltstreich**, -zhträēch, m. violent, illegal measure, violence. **Gewaltsthat**, -tät, f. violent act, violence; pl. acts of violence. **Gewaltthätig**, -tätig, a. av. violent, forcible, av. -ly; **-feit**, -kāēt, f. violence, despotic disposition. **Gewaltig**, geval'tich, a. powerful, mighty; vast; av. -ly. **Gewaltsam**, -sam, a. forcible, violent, unnatural, av. -ly; **-feit**, -kāēt, f. force, violence.
Gewand, gevant', n. pl. Gewänder, garment, raiment; champ (Arch.).
Gewandt, gevant', a. quick, active, adroit, dexterous, expeditious; versatile, easy; av. -ly. **Gewandtheit**, -hāēt, f. quickness, activity, adroitness; versatility.
Gewärtig, gevèr'tig, a. expecting, expectant; — fein, gewärtigen, vi. to expect.
Gewäsch, gevēsh', n. idle talk, nonsense.
Gewässer, gevēs'ser, n. water, flood.
Gewebe, gevā'be, n. weft, web, stuff, texture.
Gewehr, gevā-r', n. gun, musket; arms.
Geweih, gevēī', n. horns, antlers.
Gewerbe, gevèr'be, m. trade, profession, business; — treiben, to carry on a trade. **Gewerbfleiß**, gevèrp'flēīss, m. industry. **Gewerbsam**, -sam, a. industrious. **Gewerbschule**, -shyle, f. school for artisans; industrial school; höhere —, polytechnical institution. **Gewerblich**, -lich, a. industrial.
Gewerk, gevèrk', n. guild; corporation; work.
Gewicht, n. **Gewichtigkeit**, gevichtigkāēt, f. weight; importance; stress. **Gewichtig**, a. weighty, ponderous; av. -ly.
Gewillt, gevillt', a. inclined, disposed; — fein, to intend.
Gewimmel, gevim'mel, n. swarm, throng; moving to and fro.
Gewinde, gevin'de, n. winding, twisting, maze; coiling, twisting, spire, worm, thread.

Gewinn, gewinn', *m.* gain, profit, produce, acquisition, advance, return, proceeds. **Gewin'nen,** *vt.* to win, gain, obtain, get, earn. **Gewin'ner,** *m.* gainer. **Gewinnst,** gewinnzht', *m.* gain. **Gewinnsucht,** gewinn'sucht, *f.* avarice, greediness. **Gewinnsüchtig, -süchtig,** *a.* avaricious, greedy, *av.* -ly, greedy for gain.
Gewinsel, gewin'sel, *n.* whimpering, whining; moaning.
Gewirbel, gewirr'bel, *n.* whirling; rolling; warbling.
Gewirk, gewirrk', *n.* texture, web; working.
Gewirr, gewirr', *n.* complication, confusion, entanglement, maze of words.
Gewiß, gewiss', *a.* certain, sure, settled, *av.* -ly. **Gewissen,** gewis'sen, *n.* conscience. **Gewissenhaft, -haft,** *a.* conscientious, scrupulous; *av.* -ly; *igkeit,* -këet, *f.* conscientiousness. **Gewissenlos, -lös,** *a.* unscrupulous, unprincipled; *igkeit,* -këet, *f.* unscrupulousness, want of principle. **Gewissensangst,** gewis'sensangzht, *f.* anguish, remorse. **Gewissensbiß, -biss,** *m.* basf. **Gewissensskrupel, -zhrupel,** *m.* qualm, scruple of conscience. **Gewissermaßen, -mässen,** *av.* in a certain degree, in some respect, manner. **Gewißheit, -hëet,** *f.* certainty, surety. **Gewißlich, -lich,** *av.* certainly.
Gewitter, gewit'ter, *n.* thunderstorm, storm. **Gewitterwind, -vind,** *m.* tempest. **Gewitterwolke, -völke,** *f.* thunder-cloud.
Gewitzigt, gewits'icht, *a. av.* rendered wise, taught wisdom by.
Gewoben, gewö'ben, *pp. v.* Weben.
Gewoge, gewö'ge, *n.* waving, rolling: wave.
Gewogen, gewö'gen, *a.* well disposed, favorable, kind, *av.* -ly; — sein, to bear good will towards; *heit,* -hëet, *f.* favor, kindness.
Gewöhnen, gewöh'nen, *vt.* to accustom, inure one's self. **Gewohnt,** gewönt', *a. av.* usual; — sein, to be wont, accustomed, in the habit of, inured to. **Gewöhnen,** gewöh'nen, *vt.* to accustom, use, habituate, inure, form, mould. **Gewohnheit,** gewön'hëet, *f.* habit, custom, use; zur Gewohnheit werden, to grow into habit. **Ge-**

wöhnlich, gewöhn'lich, *a.* customary, usual, ordinary, habitual; *av.* -ly.
Gewölbe, gewöl'be, *n.* vault, arch warehouse; *pfeiler,* -pfëiler, *m.* buttress; *stein,* -zhtëin, *m.* voussoir, archstone, keystone.
Gewölf, gewölk', *n.* clouds.
Gewonnen, gewön'nen, *pp. v.* Gewinnen.
Geworben, gewor'ben, *pp. v.* Werben.
Geworden, gewor'den, *pp. v.* Werden.
Geworfen, gewor'fen, *pp. v.* Werfen.
Gewüchs, gewühks', *n.* growth.
Gewühl, gewühl', *n.* rooting, turning up; bustle, throng, crowd.
Gewürm, gewürm', *n.* worms, vermin; rabble.
Gewürz, gewürts', *n.* spice; *pl.* -e, aromatics. **Gewürzartig, -artig,** **Gewürzhaft, -haft,** *a.* spicy, aromatic. **Gewürzbüchse,** gewürts'büxe, *f.* spice-box. **Gewürzhändler, -hent-** ler, *m.* spicer, grocer. **Gewürzkram, -kräm,** *m.* retail of spices. **Gewürznelke, -nëlke,** *f.* **Gewürznägelein, -nägelkën,** *n.* clove. **Gewürzwein, -vëen,** *m.* spiced wine.
Gezäh, getsä', **Gezäu,** getsäü, *n.* tools, implements (Min.).
Gezänk, getsenk', *n.* quarrel, wrangle, dispute.
Gezelt, getsëlt', *n.* tent.
Gezeug, getsëüg', *n.* tool, instrument.
Geziefer, getsïï'fer, *n.* vermin, insects.
Geziemen, getsï'men, *vt.* to beseem, become, befit, suit. **Geziemend,** getsï'ment, *a.* befitting, becoming, proper, due.
Geziert, getsïrt', *a.* decorated, ornamented; affected. **Geziertheit, -hëet,** *f.* affectation, affectedness.
Gezisch, getsish', *n.* hissing.
Gezogen, getsö'gen, *pp. v.* Ziehen, rifled; clarified (quill), dipped (candle).
Gezücht, getsücht', *n.* brood, breed; set.
Gezweig, getsvëig', *n.* branches, ramage.
Gezweit, getsvëit', *a.* binary, double.
Gezwitscher, getsvit'sher, *n.* chirping, warbling.
Gezwungen, getsvung'en, *pp.* von Zwingen, forced, unnatural, affected.
Gicht, gicht, *f. pl.* -en, mouth of a furnace.

Gicht, gicht, *f.* gout. **Gicht'bruch**, -bruch, *m.* palsy. **Gicht'brüchig**, -brüchig, *a. u. s.* palsied, paralytic. **Gicht'isch**, -isch, *a.* gouty. **Gicht'schmerz**, -shmērts, *m.* pain of the gout. **Gicht'taffet**, -taffet, *m.* antiarthriticated taffeta.

Gichtrose, gicht'rō-se, *f.* peony.

Giebel, gī'ble, *m.* gable, gable-end; pediment, fronton.

Gieke, gī'ke, *f.* foot-stove.

Giekbaum, gīk'baŭm, *m.* main boom.

Giekſegel, gīk'sāgl, *n.* long boomsail.

Gier, gīr, *f.* **Gier'be**, -de, *f.* strong desire, greediness, eagerness. **Gieren**, gī'ren, *vi.* to long for; to yaw, fall off. **Gierig**, gī'rich, *a.* greedy, covetous, eager, *av.* -ly; *-keit*, -kāet, *f.* greediness, eagerness. **Gierſchlag**, gīr'shläkg, *m.* falling off. **Gierwinde**, gīr'vin-de, *f.* adjusting windlass.

Gießen, gīs'sen (goß, gegoſſen), *vt.* to pour, to spill, to throw water; to cast; diffuse, spread.

Gießbach, gīs'bach, *m. pl.* **Gießbäche**, torrent. **Gießbecken**, gīs'becken, *n.* wash-hand-basin. **Gießer**, gīs'er, *m.* founder; skeet. **Gießerei**, -erei', *f.* foundry. **Gießkanne**, -kanne, *f.* watering-pot. **Gießloch**, -loch, *n.* runner. **Gießlöffel**, -löffel, *m.* casting-ladle. **Gießmeister**, -mäezhter, *m.* master founder.

Gift, gift, *f. pl.* -en, gift, present, donation.

Gift, gift, *n.* poison, venom. **Giftarzenei**, giftartsenēī', *f.* antidote, remedy against poison. **Gift'becher**, -becher, *m.* poison-cup. **Gift'erz**, -ärts, *n.* arsenic-ore. **Gift'hauch**, -hauch, *m.* blight. **Gift'ig**, *a.* poisonous, venomous, *av.* -ly. **Gift'kies**, kīs, *m.* arsenical pyrites. **Giftkraut**, gift'krout, *n.* poisonous herb. **Gift'miſcher**, -misher, *m.* poisoner. **Giftmiſcherei**, -rēī', *f.* poisoning. **Gifttrunk**, trunk, *m.* poison-draught.

Gilbe, gil'be, *f.* yellow color.

Gilde, gil'de, *f.* guild, corporation, society.

Gimpel, gim'pel, *m.* chaffinch; blockhead.

Ginst, ginzh **Ginster**, ginzht'er, *m.* broom.

Gipfel, gip'fel, *m.* top, summit, peak, brow, pinnacle.

Gips, gips, *m.* gypsum. **Gips'abbruck**, -apdryck, *m.* plaster-cast; *arbeit*, -arbaët, *f.* plastering, stucco-work. **Gips'bild**, -bilt, *n.* figure in plaster. **Gips'bruch**, -bruch, *m.* **Gips'grube**, -grube, *f.* plaster-quarry. **Gips'decke**, -decke, *f.* stucco-ceiling; plastered ceiling. **Gipſen**, *vt.* to plaster. **Gip'ſer**, **Gips'gießer**, -gīsser, *m.* plasterer. **Gips'form**, -form, *f.* plaster-mould.

Giraffe, gir'affe, *f.* giraffe, camelopard.

Giriren, gīrī'ren, *vt.* to endorse, circulate (a bill of exchange).

Girren, gir'ren, *vi.* to coo, sigh, complain tenderly.

Giſcht, gisht, *m.* froth, foam, spray.

Giſſen, gis'sen, *vi.* to guess, to estimate by guess; *s. auch* **Giſſung**, -ung, *f.* dead reckoning.

Gitter, git'ter, *n.* trellis, gate, railing, lattice, cross-bars; *-fenſter*, -fenzhter, *n.* lattice-window; *-ſtange*, -zhtange, *f.* grate-bar. **Git'terthor**, -tōr, *n.* trellised gate. **Git'terzaun**, -tsaŭn, *m.* trellis-fence. **Git'tern**, *vt.* to lattice, cross-bar, to rail.

Glanz, glants, *m.* lustre, brightness, splendor; glory; *-bürſte*, -bürzhte, *f.* polishing-brush; *-hammer*, -hammer, *m.* polishing-hammer. **Glänzen**, glent'sen, *vi.* to shine, sparkle, glitter. **Glänz'end**, *a.* bright, glossy, *av.* -ly; — *machen*, to polish, burnish. **Glanzleinwand**, glants'lnēnvant, *f.* glazed linen. **Glanzruß**, glants'rŭss, *m.* shining soot. **Glanzwichſe**, glants'vixe, *f.* shoe-blacking.

Glas, gläs, *n.* glass; zu **Glas machen**, *werden*, vitrify. **Glas'artig**, *a.* **Glas'icht**, -icht, **Glas'ig**, -ich, glassy, vitreous. **Glasauge**, gläs'auge, *n.* glass-eye. **Glas'bläſer**, -bläser, *m.* glass-blower, glass-maker. **Glaſer**, gläs'er, *m.* glazier. **Glaſern**, *a.* glassy, vitreous. **Glaſerkitt**, -kitt, *m.* putty. **Glasfaden**, -faden, *m.* glass-thread. **Glasfabrik**, -fabrik, *f.* **Glashütte**, -hütte, *f.* glass-house, glass-work, glass-manufactory. **Glasflüchtigkeit**, glasflüchtigkeit. **Glasflüſſigkeit**, *f.* viskosët, vitreous humor. **Glasfluſſ**, -fluss.

f. glass-bottle. Glas'gasse, -galle, f. sandever. Glas'glocke, -glocke, f. glass-bell. Glashaus, -höys, n. green-house. Glas'händler, -händler, m. dealer in glass. Glas'rei, -fren, vt. to glaze. Glas'topf, -kopf, m. fibrous red-iron ore. Glas'fitt, -kitt, m. putty. Glas'maler, -mäler, m. glass-painter, annealer, painter on glass; -ei, -ei', f. glass-painting, anstic painting, annealing. Glas'= ofen, -öfen, m. glass-furnace. Glas'= scheibe, -scheibe, f. pane of glass. Glas'schleifer, -schleifer, m. glass-grinder. Glas'schneider, -schneider, m. glass-cutter. Glasur, glasür', f. glazing; enamel; ice; varnish. Glaswaare, gläs'väre, f. glass-ware.

Glatt, glatt, a. smooth, even, sleek, slippery, polished; plain; av. -ly. Glätte, glet'te, f. smoothness, slipperiness; litharge. Glatteis, glatt'is, a. sleet, glazed frost. Glätten, glet'ten, vt. to smooth, burnish, polish. Glatt'heit, -hëet, f. f. Glätte. Glatt'hobel, -hōbel, m. smoothing-plane. Glättstahl, glet'zhtäl, m. burnisher. Glattzange, -tzange, f. polisher. Glatt'zahn, -tsän'm. burnisher; wolf's tooth, boar's tusk. Glättstein, glet'zhtëen, m. sleek-stone.

Glatze, glat'se, f. baldness, calvity. Glatzkopf, glats'kopf, m. bald-head. Glaube, glāu'be, m. belief, faith, creed, religion, credit; auf Glauben, on trust; Glauben beimessen, schenken, to give credit. Glauben, glāu'ben, vt. to believe, have faith; to think, suppose, imagine. Glau'bensbekenntniß, -bekentniss, n. creed, confession of faith; apostolisches —, Angsburg Confession. Glau'kreuzbote, -bōte, m. apostle, missionary. Glau'bensfreiheit, -frëi-hëet, f. religious liberty. Glau'bensgenoß, -gen-oss, m. one of the same faith. Glau'benslehre, -läre, f. doctrine of faith, system of religion. Glau'benslaß, -satz, m. dogma. Glau'benszeuge, -tsöyge, m. martyr. Glaub'haft, -haft, a. credible, authentic, trustworthy, av. -ly; -igkeit, -këet, f. credibility, reliability, trustworthiness. Gläubig,

gläu'bich, a. believing, faithful; s m. u. f. believer, faithful. Gläubiger, -biger, m. creditor. Glaublich, gläub'lich, a. credible, creditable, av. -ly; -keit, -këet, f. credibility. Glaub'würdig, -vürdich, a. trustworthy, reliable, credible; -keit, -këet, f. credibility, trustworthiness, reliability.

Glauch, glāuch, a. bright, smooth, pretty; bluish; sterile, dead (vein or lode).

Gleich, glëich, a. even, smooth; equal; just, equitable; same, similar; equivalent, uniform; av. -ly; equally; immediately, at once; von gleichem Werth, at par; ob, wenn gleich, although. Gleich'artig, -ärtich, a. homogeneous; -keit, -këet, f. homogeneousness. Gleich'bedeutend, -bedēütent, a. synonymous, av. -ly, of the same meaning. Gleich'e, f. evenness, equality; straightness. Gleichen, glēi'chen, vt. to equal, match; to resemble, be like; vt. to equalize, to resemble. Gleich'er, m. equator. Gleichfalls, glëich'falls, av likewise, also. Gleich'förmig, -förmich, a. uniform, conformable; -keit, -këet, f. uniformity, conformity. Gleich'geltend, -geltent, a. equivalent. Gleich'gesinnt, -gesinnt, a. of the same mind. Gleich'gestaltet, -gezhtaltet, a. equal in form. Gleich'gestimmt, -gezhtimmt, a. equally tuned; congenial. Gleich'gewicht, -gevicht, n. equilibrium, equipoise, balance; in's Gleichgewicht bringen, to balance. Gleich'gewichtslage, -lāge, f. trim (of a ship). Gleich'gewichtslehre, -läre, f. statics. Gleich'gewichtspunkt, -punkt, m. centre of gravity. Gleich'giltig, -giltich, a. equivalent; indifferent, av. -ly; -keit, -këet, f. equivalence; indifference. Gleich'heit, -hëet, f. equality, equalness, purity; likeness, resemblance; evenness. Gleich'heitszeichen, -tsëchen, n. sign of equality. Gleich'klang, -klang, m. unison: consonance. Gleich'laufend, -lāufent, a.av. parallel. Gleich'laut, -löyt, m. unison: consonance; assonance; paronomasia; -end, -ent, a. unisonous; consonant, assonant; of the same sound: of the same tenor contents; — Abschrift, duplicate. **Gleich'lastig**, -lazhtich, a. upon an even keel. **Gleich'machen**, -machen, rt. to level, equalize; to smooth. **Gleich'maß**, -mass, n. proportion, symmetry. **Gleich'mäßig**, -mässich, a. equal, symmetrical, similar; av. -ly; likewise; -keit, -käet, f. similarity. **Gleich'muth**, -mut, m. **Gleich's müthigkeit**, -müthichkäet, f. equanimity, indifference, calmness. **Gleich'müthig**, -mühtich, a. eventempered, calm, cool, av. -ly. **Gleich's namig**, -nämich, a. homonymous; -keit, -käet, f. sameness of name. **Gleich'niß**, -niss, n. likeness, image; comparison, similitude; simile; parable; -rede, -rädę. f. allegory. **Gleich'jam**, -sam, av. as it were, as if, like as if. **Gleich'schenkelig**, -shenkelich, a. isosceles. **Gleich'seitig**, -seïtich, a. equilateral; -keit, -käet, f. equilateralness. **Gleich'sinn**, -sinn, **Gleich'sinnig**, f. Gleichmuth. **Gleich's stellen**, -zhtellen, vt. to compare, equal. **Gleich'stellung**, -yng, f. comparison, equalization. **Gleich'stimmig**, -zhtimmich, a. consonant, harmonious, accordant, unanimous, av. -ly. **Gleich'theilig**, -täelich, a. isomeric. **Gleich'ung**, -yng, f. equalization; equation. **Gleich'viel**, -fil, av. as much. **Gleich'weit**, -veit, a. equidistant, av. to an equal distance. **Gleichwie**, -vī', av. just as, like. **Gleich'winkelig**, -vinkelich, a. equiangular, av. -ly. **Gleich'wohl**, -vōl, a. nevertheless; however, yet, for all that. **Gleich'zeitig**, -tseïtich, a. simultaneous, coeval, contemporary; synchronous, isochronal; -keit, -käet, f. simultaneousness, synchronism.

Gleis, geläss', n. pl. -e, rut, track. **Gleisen**, gläes'en, vt. to keep the track.

Gleißen, gleïs'sen. vi. to glisten, glitter, shine. **Gleißend**, gleïs'sent, a. deceitful, hypocritical, av. -ly. **Gleißner**, gleïss'ner, m. hypocrite, dissembler. **Gleißnerei**, -reï', f. hypocrisy. **Gleiß'nerisch**, -ish, a. hypocritical.

Gleitbahn, gleït'bân, f. slide, slidingplace.

Gleiten, gleï'ten (glitt, geglitten), vi. to glide, slide, slip.

Gletscher, glèt'sher, m. glacier.

Glied, glīd, n. limb, member; link; rank, file; degree of relationship; term; male member. **Glie'derbau**, -bôy, m. structure (of the limbs). **Glie'derkrankheit**, -krankhäet, f gout, arthritis. **Glie'derlahm**, -läm, a. paralytic, palsied, av. -ly. **Glie's dermann**, -n.ann, m. puppet, layman. **Gliedern**, glī'dern, vt. to furnish with limbs; articulate; to arrange, organize; to form into files. **Glie'derreißen**, -reïssen. n. **Glie'derschmerz**, -shmèrts, m. **Glie'derweh**, -vä, n. pains in the limbs, arthritis, gout. **Gliedmaß**, glīd'mäss, n. limb. **Glied'schwamm**, -shvamm, m. white swelling. **Glied'weise**, **Glie'derweise**, -vëlse, av. by limbs; by ranks.

Glimmen, glimm'en (glomm. geglommen), vi. to glimmer, glow, gleam; to burn faintly; —de Äsche, embers. **Glim'mer**, m. gleam, glimmer, glow; mica; -artig, -ärtich, a. micaceous. **Glim'mererde**, -ërde, f. micaceous earth. **Glim'merig**, -ich, a. glimmering, micaceous. **Glim'mern**, vi. to gleam. **Glim'merschiefer**, -shīfer, m. mica-slate.

Glimpf, glimpf, m. forbearance, mildness, gentleness. **Glimpf'lich**, -lich, a. gentle, forbearing.

Glitschen, glit'shen, vi. to slide, glide, slip.

Glitt, glitt, pp. v. Gleiten.

Glittern, glitt'ern, vi. to glitter, sparkle, shine.

Glocke, glock'ę, f. bell; receiver. **Glöckchen**, glöck'chen, **Glöck'lein**, -läen, n. little bell; bell-flower. **Glockenblume**, glock'enblumę, f. blue bell. **Gloc'kenförmig**, -förmich, a. bell-shaped. **Gloc'kengeläute**, -geleïtę, n. ringing of bells. **Gloc's engießer**, -gisser, m. bell-founder. **Gloc'kengut**, -gut, n. bell-metal **Gloc'kenklang**, -klang, m. chiming of bells. **Gloc'kenklöppel**, -klöppel, m. bell-clapper. **Gloc'kenschlag**, -shläk, m. stroke of the clock, bell. **Gloc'kenschwengel**, -shvengel, lever of the bell. **Gloc'kenspiel**, -shpīl, n. chime. **Gloc'kenstube**, -shtubę, f. **Gloc'kenstuhl**, -zhtyl, m. belfry. **Gloc'kenthurm**, -tyrm, m. steeple. **Gloc'kentaufe**, -taufę, f. benediction of a bell, and **Gloc'kenweihe**, -veihę. **Gloc'kenzug**, -tsyk, m. bell-rope;

Glo 145 **Gol**

ringing of the bell. **Glöckner,** glöck'-ner, m. bell-ringer, sexton.
Glomm, glomm, v. Glimmen.
Glorie, glō'rĭy, f. glory, halo. **Glorreich,** -reĭch, **Glorwürdig,** -vürdĭch, a. glorious, illustrious, ae. -ly. **Glo'riren,** vt. to glory in.
Glossarium, glossā'rĭyum, n. glossary. **Glosse,** glos'sĕ, f. comment, gloss. **Glossator,** glossā'tŏr, m. glosser, commentator.
Glotzen, glŏt'sen, vi. to stare at. **Glotzauge,** -ăoge, n. goggle-eye. **Glotzaugig,** -ăogĭch, a. goggle-eyed. **Glotzer,** m. starer.
Gluchzen, glych'tsen, vi. to hiccough; cluck.
Gluck, glyck, a. clucking, gurgling, goggling. **Glucken,** glyck'en, vi. to cluck, gurgle. **Gluck'e, Gluckhenne,** glyck'hennĕ, f. clucking hen; Pleiads.
Glück, glück, n. luck, fortune, happiness, felicity; success, prosperity, chance; — haben in, to succeed, to be lucky; — münschen, to congratulate; zum Glücke, fortunately; zu seinem Glücke, luckily for him. **Glücken,** glück'en, vi. to succeed. **Glück'lich,** -lĭch, a. happy, lucky, fortunate, successful; -keit, -kaet, f. happiness. **Glück'selig,** -sālĭch, a. happy, felicitous; -keit, -kaet, f. happiness, felicity, bliss. **Glücks'fall,** -fall, m. windfall, godsend. **Glücks'güter,** -güter, f. blessings, possessions. **Glücks'hande,** -häobe, f. caul. **Glücks'jäger,** -yäger, **Glücks'ritter,** -ritter, m. adventurer, fortune-hunter. **Glücks'kind,** -kĭnt, n. lucky man. **Glücks'pilz,** -pilts, m. upstart. **Glücks'rad,** -rät, n. wheel of fortune. **Glücks'ruthe,** -ryte, f. fortune's wand. **Glücks'spiel,** -shpĭl, n. game of hazard. **Glücks'stand,** -shtant, m. state of fortune, circumstances; happy state. **Glücks'stern,** -shtĕrn, m. lucky star. **Glücks'topf,** -topf, m. fortune's urn. **Glücks'wurf,** -vyrf, m. hit, lucky throw. **Glücks'zug,** -tsyk, m. lucky move. **Glücks'wunsch,** -vynsh, m. congratulation. **Glücks'wunschschreiben,** -shreiben, n. congratulatory letter.
Glüh, glüh, (**Gluh,**) a. ae. glowing, red-hot; — hitze, red heat. **Glüh'e,** f. glow. **Glühen,** glüh'en, vi. to glow, be red-hot, be red with heat. **Glüh'end,** -ent, a. glowing, red-hot; fervent, ardent, ae. -ly. **Glüh'ofen,** -öfen, hot-shot-furnace. **Glüh'wein,** -väen, m. mulled wine. **Glüh'wurm** -vyrm, m. glow-worm.
Glut, glyt, f. glow, fire, heat; fervor ardor, flame. **Glut'pfanne,** -pfannĕ, f. brazier, chafing-dish.
Gnade, gĕnā'dĕ, f. grace, favor, mercy, pardon; **Euer Gnaden,** your grace, your honor. **Gna'denbezeigung,** -betsēīgung, f. favor, grace. **Gna'denbild,** -bĭlt, n. wonder-working image. **Gna'denbrief,** -brĭf, m. charter, brevet. **Gna'denbrod,** -brōt, n. sustenance given by favor. **Gna'denfrist,** -frĭsht, f. reproof, respite. **Gna'denstoss,** -zhtöss, m. finishing blow. **Gna'denstuhl,** -zhtyl, m. propitiatory. **Gna'denwahl,** -väl, f. election, predestination. **Gnädig,** gĕnā'dĭch, a. gracious, merciful, kind, ae. -ly.
Gneis, gĕnēs', m. gneiss.
Gold, gŏlt, n. gold. **Gold'ader,** -äder, f. vein, lode of gold; hemorrhoids, piles. **Gold'apfel,** -apfel, m. golden pippin, tomato. **Gold'arbeiter,** -arbäeter, m. goldsmith. **Gold'bergwerk,** -bergvĕrk, n. gold-mine. **Gold'blatt,** -blatt, n. gold-leaf. **Gold'blech,** -blĕch, n. plate of gold. **Gold'draht,** -drät, m. gold-wire. **Golden,** gŏlt'en, a. golden. **Gold'erz,** gŏlt'ärts, n. gold-ore. **Gold'faden,** -fāden, m. gold-thread. **Gold'farbig,** -farbĭch, a. gold-colored. **Gold'fasan,** -fāsān, m. gold-pheasant. **Gold'finger,** -fĭng-er, m. ring-finger. **Gold'fink,** -fĭnk, n. goldfinch. **Gold'fisch,** gŏlt'fish, m. goldfish. **Gold'gelb,** gĕlp, a. gold-colored. **Gold'fuchs,** -fyks, m. pl. -füchse, yellowdun horse; yellow birds (gold coin). **Gold'gewicht,** -gyvicht, Troy weight. **Gold'grube,** -grybe, f. gold-mine, source of wealth. **Gold'haltig,** -haltĭch, a. auriferous. **Gold'käfer,** -käfer, m. rose-chafer. **Gold'kalk,** -kalk, m. calcined gold. **Gold'kind,** -kĭnt, n. jewel; darling. **Gold'küste,** -küzhtĕ, f. gold-coast. **Gold'lack,** -lack, f. wall-flower; gold varnish; gold-colored sealing-wax. **Gold'macher,** -macher, m. alchymist. **Gold'münze,** -müntsĕ, f. gold-coin, gold-

49

Gol 146 **Göt**

medal. **Gold'oryd,** -öxīt, n. oxide of gold. **Gold'papier,** -piple, n. gold paper. **Gold'pappe,** -pappe, f. gilt pasteboard. **Gold'plattirt,** -plattirt, a. gold plated. **Gold'purpur,** -purpur, m. purple of Cassius. **Gold'reich,** -rēīch, a. auriferous, rich in gold. **Gold'salpeter,** -salpäter, m. nitrate of gold. **Gold'salz,** -salts, n. aurate. **Gold'säure,** -seüre, f. auric acid. **Gold'scheider,** -shäeder, m. gold-refiner. **Gold'schläger,** -shläger, m. goldbeater. **Gold'schmied,** -shmīt, m. goldsmith. **Gold'sohn,** -sōn, m. dear boy, darling. **Gold'staub,** -zhtǎūp, m. gold-dust. **Gold'stoff,** -zhtoff, m. gold-brocade. **Gold'streichstein,** -zhtreīchzhtäen, m. touchstone. **Gold'stück,** -zhtück, m. gold-coin. **Gold'stufe,** -zhtufe, f. piece of gold ore. **Gold'talk,** -talk, m. yellow-talk. **Gold'tochter,** -tochter, f. dear child, daughter, darling. **Gold'tresse,** -trèsse, f. gold-lace. **Goldvitriol,** golt'fitrīōl, m. sulphate of gold. **Gold'wage,** -vāge, f. gold-balance. **Gold'wäscher,** -vesher, m. gold-washer; -ei, -ēī, f. gold-washing. **Gold'wirker,** -vīrrker, m. gold-weaver. **Gold'wolf,** -volf, m. jackal.

Golf, golf, m. gulf. **Golfstrom,** golf'-zhtrom, m. gulf-stream.

Gondel, gon'del, f. gondola; pleasure-boat. **Gondolier,** gondolīr', m. gondolier.

Gönnen, gön'nen, vt. not to envy, not to grudge; permit, allow; nicht —, to grudge, envy. **Gönner,** m. patron; -in, f. patroness. **Gönnerschaft,** gön'nershaft, f. patronage, auspices.

Göpel, göp'pel, m. winch, lever, gin.

Gording, gor'ding, f. bunt and leech lines (Mar.).

Gordisch, gor'dish, a. Gordian.

Gosch, gösh, f. jack, jack-flag.

Gosche, gosh'e, f. gutter, drain, ditch.

Goßstein, -zhtāen, m. gutter-stone.

Gothisch, gō'tish, a. Gothic; —e Schrift, black letter.

Gott, gott, m. pl. **Götter,** God. **Gott bewahre,** — behüte, God forbid. **Gott gebe,** would to God; so wahr mir **Gott helfe,** so help me God. **Gottlob!** **Gott sei Dank!** thank God! mein **Gott!** good God! **Götterbild,**

göt'terbilt, n. idol, image of a god. **Gott'terbote,** -bōte, m. messenger of the gods. **Gött'terdienst,** -dīnzht, m. idolatry. **Gött'terlehre,** -lāre, f. mythology. **Gött'terspeise,** -zhpēīse, f. ambrosia. **Gött'terspruch,** -zhpruch, m. oracle. **Gött'tertrank,** -trank, m. **Gött'tertwein,** -vāen, m. nectar. **Gottesacker,** gott'tesacker, m. churchyard, cemetery. **Gottesdienst,** gott'-tesdinzht, m. devotion, divine service; -lich, -lich, a. devotional. **Gottesfurcht,** -furcht, f. fear of God; piety. **Gott'tesfürchtig,** -fürchtig, a. godly, pious. **Gott'tesgelahrtheit,** -gelärthäet, f. theology, divinity. **Gott'tesgericht,** -gericht, n. judgment of God, ordeal. **Gott'teshaus,** -hōūs, n. church. **Gott'teskasten,** -kazhten, m. poor-box. **Gott'teslästerer,** -lezh-terer, m. blasphemer. **Gott'teslästerlich,** -lich, a. blasphemous, av. -ly. **Gott'teslästerung,** -ung, f. blasphemy. **Gott'tesläugner,** -leügner, m. atheist; -isch, -ish, a. atheistic. **Gott'tesläugnung,** -nung, f. denial of God, atheism. **Gott'testisch,** -tish, m. communion-table. **Gott'tesurteil,** -ūrtāel, n. ordeal. **Gott'tesverehrer,** -ferärer, m. worshipper of God. **Gott'tesverehrung,** -ung, f. worship. **Gott'tesvergessen,** -fergessen, a. impious, wicked; **heit,** -hāet, f. impiety, wickedness. **Gott'teswelt,** -velt, f. world, universe. **Gott'teswillen,** -villen, m. with the will of God; um — , for the sake of God. **Gott'heit,** -hāet, f. deity, godhead, divinity; goddess. **Göttin,** göt'tin, f. goddess. **Gött'lich,** -lich, a. av. divine, godlike, godly; **-keit,** -kāet, f. divinity. **Gott'los,** -lōs, a. ungodly, impious, godless, wicked; av. -ly; **-igkeit,** -kāet, f. ungodliness, impiousness. **Gott'mensch,** -mènsh, m. God incarnate, God made flesh. **Gottseibeiuns,** -sāebēīūns, m. the evil one, fiend, devil. **Gott'selig,** -sēlich, a. godly, devout, pious, av. -ly; **-keit,** -kāet, f. godliness, piety, devoutness. **Gott'vergessen,** -fergessen, a. impious, ungodly, av. -ly; **-heit,** -hāet, f. impiety, wickedness. **Götze,** göt'se, m. idol, deity; einen **Götzen machen aus,** idolize. **Götzenbild,** -bilt, n. idol. **Götzendiener,** -dīner, m. idolater; -ei, f. idola-

tress. **Göt'endienſt**, -dīnzht, *m.* idolatry. **Göt'enopfer**, -opfer. *n.* idolatrous sacrifice. **Göt'enprieſter**, -prīzhter, *r.* idolatrous priest. **Göt'entempel**, -tempel, *n* temple of an idol.
Gourmand, gyr'man, *m.* gourmand.
Gouvernante, guvernan'te, *f.* governess. **Gouvernement**, guvern'man(g), *n.* government. **Gouverneur**, guvernöhr', *m.* governor.
Grab, gräp, *n.* grave, tomb, sepulchre; ruin, destruction. **Grab'eiſen**, -eīsen, *n.* spade. **Graben**, grä'ben, *m.* ditch, trench, moat; furrow; drain; sewer; *vt.* (grub, gegraben,) to dig, cut, engrave, carve. **Gräber**, grä'ber, *m.* digger. **Grabesnacht**, grä'besnacht, *f.* darkness, night of the grave. **Grab'geläute**, -geläute, *n.* knell. **Grab'gesang**, -gesang, *m.* dirge, funeral song. **Grab'hügel**, -hühgel, *m.* mound. **Grab'legung**, -lägung, *f.* sepulture, interment. **Grab'lied**, -līt, *n.* dirge, funeral song. **Grab'mal**, -mäl, *n.* monument, sepulchre, tomb. **Grab'rede**, -räde, *f.* funeral sermon. **Grab'ſchrift**, -shrift. *f.* epitaph. **Grab'ſtätte**, -zhtette, *f.* grave, tomb. **Grab'ſtein**, zhtaēn, *m.* tombstone. **Grab'ſtichel**, -zhtīchel, *m.* graver, burin, engraving tool, pointrel. **Grabtuch**, gräp'tuch, *n.* pall.
Grad, Grade, *f.* Gerade.
Grabheit, *f.* Geradheit.
Grad, gräd, *m.* pace, step; degree. **Gradation**, gradatsiōn', *f.* gradation. **Gradiren**, grädī'ren, *vt.* to graduate, refine. **Graduiren**, grädūī'ren, *vi.* to graduate. **Graduirter**, *m.* graduate. **Grad'weiſe**, -vēīse, *a. av.* by degrees, gradual, *av.* -ly.
Graf, gräf, *pl.* -en, count, earl. **Gräfin**, grä'fin, *f.* countess. **Gräflich**, gräf'lich, *a. av.* of a count *or* countess. **Graffſchaft**, -shaft, *f.* county, earldom.
Gram, gräm, *a,* angry, averse; -ſein, to dislike, to bear a grudge, to hate.
Gram, gräm, *m.* grief, affliction, sorrow. **Grämen**, grä'men, *vr.* to grieve, fret, pine, be afflicted; ſich zu Tod grämen, to pine away, to die with grief. **Gräm'lich**, -lich, *a.* morose,

peevish, sullen, sulky, ill-humored, *av.* -ly. **Gram'los**, -lōs, *a.* free from grief.
Grammatik, grammai'īk, *f.* grammar; *er, m.* grammarian **Grammat'iſch**, -ish. **Grammatikaliſch**, -i:ä-lish, *a.* grammatical, *a.* -ly, *av.*
Gran, grän, *m.* grain.
Granat, granät', *m.* garnet; *te, f.* granate; pomegranate; grenade.
Grande, gran'de, *m.* Spanish nobleman, grandee.
Granit, granīt', *m.* granite.
Granuliren granȳlī'ren, *vt.* to granulate.
Gränze, grent'se, *f.* border, limit, boundary, frontier. **Grän'zen**, *vi.* to border, bound. **Grän'zenlos**, -lōs, *a.* boundless, illimitable, unbounded; *av.* -ly; -igkeit, -kaēt, *f.* boundlessness, unlimitedness. **Gränzeſtung**, grents'feshtung, *f.* frontier fortress. **Gränz'linie**, -līnīe. *f.* boundary line, line of demarcation. **Gränz'nachbar**, -nachbär, *m.* confiner, borderer; -ſchaft, -shaft, *f.* confinity. **Gränz'ſtadt**, -zhtät, *f.* frontier-town. **Gränz'ſtein**, -zhtaēn, *m.* landmark. mere-stone.
Grapen, gra'pen, *m.* cast-iron pot, metal-pot.
Grapſe, grap'se, *f.* snatching; in die Grapſe geben, to make a scramble for. **Grap'ſen**, *vt.* to catch at, to snatch up.
Gras, gräs, *n.* grass. **Gräschen**, gräs'chen, **Gräslein**, gräs'laēn, *n.* small blade of grass. **Grasanger**, gräs'ang-er, *m.* pasture-ground. **Gras'artig**, -artig, *a.* gramineous. **Gras'bauf**, -bank, *f.* turf-covered seat. **Gras'boden**, -bōden, *m.* meadowland. **Graſen**, grä'sen, *vt.* to graze. **Gras'fleck**, -fleck, *m.* grass-plot. grass-patch. **Gras'freſſend**, -fress, *nt. a.* graminivorous. **Gras'froſch**, -frosh, *m.* green-frog. **Gras'garten**, -garten, *m.* grass-garden, orchard. **Gras'grün**, -grün, *a.* grass-green. **Gras'halm**, -halm, *m.* blade of grass. **Gras'hüpfer**, -hüpfer. *m.* grass-hopper. **Gras'ig**, *a.* grassy. **Gras'icht**, -icht, *a.* gramineous. **Gras'land**, -lant, *n.* pasture-ground, grass-land. **Gras'mücke**, -mük-e. *f.* warbler; hedge-sparrow. **Gras'pferd**, -pfert, *n.* grasshopper. **Gras'reich**, -raēch, *a*

a. grassy. **Gräswuchs**, -wuks, *m.* growth of grass; meadow. **Gras'wüste**, -vühste, *f.* prairie.

Graß, grass, **Gräßlich**, gräss'lich, *a.* shocking, horrible, *av.* -ly.

Grassiren, grassī'ren, *vi.* to rage, prevail, spread.

Grat, grāt, *m.* ridge, edge; hip (Arch.); **‑sparren**, -zhparren, *m.* hip-rafter. **Gratziegel**, grāt'tsīgel, *m.* hip-tile.

Gräte, grä'te, *f.* fish-bone. **Grätig**, grät'ich, *a.* bony, full of fish-bones; irritable.

Grätscheln, gret'sheln, *vi.* to straddle. **Gratuliren**, gratylī'ren, *vi.* to congratulate. **Gratulant**, -lant, *m.* congratulator, well-wisher. **Gratulation**, gratylatsiōn', *f.* congratulation.

Grau, grau, *a.* gray, grizzled; *s. n.* auch **Graue**, *n.* oder *f.* gray. **Grau'äugig**, -öjgich, *a.* gray-eyed. **Grau'bart**, -bärt, *m.* gray-beard. **Grau'blau**, -blāu, *a.* grayish-blue. **Grau'en**, *vi.* to turn gray, dawn; *s. n.* dawning. **Grau'haarig**, -härich, *a.* gray-haired, hoary. **Grau'lich**, -lich, *a.* grayish.

Gräuel, gröǐ'el, *m.* horror, abomination; detestation; atrocity, enormity, outrage. **Gräu'elhaft**, -haft, **Gräu'lich**, -lich, **Gräu'elvoll**, -foll. *a.* horrid, horrible, enormous, *av.* -ly.

Grauen, gröy'en, *vi.* to dread, to fear, to have a horror of; to be seized with horror. **Grau'enhaft**, -haft, **Grau'envoll**, -foll, *a.* horrid, appalling.

Graupe, gröy'pe, *f.* peeled *or* hulled oats, wheat *or* barley; sleet; granulated *or* pounded ore. **Grau'peln**, *vi.* to sleet, drizzle.

Graus, gröys, *n.* horror, shudder, fright.

Grausam, gröy'sam. *a.* cruel, fierce, fell; **‑keit**, -kāet, *f.* cruelty, barbarity, outrage.

Grausen, gröy'sen, *vi.* to shudder, shiver, to be afraid; to be frightful; *s. n.* horror, awe, dismay. **Grau'senhaft**, -haft, **Grau'senvoll**, -foll, **Grau'sig**, -sich, *a.* awful, horrible, dismal, striking with terror.

Grauwacke, gräu'vakke, *f.* graywacke.

Graveur, gravöhr', *m.* engraver. **Graviren**, grävī'ren, *vt.* to engrave; aggravate. **Gravität**, gravität', *f.* gravity, solemnity of deportment. **Gravitätisch**, gravitä'tish, *a.* grave, solemn. **Gravitation**, gravitatsiōn'. *f.* gravitation.

Grazie, grä'tsie, *f.* grace. **Graziös**, gratsiöhs', *a.* graceful.

Greeb, grāp, *n.* cutwater (Mar.).

Greif, grëif, *m.* griffin, griffon; **‑geier**, *m.* condor. **Greif'klaue**, -kläu-e, *f.* griffin's claw.

Greifen, grëi'fen (griff, gegriffen), *vt.* to gripe, grasp, lay hold of, catch, seize, apprehend, snatch. **Greif'bar**, -bär, *a.* seizable, tangible.

Greinen, grëi'nen, *vi.* to grumble, growl.

Greis, grëis, *a.* gray, hoary, aged, old; *s. m.* old man. **Grei'senalter**, -alter, *n.* senility, old age.

Grell, grell, *a.* glaring, dazzling, bright; hard, stiff; shrill. **Grell'heit**, -hāet, *f.* glaringness, stiffness.

Grenadier, grenadīr', *m.* grenadier; **‑block**, -block, *m.* monkey-block (Mar.).

Gries, grīs, *m.* core of the fruit.

Gries, grīs, *m.* coarse sand; gravel; groats, grits. **Gries'brei**, -brēǐ, *m.* gruel. **Gries'mehl**, -māl, *n.* farina, coarse flour.

Griesseln, grī'seln, *vi.* to shudder, shiver.

Grieseln, grī'seln, *vt. i.* to crumble.

Griesen, grī'sen, *vt.* to grind into grit.

Griesgram, grīs'grām, *m.* grumbler, growler; *a.* peevish, grumbling; **‑sen**, -en, *vi.* to be peevish, to grumble.

Griff, grif, *prt. v.* **Greifen**.

Griff, grif, *m.* gripe, grasp; touch; handful; trick, knack; handle, ear. **Griff'brett**, -brět, *n.* finger-board.

Griffel, grif'fel, *m.* style, pointel; slate-pencil.

Grille, gril'le, *f.* caprice, whim, freak, fancy. **Grill'enfang**, -fang, *m.* freakishness, whimsicalness. **Grill'enfänger**, -fenger, *m.* fancy-monger, fanciful person; **‑ei**, -ēǐ', *f.* whimsicalness. **Grill'enhaft**, -haft, *a.* capricious, freakish, crotchety.

Grimasse, grimas'se, *f.* grimace, wry face.

Grimm, grim, *m.* fury, rage, anger, wrath, passion; *a.* und **Grim'mig**, furious, enraged, ferocious, wild, excessive, exceeding, *av.* -ly. **Grimm'darm**, -darm, *m.* colon. **Grim'men**, *vi.* gripe. **Grim'migfeit**, -kēet, *f.* ferocity, ferociousness. **Grind**, grint, *m.* scurf, scab; scalp; **-kopf**, -kopf, *m.* scab-head. **Grind'köpfig**, -köpfich, *a.* scurvy, scab-headed. **Grinsen**, grin'sen, *vi.* to grin, sneer; *s. n.* grin, sneer. **Grob**, gröp, *a.* coarse, gross, thick; rude, rough; strong; grobes Geschütz, heavy artillery; grobe Schrift, large-sized letters. **Grobhäutig**, gröb'-hõütich, *a.* coarse-skinned. **Grob'heit**, -hēet, *f.* coarseness, roughness, rudeness, insolence; ill-breeding; *pl.* -en, abusive words, coarse language. **Grobian**, gröb'iān, *m.* rude, coarse, ill-bred, insolent fellow. **Gröblich**, gröb'lich, *a.* coarse, rough, rude; *av.* -ly. **Grobschmied**, gröp'-shmīt', *m.* blacksmith, farrier. **Grobstahl**, -zhtyl, *m.* stretcher. **Grobs**, gröps, *f.* Griebs. **Grog**, grog, *m.* grog. **Groll**, groll, *m.* grudge, ill will, rancor, resentment. **Grollen**, grol'-len, *vi.* to bear a grudge, ill will. **Groschen**, grosh'en, *m.* grosh, groschen (two cents). **Gross**, gröss, *a.* great, large, big, tall, grand; major (Mus.); gross thun, sich gross machen, to brag, boast; to talk big. **Großantiqua**, grössan-ti'kvä, *f.* great primer (Print.). **Grosseltern**, -eltern, *s. pl.* grandparents. **Großartig**, -ärtich, *a.* grand, vast, imposing; **-keit**, -kēet, *f.* grandeur. **Größe**, grüh'se, *f.* greatness, magnitude, size, height. **Großenkel**, gröss'eukel, *m.* great-grandson; **-in**, *f.* great-granddaughter. **Großentheils**, -tēels, *a.* in a great measure. **Großfürst**, -fürzht, *m.* grand-duke; **-in**, *f.* grand-duchess. **Großfürstenthum**, -tym, *m.* grand-duchy. **Großfürstlich**, -fürzhtlich, *a.* grand-ducal. **Großgliederig**, -glitrich, *a.* large-limbed. **Groß'händel**, -handel, *m.* wholesale. **Großhändler**, -hendler, *m.* wholesale dealer. **Großhandlung**, -hantlyng, *f.* wholesale establishment. **Großherzig**, -hertsich, *a.* generous, magnanimous, *av.* -ly; **-keit**, -kēet, *f.* generosity, magnanimity. **Groß'-herzog**, -hertsog, *m.* grand-duke; **-in**, *f.* grand-duchess; **-thum**, -tym, *n.* grand-dukedom, grand-duchy. **Großjährig**, -yärich, of age. **Großköpfig**, -köpfich, *a.* large-headed. **Großkreuz**, -krőits, *n.* grand-cross. **Großmächtig**, -mechtig, *f.* great powers. **Großmächtig**, -mechtig, *a.* high and mighty. **Großmaul**, -mõyl, *n.* braggart, boaster. **Großmäulig**, -mēülich, *a.* big-mouthed, bragging. **Großmuth**, -myt, *f.* magnanimity. **Großmutter**, -mytter, *f.* grandmother. **Großoheim**, -ohēem, *m.* grand-uncle. **Großpapa**, -papa, *m.* grandpa. **Großprahler**, -prāler, *m.* braggart, boaster. **Großpahlerei**, -prālerei', *f.* bragging. **Großregal**, -regāl, *n.* imperial paper. **Großsprechen**, -zhprechen, *vi.* to talk big, brag, boast. **Großsprecher**, *m.* braggadocio, boaster, swaggerer; **-ei**, -ey', *f.* bragging, boasting, rodomontade. **Großsprecherisch**, -ish, *a.* vainglorious, boastful, *av.* -ly. **Großsultan**, -syltän, *m.* grand-sultan, grand-turk. **Großtante**, -tante, *f.* great-aunt. **Großthat**, -tāt, *f.* exploit, grand achievement. **Großurenkel**, -yrenkel, *m.* great-great grandson. **Großvater**, -fater, *m.* grandfather. **Großvaterstuhl**, -zhtyl, *m.* elbow-chair, arm-chair. **Großvatertanz**, -tants, *m.* grandfather's dance. **Groß**, gröss, *n.* gross, twelve dozen. **Grot**, gröt, *m.* groat. **Grotesk**, grotēsk', *a.* wildly formed, grotesque, *av.* -ly. **Grotte**, grot'te, *f.* grotto. **Grotzen**, grot'sen, *m.* back of a fur. **Grube**, gry'be, *f.* pit, hole, cavity, mine. **Grübchen**, grüb'ch n, *n.* little cavity, dimple. **Grubenbau**, gry'-lenbőy, *m.* working of mines. **Grubenlampe**, -lampe, *f.* miner's lamp. **Grubenjahren**, -fāren, *n.* descent into mines. **Grubengezäh**, -gytsä, *n.* miner's tools. **Grubenkompaß**, -kompass, *m.* miner's compass. **Grübeln**, grüh'beln, *vi.* to grub, dig; meditate closely, muse. **Grübelei**, -lēy', *f.* musing, meditation; scrutiny. **Grübler**, *m.* muser, meditator. **Gruft**, gruft, *f.* pit, hole, tomb, vault, sepulchre; in eine Gruft sen-

13*

ien, entomb. **Gruftgewölbe**, -gewölbe, n. vaulted tomb, sepulchre.
Grummet, grŭm′met, n. **Grum′metheu**, n. second crop of hay.
Grün, grün, a. green, verdant, fresh, unripe. **Grüne**, grü′ne, n. unb f. verdure; green grass. **Grün′bonnerstag**, -donnerstäg, m. Maundy-Thursday. **Grü′ner**, m. greenhorn. **Grün′lich**, -lich, a. greenish. **Grün′span**, -zhpän, m. verdigris. **Grün′specht**, -zhpècht, m. green woodpecker. **Grün′schnabel**, -shnabel, m. greenhorn.
Grund, grŭnt, m. ground, soil, bottom; valley, dale; foundation; background; priming; reason; motive; **zu Grunde gehen**, to founder, to go to ruins. **Grund′bedingung**, -bedingung, f. principal condition. **Grundbegriff**, -begriff, m. fundamental notion. **Grund′besitzer**, -besitzer, n. landed proprietor; landlord. **Grund′ehrlich**, -ärlich, a. thoroughly honest, downright. **Grund′eigenthum**, -ägentum, n. landed property. **Grund′eis**, -ēis, n. floating ice. **Gründen**, grün′den, vt. to fathom; to ground, to lay the foundation; to prime. **Gründer**, m. founder. **Grundfalsch**, grunt′falsh, a. radically false. **Grund′farbe**, -farbe, f. primitive color; priming. **Grund′feste**, -feste, f. **Grund′lage**, -lage, f. foundation, basis. **Grund′firniß**, -firniss, m. priming varnish. **Grund′form**, -form, f. primitive form. **Grund′gesetz**, -gesetz, n. fundamental law. **Grundiren**, -i′ren, vt. to ground, prime. **Grundi′rung**, -ung, f. priming. **Grund′lage**, -lage, f. foundation, basis. **Grund′last**, -lazht, f. passive servitude. **Grund′legung**, -lēgung, f. foundation. **Grund′lehre**, -lāre, f. fundamental doctrine. **Gründlich**, -lich, a. thorough; fundamental; profound, radical; well grounded, clear; av. -ly; **-keit**, -kāet, f. thoroughness, solidity, profoundness. **Gründling**, -ling, m. gudgeon, groundling. **Grund′linie**, -linle, f. basis, baseline; outline. **Grund′los**, -lōs, a. bottomless, fathomless; impassable; unbounded: groundless, unfounded; **sigkeit**, -kāet, f. fathomlessness; groundlessness, unfoundedness.

Grund′recht, -rècht, n. seigneurial right; fundamental right. **Grund′riß**, -riss, m. outline, sketch, plan, ground-plan. **Grund′satz**, -sats, m. principle, maxim; axiom. **Grund′schoß**, -shoss, m. land-tax. **Grund′stein**, -zhtāen, foundation-stone, corner-stone. **Grund′steuer**, -zhtö′er, f. land-tax. **Grund′stoff**, -zhtoff, m. element, radical. **Grund′strich**, -zhtrich, m. principal stroke. **Grund′stück**, -zhtück, n. real estate. **Grund′suppe**, -suppe, f. dregs, sediment. **Grund′talje**, -talye, f. steering-tackle, rudder-tackle. **Grund′takellage**, -takellage, f. ground-tackle. **Grund′tau**, -tāu, n. relieving tackle. **Grund′text**, -tèxt, m. text, original text. **Grund′ton**, -tön, m. key-note, tonic. **Grund′trieb**, -trīp, m. fundamental impulse. **Grund′übel**, -übbel, n. root of all evil. **Grund′ursache**, -ursache, f. primitive cause; principal reason. **Grund′wahrheit**, -värhāet, f. fundamental truth. **Grund′zins**, -tsins, m. ground-rent. **Grund′zug**, -tsug, m. characteristic.
Grunzen, grunt′sen, vi. to grunt.
Gruppe, grŭp′pe, f. group. **Grup′piren**, vt. to group. **Gruppi′rung**, -ung, f. grouping.
Gruß, gruhss, m. pl. **Grüße**, greeting, salutation, compliments; salute. **Grüßen**, grüh′sen, vt. to greet, salute: **jemand grüßen lassen**, to send one's compliments, love.
Grütze, grüt′se, f. grit, groats. **Grütz′mühle**, -mühle, f. grit-mill.
Gucken, guck′en, vi. to look, to peep. **Guckkasten**, guck′kazhten, m. rare-show.
Guhr, guhr, f. pl. -en, fermentation; gur.
Guillotine, gillotī′ne, f. guillotine.
Guinee, f. guinea.
Guitarre, gittarr′, f. guitar.
Gulden, gul′den, **Gülden**, gül′den, m. florin (40 cents), gilder. guilder.
Gülden, gül′den, a. golden.
Gültig, gül′tich, a. valid, current, good, passable; legal, lawful; **-keit**, -kāet, f. validity; currency; lawfulness.
Gummi, gum′mi, m. gum; —arabicum, gum arabic; —elasticum caoutchouc. **Gummigut**, gummi′gut,

Gum 151 **Gyp**

a. gamboge. **Gum'mig, Gummicht, gum'micht,** a. gummy. **Gum'mi-harz,** -harts, n. gum-resin. **Gum'milch,** -lack, f. lac. **Gum'miwaſſer,** -vasser, n. gum-water. **Gum'miren,** vt. to gum.

Gunſt, guunzht, f. favor, good will, affection; leave. **Gunſtbezeigung,** -betseīgung, f. favor, kindness. **Günſtig,** günzh'tich, a. favorable, propitious; auspicious; friendly. **Günſtling,** -ling, m. favorite, minion.

Gurgel, gur'zel, f. gorge, throat, gullet; — zuſchnüren, to throttle, strangle. **Gurgeln,** gur'geln, vi. gargle; warble; to gurgle.

Gurke, gur'ke, f. cucumber, gherkin. **Gurkenbogen,** -bōgen, m. arch of a cylindrical vault. **Gurkenſalat,** -salat, m. cucumber-salad.

Gurren, gur'ren, vi. to coo; flatter.

Gurt, gurt, m. girth, girt. **Gürtel,** gür'tel, m. girdle; belt, sash, zone. **Gürtelthier,** -tīr, n. armadillo. **Gürten,** vt. to gird. **Gurtholz, gurt'holts,** n. wale. **Gürtler,** gürt'ler, m. beltmaker, girdler.

Guß, guss, m. pl. **Güſſe,** casting, founding; gush; font, fount, m. (Print.) **Gußabdruck,** -apdryck, m. plate for printing. **Gußeiſen,** -ēīsen, n. cast-iron. **Gußform,** -form, f. casting-mould. **Gußnaht,** -nāt, f. seam of casting. **Gußregen,** -rāgen, m. shower. **Gußröhre,** -rōhre, f. spout, spray (Mech.). **Gußſtahl,** -zhtāl, m. cast-steel. **Gußſtein,** -zhtāēn, m. sink, drain, gutter.

Gut, gut, a. av. good, well, sufficient, av. -ly; kind; es iſt gut, it is enough; es gut haben, to be well off: gut machen, to compensate; gut ſein einem, to like one; gut ſchreiben Einem, to place to one's credit; gut ſagen für, answer for; s. n. pl. **Güter,** goods, property, estate; ware, commodity. **Gutachten,** gut'achten, n. opinion,

judgment. **Gutartig,** -ārtich, a good-natured, well-disposed; not malignant. **Gutbefinden,** -befīnden, n. approbation; good health. **Gutsdenkend,** -denkent. a. well-disposed, thinking no ill. **Gutdünken,** -dün ken, n. good pleasure; opinion. **Güte,** gūh'te, f. goodness, kindness, purity, genuineness, quality; in **Güte,** amicably. **Güterzug,** gūh'tertsug, m. freight-train. **Gutshaben,** gut'haben, n. credit. **Gutheißen,** -hāēssen, n. **Gutheißung,** -ung, f. approbation, consent. **Gutherzig,** -hērtsich, a. kind-hearted, good-natured; **Gutheit,** -kāēt, f. good nature. **Gütig,** gūh'tich, a. kind, good; **Gutheit,** -kāēt, f. kindness, goodness, benignity. **Gütlich,** -lich, a. amicable, av. -bly; friendly; — thun, to feast, feed luxuriously; ſich gütlich thun, to indulge, pamper, enjoy one's self. **Gutmachen,** -machen, n. reparation. **Gutmüthig,** -mūhtich, a. good-natured, kind, av. -ly: **Gutheit,** -kāēt, f. good nature, kind. **Gutſagen,** -sāgen, n. security, responsibility. **Gutsbeſitzer,** -besitser, **Gutsherr,** -hērr, m. proprietor of an estate; lord of a manor. **Gutthat,** -tāt, f. benefit, kindness. **Gutthäter,** -tāter, m. benefactor. **Gutthätig,** -tātich, a. beneficent, charitable. **Gutthätigkeit,** -kāēt, f. beneficence, charitableness. **Gutwillig,** -villich, a. obliging, complaisant; voluntary; av. -ly. **Gutwilligkeit,** -kāēt, f. obligingness, willingness, readiness. **Gutturalbuchſtabe,** gutturāl'buchzhtābe, m. guttural letter.

Gymnaſiaſt, gimnāsiazht', m. student. **Gymnaſium,** gimnā'sium, n. gymnasium, high school, college. **Gymnaſt,** gimnāzht', m. gymnast. **Gymnaſtik,** gimnāzh'tik. f. gymnastics. **Gymnaſtiſch,** gimnāzht'ish, a. gymnastic.

Gyps, f. **Gips.**

Ha! häi *ij.* ha!

Haar, här, *n.* hair; nap; auf ein Haar, to a hair, to a dot; um ein Haar, within a hair's-breadth; um fein Haar beffer, not one jot better; bei den Haaren herbeiziehen, to bring in head and shoulders (forcedly); Haare laſſen müſſen, to be fleeced. **Haarbeutel,** här'beütel, *m.* hair-bag; a drop too much. **Haar'breit,** -bräet, *a.* hairbreadth. **Haarbürſte,** här'bürzhte, *f.* hair-brush. **Haar'eiſen,** -eīsen, *n.* scraper; curling-tongs. **Haaren,** här'en, **Hären,** här'en, *vt.* to loose, shed the hair; *vt.* to scrape off the hair; *a.* hairy, made of hair. **Haar'flechte,** -flĕchte, *f.* braid, plait of hair. **Haar'hemd,** -hĕmt, *n.* hair-shirt. **Haar'ig,** *a.* hairy. **Haar'klein,** -cläen, *a.* fine as hair, to a hair. **Haarkräusler,** här'kröisler, *m.* **Haar'künſtler,** -künzht-ler, *m.* hairdresser. **Haarloste,** här'lŏcke, *f.* lock, curl of hair. **Haar'nabel,** -nädel, *f.* hair-pin. **Haar'röhre,** -röhre, *f.* **Haar'röhrchen,** *n.* capillary tube. **Haar'ſalbe,** -sălbe, *f.* pomatum. **Haar'ſalz,** -sălts, *n.* hair-salt. **Haar'ſcharf,** -sharf, *a.* very sharp. **Haar'ſchmuck,** -shmuck, *m.* hair ornaments. **Haar'ſchopf,** -shopf, *m.* tuft of hair. **Haar'ſeil,** -sēl, *n.* seton. **Haar'ſieb,** -sīb, *n.* hair-sieve. **Haar'ſohle,** -sōle, *f.* hair-sole. **Haar'ſpalter,** -zhpalter, **Haar'klauber,** -klöyber, hair-splitter, fault-finder. **Haar'ſpitze,** -zhpitse, *f.* end of the hair. **Haar'ſtrich,** -zhtrich, *m.* hair-stroke. **Haar'tuch,** -tŭch, *n.* hair-cloth. **Haar'wickel,** -vickel, *m.* hair-roller. **Haar'wuchs,** -vŭks, *m.* growth of hair. **Haar'wurzel,** -vurtsel, *f.* root of the hair. **Haar'zange,** -tsange, *f.* tweezers. **Haar'zirkel,** -tsirkel, *m.* fine compasses. **Haar'zopf,** -tsopf, *m.* braid of hair; cue, pigtail.

Habe, hä'be, *f.* property, goods, effects; fahrende —, chattels, movables; liegende —, immovables; Hab und Gut, goods and chattels. **Haben,** hä'ben (hatte, gehabt), *vt.* to have, possess, enjoy; gern haben, to like; Recht haben, to be right; Unrecht haben, to be wrong, auf ſich haben, to be of consequence. **Ha'benichts,** -nĭchts, *m.* poor devil. **Hab'gier,** -gīr, *f.* greediness, covetousness; -ig, -ĭch, *a.* covetous, greedy **Hab'haft,** -haft, *a.* having, possessing; — werden, to get hold, possession of; to seize.

Haber, hä'ber, *m.* oats.

Habicht, hab'ĭcht, *m. pl.* -e, hawk; kite; —e Naſe, hooked nose, aquiline nose.

Habit, habit', *m.* habit, garment, dress, garb.

Habſeligkeit, häb'sälichkäet, *f.* property. **Hab'ſucht,** -sŭcht, *f.* avarice, covetousness. **Hab'ſüchtig,** -süchtig, *a.* avaricious, covetous.

Hack, hak, *m.* hacking. **Hack'beil,** -bēil, *n.* chopper, cleaver. **Hack'block,** -block, *m.* chopping-block. **Hack'bord,** -bord, *m.* taffrail. **Hack'brett,** -bret, *n.* chopping-board; dulcimer. **Hacke,** hak'ke, *f.* hoe, mattock. **Hack'en,** *vt.* to hoe, hack, chop, mince, hash, cleave, grub. **Hack'er,** *m.* chopping. **Häckerling,** hĕck'erling, *m.* chopped straw, chaff. **Häckerlingsbank,** -bank, *f.* straw-cutter. **Hack'meſſer,** -mĕsser, *n.* chopping-knife. **Häckſel,** hĕk'sel, *f.* Häckerling.

Hader, hä'der, *m.* rag, tatter. **Hader,** hä'der, *m.* quarrel, contention, squabble, brawl. **Ha'derbalg,** -balk, *m.* **Ha'derkatze,** -katse, *f.* **Ha'derer,** *m.* squabbler, brawler, quarreler, wrangler. **Hadern,** hä'dern, *vi.* to quarrel, brawl, wrangle. **Haderſüchtig,** hä'dersüchtig, *a.* quarrelsome.

Hafen, hä'fen, *m.* port, harbor, haven; pot, glass pot. **Ha'fenauſſeher,** -öyfsäer, *m.* **Ha'fenmeiſter,** -māeshter, *m.* harbor-master. **Hafenſtadt,** hä'fenshtat, *f.* seaport, sea-town, port-town.

Hafer, hä'fer, *m.* oats. **Ha'fergrütze,** -grütse, *f.* groats. **Ha'ferkaſten,** -kazhten, *m.* oat-bin. **Ha'fermehl,** -māl, *n.* oat-meal. **Ha'ferſack,** -säck, *m.* sack for oats. **Ha'ferſtroh,** -st:ō, *n.* oat-straw.

Hafner, häf'ner, *m.* potter.

Haft, haft, *f.* hold; custody, prison, arrest, confinement; **-befehl,** -befāl *m.* -brief, -brīf, *m.* warrant. Haften, häf'ten, *v.* to cleave, cling, stick; to be fixed, remain ; to be bail, responsible.

Hag, hāg, *m.* hedge; coppice. Hagebuche, hā'gebŭche, *n.* hornbeam. Hagebutte, -butte, *f.* hip, haw. Hagebuttenstrauch, -ströŭch, *m.* dogrose tree. Hagedorn, hā'gedorn, *m.* hawthorn. Hagerose, -röse, *f.* wild briar.

Hagel, hā'gel, *m.* hail; small shot. Hagelicht, -dicht, *a.* thick as hail. Hagelkorn, -korn, *n.* hailstone; Hageln, hā'geln, *v.* to hail. Hagelschauer, -shŏuer, *m.* hailshower. Hagelsturm, -zhtūrm, *m.* Hagelwetter, -vetter, *n.* hailstorm. Hagelschlag, hägel'shläg, *m.* hail, damage by hail.

Hägen, hā'gen, *v.* to hedge in, fence in.

Hager, hā'ger, *a.* haggard, lean. Hagerkeit, -käet, *f.* leanness.

Hagestolz, hā'gezhtolts, *m.* old bachelor.

Haha, hähä', *ij.* haha! hoho!

Häher, hā'er, *m.* jay.

Hahn, hān, *m. pl.* Hähne, cock; stopcock. Hähnchen, hān'chen, *n.* cockerel. Hahnenfuß, hā'nenfŭss, *m.* crowfoot. Hahnenkamm, -kamm, *m.* cock's-comb; lousewort. Hahnenkampf, -kampf, *m. pl.* -kämpfe. Hahnengefecht, -gefecht. *n.* cockfight. Hahnenruf, -ryf, *m.* Hahnenschrei, -shrae, *m.* Hahnengeschrei, -geshräë, *n.* cock-crowing. Hahnentritt, -trit, *m.* tread, treadle. Hahnrei, -rēe, *m.* cuckold; zum Hahnrei machen, to cuckold. Hahnreischaft, -shaft, *f.* cukoldom.

Hai, häē, *m.* Haifisch, -fish, *m.* shark.

Hain, haēn, *m.* grove, wood.

Häkchen, häk'chen, *n.* little hook; crotchet; apostrophe. Häkeln, hā'keln, *v.* crotchet; hook; tease. Haken, hā'ken, *m.* hook; clasp; crotchet; *v.* to hook, grapple. Hakenbalzen, -boltsen, *m.* hook-bolt. Hakig, häk'ig, Hakicht, häk'icht, *a.* hooked.

Halb, halp, *a. av.* half, by halves; ein halber Thaler, half a dollar; der halbe Ton, semitone; auf halber Stange, at hal'-staff; für halbe Rechnung, for join; account; halb eins, half-past twelve; noch ein halb was so groß, half as big again; halb thun, to do by halves. Halb'bier, -bīr, *n.* small-beer. Halb'bruder, -bryder, *m.* half-brother. Halb'beck, -děck, Halb'verdeck, -ferdeck, *n.* quarter-deck. Halb'dunkel, -dunkl, *a.* dusky, dim; *s. n.* dusk, gloom, dawn. Halben, Halber, *p.* on account of, for the sake of, by reason of. Halb'franz, -frants, *a.* half-calf. Halbgeschwister, halp'geshvizhter, *f.* half-brothers and sisters. Halb'gesicht, -sicht, *n.* profile. Halb'gott, -gott, *m.* demi-god. Halb'heit, -hāet, *f.* lukewarmness, incompleteness, ambiguity. Halb'insel, -insel, *f.* peninsula. Halbiren, -īren, *v.* to halve. Halbirung, -ŭng, *f.* halving. Halb'jahr, -yār, *n.* half-year, six months. Halb'jährig, -yārich, *a.* of six months. Halb'jährlich, -yārlich, semi-annual. Halb'kreis, -krāes, *m.* semicircle. Halb'kugel, -kŭgel, *f.* hemisphere. Halb'laut, -lŏut, *a. av.* in an undertone. Halb'mensch, -mensh, *m.* monster, demi-man. Halb'messer, -messer, *m.* radius. Halb'metall, -metall, *n.* semi-metal. Halb'mond, -mond, *m.* half-moon; crescent; förmig, *a.* crescent-shaped. Halb'schatten, -shatten, *m.* penumbra; partial shade. Halb'schlägig, -shlägig, *a.* mongrel. Halb'schwester, -shvezhter, *f.* stepsister. Halb'seiden, -sēīden, *a.* half-silk. Halbstiefel, halp'zhtīfel, *m.* bootee. Halb'stündig, -zhtündich, *a.* half an hour's. Halb'stündlich, *a.* half-hourly. Halb'tägig, -tägich, *a.* lasting half a day. Halbtodt, -tōt, *a.* half dead. Halb'ton, -tōn, *m.* semitone. Halb'trauer, -trŏuer, *f.* second mourning. Halb'tuch, -tŭch, *n.* cassimere. Halb'wach, -vach, *a.* half-awake. Halb'wegs, -vāgs, Halb'wege, -vā-ge, *av.* half-way: tolerably. Halb'wisser, -visser, *m.* smatterer; *vi. ēī', f.* smattering. Halb'wüchsig, -vüchseich, *a.* half-grown. Halb'zirkel, -tsirrkel, *m.* semi-circumference; semicircle; -ig, -ich, *a.* semicircular.

Halde, hal'de, *f.* hill, hill-side, steep declivity, mountain-side; heap of dead ore (Min.).

Halen, hā'len, *v.* to haul, hale.

Häl 154 **Han**

Hälfte, helfte, f. half, moiety, middle; **zur Hälfte geben mit,** to go halves: **um die Hälfte,** by half; **beffere Hälfte,** better half.
Halfter, half'ter, n. halter. **Halfteru,** vt. to halter.
Hall, hall, m. sound, noise.
Halle, hal'le, f. hall, porch.
Hallelujah, hallelu'yäh, n. hallelujah.
Hallen, hal'len, vt. to resound.
Halloh! balloh'! ij. balloo. **Halloh'rufen,** -rufen, vt. to halloo.
Hallunke, hall'unke, m. rascal, scoundrel.
Halm, halm, m. blade, culm, stalk.
Hals, hals, m. neck, throat; collar; tack; **Hals über Kopf,** headlong, helter-skelter. **Hals'ader, -ader,** f. jugular artery. **Hals'band,** -bant, collar, necklace. **Hals'binde,** -binde, f. necktie, cravat. **Hals'bräune,** -bröüne, f. quinsy. **Hals'brechend,** -brechend, a. dangerous. **Halfen,** hal'sen, vt. to veer. **Hals'entzündung,** -ntsündung, f. inflammation of the throat. **Hals'gut, -güt,** n. hole of the chess-tree. **Hals'gericht,** -gericht. n. criminal court. **Hals'geschmeide,** -geshmeide, n. neck jewels. **Halskette,** hals'kette. f. necklace. **Halskragen,** hals'krägen, m. collar. **Hals'krause, -krouse,** f. ruff. **Halsschmuck,** hals'shmuck, m. necklace.
Halsstarrig, hals'zhtarrig, a. stiffnecked, obstinate: **-keit, -käet,** f. obstinacy. **Hals'talje, -tälye,** f. tack-tackle. **Hals'tuch, -tuch,** n. pl. **Halstücher,** neckcloth, cravat. **Halsweh,** hals'vä, n. pain in the throat.
Halt, halt, m. hold, halt, stoppage; support; **Halt machen,** to halt, stop. **Haltbar,** -bär, a. tenable: **-keit, -käet,** f. tenableness. defensibility. **Halten,** hal'ten (hielt, gehalten), vt. to hold, keep; contain: support; maintain: to stop; think; to celebrate; **frei halten,** to treat; **dafür halten,** to be of opinion; **es mit Einem halten,** to side with. **Halt'ung, -ung,** f. bearing, deportment, carriage.
Hamen, ha'men, m. drag-net.
Hämisch, hä'mish, a. malicious, knavish, spiteful, av. -ly.
Hammel, ham'mel, m. wether, mutton. **Ham'melbraten, -brätten,** m. roast of mutton. **Ham'melfleisch,** -fläësh, n. mutton. **Ham'melsteule, -köüle.** f. leg of mutton. **Hammeln,** ham'meln, vt. to geld, castrate rams.
Hammer, ham'mer, m. hammer. **Hämmerchen,** hem'mörchen, n. little hammer. **Hammerarbeit,** ham'merärbet, f. hammered, raised work. **Hämmerbar,** hem'merbär, a. malleable; **-keit, -käet,** f. malleability, **Hämmern,** hem'mern, vt. to hammer. **Hammerschlag,** ham'mershläg, m. stroke of the hammer; scale-chip. **Hammerwerk,** ham'mervörk, n. forge.
Hämorrhoidal, hämorridäl', **Hämorrhoidalisch,** a. hemorrhoidal. **Hämorrhoidalfasten,** -knöten, m. piles. **Hämorrhoiden,** hämorrhol'den, n. hemorrhoids.
Hampelmann, hamp'lman, m. punch, puppet.
Hamster, ham'ster, m. hamster, marmot.

Hand, hant, f. pl. **Hände,** hand, handwriting, direction: **hohle Hand,** hollow of the hand; **flache Hand,** palm; **todte Hand,** mortmain; **die Hand drücken,** to shake hands; **Hand legen an,** to lay violent hands on; **die Hand anlegen,** to apprehend, to seize; **die letzte Hand anlegen,** to give a finishing stroke; **zur Hand, bei der Hand,** at hand; **nicht bei der Hand sein,** to be out of the way; **unter der Hand,** underhand, secretly; **vor der Hand,** at present, just now. **Handarbeit,** hant'arbäet, f. handiwork, handicraft. **Hand'arbeiter,** -arbäeter, m. workman, handicraftman. **Hand'becken,** -becken, n. wash-basin. **Hand'beil,** -bäil, n. hatchet. **Hand'breit,** -bräet, a. of a hand's-breadth. **Hand'buch, -buch,** n. manual, compendium. **Händedruck,** hen'dedryck, m. shaking, pressing of the hand. **Handeisen,** hant'äisen. n. manacles. **Hand'fessel, -fessel,** f. manacles, shackles. **Händeklatschen,** hen'deklatshen, n. applause.

Handel, hand'el, m. traffic, business affair, commerce, trade, bargain; quarrel; — **treiben,** to trade, traffic; **Händel anfangen,** to pick a quarrel. **Handeln,** han'deln, vt. to trade, bargain, traffic, deal in; to act; **Han-**

bein um, to bargain for, hackle; to treat of; to be the question. **Handelsangelegenheit**, hand'elsan-gelägenhäet, *f.* commercial affair. **Handelsartikel**, -artickel, *m.* article of trade. **Handelsbrief**, -brīf, *m.* mercantile letter. **Handelsdiener**, -dīner, *m.* clerk, merchant's clerk. **Handelsflotte**, -flotte, *f.* commercial navy. **Handelsfreiheit**, -freïhäet, *f.* free trade. **Handelsfreund**, -fröünt, *m.* correspondent, business friend. **Handelsgeschäft**, -gäscht, *m.* turn for trade. **Handelsgenoss**, -genoss, *m.* partner; **-schaft**, -shaft, *f.* partnership. **Handelsgericht**, -gericht, *n.* board of trade, commercial court. **Handelsgesellschaft**, -gesellshaft, *f.* trading company; partnership. **Handelsgesetz**, -gesetz, *n.* commercial law. **Handelshaus**, -hōus, *n.* firm, trading house, commercial house. **Handelsmann**, -mann, *m.* merchant, shopkeeper. **Handelsplatz**, -plats, *m.* emporium, commercial town, mart. **Handelspolitik**, -politik, *f.* policy of trade. **Handelsschaft**, -shaft, *f.* trade, traffic. **Handelsschiff**, *n.* merchantman, trading-vessel. **Handelsstadt**, *f. pl.* -städte, commercial town. **Handelsstand**, -shtant, *m.* trading-class, the merchants. **Handelsverkehr**, -ferkär, *m.* commercial intercourse. **Handelsvertrag**, -ferträg, *m. pl.* -verträge, commercial treaty. **Handelszweig**, -tsveïg, *m.* branch of trade. **Handfest**, hant'fesht, *a.* stout, strong, *av.* -ly. **Handgeld**, -gëlt, *n.* earnest-money. **Handgelenk**, -gelenk, *n. pl.* -e, wrist. **Handgelübnis**, -gelübpniss, *n.* **Handgelübde**, -gelüpde, *n.* solemn promise. **Handgemein**, -gemään, *a.* in close quarters; — **werden**, to close in battle, to get hand to hand. **Handgemenge**, -gemeng-e, *n.* close fighting, fray, scuffle, contest. **Handgicht**, -gicht, *f.* chiragra, gout in the hands. **Handgreiflich**, -gröïflich, *a.* palpable, evident, manifest; **-keit**, -käet, *f.* palpableness, evidentness. **Handgriff**, -griff, *m.* handle; grasp, manipulation, knack, sleight. **Handhabe**, -häbe, *f.* handle, ear. **Handhaben**, *vt.* to handle, administer, manage. **Handhabung**, -häbung, *f.* handling.

management. **Handkauf**, -kāūf, *m.* selling off-hand; retail. **Handkorb**, *m. pl.* -körbe, basket; basket-hilt (of *a* sword). **Handkuss**, -kuss, *m.* kissing the hand. **Handlanger**, -langer, *m.* hodman; understrapper; assistant workman, underworker. **Händler**, hent'ler, *m.* trader, dealer monger. **Handleuchter**, hant'löichter, *m.* hand candlestick. **Handlich**, -lich, *a.* handy, tolerable. **Handlung**, hant'lung, *f.* action, act, deed; trade, commerce; trading-house. **Handlungsdiener**, -dīner. *m.* clerk of a merchant's house. **Handlungsweise**, -veīs-e, *f.* way of acting, conduct, habits. **Handpferd**, -pfärt, *n.* led-horse. **Handpresse**, -press-e, *f.* hand-press. **Handquelle**, -kväle, *f.* **Handtuch**, -tych, *n.* towel. **Handramme**, -ramme, *f.* beetle, rammer. **Handreichung**, -räechung, *f.* help, assistance, charity. **Handsäge**, -säge, *f.* hand-saw. **Handschelle**, -shelle, *f.* handcuff. **Handschlag**, -shläg, *m.* joining of hands, shaking of the hands. **Handschrift**, -shrift, *f.* hand-writing, manuscript; **-lich**, -lich, *a. av.* in writing, (in) manuscript. **Handschuh**, -shy, *m.* glove; **-macher**, -macher, *m.* glover. **Handsiegel**, -sīgel, *n.* seal manual. **Handtieren**, -tīren, *vt.* to handle, manage, wield; to work, make a noise, bustle. **Handtierung**, -tīrung, *f.* trade, profession, business; — **treiben**, to follow a profession. **Handvoll**, hant'-foll, *m.* handful. **Handwerk**, -vërk, *n.* trade; **-er**, -er, *m.* **Handwerksmann**, -mann, *m.* mechanic. **Handwerksbursch**, -bursh, *m. pl.* -burschen, traveling journeyman. **Handwerksgesell**, -gesell, *m.* journeyman. **Handwerksmässig**, -mässig, *a.* mechanical, professional; — **treiben**, to make a trade of. **Handwerkszeug**, -tsöïg, *n.* a set of tools *or* implements. **Handwerkszunft**, hant'vërks-tsynft, *f.* guild; corporation; company.

Hanf, hanf. *m.* hemp. **Hanfacker**, -acker, *m.* **Hanffeld**, -felt, *n.* hemp-field. **Hanfbreche**, -breche, *f.* hemp-break. **Hanfdarre**, -darre, *f.* hemp kiln. **Hänfen**, hen'fen, *a.* hempen cannabine. **Hänfling**, henf'ling, *m.*

linnet. **Hanffamen,** han'sămen, *m.* hemp-seed.

Hang, hang, *m.* declivity; proneness, bent, bias, propensity, inclination. **Hängebrücke,** hĕng'ebrükke, *f.* suspension-bridge. **Häng'ekampaß,** -kompäss, *m.* miner's compass. **Häng'ematte,** -matte, *f.* hammock. **Hangen,** hang'en (**hing, gehangen**), *vi.* to hang, to be suspended, droop, dangle, to adhere, cling, cleave, stick. **Hängen,** hĕng'en. *vt.* to hang, suspend; cleave to. **Häng'efänle,** -säule, *n.* queen post. **Häng'efchloß,** -shloss, *n.* padlock.

Hänfeln, hĕn'seln, *vt.* to initiate; to tease, vex, fool.

Hanswurft, hans'vurzht, *m. pl.* **Hanswürfte,** clown, merry-andrew; buffoon; **mäßig,** -mässig. *a.* buffoonish, clownish.

Hapern, ha'pern, *vi.* to break down; **es hapert ihm,** he is at a loss; to be stumped; **da haperts,** there's the rub.

Hären, hăr'en, *a.* made of hair.

Harfe, bar'fe, *f.* harp. **Harfner,** harf'ner, *m.* **Harfenspieler,** -zhpïler, *m.* harper, harpist.

Häring, hă'ring, *m.* herring. **Hä'ringsnase,** -nase, *f.* flat nose.

Harlefin, harr'lĕkin, *m.* harlequin, buffoon.

Harm, harm, *m.* sorrow, grief. **Härmen,** her'men, *vi.* **fich —,** to grieve. **Harm'los,** -lōs, *a.* harmless, inoffensive.

Harmonie, harmonÿ', *f.* harmony, concord. **Harmoniren,** harmonÿ'ren, *vi.* to harmonize. **Harmonisch,** harmo'nish, *a.* harmonious, harmonic.

Harn, harn. *m.* urine. **Harn'blafe,** -blāse, *f.* bladder. **Harnen,** hăr'nen, *vi.* to urinate, to make water, piss.

Harnisch, har'nish, *m.* harness, armor; **in Harnisch bringen,** to enrage.

Harnröhre, harn'röhre, *f.* urethra. **Harnsäure,** harn'säure, *f.* uric acid. **Harn verstopfung,** -ferzhtopfung, *f.* retention of urine. **Harnsäures Salz,** urate. **Harnstoff,** harn'zhtoff, *m.* urea; **-strenge,** -zhtrenge, dysury.

Harpune, harpÿ'ne, *f.* harpoon. **Harpunen,** harpÿ'nen, *vt.* to harpoon.

Harren, har'ren, *vi.* to wait, stay, tarry, abide; to hope.

Harsch, harsh, *a.* rough, hard. **Hart,** hart, *a.* hard; hardened, unfeeling. **Harte,** her'te, *f.* **Hartheit,** hart'hăet, **Härtigkeit,** her'tichkăet, *f.* hardness. **Härten,** her'ten, *vt.* to harden. **Hartherzig,** hart'hertsig, *a.* hard-hearted; **-feit,** -kăet, *f.* hard-heartedness. **Harthörig,** hart'höhrig, *a.* hard, dull of hearing; **-feit,** -kăet, *f.* hard-hearing. **Hartköpfig,** -köpfig, *a.* hard-headed, stubborn; slow to learn. **Hartleibig,** -leibig, *a.* costive; **-feit,** -kăet, *f.* costiveness. **Hartmäulig,** -mäulig, *a.* hard-mouthed; **-feit,** -kăet, *f.* unruliness. **Hartnäckig,** -neckig, *a.* stiff-necked, headstrong; **-feit,** -kăet, *f.* stubborness, obstinacy.

Harz, hărts, *n.* resin, rosin. **Harzig,** *a.* resinous; resiniferous. **Harzicht,** -icht, *a.* resinous.

Hasardspiel, hasart'zhpĭl, *n.* game of chance.

Haschen, hash'en, *vt.* to catch, snatch, apprehend, seize; **— nach,** to run after. **Häscher,** hăsh'er, *m.* constable, myrmidon.

Hase, hă'se, *m.* hare; **junger Hase,** leveret.

Hasel, hă'sel, *m.* hazel. **Ha'felhuhn,** -hyn, *n.* heath-cock. **Ha'selnuß,** -nyss, *f. pl.* **-nüsse,** hazlenut. **Ha'selstaude,** -zhtowde, *f.* **Ha'selstrauch,** -zhtrŏgch, *m.* hazel.

Hasenfuß, hă'senfyss, *m.* hare's foot; coward. **Ha'fenherz,** -herts, *n.* cowardice. **Ha'fenjagd,** -yacht, *f.* harehunting. **Ha'fenpanier,** -panihr, *n.* flight; **das — ergreifen,** to take to one's heels. **Ha'fenfcharte,** -sharte, *f.* harelip.

Haspel, hash'pel, *m.* reel, windlass, winch. **Haspeln,** hash'peln, *vt.* to reel.

Haß, hass, *m.* hatred, hate. **Hassen,** has'sen, *vt.* to hate. **Hasser,** has'ser, *m.* hater. **Häßlich,** hess'lich, *a.* ugly; **-feit,** -kăet, *f.* ugliness.

Haft, hasht, *f.* haste, hurry, precipitation. **Haften,** hasht'en, *vt.* to require hurry; to hasten. **Haftig,** hasht'ich, *a.* hasty, hurried, passionate, *av.* -ly; **-feit,** -kăet, *f.* hastiness, rashness, precipitation.

Hätscheln, hătsh'eln, *vt.* to caress, to dandle, pet.

Hatz, hats, *f.* baiting, hunting; pack

Hau, häü, *m.* act or place of felling wood.

Haube, hŏy'bə, *f.* cap, coif, hood.

Haub'enkopf, -kŏpf, *m.* **Haub'enſtock,** -ſtŏck, *m.* milliner's block.

Haubiꜩe, hāu'bĭtse, *f.* howitzer.

Hauch, hŏyḣ, *m.* breath; breeze; aspiration (Gram.) **Hauch'buchſtabe, -buchſtabe,** *m.* **Hauch'laut,** -lŏyt, *m.* aspirate.

Haudegen, hǎü'dāgen, *m.* broad-sword; swordsman; bully; blade.

Haue, hǎü'ə, *f.* hoe, mattock. **Hauen,** hǎü'ən (hieb, gehauen), *vt.* to hew, chop, lash; über die Schnur hauen, to transgress. **Haubajonett,** hǎü'-bayonĕt, *n.* sword-bayonet. **Hauer,** hǎü'er, *m.* cutter, hewer; wild boar; boar's tusk.

Haufe, hŏy'fe, *m.* heap, pile; crowd, multitude, number, troop, gang. **Häufeln,** hŏü'feln, *vt.* to make small heaps; to hill. **Häufen,** hŏü'fen, *vt.* to heap, accumulate, to pile up. **Haufenweiſe,** hŏy'fenveǐse, *av.* in heaps, crowds, in great numbers. **Häufig,** hŏü'fĭḣ, *a.* frequent; *av.* -ly.

Haupt, hǎüpt, *n.* head; chief.

Haupt, hǎüpt, *a.* chief, principal, main. **Haupt'abſicht,** -apsĭḣt, *f.* chief design. **Haupt'ader,** -āder, *f.* cephalic vein. **Haupt'altar,** -altār, *m.* high-altar. **Haupt'erbe,** -ĕrbe, *m.* chief heir. **Haupt'farbe,** -farbe, *f.* main color. **Haupt'figur,** -fĭgūr, *f.* principal figure. **Haupt'geſchäft,** -gesḣäft, *n.* main business. **Haupt'grund,** -grŭnt, *m.* principal reason. **Haupt'haar,** -hār, *n.* hair of the head. **Haupt'kirche,** -kĭrḣe, *f.* cathedral, metropolitan church. **Haupt'mann,** -mann, *m.* captain; **-ſchaft,** -shaft, *f.* captaincy. **Haupt'maſt,** -mazht, *m.* mainmast. **Haupt'nenner,** -nĕnner, *m.* common denominator. **Haupt'ort,** -ŏrt, *m.* chief place. **Haupt'perſon,** -pĕrson, *f.* chief person, leader. **Haupt'punkt,** -pŭnkt, *m.* chief point, main point. **Haupt'quartier,** -kvartīr *n.* headquarters. **Haupt'rolle,** -rŏlle, *f.* principal part. **Haupt'ſache,** -saḣe, *f.* main point. **Haupt'ſächlich,** -sěḣlĭḣ, *a.* chief, essential, principal; *av.* -ly. **Haupt'ſaꜩ,** -saꜩ, *m.* main proposition; principal sentence (Gram.). **Haupt'ſegel,** -sēgl, *n.* mainsail.

Haupt'ſtadt, -shtat, *f. pl.* **-ſtädte** capital, chief city. **Haupt'ſtärke,** -shtěrke, *f.* chief strength, strong point, forte. **Haupt'ſtraße,** -shtrāsse, *f.* main street, main road. **Haupt'ſtück,** -zbtück, *n.* chief part; chapter. **Haupt'ton,** -tōn, *m.* key-tone; principal accent. **Haupt'tugend,** -tūgent, *f.* cardinal, principal virtue. **Haupt'unterſchied,** -ŭntershīd, *m.* essential difference, principal difference. **Haupt'wache,** -vaḣe, *f.* guard-house; main-guard. **Haupt'werk,** -vĕrk, *n.* chief work. **Haupt'wind,** -vĭnnt, *m.* cardinal wind; prevailing wind. **Haupt'zug,** -tsug, *m. pl.* -züge, main feature. **Haupt'zweck,** -tsvĕck, *m.* main end, principal aim.

Haus, hŏys, *n. pl.* **Häuſer,** house; family; household; shell, case; firm; von Haus, from home; zu Hauſe, at home; nach Hauſe, home, homeward; von Haus aus, originally; zu Hauſe ſein, in, to be at home, familiar with, master of. **Haus'andacht,** hŏys'ăndaḣt, *f.* private devotion. **Haus'apotheke,** -apotāke, *f.* medicine box, house dispensary. **Haus'arreſt,** -arrĕst, *m.* confinement at one's house; — haben, to be a prisoner at one's house. **Haus'arzt,** -artst, *m.* family-physician. **Haus'backen,** -backen, *a.* home-made; plain. **Haus'beſiꜩer,** -besĭtser, *m.* landlord. **Haus'brod,** -brōt, *n.* homebaked bread. **Haus'drache,** -draḣe, *m.* shrew, scold, termagant. **Haus'ehre,** -ēre, *f.* honor of the house. **Hauſen,** hŏy'sen, *vt.* to dwell, live in; rage.

Hauſen, hŏy'sen, *m.* sturgeon. **Hauſenblaſe,** -blāse, *f.* isinglass. **Hauſenrogen,** -rōgen, *m.* caviar.

Hausflur, hŏys'flūr, *f.* entry, hall, vestibule, passage. **Haus'frau,** -frǎü, *f.* lady of the house, housewife. **Haus'freund,** -frŏünt, *m.* friend of the family. **Haus'frieden,** -frīden, *m.* domestic peace. **Haus'geflügel,** -geflügel, *n.* poultry. **Haus'genoß,** -genoss, *m.* inmate of a house, lodger; **-ſchaft,** -shaft, *f.* family, household. **Haus'gerät,** -gerät, *n.* furniture. **Haus'geſinde,** -sĭnnde, *n.* domestics. **Haus'gott,** -gŏtt, *m.* household god. **Haus'gottesdienſt,**

-dinzht, m. family worship. **Haus'-**
hahn, -hän, m. cock, rooster. **Haus'-**
halt, -halt, m. housekeeping. **Haus'-**
hälter, -hälter, m. housekeeper: **-in**,
f. (female) housekeeper. **Haus'häl-**
terisch, -hĕlterish, a. economical.
Haushaltung, -haltung, f. house-
keeping, household. **Haus'herr,**
-hĕrr, m. landlord. **Haus'hofmeister,**
-höfmäezhter, m. steward. **Haus'-**
hoch, -hōch, a. as high as a house.
Haus'hund, -hunt, m. watch-dog.
Haus'ren, -īren, vt. to hawk. **Hau-**
s'rer, -īrer, m. hawker, peddler.
Hauskleid, -klăet, n. house-dress,
wrapper. **Hausknecht**, -knĕcht, m.
hostler, menial. **Haus'kost**, -kozht,
f. household fare. **Haus'kreuz,**
krŏŭts, n. domestic affliction: scold,
shrew. **Haus'krieg**, -krīg, m. domestic discord, warfare. **Haus'lehrer,**
-lărer, m. family tutor; **-stelle**,
-zhtelle, f. place of family tutor.
Hausleinwand, -līnĕnvant, f. home-
spun linen. **Häuslich**, hŏŭs'lich, a
domestic; frugal, economical; thrif-
ty; **-keit**, -kāĕt, f. domesticity, domestic life, economy, thriftiness.
Hausmädchen, hŏŭs'mĕdchen, n.
Haus'magd, -māgt, f. **Haus'mamsell,**
-mamsell, f. housemaid. **Haus'-**
mannskost, -mannskozht, f. household fare. **Haus'mittel**, -mittel, n.
domestic remedy. **Haus'mutter,**
-mutter, f. matron; mother of a
family. **Haus'plage**, -plāge, f. shrew,
scold. **Haus'rath**, -rāt, m. household furniture. **Haus'ratte**, -ratte,
f. common rat. **Haus'recht**, -rĕcht,
n. domestic authority. **Hausschlüs-**
sel, -shlüssel, m. night-key; house-
key. **Haus'segen**, -sāgen, m. domestic blessing; children. **Haus'steuer,**
-zhtŏĭer, f. house-tax. **Haus'thier,**
-tīr, n. domestic animal. **Haus'thür,**
-tūhr, f. street-door. **Haus'trauung,**
-trŏŭng, f. private wedding. **Haus'-**
trunk, -trŭnk, m. family beverage.
Haus'truppen, -truppen, f. life-
guards. **Haus'übel**, -ūbbel, n. family affliction. **Haus'vater**, -fater,
m. father of the family. **Haus'ver-**
walter, -fĕrvalter, m. **Haus'vogt,**
-fōkt, m. steward. **Haus'wesen,**
-vāsen, n. domestic concerns, household. **Haus'wirth**, -virrt, m. husband; landlord; **-in**, f. mistress of
a house; landlady. **Haus'wirth-**
schaft, -shaft, f. housekeeping.
Hauszins, hŏŭs'tsins, m. house
rent.

Haut, hŏŭt, f. pl. **Häute**, hide, skin,
cuticle; **aus der Haut fahren vor
Freude**, to jump out of one's skin for
joy; **aus der Haut fahren vor Zorn,**
to burst with anger; **die Haut über
die Ohren ziehen**, to flay, to fleece;
mit Haut und Haaren, altogether;
neck and crop. **Häuten**, hŏŭ'ten,
vt. to skin, flay; **— sich**, to peal, to
cast one's skin, slough. **Häutig,**
hŏŭ'tig, a. skinny; membran-
ous. **Häuticht**, hŏŭticht, a. mem-
braneous.

Haverie, hāvęrī', **Haverei**,-rēī', s. average.

He! Heh! hā, Ij. ha! **Heda!** hā'da,
Ij. heigh! ho there! halloo!

Hebamme, hāb'amme, f. midwife.
Hebarzt, hāb'ārtst, m. man-mid-
wife.

Hebe, hā'be, f. lifting up; lever; pulley; **-balken**, -balken, m. **-baum,**
-bąŭm, m. lever; heaver. **Hebel,**
hā'bel, m. lever. **Heben**, hā'ben (hob,
gehoben), vt. to heave, raise, lift, elevate. **Heber**, m. lever, elevator;
siphon. **Hebung**, -ung, f. raising,
lifting; elevating; gathering, levy;
removal.

Hechel, hęch'el, f. hatchel. **Hecheln,**
hęch'eln, vt. to hatchel; to lash, censure. **Hechler**, hęch'ler, m. **-in**, f.
hatcheler.

Hecht, hęcht, m. pl. **-e**, pike; **-chen**, n.
small pike, pickerel.

Heckdorn, hęck'bort, n. tafferel.

Hecke, hęk'e, f. hatching, hatch; breeding; aviary.

Hecke, hęk'e, f. hedge, fence.

Hecken, hęk'en, vt. to hatch, breed.

Heckenrose, hęk'enrōse, f. wild rose.

Heckenzaun, hęk'entsąŭn, m. encic-
sure.

Hede, hā'de, f. tow, oakum.

Hederich, hā'dęrich, m. hedge-mus-
tard.

Heer, hēr, n. army, host; multitude,
great number; **wildes Heer**, Arthur's
chase, wild chase. **Heerbann**, hēr'-
ban, arriere-ban. **Heer'biene**, -bīne,
f. predatory, thieving bee.

Heerd, hārt, m. hearth.

Heerde, hār'de, f. flock, herd, drove-crowd, multitude. **Heerdenweise,** härt'envēlse, *av.* in herds, flocks, droves.

Heeresmacht, hēr'esmacht, *f.* forces, troops, army. **Heerflüchtig,** -flüchtig, *a.* deserting. **Heerflüchtiger,** -flüchtiger, *m.* deserter. **Heerführer,** -führer, *m.* commander-in-chief, general. **Heergeräth,** -gerät, *n.* baggage, train. **Heerhaufen,** -hóyfen, *m.* corps, division. **Heerpauke,** -pòyke, *f.* kettle-drum. **Heerschwarz,** -bär, *f.* legion, host. **Heerschau,** -shao, *f.* review. **Heerstrasse,** -strässe, *f.* military road. **Heerzug,** -tsuk, *m.* march of an army.

Hefe, hef'fe, *f.* barm, yeast; dregs, lees. **Hefenbrot,** hef'enbrōt, *n.* leavened bread. **Hefigt,** hef'icht, *a.* yeasty, barmy.

Heft, heft, *n.* handle, haft, hilt.

Heft, heft, *n. or m.* book, paper-book, part, number; in **Heften,** in numbers. **Hefteisen,** -ēisen, *n.* punt. **Heftel,** *m. or n.* clasp, hook, pin. **Heften,** hef'ten, *vt.* to clasp, fasten. **Heften,** hef'ten, *vt.* to fasten, stitch, sew, fix.

Heftig, hef'tich, *a.* vehement, violent, sharp, passionate, bitter, *av.* -ly. **Heftigkeit,** -kāet, *f.* vehemence, violence, impetuosity, intensity.

Heftnadel, heft'nādel, *f.* stitching-needle.

Heftpflaster, heft'pflazhter, *n.* sticking-plaster.

Hegen, hā'gen, *vt.* to foster, cherish, entertain, harbor, bear, have.

Hehl, hāl, *n.* secrecy, concealment; **Hehl haben,** to conceal, deny. **Hehlen,** hā'len, *vt.* to conceal, secrete; receive. **Hehler,** *m.* receiver, concealer (of stolen goods).

Hehr, hēr, *a.* august, sublime, elevated, *av.* -ly.

Hei, hēi, *ij.* ho! huzzah!

Heide, hai'de, *f.* heath.

Heide, hai'de, *m.* heathen, pagan, gentile.

Heideblume, hai'deblume, *f.* heide-kraut, -krōyt, *n.* heath.

Heidegrütze, hai'degrütse, *f.* buckwheat-grit. **Heidekorn,** -korn, *n.* buck-wheat.

Heidelbeere, hai'delbēre, *f.* huckleberry, bilberry.

Heidenthum, hai'dentum, *n.* paganism, heathenism. **Heidnisch,** -nish, *a.* heathenish.

Heikelig, hāe'kelich, *a.* fastidious, particular.

Heil, hāel, *a.* whole, sound, unhurt, well; *s. n.* welfare, prosperity, salvation; **Heil dem!** long live! hail to! **Heiland,** hāe'land, *m.* Saviour. **Heilanstalt,** -anzhtalt, *f.* hospital, infirmary. **Heilart,** -ärt, *f.* method of curing. **Heilbrunnen,** -brunnen, *m.* mineral springs. **Heilbar,** -bär, *a.* curable; -keit, -kāet, *f.* curableness. **Heilen,** hāe'len, *vt.* to cure, heal, make whole. **Heilig,** hāe'lich, *a.* holy, sacred; — sprechen, to canonize. **Heiligen,** hāe'lichen, *vt.* to hallow, sanctify. **Heiligenbild,** -bilt, *n.* image of a saint. **Heiligenschein,** -shaen, *m.* glory, halo. **Heiliger,** *m.* saint. **Heiligkeit,** -kāet, *f.* holiness, sanctity, sacredness, inviolability. **Heiligsprechung,** -zhprechung, *f.* canonization. **Heiligthum,** -tum, *n.* sanctuary; relic. **Heilkraft,** -kraft, *f.* healing power. **Heilkraut,** -krōyt, *n.* medicinal herb. **Heilkunde,** -kunde, *f.* medical science. **Heilkundig,** -kundich, *a.* skilled in medicine. **Heillos,** -lōs, *a.* wicked; baleful; dismal, outrageous; villainous, atrocious; -keit, -kāet, *f.* wickedness. **Heilsam,** -sam, *a.* wholesome, salutary; -keit, -kāet, *f.* wholesomeness; salubrity. **Heilung,** -ung, *f.* cure, healing.

Heim, hāem, *av.* home, homeward. **Heimath,** hāe'mat, *f.* home, native place. **Heimathlich,** -lich, *a.* native. **Heimathlos,** hāe'matlōs, *a.* homeless. **Heimbringen,** -bringen, *vt.* to bring home.

Heimchen, hāem'chen, *n.* cricket.

Heimfahrt, hāem'tärt, *f.* return. **Heimfall,** -fall, *m.* reversion, escheat. **Heimfallen,** *vi.* to escheat. **Heimfällig,** -fällich, *a.* reversionary, escheatable. **Heimführen,** -führen, *vt.* to lead home; to bring home (a bride). **Heimgang,** -gang, *m.* decease. **Heimgehen,** -gāen, *vi.* to go home. **Heimholen,** -hōlen, *vt.* to take home. **Heimisch,** -ish, *a.* domestic, home, native, national; comfortable, *av.* -ly, at home. **Heimkehr,** -kār, *f.* **Heimkunft,** -kunft, *f.* return home. **Heimkehren,** -kāren,

Heim'kommen, -kŏmmen, *vi.* to return home.
Heim'lich, häĕm'lich, *a.* secret, concealed, underhand, clandestine, *av.* -ly; **-keit**, -kāĕt, *f.* secrecy, secret, concealment.
Heimreise, häĕm'rēise, *f.* homeward journey. **Heim'schicken**, -shicken, *vt.* to send home; to rebuke; to send packing.
Heimsuchen, häĕm'sychen, *vt.* to visit, afflict. **Heim'suchung**, -yng, *f.* visitation.
Heimtücke, häĕm'tücke, *f.* malice; underhand trick. **Heim'tückisch**, -tückish, *a.* malicious, mischievous, treacherous.
Heimwärts, häĕm'vērts, *av.* homeward.
Heimweg, häĕm'vāg, *m.* way home; return home.
Heimweh, häĕm'vā, *n.* homesickness; — haben, to be homesick.
Heimziehen, häĕmtsī'en, *vi.* to return home.
Heirath, hēi'rāt, *f.* marriage, match. **Heirathen**, hēi'rāten, *vt.* to marry, take in marriage; reich —, to marry a fortune. **Hei'rathsantrag**, -antrāk, *f.* proposal. **Hei'rathsfähig**, -fāich, *a.* marriageable. **Hei'rathsgut**, -gyt, *n.* dower, portion. **Hei'rathsstifter**, -shtifter, *m.* sin, *f.* match-maker. **Hei'rathsvertrag**, -fērträk, *m.* marriage-articles.
Heisa! Heißa! hēi'ssa', *ij.* heyday! huzzah! hurrah!
Heischen, hāĕsh'en, *vt.* to ask, require, demand, claim.
Heiser, hāĕss'er, *a.* hoarse; **-keit**, -kāĕt, *f.* hoarseness.
Heiß, hāĕss, *a.* hot, torrid; ardent, passionate; glühend heiß, red hot.
Heißen, hāĕssen (hieß, geheißen), *vt.* to call, name, bid, command, order; *vi.* to be called, named; to mean, signify, be; willkommen heißen, to bid welcome; gut heißen, to sanction, approve; wie heißen Sie? what is your name? das heißt, that is; es heißt, it is reported. **Heißhunger**, hāĕss'hynger, *m.* ravenous appetite; **-ig**, *a.* voracious, greedy; very hungry; very eager.
Heiter, hāĕ'ter, *a.* serene, bright, cheerful, merry; **-keit**, -kāĕt, *f.* cheerfulness; hilarity, merriness, serenity.
Heizbar, hāĕts'bār, *a.* that may be heated, with a fireplace, stove.
Heizen, hāĕt'sen, *vt.* to heat, make a fire. **Heiz'er**, *m.* stoker, fireman. **Heiz'raum**, -räum, *m.* firebox; hypocaust. **Heizung**, hāĕts'yng, *f.* heating.
Hektisch, hĕk'tish, *a.* hectic.
Held, helt, *m. pl.* -en, hero. **Hel'dengedicht**, -gedicht, *n.* epic poem. **Hel'dengeist**, -gāĕzht, *m.* heroism, heroic spirit. **Hel'denmäßig**, -mässich, *a.* heroic. **Hel'denmuth**, -myt, *m.* heroic daring, heroism. **Hel'denruhm**, -rym, *m.* a hero's fame. **Hel'densage**, -sāge, *f.* heroic legend. **Hel'denthat**, -tāt, *f.* exploit, heroic feat. **Held'in**, *f.* heroine.
Helfen, hĕl'fen (half, geholfen), *vt.* to help, aid, succor, assist, support, relieve; *vi.* to avail, to do good; to remedy, save; was hilft's, what avails it. **Helfer**, hĕl'fer, *m.* helper, aider; assistant. **Hel'fershelfer**, *m.* accomplice.
Heliotrop, hēl'iotrōp, *m. u. n.* heliotrope, turnsole; blood-stone (Min.).
Hell, hĕll, *a.* bright, light, clear; *av.* -ly. **Hell'blau**, -blāu, *a.* light-blue. **Hell'braun**, -brāun, *a.* light-brown. **Helldunkel**, hĕll'dynkel, *s.* chiaroscuro; twilight. **Hell'e**, *f.* brightness, clearness.
Hellebarde, hĕllebard'e, *f.* halberd.
Heller, hĕl'ler, *m.* penny, farthing; der letzte Heller, the last farthing.
Hellig, hĕl'lich, *a.* bright, clear; *-keit*, -kāĕt, *f.* brightness, clearness. **Hell'sichtig**, -sichtig, *a.* clairvoyant, clear-sighted; *-keit*, -kāĕt, *f.* clairvoyance, clear-sightedness.
Helm, hĕlm, *m.* helmet. **Helm'busch**, -bush, *m.* crest.
Helvin, hĕl'fin, *m.* helvine.
Hemd, hĕmt, *n.* shirt; smock, shift, chemise.
Hemisphäre, hĕmisfä're, *f.* hemisphere.
Hemmen, hĕm'men, *vt.* to stop, check; to trig; to hinder, prohibit. **Hemm'kette**, -kette, *f.* lock-chain, skid. **Hemmschuh**, hĕm'shy, *m.* trigger, tricker.
Hengst, hĕngzht, *m.* stallion.

Hen 161 **Her**

fohlen, -folen, **Hengſtfüllen,** -füllen, n. male-colt.
Henkel, hĕn'kĕl, m. ear, handle, hook, ring; **-korb,** -kŏrb, m. handle-basket. **Hen'keln,** vt. to furnish with a handle, ear.
Henken, hĕn'ken, vt. to hang. **Hen'ker,** m. hangman, executioner. **Henkermahl,** hĕn'kĕrmāl, n. last meal. **Hen'kersknecht,** -knĕcht, m. hangman's assistant.
Henne, hĕn'nĕ, f. hen, chicken.
Hennegat, hĕn'nĕgăt, n. helm-port.
Her, hăr, a. hither, here.
Herab, hĕrăb', av. down here. **Herab'blicken,** -blicken, vi. to look down. **Herab'bringen,** -bringen, vt. to bring down. **Herab'kommen,** -kŏmmen, vi. to come down; to be reduced, straitened. **Herab'laſſen,** -lăssen, vt. to let down; — ſich, condescend. **Herab'laſſung,** -ŭng, f. condescension. **Herab'ſehen,** -sĕen, vi. to look down. **Herab'ſetzen,** -sĕtsen, vt. to lower; depreciate; undervalue, degrade. **Herab'ſtürzen,** -zhtŭrtsen, vt. to precipitate; vi. to fall down.
Heraldik, hĕrăl'dĭc, f. heraldry.
Heran, hĕrăn', av. near, hither, hither on. **Heran'kommen,** -kŏmmen, vi. to come on. **Heran'nahen,** -nä-en, vi. to approach. **Heran'rücken,** -rücken, vi. approach. **Heran'wachſen,** -vaksen, vi. to grow up.
Herauf, hĕrŏŭf', av. upwards, up hither, up here, up. **Herauf'ſteigen,** -zhtēĭgen, vi. to ascend hither.
Heraus, hĕrŏŭs', av. out, out hither, out here; **Heraus damit!** Out with it! Speak out! **gerade heraus,** av. straightforward, frankly, downright. **Heraus'begeben,** -gāben. vr. ſich,—, to go out. **Heraus'bekommen,** -kŏmmen, vt. to receive (change); to get out. **Heraus'fahren,** -fāren, vi. to drive out; to slip out. **Heraus'finden,** -fĭnden, vt. to find out. **Heraus'fordern,** -fŏrdern. vt. to challenge; to defy. **Heraus'forderung,** -ŭng, f. challenge. **Heraus'gabe,** -gābe, f. delivery; publication. **Heraus'geben,** -gāben, vt. to deliver up; to give the change; to publish. **Heraus'geber,** -gāber, m. publisher; editor. **Heraus'helfen,** -hĕlfen, vi. to help out; to assist. **Heraus'kommen,** -kŏmmen, vi. to come out;

proceed; to result. **Heraus'laſſen,** -lăssen, vt. to let out. **Heraus'leſen,** -lāsen, vt. to pick out, select. **Heraus'locken,** -lŏcken, vt. to draw out. **Heraus'plaudern,** -plŏŭdern, vt. to blab out. **Heraus'putzen,** -pŭtsen, vt. to trick out, dress up. **Heraus'rücken,** -rücken, vt. to push out; vi. to march out; **mit der Sprache —,** to speak out. **Heraus'schießen,** -shĭssen, vi. to rush out; to shoot out. **Heraus'sprudeln,** -shrŭdĕln, vi. to gush out; vt. to throw out. **Heraus'stürmen,** -zhtürmen, **Heraus'stürzen,** -zhtŭrtsen, vi. to rush out; to precipitate one's self. **Heraus'treten,** -trāten, vi. to step out. **Heraus'werfen,** -vĕrfen, vt. to throw out. **Heraus'wickeln,** -vickeln, **Heraus'winden,** -vĭnnden, vr. ſich —, to extricate one's self, to get out of. **Heraus'ziehen,** -tsīen, vt. to draw, pull out.
Herb, hĕrp, a. harsh, acerb, bitter, sour, tart; sullen, austere, grim, gruff. **Her'be, Herb'heit,** -hāĕt, f. harshness, tartness; austerity.
Herbei, hĕrbēī', av. hither, near. **Herbei'bringen,** -bringen, vt. to bring on, along; to produce. **Herbei'holen,** -hōlen, vt. to bring along; to endeavor to reach. **Herbei'kommen,** -kŏmmen, vi. to approach. **Herbei'rufen,** -rŭfen, vt. to call hither. **Herbei'schaffen,** -shaffen, vt. to produce, procure. **Herbei'springen,** -zhpringen, vi. to run near. **Herbei'strömen,** -zhtrōmen, vi. to pour, stream, flock around. **Herbei'stürzen,** -zhtŭrtsen, vi. to rush near. **Herbei'ziehen,** -tsīen, vt. to draw, pull near; to attract.
Herbemühen, hăr'bĕmŭh-en, vt. to trouble any one to come.
Herberge, hăr'bĕrgĕ. f. lodging, harbor. inn: public-house; shelter; — einer Zunft, meeting-house of a guild: **Herberge geben,** **Herbergen,** vt. to lodge, shelter. **Her'bergsmutter,** -mŭtter, f. hostess. **Her'bergsvater** -fāter. m. host.
Herbestellen, hăr'bĕzhtĕllen, vt. to appoint. **Herbeten,** hăr'bāten, vt. to rehearse, to drawl out a prayer; — einen Rosenkranz, to tell one's beads.
Herbheit, hărb'hāĕt, f. ſ. **Herbe.**

14*

Herbitten, hår'bitten, *vt.* to invite, to desire one to come hither.
Herbringen, hår'bringen, *vt.* to bring (hither).
Herbst, herpzht, *m.* fall, autumn; harvest. **Herbst'en**, *vt.* to gather in. **Herbst'lich**, -lich, *a.* autumnal. **Herbst'luft**, -luft, *f.* autumnal air. **Herbst'monat**, -mönat, *m.* September. **Herbst'zeit**, -tseït, *f.* harvest time.
Herde, hård, **Herbe**, hår'de, *f.* Heerd, Heerde.
Herein, herkën', *av.* in, into; *Ij.* Walk in! Enter! **Herein'kommen**, -kommen, *vi.* to come in.
Hererzählen, hår'ertsälen, *vi.* to relate.
Herfahren, hår'fåren, *vi.* to ride, drive hither, to come here.
Herfallen, hår'fallen, *vi.* to fall upon, to pounce down, upon; to attack, assail.
Herführen, hår'führen, *vt.* to lead hither, to bring here.
Hergang, hår'gang, *m.* proceeding, detail, event.
Hergeben, hår'gåben, *vt.* to give away; to furnish; to give, hand, deliver; sich — zu, to lend one's self.
Herhalten, hår'halten, *vt.* to offer, tender; *vi.* to submit, suffer; to pay for.
Herholen, hår'hölen, *vt.* to fetch, to bring; weit hergeholt, far-fetched.
Herkommen, hår'kommen, *vi.* to advance, approach, proceed; to descend, originate; *s.* origin, source, descent, extraction; custom, use. **Herkömmlich**, -kümlich, *a.* customary, usual. **Herkunft**, -kunft, *f.* origin, extraction.
Herlallen, hår'lallen, *vt.* to stammer, stutter.
Herlassen, hår'lassen, *vt.* to let in, to let enter.
Herlaufen, hår'läufen, *vi.* to run in.
Hergelaufen, *n.* vagabond.
Herlesen, hår'låsen, *vt.* to read off, to recite.
Herlitze, her'litse, *f.* cornel, cornel-cherry.
Hermelin, hermęlĭn', *n.* ermine.
Hermeneutik, hermęnëu'tīk, *f.* hermeneutics.
Hermetisch, hermęt'ĭsh, *a.* hermetic; *av.* hermetically.

Hermurmeln, hår'murmeln, *vt.* to mutter, murmur.
Hernach, hernåch', *av.* after, afterwards.
Hernehmen, hår'nåmen, *vt.* to get, deduce; to bring from; to take in.
Hernennen, hår'nęnnen, *vt.* to call over, name, recite.
Hernieder, hernĭ'der, *av.* down.
Heroisch, hårō'ish, *a.* heroic. **Heroismus**, -is'mus, *m.* heroism.
Herold, hår'old, *m.* herald; harbinger. **Her'oldsamt**, -amt, *m.* heraldship, herald's office.
Herplappern, hår'plappern, *vt.* to prattle out, blab; repeat.
Herr, herr, *m.* master, proprietor; lord; gentleman; sir; Lord. **Herrchen**, herr'chen, *n.* little master; spark.
Herrechnen, hår'rechnen, *vt.* to reckon up.
Herreichen, hår'rächen, *vt.* to hand out, pass; to reach.
Herreise, hår'råëse, *f.* journey hither. **Her'reisen**, *vi.* to journey hither.
Herrenbank, her'renbank, *f.* bench of lords. **Her'rendienst**, -dinst, *m.* service. **Her'rengunst**, -gunst, *f.* a great man's favor. **Her'renhand**, -hant, *f.* a great man's power. **Her'renhaus**, -hôys, *n.* mansion, manor-house. **Her'renhof**, -höf, *m.* same. **Her'renleben**, -låben, *n.* high life. **Her'renlos**, -lös, *a.* out of service; stray, vagabond; derelict.
Herrin, her'rin, *f.* mistress, lady.
Herrisch, her'rish, *a.* imperious, overbearing, domineering.
Herrlich, herr'lich, *a.* magnificent, glorious, splendid; delicious, excellent; most beautiful; delightful, charming; -keit, käët, *f.* glory, lustre, magnificence, splendor; excellency, highness.
Herrschaft, herr'shaft, *f.* dominion, mastery, sway, empire; sovereign, lord; master, mistress; estate, barony; -lich, -lich, *a.* belonging to a sovereign, state, public.
Herrschbegierde, herrsh'begïrde, *f.* ambition, thirst of power; love of ruling. **Herrschen**, herr'shen, *vt.* to rule, reign, govern, prevail. **Herrschend**, *a.* established, prevalent, prevailing. **Herrscher**, herr'sher, *m.* ruler, sovereign, governor, master.

Herr'ſchſucht, -ſucht, f. ambition, lust of power. Herrſch'ſüchtig, -ſüchtig. a. ambitious, imperious, domineering.
Herrufen, hār'rufen, vt. to call.
Herrühren, hār'rühren, vi. to originate, come from.
Herſagen, hār'sägen, vt. to recite, rehearse.
Herſchaffen, hār'shaffen, vt. to procure, furnish, supply; to convey.
Herſchicken, hār'shicken, vt. to send to.
Herſchießen, hār'shīssen, vt. to shoot hither; to rush on; to advance (money).
Herſchleppen, hār'shleppen, vt. to drag hither, to drag in.
Herſtellen, hār'zhtellen. vt. to place, put in; to restore, repair, cure. Her'ſtellung, -yng, f. reparation, restoration, recovery.
Herwinken, hār'vīnken, vt. to beckon in.
Herüberhängen, hārüh'berhengen, vi. to hang over.
Herüber, hārüh'ber, av. over, across.
Herü'berkommen, -kommen, vi. to come over, cross. Herü'berziehen, -tsīen, vt. to draw, pull over; to cheat.
Herum, hērym', av. around, about, round-about. Herum'balgen, -balgen, vr. ſich —, to wrestle, fight with. Herum'betteln, -betteln, vi. to go begging. Herum'bringen, -bringen, vt. to carry around, to bring over, convince. Herum'irren, -Irren, vi. to stray about, to wander about, rove, ramble. Herum'laufen, -läufen, vi. to rove. Herum'ſpazieren, -zhpatsīren, vi. to walk, saunter about. Herum'ziehen, -tsīen, vi. to stray about, rove.
Herunter, hēryn'ter. av. down, downward. Herun'terbringen, -bringen, vt. to bring down, reduce, lower.
Herun'terkommen, -kommen, vi. to come down: to decay, sink; to get low, to decline. Herun'tergekommen, -gekommen. a. reduced. Herun'termachen, -machen, vt. to bring down; to reprimand, upbraid.
Herun'terſetzen, -setsen, vt. to put down, reduce, lower, depreciate.
Herun'terreißen, -reīssen, vt. to pull down, tear down. Herun'terſteigen, -zhtālgen, vi. to descend. Herun'terſtoßen, -zhtōssen, vt. to thrust down.

Hervor, hērfōr', av. forth, out. Hervor'blicken, -blicken, vi. to look forth, to look out. Hervor'brechen, -brēchen, vi. to burst forth, sally. Hervor'bringen, -bringen, vi. to bring forth, produce, create; utter, emit. Hervor'gehen, -gā-en, vi. to go forth, to come off; to follow, to result. Hervor'heben, -hāben, vt. to raise up; to give relief to, to render prominent, to lay stress on. Hervor'kommen, -kommen, vi. to come forth. Hervor'ragen, -rāgen, vi. to project, stand out; to be prominent. Hervor'rufen, -rufen, vt. to call forth, elicit. Hervor'ſpringen, -zhpringen, vi. to gush forth; to project; to follow, to spring from; -b, a. salient. Hervor'ſpritzen, -zhpritsen, vi. to spout out. Hervor'ſproſſen, -zhprossen, vi. to sprout out. Hervor'ſprudeln, -zhprydeln, vi. to bubble forth. Hervor'ſtechen, -zhtēchen, vi. to be prominent, to surpass; -b, a. prominent, eminent. Hervor'ſtehen, -zhtā-en, vi. to stand out; to project. Hervor'thun, -tyn, vi. to put forth; ſich —, to distinguish one's self. Hervor'treten, -trāten, vi. to step forward, come forward; to stand out, appear. Hervor'ziehen, -tsīen, vt. to draw forth.
Herwärts, hār'vērts, av. hither, hitherward.
Herweg, hār'vāg, m. way hither.
Herwünſchen, hār'vünshen, vt. to wish one to come.
Herz, hērts, n. heart, breast; courage; zu Herzen nehmen, to take to heart; ein Herz faſſen, to take courage; kein Herz haben, to have no hearts (card playing).
Herzählen, hār'tsālen, vt. to enumerate.
Herzbrechend, hērts'brēchent, a. heartbreaking, heart-rending. Herz'bube, -bybe, m. knave of hearts. Herz'eleid, -leīd, n. sorrow, affliction. Herzen, hērt'sen, vt. to fondle, caress. Herz'enſangſt, -angzht. f. anguish. Herz'ensfreude, -freüde, f. joy of the heart. Herz'ensgüte, -güte, f. kindness of heart, benevolence. Herz'ensmeinung, -meinyng, f. true

-**ment**, mind. **Herz'ergreifend,
-greifent,** a. affecting, heart-stirring.
Herz'erhebend, -häbent, a. elevating
the heart. **Herz'gespann,** -gezhpann,
n. cardialgy. **Herz'grube,** -grübe, f.
pit of the stomach. **Herz'haft, -haft,**
a. stout-hearted, bold, daring, courageous; **-igkeit, -käet,** f. courage,
bravery, gallantry.
Herziehen, här'tsīen, vi. to draw hither, to move, march hither, to draw
near.
Herzig, hërt'sich, a. pretty, charming,
lovely. **Herzinnig,** hërt-in'nich, a.
hearty, heartfelt, fervent. **Herz'-
kirsche,** -kîrshe, f. heart-cherry.
Herz'klopfen, -klopfen, n. palpitation, throbbing. **Herz'lich, -lich, a.**
hearty, heartfelt, cordial, affectionate, warm; av. -ly; **-keit, -käet,** f.
heartiness, cordiality. **Herz'los, -lōs,**
a. heartless, unfeeling; **-igkeit,
-käet,** f. heartlessness, unfeelingness.
Herzog, her'tsog, m. duke; **-in, -in,** f.
duchess. **Her'zoglich, -lich,** a. ducal.
Her'zogthum, -tum, n. dukedom,
duchy.
Herzschlächtig, hërts'shlächtig, a. broken-winded.
Herzschlag, hërts'shlāg, m. palpitation,
beating of the heart.
Herzu, hërtsu', av. hither, near. **Her-
zutreten,** hërtsu'trāten, vi. to come
near.
Herzzerreißend, hërts'tsërrëissent, a.
heart-rending.
Heterodox, heterodox', a. heterodox.
Heterogen, heterogān', a. heterogeneous.
Hetze, hët'se, f. magpie.
Hetze, hët'se, f. chase, hunting; pack.
Hetzen, het'sen, vt. to hunt, bait; to
set on. **Hetz'hund,** -hunt, m. hound.
Hetz'jagd, -yacht, f. hunt. **Hetz'peit-
sche,** -pêitshe, f. hunting-whip.
Heu, häe, n. hay. **Henärnte,** hâë'ärnte, f. hay-making. **Heu barn, -bärn,
m. heu'bucht, -bucht,** f. bay (for
hay). **Heu'baum, -bäum,** m. hay-
pole. **Heu'boden, -bōden,** m. hay-
loft. **Heu'bund, -bunt,** m. bundle
of hay.
Heuchelei, häücheli', f. hypocrisy.
Heucheln, hëüch'eln, vi. to play the
hypocrite, feign, dissimulate, pretend. **Heuchler,** hëüch'ler, m. -in, f.

164

hypocrite. **Heuchlerisch, -ish,** a.
hypocritical, canting, affected,
false.
Heuen, häë'en, vt. to make hay.
Heuer, hëü'er, av. this year.
Heuern, hëü'ern, vt. to hire, rent.
Heulen, hëü'len, vi. to howl, cry; to
wail; to roar. **Heu'lend,** a. howling, crying.
Heurig, hëü'rich, a. of this year.
Heumarkt, häë'markt, m. hay-market.
Heupferd, hâë'pfârt, n. **-chen,** n.
grasshopper. **Heuschober, -shōber,
m.** hay-stack. **Heu schoppen, -shop-
pen, m.** shed for hay.
Heuschrecken, häë'shrecken, m. grass-
hopper, locust. **Heu'speicher, -zhpäe-
cher, m.** hay-loft.
Heute, hëü'te, av. to-day, this day;
Heute früh, heute morgen, this morning; **Heute Abend,** this evening;
Heute Nacht, to-night; **Heute vor acht
Tagen,** this day se'nnight; **Heute
über vierzehn Tage,** this day fortnight. **Heu'tig,** a. to-day's, of this
day; present, modern; **Heutigen
Tages,** now-a-days.
Heuwage, häë'väge, f. hay-scales.
Hexe, hëk'se, f. witch, sorceress; hag.
Hex'en, vi. to practice witchcraft.
Hexenmeister, hëk'senmäezhter, m.
sorcerer. **Hexerei,** hëkserēi', f.
witchcraft, witchery, tricks.
Hieb, hīp, m. stroke, blow, cut, scar;
hit, sarcasm; right of felling wood.
Hieb'wunde, -vunde, f. wound from
a cut.
Hiefhorn, hîf'horn, n. hunting-horn;
bugle.
Hiefür, hī'führ. **Hie'her,** f. **Hierfür.**
Hienieden, bīnī'den, av. here, below.
Hier, hīr, av. here; **Hier zu Lande,** in
this country; **hier und da,** here and
there. **Hieran,** av. at this, on this,
by this. **Hieraus, -âus',** av. hereon,
hereupon. **Hieraus, -âus',** av. out
here, hence, from this, hereby.
Hierbei, hîrbēi', av. hereby, herewith; with this, in this. **Hierdurch,
-durch',** av. by this, hereby. **Hierein,
-ēin',** av. hereinto, into this. **Hierfür, -führ',** av. for this, for it. **Hier-
her, -här',** av. hither, here, this way.
Hierherum, hīrhërùm', av. hereabouts, about here. **Hierhin, -hīn,**
av. to this place. **Hierhinein, -hīn-
ëin',** av. in here, into this place

Hierin, hīrin', *av.* herein; in this.
Hiermit, -mit', *av.* herewith, by this.
Hiernach, -nāch', *av.* after this, according to this.
Hiernächst, -nexht, *av.* next to this.
Hierneben, -nā'ben, *av.* close by, next to this.
Hierüber, -ü'ber, *av.* over here, about this.
Hierum, hīrum', *av.* hereabout, about this.
Hierunten, -un'ten, *av.* below here.
Hierunter, *av.* under this, underneath this; among; by this.
Hiervon, -fon, *av.* hereof, from this.
Hierzu, -tsu', *av.* hereto, to this.
Hierzwischen, hīrtsvish'en, *av.* between this.
Hiesig, hī'sich, *a.* of this place.
Hifthorn, hift'horn, *f.* Hifthorn.
Hilfe, hil'fe, *f.* Hülfe.
Himbeere, him'bēre, *f.* raspberry; **-saft,** -saft, *m.* raspberry-juice; **-staude,** -shtöude, *f.* **-strauch,** -strouch, *m.* raspberry-bush.
Himmel, him'mel, *m.* sky, heaven, heavens; canopy, tester; roof; climate, zone. **Himmelan,** him'melān, *av.* heavenward. **Him'melbett,** -bet, *n.* bed with a tester. **Him'melblau,** -blāu, *n. u. a.* sky-blue, azure; **-farben,** azure. **Him'melfahrt,** -fārt, *f.* ascension; — **Maria,** assumption. **Him'melfahrtsfest,** -fesht, *n.* Ascension-day. **Him'melhoch,** -hōch, *a.* as high as heaven. **Him'melreich,** -rīch, *n.* kingdom of heaven; heaven, bliss. **Him'melsbewohner,** -bevōner, *m.* celestial. **Him'melschreiend,** -shrēẽnt, *a.* crying to heaven, atrocious, flagrant. **Him'melsfeste,** -feshte, *f.* firmament. **Him'melsgegend,** -gägent, *f.* quarter, region. **Him'melskörper,** -körper, *m.* heavenly body. **Him'melskugel,** -kugel, *f.* celestial globe, sphere. **Him'melspforte,** -pforte, *f.* portal of heaven. **Him'melspunkt,** -punkt, *m.* zenith. **Him'melstrich,** -shtrich, *m.* climate, zone, latitude. **Him'melszeichen,** -tsīchen, *n.* sign (Astr.). **Him'melszelt,** -tsëlt, *n.* heavenly vault, canopy of heaven. **Him'melwärts,** -vērts, *a.* towards heaven. **Him'melweit,** -vīt, *a. u.* wide, widely, as distant as heaven from earth. **Him'mlisch,** -lish, *a. u.* celestial, heavenly.
Hin, hin, *av.* thither, away, along; gone, lost; **hin und her,** to and fro.
Hinab, hīnab', *av.* on down, down.

Hinabsteigen, -shtēīgen, *vi.* to descend. **Hinab'wärts,** -verts, *av.* downward(s).
Hinan, hīnān, *av.* up, up to. **Hinan'reichen,** -rīchen, *vi.* to reach up. **Hinan'steigen,** -shtēīgen, *vi.* to ascend, mount.
Hinarbeiten, hīn'arbēīten, *vi.* — **auf** to aim at.
Hinauf, hīnōuf', *a.* up, up to, on up. **Hinauf'steigen,** -shtēīgen, *vi.* to step up; to mount. **Hinauf'wärts,** -vērts, *av.* upward(s).
Hinaus, hīnōus', *av.* out, on out. **Hinaus'führen,** -führen, *vi.* to lead out; to execute, perform, bring to an end. **Hinaus'jagen,** -yāgen, *vt.* to drive out, expel. **Hinaus'können,** -können, *vi.* to be able to go out. **Hinaus'scheren,** -shāren, *vr.* sich —, to get out, to be off. **Hinaus'laufen,** -lāufen, *vi.* to run out; — auf eins, to be the same thing. **Hinaus'werfen,** -vërfen, *vi.* to throw out, expel; — zur Thüre, to turn out of doors. **Hinaus'wollen,** -vollen, *vi.* to wish to go out, tend; hoch —, to aim high, to be proud.
Hinblick, hin'blick, *m.* look towards, regard; **sen,** *vi.* to look towards.
Hinbringen, hin'bringen, *vt.* to bring, carry to; to spend, pass (time).
Hinderlich, hinn'derlich, *a.* hindering, embarrassing, troublesome. **Hindern,** hinn'dern, *vt.* to hinder, impede, prevent, to cross, obstruct. **Hinderniss,** hinn'derniss, *n.* hindrance, impediment, obstacle. **Hinderung,** -ung, *f.* hindrance.
Hindurch, hindurch', *av.* through, throughout, across, quite through.
Hinein, hinēn', *av.* in, into. **Hinein'dürfen,** -dürfen, *vi.* to be allowed to enter. **Hinein'gehen,** -gāen, *vi.* to go in, enter. **Hinein'lassen,** -lassen, *vt.* to let in. **Hinein'schaffen,** -shaffen, *vt.* to bring in; to work in.
Hinfahren, hin'fāren, *vi.* to drive to; to pass on, over. **Hin'fahrt,** -fart, *f.* riding, driving to a place.
Hinfallen, hin'fallen, *vi.* to fall down. **Hin'fällig,** -fellich, *a.* frail, perishable, feeble; **-keit,** -kāēt, *f.* frailty, weakness, decrepitude.
Hinfliessen, hin'flīessen, *vi.* to flow on, to flow towards.

Hinfort, hinfort', *av.* henceforth; in future.
Hinfracht, hin'fracht, *f.* outward freight.
Hinführen, hin'führen, *vt.* to conduct, lead, bring, take, convey to a place.
Hingang, hin'gang, *m.* decease.
Hingeben, hin'gäben, *vt.* to give a way; to give up, yield, surrender, lay down; — sich, to devote one's self; to indulge in. **Hin'gebung**, -ung, *f.* devotion, devotedness, resignation; indulgence.
Hingegen, hingä'gen, *av.* on the contrary; whereas.
Hingehen, hin'gäen, *vi.* to go there, repair to; to pass; leicht hingehen über, to skim, slide; to pass over; hingehen lassen, to pass over, suffer; to allow to pass; to tolerate.
Hinhalten, hin'halten, *vt.* to hold out; to keep alive; to defer, put off. **Hin'haltung**, -ung, *f.* delay, putting off.
Hinken, hink'en, *vi.* to halt, limp, hobble; to be imperfect.
Hinlangen, hin'lang-en, *vi.* to reach. **Hin'länglich**, -lenglich, *a.* sufficient; -keit, -käet, *f.* sufficiency.
Hinlassen, hin'lassen, *vt.* to admit, to give access.
Hinleben, hin'läben, *vi.* to pass one's life, to live on.
Hinlegen, hin'läg-en, *vt.* to lay, put down; — sich, to lie down.
Hinleiten, hin'leiten, *vt.* to lend out.
Hinleiten, hin'läeten, *vt.* to lead to; to conduct to.
Hinmachen, hin'machen, *vt.* to fasten to; (vulg.) to destroy; — sich, to repair, resort to.
Hinmarsch, hin'marsh, *m.* march to, march there.
Hinmorden, hin'morden, *vt.* to slaughter.
Hinmüssen, hin'müssen, *vi.* to be obliged to go thither; to have to go.
Hinnehmen, hin'nämen, *vt.* to receive; bear, suffer; to put up with; submit to.
Hinneigen, hin'näegen, *vi. r.* to incline to. **Hin'neigung**, -ung, *f.* inclination.
Hinnen, hin'nen, *av.* von hinnen, hence.

Hinopfern, hin'opfern, *vt.* to sacrifice to make away with.
Hinraffen, hin'raffen, *vt.* to snatch, sweep, take away.
Hinreichen, hin'räechen, *vt.* to reach, hand over; to reach, extend to, suffice. **Hin'reichend**, -räechent, *a.* sufficient.
Hinreise, hin'rääse, *f.* journey to. **Hin'reisen**, *vi.* to travel thither.
Hinreißen, hin'rēissen, *vt.* to tear along, snatch away; to transport, enrapture.
Hinrichten, hin'richten, *vt.* to execute. **Hin'richtung**, -ung, *f.* execution.
Hinrücken, hin'rükken, *vt.* to move, march thither.
Hinschaffen, hin'shaffen, *vt.* to bring, convey to.
Hinscheiden, hin'shääden, *vi.* to die; hingeschieden, *a.* decensed.
Hinschieben, hin'shiben, *vt.* to shove thither.
Hinschiffen, hin'shiffen, *vi.* to sail to.
Hinsehen, hin'sä-en, *vi.* to look to, towards.
Hinsein, hin'säen, *vi.* to be gone; to be lost, ruined.
Hinsenden, hin'senden, *vt.* to send to.
Hinsetzen, hin'setsen, *vt.* to put down, in: — sich, to sit down.
Hinsicht, hin'sicht, *s.* regard, respect: in Hinsicht, in respect or in regard to; in jeder Hinsicht, in every respect; -lich, -lich, *a.* with regard to, as regards.
Hinsiechen, hin'sichen, *vi.* to pine away.
Hinsinken, hin'sinken, *vi.* to sink down.
Hinstellen, hin'zhtellen, *vt.* to put down; to place.
Hinstrecken, hin'zhtrecken, *vt.* to stretch out; to prostrate. **Hin'streckung**, -ung, *f.* prostration.
Hintan, hintän', *av.* after, behind. **Hintansetzen**, -setsen, *vt.* to slight, neglect. **Hintan'setzung**, -ung, *f.* slight, neglect; mit Hintansetzung, without regard to.
Hinten, hin'ten, *av.* behind. **Hin'tennach**, -nach, *av.* last, behind.
Hinter, hin'ter, *pr.* behind: *a.* or back, hinder, hind.
Hinterachse, hin'teraxe, *f.* hind-axle tree.
Hinterbaum, hin'terbaum, *m.* warp beam.

Hinterbein, hin'terbān, n. hind leg.
Hinterbleiben, hinterblēī'ben, vi. to stay behind, to be left. **Hinterbliebene,** -bli'bęne, s. those left behind, survivors, heirs; — **Wittwe,** relict.
Hinterbringen, hinterbring'en, vt. to give notice of, to apprise, inform of. **Hinterbringer,** m. -in, f. informant, informer, tale-bearer. **Hinterbringung,** -ung, f. report, information.
Hinterbug, hin'terbug. m. f. **Bug.**
Hintercastell, hin'terkazhtell, n. poop of a ship.
Hinterdeck, hin'terdeck, n. poop.
Hintere, hin'tere, a. back, hind; m. posteriors, buttocks.
Hinterfuß, hin'terfuss, m. hind foot, hind leg; sich auf die Hinterfüße stellen, to prance, rear.
Hintergebäude, hin'tergebȯüde, n. back building, out-house.
Hintergehen, hintergā'en, vt. to deceive. **Hintergehung,** -ung, f. deception, deceit, fraud.
Hintergestell, hin'tergezhtell, n. hindcarriage.
Hintergrund, hin'tergrunt, m. background.
Hinterhalt, hin'terhalt, m. ambush, ambuscade; reserve; in Hinterhalt legen, to ambush; im Hinterhalt liegen, lauern, to lie in ambush, to lurk, to lie in wait.
Hinterhand, hin'terhant, f. younger hand, whip hand.
Hinterhaupt, hin'terhäupt, n. occiput; -muskel, -muskel, f. occipital muscle.
Hinterhaus, hin'terhous, f. **Hintergebäude.**
Hinterher, hin'terhār, av. behind; after, afterwards.
Hinterhof, hin'terhöf, m. back yard.
Hinterlage, hin'terlȧge, f. deposit.
Hinterlassen, hinterlas'sen, vt. to leave (behind), bequeathe; -schaft, -shaft, f. bequest, inheritance.
Hinterlegen, hinterlā'gen, vt. to deposit, consign.
Hinterlist, hin'terlizht, f. cunning, fraud, deceit; -ig, a. cunning, fraudulent, deceitful, insidious.
Hintermast, hin'termazht, m. mizzenmast.
Hinterpforte, hin'terpforte f. backgate: stern-port.

Hinterrücks, hin'terrüks, av. backwards, from behind.
Hinterschiff, hin'tershiff, n. hind-part of a ship.
Hintersegel, hin'tersāgl, n. after-sail.
Hintersitz, hin'tersits, m. hind-seat.
Hinterst, hin'terzht, a. av. hindmost, last.
Hintersteven, hin'terzhtāfen, m. stern-post.
Hinterstube, hin'terzhtube, f. backroom.
Hinterstück, hin'terzhtück, n. hinder part; stern-chase.
Hinterthor, hin'tertör. n. back-gate.
Hinterthür, hin'tertühr, f. back-door.
Hintertreffen, hin'tertreffen, n. rear of an army, reserve.
Hintertreiben, hintertrēī'ben, vt. to prevent, to thwart, frustrate; to counteract. **Hintertreibung,** -ung, f. thwarting, frustration.
Hinterwärts, hin'tervērts, av. backwards, behind, from behind.
Hintragen, hin'trägen, vt. to carry there, convey.
Hinthun, hin'tụn. vt. to put there.
Hintreiben, hin'trēīben, vt. to drive to.
Hinüber, hinüh'ber. av. over, across.
Hinüberblicken, hinüh'berblicken, vi. to look over.
Hinüberbringen, hinüh'berbringen, vt. to bring on, over, to convey across.
Hinum, hinụm', av. about there.
Hinunter, hinụn'ter, av. down, on down; -wärts, -vērts, av. downwards.
Hinwärts, hin'vērrts, av. thitherwards.
Hinweg, hin'vāg, m. way thither.
Hinweg, hinvēg', av. away, off; ij. begone! off!
Hinwegraffen, hinvēg'raffen, vt. to snatch away, sweep off.
Hinweggehen, hinvēg'sāen, vi. to overlook, take no notice of.
Hinweisen, hin'vēīsen (hinweis, hingewiesen), vt. to point to, to refer.
Hinweisung, -ung, hint, reference.
Hinwerfen, hin'verfen (hinwarf, hingeworfen), vt. to throw down; to sketch hastily.
Hinwürgen, hin'vürgen, vt. to butcher, slaughter.
Hinzählen, hin'tsālen, vt. to count down.

Hin 168 **Hoch**

Hinzaubern, hīn'tsäubern, *vt.* to produce as if by magic.
Hinzu, hīntsụ́, *av.* to, toward, thither, near up.
Hinzudenken, hīntsụ'dęnken (-dachte, -gedacht), *vt.* to add in thought, to imagine.
Hinzudichten, hīntsụ'dichten, *vt.* to add, forge, invent.
Hinzufügen, hīntsụ'fügen, *vt.* to add, adjoin, annex, join. **Hinzufügung,** -ụng, *f.* addition.
Hinzukunft, hīntsụ'kụnft, *f.* accession.
Hinzulassen, hīntsụ'lassen (-ließ, -gelassen), *vt.* to admit, allow access.
Hinzuthun, hīntsụ'tụn, *vt.* to add, adjoin, annex.
Hinzutreten, hīntsụ'trēten (hinzutrat hinzugetreten), *vi.* to step up, approach; accede. **Hinzutritt,** -trit, *m.* accession.
Hiobspost, hī'obspọzht, *f.* bad news (Job's post).
Hippe, hip'pẹ, *f.* scythe, sickle; bill, pruning-bill.
Hippe, hip'pẹ, *f.* waffle; wafer. **Hip'peneisen,** -eīsen, *n.* wafer-iron.
Hippursäure, hippụr'seūrẹ, *f.* hippuric acid.
Hirn, hīrn, *n.* brain, brains; — einschlagen, to beat one's brains out. **Hirn'entzündung,** -enttsündụng, *f.* inflammation of the brain. **Hirn'gespinnst,** -gezhpīnzht, *n.* fancy, chimera, phantom. **Hirn'los,** -lōs, *a.* brainless, silly, *av.* -ly; **Hirnleit,** -kēet, *f.* want of intellect. **Hirn'schädel,** -shādl, *m.* **Hirn'schale,** -shāle, *f.* skull, brain-pan, cranium. **Hirn'wut,** -vụt, *f.* frenzy, madness.
Hirsch, hīrsh, *m.* stag, hart; deer. **Hirsch bock,** -bock, *m.* stag. **Hirsch'brunft,** -brụnft, *f.* rut *or* rutting season of deer. **Hirsch fänger,** -fęnger, *m.* hanger. **Hirsch farben,** -farben, *a.* fallow; fawn-colored. **Hirsch'fell,** -fell, *n.* deer-skin. **Hirsch horn,** -horn, *n.* hartshorn; **geist,** -gheīzht, *m.* spirit of hartshorn. **Hirsch geweih,** -gevēī, *n.* antlers. **Hirsch'haut,** -hoyt, *f.* deer-skin. **Hirsch'jagd,** -yagt, *f.* stag-chase, deer-hunt. **Hirsch'käfer,** -käfer, *m.* stag-beetle, horn-beetle. **Hirsch'kalb,** -kalp, *n.* fawn. **Hirsch'fuß,** -kụ, *f.* hind. **Hirsch'lauf,** -lāuf, *m.* foot *or* leg of a deer. **Hirsch'leder,** -lādr, *n.*

buckskin. **Hirschwildbret,** -vīldbret, *n.* venison. **Hirsch'ziemer,** -tsēmer, *m.* saddle of venison.
Hirse, hīr'sẹ, *f.* **Hirsen,** *m.* millet. **Hir'senbrei,** -breī, *m.* millet-porridge. **Hir'sefieber,** -fīber, *n.* miliary fever, purples.
Hirt, hīrt, *m.* herdsman, shepherd, pastor. **Hir'tengedicht,** -gedicht, *n.* pastoral poem; bucolic. **Hir'tengespräch,** -gezhpräch, *n.* eclogue. **Hir'tengott,** -gott, *m.* Pan. **Hir'tenjunge,** -yụnge, *m.* **Hir'tenknabe,** -kenäbẹ, *m.* shepherd's boy. **Hir'tenleben,** -lāben, *n.* pastoral life. **Hir'tenlied,** -līd, *n.* pastoral-song. **Hir'tenstab,** -zhtāb, *m.* shepherd's crook; bishop's crosier. **Hir'tentasche,** -tashẹ, *f.* shepherd's pouch, scrip. **Hir'tenvolk,** -folk, *n.* pastoral tribe; *pl.* nomads. **Hir'tenwelt,** -velt, *f.* pastoral life.
Hirtin, bīr'tīn, *f.* shepherdess.
Hisse, his'sẹ, *f.* windlass. **Hissen,** his'sen, *vt.* to hoist. **Hiß'tau,** -tāū, *n.* halyard.
Historie, hīstō'rīe, *f.* story, tale, narrative; history. **Historiker,** hīstō'rīker, *m.* historian, historiographer. **Historisch,** hīstō'rish, *a.* historic, *av.* historically.
Hitze, hit'sẹ, *f.* heat; a baking of bread, batch. **Hitzen,** hit'sen, *vi.* to be hot; *vt.* to heat. **Hitzegradmesser,** hit'sęgrādmēser, *m.* pyrometer. **Hitzig,** hit'sich, *a.* hot, heating; inflammatory; passionate, hasty, eager; *av.* -ly.
Hobel, hō'bel, *m.* plane. **Ho'belbank,** -bank, *f.* work-bench, carpenter's bench. **Ho'belspan,** -zhpān, *m.* shaving. **Hobeln,** hō'beln, *vt.* to plane.
Hoboe, hō'bo͞e, *f.* haut-boy. **Hoboist,** hōbo͞izht', *m.* haut-boyist.
Hoch, hoch (*comp.* höher, *sup.* höchst), *a.* high, elevated, sublime, eminent, transcendent; dear; holy, solemn. **Höher,** hö'her, *a.* higher, superior, upper; höhere Wissenschaften, abstruse sciences; höhere Geometrie, transcendental geometry. **Hoch'achten,** -achten, *vt.* to esteem, honor, respect. **Hoch'achtung,** -ụng, *f.* esteem, respect; **-voll,** -foll, *a.* respectful; *av.* -ly. **Hoch'altar,** -altār, *m.* high-altar. **Hoch'amt,** -amt, *n.* high-mass;

— halten, to say high mass. Hoch'-
begabt, -begabt, a. highly gifted,
endowed. Hoch'beglückt, -beglükt,
a. most happy. Hoch'bejahrt, -be-
yärt, a. aged, stricken with years. Hoch'boots-
mann, -mann, m. boatswain. Hoch'-
bord, hōch'bord, m. high-built vessel,
sail-ship. Hoch'brüstig, -brüzhtig,
a. high-breasted; proud. Hoch'-
deutsch, -doitsh, a. av. high-german.
Hoch'ehrwürdig, -ärvürdich, a. right
reverend. Hoch'entzückt, -entsükt,
a. entranced, enraptured. Hoch'-
fahrend, -farent, a. lofty, high-flown;
haughty. Hoch'geboren, -gebören,
a. high-born, right honorable. Hoch'-
genuß, hoch'genuss, m. high enjoyment, delight. Hoch'gericht, -gericht,
n. place of execution. Hoch'gesang,
-gesang, m. hymn, ode. Hoch'ge-
schätzt, -geshētst, a. highly valued,
esteemed. Hoch'geschmack, -geshmak,
m. fine-savor. Hoch'gesinnt, -sinnt,
Hoch'herzig, -hertsich, a. high-min-
ded. Hoch'heimer, -haemer, m. hock.
Hoch'klingend, -klingent, a. high-
sounding, pompous. Hoch'land,
-lant, n. highland, upland. Hoch'-
länder, -lender, m. highlander,
mountaineer. Höch'lich, höch'lich,
av. highly; grievously; — erfreut,
overjoyed. Hoch'muth, hōch'mūt, m.
haughtiness, pride. Hoch'müthig,
-müthich, a. haughty, proud, arrogant. Hoch'priester, -prēster, m.
Hohepriester, hōhepri'zh'ter, m.
high-priest, pontiff; römischer —,
pope. Hoch'priesteramt, -amt, n. pon-
tificate. Hoch'priesterlich, -lich, a. av.
pontifical. Hoch'roth, -rōt, a. deep
red, vivid red color; crimson. Hoch'-
rund, -rqnt, a. convex. Hoch'schätzen,
-shētsen, vt. to esteem highly. Hoch'-
schätzung, -shētzung, f. high esteem.
Hoch'schwanger, -shvanger, a. far advanced in pregnancy. Hoch'selig,
sēlig, a. deceased, late. Hoch'st,
höchst, a. av. highest, most supreme.
av. -ly. Hoch'sinn, hōch'sinn, m. loftiness, pride. Hoch'sinnig, -ich, a.
lofty. Hoch'stämmig, -shtemmich, a.
high, of lofty stature. Höchstens,
hōch'stens, av. at best, at most.
Hoch'stift, -shtift, n. chapter of a
cathedral. Hoch'stimme, -shtimme,
f. soprano, treble. Hoch'streben,
-zhträbent, a. soaring high, aspiring,
high. Hoch'tönend, -tōnent, a.
high-sounding, grandiloquent. Hoch'-
trabend, -träbent, a. high-flown,
pompous, high-sounding, bombastic. Hoch'verdient, -ferdint, a. highly
meritorious. Hoch'verrath, -ferrāt,
m. high-treason. Hoch'verräther,
-ferräter, m. one guilty of high-
treason. Hoch'verrätherisch, -ish, a.
treasonable. Hoch'wichtig, -vichtig,
a. very important. Hoch'wild, -vīlt,
n. venison (deer and boars). Hoch'-
würdig, -vūrdich, a. reverend; right
reverend. Hoch'zeit, -tsēīt, f. wedding, nuptials, marriage; wedding-
feast. Hoch'zeitbett, -bet, n. bridal-
bed. Hoch'zeiter, -tsēīter, m. bridegroom. Hoch'zeiterin, -in, f. bride.
Hoch'zeitgabe, -gābe, f. Hoch'zeitge-
schenk, -geshenk, n. bridal-present,
wedding-present. Hoch'zeitgast,
-gasht, m. bridal-guest, wedding-
guest. Hoch'zeitgedicht, -gedicht, n.
nuptial poem, epithalamium. Hoch'-
zeitlich, -lich, a. bridal, nuptial.
Hoch'zeitmahl, -māl, n. wedding-
banquet, nuptial-feast.

Hock, hokk, n. mast-pond; pen.
Hocke, hok'ke, f. heap (of sheaves);
back.
Hocken, hok'ken, vt. to set in heaps,
to take on one's back; vi. to cower
down, to squat down.
Höcker, hök'ker, m. hunch, hump.
Höck'ericht, -icht, a. like a hunch or
knob. Höck'erig, a. rough, uneven,
rugged; hunchbacked, humpbacked.
Hode, hō'de, f. testicle, stone. Ho'-
denbruch, -bruch, m. scrotocele. Ho'-
densack, -sack, m. scrotum.
Hof, hōf, m. yard, court-yard; court;
farm; halo, crown. Hofarzt, höf-
artst, m. physician to the court.
Hof'dame, -dāme, f. court-lady.
Hoffähigkeit, höf'fähigkeit, f. right
of admission to court.
Hoffen, hof'fen, vi. to hope, expect.
Hoff'entlich, -lich, av. to be hoped,
what may be hoped. Hoff'nung,
-nung, f. hope, expectation. Hoff'-
nungslos, -lōs, a. hopeless; av. -ly.
Hoff'nungsvoll, -foll, a. hopeful;
av. -ly.
Hofgebrauch, hōf'gebrŏych, m. court-
fashion, court-etiquette. Hof'gesin—

be, -sinnde, *n.* persons belonging to a court; farm-servants. **Hof'gunst, -gunbft,** *f.* court-favor. **Hof'haltung, -haltyng,** *f.* court, household of a prince. **Hof'hund, -hunt,** *m.* watch-dog, house-dog. **Hof'iren,** -Iren, *vt.* to court. **Hof'junfer, -yunker,** *m.* page, equery. **Hof'fleib, -klĕet,** *n.* court-dress. **Hof'füche, -kliche,** *f.* prince's kitchen; prince's cooks. **Hof'fünfte, -künzhte,** *f.* court tricks, intrigues. **Hof'lager, -läger,** *n.* place of residence of a prince, court. **Höflich, höf'lich,** *a.* courteous, polite. **Höflichfeit, -kĕet,** *f.* courteousness, courtesy, politeness. **Höfling, -ling,** *m.* courtier. **Hofmann, hof'mann,** *m.* courtier. **Hof'marſchall, -marshall,** *m.* marshal to the court. **Hof'meiſter, -măezhter,** *m.* tutor, governor. **Hof'meiſtern,** *vt.* to tutor, lecture; to censure; to play the pedant. **Hof'narr, -narr,** *m.* court-jester, court-fool. **Hof'rath, -rät,** *m.* counsellor of the court; aulic counsellor. **Hof'ſchranze, -shrantse,** *m.* (contemptible) courtier. **Hof'fitte, -ſitte,** *f.* etiquette. **Hof'ſtaat, -zhtăt,** *m.* household of a prince; court-dress. **Hof'tag, -tăg,** *m.* court-day; reception-day, gala-day. **Hof'theater, -theāter,** *n.* a prince's theatre.

Höhe, hö'he, *f.* height, altitude, depth of a battalion; elevation; auf der Höhe ſein, to be off; in die Höhe, aloft, upward(s); in der Höhe, on high, aloft. **Hö'her, ſ. Hoch.**

Hoheit, hō'hĕit, *f.* highness; elevation; majesty; sovereignty. **Ho'helied, -līt,** *n.* canticle. **Hoherpriester, hō'herprīzhter,** *m.* high priest.

Hohl, hōl, *a.* hollow. **Hohl'äugig, -ĕügig,** *a.* hollow-eyed. **Hohl'bohrer, -bōrer,** *m.* taper-bit. **Höhle, höh'le,** *f.* cavern; cavity, hollow. **Höhlen, höh'len,** *vt.* to hollow out. **Hohlheit, hōl'hĕit,** *f.* hollowness; emptiness. **Hohl'fehle, -kāle,** *f.* quirk-bead. **Hohl'fugel, -kygl,** *f.* shell, bomb. **Hohl'leiſte, -līszhte,** *f.* cyma-reversa. **Hohl'meißel, -mĕesl,** *m.* turning-gouge, gouge. **Hohl'rinne, -rinne,** *f.* trochilus. **Hohl'rund, -rynd,** *a.* concave. **Hohl'ſpiegel, -zhpīgl,** *m.* concave mirror.

Höhlung, höhl'yng, *f.* excavation, cavity, hollow; hollowness, concavity. **Hohlweg, hōl'vāg,** *m.* defile, narrow pass. **Hohl'ziegel, -tsīgl,** *m.* hollow-tile, gutter-tile.

Hohn, hōn, *m.* scorn, scoff, disdain, insult. **Höhnen, höh'nen,** *vt.* to scoff, mock, insult, scorn, sneer. **Hohngelächter, hōn'gelĕchter,** *n.* **Hohn'lache, -lache,** *n.* scornful laughter. **Hohn'niſch, höhn'ish,** *a.* scornful, jeering. **Hohn'lächeln, -lĕcheln, Hohn'lachen, -lachen,** *vi.* to laugh in scorn, to smile contemptuously; *s. n.* contemptuous smile. **Hohnneſſen, höhn'neken,** *vt.* to jeer, mock; *s.* jeering, mockery.

Höke, hö'ke, *m.* **Höfer,** *m.* **Höferin,** *f.* huckster, peddler. **Hö'fen,** *vi.* to peddle, higgle, huckster.

Hold, holt, *a.* lovely, lovable, graceful, sweet, gracious, affectionate, kind; loyal; *s. m. u. f.* friend, loved one. **Hold'ſelig, -sālig,** *a.* lovable, graceful, lovely, sweet, kind; ſreit, -kĕet, *f.* sweetness, loveliness, kindness. **Holdin, holt'in,** *f.* loved one, mistress.

Holder, holt'er, *m. f. Holunder.*

Holen, hō'len, *vt.* to go for, to fetch; Athem —, to draw breath; holen laſſen, to send for.

Holſter, holſ'ter, *f.* holster.

Holla, hol'la, *i.* holla! hullo!

Holländer, hol'lender, *m.* Dutchman; cylindrical paper-mill, washer.

Hölle, höl'le, *f.* hell. **Höl'lenangſt, höl'lenangsht,** *f.* mortal fright, anguish. **Höl'lenbrut, -brut,** *f.* hellish brood. **Höl'lenfeuer, -feüer,** *n.* hell-fire, infernal flame. **Höl'lenfluß, -flyss,** *m.* styx, phlegethon. **Höl'lenhund, -hunt,** *m.* hell-hound, cerberus. **Höl'lenmaſchine, höl'lenmashīne,** *f.* infernal machine. **Höl'lenpein, -pĕin,** *f.* torments of hell. **Höl'lenpforten, -pforten,** *f.* gates of hell. **Höl'lenrachen, -rachen,** *m.* jaws of hell. **Höl'lenreich, -reīch,** *n.* infernal kingdom. **Höl'lenſchlund, -shlunt,** *m.* jaws of hell, infernal gulf. **Höl'lenſtein, -shtĕin,** *m.* nitrate of silver, lunar caustic. **Höl'liſch, höl'lish,** *a.* hellish, infernal; *a.* -ly, *av.*

Holm, holm, *m.* cross-beam, rail; wale-piece.

Holm — **Hof**

Holm, holm, *m.* hill; little island, islet; river-isle; dock-yard.
Holper, hol'per, *m.* small hillock.
Holperig, hol'perig, rugged, rough, uneven; auch **holpericht**.
Holunder, hol'under, *m.* elder; (zusammen —), lilac. **Holunderbaum, -baum,** *m.* elder-tree. **Holunderblüthe, -blüthe,** *f.* elder-flowers.
Holz, holts, *n. pl.* **Hölzer,** wood; *pl.* **fel, -apfel,** *m.* wild-apple, crab; **arbeiter, -arbäeter,** *m.* worker in wood; **-arm, -arm,** *a.* destitute of wood; **artig, -ärtig,** *a.* ligneous, woody; **äsche, -äshe,** *f.* wood-ashes; **bau, -bou,** *m.* cultivation of wood; timber-work; **-birne, -birne,** *f.* wild pear; **-birnbaum, -birnbäum,** *m.* wild pear-tree; **-bock, -bokk,** *m.* jack horse; **-boden, -boden,** *m.* woodloft. **holzen,** holt'sen, *vt.* to cut wood; to climb a tree; *vt.* to line with wood; to fill with wood. **hölzern,** hölt'tern, *a. ærc,* wooden, of wood. **Holz essig, -essid,** *m.* pyroligneous acid, wood-vinegar. **Holzfaser, -fäser,** *f.* ligneous fibre. **Holzfeile, -feile,** *f.* rasp. **Holzfuhre, -fuhre,** *f.* cart-load of wood. **Holzgefälle, -gefelle,** *s. pl.* revenues from forests. **Holzhacker, -hacker,** *m.* **Holzhauer, -höger,** *m.* wood-cutter. **Holzhändler, -hendler,** *m.* dealer in wood. **Holzkohle, -köle,** *f.* charcoal. **Holzlager, -läger,** *n.* **Holzlege, -läge,** *f.* **Holzhof, -höf,** *m.* wood-yard; timber-yard. **Holzsäge, -säge,** *f.* wood-saw. **Holzsäure, -säuræ,** *f.* pyroxylic acid, pyroligneous acid. **Holzschnitt, -shnitt,** *m.* wood-cut. **Holzschneider, -shneïder,** *m.* wood cutter; engraver in wood. **Holzschuppen, -shuppen,** *m.* **Holzschuppen, -shuppen,** *m.* wood-shed. **Holzstatter, -shpälter,** *m.* wood-splitter. **Holzstall, -shtall,** *m.* wood-house. **Holzweg, -väg,** *m.* wood-road; wrong track.
Homogen, homogän', *a.* homogeneous, *æ. -ly.*
Homöopath, homöopäth', *m.* homœopathist. **Homöopathie,** homöopathï', *f.* homœopathy. **Homöopathisch,** *æ. a.* homœopathic.
Honig, hö'nig, *m.* honey. **Honigapfel, -apfel,** *m.* honey-apple. **Honigbirne, -birne,** *f.* honey-pear. **Honigkuchen, -kuchen,** *m.* ginger-bread.
Honigsäure, -säure, *f.* oxymel. **Honigscheibe, -sheïbe,** *f.* honeycomb. **Honigsüß, -süss,** *a.* sweet as honey. **Honigzelle,** hö'nigtsëlle, honey-cell.
Honnet, honnêt', *a.* fair, gentleman-like. **Honneurs,** honnöhrs', *s. pl.* honors. **Honorar,** honörär', *n.* fee; honorary salary. **Honorationen, -honorätslör'en,** *s. pl.* gentry.
Hop, hopp, *ij.* hop! **Hopsa,** hopp'sa, hey-day!
Hopfen, hop'fen, *m.* hops. **Hopfenacker, -acker,** *m.* **Hopfengarten, -garten** *m.* hop-field, hop-garden. **Hopfenbau, -bou,** *m.* culture of hops. **Hopfenstange,** hop'fenshtange, *f.* hop-pole.
Hörbar, höhr'bär, *a.* audible, *æ. -ly.*
Horchen, hor'chen, *vi.* to hearken, listen, to overhear, eavesdrop. **Horcher,** *m.* listener, eavesdropper.
Horde, hor'de, *f.* horde, tribe, gang.
Hören, höh'ren, *vt. i.* to hear, to give ear; **hören auf,** to obey. **Hörer,** *m.* **-in,** *f.* hearer, listener. **Höriger,** höh'riger, *m.* bondman.
Horizont, hörïtsont', *m.* horizon; **-al, -äl,** *a.* horizontal.
Horn, horn, *n. pl.* **Hörner,** horn, bugle. **Hornarbeiter, -arbäeter,** *m.* worker in horn. **Hornbläser, -bläser,** *m.* bugler; cornist. **Hornblende, -blënde,** *f.* hornblende. **Hörnchen,** hörn'chen, *n.* cornicle. **Hörnerklang,** hör'nerklang, *m.* bugle sound. **Hörnern,** hör'nern, *a.* horny, of horn. **Hornhaut,** horn'häut, *f.* cornea.
Hornist, hornïst', *m.* cornist.
Horniß, hor'niss, *f.* hornet.
Hornvieh, horn'ïfh, *n.* horned cattle.
Hornung, hor'nyng, *m.* February.
Horrohr, höhr'röhr, *n.* ear-trumpet.
Hörsaal, hör'säl, *m.* auditory.
Horst, horsht, *m.* eyrie, nest of birds of prey. **Horsten,** horsht'ten, *vi.* to build an eyrie; to nest.
Hort, hort, *m.* place of security, refuge, asylum, rock.
Hort, hort, *m.* treasure.
Hose, hö'se, *f.* (dim. **Höschen**) pants, trowsers. **Hosenband,** hö'senbant, *n.* (order of the) garter. **Hosenträger,** hö'senträger, *m.* suspender, gallows.
Hospital, hozhpïtäl', *n. pl.* **Hospitäler,** hospital. **Hospitalschiff, -shiff,** *n.* hospitalship.

Hoſt́ie, hochtie, f. host, consecrated wafer.
Hott! hott, Cj. ho! geeho!
Hub, hup, m. lifting up; stroke.
Hübſch, hüpzsh, a. pretty, nice, handsome, genteel, av. -ly; -keit, -käet, f. prettiness, handsomeness.
Huddeln, huʼdeln, vt. huddle, bungle; trouble.
Huf, huf, m. hoof. Hufbeſchlag, -bęshläg, m. shoeing, horse-shoe.
Hufe, huʼfe, f. measure of land (commonly 30 acres).
Hufeiſen, hufʼëisen, n. horse-shoe.
Hufhammer, -hammer, m. shoeing-hammer. Hufſchlag, hufʼshläg, m. tramp, clatter of horses' hoofs.
Hufſchmied, hufʼshmit, m. farrier, blacksmith.
Hüftbein, hüftʼbẹen, n. hip-bone.
Hüfte, hüfʼte, f. hip, haunch; quarter (of a ship). Hüftenlahm, -läm, a. hip-shot. Hüftweh, hüftʼvā, n. pain in the hip; sciatica.
Hügel, hühʼgel, m. hill; knob, boss; pimple; kleiner —, hillock. Hügelig, hühʼgelig, a. hilly, undulating.
Huhn, hun, n. pl. Hühner, hen, fowl, poultry. Hühnerauge, hühʼnerāuge, n. corn. Hühnerbraten, -brāten, m. roast fowl. Hühnerhändler, -hendler, m. poultry-dealer. Hühnerhof, -hōf, m. poultry-yard. Hühnerpaſtete, -pazhtäet, f. chicken-pie. Hühnerſtall, -zhtall, m. Hühnerhaus, -hōus, n. chicken-coop, hen-roost. Hühnerſtange, -zhtange, f. perch, roost. Hühnerzucht, -tsųcht, f. rearing of chickens.
Hui! hųi, Ij. quick! on! huzza! s. instant, moment; in einem Hui, in a trice.
Huld, hųlt, f. grace; favor, kindness.
Huldgöttin, hųltʼgöttin, Huldin, f. Grace. Huldreich, -rēich, a. gracious, kind. Huldigen, hųlʼdigen, vi. to do homage. Huldigungseid, -ęsʼid, -ket, m. oath of allegiance. Huldreich, Huldvoll, -fell, a. gracious.
Hülfe, hülʼfe, f. aid, help, assistance, succor; zu — eilen, to run to one's assistance: — leiſten, to help, succor. Hülfleiſtung, -läezhtung, f. rendering of assistance. Hülflos, -lös, a. helpless. Hülfloſigkeit, -käet, f. helplessness. Hülfreich,

-rēich, a. obliging, benevolent; — Hand leiſten, to lend a helping hand, to bring relief. Hülfsbedürftig, hilfsʼbędürftich, a. in want of help; -keit, -käet, f. indigence. Hülfsmittel, -mittel, n. remedy, expedient. Hülfsquelle, -kwellę, f. resource. Hülfstruppen, -truppen, Hülfsvölker, -fölker, s. pl. auxiliary troops, forces. Hülfswiſſenſchaft, -vissenshaft, f. auxiliary science. Hülfszeitwort, -tsëltvort, n. auxiliary verb.
Hülle, hülʼle, f. cover, case, integument, veil, envelope; Hülle und Fülle, plenty, abundance. Hüllen, hul'len, vt. to envelop, cover, veil, wrap, hide.
Hülſe, hülʼsę, f. hull, skin, glume, pod, husk, shell. Hülſenfrucht, hülʼsenfrųcht, f. pulse, legume. Hülſengewächs, -geveks, n. leguminous plant. Hülſen, hülʼsen, vt. to shell, hull, husk; vi. to cast the shell. Hülſig, hülʼsich, a. leguminous; husked.
Human, humän', a. humane, kind, affable. Humaniora, humauiōʼra, s. pl. classic lore or learning.
Hummel, humʼmęl, f. bumble-bee; drone.
Hummen, hųmʼmen, vi. to hum.
Hummer, humʼmer, m. lobster.
Humor, humōrʼ, m. humor, drollery. Humoriſt, humōrizht', m. humoriſt. Humoriſtiſch, humōrizhʼtish, a. humorous.
Humpeln, hųmʼpeln, vi. to hobble, limp; vt. to bungle, botch.
Humpen, hųmʼpen, m. large cup, goblet, bowl.
Hund, hųnt, m. dog, hound, cur; miner's cart. Hundeichen, hųnʼdełeben, n. wretched life.
Hundert, hųnʼdęrt, a. s. a hundred. Hunderterlei, -läeʼ, g. of a hundred different sorts. Hundertſt, hunʼdęrtzht, a. hundredth. Hunderttel, -zhtel, s. a hundredth.
Hündin, hünʼdinn, f. bitch. Hündiſch, hünʼdish, a. doggish, currish, canine. Hundsbiß, hųndsʼbiss, m. bite of a dog. Hundsfott, -fott, m. scoundrel. Hundsfottiſch, -ish, a. rascally. Hundsſtern, -zhtern, m. dog-star. Hundstag, -tag, m. dog-day. Hundswuth, -vųt, f. hydro-

phobia; canine madness. **Hunds'-**
zahn, -tsän, *m.* dog's tooth; eye-
tooth.

Hunger, hŭng'er, *m.* hunger, appetite,
famine; Hungers sterben, to starve,
die with hunger. **Hungerleider,**
-lŏīdẹr, *m.* needy wretch; niggardly
miser. **Hungerleiderei,** -rēī', *f.* stinginess, niggardliness. **Hungern,**
vi. to hunger, be hungry. **Hungers-**
ersnoth, -nōt, *f.* famine, dearth.
Hungertod, -tōt, *m.* starvation.
Hungrig, hŭng'riḥ, *a.* hungry;
stingy; sehr —, famished.

Hüpfen, hüp'fen, *vi.* to hop, skip,
jump.

Hürde, hür'dẹ, *f.* hurdle; fold, pen.
Hürden, *vt.* to hurdle, pen. **Hür-**
denschlag, hür'denshläg, *m.* fold-
age.

Hure, hŭ'rẹ, *f.* whore, strumpet, prostitute harlot. **Hu'ren,** *vi.* to whore.
Hurenbalg, -balk, *m.* whore; bastard. **Hurenhaus,** -hōṳs, *n.* brothel.
Hurenkind, -kint, *n.* bastard. **Hu-**
renpack, -pakk, *n.* lewd *or* whorish
rabble. **Hurenweib,** -vēīp, *n.* lewd,
profligate woman. **Hurenwirth,**
-virt, *m.* pander, pimp. **Hurenwir-**
thin, -virtin, *f.* procuress. **Hurer,**
hŭ'rer, *m.* whoremonger, fornicator.
Hurerei, -ēī', *f.* whoredom, fornica-
tion, harlotry. **Hurerisch,** hŭ'rerish,
a. whorish; *av.* -ly. **Hurkind,** -kint,
n. bastard.

Hurrah! hŭr'rä, *Ij.* hurrah! huzzah!
hurrah!

Hurtig, hŭr'tiḥ, *a.* nimble, swift,
speedy; *av.* -ly. **Hurtigkeit,** -kkēt,
f. nimbleness, quickness.

Husar, hŭsär', *m.* hussar.

Husch, hŭsh, *Ij.* quick! **Huschen,**
hŭsh'en, *vi.* to slide by, slip by, pass
quickly.

Hüsing, hüh'sĭng, *f.* houseline, housing.

Hussa! huzzä', **Hussah,** *Ij.* huzza.
Hussahen, *vi.* to huzza.

Husten, hŭzh'ten, *vi.* to cough; *s. m.*
cough.

Hut, hŭt, *m.* (dim. Hütchen) hat.

Hut, hŭt, *f.* herd, guard; protection;
feeding, pasture: auf der Hut sein,
to be upon one's guard. **Hüten,**
vt. to watch, guard: keep,
feed, tend; — sich, to take care not
to; beware; to be sure not to. **Hü-**
ter, hüh'ter, *m.* keeper, herdsman
watch, guard.

Hutform, hŭt'form, *f.* hat-block; hat-
form. **Hutfutter,** -fŭtter, *n.* lining
of a hat. **Hutkrämpe,** -krempẹ, *f.*
brim, flap of a hat. **Hutmacher,**
-mäḥer, *m.* hatter. **Hutschachtel,**
-shaḥtel, *f.* hat-case.

Hutsche, hŭt'shẹ, *f.* footstool

Hutschleife, hŭt'shlāīfẹ, *f.* loop on a
hat. **Hutschnur,** -shnŭr, *f.* hat-
band, hat-string. **Hutstaffirer,** hŭt'-
shtaffĭrer, **Hutstepper,** -zhtepper,
m. hat-dresser.

Hütte, hüt'tẹ, *f.* hut, cottage, cot;
hovel; tabernacle; shop, foundry,
kiln, forge; poop. **Hüttenkunde,**
-kundẹ, *f.* metallurgy. **Hüttenmeis-**
ter, -māēzhter, *m.* overseer of a
foundry. **Hüttenrauch,** -rāṳḥ, *m.*
cottage-smoke; flowers of arsenic.
Hüttenschreiber, -shrēīber, *m.* clerk
of a foundry. **Hüttenhaus,** -hōṳs,
n. foundry, forge, smelting-house.

Hutung, hŭt'ŭng, *f.* pasture.

Huzel, hŭts'el, *f.* dried pear.

Hyacinthe, hĭatsĭn'tẹ, *f.* hyacinth.

Hyäne, hĭä'nẹ, *f.* hyena.

Hyder, hŭh'der, *f.* hydra.

Hydrat, hĭdrät', *s.* hydrate.

Hydraulik, hĭdrōy'lĭk, *f.* hydraulics.

Hydraulisch, hĭdrōy'lish, *a.* hydraulic.

Hydrogen, hĭdrōgēn', *n.* hydrogen.

Hydropathie, hĭdrōpathī', *f.* hydro-
pathy.

Hydrostatik, hĭdrōzhtat'ĭk, *f.* hydro-
statics. **Hydrostatisch,** hĭdrōzhtat'-
ish. *a.* hydrostatic, *av.* -al.

Hymen, hĭ'men, *m.* hymen; marriage.

Hymne, hĭm'nẹ, *f.* hymn.

Hyperbel, hĭbber'bel, *f.* hyperbola;
hyperbole.

Hypochonder, hĭppoḥon'der, *m.* hypochondriac. **Hypochondrie,** hĭppo-
ḥondrī', *f.* hypochondria. **Hypo-**
chondrisch, -drish, *a.* hypochondriac.

Hypotenuse, hyppoteny'zẹ, *f.* hypo-
thenuse.

Hypothek, hyppothāk', *f.* mortgage.

Hypothese, hyppothā'zẹ, *f.* hypothesis.

Hypothetisch, hyppotēt'ish, *a.* hypo-
thetical.

Hysterie, hyzhtērī', *f.* hysterics. **Hy-**
sterisch, hyzhtā'rish, *a.* hysteric.

Ich, Ich̄, (G. meiner, mēē'ner, D. mir, mīr, A. mich, mich̄,) *pn.* 1; ich̄ selbst, I myself; mein anderes Ich̄, my other self.
Ideal, iddēal', *n.* ideal, ideal image.
Idee, Idē', *f.* idea.
Ideell, Iddēēll', *a.* ideal.
Identifiziren, Identifītsĭl'ren, *vt.* to identify. **Identisch**, iddent'ish, *a.* identical. **Identität**, iddentītāt', *f.* identity, sameness; seine — darthun, to identify one's self.
Idiom, Idiōm', *n.* idiom.
Idiot, Idjōt', *m.* idiot. **Idiotisch**, -ish, *a.* idiotic.
Idol, iddōl', *n.* idol.
Idyll, iddĭll'. *n.* **Idylle**, *f.* idyl. **Idyllisch**, -ish, *a.* idyllic, pastoral.
Igel, Ig'el, *m.* hedge-hog, urchin.
Ignoriren, ignorī'ren, *vt.* to ignore, pass over.
Ihm, Im (*dat. of* er), *pn.* to him. **Ihn**, In (*ac. of* er), him. **Ihnen**, I'nen, *pn.* to them, to you. **Ihr**, Ir. *pn.* to her; her; their; your. **Ihrethalben**, I'rēthalben, **Ihretwegen**, I'retvägen, **Ihretwillen**, -villen, *av.* for her, their, your sake; on — account. **Ihrig**, Ir'ich̄, *pn. a.* hers; theirs, yours. **Ihr**, Ir, *pn.* your; his; her.
Illegal, illegāl. *a.* illegal. **Illegalität**, illegālltāt', *f.* illegality.
Illegitim, illegĭtīm', *a.* illegitimate; **sität**, illegĭtīmĭtāt', *f.* illegitimacy.
Illiberal, il'lībĕrāl, *a.* illiberal.
Illumination, illuminātsiōn', *f.* illumination. **Illuminiren**, illumīnīr'en, *vt.* to illuminate, color.
Illusion, illusiōn', *f.* illusion.
Iltis, il'tiss, *m. or n.* fitchet, pole-cat.
Im, Im. for in tem. in the.
Imaginär, imagĭnār', *a.* imaginary. **Imagination**, Imăgĭnătsiōn', *f.* imagination.
Imbiß, im'biss, *m.* luncheon.
Immer, im'mer. *av.* ever, always. **Immerdar**, -dār, **Immerfort**, -fort, *av.* always, continually, constantly. **Immergrün**, -grün, *n.* evergreen. **Immerhin**, -hin, *av.* no matter, never mind, well and good. **Immers mermehr**, -mār, *av.* more and more. **Immerwährend**, -vārent, *av.* everlasting.

Imperativ, im'pĕrătīf, *m.* imperative mood.
Imperfekt, im'pĕrfĕct, *n.* imperfect tense.
Imperial, impĕrĭăl', *a.* imperial; **papier**, -păpīr, *n.* imperial paper.
Impertinent, impĕrtĭnĕnt', *a.* impudent, rude. **Impertinenz**, *f.* rudeness.
Impfen, imp'fen, *vt.* to graft, ingraft; to vaccinate. **Impfstoff**, impf'zhtoff, *m.* vaccine matter. **Impfung**, -ung, *f.* grafting; inoculation, vaccination.
Imponiren, impŏnī'ren, *vi.* to overawe, awe, impose. **Imposant**, imposant', *a.* imposing, striking.
Impotent, im'potĕnt, *a.* impotent. **Impotenz**, im'potens, *f.* impotence.
Impuls, Impŭls', *m.* impulse.
In, In, *pr.* in, into.
Inauguration, inŏggŭrătsiōn', *f.* inauguration. **Inaugurieren**, inŏggŭrī'ren, *vt.* to inaugurate.
Inbegriff, in'begrĭff, *m.* summary, abstract; contents, tenor.
Inbrunst, in'brunzht, *f.* fervor, ardor. **Inbrünstig**, in'brünzhtich̄, *a.* ardent, fervent.
Indem, indām', *Cj.* while, as, since, because.
Indeß', **Indessen**, indĕs'sen, *av. cj.* in the mean time, meanwhile, however, yet.
Indicativ, in'dĭkătīf, *m.* indicative mood. **Indicator**, indĭkā'tor, *m.* indicator.
Indifferent, in'dĭffĕrĕnt, *a.* indifferent. **Indifferentismus**, -tis'mus, *m.* indifference.
Indig, in'dich̄, *m.* indigo.
Indigenat, indĭgĕnāt', *n.* naturalization.
Indignation, indignātsiōn', *f.* indignation.
Indigo, in'dĭgo, *m.* indigo. **Indigoblau**, -blāu. *n.* indigo-blue.
Indirekt, in'dĭrĕkt, *a.* indirect.
Indiskret, in'dĭskrĕt, *a.* indiscrete. **Indiskretion**, indiscrĕtiōn', *f.* indiscretion.
Individualisiren, indĭfīdgŭalĭsīr'en, *vt.* to individualize. **Individualität**, -tāt', *f.* individuality. **Individuum**, indĭvīd'ŭum, *a.* individual.

Indolent, indolent', *a.* indolent, *av.* -ly. **Indolenz**, indolents', *f.* indolence.
Indossiren, indossī'ren, *vt.* to indorse.
Industrie, industrī', *f.* industry. **Industriell**, indŭzhtriĕll', *a.* industrial.
Infam, infām', *a.* infamous. **Infamie**, infāmī', *f.* infamy.
Infant, infant', *m.* infante; *sin, f.* infanta.
Infanterie, in'fantery, *f.* infantry, foot. **Infanterist**, in'fanterizht, *m.* foot-soldier.
Infernal, infērnāl', *a.* infernal.
Infinitiv, in'finītīf, *m.* infinitive mood.
Infusion, infusiōn', *f.* infusion. **Infusionsthierchen**, -tīrchen, **Infusorien**, infusoria.
Ingenieur, inzhenī'ör, *m.* engineer; **-kunst**, -kŭnzht, *f.* engineering.
Ingleichen, inglēich'en, *cj.* as also, likewise.
Ingrediens, ingredĭents', *f.* ingredient.
Ingrimm, in'grimm, *m.* anger, virulence. **Ingrimmig**, -mich, *a.* angry.
Ingwer, in'gwer, **Ingber**, in'ber, *m.* ginger.
Inhalt, in'halt, *m.* contents; purport; körperlicher —, volume.
Inholz, in'holtz, *m.* timber (Mar.).
Injurie, in'yu'rĭe, *f.* offence, insult; **-klage**, -klage, *f.* action for insult, for libel. **Injuriren**, inyurī'ren, *vt.* to insult.
Inlage, in'lāge, *f.* inclosure; inclosed.
Inland, in'land, *n.* (native) country.
Inländer, in'lender, *m.* inlander, native. **Inländisch**, in'lendish, *a.* domestic, indigenous, inland.
Inliegend, in'līgent, *a.* inclosed.
Inne, in'ne, *av.* within, at home; — haben, to possess, hold; — halten, to stop, pause; — werden, to perceive, to become aware. **Innen**, *av.* within. **Inner**, in'ner, *pr.* within; *a.* inner, internal, intrinsic; home. **Innerhalb**, in'nerhalp, *av.* within, on the inside. **Innerlich**, in'nerlich, *a.* inward, internal, interior; earnest, *av.* -ly. **Innerst**, in'nerzht, *a.* inmost. **Innig**, in'nich, *a.* intimate, hearty, heartfelt; ardent, devout; **-keit, -kĕt,** *f.* ardentness, heartiness, fervor, ardor. **Inniglich**, *av.* intimately; ardently heartily. **Innung**, -ŭng, *f.* guild, corporation.
Inquisition, inquisitsiōn', *f.* inquisition. **Inquisitor**, ingwisī'tor, *m.* inquisitor. **Inquisitorisch**, -ish, *a.* inquisitorial.
Ins, ins, for in das, into the; **ins besondere**, *av.* particularly.
Inschrift, in'shrift, *f.* inscription.
Insekt, insekt', *n.* insect.
Insel, in'sel, *f.* island, isle. **Inselbewohner**, -bevōner, *m.* islander. **Inselchen**, *n.* islet.
Insgeheim, ins'gehēm, *av.* secretly, privately.
Insgesammt, ins'gesamt, *av.* altogether.
Insignien, insign'īen, *s. pl.* insignia.
Insinuation, insinuatsiōn', *f.* insinuation; handing. **Insinuiren**, -ir'en, *vt.* to insinuate; hand, deliver.
Insofern, insofērn', *av. u. cj.* so far, in as far as.
Insolent, insolent', *a.* insolent. **Insolenz**, insolents', *f.* insolence.
Insolvent, insolfent', *a.* insolvent. **Insolvenz**, insolfents', *f.* insolvency.
Insonderheit, inson'derhēt, **Insonders**, -ders, *av. u. cj.* especially, particularly.
Inständig, in'zhtendich, *a.* instant, urgent, earnest, *av.* -ly.
Instanz, inshtants', *f.* resort, appeal; court.
Instinkt, in'stinct', *m.* instinct.
Institut, instĭtyt', *n.* institution, establishment.
Instruktion, instructiōn', *f.* instruction. **Instruiren**, -īr'en, *vt.* to instruct, prepare.
Instrument, instrŭment', *n.* instrument, document.
Insubordination, insŭbordināstiōn', *f.* insubordination.
Insulaner, insulā'ner, *m.* islander.
Insurgent, insurgent', *m.* insurgent. **Insurrektion**, insŭrrectsiōn', *f.* insurrection.
Integral, integrāl', *a.* 'ntegral. **Integralrechnung**, -rĕchnŭng, *f.* integral calculus. **Integraltheil**, -tēil *f.* integer. **Integriren**, integrī'ren, *vt.* to integrate. **Integrirend**, *a.*

integraut. **Integrität,** integrität, f. integrity.
Intellectuell, intĕllĕctuĕl', a. intellectual, mental. **Intelligent,** a. intelligent. **Intelligenz,** intĕllĭgĕnts', f. intelligence; **-blatt,** -blat. n. advertiser, intelligencer. **Intelligenz's komptoir,** -komptoär, n. office of intelligence.
Interessant, interĕssant', a. interesting. **Interesse,** interĕs'sę, n. interest; **Interessen tragend,** bearing interest. **Interessent,** m. sharer, partaker. **Interessiren,** -ïr'en, vt. to interest, concern; **sich — für,** to take interest in.
Interimistisch, interĭmĭzh'tĭsh, a. provisional, av. -ly; in the interim.
Interjection, interyĕcktsĭōn', f. interjection.
Interlinear, interlïnĕär', a. interlineary.
Intermezzo, intermĕt'sō, n. interlude.
Interpunktion, interpunctsĭōn', f. punctuation.
Intolerant, in'tolerant, a. intolerant.
Intoleranz, in'tolerants, f. intolerance.
Intransitiv, in'transĭtïv, a. intransitive.
Intrigant, intrïgant', a. intriguing; s. intriguer. **Intrige,** intrï'ge, f. intrigue, plot. **Intrigiren,** vi. to plot, intrigue.
Invalid, invalïd', a. invalid, disabled; s. invalid.
Inventar, inventär', n. inventory.
Inwärts, in'verts, av. inwards.
Inwendig, in'vendich, a. inward, interior, internal.
Inzwischen, intsvish'en, av. in the mean time.
Jod, iod, n. iodine. **Jodmetall,** -metall, n. iodite. **Jodsäure,** -söüre, f. iodic acid.
Jonisch, yōn'ish, a. Ionian.
Irden, irr'den, a. earthen. **Irdisch,** -dish, a. earthly, terrestrial, sublunary.
Irgend, ir'gent, av. any, some; **Irgend ein anderer,** any one else. **Irgendwo,** -vō, av. somewhere, anywhere; **-hin,** -hīn, av. somewhere.

Irgendwie, -vī, av. somehow, anyhow. **Irgendetwas,** -ĕtvas, s. anything, something.
Iridium, irid'yum, s. iridium.
Ironie, ïronï', f. irony. **Ironisch,** -ish, a. ironical; av. -ly.
Irre, ir're, a. astray, wrong; av. -ly; out of the right way; s. f. wandering, mistaken way; m. u. f. madman, mad-woman; **in der Irre gehen,** to wander; **Irre werden,** to rave; **Irre führen,** to lead astray.
Irregulär, ir'regulär, a. irregular, av. -ly.
Irreligiös, ir'religĭös, a. irreligious. **Irreligiosität,** ir'religĭösität', f. irreligion, irreligiousness.
Irren, ir'ren, vi. to err, go astray; to be wrong; **sich —,** to mistake, be mistaken. **Irrenhaus,** -hóus, n. mad-house, lunatic asylum. **Irrereden,** ir'rerāden, n. raving. **Irrfahrt,** -färt, f. wandering. **Irrgang,** -gang, m. labyrinth, maze. **Irrgläubig,** -glöübich, a. heterodox; **-keit,** -kāĕt, f. **Irrglaube,** -glöübe, m. heterodoxy. **Irrig,** ir'rich, a. false, wrong, erroneous, mistaken; **-keit,** -kāĕt, f. falseness, erroneousness. **Irrlehre,** irr'lāre, f. false doctrine, heresy. **Irrlicht,** -licht, n. will o' the wisp, Jack a-lantern, ignis fatuus. **Irrsal,** -säl, n. error. **Irrsinn,** -sinn, m. madness, insanity. **Irrstern,** -zhtĕrn, m. wandering star, comet. **Irrthum,** -tum, m. error, mistake, erroneous notion. **Irrung,** -ung, f. error, mistake. **Irrwahn,** -vän, m. delusion. **Irrweg,** -wäg, m. wrong way. **Irrwisch,** -vish, m. will o' the wisp, ignis fatuus.
Isabellfarbe, ī'säbĕlfarbe, f. isabel color; yellow-dun color.
Isegrimm, ï'segrim, m. wolf; ogre, surly fellow.
Isoliren, ïsolï'en, vt. to isolate, insulate. **Isolirjuwel,** -shämĕl (**Isolator**), m. insulator. **Isolirung,** -ung, f. insulation, isolation.
Isomorph, ïsōmorf, a. isomorphous.
Isop, ï'sōp, m. hyssop.
Itzt, itzt' f. **Jetzt,** av. now.

Ja, yä, *ar.* yes, aye, yea; ja freilich, to be sure; ja nicht, on no account; ja wahrlich, ja wohl, certainly, to be sure.

Jacht, yacht, *f.* yacht.

Jacke, yak'ke (dim. Jäckchen), *n.* jacket.

Jagd, yagt, *f.* chase, hunt, hunting: auf die Jagd gehen, to go a hunting; Jagd machen auf, to hunt after. **Jagdbar**, yagt'bär, *a.* chasable. **Jagdflinte**, -flinte, *f.* shot-gun, fowling-piece. **Jagdhorn**, -horn, *n.* bugle, hunting-horn. **Jagdhund**, hunt, *m.* hound; setter, pointer. **Jagdlust**, -lyzht, *f.* sport. **Jagdpartie**, -partī, *f.* hunting-party, shooting-party. **Jagdtasche**, -tashe, *f.* game-bag. **Jagdwesen**, -vāsen, *n.* venery, huntsmanship.

Jagen, yä'gen, *vi.* to chase, hunt; to course; to ride, drive quickly; in die Flucht —, to put to flight; *v.* hunting. **Jäger**, yä'ger, *m.* hunter, huntsman, sportsman, ranger. **Jägerei**, yägerēī', *f.* venery; gamekeeper's house. **Jägerin**, *f.* huntress. **Jägerhorn**, -horn, *n.* bugle. **Jägerkunst**, -kynst, *f.* woodcraft, huntsmanship.

Jäh, yä, *a.* steep, precipitous; *av.* -ly. **Jähe**, yä'e. *f.* steepness, abrupt descent, precipice. **Jählings**, yä'lings, *a.* precipitous, steep; *av.* -ly, suddenly, precipitously, steeply.

Jahr, yär, *n.* year; Jahr aus, Jahr ein, all the year around. **Jahrbuch**, -buch, *n.* chronicle; *pl.* annals. **Jahresfrist**, -frizht, *f.* a year's time. **Jahreszeit**, -tseīt, *f.* season. **Jahrgang**, -gang, *m.* annual set. **Jahrgehalt**, -gehalt, *m.* salary. **Jahrhundert**, -hundert, *n.* century. **Jährig**, yä'rich, *a.* a year old, lasting a year. **Jährlich**, yär'lich, *a. av.* annual, yearly. **Jahrmarkt**, yär'markt, *m.* fair. **Jahrstag**, -tāg, *m.* anniversary day. **Jahrtausend**, -tōu'sent, *n.* millennium. **Jahrweise**, -vēīze, *av.* annually. **Jahrzahl**, -tsäl, *f.* year, date. **Jahrzehnt**, -tsā-ent, *n.* decennium.

Jähzorn, yä'tsorn, *m.* passion, rage, violent anger. **Jähzornig**, -tsornich, *a.* passionate, given to anger.

Jammer, yam'mer, *m.* lament, misery, lamentation. **Jammergeschrei**, -geshrēī, *n.* cry of lamentation. **Jämmerlich**, yem'merlich, *a.* miserable, lamentable; wretched; *-keit*, -kāet, *f.* wretchedness. **Jammern**, yam'mern, *vi.* to lament, wail, mourn; er jammert mich, I pity him. **Jammerthal**, -täl, *n.* valley of tears; abode of misery. **Jammervoll**, -foll, *a.* lamentable, wretched, miserable.

Jänner, yen'ner, *m.* **Januar**, yänyär', *m.* January.

Jasmin, yasmīn', *n.* jasmine, jessamine.

Jaspis, yas'pīs, *m.* jasper. **Jaspisachat**, -achat, *m.* agate jasper.

Jäten, yä'ten, *vt.* to weed.

Jauche, yōu'che, *f.* liquid manure; suds.

Jauchert, yōu'chert, *n.* acre.

Jauchzen, yōuch'tsen, *vi.* to shout, exult. **Jauchzer**, *m.* exulter, shouter of joy.

Jawort, yä'vort, *n.* consent.

Je, yä, *ar.* ever, always; von je her, at all times; je nachdem, according as: je — desto, the more — the more.

Jedenfalls, yā'denfalls, *av.* at all events, in any case. **Jeder**, yā'der, *pn.* every, each. **Jedermann**, yä'dermann, *pn.* every one, every body. **Jederzeit**, -tsēīt, *av.* at any time, always. **Jedesmal**, yā'desmäl, *av.* every time. **Jedesmalig**, *a.* actual, existing. **Jedoch**, yädoch', *lj.* however, yet, nevertheless. **Jedweder**, yäd'väder, *pn.* each, every one. **Jeglicher**, yäg'līcher, *pn.* each, every one. **Jemals**, yā'mäls, *av.* ever, at any time. **Jemand**, yā'mant, *pn.* somebody, anybody, one, any.

Jener, yä'ner, *pn.* that, the former yon, yonder. **Jenseit**, yän'sēīt, *pr* beyond, on the other side of. **Jenseitig**, *a. av.* further, beyond, opposite, ulterior. **Jenseits**, *av.* on the other side, in the other world.

Jesuit, yäsyīt', *m.* Jesuit. **Jesuitenpulver**, yäsyīt'enpulfer, *n.* powdered Peruvian bark. **Jesuitisch**, -ish, a Jesuitic, -ally, *ar.* **Jesuitismus**, -ismus, *m.* Jesuitism.

Jetzig, yets'ich, *a.* present, now existing, actual; in der jetzigen Zeit, now-a-days. Jetzt, yetst, *av.* now, at present; gerade jetzt, just now. Jetzt, *s.* the present time; bis jetzt, hitherto; von jetzt an, henceforth.

Joch, yoch, *n.* yoke; stanchion, arch.

Jockei, yockäi', *m.* jockey.

Johannisbeere, yohann'isbāre, *f.* currant; -saft, -saft, *m.* currant-juice; -strauch, -zhtrouch, *m.* currant-bush. Johannisbrod, -brōt, *n.* carob. Johannisfest, -fĕzht, *n.* St. John's day. Johanniswürmchen, -vürmchen, *n.* glowworm.

Jolle, yol'le, *f.* yawl; jolly-boat.

Journal, zhurnäl', *n.* journal; -ist, -ist, *s.* journalist.

Jubel, yū'bel, *m.* jubilation, joyous shout; rejoicing; -feier, -feier, *f.* jubilee. Ju'belfest, *n.* do. Jubeln, yū'beln, *vi.* to shout with joy, rejoice. Jubiläum, yubllä'um, *n.* jubilee.

Juch! Juchhe! yū'chā, Juchhei! Juch-heisa! yuchhäi'sa, hurrah! huzzah!

Juchzen, yuchět'en, *vi.* to huzza, shout.

Jucken, yuk'ken, *vi.* to itch; *s.* itch, itching.

Juchtenleder, yuch'tenläder, *n.* russia-leather, muscovy hide.

Jude, yū'de, *m.* Jew; miser, extortioner; ewiger —, wandering Jew. Jüdeln, yü'deln, *vi.* to act the Jew; to deal like a Jew. Judenhart, yū'denhärts, *n.* Ju'denpech, -pĕch, *n.* Jew's-pitch, asphaltum. Ju'denschule, -shule, *f.* synagogue. Ju'denstein, -zhtāĕn, *m.* Jew's-stone. Ju'denthum, -tum, *n.* judaism. Jüdin, yüh'din, *f.* Jewess. Jüdisch, yüh'dish, *a.* Jewish, ar. -ly.

Jugend, yū'gent, *f.* youth; prime; young people; von Jugend auf, from one's infancy, childhood, youth. Ju'gendblüthe, -blüte, *f.* prime, bloom of youth. Ju'gendlich, -lich, *a.* youthful, juvenile; *av.* -ly. Ju'gendstreich, -zhträch, *m.* youthful frolic, prank. Ju'gendzeit, -tsĕit, *f.* youth, time of youth.

Jung, yung, *a.* young, new, fresh, youthful, *av.* -ly. Junge yung'e, *m.* boy, lad; apprentice; *n.* young (animal), cub, whelp. Jung'en, *vi.* to bring young. Jünger, yüng'er, *m.* disciple. Jungfer, yung'fer, *f.* virgin, maid, maiden. Jüng'ferlich, -lich, *a.* virgin; prim, bashful, coy. Jung'ferukranz, -krants, *m.* bridal wreath. Jung'ferschaft, -shaft, *f.* virginity, maidenhead. Jungfrau, yung'frāū, *f.* virgin, maid, maiden. Jung'fräulich, -fräülich, *a.* virgin, maidenly. Jung'fräulichkeit, -käět, *f.* maidenliness. Jung'frauschaft, -shaft, *f.* virginity, maidenhead. Jung'geselle, -gesĕll, *m.* bachelor; -enschaft, -shaft, *f.* bachelorship. Jüngling, yüng'ling, *m.* youth, young man; -alter, -alter, *n.* adolescence, youth. Jüng'lingsjahre, -yāre, *f.* years of youth. Jüngst, yüngzht, *av.* lately, the other day; *a.* youngest, last, most recent; jüngster Tag, doomsday, judgment day; jüngstes Gericht, last judgment.

Juni, yū'ni, *m.* Junius, yū'nlus, *m.* June.

Junke, yun'ke, *f.* junk.

Junker, yun'ker, *m.* young nobleman; -mäßig, -mässich, *a.* haughty, cavalier; *av.* -ly.

Jurisprudenz, yurisprudents', *f.* jurisprudence. Jurist, yurizht', *m.* juris-consult, lawyer. Juristisch, -ish, *a.* legal, law —.

Jury, zhūr'ī, *f.* jury.

Just, yuzht, *av.* just, but just, exactly. Justiren, yuzhtī'ren, *vt.* adjust; justify (Print.). Justirer, -yuzhti'rer, *m.* justifier; adjuster. Justiz, *f.* justice; administration of the law; -rath, -rāt, *m.* counsellor of justice; -wesen, -vāsen, *n.* administration of justice.

Juwel, yuvāl', *n.* Juwele, yuvā'le, *f.* jewel. Juwelenhandel, yuvā'lenhandel, *m.* jeweller's trade. Juwelenhändler, yuvā'lenhendler, *m.* jeweller. Juwelenkästchen, yuvā'lenkĕzhtchen, *n.* jewel-box. Juwelier, yuvelīr', *m.* jeweller.

Jux, yux, *m.* joke, jest, merry trick.

Kabel, kā'bẹl, *n. u. f.* cable. **Kabelaar**, kā'belār, *f.* voyol, viol, messenger.

Kabeljau, kä'belyäū, *m.* codfish.

Kabeltau, kä'beltāū, *n.* cable.

Kachel, kach'ẹl, *f.* dutch tile, earthen pane; broad earthen pot; **-ofen**, -ōfen, *m.* stove of Dutch tiles, Russian stove.

Käfer, kā'fer, *m.* beetle, chafer, bug.

Kaffee, kaffā', *m.* coffee; **-baum**, -bāūm, *m.* coffee-tree; **-bohne**, -bōne, *f.* coffee-berry, coffee-bean. **Kaffee's breit**, -brāt, *n.* tea-board; coffee-tray. **Kaffeehaus**, -hōūs, *n.* coffee-house. **Kaffeekanne**, -kanne, *f.* coffee-pot. **Kaffee kessel**, -kessel, *m.* coffee-kettle. **Kaffeemühle**, caffā'mühle, *f.* coffee-mill. **Kaffee röster**, -röhster, *m.* coffee-roaster, coffee-drum. **Kaffeeschale**, -shāle, *f.* **Kaffeetasse**, -tasse, *f.* coffee-cup, tea-cup. **Kaffeetisch**, -tish, *m.* coffee-table, tea-table. **Kaffeetrommel**, -trommel, *f.* coffee-drum. **Kaffeezeug**, -tseūk, *n.* coffee-service, tea-service. **Kafeïne**, -eine, *f.* caféine.

Käfig, kā'fig, *m.* **Käfich**, -ich, *m.* cage, bird's cage.

Kahl, käl, *a.* bald; bare, naked, barren. **Kahlheit**, -häet, *f.* baldness, bareness. **Kahlkopf**, -kopf, *m.* baldhead. **Kahlköpfig**, käl'köpfig, *a.* bald-headed.

Kahm, käm, *m.* mould. **Kahmen**, kä'men, *vi.* to mould. **Kahmig**, -mich, *a.* moldy.

Kahn, kän, *m.* boat, skiff; canoe.

Kai, käl, *n.* key, quay, wharf, mole. **Kaien**, käl'en, *vt.* to brace. **Kai geld**, -gäet, *n.* wharfage.

Kaiser, käe'sẹr, *m.* emperor. **Kaiserin**, käe'serin, *f.* empress. **Kaiserlich**, -lich, *a.* imperial. **Kaiserreich**, -räich, *n.* empire. **Kaiserschnitt**, -shnitt, *m.* Cesarean operation. **Kaiserstaat**, -stāt, *m.* **Kaiserthum**, -tum, *n.* empire. **Kaiserwürde**, -vürde, *f.* imperial dignity.

Kajüte, kayüt'tẹ, *f.* cabin; große **—**, state-room; ward-room.

Kakerlak, kä'kerlak, *m.* albino, white moor; moth, insect.

Kalb, kalb, *n.* calf. **Kalben**, kal'ben, *vi.* to calve. **Kälberbraten**, kel'ber-brāten, *m.* **Kalbsbraten**, kalbs'brāten, *m.* roast veal. **Kälbern**, kel'bern, *vi.* to calve; frisk, romp. **Kalbfell**, kalp'fell, *n.* calfskin. **Kalbfleisch**, kalp'fläesh, *n.* veal. **Kalbsleder**, -lāder, *n.* calfskin, calf-leather. **Kalbsbrust**, -bryzht, *f.* calf's-breast. **Kalbskeule**, kalps'köūle, *f.* **Kalbsschlägel**, -shlägl, *m.* leg of veal. **Kalbskopf**, kalps'kopf, *m.* calf's-head; blockhead, sheep's-head.

Kaldaunen, kaldōū'nen, *s. pl.* tripe, entrails.

Kalender, kalen'dẹr, *m.* calendar, almanac.

Kalesche, kaläesh'ẹ, *f.* calash.

Kalfaterer, kalfā'terẹr, *m.* calker. **Kalfatern**, kalfā'tern, *vt.* to calk.

Kali, kā'lī, *n.* kali, potassa. **Kalium**, kāl'yum, *n.* potassium.

Kaliber, kal'bẹr, *n.* caliber.

Kalk, kalk, *m.* lime. **Kalkartig**, -ärtig, *a.* calcareous. **Kalkbrenner**, -brenner, *m.* lime-burner. **Kalksteinbruch**, -bruch, *m.* **Kalksteinbruch**, -zhtäenbruch, *m.* limestone-quarry, limestone-pit. **Kalkerde**, -ẹrdẹ, *f.* calcareous earth. **Kalkgrube**, -grube, *f.* lime-pit. **Kalkhütte**, -hüttẹ, *f.* limekiln. **Kalkicht**, -icht, *a.* resembling lime. **Kalkig**, -ich, *a.* limy, calcareous. **Kalkspath**, -zhpät, *m.* calcareous-spar, lime-spar. **Kalkstein**, -zhtäen, *m.* limestone. **Kalkwasser**, -vasser, *n.* lime-water.

Kalmus, kal'mys, *m.* sweet flag.

Kalomel, kal'omẹl, *n.* calomel.

Kalt, kalt, *a.* cold, chill, frigid; *av.* -ly. **Kaltblütig**, -blühtig, *a.* cold-blooded; *av.* coldly, in cold blood; **-keit**, -käet, *f.* cold blood, presence of mind. **Kaltbrüchig**, -brüchig, *a.* cold-short. **Kälte**, kel'tẹ, *f.* cold, coldness, frigidity, chilliness; cold weather. **Kälten**, kel'ten, *vt.* to chill, **Kaltherzig**, kalt'hertsich, *a.* cold-hearted, unfeeling. **Kaltsinn**, -sinn, *m.* coldness, frigidity. **Kaltsinnig**, -ich, *a.* cold, frigid; **-keit**, -käet, *f.* coldness, indifference.

Kalziniren, kal'tsinīren, *vt.* to calcine.

Kamasche, kamā'shẹ, *f.* galoche, gaiters.

Kameel, kamāl', *n.* camel. **Kameel'garn**, -garn, *n.* mohair-yarn. **Kameel'haar**, -hār, *n.* camel's hair. **Kameel'ziege**, -tsīgę, *f.* Angora-goat; lama.
Kamille, kamil'lę, *f.* chamomile.
Kamin, kamīn', *n. u. m.* chimney; fire-place. **Kamin'feger**, -fāgęr, *m.* chimney-sweeper. **Kamin'gesimse**, -simsę, chimney-piece, mantelpiece.
Kamisol, kamīsōl', *n.* jacket.
Kamm, kam, *m.* comb; crest; ridge; cog; reed, sley; der Kamm schwillt ihm, he bristles up. **Kämmen**, kem'men, *vt.* to comb.
Kammer, kam'mer, *f.* chamber, bedchamber; room, apartment; office, board, exchequer; hollow, cavity. **Kammerdiener**, kam'merdīner, *m.* valet-de-chambre; waiting-man. **Kämmerer**, kem'merer, *m.* chamberlain; treasurer. **Kammerfrau**, kam'merfrāu, *f.* lady's-maid. **Kam'merfräulein**, -frāilīn, *n.* maid of honor. **Kam'mergericht**, -gericht, *n.* supreme court; exchequer. **Kam'merherr**, -herr, *m.* chamberlain. **Kam'merjungfer**, -yungfęr, *f.* waiting-maid. **Kam'mermädchen**, -mādchen, *n.* do. **Kam'merrath**, -rāt, *m.* counsellor of finances. **Kammersitze**, kam'mertsöfę, *f.* chambermaid.
Kammförmig, kam'förmich, *a.* comblike. **Kamm'garn**, -garn, *n.* worsted yarn; -spinnerei, -spinnęrēī, *f.* worsted spinning. **Kamm'macher**, -macher, *m.* comb-maker. **Kamm'rad**, -rāt, *n.* cog-wheel.
Kampf, kampf, *m. pl.* Kämpfe, combat, conflict, struggle. **Kämpfen**, kemp'fen, *vt.* to combat, struggle, fight. **Kämpfer**, kemp'fer, *m.* combatant, fighter. **Kampfhahn**, kampf'hān, *m.* game-cock, fighting-cock. **Kampflustig**, -luzhtich, *a.* eager for fight. **Kampf'platz**, -plats, *m.* battle-field. **Kampf'preis**, -prēis, *m.* prize. **Kampf'richter**, -richter, *m.* umpire, judge of the combat. **Kampf'spiel**, -zhpīl, *n.* tilting.
Kampher, kam'pfer, *m.* camphor.
Kanal, kanāl', *m.* canal, channel.
Kanapee, kan'āpe, *n.* lounge, sofa, settee.
Kanarienvogel, kānā'rīenfōgl, *m.* canary-bird.

Kaninchen, kanīn'chen, *n.* rabbit, coney.
Kanne, kan'nę, *f.* can, tankard, pot. **Kan'nengießer**, -gīser, *m.* would-be politician. **Kan'negießern**, *vi.* to talk of politics. **Kannibal**, kannībāl', *m.* cannibal, savage.
Kannonade, kanōnād'ę, *f.* cannonade. **Kanone**, kanōn'ę, *f.* cannon, gun. **Kanon'enboot**, -bōt, *n.* gun-boat. **Kanon'enkugel**, -kugl, *f.* cannon-ball, shot. **Kanon'enschuß**, -shuss, *m.* cannon-shot.
Kante, kan'tę, *f.* edge, corner, ledge, brim, selvage. **Kanten**, kan'ten, *vt.* to tilt. **Kantig**, kan'tich, *a.* angular, cornered.
Kanzel, kan'tsel, *f.* pulpit; — beredtsamkeit, pulpit-eloquence.
Kanzelei, kantselēī', **Kanzlei**, kantslēī', *f.* chancery. **Kanzelist**, -izht', *m.* chancery-clerk. **Kanzelrede**, kan'tselrādę, *f.* sermon. **Kan'zelredner**, -rādner, *m.* preacher, pulpit-orator.
Kanzleidirector, kantslēī'dīrectōr, *m.* director of the chancery. **Kanzlei'papier**, -papīr, *n.* sort of fine paper. **Kanzleirath**, -rāt, *m.* counsellor of the chancery. **Kanzlei'schreiber**, -shrāiber, *m.* chancery-clerk. **Kanzlei'schrift**, -shrift, *f.* engrossing hand, court-hand. **Kanzlei'siegel**, -sīgęl, *m.* great seal. **Kanzlei'stil**, -zhtīl, *m.* law-style; court-style. **Kanzler**, kants'ler, *m.* chancellor. **Kanz'leramt**, -amt, *n.* chancellorship.
Kaolin, kaolīn', *m.* kaoline, kaolin.
Kap, kāp, *n.* cape.
Kapaun, kapāun', *m.* capon.
Kapelle, kapēl'lę, *f.* chapel; test, cupel. **Kapell'meister**, -mēīzater, *m.* director of an orchestra.
Kaper, kā'per, *m.* privateer, corsair. **Kaper**, kā'per, *f.* caper; -brühe, -brühę, *f.* caper-sauce.
Kaperei, kaperēī', *f.* piracy. **Kapern**, ka'pern, *vt.* to capture, make a prize of. **Kaperschiff**, ka'pershiff, *n.* privateer.
Kapitän, kapītān', *m.* captain.
Kapital, kapītāl', *n.* capital.
Kapitel, kapīt'el, *n.* chapter.
Kappe, kap'pę, *f.* cap, hood, cowl; dome (of a retort). **Kappen**, kap'-

pen, *vt.* to cover; to top (boots); to tread (a hen).
Kappen, kap'pen, *vt.* to lop, cut off.
Kapphahn, kap'hän, *n.* capon. **Kapp´messer**, -messer, *n.* chopping-knife; cane-bill. **Kapp´zaum**, -tsaŭm, *m.* cavesson, cavezon.
Kapsel, kap'sèl, *f.* case, box, cover, capsule.
Kaputze, kapŭt'sę, *f.* cowl, capoch, cape. **Kapuziner** kapŭtsī'ner, *m.* capuchin.
Kapwein, käp'vặn, *m.* cape wine.
Karat, karät', *n.* carat.
Karawane, karavä'nę, *f.* caravan.
Kardätsche, kardät'shę, *f.* card; curry-comb. **Kardätschen**, kardät'shen, *vt.* to curry; to card.
Karde, kar'dę, *f.* **Kardenbistel**, kar'dendizhtèl, *f.* teasel card, fuller's thistle. **Karden**, kar'den, *vt.* to card.
Kardeel, kardäl', *n.* hawser.
Karfunkel, karfŭn'kèl, *m.* carbuncle.
Karg, kark, *a. u. av.* niggardly, stingy, miserly; parsimonious; poor. **Kargen**, kar'ken, *vi.* to be stingy, sordidly parsimonious. **Kargheit**, -hèt, *f.* stinginess, parsimony, sterility. **Kärglich**, kèrk'liḥ, *a.* poor, scanty, parsimonious.
Karpfen, karp'fen, *m.* carp; *teich*, -tệiḥ, *m.* carp-pond.
Karre, kar'rę, *f.* wheelbarrow. **Karren**, kar'ren, *m.* cart; cart-load; carriage (Print.). **Karrengaul**, -gŏyl, *m.* cart-horse. **Kärner**, kèrr'ner, *m.* carter, teamster.
Karst, kärzht, *m.* mattock, hoe. **Karsten**, kärzh'ten, *vt.* to hoe.
Kartätsche, kartät'shę, *f.* canister-shot; case-shot.
Karte, kar'tę, *f.* card; map, chart. **Karten**, kar'ten, *vi.* to play at cards; *vt.* to contrive. **Kar'tenblatt**, -blat, *n.* single card. **Kar'tenhaus**, -häŭs, *n.* house of cards. **Kar'tenschlagen**, -shlägen, *n.* telling fortunes by cards. **Kar'tenspiel**, -zhpīl, *n.* game of cards, playing at cards. **Kar'tenspieler**, -zhpīler, *m.* card-player. **Kar'tenstecher**, -zhtècher, *m.* engraver of charts, maps.
Kartoffel, kartof'fèl, *f.* potato; *krankheit*, -krankhèt, *f.* potato-disease.

Käse, kä'sę, *m.* cheese; *form*, -form, *m.* cheese-mould; *händler*, -hendler, *m.* cheese-monger; *kuchen*, -kuchen, *m.* cheesecake; *lab*, -läb *n.* rennet; *made*, -mäde, *f.* cheese-maggot. **Käsen**, kä'sen, *vt. i.* to curdle; to turn into cheese.
Kasse, kas'sę, *f.* money-box; cash; die Kasse führen, to keep the cash; nicht bei Kasse sein, to be out of cash, short of money. **Kassenanweisung**, kas'sennänvēsŭng, *f.* treasury-bill. **Kas´senbestand**, -bezhtant, *m.* clear amount. **Kas´sendieb**, -dīp, *m.* embezzler, peculator. **Kas´sendiebstahl**, -zhtäl, *m.* embezzlement, peculation. **Kas´senführer**, -führer, *m.* **Kassier**, kassīr', *m.* cashier, treasurer. **Kassiren**, kassī'ren, *vt.* to cashier; to annul. **Kassi´rung**, -ŭng, *f.* cassation.
Kastanie, kazhtä'niẹ, *f.* chestnut. **Kastan'ienbaum**, -bŏum, *m.* chestnut-tree. **Kastan'ienbraun**, -brŏun, *a.* chestnut. **Kastan'ienwald**, -vald, *m.* chestnut grove.
Kästchen, kèzht'ḥen, *n.* little box, little chest.
Kaste, kazh'tę, *f.* caste.
Kasteien, kazhtệī'en, *vt.* to mortify, macerate, chastise. **Kastei´ung**, -ŭng, *f.* mortification, castigation.
Kasten, kazh'ten, *m.* chest, box, trunk, coffer; ark; frame, cist.
Kastengeist, kazh'tengẹ̈zht, *m.* spirit of caste, exclusiveness.
Kasuar, kä'sŭär, *m.* cassowary.
Kat, kat, *f.* cat (vessel); *m.* bollard.
Kat´anker, -änker, *m.* kedge.
Katarakt, kat'arakt, *m.* cataract.
Katarrh, katarr', *m.* catarrh, rheum.
Katastrophe, katazhtrō'fę, *f.* catastrophe.
Katechismus, katechīs'mŭs, *m.* catechism.
Kategorie, katègorī', *f.* category. **Kategorisch**, katègō'rish, *a.* categoric; *av.* categorically.
Kater, kä'ter, *m.* male-cat, tom-cat.
Katheder, katä'der, *m.* lecturing desk, cathedra.
Kathedrale, katädrä'lę, *f.* cathedral.
Katheter, katä'ter, *m.* catheter.
Katholicismus, katolitsīsmŭs, *m.* catholicism. **Katholik**, katolīk', *m.* *in*, *f.* catholic. **Katholisch**, katō'lish, *a.* catholic.

Kattun, kåttyn′, *m.* calico. **Kattun'sdruck**, -drŭck. *m.* calico-printing. **Kattundrucker**, -drŭckẹr, *m.* calico-printer. **Kattunfabrik**, -făbrĭk, *f.* calico-manufactory.
Katblock, kåts′blŏkk, *m.* **Kat'bloď**, *m.* cat-block.
Kätzchen, kĕts′çĕn, *n.* kitten; catkin, aments (Bot.). **Katze**, kåt′sẹ, *f.* cat; cat (vessel). **Katzenäugig**, -äŭgĭç, *a.* cat-eyed. **Katzengelb**, -gĕlt, *n.* yellow mica. **Katzenjammer**, -yammer, *m.* sickness after a spree. **Katzenmusik**, -mŭsĭk, *f.* charivari, mock-serenade. **Katzenschwanz**, -shvants, *m.* cat's-tail.
Kaudern, kŏy′dẹrn, *vi.* to gobble, gabble. **Kauderwelsch**, kŏy′dẹrvĕlsh, *n.* gibberish. **Kauderwälschen**, kŏy′dẹrvĕlshen, *vi.* to gabble, chatter, jabber.
Kauen, kåŭ′en, *vt.* to chew, masticate.
Kauern, kåŭ′ern, *vi.* to cower, squat.
Kauf, kåŭf, *m.* bargain, purchase; price; einen Kauf schließen, to make a bargain: in den Kauf, to boot; leichten Kaufs, with trifling loss; -anschlag, -ănshlåk, *m.* estimate; -brief, -brĭf, *m.* bill of sale. **Kaufen**, kåŭ′fen, *vt.* to buy, purchase. **Käufer**, kåŭ′fer, *m.* -in, *f.* purchaser, buyer; vender. **Kauffahrer**, kåŭf′fårẹr, *m.* merchant-man, trading-vessel. **Kauffahrtei**, kåŭffartī′, *f.* navigation for the sake of commerce; -schiff, -shĭff, *n.* merchant-man. **Kaufladen**, -lådẹn, *m.* store, shop. **Käuflich**, kåŭf′lĭç, *a.* for sale; bribable; *av.* by purchase; -keit, -kåĕt. *f.* corruptibility. **Kaufmann**, kåŭf′man, *m. pl.* **Kaufleute**, merchant, tradesman. **Kaufmännisch**, -mennish, *a.* mercantile. **Kaufmannschaft**, -mannshaft, *f.* body of merchants. **Kaufmannsgut**, -gŭt, *n. pl.* -güter, merchandise. **Kaufmannsstand**, -zhtant, *m.* rank, condition of a merchant. **Kaufpreis**, -prīs, *m.* price, purchase-money. **Kaufschilling**, kåŭf′shilling, *m.* earnest-money.
Kaum, kåŭm, *av.* scarcely, hardly.
Kautsche, kŏy′shẹ, *f.* thimble, bull's eye.
Kautabak, kåŭ′tåbak *m.* chewing-tobacco.

Kauz, kŏyts, *m.* screech-owl; odd fellow.
Kauzen, kŏyt′sẹn, *vi.* to stoop, duck.
Kebse, kĕbs′ẹhẹ, *f.* concubinage. **Kebsweib**, -vīp, *n.* concubine.
Keck, kĕck, *a.* bold, forward, daring, pert; -heit, -håĕt, *f.* pertness, boldness, assurance. **Kecklich**, -lĭç, *av.* boldly; freely.
Keffer, kĕf′fer, *m.* granulous tin-ore.
Keffer, kĕf′fer, *m.* crane.
Kegel, kā′gel, *m.* cone; weder Kind noch Regel, neither kith nor kin; Kegel schieben, to play at nine-pins (ten-pins). **Kegelbahn**, -bån, *f.* bowling-alley. **Kegelgestalt**, -zhtalt, *f.* conical form. **Kegelförmig**, -förmĭç, *a.* conical. **Kegelkugel**, kā′gelkŭggl, *f.* bowl. **Kegelschieben**, -shĭben, *n.* bowling. **Kegelschnitt**, -shnitt, *m.* conic section.
Kehlader, kāl′ådẹr, *f.* jugular vein. **Kehlbuchstabe**, -bŭçzhtåbẹ, *m.* guttural letter. **Kehldeckel**, -dẹkl, *m.* epiglottis. **Kehle**, kā′lẹ, *f.* throat, gorge. **Kehlen**, *vt.* to flute, hollow, groove. **Kehlkopf**, kāl′kŏpf, *m.* **Kehlkopf**, -kŏpf, *m.* larynx. **Kehllaut**, -lŏyt, *m.* guttural sound. **Kehlsparren**, -zhparren, *m.* valley-rafter. **Kehlzäpfchen**, -tsĕpfçẹn, *n.* uvula. **Kehlziegel**, -tsĭgl, *m.* guttertile.
Kehrbesen, kār′bāsẹn, *m.* broom.
Kehren, kā′ren, *vt.* to turn, face about; to sweep, brush; to care for; rechtsum kehrt Euch! right about face! das Oberste zu Unterst kehren, to turn topsy-turvy, upside down; zum Besten kehren, to give a good turn. **Kehricht**, -ĭçt, *n.* sweepings. **Kehrseite**, -sāĕtẹ, *f.* reverse side; reverse, backside. **Kehrwisch**, -vish, *m.* whisk, brush, duster.
Keichen, kāĕ′çẹn, *f.* Keuchen.
Keifen, kāĕ′fen, *vi.* to chide, upbraid.
Keifisch, kāĕ′fish, *a.* shrewish.
Keil, kāĕl, *m.* wedge; quoin. **Keilen**, kāĕ′len, *vt.* to wedge, drive in, fasten; to thrash, beat.
Keiler, kāĕ′ler, *m.* wild boar.
Keilförmig, kāĕl′förmĭç, *a.* cuneiform, cuneated. **Keilschrift**, -shrĭft, *f.* arrow headed writing, wedge-writing.
Keim, kāĕm, *m.* germ, bud, sprout, first shoot. **Keimen**, kāĕm′en, *vi.*

to germinate, sprout, bud, shoot, spring up; to dawn.
Kein, kīn, *a. u. s.* not any, no, no one, none, nobody: keiner von beiden, neither. **Keinerlei**, kī'nerlī, *a.* of no sort; auf keinerlei Weiſe, in no way. **Kei'neswegs**, -vĕgs, *av.* by no means, not at all. **Kein'mal**, -mäl, *av.* not once, never.
Kelch, kĕlċh, *m.* cup, chalice; bowl; calyx. **Kelch'förmig**, -förmiċh, *a.* cup-shaped. **Kelch'glas**, -gläs, *n.* large cup.
Kelle, kĕl'le, *f.* trowel; scoop, ladle.
Keller, kĕl'ler, *m.* cellar, vault. **Kel'lerhals**, -hals, *m.* entrance of a cellar. **Kel'lerloch**, -loċh, *n.* cellar-hole, air-hole. **Kel'lermeiſter**, -mīszhter, *m.* butler, head-butler. **Kel'lerthür**, -tühr, *f.* cellar-door. **Kellner**, kĕll'ner, *m.* butler; waiter. **Kell'nerin**, *f.* bar-maid.
Kelter, kĕl'ter, *f.* wine-press. **Kel'terhaus**, -hŏus, *n.* press-house. **Keltern**, kĕl'tern, *vt.* to press, tread grapes. **Kel'tertreter**, -träter, *m.* press-treader.
Kennbar, kĕn'bär, *a.* discernible, distinguishable. **Kennen**, kĕn'nen (kannte, gekannt), *vt.* to know, be acquainted with; kennen lernen, to become acquainted with; nicht —, to be unacquainted with; to be ignorant of. **Kenner**, kĕn'ner, *m. sin, f.* connoisseur, judge, knower. **Ken'nerauge**, -ŏuge, *n.* a connoisseur's eye. **Ken'nerblick**, -blick, *m.* look of a connoisseur. **Ken'nermiene**, -mīne, *f.* air of a connoisseur, judge. **Kenntlich**, -liċh, *a.* recognizable, distinguishable. **Kenntniß**, -niss, *f.* knowledge, acquaintance with; acquirement,—nehmen von, to take notice, cognizance of. **Kennt'nißlos**, -lōs, *a.* destitute of knowledge, ignorant. **Kenn'zeichen**, -tsīċhen, *n.* mark, sign, badge, characteristic.
Kerbe, kĕr'be, *f.* notch, incision, score.
Kerbel, kĕr'bĕl, *m.* chervil.
Kerben, kĕr'ben, *vt.* to notch, score. **Kerb'holz**, -hŏlts, *n.* notched stick, tally. **Kerbig**, kĕr'biċh, *a.* notched, indented.
Kerker; kĕr'ker, *m.* prison, dungeon, jail; **-meiſter**, kĕr'kermīszhter, *m.* jailer.

Kerl, kĕrl, *m.* fellow, man; churl, wretch. **Kerlchen**, kĕrl'ċhen, *n.* little fellow.
Kern, kĕrn, *m.* kernel; core; stone, seed, heart; best part, choice, flower pith, marrow; grain; mould; bore. **Kernen**, kĕr'nen, *vt.* to granulate. **Kern'haft**, -haft, **Ker'nig**, *a.* substantial, solid, pithy. **Kernspruch**, kĕrn'zhpruċh, *m.* pithy sentence.
Kerze, kĕrt'se *and* kęr'tse, *f.* wax-candle, taper, candle. **Ker'zengerade**, -gerāde, *a.* straight as a taper. **Ker'zengießer**, -glasser, **Ker'zenzieher**, -tsīer, *m.* chandler.
Keſſel, kĕs'sel, *m.* kettle, caldron; bore (of a cannon); bell (of a column); burrow, cover; pit. **Keſ'ſelflicker**, -flicker, *m.* tinker. **Keſ'ſelpauke**, -pŏuke, *f.* kettle-drum.
Kette, kĕt'te, *f.* chain; ridge, range; line, cordon; train, concatenation; *pl.* chains, fetters, bondage. **Ketten**, kĕt'ten, *vt.* to chain; to connect. **Ket'tenanker**, -anker, *m.* mooring. **Ket'tenbrücke**, -brücke, *f.* suspension-bridge. **Ket'tengarn**, -garn, *n.* warp. **Ket'tengelenk**, -gelenk, *n.* **Ket'tenglied**, -glīt, *n.* link of a chain. **Ket'tenhund**, -hund, *m.* bandog, watch-dog. **Ket'tenrechnung**, -reċhnung, *f.* **Ket'tenregel**, -rāgl, *f.* double rule of three. **Ket'tenschluß**, -shlüss, *m.* sorites. **Ket'tenstich**, -stiċh, *m.* chain-stitch; chain-knot. **Ket'tenstrafe**, -strāfe, *f.* confinement in irons. **Ket'tentau**, -tŏu, *n.* chain-cable.
Ketzer, kĕt'ser, *m.* heretic. **Ketzerei**, -ī', *f.* heresy. **Ket'zerisch**, -ish, *a.* heretical.
Keuchen, kŏiċh'en, *vi.* to pant, gasp; to breathe hard. **Keuch'huſten**, -huzhten, *m.* whooping-cough. **Keucher**, kŏiċh'er. *m.* one who gasps *or* pants for breath.
Keule, kŏi'le, *f.* club; pestle: brayer (Print.); hind leg, leg. **Keu'len**, *vt.* to strike with a club.
Keusch, kŏish, *a.* chaste; **-heit**, -hīst, *f.* chastity.
Kibitz, kī'bits, *m.* lapwing.
Kichern, kiċh'ern, *vi.* to titter.
Kiefer, kī'fer, *f.* pine, fir.
Kiefer, kī'fer, *f.* gill (of a fish).
Kiefer, kī'fer, *m.* jaw.

Kiel, kīl, m. quill; keel. **Kielen**, kī'len, vt. to furnish with a new keel. **Kielholen**, -hōlen, vt. to careen; to keelhaul. **Kielrecht**, -recht, n. koelage. **Kieltau**, -tau, n. keelrope. **Kielwasser**, -vasser n. dead water, wake

Kirme, kīr'me, f. gill.

Kien, kīn, m. light-wood, p'ne-wood. **Kienbaum**, -baum, m. pine-tree. **Kienfackel**, -fackel, f. torch of pinewood. **Kienruß**, -russ, m. lampblack.

Kies, kīs, m. gravel; mit Kies bestreuen, to gravel.

Kiesel, kī'sel, m. **Kieselstein**, -zhtäen, m. flint, pebble. **Kieselartig**, -artich, a. siliceous. **Kieselhart**, -hart, a. flinty.

Kiesen, kī'sen, vt. to choose; einen Hafen —, to put into a port.

Kiesicht, kī'sicht, **Kiesig**, a gravelly. **Kiessand**, -sänd, m. gravelly, coarse sand. **Kiesweg**, kīs'väg, m. gravelled way.

Kimme, kim'me, f. edge, border; floorheads; — eines Fasses, chimb.

Kind, kīnt, n. child, infant, baby; -bett, -bet, n. child-bed, confinement; -betterin, kīnt'betterin, f. a woman lying in, woman in child-bed. **Kindchen**, kīnt'chen, n. babe, baby. **Kinderblattern**, kīn'derblattern, s. pl. small-pox. **Kinderei**, -ēī', f. childishness. **Kinderfreund**, kīn'derfreünd, m. the children's friend; the child's own book. **Kinderlehre**, -läre, f. religious instruction of children. **Kinderlos**, -lōs, a. childless. **Kindermord**, -mort, m. infanticide. **Kindermörder**, -mörder, m. -in, f. infanticide. **Kinderpocken**, -pocken, f. s. pl. small-pox. **Kinderpossen**, -posse, f. childish trick. **Kinderrand**, -räup, m. kidnapping. **Kinderräuber**, -räüber, m. kidnapper. **Kinderschrift**, -shrift, f. book for children. **Kinderschuh**, -shu, s. pl. children's shoe. **Kinderspiel**, -zhpīl n. childish play. **Kinderstube**, -zhtube, f. nursery. **Kindertaufe**, -täufe, f. baptism of children. **Kinderzucht**, -tsucht, f. government of children. **Kindesbeine**, kīn'desbēne, s. pl. von Kindes Beinen an, from the cradle. **Kindeskind**, -kīnt, n. grandchild. **Kindesnöthet**, -nöhte, s. pl. travail, labor; in Kindesnöthen sein, to be in travail. **Kindestheil**, -tāēl, m. child's portion. **Kindheit**, kīnd'hāēt, f. childhood. **Kindisch**, -ish, a. childish; — werden, to dote. **Kindlein**, -lāēn, n. babe, little child. **Kindlich**, -lich, a. filial; child-like; -keit, -kāēt, f. childlike innocence. **Kindschaft**, -shaft, f. adoption; a child's relation. **Kindskopf**, -kopf, m. childish, puerile person. **Kindsmädchen**, -mēdchen, n. nurse. **Kindtaufe**, -täufe, f. christening of a child; christening-feast. **Kindzeug**, -tsëuk, n. child's apparel.

Kink, kink, m. kink, coiling.

Kinn, kīn, n. chin; -backen, kīn'backen, m. jaw, jaw-bone: forefoot, head of the keel. **Kinnbackenkrampf**, -krämpf. **Kinnbackenzwang**, -tsvang, m. lock-jaw. **Kinnbart**, -bärt, m. chin-tuft. **Kinnkette**, kīn'kette, f. curb; — anlegen, to curb. **Kinnlade**, -lāde, f. jaw-bone.

Kippe, kip'pe, f. edge, brink; auf der — stehen, to be in imminent danger. **Kippen**, vt. to tilt over; to tilt: to fish (the anchor); vi. to lose balance.

Kirchdieb, kirch'dīp, m. church-robber; -stahl, -zhtäl, m. sacrilege. **Kirche**, kīr'che, f. (dim. Kirchlein), church. **Kirchenältester**, -ēltezhter, m. elder, church-warden, vestry-man. **Kirchenbann**, -bann, m. excommunication, interdict; in den — thun, to excommunicate, interdict. **Kirchenbuch**, -buch, n. agenda, parochial register. **Kirchenbuße**, -busse, f. church-penance. **Kirchendiener**, -diner, m. sexton, sacristan. **Kirchendienst**, -dinzst, m. church service. **Kirchenfuch**, -fluch, m. anathema. **Kirchengänger**, -genger, **Kirchgänger**, m. church-goer. **Kirchengebet**, -gebēt, n. church-prayer, common-prayer. **Kirchengemeinde**, -gemäende, f. parish, community. **Kirchengeräth**, -gerāt, n. sacred utensils, vessels. **Kirchengesang**, -sang, m. sacred song, sacred music. **Kirchlich**, -lit, a. hymn, church-hymn. **Kirchenmusik**, -mosīk, f. church-music. **Kirchenrath**, -rāt, m. consistory; ecclesiastical counsellor. **Kirchenraub**, -räup, m.

sacrilege. **Kirchenrecht**, -recht, *n.* canon-law. **Kirchenstaat**, -shtät, *m.* States of the Church; papal territory. **Kirchenstuhl**, -zhtyl, *m.* pew. **Kirchenthurm**, -tyrm, **Kirchthurm**, *m.* steeple. **Kirchenvater**, -fäter, *m.* father, apostolic father. **Kirchenverbesserung**, -fĕrbesserung, *f.* reformation. **Kirchenversammlung**, -fĕrsammlung, *f.* council; synod; vestry-meeting. **Kirchenvorsteher**, -förzhtäher, *m.* church-warden, presbyter. **Kirchenwesen**, -väsen, *n.* ecclesiastical affairs. **Kirchenzucht**, -kirchentsucht, *f.* ecclesiastical discipline.

Kirchfahrt, kirch'färt, *f.* procession to church; parish. **Kirchgang**, -gang, *m.* church-going; procession to church. **Kirchhof**, -höf, *m.* churchyard, cemetery. **Kirchlich**, -lich, *a.* ecclesiastical, church —; **Kirch'messe**, -messe, **Kirchweihe**, -vëie, *f.* church-ale; wake; church-fair. **Kirchner**, -ner, *m.* sexton. **Kirchspiel**, -zhpil, *n.* parish. **Kirchsprengel**, -zhprengel, *m.* diocese. **Kirchstock**, -zhtokk, *m.* church-box, poor-box. **Kirchstuhl**, -zhtyl, *m.* pew.

Kirre, kir're, *a.* tame, tractable; — machen, to tame; *s.* auch **Kirrheit**, -häet, *f.* tameness. **Kirren**, *vt.* to tame, subdue; *vi.* to cluck; to coo; to allure, attract. **Kirrung**, -ung, *f.* baiting, allurement.

Kirschbaum, kirsh'baum, *m.* cherry-tree. **Kirschbranntwein**, -brantvaen, *m.* cherry-brandy. **Kirsche**, *f.* cherry. **Kirschgeist**, -gäezht, *m.* **Kirschwasser**, -vasser. *n.* cherry-brandy. **Kirschkern**, -kĕrn, *m.* cherry stone.

Kissen, kis'sen, *n.* pillow, cushion; doublet (Mar.); rubber (Mech.); **Überzug**, -ühbertsug, *m.* **Zieche**, -tsĕche. *f.* pillow-case.

Kiste, kizh'te, *f.* box, chest.
Kits, **Kitz**, kits, *f.* ketch.
Kitt, kitt. *m.* cement; putty; lute.
Kittel, kit'tel, *m.* frock, smock-frock.
Kitten, kit'ten, *vt.* to cement; to putty.
Kitze, kit'se, *f.* kid.
Kitzel, kit'sel, *m.* titillation, tickling; itching. **Kitzelig**, kit'selich, *a.* ticklish; critical, nice, delicate; touchy.

Kitzeln, kit'seln, *vt.* to titillate, tickle.
Klaffen, klaf'fen, *vi.* to gape, yawn, to be ajar.
Klaffen, klaf'fen, *vi.* to chatter.
Kläffen, kläf'fen, *vi.* to bark, yelp; to bawl, scold. **Kläffer**, *m.* yelping dog; clamorous fellow.
Klafter, kläf'ter, *n.* fathom; cord (of wood); **-holz**, -holts, *n.* cord-wood; **-maass**, -mäs, *n.* cord-measure, wood-measure. **Klaftern**, -tĕrn, *vi.* to cord, to stack up. **Klafterweise**, -väse, *av.* by the cord.

Klagbar, kläg'bär, *a.* actionable, accusable; — anbringen, to bring before a court of law; — werden, to go to law.

Klage, klä'ge, *f.* complaint, lament; action, suit; — führen, to complain; **-gedicht**, -gedicht, *n.* **-gesang**, -gesang, *m.* **-lied**, -lït, *n.* elegy, lamentation. **Klagen**, klä'gen, *vi.* to complain, lament, moan; to sue at law; *vt.* to deplore, regret; lament. **Kläger**, klä'ger, *m.* plaintiff. **Klägerisch**, -ish, *a..av.* plaintiff's complaint. **Klageschrift**, klä'geshrift, *f.* action, bill of complaint; zweite —, replication; britte —. triplication. **Klagetön**, -tön, *m.* plaintive tone. **Klagegesang**, klä'gesang, *m.* efegy. **Kläglich**, kläg'lich, *a.* lamentable, wretched, miserable, deplorable; plaintive, mournful; *av.* -ly.

Klamm, klamm, *a.* tight, close, narrow, scarce, numb. **Klammer**, klam'mer, *f.* clamp, brace; brackets, hook. **Klammern**, *vi.* to clamp, grasp, fasten, pinch. **Klampe**, klam'pe, *f.* clamp, clinch.

Klang, klang, *m. pl.* **Klänge**, clang, sound, tone, ringing sound; **-boden**, -böden, *m.* sound-board. **Klanglos**, -lös, *a.* soundless. **Klangvoll**, -foll, *a.* full-sounding; tuneful.

Klapp, klapp, *ij.* clap! clack! slap! *s.* smack.

Klappe, klap'pe, *f.* lid; valve; falling-board. **Klappen**, klap'pen, *vi.* to clap, fit, suit; rattle. **Klapper**, *f.* rattle, clatter; **-dürr**, -dürr, *a.* very lean, skeletonous; **-mühle**, -mühle, *f.* clacking-mill. **Klappern**, *vi.* to rattle, clack. **Klapperrose**, -röse, *f.* corn-puppy. **Klapperschlange**, -shlange, *f.* rattle-

16*

snake. **Klapps**, klaps, *m.* smack, slap. **Klapp'stiefel**, -zhtĭfẹl, *m.* topboot. **Klap'ventil**, -ventĭl, *n.* leaf-valve, flap-valve. **Klappen**, klap'sen, *vt. i.* to box; to smack. **Klapptisch**, klap'tĭsh, folding-table.
Klar, klär, *a.* clear, limpid, pure; bright, light; transparent; — machen, to clear: sich — machen, to prepare for sailing. **Klären**, klä'ren, *vt.* to clear, clarify: — sich, to grow clear. **Klaren**, klär'en, *vt.* to prepare, make ready. **Klar'heit**, -hāĕt, *f.* **Klar'e**, *n.* **Kläre**, klä're, *f.* clearness, brightness, glory: purity, fineness; distinctness. **Klariren**, klärĭ'ren, *rv.* to clear. **Klärlich**, klär'lich, *a.* clear; *av.* clearly.
Klasse, klä-'sẹ, *f.* class, f. **Classe**.
Klatsch, klatsh. *m.* clap, slap, smack; gossip. **Klatsche**, klat'shẹ, *f.* fly-flap: tell-tale, gossip. **Klatschen**, klat'shen, *vi.* to clap: clack, smack; to chatter, tattle. **Klätscher**, 'klĕt'-sher, *m.* tattler, clatterer; smiter. **Klatscherei**, klatsherĕï'. *f.* gossiping, tale-bearing. **Klatsch'haft**, -haft, **Klatsch haftig**, -ĭch, *a.* gossiping, babbling; **-keit**, klatsch'haftichkāĕt, *f.* gossiping. **Klatsch'maul**, môul, *m.* chatter-box, tell-tale. **Klatsch'rose**, -rôsẹ, *f.* poppy.
Klauben, klŏu'ben, *rf.* to pick, select; to work at, sift, ponder.
Klaue, klŏu'ẹ, *f.* claw, talon; hoof; paw; fluke.
Klause, klŏu'sẹ, *f.* cell. hermitage; hole, pit. **Klausner**, klŏus'nẹr, *m.* hermit, anchorite.
Klavier, klaffr', *n.* piano, piano-forte. **Klavier'kasten**, -kazhten, *m.* case of a piano. **Klavier'lehrer**, -lärer, *m.* music-teacher. **Klavier'schule**, -shu-lẹ, *f.* exercises for the piano. **Klavier'spieler**, -zhpīlér, *m.* pianist, piano-player. **Klavier'stimmer**, -zhtimmer, *m.* piano-tuner.
Kleben, klä'ben, *vi.* to cleave, cling, stick, adhere; *vt.* to stick, paste, glue. **Kleber**, klä'ber, *m.* gluten; gum. **Kle'bericht**, -ĭcht, **Kle'berig**, -ĭch, *a.* glutinous, viscous, sticky; adhesive; **-keit**, -kāĕt, *f.* viscosity, stickiness.
Kleck, klĕk, *m.* **Kleckś**, klĕks, *m.* blot, blur. **Klecken**, **Klecksen**, *vt. i.* to blot, blur. daub, scrawl.

Klee, klā, *m.* clover, trefoil: **-blatt**, -blat, *n.* leaf of trefoil; triplet of friends; **-salz**, -zalts, *n.* salt of sorrel; **-säure**, -sēürẹ, *f.* oxalic acid.
Klei, klāī, *m.* clay, loam.
Kleiben, klīĕ'ben, *vt. i.* to glue, paste, fasten.
Kleid, klāĕt, *n.* raiment, clothing, covering; dress, robe, gown. **Kleiden**, klāĕ'den, *vt.* to clothe, dress, adorn. **Klei'derbesen**, -bäsen, *m.* whisk. **Klei'derhändler**, -hendler, *m.* merchant-tailor, dealer in clothes. **Klei'derkammer**, -kammer, *f.* wardrobe. **Klei'dermacher**, -macher, *m.* **-in**, *f.* dress-maker. **Klei'derordnung**, -ordnung, *f.* sumptuary law. **Klei'derrechen**, -rĕchẹn, *m.* clothes-horse. **Klei'derschrank**, -shrank, *m.* press for clothes. **Klei'dung**, -dyng, *f.* clothing, clothes; dressing, dress; **-stücke**, -zhtükkẹ, *f.* clothes.
Kleie, klēī'ẹ, *f.* bran. **Klei'enbrod**, -brōt, *n.* bran-bread. **Klei'ig**, -ĭch, *a.* branny.
Klein, klāĕn, *a. u. av.* little, small, petty, low, short; young; **kleines Geld**, change. **Klein'e**, *s. n.* little one, little child. **Klein'heit**, -hāĕt, *f.* littleness, smallness. **Klein'griff**, -gĭĕzht, *m.* narrow mind; **-erisch**, -ĕrish, *a.* little-minded, trivial. **Klein'gläubig**, -glāūbĭg, *a.* of little faith. **Klein'händler**, -hendler. *m.* retailer. **Klein'igkeit**, -kāĕt, *f.* small matter, trifle, circumstance: **-geist**, -gāĕzht, *m.* frivolousness; **-krämer**, -krämer, *m.* one who stands upon trifles. **Klein'lich**, -lich, *a. u. av.* petty, paltry, mean, little; **-keit**, -kāĕt, *f.* paltriness. **Klein'muth**, -mŭt, *m.* dejection, desponding. **Klein'müthig**, -mŭhtĭch, desponding, dejected; **-keit**, -kāĕt, *f.* despondency. **Kleinod**, klāĕn'ōt, *n.* jewel, gem; trinket, prize; *pl.* insignia. **Kleinstädtisch**, klāĕn'zhtĕtĭsh, *a.* countrified, provincial: narrow-minded. **Kleinvieh**, klāĕn'fī, *n.* small cattle.
Kleister, klēīzh'tẹr, *m.* paste. **Kleistern**, klēīzh'tern, *vt.* to paste.
Klemm, klẹm, *a.* scarce, close; **klemme Zeiten**, hard times. **Klemme**, klẹm'mẹ, *f.* pincers, clamp, cramp; strait, distress, dilemma, pinch; in

Kle 187 **Kna**

ber Klemme fein, to be in great straits. **Klemmen,** klĕm′men, *vt.* to clamp, pinch; squeeze, press; compress.
Klempner, klĕmp′ner, *m.* tin-man.
Klepper, klĕp′per, *m.* nag; hackney.
Klette, klĕt′te, *f.* bur, burdock.
Kletterer, klĕt′terer, *m.* climber. **Klettern,** klĕt′ern, *vi.* to climb, clamber, scramble. **Klet′terstange,** -zhtange, *f.* climbing-pole.
Klick, Klicks, klicks, *m.* after-piece or keel of a rudder.
Klieben, klī′ben, *vt.* to cleave, split.
Klima, klī′ma, *m.* climate. **Klima′tisch,** -tish, *a.* climatic.
Klimax, klī′max, *f.* climax.
Klimmen, klim′men (klomm, geklommen), *vi.* to climb.
Klimpern, klĭm′pern, *vi.* to chinkle, tinkle; thrum, strum.
Klinge, klīng′e, *f.* blade: vor bie Klinge forbern, to challenge; über bie Klinge springen lassen, to put to the sword.
Klinge, klīng-e, *f.* gorge, ravine, narrow valley.
Klingel, klīng′el, *f.* small bell; **beutel,** -bö‥tel, *m.* alms-bag. **Klingeln,** klīng′eln, *vi.* to ring, sound a small bell. **Klingen,** klīng′en (klang, geklungen), *vi.* to sound, chink; *vt.* to sound, jingle, tinkle; — laffen, to jingle; mit klingenbem Spiel, drums beating; klingenbe Münze, *f.* ready money. **Kling′klang,** klīng′klang, *m.* clang, jingle, tinkle.
Klinik, klīn′ĭk, *s.* clinical medicine
Klinikum, klīn′ĭkųm, *n.* clinical hospital.
Klinke, klink′-e, *f.* latch.
Klippe, klip′pe, *f.* cliff, rock, crag.
Klippig, klip′pich, *a.* craggy, rocky.
Klirren, klir′ren, *vi.* to clack, rattle, jingle, clash.
Klitsch, klitsh, *m.* slap, smack.
Kloben, klō′ben, *m.* lump, bundle, mass, clew.
Kloben, klō′ben, *m.* pulley, block; **säge,** -sä-ge, *f.* large saw.
Klopfe, klŏp′fe, *f.* beating, knocking.
Klopfel, klŏp′fel, **Kläpfel,** *m.* beater, knocker, rapper; clapper, tongue; drumstick. **Klopfen,** klŏp′fen, *vt.* to knock, rap, strike, beat. **Klopffechter,** klŏp′fechter, *m.* pugilist, boxer, prize-fighter. **Klopfi-**

fechterei, -ei′, *f.* pugilism, fighting prize-fighting; gelehrte —, literary controversy. **Klopfhengst,** klŏp′hengzht, *m.* gelding. **Klopfstein,** -zhtäen, *m.* lapstone.
Klöppel, klöp′pel, *m. f.* Klöpfel. **Klöp′pelkissen,** -kissen, *n.* laced pillow.
Klöppellade, -lade, *f.* lace-box.
Klöppeln, *vi.* to make lace. **Klöppelspitze,** -zhpitze, *f.* bone-lace. **Klöppelzwirn,** -tswirrn, *m.* thread for lace.
Kloß, klōss, *m.* clod; clot; lump; dumpling. **Kloßig,** -ich, *a.* cloddy, clotty.
Kloster, klōzh′ter, *n.* cloister, convent, monastery; **bruder,** klōzh′terbruder, *m.* lay-brother; **frau,** -frāu, *f.* nun; **leben,** -läben, *n.* monastic life. **Klösterlich,** klōzh′terlich, *a.* monastic, cloistral. **Klosterschwester,** klōzh′tershvester, *f.* lay-sister. **Klosterzucht,** klōzh′tertsųcht, *f.* monastic discipline.
Klotz, klots, *m.* block, log, stock; blockhead. **Klotzig,** klŏt′sich, *a.* blockish; awkward.
Klubb, klųbb, *m.* club.
Kluft, klųft, *f.* cleft, gap, gulf, abyss.
Klüftig, klüft′ich, *a.* full of clefts.
Klug, klųk, *a.* prudent, sensible, intelligent; shrewd, artful. **Klügelei,** klügelei′, *f.* subtility, affected intelligence. **Klügeln,** kl..b′geln, *vi.* to pretend intelligence; subtilize
Klugheit, klųk′hāet, *f.* prudence shrewdness, intelligent, discretion policy. **Klüglich,** klüg′lich, *a. av.* prudent, -ly; shrewdly.
Klump, *m.* **Klumpen,** klųmp′en, *m.* lump, clot, mass. **Klump′rig, -rich, Klumpig,** -ich, *a.* clodded, cloddy, clotty. **Klumpfuß,** -fųss, *m.* club foot.
Klunker, klųn′ker, *m.* clot; tassel.
Klunkerig, -rich, *a.* raggedly dressed; dirty.
Kluppe, klųp′pe, *f.* clamp.
Klüver, klü′ver, *m.* jib.
Klystier, klïzhtīr′, *n.* clyster; **spritze,** -zhpritze, *f.* syringe.
Knabe, knā′be, *m.* boy, lad. **Knabenalter,** -alter, *m.* boyhood. **Knabenhaft,** -haft, *a.* boyish **Knabenschänder,** -shender, *m.* sodomite.
Knack, knakk, *b.* crack; *s. m.* crack; *vt.* to crack; *vi.* to break. **Knacker,** *m.* cracker. **Knackmandel,** -mandel,

f. almond in the shell. **Knallwurst**, -wurzel, *f.* smoked sausage.
Knall, kenall, *m.* crack, clap, report, detonation; **Knall und Fall**, on a sudden. **Knallen**, *vi.* to crack, clap; detonate. **Knallerbse**, -erbse, *f.* torpedo. **Knallgold**, -gold, *n.* fulminating gold. **Knallpulver**, -pulfer, *n.* fulminating powder. **Knallsäure**, -säure, *f.* fulminic acid. **Knallsilber**, -silber, *n.* fulminating silver.
Knapp, kenapp, *a.* close, tight, scarce, scanty; *av.* -ly.
Knappe, kenap'pe, *m.* esquire, journeyman; miner.
Knarren, kenar'feln, **Knarrpeln**, *vi.* to crunch.
Knarren, kenar'ren, *vi.* to creak, grumble.
Knaster, kenazh'ter, *m.* canaster; -bart, -bärt, *m.* grumbler. **Knastern**, kenazh'tern, **Knattern**, ke attern, *vi.* to crackle.
Knäuel, kenöi'el, *m.* clew, ball, coil.
Knauf, kenäuf, *m.* knob, pommel; head, top, capital.
Knaupeln, kenöü'peln, *vi.* to gnaw, pick, crunch.
Knauser, kenöy'ser, *m.* -in, *f.* niggard; -ei, -ēi, *f.* niggardliness. **Knauserig**, kenöy'serich, *a.* niggardly. **Knausern**, kenöy'sern, *vi.* to be stingy, niggardly.
Knebel, kenä'bel, *m.* gag; packing-stick; -bart, -bärt, *m.* moustache, mustache; -holz, -holts, *n.* gagging-stick. **Knebeln**, kenä'beln, *vi.* to gag.
Knecht, kenecht, *m.* servant, workman; bondman, slave. **Knechten**, kenech'ten, *vi.* to enslave, tyrannize. **Knechtisch**, -ish, *a.* slavish, servile. **Knechtschaft**, -shaft, *f.* bondage, servitude, thraldom, slavery.
Kneif, kenelf, *m.* pocket-knife; cutting-knife. **Kneifen**, keneif'en, *vi.* to pinch, nip; — den Wind, to keep close to the wind.
Kneipe, kenei'pe, *f.* pincers; inn, grog-shop. **Kneipen**, keneip'en, *vi.* to pinch, gripe. **Kneipzange**, -tsange, *f.* pincers.
Kneten, kenä'ten, *vt.* to knead.
Knick, kenick, *m.* crack, flaw, breach. **Knicken**, kenick'en, *vi.* to crack, flaw, break. **Knicker**, -er, *m.* -in,

f. niggard. **Knickerei**, -rēi', *f.* niggardliness. **Knickerig**, -ich, *a.* niggardly. **Knickern**, -ern, *vi.* to haggle, higgle.
Knicks, kenicks, *m.* crack, flaw; bow, courtesy. **Knicksen**, kenick'sen, *vi.* to bow, to courtesy.
Knie, keni, *n.* knee; -band, -bant, *n.* garter. **Knieen**, keni'ent, *vi.* to kneel. **Kniegicht**, -gicht, *f* quaegra **Kniekehle**, -käle, *f.* hook **Kniescheibe**, keni'sheibe, *f.* kneepan.
Kniff, kenif, *m.* pinch; trick, stratagem.
Knipp, **Knipps**, kenipps, *m.* fillip, snap. **Knippsen**, kenipp'sen, *vi.* to fillip.
Knirps, kenirps, *m.* manikin, little fellow, pigmy, pygmy.
Knirschen, kenir'shen, *vi. i.* to gnash, crash.
Knistergold, kenizh'tergolt, *n.* tinsel. **Knistern**, kenizh'tern, *vi.* to crackle, crepitate.
Knitter, kenit'ter, *m.* wrinkle. **Knitterig**, -ich, *a.* wrinkled.
Knoblauch, kenōb'läuch, *m.* garlic; -zehe, -tsähe, *f.* clove of garlic.
Knöchel, kenöch'el, *m.* knuckle, anklejoint. **Knöcheln**, -eln, *vi.* to play with dice.
Knochen, kenoch'en, *m.* bone; -band, -bant, *m.* ligament; -bruch, -bruch, *m.* fracture; -fäule, -fäule, *f.* -fraß, -fräss, *m.* -krebs, -krebs, *m.* caries; -haus, -hōys, charnel-house; -mann, -mann, *m.* death. **Knöchern**, kenöch'ern, *a.* bone. **Knochicht**, kenoch'icht, *a.* bonelike. **Knochig**, kenoch'ig, *a.* bony.
Knödel, kenöh'del, *m.* dumpling.
Knollen, kenol'len, *m.* clot; tuber; -gewächs, -gevēks, *n.* tuberous plant. **Knollig**, kenol'lich, *a.* clotty; tuberous.
Knopf, kenopf, *m.* button; knob; pummel. **Knöpfchen**, kenöpf'chen, *n.* little button. **Knöpfen**, *vt.* to button. **Knopfform**, kenopf'form, *f.* button-mould. **Knopfloch**, -lch, *n.* button-hole.
Knorpel, kenor'pēl, *m.* cartilage, gristle. **Knorpelig**, -ich, *a.* cartilaginous, gristly. **Knorpeln**, kenor'peln, *vi.* to crunch.
Knorren, kenor'ren, *m.* knot, protu

Knu 189 **Köu**

berauce, excrescence, gnarl. **Knur′rig**, a. knotty.

Knorrj, knorrts, m. gnarled, knotty piece of wood; snob.

Knospe, knosh′pe, f. bud, sprout. **Knos′pen**, vi. to bud. **Knos′pig**, a. full of buds.

Knote, kno′te, m. **Kno′ten**, m. knot, excrescence; hitch; plot; boor; journeyman. **Knotig**, kno′tich, a. knotty, nodose, knobby.

Knüllen, knül′len, vt. to rumple, pucker.

Knüpfen, knüp′fen, vt. to tie, bind, knit, fasten.

Knüppel, knüp′pl, m. stick, fagot, clog, cudgel; vt. to cudgel.

Knurren, knur′ren, vt. to growl, snarl; to grumble. **Knur′rig**, -ich, a. grumbling, peevish.

Knute, knu′te, f. knout. **Knuten**, knu′ten, vt. to flog with the knout.

Knüttel, knüt′tel, m. cudgel; »reim, -räom, m. vers, -fers, m. doggerel.

Kobalt, ko′balt, m. cobalt.

Koben, ko′ben, m. pig-sty.

Kober, ko′ber, m. basket, panier.

Kobold, ko′bolt, m. goblin, hobgoblin.

Koch, koch, m. cook. **Koch′buch**, -buch, n. cookery-book. **Kochen**, koch′en, vt. i. to cook; boil; to ripen.

Köcher, küch′er, m. quiver.

Kocherei, kocherël′, f. cookery. **Köchin**, köch′in, f. cook. **Kochkunst**, koch′kunzht, f. culinary art. **Koch′löffel**, -leffel. m. ladle. **Koch′ofen**, -öfen, m. cooking-stove. **Koch′salz**, -salts, n. cooking-salt. **Koch′topf**, -topf, m. kitchen-pot.

Köder, köh′der, m. bait, lure, allurement, enticement. **Kö′dern**, vt. to bait; to entice.

Kofent, kofënt′, m. small-beer.

Koffer, kof′fer, m. trunk, box.

Kohl, köl, m. cabbage.

Kohle, kö′le, f. coal: charcoal. **Kohlen**, kö′len, vt. to make charcoal, to char. **Koh′lenbecken**, -bekken, n. coal-pan. **Koh bergwerk**, -bërkwerk, n. coal-mine. **Koh′lenbrenner**, -brenner, m. charcoal-burner. **Koh′lenfeuer**, -feüer, n. coal fire. **Koh′lengrube**, -grube, f. coal-pit. **Koh′lenpfanne**, -pfanne, f. coal-pan. **Koh′lensäure**, -seüre, f. carbonic acid;

kohlensaures Salz, carbonate. **Koh′lenschaufel**, -shoüfel, f. coal-shovel. **Koh′lenschiff**, -shiff, n. collier; coal-ship. **Koh′lenstaub**, -zhtäub, m. coal-dust. **Koh′lenstoff**, -zhtoff, m. carbon. **Koh′lenwasserstoffgas**, -vasserzhtoffgäs, n. carbureted hydrogen gas. **Köhler**, köh′ler, m. charcoal-burner. **Köh′lerglaube**, -gläube, m. implicit faith, blind faith. **Köhlerhütte**, köh′lerhütte, f. charcoal-burner's hut.

Kohlgarten, köl′garten, m. kitchen-garden. **Kohlrabi**, -rä′bl, m. cole-rabi. **Kohl′rübe**, -rühbe, f. turnip-rooted cabbage.

Koje, kö′ye, f. berth, cabin.

Koker, kö′ker, m. wooden case; coursey.

Kokett, kokett′, a. coquettish, ar. -ly. **Kokette**, koket′te, f. coquette, flirt. **Koketterie**, -erī′, f. coquetry, flirtation. **Kokettiren**, -īren, vi. to coquet, flirt.

Kokosnuss, kō′kōsnuss, f. cocoa-nut.

Kolbe, kol′be, f. **Kolben**, kol′ben, m. club; ear of corn; spadix; alembic, cucurbit; piston; pate.

Kolibri, ko′librī, m. humming-bird.

Kolik, kō′lic, f. colic, gripes.

Koller, kol′ler, m. collar; cape; doublet.

Koller, kol′ler, m. choler; rage, madness.

Kollern, kol′lern, vi. to roll, tumble; rumble; gobble.

Koloss, koloss′, m. colossus. **Kolossal**, -äl′, a. huge, colossal.

Komet, komāt′, m. comet. **Kometenschweif**, komāt′enshvëïf, m. tail of a comet.

Komiker, -köm′īker, m. comedian; writer of comedies. **Komisch**, kō′mish, a. comic, -al; funny.

Komma, kom′ma, n. comma.

Kommen, kom′men (kam, gekommen), vi. to come, arrive; — auf, to hit upon; to think of: gelaufen —, to come running; — lassen, to send for, import; to let run; kommen um, to lose.

Komödiant, komöhdīant′, m. comedian, actor; »in, f. actress. **Komödie**, komöh′die, f. comedy, play; »haus, -hoüs, n. play-house.

Kompass, kom′pass, m. compass.

König, köh′nich, m. king; »in, f.

queen. **Königlich,** -lich, *a.* royal, kingly, regal. **Königreich,** -reich, *n.* kingdom, realm. **Königsmord,** -mort. *m.* **Königsmörder,** -mörder, *m.* regicide. **Königsohn,** -sön, *m.* prince. **Königswürde,** -vürde, *f.* royalty, royal dignity. **Königthum,** -tųm, *n.* kingdom

Können, kön'nen (konnte, gekonnt), *vi.* can, may; to be able: to know.

Köper, köp'per, *m.* buckaback; twill. **Köpern,** *vt.* to twill.

Kopf, kepf, *m.* head; top, peak, crown; mind; **aus dem Kopf,** by heart. **Kopfarbeit,** -arbäet, *f.* head-work. **Kopfband,** -bant, *n.* bandeau. **Kopfbedeckung,** -bedęckųng, *f.* covering for the head. **Kopfbrechen,** -brechen, *n.* racking of the brain. **Kopfbürste,** -bürzhte, *f.* hair-brush. **Köpfchen,** köpf'chen, *n.* little head. **Köpfen,** kop'fen, *vt.* to form heads, to cabbage. **Köpfen,** köp'fen, *vt.* to behead, decapitate. **Kopfgeld,** -kopfgëlt, *n.* poll-tax. **Kopfgrind,** -grint, *m.* scab, scurf on the head. **Kopfhänger,** -henger. *m.* sin, *f.* devotee, hypocrite. **Kopfkissen,** -kissen, *n.* pillow. **Kopfkohl,** -köl, *n.* headed cabbage. **Kopflos,** -lös, *a.* headless. **Kopfputz,** -pųts, *m.* head-dress. **Kopfrechnen,** -rechnen, *n.* mental arithmetic. **Kopfsalat,** -sälät, *m.* headed lettuce. **Kopfschmerz,** -shmërts, *m.* headache; **einseitiger —,** megrim. **Kopfschmuck,** -shmųck, *m.* ornament for the head. **Kopfschütteln,** -shütteln, *n.* shake of the head. **Kopfsteuer,** -shtöüer, *f.* capitation tax. **Kopfstück,** -zhtück, *n.* headpiece. **Kopfwassersucht,** -vassersųcht, *f.* dropsy in the head. **Kopfweh,** -vä. *n.* headache. **Kopfzerbrechen,** -tserbrechen, *n.* racking of the brain.

Koppel, kop'pël, *f.* couple; tie, belt. **Koppeln,** kop'pëln, *vt.* to couple; **Weide,** -veïde, *f.* trailing willow; common pasture.

Koppen, kop'pen, *vt.* to lop; top.

Koralle, koral'lę, *f.* coral. **Korallenfischer,** -fisher, *m.* coral-fisher; **-ei,** -ëi', *f.* coral-fishery. **Korallenschnur,** -shnųr, *f.* coral-string.

Koran, ko'rän, *m.* coran.

Koranzen, koran'tsen, *vt.* to beat, cudgel.

Korb, korp, *m.* basket; **einem den — geben,** to give the mittens to; **einen — bekommen,** to meet with a refusal. **Körbchen,** körb chen, *n.* little basket. **Korbflechter,** korb'flechter, *m.* **Korbmacher,** -macher, *m.* basket-maker.

Korinthe, korin'tę, *f.* currant.

Kork, kork, *m.* cork: **-baum,** -bäum, *m.* cork-tree; **-pfopfel,** -zhtöpsel, *m.* cork-stopper; **-säure,** -säürę, *f.* suberic acid; **-saures Salz,** suberate. **Korkschwärze,** -shvęrtsę, *f.* Spanish black; **-zieher,** tsïher, *m.* cork-screw; **Korken,** kor'ken, *vt.* to cork.

Korn, korn, *n. pl.* **Körner,** grain, corn; rye; sight on a gun; vaine; **Körner ansetzen,** to grain; **-ähre,** -ä-rę, *f.* ear of corn, rye; **-bau,** -bóu, *m.* — cultivation; **-boden,** -böden, *m.* granary; **-blume,** -blųme, *f.* blue-bottle; **-brand,** -brant, *m.* blast, blight in grain; **-branntwein,** -brantvęin, *m.* rye-whisky. **Körnchen,** kürn chen, *n.* granule. **Körnen,** kör'nen, *vt.* to granulate; to bait. **Kornfeld,** kern'fëlt, *n.* field of grain, corn-field. **Kornhandel,** -handel, *m.* corn-trade. **Kornhaus,** -hóus, *n.* granary. **Körnig,** kör'nich, *a.* granulary. **Körnig,** kör'nich, *a.* grained, granulous. **Kornjahr,** kern'yär, *n.* corn-year. **Kornjube,** korn'ypde, *n.* corn-jew. **Kornland,** -lant, *n.* country rich in corn. **Körnlein,** körn'lęin, *n.* granule. **Kornmarkt,** korn'markt, *m.* grain-market. **Kornmehl,** -mäl, *n.* rye-flour. **Körnung,** körn'ųng, *f.* granulation. **Kornzehnter,** korn'zęhnter, *f.* corn-duty. **Kornwuchęrer,** -vųchęrer, *m.* corn-jew.

Körper, kör'per, *m.* body; **-bau,** -bóu, *m.* **-bildung,** -bildung, *f.* **-gestalt,** -gęzhtalt, *f.* structure, build of the body; **-beschaffenheit,** -beshaffenheit, *f.* constitution. **Körperlich,** -lich, *a.* bodily, corporeal; material, solid; corpuscular; **-feit,** -keït, *f.* corporality, corporeity. **Körperschaft,** kör'pershaft, *f.* corporation, body.

Koryphäe, korüpfä'ę, *m.* leader, master-mind.

Kosak, kösak', *m.* cossack.

Kosen, kö'sęn, *vt.* to caress; to chat. **Kosmisch,** kos'mish. *a.* cosmical. **Kosmopolit,** -mopölit', *m.* cosmopolitan

Kost, kozht, *f.* fare, food; diet; board in die Kost geben, to board.
Kost, kozht, *f.* cost, expense; -bar, *a.* precious, costly; expensive; -barkeit, *f.* preciousness; jewel. **Kosten**, kozh'ten, *vi.* to cost, to come to, require.
Kosten, kozh'ten, *vt.* to taste, try.
Kostenfrei, kozh'tènfrèl, *a.* free of expense, gratis.
Kostgänger, kozht'genger, *m.* boarder. **Kostgeld**, -gelt. *n.* board. **Kosthaus**, -hōns, *n.* boarding-house.
Köstlich, közht'lich, *a.* costly, precious, delicious, delicate; -keit, -kāet, *f.* preciousness, choiceness. **Kostspielig**, kozht'zhpīlich, *a.* expensive, costly; -keit, -kāet, *f.* expensiveness. **Kostverächter**, kozht'ferèchter, *m.* -in, *f.* dainty person.
Köter, köh'ter, *m.* cur.
Kot, köt, *m.* mire, mud, dirt; excrement.
Köthe, köh'te, *f.* fetlock-joint.
Kothig, köt'ich, *a.* muddy, miry, dirty.
Kotzen, kot'sen, *vi.* to spue, vomit.
Krabbe, krab'he, *f.* crab, shrimp.
Krabbeln, krab'beln, *vi.* to crawl, grope; itch.
Krach, krach, *m.* crack, crash. **Krachen**, krach'en, *vi.* to crack, crash. **Krachmandel**, -mandel, *m.* shell-almond.
Krächzen, krëch'tsen, *vi.* to croak, groan.
Kracke, krack'e, *f.* jade.
Kraft, kraft, *f.* strength, force, power, vigor, energy; *pr.* by, in virtue of; -anstrengung, -anzhtrengung, *f.* exertion of power, strength; -ausdruck, -ōysdruck, *m.* pithy expression. **Kraftbrühe**, kraft'brühe, *f.* strengthening broth. **Kräftemesser**, krëf'temesser, *m.* dynameter, dynamometer. **Kräftig**, krëf'tich, *a.* strong, vigorous, powerful. **Kräftigen**, krëf'tichen, *vt.* to strengthen, invigorate. **Kräftiglich**, -lich, *a.* powerfully, vigorously. **Kräftigung**, -ung, *f.* invigoration. **Kraftlos**, kraft'lös *a.* weak, languid, feeble; invalid; -igkeit, -igkāet, *f.* weakness; invalidity; languor.
Kraftvoll, -foll, *a.* vigorous, pithy, energetic.
Kragen, krä'gen, *m.* collar, cape;

neck; coat (Mar.); am Kragen nehmen, to collar. **Kragstein**, -zhtāen, *m.* bracket, socle.
Krähe, krä'he, *f.* crow. **Krähen**, krä'hen, *vi.* to crow; croak. **Krähenauge**, -āuge, *n.* crow's-eye; nux vomica. **Krähenfuss**, -fyss, *m.* crowfoot; scrawl.
Krahn, krān, *m.* crane; vor den Krahn winden, to cat.
Krakeel, krakāl', *m.* racket, uproar. **Krakeelen**, *vi.* to quarrel.
Kralle, kral'le, *f.* claw, talon; clutch. **Krallen**, kral'len, *vt.* to scratch, claw.
Kram, kräm, *m.* retail, shop; goods; -bude, -byde, *f.* booth, stall; -en, *vt. i.* to retail.
Krämer, krä'mer, *m.* retailer, retail-dealer; -geist, -gāezht, *m.* grasping spirit; -gewicht, -gevicht, *n.* avoirdupois weight.
Kramladen, kram'läden, *m.* retail-shop; grocery.
Krampe, kram'pe, *f.* cramp, cramp-iron; staple; clasp.
Krämpe, krëm'pe, *f.* flap of a hat.
Krämpel, krëm'pel, *f.* card, carding-comb. **Krämpeln**, krëm'peln, *vt.* to card.
Krämpen, krëm'pen, *vt.* to bend, to turn up.
Krampf, krampf, *m.* cramp, spasm, convulsion. **Krampfen**, kramp'fen, *vt.* to cramp, convulse. **Krampfhaft**, -haft, *a.* spasmodic, convulsive.
Kranich, kran'ich, *m.* crane.
Krank, krauk, *a.* sick, diseased, ill; — werden, to fall sick, der, die Kranke, *s.* patient, sick person.
Kränkeln, krën'keln, *vi.* to be sickly.
Kranken, kran'ken, *vi.* to be sick.
Kränken, krën'ken, *vt.* to injure, grieve, vex, mortify.
Krankenbett, kran'kenbett, *n.* sick-bed. **Kran'kenhaus**, -hōys, *n.* infirmary, hospital. **Kran'kenlager**, -läger, *n.* sick-bed. **Kran'kenstube**, -zhtybe, *f.* **Kran'kenzimmer**, -tsimmer, *n.* sick-room. **Kran'kenwärter**, -vërter, *m.* -in, *f.* nurse. **Krankhaft**, krank'haft, *a.* sickly, morbid. **Krankheit**, -hāet, *f.* disease, sickness, illness, malady, distemper.
Kränklich, krënk'lich, *a.* sickly; -keit, -kāet, *s.* sickliness **Kränkung**,

-ung, f. mortification, vexation, insult.

Kranz, krants, m. wreath, garland; cincture, fillet; cornice; capital; ring, crown. **Kränzchen**, krents'chen, n. little wreath; little circle. **Kränzen**, krent'sen, vt. i. to wreathe.

Krapf, krapf, m. **Kräpfchen**, kröpf'chen, n. fritter.

Krapp, krap, m. madder.

Kraß, kras, a. gross: hard, cruel.

Krater, krä'ter, m. crater.

Kratzbürste, krats'bürzhte, f. scraper.

Krätze, krėt'se, f. scrapings.

Krätze, krėt'se, f. itch.

Kratzen, krat'sen, vt. to scrape, scratch; to card. **Kratzer**, krėt'ser, m. scraper; bad wine. **Kratzing**, krats'fuss, m. chicken; scrape. **Krätzig**, krėt'sich, a. itchy. **Krätzsalbe**, kräts'salbe, f. salve for the itch.

Krauen, krŏu'en, vi. to scratch softly.

Kraus, krŏus, a. frizzled, curled, curly; crisp. **Krause**, krŏu'se, f. curliness; ruff, frill. **Kräuseln**, krëŭ'seln, vt. to frizzle, curl; ruffle, crisp. **Kräusen**, krëŭ'sen, vt. to lay in folds, to curl, ruffle. **Krauskohl**, krŏus'kōl, m. crisped, curled cabbage. **Kraussalat**, -sälät, m. crisped lettuce.

Kraut, krŏut, n. herb, plant; cabbage. **Krauten**, krŏu'ten, vt. to weed. **Kräuterarzt**, krëŭ'terärtst. m. herb-doctor. **Kräuterbuch**, -buch, n. herbal. **Kräuterfressend**, -fressent. a. herbivorous. **Kräuterkäse**, -käse, m. sage-cheese. **Kräuterkenner**, -kenner, m. herbalist. **Kräuterkunde**, -kunde, f. botany. **Kräutersammler**, -sammler, m. herb-man, herbalist. **Kräutersammlung**, -samlung, f. herbarium. **Krautjunker**, krŏut'yunker, m. country-squire.

Kreatur, krėätyr', f. creature.

Krebs, krėbs, m. crawfish, crab; cancer; **-auge**, -äu-ge, m. crab's-eye; **-butter**, -butter, f. crab's-butter. **Krebsen**, krėb'sen, vt. to catch crawfish; fig. to grope. **Krebsgang**, -gang, m. retrogression; den — gehen, to go backwards. **Krebs'schaden**, -shäden, m. cancer. **Krebsscheere**, -shẹre, f. claw of a crawfish.

Kredenzen, krėdent'sen, vt. to present to hand (a cup).

Kreide, krī'de, f. chalk; crayon. **Kreiden**, krī'den, vt. to chalk, crayon. **Kreidig**, krī'dich, a. chalky.

Kreis, krīs, m. circle, orbit; sphere; district; **-abschnitt**, -abshnitt, n. segment; **-amt**, -amt, n. bailiwick; **-ausschnitt**, -ŏusshnitt, m. sector; **-bewegung**, -beväguŋg, f. gyration, revolution, circular motion; **-bogen**, -bōgen, m. quadrant, quarter of a circle.

Kreischen, krī'shen, vi. to scream, shriek, screech.

Kreisel, krī'sel, top, gig; den — treiben, to spin the top. **Kreiseln**, krī'seln, vi. to whirl; vt. to spin a top. **Kreiselrad**, -räd, n. turbine. **Kreisen**, krī'sen, vi. to circle, gyrate; to turn around, revolve. **Kreisförmig**, krīs'förmich, a. circular. **Kreislauf**, -lŏuf, m. circulation, revolution; succession.

Kreißen, krīs'sen, vi. to travail, be in labor. **Kreißerin**, -erin, f. woman in labor.

Krepp, krep, m. **Kreppflor**, -flōr, m. crape.

Kresse, krės'se, f. cress, cresses.

Kreuz, krëŭts, n. cross, crucifix; croup; crupper; rump, back; tribulation, trouble; **-band**, -bant, n. paper cover; **-brav**, -bräf. a. downright good; **-bube**, -bybe, m. knave of clubs; **-dame**, -däme, f. queen of clubs. **Kreuzen**, krëŭt'sen, vt. i. to cross; to cruise; ein Tau —, to rack.

Kreuzer, krëŭt'ser, m. kreutzer (two thirds of a cent).

Kreuzer, krëŭt'ser, m. cruiser. **Kreuzfahrer**, -färer, m. crusader. **Kreuzfahrt**, -färt, f. crusade. **Kreuzgang**, -gang, m. cross-passage (in a cloister). **Kreuzigen**, krëŭ'tsigen, vt. to crucify. **Kreuzigung**, -ung, f. crucifixion. **Kreuzlahm**, -lām, a. broken-backed, lame in the hip. **Kreuzritter**, -ritter, m. knight of the cross. **Kreuzschwester**, -shvester, f. fellow sufferer. **Kreuzsegel**, -sägl, n. top-sail. **Kreuzspinne**, -shpinne, f. garden-spider. **Kreuzsprung**, krëŭts'shprung m. capriole, caper. **Kreuzverhör**, -ferhör, m. cross-examin tion. **Kreuzweg,** -wäg, m. cross-road. **Kreuzweise,** -weise, a. av. across, cruciform; sich kreuzweis durchschneiben, to cross. **Kreuzzeichen,** -tsäichen, n. sign of the cross; das — annehmen, to take the cross. **Kreuzzug,** -tsuk, m. crusade.

Kribbeln, krib'beln, **Kriebeln,** krī'beln, vi. to crawl, swarm; to bite, itch, to rub, scratch gently.

Kriechen, krī'chen (kroch, gekrochen), vi. to creep, crawl; to cringe, crouch. **Kriecher,** krī'cher, m. creeper, cringer. **Kriecherei,** -ī', f. cringing, fawning.

Krieg, krīk, m. war, contest; — führen, to wage war. **Kriegen,** krī'gen, vi. to wage war; struggle.

Kriegen, krī'gen, vt. to get, catch, receive, obtain.

Krieger, krī'ger, m. warrior, soldier; **-isch,** -ish, a. warlike, military, martial; av. -ly. **Kriegführend,** -führent, a. belligerent. **Kriegsangelegenheit,** krīgs'angelägenhäit, f. military affair. **Kriegsartikel,** -artĭkel, m. article of war. **Kriegsdienst,** -dīnzht, m. military service. **Kriegserklärung,** -erklärung, f. declaration of war. **Kriegsflotte,** -flotte, f. fleet, navy. **Kriegsgefangen,** -gefangen, a. taken in war. **Kriegsgefangener,** -er, z. prisoner of war. **Kriegsgericht,** -gericht, n. court-martial. **Kriegsglück,** -glükk, n. fortune, chance of war. **Kriegsheer,** -hēr, n. army. **Kriegsheld,** -helt, m. great warrior, hero. **Kriegskamerad,** kamerät, m. fellow-soldier, brother-in-arms. **Kriegskasse,** -kasse, f. military chest. **Kriegsknecht,** -knecht, m. soldier. **Kriegskosten,** -kozhten, f. expenses of war. **Kriegskunst,** -kunzht, f. military science. **Kriegslied,** -līd, n. war-song. **Kriegslist,** -lizht, f. stratagem. **Kriegsmacht,** -macht, f. military power, forces. **Kriegsmann,** -mann, m. soldier; **-schaft,** -shaft, f. soldiery, forces, troops. **Kriegsminister,** -minīzhter, m. minister of war; secretary-of-war. **Kriegsministerium,** -īum, n. war-office. **Kriegsrath,** -rät, n. council of war; counsellor-of-war. **Kriegsrecht,** -recht, n. martial-law. **Kriegsruhm,** -rum, m. military glory. **Kriegsrüstung,** -rüzhtung, f. preparation for war. **Kriegsschaar,** -shär, f. body of soldiers. **Kriegsschiff,** -shiff, n. man-of-war. **Kriegsschule,** -shule, f. military-school. **Kriegsvolk,** -folk, n. soldiery. **Kriegswesen,** -wäsen, n. military affairs. **Kriegswissenschaft,** -vissenshaft, f. military science. **Kriegszucht,** -tsucht, f. military discipline. **Kriegszug,** krīgs'tsug, m. expedition, campaign.

Kriminalamt, krimīnäl'amt, n. **Kriminalgericht,** -gericht, n. criminal court. **Kriminalprozeß,** -prōtsess, m. criminal case, suit. **Kriminalgesetz,** -gesets, n. criminal law; **-buch,** -buch, n. criminal code. **Kriminalverfahren,** -ferfären, n. criminal prosecution.

Kriminell, krimīnell', a. criminal.

Krippe, krip'pe, f. manger, crib.

Krise, krī'se, **Krisis,** krī'sis, f. crisis.

Krystall, krizhtall', **Kristall,** m. crystal. **Krystallen,** -len, a. crystalline, crystal. **Krystallhell,** -hell, a. bright, clear as crystal, crystalline.

Kritik, krītīk', f. criticism, critique.

Kritiker, krīt'iker, m. critic.

Kritisch, krīt'ish, a. critical.

Kritisiren, kritīsī'ren, vt. to criticise, review, comment upon.

Krittelei, krittelēī', f. fault-finding; over-nice criticism. **Kritteln,** krittĕln, vt. to criticise, carp at; to find fault. **Krittler,** krittˈler, m. over-nice critic, fault-finder.

Kritzeln, krit'seln, vi. to scrawl, scribble, scratch.

Krokodil, krokōdīll', n. crocodile; amerikanisches —, alligator, cayman. **Krokodilsthräne,** -träne, f. false, hypocritical tear.

Kronanwalt, krōn'änvalt, m. attorney general. **Kronbeamter,** -beamter, m. officer of the crown. **Krone,** krōn'e, f. crown; coronet, head, top. **Krönen,** krön'nen, vt. to crown, wreathe; to award the prize; to adorn, complete. **Kronerbe,** krōnˈerbe, m. heir to the crown. **Kronleuchter,** -löuchter, m. chandelier, lustre. **Kronprinz,** krōn'prints, m. prince royal. **Kronprinzessin,** -prīntsessin, f. princess royal. **Kronrad,** -räd, n. crown-wheel. **Krönung,** krön'ung, f. coronation.

Kro   194   **Kuu**

Kropf, kropf, *m.* craw, crop; wen, struma, bronchocele, goitre; excrescence; head, bow (of a ship). **Kropf= gans,** kropf'gans, *f.* pelican.
Kröſchen, krösh'en, *vt.* to broil; to hiss, crackle.
Kröte, kröh'te, *f.* toad.
Krücke, krük'ke, *f.* crutch; scraper; **-nſtock,** krük'kenzhtock, *m.* crutchstick.
Krug, krug, *m.* pitcher; jug, jar.
Krümchen, krühm'chen, *n.* little crumb. **Krume,** *f.* crum, crumb. **Krü= meln,** krü'meln, *vt.* to crumble.
Krumm, krumm, *a.* crooked, curved, bent. wry; frumme Linie, curve; **-bein, -baen.** *n.* crook-shanks; **-ig, -ich,** *a.* bow-legged.
Krümme, krüm'me, *f.* crookedness, bent, turning, winding, intricacy. **Krümmen,** krüm'men, *vt.* to crook, curve, wind, bend. **Krüm'mung,** -ung, *f.* bend, curve.
Krüppel, krüp'pel, *m.* cripple; zum — machen, to cripple, lame: zum — werden, to be crippled. **Krüp'pelig, -ich, Krüp'pelhaft, -haft,** *a.* maimed, lame.
Kruſte, kruzh'te, *f.* crust; — bekommen, to crust. **Kru'ſtenthier, -tĭr,** *n.* crustacean. **Kruſtig,** kruzht'ich, *a.* crusty.
Kryſtall, krĭzh'tall, etc., f. **Kriſtall.**
Kübel, küh'bel, *m.* bucket. pail; tub.
Kubik, kubĭk', *a. av.* cubic, cubically; **-fuß, -fyss,** *m.* cubic foot; **-maaß, -mäss,** *n.* cubic measure; **-meile, -mēīle,** *f.* cubic mile; **-wurzel, -vyr- tsel,** *f.* cubic root; **-zahl, -tsäl,** *f.* cube (number). **Kubiſch, -bĭsh,** *a.* cubic; *av.* cubically. **Kubus,** ky'- bys, *m.* cube.
Küche, küch'e, *f.* kitchen; **kalte —,** cold meat.
Kuchen, ky'chen, *m.* cake, pie, pastry; **-bäcker,** ky'chenbekker, *m.* pastrycook.
Küchengarten, küch'engarten, *m.* kitchen-garden. **Küch'engeschirr, -ge- shirr,** *n.* kitchen furniture. **Küch'en- herd, -härt,** *m.* kitchen-hearth. **Küch'enmagd, -magt,** *f.* kitchenmaid. **Küch'enschrank, -shrank,** *m.* larder. **Küch'enzettel, -tsettel,** *m.* bill of fare.
Kuckuck, kuk'uk, **Kukuk,** *m.* cuckoo.
Kufe, ky'fe, *f.* vat, tub; large beer- barrel. **Küfner,** kühf'ner, **Küfer,** küh'fer, *m.* cooper.
Kugel, ky'gel, *f.* bullet, ball, shot; bowl; globe, sphere. **Ku'gelfeſt, -fezht,** *a.* shot-proof. **Ku'gelförmig, -förmĭch, Ku'gelicht, -ĭcht, Ku'gelig,** *a.* spherical, globular. **Kugeln,** ky'- geln, *vt.* to roll, tumble; to assume a globular form, to round. **Ku'gel= rund,** -rund, *a.* round as a ball.
Kuh, ky, *f.* cow; hind; junge **Kuh,** heifer; blinde **Kuh,** blind-man's-buff; **-brücke, -brükke,** *f.* orlop-deck; **-eu- ter, -ūter,** *f.* cow-udder. **Kuh'fla= den, -fläden,** *m.* cow-dung. **Kuh'= fleiſch, -flāesh,** *n.* cow-flesh. **Kuh= hirt,** ky'hĭrt, *m.* cowherd, neatherd.
Kühl, kühl, *a.* cool, fresh; *av.* -ly. **Kühle,** küh'le, *f.* coolness. **Küh= len,** küh'len, *vt.* to cool; *vi.* to be cool.
Knhle, kuh'le, *f.* waist (Mar.).
Kühlfaß, kühl'fass, *n.* cooling-vat. **Kühl'ofen, -öfen,** *m.* cooling-furnace, annealing-furnace. **Kühlte,** kühl'te, *f.* wind, gale. **Kühl'ung,** -ung, *f.* cooling; coolness; refrigeration.
Kuhmilch, ky'mĭlch, *f.* cow's milk.
Kühn, kühn, *a.* bold, daring, dauntless. **Kühn'heit, -hāet,** *f.* boldness, hardiness, daring. **Kühn'lich, -lĭch,** *av.* boldly, daringly.
Kuhpocke, ky'pokke, *f.* cow-pox. **Kuh= reigen,** ky'rāegen, ranz-des-vaches. **Kuh ſtall,** -zhtall, *m.* cow-house.
Kukummer, kukum'mer, *f.* cucumber.
Kulminiren, kulmĭnī'ren, *vi.* to culminate.
Kümmel, küm'mel, *m.* caraway-seed; cumin; **-brod, -bröt,** *n.* bread with caraway-seeds; **-waſſer, -vasser,** n. cumin-brandy.
Kummer, kum'mer, *m.* grief, sorrow, distress. **Kümmerlich,** küm'merlĭch, *a.* needy, destitute, distressed, &c. -ly: — leben, to live poorly. **Küm= mern,** küm'mern, *vt. i.* to grieve, afflict; to distress (Law); to care for; to concern. **Küm'merniß, -nĭss,** *f.* grief, sorrow. **Kum'mervoll, -fall,** *a.* sorrowful.
Kummet, kum'mĕt, *n.* horse-collar.
Kumpan, kumpän', *m.* companion; fellow.
Kund, kunt, *a.* known. **Kund'bar,**

-bär, *a. av.* known, notorious; — machen, to publish, divulge. Kunde, kun'de, *f.* knowledge; tidings; *m.* customer. Künden, kün'den, *vt.* to announce. Kundig, kun'dich, *a.* acquainted with, skilled in; expert. Kündigen, kün'dichen, *vt.* to give warning. Kundschaft, kund'shaft, *f.* custom, customers; information, knowledge; —einziehen, to get information; auf —ausgehen, to go out scouting; auf — sein, to reconnoitre. Kundschaften, -en, *vt.* to spy, scout. Kundschafter, -er, *m.* spy.
Künftig, künf'tich, *a.* future, to come, *av.* in future.
Kunkel, kun'kel, *f.* distaff; Lehen, -lä-en, *n.* female fief.
Kunst, kunzht. *f. pl.* Künste, art; skill; trick; die freien Künste, liberal arts; schöne Künste, fine arts; anlage, -änlage, *f.* pleasure-ground; ausdruck, -öysdruck, *m.* technical term; ausstellung, -zhtellung, *f.* exhibition (of fine arts). Künstelei, künzhtelēī', *f.* artificiality; affectation. Künsteln, künzh'teln, *vi.* to subtilize, affect. Kunstfähigkeit, kunzht'faigkäet, *f.* talent for art. Kunstfertig, -fertich, *a.* expert, skilled. *av.* -ly; -keit, -käet, *f.* skill, expertness. Kunstfleiss, -flēīss, *m.* industry. Kunstfreund, -frēünt, *m.* -in, *f.* amateur, dilettant. Kunstgärtner, -gertner, *m.* horticulturist. Kunstgriff, -grif, *m.* artifice, trick, knack. Kunsthandel, -handel, trade in works of art. Kunsthändler, -hendler, *m.* picture-dealer. Künstler, künzht'ler, *m.* artist. Künstlerisch, -ish, *a.* artistical. Künstlich, -lich, *a.* artificial. Kunstliebhaber, kunsht'lēēhaber, amateur. Kunstlos, -lōs, *a.* artless. Kunstmässig, -mässich, *a.* according to the rules of art. Kunstreich, -reich, *a.* skillful, ingenious. Kunstrichter, -richter, *m.* critic. Kunstsammlung, -samlung, *f.* gallery, collection of works of art. Kunstschule, -shule, *f.* academy of arts; style *or* school of art. Kunstsinn, -sinn, *m.* taste for art. Kunstsprache, -zhprache, *f.* technical language. Kunststück, -zhtük, *n.* work of art; trick, artifice. Kunsttischler, -tishler, *m.* cabinet-maker. Kunsttrieb, -trīp. *m.* innate love of art; mechanical instinct. Kunstverständiger, -ferzhtendiger, *m.* connoisseur. Kunstwerk, -verk, *n.* work of art. Kunstwort, -vort, *n.* technical term.
Kupe, ku'pe, *f.* vat, boiler.
Kupfer, kup'fer, *n.* copper; copperplate; bergwerk, -bergverk, *n.* copper-mine. Kupfererz, -erts, *n.* copper-ore. Kupfergrün, -grün, *n.* verditer. Kupferhaltig, -haltich. Kupferig, -ich, *a.* coppery. Kupferhammer, -hammer, *m.* copper-work, copper-mill. Kupferkiese, -hīkē, Kupferkies, -kīs, *m.* mountain-green; copper-pyrites. Kupferkönig, -köhnich, *m.* regulus of copper. Kupfern, -fern, *a.* made of copper; Kupferschmied, -shmīt, *m.* brazier. Kupferstecher, -zhtecher, *m.* engraver in copper. Kupferstich, -zhtich, *m.* Kupfertafel, -täfel, *f.* copperplate, engraving. Kupferstufe, -zhtufe, *f.* piece of copper-ore. Kupfervitriol, -fītrīōl, *m.* blue vitriol. Kupferwasser, -vasser, *n.* solution of blue vitriol.
Kuppe, kup'pe, *f.* top, summit, head, point, knob.
Kuppel, kup'pel, *f.* cupola, dome.
Kuppelei, kuppelēī', *f.* coupling, match-making, procuring. Kuppeln, kup'peln, *vt.* to couple; to make a match; to pimp, procure. Kuppelpelz, -pelts, *m.* reward for making a match.
Kuppen, kup'pen, *vt.* to top, lop.
Kuppler, kup'ler, *m.* -in, *f.* matchmaker; pimp, procurer, pander, procuress, bawd.
Kur, kur, *f.* election; electorate.
Kuranzen, kurant'sen, *vt.* to beat, chastise.
Kürass, küh'rass, *m.* cuirass. Kürassier, -sīr', *m.* cuirassier.
Kurbe, kur'be, Kurbel, kur'bel, *f.* wench, handle, windlass.
Kürbiss, kür'biss, *m.* pumpkin, gourd.
Küren, kūh'ren (for geforen), *vt.* to chose, elect. Kurfürst, kur'fürst, *m.* elector; enthum, -tym, *n.* electorate; lich, -lich, *a.* electoral. Kurfürstenwürde, -vürde, *f.* electoral dignity.
Kürschner, kürsh'ner, *m.* furrier; ei, -ēī', *f.* furrier's trade.

Kurz, kurtz, *a.* short, brief, *av.* -ly; in short; in Kurzem, shortly, in a short time; kurz und gut, in a word; über kurz oder lang, sooner or later; kurz abfertigen, to be short with; kurz halten, to be strict with; den Kürzern ziehen, to be worsted; **-athmig**, -ätmig, *a.* asthmatic. **Kürze**, kürt'ze, *f.* shortness. **Kürzen**, kürt'sen, *vt.* to shorten. **Kürzlich**, -lich, *av.* lately. **Kurzsichtig**, kurts'sichtig, *a.* short-sighted, near-sighted; **-keit**, *f.* short-sightedness. **Kurz'sum**, -umm, *av.* — machen, to turn short. **Kurzweile**, -veĭle, **Kurz'weil**, *f.* pastime, amusement; **sen**, *vr.* to divert, amuse one's self. **Kurz'weilig**, -veĭlig, *a.* facetious, amusing.

Kuß, kuss, *m. pl.* Küsse, kiss, buss; — zuwerfen, to kiss one's hand to. **Küssen**, küs'sen, *vt.* to kiss. **Kuß'hand**, kuss'hant, *f.* **Kuß'händchen**, -hendchen, *n.* kissing one's hand to.

Küste, küzh'te, *f.* coast; **-fahrer**, -fārer, *m.* coaster; **-fahrt**, -fārt, *f.* coasting; **-handel**, -handel, *m.* coasting-trade.

Küster, küzhter, *m.* sexton, sacristan.

Kutschbock, kutsh'bokk, *m.* coach-box. **Kutsche**, kut'she, *f.* coach, carriage; **-schlag**, -shlak. *m.* coach-door. **Kutschentritt**, -tritt. **Kutsch'tritt**, *m.* foot-board. **Kut'scher**, *m.* coachman, carriage-driver; **-sitz**, -sits, *m.* driver's seat. **Kutschieren**, kutshī'ren, *vi.* to drive in a coach.

Kutte, kut'te, *f.* cowl, capoche.

Kuttel, kut'tel, *f.* tripe. **Kut'telflecke**, -flēcke, *m.* tripe, chitterlings.

Kutter, kut'ter, *m.* cutter (Mar.).

L

Lab, läp, *n.* runnet, rennet.

Labben, lab'ben, *vi.* to lap; to twaddle.

Labe, lä'be, *f.* refreshment. **Laben**, lä'ben, *vt.* to refresh, quicken, recreate.

Laberdan, lä'berdän, **Labberdan**, lab'berdän. *m.* salted codfish.

Labetrunk, lä'betrunk, *m.* **La'betrunk**, -trunk. *m.* refreshing draught.

Labial, labiäl', *m.* **Labialbuchstabe**, -buchstäbe, *m.* labial.

Laboratorium, laborätō'rium, *n.* laboratory. **Laboriren**, laborī'ren, *vi.* to labor.

Labsal, läb'säl, *n.* **Lab'ung**, -ung, *f.* refreshment.

Labyrinth, labyrint', *n.* labyrinth, maze.

Lache, lach'e, *f.* pool, slough.

Lache, lach'e, *f.* blaze, mark cut in a tree.

Lache, lach'e, *f.* laughter; — aufschlagen, to break out into laughter. **Lächeln**, lĕch'eln, *vi.* to smile; böhnisch —, to sneer. **Lachen**, lach'en, *vi.* to laugh.

Lachen, lach'en, *vt.* to blaze, to make a cut in a tree.

Lacher, lach'er, *m.* laugher. **Lächerlich**, lĕch'erlich, *a.* ridiculous, laughable, ludicrous; — machen, to ridicule; — werden, to fall into ridicule; **-keit**, -kĕĭt, *f.* ludicrousness, ridiculousness. **Lächern**, lĕch'ern. *vt.* to make laugh. **Lachlustig**, lach'lynhtig, *a.* fond of laughing, merry.

Lachs, laks, *m. pl.* Lachse. salmon. **Lachsfang**, -fang, *m.* **Lachs'fischerei**, -fisherĕī', *f.* salmon-fishery. **Lachs'forelle**, -forĕlle, *f.* sea-trout, salmon-trout.

Lachter, lach'ter, *f.* fathom.

Lack, lack, *m.* lac, gum-lac; wallflower.

Lackei, lackäī', *m.* lackey, footman. **Lacken**, lac'ken. **Lackiren**, lakkī'ren, *vt.* to lacquer, varnish, japan. **Lackī'rer**, *m.* varnisher.

Lackmus, lack'mys, *m.* litmus.

Lade, lä'de, *f.* box, chest; lathe. **Laben**, lä'den, *m.* shutter; store, shop.

Laden, lä'den (lub, gelaben), *vt.* to lade, load, charge; freight; to cite, summon, invite.

Ladenbank, lä'denbank, *m.* counter. **La'denbiener**, -diner, *m.* shop-man, clerk. **La'benfenster**, -fenzhter, *n.* shop-window. **La'benhüter**, -hüter, *m.* unsalable goods. drug. **La'benmädchen**, -mĕdchen, *n.* shop-girl. **La'denpreis**, -prĕīss. *m.* selling-price. **La'denschwengel**, -shvengel, *m.* counter-jumper, clerk.

Ladestock, lä'dezhtock, *m. pl.* Ladestöcke, ramrod, rammer.

Lädiren, lädī'ren, *vt.* to injure, hurt.

Ladung, lä'dung, *f.* lading; load, freight, cargo; charge; summons. **La'dungsplatz**, -plats, *m.* place of

lading. **Ladungschein**, -sch**en**, *m.* bill of lading.
Laffe, laf'fe, *m.* fop, puppy, dandy.
Läffeln, läf'feln, *vt.* to caress, fondle, dally.
Laffete, laffā'te, *f.* carriage (of a gun).
Lage, lā'ge, *f.* situation, site, position; stratum, layer, tier.
Lägel, lā'gel, *n.* small barrel, keg; cringle (Mar.).
Lager, lā'ger, *n.* couch, bed; lair; camp, encampment; **-baum**, -b**au**m, *m.* **-balken**, -balken, *m.* gauntree; **-bier**, -bīr, *n.* lager-beer; March-beer; **-haus**, -h**ou**s, *n.* warehouse, storehouse; **-hütte**, -hütte, *f.* camp-hut, barrack; **-kunst**, -kunzht, *f.* castrametation; **-miethe**, -mīte, *f.* storage. **Lagern**, lā'gern, *vt. i.* to lay, store; to encamp, be encamped; to rest. **Lagerstätte**, -zhtette, **Lagerstelle**, -zhtelle, *f.* resting-place, couch, bed. **Lagerwache**, -vach-e, *f.* camp-guard. **Lagerzins**, -tsins, *m.* storage.
Lagune, lagū'ne, *f.* lagoon.
Lahm, lām, *a.* lame, halt. **Lähme**, lā'me, *f.* lameness. **Lahmen**, lā'men, *vi.* to be lame, to halt. **Lähmen**, lā'men, *vt.* to lame, paralyze. **Lahmheit**, lām'hāet, *f.* lameness. **Lähmung**, lām'ụng, *f.* laming, palsy, paralysis, lameness.
Lahn, lān, *m.* tinsel.
Laib, lāep, *m.* loaf.
Laich, laech, *m.* spawn. **Laichen**, *vi.* to spawn. **Laiche**, lāech'e, *f.* spawning-time.
Laie, lāe'e, *m.* layman; *pl.* laity; ignorant of. **Laienbruder**, -bruder, *m.* lay-brother. **Laienschwester**, -shvezhter, *f.* lay-sister.
Lake, lā'ke, *f.* brine, pickle.
Laken, lā'ken, *n.* sheet.
Lakonisch, lakō'nish, *a.* laconic.
Lakritze, lakrit'se, *f.* licorice.
Lallen, lal'len, *vi.* to stammer, lisp.
Lambertnuss, lam'bērtnụss, *f.* filbert.
Lamentiren, lamentī'ren, *vi.* to lament.
Lamento, lamentō, *n.* lament.
Lamm, lam, *n. pl.* **Lämmer**, lamb, ewe. **Lämmergeier**, lēm'mergēer, *m.* golden vulture. **Lammfleisch**, lam'flaesh, *n.* lamb. **Lammfromm**, -from', *a.* gentle as a lamb. **Lämmchen**, lēm'chen, *n.* **Lämmlein**, -l**ae**n,

n. lambkin. **Lammsbraten**, lam'brāten, *m.* roasted lamb. **Lammzeit**, tsāet, *f.* ewing-time.
Lampe, lam'pe, *f.* lamp; **-docht**, lempendocht, *m.* lamp-wick; **-licht**, -licht, *n.* lamp-light; **-mann**, -man, *m.* lamp-lighter; **-russ**, -russ, *m.* lamp-black; **-nschein**, -sh**ae**n, *m.* light of lamps.
Lamprete, lamprā'te, *f.* lamprey.
Land, lant, *n. pl.* land, country; **-adel**, lant'ādl, *m.* country-nobility; **-ammann**, -amman, *m.* landamman; **-bau**, -b**ou**, *m.* agriculture; **-bauer**, -b**ou**er. *m.* husbandman, farmer; **-besitzer**, land'bezitser, *m.* landed proprietor: **-edelmann**, -ādelman, *m.* country-squire. **Landen**, lan'den, *vt. i.* to land. **Landenge**, land'enge, *f.* isthmus. **Länderei**, lenderē'ī, *f.* lands, territory. **Landesfürst**, lan'desfürzht, *m.* reigning prince. **Landesherr**, -hērr, *m.* sovereign. **Landesherrlich**, -lich, *a.* sovereign. **Landesherrlichkeit**, -kāet, *f.* **Landeshoheit**, -hōhāet, *f.* sovereignty. **Landesobrigkeit**, -ōbrigkāet, *f.* government, authorities. **Landesordnung**, -ōrdnụng, *f.* law, regulation. **Landespolizei**, -pōlitsāī, *f.* police of a country. **Landesregierung**, -regīrụng, *f.* government of a country. **Landessprache**, -zhprāche, *f.* vernacular tongue; language of a country. **Landestracht**, -tracht, *f.* national costume. **Landflüchtig**, land'flüchtig, *a.* fugitive. **Landfriede**, -frīde, *m.* public peace. **Landgeistliche**, -g**ae**zhtliche, *m.* country-clergyman. **Landgericht**, -gericht, *n.* provincial court of justice. **Landgraf**, -grāf, *m.* landgrave. **Landgräfin**, -grāfin, *f.* landgravine. **Landgrafschaft**, -shaft, *f.* **Landgrafthum**, -tụm, *n.* landgraviate. **Landgränze**, grentse, *f.* border, boundary. **Landgut**, -gụt, *n.* country-seat, estate. **Landhandel**, -handel, *m.* inland trade. **Landhaus**, -h**ou**s, *n.* country-house **Landheer**, -hēr, *n.* land-forces. **Landjunker**, -yụnker, *m.* country-puppy. **Landkarte**, -karte, *f.* map. **Landkundig**, -kụndich, *a.* acquainted with the country; notorious. **Landkutsche**, -kụtshe, *f.* private-coach; stagecoach. **Landläufer**, -l**oi**fer, *f.* va-

grant, vagabond. **Land'läufig,** -läufich, a. current. **Land'leben,** -lebens, n. country-life. **Land'leute,** -leute, s. pl. country people. **Länd-lich,** lend'lich, a. rural; -keit, -kät, f. ruralness. **Landmacht,** land'macht, f. land-forces. **Land'mädchen,** -mäd-chen, n. country-girl. **Land'mann,** -man, m. peasant. **Land'mark,** -mark, f. boundary of a country. **Land'markt,** -markt, f. landmark. **Land'messer,** -mässer, m. surveyor; geometer. **Land'messung,** -ung, f. surveying. **Land'miliz,** -milits, f. militia. **Land'partie,** -partī, f. picnic. **Land'pfarre,** -pfarre, f. country-parsonage. **Land'pfarrer,** -pfarrer, **Land'prediger,** -prädiger, m. country-parson. **Land'plage,** plage, f. public calamity. **Land'rat,** -rāt, m. deputy of a province; counsellor of a canton. **Land'ratte,** -ratte, f. land-rat. **Land'recht,** -recht, n. common-law; country-law. **Land'regen,** -rägen, m. general rain. **Land'reise,** -rāise, f. journey by land. **Land'richter,** -richter, m. country-justice. **Land'sass,** -sāss, m. freeholder. **Landschaft,** -shaft, f. landscape; province. **Landschaftlich,** -lich, a. provincial. **Landschaftsmaler,** -māler, m. landscape-painter. **Land'scheide,** -shāede, f. boundary of a country. **Land'schule,** -shule, f. country-school. **Land'see,** -sā, m. lake. **Land'seuche,** -söuche, f. epidemic. **Land'sitz,** -sits, m. country-seat. **Landskind,** -kint, **Landeskind,** lan'deskint, n. native of the country. **Landsmann,** lands'man, m. countryman. **Landsmännin,** -mennin, f. country-woman. **Land'spitze,** -spitse, f. cape, promontory. **Landstadt,** -shtāt, f. provincial town; inland town. **Land'stand,** -shtant, m. member of the states of a country. **Land'strasse,** -shtrāsse, f. highway; high-road. **Land'streicher,** -shtrëicher, m. vagabond; -rei, -ēī, f. vagrancy. **Landstrich,** -shtrich, m. tract of land, district; climate. **Land'sturm,** -shtyrm, m. general levy; storm on land. **Land'sturz,** -shtyrts, m. land-slip, land-slide. **Land'tag,** -tāg, m. diet, assembly of the states; **-abschied,** landtāgs'-apshīd, m. dismissal of the states.

Land'thier, -tīr, n. terrestrial animal. **Land'trauer,** -tröuer, f. public-mourning. **Land'truppen,** -troppen, s. pl. land-forces. **Land'üblich,** -üblich, a. national. **Land'ung,** -ung, f. landing. **Land'vogt,** -fogt, m. governer. **Land'volk,** -fōlk, n. country-people, peasantry. **Land'wärts,** -verts, av. landward. **Land'wehr,** -vēr, f. militia. **Land'wein, -wēn,** m. home-grown wine; country-wine. **Land'wind,** -vint, m. land-wind, land-breeze. **Land'wirth,** -veert, m. husbandman, farmer; landlord; -in, f. landlady. **Land'wirthschaft,** -shaft, f. husbandry, farming; -lich, -lich, a. agricultural. **Land'zunge,** -tsynge, f. neck of land.

Lang, lang, a. av. long, tall; long-sighted; eine Woche lang, for a week; Stundenlang, for hours. **Lang'beinig,** -bänig, a. long-legged. **Lange,** lan'ge, av. long, a long while, a good while; lange her, of old standing; lange machen, to be long in doing; lange nicht, far from, anything but. **Länge,** leng'e, f. length, longitude. **Langen,** lang'en, vi. to reach, to stretch one's hand; to suffice. **Längen,** leng'en, vt. to lengthen, stretch. **Länger,** leng'er, a. longer; — machen, to lengthen; — werden, to grow longer. **Länglich,** leng'lich, a. oblong; -rund, -runt, a. oval, elliptical. **Lang'muth,** -myt, f. **Lang'müthigkeit,** -müthichkāīt, f. forbearance, patience. **Langmüthig,** -müthich, a. long-suffering, forbearing, patient. **Lang'nasig,** -nāsich, a. long-nosed. **Langohr,** -ōr, n. jackass. **Längs,** lengs, pr. along. **Langsam,** lang'sam, a. slow; -keit, -kāīt, f. slowness. **Lang'schenkelig,** -shenkelich, a. long-shanked. **Lang'schläfer,** -shlāfer, m. lie-abed, sluggard. **Längst,** lengkht, av. long ago, long since. **Längstens,** leng'shtens, av. at the latest, at the farthest. **Lang'weile,** lang'vēīle, f. **Lang'weile,** f. tediousness, ennui. **Lang'weilen,** vt. to tire, to cause tediousness, to bore; — sich, to feel tired, bored. **Lang'weilig,** -vēīlich, a. tedious, tiresome, irksome, dull; -keit, -kāīt, f. tiresomeness, tediousness. **Lang'wierig,** lang'vīrich, a. protracted, tedious; -keit, -kāīt, f. tediousness.

Lan 199 **Lau**

Langsichtig, lang'sichtig, long-sighted, far-sighted; of long date. **Langsilbig,** -silbich, a. consisting of a long syllable.
Lanze, lan'tse, f. lance, spear; — einlegen, to couch the lance;— brechen, to break a lance. **Lanzknecht,** lants'-kenècht, m. foot-soldier (of the middle ages).
Lapp, lap, a. slack, flappy.
Läppalie, lappä'lie, f. **Lapperei,** -rī', f. trifle.
Lappen, lap'pen, m. rag, patch; flap; botch.
Läppern, lëp'pern, vi. to lap, sip; to collect. **Läpperschulden,** -shulden, s. pl. driblets, dribbling debts.
Lappicht, lap'picht, a. flappy. **Lappig,** a. ragged.
Läppisch, lëp'pish, a. silly, awkward.
Lärche, lër'che, f. larch, larch-tree.
Larifari, lärifä'rī, f. fiddle-faddle.
Lärm, lërm, m. noise; tumult, alarm; ado. **Lärmen,** lër'men, vi. to make a noise; to bluster; to brawl, quarrel. **Lärmglocke,** -glocke, f. alarm-bell.
Larve, lar'fe, f. mask; spectre, ghost; larva, larve, caterpillar.
Lasche, lash'e, f. flap; groove.
Laß, lass, a. relaxed, weary, tired; indolent.
Lassen, (ließ, gelassen), to let; to leave; to permit, allow, grant;— machen, to get made; Aber lassen, to bleed, let blood; Wasser —, to make water; drucken lassen, to have printed; in Ruhe lassen, to leave alone.
Lässig, las'sich, a. lazy, sluggish; steif, -käet, f. sluggishness.
Last, lasht, f. pl. Lasten, load, burden. **Lastbar,** -bär, a. intended to bear. **Lasten,** lazh'ten, vi. to weigh, press (heavy); encumber.
Laster, lazh'ter, n. vice, crime. **Lästerer,** lezh'terer, m. slanderer, calumniator. **Lasterhaft,** lazh'terhaft, a. vicious; -eigkeit, -käet, f. viciousness. **Lästerlich,** lezh'terlich, a. shameful, av. -ly. **Lästermaul,** -lezh'termouil, n. pl. Lästermäuler, **Lästerzunge,** -tsunge, f. slanderer. **Lästern,** lezh'tërn, vt. to slander, revile, defame. **Lästerschrift,** -shrift, f. libel. **Lästersucht,** -sucht, f. calumnious disposition. **Lästerung,** -ung, f. slander, backbiting.

Lästig, lëzh'tich, a. burdensome, troublesome; -keit, -käet, burdensomeness. **Laßigkeit,** lazh'tichkäet, f. tonnage, burden.
Lasurblau, lä'surblän, a. azure. **Lasurfarbe,** -farbe, f. azure-color. **Lasurstein,** -zhtäen, m. lapis lazuli.
Latein, latäin', n. Latin language. **Lateiner,** latäi'ner, m. Latin scholar. **Lateinisch,** -ish, a. Latin; auf —, in Latin.
Laterne, latër'ne, f. lantern; lamp. **Laternenpfahl,** -pfäl, m. pl. Pfähle, lamp-post.
Latschen, lat'shen, vi. to shuffle, walk slovenly. **Latschig,** lät'shig, a. shuffling; sloven; av. -ly.
Latte, lat'te, f. lath. **Latten,** lat'ten, vt. to lath; swerk, -vërk, n. lathwork.
Lattich, lat'tich, a. lettuce.
Latwerge, lat'vërge, f. electuary.
Latz, lats, m. flap; stomacher, bodice; waistcoat.
Lau, läu, a. lukewarm, tepid; slack, cold.
Laub, läup, n. foliage, leaves. **Laube,** läu'be, f. arbor, bower.
Laubhütte, läu'berhütte, f. **Laubshütte,** f. bower, arbor. **Laubhüttenfest,** läub'hüttenfëzht, n. feast of tabernacles. **Laubfrosch,** -frosh, m. pl. -frösche, green-frog, tree-frog. **Laubicht,** -icht, a. like foliage, like an arbor. **Laubig,** läu'bich, a. leafy.
Laubwerk, läup'vërk n. foliage.
Lauch, läuch, m. leek.
Lauer, löy'er, f. lurking, ambush. **Laurer,** löy'erer, m. spy, lurker. **Lauern,** löy'ërn, vi. to lurk; lie in wait, in ambush; to be on the watch.
Lauf, läuf, m. pl. Läufe, course, run, speed; barrel; sbahn, -bän, f. course. **Laufbrett,** -brët, n. plant, carriage (Print.); sbrief, -brīf, m. circular. **Laufbrücke,** -brükke, f. foot-bridge. **Laufbursche,** -burshe, m. errand-boy. **Laufen,** läu'fen, vi. to run; to flow; Gefahr laufen, to run a risk. **Läufer,** läu'fer, m. runner; roulade; upper mill-stone; slider. **Laufeuer,** läuf'föüer, m. running fire. **Laufgraben,** -gräben, m. trench. **Läufig,** leü'fich, **Läufisch,** -fish, a. ruttish, at heat. **Laufpaß,**

-paß, m. dismission; — geben, to turn out. Laufplanken, -planken, s. pl. gangway. Laufwagen, -vägen, m. go-cart. Laufzeit, -tsēīt, f. rut-time.
Lauge, lāū'ge, f. lye, buck. Laugen, vt. to buck. Laugenartig, lāū'genärtich, a. lixivial, alkaline. Laugensalz, -salts, n. alkaline salt.
Laugnen, laūg'nen, vt. to deny, disown.
Lauigkeit, lāū'ichkāēt, f. lukewarmness.
Laulich, lāū'lich, a. lukewarm; -keit, -kāēt, f. lukewarmness.
Laune, lau'ne, f. whim, caprice, humor. Launenhaft, Launisch, lau'nish, a. capricious, peevish. Launig, lau'nich, a. humorous; -keit, -kāēt, f. humorousness.
Laus, lōūs, f. louse, pl. Läuse, lōū'se, lice.
Lausche, lōū'she, f. listening. Lauschen, lōū'shen, vi. to listen, lurk. Lauscher, -sher, m. listener, eavesdropper.
Läusekamm, lōū'sekamm, m. fine-comb. Läusekrankheit, -krankhāēt, f. Läusesucht, lōū'sesucht, f. phthiriasis.
Lausig, lōū'sich, a. lousy; sordid, mean.
Laut, lōūt, m. sound, tone; noise; a. loud; noisy, boisterous, av. -ly; pr. according to; laut werden, to become public.
Laute, lōū'te, f. lute.
Lauten, lōū'ten, vi. to sound, run. Läuten, lōū'ten, vt. to ring, toll; to peal: s. peal, ringing, tolling.
Lautenschläger, lōū'tenshläger, Lautenspieler, lōū'tenzpīler, m. luteplayer.
Lauter, lōū'ter, a. pure, clear; mere, nothing but, none but, only; -keit, -kāēt, f. purity; integrity. Läutern, lōū'tern, vt. to purify, clear, refine. Läuterasen, -ōfen, m. refining furnace. Läutertuch, -tuch, n. filtering cloth. Läuterung, -ung, f. purification, refining.
Lautlos, lōūt'lōs, a. silent, mute.
Lauwarm, lāū'varm, a. lukewarm.
Lava, lā'fā, f. lava.
Lavendel, lafen'del, m. lavender.
Laviren, lafī'ren, vi. to tack.
Lawine, lavī'ne, f. pl. -n. avalanche.

Laxir, laxīr', s. pl. -e, purgative, purge Laxiren, laxī'ren, vi. i. to purge.
Lazareth, latsarāt', n. -es, pl. -e, lazaret, hospital, infirmary.
Lebehoch, lābehōch', n. cheering, toast. Leben, lā'ben, vi. to live, to be alive. Lebe wohl! long live! hurrah for—! lebe wohl! good bye! farewell! adieu! Leben, s. n. -s, life. Lebend, lā'bent, a. living. Lebendig, -dich, a. living, alive, lively, quick; -keit, -kāēt, f. liveliness, quickness. Lebensart, -ärt, f. pl. -en. way of life, manner of living; good breeding. Lebensbedürfnisse, -bedürfnisse, s. pl. necessaries. Lebensbeschreibung, -beshrēibung, f. pl. -en, biography, life. Lebensgefahr, -gefār, f. pl. -en, danger of life. Lebensgröße, full length. Lebenskraft, -kraft, f. pl. -kräfte, vital power. Lebenslang, -lang, a. lifelong; av. through life. Lebenslauf, -lāūf, m. -s, pl. -läufe, career, career of life; life, biography. Lebenslicht, -licht, n. -s, light of day; life. Lebensluft, -luft, f. pl. -lüfte, vital air. Lebenslust, -lŭzht, f. enjoyment of life. Lebensmittel, -mittel, s. pl. victuals, provisions, food. Lebensordnung, -ordnung, f. diet, regimen. Lebensregel, -rāgel, f. pl. -n, rule of life. Lebensstrafe, -shträfe, f. pl. -n, capital punishment. Lebenstheile, -tāēle, s. pl. vitals. Lebensunterhalt, -ynterhalt, m. -es, livelihood, subsistence, sustenance. Lebensversicherung, -fersicherung, f. life-insurance. Lebenswandel, -vandel, m. -s, course of life, conduct. Lebenswärme, -verme, f. vital warmth. Lebensweise, -vēīse, f. way of life. Lebensweisheit, -vēīshāēt, f. practical wisdom, worldly wisdom. Lebenszeichen, -tsāēchen, n. -s, sign of life. Lebenszeit, -tsāēt, f. lifetime. Lebensziel, -tsīl, n. -s, aim or object of one's life.
Leber, lā'ber, f. pl. -n, liver; von der — weg sprechen, to speak openly.
Leberbrand, -brand, m. -es, distemper, inflammation of the liver (of sheep, etc.). Leberentzündung, -entsündung, f. hepatitis, inflammation of the liver. Leberherz, -erts, n. -es, pl. -e, reddish ore (of copper mercury or iron). Leberfarbe,

-farbe, f. liver-color. Le'berfar-
ben, Le'berfarbig, a. liver-colored.
Le'berflecken, -flecken, m. -s, mole,
freckle. Le'berlies, -ks, m. -es, pl.
-e, hepatic pyrites. Le'berkrankheit,
-krankhäet, f. pl. -en, liver complaint. Le'berreim, -räem, m. -s,
pl. -e, doggerel verse. Le'berflein,
-catken, m. hepatite. Le'bertran,
-trän, liver-oil. Le'berwurft, -vyrzht,
f. liver-pudding.
Lebewohl, lābevōl', n. -s, farewell.
Lebhaft, lāb'haft, a. lively, vivacious,
sprightly, bright; -igkeit, -käet, f.
liveliness, vivacity.
Lebkuchen, lēb'kuchen, m. honey-cake,
ginger-bread.
Leblos, lēb'lōs, a. lifeless. Leb'zeiten,
-tseīten, s. pl. lifetime.
Lechzen, lech'tsen, vi. to pant, thirst;
to gape from heat.
Leck, lěck, a. av. leaky; m. -es, pl. -e,
leak; einen — bekommen, to spring
a leak. Leckage, lěcka͞zī', f. leak-
age. Lecken, lěk'ken, vt. to leak.
Lecken, lěk'ken, vi. to lick. Lecker,
lěk'ker, m. -s, licker; dainty person; tongue; a. delicate, delicious,
dainty; lickerish. Lecferbissen,
-bissen, m. -s, dainty; tidbit; delicacy; sweetmeat. Leckerhaft, -haft,
a. dainty, lickerish; -igkeit, -käet,
f. daintiness. Leckermaul, -möul,
n. -es, pl. -mäuler, Lecferzahn, -tsān,
m. -s, dainty person, Epicure.
Lection, lěktsion', f. pl. -en, lesson.
Lecture, lěktū're, f. pl. -en, reading.
Leder, lē'der, s. leather. Le'derband,
-band, m. -s, pl. -bände, binding in
leather, book bound in leather. Le'-
derbereiter, -beräeter, m. currier, lea-
ther-dresser. Le'derhandel, -handel,
m. -s, leather-trade. Le'derhändler,
-hendler, m. -s, dealer in leather.
Le'derhandschuh, -handshy, m. -es,
pl. -e, leather-glove. Le'der-
hosen, s. pl. leather-breeches. Le'-
dern, lē'dern, a. leathern, of leather;
vt. to cover with leather; to curry,
drub. Le'derwerk, -věrk, n. -s, lea-
ther-work.
Ledig, lā'dich, a. empty, vacant, free,
loose; single, unmarried; lediger
Stand, Le'digkeit, -käet, f. unmarried state. Le'diglich, -lich, av. solely,
entirely.

Lee, lā, n. -s, lee; leeside. Leebord,
lā'bord, n. -s, larboard.
Leer, lēr, a. empty, void, blank, vacant. Leere, lē're, f. Leerheit, lēr'-
häet, f. emptiness, vacuum. Leeren,
lē'ren, vt. to empty, evacuate,
clear.
Leesegel, lā'sēgel, n. -s, studding-sail.
Lee'seite, -sēte, f. leeside. Lee'wärts,
-vërts, av. leeward.
Lefze, lěf'tse, f. pl. -n, lip.
Legal, legāl', a. legal. Legalisiren,
legalis'ren, vt. to legalize. Legalität, legalität', f. legality.
Legat, legāt', m. -en, pl. -en, legate.
Legat, legāt', n. -es, pl. -e, legacy,
bequest.
Legation, legatsiōn', f. pl. -en. legation; -strath, -rāt, m. counsellor of
embassy; -sekretär, -sekretär, m.
secretary to an embassy.
Legen, lā'gen, vt. to lay, place, put;
nahe legen, to give a hint; Hand legen an, to lay hands on; to do violence to; an den Tag —, to make
manifest; sich —, to abate; to go to
bed; sich — auf, to apply one's self
to; sich ins Mittel —, to interpose.
Legende, legen'de, f. legend.
Leger, lāger, m. layer.
Leghuhn, lāg'hyn, n. -es, pl. -hühner,
layer, laying-hen.
Legion, legiōn', f. pl. -en, legion.
Legiren, legīr'en, vt. to alloy. Legi-
rung, legīr'yng, f. alloy.
Legitim, legitīm', a. lawful, legitimate.
Legitimiren, legitimīr'en, vt. to legitimate. Legitimität, legitimität',
f. legitimacy.
Lehde, lā'de, f. pl. -n, waste land.
Lehen, lā'en, n. -s, fief.
Lehm, lām, m. -es, pl. -e, clay, loam.
Lehmen, lām'en, vt. to daub with
clay. Lehmern, lā'mern, a. clayey.
Lehmgrube, -grybe, f. pl. -n, clay-
pit.
Lehnbank, lān'bank, f. pl. -bänke, set-
tee.
Lehnbar, lān'bār, a. feudal; -keit,
-käet, f. feudalism. Lehndienst,
lān'dīnst, m. -es, pl. -e, feudal ser-
vice.
Lehne, lā'ne, f. pl. -n, support, railing; slope, declivity. Lehnen, lān'-
en, vt. v. r. to lean against or upon.
Lehnrecht, lān'recht, n. feudal law.

Lehnſeſſel, lān'sössel, m. -s, **Lehnſtuhl,** lān'zhtyl, m. -s, pl. -ſtühle, armchair.

Lehnsherr, lāns'hĕrr, m. -n, pl. -n, liege-lord. **Lehnsrecht,** -recht, n. feudal right.

Lehramt, lēr'amt, n. office, profession of a teacher. **Lehr'anſtalt,** -anzhtalt, f. pl. -en, school, institution, academy. **Lehr'art,** -ärt, f. pl. -en, method of teaching. **Lehr'bogen,** -bōgen, centre of, centering. **Lehr'brief,** -brīf, m. -s, pl. -e, indenture. **Lehr'buch,** -bych, n. -s, pl. -bücher, manual, compendium. **Lehr'burſche,** -burshe, m. -n, pl. -n, apprentice. **Lehre,** lā're, f. pl. -n, doctrine, dogma, rule, precept; model; pattern; in die — thun, to apprentice, to bind an apprentice. **Lehren,** lēr'en, vt. to teach, instruct, profess. **Lehrer,** lēr'er, m. -s, teacher, instructor, professor; -in, f. pl. -innen, teacher, instructress. **Lehrfach,** lēr'fach, n. -es, pl. -fächer, department of teaching. **Lehrform,** -form, f. pl. -en, didactic form. **Lehrgedicht,** -gedicht, n. -es, pl. -e, didactic poem. **Lehrgeld,** -geld, n. apprentice-fee; experience bought by losses. **Lehrherr,** -hĕrr, m. -n, pl. -n, master, boss. **Lehrjahre,** -yäre, s. pl. years of apprenticeship. **Lehrjunge,** lēr'yunge, m. -n, pl. -n, **Lehrling,** -ling, m. -s, pl. -e, apprentice. **Lehrmeiſter,** -māchter, m. -s, teacher, master, instructor. **Lehrreich,** -rīch, a. instructive. **Lehrſaal,** -sāl, m. -es, pl. -ſäle, auditory. **Lehrſatz,** -sats, m. -es, pl. -ſätze, theorem, tenet, dogma. **Lehrſpruch,** lēr'zhpruch, m. -es, pl. -ſprüche, maxim, aphorism. **Lehrſtand,** -shtant, m. body of teachers; profession of a teacher. **Lehrſtelle,** -shtelle, f. pl. -n, situation of a teacher. **Lehrſtube,** -zhtybe, f. pl. -n, school-room. **Lehrſtuhl,** -zhtyl, m. -es, pl. -ſtühle, professor's chair. **Lehrton,** -tōn, m. -es, dogmatic tone or style. **Lehr'zeit,** -tsēīt, f. time of apprenticeship.

Leib, līb, m. -es, pl. -er, body, belly, waist (dress); body: wohl bei Leibe, fat, corpulent; bei Leibe nicht, not on your life. **Leibarzt,** līb'artst, m. -es, pl. -ärzte, physician-in-ordinary to (the king, etc.). **Leib'binde,** -bīnde, f. pl. -n, binder; scarf. **Leib'chen,** -chen, -s, bodice. **Leib'chirurg,** -chirurg, m. -en, pl. -en, surgeon-in-ordinary. **Leibeigen,** līb'īgen, a. bond. **Leib'eigener,** -īgener, m. -n, pl. -n, serf, bondsman. **Leib'eigenthum,** -īgentym, n. serfdom. **Leiben,** līb'ben, vi. to appear, live, to be bodily; wie er leibt und lebt, his very self. **Leibesbeſchaffenheit,** -esbeshaffenhāīt, f. bodily constitution. **Leib'esfrucht,** -frycht, f. offspring; fœtus. **Leib'esgeſtalt,** -gezshtalt, f. pl. -en, figure, form. **Leib'esgröße,** -gröhse, f. stature. **Leib'eskraft,** -kraft, f. pl. -eskräfte, bodily strength; aus Leibeskräften, with might and main. **Leib'esleben,** -lēben, n. -s, lifetime; bei —, while alive. **Leib'esnahrung,** -nārung, f. nourishment. **Leib'eſſen,** -essen, n. **Leib'gericht,** -gericht, n. pl. -e, favorite dish. **Leib'esſorge,** -sorge, f. pl. -n, care of the body. **Leib'esſtrafe,** -shtrafe, f. pl. -n, corporal punishment. **Leib'esübung,** -ühbung, f. pl. -en, bodily exercise; pl. gymnastic exercises. **Leib'farbe,** -farbe, f. pl. -n, favorite color. **Leib'gedinge,** -gedinge, n. -s, appanage. **Leib'gurt,** -gurt, m. -es, pl. -e, **Leib'gürtel,** -gürtel, m. -s, belt, waistbelt. **Leib'haft,** -haft, **Leib'haftig,** -haftig, a. bodily, visible, real, incarnate. **Leib'koch,** -kŏch, m. -s, pl. -köche, cook to (a prince, etc.). **Leiblich,** -lich, a. bodily. **Leib'rente,** -rente, f. pl. -n, annuity, life-rent. **Leib'ſchneiden,** -shnēīden, n. -s, griping. **Leib'ſpruch,** -zhpruch, m. favorite maxim. **Leib'wache,** -vache, f. pl. -n, body-guard.

Leich, lǣch, m. -es, spawn.

Leichdorn, lēīch'dorn, m. -s, pl. -e, corn.

Leiche, lēī'che, f. pl. -n, corpse, dead body; funeral.

Leichenacker, lēī'chenaker, m. -s, burying-ground. **Lei'chenartig,** -ārtich, **Lei'chenhaft,** -haft, a. corpse-like, cadaverous, ghastly; funereal. **Lei'chenbegängniß,** -begängniss, n. -niſſes, pl. -niſſe, funeral. **Lei'chenbeſtattung,** -gšētung, f. pl. -en, funeral-train. **Lei'chenbeſorger,** -besorger, m. -s, undertaker. **Lei'chen-**

Leiблаß, -blaß, *a.* as pale as death. **Lei'chendieb**, -dīb. *m. -s, pl. -e,* resurrection-man. **Lei'chengedicht**, -gedicht, *n. -es, pl. -e,* elegy, funeral poem. **Lei'chengruft**, -gruft, *f. pl.* -grüfte, vault, burial-vault, family-vault. **Lei'chenkosten**, -kŏzhten, *s. pl.* funeral expenses. **Lei'chenmahl**, -māl, *n. -es, pl. -e,* funeral meal. **Lei'chenmusik**, -mŭsīk, *f.* funeral music. **Lei'chenrede**, -rāde, *f. pl. -n,* funeral sermon or oration. **Lei'chenschau**, -shŏu, *f.* inquest. **Lei'chenstein**, -zhtīīen, *m. -s, pl. -e,* tomb-stone. **Lei'chentuch**, -tŭch, *n. -s, pl.* -tücher, shroud; pall. **Lei'chenwagen**, -vāgen, *m. -s, pl.* -wägen, hearse. **Lei'chenzug**, -tsŭg, *m. -s, pl.* -züge, funeral procession. **Leichnam**, leīch'nām, *m. -s, pl. -e,* corpse, dead body. **Leicht**, leīcht, *a.* light, easy, unimportant, thin, slight, *av.* easily. **Leicht'bewaffnet**, -bevaffnet, *a.* light-armed. **Leicht'blütig**, -blūtich, *a.* sanguine, cheerful, hopeful. **Leicht'fertig**, -fertich, *a.* frivolous, wanton; -keit, -kāet, *f.* frivolity. **Leicht'füßig**, -fūhssich, *a.* light-footed. **Leicht'gläubig**, -glŏibich, *a.* credulous; *av. -ly.* **Leicht'gläubigkeit**, -kāet, *f.* credulity. **Leicht'igkeit**, -ichkāet, *f.* lightness, swiftness, ease, easiness. **Leicht'sinn**, -sinn, *m.* levity, frivolity. **Leicht'sinnig**, -sinnich, *a.* giddy, heedless. **Leid**, līēd, *n.* hurt, harm, grief, sorrow; sorry, unpleasant: leid thun, to cause sorrow; es ist mir leid, I am sorry for. **Leiden**, leī'den (litt, gelitten), *vt.* to suffer, endure, bear, undergo; to like; *s. n.* suffering, affliction, passion. **Leidend**, leīd'end, *a.* suffering, sick; passive. **Leid'enschaft**, -shaft, *f.* passion: -lich, -lich, *a.* passionate, impassioned; -keit, -kāet, *f.* passionateness, vehemence. **Leid'ensgefährte**, -gefārte, *m. -n,* **Leid'ensgenosse**, -nosse, *m. -n,* fellow-sufferer. **Leid'ensgeschichte**, -geschichte, *f.* history of the sufferings. **Leid'enskelch**, -kelch, *m.* cup of sorrow. **Leid'entlich**, -entlich, *a.* tolerable; passive. **Leider**, līēd'er, *av.* unfortunately, alas. **Leidig**, līēd'ich, *a.* unfortunate, disagreeable. **Leidlich**, līēd'lich, *a.* passable,

tolerable, pretty well. **Leidwesen**, līēd'vēsen, *n.* sorrow, affliction, grief, regret.
Leier, leī'er, *f.* lyre: alte —, old tune, the same thing. **Leiern**, leī'ern, *vt.* to play on the lyre; to drawl.
Leihbank, leī'bank, *f.* accommodation-bank, loan-office; pawn-house. **Leih'bibliothek**, -bibliotāk, *f.* circulating library. **Leihen**, leī'en (lieh, geliehen), *vt.* to lend, loan; borrow.
Leik, leīk, *n. pl.* **Leike**, hull; bolt-rope.
Leilacken, leī'lacken, *n.* sheet.
Leim, leīm, *m. pl. -e,* glue, lime; clay. **Leimen**, leīm'en, *vt.* to glue; to size. **Leim'ig**, -ig, **Leim'icht**, -icht, *a.* gluey, viscous; clayey. **Leim'ruthe**, -rute, *f.* lime-twig. **Leim'sieder**, -sīder, *m.* glue-boiler. **Leim'wasser**, -vasser, *n.* glue-water, size.
Lein, leīn, *m.* flax; linen. **Leine**, leī'ne, *f.* line, cord, small rope. **Lein'en**, *a.* linen; *s.* linen-cloth, linen-yarn, linen. **Lein'tuch**, -tŭch, *n.* sheet. **Lein'wand**, -vand, *f.* linen. **Lein'weber**, -vēber, *m.* linen-weaver; -ei, -eī', *f.* trade of a linen-weaver; manufacturer of linen. **Lein'weberstuhl**, -zhtŭl, *m.* linen-weaver's loom. **Lein'zeug**, -tseūg, *n.* linen.
Leise, leī'se, *a.* low, soft, still, gentle, *av. -ly*; nicely.
Leistbar, leīst'bār, *a.* practicable; -keit, -kāet, *f.* practicability. **Leiste**, leī'ste, *f.* ledge, border, bracket; fillet, listel; list; tail-piece (Print.); edge, border; groin. **Leisten**, leī'sten, *m.* last, model. **Leisten**, leī'sten, *vt.* to perform, accomplish, render, afford; Gesellschaft —, to keep one's company; Gehorsam —, to obey; Eid —, to take an oath. **Leistenband**, leī'stenband, *n.* inguinal ligament. **Leistenbeule**, -beūle, *f.* bubo. **Leistung**, leī'stung, *f.* performance.
Leiten, leī'ten, *vt.* to lead, guide, direct. **Leiter**, leī'ter, *m.* leader, guide; conductor; ladder; scale; stay-sail. **Lei'terbaum**, -baūm, *m. pl.* -bäume, ladder-beam. **Lei'terstraße**, -zhprosse, *f.* round of a ladder, rundle. **Lei'terwagen**, -vägen, *m. pl.* -wagen, wagon with racks.
Leitfaden, leīt'fāden, *m. pl.* -fäden,

Leu 204 Lie

leading-line; guide, manual. **Leit's hammel,** -hammel, *m.* bell-wether. **Leitseil,** -säel, *n. pl.* -e, leash. **Leitstern,** -zhtërn, *m. pl.* -e, guiding-star, load-star, pole-star. **Leittau,** -täu, *n. pl.* -e, ladder-rope, man-rope. **Leitung,** -ung, *f.* leading, guidance, direction, management; **sdraht,** -drät, *m. pl.* -brähte, voltaic wire; **sröhre,** -röre, *f.* conduit-pipe. **Leitwagen,** -vägen, *m.* sweep.
Lende, lęn'dę, *f.* loin. **Lendenbraten,** -bräten, *m.* surloin. **Lendengicht,** -gicht, *f.* sciatic, hip-gout. **Lendengries,** -grīs, *m.* gravel in the kidneys. **Lendenlahm,** -läm, *a.* hipshot; sluggardly. **Lendenschmerz,** -shmērts, *m.* -ęs, *pl.* -en. **Lendenweh,** lęn'denvä, *n.* lumbago, sciatica.
Lenken, lęnk'en, *vt.* to turn, bend, guide, direct, steer, rule, manage. **Lenker,** lęnk'ęr, *m.* guider; ruler. **Lenkriemen,** -rīmen, *m.* rein. **Lenksam,** -sam, *a.* tractable, manageable; **-keit,** -kãet, *f.* tractableness, manageableness. **Lenkscheit,** -shãit, *n. pl.* -e, sway-bar. **Lenkschnur,** shngr, *f. pl.* -schnüre. **Lenkseil,** -sãel, *n. pl.* -e, line, rein. **Lenkung,** -ung, *f.* direction, management, steering.
Lenz, lęnts, *m. pl.* -e, spring.
Leopard, lã'opard, *m.* leopard.
Lerche, lęrd'ę, *f.* lark; larch.
Lernbegierde, lērn'bęgïrdę, *f.* desire of learning. **Lernen,** lēr'nen, *vt.* to learn; to teach, to apprentice; auswendig —, to learn by heart, to commit to memory; **lennen** —, to become acquainted with.
Lesart, lēs'ärt, *f.* reading. **Lesbar,** -bär, *a.* legible, readable; *av.* legibly; **-keit,** -kãet, *f.* legibility. **Lese,** lã'sę, *f.* cleaning, gathering, vintage. **Lesebuch,** -buǵ, *n. pl.* -bücher, reader, manual. **Lesekreis,** -krães, *m. pl.* -e, (circle of) readers. **Leser,** lã'sęr, *m.* reader. **Leserlich,** -lich, *a.* readable, legible. **Leseübung,** -übung, *f.* reading-exercise. **Lesezeichen,** -tsãechen, *n.* bookmark; dog's ear. **Lesung,** lã'sung, *f.* reading.
Lethargie, lętargï', *f.* lethargy.
Letten, lęt'ten, *m.* clay, potter's clay.
Lettig, lęt'tich, *a.* clayey.
Letzt, lętst, *a.* last, *av.* lastly; **letzte**

Ölung, extreme unction. **Letzte,** lęts'tę, *f.* the end. **Letzthin,** -hïn, **Letztlich,** -lich, *av.* lately, the other day.
Leu, lẽü, *m.* -en, *pl.* -en, lion. **Leuchte,** lẽüch'tę, *f.* light, lamp, lantern. **Leuchten,** lẽüch'ten, *vi.* to shine, to light, flash. **Leuchtend,** *a.* shining; glorious, bright. **Leuchter,** lẽüch'tēr, *m.* candlestick. **Leuchtfeuer,** -fẽüēr, *n.* beacon. **Leuchtkäfer,** -kãfēr, *m.* glowworm. **Leuchtstein,** -zhtãen, *m. pl.* -e, Bolognian stone. **Leuchtthurm,** -tųrm, *m. pl.* -thürme, pharos, light-house.
Leumund, lẽü'mund, *m.* repute, reputation, name.
Leute, lẽü'tę, *z. pl.* people, folks, persons.
Leutschen, lẽüt'shēll, *a.* bashful, shy. **Leutselig,** -sēlich, *a.* affable, condescending; **-keit,** -kãet, *f.* affability, kindness.
Levkoje, lefkoi'yę, *f.* stock-gilliflower. **Lexikon,** lex'ikon, *n. pl.* Lexika, dictionary.
Linstall, li'aaskalk, *m. pl.* -e, lias.
Libell, libēll', *n. pl.* -e, libel.
Liberal, liberäl', *a.* liberal; *av.* liberally. **Liberaler,** liberäl'ēr, *m.* liberal. **Liberalismus,** liberalīs'mus, *m.* liberalism.
Licenz, litsęnts', *f.* license.
Licht, licht, *n. pl.* -er, light, candle; luminary; *a.* light, bright. **Lichten,** lich'ten, *vt.* to brighten; to clear up; to thin out.
Lichten, lich'ten, *vt.* to lighten; to heave up; den Anker —, to weigh anchor.
Lichterloh, lich'tērlõ, *av.* blazing, in bright flames. **Lichterhalter,** -halter, *m.* saveall. **Lichthut,** licht'hųt, *m. pl.* -hüte, jesuit, extinguisher. **Lichtmess,** licht'mēss, *f.* Candlemas. **Lichtmesser,** -mēssēr, *m.* photometer. **Lichtputze,** -pųtsę, *f.* **Lichtscheere,** -shērę, *f.* snuffers. **Lichtscheu,** -shẽü, *a.* shunning the light. **Lichtschirm,** -shïrm, *m. pl.* -e, lamp-shade, lamp-screen. **Lichtstrahl,** -zhträl, *m.* -s, *pl.* -en, ray, beam of light. **Lichtzieher,** licht'tsï-ēr, *m.* tallow-chandler.

Lieb, lïb, *a.* dear, beloved; **lieb haben,** to love, to like; **das ist mir lieb,** I am glad of it; **lieber Gott!** good God. **Liebäugeln,** -ãügęln, *vi.* to

eye fondly, to ogle. **Liebchen,** lïb'-chen, *n.* sweetheart, darling, love.
Liebe, lï'be, *f.* love, affection; charity. **Liebelei,** lïbelī', *f.* flirtation.
Liebeln, lï'beln, *vt. i,* to flirt, dally.
Lieben, lï'ben, *vt.* to love, cherish, be fond of; *vi.* to love, be in love.
Liebenswürdig, lï'bensvürdich, *a.* amiable, lovely; **-keit, -kāet,** *f.* amiableness, loveliness **Lieber,** lï'ber, *av.* rather. **Liebesabenteuer,** lï'besäbentöiliär, *n.* love-adventure.
Liebesblick, -blick, *m. pl. -e,* look of love. **Liebesbrief,** -brīf, *m. pl. -e,* love-letter. **Liebesdienst,** -dīnzht. *m. pl. -e,* kind office. **Liebeserklärung,** -ērklärung, *f.* proposal. **Liebespfeil,** -pfēīl, *m. pl. -e,* shaft of love. **Liebestrank,** -trank, *m. pl. -e,* philter, love-potion. **Liebesstern,** -chtērn, *m.* star of love. **Liebeswonne,** -vonne, *f.* delight of love.
Liebeszeichen, -tsāichen, *n.* token of love, love-favor.
Liebhaber, lïb'häber, *m. -in, f.* lover; amateur. **Liebhaberei,** -häberäī', *f.* fondness, partiality, preference.
Liebkosen, -kōsen, *vt.* to caress, fondle. **Liebkosung,** -kōsung. *f.* caress, endearment. **Lieblich,** -lich, *a.* lovely, charming, sweet, delightful; **-keit, -kāet,** *f.* loveliness, sweetness, amenity. **Liebling,** -ling, *m. pl. -e,* favorite, darling; **-gericht, -gericht,** *f.* favorite dish. **Lieblos, -lōs,** *a.* unkind, uncharitable; rough. **Lieblosigkeit,** -kāet, *f.* unkindness, unfeelingness. **Liebreich,** lïb'rēich, *a.* kind, gentle, sweet. **Liebreiz, -rāets,** *m.* charm, grace, attraction; **-end,** -ent, *a.* charming. **Liebschaft,** -shaft, *f.* amour, love-intrigue. love-affair.
Liebste, lïps'te, *f.* **Liebster,** lïps'ter, *m.* beloved one, love. **Liebthätig,** -tätich, *a.* charitable; **-keit, -kāet,** *f.* charity.
Lied, līd, *n. pl. -er,* song, lay; warbling, note, tune; hymn. **Liedchen,** -chen, *n.* ditty, little song. **Liederbuch,** -buch. *n.* song-book. **Liederkranz,** -krants, *m. pl. -kränze,* collection of songs; circle of singers, singing-club.
Liederlich, lī'dērlich, *a.* loose; disorderly, dissolute, wretched, paltry, careless; **-keit, -kāet,** *f.* looseness, dissoluteness.

Liederreich, lī'dērrēich, *a.* rich in songs.
Lief, līf, *prt. v.* **Laufen.**
Lieferant, līfērant', *m.* contractor, purveyor, furnisher. **Liefern,** lī'fern, *vt.* to deliver; to furnish. provide with. **Lieferung,** -ung, *f.* delivery, supply; furnishing; number, part (of a book).
Liegen, lī'gen (lag, gelegen), *vi.* to lie; to be situated; **vor Anker —,** to ride at anchor.
Lien, līn, *f.* line, cord, rope; **-bahn,** -bān, *f.* rope-walk.
Lieutenant, lēū'tnant, *m. pl. -e,* lieutenant.
Lila, lī'lä, **Lilaf,** lī'lack, *m.* lilac.
Lilafarben, -farben, *a.* lilac-colored.
Lilie, lī'li-e, *f.* lily. **Lilienweiss,** -vēīs, *a.* lilywhite, white as a lily.
Limonade, limōnä'de, *f.* lemonade.
Limone, limō'ne, *f.* lemon.
Lind, Linde, lin'de, *a.* soft, mild, *av.* -ly, gently.
Linde, lin'de, *f.* lind, linden (tree), **Lindenbaum,** *a.* linden.
Lindern, lin'dērn, *vt.* to mitigate, soften, soothe. **Linderung,** -ung. *f.* mitigation, alleviation; **-mittel,** -mittel, *n.* palliative. **Lindigkeit,** -dichkāet, *f.* lenity, mildness, softness.
Lindwurm, lind'vŭrm, *m. pl. -würmer,* dragon.
Lineal, line-äl', *n. pl. -e,* rule, ruler.
Lineament, line-ament', *n. pl. -e,* feature, lineament.
Linguist, linguist', *m. -en, pl. -en,* linguist.
Linie, lī'nī-e, *f.* line, lineage. **Liniensschiff,** -shiff', *n. pl. -e,* ship of the line. **Linientruppen,** -trŭppen, *s. pl.* regulars.
Liniren, linī'ren, *vt.* to rule.
Linke, lin'ke. *a.* left-handed; *s.* left hand; **zur Linken,** on the left. **Linkisch,** link'ish, *a.* awkward. **Links,** links, *av.* on the left, to the left side; awkward; **— sein,** to be left-handed. **Linksum, -ŭm,** *av.* to the left, left.
Linnen, lin'nen, *n.* linen; **-zeug,** -tsēūg, *n.* linen.
Linon, lin'ong, *m.* lawn.
Linse, lin'se, *f.* lentil; lens; **-gericht,** -gericht, *n. pl. -e,* dish of lentils
Linsenglas, -gläs, *n.* lens.

18

Lippe, lip'pe, f. lip. **Lip'penbuchstabe**, -buchztābe, m. -n, pl. -n, labial (letter).
Liquidiren, liquidī'ren, vt. to clear, settle (accounts).
Lispeln, lis'pelu, vi. to lisp, whisper; s. n. lisp, whisper.
List, list, f. art, craft, stratagem, cunning, artifice.
Liste, lis'te, f. list, roll, catalogue.
Listig, lis'tig, a. artful, cunning, crafty, sly.
Litanei, litanēī', f. litany.
Literarisch, litērär'ish, a. literary. **Literat**, litērāt', m. -en, pl. -en, man of letters. **Literatur**, litērātūr', f. literature.
Lithograph, litogräf', m. -en, pl. -en, lithographer. **Lithographie**, litogrāfī', f. lithography.
Liturgie, liturgī', f. liturgy.
Litze, lit'se, f. lace, bobbin, cord.
Livree, livrā', f. livery.
Lob, lōb, n. praise, commendation; Gott lob! thank God! **Loben**, lō'ben, vt. to praise. **Lo'benswerth**, -vert, a. praiseworthy. **Lo'beserhebung**, -ērhäbung, f. praise; encomium. **Lobgesang**, -gesang, m. pl. -gesänge, **Loblied**, lōb'līd, n. pl. -er, hymn, song of praise. **Lobhudelei**, lōb'hudelēī, f. fulsome praise. **Löblich**, lōb'lich, a. laudable, commendable; -keit, -kāēt, f. laudableness. **Lobpreisen**, lōb'prēīsen, vt. to praise, exalt, extol. **Lobrede**, lōb'rāde, f. eulogy, encomium, panegyric. **Lob'redner**, -rādner, m. panegyrist. **Lob'singen**, -singen, vt. to sing, praise; to extol. **Lobspruch**, -zhpruch, m. pl. -sprüche, panegyric, encomium.
Local, lokāl', a. local; s. n. pl. -e, locality, apartments. **Localität**, -itāt', f. locality.
Loch, loch, n. pl. **Löcher**, hole; opening; pore; jail, dungeon; -beutel, -bōītel, m. mortise-chisel; -eisen, -ēīsen, n. punch; -feile, -fēīle, f. round file. **Locher**, loch'er, m. large gimlet. **Löcherig**, loch'erig, a. full of holes, perforated; porous. **Lochring**, loch'ring, m. **Lochscheibe**, -shēībe, f. ringstand. **Lochsäge**, loch'säge, f. fretsaw.
Lociren, lotsī'ren, vt. to rank, locate.
Locke, lock'e, f. curl, ringlet. **Locken**, lock'en, vt. to curl.
Locken, lock'en, vt. to call, allure, entice, draw on.
Lockenkopf, lock'enkopf, m. curly head.
Locker, lock'er, a. loose, spongy; slack; extravagant, dissolute; -heit, -hāēt, f. looseness. **Lockern**, lock'ern, vt. to loosen, relax.
Lockig, lock'ich, a. curled, curly.
Lockpfeife, lock'pfēīfe, f. bird-call. **Lockspeise**, -zhpēīse, f. bait, decoy. **Lockung**, -ung, f. allurement, enticement. **Lockvogel**, -fōgel, m. pl. -vögel, decoy-bird.
Locomotive, lokomotī've, f. locomotive (engine). **Locomotivpfeife**, -prēīfe, f. steam-whistle.
Lodern, lō'dērn, vi. to blaze, flame, flare.
Löffel, löf'fel, m. spoon, ladle; -gans, -gants, f. pl. -gänse, spoon-bill, pelican. **Löffeln**, vt. to eat with a spoon; to ladle. **Löffelstiel**, -zhtīl, m. handle of a spoon.
Log, lōg, m. und n. -es, pl. -e, log (Mar.).
Logarithme, logarit'me, f. logarithm.
Logbuch, lōg'buch, n. pl. -bücher, log-book.
Loge, lō'zhe, f. lodge; box.
Loggen, log'gen, vt. to (heave the) log.
Logik, lō'gik, f. logic.
Logiren, lozhī'ren, vt. to lodge, reside.
Logis, lozhī', n. lodging.
Logisch, lō'gish, a. logical; av. logically.
Logleine, lōg'lāēne, f. log-line. **Log'rolle**, -rolle, f. roll of the log.
Loh, lō, a. blazing, flaming; av. -ly.
Lohbeize, lō'bāētse, f. tanning; tanpit; ooze. **Lohe**, lō'e, f. tan.
Lohe, lō'e, f. blaze, flame. **Lohen**, lō'en, vi. to blaze.
Lohen, lō'en, vt. to tan. **Lohfarbe**, -farbe, f. tan-color. **Lohfarben**, **Lohfarbig**, -farbich, a. tancolored. **Lohgar**, lō'gär, a. tanned. **Lohgerber**, lō'gērber, m. tanner. **Lohgerberei**, -ēī', f. tannery. **Loh'mühle**, -mühle, f. tan-mill.
Lohn, lōn, m. hire, pay, wages; reward. **Lohnarbeiter**, -ärbāēter, m. jobber, laborer. **Lohnen**, lōn'en, vt. to pay, to requite, recompense, reward; vr. to pay, to be worth while. **Lohnend**, a. remunerative. **Lohn'kutsche**, -kutshe, f. hackney-coach

Löhnung, lön'ụng, *f.* pay, payment; **-stag**, -täg, *m. pl. -e*, pay-day.

Loos, lōs, *n. pl. -e*, lot, allotment; share; fate. **Loosen**, lōs'ẹn, *vi.* to draw lots, to cast lots; — um to raffle. **Loos'ung**, -ụng, *f.* casting lots, raffling; watchword; **-wort**, -vort, *n. pl. -e*, watchword.

Lootse, lōt'sẹ, *m.* pilot. **Loot'sen**, *vt.* to pilot.

Lorbeer, lōr'bär, *m.* laurel, bay; **-baum**, -bäum, *m. pl. -bäume*, laurel-tree, bay-tree. **Lor'beerblatt**, -blatt, *n. pl. -blätter*, laurel-leaf. **Lor'beergrün**, -grün, *n.* laurel-green. **Lor'beerkranz**, -krants, *m. pl. -kränze*, **Lor'beerkrone**, -krōnẹ, *f.* laurel-wreath, crown of laurel.

Lorgnette, lornèt'tẹ, *f.* lorgnette, opera-glass.

Los, lōs, *a.* loose, slack, flowing, free, untied; — sein, to be loose, to be rid of; — werden, to get rid of; *av.* on, forward. **Los'brechen**, -brechen, *vi.* to break off; to break out.

Löschblatt, lösh'blatt, *n. pl. -blätter*, blotting-paper. **Löschen**, lösh'en, *vt.* to quench, extinguish, slake; to light, unload, land; to blot out, cancel. **Lösch'papier**, -papīr, *n.* blotting-paper. **Lösch'platz**, -plats, *m.* wharf. **Lösch'ung**, -ụng, *f.* quenching; discharging, unloading; **-hafen**, -häfen, *m.* port of delivery.

Losdrücken, lōs'drücken, *vt.* to discharge, fire off.

Lose, lō'sẹ, *a.* loose, vagrant; dissolute, wanton, mischievous, playful; base, wicked.

Lösegeld, löh'segeld, *n. pl. -er*, ransom.

Lösen, löh'sẹn, *vt.* to loose, unravel; uncouple; to free, redeem; to solve, find out; to receive, make (money); to dung.

Losgeben, lōs'gēben, *vt.* to release, discharge; emancipate.

Losgehen, lōs'gā-ẹn, *vi.* to go off; — auf, to go towards, to charge.

Loskaufen, lōs'käufen, *vt.* to redeem, ransom; to exempt.

Loskommen, lōs'kommen, *vi.* to get off, to get away, escape.

Loslassen, lōs'lassen, *vt.* to let go, release, discharge.

Losmachen, lōs'machen, *vt.* to loosen, disengage, detach; to clear from.

Losreißen, lōs'reīssen, *vt.* to tear off, pull away; sich —, to tear one's self away.

Losschießen, lōs'shīssen, *vt.* to discharge, fire off; *vi.* to rush upon.

Losschlagen, lōs'shlāgen, *vt.* to knock off; to sell (at a loss).

Losschnallen, lōs'shnallen, *vt.* to unbuckle.

Losschnüren, lōs'shnüren, *vt.* to unlace, untie.

Lossprechen, lōs'zhprechen, *vt.* to absolve, acquit; to free.

Lossprengen, lōs'zhpreng-ẹn, *vi.* to rush upon; to blast off.

Losspringen, lōs'zhpring-ẹn, *vi.* to fly off; — auf, to rush upon, to fly at.

Lostrennen, lōs'trennen, *vt.* to rip off; to separate.

Losung, lōs'ụng, *f. s.* Loosung, cash-box; dung.

Lösung, löhs'ụng, *f.* solution, redemption; discharge.

Loswickeln, lōs'vickeln, *vt.* to unravel, extricate, unwind.

Loswinden, lōs'vinden, *vt.* to unwind; to tear away.

Loth, lōt, *n. pl. -e*, half an ounce; plummet, lead.

Löthe, löh'tẹ, *f.* solder. **Löthen**, löh'ten, *vt.* to solder.

Lothen, lō'ten, *vi.* to sound; to plumb.

Löthig, löh'tich, *a.* of half an ounce.

Löthkolben, löht'kolben, *m.* soldering-iron.

Lothrecht, lōt'recht, *a.* perpendicular; *av.* -ly.

Löthrohr, löht'rōr, *n.* blow-pipe.

Lotte, lot'tẹ, *f.* water-pipe; air-shaft (Min.).

Lotterbube, lot'terbube, *m.* scoundrel, vagabond.

Lotterie, lotterī', *f.* lottery; **-gewinnst**, -gevinzht, *m. pl. -e*, prize.

Lotterig, lot'terich, *a.* loose, shaky. **Lottern**, lot'tern, *vi.* to be loose.

Löwe, löh'vẹ, *m. -n, pl. -n*, lion; junger —, lion's whelp; **-grube**, -grubẹ, *f.* lion's den. **Lö'wenherz**, -herts, *n. -ens, pl. -en*, lion's heart. **Lö'wenstark**, -zhtark, *a.* strong as a lion. **Löwin**, löh'vin, *f. pl. -innen*, lioness.

Luchs, lyx, *m. -e*, lynx; **-auge**, -äugẹ, *n. -s, pl. -n*, lynx's-eye.

Lücke, lück'ẹ, *f.* gap, chasm, notch; blank, white (Print.). **Lück'enbüßer**,

-büſſer, m. makeshift. **Lück'enhaft**, -haft, **Lück'ig**, -ich, a. defective, incomplete. **Lück'enhaftigkeit**, -haftichkeit, f. defectiveness, incompleteness.

Luder, lŭ'dĕr, n. carrion; decoy, bait; debauchery; jade. **Lu'derleben**, -lĕben, n. debauchery. **Lüderlich**, lüh'dĕrlich, a. dissolute, immoral, disorderly, riotous, lewd.

Luf, lŭf, f. loof, luff, weatherside.

Luft, lŭft, f. air; breeze, wind; friſche —, fresh air; — ſchöpfen, to take the air; — machen, to give vent. **Luftart**, lŭft'ärt, f. gas. **Luſtballon**, -ballōn, m. pl. -e, balloon. **Luft'bild**, -bilt, n. phantom. **Luft'blaſe**, -blāse, f. bubble. **Lüften**, lüf'ten, vt. to air; to raise up, lift. **Lufterſcheinung**, lŭft'ersheûung, f. phenomenon, meteor. **Luft'fahrt**, -färt, f. aeronautic excursion. **Luft'gehalt**, -gezhalt, f. phantom. **Luft'sheizung**, -häetsung, f. heating with hot air. **Luftig**, lŭft'ich, a. airy, aerial, lofty, light, flighty. **Luft'klappe**, -klappe, f. air-valve. **Luft'kreis**, -krēs, m. atmosphere. **Luft'loch**, loch, n. pl. -löcher, air-hole, vent. **Luft'leer**, -lēr, a. void of air. **Luft'pumpe**, -pumpe, f. air-pump. **Luft'röhre**, -röhre, f. air-tube, wind-pipe. **Luftſchiffer**, -shiffēr, m. aeronaut. **Luft'ſchloß**, -shloss, n. pl. -ſchlöſſer, castle in the air. **Luft'ſpiegelung**, -zhpigĕlung, f. mirage. **Luft'ſprung**, -zhprŭng, m. pl. -ſprünge, caper. **Luft'ventil**, -fentīl, n. pl. -e, reverse-valve, vacuum-valve.

Lug, lŭg, m. pl. -e, lie; fraud. **Lüge**, lü'gẹ, f. lie, falsehood; — ſtrafen, to give the lie to. **Lü'gen**, vi. to lie, to speak a falsehood; to deceive; simulate. **Lü'genhaft**, -haft, a. lying, false; -igkeit, -ichkäet, f. lying disposition, deceitfulness. **Lü'genmaul**, -möyl, n. pl. -mäuler, **Lüg'ner**, lühg'nēr, m. liar, deceiver. **Lüg'neriſch**, -ish, a. lying, false.

Luke, lŭ'ke, f. hatch.

Lullen, lŭl'len, vi. to hum, lull; to suckle.

Lümmel, lüm'mĕl, m. lubber, clown; -haft, -haft, a. clumsy, lubberly.

Lump, lŭmp, m. pl. -e, ragamuffin. **Lumpen**, lŭm'pen, vt. to treat as a ragamuffin; s. m. rag; -geld, -gĕlt, n. trifling expense, trifle. **Lum'pengeſindel**, -gesindĕl, n. **Lum'penpack**, -pack, n. rabble. **Lum'penhandel**, -handel, m. trade in rags; trade in trash. **Lum'penhund**, -hŭnt, m. pl. -e. **Lum'penkerl**, -kĕrl, m. shabby fellow, scoundrel.

Lumpenzucker, lŭm'pentsyckēr, m. lump-sugar.

Lumperei, lŭmpĕrēy', f. trumpery, paltry concern. **Lump'icht**, -icht, a. paltry. **Lumpig**, lŭmp'ich, a. raggy, shabby.

Lunge, lŭng'ẹ, f. lungs. **Lung'enentzündung**, -entsündung, f. inflammation of the lungs. **Lung'enflügel**, -flühgel, m. lobe of the lungs. **Lun'genſucht**, -sucht, f. phthisis, pulmonary consumption. **Lung'enſüchtig**, -süchtig, a. consumptive.

Lungern, lŭng'ĕrn, vi. to long after.

Lünn, lünn, **Lünſe**, lün'se, f. linch-pin.

Lunte, lŭn'tẹ, f. match, lunt; die — riechen, to smell a rat. **Lun'tenſtock**, -zhtock, m. pl. -ſtöcke, linstock.

Lupfen, lŭp'fen, vt. to lift, raise.

Luſt, lŭst, f. pl. Lüſte, pleasure, enjoyment, joy; desire, longing, mind; fancy. **Luſt'barkeit**, -barkĕet, f. amusement, diversion. **Luſt'dirne**, -dīrnẹ, f. prostitute. **Lüſten**, lüs'ten, vi. to lust after. **Lüſtern**, lüs'tĕrn, a. lusting, louging; lascivious. **Lüſ'ternheit**, -hĕet, f. lustfulness, lasciviousness; concupiscence. **Luſt'fahrt**, lŭst'fart, f. pleasure excursion. **Luſtig**, lŭst'ich, a. merry, jolly, jovial, gay; ſich — machen über, to ridicule, banter any one; -keit, f. gayety, merriness. **Lüſtling**, lüst'ling, m. pl. -e, debauchee, profligate. **Luſtort**, lŭst'ort, m. pl. -e, pleasure-ground. **Luſt'ſchloß**, -shloss, country-seat, villa. **Luſt'ſeuche**, -söůchẹ, f. venereal disease; syphilis. **Luſt'ſitz**, -sits, m. pl. -e, country-seat. **Luſt'ſpiel**, -zhpīl, n. pl. -e, comedy. **Luſt'wald**, -valt, m. **Luſt'wäldchen**, -vĕltchen, n. park, grove. **Luſt'wandeln**, -vandĕln, vi. to promenade, take a walk for amusement.

Luth, lŭt, f. boom.

Lutter, lŭt'tĕr, m. thin brandy.

Luxuriös, luxuriöhs', a. luxurious.

Luxus, lŭx'ŭs, m. luxury.

Lymphatiſch, lĭmfat'ish, a. lymphatic.

Lymphe, lŭm'fe, *f.* lymph. **Lymphgefäße**, lĭmpf'gefässe, *s. pl.* lymphatics.
Lyriker, lī'rĭker, *m.* lyric, lyric poet.
Lyrisch, lī'rĭsh, *a.* lyric, lyrical.

M

Maat, mät, *m. pl. -e.* mate.
Mache, mach'e, *f.* making. **Machen**, mach'en, *vt.* to make, fabricate, produce, render; to make up, constitute; to do: — **laffen**, to order, to have made. **Macherlohn**, mach'ĕrlōn, *n. u. m.* pay for making.
Machination, mächinatsiōn', *f.* intrigue, plot.
Macht, macht, *f. pl.* **Mächte**, might, power. **Machtgeber**, -gēber, *m.* constituent. **Machtgebot**, -gebŏt, *n. pl.* -e, dictation. **Machthaber**, -häber, *m.* potentate. **Mächtig**, mech'tig, *a.* mighty, powerful, strong; master of. **Mächtigkeit**, -käet, *f.* thickness, breadth, richness (of a vein). **Machtlos**, macht'lōs, *a.* powerless, impotent. **Machtspruch**, -zhpruch, *m. pl.* -sprüche, command, dictatorial sentence. **Machtvollkommenheit**, -foll kommenhäet, *f.* absolute, sovereign power. **Machtwort**, -vort, *n. pl. -e*, dictate, word of command.
Machwerk, mach'vĕrk, *n. pl. -e*, botch; performance.
Maculatur, maku̇latyr', *f.* waste paper.
Madame, madam', *f.* madam, Mrs.
Mädchen, mäd'chen, *n.* girl, maiden. **Mädchenhaft**, -haft, *a.* maidenly; -**igkeit**, -ĭchkäet, *f.* maidenliness, bashfulness. **Mädchenschule**, -shyle, *f.* school for girls.
Made, mä'de, *f.* maggot; skipper.
Magazin, magatsīn', *n. pl. -e*, magazine, warehouse, store-house; review.
Magd, makt, *f. pl.* **Mägde**, girl; servant, maid. **Mägdlein**, mĕkt'läen, *n.* little girl.
Magen, mä'gen, *m. pl.* **Mägen**, stomach: msw. **Magenblähung**, -bläung, *f.* flatulence. **Magenbrennen**, -brennen, *n.* heart-burn. **Magenentzündung**, -enttsündung, *f.* inflammation of the stomach. **Magenkrampf**, -krampf, *m.* cardialgy. **Magensaft**, -saft, *m. pl.* -säfte, gastric juice. **Magenstärkung**, -zhterkung, *f.* cordial for the stomach.
Mager, mä'gĕr, *a.* meagre, lean, thin, slender; poor, barren; -**keit**, -käet, *f.* meagreness, leanness.
Magie, magī', *f.* magic. **Magisch**, mä'gish, *a.* magical.
Magister, magĭs'ter, *m.* master of arts.
Magistrat, magĭzhträt', *m.* magistracy; -**sperson**, -persōn, *f.* magistrate.
Magnesia, mang-nā'siä, *f.* magnesia.
Magnet, mag-nāt', *m.* magnet, loadstone. **Magnetisch**, mang-ne̱t'ish, *a.* magnetic. **Magnetisiren**, mang-ne̱tisī'ren, *vt.* to magnetize. **Magnetismus**, -tĭs'mu̇s, *m.* magnetism. **Magnetnadel**, -nädel, *f.* magnetic-needle, compass-needle.
Mahagoni, mahagō'nī, *n.* mahogany.
Mahd, mäd, *f.* mowing. **Mähder**, mä'dĕr, **Mäher**, mä'ĕr, *m.* mower. **Mähen**, mä-en, *vt.* to mow.
Mahl, mäl, *n. pl. -e,* oder **Mähler**, meal, repast.
Mahl, mäl, *n. pl. -e,* oder **Mähler**, sign, token, mark; mole.
Mahlen, mä'len (*Prt.* mahlte (mahl), *Pp.* gemahlen), to grind. **Mahlgang**, mäl'gang. *m. pl.* -gänge, set of stones. **Mahlgeld**, -gĕlt, *n.* miller's fee. **Mahlmühle**, -mühle, *f.* mill, grist-mill. **Mahlschatz**, -shats, *m.* dowry, portion. **Mahlstein**, -stäen, *m. pl. -e,* landmark. **Mahlstrom**, -zhtrōm, *m. pl.* -ströme, whirlpool. **Mahlzeichen**, mäl'tsäechen, *n.* mark, sign.
Mahlzeit, mäl'tsäet, *f.* meal, repast.
Mähne, mä'ne, *f.* mane.
Mahnen, mä'nen, *vt.* to remind, admonish; dun. **Mahner**, män'ĕr, *m.* admonisher; dun. **Mahnung**, -ung, *f.* monition, warning; dunning.
Mähr, **Mähre**, mä're, *f.* tiding, tale. **Mährchen**, mär'chen, *n.* legend, fairy tale; fb. **Mährchenhaft**, -haft, *a.* fictitious, legendary; fabulous; -**igkeit**, -ĭchkäet, *f.* fictitiousness.
Mähre, mä're, *f.* horse; jade; mare.
Mai, mäe, *m.* May. **Maibaum**, mäe'baum, *m. pl.* -bäume, May-pole. **Maiblume**, -blyme, *f.* May-flower. **Maie**, mäe'ye, *f.* birch, birch-branch. **Maikäfer**, -käfer, *m.* May-bug cockchafer. **Mailuft**, -lyft, *f. pl.*

Mai 210 **Man**

-lüfte, vernal air. **Mai'monb,** -mont, m. month of May.
Mais, mäes, m. maize, Indian-corn.
Maische, mäe'she, f. mash.
Maitag, mäe'täg, m. May-day.
Majestät, ma-yezhtät', f. majesty. **Majestätisch,** -isch, a. majestic; av. -ally. **Majestätsverbrechen,** -ferbrechen, n. high-treason.
Major, ma-yōr', m. major.
Majoran, ma-yorän', m. marjoram.
Majorat, ma-yorät', n. pl. -e, majorat, entail.
Majorenn, ma-yorenn, a. of age.
Majorennität, ma-yorennität', f. majority, full age.
Makel, mak'kel, m. stain, blot, fault.
Mäkelei, mekèlēī', f. fault-finding.
Makellos, mak'kellōs, a. spotless, faultless. **Mäkeln,** mèk'keln, vt. i. to find fault.
Mäkeln, mèk'keln, vi. to broke, to act the broker. **Mäkler,** mèk'klèr, m. broker.
Makrele, makrā'le, f. mackerel.
Makrone, makrō'ne, f. macaroon.
Mal, mäl, n. -e, time; einmal, once: noch ein mal, once more; ein für alle Mal, once for all.
Malen, mä'len, vt. to paint, represent, depict; to describe. **Maler,** mäk'ler, m. painter, artist; -ei, -eī', f. painting, picture. **Malerisch,** -isch, a. picturesque. **Ma'lerkunst,** -kunzht, f. art of painting.
Mall, mall, f. model, form.
Malter, mal'tèr, n. a corn measure (about 12 bushels).
Malve, mal'fe, f. mallow.
Malz, malts, n. malt; -boden, -bōden, m. malt-loft. **Malzbarre,** -darre, f. malt-kiln, ost. **Malzen,** mal'tsen, vt. to malt.
Mamma, mam'mä, f. mamma, ma.
Mammon, mam'mōn, m. mammon, pelf.
Mamsell, mam'sèll, f. pl. -s, Miss.
Man, man, pn. a man, one, they, people, you.
Mancher, man'chèr, m. manche, f. manches, n. m. many a, some; many a man; many a thing; pl. some, several, many. **Mancherlei,** -läē', a. of several sorts, divers, various.
Manchmal, manch'mäl, av. many a time.

Manchester, man'tshèstèr, m. cotton-velvet, velveteen, fustian.
Mandat, mandät', n. pl. -e, mandate
Mandatar, mandatär', m. proxy, attorney.
Mandel, man'del, f. number of fifteen.
Mandel, man'del, f. almond; -baum, -baūm, m. pl. -bäume, almond-tree. **Mandelbrei,** -brēi, m. **Mandelmilch,** -myss, n. almond-pap. **Mandelmilch,** -milch, f. almond-milk, emulsion of almonds. **Mandelöl,** -ōhl, n. almond-oil. **Mandelseife,** -säfe, f. almond-soap. **Mandelstein,** -shtäen, m. pl. -e, amygdaloid. **Mandeltorte,** -torte, f. almond-tart.
Mandoline, mandelī'ne, f. mandolin.
Mangan, man-gän', m. manganese.
Mangansäure, -säūre, f. manganic acid.
Mange, mang'e, f. mangle.
Mangel, mang'el, m. pl. **Mängel,** want, scarcity; defect, fault. **Mangelhaft,** -haft, a. defective, deficient, imperfect; -igkeit, -ichkäet, f. defectiveness, imperfection. **Mangeln,** mang'eln, vt. to want, to be in want of, to be deficient; to fail, lack.
Mangen, mang'en, vt. to mangle.
Mangold, mang'gelt, m. mangold, mangel-wurzel, beet.
Manie, manī', f. mania, madness.
Manierirt, manīrīrt', a. affected.
Manier, manīr', f. manner. **Manierlich,** -lich, a. mannerly; -keit, -käet, f. good breeding.
Mann, mann, m. pl. **Männer** (Mannen, vassals,) man, person; husband; auf den Mann, a head, a piece; bis auf den letzten Mann, to a man; Manns genug sein, to be a match for. **Mannbar,** -bär, a. marriageable; -keit, -käet, f. puberty. **Männchen,** men'chen, n. little man, manikin; the male. **Mannesalter,** man'nesalter, n. manhood. **Mannshaft,** -haft, a. manly; -igkeit, -käet, f. manliness, manhood. **Mannheit,** -häet, f. manhood; virility.
Mannigfach, man'nichfach, a. manifold, repeated. **Mannigfalt,** -falt, m. pl. -e, tripe, third stomach of ruminating animals. **Mannigfaltig,** -feltich, a. various, divers, manifold; -keit, -käet, f. variety, diversity, multifariousness.

Männiglich, mĕn'niglĭch, *pn.* each and every one. **Männin,** mĕn'nĭn, *f.* virago. **Männisch,** mĕn'nish, *a.* masculine. **Männlich,** mĕn'lĭch, *a.* manly, brave, courageous, resolute; male, masculine, virile; —**es Glied,** penis. **Männlichkeit,** -kĕet, *f.* manliness, boldness, manly character. **Mannsbild,** mans'bĭlt, *n. pl.* -er, male person, man, fellow. **Mannschaft,** man'shaft, *f.* crew; men; troops. **Mannshand,** mans'hant, *f. pl.* -hände, man's hand, man's handwriting. **Mannshemd,** -hĕmt, *n. pl.* -en, shirt. **Mannshoch,** -hōch, *a.* of a man's height. **Mannskerl,** -kĕrl, *m.* young fellow. **Mannsleute,** -löĭte, *s. pl.* men, males. **Mannsname,** -nāme, *m.* -ens, *pl.* -n, name of a male person; man, male. **Mannsschneider,** -shnēĭdĕr, *m.* tailor for men. **Mannsstamm,** -zhtamm, *m.* male line. **Mannsstimme,** -zhtĭmme, *f.* male voice. **Mannstief,** -tīf, *a.* fathom-deep. **Mannsucht,** man'sycht, *f.* **Mannstollheit,** -tollhĕet, *f.* nymphomania. **Mannszucht,** -tsycht, *f.* discipline.
Manometer, manomā'ter, *m.* manometer.
Manschen, man'shen, *vi.* to dabble, paddle.
Manchester, manches'ter, [. Manchester.
Mantel, man'tel, *m.* mantle; (steam) jacket; coat; crown (of a bell); cage (of a staircase); runner (Mar.). **Mantelkind,** -kĭnt, *n. pl.* -er, child born before marriage. **Manteltragen,** -krägen, *m.* cape. **Mantelsack,** -sack, *m. pl.* -säcke, valise, carpetbag.
Manual, manyăl', *n. pl.* -e, note-book (Com.): key-board.
Manufaktur, manufaktyr', *f.* manufactory.
Manuskript, manyskrĭpt', *n. pl.* -e, manuscript.
Mappe, map'pe, *f.* portfolio; map.
Marder, mar'der, *m.* martin.
Marginalie, marginā'lĭ-e, *f.* marginal note.
Marienbild, marī'enbĭlt, *n. pl.* -er, image of the virgin.
Marine, marī'ne, *f.* marine, navy.
Mariniren, marinī'ren, *vt.* to pickle, cure.

Marionette, marionĕt'te, *f.* puppet.
Marionettenspiel, -zhpīl, *n. pl.* -e, **Marionettentheater,** -tāā'ter, *n.* puppet-show.
Mark, mark, *m.* mark, *n.* marrow; pith; pulp.
Mark, mark, *f.* boundary, border; mark; marches.
Mark, mark, *f.* mark (33 cts.), (gold) weight.
Markasit, markasīt', *m.* marcasite.
Markbein, mark'bēĭn, *n. pl.* -e, marrow-bone.
Marke, mar'ke, *f.* mark, token, check, stamp.
Marketender, marketen'der, *m.* sutler; -bube, -byde, *f.* sutler's shop.
Markgraf, mark'grāf, *m.* -en, *pl.* -en, margrave (marquis). **Markgräfin,** -gräfĭn, *f.* margravine (marchioness). **Markgrafschaft,** -shaft, *f.* margraviate (marquisate).
Markicht, markĭcht, *a.* medullary.
Markig, mark'ĭch, *a.* marrowy; pithy.
Markstein, mark'zhtēĭn, *m. pl.* -e, landmark, boundary-stone.
Markt, markt, *m. pl.* **Märkte,** market, mart; fair; market-place; -bude, -byde, *f.* market-booth, stand, stall. **Markten,** mark'ten, *vt.* to market; to bargain, to haggle; to sell. **Marktflecken,** -flĕcken, *m.* market-town. **Marktgeld,** -gĕlt, *n. pl.* -er, marketing-money. **Marktmeister,** -mēĭzhter, *m.* **Marktvogt,** -fockt, *m. pl.* -e, inspector of the market. **Marktplatz,** -plats, *m. pl.* -plätze, market-place. **Marktpreis,** -prēĭs, *m. pl.* -e, market-price. **Marktrecht,** -rĕcht, *n. pl.* -e, market-law. **Marktschreier,** -shrēĭer, *m.* mountebank, quack, charlatan; -ei, -ēĭ', *f.* quackery. **Marktschreierisch,** -ish, *a.* quackish, puffing.
Markung, mark'yng, *f.* boundary.
Marmelade, marmelā'de, *f.* marmalade.
Marlen, mar'len, *vt.* to marl; -schlag, -shlāg, *m. pl.* -schläge, marling-knot.
Marmor, mar'mor, *m.* marble; -arbeit, -arbēĭt, *f.* work in marble. **Marmorbild,** -bĭlt, *n. pl.* -er, statue in marble. **Marmorbruch,** -bryʊch, *m. pl.* -brüche, marble-quarry. **Marmoriren,** marmorī'ren, *vt.* to marble.

Mar   212   **Mas**

Marmorn, mar'morn, *a.* of marble.
Mar'morplatte, -platte, *f.* slab of marble. **Mar'morsaal,** -säl, *m. pl.* -säle, *f.* marble-hall. **Mar'mortafel,** -täfel, *f.* marble-slab. **Mar'mortisch,** -tish, *m. pl.* -e, marble-table. **Mar'morwand,** -vant, *f. pl.* -wände, marble-wall.

Marsbeur, marsdöhr', *m.* marauder, straggler. **Marsbiren,** marsdī'ren, *vt.* to maraud, plunder.

Maroquin, marokään', *m.* morocco-leather.

Mars, märs, *m.* Mars; top, scuttle; großes —, maintop.

Marsch, marsh, *m. pl.* **Märsche,** march.

Marschall, mar'shall, *m. pl.* **Marschälle,** marshal; -amt, -amts, *n.* -würde, -würde, *f.* marshalship. **Marschallstab,** -zhtäb, *m.* marshal's-staff, baton.

Marschfertig, marsh'fertich, *a.* ready to march. **Marschiren,** -ī'ren, *vi.* to march.

Marschland, marsh'lant, *n. pl.* -länder, moor-land, marshy land.

Marschlinie, marsh'līni-e, *f.* line of march. **Marschordnung,** -ordnung, *f.* order of march.

Marsraa, mars'rä, *f.* topsail-yard. **Marssegel,** -segel, *n.* topsail.

Marstall, mar'zhtäl, *m. pl.* -ställe, royal stable, equery.

Marter, mar'ter, *f.* torment, torture, rack; -bank, -bank, *f. pl.* -bänke, rack. **Marterer,** mar'terer, *m.* tormentor. **Martern,** mar'tern, *vt.* to torture, rack. **Marterwoche,** -voche, *f.* passion week. **Martertum,** -tum, *n.* martyrdom.

Märtyrer, mer'tīrer, *m.* martyr. **Märtyrerkrone,** -krōne, *f.* crown of martyrdom. **Märtyrertum,** -tum, *n.* martyrdom. **Märtyrtod,** -tōt, *m.* martyr-death.

Märj, merts, *m.* March; -bier, -bīr, *n.* March-beer.

Marzipan, martsipän', *m.* marchpane.

Masche, mash'e, *f.* mesh, stitch.

Maschine, mashī'ne, *f.* machine, engine. **Maschinerie,** mashīnerī', *f.* machinery. **Maschinist,** mashīnist', *m.* engineer.

Maser, mä'ser, *f.* spot, streak; *pl.* measles. **Maserig,** mä'serich, *a.* spotted; having the measles.

Maske, mas'ke, *f.* mask; masked person: — abnehmen, to unmask. **Maskenball,** mas'kenball, *m. pl.* -bälle, masquerade. **Maskiren,** maskī'ren, *vt.* to mask.

Maß, mäs, *n. pl.* -e, measure (of); liquid measure (about two quarts); bound, limit; size; degree; proportion, moderation; in dem **Maße als,** according as. **Maße,** mäs'se, *f.* measure, proportion; manner.

Masse, mas'se, *f.* mass, bulk, lump, multitude; body, substance. **Massenhaft,** -haft, *a.* massy, bulky. **Massenweise,** -vēise, *av.* in mass, by the bulk.

Maßgabe, mäs'gäbe, *f.* proportion, measure; nach —, according to, in proportion to.

Mäßig, mäs'sich, *a.* moderate, temperate; sober, frugal; middling; *av.* -ly. **Mäßigen,** mäs'sichen, *vt.* to moderate, temperate, mitigate, lessen, restrain, lower. **Mäßigkeit,** mäs'sichkäet, *f.* moderation, temperance. **Mäßigung,** -ung, *f.* moderation.

Massiv, massīf', *a.* massive, massy; coarse, rude.

Maßlos, mäss'lōs, *a.* unbounded; signifies, -ichkäet, *f.* unboundedness. **Maßregel,** mäs'rägel, *f.* measure; — ergreifen, to take measures. **Maßstab,** mäs'zhtäb, *m. pl.* -stäbe, scale, proportion, rule; measure; verjüngter —, reducing scale, reduced scale.

Mast, mast, *m.* -es, *pl.* -en, mast; ship.

Mast, mast, *f.* mast; in die — thun, to set to fatten.

Mastbaum, mäst'baum, *m.* mast.

Mastdarm, mäzht'darm, *m. pl.* -därme, rectum.

Mästen, mes'ten, *vt.* to fatten.

Mastix, mas'tix, *m.* mastic, mastich.

Mastkorb, mast'korb, *m. pl.* -körbe, scuttle, top of the mast. **Mastlos,** -lōs, *a.* mastless; — machen, dismast.

Mastochs, mast'ox, *m.* -en, *pl.* -en, fatted ox. **Mastschwein,** -shvaēn, *n. pl.* -e, fatted hog. **Mastung,** -ung, *f.* fattening; mast.

Masurka, masur'kä, *f.* mazurka.

Material, material', *n. pl.* -ien, material. **Materialist,** materialist', *m.*

Mat   213   **Mec**

druggist; materialist. **Materialismus**, matāriālls'mus, m. materialism. **Materie**, matā'ri-e, f. material, stuff; pus. **Materiell**, materiēl', a. material.
Mathematik, matemat'ick, s. mathematics. **Mathematiker**, -mat'icker, m. mathematician. **Mathematisch**, -ish, a. mathematic, -al, av. -ally.
Matrate, matrat'se, f. mattress.
Matrikel, matrick'el, f. register, roll; in die — einschreiben, vt. to matriculate.
Matrize, matrit'se, f. matrix, mater.
Matrose, matrō'se, m. -n. pl. -n, mariner, sailor, seaman, tar.
Matsch, matsh, m. pl. -e, capot; — machen, to capot. **Matschen**, mat'shen, vt. to capot: squash.
Matt, matt, a. faint, feeble, weary, languid, dull, dead; stale; dim; — machen, to mate.
Matte, mat'te, f. mat; meadow, mead.
Mattheit, mat'hāet, f. dulness, dimness, deadness. **Mattigkeit**, mat'tichkāet, f. faintness, weakness, weariness; dimness: exhaustion.
Matz, mats, m. pl. Mätze, blockhead.
Mauen, māu'en, vi. to mew, caterwaul.
Mauer, mōu'ēr, f. wall; -brecher, -brecher, m. battering-ram. **Mauerkalk**, -kalk, m. mortar. **Mauerkelle**, -kelle, f. trowel. **Mauermeister**, -māezhter, m. master-mason. **Mauern**, mōu'ērn, vt. to build (with stone or brick). **Mauerquadrant**, -quadrant, m. mural quadrant. **Mauerstein**, -zhtāen, m. pl. -e, **Mauerziegel**, -tsigel, m. brick. **Mauerwerk**, -verk, n. masonry, walls; raubes —, rubble-work; glattes —, plain work.
Maufe, mōu'ke, f. malanders.
Mauke, mōu'ke, f. hoard (of money, fruit).
Maul, moyl, n. pl. Mäuler, mouth, jaw, chops; raffe, -affe, m. gaper.
Maulbeer, mōyl'bār, f. mulberry; -baum, -bāum, m. pl. -bäume, mulberry-tree.
Mäulchen, mōūl'chen, n. little mouth, kiss. **Maulen**, mōyl'en, vi. to pout, to be in the sulks.
Maulesel, mōyl'āsel, m. mule.
Maulfaul, mōyl'fōyl, a. averse to speaking, mum. **Maulhänger**, -henger, m. pouter, sulky person. **Maulklemme**, -klemme, f. lock-jaw. **Maulkorb**, -korb, m. pl. -körbe, muzzle; — anlegen, to muzzle. **Maulschelle**, -shelle, f. box, blow on the mouth.
Maulthier, mōyl'tīr, n. pl. -e, mule.
Maultrommel, mōyl'trommel, f. Jew's-harp. **Maulwerk**, -verk, n. gift of gab.
Maulwurf, mōyl'vurf, m. pl. -würfe, mole; -hügel, -hühgel, m. molehill.
Maurer, mōy'rēr, m. mason; -gesell, -gesell, m. -en, pl. -en, journeyman-mason. **Maurerhandwerk**, -hautverk, n. masonry. **Maurermeister**, -māezhter, m. master-mason.
Maus, mōus, f. pl. Mäuse, mouse; muscle; -ader, -āder, f. nasal vein. **Mäuschenstill**, mēü'chēnzhtill, **Mausestill**, mōy'sezhtill, a. still, quite hushed.
Mauschel, mōy'shel, m. Jew. **Mauscheln**, mōy'sheln, vi. to deal like a Jew.
Mause, mōy'se, f. moulting; moulting season; auch **Mausezeit**, mōy'setsāet, f.
Mausefahl, mōy'sefāl, a. mouse-gray. **Mausefalle**, mōy'sefalle, f. mousetrap. **Mausegift**, -gift, n. pl. -e, **Mauseloch**, -loch, n. pl. -löcher, mouse-hole. **Mausen**, mōy'sen, vi. to mouse, pilfer.
Mausen, mōy'sen, rr. to moult. mew; to cast the feathers, shell, skin.
Mauseohr, mēü'se-ōr, n. -es, pl. -en, mouse-ear; name of various plants. **Mauser**, mōy'ser, m. pilferer. **Mausig**, mōy'sich, a. pert, saucy; sich — machen, to give one's self airs.
Mausoleum, mōy'sōle'ym, n. mausoleum.
Mauth, mōyt, f. custom-house: custom, excise, duty; -amt, -amt. n. pl. -ämter, custom-house. **Mauth's-beamter**, -beamter, m. **Mauthein-nehmer**, -ēinnāmēr, m. **Mauthner**, mōyt'nēr, m. custom-house officer.
Mauthwage, mōyt tāge, f. weigh-bridge.
Maxime, maxī'me, f. maxim.
Maximum, max'imym, n. maximum.
Mechanik, mechān'ik, f. mechanics.
Mechaniker, -ēr, m. mechanician

mechanist. **Mechanisch**, -ish, *a.* mechanical. **Mechanismus**, -is'mus, *m.* mechanism, machinery.
Meckant, moshant', *a.* wicked, mean.
Meckern, měck'ĕrn, *vi.* to bleat.
Medaille, medall'ye, *f.* medal. **Medaillon**, medallyōn', *n.* medallion, locket.
Median, mēdiän', *a.* medium (paper); of middle size. **Medianform**, -form, *f.* medium.
Mediatisiren, mēdiatiz'ren, *vt.* to mediatize.
Medizin, meditsīn', medicine, physic, science of medicine. **Medicinal-Collegium**, meditsinäl' kollā'gium, *n.* board of health. **Medizinalrath**, -rät, *m. pl.* -räthe, medical counsellor. **Mediziner**, meditsī'nĕr, *m.* medical student. **Medizinisch**, -ish, *a.* medical, medicinal.
Meer, mär, *n.* sea, ocean; lake: **busen**, -busen, *m.* bay, gulf. **Meerenge**, -enge, *f.* strait, straits. **Meeresstille**, -sztille, *f.* calm. **Meeresstrand**, -zhtrant, *m.* sea-shore. **Meereswoge**, -vōge, *f.* billow. **Meerfrau**, mär'frau, *f.* mermaid, siren. **Meergrün**, -grün, *a.* sea-green. **Meerkrebs**, -krĕbs. *m.* lobster. **Meermädchen**, mär'mĕdchen, *n.* mermaid. **Meernessel**, -nessel, *n.* sea-nettle. **Meerrettig**, -rĕttich. *m.* horse-radish. **Meerschaum**, -shaŭm, *m.* meerschaum. **Meerschwein**, -zhvĕen, *n. pl.* -e, porpoise; **chen**, *n.* guinea-pig. **Meerweib**, -vĕib, *n. pl.* -er, mermaid. **Meerwunder**, -vŭnder, *n.* sea-monster; a great miracle.
Mehl, māl. *n.* flour; meal; dust: **brei**, -brĕi. *m.* pap. **Mehlfass**, -fass. *n. pl.* -fässer, flour-barrel. **Mehlhandel**, -handel, *m.* trade in flour. **Mehlhändler**, -hentler, *m.* dealer in flour. **Mehlig**, māl'ich, *a.* farinaceous; mealy. **Mehlkasten**, -kazhten, *m.* bolting-hutch. **Mehlkloß**, -klōss, *m.* dumpling. **Mehlloch**, -loch, *n. pl.* -löcher, scuttle. **Mehlsack**, -sack. *m. pl.* -säcke, flour-bag. **Mehlspeise**, -zhpĕise. *f.* farinaceous food **Mehlthau**, -täū, *m.* mildew, blight, blast. **Mehlwurm**, -vurm, *m. pl.* -würmer meal-worm. **Mehlzucker**, -tsycker, *m.* pulverized sugar.
Mehr, mār, *a. av.* more, the greater number, better; else; *pl* **mehrere**,

several. **Mehren**, mēr'en, *vt.* to increase, augment. **Mehrentheils**, -täels, *av.* for the greater part. **Mehrer**, mēr'er, *m.* multiplicator. **Mehrheit**, -hĕit, *f.* majority, plurality; multiplicity: plural number. **Mehrmalig**, -mälich, *a.* repeated, reiterated. **Mehrmals**, -mäls, *av.* several times. **Mehrsilbig**, -silbich, *a.* polysyllabic. **Mehrung**, -yng, *f.* increase, multiplication. **Mehrzahl**, -tsäl, *f.* plurality, majority; plural number.
Meiden, mēi'den, *vt.* to avoid, shun, fly, shrink from.
Meier, mĕe'er, **Maier**, *m.* farmer. **Meierei**, -ĕi', *f.* **Meierhof**, -hōf, *m. pl.* -höfe, farm.
Meile, mēi'le, *f.* mile: **deutsche** —, nearly five English miles. **Meilenstein**, -zhtĕen, *m.* milestone, and **Meilenzeiger**, -tsēiger, *m.*
Meiler, mēi'lĕr, *m.* charcoal-kiln.
Mein, mĕen, *pn.* my, mine, of me.
Meineid, mĕen'ĕed, *m. pl.* -e, perjury, false oath; — schwören, to perjure one's self, to forswear: **sig**, -ich, *a.* perjured; **ziger**, *m.* forswearer. **Meineidigkeit**, -kĕit, *f.* perjury, perfidiousness.
Meinen, mĕen'en, *vt.* to think; to mean, intend.
Meiner, mĕen'er, *pn.* of me; **seits**, -sĕits, *av.* for my part, as for me.
Meinethalben, mĕe'net-halben, **Meinetwegen**, -vägen, **Meinetwillen**, -villen, *av.* on my account, for my sake.
Meinig, mĕen'ich, *a.* mine.
Meinung, mĕen'yng, *f.* meaning, intention; opinion.
Meisch, mĕesh, *m.* mash. **Meischen**, mĕesh'en, *vt.* to mash.
Meise, mĕe'se, *f.* titmouse, tomtit.
Meissel, mĕe'sel, *m.* pledget.
Meissel, **Meißel**, mĕes'sel, *m.* chisel. **Meißeln**, mĕes'sĕln, *vt.* to chisel, to cut, cut off, crop.
Meist, mĕezht, *a. av.* most; greatest; almost; am meisten, most; **bietsub**, -bī'tent, *a.* bidding most; s. highest bidder. **Meistens**, mĕezh'tens, *av* mostly. **Meistentheils**, -täels, *av* for the most part, generally.
Meister, mĕezh'tĕr, *m.* master; — werden über, to master. **Meisterhaft**, -haft, *a.* masterly *av.* in a masterly

manner. **Meiſt'erhand**, -hant, f. pl. -hände, a. master's hand. **Mei'ſterlich**, -lich, a. av. masterly. **Meiſtern**, mīezh'tĕrn, vt. to subdue, muster, control, command; to censure, tutor, find fault with. **Mei'ſterſänger**, -sęngĕr, m. minstrel. **Mei'ſterſchaft**, -shaft, f. mastery, mastership; (body of) masters.

Melancholie, melancholī', f. melancholy. **Melancho'liſch**, -lish, a. melancholic.

Melden, mĕl'den, vt. to announce, advise, notify, send word, write: to usher in; ſich — laſſen, to send in one's name; ſich —, to address, apply one's self to. **Mel'dung**, -ung, f. announcement, advise, information.

Meliren, melī'ren, vt. to mix, mingle.

Melkeimer, melk'ȝēmĕr, m. milk-pail. **Melken**, melk'en, vt. to milk. **Melkerei**, melkĕrēī', f. dairy.

Melodie, melōdī', f. melody. **Melo'diſch**, -ish, a. melodious.

Melone, melō'ne, f. melon. **Melo'nengarten**, -garten, n. pl. -gärten, melon-patch.

Memme, męm'mę, f. coward, poltroon.

Memorandum, memōran'dum, n. pl. -da, memorandum.

Memoriren, memōrī'ren, vt. to learn by heart.

Menagerie, menazhĕrī', f. menagerie.

Menge, męng'ę, f. multitude; plenty, great deal.

Mengen, meng'en, vt. to mingle, blend, mix. **Meng'futter**, -futtĕr, n. mash (for horses, etc.). **Meng'ung**, -ung, f. mingling, mixing.

Mennig, men'nich, m. **Men'nige**, f. red lead.

Menſch, mensh, m. -en, pl. -en, man, human being, person; fellow; kein —, nobody.

Menſch, mensh, n. -en, pl. -er, wench, jade, hussy. **Men'ſchenalter**, -altĕr, m. age, generation. **Men'ſchendieb**, -dīb, m. pl. -e, kidnapper. **Men'ſchenfeind**, -fīent, m. pl. -e, misanthrope; -lich, -lich, a. misanthropic. **Men'ſchenfreſſer**, -freſsĕr, m. cannibal. **Men'ſchenfreund**, -freünd, m. pl. -e, philanthropist; -lich, -lich, a. philanthropic, humane; -lichkeit, f. humaneness, philanthropy, humanity. **Men'ſchengedenken**, -gedenken, n. memory of man; ſeit —, in the memory of man; über —, since immemorial times. **Men'ſchenhand**, -hant, f. pl. -hände, the hand of man. **Men'ſchenkenntniß**, -kenntniss, f. knowledge of human nature. **Men'ſchenkind**, -kint, n. pl. -er, human being. **Men'ſchenleben**, -lēben, n. human life. **Men'ſchenleer**, -lēr, a. unpeopled, deserted. **Men'ſchenliebe**, -lībe, f. charity, philanthropy. **Men'ſchenmöglich**, -möglich, a. possible for human power. **Men'ſchenpflicht**, -pflicht, f. duty of man. **Men'ſchenraub**, -rāub, m. kidnapping. **Men'ſchenräuber**, -rāubĕr, m. kidnapper. **Men'ſchenrecht**, -recht, n. right of man. **Men'ſchenſatzung**, -satzung, f. tradition, human ordinance. **Men'ſchenſchen**, -sheü, f. misanthropy, unsociableness. **Men'ſchenſeele**, -sēlę f. human soul. **Men'ſchenverſtand**, -fĕrzhtant, m. common sense. **Men'ſchenwerk**, -vĕrk, n. work of man. **Menſchheit**, mensh'hāet, f. human race, humanity. **Menſch'lich**, -lich, a. human; humane; -keit, -kāet, f. humanity, humaneness. **Menſch'werdung**, mensh'vĕrdung, f. incarnation.

Menuet, menųĕt' n. pl. -ette, minuet.

Mercantil, mĕrkantīl', -iſch, a. mercantile.

Mercur, mĕrkųr', m. mercury.

Mergel, mĕr'gel, m. marl; -ig, -ich, a. marly. **Mergeln**, mĕr'geln, vt. to marl.

Merk, merk, n. mark, sign; -bar, -bār, a. perceptible. **Merken**, mer'ken, vt. to perceive, observe, mark, note; ſich — laſſen, to betray. **Merk'lich**, -lich, a. perceptible. **Merk'mal**, -māl, n. pl. -e, mark, sign, characteristic. **Merks**, merks, m. wits, caption. **Merk'würdig**, -vürdich, a. remarkable, curious; -keit, -kāet, f. curiosity, remarkable object. **Merk'zeichen**, -tsāechen, n. mark, characteristic.

Meßamt, mess'amt, n. pl. -ämter, mass.

Meßband, mess'bant, n. pl. -bänder, tape-line. **Meß'bar**, -bār, a. measurable; -keit, -kāet, f. measurableness. **Meß'brief**, -brīf, m. pl. -e, bill

Meſ 216 **Mig**

of tonnage. **Meß'buch,** -buch, n. pl. -bücher, mass-book, missal. **Meſſe,** mës'ſe, f. mass; — leſen, to say or read mass.
Meſſe, mës'ſe, f. fair, market.
Meſſen, mës'ſen (maß, gemeſſen), vt. to measure. **Meſſer,** mës'ſër, m. measurer.
Meſſer, mës'ſër, n. knife. **Meſſer beſteck,** mës'sërbështëck, n. knife-case. **Meſſerklinge,** -klinge, f. blade of a knife. **Meſſerrücken,** -rücken, m. back of a knife. **Meſſerſcheibe,** -shëïde, f. sheath or case of a knife. **Meſſerſchmied,** -shmïd, m. cutler. **Meſſerſchneide,** -shnëïde, f. blade of a knife. **Meſſerſpitze,** -zhpitse, f. point of a knife.
Meßgeld, mës'gëlt, n. pl. -er, metage, guger's fees. **Meß'gut,** -gut, n. pl. -güter, goods destined for a fair.
Meſſing, mës'sing, n. brass; -blech, -blëch, n. sheet-brass, latten; -draht, -drät, m. pl. -drähte, brass-wire.
Meſſingen, mës'singen, a. brazen, brass, of brass.
Meßinſtrument, mës'inzhtrument, n. surveying instrument.
Meßkette, mës'kette, f. surveyor's chain. **Meß'kunſt,** -kunzht, f. surveying.
Meßner, mës'nër, n. sexton, sacristan.
Meßruthe, mës'rute, f. surveyor's rod. **Meß'tiſch,** -tish, m. pl. -e, plane-table.
Meßwaare, mës'väre, f. goods for a fair.
Metall, metall', n. metal; -ſen, -en, a. metal, brazen. **Metalliſch,** metall'-ish, a. metallic. **Metalloid,** metall-oïd', n. pl. -e, metalloid. **Metalloxyd,** metall'oxïd', n. metallic oxide. **Metallurgie,** metallurgï', f. metallurgy.
Metamorphoſe, metamorfō'se, f. metamorphosis.
Metapher, metaf'ër, m. metaphor.
Metaphyſik, metafisïk', f. metaphysics.
Meteor, mäte-ōr', m. pl. -e, meteor. **Meteorologie,** mäte-orologï', f. meteorology.
Meth, mät, a. mead.
Methode, metō'de, f. method. **Methodiſch,** metō'dish, a. methodical.
Methodiſt, netōdist', m. -en, pl. -en, methodist

Metrum, mä'trum, n. metre.
Mette, mët'te, f. matins.
Mettwurſt, mëtt'vurzht, f. pl. -würſte, pork-sausage.
Metze, mët'se, f. jade, strumpet.
Metze, mët'se, f. peck.
Metzelei, metselëï', f. butchery, slaughter, massacre. **Metzeln,** mët'seln, vt. to butcher, slaughter, massacre.
Metzge, mëts'ge, f. shambles. **Metzgen,** mëts'gen, vt. to butcher, slaughter. **Metz'gern,** -gërn, vt. to butcher, slaughter. **Metz'gerbeil,** -bëïl, n. butcher's cleaver. **Metz'gerhund,** -gerhunt, m. pl. -e, butcher's dog, mastiff. **Metz'gerknecht,** -knëcht, m. pl. -e, butcher's man.
Meuchelmord, mëü'chelmort, m. pl. -e, assassination. **Meu'chelmörder,** -mörder, m. assassin; -iſch, -ish, a. assassin-like: — umbringen, to assassinate. **Meucheln,** mëü'cheln, vt. to plot against, cavil; assassinate.
Meuchleriſch, mëüch'lerish, a. insidious, assassin-like. **Meuchliſch,** mëüch'-lish, av. insidiously.
Meute, mëü'te, f. mutiny; pack of hounds. **Meuterei,** -rëï', f. mutiny.
Meuterer, mëü'tërër, m. mutineer.
Mewe, mä've, f. mew, gull.
Miauen, miäü'en, vi. to mew.
Mich, mich, pn. me.
Michaelisfeſt, micha-ä'lisfëzht, n. Michael's-mass.
Mied, mïd, Prt. v. Meiden.
Mieder, mï'dër, n. bodice.
Miene, mï'ne, f. mien, air, look; — machen, to do as if; to pretend; finſtere —, frown. **Mienenſpiel,** -shpïl, n. pantomime.
Miethcontrakt, mït'kontrakt, **Miethvertrag,** -fërträg, m. pl. -verträge, lease, tenure.
Miethe, mï'te, f. hire, rent. **Miethen,** mï'ten, vt. to rent, to hire. **Miether,** mït'ër, m. hirer, lodger, tenant.
Miethkutſche, -kutshe, f. hack, hackney-coach. **Miethleute,** -lëü'te, s. pl. lodgers, tenants. **Mieth'ling,** -ling, m. pl. -e, hireling. **Mieth'pferd,** -pfërt, n. pl. -e, hack, hackney-horse. **Miethtruppen,** -truppen, s. pl. mercenary troops. **Mieth'weiſe,** -vëïſe, av. by lease, by hiring. **Mieth'zins,** -tsins, m pl. -en, house-rent.
Mieze, mï'tse, f. puss, cat.
Migräne, mï'grä'ne, f. megrim.

Mik   217   **Miß**

Mikrokosmus, mikrokos'mus, *m.* microcosm.
Mikrometer, mikromä'tĕr, *m.* micrometer.
Mikroskop, mikroskōp', *m.* microscope.
Milbe, mil'be, *f.* mite.
Milch, milch, *f.* milk; milt, soft roe. **Milch'ader**, -āder, *f.* lacteal vein. **Milch'bart**, -bärt, *m. pl.* -bärte, down; milkshop. **Milch'brei**, -brei, *m.* milk-pap. **Milch'brod**, -brōd, *n.* French roll. **Milch'bruder**, -brudĕr, *m. pl.* -brüder, foster-brother. **Milch'er**, **Milch'ner**, **Milch'ling**, *s.* milter. **Milch'farben**, -farben, *a.* milk-colored. **Milch'friesel**, -frīsel, *n.* miliary fever. **Milch'hafen**, -häfen, *m. pl.* -häfen, milk-pot. **Milch'kalb**, -kalp. *n. pl.* -kälber, sucking-calf. **Milch'kuh**, -kụ, *f. pl.* -kühe, milch-cow; **Milchſaures Salz**, lactate. **Milch'säure**, -säure, *f.* lactic acid. **Milch'stein**, -zhtäen, *m. pl.* -e, galactite. **Milch'straße**, -zhträsse, *f.* galaxy, milky way. **Milch'topf**, -topf, *m. pl.* -töpfe, milk-pot. **Milch'wirthſchaft**, -virrtshaft, *f.* dairy. **Milch'zahn**, -tsän, *m. pl.* -zähne, milk-tooth. **Milch'zucker**, -tsuckĕr, *m.* sugar of milk; **-säure**, -säure, *f.* saccholactic acid.
Mild, milt, *a.* mild, soft, tender, gentle, sweet, liberal, charitable. **Milde**, mil'de, *f.* mildness, softness, tenderness; kindness, liberality. **Mildern**, mil'dĕrn, *vt.* to soften, mitigate, temper, alleviate, soothe, lessen, extenuate. **Mil'derung**, -ụng, *f.* mitigation; relief; **-wort**, -vort, *n. pl.* -wörter, euphemism. **Mild'herzig**, -hĕrtsich, *a.* kind-hearted, benevolent, charitable; **-keit**, -käet, *f.* benevolence, charitableness. **Mildigkeit**, mil'dichkäet, *f.* kindness, benevolence. **Mildthätig**, mild'tätich, *a.* charitable; **-keit**, -käet, *f.* charity.
Militär, militär', *n.* military, soldiery. **Militärisch**, militär'ish, *a.* military, soldierly. **Miliz**, milits', *f.* militia.
Million, milliōn', *f.* million. **Millionär**, -när', *m.* millionaire.
Milz, milts, *f.* milt, spleen. **Milz'entzündung**, -enttsündụng. *f.* inflammation of the spleen, splenitis. **Milzſucht**, -sụcht, *f.* hypochondriasis,

spleen. **Milzſüchtig**, -süchtig, *a.* splenetic, hypochondriac.
Minder, min'dĕr, *a. av.* less, smaller; **-heit**, -häet, *f.* minority. **Min'derjährig**, -yärich, *a.* minor, under age; **-keit**, -käet, *f.* minority. **Min'dern**, -dĕrn, *vt.* to diminish, lessen; **ſich** —, to grow less, decay, decrease. **Min'derung**, -ụng, *f.* diminution. **Min'derzahl**, -dĕrtsäl, *f.* minority. **Mindest**, min'dĕst, *a. av.* least; **-ens**, -ens, *av.* at least.
Mine, mi'ne, *f.* mine; — **ſpringen laſſen**, to spring a mine. **Minengang**, mī'nengang, *m. pl.* -gänge, entrance of a mine. **Mi'nengräber**, -gräbĕr, *m.* miner, sapper, pioneer. **Mi'nenkammer**, -kammĕr, *f.* chamber of a mine.
Mineral, minĕräl', *n. pl.* -ien, mineral; **-waſſer**, minĕräl'vassĕr, *n.* mineral water.
Miniatur, miniatụr', *f.* miniature; auch **Miniaturgemälde**, -gemälde, *n.*
Minimum, mī'nimụm, *n. pl.* **Minima**, minimum.
Miniren, minī'ren, *vt.* to mine.
Minister, minis'tĕr, *m.* minister. **Ministeriell**, ministeri-ell', *a.* ministerial. **Ministerium**, minizhtä'riụm, *n.* ministry.
Minne, min'ne, *f.* love. **Min'nelohn**, -lōn, *m.* love returned; swain's reward. **Minnen**, min'nen, *vt.* to love. **Minnesänger**, min'nesengĕr, *m.* minstrel.
Minute, minụ'te, *f.* minute; **-zeiger**, -tsäegĕr, *m.* minute-hand.
Mir, mīr, *pn.* to me, for me.
Mirakel, mīrack'el, *n.* miracle, prodigy.
Misanthrop, misantrōp', *m.* -en, *pl.* -en, misanthrope.
Mischbar, mish'bär, *a.* mixable. **Miſchen**, mish'en, *vt.* to mix, to mingle; to shuffle (the cards); **ſich** — in, to meddle with, interpose. **Miſch'ling**, -ling, *m.* mongrel. **Miſch'maſch**, -mash, *m.* medley, hodgepodge. **Miſch'ung**, -ụng, *f.* mixture, medley.
Mispel, mis'pel, *m.* medlar; **-baum**, -baum, *m. pl.* -bäume, medlar, medlar-tree.
Mißachten, missach'ten, *vt.* to slight, despise, esteem lightly.
Mißärnte, miss'ärnte, *f.* bad crop

Mißbehagen, miss'behägen, *vi.* to displease, dissatisfy; *s.* dissatisfaction, displeasure, discomfort.
Mißbilligen, missbill'ichen, *vt.* to disapprove. **Mißbilligung**, -ung, *f.* disapprobation.
Mißbrauch, miss'brōych, *m.* abuse, misuse; **sen**, *vt.* to abuse, misuse, take in vain; to seduce, debauch. **Miß'bräuchlich**, miss'brōychlich, *a.* abusive.
Mißdeuten, missdöü'ten, *vt.* to misinterpret, misconstrue. **Miß'beutung**, -ung, *f.* misconstruction.
Mißen, mis'sen, *vt.* to miss, to be without.
Mißethat, mis'setät, *f.* misdeed, crime. **Mis'sethäter**, -tätèr, *m.* malefactor, criminal.
Mißfallen, missfall'en (**mißfiel**, **mißfallen**), *vi.* to displease; *s. n.* displeasure, dislike. **Mißfällig**, miss'fellich, *a.* unpleasant, displeasing, offensive.
Mißgeburt, miss'gebyrt, *f.* miscarriage, abortion: monster.
Mißgeschick, miss'geshick, *m.* disaster, fatality.
Mißgestalt, miss'gezhtalt, *f.* deformity; **en**, miss'gezhtalten, *vt.* to deform, misshape.
Mißglücken, missglück'en, *vi.* to fail, miscarry.
Mißgönnen, missgön'nen, *vt.* to envy, grudge.
Mißgreifen, miss'greifen (**mißgriff**, **mißgegriffen**), *vt.* to mistake. **Miß'griff**, -griff. *m. pl.* -e, mistake, failure, blunder.
Mißgunst, miss'gunzht, *f.* envy. **Miß'günstig**, -günzhtich, *a.* envious, jealous.
Mißhandeln, misshan'deln, *vt.* to illtreat, abuse, maltreat. **Mißhandlung**, -band'lung, *f.* ill-treatment, abuse.
Mißheirath, miss'heīrāt, *f.* misalliance; **en**, *vt.* to marry below one's self.
Mißhellig, miss'hellig, *a.* dissonant, discordant, unharmonious; — **sein**, to be at variance; **keit**, -kāet, *f.* dissension.
Mission, missiōn', *f.* mission; **är**, -är', *m.* missionary. **Missionsgesellschaft**, missiōns'gesellshaft, *f* missionary society.

Mißjahr, miss'yär, *n.* sterile year.
Mißklang, miss'klang, *m. pl.* -klänge, dissonance; disharmony.
Mißkleiden, misskläö'den, *vt.* to dress badly, disfigure.
Mißklingen, misskling'en (**mißklang**, **mißgeklungen**), *vi.* to be dissonant; to sound ill.
Mißlaut, miss'loüt, *m. pl.* -e, discordant sound, inharmonious sound, dissonance; **en**, *vi.* to sound unharmonious, badly.
Mißleiten, misskläö'ten, *vt.* to mislead, lead astray.
Mißlich, miss'lich, *a.* critical, dangerous; **keit**, -kāet, *f.* difficulty, danger, risk.
Mißlingen, missling'en (**mißlang**, **mißlungen**), *vi.* to fail, miscarry, to prove abortive; *s. n.* ill success, failure, mischance.
Mißmuth, miss'mut, *m.* ill humor, discontentedness. **Miß'müthig**, -mülhtich, **Miß'muthig**, -mytich, *a.* discontented, displeased.
Mißrathen, miss'rāt'en (**mißrieth**, **mißrathen**), *vi.* to fail, miscarry; *vt.* to dissuade.
Mißstand, miss'zhtant, *m.* inconvenience, nuisance.
Mißstimmen, misszhtim'men, *vt.* to put out of tune, to put out of humor; to put into an ill humor. **Mißstim'mung**, -ung, *f.* dissonance; ill humor.
Mißton, miss'tōn, *m.* false sound: discord. **Miß'tönen**, -töhnen, *vi.* to sound wrong, to be dissonant.
Mißtrauen, miss'troÿen, *vt.* to distrust; *s. n.* distrust, diffidence, suspicion; — **setzen in**, to distrust, suspect. **Miß'trauisch**, -troÿ-ish, *a.* suspicious, distrustful.
Mißtritt, miss'tritt, *m. pl.* -e, false step; error.
Mißvergnügen, miss'fergnühgen, *n.* dissatisfaction, discontent, displeasure. **Miß'vergnügt**, -fergnühkt, *a.* dissatisfied, displeased, **ser**, **-er**, *s.* malcontent.
Mißverhältniß, miss'ferheltniss *n pl.* -e, disproportion.
Mißverstand, miss'ferzhtant, *m.* misunderstanding. **Miß'verständniß**, -zhtendniss, *n.* misunderstanding.
Mißverstehen, -zh'ä'en, *vt.* to misunderstand, misapprehend.

Mißwachs, miss'vax, m. scarcity, failure of the crops.
Mist, mizht, m. dung, manure, dirt; -beet, -bāt, n. pl. -e, hot-bed.
Mistel, mizh'tel, f. mistletoe.
Misten, mizh'ten, vt. to dung, manure; vi. to clear of dung.
Mistgabel, mizht'gäbel, f. dung-fork.
Mistgauche, mizht'goŭçhe, **Mistlache**, -lache, f. drainings of a stable, dung-water. **Mistgrube**, -grŭbe, f. dung-pit. **Misthaufen**, -hoŭfen, m. dung-hill. **Mistig**, -ich, a. dungy. **Mist's käfer**, -käfer, m. dung-beetle. **Mist's wagen**, -vägen, m. dung-cart.
Mit, mit, pr. with, at.
Mitarbeiter, mit'arbäëtěr, m. fellow-laborer.
Mitbesitzer, mit'bĕsitsĕr, m. joint-possessor.
Mitbeten, mit'bēten, vi. to join in prayer.
Mitbewerben, mit'bĕvĕrben, vi. to compete with, to contend for. **Mit's bewerber**, m. competitor. **Mit'bewerbung**, -ŭng, f. competition.
Mitbringen, mit'bring-ĕn, vt. to bring along with.
Mitbruder, mit'brŭdĕr, m. brother, colleague.
Mitbürger, mit'bürgĕr, m. fellow-citizen.
Mitbürgschaft, mit'bŭrgshaft, f. joint-bail.
Miteinander, mitæĕnan'dĕr, av. together.
Mitempfinden, mit'empfinden, vi. to sympathize, to feel in common with.
Miterbe, mit'erbĕ, m. coheir; joint heir. **Miterben**, vi. to be coheir, coheiress. **Mit'erbschaft**, -shaft, f. joint inheritance.
Mitessen, mit'ĕssen, vi. to eat with.
Mitfahren, mit'fären, vi. to ride with, drive with.
Mitgabe, mit'gäbe, f. portion, dower. **Mit'geben**, -gēben, vt. to endow, portion.
Mitgefangener, mit'gĕfangenĕr, m. fellow-prisoner.
Mitgehülfe, mit'gehilfe, m. assistant.
Mitgeschöpf, mit'gĕshöpf, n. fellow-creature.
Mitgift, mit'gift, f. portion, dowry.
Mitglied, mit'glid, n. pl. -er, member, fellow; -schaft, -shaft, f. membership.

Mithandeln, mit'handĕln, vi. to cooperate.
Mithin, mit'hin, Cj. consequently, therefore.
Mithilfe, mit'hilfe, f. assistance.
Mitkämpfer, mit'kempfĕr, m. fellow-combatant.
Mitkläger, mit'klägĕr, m. joint-plaintive.
Mitkommen, mit'kommen, vi. to come along with.
Mitkönnen, mit'können, vi. to be able to go along with.
Mitlauter, mit'loŭtĕr, m. consonant.
Mitleid, **Mitleiden**, mit'lëïden, n. compassion, pity, mercy, sympathy.
Mitleidig, mit'lëïdich, a. compassionate: -keit, -käet. f. compassionate-ness. **Mit'leidsbezeigung**, -bętsëïgung, f. condolence.
Mitmachen, mit'machen, vt. to join in, to go along with; to make one at a party.
Mitmensch, mit'mensh, m. -en, pl. -en, fellow-man.
Mitnehmen, mit'nämen, vt. to take along with; to criticise; hart —, to handle roughly, to cut up.
Mitregent, mit'regent, m. co-regent.
Mitschuld, mit'shŭlt, f. participation in guilt; -ig, -ich, a. accessory.
Mitschüler, mit'shŭlĕr, m. school-fellow.
Mitschwester, mit'shvęzhtĕr, f. fellow-sister.
Mitspielen, mit'shpilen, vi. to join in play; übel —, to treat ill. handle roughly. **Mit'spieler**, m. partner (in a game).
Mitstand, mit'zhtant, m. pl. -ständĕ, co-estate.
Mittag, mit'täg, m. pl. -e, midday, noon, south, meridian; zu — essen. speisen, to dine; — machen, to stop, halt for dinner; zu — bleiben, to stay for dinner.
Mittägig, mit'tägich, a. happening at noonday. **Mit'täglich**, -lich, a. south, southern, meridional.
Mittags, mit'tägs, av. at noon, at twelve o'clock; -essen, -ĕssen, n. -mahl, -mäl, n. dinner; -gegend, -gägend, f. southern, meridional region, country; -glocke, -glockĕ, f. noon-bell; -kreis, -kräës, m. pl. -e, meridian; -ruhe, -ry-ĕ, f. noon-rest, nap; -seite, -säïte, f. South side;

Mit   220   **Mod**

auf der — liegen, to lie towards the South; **-tisch**, -tish, *m.* dinner; **-zeit**, -tsĕīt, *f.* noontide.
Mitte, mit'tĕ, *f.* middle, midst, centre.
Mittel, mit'tel, *n.* midst, middle; **ins — treten**, to interpose, intercede, interfere.
Mittel, mit'tel, *a.* middle.
Mittelweise, mit'tĕrveīlĕ, *av.* in the mean time.
Mittel, mit'tel, *n.* means, medium, remedy.
Mittelalter, mit'telaltĕr, *n.* middle ages.
Mittelbar, mit'tĕlbär, *a.* mediate, indirect.
Mittelding, mit'telding, *n.* (something) intermediate.
Mittelfinger, mit'telfingĕr, *m.* middle finger.
Mittelgebäude, mit'telgĕbŏūdĕ, *n.* centre-building.
Mittelgattung, mit'telgattung, *f.* middling sort.
Mittelgut, mit'telgut, *a.* second-rate.
Mittelländisch, mit'tellĕndish, *a.* mediterranean; **-es Meer**, mediterranean.
Mittelmässig, mit'telmāssich, *a.* moderate, mediocre; **-keit**, -kāĕt, *f.* mediocrity.
Mittellos, mit'tellōs, *a.* without means, indigent.
Mittelmeer, mit'telmār, *n.* Mediterranean.
Mittelpreis, mit'telprĕīs, *m.* average price.
Mittelpunkt, mit'telpunkt, *m. pl.* **-e**, centre.
Mittels, **Mittelst**, mit'tĕlzht, *pr.* by means of, by the instrumentality of.
Mittelsperson, mit'telspĕrsōn, *f.* **Mittelsmann**, -man, *m.* mediator, agent, go-between.
Mittelst, mit'telzht, *a.* middlemost, midmost.
Mittelstand, mit'telzhtant, *m.* middle classes.
Mittelstrasse, mit'telzhträssĕ, *f.* middle way; **die — gehen**, to observe the golden mean.
Mitteltreffen, mit'teltrĕffen, *n.* centre (of an army).
Mittelweg, mit'telvĕg, *m. pl.* **-e**, middle road; **den — einschlagen**, to observe the mean.
Mitten, mit'ten, *a.* in the midst or middle of, in the heart of, amidst, recht —, in the very middle; — unter, among; into the midst; — am Tage, in the broad daylight; — in der Nacht, at midnight.
Mitternacht, mit'tĕrnächt, *f. pl.* **-nächte**, midnight, north. **Mitternachts**, av. at midnight. **Mitternächtlich**, -nĕchtlich, **Mitternächtig**, -nĕchtig, *a.* septentrional, northern; midnight.
Mitternachtspunkt, -punkt, *m. pl.* **-e**, northern point.
Mittheilbar, mit'tāelbär, *a.* communicable; **-keit**, -kāĕt, *f.* communicableness. **Mittheilen**, mit'tāelen, *vt.* to communicate, impart. **Mittheilung**, -ung, *f.* communication, information, notice; — machen, to give notice, inform.
Mittler, mit'ler. *m.* (*f.* Mittel), mediator; **-amt**, -amt, *n.* mediatorship.
Mittwoch, mitt'voch, *m.* **Mittwoche**, *f.* Wednesday.
Miturfache, mit'ursachĕ, *f.* concurrent cause.
Mitverschworner, mit'fĕrshvörnĕr, *m.* fellow-conspirator.
Mitwirken, mit'virken, *vi.* to cooperate in. **Mitwirkung**, -ung, *f.* cooperation.
Mitwissen, mit'vissen, *vi.* to be privy to, informed of; *s. n.* privity. **Mitwisser**, -vissĕr, *m.* accessory, one privy to.
Mitziehen, mit'tsī-en, *vi.* to draw along with.
Mixtur, mixtur', *f.* mixture.
Möbel, mö'bel, *n.* furniture, piece of furniture.
Mobil, mobīl', *a.* movable; — machen, to put in motion, to equip; to call into active service.
Mobiliar, mobiliär', *n.* **Mobilien**, mobīl'i-en, *s. pl.* movables, furniture; chattels.
Möbliren, möblī'ren, *vt.* to furnish. **Möblirer**, möblīr'ĕr, *m.* upholsterer.
Mode, mō'dĕ, *f.* fashion; nach der —, fashionably; fashionable: in der —, in fashion, fashionable. **Modehändler**, -hĕndlĕr, *m.* **-in**, *f.* milliner. **Modehandlung**, -handlung, *f.* milliner's-shop.
Model, mō'del. *m.* mould, form.
Modell, modĕll', *n.* model, pattern.
Modelliren, -ī'ren, *vt.* to model

form, mould. **Modeln**, mō'děln, *vt.* to mould, form.
Moder, mō'děr, *m.* mould, rottenness, putrefaction. **Moderig**, mō'děrich, **Mo'drig**, *a.* mouldy, musty.
Modern, mō'děrn, *vi.* to moulder, decay, putrefy.
Modern, mōdĕrn', *vi.* modern, fashionable. **Mo'dewaare**, -vāre, *f.* fancy-goods. **Mo'disch**, -dish, *a.* fashionable, modish.
Modulation, mŏdulatsi-ōn', *f.* modulation.
Mögen, möh'gen (mochte, gemocht), *vt.* to like, to wish; **Ich mag**, I may, I can; **ich möchte lieber sterben**, I had rather die; **möchte der Himmel**, would that heaven! **Möglich**, möhg'lich, *a.* possible; **-keit**, -kāet, *f.* possibility.
Mohn, mōn, *m. pl.* -e, poppy. **Mohn'saft**, -saft, *m.* poppy-juice, opium.
Mohr, mōr, *m.* -en, *pl.* -en, moor, negro.
Mohr, mōr, *m. pl.* -e, tabby, moire, mohair: **wollener —**, noreen.
Möhre, möh're, *f.* carrot.
Mohren, mō'ren. **Moiriren**, moarī'ren, *vt.* to tabby, to cloud, water.
Moirisch, mōr'ish, *a.* moorish.
Molch, molch, *m. pl.* -e, salamander.
Molke, mol'ke, *f.* **Mol'fen**, *m.* whey. **Mol'kensäure**, -sēüre, *f.* acid of milk. **Molkicht**, molk'icht, *a.* resembling whey. **Mol'fig**, *a.* wheyey.
Moll, moll, *n.* minor.
Molluske, molus'ke, *f.* mollusk.
Molybdän, molibdān', molybden (*a*); **-säure**, -sēüre, *f.* molybdic acid. **Molybdensaures Salz**, molybdate.
Moment, moment', *m.* moment. **Momentan**, momentān', *a.* momentary.
Monade, monā'de, *f.* monad. atom.
Monarch, monarch', *m.* monarch. **Monarchie**, monarchī', *f.* monarchy. **Monarch'isch**, -ish, *a.* monarchical; *av.* monarchically.
Monat, mō'nat, *m. pl.* -e, month. **Monatlich**, mō'natlich, *a.* monthly. **Mo'natliches**, *m.* **Monatliche Reinigung**, **Mo'natsfluss**, -fluss. *m.* monthly courses. **Mo'natschrift**, -shrift, *f.* monthly (magazine). **Mo'natsweise**, -vēīse, *av.* by the month.
Mönch, mönch, *m.* monk. **Mönch'isch**, -ish, *a.* monkish. **Möncherei**, -erēī', *f.* monkery. **Mönchs'kappe**, -kappe,

f. monk's hood. **Mönchs'kloster**, -klōzhter, *n. pl.* -klöfter, monastery **Mönchs'kolben**, -kölben, *m.* plunger (Mech.). **Mönchs'kutte**, -kutte, *f.* capouche. **Mönchs'leben**, -lēben, *n.* monastic life. **Mönchs'orden**, -orden, *m.* monastic, religious order **Mönch'thum**, -tum, *n.* monachism, monkery.
Mond, mont, *m. pl.* -e, moon; month; lune, lunette. **Mond'blind**, -blint, *a.* moon-blind. **Mond'enjahr**, **Mond'sjahr**, -yăr, *n. pl.* -e, lunar year. **Mond'finsterniss**, -finsterniss, *f. pl.* -nisse, eclipse of the moon. **Mond'salb**, -kalp, *n.* moon-calf. **Mond'licht**, -licht, *n.* moonlight. **Mond'scheibe**, -sheibe, *f.* disc of the moon. **Mond'schein**, -shāen, *m.* moonshine. **Mond'sichel**, -sichel, *f.* crescent. **Mond'stein**, -shtāen, *m. pl.* -e, selenite. **Mond'sucht**, -sucht, *f.* somnambulism. **Mond'süchtig**, -süchtig, *a.* somnambulist, moon-struck; **-er**, -er, *m.* somnambulist.
Monopol, monopōl', *n.* monopoly.
Monotonie, monotonī', *f.* monotony.
Monstranz, monzhtrans', *f.* pyx.
Monströs, monzhtrös', *a.* monstrous.
Montag, mon'tăg. *m. pl.* -e, Monday; blauer **—**, Sanct-Monday.
Montiren, montī'ren, *vt.* to clothe in regimentals, to uniform; to set up (machinery). **Montur**, -tyr, *f.* uniform, regimentals.
Monument, monument', *n. pl.* -e, monument.
Moor, mōr, *n. pl.* -e, moor, fen, bog. **Moor'grund**, -grunt, *m. pl.* -gründe, moor, swampy ground. **Moorig**, mōr'ich. *a.* boggy, moory.
Moos, mōs, *n. pl.* -e, moss; **-icht**, -icht, *a.* resembling moss. **Moosig**, mōs'ich, *a.* mossy. **Moos'rose**, -röse, *f.* moss-rose.
Mops, mops, *m. pl.* **Möpse**, pug-dog.
Moral, morāl', *f.* moral, morals, ethics; **-isch**, -ish, *a.* moral. **Moralisiren**, morālisī'ren, *vi.* to moralize. **Moralität**, moralität', *f.* morality.
Morast, morazht', *m. pl.* **Moräste**, morass, marsh; **-ig**, -ich, *a.* marshy, boggy.
Morchel, mor'chel, *f.* moril, morel.
Mord, mort, *m. pl.* -e, murder. **Mordbrand**, mort'brant, *m. pl.* -bränds

arson. **Mord'brenner**, -brennĕr. m. incendiary; **-ei**, -ĕi', f. incendiarism arson. **Morden**, mör'den, vt. to murder. **Mörder**, mör'der, m. murderer, assassin; **-isch**, -ish, a. murderous, deadly. **Mörderlich**, -lich, a. murderous, violent. **Mordgeschrei**, mort'geshrĕe, n. cry of murder. **Mordgewehr**, -vār, n. pl. -e, murderous weapon. **Mordgier**, -gīr, f. thirst of blood; **-ig**, -ich, a. bloody, blood-thirsty. **Mordio**, mor'dĭō, n. cry of murder; — **schreien**, to cry murder. **Mordthat**, mort'tät, f. murder.

Morelle, morĕl'le, f. morello.
Morgen, mor'gen, m. acre.
Morgen, mor'gen, m. morning; east; **heute —**, this morning; av. to-morrow; **-andacht**, -andacht, f. morning-devotion; **-besuch**, -besuch, m. pl. -e, morning-call; **-blatt**, -blatt, n. pl. **-blätter**, morning-paper; **-brod**, -brōt, n. breakfast. **Morgend**, mor'gent, a. to-morrow's. **Morgendämmerung**, mor'gendemmĕrung, f. dawn. **Morgengebet**, -gebĕt, n. morning-prayer. **Morgenland**, -lant, n. pl. -länder, orient, eastern country, Levant. **Morgenländer**, -lĕndĕr. m. **-sin**, f. oriental. **Morgenlied**, -līd, n. pl. -er, morning-song, morning-hymn. **Morgenroth**, -rōt, n. **Morgenröthe**, -rö̆te, f. aurora, dawn; prime, bloom, morning. **Morgens**, mor'gens, av. in the morning; — früh, early in the morning. **Morgenstern**, -zhtĕrn, m. pl. -e, morning-star. **Morgenstunde**, -zhtunde, f. morning-hour.

Morgig, morg'ich, a. to-morrow's.
Morphin, morfīn', m. morphine.
Morsch, morsh, a. brittle, rotten, worm-eaten; carious.
Mörsel, mör'sel, **Mörser**, mör'sĕr, m. mortar; mortar (Art.). **Mörserkeule**, -kā'le, f. pestle.
Mörtel, mör'tel, m. mortar, plaster; — **anmachen**, to temper mortar; **-kelle**, -kelle. f. trowel; **-trage**, -trägĕ, f. hod, tray; **-träger**, -trägĕr, m. hodman.
Mosaik, mosä'ik. f. mosaic, mosaicwork; — **Fußboden**, tesselated pavement.
Moschee, moshā'. f. mosque.
Moschratte, mosh'ratte, f. musk-rat.

Moschrose, mosh'rōse, f. musk-rose.
Moschthier, mosh'tīr, n. pl. -e, musk-deer; Thibet-musk.
Moschus, mō'shuss, m. musk.
Most, mozht, m. pl. -e, must; cider. **Mosten**, mozh'ten, vt. to make cider, must, perry. **Mostpresse**, -presse, f. wine-press; cider-press.
Motion, motsiōn', f. motion; exercise; — **machen**, to make a motion; **sich —** machen, to take exercise.
Motiv, motīf', n. pl. -e, motive. **Motiviren**, motifī'ren, vi. to state the reasons of.
Motte, mot'te, f. moth.
Mücke, mück'e, f. fly; gnat.
Mucken, muck'en, **Mucksen**, vi. to open one's mouth.
Muckisch, muck'ish, a. whimsical, capricious.
Muddern, mud'dĕrn, vi. to make foul water.
Müde, mü'de, a. weary, tired. **Müdigkeit**, -dichkāĕt, f. weariness, fatigue.
Muff, muff, m. pl. **Müffe**, muff.
Muff, muff, m. mouldiness, mustiness. **Müffeln**, muffĕln. vi. to smell musty or rank. **Muffig**, muf'fich, a. musty, rank.
Muffig, muf'fich, a. sullen, sulky.
Mühe, mü'e, f. trouble. pains. **Mühen**, mü'en, vt. to trouble; **sich —**, to trouble one's self. **Mühevoll**, -foll, a. troublesome, toilsome.
Mühlbach, mūl'bach, m. mill-brook. **Mühle**, mü'le, f. mill. **Mühlenrad**, -rät, n. mill-wheel. **Mühlgang**, -gang, m. pl. -gänge, set of millstones. **Mühlgerinne**, -gerinne. n. mill-race. **Mühlrad**, -rät, n. pl. -räder, mill-wheel. **Mühlstein**, -zhtĕin, m. pl. -e. mill-stone: **oberer —**, runner. **Mühlwehr**, -vār, n. mill-dam. **Mühlwerk**, mūl'vĕrk, n. mill, mill-work.
Muhme, mu'me, f. aunt; cousin, female relation.
Mühsam, mü'sam, a. troublesome, toilsome, painful; av. -ly: **-keit**, -kāĕt. f. troublesomeness, difficulty. **Mühselig**, -sēlich, a. laborious, toilsome, troubled; **-keit**, -kāĕt, f. laboriousness, painfulness. **Mühwaltung**, -valtung, f. trouble. **Mühvoll**, mū'foll, a. troublesome, laborious.

Mulde, mŭl'de, *f.* tray.
Müller, mŭl'ler, *m.* miller. **Müllerin, Müllerin,** mŭl'lĕrin, *f.* miller's wife.
Multiplikation, multiplikatsiōn', *f.* multiplication. **Multiplizieren,** multiplitsī'ren, *vt.* to multiply.
Mumie, mŭ'mi-e, *f.* mummy.
Mumme, mŭm'me, *f.* mum (beer).
Mumme, mŭm'me, *f.* mask.
Mummeln, mŭm'mĕln, *vi.* to mumble.
Mummerei, mŭmmĕrī', *f.* mummery, masking, disguise; hypocrisy.
Mund, mŭnt, *n. pl.* **Münde(r),** mouth; orifice; **reinen — halten,** to keep a secret; **kein Blatt vor den — nehmen,** to speak openly; **— und Nase aufsperren,** to stand staring and gaping; **-art, -ärt,** *f.* dialect; **-bedarf, -bedarf,** *m.* victuals, provisions.
Mündel, mŭn'del, *n.* ward.
Munden, mŭn'den, *vi.* to relish.
Münden, mŭn'den, *vt.* to empty, discharge itself.
Mundfäule, mŭnt'foile, *f.* scurvy in the gums.
Mündig, mŭn'dich, *a.* of age; **-keit, -käet,** *f.* full age, majority.
Mundklemme, mŭnt'klemme, *f.* lockjaw.
Mündlich, münt'lich, *a.* oral, verbal, *av.* -ly; **-es Verfahren,** oral pleading.
Mundrecht, mŭnt'recht, *a.* palatable.
Mundschenk, mŭnt'shenk, *m. -en, pl. -en,* cup-bearer.
Mundstück, mŭnt'zhtück, *n. pl. -e,* mouthpiece, orifice.
Mündung, mŭn'dŭng, *f.* mouth; orifice; muzzle.
Mundvoll, mŭnt'fŏll, *av.* mouthful.
Mundwerk, mŭnt'vĕrk, *n.* mouth; volubility.
Munition, munitsiōn', *f.* ammunition.
Munizipalität, munitsipalitāt', *f.* municipality.
Munkeln, mŭn'kĕln, *vi.* to act clandestinely; to be whispered; to be gloomy.
Münster, mŭn'zhtĕr, *m.* minster, cathedral.
Munter, mŭn'tĕr, *a.* awake; lively, brisk, sprightly, cheerful; **-keit, -käet,** *f.* watchfulness, sprightliness, cheerfulness

Münze, mŭn'tse, *f.* coin, money change; mint. **Münzen,** mŭn'tsen, *vt.* to coin, mint. **Münzer,** mŭn'tsĕr, *m.* coiner. **Münzfälscher,** -fĕlsher, *m.* counterfeiter. **Münzfuß,** -fŭss, *m.* standard of coinage. **Münzhaus,** -hōŭs, *n. pl.* -**häuser,** mint. **Münzkunde,** -kŭnde, *f.* numismatics. **Münzmeister,** -mĕezhtĕr, *m.* mint-master. **Münzrecht,** -recht, *n.* right of coinage. **Münzschlag,** -shläg, *m.* coining. coinage. **Münzsorte,** -sorte, *f.* species of coin. **Münzwardein,** -vardāēn. *m.* mint-warden; assaymaster **Münzwesen,** münts'vēsen, *n.* coinage.
Mürbe, mŭr'be, *a.* tender, mellow, brittle; *s. f.* mellowness, tenderness.
Murmeln, mŭr'mĕln, *vt. i.* to murmur, mutter, grumble.
Murmeltier, mŭr'mĕltīr, *n.* marmot.
Murren, mŭr'ren, *vi.* to mutter, grumble, murmur.
Mürrisch, mŭr'rish, *a.* surly, sulky, sullen, peevish.
Murrkopf, mŭrr'kopf, *m. pl. -köpfe,* grumbler.
Mus, mŭs, *n. pl. -e,* pap, mush.
Muschel, mŭsh'el, *f.* shell; muscle, shellfish; **-schale, -shale,** *f.* shell of a muscle; **-kalk, -kalk,** *m.* shell-lime.
Muse, mŭ'se, *f.* muse. **Musensohn,** -sōn, *m. pl. -söhne,* student.
Museum, musā'um, *n.* museum.
Musizieren, musitsī ren, *vi.* to make or practise music. **Musik,** musīk', *f.* music; **-alisch, -āl'ish,** *a.* musical. **Musikant,** musikant', *m. -en, pl. -en.* **Musiker,** mu'sikĕr, *m.* musician. **Musiklehrer,** -lērēr, *m.* music-teacher. **Musikstunde,** -zhtŭnde, *f.* music-lesson.
Musivarbeit, musīf'arbäet, *f.* mosaic, mosaic work.
Muskatenblüthe, muskāt'enblüte, *f.* mace. **Muskatnuß,** -nŭss, *f. pl. -nüsse,* nutmeg.
Muskel, mŭs'kel, *f.* muscle. **Muskelig,** mŭs'kelich, *a.* muscular. **Muskelstärke,** -zhtĕrke, *f.* muscular strength.
Muskete, muskā'te, *f.* musket. **Musketenfeuer,** -fŏī-ēr, *n.* **Musketensalve,** -salfe, *f.* musketry, volley of

musket-shot. **Musketier,** mŭsketīr', m. musketeer.
Muskulös, mŭskŭlös', a. muscular.
Muß, mŭs, n. pap, mush, porridge.
Muß, mŭse, n. necessity.
Muße, mŭse, f. leisure; — haben, to be at leisure; **-stunde,** -zhtŭnde, f. leisure-hour.
Müssen, müs'sen (mußte, gemußt), ich muß, I must, am obliged to.
Müßig, müs'sich, a. unemployed, idle, leisurely; — gehen, to idle; **-gang,** -gang, m. idleness. **Müß'iggänger,** -genger, m. idler.
Mussiren, mŭssī'ren, vi. to sparkle, froth.
Muster, mŭzh'tĕr, n. pattern, sample; type, ideal, paragon; **-haft,** -haft, a. exemplary; **-hastigkeit,** -ichkāēt, f. exemplariness. **Must'erkarte,** -karte, f. pattern-card.
Mustern, mŭzh'tĕrn, vt. to review, muster, view; figure; gemustert werden, to pass muster. **Must'errolle,** -rolle, f. muster-roll. **Mus'erung,** mŭzh'tĕrŭng, f. muster, review.
Muth, mŭt, m. courage; mind, state of mind, disposition; — machen, to encourage; **-ig,** mŭt'ich, a. courageous, brave, spirited, fiery. **Muth'los,** -lōs, a. coward, discouraged, disheartened; **-igkeit,** -ichkāēt, f. want of courage, dejection. **Muth'maßen,** -mässen, vt. to conjecture, presume, suppose. **Muth'maßlich,** -mässlich, a. presumptive, conjectural. **Muth'maßung,** -mässung, f. conjecture, presumption, supposition. **Muth'voll,** -foll, a. courageous. **Muth'wille,** -ville, **-ns,** m. wantonness, petulance, roguery, prank. **Muthwillig,** mŭt'villich, a. wanton, petulant.
Mutter, mŭt'tĕr, f. mother; matron; womb; **-beschwerde,** -beshvērde, f. hysterical affection, hysterics. **Mutterbiene,** mŭt'tĕrbīne, . queen-bee.

Mut'terbrust, -brŭzht. f. pl. -brüste bosom of a mother; affection of a mother. **Mut'terfüllen,** -füllen, n. filly. **Mut'terherz,** -hĕrts, -ens, pl. -en, mother's heart; maternal affection. **Mut'terkrampf,** -krampf, m. pl. -krämpfe, hysterical spasms. **Mut'terkrebs,** -krēps, m. cancer of the womb. **Mut'terlamm,** -lamm, n. pl. -lämmer, ewe-lamb. **Mut'terlauge,** -lāŭge, f. mother-lye. **Mut'terleib,** -lēīb, m. womb; von — an, from one's birth. **Mütterlich,** mŭtt'tĕrlich, a. motherly. **Mutterlos,** mŭt'tĕrlōs, a. motherless. **Mut'termahl,** -māl, n. mole. **Mut'termilch,** -milch, f. mother's milk. **Mut'termord,** -mort, m. matricide. **Mut'termörder,** -mörder, m. -in, f. matricide. **Mut'ternackt,** -nackt, a. stark naked. **Mut'terpferd,** -pfērt, n. pl. -e, mare. **Mut'terschaf,** -shāf, n. pl. -e, ewe. **Mut'terschaft,** -shaft, f. maternity. **Mut'terschoß,** -shōs, m. mother's lap. **Mut'terschwein,** -shvēīn, n. pl. -e, sow. **Mut'terschwester,** -shvezhter, f. mother's sister, aunt. Mutterseelen allein, quite alone. **Mut'tersprache,** -shprache, f. mother-tongue; native language. **Mut'terwitz,** -vits, m. common sense, mother-wit.
Mutz, mŭts, m. pl. -e, curtail; bobtail.
Mütze, müt'se, f. cap, bonnet.
Mutzen, mŭt'sen, vi. to curtail, clip, dock, crop.
Myriade, mĭrīā'de, f. myriad.
Myricin, mĭrītsīn', n. myricine.
Myrrhe, mĭr're, f. myrrh.
Myrte, mĭr'te, f. myrtle.
Mysterien, misiā'rī-en, f. mysteries.
Mysticismus, mistītsīs'mŭss, m. **Mystik,** nis'tic, f. mysticism.
Mystisch, mis'tish, a. mystic.
Mythe, mī'te, f. fable, myth.
Mythisch, mīt'ish, a. mythical.
Mythologie, mĭtŏlŏgī', f. mythology.

Rabe, nā′bẹ, *f.* nave. **Ra′benbüchſe**, -büxẹ. *f.* nave-box.

Rabel, nā′bel, *m.* navel, boss. **Ra′belſchnur**, -ṡhnṇr, *f.* **Ra′belſtrang**, -ẓhtrang, *m. pl.* -ſtränge, umbilical cord; navel-string.

Rach, nāch, *av. u. pr.* after, past, behind; according to, in: of; to, for; — der Reihe, in turn; Einer nach dem andern, one by one: riechen nach, to smell of; nach der Natur, from nature.

Rachäffen, nāch′ĕffen, *vt.* to ape, imitate.

Rachahmen, nāch′ämen, *vt.* to imitate.

Rachbar, nach′bar, *m.* -n, *pl.* -n, neighbor; -in, *f. pl.* -innen, neighbor. **Rach′barlich**, -barlich, *a.* neighborly, neighboring. **Rach′barſchaft**, -ṡhaft, *f.* neighborhood, vicinity; neighbors.

Rachbellen, nāch′bellen, *vi.* to bark after.

Rachbeten, nāch′bēten, *vt.* to echo (another), to repeat mechanically.

Rachbild, nāch′bilt, *n. pl.* -er, copy, imitation. **Rachbilden**, nach′bilden, *vt.* to copy, imitate, to form after. **Rach′bildung**, -ụng, *f.* imitation; copy, fac-simile.

Rachbleiben, nāch′blĕïben, *vi.* to be left, to remain behind.

Rachblicken, nāch′blicken, *vi.* to look after.

Rachblühen, nāch′blü-en, *vi.* to bloom a second time.

Rachbringen, nāch′bring-ẹn, *vt.* to bring after, to fetch up.

Rachbürge, nāch′bürge, *m.* second bail or security.

Rachdatiren, nāch′datīren, *vt.* to postdate.

Rachdem, nāchdām′, *Cj.* after (that), when.

Rachdenken, nāch′denken (nachbachte, nachgedacht), *vi.* to reflect, meditate; *s. n.* reflection, meditation, consideration. **Rach′denklich**, -denklich, *a.* thoughtful, meditative.

Rachdrängen, nāch′dreng-ẹn, *vt.* to press after, to crowd after.

Rachdringen, nāch′dring-ẹn, *vi.* to press after, pursue.

Rachdruck, nāch′drụck, *m.* energy, stress, force, emphasis; pirated edition, piracy; — legen auf, to emphasize. **Rach′drucken**, -ẹn, *vt.* to piratic. **Rach′drücklich**, -drücklich, *a.* emphatic, energetic, forcible.

Racheifer, *m.* **Racheiferung**, nāch′ëïferụng, *f.* emulation. **Rach′eiferer**, -ër, *m.* emulator, rival. **Rach′eifern**, *vi.* to emulate, rival.

Racheilen, nāch′ëïlen, *vi.* to hurry, hasten after.

Rachen, nach′en, *m.* boat, skiff, canoe.

Racherbe, nāch′erbe, *m.* -n, *pl.* -n, second heir, after-heir.

Racheſſen, nāch′ë-ssen, *n.* dessert.

Rachfahren, nāch′fāren, *vi.* to ride after. follow after.

Rachfolge, nāch′folgẹ, *f.* following after, imitation, succession; consequence. **Rach′folgen**, -folgen, *vi.* to follow after, to succeed; to imitate. **Rach′folger**, -folger, *m.* successor; follower, imitator.

Rachforſchen, nāch′forshen, *vi.* to inquire, search into. **Rach′forſcher**, -forsher, *m.* searcher, inquirer. **Rach′forſchung**, -ụng, *f.* inquiry, search, investigation.

Rachfrage, nāch′frägẹ, *f.* inquiry, demand. **Rach′fragen**, *vi.* to inquire after, ask after.

Rachfüllen, nāch′füllen, *vt.* to fill up, to add.

Rachgeben, nāch′gēben, *vi.* to yield, to give way, slacken; to comply; to be inferior to.

Rachgeboren, nāch′gẹbören, *a.* posthumous. **Rach′geburt**, -burt, *f.* afterbirth, secundines.

Rachgedanke, nāch′gẹdankẹ, *m.* -n, *pl.* -n, after-thought.

Rachgehen, nāch′gä-ẹn, *vi.* to go after, to follow after, to attend to; to be too slow; auf dem Fuße —, to dog one; der Spur —, to trace. **Rach′gehend**, nāch′gä-ẹnds, *av.* afterwards.

Rachgeſchmack, nāch′gẹshmack, *m.* after-taste.

Rachgiebig, nāch′gībich, *a.* yielding, complying; -keit, -kĕit, *f.* yielding disposition.

Rachgrübeln, nāch′grübeln, *vi.* to ponder, muse over.

Rachgrummet, nāch′grụmmẹt, *n.* third crop of hay.

Nach 226 **Nach**

Nachhall, nāch'hall, *m. -e,* echo, reverberation. **Nach'hallen,** -hallen, *vi.* to echo, resound.

Nachhängen, nāch'hengen, *vi.* to indulge in, to give way to.

Nachhelfen, nāch'helfen, *vi.* to help forward, to assist.

Nachher, nāch'hēr, *a.* afterwards, subsequently.

Nachherbst, nāch'herpst, *m. pl. -e,* Indian-summer.

Nachherig, nāch'hērich, *a.* subsequent.

Nachhetzen, nāch'hetsen, *vt.* to set (the dogs) on.

Nachhinken, nāch'hinken, *vi.* to hobble, limp after.

Nachholen, nāch'hōlen, *vt.* to bring up, to make up.

Nachhut, nāch'hut, *f.* rearguard.

Nachjagen, nāch'yāgen, *vt.* to pursue, chase, to give chase, to hunt (after); to follow after.

Nachklang, nāch'klang, *m. pl. -klänge,* echo, (faint) re-echo. **Nach'klingen,** -klingen, *vi.* to echo.

Nachkomme, nāch'komme, *m. gew. pl. -n,* descendant, progeny. **Nach'kommen,** -kommen, *vi.* to come after, to come up; to comply with; *-schaft, f.* progeny, posterity. **Nach'kömmling,** -kömmling, *m. pl. -e,* progeny, offspring.

Nachlaß, nach'lass, *m.* intermission; abatement; inheritance. **Nach'lassen,** -lassen (nachließ, nachgelassen), *vt.* to leave; to slacken, to loosen, to ease; to abate, diminish; *vi.* to decrease, abate, subside, cease. **Nach'lässig,** -lässich, *a.* negligent; *-keit, -kēet, f.* negligence, carelessness. **Nach'lassung,** -ung, *f.* remission.

Nachlaufen, nāch'laufen (nachlief, nachgelaufen), *vt.* to run after; to pursue.

Nachleben, nāch'lēben, *vi.* to follow one's example.

Nachliegen, nāch'lāgen, *vt.* to lay on more.

Nachlese, nāch'lēse, *f.* gleaning; — halten, to glean. **Nach'lesen,** -lēsen, *vt.* to glean; to read after; to verify.

Nachmachen, nāch'machen, *vt.* to imitate.

Nachmalen, nāch'mālen, *vt.* to copy, to paint; to imitate.

Nachmittag, nach'mittāg, *m. pl. -e,* afternoon. **Nach'mittägig,** -tāgich, *a.* of the afternoon. **Nach'mittäglich,** -tāglich, *a.* afternoon. **Nach'mittags,** -mittāgs, *av.* in the afternoon.

Nachmodeln, nāch'mōdeln, *vt.* to mould, cast after.

Nachnahme, nāch'nāme, *f.* cash on delivery. **Nach'nehmen,** -nāmen, *vt.* to cash on delivery.

Nachrechnen, nāch'rechnen, *vt.* to examine accounts.

Nachrede, nāch'rāde, *f.* report; üble —, bad reputation; blame, censure. **Nach'reden,** -rāden, *vt.* to impute to; Böses —, to asperse one.

Nachreiten, nāch'reiten (nachritt, nachgeritten), *vt.* to ride after.

Nachrennen, nāch'rennen (nachrannte, nachgerannt), *vt.* to run after.

Nachricht, nāch'richt, *f.* information, advice; — geben, to inform, to give notice of; — bekommen, to receive news from.

Nachrichter, nāch'richtēr, *m.* executioner.

Nachrufen, nāch'rufen (nachrief, nachgerufen), *vt.* to call after.

Nachruhm, nāch'rum, *m.* posthumous fame, praise after death.

Nachsagen, nāch'sāgen, *vt.* to say after one; to slander, backbite.

Nachsatz, nāch'sats, *m. pl. -sätze,* apodosis, conclusion.

Nachschallen, nāch'shallen (nachscholl, nachgeschallt), *vi.* to echo, resound.

Nachschauen, nāch'shāū-en, *vi.* to look after.

Nachschicken, nāch'shicken, *vt.* to send after.

Nachschießen, nāch'shīssen (nachschoß, nachgeschossen), *vi.* to run after; to shoot after.

Nachschlagen, nāch'shlāgen (nachschlug, nachgeschlagen), *vt.* to take after, to resemble; to consult (a book).

Nachschleichen, nāch'shleichen (nachschlich, nachgeschlichen), *vi.* to sneak after; to follow stealthily.

Nachschleifen, nāch'shlāfen, *vt.* to drag after.

Nachschleppen, nāch'shleppen, *vt.* to drag after.

Nachschlüssel, nāch'shlüssel, *m.* false key.

Nachschmecken, nāch'shmecken, *vi.* to taste after, to leave a taste.

Nachschreiben, năch'shrēīben (nach-
schrieb, nachgeschrieben), *vt.* to copy,
to write off; to write after.
Nachschreien, năch'shrēīen (nachschrie,
nachgeschrien), *vt.* to cry after.
Nachschrift, năch'shrift, *f.* postscript;
copy.
Nachschüren, năch'shüren, *vt. i.* to add
fuel.
Nachschuß, năch'shuss, *m.* after-pay-
ment; subsequent shot.
Nachschütten, năch'shütten, to pour in
subsequently, to add.
Nachschwimmen, năch'shvimmen (nach-
schwamm, nachgeschwommen), *vi.* to
swim after.
Nachsehen, năch'sē-en (nachsah, nachge-
sehen), *vt.* to look after; to overlook,
pardon; *s. n.* das — haben, to be
disappointed.
Nachsenden, năch'senden (nachsandte,
nachgesandt), *vt.* to send after.
Nachsetzen, năch'setsen, *vi.* to pursue,
run after; to slight. **Nachsetzung,**
-ung, *f.* pursuit; slight.
Nachsicht, năch'sicht, *f.* forbearance, indulgence. **Nachsichtig,** *a.* forbearing,
indulgent; -keit, -kĕĕt, *f.* forbearance. **Nachsichtsvoll,** -foll, *a.* indulgent.
Nachsilbe, năch'silbe, *f.* suffix.
Nachsingen, năch'singen (nachsang,
nachgesungen), *vi.* to sing after.
Nachsinnen, năch'sinnen (nachsann,
nachgesonnen), *vi.* to muse, meditate,
reflect; *s. n.* meditation, reflection,
musing. **Nachsinnend,** năch'sinnend,
a. meditating, reflective, thoughtful.
Nachspähen, năch'spä-en, *vi.* to spy; to
search, explore. **Nachspähung,** -ung,
f. investigation, search.
Nachspiel, năch'zhpīl, *n. pl.* -e, after-
play, farce. **Nachspielen,** -zhpīlen,
vi. to imitate; to play after; — nach
dem Gehör, to play by ear.
Nachsprechen, năch'zhprechen (nach-
sprach, nachgesprochen), *vt.* to repeat
the words of another.
Nachsprengen, năch'zhprengen, *vi.* to
gallop after.
Nachspringen, năch'zhpring-en (nach-
sprang, nachgesprungen), *vi.* to run
after, to jump after.
Nachspüren, năch'zhpüren, *vi.* to dive
into, search into, investigate. **Nach'-
spürung,** -ung, *f.* investigation.

Nächst, nĕxt, *a. av.* next, nearest, next
to; mit nächstem, *av.* soon. **Nächst'-
beste,** -beste, *m.* second-best. **Nächste,**
nĕx'te, *a.* next, nearest; der — beste,
the first comer.
Nachstehen, năch'zhtā-en (nachstand,
nachgestanden), *vi.* to stand after; to
be inferior to.
Nachstellen, năch'zhtellen, *vt.* to put
behind, to place after; to lay snares;
to waylay, lie in wait for. **Nach'-
stellung,** -ung, *f.* snares, plot, way-
laying.
Nächstenliebe, nĕxt'enllbe, *f.* charity,
neighborly love. **Nächstens,** nĕx'-
tens, *av.* soon. **Nächster,** nĕx'ter, *m.*
neighbor.
Nachstreben, năch'zhtrēben, *vi.* to strive
after, for; to emulate. **Nach'stre-
bung,** năch'zhtrēbung, *f.* emulation.
Nachströmen, năch'zhtrömen, *vi.* to flow
after, to gush out.
Nachstürmen, năch'zhtürmen, *vi.* to
rush after.
Nachstürzen, năch'zhtürtsen, *vi.* to rush
after, run after; *vt.* to precipitate
after; to throw down.
Nachsuchen, năch'suchen, *vi.* to search
after; to apply for. **Nachsuchung,**
-ung, *f.* search, inquiry.
Nacht, nacht, *f. pl.* Nächte, night;
darkness; bei —, at night: über —,
during the night; mit einbrechender
—, at nightfall; des Nachts, at
night. **Nachtarbeit,** -arbĕĕt, *f.*
night-work, lucubration. **Nachten,**
nach'ten, *vi.* to grow night; to be
night. **Nachtessen,** -essen, *n.* supper.
Nachteule, -eule, *f.* screech-owl,
owlet.
Nachtfalter, nacht'falter, *m.* night-but-
terfly.
Nachthaube, nacht'hoube, *f.* night-cap.
Nachtheil, năch'tĕĕl, *m.* disadvantage,
detriment, prejudice; im —e sein, to
have the worst. **Nach'theilig,** -tĕĕ-
lich, *a.* disadvantageous, prejudicial, derogatory, injurious, unfavorable.
Nachthun, năch'tun (nachthat, nachge-
than), *vi.* to do after; to copy, imitate; to come up with.
Nachtigall, nach'tigall, *f.* nightin-
gale.
Nachtisch, năch'tish, *m.* dessert; — auftragen, to serve the dessert.

Nach   228   **Nag**

Nachtkerze, nacht'kĕrtse, f. rush-light. **Nacht'kleid**, -klĕed, n. pl. -er, nightgown. **Nacht'lager**, -lägĕr, n. night's lodging. **Nacht'lampe**, -lampe, f. night-lamp. **Nächtlich**, něcht'lich, a. av. nightly, nocturnal; at night. **Nachtlicht**, nacht'licht, n. pl. -er, rush-light, night-candle. **Nacht'mahl**, -mäl, n. Holy Supper. **Nacht'musik**, -musik, f. serenade. **Nacht'mütze**, -mütse, f. night-cap.

Nachtönen, nāch'tōnen, vi. to prolong a sound; vt. to resound.

Nachtquartier, nacht'quartīr, n. night's lodging.

Nachtrab, nāch'trāb, rear, rearguard. **Nach'traben**, -trāben, vt. to trot after.

Nachtrachten, nāch'trachten, vi. to aspire to, to strive after.

Nachtrag, nāch'trāg, m. pl. -träge, supplement, appendix. **Nach'tragen**, -trägen (nachtrug, nachgetragen), vt. to carry after, behind; to bear a grudge; to add to. **Nach'träglich**, -träglich, a. additional, further, in addition.

Nachtreten, nāch'trēten (nachtrat, nachgetreten), vi. to follow servilely. **Nach'treter**, -trāter, m. follower.

Nachtrieb, nāch'trīb, m. pl. -e, aftershoot.

Nachtriegel, nacht'rīgel, m. night-bolt. **Nachts**, nachts, av. in the night. **Nachtschatten**, n cht'shatten, m. nightshade. **Nacht'schwärmer**, -shvermĕr, m. night-reveller. **Nacht'schweiß**, -shvīss, m. nocturnal sweat or perspiration. **Nacht'stück**, -zhtück, n. pl. -e, night-piece, night-scene. **Nacht'stuhl**, -zhtyl, m. pl. -stühle, stool, close-stool. **Nacht'tisch**, -tish, m. pl. -e, toilet, dressing-table. **Nacht'topf**, -topf, m. pl. -töpfe, chamber-pot. **Nacht'wache**, -vache, f. nightwatch. **Nacht'wächter**, -vēchtĕr, m. watchman, night-watch. **Nacht'wandeln**, -vandĕln, vi. to walk in one's sleep. **Nacht'wandler**, -vandlĕr, m. sleep-walker, somnambulist. **Nachtzeit**, nacht'tsēit, f. night-time. **Nacht'zug**, -tsyk, m. night-train; nocturnal procession.

Nachwachsen, nāch'vaksen (nachwuchs, nachgewachsen), vi. to grow after.

Nachwagen, nāch'vāgen, vt. to weigh over or again.

Nachwälzen, nāch'vęltsen, vt. i. to roll after.

Nachwandeln, nāch'vandeln, vi. to follow after, walk after.

Nachweh, nāch'vā, n. pl. -en, afterpain; evil consequence.

Nachwein, nāch'vęēn, m. pl. -e, bad wine; wine of the second press.

Nachweisen, nāch'vēisen (nachwies, nachgewiesen), vt. to point out, show. **Nach'weisung**, -yng, f. direction, proof, demonstration.

Nachwelt, nāch'vęlt, f. posterity.

Nachwerfen, nāch'vērfen (nachwarf, nachgeworfen), vt. to throw after.

Nachwirken, nāch'vīrken, vi. to operate or work subsequently.

Nachwuchs, nāch'vųx, m. after-growth; progeny.

Nachzahlen, nāch'tsālen, vt. to pay in addition.

Nachzählen, nāch'tsēlen, vt. to count over.

Nachzahlung, nāch'tsālyng, f. afterpayment.

Nachzeichnen, nāch'tsēēchnen, vt. to draw after. **Nach'zeichnung**, -yng, f. copy (of a drawing).

Nachziehen, nāch'tsī-en (nachzog, nachgezogen), vt. to draw after; vi. to march after, follow after.

Nachzucht, nāch'tsucht, f. after-swarm. **Nachzug**, nāch'tsyk, m. pl. -züge, rear. **Nach'zügler**, -tsühklĕr, m. straggler, marauder.

Nacken, nack'en, m. neck, nape. **Nackt**, nackt, a. naked, bare. **Nackt'heit**, -hēet, f. nakedness, nudity, bareness.

Nadel, nā'del, f. needle; pin. **Na'delbrief**, -brīf, m. pl. -briefe, paper of pins. **Na'delbüchse**, -büxe, f. needlecase. **Na'delgeld**, -gĕlt, n. pl. -er, pin-money. **Na'delkissen**, -kissen, n. pin-cushion. **Na'delkopf**, -kopf, m. pl. -köpfe, head of a pin. **Na'delöhr**, -ör, n. pl. -e, eye of a needle. **Na'delspitze**, -zhpitse, f. point of a needle or pin. **Na'delstich**, -zhtich, m. pl. -e, prick of a needle; stitch. **Nadler**, nād'lĕr, m. needler, pinmaker.

Nagel, nā'gel, m. nail; pin. peg. **Na'gelbank**, -bank, m. pl. -bänke, range. **Na'gelbohrer**, -börĕr, m. gimlet. **Na'geleisen**, -ēisen, n. nail-rod. **Na'gelfest**, -fĕsht, a. nailed, immovable.

Ra'gelform, -form, *f.* nail-mould.
Ra'gelgeschwür, -geshvühr, *n. pl.* -e, whitlow. **Ra'gelkopf,** -kopf, *m. pl.* -köpfe, nail-head. **Ragen,** nä'geln, *vt.* to nail, spike. **Ra'gelneu,** -neü, *a.* bran-new, span-new. **Ra'gelschmied,** -shmīd, *m. pl.* -e, nailsmith.

Ragen, nä'gen, *vt.* to gnaw, pick, nibble.

Ragethier, nä'getīr, *n. pl.* -e, rodent.

Rahe, nä'e, **Räher,** nä'er, *a.* nigh, near, nearer; close at hand, imminent, impending; nah und fern, far and wide, far and near. **Rähe,** nä'e, *f.* nearness, proximity, neighborhood, vicinity; in der —, near at hand. **Rahen,** nä'en, *vi. u. r.* to approach, to draw near.

Rähen, nä'-en, *vt. i.* to sew, stitch; to do needle-work.

Räherei, nä-ērī', *f.* sewing, needlework.

Räheres, nä'ēres, *n.* particulars, details.

Räherin, nä'ērin, *f.* seamstress.

Rähern, nä'ērn, *vr.* to approach, approximate, draw near; sich dem Ende —, to draw to a close.

Rähkasten, nä'kazhten, *m.* **Rät'lästchen,** -kezhtchen, *n.* work-box. **Räh'kissen,** -kissen, *n.* pin-cushion. **Räh'korb,** -korp, *m. pl.* -körbe, work-basket. **Rähmädchen,** nä'mēdchen, *n.* seamstress. **Räh'nadel,** -nädel, *f.* sewing-needle. **Räh'ramen,** -rämen, *m.* frame for needle-work.

Rähren, nä'ren, *vt.* to nourish, foster, feed, support, entertain; sich — mit, to live by, to make one's living by. **Rahrhaft,** när'haft, *a.* nutritious, nourishing, substantial; -igkeit, -ichkäet, *f.* nutritiousness.

Rähring, nä'ring, *m. pl.* -e, sewing-ring.

Rährstand, när'zhtant, *m.* laboring-class.

Rahrung, när'ung, *f.* nourishment, food, nutriment; -smittel, -mittel, *f.* means of subsistence, provisions. **Rah'rungssorgen,** -sorgen, *s. pl.* cares for subsistence.

Rähschule, nä'shule, *f.* sewing-school. **Raht,** nāt, *f. pl.* Rähte, seam; suture. **Rähterin,** nä'tērin, *f.* seamstress. **Rähtzug,** nä'tsöuk, *n.* work, sewing, sewing-implements.

Raiv, na-īf, *a.* natural, unaffected; naive; artless. **Naivetät,** nä-īfetät', *f.* naiveté, artlessness.

Name, nä'me, *m.* -ns, *pl.* -n, name; dem — nach, *a.* nominally. **Ra'menlos,** -lōs, *a.* nameless, anonymous; unutterable. **Ra'mentlich,** -lich, *a.* namely, especially. **Ramhaft,** nām'haft, *a.* celebrated, far-famed; considerable; — machen, to name. **Rämlich,** näm'lich, *av.* namely, to wit; *a.* same.

Rapf, napf, *m. pl.* Näpfe (*dim.* Näpfchen), bowl, cup.

Raphtha, naf'tä, *n.* naphtha. **Raphthalin,** naf'talīn, *n.* naphthaline.

Rarbe, nar'be, *f.* scar, mark; stigma. **Rarben,** när'ben, *vi.* to scar; *vt.* to grain. **Rarbig,** nar'bich, *a.* scarred; grained.

Narcein, nartse-īn', *n.* narceine.

Narcisse, nartsis'se, *f.* narcissus.

Rarde, nar'de, *f.* nard, spikenard.

Rarkotin, narkotīn', *n.* narcotine.

Rarkotisch, narkot'ish, *a.* narcotic.

Rarr, narr, *m.* -en, *pl.* -en, (*dim.* Närrchen,) fool, buffoon. **Rarren,** när'ren, *vt.* to fool, make a fool of, banter. **Rar'renhaus,** -hőus, *n.* insane-asylum; mad-house, bedlam. **Rar'renkappe,** -kappe, *f.* fool's-cap. **Rar'renposse,** -posse, *f.* foolery. **Rar'renstreich,** -zhtrēch, *m. pl.* -e, foolish trick. **Rarrheit,** narr'hāet, *f.* foolishness, folly, foolery. **Närrin,** nër'rin, *f. pl.* -innen, foolish woman, fool. **Närrisch,** nër'rish, *a.* foolish, ridiculous, insane.

Narcisse, nartsis'se, *f.* narcissus.

Rasal, nasäl', *m. pl.* -en, **Rasal'laut,** -lőut, *m. pl.* -e, nasal sound.

Raschen, nash'en, *vt. i.* to nibble, to gormandize, to eat (dainties) by stealth; to enjoy illicitly. **Räscher,** nësh'ër, *m.* dainty mouth, nibbler, junketing person. **Räscherei,** -ēī', *f.* titbit, dainty; junketing. **Raschhaft,** nash'haft, *a.* fond of dainties, dainty; gormandizing. **Rasch'haftigkeit,** -ichkäet, *f.* fondness for gormandizing, junketing. **Rasch'werk,** -vërk, *n. pl.* -e, sweetmeats, titbits.

Rase, nä'se, *f.* nose; horn (of a plane); hook (of a tile); scent; reprimand; die — hochtragen, to carry a high head; to nose. **Räseln,** nä'seln, *vt.*

to utter through the nose; to nose, to snuffle. **Nasenband,** nä′senbant, *n. pl.* -bänder, nose-band, musrol. **Na′seubein,** -bēn, *n.* bridge of the nose. **Na′senbluten,** -blŭten, *n.* bleeding of the nose. **Na′senlaut,** lǭut, *m. pl.* -e, nasal sound. **Na′senloch,** -loch, *n. pl.* -löcher, nostril. **Na′senschleim,** -shlāum, *m. pl.* -e, mucus. **Na′senspitze,** -zhpitse, *f.* tip of the nose. **Na′senstüber,** -zhtüber, *m.* fillip; einen — geben, to fillip. **Na′senton,** -tōn, *m. pl.* -töne, nasal sound. **Na′senwurzel,** -vŭrtsel, *f.* root of the nose. **Na′seweis,** -vēīs, *a.* pert, malapert; **-heit,** -hāet, *f.* pertness. **Nas′horn,** -horn, *n. pl.* -hörner, rhinoceros. **Nas′tuch,** -tŭch, *n. pl.* -tücher, handkerchief.

Nass, nass, *a.* wet, moist; *s. n.* wetness, wet, moisture. **Nässe,** nes′se, *f.* dass. **Nässen,** nes′sen, *vt.* to wet. **Nasskalt,** nass′kalt, *a.* damp and cold. **Nässlich,** ness′lich, *a.* damp, moist.

Nation, natsiōn′, *f.* nation. **National,** natsionäl′, *a.* national. **Nationalisiren,** natsionalisī′ren, *vt.* to nationalize. **Nationalität,** -ität′, *f.* nationality, national character.

Nativität, natifität′, *f.* nativity; horoscope.

Natrium, nä′trium, *n.* **Na′triummetall,** -metall, *n.* sodium. **Natron,** nä′tron, *n.* soda. **Na′tronlaun,** -alǭun, *m.* soda-alum.

Natter, nat′ter, *f.* viper.

Natur, natŭr′, *f.* nature; constitution; von —, of nature, naturally; zur andern — werden, to grow into habit; in —, (in nature), in kind. **Naturalien,** natŭrä′lien, *s. pl.* natural products or curiosity; **-kabinet,** -kabinet, *n.* museum of natural curiosities. **Naturalisiren,** -isī′ren, *vt.* to naturalize. **Naturalist,** naturalist, *m.* -en. *pl.* -en. naturalist. **Naturell,** natŭrell′, *n.* temper, nature. **Naturforscher,** natŭr′forsher, *m.* naturalist, natural philosopher. **Naturgabe,** -gäbe, *f.* natural endowment, native talents. **Naturgeschichte,** -geshichte, *f.* natural history. **Naturgesetz,** -geseẓ, *n. pl.* -e, law of nature. **Naturkraft,** -kraft, *f. pl.* -kräfte, power of nature. **Naturkunde,** -kŭnde, *f.* physics, natural philosophy. **Naturkundiger,** -kŭndiger, *m.* natural philosopher. **Naturlehre,** -lēre, *f.* physics. **Natürlich,** natührlich, *a.* natural, artless; **-keit,** -kāet, *f.* naturalness, ingenuousness, artlessness. **Naturprodukt,** -produckt, *n. pl.* -e, natural production. **Naturrecht,** -recht, *n.* right by nature. **Naturreich,** -rēīch, *n. pl.* -e, natural kingdom. **Naturtrieb,** -trīp, *m. pl.* -e, instinct. **Naturwidrig,** -vīdrich, *a.* contrary to nature, unnatural, abnormal; **-keit,** -kāet, *f.* irregularity, abnormity. **Naturwissenschaft,** -shaft, *f.* natural sciences. **Naturzustand,** -tsŭzhtant, *m.* state of nature.

Nautisch, nǭu′tish, *a.* nautic.

Neapelgelb, neap′elgelp, *n.* Naples-yellow.

Nebel, nē′bel, *m,* fog, mist, haze. **Nebelbank,** -bank, *f. pl.* -bänke, fog-bank. **Ne′belferne,** -ferne, *f.* hazy distance. **Ne′belfleck,** -fleck, *m.* -en, *pl.* -en, nebula. **Ne′belgestalt,** -gestalt, *f.* airy phantom. **Ne′belgrau,** -grǭu, *a.* foggy, hazy. **Ne′belkappe,** -kappe, *f.* magic cap. **Nebelig,** nē′belich, *a.* foggy, misty. **Ne′belkrähe,** -krä-e, *f.* hooded crow. **Nebeln,** nē′beln, *vi.* to be foggy, misty.

Neben, nē′ben, *pr.* by the side of, besides, near, close by. **Ne′benabsicht,** -absicht, *f.* secondary intention. **Ne′benan,** -än, *av.* close by. **Ne′benbegriff,** -begriff, *m. pl.* -e, accessory idea, secondary notion. **Ne′benbei,** -bēī, *av.* close by. **Ne′benbuhler,** -būler, *m.* sin, *f.* rival, competitor. **Nebenbuhlerei,** -būlerēī′, *f.* rivalry. **Ne′benbuhlerisch,** -ish, *a.* rival. **Ne′beneinanderstellung,** -āenanderstellŭng, *f.* juxtaposition. **Ne′beneinkünfte,** -āenkünfte, *s. pl.* perquisites, fees. **Ne′bengasse,** -gasse, *f.* by-street, lane, alley. **Ne′bengebäude,** -gebāude, *n.* adjoining building, out-building. **Ne′bengedanke,** -gedanke, *m.* -ns. *pl.* -e, secondary thought, by-thought. **Ne′bengewinnst,** -gevinst, *m.* accidental profit, extra profit; secondary prize. **Ne′bengruppe,** -gruppe, *f.* accessory group. **Ne′benhandlung,** -handlŭng, *f.* episode. **Ne′benher,** -hēr, *a.* by the side; besides; independently. **Ne-**

benidee, -idă, f. accessory idea. Re's
benmann, -man, m. pl. -männer,
next man, neighbor. Re'benmenſch,
mensh. m. -en, pl. -en, fellow-man,
fellow-creature. Re'benmond, -mont,
m. mock-moon, paraselene. Re'ben-
punkt, -pynkt, m. pl. -e, secondary
point. Re'benrolle, -rolle, f. subordinate part. Re'benſache, -ache, f.
secondary consideration, trifle. Re's
benſatz, -sats, m. pl. -ſätze, subordinate clause. Re'benſonne, -sonne,
f. parahelion. Re'benſtraße, -zhträ-
se, f. by-street. Re'benſtunde,
-zhtynde, f. leisure-hour. Re'ben-
tiſch, -tish, m. pl. -e, side-table. Re's
benumſtand, -ymzhtant, m. pl.
-ſtände, accessory circumstance.
Re'benurſache, -yrsache, f. secondary
cause. Re'benverdienſt, -ferdĭenzht,
m. pl. -e, perquisite. Re'benweg,
-vēg, m. pl. -e, by-way, by-path.
Re'benwort, -vort, n. pl. -wörter, adverb. Re'benzimmer, -tsimmer, n.
Re'benſtube, -zhtybe, f. adjoining
room. Re'benzweg, -tsvěck, m. pl.
-e, subordinate aim or end.
Rebſt, nepzht, av. together with.
Recken, něk'ken, vt. to tease, banter,
vex. Reckerei, neckěrei', f. teasing,
bantering, raillery. Reckiſch, neck'-
ish, a. teasing; droll, funny.
Reffe, něf'fe, m. -n, pl. -n, nephew.
Relation, negatsion', f. negation.
Regativ, neg'atīf, a. negative; resinous.
Reger, nā'ger, m. negro. Re'gerin, f.
negress.
Regiren, näg'I'ren, vt. to deny.
Regligee, neglizhā', n. negligée.
Rehmen, nā'men, (nā'men) (nahm,
genommen), vt. to take; to accept,
receive; mit ſich —, to take along
with; leicht —, to make light of;
Anfang —, to begin; Ende —, to
end, finish; Schaden —, to suffer
damage; Wunder —, to surprise.
Reib, neid, m. envy, grudge, jealousy.
Reid'er, m. Reidhammel, -hammel,
n. pl. -hämmel, envious person,
grudger. Reidig, neid'ich, Reid'iſch,
-ish, a. envious, jealous.
Reige, näe'ge, f. decline; dregs: auf
die — gehen, to be on the decline.
Reigen, näe'gen, vt. to incline, bend;
to lower; vr. to bow; to slope, dip;
to decline; to draw to a close; ſich

— zu, to incline towards. Rei'gung,
-yng, f. inclination, disposition,
bias, propensity; affection; — faſ-
sen zu, to take a fancy to.
Rein, nšen, av. no, nay; mit — antworten, to answer in the negative.
Rektar, něk'tar, m. nectar.
Relke, něl'ke, f. pink.
Rennen, nen'nen, vt. to name, call;
mention. Renn'ner, m. denominator.
Renn'ung, -yng, f. naming, mention. Renn'werth, -vērt, m. nominal
value. Renn'wort, -vort, n. pl. -wör-
ter, noun.
Rerve, něr'fe, f. -n, pl. -n, nerve.
Rer'venfieber, -fībēr, n. nervous fever. Rer'venkrank, -krank, a. nervous; -heit, -häet, f. nervous disorder. Rervig, něr'fich, a. nervous,
sinewy, brawny.
Reſſel, nes'sel, f. nettle. Reſſelfieber,
-fībēr, n. Reſſelſucht, -sycht, f. nettle
-rash. Reſſeltuch, nes'seltych, mus-
lin.
Reſt, nest, n. pl. -er, nest, bed.
Reſtel, nes'tel, m. lace, shoe-lace. Reſ'-
teln, vt. to lace.
Rett, nětt, a. neat, pretty; exact.
Ret'tigkeit, -ichkäet, f. neatness,
prettiness.
Retz, nets (nēts), n. net.
Retzen, net'sen, vt. to wet, moisten.
Retzförmig, nets'förmich, a. reticular,
retiform. Retz'werk, -věrk, n. pl. -e
net-work.
Reu, neü, a. fresh, new; recent; aufs
Reue, anew, afresh. Reu'backen,
-backen, a. new-baked. Reu'erdings,
-ěrdings, Reu'erlich, -lich, av. newly,
lately. Reuerer, neü'ērěr, m. inno-
vator. Reu'erung, -yng, f. innova-
tion. Reu'geboren, -gēbōren, a. new-
born. Reu'gier, -gīr, f. curiosity.
Reu'gierig, -ich, a. inquisitive, curious. Reu'heit, -häet, f. newness,
novelty. Reuigkeit, neü'ichkäet, f.
news. Reu'jahr, -yār, n. new year.
Reu'jahrsgeſchenk, -gshenk, p. pl.
-e, new-year's gift. Reu'jahrsnacht,
-nacht, f. pl. -nächte, new-year's
night. Reu'jahrswunſch, -vynsh, m.
pl. -wünſche, congratulation for the
new year. Reu'modiſch, -mōdish, a.
new-fashioned. Reu'mond, -mont,
m. new-moon.
Reun, nšen, a. u s. f. nine. Reun'-
ed, -eck, n. pl. -e, nonagon. Reun'-

erlei, -ĕrlĕĭ, a. of nine sorts. **Neun's-fach**, -fach. **Neun'fältig**, -fĕltĭch, a. ninefold. **Neun'jährig**, -yärĭch, a. nine years old. **Neun'mal**, -mäl, av. nine times. **Neun'stimmig**, -zhtĭmmĭch, a. for nine voices. **Neun'stündig**, -zhtündĭch, a. of nine hours. **Neun'tägig**, -tägĭch, a. of nine days, nine days old. **Neunte**, nöĕn'tĕ, a. ninth. **Neun'tel**, -tel, n. ninth (part). **Neun'tens**, -tens, a. ninthly. **Neun'zehn**, -tsän, a. nineteen. **Neun'zehnt**, -tsänt, a. nineteenth. **Neun'zig**, -tsĭch, a. ninety. **Neunzigst**, -tsĭkst, a. ninetieth. **Neun'zigstel**, -tsĭkstel, n. ninetieth part.

Neutral, nöüträl', a. neutral. **Neutralisiren**, -isī'ren, vt. to neutralize. **Neutralität**, -ĭtät', f. neutrality.

Neutrum, nöü'trum, n. neuter.

Nicht, nĭcht, av. not; noch —, not yet; — einmal', not even: durchaus —, not at all; z. zu Nichte machen, to annihilate; mit Nichten, by no means. **Nichtachtung**, nĭcht'achtŭng, f. disregard.

Nichte, nĭch'tĕ, f. niece.

Nichtig, nĭch'tĭg, a. null, void, invalid; -keit, nĭch'tĭchkĕĭt, f. nullity, invalidity.

Nichts, nĭchts, z. n. und pl. -e, nothing, naught; — bestoweniger, nevertheless, notwithstanding. **Nichts'nutzig**, -nutzĭch, a. of no use, useless; -keit, -kĕĭt, f. worthlessness. **Nichts'sagend**, -sägent, a. insignificant. **Nichts'würdig**, -vürdĭch, a. worthless; -keit, -kĕĭt, f. worthlessness.

Nick, nick, m. pl. -e, nod, wink.

Nickel, nick'el, m. nickel.

Nicken, nick'en, vi. to nod, wink.

Nie, nī, av. never.

Nieder, nī'dĕr, av. down; a. low, lower, inferior; auf und nieder, up and down.

Niederbeugen, nī'dĕrböügen, vt. to bow down, bend down.

Niederbiegen, nī'dĕrbīgen (-bog, -gebogen), vt. to bow down.

Niederbrennen, nī'dĕrbrennen, vt. i. to burn down.

Niederbücken, nī'dĕrbücken, vt. to stoop, to bend down.

Niederdrücken, nī'dĕrtrücken, vt. to press down.

Niederfahren, nī'dĕrfären (-fuhr, -gefahren), vt. to soar down, rush down.

Niederfallen, nī'dĕrfallen (-fiel, -gefallen), vi. to fall down.

Niedergeschlagen, nī'dĕrgeshlägen, a. dejected, depressed; -heit, -hĕĭt, f. dejection, dejectedness.

Niederhalten, nī'dĕrhalten (-hielt, -gehalten), vt. to hold down, keep down.

Niederhangen, nī'dĕrhang-en (-hing, -gehangen), vi. to hang down.

Niederhauen, nī'dĕrhäü-en (-hieb, -gehauen), vt. to cut down, to fell.

Niederknien, nī'dĕrkni-en, vi. to kneel down.

Niederkommen, nī'dĕrkommen (-kam -gekommen), vi. to come down; to be delivered (of a child).

Niederkunft, nī'dĕrkunft, f. coming down; delivery, lying-in.

Niederlage, nī'dĕrläge, f. depository, depôt; defeat, rout.

Niederland, nī'dĕrlant, n. pl. -e, lowland; pl. Netherlands.

Niederlassen, nī'dĕrlassen (-ließ, gelassen), vt. to let down; vr. to sit down. **Nie'derlassung**, -ŭng, f. settlement.

Niederliegen, nī'dĕrlägen, vt. to lay down; vr. to lie down, to go to bed.

Niedermachen, nī'dĕrmachen, vt. to cut down, put to the sword.

Niedermetzeln, nī'dĕrmetseln, vt. to massacre.

Niederneigen, nī'dĕrnäĭgen, vt. u. r. to bend down, bow down.

Niederrauschen, nī'dĕrröüshen, vi. to rush down; to rustle down.

Niederreißen, nī'dĕrrĕĭssen, vt. to pull down, demolish.

Niederschießen, nī'dĕrshĭssen (-schoß, -geschossen), vt. to shoot down, to batter down; vi. to rush down.

Niederschlag, nī'dĕrshläg, m. precipitate. **Nie'derschlagen**, -en (-schlug, -geschlagen), vt. to strike down; to precipitate. **Nie'derschlagung**, -ŭng, f. precipitation.

Niederschreiben, nī'dĕrshrĕĭben, vt. to write down.

Niedersehen, nī'dĕrsĕ-en (-sah, -gesehen), vt. to look down.

Niedersenken, nī'dĕrsenken, vt. to lower.

Niedersetzen, nī'dĕrsetsen, vt. to set down; to appoint; sich niederf setzen, to sit down.

Nie 233 **Not**

Niedersinken, nī'dĕrsinken (-sank, -gesunken), vt. to sink down.
Niedersitzen, nī'dĕrsitsen (-saß, -gesessen), vi. to sit down.
Niederstechen, nī'dĕrshtĕchen (-stach, -gestochen), vt. to stab.
Niedersteigen, nī'dĕrshtīgen, vi. to step down, to descend.
Niederstimmen, nī'dĕrshtimmen, vi. to vote down; to depress.
Niederstoßen, nī'dĕrshtossen (-stieß, -gestoßen), vt. to stab; to knock down, to kill.
Niederstrecken, nī'dĕrshtrecken, vt. to strike down (dead).
Niederstürzen, nī'dĕrshtürtsen, vi. to fall headlong; vt. to precipitate.
Niederträchtig, nī'dĕrtrĕchtig, a. base, abject, vile; -keit, -kāĕt, f. baseness, meanness.
Niedertreiben, nī'dĕrtrīben (-trieb, -getrieben), vt. to drive down; vi. to float down.
Niedertreten, nī'dĕrtrēten (-trat, -getreten), vt. to tread down.
Niederung, nī'dĕrung, f. low-land. low-ground.
Niederwärts, nī'dĕrvĕrts, av. downwards.
Niederwerfen, nī'dĕrvĕrfen (-warf, -geworfen), vt. to throw down; sich — vor, to prostrate one's self before.
Niederziehen, nī'dĕrtsīen (-zog, -gezogen), vt. to draw down, bend down.
Niedlich, nīt'lich, a. neat, pretty, nice; -keit, -kāĕt, f. neatness.
Niedrig, nī'drich, a. low; base, mean; -keit, -kāĕt, f. lowness, depression; baseness, meanness.
Niemals, nī'mäls, av. never.
Niemand, nī'mant, n. nobody, no one.
Niere, nī're, f. kidney; pl. reins. **Nie'renbraten,** -brāten, m. roustloin. **Nie'renentzündung,** -entsündung, f. nephritis, inflammation of the kidneys. **Nie'renfett,** -fett, n. suet. **Nie'renstück,** -zhtück, n. loin of veal with kidney.
Niesen, nī'sen, vi. to sneeze. **Nie'sewurz,** -vurts, f. hellebore.
Nießbrauch, nīs'brōuch, m. usufruct.
Niet, nīt, n. rivet; auch **Nie'te,** f.; niet und nagelfest, clinched and riveted.
Niete, nī'te, f. blank (in lotteries).

Nieten, nī'ten, vt. to rivet, clinch **Riet'nagel,** -nāgel, m. pl. -nägel, rivet; hang-nail. **Niet'pfeife,** -pfīfe, m. **Riet'meißel,** -mäŏssel, m. riveting-punch.
Nilpferd, nīl'pfĕrt, n. pl. -e, hippopotamus.
Nimmer, nim'mĕr, av. never; -mehr, -mĕr, ar. nevermore.
Nippen, nip'pen, vi. to sip; tipple.
Niß, niss, f. pl. **Nisse,** nit.
Nisten, nis'ten, vi. to nest, nestle.
Nixe, nix'e, f. water-nymph.
Noch, noch, av. still, yet; weder ... noch, neither ... nor. **Noch'malig,** -mälich, a. repeated. **Noch'mals,** -mals, av. once more.
Nock, nock, n. pl. -e, yard-arm. **Nock'bändsel,** -bintsel, n. earing (Mar.).
Nomade, nomā'de, f. -n, pl. -n. nomad.
Nominal, nominäl', **Nominell,** nominĕll', a. nominal.
Nominativ, no'minatīf, m. nominative.
Nonne, non'ne, f. nun; moth; funnel.
Nonpareil, nonparĕll', f. nonpareil.
Noppe, nop'pe, f. knot, burl. **Noppen,** nop'pen, vt. to burl.
Nord, nort. m. **Norden,** nor'den, m. North. **Nordisch,** nor'dish, a. northern, northerly. **Nördlich,** nörd'lich, a. northerly; av. northward. **Nordlicht,** nord'licht, n. pl. -er, aurora borealis, northern light. **Nord'meer,** -mār, n. pl. -e, Arctic Ocean. **Nordost,** -ozht', m. northeast. **Nordöstlich,** -özht'lich, a. northeasterly. **Nord'pol,** -pōl, m. north pole. **Nord'polarkreis,** -polärkrīes, m. Arctic circle. **Nord'see,** -sā, f. North Sea. **Nord'stern,** -zhtĕrn, m. pole-star. **Nordwest,** nord'vĕst, m. northwest. **Nord'wind,** -vint, m. pl. -e, north wind.
Nörgeln, nör'geln, vi. to grumble, to be sulky: to tease.
Norm, norm, f. rule, norm. **Normal,** normäl', a. normal. **Normiren,** normī'ren, vt. to rule, direct.
Nössel, nös'sel, n. pint.
Notar, notär', m. pl. -e, notary. **Notariat,** notariät', n. pl. -e, office of a notary.
Note, nō'te, f. note, bill, note (Mus.). **No'tenbuch,** -buch, n. pl. -bücher, mu-

sic-book. **Nŏ'tenpapier**, -papīr, *n.* music-paper, note-paper. **Nŏtenpult**, nŏ'tenpŭlt, *m. pl.* -e, music-desk.

Noth, nōt, *f.* need, distress, trouble, pain, difficulty, want, necessity; in **Nöthen sein**, to be distressed; **von Nöthen**, needed; **zur Noth**, if necessary. **Noth'anker**, -anker, *m.* sheet-anchor. **Noth'behelf**, behelf, *m. pl.* -e, makeshift. **Noth'durft**, -dŭrft, *f.* sufficiency; necessity; poverty; **seine — verrichten**, to ease one's self. **Nothdürftig**, -dürftich, *a.* indigent, scanty; *av.* barely, hardly: poorly; **-keit**, -kāet, *f.* indigence. **Noth'fall**, -fall, *m.* case of need, case of necessity. **Nöthig**, nöt'ich, *a.* necessary, needed. **Nöthigen**, nö'tichen, *vt.* to compel, necessitate, oblige. **Nöthi'gung**, -ŭng, *f.* pressing invitation; compulsion. **Nothleidend**, nōt'leïdent, *a.* suffering want. **Noth'lüge**, -lüge, *f.* white lie. **Nothmast**, nōt'mazht, *m.* -es, *pl.* -en, jury-mast. **Noth'schuß**, -shŭss, *m. pl.* -schüsse, signal of distress. **Noth'stall**, -zhtall, *m. pl.* -ställe, trave. **Noth'stand**, -zhtaut, *m.* need, distress. **Noth'wehr**, -vär, *f.* self-defence. **Noth'wendig**, -vendich, *a.* necessary, *av.* necessarily; **-keit**, -kāet, *f.* necessity. **Noth'zucht**, -tsŭcht, *f.* violation, rape. **Noth'züchtigen**, -tsüchtigen, *vt.* to ravish, commit a rape. **Noth'züchtigung**, -ŭng. *f.* rape, ravishment.

Notiren, notī'ren, *vt.* to note, book. **Notiz**, notīts', *f.* notice; **— nehmen**, to notice.

Notorisch, notō'rish, *a.* notorious; *av.* notoriously.

Novelle, novèl'lę, *f.* novel. **Novellist**, novèllizht', *m.* -en, *pl.* -en, novel-writer, novelist.

November, noṣem'bèr, *m.* November.

Nu, nŭ, *n.* (das Nu, etc.) moment; **im Nu**, in a trice, in a twinkling.

Nüchtern, nüch'tèrn, *a.* fasting; sol r;
witless; **-keit**, -kāet, *f.* sobriety, soberness.

Nudel, nŭ'del, *f.* vermicelli. **Nu'delbrett**, -brĕt, *n. pl.* -er, vermicelli-board. **Nu'delholz**, -holts, *n. pl.* -hölzer, rolling-pin.

Null, nŭll, *a.* null; *s. f.* zero, naught, cipher.

Nummer, nŭm'mèr, *f.* number. **Nummeriren**, nŭmmerī'ren, *vt.* to number, to cipher, to mark with number.

Nun, nŭn, *av.* now, at present; well, well then; **von nun an**, henceforth.

Nunmehr, nŭn'mèr, *a.* now, henceforth. **Nun'mehrig**, -ich, *a.* present, actual.

Nur, nŭr, *av.* only, but; **wenn nur**, would that; provided that; **wer nur**, whosoever.

Nuß, nŭss, *f. pl.* Nüsse, nut; whirl (Mech.), notch (of a cross-bow); **welche Nuß**, walnut. **Nuß'baum**, -baŭm, *m.* walnut-tree : **-holz**, -holts, *n.* walnut-wood. **Nuß'braun**, -braŭn, *a.* nut-brown. **Nuß'kern**, -kèrn, *m. pl.* -e, kernel of a nut. **Nuß'knacker**, -knacker, *m.* nut cracker. **Nuß'öl**, -öl, *n.* nut-oil. **Nuß'schale**, -shāle, *f.* nut-shell.

Nüster, nüzh'ter, *f.* nostril.

Nuth, nŭt, *f.* groove, rabbet, joint, gutter; key-bed. **Nuth'hobel**, -hōbel, *m.* grooving-plane, plough.

Nutz, nŭts, *a.* useful, of use ; **nichts nutze**, of no use. **Nutz**, **Nutzen**, nŭt'sen, *m.* use; **zu Nutze machen**, to turn to advantage, to avail one's self of. **Nutzanwendung**, nŭts'anvendŭng, *f.* moral, application. **Nutzbar**, nŭts'bär, *a.* useful; **-keit**, -kāet, *f.* usefulness. **Nutzen**, **Nützen**, nŭt'sen, *vi.* to be of use. **Nütz'lich**, -lich. *a.* useful, of use, conducive; **-keit**, -kāet, *f.* usefulness, utility, advantage. **Nutzlos**, nŭts'lōs, *a.* useless; **-keit**, -ichkāet, *f.* uselessness. **Nutznießung**, nŭts'nisŭng. *f.* usufruct. **Nutzung**, -ŭng, *f.* use.

Nymphe, nim'fę, *f.* nymph; chrysalis

O, ō, ŋ. oh! o!

Oaſe, o-ā'ṣe, f. oasis.

Ob, ŏb, Cj. if, whether; als ob, as if; ar. above. over; pr. on account of.

Obacht, ŏb'acht, f. heed, care.

Obdach, ŏb'dach, n. shelter, lodging.

Oben, ŏb'en, av. above, on high; overhead, on the surface, up-stairs; before; von oben, from above; oben auf, uppermost; oben hin, superficially; oben aus, high-flown; **Obendrein**, ŏ'bendrēn, av. over and above, besides.

Ober, ŏ'bēr, a. upper, higher, superior.

Oberamt, ŏ'bēramt, n. upper bailiwick: -mann, -manu, m. pl. -männer, or -leute. bailiff.

Oberarm, ŏ'bērarm, m. pl. -e, upper arm.

Oberaufſeher, ŏ'bēröyfsē-ēr, m. superintendent. **Oberaufſicht**, -sicht, f. superintendence.

Oberbefehl, ŏ'bērbefēl, m. chief command: -shaber, -häber, m. commander-in-chief.

Oberbergamt, ŏ'bērbērkamt, n. pl. -ämter, mining-bureau.

Oberbramſegel, ŏbērbräm'sēgel, n. royal.

Obercommando, ŏbērcommandō, n. chief command.

Oberdeck, ŏ'bērdeck, n. pl. -e, upper deck.

Oberdeutſch, ŏ'bērdöytsh, a. peculiar to southern Germany.

Obereinnehmer, ŏ'bērṣennämēr, m. collector-general.

Oberer, ŏ'bērēr, m. chief, superior.

Oberfeldherr, ŏ'bērfēlthērr, m. -n, pl. -n, commander-in-chief.

Oberfeuerwerker, ŏ'bērföyērvērkēr, m. chief gunner.

Oberfläche, ŏ'bērflēche, f. surface, outside. **Oberflächlich**, -lich, a. superficial. av. -ly.

Oberförſter, ŏ'bērförstēr, m. upper forester.

Obergeſenk, ŏ'bērgesenk, n. top swage.

Obergewalt, ŏ'bērgevalt, f. sovereignty.

Obergurt, ŏbērgurt, f. pl. -e, wanty.

Oberhalb, ŏ'bērhalp, pr. u. av. above; superiorly.

Oberhand, ŏ'bērhant, f. upperhand,
ascendency, superiority, predominance; — haben, to sway, prevail.

Oberhaupt, ŏ'bērhäupt, n. head, chief chieftain.

Oberhaus, ŏ'bērhöys, n. house of lords.

Oberherr, ŏ'bērhērr, m. -n, pl. -n, sovereign. **Oberherrlich**, ŏ'bērhērrlich, a. sovereign; -keit, -kāet, f. sovereignty. **Oberherrſchaft**, -shaft, f. sovereignty, supremacy.

Oberhofgericht, ŏbērhŏf'gericht, n. supreme court, high court.

Oberhofmarſchall, ŏbērhŏf'marshal, m. grand marshal.

Oberhoheit, ŏbērhŏ'hāet, f. sovereignty.

Oberkellner, ŏ'bērkēllnēr, m. chief butler, head waiter.

Oberküchenmeiſter, ŏ'bērküchenmāstēr, m. head cook, master of the household.

Oberland, ŏ'bērlant, n. pl. -e, upland.

Oberlehnsherr, ŏbērläns'hērr, m. suverain.

Oberleib, ŏ'bērlēib, m. upper part of the body.

Oberleif, ŏ'bērlēik, pl. -e, head rope.

Oberlieutnant, ŏ'bērlētnant, m. pl. -e, first lieutenant.

Oberlippe, ŏ'bērlippe, f. upper lip.

Oberlitze, ŏ'bērlitse, f. sleeper (in weaving).

Obermann, ŏ'bērmann, m. pl. -männer, top-man, foreman.

Oberofſizier, ŏ'bēroffitsīr, m.pl. general officer.

Oberpfarrer, ŏ'bērpfarrēr, m. rector, chief minister.

Oberpoſtmeiſter, ŏbērpost'māstēr, m. postmaster-general.

Oberrichter, ŏ'bērrichtēr, m. chief judge.

Oberrock, ŏ'bērrock, m. pl. -röck, overcoat, greatcoat.

Oberſatz, ŏ'bērsats, m. pl. -sätze, major, first proposition.

Oberſchale, ŏ'bērshäle, f. cup.

Oberſchenkel, ŏ'bērshenkel, m. upper part of the thigh.

Oberſchlächtig, ŏ'bērshlēchtich, a. overshot.

Oberſchule, ŏ'bērshule, f. high school.

Oberſchulrath, -rath, m. board of

Obe 236 **Ofe**

public instruction; one of its members.
Oberſchwelle, ō'bĕrshvĕlle, f. lintel.
Oberſegel, ō'bĕrsēgel, n. topsail.
Oberſt, ō'bĕrst, a. uppermost, highest, supreme; s. m. auch **Obriſt,** colonel.
Oberſtallmeiſter, ōbĕrstall'māĕster, m. master of the horse, equerry.
Oberſtimme, ō'bĕrstimme, f. soprano, treble.
Oberſtlieutnant,ō'bĕrstlöutnant, m. pl. -e, lieutenant-colonel.
Oberſtube, ō'bĕrstube, f. upper room; dim. **-ſtübchen,** upper story (the brain).
Obertaſſe, ō'bĕrtasse, f. cup.
Obertheil, ō'bĕrtāĕl, m. upper part; top swage.
Obervormund, ō'bĕrformunt, m. chief guardian.
Oberwärts, ō'bĕrvĕrts, av. upward.
Oberwaſſer, ō'bĕrvassĕr, n. freshet.
Oberwelt, ō'bĕrvelt, f. upper world.
Oberzahn, ō'bĕrtsān, m. upper tooth.
Obgedacht, ōb'gedacht, a. above-said.
Obgemeldet, ōb'gemĕldĕt, a. above-mentioned.
Obgenannt, ōb'genannt, a. aforesaid.
Obgleich, ōbglēich', Cj. though, although.
Obhut, ōb'hut, f. protection, care, charge.
Obig, ōb'ich, a. above-said, former.
Objekt, obyĕkt'. n. pl. -e, object. **Ob-jektiv,** obyĕktīf', a. objective; **-glas,** -gläs. n. pl. **-gläſer,** object-glass.
Objektivität, -tiftāt', f. objectivity.
Oblate, ōb'late, f. wafer.
Obliegen, ōb'līgen, vi. to attend to, pursue, to apply one's self to: einem —, to be incumbent on. **Obliegen-heit,** ōb'līgenhāĕt, f. duty, incumbency, obligation. [bond.
Obligation, obligatsiōn', n. obligation.
Obmann, ōb'mann, m. pl. **Obmänner,** president; foreman (of a jury); umpire.
Obrigkeit, ōb'richkāĕt, f. authority, magistracy, government; **-lich,** -lich, a. official, magisterial.
Obriſt, ō'brist m. en, pl. -en, colonel.
Obſchon, obshōn', Cj. although, albeit.
Obſchweben, ōb'shvēben, vi. to be pendent.
Obſcän, obstsän', a. obscene.
Obſequien, obsā'qui-en, s. pl. obsequies.

Obſervanz, obsĕrfants', f. custom, usage. **Obſervatorium,** obsĕrfatō'-rium, n. pl. -rien, observatory.
Obſiegen, ob'sīgen, vi. to overcome, triumph.
Obſt, ōpst, n. pl. -e, fruit, fruits, fruit-age; **-bau,** -bŏy, m. culture of fruits, horticulture; **-baum,** -baŭm, m. fruit-tree; **-barre,** -darre, f. fruit-kiln; **-garten,** -garten, m. pl. **-gärten,** orchard; **-händler,** -hĕntlĕr, m. -in, f. fruit-seller, fruiterer; **-jahr,** -yār, n. pl. -e, fruit-year; **-kammer,** -kammĕr, f. fruit-room, fruit-loft. **-korb,** -korp, m. pl. **-körbe,** fruit-basket; **-markt,** -markt, m. pl. **-märkte,** fruit-market; **-moſt,** -most, m. pl. -e, cider; new cider; **-wein,** -vāĕn, m. cider.
Obwalten, ōb'valten, vi. to prevail, rule, to have sway.
Obwohl, obvōl', Cj. although, though, albeit.
Occident, ok'tsident, m. occident, west, western countries.
Ocean, ō'tsēān, m. ocean, sea.
Ocher, ōch'ĕr, m. ochre.
Ochs, oks, m. -en, pl. -en, ox; **-fleiſch,** -flāĕsh, n. beef; **-händler,** -hĕntlĕr, m. drover; **-haut,** -hŏyt, f. pl. **-häute,** ox-hide; **-hirt,** -hīrt, m. -en, pl. -en, neat-herd, cow-herd; **-horn,** -horn, m. pl. **-hörner,** bull's-horn; **-kopf,** -kopf, m. pl. **-köpfe,** bull's-head; **-ſtall,** -stall. m. pl. **-ſtälle,** ox-stable; **-zunge,** -tsunge, f. beef-tongue.
Ocker, ok'kĕr, m. ochre.
October, ok'tāŏdĕr, m. octahedron.
Octav, oktāf', a. octave. **Octav'band,** -bant, m. pl. **-bände,** octavo volume. **Octave,** oktā'fe, f. octave, diapason.
October, oktō'bĕr, m. October.
Octroiren, oktro-ī'ren, vt. to grant.
Oculiren, okulī'ren, vt. to inoculate, bud.
Ode, ōh'de, a. void, waste, empty, deserted; dreary; s. f. waste, desert.
Ode, ōde, f. ode.
Odem, ō'dem, m. breath.
Oder, ō'dĕr, Cj. or.
Ofen, ō'fen, m. pl. **Öfen,** stove, oven, kiln, furnace. **O'fenkachel,** -kachel, f. stove-tile. **O'fenloch,** -loch, n. pl. **-löcher,** mouth of a stove, **O'fen-rohr,** -rōr, n. stove-pipe. **O'fen-ſchirm,** -shirm, m. pl. -e, fire-screen. **O'fenthür,** -tür, f. stove-door.

Offen, off'n, *a.* open; frank; vacant; loose; clear; offene See, offing; **-bar,** -bär, *a.* manifest, evident, obvious, *av.* -ly; **-baren,** -bären, *vt.* to manifest, reveal; **-barung,** -bärung, *f.* revelation; manifestation, disclosure; Apocalypse; **-heit,** -hāēt, *f.* openness, candor; **-herzig,** -hērt-sich, open-hearted, frank, candid, ingenuous; **-herzigkeit,** *f.* candor, ingenuousness; **-kundig,** -kŭndich, *a.* notorious.

Offensiv, offensīfw', *a.* offensive; **Offensive,** *f.* offensive.

Öffentlich, öf'fentlich, *a.* public; **-keit,** kāēt, *f.* publicity.

Offeriren, offēri'ren, *vt.* to offer. **Offerte,** offēr'te, *f.* offer.

Officiant, offitsi-ant', *m.* -en, *pl.* -en, officer. **Officiell,** offitsi-ēll, *a.* official. **Officier,** offitsīr', **Offizier,** *m. pl.* -e, officer.

Officin, offitsīn', *f.* workshop, apothecary's shop.

Öffnen, öff'nen, *vt.* to open. **Öffnung,** öff'nŭng, *f.* opening, aperture; undoing; dissection; stool.

Oft, oft, *av.* often, oft. **Öfter,** öf'ter, *a.* repeated, frequent. **Öfters,** öf'ters, *av.* frequently, often. **Oftmalig,** oftmälich, *a.* repeated, frequent. **Oftmals,** -mäls, *av.* oftentimes.

Oh, ō, *ij.* oh! o! **Oho,** ohō, *ij.* oh! oho!

Oheim, ō'hāēm, *m. pl.* -e, uncle.

Ohne, ō'ne, *pr.* without, except, save. **Ohne das, Ohne dem, Ohnehin,** ōnehīn', *av.* without this, besides.

Ohnmacht, ōn'macht, *f.* impotency; swoon: in — fallen, to swoon, faint. **Ohnmächtig,** -mēchtich, *a.* impotent; fainting, swooning.

Ohr, ōr, *n. pl.* -e, eye (of a needle).

Ohr, ōr, *n.* -es, *pl.* -en, ear; hearing; vor einem Ohren, in one's hearing; die Ohren spitzen, to prick one's ears. **Ohrenbeichte,** ō'renbēīchte, auricular confession. **Ohrenbläser,** -bläser, *m.* whisperer, tell-tale. **Ohrenbrausen,** -brŏusen, *n.* humming, ringing in the ear. **Ohrenklingen,** -kling-en, *n.* ringing, tingling in one's ear. **Ohrenschmalz,** -shmälts, *n.* ear-wax. **Ohrenschmaus,** -shmŏus, *m.* feast for the ear. **Ohrenschmerz,** -shmērts, *m.* -es, *pl.* -en, ear-ache. **Ohrenzeuge,** -tsēūge, *m.* ear-witness, auricular witness. **Ohreule,** ōr'ōūle, *f.* horned owl. **Ohrfeige,** ōr'fēīge, *f.* box on the ear; — geben, to box one's ears. **Ohrläppchen,** -lēpchen, *n.* flap of the ear. **Ohrlöffel,** löf'fel, *m.* ear-picker. **Ohrring,** -ring, *m. pl.* -e, ear-ring. **Ohrwurm,** -vŭrm, *m. pl.* -würmer, ear-wig.

Öse, ō'se, *f.* eye, shank (of a button).

Ökonom, ökonōm', *m.* -en, *pl.* -en, husbandman; economist. **Ökonomie,** ökonomī', *f.* husbandry, economy. **Ökonomisch,** ökonō'mish, *a.* argricultural, economical.

Oktober, oktō'ber, *m.* October or Tenth month.

Öl, öl, *n. pl.* -e, oil; **-baum,** bäūm, *m. pl.* -bäume, olive-tree; **-berg,** -bērk, *m.* mount of olives.

Oleander, oleän'der, *m.* rose-bay, oleander.

Ölen, ō'len, *vt.* to oil. **Ölfarbe,** *f.* oil-color; **-gemälde,** -gemälde, *n.* **-bild,** -bilt, *n. pl.* -er, oil-painting; **-handel,** -handel, *m.* oil-trade; **-händler,** -hēntler, *m.* dealer in oil, oil-merchant; **-icht,** öl'icht, **-ig,** -ich, *a.* unctuous.

Oligarchie, oligarchī', *f.* oligarchy.

Olive, o'līfe, *f.* olive; **-farbig,** -fārbich, **-grün,** -grün, *a.* olive-green, olive, tawny.

Ölkuchen, -kuchen, *m.* oil-cake, linseed-cake; **-lampe,** -lampe, *f.* oil-lamp; **-malerei,** -mālērēī', *f.* oil-painting; **-mühle,** -mühle, **-presse,** -presse, *f.* oil-press; **-palme,** -palme, *f.* oil-palm; **-same,** -säme, *m.* seeds from which oil is obtained; **-säure,** -sēūre, *f.* oleic acid; **-saures Salz,** *n.* oleate; **-ung,** -ŭng, *f.* oiling; letzte —, extreme unction; **-süss,** -sūs, *n.* glycerine; **-zweig,** -tvāīg, *m. pl.* -e, olive-branch.

Omet, ō'met, *n.* after-math.

Ominös, ominōs', *a.* ominous.

Omnibus, om'nibŭss, *m. pl.* -e, omnibus.

Onkel, on'kel, *m.* uncle.

Onyx, ō'nix, *m.* onyx.

Opal, opāl', *m. pl.* -e, opal.

Oper, ō'per, *f.* opera.

Operation, operatsiōn', *f.* operation. **Operiren,** opēri'ren, to operate.

Operngucker, o'pērngŭcker, *m.* opera-glass; **-haus,** -hōūs, *n. pl.* -häuser,

opera-house: **Sänger,** -sing-ẽr, *m.*; **Operist,** opērist', *m.* opera-singer.
Opfer, op'fēr, *n.* offering, sacrifice; victim; **Fest,** -fest, *n. pl. -e,* sacrificial feast; **Herd,** -hĕrd, *m. pl. -e,* altar. **Opfern,** op'fērn, *vt.* to sacrifice, immolate. **Opferpriester,** op'fērprīstēr, *m.* sacrificer; **Thier,** -tīr, *n. pl. -e,* victim; **Tod,** -tōd, *m.* expiatory death; **-ung,** -yng, *f.* offering, immolation.
Ophit, ofīt', *m.* serpentine, green porphyry.
Opiat, opiät', *n. pl. -e,* opiate.
Opium, ō'pĭym, *n.* opium.
Opposition, oppositsiōn', *f.* opposition.
Optativ, op'tatīf, *m.* optative.
Optik, op'tik, *f.* optics. **Optiker,** op'tikēr, *m.* optician. **Optisch,** op'tish, *a.* optic, -al.
Orakel, orack'el, *n.* oracle.
Orange, orän'zhe, *f.* orange. **Orangenbaum,** orän'zhenbaum, *m. pl. -bäume,* orange-tree. **Orangenblüthe,** -blüte, *f.* orange-blossom. **Orangerie,** orănzhĕrī', *f.* orangery.
Orchester, orches'tēr, *n.* orchestra.
Orden, or'den, *m.* order. **Ordensband,** -bant, *n. pl. -bänder,* ribbon (badge) of an order. **Ordensgeistlicher,** -gäestlichēr, *m.* priest of an order. **Ordenskreuz,** -kröŭts, *n. pl. -e,* cross of an order. **Ordensritter,** -rittēr, *m.* knight of an order. **Ordenszeichen,** -tsäechen, *n.* badge of an order.
Ordentlich, or'dentlich, *a.* orderly, regular, ordinary.
Order, or'dēr, *f.* order.
Ordinalzahl, ordĭnäl'tsäl, *f.* ordinal number.
Ordination, ordĭnatsiōn', *f.* ordination. **Ordiniren,** ordinī'ren, *vt.* to ordain.
Ordnen, ord'nen, *vt.* to order, arrange; regulate, dispose.
Ordnung, ord'nyng, *f.* order, arrangement. **Ordnungsmässig,** -mässich, *a.* orderly, regular.
Ordonnanz, ordonnants', *f.* order, command; orderly.
Organ, orgăn', *n. pl. -e,* organ. **Organisation,** organisatsiōn', *f.* organization. **Organisch,** orgăn'ish, *a.* organic. **Organisiren,** organisī'ren, *vt.* to organize. **Organismus,** organis'mus, *m.* organism

Organist, organist', *m. -en, pl. -en,* organist.
Orgel, or'gel, *f.* organ. **Orgelbalg,** -balk, *m. pl. -bälge,* bellows of an organ. **Orgelbauer,** -bóyēr, *m.* organ-builder. **Orgeln,** or'geln, *vi.* to play the organ. **Orgelpfeife,** -pfeife, *f.* organ-pipe. **Orgelspieler,** *m.* organist.
Orgien, or'gi-en, *s. pl.* orgies.
Orient, ō'ri-ent, ori-ent', *m.* orient. **Orientalisch,** ōri-entăl'ish, *a.* oriental. **Orientiren,** ōri-entī'ren, *vt.* to set right, to orient, to ascertain the bearings.
Oriflamme, o'riflamme, *f.* oriflamb.
Original, originäl', *a.* original; *s. n. pl. -e,* or -ien, original, original document, original text. **Originalität,** originalitāt, *f.* originality. **Originell,** originĕll. *a.* original, eccentric.
Orkan, orkān', *m. pl. -e,* hurricane.
Ort, ort, *m. pl.* Oerter, Orte, place, region; village.
Orthodoxie, ortodoxī', *f.* orthodoxy.
Orthographie, ortografī', *f.* orthography. [*f.* locality.
Ortlich, ört'lich, *a.* local; **-keit,** -käet, **Ortsbeschreibung,** orts'beshrēībyng, *f.* topography. **Ortschaft,** ort'shaft, *f.* community; township. **Ortscheit,** -shăIt, *n. pl. -e,* single tree.
Os, Osten, ost'en, *m.* east.
Osterabend, ōs'terăbent, *m. pl. -e,* Easter-eve. **Osterei,** -āe, *n. Easter-egg.* **Osterfest,** -fest, *n.* **Ostern,** *s. pl.* Easter, passover. **Osterlamm,** -lamm, *n. pl. -lämmer,* paschal lamb.
Osterlich, ö'sterlich, *a.* Eastern, paschal, Easter. **Ostermonat,** -vochĕ, *f.* Easter-week.
Östlich, öst'lich, *a.* eastern, easterly; oriental. **Ostsee,** ost'sā, *f.* Baltic Sea. **Ostwind,** öst'vint, *m. pl. -e,* east wind.
Otter, ot'tēr, *f.* viper, adder.
Otter, ot'tēr, *m.* otter; **-balg,** -balk, *m. pl. -bälge,* **-fell,** -fell, *n. pl. -e,* skin of an otter.
Ouvertüre, yvertü're, *f.* overture.
Oval, ofäl', *a.* oval.
Oxhoft, ox'hoft, *n. pl. -e,* hogshead.
Oxyd, oxīd', *n. pl. -e,* oxide. **Oxydiren,** oxidī'ren, *vt.* oxidize, oxidate. **Oxydirung,** oxidī'ryng, *f.* oxidation. **Oxygen,** ox'igăn, *m.* oxygen.
Ocean, ō'tseăn, *m.* ocean.

Paar, pär, *n. pl.* -e, pair, couple, brace, match; ein Paar, a pair, a few; ju Paaren treiben, to rout. **Paaren,** pär'en, *vt.* to couple, pair off, match; fich —, to copulate. **Paarung,** pär'ung, *f.* copulation; matching. **Paarweise,** -vēlse, *av.* by pairs.

Pacht, pacht, *f.* lease, tenure, rent; in — geben, to let out, to lease. **Pacht- brief,** -brīf, *m. pl.* -e, lease. **Pach- ten,** pach'ten, *vt.* to rent. **Pächter,** pach'ter, **Pächter,** pěch'ter, *m.* -in, *f.* farmer, tenant, lessee. **Pachtgeld,** pacht'gělt, *n. pl.* -er, rent. **Pacht- herr,** -hěrr, *m.* -en, *pl.* -n, lessor, landlord. **Pachtung,** -ung, *f.* renting, farming.

Pack, pack, *m.* rabble, mob.

Pack, pack, *m. u. n. pl.* Päcke, pack, package. **Päckchen,** pěck'chen, *n.* little package, parcel; mit Sack und Pack, with bag and baggage. **Packen,** pack'en, *vt.* to pack; to seize, lay hold of; fich —, to be off. **Packer,** pack'er, *m.* packer; bear-hound. **Packesel,** -āsel, *m.* sumpter-ass; drudge. **Packet,** packet', *n.* f. **Paket. Packleinwand,** -lēinvant, *f.* pack- cloth. **Packpapier,** -papīr, *n.* wrap- ping-paper. **Packpferd,** -pfērt, *n. pl.* -e, pack-horse, sumpter-horse. **Packpresse,** -prěsse, *f.* packing-press. **Packsattel,** -sattel, *m. pl.* -sättel, pack-saddle. **Packtuch,** -tuch, *n. pl.* -tücher, pack-cloth. **Packwagen,** -vägen, *m.* baggage-wagon.

Pact, pakt, *m. pl.* -e, compact, agreement.

Pädagog, pēdagōg', *m.* pedagogue. **Pädagogik,** -gō'gik, *a.* pedagogics. **Pädagogisch,** pēdagō'gish, *a.* peda- gogic.

Paff, paff, *Ij.* bang! puff! whiff! **Paffen,** paf'fen, *vi.* to puff, whiff.

Page, pä'zhe, *m.* -n, *pl.* -n, page.

Pah, pä, *Ij.* pooh! bah.

Pair, pär, *m.* -s, *pl.* -s, peer.

Paket, paket', *n. pl.* -e, packet, package, parcel.

Paketboot, packet'bōt, *n. pl.* -e, packet.

Palast, palazht', *m. pl.* Paläste, palace.

Paletot, pa'letō, *m.* -s, *pl.* -s, paletot, overcoat.

Palette, palět'te, *f.* palette.

Palissade, palissä'de, *f.* palisade.

Pallasch, pall'ash, *m. pl.* -e, falchion broadsword.

Palliativ, palliatīf', *n.* palliative.

Palmbaum, palm'bäum, *m. pl.* -bäume. **Palme,** pal'me, *f.* palm, palm- tree. **Palmöl,** -öl, *n.* palm-oil. **Palmsonntag,** -sonntäg, *m. pl.* -e, Palm-Sunday. **Palmwoche,** -voche, *f.* Passion-week. **Palmzweig,** -tsvēlg, *m. pl.* -e, palm-branch.

Pamphlet, pamflět', *n. pl.* -e, pam- phlet.

Pandekten, panděk'ten, *s. pl.* pan- dects.

Panier, panīr', *n. pl.* -e, banner, stan- dard.

Panisch, pä'nish, *a.* panic; panischer Schrecken, panic.

Panschen, pan'shen, *vt.* to slap, whip.

Panster, pan'zhtěr, *n.* large undershot wheel.

Pantalons, pan'talōn', *s. pl.* pants.

Panther, pan'těr, *m.* panther.

Pantoffel, pantof'fel, *m. pl.* -el, or -ein, slippers; unter dem — stehen, to be henpecked.

Pantomime, pantomī'me, *f.* panto- mime. **Pantomimisch,** -mīm'ish, *a.* pantomimic.

Panzer, pan'tsěr, *m.* coat of mail; **-handschuh,** -hantshu, *m. pl.* -e, gauntlet. **Panzerhemd,** -hěmt, *n. pl.* -en, coat of mail. **Panzerthier,** -tīr, *n. pl.* -e, armadillo.

Papa, pap'pä, *m.* papa.

Papagei, pap'pagäe, *m. pl.* -e, or -en, parrot.

Papier, papīr', *n. pl.* -e, paper; docu- ment, certificate. **Papieren,** papī'ren, *a.* paper. **Papiergeld,** -gělt, *n.* paper-money. **Papierhandel,** -han- del, *m.* paper-trade. **Papierhändler,** -hěndlěr, *m.* stationer. **Papier- handlung,** -hantlyng, *f.* stationery. **Papiermasse,** -masse, *f.* paper-pulp. **Papiermühle,** -mūle, *f.* paper-mill. **Papiermüller,** -müllěr, *m.* manu- facturer of paper. **Papierscheere,** -shēre, *f.* paper-shears. **Papier- schirm,** -shīrm, *m. pl.* -e, paper- screen. **Papierschnitzel,** -shnitsel, *m.* scrap of paper. **Papierstaude,** -zhtöude, *f.* papyrus.

Papillote, papılyot'tę, *f.* curling-paper.
Papist, papizht', *m.* -en, *pl.* -en, papist.
Pappband, pap'bant, *m.* binding in boards.
Pappe, pap'pę, *f.* pasteboard; in **Pappe**, in boards.
Pappel, pap'pel, *f.* poplar; **-holz**, -holts, *n.* poplar-wood.
Pappen, pap'pen, *vt.* to paste: *vi.* to eat pap. **Pap'pendeckel**, -deckel, *m.* pasteboard. **Pappig**, pap'piʃ, *a.* pasty, sticky.
Papst, päpzht, *m. pl.* **Päpste**, pope. **Päpstler**, päpzht'lêr, *m.* papist. **Päpst'lich**, -liʃ, *a.* papal. **Papstthum**, papzht'tųm, *n.* papacy, popery.
Parabel, parä'bel, *f.* parable; parabola.
Parade, parä'dę, *f.* parade.
Paradies, paradīs', *n. pl.* -e, paradise. **Paradies'apfel**, -apfel, *m. pl.* -äpfel. paradise-apple, June-apple. **Paradies'isch**, -ish, *a.* paradisiacal. **Paradies'vogel**, -fögel, *m. pl.* -vögel, bird of paradise.
Paradiren, paradī'ren, *vi.* to parade.
Paradox, paradox', *a.* paradoxical. **Paradox'on**, -ōn, *n. pl.* -xen, paradox.
Paragraph, paragräf', *m.* -en, *pl.* -en, paragraph.
Parallaxe, paralax'ę, *f.* parallax.
Parallel, paralāl', *a.* parallel. **Parallele**, paralę'lę, *f.* parallel. **Parallelismus**, paralēlīs'mųss, *m. pl.* -ismen, parallelism. **Parallelogramm**, -logram', *n. pl.* -e, parallelogram.
Paralysiren, paralisī'ren, *vt.* to paralyze.
Paraphrase, parafrä'sę, *f.* paraphrase.
Parasol, parasōl', *m. pl.* -e, parasol.
Parcelle, partsēl'lę, *f.* parcel. **Parcelliren**, partsēllī'ren, *vt.* to parcel.
Pardel, par'del, *m.* panther.
Pardon, pardōn', *m.* pardon; **-iren**, -ī'ren. *vt.* to pardon.
Parenthese, parentä'sę, *f.* parenthesis.
Parfümerie, parfümērī', *f.* perfume, perfumery.
Parfümiren, parfümī'ren, *vt.* to perfume.

Pariren, parī'ren, *vi.* to obey.
Pariren, parī'ren, *vt.* to parry.
Park, park, *m. pl.* -e, park.
Parlament, parlament', *s. pl.* -e, parliament. **Parlamentär**, -tär', *m. pl.* -e, officer with a flag of truce. **Parlamentiren**, parlamentī'ren, *vi.* to parley.
Parodie, parodī', *f.* parody. **Parodiren**, -dī'ren, *vt.* to parody.
Parole, parō'lę, *f.* watchword; parole.
Part, part, *m. pl.* -e, part. **Partei**, partēī', *f.* party, part; **-gänger**, -gęngêr, *m.* partisan. **Parteigeist**, -gäszht, *m.* party-spirit. **Parteiisch**, -ish, **Partei'lich**, -liʃ, *a.* partial; **-keit**, -käšt, *f.* partiality. **Parteilos**, -lōs, *a.* impartial, neutral; **-igkeit**, -iʃkäšt, *f.* impartiality, neutrality.
Parterre, partêrr', *n. pl.* -e, ground-floor; pit (of a theatre); parterre.
Particip, partitsip', *n. pl.* -e, *or* -ien, participle. **Participial**, -tsipīäl', *a.* participial.
Parthie, partī', *f.* parcel, lot; party, game; match, marriage; excursion: part; **gute — machen**, *vi.* to marry a fortune. **Partiell**, partsi-ēll', *a.* partial.
Partikel, partik'kel, *m.* particle.
Partitur, partitųr', *f.* score (Mus.).
Pasch, pash, *m.* doublet, triplet (at dice).
Pasquill, pasquill', *n. pl.* -e, pasquil.
Paß, pass, *m. pl.* **Pässe**, pace, amble; pass, passage; passport. **Passage**, passä'zhę, *f.* passage. **Passagier**, passazhīr', *m.* passenger: **-gut**, -gųt, *n. pl.* -güter, baggage. **Passatwind**, passät'vint, *m. pl.* -e, trade-wind.
Passen, pas'sen, *vi.* to fit; to attend to, to wait for. **Passend**, pas'sent, *a.* fit, suitable, just.
Paßgang, pass'gang, *m.* amble, pace. **Paß'gänger**, -gęngêr, *m.* pacer.
Passion, passiōn', *f.* passion.
Passiren, passī'ren, *vi.* to pass, to be tolerable, to do; to come to pass. **Passirzettel**, -tsēttel, *m.* pass, permit.
Passiv, passīf', pas'sif, *a.* passive.
Pastell, pazhtēll', *n. pl.* -e, pastol, crayon.
Pastete, pastä'tę (*dim.* **Pastetchen**). *a* pastry, pasty, pie. **Paste'tenbäcker** -becker, *m.* pastry-cook.

Paſtille, pazhtil'le, *f.* pastil.
Paſtinake, *f.* **Paſtinaf**, pazhtinkk', *m. pl.* -e, parsnip.
Paſter, pazh'tör, pazhtōr', *m. pl.* -en. *or* **Paſtöre**. pastor, parson; -in, *f.* pastor's wife.
Patent, patent', *n.* patent; license; commission. **Patentiren**, -tī'ren, *vt.* to patent.
Paternoſter, pa'ternzhter, *m.* paternoster.
Pathe, pä'te, *m. u. f.* godfather, godmother; godchild.
Pathetiſch, patet'ish, *a.* pathetic; *av.* -ally. **Pathos**, pä'tōs, *m.* pathos.
Patient, patsi-ent', *m.* -en, *pl.* -en, patient.
Patriarch, patriarch', *m.* -en, *pl.* -en, patriarch.
Patrizier, patrī'tsi-ēr, *m.* patrician.
Patriot, patri-ot', *m.* -en, *pl.* -en, patriot; -iſch, -ish, *a.* patriotic. **Patriotismus**, -otīs'muss, *m.* patriotism.
Patrize, patrit'se, *f.* punch.
Patrolle, patrol'le, **Patrouille**, patrull'ye, *f.* patrol. **Patrolliren**, -lī'ren, *vt.* to patrol.
Patron, patrōn', *m.* patron, protector; fellow.
Patrone, patrō'ne, *f.* pattern, cartridge. **Patronentaſche**, -tashe, *f.* cartridge-box.
Patſch, patsh, *m. pl.* -e, clap, slap, smack. **Patſche**, pat'she. *f.* hand, palm; difficulty. **Patſchen**, pat'shen, *vt.* to splash, smack, slap.
Patzig, pats'ich, *a.* snappish, impertinent.
Pauke, pöy'ke, *f.* kettle-drum. **Pauken**, pöy'ken, *vt.* to beat the kettle-drum; to cudgel.
Pausbäckig, pöys'bĕckich, *a.* chub-faced.
Pauſe, pöy'se, *f.* pause. **Pauſiren**, pöysī'ren, *m.* to pause.
Pavian, pä'fiän, *m.* baboon.
Pavillion, pavill'yōn, *m.* pavilion.
Pech, pĕch. *n.* pitch; difficulty. **Pechfackel**, pĕch'fackel. *f.* torch, pine-torch. **Pechicht**, pĕch'icht, **Pechig**, pĕch'ich, *a.* pitchy. **Pechfohle**, -kōle, *f.* bituminous coal, pitch-coal; jet. **Pechfranz**, -krants, *m. pl.* -fränze, pitch-ring. **Pechpfanne**, -pfanne, *f.* pitch-par **Pechſchwarz**, -shvarts, *a.* black as pitch. **Pechtanne**, -tanne, *f.* pitch-pine.
Pectin, pĕktın', *n.* pectine.
Pedal, pedäl', *n. pl.* -e, pedal.
Pedant, pedant', *m.* -en, *pl.* -en, pedant; -iſch, -ish, *a.* pedantic.
Pedell, pedĕll', *m. pl.* -e, beadle.
Pegel, pā'gel, *m.* water-gauge.
Peil, pĕil, *n. pl.* -e, water-gauge. **Peilen**, pĕil'len, *vt.* to gauge.
Pein, päen, *f.* pain, torment, torture; -igen, päen'ichen, *vt.* to pain, torment. **Peiniger**, päen'icher, *m.* tormentor. **Peinigung**, -ung, *f.* tormenting. **Peinlich**, päen'lich, *a.* painful, tormenting; criminal, capital.
Peitſche, pĕï'tshe, *f.* whip, scourge. **Peitſchen**, pĕï'tshen, *vt.* to scourge, whip; -hieb, -hīb, *m. pl.* -e, lash. **Peitſchenſtock**, -zhtock, *m. pl.* -ſtöcke, whip-stick.
Pelikan, pä'likän, *m.* pelican.
Peloton, pelotōn', *n. pl.* -e, platoon; -feuer, -feü-ĕr, *n.* firing by platoons.
Pelz, pelts, *m.* fur, pelt; -futter, -futter, *n.* lining of fur. **Pelzhandel**, pelts'handel, *m.* fur-trade. **Pelzhändler**, -hentlĕr, *m.* fur-trader, furrier. **Pelzhandſchuh**, -hantshu, *m. pl.* -e, fur-glove. **Pelzkragen**, -krägen, *m.* fur-cape, fur-collar. **Pelzmütze**, -mütse, *f* fur-cap. **Pelzrock**, -rock, *m. pl.* -röcke, fur-coat. **Pelzſchuh**, -shu, *m. pl.* -e, fur-shoe. **Pelzſtiefel**, pelts'zhtīfel, *m.* fur-boot. **Pelzwerk**, pelts'vĕrk, *n.* furs, peltry.
Pendel, pen'del, *n.* pendulum.
Penſion, pensi-ōn', *f.* pension; boarding-school. **Penſionär**, pensionär', *m. pl.* -e, pensioner. **Penſioniren**, pensionī'ren, *vt.* to pension.
Peremptoriſch, perempto'rish, *a.* peremptory.
Perfekt, pĕrfĕkt', *a.* perfect. **Perfekt**, perfect (tense).
Perfidie, pĕrfidī', *f.* perfidy.
Pergament, pergament', *n. pl.* -e, parchment.
Periode, peri-ō'de, *f.* period (Math.); repetend. **Periodiſch**, periō'dish, *a.* periodical.
Peripherie, periferī', *f.* periphery, circumference.
Perlaſche, pĕrl'ashe, *f.* pearl-ashes

Per 242 **Pfa**

Perle, pĕr'lĕ, f. pearl, bead. **Perlen**, pĕr'len, vi. to bubble, sparkle, purl.
Perlenfischer, -fishēr, m. pearl-fisher.
Perlenmutter, **Perlmutter**, pĕrl'muttẹr, f. mother-of-pearl. **Perlenschnur**, -shnur, f. pl. -schnüre, string of pearls. **Perlfarbig**, pĕrl'farbiğ, a. pearl-colored. **Perlhuhn**, -hụn, n. pl. -hühner, guinea-fowl. **Perlstein**, pĕrl'zhtān, m. pl. -e, pearl-stone.
Permanent, pērmanent', a. permanent, lasting.
Perpendikel, pĕrpendick'el, m. pendulum, plummet-line. **Perpendikulär**, pĕrpendikulâr', a. perpendicular.
Perrücke, pērrück'ẹ, f. periwig, wig. **Perrückenmacher**, -macher, m. wig-maker, hair-dresser. **Perrückenstock**, -zhtock, m. pl. -stöcke, block for wigs.
Persico, pĕr'siko, m. persecot, persicot.
Person, pērsōn', f. person, personage. **Personalität**, pērsonalitāt', f. personality. **Personifikation**, pērsonifikatsiōn', f. personification. **Personifiziren**, pērsonifitsī'ren, vt. to personify. **Persönlich**, pērsön'liḉ, a. personal; -keit, -kāt, f. personality: person.
Perspektiv, pērzhpektīf', n. spy-glass. **Perspektive**, -tī'fẹ, f. perspective; -ista. **Perspektivisch**, -tī'fish, a. perspective.
Perücke, pērück'ẹ, f. s. **Perrücke**.
Peristyl, pēristīl', n. pl. -e, peristyle.
Pest, pēzht, f. pest, pestilence, plague, bane: -artig, -ärtiğ, a. pestilential. **Pestbeule**, -bēulẹ, f. **Pestblatter**, -blattēr, f. plague-ulcer, plague-spot. **Pestflecken**, -flecken, m. plague-spot. **Pestilenz**, pēzhtilents', f. pestilence, plague; -ialisch, -iāl'ish, a. pestilential. **Pestkrank**, pēzht'krank, a. infected with the plague. **Pestluft**, -luft, f. pestilential air. **Pestzeit**, -tsāt, f. time of the plague.
Petersilie, pātērsī'li-ẹ, f. parsley.
Petition, pẹtitsiōn', f. petition. **Petitioniren**, pẹtitsioni'ren, vt. to petition.
Petschaft, pĕt'shaft, n. pl. -e, seal, signet.
Petschiren, pẹtshī'ren, vt. to seal.
Petto, pĕt'tō, breast; in **Petto**, in reserve.

Petz, pēts, m. pl. -e, bear, bruin.
Petze, pĕt'sẹ, f. bitch; strumpet.
Pfad, pfād, m. path, way. **Pfadlos**, -lōs, a. pathless.
Pfaffe, pfaf'fẹ, m. priest, parson, monk. **Pfaffenbischen**, pfaf'fenbisschen, n. **Pfaffenschnitt**, -shnitt, m. best cut of a joint. **Pfaffenthum**, -tụm, n. priesthood, monkery; priestcraft, auch **Pfafferei**, pfafferēī'. **Pfäffisch**, pfĕf'fish, a. monkish, priestly.
Pfahl, pfāl, m. pl. **Pfähle**, stake, pole, pale, pile, post. **Pfählen**, pfä'len, vt. to stake; to empale. **Pfahlramme**, pfāl'rammẹ, f. pile-driver. **Pfahlwerk**, pfāl'vērk, n. pl. -e, stockade.
Pfalzgraf, pfalts'grāf, m. pl. -en, count palatine; -schaft, -shaft, f. palatinate.
Pfand, pfant, n. pl. **Pfänder**, pawn, pledge, mortgage; forfeit. **Pfandbrief**, -brīf, m. pl. -e, mortgage. **Pfänden**, pfen'den, vi. to distrain, seize. **Pfänderspiel**, pfen'dērzhpīl, n. **Pfandspiel**, pfant'zhpīl, n. game of forfeits. **Pfandhaus**, -hōụs, n. pl. -häuser, lombard, pawn-house. **Pfändung**, pfend'ụng, f. seizure, distraint.
Pfanne, pfan'nẹ, f. pan: socket: step (Mech.). **Pfannenstein**, pfan'neuzhtān, m. pan-scales, fur of a pan. **Pfannenstiel**, -zhtīl, m. pl. -e, pan-handle.
Pfannkuchen, pfann'kụchen, m. pancake.
Pfarramt, pfarr'amt, n. pl. -ämter, pastorship, curacy. **Pfarre**, pfar'rẹ, **Pfarrei**, pfar'rēī', f. parsonage, curacy. **Pfarrer**, pfar'rēr, m. parson, minister: -in, f. parson's wife. **Pfarrhaus**, pfarr'hōụs, n. pl. -häuser, parsonage. **Pfarrgemeinde**, -gemāndẹ, f. parish. **Pfarrgenoss**, -genoss, m. -en, pl. -en. **Pfarrkind**, -kint, n. pl. -er, parishioner. **Pfarrkirche**, -kirchẹ, f. parish-church. **Pfarrstelle**, -zhtellẹ, f. living, benefice. **Pfarrwohnung**, -vōnụng, f. parsonage.
Pfau, pfāụ, -en, or -es, pl. -e, or -en, peacock. **Pfauenfeder**, pfāụ'enfēdēr, f. peacock's feather. **Pfauenschwanz**, -shvants, m. pl. -schwänze, peacock's-tail. **Pfauhahn**, pfāụ'hān,

m. pl. -hähne, peacock. **Pfau'henne,** -henne, *f.* pea-hen.
Pfeffer, pfĕf'fĕr, *m.* pepper. **Pfef'ferbaum,** -baŭm, *m. pl.* -bäume, pepper-tree. **Pfef'ferbüchſe,** -büxe, *f.* pepper-box. **Pfef'fergurke,** -gŭrke, *f.* pepper-gherkin; pickled gherkin. **Pfef'ferkorn,** -korn, *n. pl.* -körner, pepper-corn. **Pfef'ferkuchen,** -kŭchen, *m.* gingerbread. **Pfef'fermünze,** -münt-ẹ *f.* peppermint. **Pfeffern,** pfĕf'fĕrn, *vt.* to pepper. **Pfeffernuß,** pfĕf'fĕrnŭss. *m. pl.* -nüſſe, gingerbread-nut. **Pfef'ferſtrauch,** -zhtroŭch, *m. pl.* -ſträuche, pepper-tree.
Pfeife, pfẽī'fẹ, *f.* pipe; fife; whistle; tube. **Pfeifen,** pfeĭ'fen, *vi.* to pipe, whistle; whiz; **-deckel,** -deckel. *m.* pipe-lid. **Pfei'fenerde,** -ĕrdẹ, *f.* pipeclay. **Pfei'fenkopf,** -kopf. *m. pl.* -köpfẹ, pipe-bowl. **Pfei'fenräumer,** -raŭmĕr. *m.* pipe-cleaner. **Pfei'fenrohr,** -rōr. *n. pl.* -röhrẹ, pipe-tube. **Pfei'fenſpitze,** -zhpitsẹ, *f.* mouthpiece of a pipe.
Pfeifer, pfēī'fĕr, *m.* piper, fifer; whistler.
Pfeil, pfeīl. *m. pl.* -ẹ, arrow.
Pfeiler, pfeīl'ĕr, *m.* pillar, pier. **Pfei'lerſpiegel,** -zhpīgel, *m.* pier-glass.
Pfeilſchnell, pfeīl'shnell, *a.* swift as an arrow. **Pfeil'ſchütze,** -shütsẹ, *m.* archer. **Pfeil'ſtein,** -zhtein, *m. pl.* -ẹ, arrow-stone, belemnite.
Pfennig, pfen'nich, *m. pl.* -ẹ, penny; farthing.
Pferch, pferch. *m. pl.* -ẹ, fold, sheepcot, pen. **Pferchen,** pferch'en, *vt.* to pen; to manure.
Pferd, pfĕrt. *n. pl.* -ẹ, horse. **Pferdearbeit,** pfĕr'dẹ arbĕĕt, *f.* horse-labor. **Pfer'dearzt,** -artst, *m. pl.* -ärzte, farrier, horse-leech. **Pfer'dedieb,** -dīb, *m. pl.* -ẹ, horse-thief. **Pfer'dehaar,** -hār, *n. pl.* -ẹ, horse-hair. **Pfer'dehändler,** -hentlĕr, *m.* horse-dealer. **Pfer'dekraft,** -kraft, *f. pl.* -kräftẹ, horse-power. **Pfer'demähne,** -mänẹ, *f.* mane of a horse. **Pfer'demarkt,** -markt, *m.* horse-mart, horse-fair. **Pfer'deſtall,** -zhtall, *m. pl.* -ſtälle, horse-stable. **Pfer'deſtein,** -zhteĭn, *m. pl.* -ẹ, hippolith.
Pfiff, pfiff, *m.* whistle; trick.
Pfifferling, pfif'fĕrling, *m. pl.* -ẹ, toadstool; trifle.
Pfiffig, pfif'fich, *a.* cunning, artful;

sly; **-keit,** -kĕĕt, *f.* cunning, shrewdness.
Pfingſtabend, pfingzht'äbent. *m. pl.* -ẹ, Pentecost-eve. **Pfingſten,** pfingzh'ten, *s. pl.* Whitsuntide. **Pfingſt'feiertage,** -fĕĕrtägẹ. *s. pl.* Whitsunweek holidays. **Pfingſt'feſt,** -fĕzht, *n. pl.* -ẹ, Whitsuntide. **Pfingſt'zeit,** -tsĕĭt. *f.* Whitsuntide-season.
Pfirſich, pfĭr'sich, *m. pl.* -ẹ, **Pfir'ſiche,** *f.* peach. **Pfir'ſichbaum,** -baŭm, *m. pl.* -bäume, peach-tree. **Pfir'ſichblüthe,** -blütẹ, *f.* peach-blossom. **Pfir'ſichbranntwein,** -bra tvĕĕn, *m. pl.* -ẹ, peach-brandy. **Pfir'ſichkern,** -kĕrn, *m. pl.* -ẹ, kernel of a peach. **Pfir'ſichſtein,** -zhtĕĕn, *m. pl.* -ẹ, peach-stone.
Pflanze, pflan'tsẹ, *f.* plant. **Pflanzen,** pflan'tsen, *vt.* to plant, to set out; to place, to fix. **Pflan'zenfaſer,** -fāsĕr, *f.* vegetable fibre. **Pflan'zenforſcher,** -forshĕr, *m.* botanist. **Pflan'zengarten,** -garten, *m. pl.* -gärten, botanical garden. **Pflan'zer,** pflan'tsĕr, *m.* planter. **Pflanzſchule,** pflants'shŭlẹ, *f.* nursery; seminary. **Pflanzſtadt,** -zhtatt, *f. pl.* -ſtädtẹ, colony, settlement. **Pflanzung,** pflants'ŭng, *f.* plantation; planting, settlement.
Pflaſter, pflazht'ĕr, *n.* pavement; plaster. **Pflaſtern,** pflazh'tĕrn, *vt.* to pave; to lay on plasters. **Pfla'ſterſtein,** -zhtĕĕn, *m. pl.* -ẹ, paving-stone.
Pflaume, pflaŭ'mẹ, *f.* plum. **Pflau'menbaum,** -baŭm, *m. pl.* -bäume, plum-tree. **Pflau'menkern,** -kĕrn, *m. pl.* -ẹ, plum-stone; kernel of a plum-stone. **Pflau'menmuß,** -mŭs, *n.* plum-jam.
Pflege, pflĕ'gẹ, *f.* nursing, care; cultivation. **Pfle'geeltern,** -eltĕrn. *s. pl.* foster-parents. **Pfle'gekind,** -kint, *n. pl.* -er, foster-child. **Pfle'gemutter,** -mŭttĕr, *f. pl.* -mütter, foster-mother. **Pflegen,** pflĕ'gen, *vt.* to attend to, to nurse; to cultivate; *vi.* to be wont, to be in habit of; to use; er pflegte zu ſagen, he would say. **Pfleger,** pflĕ'gĕr, *m.* sin, *f.* guardian, nurse, attendant. **Pfle'geſohn,** -sŏn, *m. pl.* -ſöhnẹ, foster-son. **Pfle'getochter,** -tochtĕr. *f. pl.* -töchter, foster-daughter. **Pfle'gevater,** -fātĕr, *m.* foster-father. **Pflege**

Pfli   244   **Pho**

ling, pflēg'ling. m. pl. -e, ward. **Pfleg'ſchaft**, -shaft, f. guardianship. **Pflegung**, pflēg'ung, f. tending, nursing.
Pflicht, pflicht, f. duty, obligation. **Pflicht'anker**, -ankēr, m. sheet-anchor. **Pflicht'gefühl**, -gefühl, n. sense of duty. **Pflicht'gemäß**, -gemäse, **Pflicht'mäßig**, -mässich, a. av. in duty bound, in accordance with duty. **Pflichtig**, pflicht'ich, a. bound, obliged. **Pflicht'lich**, -lich, a. dutiful, av. -ly. **Pflicht'leiſtung**, -lāeshtung, f. performance of duty; oath of allegiance. **Pflicht'ſchuldig**, -shuldich, a. bound in duty. **Pflicht'theil**, m. legitimate portion, lawful share. **Pflicht'vergeſſen**, -fergēssen, a. unmindful of one's duty, faithless, false; -heit, -hāēt, f. faithlessness, falseness. **Pflicht'widrig**, -vīdrich, a. contrary to duty, opposed to duty.
Pflock, pflock, m. pl. **Pflöcke**, plug, peg, pin, stake. **Pflöcken**, pflöck'en, vt. to peg, pin, stake.
Pflücken, pflück'en, vt. to pluck, gather, pick.
Pflug, pflūg, m. pl. **Pflüge**, plough, plow. **Pflug'eiſen**, -āēsen, n. colter. **Pflügen**, pflü'gen, vt. to plow, plough. **Pflüger**, pflü'gēr, m. plower, ploughman. **Pflugpferd**, pflug'pfērt, n. pl. -e, plough-horse. **Pflugſchar**, pflug'shār, f. ploughshare. **Pflugſterze**, -zhtērtse, f. plow-handle.
Pfortader, pfort'ādēr, f. vena portæ, mesenteric vein.
Pforte, pfor'te, f. gate, wicket, door; gun-port: bobe —, (sublime) Porte. **Pfortgat**, pfort'gat, n. pl. -e, port-hole. **Pfort'luke**, -lūke, f. port-lid. **Pfort'talje**, -talye, f. port-tackle. **Pförtner**, pfört'nēr, m. door-keeper, porter.
Pfoſte, pfozh'te, f. **Pfoſten**, m. post, stake, pale.
Pfote, pfō'te, f. paw. **Pfötchen**, pföt'chen, little paw.
Pfriem, pfrīm, m. pl. -e, **Pfriemen**, pfrī'men, m. **Pfrieme**, pfrī'me, f. awl, punch.
Pfropf, pfropf, m. **Pfröpfe**, pfröp'fe, f. **Pfropfen**, pfrop'fen, m. cork, stopper: graft.
Pfropfen, pfropf'en, vt. to cork; to

cram; to graft. **Pfropf'reis**, -rīs, n. pl. -er, graft. scion. **Pfropf'zieher**, -tsī-ēr, m. cork-screw.
Pfründe, pfrün'de, f. benifice, living, prebend. **Pfründner**, pfründ'nēr, m. prebendary, beneficiary.
Pfuhl, pfūl, m. pl. -e, pool, puddle, slough.
Pfühl, pfūl, m. u. n. pl. -e, pillow, cushion.
Pfui, pfū-i, ij. fy! foh! shame!
Pfund, pfunt, n. pl. -e, pound: talent. **Pfündig**, pfün'dich, a. weighing one pound. **Pfundweiſe**, pfunt'vēse, ar. by the pound.
Pfuſchen, pfush'en, vi. to bungle, dabble, botch. **Pfuſcher**, pfush'ēr, m. bungler, dabbler. **Pfuſcherei**, pfushērēī', f. bungling, dabbling.
Pfütze, pfüt'se, f. pool, puddle, slough.
Phänomen, fēnōmān', n. pl. -e, phenomenon.
Phantaſie, fantasī', f. phantasy, fancy, imagination. **Phantaſiren**, fantasī'ren, vi. to rave. **Phantaſt**, fantazht', m. visionary, dreamer. **Phantaſtiſch**, -ish, a. fantastical, fanciful, visionary, chimerical. **Phantom**, fantōm', n. phantom.
Phariſäiſch, farisā'ish, a. pharisaical, hypocritical.
Pharmaceut, farmatsēūt', m. -en, pl. -en, apothecary. **Pharmacie**, farmatsī', f. pharmaceutics, pharmacy.
Phaſe, fā'se, f. phase.
Philanthrop, filantröp', m. philanthropist. **Philanthropie**, -trōpī', f. philanthropy. **Philanthropiſch**, -pish, a. philanthropic.
Philiſter, filizh'tēr, m. philistine; old fogy; cit; cockney.
Philolog, filolōg'. m. philologer, philologist. **Philologie**, filolōgī', f. philology. **Philologiſch**, filolō'gish, a. philologic.
Philoſoph, filosōf', m. -en, pl. -en, philosopher. **Philoſophie**, filosofī', f. philosophy. **Philoſophiren**, filosofī'ren, vi. to philosophize. **Philoſophiſch**, filosō'fish, a. philosophic, ar. -ally.
Phlegma, flēg'mā. n. phlegm, dulness. **Phlegmatiſch**, flēgmat'ish, a. phlegmatic.
Phoſphor, fos'for, m. phosphorus

Pho 245 **Pla**

Phosphoresciren, fosforestsī'ren, vi. to phosphoresce. **Phosphorsäure**, -säure, f. phosphoric acid. **Phosphorsaures Salz**, phosphate. **Phosphorig**, fosfō'riċh, a. phosphorous.
Photograph, fotogrāf', m. photographer. **Photographie**, -gra'ī', f. photography; photograph. **Photographiren**, -firen, vt. to photograph.
Phrase, frä'se, f. phrase.
Phrenologie, frenologī', f. phrenology.
Physik, fisīk', f. physics, natural philosophy.
Physiognomie, fisiognomī', f. physiognomy.
Physiologie, fisiologī', f. physiology.
Physisch, fī'sish. a. physical.
Pianist, pianizht', m. -en, pl. -en, pianist. **Piano**, piä'nō, n. piano, piano-forte.
Pichen, piċh'en, vt. to pitch.
Pick, pick, m. pl. -e, tick; picking.
Picke, pick'e, f. pick-axe, pick.
Pickelhaube, pik'kelhŏybe, f. helmet.
Picken, pick'en, vt. i. to peck; to pick; to tick.
Picknick, pick'enick, n. picnic.
Pietist, pietizht', m. -en, pl. -en, pietist, devotee.
Pik, pīk, n. spade (in cards); grudge.
Pike, pī'ke, f. pike.
Pilger, pil'gĕr, m. **Pilgrim**, pil'grim, m. pl. -e, pilgrim. **Pilgerfahrt**, pil'gĕrfärt, f. pilgrimage. **Pilgern**, pil'gĕrn, vi. to make a pilgrimage.
Pille, pil'le, f. pill, pellet.
Pilot, pilōt', m. -en. pl. -en, pilot.
Pilz, pilts, m. pl. -e, mushroom.
Piment, piment', m. allspice.
Pinguin, pinguīn', m. pl. -s, penguin.
Pinie, pī'ni-e, f. sweet pine.
Pinne, pin'ne, f. pin, peg, pike; tenon, spindle (Mar.).
Pinsel, pin'sel, m. pencil, paint-brush; simpleton, blockhead. **Pinseln**, pin'seln, vt. to paint, pencil.
Pinte, pin'te, f. pint.
Pionier, pionīr', m. pl. -e, pioneer.
Piepen, pī'pen, vi. to pip, chirp.
Pisang, pī'sang, m. banana.
Pissen, pis'sen, vi. to piss, urinate.
Pistazie, pizhtā'tsi-e, f. pistachio-nut.
Pistill, pizhtil', n. pl. -e, pistil.
Pistol, pistōl'. n. pl. -en, **Pistole**, pistō'le, f. pistol.

Pistole, pistō'le, f. pistole.
Pistolenhalfter, pistō'lenholftĕr, f. holster.
Placat, placāt', n. pl. -e, placard, poster.
Placken, pläck'en, vt. to vex, harass.
Plackerei, plackerēī', f. turmoil, vexation, trouble.
Plädiren, plēdī'ren, vi. to plead.
Plage, plä'ge, f. plague, trouble, vexation. **Plagegeist**, plä'gegĕzhe, m pl. -er, tormenter **Plagen**, plä gen, vt. to plague, trouble.
Plan, plän, a. plain.
Plan, plän, m. plan, design. **Planconvex**, plänkonkäf', m. plano-concave. **Planconvex**, plänkonfex', a. plano-convex.
Plane, plä'ne, f. tilt, awning, linen cover.
Pläne, plä'ne, f. plain.
Planet, planät', m. -en, pl. -en, planet. **Planetenbahn**, planä'tenbän, f. planetary orbit.
Planiren, planī'ren, vt. to plane, smooth; to glue, size.
Planke, plan'ke, f. plank, board.
Plänkeln, plen'keln, vi. to skirmish. **Plänkler**, plenk'lĕr, m. skirmisher. **Plänkelei**, plenkelēī', f. skirmishing.
Planlos, plän'lōs, a. planless, without end. **Planmäßig**, -mässiċh, a. systematic; concerted.
Plantage, plantä'zhe, f. plantation.
Plappern, plap'pĕrn, vi. to babble, chat.
Plärren, pler'ren, vi. to bawl, bleat.
Platane, platä'ne, f. plane-tree.
Platin, platīn', n. **Platina**, plä'tīnä, n. platinum.
Plätschen, plat'shen, **Plätschern**, plät'shĕrn, vi. to splash, dabble, dash.
Platt, platt, a. flat, plain, even; downright; — schlagen, to flatten. **Plattdeutsch**, -dĕütsh, a. low German. **Platte**, plat'te, f. plate, slab; plate, charger; bald pate. **Platteisen**, -eisen, n. smoothing-iron goose. **Plätten**, plet'ten, vt. to flatten, smooth, iron. **Platterdings**, platterdings', ar. by all means. **Plattheit**, -hāēt, f. flatness, dulness; platitude. **Plattung**, plat'ting, n. pl. -e, sennit. **Plattiren**, plattī'ren, vt. to plate.
Platz, plats, m. smash, crack.

21*

Plaz, plats. m. pl. **Plätze**, place, space; seat; room; — **nehmen**, to sit down.
Platzcommandant, -kommandant, m. -en, pl. -en, commander of a post.
Platzen, plat'sen, vi. to burst, smash.
Platzregen, plats'regen, m. heavy shower.
Plauderei, plöŋdĕrēī', f. chatting, babbling. **Plauderer**, plöŋ'dĕrĕr, m. babbler, chatterer. **Plauderhaft**, -haft, a. talkative, chattering. **Plaudern**, plöŋ'děrn, vi. to chat, prattle, babble.
Plaut, plôųts. Ij. plump! bounce!
Plebejer, plĕbä'yĕr. m. plebeian.
Plombiren, plembī'ren, vi. to seal with lead; to plug.
Plotz, plots. m. clap. bounce; auf den —, on a sudden. **Plötzlich**, plęts'-lich, av. a. suddenly.
Plump, plụmp, ij. plump! clap!
Plump, plụmp, a. plump, clumsy, awkward, coarse. **Plumpsen**, plụm'psen, vi. to plump, fall heavily. **Plumpheit**, -häēt, f. plumpness, clumsiness.
Plunder, plụn'dĕr, m. lumber, trash, trumpery.
Plünderei, plündĕrēī', f. plunder, pillage. **Plünderer**, plün'dĕrĕr, m. plunderer. **Plündern**, plün'děrn, vt. to pillage, plunder. **Plünderung**, -ŭng, f. plundering, pillaging.
Plural, plụ'räl, m. plural.
Plüsch, plush. m. pl. -e, plush.
Plusquamperfect, plụs'qųampĕrfĕkt, n. pl. -e, pluperfect.
Pöbel, pö'bel. m. populace, rabble, mob. **Pöbelhaft**, -haft, a. plebeian, low.
Pochen, poch'en, vi. to knock, beat; to boast. **Pochwerk**, -vĕrk, n. stamping-mill.
Pocken, pock'en, s. pl. small-pox.
Podagra, pō'dagrä, f. gout (in the feet).
Poesie, po-esī', f. poetry; poesy.
Poet, po-ēt', m. -en, pl. -en, poet. **Poetin**, poāt'in, f. poetess. **Poetisch**, poāt'ish. a. poetic, -al.
Pokal, pokäl', m. pl. -e, bumper, bowl, cup.
Pökel, pöck'el, m. pickle. **Pökelfleisch**, -flēēsh. n. salt-meat. **Pökelhäring**, -häring, m. pl. -e, pickled herring. **Pökeln**, pö'keln, vt. to pickle, salt, corn.
Pol, pōl', m. pl. -e, pole. **Polarbär**, pōlar'bär, m. -en. pl. -en, white bear. **Polarisch**, polār'ish, a. polar. **Polarität**, polaritāt', f. polarity. **Polarkreis**, -krēes, m. pl. -e, polar circle. **Polarstern**, -zhtĕrn, m. pl. -e, pole-star.
Polei, po'lāē, m. penny-royal.
Police, polīs'. f. policy.
Poliren, polī'ren, vt. to polish, burnish. **Polirstahl**, -zhtäl. m. polisher, burnisher. **Polirzahn**, -tsän, m. pl. -zähne, polishing tooth.
Politif, politīk', f. politics. **Politiker**, polit'ikĕr, m. politician. **Politisch**, polit'ish, a. politic.
Politur, politụr', f. polish.
Polizei, politsēī', f. police. **Polizeidiener**, -dīner, m. policeman. **Polizeilich**, poli'tsēllich, a. of the police.
Polster, pol'zhtĕr, n. bolster, cushion **Polstern**, pol'zhtĕrn, vt. to stuff, quilt.
Polterabend, pol'tĕräbent. m. pl. -e nuptial-eve. **Poltergeist**, -gäēzht, m. pl. -er, hobgoblin. **Poltern**, pol'tĕrn, vi. to rattle, clatter; to be noisy. **Polterkammer**, -kammĕr, f lumber-room.
Polygamie, polịgamī', f. polygamy.
Polygon, polī'gon. n. pl. -e, polygon.
Polyheder, polihä'dĕr. n. polyhedron.
Polyp, polīp', m. -en, pl. -en, polypus.
Polytechnisch, politech'nish, a. polytechnic.
Polytheismus, politę-īs'mụs, m. polytheism.
Pomade, pomā'de, f. pomatum.
Pomeranze, pomĕrant'se. f. orange. **Pomeranzenbaum**, -baum, m. pl. -bäume, orange-tree. **Pomeranzenfarben**, pomĕrant'senfarben, a. orange-colored.
Pomp, pomp, m. pomp, splendor. **Pomphaft**, -haft, a. pompous.
Ponton, pŏn'tŏn, n. pl. -s, pontoon.
Popanz, popants', m. pl. -e, bugbear.
Populär, populär', a. popular. **Popularität**, popularitāt', f. popularity.
Pore, pō'rẹ, f. pore. **Porös**, perös', a. porous. **Porosität**, pörositāt', f porosity.

Por   247   **Pra**

Porphyr, porfīr′, *m. pl.* -e, porphyry.
Port, port. *m. pl.* -e, port, harbor.
Portal, portäl′, *n. pl.* -e, portal.
Portier, por′ti-ā, *m.* porter, doorkeeper.
Portion, portsiōn′, *f.* portion, share, ration.
Porto, por′tō, *n.* postage. **Portofrei,** -frēī, *a.* post-paid, franked.
Portrait, por′trā. *n. pl.* -e, portrait. **Portraitiren,** portrētī′ren, *vt.* to portray.
Porzulak, por′tulak, *m.* purslain.
Portwein, port′vēīn, *m.* port wine.
Porzellan, portse̥län′, *n.* porcelain, china. **Porzellan'en,** *a.* china. **Porzellanfabrik,** -fabrik, *f.* china-manufactory. **Porzellanhandlung,** -hantlung, *f.* china-store.
Posamentirer, po-amentī′rer, *m.* lacemaker, fringe-maker.
Posaune, posḁū′ne̥, *f.* trombone, trumpet. **Posaunen,** posḁū′nen, *vi.* to trumpet.
Position, positsiōn′, *f.* position.
Positiv, pos′itīf, *a.* positive, *av.* -ly; *s. m.* positive (degree).
Positur, positṳr′, *f.* posture, position.
Posse, pos′se̥, *f.* drollery, fun, burlesque; farce. **Possenhaft,** -haft. *a.* droll, funny. **Possenreisser,** -rēīs-ser, *m.* buffoon. **Possenspiel,** -zhpīl, *n. pl.* -e, farce. **Possirlich,** -sīrlich, *a.* droll, funny, comic, ridiculous; -keit, -kāēt, *f.* drollery.
Post, pozht. *f.* mail; post-office. **Postamt,** pozht′amt, *n. pl.* -ämter, post-office.
Posten, pozh′ten, *m.* post, station; item.
Postfrei, pozht′frēī, *a.* post-paid, free of postage. **Postgeld,** -gelt, *n. pl.* -er, postage. **Posthalter,** -halter, *m.* postmaster. **Posthaus,** -hōus, *n. pl.* -häuser, post-office. **Posthorn,** -horn, *n. pl.* -hörner, postilion's horn. **Postillion,** pozhtillyōn′, *m. pl.* -e, postillion.
Postiren, pozhtī′ren, *vt.* to post.
Postknecht, pozht′knecht, *m.* postilion. **Postkutsche,** -kutshe̥, *f.* mail-coach. **Postmeister,** -māēzhter, *m.* postmaster. **Postpapier,** -papīr, *n.* letter-paper. **Postpferd,** -pfert, *n. pl.* -e, post-horse. **Poststall,** -zhtall, *m. pl.* -ställe, stable for post-horses.

Poststation, -zhtatsiōn, *f.* stage-station. **Poststrasse,** -zhträsse, *f.* stage-road. **Posttag,** -tāg, *m. pl.* -e, mail-day. **Postwagen,** -vāgen, *m.* stage-coach. **Postwechsel,** -vexel, *m.* change of horses.
Potasche, pō′tashe̥, *f.* potash.
Potentat, potentät′, *m.* -en, *pl.* -en, potentate.
Potenz, potents′, *f.* power (Math.); potency.
Pot, pots, *ij.* zounds! odds!
Poussiren, pussī′ren, *vt.* to model; to push forward.
Präceptor, prētsep′tor, *m.* preceptor, teacher.
Pracht, pracht, *f.* splendor, brightness, magnificence. **Prachtausgabe,** -ōusgäbe̥, *f.* splendid edition. **Prächtig,** prech′tich, *a.* splendid, gorgeous. **Prachtvoll,** pracht′foll, *a.* grand, gorgeous, magnificent.
Präcipitat, prētsipitāt′, *n.* precipitate. **Präcipitiren,** prētsipitī′ren, *vt.* to precipitate.
Prädestination, prēdezhtinatsiōn′, *f.* predestination.
Prädikat, prēdikāt′, *n. pl.* -e, predicate.
Prägeln, prā′geln, *vt.* to fry.
Prägen, prā′gen, *vt.* to coin; stamp, impress. **Prägewerk,** prā′gewerk, -verk, *n. pl.* -e, coining-press.
Pragmatisch, pragmat′ish, *a.* pragmatical.
Prägnant, pregnant′, *a.* pregnant.
Prahlen, prā′len, *vi.* to shine; to brag, boast. **Prahler,** prā′ler, *m.* braggart, boaster. **Prahlerei,** prālerēī′, *f.* boasting, ostentation. **Prahlerisch,** -ish, *a.* boasting, boastful. **Prahlhans,** -hans, *m. pl.* -hänse, braggadocio. **Prahlsucht,** -sycht, *f.* boastfulness.
Prahm, präm, *m. pl.* -e, pram, flat.
Praktikant, praktikant′, *m. pl.* -en. **Praktikus,** -kus, *m.* practitioner. **Praktisch,** prak′tish, *a.* practical. **Praktiziren,** praktitsī′ren, *vt.* to practise.
Prälat, prēlät′, *m.* -en, *pl.* -en, prelate.
Prall, prall. *m. pl.* -e, rebound; *a.* elastic. **Prallen,** prall′en, *vi.* to rebound, bound. **Prallkraft,** -kraft, *f.* elasticity. **Prallschuss,** -shyss, *m. pl.* -schüsse, ricochet-shot.

Prä   248   **Pre**

Präludiren, prēlyḍ'ren, *vi.* to prelude.
Prämie, prā'mĭ-ẹ, *n. pl.* -n, premium, prize.
Prämisse, prĕmĭs'sẹ, *f.* premise.
Prangen, prang'en, *vi.* to shine, glitter; to make a show.
Pranger, prang'-er, *m.* pillory.
Pränumerant, prănŭmerant', *m.* -en, *pl.* -en, one who prepays; subscriber.
Pränumeration, -mĕratsiōn', *f.* payment in advance. **Pränumeriren,** -mĕrī'ren, *vi.* to prepay.
Präpariren, prĕparī'ren, *vi.* to prepare.
Präsent, prĕsent', *n. pl.* -e, present, gift. **Präsentiren,** prĕsentī'ren, *vi.* to present.
Präsident, prĕsident', *m.* -en, *pl.* -en, president; chairman. **Präsidentschaft,** -shaft, *f.* presidency. **Präsidiren,** prĕsidī'ren, *vi.* to preside.
Prasseln, pras'seln, *vi.* to crackle.
Prassen, pras'sen, *vi.* to riot, to be profuse, to lavish. **Prasser,** pras'ser, *m.* spendthrift.
Präsumiren, prĕsumī'ren, *vi.* to presume.
Prätendent, prĕtendent', *m.* -en, *pl.* -en, pretender.
Präteritum, prĕta'rĭtŭm, *n.* preterit.
Praxis, prax'ĭs, *f.* practice.
Predigen, prā'dĭḡen, *vi.* to preach. **Prediger,** prā'dĭḡĕr, *m.* preacher, minister; ecclesiastic. **Predigt,** prā'dĭkt, *f.* sermon.
Preis, prĕis, *m. pl.* -e, price, cost, rate; reward, prize; praise; — geben, to expose, give up. **Preisaufgabe,** -ŏufgābe, *f.* **Preisfrage,** -frāge, *f.* prize-question. **Preisen,** prĕi'sen (pries, gepriesen), *vt.* to praise. **Preiswürdig,** -vürdiḡ, *a.* praiseworthy; **-feit,** -kĕit, *f.* praiseworthiness.
Preißelbeere, prĕi'selbāre, *f.* cranberry.
Prekär, prekār', *a.* precarious, *av.* -ly.
Prellen, prel'len, *vt.* to toss; to cheat, to dupe. **Prellerei,** prellerā', *f.* imposition. **Prellschuß,** -shŭss, *m. pl.* -schüsse, glancing-shot.
Premierminister, premīr'minĭzhtĕr, *m.* prime-minister.
Pressant, prĕssant', *a.* pressing, urging. **Pressiren,** prĕssī'ren, *vi.* to be in a hurry, to hasten.

Preßbar, press'bär, *a.* compressible.
Presse, pres'se, *f.* press. **Pressen,** pres'sen, *vt.* to press, squeeze. **Preßfreiheit,** press'frēihĕit, *f.* liberty of the press. **Preßkopf,** -kopf, *m.* **Preßtöpfe,** piz's-head-cheese.
Prickle, prick'e, *f.* lamprey.
Prickeln, prik'keln, *vi.* to prick, prickle.
Priester, prī'zhtĕr, *m.* priest. **Priesterin,** *f.* priestess. **Priesterlich,** -ĕrlĭḡ, *a.* priestly, sacerdot. **Priesterstand,** -zhtant, *m.* **Priesterthum,** -tŭm, *n.* priesthood. **Priesterweihe,** -vēi-ẹ, *f.* ordination, consecration.
Primas, prī'mass, *m. pl.* **Primaten,** primate.
Prime, prī'mẹ, *f.* prime.
Primel, prī'mel, *f.* primrose.
Primitiv, primitīf', *a.* primitive.
Princip, printsīp', *n. pl. or* -ien, principle. **Principal,** printsipāl', *m. pl.* -e, principal, master.
Prinz, prints, *m.* -en, *pl.* -en, prince. **Prinzessin,** printsĕs'sin, *f.* princess. **Prinzlich,** -lĭḡ, *a.* princely.
Prior, prī'ōr, *m.* -s, *pl.* -en, prior. **Priorin,** priō'rin, *f.* prioress. **Priorität,** priorĭtāt', *f.* priority.
Prise, prī'sẹ, *f.* prize; booty; pinch.
Prisma, pris'mä, *n. pl.* -men, prism.
Pritsche, prit'she, *f.* wooden couch, camp-bed; backseat.
Pritschen, prit'shen, *vt.* to slap, smack.
Privat, prifāt', *a.* private. **Privatabsicht,** -apsiḡt, *f.* private end. **Privatisiren,** prifātisī'ren, *vi.* to live as a private citizen. **Privatleben,** -lēben, *n.* private life. **Privatmann,** -man, *m. pl.* **Privatleute,** private citizen, private man. **Privatstunde,** -zhtundẹ, *f.* private lesson.
Privilegiren, prifilegī'ren, *vt.* to privilege; to patent. **Privilegium,** prifīlā'gium, *n.* privilege; patent.
Probat, probāt', *a.* tried; approved.
Probe, prō'bẹ, *f.* prove, trial, experiment, test; rehearsal; sample. **Probeblatt,** -blatt, *n. pl.* -blätter, proof-sheet. **Proben,** prō'ben, *vt.* to prove, try, test. **Probestein,** -zhtēin, *m. pl.* -e, touchstone. **Probestück,** -zhtück, *n. pl.* -e, sample. **Probezeit,** prō'betsĕit, *f.* time of probation.

Probiren, probī'ren, *vt.* to try, test, prove; to assay. **Probirstein,** -zhtăen, *n. pl.* -e, touchstone.
Problem, problām', *n. pl.* problem. **Problematisch,** -mat'ish, *a.* doubtful.
Procent, protsent', *m. f.* Prozent.
Proceß, protsess', *m.* siehe Proz...
Procura, prokū'rä, *f.* procuration; power of attorney.
Producent, produtsent', *m.* -en, *pl.* -en, producer.
Product, produkt', *n. pl.* -e, product, production, produce. **Production,** produktsiōn', *f.* production. **Productiv,** produktīv', *a.* productive. **Produciren,** produtsī'ren, *vt.* to produce.
Profan, profān', *a.* profane. **Profaniren,** pro anī'ren, *vt.* to profane.
Profession, profession', *f.* profession. **Professor,** professor, *m.* -s. *pl.* -en, professor. **Professur,** professūr', *f.* professorship.
Profil, pro īl', *n. pl.* -e. profile.
Profit, p ofīt', *m.* profit. **Profitiren,** profitī'ren, *vt. i.* to profit.
Profoß, profōs'. *m. pl.* -e, provost.
Programm, program', *n. pl.* -e, programme.
Progression, progression', *f.* progression: geometrische —, geometrical progression; arithmetische —, arithmetical progression.
Project, pro-yekt', *n. pl.* -e, project. **Projection,** pro-yektsiōn'. *f.* projection. **Projectiren,** pro-yektī'ren, *vt.* to project; to intend.
Proletarier, proletāri-ĕr, *m.* proletary.
Promenade, promenä'de, *f.* promenade.
Promotion, promotsiōn', *f.* promotion. **Promoviren,** promovī'ren, *vt.* to promote.
Prompt, prompt, *a.* prompt.
Pronomen, pronō'men, *n. pl.* -nomina, pronoun. **Pronominal,** -nominäl', *a.* pronominal.
Prophet, profēt', *m.* -en, *pl.* -en, prophet: -in, *f.* prophetess. **Prophetisch,** -ish. *a.* prophetic. **Prophezeien,** prophetseī'en, *vt.* to prophesy. **Prophezeiung,** prophetseī'ung, *f.* prophecy.
Proportion, proportsiōn', *f.* proportion.

Propst, propzht, *m. pl.* Pröpste, provost (of a chapter).
Prosa, prō'sä, *f.* prose, prose composition. **Prosaiker,** prosǟ'ikĕr, *m* prose writer. **Prosaisch,** prosǟish, *a.* prosaic, prose.
Proselyt, pro-elīt', *m.* proselyte.
Prosit, prō'sit, *ij.* May it do yor good!
Prosodie, prosodī', *f.* prosody.
Prospect, prospěkt', *m.* prospect, view; prospectus.
Prostituiren, prostituī'ren, *vt.* to prostitute. **Prostitution,** prozhtitutsiōn', *f.* prostitution.
Protest, protězht'. *m. pl.* -e, protest; unter —, mit —, protested, dishonored.
Protestant, protězhtant', *m.* -en, *pl.* -en, protestant. **Protestantisch,** -ish, *a.* protestant. **Protestiren,** protězhtī'ren, *vt.* to protest.
Protokoll, protokoll', *n.* minutes, record. **Protokolliren,** -ī'ren, *vt.* to record, register.
Protoxyd, protoxīd', *n. pl.* -e, protoxide.
Protze, prot'se, *f.* front part of a gun-carriage.
Proviant, profiant', *m.* provision, supply.
Provinz, profīnts', *f.* province.
Provision, profisiōn', *f.* provision; commission.
Provisor, profī'sor, *m.* provisor; -isch, -ish, *a.* provisory; temporary.
Prozent, protsent', *m. pl.* -e, per cent., percentage.
Prozeß, prot-ěss', *m. pl.* -e, process law-suit, action.
Prozession, protsession', *f.* procession
Prozessiren, protsess-ī'ren, *vi.* to be a law with.
Prüfen, prü'fen, *vt.* to prove, try, test examine. **Prüfstein,** prüf'zhtǟen *m. pl.* -e, touchstone. **Prüfung,** -ung, *f.* trial, examination; temptation.
Prügel, prüh'gel, *m.* cudgel, stick; cudgelling: — bekommen. to be cudgelled. **Prügelei,** prügelǟ', *f.* fight, row. **Prügeln,** prü'geln, *vi.* to cudgel, drub, thrash.
Prunk, prunk, *m.* show. ostentation. splendor. **Prunken,** prun'ken. *vi.* to display, make a show. **Prunk'**

Pſa   250   **Pyr**

gemach, -gemach, *n. pl.* -gemächer, apartment of state. **Prunkhaft,** -haft, *a.* ostentatious, showy. **Prunklos,** -lōs, *a.* unostentatious.
Pſalm, psalm, *m. pl.* -e, psalm. **Pſalmiſt,** psalmizht', *m.* -en, *pl.* -en, psalmist. **Pſalter,** psal'ter, *m.* psalter, psaltery.
Pſt, *ij.* Hist! Hush!
Pſychologie, psichologī', *f.* psychology.
Publikum, pŭ'blikŭm, *n.* public.
Publiziren, publitsī'ren, *vt.* to publish.
Pudding, pŭd'ding, *m. pl.* -e, *n*, pudding.
Pudel, pū'del, *m.* poodle: blunder. **Pudeln,** pū'deln, *vi.* to blunder.
Puder, pū'der, *m.* (hair) powder. **Pu'derbeutel,** -beutel, *m.* powder-bag. **Pu'derig,** -ich, *a.* powdery.
Puff, puff, *ij.* bang! puff! *s. m. pl.* **Püffe,** puff, thump. **Puffen,** pŭf'fen, *vt.* to puff; to cuff, thump. **Puffer,** pŭf'fer, *m.* pocket-pistol.
Puls, pŭls, *m.* pulse. **Puls'ader,** -äder, *f.* artery. **Pulsiren,** pŭlsī'ren, *vi.* to beat, throb, pulsate. **Puls'ſchlag,** -schläg, *m. pl.* -ſchläge, beating of the pulse.
Pult, pult, *m. pl.* -e, desk. **Pult'dach,** -dach, *n. pl.* -dächer, lean-to.
Pulver, pul'fer, *n.* powder, gunpowder: — und Blei, powder and shot. **Pul'verdampf,** -dampf, *m.* smoke (from powder). **Pul'verflaſche,** -flasche, *f.* **Pul'verhorn,** -horn, *n. pl.* -hörner, powder-flask. **Pul'verig,** -ich, *a.* powdery. **Pulveriſiren,** pulferisī'ren, *vt.* to pulverize. **Pulverkammer,** pul'ferkammer, *f.* powder-room. **Pul'vermagazin,** -magatsīn, *n. pl.* -e, powder-magazine. **Pul'vermühle,** -mühle, *f.* powder-mill. **Pulvern,** pul'fern, *vt.* to pulverize. **Pul'verthurm,** -turm, *m. pl.* -thürme, powder-magazine. **Pul'verwagen,** -fervagen, *m.* powder-wagon, ammunition-wagon; auch **Pul'verkarren,** -karren, *m.*
Pump, pump, *m.* credit.
Pumpbrunnen, pump'brunnen, *m.* **Pumpe,** pum'pe, *f.* pump. **Pumpen,** pum'pen, *vt.* to pump; to take on credit. **Pum'venbohrer,** -bōrer, *m.* pump-borer. **Pum'penkaſten,** -kazhten, *m.* case of a pump. **Pum'pen-**

klappe, -klappe, *f.* pump-valve. **Pum'penſchwengel,** -shvengel, *m.* handle of a pump.
Pumpernickel, pŭm'pĕrnickel, *m.* pumpernickel, rye-bread.
Pumphoſen, pump'hōsen, *s. pl.* wide trowsers.
Pumpwerk, pump'vĕrk, *n.* pump-gear.
Punkt, punkt, *m. pl.* -e, point, dot, period; article; auf den —, exactly. **Punktiren,** punktī'ren, *vt.* to punctuate; to dot. **Pünktlich,** pünkt'lich, *a.* punctual, exact, accurate; -keit, -kēĕt, *f.* punctuality, exactness, accuracy. **Punktur,** punktūr', *f.* puncture; points (Print.); -loch, -loch, *n. pl.* -löcher, point hole.
Punſch, punsh, *m.* punch. **Punſch'bole,** -bōle, *f.* punch-bowl. **Punſch'löffel,** -lŭffel, *m.* punch-ladle.
Punzen, pŭnt'sen, *m.* punch (Mech.)
Pupille, pupil'le, *f.* pupil.
Puppe, pŭp'pe, *f.* doll, puppet, chrysalis. **Pup'penſpiel,** -zhpīl, *n. pl.* -e, puppet-show.
Pur, pūr, *a.* pure, unmixed.
Purgans, purgants', *f.* purgative. **Purgiren,** purgī'ren, *vt.* to purge. **Purgirmittel,** -gir'mittel, *n.* purgative.
Puritaner, puritän'ĕr, *m.* puritan.
Purpur, pur'pur, *n.* purple, scarlet; purple-robe; -farben, -farben, *a.* purple, purple-colored. **Pur'purmantel,** -mantel, *m.* purple-robe, scarlet-mantle. **Purpurn,** pur'purn, *a.* purple-colored. **Pur'purſchnecke,** -shnĕcke, *f.* purple, purple-shell-fish.
Puſten, pŭzh'ten, *vi.* to blow, breathe.
Pute, pū'te, *f.* turkey-hen. **Puter,** pū'tĕr, *m.* turkey-cock, gobbler.
Putting, pŭt'ting, *f.* chains of the dead-eye. **Put'tingtau,** -tau, *f. pl.* -e, futtock.
Putz, puts, *m.* dress, attire, finery. **Putzen,** put'sen, *vt.* to attire, dress; to trim, clean; to snuff. **Putz'händler,** -hendlĕr, *m.* sin, *f.* milliner. **Putz'macherin,** -macherin, *f. pl.* -innen, milliner. **Putz'tiſch,** -tish, *m. pl.* -e, dressing-table, toilet. **Putzwaaren,** puts'vāren, *s. pl.* millinery.
Pyramide, piramī'de, *f.* pyramid.
Pyrit, pirit, *m.* pyrite.

Pyr 251 **Qui**

Pyrogallussäure, pirogal'lyssöüre, f. pyrogallic acid.
Pyrometer, pirom̄ā'tĕr, m. pyrometer.
Pyrotechnik, pirotĕch'nik, f. pyrotechnics.

Quabbe, quab'be, f. dew-lap. **Quabbelig**, quab'belich, a. shaky, quivering, plump, fat. **Quabbeln**, quab'beln, vi. to quiver, shake.
Quacksalber, quack'salbĕr, m. quack, mountebank. **Quacksalberei**, -rēī', f. quackery. **Quacksalbern**, quack'salbĕrn, vi. to act as quack, to quack.
Quader, quä'dĕr, m. **Quaderstein**, -zhtaĕn, m. pl. -e, freestone, squarestone.
Quadrant, quadrant', m. quadrant.
Quadrat, quadrät', n. square. quadrate; second power. **Quadratfuß**, -fuss, n. pl. -e, square foot. **Quadratisch**, -ish, a. quadratic. **Quadratmeile**, -mēile, f. square mile. **Quadratur**, quadratyr', f. quadrature. **Quadratwurzel**, -vyrtsel, f. square root.
Quadrille, kadril'ye, f. quadrille.
Quadriren, quadri'ren, vi. to square.
Quaken, quä'ken, vi. to croak; quack.
Quäken, quä'ken, vi. to scream; to squeal.
Quäker, quä'kĕr, s. Quaker, Friend.
Qual, quäl, f. pain, torment. **Quälen**, quä'len, vt. to torment, torture; to plague, pester. **Quäler**, quä'lĕr, **Quälgeist**, quäl'gaĕzht, m. pl. -er, tormentor, teaser.
Qualifiziren, qualifitsī'ren, vt. to qualify, fit.
Qualität, qualität', f. quality.
Quall, quall, m. gushing forth.
Qualm, qualm, m. thick vapor, smoke.
Qualmen, qual'men, vi. to steam; to smoke; vt. to fill with smoke.
Qualmig, qual'mich, a. smoky, vapory.
Qualster, qual'zhtĕr, m. phlegm.
Qualstern, qual'zhtĕrn, vi. to spit phlegm.
Quantität, quantität', f. quantity.
Quappe, quap'pe, f. eel-pout; tadpole.
Quarantaine, karantä'ne, f. quarantine.

Quark, quark, m. curds; trash, dirt, lumber.
Quarkkäse, quark'käse, f. whey-cheese.
Quart, quart, n. pl. -e, quarter, quart; quarto.
Quartal, quartäl', n. pl. -e, quarter (of a year), term.
Quartanfieber, quartän'fībĕr, n. quartan fever.
Quartant, quartant', m. -en, pl. -en, quarto.
Quarte, quar'te, f. quart; fourth.
Quartett, quartet', n. quartet.
Quartier, quartīr', n. pl. -e, quarter; lodging.
Quartiermeister, quartīr'maĕzhtĕr, m. quartermaster.
Quarz, quärts, m. quartz.
Quarzsinter, quärts'sintĕr, m. quartzsinter.
Quasi, quä'si, av. as it were, quasi.
Quassie, quas'si-e, f. quassia.
Quast, quazht, m. pl. -e, tassel.
Queck, queck'e, f. conch-grass.
Quecksilber, queck'silbĕr, n. quicksilver, mercury. **Quecksilbersalbe**, -salbe, f. mercury-salve.
Quehle, quē'le, f. towel.
Quell, quell, m. pl. -e, **Quelle**, quell'e, f. spring, fountain, source. **Quellen**, quěl'len, vi. to gush, flow, spring forth.
Quellwasser, quell'vassĕr, n. springwater.
Quendel, quen'del, m. wild thyme.
Quent, quent, n. pl. -e, **Quentchen**, quent'chen, n. one eighth of an ounce, two drams.
Quer, quēr, a. av. across, athwart, cross. **Queraxt**, -axt, f. holing-axe.
Querbalken, quēr'balken, m. crossbeam, transom. **Quere**, quē're, f. cross direction; in die —, across.
Querfeldein, quērfeltaěn', av. across the field. **Quergasse**, -gasse, f. cross-lane. **Querholz**, -holts, n. pl. -hölzer, cross-bar.
Querl, quěrl, **Quirl**, quirl, m. pl. -e, twirling-stick; whorl. **Querlen**, quěr'len, vt. to twirl.
Quetsche, quet'she, f. squeezing-tool; a tight place. **Quetschen**, quet'shen, vt. to squeeze, bruise. **Quetschung**, quet'shung, f. squeezing, crushing; contusion. **Quetschwunde**, -vynde f. contusion.
Quick, quick, m. native quicksilver

Quieken, qui'ken, *vi.* to squeak, squeal.
Quinte, quin'te, *f.* fifth; quint.
Quintessenz, quin'tĕ·sents, *f.* quintessence.
Quintett, quintĕtt', *n. pl. -e,* quintet.
Quitt, quitt, *a.* quit, quits, clear.
Quitte, quit'te, *f.* quince. **Quittenbaum,** quit'tenbaum, *m. pl. -bäume,* quince-tree. **Quittensaft, -saft,** *m.* juice of quinces.
Quittiren, quittī'ren, *vt.* to quit; to receipt, acquit.
Quittung, quit'tụng, *f.* receipt, acquittance.
Quote, quō'te, *f.* quota, share.
Quotidianfieber, quotidiăn'fīber, *n.* quotidian fever.
Quotient, quotsi-ent', *m.* quotient.

Raa, rä, *f.* **Rahe,** rä·e, *f.* yard; große —, main yard. **Raasegel, -sē**gel, *n.* yard-sail.
Rabatt, rabatt', *m.* discount, deduction.
Rabatte, rabat'te,*f.* facing (of a dress); border-bed.
Rabbiner, rabī'nēr, *m.* rabbi.
Rabe, rä'be, *m. -n, pl. -n,* raven (crow). **Ra'benaas, -äs,** *n. pl. -äser,* carrion. **Ra'benfeder, -fēder,** *f.* raven-quill. **Ra'benmutter,** -mụtter, *f. pl. -mütter,* unnatural mother. **Ra'benschwarz,** -shvarts, *a.* black as a crow. **Ra'benstein,** -zhtṣĕn, *m. pl. -e,* place of execution. **Ra'benvater, -fātēr,** *m. pl. -väter,* unnatural father.
Rabulist, rabụlizht', *m. -en, pl. -en,* pettifogger.
Rache, rä'ch̭e, *f.* vengeance, revenge. **Rächen,** rä'ch̭en, *vt.* to avenge, revenge.
Rachen, rach̭'en, *m.* throat, mouth, jaws.
Rächer, rä'ch̭ēr, *m.* avenger.
Rachgier, räch̭'gīr, *f.* vindictiveness, revengefulness. **Rach̭'gierig, -ich̭,** *a.* vindictive, revengeful. **Rach̭'sucht, -sụch̭t,** *f.* vindictiveness. **Rach̭'süch̭tig, -süch̭tich̭,** *a.* vindictive, revengeful.
Rack, rack, *n. pl. -e,* rack (Mar.); **-talje, -talye,** *f.* truss-tackle.
Rad, räd, *n. pl.* **Räder,** wheel; rowel. **Rad'achse, -***xe, *f.* axle-tree. **Rad's-**

---

bärge, -bērge, *f.* wheel-barrow.
Radebrechen, rä'debrěch̭en, *vt.* to mangle, to speak broken words.
Ra'dehacke, -hacke, *f.* **Ra'dehaue,** -haü·e. *f.* mattock.
Rädelsführer, rä'delsfürer, *m.* ringleader.
Rademacher, rä'demach̭er, *m.* wheelwright.
Rädern, rä'dērn, *vt.* to break on the wheel.
Räderwerk, rä'dērvĕrk, *n. pl. -e,* wheelwork.
Radikal, radikäl', *a.* radical, *ar. -ly* **Radikalismus,** radīkalīs'mụs, *m.* radicalism.
Radieschen, radīs'ch̭en, *n:* radish.
Radiren, radī'ren, *vt.* to erase, to scrape out; to etch. **Radir'kunst,** -kụnzht, *f.* etching. **Radir'messer,** -messĕr, *n.* knife for erasing. **Radir'nadel, -nädel,** *f.* etching-needle, etching-pin. **Radir'ung, -ụng,** *f.* erasure.
Radius, rä'diụss, *m. pl.* **Radien,** radius, semi-diameter.
Radkasten, räd'kazhten, *m.* wheel-box. **Rad'scheibe,** -shēïbe, *f.* ram's-block. **Rad'schiene, -shīne,** *f.* cart-tire. **Rad'speiche, -späech̭e,** *f.* spoke. **Rad'spur,** -zhpụr, *f.* track-rut.
Raffel, raff'el, *f.* ribble; scold, shrew.
Raffen, raff'en, *vt.* to snatch up, seize.
Raffinade, raffīnā'de, *f.* refining of sugar; refined sugar. **Raffiniren,** raffīnī'ren, *vt.* to refine.
Raffzahn, raff'tsän, *m. pl. -zähne,* projecting tooth: fore-tooth.
Ragen, rä'gen, *vi.* to project, to rise up: to be eminent.
Ragout, ragụ', *m.* ragout.
Rahm, räm, *m.* cream.
Rahmeisen, räm'ēīsen, *n.* chase-bar.
Rahmen, rä'men, *vt. i.* to cream; to skim.
Rahmen, rä'men, *m.* frame; form, chase: rim, edge; welt.
Rahmhobel, rämhō'bel, *m.* notching-plane.
Rahmkäse, räm'kāse, *f.* cream-cheese.
Rahmlöffel, räm'löffel, *m.* cream-ladle.
Rain, rṣĕn, *m. pl. -e,* balk, boundary.
Rainen, rṣĕn'en, *vi.* to border on.
Raisoniren, resonī'ren, *vi.* to reason, to censure, find fault.
Rakete, rakā'te, *f.* rocket, sky-rocket

Rammblad, ramm'block. *m. pl.* -blöde.
Ramme, ram'me, *f.* **Rammel,** ram'mel, *f.* ram, paving-beetle, pile-driver. **Rammeln,** ram'meln, *vi.* to ram; to rut, couple. **Rammen,** ram'men, *vt.* to ram, to drive in.
Rand, rant. *m. pl.* Ränder, edge, brink, brim, ledge, margin. **Rand'bemertung,** -bemerkung, *f.* **Rand'gloße,** -glosse, *f.* marginal note, gloss. **Rän'dern, Rän'deln, Rän'den,** ren'den, *vt.* to edge, border; mill (coins).
Ranft, ranft, *m. pl.* Ränfte, crust.
Rang, rang. *m.* rank, order, precedence, dignity; den — ablaufen, to get the better of.
Rangordnung, rang'ordnung, *f.* order of rank.
Rank, rank, *m. pl.* Ränke, trick, intrigue; — schmieden, to intrigue.
Ranke, ran'ke, *f.* tendril, runner, twig, vine.
Ranken, ran'ken, *vi.* to run, shoot, climb.
Ränkevoll, ren'kefoll, *a.* tricky, intriguing.
Ranunkel, ranun'kel, *m.* ranunculus.
Ranzen, ran'tsen, *m.* **Ränzel,** ren'tsel, *n.* belly; knapsack.
Ranzen, ran'tsen, *vi.* to rove about; to couple.
Ranzig, ran'tsich. *a.* rancid, rank.
Ranzion, rantsion'. *f.* ransom. **Ranzioniren,** rantsioni'ren, *vt.* to ransom, redeem.
Rappe, rap'pe, *m.* -n, *pl.* -n, **Rap'pen,** *m.* black horse.
Rappel, rap'pel. *m.* craziness, hotheadedness. **Rap'pelköpfisch,** -köpfisch. *a.* crazy, crackbrained, mad.
Rappell, rappell', *m.* recall.
Rappeln, rap'peln, *vi.* to rattle, to stir, to be in a hurry; to be crazy.
Rappier, rappīr'. *n. pl.* -e, foil.
Rapport, rapport', *m. pl.* -e, report, account. **Rapportiren,** rapportī'ren, *vt.* to report.
Rappuse, rappu'se, *f.* scramble, seizure: in die — geben, to deliver up to pillage.
Raps, raps, *m.* rape-seed.
Rapunzel, rapun'tsel, *m.* rampion.
Rar, rär, *a.* rare, scarce, exquisite. **Rarität,** rärität', *f.* rarity, curiosity.
Rasch, rash, *a.* fast quick, swift, prompt; *av.* -ly; zu rasch, rash, hasty.
Rasch, rash, *m. pl.* -e, serge.
Rascheln, rash'eln, *vi.* to rustle.
Raschheit, rash'hēët, *f.* swiftness promptness.
Rasen, rä'sen, *m.* turf, sod.
Rasen, rä'sen, *vi.* to rage, to rave, to rant.
Rasenbank, rä'senbank, *m. pl.* -bänke, seat of turf.
Rasend, rä'sent, *a.* raving, raging, furious: — werden, to run mad.
Rasenplatz, rä'senplats, *m. pl.* -plätze, grass-plot, green.
Rasensitz, rä'sensits, *m. pl.* -e, seat of turf. **Rasenweg,** -wēg, *m. pl.* -e, turfed way.
Raserei, räserēī', *f.* raving, raging, delirium, madness.
Rasiren, rasī'ren, *vt.* to shave. **Rasir'messer,** -messer, *n.* razor.
Raspel, ras'pel, *f.* rasp. **Raspeln,** ras'peln, *vt.* to rasp.
Raß, räs, *a.* sharp, acrid, sour, strong.
Rasse, ras'se, *f.* race.
Rassel, ras'sel, *f.* rattle. **Rasseln,** ras'seln, *vi.* to rattle, clatter.
Rast, rast, *f.* rest, repose. **Rasten,** ras'ten, *vi.* to rest, repose. **Rast'los,** -lōs, *a.* restless: **igkeit,** -ĭchkēët, *f.* restlessness. **Rast'tag,** -tāg, *m. pl.* -e, day of rest.
Rate, rä'te, *f.* rate; instalment.
Rath, rāt, *m.* advice, counsel; council; zu Rathe ziehen, to consult; councilor, counselor. **Rathen,** rä'ten (rieth, gerathen), *vt.* to advise, counsel; to guess. **Rath'fragen,** -frägen, *vt.* to consult. **Rath'geber,** -gēber, *m.* counselor. **Rath'haus,** -hōys. *n. pl.* -häuser, court-house, town-hall. **Räthlich,** rät'lich, *a.* expedient, advisable; suitable, *ar.* -ly; **-keit,** -kēët, *f.* expediency. **Rathlos,** rāt'lōs, *a.* perplexed, desponding, at a loss; **igkeit,** -ĭchkēët, *f.* bewilderment, perplexity. **Rath'sam,** -sam, *a.* advisable, expedient, useful. **Rath'schlag,** -shlāg, *m. pl.* -schläge, counsel, advice. **Rath'schlagen,** -shlägen, *vi.* to consult, deliberate. **Rath'schluß,** -shluss, *m. pl.* -schlüsse, decree. **Rathscollegium,** -kollāgium, *n. pl.* -ien, council. **Räthsel,** rät'sel, *n.* riddle, enigma. **Räthselhaft,** -haft, *a.* enigmatical,

Rat 254 **Rau**

mysterious; **=igfeit**, -kāėt, f. mystery, strangeness. **Rathsherr**, räts'hèrr, m. -n, pl. -n, councilor, senator, councilman. **Rathsſchluß**, -shlyss, m. pl. -ſchlüſſe, decree of a council. **Rathsſchreiber**, -shrēībėr, m. recorder. **Rathsſtube**, -zhtybẹ, f. council-room, council-chamber. **Rathstag**, -tāg, m. pl. -e, council-day.
Ratifiziren, ratifitsī'ren, vt. to ratify.
Ration, ratsiōn', f. ration, allowance.
Rationalismus, ratsionalīs'mŭs, m. rationalism.
Rationaliſt, ratsionalīzht', m. -en, pl. -en, rationalist.
Rationell, ratsionėll', a. rational.
Ratte, rat'tẹ, **Ratze**, rat'sẹ, f. rat. **Rattenfalle**, -fallẹ, f. rat-trap. **Rattenfänger**, -fēngėr, m. rat-catcher. **Rattengift**, -gift, n. pl. -e, rat-bane. **Rattenkönig**, -köniḡ, a. rat's-king. **Rattenſchwanz**, rat'tenshvants, m. rat-tail.
Raub, rǎŭb, m. robbery, rapine; spoil, booty. **Rauben**, rǎŭ'bėn, vt. to rob, take away, seize. **Räuber**, rǎŭ'bėr, m. robber, highwayman, brigand; thief (in a candle). **Räuberbande**, -bandẹ, f. gang of robbers. **Räuberei**, -rēī', f. robbery. **Räuberhauptmann**, -haŭptmann, m. leader of robbers. **Räuberhöhle**, -hȫlẹ, f. den of robbers. **Räuberiſch**, -ish, a. rapacious, thievish. **Raubfiſch**, rǎŭb'fish, m. fish of prey. **Raubgier**, -gīr, f. rapacity; **=ig**, -iḡ, a. rapacious. **Raubſchiff**, -shiff, n. pl. -e, pirate. **Raubſchloß**, -shloss, n. pl. -ſchlöſſer, castle of knight-robbers. **Raubſtaat**, -zhtāt, m. -e, pl. -en, piratical state. **Raubthier**, -tīr, n. pl. -e, beast of prey: **Raubvogel**, -fōgel, m. pl. -vögel, bird of prey.
Rauch, rǎŭch, a. hairy, shaggy, rough.
Rauch, rǎŭch, m. smoke, fume; steam; in — aufgehen, to burn down, to be consumed. **Rauchen**, rǎŭ'chen, vi. to smoke. **Raucher**, rǎŭ'chėr, m. smoker. **Räucherin**, rǎŭ'chėrin, a. **Rauchicht**, rǎŭch'icht, a. smoky. **Räucherkerze**, rǎŭ'chėrkertsẹ, f. pastil. **Räuchern**, rǎŭ'chėrn, vt. to smoke. **Räucherpfanne**, -pfannẹ, f. censer. **Räucherpulver** -pulfėr,

n. fumigating powder. **Räucherung**, -ŭng, f. fumigation. **Rauchfang**, rǎŭch'fang, m. pl. -fänge, chimney; hearth. **Rauchfaß**, -fass, n. pl. -fäſſer, censer.
Rauchhandel, rǎŭch'handel, m. fur-trade. **Rauchhändler**, -hendlėr, m. furrier, dealer in furs.
Rauchkammer, rǎŭch'kammer, smoke-house. **Rauchſäule**, -sēŭlẹ, f. pillar of smoke. **Rauchtabak**, -taback, m. pl. -e, tobacco for smoking.
Rauchwaare, rǎŭch'vārẹ, f. peltry, furs.
Räude, rȫŭ'dẹ, **Raude**, rǒŭ'dẹ, f. itch; mange. **Räudig**, rȫŭ'diḡ, a. itchy; mangy, scurfy.
Raufbold, rǎŭf'bolt, m. pl. -e, bully, brawler.
Raufe, rǎŭ'fẹ, f. crate, rack; flax-comb, breaker. **Raufen**, rǎŭ'fen, vt. to pull, pluck. **Raufer**, rǎŭf'ėr, m. brawler. **Rauferei**, rǎŭfėrēī', f. fighting, brawl.
Rauh, rǒŭ, a. rough, raw, hoarse, rude. **Rauhdiſtel**, -dizhtel, f. teazle. **Rauhheit**, -hāėt, f. roughness, hoarseness, rudeness. **Rauhhobel**, -hōbel, n. fore-plane. **Rauhreif**, -rēīf, m. hoar-frost.
Raum, rǎŭm, m. pl. **Räume**, space, room; hold (Mar.); opportunity; leerer —, empty space, vacuum. **Raumanker**, -anker, m. spare-anchor. **Räumen**, rȫŭ'men, vt. to clear out, empty; to quit, evacuate; to veer aft (Mar.). **Räumer**, rȫŭ'mėr, m. cleaner; crooked file. **Räumlichkeit**, rȫŭm'lichkāėt, f. room. **Räumung**, -ŭng, f. clearing up, evacuation.
Raunen, rǎŭ'nen, vi. to whisper.
Raupe, rǒŭ'pẹ, m. -n, pl. -n, caterpillar. **Raupen**, rǒŭ'pen, vi. to clean of caterpillars. **Raupenneſt**, -nėzht, n. pl. -er, nest, web of caterpillars.
Rauſch, rǒŭsh, m. pl. **Räuſche**, fit: intoxication, drunkenness, spree; drunken fit. **Räuſchchen**, rȫŭsh'chen, n. spree, slight intoxication; ein — haben, to be tipsy.
Rauſchen, rǒŭsh en. vi. to rush, to rustle, roar.
Rauſchgold, rǒŭsh'golt, n. gold-tinsel, gold-foil. **Rauſchſilber**, -silbėr, n silver-foil.

Räuspern, rŏŭs'pėrn, *vr. u. i.* to hawk, to clear the throat.
Raute, rŏṷ'tẹ, *f.* rue.
Raute, rŏṷ'tẹ, *f.* lozenge, rhomb, diamond; rhomboid. **Rautenförmig,** -tenförmiǵ, *a.* rhombic, lozenged; rhomboidal.
Reaktion, rẹ-aktiōn', *f.* reaction.
Reagentie, rẹ-agẹn'tsi-ẹ, *f.* test, reagent.
Real, rẹ-ál', *a.* real. **Realiſiren,** realiṡī'ren, *vt.* to realize. **Realität,** rẹ-alität', *f.* reality. **Realſchule,** rẹ-ál'shųlẹ, *f.* practical school.
Rebe, rá'bẹ, *f.* vine, vine-branch.
Rebell, rẹbėll', *m.* -en, *pl.* -en. rebel. **Rebellion,** rẹbėlliōn', *f.* rebellion. **Rebelliren,** rẹbėllī'ren, *vi.* to rebel. **Rebelliſch,** rẹbėll'ish, *a.* rebellious.
Rebenſaft, rā'bensaft, *m.* juice of the vine. **Re'benſtock,** -zhtock, *m. pl.* -ſtöcke, vine.
Rebhuhn, rĕb'hųn, *n. pl.* -hühner, partridge.
Recapituliren, rẹkapitųlī'ren, *vt.* to recapitulate.
Recenſent, rẹtsẹnsent', *m.* -en, *pl.* -en. critic, reviewer. **Recenſion,** rẹtsẹnsiōn', *f.* review, criticism. **Recenſiren,** rẹtsẹnsī'ren, *vt.* to criticise, review.
Recept, rẹtsėpt', *n. pl.* -e. prescription, recipe.
Receß, rẹtsėss'. *m. pl.* -eſſe, compromise; arrears.
Rechen, rėch'en, *m.* rake; clothes-rack; grate; ratchet; *vt.* to rake.
Rechenbrett, rėch'enbrĕt, *n.* counting-board.
Rechenbuch, rėch'enbųch, *n. pl.* -bücher, ciphering-book, arithmetic. **Rechenkunſt,** rėch'enkųnzht, *f.* arithmetic. **Rech'enlehrer,** -lėrėr, *m.* teacher of arithmetic. **Rech'enmeiſter,** -mäezhter, *m.* arithmetician. **Rech'enpfennig,** -pfenniǵ, *m. pl.* -e, counter.
Rech'enſchaft, -shaft, *f.* account; — geben, to give an account, to explain; zur — ziehen, to demand an account. **Rech'entafel,** -täfel, *f.* slate.
Rechnen, rėch'nen, *vi.* to count, reckon, calculate, cipher; — unter, to class with; — auf, to count, depend on. **Rech'nung,** -nųng, *f.* reckoning, account, calculation; — machen auf, to depend, rely upon. **Rech'nungsabſchluß,** -apshlųss, *m.* closing of accounts. **Rechnungsführer,** rėch'nųngsführėr, *m.* book-keeper, accountant.
Recht, rėcht, *a.* right, just, proper, true, real, genuine, correct, legitimate. *av.* -ly, well; *s. n. pl.* -e, right, law, justice; privilege; — haben, to be right; von Rechtswegen, by right; es iſt ihm — geſchehen, he is served right.
Rechte, rėch'tẹ, *f.* right hand.
Rechteck, rėcht'ėck, *n. pl.* -e, rectangle. **Rechteckig,** -iǵ, *a.* rectangular.
Rechten, rėch'ten, *vi.* to dispute, expostulate; to go to law with, to plead.
Rechtfertigen, rėcht'fẹrtiǵen, *vt.* to justify. **Recht'fertigung,** -ųng, *f.* justification, vindication.
Rechtgläubig, rėcht'gläübiǵ, *a.* orthodox; -keit, -käėt, *f.* orthodoxy.
Rechthaberei, rėcht'hȧberėī', *f.* dogmaticalness. **Recht'haberiſch,** -ish, *a.* dogmatical.
Rechtlich, rėcht'lich, *a.* righteous, just, honest; lawful; -keit, -käėt, *f.* righteousness, integrity, lawfulness.
Rechtlos, rėcht'lōs, *a.* illegal; outlawed. **Recht'loſigkeit,** -ichkäėt, *f.* illegality; condition of an outlaw.
Rechtmäßig, rėcht'mässich, *a.* lawful, legitimate; -keit, -käėt, *f.* lawfulness, legality.
Rechts, rėchts, *av.* on the right; to the right hand.
Rechtsanſpruch, rėchts'anzhprųch, *m.* -ſprüche, legitimate claim.
Rechtsbefliſſen, rėchts'beflissen, studying law.
Rechtsbeſtändig, rėchts'bezhtẹndich, *a.* legal, in due form.
Rechtſchaffen, rėcht'shaffen, *a.* righteous, honest; -heit, -häėt, *f.* righteousness, honesty.
Rechtſchreibung, rėcht'shrėībųng, *f.* orthography.
Rechtsfall, rėchts'fall, *m. pl.* -fälle, case in law.
Rechtsgelehrter, rėchts'gelėrtėr, *m.* lawyer.
Rechtsgelehrtheit, rėchts'gel'rthäėt, *f.* jurisprudence.
Rechtsgrund, rėchts'grųnd, *m. pl.* -gründe, legal ground.
Rechtsgültig, rėchts'gültich, **Rechtskräftig,** -kręftich, *a.* legal, valid; -keit, -käėt, *f.* legality, validity.

Rechtshandel, rĕchts'handel, m. pl. -bändel, lawsuit.
Rechtsher, rĕchts'hēr, av. from the right.
Rechtskundig, rĕchts'kŭndich, a. versed in law.
Rechtslehre, rĕchts'lēre, f. jurisprudence.
Rechtsmittel, rĕchts'mittel, n. legal means.
Rechtspflege, rĕchts'pflēge, f. administration of justice.
Rechtssache, rĕchts'sache, f. lawsuit.
Rechtsspruch, rĕchts'zhpruch, m. pl. -sprüche, decree, decision, verdict.
Rechtsstreit, rĕchts'zhtrĕīt, m. lawsuit.
Rechtsungültig, rĕchts'ŭngŭltich, a. invalid, illegal.
Rechtsverdreher, rĕchts'fĕrdrē-er, m. pettifogger; sophist.
Rechtsverfahren, rĕchts'fĕrfāren, n. legal proceeding.
Rechtsverständiger, rĕchts'fĕrzhtĕndicher, jurist, lawyer.
Rechtswidrig, rĕchts'vīdrich, a. contrary to law, illegal.
Rechtswissenschaft, rĕchts'vissenshaft, f. jurisprudence, science of law.
Rechtwinkelig, rĕcht'vinkēlich, a. rectangular.
Recipient, rĕtsīpi-ent', m. -en, pl. -en, recipient, receiver.
Reciprok, rĕtsiprōk', a. reciprocal, mutual.
Recitativ, rĕtsitatīf', n. pl. -e, recitative.
Recke, rĕck'e, m. -n, pl. -n, giant, hero.
Recken, rĕck'en, vt. to stretch out.
Reclamiren, rĕklamī'ren, vt. to claim, protest.
Recognosciren, rĕkong-nostsī'ren, vi. to reconnoitre, scout. **Recognosci'rung**, -tsīr'ŭng, f. reconnoissance, scouting.
Rectificiren, rĕctifītsī'ren, vt. to rectify.
Rector, rĕk'tōr, m. -s, pl. -en, rector.
Rectorat, rĕktorāt', n. pl. -e, rectorship.
Redacteur, rĕdaktör', m. pl. -e, editor.
Redaktion, rĕdaktsiōn', f. editorship.
Rede, rā'de, f. speech, language: oration; zur Rede stellen, to call to account; zur Rede stehen, to give account. **Re'defunst**, -kŭnzht, f. rhetoric, oratory.

Reden, rā'den, vi. to speak, say. **Re'densart**, rā'densārt, f. phrase. expression. **Redetheil**, rā'detāĕl, m. pl. -e, part of speech.
Redigiren, rĕdigī'ren, vt. to edit.
Redlich, rād'lich, a. honest, faithful: -feit, -kāĕt, f. honesty, faithfulness.
Redner, rād'ner, m. orator. **Rednerbühne**, rād'nerbüne, f. rostrum, tribune, platform. **Rednerisch**, rād'nerish, a. oratorical.
Redoute, rĕdu'te, f. redoubt.
Redselig, rād'sēlich, a. talkative, loquacious.
Reduktion, rĕdŭktsiōn', f. reduction.
Reduziren, rĕdŭtsī'ren, vt. to reduce.
Reell, rĕ-ĕll', a. real, sure; solid genuine.
Reep, rāp, n. pl. -e, rope.
Referent, rĕfĕrent', m. -en, pl. -en, reporter. **Referiren**, rĕfĕrī'ren, vi. to report.
Reff, rĕff, n. pl. -e, dosser.
Reff, rĕff, n. reef (Mar.). **Reffen**, rĕff'en, vt. to reef. **Reff'talje**, -talye, f. reefing-tackle.
Reffträger, rĕff'trāger, m. hawker.
Reflektiren, rĕflĕktī'ren, vt. to reflect. **Reflektor**, rĕflĕk'tor, m. -s, pl. -en, reflector. **Reflexion**, rĕflĕxiōn', f. reflexion. **Reflexions'strahl**, -zhtrāl, m. -s, pl. -en, reflected ray.
Reform, rĕform', f. reform. **Reformation**, -matsiōn', f. reformation. **Reformator**, -mā'tor, m. -s, pl. -en, reformer. **Reformiren**, -mī'ren, vt. to reform. **Reformirter**, -mīr'tĕr, m. Calvinist.
Refraktion, rĕfraktsiōn', f. refraction.
Refrain, rĕfraĕn', m. burden, refrain.
Regal, rĕgāl', a. regal, royal; s. n. pl. -ien, register; shelf; royal prerogative.
Regalpapier, rĕgāl'papīr, n. paper royal.
Rege, rā'ge, a. active, stirring; — machen, to stir up; — werden, to stir, revive.
Regel, rā'gel, f. rule; — be tri, rule of three. **Re'gellos**, -lōs, a. irregular: -heit, -heāĕt, f. irregularity. **Re'gelmäßig**, -mässich, a. regular; -keit, -kāĕt, f. regularity. **Regeln**, rā'geln, vt. to regulate, order, arrange.

Reg 257 **Rei**

Regelrecht, rä'gelrĕcht, *a.* regular, correct. **Re'gelwidrig**, -vĭdrĭch, *a.* contrary to rule; **-keit**, -kāet, *f.* irregularity.

Regen, rä'gen, to stir, move, to be stirring.

Regen, rē'gen, *m.* rain, shower; **-bogen**, -bōgen, *m.* rainbow.

Regeneration, regĕnĕratsiōn', *f.* regeneration. **Regeneriren**, -rī'ren, *vt.* to regenerate.

Regenguß, rē'genguss, *m. pl.* -güsse, shower. **Re'genmaß**, -mās, *n. pl.* -e, **Re'genmesser**, -messĕr, *n.* rain-gauge, hydrometer. **Re'genschauer**, -shŏuer, *m.* shower of rain. **Re'genschirm**, -shīrm, *m. pl.* -e, umbrella.

Regent, regent', *m.* -en, *pl.* -en, regent. **Regent'in**, *f.* regentess. **Regent'schaft**, -shaft, *f.* regency.

Regentropfen, rē'gentropfen, *m.* raindrop. **Re'genwasser**, -vassĕr, *n.* rainwater. **Re'genwetter**, -vettĕr, *n.* rainy weather. **Re'genzeit**, -tsĕīt, *f.* rainy season.

Regieren, regī'ren, *vt.* to rule, reign, govern; to manage, work, steer.

Regierung, regīr'ung, *f.* government, reign, rule. **Regier'ungsform**, -form, *f.* form of government. **Regier'ungsrath**, -rät, *m. pl.* -räthe, counselor of the government. **Regier'ungssitz**, -sits, *m. pl.* -e, seat of government.

Regiment, regiment', *n. pl.* -er, regiment, government, rule. **Regiments'arzt**, -artst, *m.* regimental surgeon. **Regiments'musik**, -musĭk, *f.* regimental band (musicians). **Regiments'tambour**, -tambŏr, *m.* drum-major. **Regiments'tisch**, -tish, *m.* mess. **Regiments'uniform**, -uniform, *f.* regimental uniform.

Region, regiōn', *f.* region.

Regisseur, rĕzhissör', *m.* (theatrical) manager.

Register, rĕgis'tĕr, *n.* register, record; index.

Registrator, rĕgisträ'tŏr, *m.* recorder. **Registratur**, rĕgisträtŭr', *f.* registry. **Registriren**, rĕgistrī'ren, *vt.* to register, record.

Regnen, rĕg'nen, *vi.* to rain. **Reg'nerisch**, -ish, *a.* rainy.

Regreß, regrĕss', *m.* recourse.

Regsam, räg'sam. *a.* active, energetic, bustling **-keit**, -kāet, *f.* activity.

Regulär, regulär', *a.* regular. **Regulator**, rĕgulä'tŏr, *m.* -s, *pl.* -en, regulator, government. **Reguliren**, rĕgulī'ren, *vt.* to regulate. **Regulirung**, rĕgulīr'ung, *f.* regulation.

Regung, rä'gung. *f.* motion, stir; emotion, agitation. **Re'gungslos**, -lōs, *a.* motionless.

Reh, rä, **Rehe**, rä'-e, *a.* foundered, disabled.

Reh, rä, *n. pl.* -e, roe, doe, deer. **Reh'bock**, -bock, *n. pl.* -böcke, roe-buck. **Reh'kalb**, -kalp, *n. pl.* -kälber, fawn. **Reh'keule**, -kĕüle, *f.* **Reh schlägel**, -shlägel, *m.* leg of venison. **Reh'wildbret**, -viltbrĕt, *n.* venison. **Reh'ziemer**, -tsīmer, *m.* saddle of venison.

Reibahle, rēīb'āle, *f.* broach.

Reibebrett, rēī'bĕbrĕt, *n. pl.* -er, rubbing-board.

Reibeisen, rēīb'ēīsen, *n.* grater.

Reiben, rēī'ben (rieb, gerieben), *vt.* to rub, grate, grind, pulverize.

Reibscheit, rēīb'shēīt, *n. pl.* -e, swaybar, sweep-bar.

Reibung, rēī'bung, *f.* rubbing, friction.

Reibungsmesser, rēī'bungsmessĕr, *m.* tribometer.

Reibzeug, rēīb'tsöüg, *n.* rubber.

Reich, rēīch, *a.* rich, wealthy; opulent, copious.

Reich, rēīch, *n. pl.* -e, realm, empire, kingdom.

Reichen, rēīch'en, *vt. i.* to reach, offer, extend, suffice.

Reichhaltig, rēīch'haltĭch, *a.* rich, copious; **-keit**, -kāet, *f.* richness, plenteousness. **Reich'lich**, -lich, *a.* abundant, copious, plentiful; *av.* -ly: **-keit**, -kāet, *f.* copiousness, plenty, abundance.

Reichsacht, rēīchs'acht, *f.* ban of the empire, outlawry.

Reichsadler, rēīchs'ādler, *m.* imperial eagle. **Reichsapfel**, rēīchs'apfel, *m. pl.* -äpfel, imperial globe. **Reichs'archiv**, -archīf, *n. pl.* -e, archives of the empire. **Reichs'graf**, -gräf, *m.* -en, *pl.* -en, count of the empire. **Reichs'gericht**, -gerĭcht, *n. pl.* -e, supreme court of the empire. **Reichs'kleinodien**, -klēnōdi-en, *s. pl.* insignia of the empire. **Reichs'stadt**, -shtatt, *f.* imperial city. **Reichs'tag**,

22*

Rei 258 Rei

-tăg, *m pl. -e*, imperial diet. **Reichs'-thaler**, -tālĕr. *m.* rix-dollar. **Reichs'-verfassung**, -fĕrfássŭng. *f.* constitution of the empire. **Reichsverweser**, -fĕrvĕsŏr, *m.* regent, administrator of the empire.

Reichthum, rīch'tŭm, *m. pl. -thümer*, riches, wealth, opulence.

Reif, rīf, *a.* ripe, mature.

Reif, rīf, *m. -es, pl. -en*, hoar frost, rime.

Reif, rīf, *m. pl. -e*, hoop, ring, wheel; crinoline.

Reife, rī'fe, *f.* ripeness, maturity.

Reifeln, rī'feln, *vt.* to chamfer, groove, flute.

Reifen, rī'fen, *vt.* to mature, ripen, grow ripe.

Reifen, rī'fen, *vt.* to hoop; to groove. **Reif'holz**, -holts. *n.* hoop-poles.

Reiflich, rīf'lich, *a.* mature. *ar. -ly*.

Reifrock, rīef'rock, *m. pl. -röde*, hoop-skirt, crinoline.

Reigen, rīe'gen, *m.* dance.

Reihe, rīe'ye, *f.* row, line, rank, file, series, succession; turn; nach der —, by turns. **Reihen**, rīe'yen, *vt.* to file, rank, string; *vr.* to follow.

Reihen, rīe'yen, *m.* dance.

Reiher, rīe'yĕr, *m.* heron.

Reiltopp, rīl'topp, *m. pl. -e*, royal pole.

Reim, rīem, *m.* rhyme. **Reimen**, rīe'men, *vt. u. r.* to rhyme; to suit, fit; to agree; *vt.* — mit. to reconcile to or with. **Reim'los**, -lōs. *a.* rhymeless.

Rein, rīen, *a.* clean, pure, clear, innocent, neat; ins Reine bringen, to settle.

Reinecke, rīen'ęcke, *m. pl. -n*, fox.

Reinheit, rīen'hīet, *f.* cleanness, purity, clearness.

Reinigen, rīen'ichen, *vt.* to clean, cleanse, purify. **Reinigung**, -ŭng, *f.* cleaning, cleansing, purification; monatliche —, monthly courses.

Reinlich, rīen'lich, *a.* cleanly, neat, *av. -ly*: -feit, -kīet, *f.* cleanliness, neatness.

Reis, rīes, *s. pl. -er*, twig, sprig.

Reis, rīes. *m.* rice.

Reisbesen, rīes'bĕsen, *m.* birch-broom.

Reisbund, rīes'bunt, *n. pl. -e*, fagot.

Reise, rīe'se, *f.* journey, travel; voyage: eine — machen, to travel. **Rei'sebeschreibung**, -beshrīebŭng, *f.* description of travel. **Rei'sebundel**, -bŭndel, *n.* bundle, luggage. **Rei's-**

sefertig, -fĕrtich, *a.* ready for traveling. **Rei'segefährte**, -gefărte. *m. -n pl. -n*, fellow-traveler. **Rei'segeld**, -gĕlt, *n. pl. -er*, traveling-money. **Rei'sekleid**, -klīed, *n. pl. -er*. traveling-dress. **Rei'sekoffer**, -koffer, *m.* traveling-trunk.

Reisen, rīe'sen, *vi.* to travel, to journey, to make a voyage, to go to. **Reisend**, rīe'sent, *a.* traveling, itinerant. **Rei'sender**, *m.* traveler. **Rei'sepaß**, -pass. *m. pl. -pässe*. passport. **Rei'seprediger**, -prĕdicher, *m.* itinerant preacher. **Rei'sesack**, -sack, *m. pl. -säde*. carpet-bag, portmanteau. **Rei'sewagen**, -vägen, *m.* traveling-carriage.

Reisholz, rīes'holts, *n.* **Reisig**, rīes'ich, *a.* brushwood.

Reisig, rīes'ich, *a.* mounted on horseback. **Reisiger**, rīes'icher, *m.* horseman, trooper.

Reisaus, rīes'ous, *m.* running away, flight; — nehmen, to take to one's heels.

Reißblei, rīess'blīel, *n.* crayon; black lead.

Reißbrett, rīess'brĕt, *n. pl. -er*, drawing-board.

Reißen, rīes'sen (riß, gerissen), *vt.* to tear, snatch, pull; to sketch; *s. n.* tearing; tearing pains.

Reißend, rīes'sent, *a.* rapid; rapacious, wild, ravenous.

Reißfeder, rīess'fĕdĕr, *f.* drawing-pen.

Reißkohle, rīes'kōle, *f.* coal for drawing.

Reißzeug, rīess'tsöuk, *n.* case of mathematical instruments.

Reitbahn, rīet'bān, *f.* manege, riding-school.

Reiten, rīe'ten, *vt.* to ride, to go on horseback: spazieren —, to take a ride: Galopp reiten, to gallop; vor Anker —, to ride at anchor, to ride hard.

Reiter, rīe'tĕr, *m.* rider, horseman. **Reiterei**, -īe', *f.* riding; cavalry, horse. **Rei'terfahne**, -fāne, *f.* banner. **Rei'terführich**, -fūnrich, *m. pl. -e*, cornet. **Rei'terpferd**, -pfĕrt, *n. pl. -e*, trooper's horse. **Rei'terregiment**, -rĕgiment, *n. pl. -er*, regiment of horse. **Rei'terstatue**, -zhātu-e. *f.* equestrian statue. **Rei'terstiefel**, -ztīfel, *m. pl. -n*. cavalry-boot, jack-boot. **Reitgerte**, rīet'gĕrte, *f.*

riding-whip. **Reit'gurt**, -gṳrt, *f.* riding-girth. **Reit'handſchuh**, -hantshṳ, *m.* gauntlet, riding-glove. **Reit'fleid**, -kläed, *n. pl.* -er, riding-habit. **Reit'knecht**, -knĕcht. *m. pl.* -e, groom. **Reit'kunſt**, -kṳnzht, *f.* horsemanship. **Reit'peitſche**, -peītshẹ, *f.* riding-whip. **Reit'pferd**, -pfert, *n. pl.* -e, saddle-horse, riding-horse. **Reit'ſattel**, -sattel. *m. pl.* -ſättel, riding-saddle. **Reit'ſchule**, -shṳlẹ, *f.* riding-school. **Reit'ſtieſel**, -zhtīfel, *m. pl.* -n, jack-boot, riding-boot.

Reiz, rīěts, *m. pl.* -e, charm, attraction, incentive; irritation; **-bar**, -bär, *a.* irritable: **-barkeit**, -käět,*f.* irritability, sensibility, nervousness. **Reizen**, rīě'tsen, *vt.* to irritate, provoke; to allure, entice, charm. **Reizend**, rīĕ'tsent, *a.* charming. **Reiz'los**, -lōs, *a.* charmless. **Reiz'mittel**, -mittel, *n.* incentive, stimulant. **Reizung**, rīĕts'ung. *f.* irritation, provocation. **Reiz'voll**, -foll, full of charms.

Rekel, rē'kel, *m.* clumsy fellow.

Rekrut, rekrṳt', *m.* -en, *pl.* -en, recruit.

Relativ, rel'atīf, *a.* relative.

Relief, rēl'yef. *n. pl.*-s, relief (Arch.).

Religion, religiōn', *f.* religion; creed, religious denomination. **Religions'freiheit**, -frēīhkēt, *f.* religious liberty. **Religions'gebrauch**, -gebrouch. *m.* rite. **Religiös**, religiōs', *a.* religious. **Religiosität**, religiositāt', *f.* religiousness.

Reliquie, reli'qui-ẹ, *f.* relic.

Rellmaus, rell'mous, *f. pl.* -mäuse, rell-mouse.

Reminiscenz, reminīstsents', *f.* reminiscence.

Remiſe, remī'sẹ. *f.* coach-house.

Remittiren, remittī'ren, *vt.* to send back, return, remit.

Remonſtriren, remonzhtrī'ren, *vt.* to remonstra e.

Remonte, remōnt' *f.* remount.

Rendezvous, rän'devṳ, *n.* rendezvous.

Renegat, renegāt', *m.* -en, *pl.* -en, renegade.

Renette, renĕt'tẹ. *f.* rennet.

Rennbahn, renn'bän, *f.* race-course, race-ground.

Rennen, ren'nen (rannte, gerannt), *vi.* te run, race, course; zu Boden — tc run down; *s. n.* race, course.

Renner, ren'nēr, *m.* runner, race horse.

Rennthier, renn'tīr, *n. pl.* -e, reindeer; **-fleche**, -flĕchtẹ, *f.* reindeer moss.

Renommee, renommā', *n.* renown.

Renommiren, renommī'ren. *vi.* to bully, hector. **Renommiſt'**, *m.* -en, *pl.* -en, bully.

Renoviren, renofī'ren, *vt.* to renovate.

Rentamt, rent'amt, *n. pl.* -ämter, board of revenue; exchequer.

Rente, ren'tẹ. *f.* rent, revenue, income; jährliche —, annuity.

Rentiren, rentī'ren, *vi.* to yield rents, to pay.

Rentner, rent'nēr, *m.* capitalist.

Reorganiſiren, reorganisī'ren, *vt.* to reorganize.

Reparatur, reparatṳr', *f.* repair.

Repariren, reparī'ren, *vt.* to repair.

Repertorium, repērtō'riṳm, *n.* repertory.

Repetiren, repetī'ren, *vt.* to repeat.

Repetiruhr, repetīr'ṳr, *f.* repeater.

Repetitionskreis, repetitsiōns'krāěs, *m. pl.* -e, repeating-circle.

Repoſitorium, repositō'riṳm, *m.* repository.

Repräſentant, reprāsentant', *m.* -en, *pl.* -en, representative.

Repräſentiren, reprāsentī'ren, *vt.* to represent.

Represſalie, repressā'li-ẹ, *f.* reprisal.

Reproduktion, reprodṳtsiōn', *f.* reproduction. **Reproduktiv**, reprodṳktīf', *a.* reproductive.

Reptilie, reptī'li-ẹ, *f.* reptile.

Republik, repṳblīk'. *f.* republic. **Republikaner**, repṳblīka'nēr. *m.* republican. **Republikaniſch**, -ish, *a.* republican. **Republikanismus**, -ĭs'mṳs, *m.* republicanism.

Reputation, repṳtatsiōn', *f.* reputation, repute.

Requiem, rä'qui-em. *n.* requiem.

Requiriren, requirī'ren, *vt.* to require.

Requiſition, requisitsiōn', *f.* requisition.

Reſeda, resā'dä. *f.* mignonette.

Reſerve, resĕr'fẹ. *f.* reserve. **Reſerviren**, -fī'ren, *vt.* to reserve.

Reſident, resident', *m.* -en, *pl.* -en, resident.

Reſidenz, residents', *f.* residence.

Reſidiren, residī'ren, *vi.* to reside.

Ref   260   **Rich**

Refignation, resignatsiōn', *f.* resignation. **Refigniren,** resigni'ren, *vi.* to resign.
Refolution, resolutsiōn', *f.* resolution, resolve. **Refolviren,** resolfi'ren, *vi.* to resolve.
Refonanzboden, resonants'boden, *m.* sounding-board.
Refpekt, respĕkt, *m.* respect, regard. **Refpektiren,** -ti'ren, *vt.* to respect. **Refpektwidrig,** -vidrich, *a.* disrespectful.
Refsource, resurs', *f.* resources.
Reft, rĕst, *m. pl. -e,* rest, remainder.
Reftauration, rĕzhtōgratsiōn', *f.* restoration; eating-house.
Refultat, resultăt', *n.* result.
Retinit, retinit', *n.* retinite.
Retirade, retirä'de, *f.* retreat. **Retiriren,** retirī'ren, *vi.* to retreat, fall back.
Retorte, retor'te, *f.* retort.
Retouchiren, retushī'ren, *vt.* to retouch.
Retour, retur', *f. -fracht,* -fracht, *f.* return-freight, home-freight.
Retten, ret'ten, *vt.* to save, rescue, deliver, preserve.
Retter, ret'tĕr, *m.* saver, preserver, deliverer.
Rettig, rĕt'tich, *m. pl. -e,* radish.
Rettung, ret'tung, *f.* salvation, preservation, rescue; ohne —, past help. **Rettungsboye,** -bō-ye, *f.* life-buoy. **Rettungsboot,** -bōt, *n. pl. -e,* life-boat. **Rettungslos,** -lōs, *a.* irretrievable, past recovery.
Reue, rōü'e, *f.* repentance, remorse. **Reuelos,** rōü'elōs, *a.* remorseless. **Reuen,** rōü'en, *vt. i.* to rue, repent, regret; sich — lassen, to repine at. **Reuvoll,** rōü'efoll, *a.* remorseful. **Reuig,** rōü-ich, *a.* repentant.
Reuse, rōü'se, *f.* weir-basket, weel.
Reuten, rōü'ten, *vt.* to clear up, root out.
Reveille, revĕll'ye, *f.* reveille.
Reverenz, referĕnts', *f.* reverence, bow.
Revers, refers', *m. pl. -e,* reverse.
Revidiren, refidī'ren, *vt.* to revise.
Revier, refīr', *n. pl. -e,* district, quarter.
Revision, refisiōn'. *f.* revision, clean proof (sheet). **Revisor** refī'sor, *m. -s, pl. -en.* revisor.
Revociren, revotsī'ren, *vt.* to call back, revoke.

Revolution, refolutsiōn', *f.* revolution.
Revolutionär, refolutsionär', *a.* revolutionary; *m. pl. -e,* revolutionist. **Revolutioniren,** refolutsioni'ren, *vt.* to revolutionize.
Revolver, revol'vĕr, *m.* revolver.
Revue, revü', *f.* review.
Rez—, *f.* Rec—.
Rhabarber, rabar'ber, *m.* rhubarb.
Rhapsodie, rapsodī'. *f.* rhapsody.
Rhede, rä'de, *f.* road, roadstead. **Rheder,** rä'dĕr, *m.* ship-owner. **Rhederei,** -rēī', *f.* fitting out (of a vessel).
Rheinwein, raēn'vaēn, *m.* Rhenish *or* Rhinish wine, Hock.
Rhetorik, retō'rik, *f.* rhetoric. **Rhetorisch,** retō'rish, *a.* rhetorical.
Rheumatism, rĕfmat'ish, *a.* rheumatic. **Rheumatismus,** rĕfmatis'muss, *m.* rheumatism.
Rhinozeros, rinō'tsĕross, *n. pl. -rosse,* rhinoceros.
Rhomboeder, rombo-ā'dĕr, *m.* rhombohedron. **Rhomboid,** rombōīd', *n. pl. -e,* rhomboid. **Rhombus,** rom'buss, *m. pl. -ben,* rhombus.
Rhumb, rump. *m.* rumb-line.
Rhythmisch, rit'mish, *a.* rhythmical.
Rhythmus, rit'muss, *m.* rhythm.
Richtbaum, richt'bäum, *m. pl. -bäume,* pulley-beam. **Richtbeil,** -bĕīl, *n. pl. -e,* executioner's ax. **Richtblei,** -blēī, *n. pl. -e,* plumb-line, plummet. **Richten,** rich'ten, *vt.* to direct, straighten; level, point; adjust, arrange; to judge: to censure. **Richter,** rich'tĕr, *m.* judge. **Richteramt,** -amt, *n. pl. -ämter,* judicature, judgeship. **Richterlich,** -lich, *a.* judicial, judiciary. **Richterspruch,** -zhpruch, *m. pl. -sprüche,* sentence, decision. **Richterstuhl,** -zhtyl, *m. pl. -stühle,* tribunal, court of justice; (judge's) bench; judgment-seat. **Richtig,** rich'tich, *a.* right, correct, just, true, fair, *av. -ly:* — machen, to adjust, settle, regulate. **Richtigkeit,** -kaēt, *f.* justness, correctness: in — bringen, to settle ; seine — haben, to be correct. **Richtloth,** -lōt, *n. pl. -e,* plumb-line. **Richtmaß,** -mäs, *n. pl. -e,* gage, level, standard, measure, rule. **Richtplatz,** -plats, *m. pl. -plätze,* place of execution. **Richtscheit,** -shēīt, *n. pl. -e,* standard, rule. **Richtschnur,** -shnur, *f.* line, rule, standard, guide. **Richt'**

Ratt, *f. pl.* -ſtätte, place of execution. **Richtung**, -ung, *f.* direction. **Richtwage**, -wäge, *f.* level.
Riechbein, riech'beĭn, *n. pl.* -e, ethmoid bone.
Riechen, rie'chen (roch, gerochen), *vt.* to smell, scent; to perceive.
Riechfläſchchen, riech'fläshchen, *n.* smelling-bottle.
Riechnerv, riech'nerf, *m.* -s, *pl.* -en, olfactory nerve.
Ried, ried, *n.* reed. **Ried'gras**, -gräs, *n. pl.* -gräſer, reed-grass, burgrass.
Rief, rief, *Prt. v.* Rufen.
Riefe, rie'fe. *f.* channel, chamfer, groove. **Riefeln**, rie'feln, *vt.* to chamfer, flute; to rifle.
Riege, rie'ge, *f.* row. line.
Riegel, rie'gel, *m.* rail, bar, bolt; crossbeam. **Riegeln**, rie'geln, *vt.* to bolt. **Riegelwand**, -vant, *n. pl.* -wände, wood-partition, nogging.
Riem, rim, *m. pl.* -e. **Riemen**, rie'men, *m.* strap, strop, strip.
Riemer, rie'mer, *m.* girdler, belt-maker.
Rieſe, rie'ſe, *m.* -n, *pl.* -n, giant; slide.
Rieſeln, rie'ſeln, *vi.* to purl, ribble; thrill, shudder. **Rieſelregen**, -rëgen, *m.* drizzling rain, drizzle.
Rieſenhaft, rie'ſenhaft, **Rieſenmäßig**, -mässich, *a.* gigantic, colossal. **Rieſig**, rie'ſich, *a.* gigantic. **Rieſin**, rie'ſin, *f.* giantess.
Rieſter, riezh'ter, *m.* patch (of a shoe); wrist, instep; handle of a plough.
Riet, riet, *n. pl.* -e, reed.
Riff, riff, *m. pl.* -e, reef, ridge.
Riffel, riff'el, **Riffe**, *f.* ripple, flaxcomb; rebuke. **Riffeleiſen**, -eiſen, *n.* **Riffelfeile**, -feile, *f.* smoothing-file. **Riffeln**, riff'eln, *vt.* to ripple (flax); to rebuke.
Rigoriſt, rigorizht', *m.* -en, *pl.* -en, precisian, formalist.
Rimeſſe, rimes'ſe, *f.* remittance.
Rind, rint, *n. pl.* -er, heifer, young bull *or* ox, horned cattle, beef, neat.
Rinde, rin'de, *f.* bark, rind; crust.
Rinderbraten, rin'terbräten, *m.* roast-beef. **Rinderheerde**, -hërde, *f.* herd of (horned) cattle. **Rinderhirte**, -hirte, *m.* -n, *pl.* -n, neat-herd. **Rindern**, rin'dern, *vi.* to long for the bull; *a.* bovine, beef. **Rindfleiſch**, -fläsh, *n.* beef.

Rindig, rin'dich, *a.* crusty, crusted.
Rindsleder, rints'lëder, *n.* neat-leather ox-skin, cow-skin. **Rindsjunge** -tsunge, *f.* beef-tongue. **Rindvieh**, -fī, *n. pl.* -e, beef, neat-cattle, horned cattle; bullhead, lubber.
Ring, ring. *m. pl.* -e, ring, circle; halo; collar; circus. **Ringel**, ring'el, *m.* ringlet; collar. **Ringelblume**, -blume, *f.* marigold. **Ringeln**, ring'-eln, *vt.* to curl; to mark with circles; *vi.* to curl; **geringelt**, annular. **Ringeltaube**, -toŭbe, *f.* ring-dove.
Ringen, ring'-en (rang, gerungen). *vi.* to wrestle, grapple, tussle, struggle, strive; to wring. **Ringer**, ring'er, *m.* wrestler, athlete.
Ringfinger, ring'finger, *m.* ring-finger. **Ringförmig**, -förmich. *a.* annular, orbicular. **Ringkragen**, -krägen, *m.* gorget. **Ringmauer**, -moŭer, *f.* (close) wall.
Rings, rings, *av.* around, roundabout, all around; **-um**, ringsum', *av.* all around.
Rinne, rin'ne, *f.* gutter, drain, furrow.
Rinnen, rin'nen (rann, geronnen), *vi.* to run, trickle, rill, gush; leak.
Rinnſtein, rinn'zhtşen, *m.* gutter; sink.
Rippe, rip'pe, *f.* rib.
Rippeln, rip'peln, *vi.* to stir, to move.
Rippen, rip'pen, *vt.* to rib: **-ſtoß**, -zhtöss, *m. pl.* -ſtöße, thump, thrust in the ribs. **Rippenſtück**, -zhtück, *n. pl.* -e, rib of meat. **Rippenweh**, -vā, *n.* pain in the ribs.
Rifiko, rī'sikō, *n.* risk. **Risfiren**, riskī'ren, *vi.* to risk.
Riſpe, ris'pe, *f.* panicle.
Riß, riss, *m. pl.* **Riſſe**, *f.* rent, tear, cleft; draft, sketch. **Riſſig**, ris'sich, *a.* full of fissures.
Riſt, rist, *m. pl.* -e, wrist; instep.
Ritt, ritt, *m.* ride. **Ritter**, rit'ter, *m.* knight, chevalier, cavalier; **-lich**, -lich, *a.* knightly, chivalrous; **-keit**, *f.* chivalrousness, chivalry. **Ritterorden**, -orden, *m.* order of knighthood. **Ritterſchaft**, -shaft, *f.* knighthood, knights, equestrian order. **Ritterſpiel**, -zhpīl, *n.* tournament, tilt. **Ritterſporn**, -zhporn, *m.* larkspur (Bot.). **Ritterſtand**, -zhtant, *m.* knighthood. **Ritters**

Rit 262 **Rof**

thum, -tŭm, n. knighthood, chivalry. **Rit'terwefen**, -vēsen, n. chivalry.
Rittmeifter, ritt'māězhter, m. captain (of cavalry).
Rih, rits, m. pl. -e, crevice, fissure, crack, chink, cleft.
Rihen, rit'sen, vt. to scratch, notch.
Rihig, rits'ich, a. cracked, chinky.
Rival, rivāl', m. rival: **-ifiren**, -isī'ren, vt. to rival. **Rivalität**, -tāt', f. rivalry.
Robbe, rob'be, m. -n, pl. -n, auch f. seal. **Rob'benfang**, -fang, m. seal-hunting.
Roche, roch'e, m. roach, ray (fish); rook, castle.
Röcheln, röch'eln, vi. to rattle (in the throat); s. n. death-rattle.
Rock, rock, m. pl. Röcke, coat; gown, robe.
Rocken, rock'en, m. distaff.
Rocktafche, rock'tashe, f. coat-pocket.
Roden, rō'den, vt. to grub, to dig up.
Rogen, rō'gen, m. roe, spawn. **Rogener**, rō'gner, m. spawner.
Rogenftein, rō'genzhtsēn, m. oolite.
Roggen, rog'gen, m. rye; **-brod**, -brōt, n. rye-bread. **Rog'genmehl**, -mēl, n. rye-flour.
Roh, rō, a. raw, rough, rude; crude; gross. **Roh'eifen**, -ēïsen, n. pig-iron. **Roh'heit**, -hēit, f. roughness, rawness, crudeness.
Rohr, rōr, n. pl. -e, auch **Röhre**, reed; tube: pipe; flue; barrel; stick. **Rohr'brunnen**, -brunnen, m. fountain. **Rohr'dommel**, -dommel, f. bittern. **Röhre**, rö're, f. pipe, tube; reed. **Röhren**, rö'ren, vi. to gather reeds: a. (of) cane, reeds.
Röhren, rö'ren, to bellow, troat, roar.
Röhrenleitung, rö'renlāëtung, f. (water)conduit. **Röh'renmeifter**, -māězhter, m. overseer of water-works.
Rohrflöte, rōr'flöte, f. reed-pipe.
Rohricht, rōr'icht, n. pl. -e, cane-brake.
Rohrfperling, rōr'zhpērling, m. pl. -e, reed-bunting, reed-sparrow.
Rohrftuhl, rōr'zhtyl, m. pl. -ftühle, cane-bottomed chair.
Rohzucker, rō'tsycker, m. raw sugar, muscovado.
Rojen, rō'yen, vt. to row, to pull.
Rollbett, roll'bett, n. bedstead with rollers or casters.

Rolle, rol'le, f. roll, scroll, roller register, catalogue; roll, part.
Rollen, rol'len, vt. i. to roll: to mangle; to couple. **Rol'lentabak**, -taback, m. roll-tobacco, twist(tobacco) **Rollftuhl**, roll'zhtyl, m. pl. -ftühle, chair with casters. **Roll'wagen**, -vägen, m. cart; go-cart.
Roman, romān', m. romance, novel **Roman'dichter**, -dichtēr, m. novelist.
Roman'haft, -haft, **Romantifch**, -tish, a. romantic. **Romanje**, tsman'tse, f. romance.
Römifch, rö'mish, a. Roman: Romish; **Römifche Kirche**, the Roman Catholic Church.
Römling, röm'ling, m. pl. -e, papist.
Rondeau, ron'dō, n. pl. -s, rondeau.
Rofa, rō'sā, a. roseate, rose-colored.
Röfch, rösh, a. (baked) brown; brittle.
Rofe, rō'se, f. rose. **Rofenblatt**, rō'senblatt, n. pl. -blätter, rose-leaf.
Ro'fenbufch, -bush, m. pl. -büfche, rose-bush. **Ro'fenfarben**, -farben, a. roseate, rosy, rose-colored. **Ro'fenhonig**, -hōnich, m. rose-honey. **Ro'fenfranz**, -krants, m. pl. -fränze, wreath of roses, rosary. **Ro'fenöl**, -öl, n. rose-oil. **Ro'fenpappel**, -pappel, rose-mallow. **Ro'fenroth**, -rōt, a. rosy, rose-colored. **Ro'fenftock**, -zhtock, m. pl. -ftöcke, **Ro'fenftrauch**, -zhtröuch, m. pl. -fträucher, rose-bush.
Rofette, rosēt'te, f. rosette. **Ro'fettenfenfter**, -fenzhtēr, n. rose-window, catharine-wheel. **Rofig**, rō'sich, a. rosy, rosente.
Rofine, rosī'ne, f. currant.
Rosmarin, rosmarīn', n. rosemary.
Rof, ross, n. pl. -e, horse, steed. **Rof'arzt**, ross'artst, m. farrier, veterinary surgeon. **Rof'bremfe**, -bremse, f. horse-fly, gad-fly. **Rof'haar**, -hār, n. horse-hair. **Rof'händler**, -hentler, m. **Rof'famm**, -kamm, m. pl. -fämme, horse-trader, jockey. **Rof'kaftanie**, -kazhtā'ni-e, f. horse-chestnut. **Rof'markt**, -markt, m. pl. -märkte, horse-market. **Rof'fchwanz**, -shvants, m. pl. -fchwänze, **Rof'fchweif**, -shvāēf, m. pl. -e, horse-tail.
Roft, rozht, m. rust, blight, mildew.
Roft, rozht, m. pl. Röfte, grate, grid iron. **Rof'braten**, -brāten, m. roast.
Röfte, rözh'te, f. roasting; steeping.

Roſten, rozh'ten, *vt.* to rust, decay.
Röſten, rözh'ten, *vt.* to broil; toast; roast. **Röſthaus**, rözht'hoŭs, *n. pl.* -häuſer, **Röſt'hütte**, -hütte, *f.* roasting-furnace (for ores).
Roſtig, rozht'ĭḣ, *a.* rusty.
Roth, röt, *a.* red; *s. n.* red color; — machen, to redden; — werden, to blush, redden; rothe Ruhr, dysentery. **Roth'bart**, -bart, *m. pl.* -bärte, red-beard. **Roth'braun**, -brăŭn, *a.* reddish-brown, bay. **Roth'buche**, -buḣe, *f.* red beech. **Röthe**, rö'te, *f.* redness, red. **Rötheiſenſtein**, rötěi'zenzhtšen, *m. pl.* -e, red oxide of iron. **Röthel**, rö'tel, *m.* red chalk, red crayon. **Röthen**, rö'ten, *vt. i.* to redden. **Rothfleckig**, röt'fleckĭḣ, *a.* red-spotted. **Roth'finf**, -fink. *m.* -en, *pl.* -en, bullfinch. **Rothfuchs**, -fŭḣs, *m. pl.* -füchſe, red fox; bay horse. **Roth'gelb**, -gělp, *a.* reddish yellow, orange. **Roth'gerber**, -gěrber, *m.* tanner. **Roth'gießer**, -gĭsěr, *m.* brazier. **Roth'haarig**, -hǟrĭḣ, *a.* red-haired. **Roth'käppchen**, -kěppḣen, *n.* red-cap. **Roth'kehlchen**, -kělḣen, *n.* robin red-breast. **Roth'lauf**, -laŭf, *m.* erysipelas. **Röthlich**, röt'lĭḣ, *a.* reddish.
Rothwelſch, röt'vělsh, cant, gibberish, slang.
Rothwangig, röt'vangĭḣ, *a.* red-cheeked.
Rothwild, röt'vĭlt, *n.* fallow deer.
Rothwildbrät, röt'vĭltbrět, *n.* venison.
Rotte, rot'te, *f.* band, pack, gang; troop; file.
Rottenmeiſter, rot'tenmǟzhter, *m.* chief, headman; sergeant.
Roz, rots, *m.* snot, snivel, mucus (from the nose); glanders. **Rozen**, rot'sen, *vi.* to snot, snivel; to have the glanders.
Roulade, rŭlä'de, *f.* roulade (Mus.).
Rouleau, rŭl'lō, *s.* (window) blind.
Routine, rŭtīn', *f.* routine.
Rübe, rü'be, *f.* turnip; rothe —, beet; gelbe —, carrot; weiße —, turnip.
Rübenzucker, rü'bentsŭckěr, *m.* beet-sugar.
Rubel, rŭ'bel, *m.* ruble (a coin).
Rubin, rŭbīn', *m.* ruby.
Rubrik, rŭbrīk', *f.* section, division, rubric.
Rübſen, rüp'sen, *n.* rape. **Rübſöl**, rŭb'öl, *n.* rape-oil.

Ruchbar, rŭḣ'bǟr, **Ruḣt'bar**, *a.* notorious; -keit, -kǟt, *f.* notoriousness.
Ruchlos, -lōs, *a.* wicked, profligate, nefarious. **Ruch'loſigkeit**, -lŏḣkǟt, *f.* profligacy, wickedness.
Ruck, rŭck, *m. pl.* -e, push, shock, jerk.
Rückblick, rŭck'blĭck, *m.* retrospect, review.
Rückbürge, rŭck'bürge, *m.* counter-security.
Rücken, rŭck'en, *vi.* to move, advance, proceed; *vt.* to push, move. **Rucken**, rŭck'en, *vt.* to jerk, snatch.
Rücken, rŭck'en, *m.* back; ridge; rear. **Rück'enmark**, -mark, *n.* spinal marrow. **Rück'enſchmerz**, -shměrts, *m. pl.* -en. **Rück'enweh**, -vā, *n.* pain in the back, lumbago. **Rückenſtück**, -zhtück, *n. pl.* -e, sirloin, chine.
Rückerinnern, rŭck'ěrĭnněrn, *vt. i.* to remind, recollect. **Rück'erinnerung**, -ŭng, *f.* recollection.
Rückfahrt, rŭck'fart, *f.* return.
Rückfall, rŭck'fall, *m. pl.* -fälle, relapse; reversion. **Rück'fällig**, -fellĭḣ, *a.* revertible, relapsing.
Rückfracht, rŭck'fracht, *f.* return-freight, home-freight.
Rückgabe, rŭck'gäbe, *f.* return.
Rückgängig, rŭck'gengĭḣ, *a.* retrogressive, retrograde; — machen, to undo, to break off, to rue (a bargain).
Rückgrat, rŭck'grät, *m. pl.* -e, spine.
Rückhalt, rŭck'halt, *m. pl.* -e, reserve; support, remnant.
Rückkauf, rŭck'kaŭf, *m. pl.* -läufe, redemption.
Rückkehr, rŭck'kǟr, *f.* return.
Rückkunft, rŭck'kŭnft, *f.* return.
Rückladung, rŭck'lädŭng, *f.* return-freight.
Rückläufig, rŭck'laŭfĭḣ, *a.* retrograde.
Rücklings, rŭck'lĭngs, *av.* backward; from behind.
Rückmarſch, rŭck'marsh, *m. pl.* -märſche, counter-march, march back.
Rücknahme, rŭck'näme, *f.* taking back.
Rückprall, rŭck'prall, *m.* rebound.
Rückreiſe, rŭck'rǟse, *f.* return, home journey.
Rückruf, rŭck'rŭf, *m.* recall.
Rückſchlag, rŭck'shläg, *m. pl.* -ſchläge, back-stroke; falling-off.

Rüdſchritt, rück'shritt, m. pl. -e, retrocession; relapse.
Rüdſeite, rück'sēite, f. back-side, back.
Rüdſicht, rück'sicht, f. respect, regard, consideration: in — auf, with respect to: — nehmen, to have regard for. **Rüdſichtlich**, -lich, av. in reference to, in respect to, considering. **Rüdſichtlos**, -lös, a. inconsiderate, injudicious; ⸱igfeit, -ichkäet, f. inconsiderateness.
Rüdſprache, rück'zhpráche, f. consultation.
Rüdſtand, rück'zhtant, m. arrears, balance.
Rüdſtändig, rück'zhtendich, a. in arrears, behindhand.
Rüdſtrahlen, rück'zhträlen, vt. to reflect.
Rüdtritt, rück'tritt, m. pl. -e, withdrawal.
Rüdwärts, rück'vērts, av. backward, back.
Rüdweg, rück'vēg, m. pl. -e, return, way back.
Rudweiſe, ruck'vēisə, av. by fits and starts, by jerks.
Rüdwirkend, rück'virkent, a. reacting. **Rüd'wirkung**, -ung, f. reaction.
Rüdzahlen, rück'tsälen, vt. to repay. **Rüd'zahlung**, -tsälung, f. repayment.
Rüdzug, rück'tsyg, m. retreat, falling back.
Rüde, rü'de, m. (male) dog, fox, or wolf.
Rudel, ry'del, n. herd, troop.
Ruder, ry'dēr, n. oar, rudder, helm; direction; scoop, ladle. **Ru'derbank**, -bank, m. pl. -bänke, rowing bench.
Ruderer, ry'dērer, m. rower, oarsman.
Rudergat, ry'dērgat, n. pl. -e, rowlock.
Rudern, ry'dērn, vi. to row.
Ruderſchiff, ry'dērshiff, n. pl. -e, galley.
Ruderſchlag, ry'dērshläg, m. pl. -ſchläge, stroke of the oar.
Ruderſtange, ry'dērzhtang-ə, f. oar.
Ruderſalje, ry'dērtalyə, f. steering-tackle.
Ruf, ryf, m. pl. -e, call, cry; vocation; rumor; repute.
Rufen, ry'fen (rief, gerufen), vt. to call, cry; — laſſen, to send for.
Rüffeln, rüf'teln, vt. to ripple (flax); to rebuke.

Rüge, rüh'gə, f. rebuke, censure; accusation. **Rügen**, rü'gen, vt. to rebuke, censure, accuse; punish.
Ruhe, ry'ə, f. rest, tranquillity, repose, quiet, peace; sleep; death; ſich zur — begeben, to go to rest, retire. **Ruh'ebank**, -bank, f. pl. -bänke, seat for resting. **Ruh'ebett**, -bett, n. -es, pl. -en, couch. **Ruh'elos**, -lös, a. restless; ⸱igfeit, -ichkäet, f. restlessness.
Ruhen, ry'en, vt. to rest, repose; to sleep. **Ruh'eplat**, -plats, m. pl. -plätze, resting-place. **Ruh'epunkt**, -pyunkt, m. pl. -e, point of rest; pause. **Ruh'eſtätte**, -zhtettə, f. place of rest. **Ruh'eſtörer**, -zhtörēr, m. disturber. **Ruh'eſtunde**, -zhtyndə, f. hour of rest.
Ruhig, ry'ich, a. tranquil, quiet, peaceable, calm.
Ruhm, rym, m. glory, fame, renown. **Ruhm'begierde**, -begīrdə, f **Ruhm'begier**, f. ambition, love of fame, thirst of glory. **Ruhm'begierig**, a. ambitious.
Rühmen, rü'men, vt. to praise, extol, vaunt; to celebrate; ſich —, to glory, boast.
Ruhmbegierig, rym'begīrich, a. ambitious.
Ruhmlich, rüm'lich, a. glorious, famous; laudable, creditable; av. -ly, with glory; ⸱feit, -käet, f. praiseworthiness, glory.
Ruhmlos, rym'lös, a. inglorious.
Ruhmredig, rym'rädich, a. vain-glorious; ⸱feit, -käet, f. vain-glory, boasting.
Ruhmſucht, rym'sycht, f. thirst of glory, ambition. **Ruhm'ſüchtig**, -süchtich, a. ambitious.
Ruhmwürdig, rym'vürdich, a. worthy of glory, glorious; ⸱feit, -käet, f. gloriousness.
Ruhr, rur, f. dysentery.
Rühren, rü'ren, vt. to stir, move; to spring from; — an, to touch.
Rührend, rü'rent, a. touching, moving.
Rührig, rü'rich, a. active, alert, industrious, nimble; ⸱feit, -käet, f. nimbleness, activity.
Rührlöffel, rür'löffel, m. ladle.
Rührung, rür'yng, f. emotion.
Ruin, ryīn', m. ruin, decay. **Ruine**, ry-in'ə, f. ruins.

Ruiniren, ruinī'ren, *vt.* to ruin, destroy.
Rülps, rülps, *m.* belch. **Rülpsen**, rülp'sen, *vi.* to belch.
Rum, rum, *m.* rum.
Rummel, rum'mel, *m.* lumber, trumpery; bustle; **den — verstehen**, to be a sly hand; **im —**, in the bulk.
Rumor, rumōr', *m.* noise, tumult.
Rumoren, rumō'ren, *vi.* to raise a row.
Rumpeln, rum'peln, *vi.* to rumble.
Rumpf, rumpf, *m. pl.* **Rümpfe**, rump, trunk, body; hopper (in a mill).
Rümpfen, rümp'fen, *vt.* to curl up, turn up.
Rund, runt, *a.* round, circular, spherical. **Runde**, run'de, *f.* round, circle. **Rünbe**, rün'de, *f.* roundness, bend. **Runden**, run'den, *vi.* to become round, circular, spherical. **Rünben**, rün'den, *vt.* to round. **Runderhaben**, runderhä'ben, *a.* convex. **Rundlich**, runt'lich, *a.* roundish; plump; globulous. **Rundum**, rundum', *av.* all around. **Rund'ung**, -ung, *f.* roundness.
Runge, rung-e, *f.* track, trigger, skid.
Runkelrübe, run'kelrübe, *f.* beet.
Runkelrübenzucker, run'kelrübenzucker, *m.* beet-root sugar.
Runzel, run'tsel, *f.* wrinkle. **Run'zelig**, -ich, *a.* wrinkled. **Runzeln**, run'zeln, *vt.* to wrinkle, shrivel; to shrink; to knit.
Rupfen, rup'fen, *vt.* to pluck, pull, pick. **Rupfwolle**, rupf'volle, *f.* lock of fine wool.
Rupie, ru'pi-e, *f.* rupee.
Ruppig, rup'pich, *a.* poor, ragged, shabby, mean.
Ruscheln, rush'eln, *vi.* to bustle, rush.
Rüschlich, rush'lich, *a.* rash, overhasty.
Ruß, rus, *m.* soot. **Rußbutte**, -butte, *f.* soot-box.
Rüssel, rüs'sel, *m.* trunk; proboscis; snout.
Rußig, rus'sich, *a.* sooty.
Rust, rust, *f.* chain-wale.
Rüstbaum, rüst'baum, *m.* scaffolding-pole.
Rüsten, rüs'ten, *vt.* to prepare, make ready; to set up a scaffolding.
Rüster, rüs'ter, *f.* elm. **Rüstern**, rüs'tern, *a.* made of elm.
Rüsthaus, rüst'hous, *n. pl.* **-häuser**, arsenal.

Rüstig, rüs'tich, *a.* alert, active, strong felt, -kät, *f.* vigorousness.
Rüstkammer, rüst'kammer, *f.* armory
Rüstung, rüs'tung, *f.* preparation, fitting out, armament, equipment; armor.
Rüstzeug, rüst'tseüg, *n. pl. -e*, instrument.
Ruthe, ru'te, *f.* rod, wand, switch; shank (of an anchor); yard (Mar.); male genitals.
Ruthenium, rutä'nium, *n.* ruthenium.
Rutsche, rut'she, *f.* slide (forward).
Rutschen, rut'shen, *vi.* to glide, slide.
Rütteln, rüt'teln, *vt.* to shake, to wag.

Sa, sä. *ħ.* eh! ho! Merry!
Saal, säl, *m. pl.* **Säle**, saloon, hall, drawing-room.
Saat, sät, *f.* sowing, seed; standing corn. **Saatbohne**, -bōne, *f.* bean for sowing. **Saatfeld**, -felt, *n.* wheat-field, corn-field. **Saatforn**, -korn, *n. pl. -körner*, seed-grain, seed-corn. **Saatkrähe**, -krä-e, *f.* rook.
Sabbath, sab'bat, *m. pl. -e*, Sabbath.
Säbel, sä'bel, *m.* sabre, sword. **Sä'belbein**, -bēn, *n. pl. -e*, bow-leg. **Säbelherrschaft**, -herrshaft, *f.* soldier-rule. **Säbelhieb**, -hīb, *m. pl. -e*, sword-cut. **Säbelklinge**, -klinge, *f.* sabre-blade. **Säbeln**, sä'beln, *vt.* to sabre. **Säbelscheide**, -shäede, *f.* sabre-sheath.
Sachdienlich, sach'dīnlich, *a.* relevant, expedient.
Sache, sach'e, *f.* matter, thing, affair, cause, concern.
Sachführer, sach'fürer, *m.* attorney, advocate.
Sachkenner, sach'kenner, *m.* connoisseur, expert.
Sachkenntniß, sach'kenntniss, *f.* knowledge, experience.
Sachkundig, sach'kundich, *a.* expert, competent.
Sachlage, sach'lāge, *f.* state of affairs.
Sächlich, sech'lich, *a.* neuter.
Sachregister, sach'regizhter, *n.* index, register of contents.
Sacht, sacht, **Sachte**, sach'te, *a. u. av.* soft, gentle, gradual, easy, *av. -ly*.
Sachverhalt, sach'ferhalt, *m.* **Sachverhältniß**, -heltniss, *a.* state of affairs.

Sachverständig, sach'fĕrzhtĕndich, a. competent, expert.
Sachverzeichniß, sach'fĕrtsīĕchnis, n. index; invoice.
Sachwalter, sach'valtĕr, m. attorney, advocate.
Sachwaltung, sach'valtung, f. management.
Sack, sack, m. pl. **Säcke**, sack, bag, pocket, poke; **mit Sack und Pack**, with bag and baggage, **Sacken**, sack'en, vt. to bag, sack. **Sackgasse**, -gasse, f. blind-valley. **Sackleinwand**, -līĕnvant, f. sackcloth, bagging. **Sackpfeife**, -pfīfe, f. bag-pipe. **Sackpistole**, -pizhtole, f. pocket-pistol. **Sackträger**, -trāger, m. sack-bearer. **Sacktuch**, -tūch, n. pl. -tücher, pocket-handkerchief; bagging. **Sackuhr**, -ūr, f. watch. **Sackzwillich**, -tsvillich, m. pl. -e, sack-drilling. **Sackzwirn**, -tsvīrn, m. pl. -e, sack-twine, sack-thread.
Sämann, sā'emann, m. pl. -männer, sower.
Särmaschine, sā'e-mashīne, f. drill, sowing-machine.
Säen, sā'en, vt. to sow; strew. **Säezeit**, -tsīt, f. seed-time.
Saffian, saffiān', m. pl. -e, morocco-leather.
Safran, safrān, m. saffron; **-gelb**, -gĕlp, a. saffron, saffrony.
Saft, saft, m. pl. **Säfte**, sap, juice. **Saftgrün**, saft'grün, a. sap-green. **Saftig**, saftich, a. juicy; succulent, sappy. **Saftlos**, saft'lōs, a. sapless, juiceless; **-igkeit**, -ichkĕit, f. saplessness. **Saftreich**, -rīch, a. rich in juice; juicy.
Sage, sā'ge, f. say, legend, tradition.
Säge, sā'ge, f. saw. **Sägeblatt**, -blat, n. pl. -blätter, saw-blade. **Sägeblock**, -block, m. pl. -blöcke, saw-block. **Sägebock**, -bock, m. pl. -böcke, sawing-jack. **Sägefisch**, -fish, m. pl. -e, saw-fish. **Sägemühle**, -mülle, f. saw-mill. **Sägen**, sā'gen, vt. to saw.
Sagen, sā'gen, vt. to say, to tell, to speak; **Dank —**, to give thanks.
Säger, sā'gĕr, m. sawyer.
Sageschlitten, sā'geshlitten, m. drag, carriage, auch **Sägewagen**, -vāgen. **Sägespäne**, -zhpäne s. pl. sawdust.

Sago, sā'go, m. sago. **Sagopalme**, -palme, f. sago-tree.
Sahling, sā'ling, f. cross-tree, trestle-tree (Mar.).
Sahlband, sāl'bant, n. pl. -bänder. **Sahlleiste**, -līĕzhte, f. selvage.
Sahne, sā'ne, f. cream.
Saite, sīĕ'te, f. cord, string, cat-gut. **Saitendraht**, -drāt, m. wire-string **Saiteninstrument**, -inzhtrument, n. stringed instrument. **Saitenspiel**, -zhpīl, n. playing on a stringed instrument.
Sakrament, sakrament', n. pl. -e, sacrament.
Sakristan, sakrizhtān', m. pl. -e, sacristan, sexton. **Sakristei**, sakrizhtĕī', f. vestry, sacristy.
Säkularisiren, sekūlarisī'ren, vt. to secularize.
Salär, salār', n. pl. -e, salary.
Salamander, salaman'dĕr, m. salamander.
Salat, salāt', m. pl. -e, salad: lettuce. **Salathaupt**, -hāŭpt, n. pl. -häupter, **Salatkopf**, -kopf, m. pl. -köpfe, head of lettuce. **Salatschüssel**, -shüssel, f. salad-dish.
Salbader, salbā'dĕr, m. gossip. **Salbadern**, salbā'dĕrn, vi. to chat, prattle, gossip.
Salbe, sal'be, f. salve, ointment.
Salben, sal'ben, vt. to salve, anoint. **Salbung**, sal'bung, f. anointing; unction.
Saldo, sal'dō, m. pl. **Saldi**, balance.
Saline, salī'ne, f. salt-works, saline.
Salm, salm, m. pl. -e, salmon.
Salmiak, salmiack', m. sal-ammoniac. **Salmiakgeist**, -gēĕzht, m. spirits of sal-ammoniac.
Salon, salōn', m. pl. -s, saloon, drawing-room.
Salpeter, salpā'tĕr, m. saltpetre, nitre. **Salpeterhütte**, -hütte, f. saltpetre-house. **Salpeterig**, -ich, a. nitrous, saltpetrous. **Salpetersalzsäure**, -saltssēŭre, f. nitro-muriatic acid. **Salpetersaures Salz**, nitrate. **Salpetersäure**, -sēŭre, f. nitric acid.
Salutiren, salūtī'ren, vt. to salute.
Salve, sal'fe, f. volley, salute.
Salz, salts, n. pl. -e, salt: **-äther**, -ātĕr, m. muriatic ether **Salzbergwerk**, -bĕrkvĕrk, n. pl. -e, salt-mine. **Salzbrühe**, -brüe, f. brine. **Salzbüchse**, -büchse, f. salt-cellar.

Sal   267   **Saf**

Salzen, sal'tsen, *vt.* to salt; to pickle, cure; gesalzenes Rindfleisch, salt beef.
Salzfaß, salts'fass, *n. pl.* -fässer, salt-cellar. **Salz'geist,** -gāezht, *m.* spirits of salt. **Salz'grube,** -grube, *f.* salt-pit, salt-mine. **Salz'gurke,** -gurke, *f.* pickled cucumber. **Salzig,** salts'ich, *a.* salt, salty, briny. **Salz'pfanne,** -pfanne, *f.* salt-pan. **Salz'quelle,** -quelle, *f.* salt-spring. **Salz'säure,** -sēūre, *f.* muriatic acid. **Salz'saures Salz,** muriate. **Salz'siederei,** -sīdĕrēī', *f.* salt-works. **Salz'sohle,** -sōle, *f.* brine. **Salz'werk,** -vèrk, *n. pl.* -e, salt-works.
Same, sä'me, -ns, *pl.* -n, **Sa'men,** -s, seed; sperm, spawn. **Sa'menbehälter,** -behelter, *m.* seminal vessel. **Sa'menfluß,** -fiuss, *m. pl.* -flüsse, gonorrhœa.
Samenhändler, sā'menhentlēr, *m.* dealer in seeds. **Sa'menkorn,** -korn, *n. pl.* -körner, seed-corn, seed-grain. **Sa'menstaub,** -zhtäub, *m.* pollen. **Sa'menstengel,** -zhteng-ĕl, *m.* seed-stalk.
Sämerei, semērēī', *f.* seeds.
Sämischgerber, sä'mishgärbĕr, *m.* chamois-dresser. **Sä'mischleder,** -lĕdĕr, *n.* chamois.
Sammeln, sam'meln, *vt.* to gather, collect, accumulate. **Sam'melplatz,** -plats. *m. pl.* -plätze, gathering-place, rendezvous. **Sam'melwort,** -vort, *n. pl.* -wörter, collective noun.
Sammet, sam'met, *m.* velvet; gerissener —, shorn velvet. **Sam'metband,** -bant, *n. pl.* -bänder, velvet-ribbon. **Sam'metpappel,** -pappel, *f.* marsh-mallow.
Sammler, samm'lēr, *m.* collector.
Sammlung, samm'lung, *f.* collection, gathering.
Sammt, sammt, *av.* together with; — und sonders, altogether, each and all.
Sammten, samm'ten. *a.* velvet.
Sämmtlich, semmt'lich, *a.* altogether, all. in a body. complete.
Samstag, sam'stäg, *m.* Saturday.
Sanct, sankt, *a.* saint.
Sand, sant, *m.* sand.
Sandale, sandä'le, *f.* sandal.
Sandarach, san'darach, *m.* sandarac.
Sandbank, saut'bank, *f. pl.* -bänke, sand-bank.

Sandboden, sant'bōden, *m.* sandy soil.
Sandel, san'del, *m.* sandal-wood.
Sanden, san'den, *vt.* to strew with sand. **Sand'fläche,** -fleche, *f.* sandy plain. **Sandig,** san'dich, *a.* sandy. **Sand'korn,** -korn, *n. pl.* -körner, grain of sand. **Sand'meer,** -mär, *n. pl.* -e, sea of sand. **Sand'mergel,** -mergel, *m.* sandy marl. **Sand'sack,** -sack, *m. pl.* -säcke, sand-bag. **Sand'schiefer,** -shīfēr, *m.* schistous, sand-stone. **Sand'stein,** -zhtšen. *m. pl.* -e, sand-stone; **bruch,** -bruch, *m. pl.* -brüche, sand-stone quarry.
Sanduhr, sant'ur, *f.* hour-glass.
Sanft, sanft, *a.* soft, mild, gentle, tender.
Sänfte, senf'te, *f.* sedan-chair, litter. **Sänftenträger,** -träger, *m.* chair-man. **Sanft'heit,** -hēēt, *f.* softness, mildness, gentleness. **Sänftigen,** senf'tichen, *vt.* to soften, mitigate. **Sänf'tigung,** -ung, *f.* softening, mitigation.
Sang, sang (*Prt. v.* Singen), *m. pl.* Sänge, song. **Sänger,** seng'er, *m.* singer, songster; bard, poet.
Sängerin, seng'erin, *f.* songstress, (opera) singer.
Sanguinisch, sanguīn'ish, *a.* sanguine.
Sank, sänk, *Prt. v.* Sinken.
Saponin, sapoūīn'. *n.* saponine.
Sappanholz, sappän'holts, *n.* sapan-wood.
Sappe, sap'pe, *f.* sap.
Sapperment, sappèrment', *Ij.* zounds!
Sappeur, sappöhr', *m.* sapper, pioneer.
Sappiren, sappī'ren, *vt.* to sap.
Sapphir, saf'fīr, *m.* sapphire.
Sardelle, sardel'le, *f.* sardine, anchovy.
Sarder, sar'dĕr, *m.* sardine, carnelian.
Sardonisch, sardō'nish, *a.* sardonic, malicious.
Sardonyx, sardō'nix. *m.* sardonyx.
Sarg, sark, *m. pl.* Särge, coffin; **tuch,** -tuch, *n. pl.* -tücher, pall.
Sarkasmus, sarkäs'mus, *m. pl.* -men, sarcasm.
Sarkastisch, sarkazh'tish, *a.* sarcastic, *av.* -ally.
Sarkophag, sarkofäg', *m. pl.* -e, sarcophagus.
Sarrass, sar'rass, *m. pl.* -e sabre.
Sarsche, sar'she, *f.* serge.
Sassafras, sas'safras, *n.* sassafras.

Saſſe, sas'ṣe, *m.* freeholder, inhabitant.
Satan, sa'tän, *m. pl. -e*, Satan. **Satanisch**, -ish, *a.* satanic, *av.* -ally; diabolical, *av.* -ly.
Satellit, satĕllīt', *m. -en, pl. -en*, satellite.
Satin, sa'tän, *m. pl. -s*, satin.
Satire, satī'rẹ, *f.* satire. **Satiriker**, satī'rikēr, *m.* satirist. **Satirisch**, -ish, *a.* satirical. **Satirisiren**, -ēī'ren, *vt.* to satirize.
Satisfaktion, satisfaktsiōn', *f.* satisfaction.
Satrap, satrap', *m. -en, pl. -en*, satrap.
Satt, satt, *a.* sated, filled, satiated, satisfied; ſich — eſſen, to eat one's full.
Sattel, sat'tel, *m.* saddle; ridge. **Sattelbaum**, sat'telbäum, *m. pl. -bäume*, saddle-tree. **Satteldecke**, -deckẹ, *f.* saddle-cloth, caparison. **Sattelfeſt**, -fezht, *a.* firm in the saddle. **Sattelgurt**, -gurt, *m. pl. -e*, girth, surcingle. **Sattelkiſſen**, -kissen, *n.* saddle-pad. **Sattelknopf**, -knopf, *m. pl. -knöpfe*, pommel. **Satteln**, sat'teln, *vt.* to saddle. **Sattelpferd**, -pfērt, *n. pl. -e*, saddle-horse. **Sattel-taſche**, -tashẹ, *f.* saddle-bags. **Sattelzeug**, -tsöüg, *n.* saddle and harness.
Sattheit, satt'häet, *f.* satiety.
Sättigen, set'tiḥen, *vt.* to fill, satisfy; saturate, impregnate.
Sättigung, set'tiḥung, *f.* satiety, satiation; satnration. **Sättigungspunkt**, -pṇnkt, *m. pl. -e*, point of saturation.
Sattler, sat'tlēr, *m.* saddler; ſin, *f.* saddler's wife. **Sattlerahle**, -ālẹ, *f.* saddler's awl. **Sattlerei**, -ēī', *f.* saddler's trade; saddler's shop.
Sattſam, satt'sam, *a.* sufficient, *av.* -ly, enough. **Sattſamkeit**, -käet, *f.* sufficiency.
Satyre, *f.* Satire.
Satz, sats, *m. pl.* **Sätzẹ**, sentence, clause; proposition; set; sediment; stake (in gambling); position; pull (Print.).
Satzung, sats'ụng, *f.* statute, law, ordinance.
Sau, sōụ, *f. pl.* **Säụe**. sow, hog, pig.
Sauber, sōụ'ber, *a.* clean neat, pretty; ſkeit, -käet, *f.* clean uess, neatness. **Säuberlich**, sēü'berliḥ, *a.* *u. a.* cleanly, neatly; gently. **Säubern**, sēü'bērn, *vt.* to cleanse, clean, clear, purify. **Säụberung**, -ụng, *f.* cleansing, clearing.
Saubohne, sōụ'bōnẹ, *f.* field-bean, broad-bean.
Saudiſtel, sōụ'dizhtel, *f.* sow-thistle.
Sauer, sōụ'ēr, *a.* sour, acid, tart, harsh. **Sauerampfer**, -ampfēr, *m.* sorrel. **Sauerbrunnen**, -brụnnen, *m.* chalybeate spring.
Sauerei, sōụēr̄ēī', *f.* hoggishness, obscenity.
Sauerklee, sōụērklā', *m.* wood-sorrel; ſſalz, -salta, *n.* binoxalate of potash. **Sauerkleeſäure**, -sēürẹ, *f.* oxalic acid.
Sauerkraut, sōụ'erkrọụt, *n.* sourkrout.
Säuerlich, sēü'ōrliḥ, *a.* sourish, acidulous, acescent.
Sauern, sōụ'ērn, *vi.* to turn sour, to sour.
Säuern, sēü'ērn, *vt.* to sour, make sour.
Sauerſtoff, sōụ'ērzhtoff, *m.* oxygen; ſgas, -gās, *n.* oxygen gas.
Sauerſüß, sōụ'ersühs, *a.* sour-sweet.
Sauerteig, sōụ'ērtāeg, *m.* leaven.
Sauertöpfiſch, sōụ'ērtöpfish, *a.* peevish, crabbed.
Säuerung, sēü'ērụng, *f.* leavening, acidification.
Sauerwaſſer, sōụ'ērvasser, *n.* chalybeate water.
Saufaus, sōụf'ōus, *m. pl. -e.* **Säuf*-brụder**, -brụdēr, *m. pl. -brüder*, tippler, sot, drunkard.
Saufen, sōụ'fen (ſoff, geſoffen), *vi.* to drink; to tipple, to get drunk.
Säufer, sēü'fēr, *m.* drinker, drunkard. **Säuferei**, sōụfērēī', *f.* immoderate drinking.
Säuferwahnſinn, sēü'fērvänsinn, *m.* delirium tremens.
Saufgelage, sōụf'gelāgẹ, *n.* drinking-bout, revel.
Saugader, sōụg'āder, *f.* absorbent, duct.
Säugamme, sōüg'ammẹ, *f.* wet-nurse.
Saugeſiſch, sōụg'gefish, *m. pl. -e*, sucking-fish, remora.
Saugen, sōụ'gen (ſog, geſogen), *vi.* to suck.
Säugen, sēüi'gen, *vt.* to suckle, give suck.

Säu 269 **Sch**

Säugethier, säü'getīr, *n. pl. -e*, mammal.
Säugling, säüg'ling, *m. pl. -e*, suckling.
Saugpumpe, sōug'pumpe, *f.* sucking-pump.
Saugröhre, sōug'rörhe, *f.* suction-tube, suction-pipe.
Saugrüsel, sōug'rühsel, *m.* proboscis, trunk.
Sauhirt, sōu'hirt, *m. -en, pl. -en*, swine-herd.
Sauhund, sōu'hunt, *m.* boar-hound; nasty dog.
Säuisch, -öü'ish, *a.* hoggish, sluttish, beastly.
Säule, sēü'le. *n.* pillar, column.
Sauleder, sōu'lēdēr, *n* hog-leather.
Säulengang, sēü'lengang, *m. pl. -gänge*, colonnade, arcade, peristyle, gallery. **Säulenhaupt**, -häupt, *n. pl. -häupter*. **Säulenknauf**, -knäuf, *m. pl. -knäufe*, capital. **Säulenordnung**, -ordnung, *f.* order. **Säulenplatte**, -platte, *f.* plinth. **Säulenschaft**, -shaft, *m. pl. -schäfte*, shaft of a pillar. **Säulenspath**, -shpät, *m.* prismatic spar. **Säulenstuhl**, -shtūl, *m. pl. -stühle*, pedestal, stereobate. **Säulenweite**, -vēite, *f.* intercolumniation.
Saum, sōum, *m. pl.* Säume. border, hem, edge, skirt.
Säumen, sēü'men, *vt.* to hem, border; *vi.* to delay, tarry.
Säumer, sēü'mēr, *m.* delayer, hemmer; beast of burden.
Säumig, sēü'mich, *a.* tardy, slow.
Säumniß, sēüm'niss, *n. pl. -e*, delay, dilatoriness.
Saumpferd, sōum'pfērt, *n.* **Saumroß**, -ross, *n. pl. -e*, sumter-horse.
Saumsattel, sōum'sattel, *m. pl. -sättel*. pack-saddle.
Saumselig, sōum'sēlich, *a.* tardy.
Saumthier, sōum'tīr, *n. pl. -e*, beast of burden.
Säure, sēü're, *f.* sourness, tartness, acidity; acid.
Saurüsel, sōu'rühsel, *m.* snout of a hog.
Saus, sōus, *m.* revel, riot. **Säuseln**, sēü'seln, *vi.* to rustle, murmur, whisper.
Sausen, sōu'sen, *vt.* to rush; to hiss, whizz, whistle.
Sauställ, sōu'zhtall, *m. pl. -ställe*, pig-sty. **Sautrog**, -trōg, *m. pl. -tröge*, pig's-trough.
Scala, skä'lä, *f.* scale.
Scandiren, skandī'ren, *vt.* to scan.
Scansion, skansiōn', *f.* scanning.
Scene, stsä'ne, *f.* scene. **Scenerie**, stsänērī', *f.* scenery.
Scepter, stsēp'tēr, *n.* sceptre, f. Sj.
Schaar, shär, *f.* troop, band, multitude, host, crowd, flock. **Schaaren**, shä'ren, *vi.* to flock together; *vt.* to form into troops; **weise**, -vēise, *av.* in bands, troops.
Schabe, shä'be, *f.* moth; cockroach.
Schabe, shä'be, *f.* scraper.
Schabe, shä'be, *f.* itch.
Schabebrett, shä'bebrēt, *n.* scraping-board. **Schabeisen**, -ēisen, *n.* scraper. **Schabemesser**, -messēr, *n.* shaving-knife. **Schaben**, shä'ben, *vt.* to scrape, to shave, grate.
Schabernack, shä'bernack, *m.* hoax, trick; einen — spielen. to play a trick.
Schäbig, shä'bich, *a.* shabby, mean; scabby, mangy.
Schablone, shablō'ne, *f.* model, pattern.
Schabrade, shabrack'e, *f.* saddle-cloth, housing.
Schach, shach, *m, pl. -e.* shah.
Schach, shach, *n.* chess; — spielen, to play chess; **brett**, -brēt, *n. pl. -er*, chess-board.
Schächer, shēch'ēr, *m.* robber, murderer.
Schacher, shach'ēr, *m.* chaffering, traffic, usury. **Schacherei**, -ēī', *f.* chaffering. **Schach'erer**, *m.* huckster, chafferer, huckstering Jew.
Schachfigur, shach'figur, *f.* chess-man. **Schach'matt**, -matt, *a.* checkmate. **Schach'spiel**, -zhpīl, *n. pl. -e*, game at chess. **Schach'spieler**, -zhpīler, *m.* chess-player. **Schach'stein**, *m. pl. -e*, chess-man.
Schacht, shacht, *m. pl.* Schächte, shaft, pit.
Schachtel, shach'tel, *f.* box; pepper-box; old woman: **deckel**, -deckel, *m.* cover, lid of a box.
Schächter, shēch'ter, Jewish butcher.
Schachzug, shach'tsug, *m.* move.
Schade, shä'de, *m. -ns*, **Schaben**, *-s, pl.* Schäden, damage, injury, loss, hurt, harm, prejudice; — thun, to hurt, damage, prejudice; — nehmen, to suffer injury.

23*

Schä 270 **Scha**

Schädel, shā'del, m. scull, cranium, brain-pan: **-bohrer,** -bōrēr, m. trepan. **Schä'delhaut,** -hout, f. pl. **-häute,** pericranium. **Schä'dellehre,** -lēre, f. phrenology. **Schä'delstätte,** -zhtętte, f. calvary.

Schaden, shā'den, vt. to hurt, harm, damage, injure: **es schadet nichts,** no matter. **Scha'denersatz,** -ērsats, m. indemnification, indemnity, amends. **Scha'denfreude,** -fräüde, f. rejoicing (over another's loss), malignity, maliciousness. **Scha'denfroh,** -frō, a. malignant, malicious. **Schad'haft,** -haft, a. damaged, injured; **-igkeit,** -kkēt, f. damaged condition. **Schädlich,** shäd'lich, a. injurious, hurtful, noxious, detrimental, prejudicial: **-keit,** -kēt, f. hurtfulness, noxiousness. **Schad'los,** -lōs, a. undamaged, uninjured: **— halten,** to indemnify. **Schad'loshaltung,-haltung,** f. indemnification, compensation. **Schad'losigkeit,** -ichkēt, f. indemnity.

Schaf, shäf, n. pl. **-e,** sheep. **Schaf's blattern,** -blattern, s.pl. chicken-pox. **Schaf'bock,** -bock, m. pl. **-böcke,** ram. **Schaf bremse,** -bremse, f. gray-fly.

Schäfer, shā'fēr, m. shepherd. **Schäferei,** -ēī', f. sheep-walk, sheep-fold. **Schä'fergedicht,** -gedicht, n. pl. **-e,** pastoral poem, eclogue, idyl. **Schä'ferhund,** -hunt, m. pl. **-e,** shepherd's dog. **Schä'ferin,** f. shepherdess. **Schä'ferleben,** -lēben, n. pastoral life. **Schä'ferlied,** -līt, n. pl. **-er,** pastoral song. **Schä'ferstab,** -zhtäb, m. pl. **-stäbe,** crook. shepherd's staff. **Schä'fertasche,** -tashe, f. shepherd's pouch.

Schaffell, shäf'fell, n. pl. **-e,** sheep-skin. **Schaffen,** shaf'fen (schuf, geschaffen), vt. to work, do, make: to create.

Schaffleisch, shaf'flāesh, n. mutton.

Schaffner, shāf'ner, m. steward, purveyor. **Schaffnerei,** -ēī', f. stewardship.

Schaffnerin, shaff'nerin, f. housekeeper.

Schaffot, shaffot', n. pl. **-e,** scaffold.

Schafgarbe, shäf'garbe, f. milfoil, yarrow.

Schafhirt, shäf'hirt, m. **-en,** pl. **-en,** shepherd. **Schafkäse,** -käse, m. cheese made of sheep's milk. **Schafleder,** shäf'lēdēr, r. sheep-skin.

Schafmäßig, shäf'mässich, a. sheepish. **Schaf'mutter,** -mutter, f. pl. **-mütter,** ewe. **Schafschur,** shäf'shur, f. sheep-shearing. **Schaffeuche,** shäf'säüche, f. sheep-rot. **Schafskopf,** -kopf, m. pl. **-köpfe,** sheep's head; blockhead. **Schafstall,** -zhtall, m. pl. **-ställe.** sheep-fold. **Schafstand,** -zhtaut, m. stock of sheep.

Schaft, shaft, m. pl. **Schäfte,** shaft, stock, stick, shank.

Schäften, shēf'ten, vt. to stock (a gun).

Schaftrift, shäf'trift, f. sheep-walk, sheep-pasturage. **Schafweide,** -vēlde, f. sheep-pasturage. **Schafwolle,** -volle, f. wool of sheep. **Schafzähne,** -tsēcke, f. sheep-tick. **Schafzucht,** -tsucht, f. breeding, raising, rearing of sheep. **Schafzüchter,** -tsüchtēr, m. raiser, breeder of sheep.

Schakal, shä'kal, m. **-e,** jackal.

Schäker, shēk'er, m. jester: jest, joke. **Schäkerei,** -ēī', f. jest, joke. **Schä'kerhaft,** -haft, a. playful. **Schäkern,** shēk'ērn, vi. to play, jest, joke.

Schal, shäl, a. stale, insipid, flat.

Schalbrett, shäl'brēt, n. slab.

Schale, shä'le, f. shell, peel, husk, scale; cup.

Schälen, shā'len, vt. to peel, pare, to shell. **Schalig,** shäl'ich, a shell; shelly.

Schalk, shalk, m. pl. **-e,** wag, rogue, fox; **-haft,** -haft, a. arch, roguish, sly: **-haftigkeit,** -ichkēt, f. roguishness. **Schalkheit,** -hēt, f. archness; subtlety. **Schalkauge,** -äüge, n. **-e,** pl. **-n,** roguish eye. **Schalksäugig,** -äügich, a. roguish, arch-eyed. **Schalksknecht,** -knēcht, m. pl **-e,** false steward. **Schalksnarr,** -narr, m. **-en,** pl. **-en,** wag, jester.

Schall, shall, m. pl. **Schälle,** sound, clangor; **-boden,** -bōden, m. sounding-board.

Schallen, shal'len (reg. or Prt. scholl), vt. to sound. **Schalllehre,** -lēre, f. acoustics. **Schallloch,** -loch, n. pl. **-löcher,** sound-hole. **Schallos,** -lōs, a. insonorous. **Schallwelle,** -velle, f. wave of sound.

Schalmei, shalmēi', f. shawm, cornet, reed-pipe.

Schalotte, shalet'te, f. shallot, scallion.

Schalt, shält, Prt. v. **Schelten.**

Schalten, shal'ten, vi. to dispose of; to act.

Schalter, shal'tĕr *m.* letter-box.
Schaltjahr, shalt yăr, *n. pl -e,* leap year, bissextile year. **Schaltmonat,** -mōnat. *m. pl. -e,* intercalary month. **Schalttag,** -täg, *m. pl. -e,* intercalary day.
Schaluppe, shalup'pe, *f.* sloop.
Scham, shäm, *f.* shame; nakedness; privy parts. **Schambein,** -bęn, *n. pl. -e* share-bone, os pubis.
Schämel, shā'mel, *m.* footstool; trestle.
Schämen, shā'men, *rr.* to be ashamed.
Schamhaft, shäm'haft, *a.* shamefaced, bashful; **-igkeit, -igkäet,** *f.* bashfulness. **Schamleiste,** -läezhte, *f.* **Schambug,** -bug, *m.* groin. **Schamlos,** -lōs, *a.* impudent, shameless. **Schamlosigkeit,** -ichkäet. *f.* shamelessness, impudence. **Schamroth,** -rōt, *a.* blushing; — machen, to put to the blush; — werden, to blush. **Schamröthe,** shäm'röhte. *f.* blush. **Schamtheile,** -täele, *f.* privy parts, nakedness.
Schandbar, shant'bär, *a.* shameful.
Schande, shan'de, *f.* shame, disgrace, infamy.
Schänden, shęn'den, *vt.* to disgrace; to violate, abuse, dishonor; to disfigure.
Schänder, shęn'dĕr, *m.* ravisher, violator; defamer, abuser.
Schandfleck, shand'fleck, *m.* stain, blemish.
Schändlich, shęnt'lich, *a.* shameful, disgraceful, infamous; **-keit,** -käet, *f.* disgracefulness, infamy.
Schandpfahl, shant'pfül, *m. pl. -pfähle,* pillory.
Schandpreis, shant'prēis. *m. pl. -e,* price far below the worth.
Schandsäule, shant'seüle, *f.* column of infamy.
Schandschrift, shant'shrift, *f.* lampoon, libel.
Schandthat, shant'tät, *f.* infamous action, indignity, atrocity.
Schändung, shęn'dung, *f.* rape, violation, deflowering; disgracing, dishonoring.
Schandwort, shant'vert, *n. pl. -e,* disgraceful language, ribaldry, obscenity.
Schank, shank, *m.* public-house, tavern, tap-house.
Schanzarbeit, shant 'arbäet, *f.* working on fortifications. **Schanze,** shan'tse, *f.* intrenchment, redoubt, fortification; quarter deck; throw (at dice). **Schanzen,** shan'tsen, *vi.* to intrench; work hard. **Schanzkorb,** -korp, *m. pl. -körbe,* gabion. **Schanzpfahl,** -pfäl, *m. pl. -pfähle,* palisade.

Schar, shär, *f. f.* **Schaar.**

Scharbock, shär'bock, *m.* scurvy.

Scharf, sharf, *a.* sharp, acrid, pungent, stinging, biting, burning; cutting, piercing, bleak; severe, harsh, rigid; acute. **Scharfblick,** -blick, *m. pl. -e,* penetration, piercing glance.

Schärfe, sherr'fe, *f.* sharpness; bleakness; strictness, acuteness; cutting edge.

Scharfeckig, sharf'eckich, *a.* sharp-cornered.

Schärfen, sherr'fen, *vt.* to sharpen, to set, to give an edge to; to emphasize; to stimulate.

Scharfrichter, sharf'richtĕr, *m.* executioner.

Scharfschütze, sharf'shütse, *m.* sharpshooter, rifleman.

Scharfsichtig, sharf'sichtich, *a.* sharp-sighted, penetrating; **-keit,** -käet, *f.* sharp-sightedness, penetration.

Scharfsinn, sharf'sinn, *m.* basf.

Scharfsinnig, sharf'sinnich, *a.* perspicacious, quick-sighted, acute.

Schärfung, sherr'fung, *f.* sharpening; brightening, heightening.

Scharlach, sharlach, *a.* scarlet, *m.* scarlet-robe. **Scharlachen,** *a.* scarlet. **Scharlachfarbe,** -farbe, *f.* scarlet. scarlet-color. **Scharlachfieber,** -fībĕr, *n.* scarlet-fever. **Scharlachroth,** -rōt, *a.* scarlet.

Scharmützel, sharmüt'sel. *n.* skirmish. **Scharmützeln,** sharmüt'seln, *vi.* to skirmish.

Scharnier, sharnīr', *n.* hinge.

Schärpe, sher'pe, *f.* scarf, sash.

Scharre, shar're, *f.* rake, scraper.

Scharren, shar'ren, *vt. i.* to scrape, scratch, rake.

Scharte, sharr'te, *f.* notch, fissure, gap. **Schartig,** shar'tich, *a.* notched, notchy.

Schatten, shat'ten, *m.* shadow, shade; gloom, darkness; *vi.* to shade; in den — stellen, to eclipse; **Bild,** -bilt, *n. pl. -er.* shade, phantom. **Schattenriss,** -riss, *m.* silhouette outline

Sch 272 **Sche**

Schat'tenseite, -seīte, f. shady side; unfavorable side, reverse. **Schat'tenspiel,** -zhpīl, n. pl. -e, magic lantern. **Schat'tenwelt,** -vĕlt, f. world of spirits.

Schattig, shat'tĭch, a. shady, umbrageous.

Schattiren, shattī'ren, vt. to shade (a drawing). **Schattirung,** -tī'rŭng, f. shading.

Schatulle, shatŭl'le, f. cash-box; casket.

Schatz, shats, m. pl. **Schätze,** treasure, store, stock; riches; **-amt,** -amt, n. pl. -ämter, treasury.

Schätzbar, shĕts'bär, a. estimable, valuable, dear; **-heit,** -kāĕt, f. value, worth, merit.

Schätzchen, shĕts'chen, n. sweetheart.

Schatzen, shat'sen, vt. to estimate, tax, assess.

Schätzen, shĕt'sen, vt. to value, estimate, esteem, appreciate; **-swerth,** -vĕrt, a. estimable, commendable.

Schätzer, shĕts'ĕr, m. assessor, estimator.

Schatzfrei, shats'frāī, a. exempt from taxes. **Schatzkammer,** -kazhten, m. strong-box, safe. **Schatzmeister,** -mäezhtĕr, m. treasurer. **Schatzung,** shats'ŭng, f. tax, taxation. **Schätzung,** shĕts'ŭng, f. appreciation, estimation, valuation; assessment.

Schau, shäū, f. show, view, sight.

Schaubrod, shäū'brōd, n. pl. -e, showbread.

Schaubühne, shäū'būhne, f. stage, theatre.

Schaub, shäūb. m. pl. -e, sheaf.

Schauder, shŏy'dĕr, m. shudder, shivering, horror; **-haft,** -haft, a. horrible, shocking, horrid. **Schaudern,** shŏy'dĕrn, vi. to shudder, shiver. **Schaudervoll,** -fŏll, a. horrid, horrible, awful.

Schauen, shäū'en, vt. i. to see, view, look; in die Zukunft —, to scan the future. **Schauer,** shäū'ĕr, m. seer; overseer.

Schauer, shŏy'ĕr, m. shower, rainstorm; shuddering, shivering, horror.

Schauer, shŏy'ĕr, m. shed.

Schauerlich, shŏy'ĕrlich, a. awful, horrible. **Schau'ern,** vi. to shudder, shiver, thrill.

Schaufel, shŏy'fel. f. shovel, paddle. scoop. **Schau'feln,** vt. to shovel. **Schau'felrad,** -rät, n. pl. -räder, paddle-wheel. **Schau'felzahn,** -tsäu, n. pl. -zähne, incisor.

Schaufenster, shäū'fenzhtĕr, n. show-window.

Schaufe, shäū'ke, f. punt, floating stage.

Schaufel, shäū'kel, f. swing; see-saw **Schau'feln,** vi. to swing, to rock. **Schau'felpferd,** -pfĕrt, n. pl. -e, rocking-horse. **Schau'felstuhl,** -zhtŭl, m. pl. -stühle, rocking-chair. **Schaufler,** shäūk'lĕr, m. rocker; see-sawer.

Schaulustig, shäū'lŭzhtich, a. fond of sight-seeing, curious.

Schaum, shäum, m. pl. **Schäume,** scum, foam, froth. **Schäumen,** shäō'men, vi. to foam, to froth; vt. to scum. **Schäumend, Schäumig,** a. frothy, foaming. **Schaumgold,** -gŏlt, n. gold-foil, tinsel. **Schaumlöffel,** -löffel, m. skimmer, skimming-ladle.

Schaumünze, shäū'mŭntse, f. medal.

Schauplatz, shäū'plats, m. pl. -plätze, scene, stage, theatre.

Schaurig, shŏy'rich, a. horrible, awful.

Schauspiel, shäū'zhpīl, n. pl. -e, play, drama; spectacle; **-dichter,** -dichtĕr, m. dramatic poet, dramatist. **Schau'spieler,** -zhpīlĕr, m. actor, player; **-in,** f. actress. **Schauspielhaus,** -hŏys, n. pl. -häuser, theatre.

Schaustellung, shäū'zhtellŭng, f. exhibition, display.

Schautragen, shäū'trägen, vt. to display.

Schebecke, shebĕck'e, f. Xebec.

Sched, shĕd, n. cutwater.

Schecke, shĕck'e, f. pied, spotted animal. **Scheckig,** shĕck'ich, a. pied, spotted.

Scheel, shāl, n. tungsten, wolfram.

Scheel, shāl, a. awry, asquint, askant, envious, jealous: **-sucht,** f. envy, jealousy. **Scheelsüchtig,** -sūchtich, a. jealous, envious.

Scheffel, shĕf'fel, m. bushel.

Scheibe, shāī'be, f. slice, cut, disk, orb, honey (comb); pane. target.

Scheibchen, shāīb'chen, n. little slice.

Scheibengat, shāī'bengat, n. pl. -e, sheave-hole. **Scheibenglas,** -gläs, n. pane. **Scheibenzucker,** -tsŭck'ĕr, n. honey comb.

Scheibenschießen, shīr'benshĭssen, n. target-practice. **Schei'benschütze**, -shütse, m. target-shooter.
Scheibig, shī'bĭch, a. orbicular.
Scheide, shāe'de, f. sheath, scabbard; spathe; vagina; -brief, -brĭf, m. pl. -e, bill of divorce.
Scheidekolben, shāe'dekolben, m. cucurbit.
Scheidekunst, shāe'dekṇnzht, f. Chemistry.
Scheidelinie, shāe'delīni-e, f. dividing line.
Scheidemünze, shāe'demüntse, f. change, small coin.
Scheiden, shāe'den (schied, geschieden), vt. to divide, separate; vi. to part, depart.
Scheidewand, shāe'devant, f. pl. -wände, partition, division-wall; septum; barrier.
Scheidewasser, shāe'devassēr, n. nitric acid, aqua-fortis.
Scheideweg, shāe'devēg, m. pl. -e, cross-road.
Scheidung, shīēd'ụng, f. division, parting, separation, divorce.
Schein, shāen, m. lustre, brightness, shining, light; aspect; appearance; receipt, certificate: -angriff, -ăngriff, m. pl. -e, mock-attack, sham-attack. **Schein'bar**, -bär, a. apparent, seeming, specious; -keit, -kāet, f. appearance. **Schein'bild**, -bĭlt, n. pl. -er, phantom. **Schein'ehe**, -ā-ye, f. mock-marriage.
Scheinen, shāen'en (schien, geschienen), vi. to shine; appear, seem; look. **Schein'grund**, -grụnt, m. pl. -gründe, seeming reason, pretense. **Scheinheilig**, shāen'hāelĭch, a. hypocritical; -keit, -kāet, f. sham-devotion. **Schein'kauf**, -kāuf, m. pl. -käufe, fictitious purchase. **Schein'tod**, -tōt, m. apparent death, asphyxy. **Scheintodt**, shāen'tōt, a. apparently dead.
Scheitegel, shāe'sēgel, n. sky-sail.
Scheiße, shāe'se, f. excrement, dirt.
Scheißen, shāe'sen (schiß, geschissen), vi. to void excrements.
Scheit, shāet, n. pl. -er or -e, billet, log.
Scheitel, shāe'tel, m. crown, top, summit head; -kreis, -krāes, m. pl. -e, vertical circle.
Scheiteln, shāe'teln, vt. to part (the hair).

Scheitelpunkt, shāe'telpụnkt, m. pl. -e, zenith.
Scheitelrecht, shāe'telrēcht, a. vertical.
Scheitelwinkel, shāe'telvinkel, m. azimuth.
Scheiterhaufen, shāe'tērhọpfen, m. funeral pile, pyre.
Scheitern, shāe'tērn, vi. to be wrecked, to founder.
Schel, shēl, a. f. **Schrel**.
Schelfe, shel'fe, f. peel, shell.
Schelle, shel'le, f. bell; manacle; box on the ear. **Schellen**, shel'len. vt to ring the bell, to tingle; to give a box on the ear. **Schel'lengeläute**, -geläute, n. ringing of bells; bell-harness. **Schel'lenschlitten**, -shlitten, m. sleigh with bells.
Schellfisch, shell'fish, m. pl. -e, haddock.
Schellack, shel'lack, m. shell-lac.
Schelm, shelm, m. pl. -e, rogne, knave; scoundrel. **Schelm'engesicht**, -gesicht, n. pl. -er, roguish face. **Schel'mensprache**, -zhprāche, f. cant. **Schel'menstreich**, -zhtrāech, m. **Schel'menstück**, -zhtück, n. pl. -stücke, roguish trick. **Schelmerei**, shelmerāī', f. roguery. **Schelmisch**, shel'mish, a. roguish.
Schelten, shel'ten (schalt, gescholten), vt. to chide, scold; to abuse; einen Schuft —, to call one a scoundrel. **Schelt'wort**, -vort, n. pl. -e, abusive word. abuse.
Schemel, shā'mel, m. footstool.
Schemen, shā'men, m. phantom.
Schenk, shenk. m. -es, pl. -en, butler; tavern-keeper. **Schenke**, shen'ke, f. tavern.
Schenkel, shen'kel, m. leg. thigh; shank; pendant (Mar.). **Schen'kelader**, -āder, f. femoral artery or vein. **Schen'kelbein**, -bāen, n. pl. -e, thigh-bone.
Schenken, shen'ken, vt. to pour (out), to fill; to give to drink; to retail liquors; to give, present; to remit. **Schenk'faß**, -fass, n. pl. -fässer, cooler. **Schenkgerechtigkeit**, -gerēchtichkāet, f. license. **Schenkstube**, -zhtụbe, f. **Schenktisch**, -tish, m. pl. -e, bar, cupboard, sideboard. **Schenkwirth**, -vĭrt, m. tavern-keeper, ale-house-keeper; -schaft, -shaft, f. beer-saloon, ale-honse.
Scherbe, shēr'be, f. pot-sherd; scari (Mar.); pot.

Schere, shē′re̥, *f.* scissors, shears, clippers; twitchers; claws; fork (of a wagon); handle (of a balance).

Scheren, shē′ren, *vt.* to shear, clip, fleece; to shave; to poll; to tease, vex; to cheat, fleece; to warp (Mech.): *vr.* to clear out, to leave. **Sche′renschleifer, -schleifer**, *m.* knife-grinder.

Schererei, shērerī′, *f.* vexation, annoyance.

Schermesser, shēr′mĕssĕr, *n.* razor.

Scherstöcke, shēr′zhtöcke̥, *s. pl.* binding strakes (of a deck).

Scherflein, shĕrf′līn, *n.* mite.

Scherge, shĕr′ge̥, *m.* -n, *pl.* -n, beadle, myrmidon.

Scherz, shĕrts, *m.* -es, *pl.* -e, jest, joke, sport, raillery. **Scher′zen**, *vi.* to jest, joke, sport. **Scherz′haft**, -haft, *a.* jesting, jocose; comic, droll: **-igkeit, -ichkāt**, *f.* sportiveness, jocoseness, drollery. **Scherz′weise**, -vēise, *av.* in fun, by way of a joke.

Scheu, shĕü, *a.* shy, timid, bashful; *s. f.* shyness, bashfulness; aversion, dislike: reverence.

Scheuche, shĕü′che̥, *f.* scare-crow, bugbear. **Scheu′chen**, *vt.* to scare, frighten (away); to drive away.

Scheuen, shĕü′en, *vt. u. r.* to be scared, frightened, to fear, shun, to be afraid of.

Scheuer, shĕü′ĕr, *f.* barn, granary.

Scheuerlappen, shĕü′erlappen, *m.* scouring-cloth: mop.

Scheuern, shĕü′ern, *vt.* to scour, rub hard, cleanse, scrub; *vr.* to chafe.

Scheuleder, shĕü′lĕdĕr, *n.* eye-flap, blinder.

Scheune, shĕü′ne̥, *f.* **Scheure**, shĕü′re̥, *f.* barn.

Scheusal, shĕü′sāl, *n.* monster, abomination.

Scheuslich, shĕüs′lich, *a.* revolting, hideous, horrible, atrocious; **-keit**, shĕüss′lichkāt, *f.* monstrosity, atrocity.

Schicht, shicht, *f.* layer, stratum, bed; inheritance. **Schichten**, shich′ten, *vt.* to put in layers; to divide, separate. **Schich′tenweise**, -vēise, *av. u. a.* in layers, stratified.

Schicken, shick′en, *vt.* to send, forward, dispatch: **sich**, to suit, become; to come to pass: **in den April —**, to make an April fool of.

Schicklich, shick′lich, *a.* proper, appropriate, suitable, becoming; **-keit, -kāt**, *f.* propriety, suitableness.

Schicksal, shick′sāl, *n.* destiny, fate.

Schickung, shick′ung, *f.* (Gottes) divine providence.

Schiebe, shī′be̥, *f.* spud; **-fenster, -fenzhtĕr**, *n.* sash.

Schieben, shī′ben (schob, geschoben), *vt.* to push, shove, stick, slide, put; **Kegel —**, to play at nine-pins.

Schieber, shī′bĕr, *m.* shover, pusher; slide, slide-valve, slide-bar.

Schiebfenster, shīp′fenzhtĕr, *n.* sash-window.

Schied, shīd (*Prt. v.* scheiden). **Schieds′gericht**, shīds′gericht, *n.* court of arbitration. **Schieds′richter, -richtĕr**, *m.* umpire, arbitrator: **-lich**, -lich, *a.* by arbitration. **Schieds′spruch**, -zhpruch. *m. pl.* -sprüche, award, arbitrament.

Schief, shīf, *a.* oblique, sloping, wry, warped; crooked, wrong, *av.* -ly; **-beinig, -bānich**, *a.* knock-kneed, bandy-legged. **Schiefe**, shī′fe̥, *f.* obliquity; slope.

Schiefer, shī′fĕr, *m.* slate; **-bruch**, -bruch. *m. pl.* -brüche, slate-quarry. **Schie′ferdach**, -dach, *n. pl.* -dächer, slate-roof. **Schie′ferdecker**, -deckĕr, *m.* slater. **Schie′ferhammer**, -hammĕr, *m. pl.* -hämmĕr, slater's hammer. **Schie′fericht, -icht, Schie′ferig**, *a.* slaty, schistous; touchy. **Schie′fern**, shī′fĕrn. *vi.* to exfoliate. **Schie′ferpfad**, shī′fĕrzhpāt, *m.* slate-spar. **Schie′ferstein**, -zhtāen, *n. pl.* -e̥, argillite; slate-rock. **Schie′ferstift**, -zhtift, *m. pl.* -e̥, slate-pencil. **Schie′fertafel**, -tāfel, *f.* slate.

Schiefheit, shīf′hāt, *f.* slope, obliquity: oddity, eccentricity, onesidedness.

Schieläugig, shīl′āügich, *a.* squinting, squint-eyed.

Schielen, shī′len, *vi.* to squint, to look asquint. **Schieler**, shī′ler, *m.* squinter.

Schiemann, shī′mann, *m.* boatswain's mate. **Schie′mannsgarn**, -garn, *n.* spun yarn or twine. **Schie′mannsmaat**, -māt, *m.* quartermaster's mate.

Schienen, shīn, *Prt. v.* scheinen.

Schienbein, shīn′bāen, *n.* shin, shinbone.

Schienbeinknochen, shīn'bānknochen, *m.* tibia. **Schienbeinmuskel**, -muskel, *f.* tibial muscle.
Schiene, shī'ne, *f.* rail, clout, splint.
Schienen, shīn'en, *vt.* to splint.
Schier, shīr, *av.* almost, nearly; *a.* clear, pure, smooth.
Schierling, shīr'ling, *m.* hemlock. **Schierlingsbecher**, -bēcher, *m.* cup of hemlock.
Schießbaumwolle, shīss'bāumvolle, *f.* gun-cotton.
Schießbedarf, shīss'bedarf, *m.* ammunition.
Schießen, shīs'sen (schoß, geschossen), *vi.* to shoot, fire, discharge; to rush, dart: in Samen —, to run to seed; — lassen, to let fly, let go; *s. n.* shooting, shooting-match.
Schießgewehr, shīss'gevär, *n.* fire-arm. **Schießhaus**, -hōus, *n. pl.* -häuser, shooting-gallery, shooting-house. **Schießloch**, -loch, *n. pl.* -löcher, loop-hole, embrasure. **Schießplan**, -plan, *m. pl.* -pläne, **Schießplatz**, -plats, *m. pl.* -plätze, shooting-ground. **Schießpulver**, -pulfer, *n.* gunpowder. **Schießscharte**, -sharte, *f.* loop-hole, embrasure. **Schießscheibe**, -shēlbe, *f.* target. **Schießstand**, -zhtant, *m. pl.* -stände, shooting-stand.
Schiff, shiff, *n. pl.* -e, ship, vessel; nave (of a church); shuttle (for weaving); zu Schiffe gehen, to take ship, to go aboard. **Schiffbar**, -bär, *a.* navigable; -keit, -kēet, *f.* navigableness. **Schiffbau**, -bōu, *m.* ship-building; -kunst, -kunzht, *f.* ship-building, naval architecture. **Schiffbaumeister**, shiff'boumäster, *m.* ship-builder, ship-wright. **Schiffbauplatz**, -plats, *m. pl.* -plätze, dock-yard. **Schiffboot**, -bōt, *n. pl.* -e, nautilus. **Schiffbruch**, -bruch, *m.* shipwreck; — leiden, to suffer shipwreck, to be wrecked. **Schiffbrüchig**, -brüchig, *a.* wrecked, cast away. **Schiffbrücke**, -brücke, *f.* pontoon. **Schiffen**, shiff'en, *vi.* to sail, go by water. **Schiffer**, shiff'er, *m.* mariner, sailor; ship-master. **Schiffersprache**, -zhprache, *f.* nautical language. **Schifffahrt**, -fart, *f.* navigation. **Schifffahrtskunde**, -kunde, *f.* art of navigation. **Schiffsherr**, -hěrr, *m.* -n, *pl.* -n, ship-owner.
Schiffsjunge, -yung-e, *m.* -n, *pl.* -n, cabin-boy. **Schiffskapitän**, -kapi tän, *m.* captain (of a ship). **Schiffskoch**, -koch, *m. pl.* -köche, crew's cook. **Schiffsleute**, -lēute, *s. pl.* crew, sailors. **Schiffspumpe**, -pumpe, *f.* pump. **Schiffsraum**, -rāum, *m.* hold. **Schiffsruder**, -räder, *m.* shipowner. **Schiffsrose**, -röse, *f.* mariner's compass. **Schiffsschnabel**, -shnäbel, peak of a vessel. **Schiffssoldat**, -soldät, *m.* -en, *pl.* -en, marine. **Schiffsuhr**, -ur, *f.* chronometer. **Schiffsvolk**, -folk, *n.* crew. **Schiffszimmermann**, -tsimmerman, *m. pl.* -zimmerleute, ship-wright. **Schiffszwieback**, -tsvīback, *m.* ship-biscuit.
Schiften, shif'ten, *vt.* to join, to bind together.
Schild, shilt, *m. pl.* -e, shield, buckler; protection; escutcheon, coat of arms: *n. pl.* -er, sign, sign-board; im Schilde führen, to intend.
Schilderhaus, shil'derhōus, *n. pl.* -häuser, sentry-box.
Schildern, shil'dern, *vt.* to paint; to describe; to stand guard.
Schilderung, shil'derung, *f.* description, delineation.
Schildknappe, shilt'knappe, *m.* -n, *pl.* -n, esquire, armor-bearer.
Schildkröte, shilt'kröte, *f.* turtle, tortoise. **Schildkrötenschale**, -shāle, *f.* tortoise-shell. **Schildkrötensuppe**, -suppe, *f.* turtle-soup.
Schildlaus, shilt'lōus, *f. pl.* -läuse, cochineal, kermes.
Schildträger, shilt'träger, *m.* shield-bearer, esquire.
Schildwache, shilt'vache, *f.* sentry, sentinel.
Schilf, shilf, *n. pl.* -e, reed, rush, bulrush; -gras, -gräs, *n.* reed-grass.
Schilfig, shilf'ig, *a.* reedy, rushy.
Schilfrohr, shilf'rōr, *n.* reed.
Schiller, shil'ler, *m.* lustre, splendor, gloss, rainbow-hue. **Schillern**, shil'lern, *vi.* to vary one's colors. **Schillerspath**, -zhpät, *a.* changeable feldspar: *a.* opaline.
Schilling, shil'ling *m. pl.* -e, shilling.
Schimmel, shim'mel, *m.* white-horse. **Schimmelfahrt**, -fart, *f.* navigation. **Schimmlig**, shim'mel, *m.* mould, mildew, mustiness. **Schimmelig**, shim'melich, *a.* mouldy, musty, mildewed **Schimmeln**, shim'meln, *vi.* to mould, mildew.

Schi 276 **Schl**

Schimmer, shim'mer, m. glitter, gleam, sparkle, dazzling, brightness.
Schimmern, shim'mern, vi. to shine, glitter, twinkle, gleam. **Schimmernd,** shim'mernd, a. glossy, shining, bright; gleaming.
Schimpf, shimpf, m. pl. -e, abuse, disgrace, insult; — anthun, to insult, affront.
Schimpfen, shim'pfen, vt. to abuse, insult, affront.
Schimpflich, shimpf'lich, a. dishonorable, disgraceful, ignominious, insulting; av. -ly; -feit, -käet, f. shame, disgracefulness.
Schimpfname, shimpf'näme, m. -ne, pl. -n, **Schimpfwort,** -vort, n. pl. -e, abuse, nickname, abusive word.
Schindaas, shind'äs, n. pl. -äser, carrion.
Schinbanger, shind'ang-er, m. flaying-place.
Schindel, shin'del, f. shingle: -dach, -dach, n. pl. -bächer, shingle-roof.
Schindelnagel, -nägel, m. pl. -nägel, shingle-nail.
Schinden, shin'den (schund, geschunden), vt. to flay, skin; to oppress; vt. i. to overwork.
Schinder, shin'der, m. flayer. **Schinderei,** -ei', f. oppression; flayer's house. **Schinderkarren,** -karren, m. flayer's-cart.
Schindluder, shind'lyder, n. carrion: — treiben, to make a fool of, to impose upon.
Schinken, shin'ken, m. ham.
Schippe, ship'pe, f. spade.
Schirm, shirm, m. shield, screen, umbrella; protection. **Schirmdach,** -dach, n. pl. -bächer, pent-house, shed; awning, shelter. **Schirmen,** shir'men, vt. to screen, protect.
Schirren, shir'ren, vt. to harness.
Schiß, shiss, m. evacuation, stool; fright (vulg.).
Schlacht, shlacht, f. battle, action; — anbieten, to offer battle.
Schlachtbank, shlacht'bank, f. pl. -bänke, shamble, slaughter-house; zur — führen, to deliver up to slaughter.
Schlachten, shlach'ten, vt. to slaughter, kill, slay, to butcher.
Schlachter, shlach'ter, m. **Schlächter,** shlech'ter, m. slaughterer, butcher.
Schlachtfeld, shlacht'felt, n. pl. -er, battle-field. **Schlachtgeschrei,** -shräe, n. battle-cry.
Schlachtmesser, shlacht'messer, n. butcher's knife.
Schlachtopfer, shlacht'opfer, n. victim.
Schlachtordnung, shlacht'ordnung, f. battle-array.
Schlachtroß, shlacht'ross, n. pl. -rosse, charger, war-horse.
Schlachtruf, shlacht'ruf, m. pl. -e battle-cry. **Schlachtstatt,** -shtatt, f. battle-field. **Schlachttag,** -täg, m pl. -e, day of battle.
Schlacke, shlack'e, f. dross, slag, scoria. **Schlacken,** shlack'en, vi. to give slags. **Schlackig,** shlack'ich, a. drossy, scorious, slaggy.
Schlaf, shläf, m. sleep, nap; temple (of the head). **Schlafbank,** -bank, f. pl. -bänke, (wooden) couch. **Schlafbringend,** -bring-ent, a. somniferous, soporific. **Schläfchen,** shläf'chen, n. nap, slumber. **Schlafen,** shlä'fen (schlief, geschlafen), vi. to sleep, slumber. **Schläfer,** shlä'fer, m. sleeper. **Schläfern,** shlä'fern, vt. to make sleepy; es schläfert mich, I am sleepy.
Schlaff, shlaff, a. slack, loose, relaxed, weary; — werden, to relax. **Schlaffheit,** -häet, f. fluccidity, slackness; laxity.
Schlafgänger, shlaf'geng-er, m. sleepwalker, somnambulist. **Schlafgemach,** -gemach, n. pl. -gemächer, bed-room, bed-chamber. **Schlafgesell,** -gesell, m. -en, pl. -en, bedfellow, chum. **Schlafhaube,** -höybe, f. night-cap; drone, sluggard. **Schlafkammer,** shlafkammer, f. bed-chamber. **Schlaflos,** -lös, a. sleepless; -säfeit, -schkäet, f. sleeplessness. **Schlafmittel,** -mittel, n. soporific. **Schlafmütze,** -mütse, f. night-cap; lazy fellow. **Schlafratte,** -ratte, **Schlafratze,** -ratse, f. marmot, dormouse; lazy fellow. **Schlafrig,** shläf'rich, a. sleepy; -feit, -käet, f. sleepiness. **Schlafrock,** shlafrock, m. pl. -rödt, dressing-gown. **Schlafsucht,** shläf'sucht, f. somnolency. **Schlaftrank,** -trank, **Schlaftrunk,** -trunk, m. sleeping draught, sleeping-potion. **Schlaftrunken,** -trunken, a. overcome with sleep, sleepy **Schlafzimmer,** -tsimmer, n. bed-room, bed-chamber.

Schla, schläg, *m. pl.* **Schläge**, blow, stroke, knock, clap, shock: twist (of a rope); palpitation, throbbing, beating; kind, sort; warble, trill; apoplexy. **Schlag'ader**, -ädēr, *f.* artery. **Schlag'baum**, -baūm, *m. pl.* -bäume, turnpike.

Schlägel, shlä'gel. *m.* mallet, beater; leg, haunch, thigh: rammer. **Schlä'gein**, *vi.* to limp, to kick.

Schlagen, shlä'gen (schlug, geschlagen), *vt.* 1. to beat, strike, dash, hit; to fell (wood); to coin, stamp; to press (oil): to warble; zu Boden —, to strike down; aus der Art —, to degenerate; sich —, to fight, combat. **Schlagend**, shlä'gent, *a.* striking.

Schläger, shlä'ger, *m.* fighter; sword. **Schlägerei**, -ēī', *f.* fight, row, scuffle.

Schlagfluß, shläg'fluss, *m. pl.* -flüsse, apoplexy.

Schlaggold, shläg'golt, *n.* leaf-gold.

Schlaglawine, shläg'lavīne, *f.* avalanche.

Schlagregen, shläg'rēgen, *m.* shower.

Schlagseite, shläg'sēite, *f.* lapside, heeling side.

Schlaguhrwerk, shläg'vērk, *n.* clockwork.

Schlamm, shlamm, *n. pl.* **Schlämme**, slime, mud, mire.

Schlämmen, shlem'men, *vt.* to separate by washing: to wash, purify, cleanse (metals); to whitewash; to gormandize.

Schlammig, shlam'mich, *a.* slimy, muddy.

Schlampe, shlam'pe, *f.* slut. **Schlam'pen**, *vt.* to lap; to draggle, to be sluttish. **Schlampig**, shlam'pich, *a.* slovenly; rainy.

Schlange, shlang'e, *f.* serpent, snake. **Schlängeln**, shleng'-ein, *vi.* to creep, meander.

Schlangenförmig, shlang'enförmich, *a.* serpentine. **Schlangengift**, -gift, *n.* venom of serpents. **Schlangenlinie**, -līni-e, *f.* serpentine line. **Schlangenstein**, -shtaēn, *m. pl.* -e, serpentine, ophite. **Schlangenstich**, -zhtich, *m. pl.* -e, **Schlangenbiß**, shlang-enbiss, *m. pl.* -e, snakebite.

Schlank, shlank, *a.* slender, tall, graceful, delicate, slight, slim; -heit, -hāet, *f.* slenderness.

Schlappe, shlap'pe, *f.* slap, stroke, smack; defect, loss. **Schlappen**, shlap'pen, *vi.* to flap; to be slovenly; to lap. **Schlappig**, shlap'pich, *a* slovenly.

Schlaraffe, shlaraf'fe, *m. -n, pl. -n,* idler, sensualist, indolent voluptuary. **Schlaraffenland**, -lant, *n.* Utopia, fool's paradise. **Schlaraf'fenleben**, -lēben, *n.* idle, voluptuous life.

Schlarfe, shlarr'fe, *f.* slipper. **Schlarfen**, shlarr'fen, *vi.* to walk slipshod.

Schlau, shlōy, *a.* sly, keen, crafty, cunning, sharp.

Schlauch, shlōych, *m. pl.* **Schläuche**, leather-bag, pipe, hose.

Schlauheit, shlōy'hāet, *f.* slyness, cunning, sharpness. **Schlaukopf**, -kopf, *m. pl.* -köpfe, sly hand, sharper, tricky fellow.

Schlecht, shlecht, *a.* bad, base, vile, mean, worthless, poor, wretched, *av.* -ly; schlecht und recht, simple and upright. **Schlechterdings**, -terdings', *av.* by all means. **Schlechtheit**, -hāet, *f.* **Schlechtigkeit**, -tichkāet, *f.* badness, meanness. **Schlechthin**, -hīn, *av.* absolutely.

Schleck, shlēck, *m.* dainty, sweetmeat. **Schlecken**, shleck'en, *vi.* to lick; to be dainty. **Schlecker**, shlēck'er, *m.* dainty feeder, Epicure. **Schleckerhaft**, -haft, *a.* dainty.

Schlehdorn, shlā'dorn, *m. pl. -en,* black thorn.

Schleiche, shlā'ye, *f.* sloe.

Schleichen, shlāi'chen (schlich, geschlichen), *vi.* to glide, creep, steal.

Schleicher, shlāich'er, *m.* sneaker. **Schleicherei**, shlāicherāi', *f.* underhand dealing, sneaking.

Schleichhandel, shlāich'handel, *m.* smuggling, contraband trade; — treiben, to carry on smuggling. **Schleichhändler**, shlāich'hentler. *m.* smuggler. **Schleichwaare**, -vāre, *f.* smuggled goods, contraband goods. **Schleichweg**, -vēg, *m. pl. -e,* by-path, secret way.

Schleie, shlāi'e, *f.* tench.

Schleier, shlāi'er, *m.* vail, veil. **Schleierflor**, -flōr, *m.* lawn, crape. **Schleiertuch**, -tūch, *n. pl.* -tücher, lawn.

Schleife, shlāi'fe, *f.* loop, bow, knot: sledge, drag. **Schleifen**, shlāi'fen, *vt. i.* to drag, draggle, trail; to raze

24

demolish; to tie a bow *or* knot; to slur (Mus.).
Schleifen, shleī'fen (schliff, geschliffen), *vt. i.* to slide, glide; to dance around; to grind, whet; to furbish, polish.
Schleifer, shleī'fer, *m.* grinder.
Schleifer, shläe'fer, *m.* slurred passage, legato.
Schleiffanne, shläef'kanne, *f.* large wooden can.
Schleifmühle, shleīf'mǜhle, *f.* mill for grinding, polishing.
Schleifstein, shleīf'zhtāen, *m. pl.* -e, grindstone.
Schleiftrog, shläef'trōk, *m. pl.* -tröge, clog, drag.
Schleim, shlaēm, *m. pl.* -e, mucilage, mucus, phlegm. **Schleim'artig,** -ärtich, *a.* mucous, mucilaginous. **Schleim'darmgicht,** -darmgicht, *f.* pituitous colic. **Schleim'haut,** -hout, *f. pl.* -häute, pituitous membrane. **Schleimig,** shlaēm'ich, *a.* pituitous, mucous. **Schleim'säure,** -söüre, *f.* mucic acid.
Schleiße, shleīs'se, *f.* splint, splinter; beard (of a feather).
Schleißen, shleīs'sen (schliß, geschliffen), *vt.* to slit, split.
Schlemmen, shlem'men, *vi.* to eat *or* drink to excess, to revel, carouse.
Schlemmer, shlem'mer, *m.* glutton, drunkard, reveller. **Schlemmerei,** -reī', *f.* gluttony, carousal, revelry.
Schlender, shlen'der, *m.* sauntering, loitering; **-gang,** -gang, *m.* sauntering gait; the old beaten track.
Schlendern, shlen'dern, *vi.* to stroll, loiter, saunter. **Schlendrian,** shlen'drian, *m.* the old beaten track.
Schlenkern, shlen'kern, *vi.* to toss about, fling about, to loiter, dangle.
Schleppe, shlep'pe, *f.* train, trail.
Schleppen, shlep'pen, *vt. i.* to drag, draggle, trail, to sweep the ground; to draw; to tow (a vessel).
Schleppend, shlep'pent, *a.* drawling, heavy, diffuse. **Schlep'penträger,** -träger, *m.* train-bearer. **Schlepperei,** -reī', *f.* heavy work, dragging. **Schlepp'fleid,** -klāed, *n. pl.* -er, dress with a train. **Schlepp'netz,** -nets, *n. pl.* -e, drag-net. **Schlepp'seil,** -säēl, *n. pl.* -er, towing-rope, tow-line. **Schlepp'tau,** -tou, *n. pl.* -e, towing-cable; in das — nehmen, to take in tow.

Schleuder, shleū'der, *f.* sling **Schleuderer,** shleū'derer, *m.* slinger.
Schleudern, shleū'dern, *vt.* to sling, hurl, throw, cast; *vi.* to sell under price. **Schleu'derstein,** -zhtāen, *m. pl.* -e, sling-stone.
Schleunig, shlaūn'ich, *a.* speedy, hasty; aufs schleunigste, most speedily, immediately.
Schleuse, shleū'se, *f.* sluice, lock, water-gate; sewer, drain. **Schleusengeld,** -gēlt, *n. pl.* -er, toll, lock-dues. **Schleusenthor,** -tōr, *n. pl.* -e, lockgate, flood-gate.
Schlich, shlich, *Prt. v.* schleichen.
Schlich, shlich, *m.* trick, artifice, secret way.
Schlich, shlich, *m* pounded ore, slich, slick; sleetch.
Schlicht, shlicht, *a.* plain, simple, flat, uncurled; natural, unpretending; schlichter Verstand, common sense. **Schlicht'beil,** -bēīl, *n.* chip-axe.
Schlichte, shlich'te, *f.* weaver's glue.
Schlichten, shlich'ten, *vt.* to straighten, smooth, plain, level; to adjust, compose, settle.
Schlichter, shlich'ter, *m.* mediator, reconciler.
Schlichtfeile, shlicht'fēīle, *f.* smoothing file. **Schlicht'hammer,** -hammer, *m. pl.* smoothing hammer. **Schlicht'heit,** -hāēt, *f.* plainness, simplicity. **Schlicht'hobel,** -hōbel, *m.* smoothing-plane. **Schlicht'ung,** -ung, *f.* settling, accommodation.
Schlid, shlick, **Schlid'grund,** -grunt, *m.* sleetch, oozy ground.
Schlief, shlīf, *Prt. v.* schlafen, slept.
Schliefen, shlī'fen (schloff, geschloffen), *vi.* to creep, slide, crawl, slip.
Schließig, shlī'fich, *a.* doughy.
Schließen, shlīs'sen (schloß, geschlossen), *vt.* to lock, shut, close; to chain; to conclude, to end; *vr.* to close, conclude; to be formed.
Schließer, shlīs'ser, *m.* jailer, turnkey; door-keeper.
Schließlich, shlīss'lich, *a.* final, definitive, final, *av.* -ly, lastly, in conclusion.
Schließung, shlīss'ung, *f.* close, shutting, closing; — eines Handels, conclusion; — einer Ehe, consummation.
Schlimm, shlimm, *a.* wrong, bad, *av.* -ly.

Schlinge, shling'-ę, *f.* snare, noose, loop, toil.
Schlingel, shling'-ęl, *m.* rascal, rogue.
Schlingelei, -ēī', *f.* roguishness.
Schlingelhaft, shling'-elhaft, *a.* roguish, rascally.
Schlingen, shling'-en (schlang, geschlungen), *vt. u. r.* to wind, to twine, twist, fold, wreathe; to wind, meander.
Schlingern, shling'-ern, *vi.* to roll, wallow (Mar.).
Schlingpflanze, shling'pflantse, *f.* climber, creeper.
Schlinkschlank, shlink'shlank, *m. pl.* -e, idler, lounger.
Schlippen, shlip'pen, *vt.* to slip (a cable).
Schlitten, shlit'ten, *m.* sleigh, sled, sledge; skid; carriage. **Schlittenbahn,** -bān, *f.* sledge-track. **Schlitt'enfahrt,** -fārt, *f.* sleigh-ride. **Schlitt'enschelle,** -shelle, *f.* sleigh-bell.
Schlittschuh, shlitt'shụ. *m.* skate; — laufen. — fahren, to skate. **Schlitt'schuhläufer,** -läufer, *m.* skater.
Schlitz, shlits, *m. pl.* -e, slit, slash, rip, cut. **Schlitzen,** shlit'sen, *vt.* to slit, slash, rip, cut. **Schlitz'ung,** -ung, *f.* slitting.
Schloß, shlōs, *Prt. v.* schließen.
Schloß, shlōss, *n. pl.* **Schlösser,** castle, citadel, palace; lock, padlock; clove-hitch; notch: lasket, latching; clasp. **Schlößchen,** shlöss'chen, *n.* small castle, small lock, locket.
Schloße, shlō'se, *f.* hail, hailstone. **Schloßen,** shlō'sen, *vi.* to hail.
Schloßenwetter, shlō'senvetter, sleet, hail-storm.
Schlosser, shlos'ser, *m.* lock-smith. **Schloss'erarbeit,** -arbāēt, *f.* locksmith's work. **Schlos'serhandwerk,** -hantverk, *n.* lock-smith's trade.
Schloßgarten, shloss'garten, *m. pl.* -gärten, castle-garden. **Schloß'graben,** -grāben, *m. pl.* -gräben, moat. **Schloß'hauptmann,** -hāuptman. *m. pl.* -männer, castellan. **Schloß'thor,** -tōr, *n. pl.* -e, castle-gate. **Schloß'thurm,** -tụrm, *m. pl.* -thürme, castle-tower.
Schlot, shlōt, *m.* chimney. **Schlot'feger,** -fēger, *m.* chimney-sweep.
Schlotterig, shlot'terich, *a. av.* dangling, -y, slovenly.

Schlottern, shlot'tern, *vi.* to flutter, dangle; to knock together (the knees).
Schlucht, shluçht, ravine, gorge, cleft.
Schluchzen, shlụçh'tsen, *vi.* to sob; to hiccough.
Schluck, shlụck, *m. pl.* -e, draught, swig, gulp. **Schlucken,** shlụck'en, *vi.* to gulp, swallow.
Schlucken, shlụck'en, *m.* hiccough.
Schlucker, shlụck'er, *m.* wretch, poor fellow, sorry fellow. **Schluck'weise,** -vēīse, *av.* by gulps.
Schlug, shlụg, *Prt. v.* schlagen.
Schlummer, shlụm'mer, *m.* slumber, doze. **Schlum'merlos,** -lōs, *a.* slumberless. **Schlummern,** shlụm'mern, *vi.* to slumber.
Schlumpe, shlụm'pę, *f.* slattern, slut. **Schlumpen,** shlụm'pen, *vi.* to dangle, trail. **Schlumpig,** shlụm'pich, *a.* slovenly, slatternly, sluttish.
Schlund, shlụnt, *m. pl.* **Schlünde,** throat, gullet; gulf, chasm, abyss; whirlpool.
Schlung, shlụng, *m. pl.* **Schlünge,** gulp.
Schlunt, shlụnt, *m. pl.* -e, dark lantern (Mar.).
Schlüpfen, shlüp'fen, *vi.* to slip, glide, slide, creep.
Schlupfer, shlụpf'er, *m.* muff. **Schlüpferig,** shlụpf'erich. *a.* **Schlüpfrig,** shlụpf'rich, *a.* slippery, dangerous; wanton, amatory; -keit, -kāēt, *f.* slipperiness; obscenity. **Schlupf'winkel,** -vinkel, *m.* hiding-place.
Schluren, shlụ'ren, *vt.* to line, measure.
Schlürfen, shlür'fen, *vi.* to trail, drag; *vt.* to sip, suck in, suck up; to inhale.
Schluß, shlụss, *m. pl.* **Schlüsse,** close, closing, shutting, conclusion, end; decision; inference, consequence; deduction: decree, resolution.
Schlußbein, shlụss'bāēn, *n. pl.* -e, hip bone.
Schlüssel, shlüs'sel, *m.* key; lasket. **Schlüsselbein,** shlüs'selbāēn, *n. pl.* -e, clavicle. **Schlüs'selblume,** -blụmę *f.* primrose. **Schlüs'selloch,** -loch, *n. pl.* -löcher, key-hole.
Schlußgerecht, shlụss'gerēcht, *a.* conclusive.
Schlüssig, shlüs'sich, *a.* resolved.
Schlußpunkt, shlụss'pụnkt, *m. pl.* -e,

Schm   280   **Schm**

full stop. **Schluß'satz**, -sates, m. pl. -sätze, conclusion; final sentence. **Schluß'stein**, -zhtäen, m. key-stone. **Schluß'wort**, -vort, n. pl. -e, concluding word, last word.
Schmach, shmäch, f. shame, dishonor, disgrace; insult, outrage.
Schmachten, shmach'ten, vi. to languish, pine away; to long for.
Schmächtig, shmëch'tich, a. slender, slim, slight; lank; -keit, -kāet, f. slenderness, slimness. **Schmachtlappen**, shmacht'lappen, m. languisher.
Schmachvoll, shmach'foll, a. shameful, disgraceful.
Schmack, shmack, m. pl. -e, sumach.
Schmackt, shmack'e, f. smack.
Schmackhaft, shmack'haft, a. savory, palatable, relishable; -igkeit, -kāet, f. savor, savoriness, palatableness.
Schmacklos, shmack'lōs, a. tasteless, unsavory, insipid; -igkeit, -ichkāet, f. tastelessness, insipidness.
Schmaddern, shmad'dern, vi. to scrawl.
Schmähen, shmä'-en, vt. to abuse, scold, revile. **Schmählich**, -lich, a. ignominious, disgraceful, av. -ly. **Schmäh'rede**, -rēde, f. abuse, invective. **Schmäh'schrift**, -shrift, f. libel. **Schmähsucht**, -sucht, f. slanderous disposition. **Schmäh'süchtig**, -süchtich, a. slanderous. **Schmäh'ung**, -ung, f. invective, abuse, insult. **Schmäh'wort**, -vort, n. pl. -e, invective abuse.
Schmal, shmāl, a. narrow, small, scanty, poor. **Schmal'backig**, -beckich, a. hollow-cheeked.
Schmälen, shmā'len, vt. i. to scold, chide.
Schmälern, shmā'lern, vt. to narrow, diminish, lessen. **Schmä'lerung**, -ung, f. diminution, curtailing; encroachment.
Schmalheit, shmāl'hāet, f. narrowness.
Schmalte, shmal'te, f. smalt.
Schmalz, shmalts, n. lard, grease, fat. **Schmalzig**, shmal'tsich, a. greasy, fat.
Schmaub, shmannt, n. loam.
Schmarotzen, shmarot'sen, vi. to sponge on. **Schmarotzer**, shmarot'ser, m. spunger, parasite; -isch, -ish, a sponging, parasitical.

Schmarotzerpflanze, shmarot'serpflanze, f. parasite.
Schmarre, shmar're, f. scar, cut, gash. **Schmarrig**, shmar'rich, a. scarred, gashed.
Schmatz, shmats, m. smack; buss, kiss. **Schmatzen**, shmat'sen, vi. to smack, buss.
Schmauch, shmäuch, m. thick smoke. **Schmauchen**, shmäuch'en, vi. to give a dank smoke; vt. to smoke. **Schmaucher**, shmäuch'er, m. smoker.
Schmaus, shmōus, m. feast, banquet. **Schmausen**, shmōu'sen, vi. to feast, banquet. **Schmauser**, shmōu'ser, m. feaster, reveler. **Schmauserei**, -ēi', f. feasting, banqueting, revelry.
Schmecken, vt. i. to taste; relish.
Schmecker, shmeck'er, m. epicure, dainty feeder: mouth.
Schmeer, shmēr, m. suet, grease, fat. **Schmeer'bauch**, -bäuch, m. pl. -bäuche, paunch. **Schmeerig**, shmēr'ich, a greasy.
Schmeichelei, shmäechelēi', f. flattery, adulation. **Schmeich'elhaft**, -haft, a. flattering. **Schmeich'elkatze**, -katse, f. wheedling puss, flatterer.
Schmeicheln, shmäech'eln, vt. to flatter, fawn upon. coax; caress. **Schmeichler**, shmäech'ler, m. flatterer, fawner, adulator; -in, f. adulatress, flatterer. **Schmeich'lerisch**, -ish, a. flattering, coaxing, wheedling, fawning.
Schmeidigen, shmēi'dichen, vt. to make pliant, supple, to soften.
Schmeißen, shmēis'sen (schmiß, geschmissen), vt. to smite; to hurl, cast, throw: to hit.
Schmeißfliege, shmäess'flīge, f. blue bottle, muck-fly.
Schmelz, shmelts, m. enamel: -arbeit, -arbāet, f. working in enamel.
Schmelzbar, shmelts'bār, a. fusible; -keit, -kāet, f. fusibility.
Schmelzblau, shmelts'bläu, n. smalt, enamel-blue.
Schmelzbutter, shmelts'butter, f. melted butter.
Schmelzen, shmel'tsen (schmolz, geschmolzen), vt. i. to melt, fuse, smelt, liquify; to blend; to enamel, vitrify; to soften; to oil, grease.
Schmelzfarbe, shmelts'farbe, f. enamel-color, vitrifiable color or pigment.

Schm.eizhaus, shmęlts'hŏus, *n. pl.* -häuser. **Schmelzhütte**, -hütte, *f.* foundery, blast-furnace.
Schmelzkunst, shmęlts'kunzht, *f.* art of smelting, of roasting metals.
Schmelzofen, shmęlts'ōfen, *m. pl.* -öfen, melting-furnace, blast-furnace.
Schmelzrohr, shmęlts'rōr, *n. pl.* -röhre, blow-pipe.
Schmelztiegel, shmęlts'tīgel, *m.* crucible, cupel.
Schmelzung, shmęlts'ung, *f.* melting.
Schmelzwerk, shmęlts'vĕrk, *n. pl.* -e, enamelled work.
Schmergel, shmĕr'gel, *m.* emery (Min.).
Schmergeln, shmĕr'geln, *vt.* to rub or polish with emery.
Schmerz, shmĕrts, *m.* -enš or -eš, *pl.* -en, pain, ache, pang, smart; grief, sorrow, anguish.
Schmerzen, shmĕr'tsen, *vt.* to pain, afflict; grieve. **Schmerzensgeld**, *n.* smart-money, indemnification.
Schmerzhaft, shmĕrts'haft, *a.* painful, aching, smarting, sore, bitter, mournful; -igkeit, -ichkĕet, *f.* painfulness. **Schmerzlich**, -lich, *a.* painful, grievous, sorrowful. **Schmerz'los**, -lōs, *a.* painless. **Schmerzstillend**, -zhtillent, *a.* soothing, anodyne. **Schmerzvoll**, -fŏll, *a.* painful, sorrowful.
Schmetterling, shmĕt'terling, *m.* butterfly.
Schmettern, shmĕt'tern, *vt. i.* to peal, bray, clang; warble; to dash, crash, hurl.
Schmied, shmīd. *m. pl.* -e, smith, blacksmith. **Schmied'bar**, -bār, *a.* malleable; -keit, -kĕet, *f.* malleability.
Schmiede, shmī'de, *f.* blacksmith's shop, smithy, forge; vor die rechte — gehen, to find the right man.
Schmiedeeisen, shmī'deēisen, *n.* malleable iron. **Schmiedesse**, -ěsse, *f.* forge. **Schmiedegesell**, -gesell, *m.* -en, *pl.* -en, **Schmiedeknecht**, -knĕcht, *m. pl.* -e, smith's journeyman. **Schmiedehammer**, -hammer, *m. pl.* -hämmer, blacksmith's hammer, sledge-hammer. **Schmiedemeister**, -mäehzhter, *m.* master-smith.
Schmieden, shmī'den, *vt.* to forge: in Eisen —, to chain, manacle; Ränke —, to intrigue, plot.

Schmiedewerkstatt, shmī'devĕrkzhtat, *f. pl.* -stätte, smithy, blacksmith's-shop. **Schmiedezange**, -tsange, *f.* blacksmith's-tongs, pincers.
Schmiege, shmī'ge, *f.* bevel; slope. **Schmiegen**, shmī'gen, *vt.* to bevel; *vr.* to nestle, to cling to; to bend to insinuate one's self. **Schmieg'sam**, -sam, *a.* pliant, supple, flexible; -keit, -kĕet, *f.* pliancy, suppleness, flexibility; submissiveness.
Schmierbuch, shmīr'buch, *n. pl.* -bücher, waste-book.
Schmiere, shmī'rę, *f.* grease, fat.
Schmieren, shmī'ren, *vt. i.* to smear, grease, oil; to scrawl, scribble; to adulterate (wine); einen —, to bribe. **Schmierer**, shmī'rer, *m.* scrawler, scribbler; greaser. **Schmiererei**, -rēī', *f.* smearing; scrawling, scribbling. **Schmierig**, -ich, *a.* greasy, dirty. **Schmierlappen**, -lappen, *m.* cleaning rag; dirty fellow.
Schminkbohne, shminǩ'bōne, *f.* kidney-bean.
Schminke, shminǩ'e, *f.* paint, rouge. **Schminken**, shmin'ken, *vt.* to paint, color.
Schmirgel, shmīr'gel, *m.* emery (Min.).
Schmiss, shmiss, *m. pl.* -e, stroke, blow.
Schmitz, shmits, *m. pl.* -e, cut, lash; stain. **Schmitze**, shmit'se, *f.* whiplash. **Schmitzen**, shmit'sen, *vt.* to whip, lash.
Schmollen, shmŏl'len, *vi.* to pout, to be sulky. **Schmoll'end**, **Schmoll'ig**, *a.* pouting, sulky. **Schmollwinkel**, -vinkel, *m.* pouting-corner.
Schmolz, shmŏlts, *Prt. v.* schmelzen.
Schmorbraten, shmōr'brāten, *m.* roast.
Schmoren, shmō'ren, *vt.* to roast, broil, fry. **Schmorpfanne**, -pfanne, *f.* frying-pan.
Schmu, shmu, *m.* (unfair) profit, gain; cheat.
Schmuck, shmuck, *a.* trim, neat, fine, spruce; *s. m. pl.* -e, ornament, finery, trim; set of jewels.
Schmücken, shmück'en, *vt.* to ornament, adorn, trim.
Schmuckkästchen, shmuck'kĕstchen, *n.* jewel-box. **Schmucklos**, -lōs, *a.* unadorned, plain, simple.
Schmuggel, shmug'gel, *m.* **Schmuggelei**, -lēī', *f.* smuggling. **Schmuggeln**, *vt. i.* to smuggle.

Schm 282 **Schn**

Schmuggler, shmŭg'gler, m. smuggler.
Schmunzeln, shmŭn'tseln, vi. to smirk, simper.
Schmutz, shmŭts, m. filth, dirt; **-buchstabe**, -bŭchzhtabe, m. -ns. pl. -n, pick. **Schmutzen**, shmŭt'sen, vi. to soil. **Schmutzfarbe**, -farbe, f. drab-color, dull, dark color; dirt-color. **Schmutzfink**, -fink, m. -en, pl. -en, dirty fellow. **Schmutzfleck**, -fleck, m. pl. -e, stain, soil. **Schmutzig**, shmŭts'ich, a. dirty, filthy, unclean. **Schmutzlappen**, -lappen, m. clout, wiper, rag. **Schmutzpapier**, -papīr, n. pl. -e, waste paper.
Schnabel, shnä'bel, m. bill, beak, nib; mouth, nozzle. **Schnäbelei**, shnäbelī', f. kissing, caressing. **Schnäbeln**, shnä'beln, vt. to bill, coo, caress. **Schnabelschiff**, shnä'belshiff, n. pl. -e, beaked ship. **Schnabelschuhe**, -shŭ-e, f. beaked or Chinese shoes. **Schnabelspitze**, -zhpitse, f. tip of a bill. **Schnabelthier**, -tīr, n. pl. -e, ornithorhynchus.
Schnake, shnä'ke, f. gnat; drollery.
Schnakisch, shnä'kish, a. droll.
Schnalle, shnal'le, f. buckle. **Schnallen**, shnal'len, vt. to buckle, strap. **Schnallenschuh**, -shŭ, m. pl. -e, shoe with buckles.
Schnalzen, shnal'tsen, vi. to smack, clack, snap, pop.
Schnapp, shnapp, shnapps, ĭj. snap! smack! m. smack, snap. **Schnappen**, shnap'pen, vi. to snap, seize. **Schnapps**, shnaps, m. pl. -e, snapping.
Schnapps, shnaps, m. pl. **Schnäpse**, brandy, whisky, dram, grog.
Schnappsbude, shnaps'bŭde, f. grog-shop.
Schnappsen, shnapp'sen, vi. to drink whisky, brandy. **Schnappsflasche**, -flashe, f. whisky-bottle.
Schnarchen, shnarr'chen, vi. to snore.
Schnarre, shnar're, f. rattle. **Schnarren**, shnar'ren, vi. to rattle, jar, creak, grate.
Schnatterhaft, shnat'terhaft, a. chattering. **Schnattern**, shnat'tern, vi. to cackle, quack; to chatter.
Schnauben, shnŏy'ben (schnob, geschnoben), vi. to snort, puff, pant, blow.
Schnaue, shnäu'e, f. snow (Mar.).
Schnaufen, shnŏy'fen, vi. to pant, breathe hard.

Schnausegel, shnäu'sēgel, n. try-sail
Schnauzbart, shnŏyts'bärt, m. pl. -bärte, mustache.
Schnauze, shnŏyt'se, f. snout, muzzle, spout, mouth, beak.
Schnauzen, shnŏy'tsen, vi. so snarl at, to snort.
Schnäuzen, shnĕll'tsen, vt. to snuff (a candle); to wipe, blow (one's nose).
Schnecke, shnĕck'e, f. snail; voluta. **Schneckenförmig**, förmich, a. spiral, conchyloid. **Schneckengang**, -gang, m. pl. -gänge, snail's pace. **Schneckenhaus**, -hŏys, n. pl. -bäuser, snail-shell. **Schneckenhorn**, -horn, n. pl. -hörner, feeler, tentackle, antenna. **Schneckenlinie**, -līnī-e, f. spiral, conchoid. **Schneckenpost**, -pozht, f. snail-coach. **Schneckentreppe**, -treppe, f. spiral staircase.
Schnee, shnä, m. snow. **Schneeball**, shnä'ball, m. pl. -bälle, snow-ball. **Schneeblind**, -blint, a. snow-blind. **Schneeflocke**, -flocke, f. snow-flake. **Schneegans**, -gans, f. pl. -gänse, snow-goose. **Schneegestöber**, -gezhtöhber, n. snow-storm. **Schneeglöckchen**, glöckchen, n. snow-drop. **Schneehuhn**, -hŭn, n. pl. -hübner, white grouse; white ptarmigan. **Schneeicht**, -icht, **Schneeig**, -ich, a. snowy. **Schneekönig**, -kömch, m. pl. -e, wren. **Schneelawine**, -lavīne, f. avalanche. **Schneelinie**, -līnī-e, f. limit of snow; snow-line. **Schneemann**, -mann, m. pl. -männer, man of snow. **Schneeschuh**, -shŭ, m. pl. -e, snow-shoe. **Schneeweiss**, -vēiss, a. snow-white, snowy.
Schneide, shnēi'de, f. edge, cutting side; energy, sharpness.
Schneidebank, shnēi'debank, f. pl. -bänke, cooper's bench.
Schneidemühle, shnēi'demühle, f. saw-mill.
Schneiden, shnēi'den (schnitt, geschnitten), vt. to cut, to saw; to mow; penetrate; castrate, geld; **Gesichter —**, to make faces.
Schneider, shnēi'der, m. cutter; tailor. **Schneiderarbeit**, -arbēit, f. tailor's work. **Schneiderei**, -ēi', f. tailor's trade. **Schneidergeselle**, -geselle, m. -n, pl. -n, tailor's journeyman **Schneiderhandwerk**, -hantverk, n. tailor's trade. **Schneidermuskel**, -myskel, f. tailor's muscle, sartorius.

Schneidern, shnei'dern, vi. to tailor.
Schneiderrechnung, -rĕchnung, f. tailor's bill. **Schneiderschere**, -shē-re, f. tailor's shears. **Schneiderseele**, -sēle, f. coward. **Schneiderzunft**, -tsunft, f. guild of tailors.
Schneidestichel, shnei'dezhtichel, m. sharp graver. **Schneidezahn**, -tsān, m. cutter, incisor. **Schneidewerkzeug**, -vĕrktsēilg, n. **Schneidezeug**, -tsēilg, n. edged tool.
Schneidig, shnei'dich, a. cutting, edged; soft (rock).
Schneien, shnei'en, vi. to snow; vt. to shower.
Schnell, shnĕll, a. swift, fast, quick, rapid, fleet, brisk. **Schnelle**, shnĕl'le, f. swiftness, rapidity.
Schnellen, shnĕl'len, vi. to fly, spring, snap; vt. to jerk, snap, let fly; to fillip; to cheat.
Schneller, shnĕl'ter, m. spring; jerk, fillip; trigger.
Schnellfüßig, shnĕll'füssich, a. swift-footed.
Schnellkraft, shnĕll'kraft, f. elasticity, springiness.
Schnellpresse, shnĕll'presse, f. steam-press, fast printing-press.
Schnellschreibekunst, shnĕll'shreibe-kunzht, f. short-hand writing, stenography. **Schnellschreiber**, -shreiber, m. short-hand writer, stenographer.
Schnellschritt, shnĕll'shritt, m. quick-step.
Schnepfe, shnĕp'fe, f. snipe, wood-cock. **Schnepfendreck**, -drĕck, m. snipe's excrement. **Schnepfenjagd**, -yacht, f. snipe-shooting. **Schnepfenzug**, -tsug, m. pl. -züge, flock of snipes.
Schnickschnack, shnick'shnack, m. tittle-tattle, prattle.
Schnieben, shni'ben (schnob, geschnoben), to blow, breathe, snuff.
Schniegeln, shnī'geln, vt. to trim up, trick out, up.
Schnipp, **Schnippchen**, shnips, m. pl. -e, snap. **Schnippchen**, shnip'chen, n. snap, small piece. **Schnippen**, vt. to snap. **Schnippisch**, shnip'pish, a. snappish, curt, flippant.
Schnitt, shnitt. m. pl. -e, cut, cutting, mowing; pruning; cutting edge. **Schnitte**, shnit'te, f. slice, chop, cut. **Schnitter**, shnit'ter, m. reaper, mower.

Schnitthandel, shnitt'handel, m. dry goods trade. **Schnitthändler**, -hent ler, m. dry-goods merchant.
Schnittlauch, shnitt'läuch, m. cives, chives.
Schnittkohl, shnitt'kōl, m. cabbage-sprouts.
Schnittlinie, shnitt'līnī-e, f. secant.
Schnittwaare, shnitt'väre, f. dry goods.
Schnittweise, shnitt'veīse, f. in slices.
Schnittwunde, shnitt'vunde, cut, gash.
Schnitz, shnits, m. pl. -e, cut, slice, chip, piece. **Schnitzarbeit**, -arbäet, f. carving in wood, etc. **Schnitzeln**, shnit'seln, vt. i. to carve, cut.
Schnitzen, shnit'sen, vt. to carve, cut.
Schnitzer, shnit'ser, m. carver, cutter; blunder, mistake. **Schnitzern**, shnit'sern, vi. to make mistakes, to blunder. **Schnitzkunst**, -kunzht, f. art of carving. **Schnitzwerk**, -vĕrk, n. pl. -e, carving, carved work.
Schnob, shnōb, I'rt. v. schnieben.
Schnöde, shnöh'de, a. scornful, contemptuous, offensive, injurious.
Schnödigkeit, shnöh'dichkēet, f. contemptuousness, indignity.
Schnobern, shnop'pern, vi. to sniff, scent, snuffle.
Schnörkel, shnör'kel, m. scroll, flourish. **Schnörkeln**, shnör'keln, vi. to flourish; to adorn with scrolls.
Schnüffeln, shnüf'feln, vi. to snuff, snuffle, scent.
Schnüffelventil, shnüf'felfentīl, n. pl. -e, snifting-valve.
Schnupfen, shnup'fen, vi. to snuff; to take snuff; m. cold, catarrh.
Schnupfer, shnup'fer, m. snuff-taker.
Schnupftaback, shnupf'taback, snuff. **Schnupftabacksdose**, -dōse, f. snuff-box.
Schnupftuch, shnupf'tuch, n. pl. -tücher, (pocket) handkerchief.
Schnuppe, shnup'pe, f. snuff (of a candle).
Schnur, shnur, f. pl. -en, daughter-in-law.
Schnur, shnur, f. pl. **Schnüre**, cord, string, line; lace. **Schnürband**, -bant, n. pl. -bänder, stay-lace, lace.
Schnürbrust, -brụzht, f. pl. -brüste, stay, bodice. **Schnüren**, shnü'ren, vt. to lace, string; to tie; to pack up; sich —, to wear stays. **Schnurgerade**, shnur'gerāde, a. straight

(as a bee line). **Schnürleib**, shnür'-
leīb, n. pl. -er, corset, bodice.
Schnürloch, shnür'loḥ, n. pl. -löcher,
eyelet-hole. **Schnürnadel**, -nädel,
f. bodkin. **Schnürnestel**, -nestel,
Schnürstift, -zhtift, m. tag.
Schnurrbart, shnurr'bärt, m. pl. -bär-
te, mustache. **Schnurrbartig**, -bär-
tiḥ, a. mustachioed.
Schnurre, shnur're, f. rattle; drollery,
joke.
Schnurren, shnur'ren vi. to buzz,
whizz, hum; to pur.
Schnurriemen, shnühr'rīmen, m.
strap.
Schnurrig, shnur'riḥ, a. droll, funny.
Schnurrpfeiferei, -pfēifĕrēī', f. trifle,
bauble, trash.
Schnurstracks, shnur'zhtracks, av.
straight, directly.
Schnürung, shnühr'ung, f. lacing,
tying up.
Schob, shōb, Prt. v. schieben.
Schober, shō'ber, m. rick, stack, heap,
pile.
Schock, shock, n. pl. -e, heap, pile, lot;
three score.
Schofel, shō'fel, a. mean, paltry; s. m.
trash.
Schöffe, shöf'fe, m. -n, pl. -n, justice,
judge, assessor.
Schokolade, shokolā'de, f. chocolate.
Schokoladentafel, -täfel, f. cake of
chocolate.
Scholar, sholār', m. -s, pl. -en,
scholar.
Scholle, shol'le, f. clod; lump; sod.
Schollern, shol'lern, rt. to fall down
(of clods); to crumble. **Schollig**,
shol'liḥ, a. cloddy.
Schon, shōn, av. already; in time;
— der Name, the bare name; — der
Gedanke, the very idea; Cj. although,
even if.
Schön, shöhn, a. beautiful, fine, fair,
handsome; das schöne Geschlecht, the
fair sex: schöne Künste, liberal arts,
belles-lettres. **Schöne**, shöh'ne, n.
the beautiful; f. the fair one, beauty. **Schönen**, shöh'nen, vt. to refine, clarify; vi. to beautify; vi. to
seem fair.
Schonen, shō'nen, vt. to spare, save,
screen, economize; to take care of.
Schoner, shō'ner, m. schooner.
Schöngeist, shöhn'gīszht, m. wit, bel-
esprit.

Schönheit, shöhn'hīēt, f. good looks
beauty.
Schönschreibekunst, shōn'shrēībĕkunst,
f. calligraphy.
Schonung, shōn'ung, f. care, management, indulgence, forbearance,
mercy. **Schonungslos**, -lōs, a. un-
sparing, relentless.
Schoos, shōs, m. womb; lap; flap,
tail (of a coat); die Hände in den —
legen, to sit with hands folded, to
idle. **Schooshund**, -hunt, m. pl. -e,
(dim. **Schooshündchen**,) lap-dog.
Schooskind, shōs'kint, n. pl. -er, darling, pet.
Schopf, shopf, m. pl. Schöpfe, m. top,
tuft, lock, hair, crest.
Schöpfbrunnen, shöpf'brunnen, m.
draw-well. **Schöpfeimer**, -ēīmer,
m. well-bucket.
Schöpfen, shöp'fen, vt. to draw, scoop,
bale; to leak; to create, make,
form; Athem —, to draw in breath,
to breathe; Argwohn —, to conceive
suspicion.
Schöpfer, shöp'fer, m. drawer, scooper;
creator, former, maker. **Schöpfe-
risch**, -ish, a. creative, creating.
Schöpflöffel, shöpf'löffel, m. ladle.
Schöpfrad, shöpf'räd, n. pl. -räder
scoop-wheel.
Schöpfung, shöpf'ung, creation, work.
Schöppe, shöp'pe, m. -n, pl. -n, justice,
alderman.
Schoppen, shop'pen, m. pint.
Schöps, shöps, m. -en, pl. -en, wether;
dunce. **Schöpsenbraten**, -brāten,
m. roast mutton. **Schöpsenfleisch**,
-flēīsh, n. mutton. **Schöpsenkeule**,
-kēūle, f. **Schöpfenschlagel**, -shlā-
gel, m. leg of mutton.
Schor, shōr, Prt. v. scheren.
Schore, shō're, f. spade; stays, up-
rights (of a ship).
Schoren, shō'ren, vi. to dig (with a
spade).
Schorf, shorf, m. pl. -e, scurf, scab.
Schorfig, shorf'iḥ, a. scurfy, mangy,
scabby.
Schornstein, shorn'zhtāēn, m. chimney. **Schornsteinfeger**, -fēger, m.
chimney-sweep.
Schoss, shōss, Prt. v. schiessen.
Schoss, shoss, m. pl. -e, shoot, sprout,
scot, tax. **Schossbar**, a. taxable.
Schossen, shos'sen, vi. to shoot up; to
pay scot.

Scho 285 **Schr**

Schoßfrei, shoss'frēī, a. scot-free.
Schoßkelle, shoss'kĕlle, f. boot (of a coach).
Schößling, shüss'ling. m. pl. -e, shoot, scion, sprout. **Schoßreis,** shoss'reīs, n. pl. -er, twig, scion, shoot.
Schote, shō'te, f. pod, cod, shell, sheath. **Schotenerbsen,** -ĕrpsen, s. pl. green peas, peas in the shell.
Schothorn, shot'horn, n. pl. -hörner, clue of a sail.
Schraffiren, shraffī'ren. vt. to hatch.
Schräg, shräg. **Schräge,** shrä'ge, a. oblique, slanting, inclined, sloping.
Schräge, f. obliquity, slope.
Schragen, shrä'gen, m. trestle, stool, horse, crane, shambles; sick-bed.
Schrägen, shrä'gen, vt. to slant, slope, bevel; vi. to slope. **Schragmaß,** -mäs, n. bevel.
Schralen, shrä'len. vi. to scant.
Schramme, shram'me, f. scratch, scar, cut. **Schrammig,** shram'mich, a. scarred.
Schrank, shrank, m. pl. **Schränke,** cupboard; press, chest, cabinet, closet.
Schranke, shran'ke, f. bar, barrier, rail, fence; limit, boundary; pl. lists.
Schrankeisen, shrenk'ēīsen, n. saw-set, saw-wrest.
Schränken, shren'ken, vt. i. to cross, lay across; to incline; to set a saw; to wind.
Schrankenlos, shran'kenlōs, a. boundless, illimitable.
Schranne, shran'ne, f. bar, barrier; corn-exchange.
Schranze, shran'tse, f. courtier.
Schraube, shröy'be, f. screw. **Schrauben,** shröy'ben, vt. i. to screw.
Schraubenbohrer, shröy'benbōrer, m. screw-tap. **Schraubenbolzen,** -boltsen, m. screw-bolt. **Schraubendampfer,** -dampfer, m. -propeller, screw-steamer. **Schraubendreher,** -drē-er, m. winch, turn-screw. **Schraubenförmig,** -förmich, a. spiral, cochleated. **Schraubengang,** -gang, m. pl. -gänge, screw-worm. **Schraubenlinie,** -līnī-e, f. spiral line, helix. **Schraubenmutter,** -mutter, f. pl. -mütter, nut, female screw. **Schraubenzieher,** -tsī-er, m. screw-driver.
Schraubstock, shröyb'zhtock, m. pl. -stöcke, vice.

Schreck, shrĕck, m. pl. -e. **Schrecken,** shrĕck'en, m. fright. terror, fear, horror; in **Schrecken setzen,** to frighten.
Schreckbild, shrĕck'bilt, n. pl. -er, fright, bugbear.
Schrecken, shrĕck'en, vt. to frighten, terrify, intimidate. scare; vi. (Prt. schra Pp. geschrocken,) to start, to be startled; to chill.
Schreckensbild, shrĕck'ensbilt, n. picture of fright, image of horror.
Schreckensbotschaft, shrĕck'ensbŏtshaft f. terrible news.
Schreckensherrschaft, shrĕck'enshĕrrshaft, f. terrorism, reign of terror.
Schreckhaft, shrĕck'haft, a. timid, fearful, skittish; terrible, appalling.
Schrecklich, shrĕck'lich, a. terrible, horrible, dreadful, atrocious; av. -ly; very.
Schrecknis, shrĕck'nīss, n. dread, fright, dismay, terror.
Schreckschuß, shrĕck'shuss, m. pl. -schüsse. alarm-shot.
Schrei, shrēī, m. scream, shriek, cry.
Schreibart, shrēīb'ärt, f. style; spelling. **Schreibbuch,** -buch, n. pl. -bücher, copy-book.
Schreiben, shrēī'ben (schrieb, geschrieben), vt. to write, pen; to compose; ins **Reine —,** to copy; sich —. to write one's name; s. n. writing, letter.
Schreiber, shrēī'ber, m. writer, clerk, secretary; copyist. **Schreiberei,** -ēī', f. writing; scribbling. **Schreibfeder,** -fēder. f. quill, pen. **Schreibfehler,** -fēler, m. mistake in spelling. **Schreibgebühren,** -gebühren, s. pl. writing-fees. **Schreibkunst,** -kunst, f. art of writing: penmanship. **Schreiblustig,** -luzhtich, **Schreibselig,** -sēlich, a. fond of writing. **Schreibmaterialien,** -materiālien, s. pl. writing-materials, stationery. **Schreibpapier,** -papīr, n. writing-paper. **Schreibschule,** -shūle, f. writing-school. **Schreibstube,** -zhtybe, f. writing-office. **Schreibtafel,** -tāfel, f. slate. **Schreibtisch,** -tish, m. pl. -e. desk. **Schreibweise,** -vēīse, f. spelling, orthography, style. **Schreibzeug,** -tsēüg, n. pl. -e, ink-stand.
Schreien, shrēī'en (schrie, geschrieen), vt to cry, shout, scream, shriek.

Schreier, shrēī'er, m. Schreihals, -hals, m. pl. -hälse, cryer, squaller, brawler.
Schrein, shrēēn, m. pl. -e, shrine, chest.
Schreiner, shrēēn'er, m. joiner, cabinet-maker. Schrein'ergeselle, -gesęllę, m. -n, pl. -n, journeyman-joiner. Schrei'nerhandwerk, -hantvĕrk, n. trade of a joiner.
Schreiten, shrēī'ten (schritt, geschritten), vi. to stride, stalk, step, walk; — zu, to proceed to.
Schrift, shrift, f. writing, book, paper; types, letter; scripture, bible.
Schrifterklärung, shrift'ĕrklärŭng, f. exegesis.
Schriftgelehrter, shrift'gęlĕrter, m. scribe.
Schriftgießer, shrift'gīser, m. type or letter-founder. Schriftgießerei, -gīsĕrāī', f. type-foundry.
Schriftkasten, shrift'kasten, m. pl. -kästen, letter-case.
Schriftkegel, shrift'kāgęl, m. body of a letter.
Schriftlich, shrift'liсh, a. u. av. in writing; by writing, written.
Schriftmäßig, shrift'mässiсh, a. scriptural.
Schriftsprache, shrift'zhprächę, f. written language.
Schriftsetzer, shrift'sętser, m. compositor, (typogr.).
Schriftstelle, shrift'zhtęllę, f. passage (in a book).
Schriftsteller, shrift'zhtęller, m. author, writer. Schriftstellerei, -lerāī', f. writing of books. Schriftstellerin, -lerin, f. pl. -nen, authoress. Schriftstellerisch, -ish, a. literary. Schriftstellern, -zhtellern, vi. to follow literary pursuits; to make books.
Schriftstempel, shrift'zhtempel, m. punch for letter-founders.
Schriftung, shrift'tsŭng, n. pl. -züge, character.
Schrill, shrill, a. shrill. Schrillen, shrill'len, vi. to (sound) shrill.
Schritt, shritt, m. pl. -e, step, stride, pace: Schritt für Schritt, Schrittweise, step by step; Schritt halten, to keep step with.
Schrobel, shrō'bel, f. fine card.
Schrobeln, shrō'beln, vi. to card (the second time).

Schroff, shroff, a. precipitous, steep, rough, rugged; gruff, harsh.
Schroffe, shroff'ę, f. Schroff'heit, -hāĕt, f. steepness, ruggedness; gruffness, harshness.
Schröpfeisen, shröpf'ēīsen, n. scarifier.
Schröpfen, shröpf'en, vt. to cup, scarify. Schröpfkopf, shröpf'kopf, m. pl. -köpfe, cupping-glass.
Schrot, shröt, n. pl. -e, slice, cut; log; small shot; groats: due weight of a coin; langrel (Mar.). Schrot'beutel, shröt'bēūtel, m. shot-pouch, groats-holder. Schrot'eisen, -ēīsen, m. chisel. Schroten, shrō'ten, vt. to cut, bruise, grind; to roll.
Schröter, shröb'ter, m. cutter; porter; stag-beetle.
Schrothobel, shröt'hōbel, m. jack-plane. Schrotkasten, -kazhten, m. bran-chest. Schrotmehl, -mĕl, n. corn-flour. Schrotmühle, -mühlę, f. crippling-mill. Schrotsäge, -säge, f. crosscut-saw. Schrotseil, -sēīl, n. pl. -e, Schrottau, -tāū, n. pl. -e, par buckle.
Schrubben, shrŭb'ben, vt. to scrub; to plane. Schrubber, shrŭb'ber, m. scrubbing-brush.
Schrumpeln, shrŭm'peln, vi. to shrivel.
Schrumpfen, shrŭmpf'en, vi. to wrinkle, shrivel, shrink. Schrumpfig, shrŭmpf'iсh, a. shrivelled, wrinkled.
Schrunde, shrŭn'dę, f. chap, scratch; flaw; crevice. Schrunden, shrŭn'den, vi. to chap, crack.
Schub, shŭb, m. pl. Schübe, shove, push; bowl; batch; hollow floor (Mar.); einen — thun. to bowl; to cut the tooth. Schub'fenster, -fenster, n. sash-window. Schub'karren, -karren. m. wheelbarrow. Schub'lade, -lādę, f. drawer. Schub'weise, -vēīsę, av. by shoves.
Schüchtern, shüсh'tern, a. timid, shy, coy; -heit, -hāĕt, f. timidity, shyness.
Schucken, shŭck'en, vt. to shove, push.
Schuft, shŭft, m. rascal, scoundrel, scamp. Schuftig, shŭf'tiсh, a. mean, vile, rascally, base; -keit, -kāĕt, f. rascality, meanness.
Schuh, shŭ, m. pl. -e, shoe; foot; nose of the lancet; socket. Schuh'bürste, -bŭrzhtę, f. shoe-brush. Schuh'flicker, -flicker, m. cobbler. Schuh'macher, -macher, m. shoemaker.

Schuhputzer, shu'pŭtser, *m.* bootblack. **Schuhriemen,** shu'rīmen, *m.* shoe-latchet. **Schuhschnalle,** -schnalle, *f.* shoe-buckle. **Schuhschwärze,** shu'shvertse, *f.* shoe-blacking. **Schuhsohle,** -sōle, *f.* shoe-sole. **Schuhzwecke,** -tsvĕcke, *f.* shoe-tack.

Schuhu, shu'hu, *m. pl.* -e, great horned owl.

Schulamt, shul'amt, *n. pl.* -ämter, school-board; employment at a school. **Schul'anstalt,** -anzhtalt, *f.* institution, school, academy. **Schul'aufseher,** -oufsē-er, *m.* school-inspector. **Schul'buch,** -buch, *n. pl.* -bücher, school-book.

Schuld, shult, *f.* guilt; fault; debt: — haben, — sein, to be in fault; die — schieben auf, to throw the blame upon.

Schuldbewußt, shult'bevusst, *a.* conscience-struck. **Schuld'brief,** -brīf, *m. pl.* -e. bond. **Schuld'buch,** -buch, *n. pl.* -bücher, account-book, debt-book.

Schulden, shul'den, *vt.* to owe. **Schul'dentilgungskasse,** -tilkungskasse, *f.* sinking-fund. **Schuldforderung,** shuld'forderung, *f.* demand, claim. **Schuld'frei,** -frī, *a.* free of guilt; free of debts.

Schuldig, shul'dich, *a.* guilty (of); in fault; culpable; due, indebted: etwas — sein, to owe. **Schuldiger,** shul'dicher, *m.* debtor, trespasser. **Schul'digkeit,** -kēt, *f.* duty, obligation; debt. **Schuld'los,** -lōs, *a.* guiltless, innocent: **-igkeit,** -ichkēt, *f.* innocence. **Schuldner,** shuld'ner, *m.* debtor. **Schuld'posten,** -posten, *m.* item (of debt); debt. **Schuld'register,** -register, *m.* register of debt. **Schuld'schein,** -shēn, *m. pl.* -e. bond, note of hand. **Schuld'thurm,** -tyrm, *m. pl.* -thürme, debtors' prison. **Schuldverschreibung,** shuld'fershrēibung, *f.* bond, note of hand.

Schule, shu'le, *f.* school; school-house: hohe —, university; academy; in die — gehen, to go to school; hinter die — gehen, to play truant; **Schule halten,** to keep school.

Schulen, shu'len, *vt.* to school, teach; to discipline: to break in, train.

Schüler, shü'ler, *m.* pupil, school-boy; disciple. **Schü'lerhaft,** -haft, **Schü'lermäßig,** -mässich, *a.* bungling, imperfect, like a school-boy.

Schulfreundschaft, shul'frūintshaft, *F.* school-friendship. **Schul'fuchs,** -fux, *pl.* -füchse. pedant. **Schul'füchserei,** -füxerēī, *f.* pedantry. **Schul'geld,** shul'gĕlt, *n. pl.* -er, school-money **Schul'gelehrsamkeit,** -gelērsamkēt, *f.* school-learning, classical learning. **Schul'gelehrter,** -gelērter, *m.* (classical) scholar. **Schul'gerecht,** -gerĕcht, *a.* regular, correct; trained. **Schul'haus,** -hōus, *n. pl.* -häuser, school-house. **Schul'jahr,** -yār, *n. pl.* -e, school-year. **Schul'jugend,** -yugent. *f.* school-boys and school-girls. **Schullehrer,** shul'lērer, *m.* schoolmaster, school-teacher.

Schulmann, shul'man, *m.* pedagogue. **Schul'mädchen,** -mēdchen. *n.* school-girl. **Schul'meister,** -mēzhter, *m.* schoolmaster. **Schul'meistern,** *vt.* to teach, tutor: to censure pedantically. **Schul'ordnung,** -ortnung, *f.* school-discipline. **Schul'prüfung,** -prüfung, *f.* examination. **Schul'rath,** -rāt, *m. pl.* -räthe, board of public instruction; school-commissioner. **Schul'sack,** -sack, *m. pl.* -säcke, school-boy's satchel; school-learning. **Schul'stube,** -zhtube, *f.* school-room. **Schul'stunde,** -zhtunde, *f.* school-hour.

Schulter, shul'ter. *f.* shoulder: **-blatt,** -blatt, *n. pl.* -blätter, shoulder-blade. **Schultern,** shul'tern, *vt.* to shoulder; **Schultert's Gewehr!** shoulder arms! **Schultheiß,** shult'hāess, *m.* mayor, chief magistrate.

Schulunterricht, shul'unterricht, *m.* education.

Schulvorsteher, shul'forshtā-er, *m.* principal (of a school).

Schulweisheit, shul'vēis-hēt, *f.* scholastic philosophy.

Schulwesen, shul'vēsen, *n.* public instruction; education.

Schulze, shul'tse, *m.* mayor, chief magistrate.

Schulzeit, shul'tsēīt, *f.* school-time.

Schulzucht, shul'tsucht, *f.* school-discipline.

Schund, shunt, *m.* refuse, rubbish, trash: filth. **Schund'fe(g)er,** -fēger, *m.* night-man. **Schund'grube,** -grube, *f.* sink.

Schuppe, shŭp'pe, f. scale.
Schüppe, shŭp'pe, f. spade, shovel, scoop.
Schuppen, shŭp'pen, m. shed, coach-house.
Schuppen, shŭp'pen, vt. to scale, unscale; to scratch. **Schuppenlos**, -lōs, a. scaleless, alepidote.
Schuppenthier, shŭp'pentīr, n. pl. -e, armadillo.
Schuppig, shŭp'pich, a. scaly, squamous.
Schur, shŭr, f. pl. -en, shearing, cropping (of cloth).
Schürbaum, shür'bȧum, m. pl. -bäume, poker, stirring-pole. **Schür'eisen**, -eīsen, n. poker. **Schüren**, shüh'ren, vt. to poke, stir, rake; to light. **Schürer**, shüh'rer, m. fireman, stoker.
Schurf, shurf, m. scurf; cut; drain, burrow (Min.).
Schürfen, shür'fen, vt. to scratch; to burrow (Min.).
Schürhaken, shühr'hāken, m. poker.
Schurigeln, shur'īgeln, vt. to worry, plague, annoy.
Schurke, shŭr'ke, m. -n, pl. -n, scoundrel, rascal, villain. **Schur'fenstreich**, -zhträëch, m. pl. -e, villany. **Schurkerei**, -reī', f. villany, roguery, rascality. **Schurkisch**, shŭrk'ish, a. roguish, knavish, rascally, mean.
Schürloch, shühr'loch, n. pl. -löcher, working hole.
Schurwolle, shŭr'volle, f. fleece-wool.
Schurz, shŭrts, m. pl. **Schürze**, apron; mantle (of a chimney). **Schürze**, shürt'se, f. (woman's) apron.
Schürzen, shür'tsen, vt. to tie; tuck up. **Schurzfell**, shŭrts'fěll, n. pl. -e, leather-apron.
Schusselig, shŭs'selich, a. bustling.
Schuss, shŭss, m. pl. **Schüsse**, shot; flow, rushing; batch.
Schüssel, shüs'sel, f. dish, platter, bowl.
Schussfertig, shŭss'fertich, a. ready for shooting. **Schussfest**, -fest, a. bullet-proof, shot-proof. **Schussloch**, -loch, n. pl. -löcher, shot-hole, loop-hole. **Schussweite**, shŭss'veīte, f. range. **Schusswunde**, -vŭnde, f. gunshot wound.
Schuster, shŭs'ter, m. cobbler, shoemaker. **Schusterahle**, -āle, f. awl. **Schusterei**, -reī' f. shoemaking,

cobbling. **Schustergesell**, -gesell, m. -en, pl. -en, journeyman-shoemaker.
Schusterkneif, -knīf, n. pl. -e, shoeknife, paring-knife. **Schusterladen**, -lāden, m. shoe-store. **Schustern**, shŭs'tern, vi. to make shoes, to cobble. **Schusterpfriem**, -pfrīm, m. pl. -e, f. punch. **Schusterschwärze**, -shvertse, f. shoemaker's ink. **Schusterzwecke**, -tsvěcke, f. tack, hob-nail.
Schutt, shŭtt, m. mound; rubbish, refuse.
Schüttboden, shütt'bōden, m. cornloft, granary. **Schütte**, shüt'te, f. bundle of straws; heap.
Schütteln, shüt'teln, vt. to shake, toss, wag, agitate; aus dem Ärmel —, to extemporize, to have at one's command.
Schütten, shüt'ten, vt. to pour, shed.
Schüttern, shüt'tern, vt. i. to shake, quake, shiver, tremble.
Schutz, shŭts, m. pl. **Schütze**, protection, shelter, defence; sluice, floodgate.
Schutzblattern, shŭts'blattern, s. pl. cow-pox.
Schutzbret, shŭts'brět, n. pl. -er, water board, wicket (in a flood-gate).
Schutzbrief, shŭts'brīf, m. pl. -e, letter of safe-conduct, safeguard.
Schutzbündniss, shŭts'büntniss, n. pl. -e, defensive alliance.
Schütze, shüt'se, m. shooter, sharpshooter, rifleman, archer, bowman; shuttle.
Schützen, shüt'sen, vt. to protect, defend, shelter, guard; to dam, shut; to stop.
Schutzengel, shŭts'eng-el, m. guardian angel.
Schützengesellschaft, shüt'sengesellshaft, f. band of sharpshooters.
Schutzgatter, shŭts'gatter, n. portcullis. **Schutzgeist**, -gēisht, m. pl. -er, guardian-genius. **Schutzgeleite**, -gelāite, n. escort, safe-conduct. **Schutzgott**, shŭts'gott, m. pl. -götter, tutelar divinity. **Schutzheiliger**, -hāiliger, m. patron saint, patron. **Schutzheilige**, f. patroness. **Schutzherr**, shŭts'hěrr, m. -n, pl. -n, patron, guardian. **Schützling**, shüts'ling, m. pl. -e, protégé, client. **Schutzlos**, -lōs, a. defenceless, unprotected; **Schutzlosigkeit**, -ichkāit, f. defenceless

Schu 289 **Schw**

ness. **Schutz'mittel,** -mittel, n. preventive. **Schutz'patron,** -patron, m. pl. -e, -in, f. pl. -innen, patron, patroness. **Schutz'pocken,** -pocken, f. cow-pox. **Schutzrede,** shuts'rāde, f. **Schutz'schrift,** -shrift, f. vindication, apology. **Schutz'waffe,** -vaffe, f. safeguard. **Schutz'waffe,** -vaffe, f. armor, defensive arms. **Schutz'wehr,** shuts'vār, f. bulwark, shelter, defence.

Schwabacher, shva'bacher, f. German Italics.

Schwabbelig, shvab'belich, a. shaky, quivering. **Schwabbeln,** shvab'beln, vi. to shake, quiver.

Schwach, shvach, a. weak, slender, feeble, flimsy, infirm. **Schwäche,** shvēch'e, f. weakness, feebleness; swoon. **Schwächen,** vt. to weaken, enfeeble; impair, unnerve; to deflour, debauch. **Schwachheit,** shvach'hāēt, f. weakness, feebleness, infirmity. **Schwach'herzig,** -hērtsich, a. faint-hearted. **Schwach'kopf,** -kopf, m. pl. -köpfe, simpleton. **Schwächlich,** shvēch'lich, a. weakly, sickly, delicate; -keit, -kāēt, f. feebleness, sickness; delicacy. **Schwäch'ling,** -ling, m. pl. -e, sickly, weakly fellow: irresolute character. **Schwachsichtig,** shvach'sichtich, a. weak-eyed. **Schwach'sinnig,** -sinnich, a. weak-minded. **Schwächung,** shvēch'ung, f. weakening, impairing, imbecility; defloration.

Schwaden, shvā'den, m. swath.

Schwaden, shvā'den, m. damp; steam.

Schwadron, shvadrōn', f. squadron, troop; -iren, -ï'ren, vt. to swagger, brag.

Schwäger, shvā'ger, m. pl. Schwäger, brother-in-law. **Schwägerin,** shvā'gerin, f. pl. -en, sister-in-law.

Schwägerschaft, shvā'gershaft, f. affinity. **Schwäher,** shvā'er, m. father-in-law.

Schwalbe, shval'be, f. swallow.

Schwalbenschwanz, shval'benshvants, m. pl. -schwänze, swallow-tail, dovetail; mit -en zusammenfügen, to dovetail.

Schwalch, shvalch, **Schwalg,** m. pl. -e. **Schwall,** shvall, m. wave, billow; throng.

Schwamm, shvam, m. pl. Schwämme sponge; mushroom, fungus.

Schwammicht, shvam'micht, **Schwammig,** a. fungous, spongy, soft.

Schwanen, shvä'nen, vi. to forebode, to have a presentiment.

Schwan, shvän, m. pl. Schwäne, swan.

Schwanenhals, shvä'nenhals, m. pl. -hälse, neck as white as a swan.

Schwa'nengesang, -gesang, m. pl. -gesänge, swan's song, dying strains.

Schwa'nenkiel, -kīl, m. pl. -e, swan's quill.

Schwang, shvang, m. swing; im — e sein, to be in vogue, in full operation.

Schwanger, shvang'er, a. pregnant, in the family way, big; — sein, — gehen, to be with child; — gehen mit, to meditate, to be hatching.

Schwängern, shvēng'ern, vt. to impregnate; to saturate. **Schwangerschaft,** shvang'-ershaft, f. pregnancy. **Schwängerung,** shvēng'-erung, f. impregnation.

Schwank, shvank, a. pliable, slender, bending.

Schwank, shvank, m. pl. Schwänke, drollery, merry story, joke, prank.

Schwanken, shvan'ken, vi. to stagger, reel, waver, hesitate, fluctuate.

Schwankend, shvan'kent, a. bending, fluctuating, wavering, uncertain, ambiguous.

Schwanz, shvants, m. pl. Schwänze, tail; train, end. **Schwanz'bein,** -bāēn, n. coccyx.

Schwänzeln, shvēn'tseln, vi. to wag the tail, to fawn; to mince.

Schwänzen, shvēn'tsen, vt. to mince, walk affectedly; to shirk (school).

Schwanzlos, shvants'lōs, a. tailless.

Schwanz'riemen, -rīmen, m. crupper. **Schwanz'säge,** -sāge, f. whipsaw; hand-saw. **Schwanz'stern,** -zhtērn, m. pl. -e, comet.

Schwapp, shvapp, **Schwapps,** ij. crack! slap!

Schwär, shvär, m. pl. -e, **Schwä'ren,** m. ulcer, boil, carbuncle.

Schwären, shvä'ren (schwor, geschworen), vi. to suppurate; s. m. suppuration.

Schwarm, shvarm, m. pl. Schwärme, swarm. **Schwärmen,** shvēr'men, vi. to swarm; to revel, carouse; to be a dreamer, enthusiast. **Schwärmer,** shvēr'mer, m. fire-cracker; moth; reveller; dreamer, enthusiast.

Schwärmerei, shvẹrmerāī', *f.* dreaminess, enthusiasm, fanaticism.
Schwärmerisch, shvẹr'merish, *a.* dreamy, enthusiastic, fanatic. **Schwärmzeit**, shvẹrm'tsēĭt, *f.* swarming-time.
Schwarte, shvar'tẹ, *f.* rind, skin, hide; slab; sward. **Schwartig**, shvar'tich, *a.* having a rind, skinny.
Schwarz, shvarts, *a.* black, dark; dirty; foul; wicked: sad; *s. n.* black, blackness; — auf Weiß, black and white, printed, written.
Schwarzamsel, shvarts'amsel, *f.* blackbird.
Schwarzäugig, shvarts'äugig, *a.* black-eyed.
Schwarzbart, shvarts'bārt, *m. pl.* -bärte. black-beard.
Schwarzblau, shvarts'blāy, *m.* black-blue.
Schwarzblei, shvarts'blēĭ, *n.* black-lead.
Schwarzblütig, shvarts'blühtich, *a.* bilious.
Schwarzbraun, shvarts'brāun, *a.* dark brown, brownish black.
Schwarzbrod, shvarts'brōt, *n.* brown bread, rye-bread.
Schwarzdorn, shvarts'dorn, *m. pl.* -en, black-thorn.
Schwarze, shvar'tsẹ, *m.* -n, *pl.* -n, black, negro.
Schwärze, shvẹr'tsẹ, *f.* blackness, blacking, black ink.
Schwärzen, shvẹr'tsen, *vt.* to blacken, black.
Schwarzgelb, shvarts'gelp, *a.* tawny.
Schwarzgrau, shvarts'grāu, *a.* dark-grey.
Schwarzgrün, shvarts'grün, *a.* dark-green.
Schwarzhaarig, shvarts'hārich, *a.* black-haired.
Schwarzkünstler, shvarts'künstler, *m.* necromancer, magician.
Schwarzkupfererz, shvarts'kupferärts, *n.* black copper ore.
Schwärzlich, shvẹrts'lich, *a.* blackish.
Schwarztanne, shvarts'tannẹ, *f.* black pine.
Schwarzwald, shvarts'valt, *m.* black forest, pine forest.
Schwarzwild, shvarts'vilt, *n.* wild boar, black-game.
Schwarzwurzel, shvarts'vurtsel, *f.* oyster-plant, salsify.

Schwatzen, shvat'sen, *vi.* to chat, talk, gossip.
Schwätzer, shvẹt'ser, *m.* -in, *f.* prattler, tattler, talker. **Schwätzerei**, -rēī', *f.* talking, babbling.
Schwatzhaft, shvats'haft, *a.* talkative, loquacious; -igkeit, -ichkēĭt, *f.* talkativeness, loquacity.
Schwebe, shvē'bẹ, *f.* suspense.
Schweben, shvē'ben, *vi.* to hover, flit; to impend; to be pending, undecided; in Gefahr —, to be in danger.
Schwefel, shvē'fel, *m.* sulphur, brimstone. **Schwefeläther**, -āter, *m.* sulphuric ether. **Schwefelblumen**, -blumen, *s. pl.* flower of sulphur. **Schwefeldampf**, -damf, *m. pl.* -dämpfe, sulphurous smoke or fumes. **Schwefelfarbig**, -farbich, **Schwefelgelb**, -gelp, *a.* brimstone-colored. **Schwefelhaltig**, *a.* sulphureous. **Schwefelhölzchen**, -höltschen, match. **Schwefelicht**, -icht, *a.* sulphurous; -e Säure, sulphurous acid. **Schwefelig**, shvē'felich, *a.* sulphury.
Schwefelkies, shvē'felkīs, *m. pl.* -e, pyrites. **Schwefelleber**, -lēber, *f.* liver of sulphur, sulphurated potash. **Schwefelmilch**, -milch, *f.* precipitated sulphur, milk of sulphur. **Schwefeln**, shvē'feln, *vt.* to smoke with sulphur, to match. **Schwefelsauer**, -sōu-er, *a.* sulphate. **Schwefelsäure**, -sēure, *f.* sulphuric acid. **Schwefelwasser**, -vasser, *n.* sulphur-water. **Schwefelwasserstoffgas**, -vasserzhtoffgās, *n.* sulphureted hydrogen.
Schweien, shvēĭ'en, *vi.* to swing (Mar.).
Schweif, shvēĭf, *m. pl.* -e, tail, train.
Schweifen, shvēĭ'fen, *vi.* to ramble, rove; *vt.* to warp; to furnish with a tail; to curve.
Schweifriemen, shvēĭf'rīmen, *m.* crupper.
Schweifung, shvēĭf'ung, *f.* curve, curving.
Schweigegeld, shvēī'gegelt, *n. pl.* -er, hush-money.
Schweigen, shvēī'gen (schwieg, geschwiegen), *vi.* to be silent, to keep silence; to hush; *s. n.* silence, stillness; — auferlegen, to impose silence; zum — bringen, to silence; to dismount.

Schweigsam, shvālg'sam, *a.* silent, taciturn; *-keit*, -kāet, *f.* taciturnity.
Schweimeln, shvāē'meln, *vi.* to be dizzy.
Schwein, shvān, *n. pl.* -e, hog, swine, pig. **Schwei'nebraten**, -braten, *m.* roast pork. **Schwei'nefett**, -fett, *n.* lard. **Schwei'nefleisch**, -flāesh, *n.* pork. **Schweinerei**, -rā', *f.* nastiness, filthiness, hoggishness.
Schweinhund, shvān'hunt, *m. pl.* -e, filthy dog. **Schwein'igel**, -Igel, *m.* porcupine. urchin; filthy, hoggish fellow. **Schweinigrlei**, -lā', *f.* hoggishness, obscenity. **Schwein'isch**, -ish, *a.* hoggish, filthy. **Schweins'leber**, -lēder, *n.* hog-leather.
Schweinftall, shvān'zhtāl, *m. pl.* ftälle, pig-sty. **Schwein'wildbrät**, -viltprēt, *n.* wild-boar-meat.
Schweiß, shvāēss, *m.* perspiration, sweat; moisture; blood: hard labor.
Schweißen, shvāēs'sen, *vi.* to bleed.
Schweißen, shvāēs'sen, *vt.* to weld, to forge together.
Schweißfuchs, shvāēss'fux, *m.* -es, *pl.* -füchse, bright bay, sorrel horse.
Schweißloch, shvāēss'loch, *n. pl.* -löcher, pore.
Schweißofen, shvāēss'ōfen, *m. pl.* -öfen, reheating-furnace, balling-furnace.
Schweißtropfen, shvāēss'tropfen, *m.* drop of sweat.
Schweißtuch, shvāēss'tuch, *n. pl.* -tücher, handkerchief.
Schweizerei, shvāītserā', *f.* dairy.
Schwelen, shvē'len, *vi.* to smoulder, to burn slowly.
Schwelgen, shvēl'gen, *vi.* to revel, carouse.
Schwelger, shvēl'ger, *m.* reveller, sot.
Schwelgerisch, -gērish, *a.* revelling, luxurious.
Schwelken, shvēl'ken, *vt.* to half-dry; *vi.* to wither.
Schwelle, shvēl'le, *f.* threshold; sill; ground-joist, raising-plate, sleeper.
Schwellen, shvēl'len, *vt.* to swell, raise, distend; *vi.* (schwoll, geschwollen,) to swell, rise, heave.
Schwemme, shvem'me, *f.* horse-pond.
Schwemmen, shvem'men, *vt.* to water, wash; to float.
Schwenden, shven'den, *vt.* to burn (new ground).

Schwengel, shveng'el, *m.* clapper, pendulum; handle; sweep (of a well). **Schweng'elbrunnen**, -brunnen, *m.* well with a sweep.
Schwengelruhe, shveng'elyr, *f.* pendulum clock.
Schwenken, shven'ken, *vt.* to swing, brandish, wave; to shake, rinse; to turn around; to wheel. **Schwenk'ung**, -ung, *f.* wheeling; flourishing.
Schwer, shvēr, *a.* heavy, weighty, ponderous; hard, difficult; severe; schwerer Athem, short breath.
Schwere, shvē're, *f.* heaviness, weight, gravity.
Schwerfällig, shvēr'fellich, *a.* heavy, clumsy; *-keit*, -kāet, *f.* heaviness, clumsiness.
Schwerhörig, shvēr'höhrich, *a.* hard of hearing.
Schwerkraft, shvēr'kraft, *f.* gravitation, force of gravity.
Schwerlich, shvēr'lich, *a.* scarcely, hardly.
Schwermuth, shvēr'mut, *f.* heaviness of heart, melancholy, the blues. **Schwer'müthig**, -mühtich, *a.* melancholy, sad, *ar.* -ly, despondingly.
Schwerpunkt, shvēr'punkt, *m. pl.* -e, centre of gravity.
Schwerspath, shvēr'zhpāt, *m.* heavy spar, barytes.
Schwerstein, shvēr'zhtāen, *m.* tungsten; säure, -säūre, *f.* tungstic acid.
Schwert, shvērt, *n. pl.* -er, sword.
Schwertfisch, shvērt'fish, *m. pl.* -e sword-fish.
Schwertlilie, shvērt'lili-e, *f.* sweet-flag.
Schwertschlag, shvērt'shläg, *m. pl.* -schläge, **Schwert'streich**, -zhträch, *m. pl.* -e, sword-cut; ohne — wegnehmen, to take without striking a blow.
Schwester, shves'ter, *f.* sister; nun; -lich, -lich, *a.* sisterly. **Schwe'sterliebe**, -lībe, *f.* sisterly love.
Schwibbogen, shvib'bōgen, **Schwieb'bogen**, *m.* arch, vault.
Schwieger, shvī'ger, *f.* mother-in-law. **Schwie'gereltern**, -eltern, *f.* father- and mother-in-law. **Schwie'germutter**, -mytter, *f.* mother-in-law. **Schwie'gersohn**, -sōn, *m. pl.* -söhne son-in-law. **Schwie'gertochter**, -tochter, *f. pl.* -töchter, daughter-in-law.

Schwiegervater, shvī'gerfāter, m. pl. -väter, father-in-law.
Schwiele, shvī'lę, f. weal, callosity, wale, streak. **Schwielig,** shvī'lich, a. horny, callous, hard.
Schwiemschlag, shvīm'shläg, m. im — liegen, to lie in the wind's eye.
Schwierig, shvī'rich, a. difficult, hard, difficile; **-keit, -kāet,** f. difficulty.
Schwichten, shvik'ten, vt. to snake two ropes together; to worm.
Schwilbe, shvil'bę, f. dead lode.
Schwimmblase, shvim'bläse, f. airbladder; swimming-bladder.
Schwimmen, shvim'men (schwamm, geschwommen), vi. to swim.
Schwimmer, shvim'mer, m. swimmer.
Schwimmfuß, shvim'fyss, m. pl. -füße, web-foot. **Schwimmhaut, -hout,** f. pl. -häute, web. **Schwimmkunst, -kunzht,** f. art of swimming.
Schwimmschule, -shu-lę, Schwimms' anstalt, -änzhtalt, f. swimmingschool.
Schwind, shvint, m. atrophy; pining away. **Schwinde,** shvin'dę, f. tetter.
Schwindel, shvin'del, m. vertigo, giddiness, dizziness. **Schwindelei, -ēl',** f. swindling, swindle.
Schwindeln, shvin'deln, vi. to whirl around, to turn; to grow giddy, dizzy, to reel.
Schwindelnd, shvin'delnt, a. dizzy.
Schwinden, shvin'den (schwand, geschwunden), vi. to vanish, disappear; to wither, shrivel; to diminish; — lassen, to resign, give up, abate.
Schwindler, shvint'ler, m. swindler, sharper.
Schwindlicht, shvind'licht, **Schwind' lig,** a. giddy, dizzy.
Schwindsucht, shvint'sucht, f. consumption, phthisis. **Schwindsüchtig, -sichtich,** a. consumptive.
Schwinge, shving'-ę, f. pinion, wing; beetle, swingle. **Schwingebrett, -brēt,** n. pl. -er, swingle, hempbrake.
Schwingel, s' ving'el, m. fescue-grass.
Schwingen, shving'-en (schwang, geschwungen), vi. to swing, vibrate, oscillate; to soar; vt. to brandish, shake, whirl; to winnow.
Schwingung, shving'yng, f. vibration, oscillation.

Schwirbeln, shvirr'beln, vi. to grow dizzy; vt. to make dizzy.
Schwirren, shvirr'en, vi. to whir, whizz; to sing.
Schwitzbad, shvits'bäd, n. pl. -bäter, steam-bath, sweating-room.
Schwitzen, shvit'sen, vi. to perspire, sweat; vt. to sweat.
Schwöbegrube, shvöh'degrubę, f. limepit.
Schwoll, shvoll, Prt. v. schwellen.
Schwören, shvöh'ren (Prt. schwor, schwur, geschworen). vi. to swear, to take an oath; vt. to swear, pledge, plight.
Schwül, shvühl, a. sultry, oppressive, sweltry. **Schwüle, -lę,** f. sultriness.
Schwulst, shvulst, f. swelling, tumor; bombast. **Schwülstig,** shvül'stich, a. bombastic, turgid, tumid, pompous; **-keit, -kāet,** f. pomposity, turgidity.
Schwung, shvyng, m. pl. **Schwünge** swing, vibration; vault, bound; flight, soaring; elevation, loftiness; impulse. **Schwungbrett, -brēt,** n. pl. -er, spring-board. **Schwungfeder, -fēder,** f. wing-feather, quill.
Schwunghaft, shvyng'haft, a. energetic, thriving, prosperous.
Schwungkraft, shvyng'kraft, a. centrifugal power. **Schwungrad, -rät,** n. pl. -räter, fly-wheel.
Schwur, shvyr, m. pl. **Schwüre,** oath; imprecation. **Schwurgericht, -gericht,** n. pl. -e, jury.
Scontro, skon'trō, f. balance.
Scorbut, skor'but, m. scurvy; **-isch, -ish,** a. scorbutic.
Secante, sękan'tę, f. secant.
Sech, sech, n. pl. -e, coulter. **Sechbolz, sech'holts,** n. pl. -hölzer, coulterbeam.
Sechs, sex, a. six. **Sechseck, -eck,** n. pl. -e, hexagon. **Sechseckig, -eckich,** a. hexagonal.
Sechser, sex'er, m. German coin (worth 4 cents).
Sechserlei, sex'erlāē, a. of six sorts or kinds. **Sechsfach, -fach,** a. sixfold, sextuple, auch **Sechsfältig, -feltich,** a. sixfold. **Sechsjährig, -yärich,** a. six years old. **Sechsmal, -mäl,** a. six times. **Sechspfünder, -pfünder,** m. six-pounder. **Sechsseitig, -sītich,** a. six-sided, hexagonal.

Sechsſpännig, sĕx'zhpennich, *a.* six-horse, drawn by six horses. **Sechs'ſtimmig**, -zhtĭmmich, *a.* for six voices. **Sechs'tägig**, -tägich, *a.* of six days.
Sechſt, sĕxt, *a.* sixth. **Sechſtehalb**, sĕxt'halp, *t.* five and a half.
Sechſtel, sĕx'tel, *n.* a sixth. **Sechſtens**, sĕx'tens, *av.* in the sixth place.
Sechzehn, sĕch'tsän, *a.* sixteen. **Sechs'zehnt**, -tsänt, *a.* sixteenth. **Sechs'zehntel**, -tsäntel, *n.* the sixteenth part. **Sechzig**, sĕch'tsich, *a.* sixty. **Sechziger**, sĕch'tsicher, *m.* sexagenarian. **Sechzigſt**, sĕch'tsixt, *a.* sixtieth. **Sechzigſtel**, sĕch'tsixtel, *n.* the sixtieth.

Seciren, setsī'ren, *vt.* to dissect.
Seckel, seck'el, *m.* purse; treasury; shekel.
Sector, sĕk'tor, *m.* -es, *pl.* -en, sector.
Sedez, sedäts', *n. pl.* -e, sedecimo.
See, sä, *m.* -s, *pl.* -n, lake.
See, sä, *f.* sea, ocean; in die — gehen, to go to sea, to stand out; die — halten, to keep out at sea. **See'anker**, -anker, *m.* sea-anchor. **See'bad**, -bäd, *n. pl.* -bäder, sea-bathing. **See'brief**, -brīf, *m. pl.* -e, sea-letter; ship's papers. **See'cadet**, -kadĕt, *m. pl.* -en, midshipman (middy). **See'dienſt**, -dĭnzht, *m. pl.* -e, naval service. **See'elephant**, -elefant, *m.* -en, *ol.* -en, sea-elephant. **See'fahrer**, -färer, *m.* navigator, mariner, seaman. **See'fahrt**, -fart, *f.* navigation, voyage. **See'fiſch**, -fĭsh. *m.* sea-fish, salt-water fish. **See'geſetz**, -gesets, *n. pl.* -e, maritime law; -buch, -bych, *n. pl.* -bücher, naval code. **See'gras**, -gräs, *n. pl.* -gräser, sea-weed. **See'hafen**, -häfen, *m. pl.* -häfen, seaport. **See'handel**, -handel, *m.* maritime commerce. **See'herrſchaft**, -hĕrrshaft, *f.* supremacy by sea. **See'hund**, -hunt, *m. pl.* -e, seal, sea-calf; -fell, -fĕll, *n. pl.* -e, seal-skin. **See'igel**, -īgel, *m.* sea-urchin; **Stein-** -zhtäen, *m. pl.* -e, echinite. **See'karte**, -karrte, *f.* sea-chart. **See'kennung**, -kennung, *f.* sea-mark. **See'krank**, -krank, *a.* sea-sick; -heit, -hät, *f.* sea-sickness. **See'krebs**, -kreps, *m. pl.* -e, lobster, sea-crab. **See'krieg**, -krĭg, *m. pl.* -e, maritime war. **Seeküſte**, sä'küzhte, *f.* sea-coast.

Seele, sā'le, *f.* soul, mind; man.
Seeleben, sä'lĕben, *n.* sea-life.
Seelenadel, sē'lenädel, *m.* nobility of soul. **See'lenamt**, -amt, *n. pl.* -ämter, requiem. **See'lenangſt**, -angzht, *f.* anguish of soul. **See'lengröße**, -gröse, *f.* greatness of soul. **See'lenlehre**, -lĕre, *f.* doctrine of the soul, psychology. **See'lenleiden**, -lēīden, *n.* anguish of soul, mental suffering. **See'lenlos**, -lōs, *a.* soulless, unfeeling. **See'lenluſt**, -lyzht, *f.* delight of the soul. **See'lenmeſſe**, -mĕsse, *f.* mass for the dead, requiem. **See'lenruhe**, -rye, *f.* peace, tranquillity of soul. **See'lenſchmerz**, -shmĕrts, *m. pl.* -en, anguish, grief of soul. **See'lenvoll**, -foll, *a.* full of soul, beaming with feeling, spiritual. **See'lenwanderung**, -vanderung, *f.* transmigration of souls, metempsychosis.

Seelöwe, sä'löhve, *m.* sea-lion.
Seelſorge, sēl'sorrge, *f.* curacy. **Seel'ſorger**, -sorrger, *m.* curate, minister.
Seemacht, sä'macht, *f.* maritime power, marine. **See'mann**, -mann, *m. pl.* **Seeleute**, seaman, mariner. **See'meile**, -mĕile, *f.* league. **See'neſſel**, -nessel, *f.* sea-nettle. **See'offizier**, -offitsīr. *m. pl.* -e, naval officer, marine officer. **See'otter**, -ŏtter, *m.* sea-otter. **See'pferd**, -pfĕrt, *n. pl.* -e, sea-horse. **See'räuber**, -räuber, *m.* pirate. **Seeräuberei**, -reī', *f.* piracy. **See'recht**, -rĕcht, *n. pl.* -e, naval law, maritime law. **See'reiſe**, -rīĕse, *f.* voyage. **See'ſalz**, -salts, *n.* sea-salt, bay-salt. **See'ſchaden**, -shäden, *m.* average. **See'ſchiff**, -shiff, *n. pl.* -e, sea-going vessel. **See'ſchlacht**, -shlacht, *f.* naval action, sea-fight. **See'ſchlange**, -shlange, *f.* sea-serpent, kraken. **See'ſoldat**, -soldät, *m. pl.* -en, marine. **See'ſprache**, -zhprache, *f.* sea-terms, seaman's language. **Seeſtaat**, sä'zhtät, *m. pl.* -en, maritime state. **See'ſtadt**, -zhtatt, *f. pl.* -ſtätte, maritime city. **See'ſturm**, -zhturm, *m. pl.* -ſtürme, storm at sea. **See'thier**, -tīr, *n. pl.* -en, marine animal. **See'ufer**, -yfer, *n.* sea-shore. **See'uhr**, -yr, *f.* chronometer. **See'ungeheuer**, -yngehöū-er, *n.* sea-monster. **See'wärts**, -vĕrts, *av.* out to

See 294 **Sei**

See, seaward. **See'waſſer,** -vaſſer, n. salt-water, brine. **See'weſen,** -vēsen, n. maritime affairs; marine. **See'wind,** -vĭnt, n. pl. -e, sea-breeze. **See'wolf,** -volf, m. pl. -wölfe, sea-wolf. **See'wörterbuch,** -vörterbŭch, n. pl. -bücher, nautical dictionary. **See'wurf,** -vŭrf, m. jetson.
Segel, sā'gel, n. sail; großes —, mainsail: unter Segel geben, to set sail. **Se'gelfertig,** -fĕrtĭch, a. ready to sail. **Se'gelmacher,** -mächer, m. sailmaker. **Segeln,** sē'geln, vi. to sail, set sail. **Se'gelſchiff,** -shĭff, n. pl. -e, sailing-vessel. **Segelſtange,** sā'gelzhtange, f. sail-yard. **Se'geltuch,** -tŭch, n. canvas (for sails), sail-cloth.
Segen, sā'gen, m. blessing, benediction; charm, spell. **Se'gensreich,** -rēĭch, **Se'gensvoll,** -foll, a. rich in blessings, blessing.
Segment, sĕkment', n. pl. -e, segment.
Segnen, sāg'nen, vt. to bless, to give the benediction: to make the sign of the cross. **Seg'nung,** -nŭng, f. blessing, benediction.
Sehen, sā'-en (sah. geſehen), vi. to see, perceive. **Sehenswerth,** sā'-ensvērt, a. worth seeing, curious.
Seher, sā'-er, m. seer, prophet; -in, f. prophetess.
Sehkraft, sā'-kraft, f. faculty of vision, sight.
Sehne, sān'e, f. sinew, nerve.
Sehnen, sān'en, vr. to long for, desire (ardently).
Sehnerv, sā'nĕrf, m. -en, pl. -en, optic nerve.
Sehnig, sān'ĭch, a. sinewy; stringy.
Sehnlich, sān'lĭch, a. longing, ardent, passionate, heartfelt, eager.
Sehnſucht, sēn'sŭcht, f. longing, ardent desire. **Sehn'ſüchtig,** -süchtĭch, a. yearning, longing, ardent, eager, av. -ly; auch **Sehn'ſuchtsvoll,** -foll, a. u. av.
Sehr, sēr, av. very, much.
Sehrohr, sē'rōr, n. pl. -röhre, telescope.
Seichen, sīch'en, vi. to piss.
Seicht, sēĭcht, a. shallow, flat, superficial; **-heit,** -hĕĭt, f. shallowness.
Seide, sēĭ'de, f. silk. **Seiden,** sēĭ'den, a. silken. **Sei'denarbeit,** -arbĕĭt, f. work in silk. **Sei'denarbeiter,** m.

worker in silk. **Sei'denfabrik,** -brĭk, f. silk-mill, silk-manufactory. **Sei'denfärber,** -fĕrber, m. dyer of silks. **Sei'denhandel,** -handel. m. silk-trade. **Sei'denhändler,** -hĕntler, m. dealer in silks, silk-mercer. **Sei'denpapier,** -papīr, n. tissue-paper. **Sei'denraupe,** -rŏŭpe, f. silkworm. **Sei'denſpinner,** -zhpinner m. silk-spinner. **Seidenſpitze,** sēĭ'denzhpitse, f. blonde, blond-lace. **Sei'denſticker,** -zhtĭcker, m. embroiderer in silk. **Sei'denwaare,** -vāre, f. silk goods. **Sei'denweber,** -vēber, m. silk-weaver. **Seidenweberei,** -ēĭ', f. silk-weaving. **Sei'denwickler,** -vickler, m. silk-reeler. **Sei'denzeug,** -tsĕŭg, m. pl. -e, silk stuff, silks. **Sei'denzucht,** -tsŭcht, f. culture of silk.
Seife, sēĭ'fe, f. soap; buddle (Mining). **Seifen,** sēĭ'fen, vt. to soap; to wash (ore), to buddle. **Sei'fenblaſe,** -blāse, f. soap-bubble. **Sei'fenerde,** -ĕrde, f. fuller's earth. **Sei'fenfabrik,** -fabrĭk, f. soap-factory. **Sei'fenpulver,** -pŭlfer, n. shaving-powder. **Sei'fenſieder,** -sīder. m. soap-boiler. **Seifenſiederei,** -ēĭ', f. soap-factory. **Sei'fenſtein,** -zhtĕĭn. m. pl. -e, soap-stone, steatite. **Sei'fenwaſſer,** -vasser, n. soap-suds.
Seige, sēĭ'ge, **Seihe,** sēĭ'-e, f. straining; colander, strainer, filter; dregs. **Seigen,** sēĭ'gen, **Seih'en,** vt. to strain, to filter. **Seiger,** sēĭ'cher, **Sei'her,** m. strainer, colander, sieve.
Seiger, sēĭ'ger, a. perpendicular.
Seigern, sēĭ'gern, vt. to refine. **Seigerofen,** sēĭ'gerōfen, m. refining furnace.
Seigerſchacht, sēĭ'gershacht, m. pl. -ſchächte, perpendicular shaft.
Seiſack, sēĭ'sack, m. pl. -ſäcke, filtering-bag.
Seil, sēĭl, n. pl. -e, cord, rope, line.
Seiler, sēĭl'er, m. rope-maker.
Seilerbahn, sēĭ'lerbān, f. rope-walk.
Seiltänzer, sēĭl'tĕntser, m. rope-dancer.
Seim, sēĭm, m. pl. -e, honey: mucilaginous fluid. **Seimen,** sēĭm'en, vt. to be mucilaginous; vt. to strain (honey). **Seim'honig,** -hōnĭch, m. strained honey. **Seimig,** sēĭm'ĭch, a. mucilaginous.

Sein, sṣön, *pron. adj.* his, its, of him, of it.

Sein, sṣön (*Prt.* war, gewesen), *vi.* to be, to exist; es sei, be it so; mag sein das sein? what does that mean? was ist Ihnen? what is the matter with you? ich bin es, it is I; *s. n.* being, existence.

Seinerseits, sṣön'erseits, *av.* as for him, for his part. Seinethalben, -halben, Sei'netwegen, -vēgen. Sei'netwillen, -villen, *av.* on his account.

Seinig, sṣön'ig, *a.* his, its; das Seinige, his own; his duty, one's duty; die Seinigen, his family, his relations.

Seisen, sēi'sen, *vt.* to lash, seize (Mar.).

Seit, sēit, *prep.* since. Seitab, sēit'ap, *av.* apart, aside. Seitdem, -dām, *av.* since.

Seite, sēi'te, *f.* side, flank; page; part, party; quarter; bei Seite, apart, aside; von meiner Seite, for my part, as for me: auf der einen Seite, on the one hand.

Seitenangriff, sēi'tenangriff, *m. pl.* -e, attack on the flank.

Seitenblick, sēi'tenblick, *m. pl.* -e, side-glance, leer.

Seitenerbe, sēi'tenerbe, *m.* -n, *pl.* -en, lateral heir.

Seitengasse, sēi'tengasse, *f.* by-street, lane, alley.

Seitengewehr, sēi'tengevār, *n. pl.* -e, side-arms.

Seitenhieb, sēi'tenhīb, *m. pl.* -e, side-cut.

Seitenlinie, sēi'tenlīni-e, *f.* collateral line.

Seitenstechen, sēi'tenzhtēhen, *n.* pleurisy.

Seitenstück, sēi'tenzhtück, *n. pl.* -e, side-piece.

Seitenthür, sēi'tentühr, *f.* side-door.

Seitenverwandter, sēi'tenfervanter, *m.* -dte, *f.* collateral relation.

Seitenweg, sēi'tenvēg, *m. pl.* -e, byway, by-path.

Seitenweh, sēi'tenvā, *n.* pain in the side.

Seither, sēit'hēr, *av.* since that time, since.

Seitwärts, sēit'vërts, *av.* sidewards, aside; Seitwärts gehen, to go aside.

Selb, selp, Selbander, se pan'der, Selbdritt, etc. together with one, two, etc.

Selber, sēl'ber, *pron.* same. Selbiger, sēl'biger, the same, that one.

Selbst, sēlpst, *pron.* self; ich selbst, I myself; *av.* even. Selbstachtung, -achtung, *f.* self-respect.

Selbstbefleckung, sēlps'befleckung, *f.* self-pollution, onanism.

Selbstbeherrschung, sēlpst'beherrshung, *f.* self-command.

Selbstbestimmung, sēlpst'bezhtimmung, *f.* self-determination; freewill.

Selbstbewusst, sēlpst'bevusst, *a.* conscious; — sein, consciousness.

Selbstdenker, sēlpst'denker, *m.* independent thinker.

Selbsteigen, sēlpst'eigen, *a.* one's own.

Selbsterhaltung, sēlpst'erhaltung, *f.* self-preservation.

Selbsterhebung, sēlpst'erhābung, *f.* self-exaltation.

Selbsterniedrigung, sēlpst'ernīdrigung, *f.* self-humiliation.

Selbstgefällig, sēlpst'gefellig, *a.* self-satisfied, self-complacent; conceited, *av.* -ly; -keit, -kāet, *f.* self-complacency.

Selbstgelehrter, sēlpst'gelērter, *m.* self-taught.

Selbstgefühl, sēlpst'gefühl, *n.* self-confidence, self-reliance.

Selbstgenügsam, sēlpst'genühksam, *a.* self-sufficient, self-satisfied.

Selbstgespräch, sēlpst'gezhpräch, *n.* monologue, soliloquy.

Selbstherrscher, sēlpst'herrsher, *m.* autocrat, absolute, sovereign.

Selbsthilfe, sēlpst'hil-fe, *f.* self-defense, lynch-law.

Selbstigkeit, sēlpst'ichkāet, *f.* egotism, selfishness. Selbstisch, -ish, *a.* selfish, egotistical.

Selbstlauter, sēlpst'lōuter, *m.* vowel.

Selbstliebe, sēlpst'lībe, *f.* self-love.

Selbstlob, sēlpst'lōb, *n.* self-praise, self-applause.

Selbstmord, sēlpst'mort, *m. pl.* -e, suicide. Selbstmörder, -mörder, *m.* suicide: -risch, -ish, *a.* suicidal.

Selbstprüfung, sēlpst'prühfung, *f.* self-examination.

Selbstrache, sēlpst räche, *f.* private vengeance.

Selbstregierung, sĕlpst'regīryng, *f.* self-government; absolute government.

Selbstruhm, sĕlpst'rum, *m.* self-applause, vainglory.

Selbständig, sĕlpst'zhtĕndich, *a.* independent; **-keit**, **-kāet**, *f.* independence.

Selbstsucht, sĕlpst'sucht, *f.* selfishness, egotism. **Selbstsüchtig, -süchtig**, *a.* selfish, egotistical. **Selbstsüchtler, -süchtler,** *m.* egotist.

Selbsttäuschung, sĕlpst'tŏushyng, *f.* self-delusion.

Selbstverachtung, sĕlpst'ferachtyng, *f.* self-contempt.

Selbstverläugnung, sĕlpst'ferläuknung, *f.* self-denial.

Selbstvertrauen, sĕlpst'fertrŏu-en, *n.* self-confidence, self-reliance, self-sufficiency.

Selbstzufriedenheit, sĕlpst'tsufrīdenhāet, self-complacency, self-satisfaction.

Selbstzweck, sĕlpst'tsvĕck, *m. pl.* **-e**, one's own aim *or* end.

Selen, selān', *n.* selenium. **Selensäure, -söure,** *f.* selenic acid.

Selenit, selenīt', *m.* selenite.

Selig, sā'lich, *a.* blessed, blissful, happy; deceased, late; **— sterben**, to die a Christian; **— sprechen**, to beatify. **Se'ligkeit**, **-kāet**, *f.* bliss, beatitude, blessed state, happiness. **Se'ligmachend, -machent**, *a.* beatific. **Se'ligmachung, -machyng**, *f.* salvation. **Se'ligsprechung, -zhprĕchyng**, *f.* beatification.

Sellerie, sĕl'lerī, *m.* celery.

Selten, sĕl'ten, *av.* seldom, rare, scarce; **-heit, -hāet,** *f.* rarity, scarcity, curiosity.

Seltsam, sĕlt'sam, *a.* strange, odd, singular; **-keit, -kāet,** *f.* oddity, strangeness, singularity.

Semester, semĕs'ter, *n.* term of six months.

Semikolon, semikō'lon, *n.* semicolon.

Seminar, seminār', *n. pl.* **-e**, seminary. **Seminarist**, seminarist', *m.* **-en**, *pl.* **-en**, seminarist.

Semmel, sĕm'mel, *m.* roll, wheat-bread. **Sem'melmehl, -mēl,** *n.* (fine) wheat-flour.

Senat, senāt', *m.* senate. **Senator, Sena'tor**, senā'tr, *m.* senator; **-isch, -ish,** *a.* senatorial.

Senden, sĕn'den (sandte, gesandt), *vt.* to send, dispatch, forward.

Sendschreiben, sĕnd'shrēīben, *n.* epistle, (circular) letter.

Sendung, sĕnd'yng, *f.* mission, transmission; consignment.

Senf, sĕnf, *m.* mustard. **Senf'korn, -korn,** *n.* mustard-seed. **Senf'pflaster, -pflazhter,** *n.* mustard-poultice.

Sengen, sĕng'-en, *vt.* to singe, burn; **— und brennen**, to lay waste with fire.

Senkblei, sĕnk'blēī, *n.* sounding-lead; plummet.

Senkel, sĕn'kel, *m.* shoe-lace; **-stift, -zhtift,** *n. pl.* **-e**, tag.

Senken, sĕn'ken, *vt.* to sink, lower, let down; plunge; to delve; to lay, make layers; **sich —**, to subside, settle, to slope.

Senker, sĕn'ker, *m.* layer.

Senkgrube, sĕnk'grube, *f.* sink-hole.

Senk'rebe, -rēbe, *f.* layer of a vine.

Senk'recht, -rĕcht, *a.* vertical, perpendicular; *av.* **-ly. Senk'schnur, -shnur,** *f. pl.* **-schnüre,** plumb-line.

Senkung, -yng, *f.* slope.

Senne, sĕn'ne, *m.* **-n,** *pl.* **-n**, Swiss herdsman. **Sennerei, -rēī',** *f.* Alpine pasture, dairy.

Sensal, sensāl', *m. pl.* **-e**, broker, agent, jobber.

Sense, sĕn'se, *f.* scythe. **Sen'senklinge, -klinge,** *f.* scythe-blade. **Sensenmann**, sĕn'senmaun, *m. pl.* **-männer**, scythe-bearer; mower; death. **Sen'senschmied, -shmīd,** *m. pl.* **-e**, scythe-smith. **Sen'senstein, -zhtāen,** *m. pl.* **-e**, whetstone, hone.

Sensibilität, sensībilitāt', *f.* sensibility.

Sensitiv, sensītīf', *a.* sensitive.

Sente, sĕn'te, *f.* ribband.

Sentenz, sentĕns', *f.* sentence.

Sentimental, sentimentāl', *a.* sentimental. **Sentimentalität, -talitāt',** *f.* sentimentality.

Sepia, sā'pīā, *f.* sepia.

September, septĕm'ber, *m.* September.

Sequester, sequĕs'ter, *m.* sequestrator. **Sequestriren, -trī'ren,** *vt.* to sequestrate.

Serail, serāēl', *m. pl.* **-e**, seraglio.

Seraph, sā'raf, *m. pl.* **-e**, seraph.

Serenade, serenā'de, *f.* serenade; **ein — bringen**, to serenade.

Ser 297 **Sie**

Sergeant, sĕrzhant', *m.* -en, *pl.* -en, sergeant.
Serie, sā'ri-e, *f.* series.
Serpent, sĕr'păn, *m. pl.* -e, serpent (Mus.).
Serpentin, sĕrpentīn', *m.* serpentine (Min.).
Service, sĕrvīs', *n.* service.
Serviette, sĕrvi-et'te, *f.* napkin.
Serviren, sĕrvī'ren, *vt.* to serve.
Servitut, sĕrvitṳt', *n. pl.* -en, compulsory service, obligation.
Sesam, sā'sam, *m.* sesam.
Sessel, sĕs'sel, *m.* chair; stool.
Seßhaft, sĕss'haft, *a.* residing, settled, stationary.
Session, sessiōn', *f.* session.
Setzbrett, sets'brĕt, *n. pl.* -er, composing board.
Setzei, sets'ẽe, *n. pl.* -er, poached egg.
Setzen, sets'en, *vt.* to set, place, put, lay, plant, raise, settle; compose; — über, to leap, pass over; sich —, to sit down; to perch; to settle, to sink: auseinander —, to explain; zur Wehr —, to resist, make resistance.
Setzer, sets'er, *m.* compositor. **Setz- kasten,** sets'kazhten, *m.* letter-case; settling-vat. **Setzkunst,** -kunzht, *f.* (art of) composition. **Setzling,** -ling, *m. pl.* -e, layer, plant, shoot, sprig, young tree; spawn; fry. **Setzreis,** sets'reīs, *n. pl.* -er, set, slip. **Setzschiff,** -shiff, *n.* galley, composing-board.
Seuche, sĕuch'e, *f.* epidemic, contagious disease.
Seufzen, sĕuf'tsen, *vi.* to sigh, groan.
Seufzer, -tser, *m.* sigh, groan.
Sextant, sĕxtant', *m.* -en, *pl.* -en, sextant.
Sexte, sĕx'te, *f.* sixth (Mus.).
Sextett, sĕxtett', *n. pl.* -e, sextet, sestetto, sestuor.
Shawl, shāl, *m. pl.* -e, shawl.
Sich, sich, *prn.* himself, herself, itself, one's self, themselves, each other.
Sichel, sich'el, *f.* sickle; crescent.
Sicher, sich'er, *a.* secure, safe, certain, sure; -heit, -hĕet, *f.* security, safety, surety, assurance. **Sicherheitsgeleite,** -geläete, *n.* safe conduct. **Sicherheitsklappe,** -klappe, *f.* **Sicherheitsventil,** -fentīl, *n. pl.* -e, safety-valve. **Sicherheitslampe,** -lampe, *f.* safety-lamp. **Sicherheitsschein,** sich'- erhāetsshāen, *m. pl.* -e, bond of security. **Sicherlich,** sich'erlich, *av.* surely, certainly. **Sichern,** sich'ern, *vt.* to secure, guarantee, assure.
Sicht, sicht, *f.* sight. **Sichtbar,** -bār, *a.* visible; *av.* -bly: -keit, -kāet, *f.* visibility, conspicuousness. **Sichtbarlich,** -lich, *av.* visibly.
Sichten, sich'ten, *vt.* to sift.
Sichtlich, sicht'lich, *a.* visible.
Sichtung, sicht'ṳng, *f.* sifting.
Sickern, sick'ern, *vt.* to ooze, trickle, drop; to leak.
Sie, sī, *pn.* she, her; they, them; ye, you.
Sieb, sīb, *n. pl.* -e, sieve. **Sieben,** *vt.* to sift, bolt.
Sieben, sīb'en, *a.* seven. **Siebeneck,** -eck, *n. pl.* -e, heptagon. **Siebenedig,** -eckich, *a.* heptagonal. **Siebenfach,** -fach, **Siebenfältig,** -fĕltich, *a.* sevenfold. **Siebengestirn,** -gezhtīrn, *n. pl.* -e, pleiades. **Siebenjährig,** -yārich, *a.* seven years old, septennial. **Siebenmal,** -māl, *av.* seven times. **Siebensachen,** -sachen, *s. pl.* bag and baggage. **Siebenschläfer,** -shlāfer, *m.* sluggard. **Siebent,** sīb'ent, *a.* seventh. **Siebentehalb,** -entehalp, *a.* six and a half. **Siebentel,** -entel, *n.* seventh (part). **Siebner,** (number) seven. **Siebnerlei,** -lĕy', *a.* of seven sorts, of seven kinds. **Siebzehn,** -tsān, *a.* seventeen. **Siebzehnt,** -tsānt, *a.* seventeenth. **Siebzehntel,** -tsāntel, *n.* seventeenth (part). **Siebzig,** -tsich, *a.* seventy. **Siebzigst,** -tsikst, *a.* seventieth.
Siech, sich, *a. av.* sick, sickly. **Siechbett,** -bett, *n.* sick-bed. **Siechen,** sich'en, *vi.* to be sickly, to languish. **Siechling,** -ling, *m. pl.* -e, sickly person. **Siechthum,** -tṳm, *n.* (prolonged) sickness, sickliness.
Siede, sī'de, *f.* boiling. **Sieden,** sī'den (sott. gesotten), *vt. i.* to seethe, boil, stew; to refine; to make (salt, soap, etc.). **Sieder,** sī'der, *m.* boiler. **Siederei,** -ĕy', *f.* boiling-house. **Siedheiß,** sīd'hāess, *a.* boiling hot.
Sieg, sīg, *m. pl.* -e, victory, triumph, conquest.
Siegel, sīg'el, *n.* seal. **Siegelbewahrer,** -bevārer, *m.* keeper of the seal. **Siegellack,** -lack, *n. pl.* -e, sealing-wax. **Siegeln,** sīg'eln, *vt.* to seal.

Sie 298 **Sim**

Sie'gelring, -ring, m. pl. -e, signet-ring. **Sie'gelstecher**, -ztechers, m. seal-engraver.
Siegen, si'gen, vi. to conquer, to get the victory.
Sieger, sīg'er, m. victor, conqueror.
Siegesbahn, sīg'esbān, f. career of victory. **Sieg'esbogen**, -bōgen, m. triumphal arch. **Sieg'esfeier**, -feī-er, f. celebration of victory. **Sie'gesgöttin**, -göttin, f. (goddess of) victory. **Sieg'esjubel**, -yūbel, m. shout of victory. **Sieg'eskranz**, -krants, m. pl. -kränze, crown of victory. **Sieg'eslauf**, -lāuf, m. career of victory. **Sieg'eslied**, -līd, n. pl. -er. triumphal song. **Sieg'espalme**, -palme, f. palm of victory. **Sieg'estaumel**, -tåumel, m. intoxication of victory. **Sie'geszeichen**, -tsīchen, n. trophy. **Sieg'reich**, -reīch, a. victorious, triumphant.
Siehe, sī'e, ij. behold! lo! see!
Sieke, sī'ke, f. ledge of sheet iron; seam (Mar.).
Siel, sīl, n. pl. -e, sluice.
Siel, sīl, n. pl. -e, harness.
Siesta, si-es'tä, f. noonday nap.
Signal, singnäl', n. pl. -e, signal, sign. **Signalisiren**, singnālisī'ren, vt. to signalize, signal. **Signiren**, singnī'ren, vt. to mark, sign.
Silbe, sil'be, f. syllable. **Sil'benmaß**, -mās, n. pl. -e, quantity (of a syllable). **Sil'benmessung**, -messung, f. prosody. **Sil'benrätsel**, -rętsel, n. charade.
Silber, sil'ber, n. silver; plate. **Sil'berarbeit**, -arbäet, f. silver-ware; silver-work. **Sil'berarbeiter**, -arbäeter, m. silversmith. **Sil'berbarren**, m. **Sil'berbarre**, -barre, f. bar of silver. **Sil'berbergwerk**, -bērkvērk, n. silver-mine. **Sil'berblatt**, -blatt, n. pl. -blätter, silver-leaf; silver-foil. **Sil'berblech**, -bléch, n. silver-leaf, silver in plates. **Sil'berbuche**, -bųche, f. white beech-tree. **Sil'berdraht**, -drāt, m. pl. -brähte, silver-wire. **Sil'berdruck**, -druck, m. pl. -e, silver-print. **Sil'bererz**, -ärts, n. silver-ore. **Sil'berfaden**, -fāden, m. pl. -fäden, silver-thread. **Sil'berfarbe**, -farbe, f. silver-color. **Sil'berfarbig**, -farbich, a. silver-colored. **Sil'berfuchs**, -fųx, m. pl. -fuchse. gray-fox. **Sil'bergeld**, -gēlt,

n. pl. -er, silver coin, money. **Sil'bergeräth**, -gerät, n. pl. -e, **Sil'bergeschirr**, -geshirr, n. pl. -e, silver-plate. **Sil'berglanz**, -glants, m. silvery brightness, lustre. **Sil'berglas**, -glās, n. pl. -gläser, **Sil'berglaserz**, -erts, n. vitreous silver ore, silver-glance. **Sil'bergrau**, -grā, a. silver-grey. **Sil'bergrube**, -grube, f. silver mine. **Sil'berhaar**, -hār, n. pl. -e, silvery hair. **Sil'berhaltig**, -haltich, a. argentiferous. **Sil'berhell**, -hell, a. silver-bright, silvery. **Sil'berkies**, -kīs, m. argentiferous pyrites. **Sil'berkönig**, -könich, m. pl. -e, silver regulus. **Sil'berlachs**, -lax, m. pl. -e, white trout. **Sil'berlicht**, -licht, n. silvery light. **Sil'bermine**, -mīne, f. silver mine. **Sil'bermünze**, -müntse, f. silver coin. **Silbern**, sil'bern, a. silvery, (made of) silver. **Sil'berpapier**, -papīr, n. silvered paper. **Sil'berpappel**, -pappel, f. white poplar. **Sil'berplatte**, -platte, f. silver-leaf, plate of silver. **Sil'berprobe**, -prōbe, f. trial, test of silver. **Sil'berquelle**, -quelle, f. silvery fountain. **Sil'berrein**, -rēn, a. pure as silver. **Sil'bersaite**, -sāte, f. silver string. **Sil'berschmied**, -shmīd, m. pl. -e, silversmith. **Sil'berschrank**, -shrank, m. pl. -schränke, buffet, closet for plate. **Sil'berstickerei**, -shtickere', f. embroidery in silver. **Sil'berstoff**, -shtoff, m. pl. -e, silver (brocade). **Sil'berstück**, -shtück, n. pl. -e, piece of silver; silver coin. **Sil'berton**, -tōn, m. pl. -töne, silvery sound. **Sil'bertresse**, -tresse, f. silver-lace. **Sil'berwaare**, -wāre, f. silver-plate. **Sil'berweiß**, -vīß, a. silver-white. **Sil'berzeug**, -tsåug, n. silver-plate.
Silge, sil'ge, f. marsh-parsley.
Silhouette, silyuett', f. profile; silhouette.
Silicat, silicāt', n. pl. -e, silicate.
Silicium, sili'tsium, n. silicon.
Similor, similōr', n. similor.
Simonie, simonī', f. simony.
Simpel, sim'pel, a. simple, plain; artless; stupid; s. simpleton.
Sims, sims, m. pl. -e, shelf, cornice. **Sims'hobel**, -hōbel, m. moulding-plane. **Sims'träger**, -träger, pl. atlantes. **Sims'werk**, n. moulding.

Sim   299   **Sit**

Simuliren, simulī'ren, *vt.* to simulate.
Singchor, sing'kōr, *m. pl.* -chöre, choir.
Sing'drossel, -drossel, *f.* song-thrush.
Singen, sing'en (sang, gesungen), *vi.* to sing, chant; nach Noten —, to sing from notes. **Singkunst,** sing'kunzht, *f.* art of singing. **Sing'lehrer,** -lērer, **Sing'meister,** -mīstzh-ter, *m.* singing-teacher. **Sing'vogel,** -fōgel, *m. pl.* -vögel, singing-bird. **Singweise,** sing'vēlse, *f.* air, melody.
Singular, sin'gulär, *m. pl.* -e, singular.
Sinken, sin'ken (sank, gesunken), *vi.* to sink; set; decrease; abate; in Ohnmacht —, to swoon; — lassen, to let down, to droop, lower; den Muth — lassen, to be discouraged.
Sinn, sinn, *m. pl.* -e, mind, sense, feeling, taste, perception: will, intention: opinion, meaning, import; im Sinne haben, to intend, to have a mind; in den Sinn kommen, to enter into one's mind; nicht bei Sinnen sein, to be out of one's wits.
Sinnbild, sinn'bilt, *n. pl.* -er, emblem, symbol; **-lich,** -lich, *a.* allegoric, symbolic.
Sinnen, sin'nen (sann, gesonnen), *vi.* to meditate, muse, speculate, reflect on, to think upon.
Sinnenlust, sin'nenlyst, *f. pl.* -lüste, sensual pleasure.
Sinnenrausch, sin'nenroush, **Sin'nentaumel,** -taumel, *m.* intoxication of one's senses.
Sinnentäuschung, sin'nentöushyng, *f.* delusion of the senses.
Sinnenwelt, sin'nenvelt, *f.* external world, world of sense.
Sinnenwerkzeug, sin'nenverktsöūg, *n. pl.* -e, organ of sense, sensorium.
Sinnesänderung, sin'nesenderyng, *f.* change of mind.
Sinnesart, sin'nesärt, *f.* temper, disposition.
Sinnig, sin'nich, *a.* thoughtful, musing, ingenious, sensible.
Sinnlich, sinn'lich, *a.* sensuous; sensitive; sensual; — wahrnehmbar, perceptible through the senses; **-keit,** -kĕet, *f.* sensuality; sensitive faculty.
Sinnlos, sinn'lōs, *a.* senseless. **Sinn'losigkeit,** sinn'lōsichkĕet, *f.* senselessness.

Sinnpflanze, sinn'pflantse, *f.* sensitive plant.
Sinnreich, sinn'rēich, *a.* ingenious, witty.
Sinnspruch, sinn'zhpruch, *m. pl.* -sprüche, maxim, sentiment.
Sinnverwandt, sinn'fervant, *a.* synonymous.
Sintemal, sin'temäl, *Cj.* whereas, since, seeing.
Sinter, sin'ter, *m.* iron-scales, dross; sinter (Min.).
Sinus, sī'nyus, *m.* sine; Sinus versus, vorsed sine.
Sipp, sipp, *m.* -en, *pl.* -e, **Sippe,** sip'pe, *f.* kinsman, relative. **Sippschaft,** -shaft, *f.* kin, kindred, relations.
Sirene, sirā'ne, *f.* siren.
Sirup, sī'ryp, *m.* syrup.
Sistiren, sistī'ren, *vt.* to inhibit, stop.
Sistir'ung, -yng, *f.* inhibition; stoppage.
Sitte, sit'te, *f.* custom, manner, usage. **Sit'tengesetz,** -gesets, *n.* moral law. **Sit'tenlehre,** -lēre, *f.* moral philosophy, ethics. **Sit'tenlehrer,** -lērer, *m.* moralist. **Sit'tenlos,** -lōs, *a.* immoral; **-igkeit,** -ichkĕet, immorality. **Sit'tenprediger,** -prädicher, *m.* moralizer. **Sit'tenrichter,** -richter, *m.* censor. **Sittenverderbniss,** sit'ten-ferderbniss, *n.* corruption of morals.
Sittig, sit'tich, *a.* modest, chaste.
Sittich, sit'tich, *m. pl.* -e, parrot.
Sittlich, sitt'lich, *a.* moral, *av.* -ly; **-keit,** -kĕet, *f.* morality.
Sittsam, sitt'sam, *a.* modest, discreet, decent; **-keit,** -kĕet, *f.* modesty.
Situation, situatsiōn', *f.* situation.
Sitz, sits, *m. pl.* -e, seat, chair, stool; residence.
Sitzen, sit'sen (saß, gesessen), *vi.* to sit; to fit; to stick fast, to be aground; to be imprisoned; — lassen, to abandon. **Sitzung,** -yng, *f.* sitting; session; assizes.
Skala, skä'lä, *f.* scale.
Skalde, skal'de, *m.* -n, *pl.* -n, scald, bard.
Skalpell, skalpĕll', *n. pl.* -e, scalpel.
Skalpiren, skalpī'ren, *vt.* to scalp.
Skandal, skandäl', *m. pl.* -e, scandal. **Skandalös,** -lōhs', *a.* scandalous.
Skelett, skelĕtt', *n. pl.* -e, skeleton.
Skepticismus, skeptitsīs'mus, *m.* scepticism.

Septiker, skĕp'tikĕr, m. sceptic.
Septisch, skĕp'tish, a. sceptic, av. -ally.
Skizze, skits'e, f. sketch. Skizziren, skittsī'ren, vt. to sketch.
Sklave, sklă'fe, m. -n, pl. -n, slave; zum Sklaven machen, to enslave, enthrall. Skla'venhandel, -handel, m. slave-trade. Sklaverei, -rēī', f. slavery. Sklavin, sklă'fĭn, f. (female) slave. Sklavisch, sklă'fish, a. slavish.
Skorbutisch, skorbyt'ish, a. scorbutic.
Skorpion, skorpiōn', m. scorpion.
Skrofel, skrŏff'el, f. scrofula.
Skrofulös, skrŏffʉlōhs', a. scrofulous.
Skrupel, skrup'el, a. scruple.
Skrupulös, skrupulōhs', a. scrupulous.
Smaragd, smarrakt', m. emerald.
Smaragden, smarrakt'en, a. (of) emerald, smaragdine.
So, sō, av. u. Cj. so, thus, if; pn. who; sowohl als auch, as well as, both.... and. Sobald, sobalt', cj. as soon as.
Sozial, sotsiäl', a. social, av. -ly.
Sozialist, sotsialist', m. -en, pl. -en, socialist.
Societät, sotsi-etät', f. society, company, partnership.
Socke, sock'e, f. sock; socle, pedestal (Arch.).
Sod, sōd, m. boiling, stew.
Soda, sō'dä. n. carbonate of soda.
Sodann, sodann', av. then, afterwards.
Sodbrennen, sōd'brennen, n. heartburn.
Sodomit, sodomīt', m. -en, pl. -en, sodomite. Sodomiterei, -miterēī', f. sodomy.
Sofa, ss'fä, n. sofa.
Sofern, sofĕrn', Cj. in as much as; in case, if.
Soff, sōf, Prt. v. Saufen, m. drinking.
Soffer, sŏf'fer, m. tippler, drunkard.
Sofort, sofort', av. forthwith, straight-way, right-away.
Sog, sōg. Prt. v. Saugen, m. pl. -e. sucking, sipping; (ship's) wake.
Sogar, sogär', av. even, moreover.
Sogen, sō'gen, vt. to drip, drain; to granulate, crystallize.
Sogleich, sō'glēich, av. immediately, instantly.
Sohle, sō'le, f. sole; sill; splint.
Sohlen, sō'len, vt. to sole.

Söhlig, söh'lich, a. horizontal, level.
Sohlleder, sōl'lĕder, n. sole-leather.
Sohn, sōn, m. pl. Söhne, son.
Söhnchen, sön'chen, n. little son.
Solch, solch, a. such. Solcherlei, -erlēi, a. of such a kind, such.
Sold, solt, m. pl. -e. pay, reward, hire.
Soldat, soldăt', m. -en, pl. -en, soldier.
Soldatenleben, -lĕben, n. military life. Soldatenrock, -rock, m. pl. -röcke, uniform-coat. Soldat'enstand, -ztant, m. the soldier's profession.
Soldateska, soldätess'kä, f. soldiery. Soldatisch, -ish, a. soldier-like.
Söldling, söld'ling, Söldner, söld'ner, m. mercenary, hireling.
Solid, solīd', a. solid, av. -ly; sterling; respectable.
Solidarisch, solidär'ish, a. bound for the whole.
Solidität, soliditat', f. solidity; integrity, respectability.
Sollen, sol'len, vt. to owe, to be to —, to be obliged; to be said to —; to be bound for —; ought, should.
Söller, söl'ler, m. balcony; platform.
Solo, sō'lo. n. solo.
Solvent, sol'fent, a. solvent, able to pay.
Solvenz, solfents', f. solvency.
Somit, sō'mĭt, ar. therefore.
Sommer, som'mer, m. summer.
Som'merabend, -abent, m. summer's evening. Som'meraufenthalt, -öufenthalt, m. Sommerwohnung, -vōnung, f. summer residence. Som'mersfleck, -fleck. m. freckle; sig.-ich, a. freckled. Som'merflur, -flyr, f. field with spring corn. Som'merfrucht, -frycht, f. summer fruit Som'merkartoffel, -kartoffel, f. early potato. Som'merlich, -lich, a. summer-like. Som'merwende, -vende, f. midsummer, summer solstice.
Sommerreise, som'merräese, f. summer tour. Som'merzeug, -tsäüg, n. summer-stuff.
Sonach, sō'näch, av. consequently, therefore.
Sonate, sonä'te, f. sonata.
Sonde, son'de, f. plummet, sounding lead; probe.
Sonder, son'der, a. seperate; pr. without; sinteresse, -interesse, n private interest.

Sonderbar, son'derbär, *a.* singular, strange, odd; **≠feit,** -käët, *f.* singularity, oddity.

Sonderlich, sond'erlich, *a. v.* particular, special; excessive, extraordinary; apart; very.

Sonderling, son'derling, *m.* strange, whimsical fellow.

Sondern, son'dern, *vt.* to separate, sever, disjoin, part; *av.* but.

Sonders, son'ders, *av.* separately; sammt und sonders, all and every one (of them).

Sonderung, sond'erung, *f.* separation.

Sondiren, sondī'ren, *vt.* to sound, fathom; probe.

Sonnabend, sonn'äbent. *m.* Saturday.

Sonne, son'ne, *f.* sun. **Sonnen,** *vt. i.* to sun; to air, bask, expose to the sun. **Sonnenaufgang,** -ŏufgang, *m.* sunrise. **Sonnenblick,** -blick, *m.* sunblink, glance of the sun. **Sonnenblume,** -blume, *f.* heliotrope. **Sonnenferne,** -ferne, *f.* aphelion. **Sonnenfinsterniß,** -finsterniss, *f.* solar eclipse. **Sonnenfleck,** -fleck, *m.* solar spot. **Sonnenjahr,** -yär, *n.* solar year. **Sonnenklar,** -klär, *a.* sun-bright, bright as the sun. **Sonnenlos,** -lōs, *a.* sunless. **Sonnennähe,** -nähe, *f.* perihelion. **Sonnenstaub,** -zhtŏub, *m.* atom. **Sonnenstich,** -zhtich, *m.* siriasis; — bekommen, to be sunstruck. **Sonnenstrahl,** -zhträl, *m.* sunbeam. **Sonnenuhr,** -ŭr, *f.* dial, sun-dial. **Sonnenuntergang,** -untergang, *m.* sunset. **Sonnenwendung,** son'nenvendung, *f.* solstice. **Sonnenzelt,** -tsëlt, *n.* awning.

Sonnett, sonnët', *n.* sonnet.

Sonnicht, son'nicht, **Sonnig,** *a.* sunny, sunlike.

Sonntag, sonn'täg, *m.* Sunday.

Sonntägig, sonn'tägich, *a.* dominical, Sunday.

Sonntagskind, sonn'tägskint, *n.* lucky or high-gifted person.

Sonntagsschule, sonn'tägsshule, *f.* Sunday-school.

Sonst, sonst, *av.* else, otherwise; formerly; besides, in other respects; — etwas, anything else; — wo, -vō, *av.* elsewhere; — nirgends, nowhere else; — woher, from so no other quarter, place.

Sanftig, sons'tich, *a.* former; existing besides.

Soole, sō'le, *f.* brine.

Sophist, sōphist', *m.* sophist; -erei, -erēī', *f.* sophistry.

Sopran, soprän', *m.* soprano, treble.

Sorge, sor'ge, *f.* care, sorrow; solicitude; — tragen, to take care.

Sorgen, sor'gen, *vi.* to care, take care; to provide for; to be afraid, apprehensive of. **Sorgenfrei,** -frēī, **Sorgenlos,** -lōs, *a.* free or exempt from care. **Sorgenstuhl,** -zhtyl, *m.* armchair, easy-chair. **Sorgenvoll,** -foll, *a.* anxious, uneasy, full of care.

Sorgfalt, sorg'falt, *f.* care, carefulness, solicitude. **Sorgfältig,** -fëltich, *a.* careful, -ly, *av.*

Sorglich, sorg'lich, *a.* anxious, uneasy, careful, critical, difficult.

Sorglos, sorg'lōs, *a.* careless, unconcerned, heedless, reckless; supine, negligent; **≠igfeit,** -ichkäët, *f.* recklessness, negligence, indolence.

Sorgsam, sorg'sam, *a.* careful, attentive, heedful: **≠feit,** -käët, *f.* carefulness, heedfulness.

Sorren, sor'ren, *vi.* to lash, moor, belay, seize. **Sorrfatt,** -katt, *f.* mooring. **Sorrflampe,** -klampe, *f.* hollow cleat. **Sorrtau,** sorr'täŭ, *n.* lashing.

Sorte, sor'te, *f.* sort, kind. **Sortiren,** sortī'ren, *vt.* to sort out, separate. **Sortirkasten,** -kazhten, *m.* sorting-chest. **Sortirsieb,** -sīb, *n.* separating sieve.

Souffleur, sufflör', *m.* prompter.

Souverän, suverän', *m.* sovereign. **Souveränität,** suveränetät', *f.* sovereignty.

Spähen, spä'hen, *vt. i.* to spy, espy; pry, explore. **Späher,** *m.* spy, scout.

Spalier, spalīr', *n.* (of trees) espalier; fence; lane.

Spalt, zhpalt, *m. pl.* **Spälte,** slit, split, cleft, chink, crack, fissure, crevice.

Spalte, zhpal'te, *f.* gap, cranny, split; column. **Spalten,** zhpal'ten, *n.* wedging.

Spalten, zhpal'ten, *vi.* to split, cleave, divide. **Spaltenweise,** -vēīse, *av.* in columns. **Spaltig,** zhpal'tich, *a.* chippy. **Spaltsäge,** -säge, *f.* long saw. **Spaltung,** -ung, *f.* splitting, rupture, disunion; schism.

Span, zhpän, *m. pl.* **Späne**, chip, splint, splinter, reglet.
Spanferkel, zhpän'ferkel, *n.* sucking-pig.
Spange, zhpang'e, *f.* buckle, bracelet, clasp.
Spanne, zhpan'ne, *f.* span. **Span'nen**, *vt.* to span, stretch, strain, bend. **Spanner**, zhpan'ner, *m.* tenter: bender. **Spann'kraft**, -kraft, *f.* elasticity.
Spannagelneu, zhpän'nägelneü, *a.* **Spannen**, zhpan'neü, *a.* spick and span new.
Spannsäge, zhpann'säge, *f.* frame-saw, tenon-saw, span-saw.
Spannstock, zhpann'zhtock, *m.* temple, templet.
Spanntau, zhpann'taü, *n.* painter.
Spannung, zhpann'ung, *f.* bending, spanning; tension; suspense.
Sparbüchse, zhpär'büxe, *f.* saving-box. **Spar'enbchen**, -endchen, *n.* save-all. **Sparen**, zhpä'ren, *vt. i.* to spare, save, reserve; to husband, economize.
Spargel, zhpar'gel, *m.* asparagus; -beet, -bét, *n.* asparagus-bed.
Spärlich, zhpär'lich, *a.* scanty, bare, meager, thin; -keit, -käet, *f.* scantiness.
Sparpfennig, zhpär'pfennich, *m.* spare-money, savings, *pl.*
Sparren, zhpar'ren, *m.* rafter, spar, sheer; einen — zu viel haben, to be crazy, to be a little cracked.
Sparrenkopf, zhpar'renkopf, *m.* modillion.
Sparrwerk, zhpärr'vérk, *n.* rafters.
Sparsam, zhpär'sam, *a.* sparing, saving, economical, parsimonious; -keit, -käet, *f.* parsimony, economy, savingness.
Spaß, zhpass, *m. pl.* **Späße**, joke, jest, sport. **Spaßen**, zhpa'sen, *vt.* to joke, jest, sport: mit sich — laßen, to take a joke. **Spaßhaft**, -haft, *a. av.* jocose, droll, sportful; funny; -igkeit, -ichkäet, *f.* sportfulness, sportiveness. **Spaßvogel**, -fogel, *m.* wag.
Spät, zhpät, *a. av.* late. **Späte**, zhpä'te, *f.* lateness. **Spät'estens**, -zhtens, *av.* at latest, farthest.
Spaten, zhpä'ten, *m.* spade.
Spath, zhpät, *m.* spar, siderite.
Spateisenstein, zhpät'äisenzhtäen, *m.*

spa.ry iron-ore. **Spatig**, zhpät'ich, *a.* sparry.
Spätjahr, zhpät'yär, *n.* autumn, fall.
Spatium, zhpä'tsium, *n. pl.* **Spatien**, space, space-line; — einsetzen, to space.
Spatz, zhpats, *m. pl.* -en. sparrow.
Spazieren, zhpatsī'ren, *vt.* to walk; — gehen, to take a walk. **Spazier=fahrt**, -fart, *f.* drive, ride, airing. **Spazier'gang**, -gang, *m.* walk. **Spazier'gänger**, -geng-er, *m.* promenader, walker. **Spazier'ritt**, -ritt, *m.* ride (for pleasure). **Spazier'rohr**, -rör, *n.* **Spazier'stock**, -zhtock, *m. pl.* -stöcke, walking-cane **Spazier'weg**, -vég, *m. pl.* -e, walk.
Special, zhpetsïäl', *a.* special; -karte, -karte, *f.* particular map, carte.
Species, zhpä'tsïes, *n. pl.* **Species**, species.
Specificiren, zhpetsïfïtsä'ren, *vt.* to specify, particularize.
Specifisch, zhpetsïfī'sh, *a.* specific.
Speck, zhpék, *m.* lard, bacon; -seite, -säïte, *f.* side of bacon. **Speck'stein**, -zhtäen, *m.* steatite.
Spectakel, zhpektä'kel, *m.* (spectacle) row, fuss.
Spectrum, zhpéct'rum, *n.* spectrum, image, representation.
Speculation, zhpeculatsïön', *f.* speculation'. **Speculiren**, -lï'ren, *vt.* to speculate.
Spediren, zhpedï'ren, *vt.* to convey, dispatch, forward.
Spediteur, zhpedïtöhr', *m.* forwarding agent, merchant, consignee.
Spedition, zhpedïtsïön', *f.* transmission; sending; -geschäft, -geshäft, *n.* forwarding-house, transmission-business.
Speer, zhpär, *m.* spear, lance. **Speer'fisch**, -fis, *m.* marcasite.
Speiche, zhpäe'ch'e, *f.* spoke.
Speichel, zhpäe'chel, *m.* spittle, saliva. **Spei'chelfluß**, -fliuss, *m.* salivation. **Spei'chellecker**, -lecker, *m.* sycophant, toad-eater.
Speicher, zhpäe'cher, *m.* store, granary, warehouse.
Speidel, zhpäel'del, *m.* wedge.
Speien, zhpäe'en (**spie**, **gespien**), *vt. i.* to vomit, spew; spit.
Speiler, zhpäe'ler, *m.* skewer.
Speinapf, zhpäe'napf, *m. pl.* -näpfe, spitting-box.

Speise, zhpēī'sẹ, f. food, aliment, meat, dish; -kammer, -kammer, f. larder; -meister, -mäëzhter, m. master of the feast, steward. Speise= opfer, -opfer, n. meat-offering.

Speiseröhre, zhpēī'sẹröhrẹ, f. œsophagus.

speisen, zhpēī'sen, vi. to eat; — zu Mittag, to dine; — zu Abend, to sup; vt. to feed, give food, to nourish.

Speisepumpe, zhpēī'sẹpumpẹ, f. feed-pump. Speisesaal, zhpēī'sẹsäl, m. dining room. Speiseschrank, zhpēī'sẹshrank, m. safe, pantry, larder. Speisewirth, -virt, m. eating-house keeper, master of an ordinary, landlord. Speisezettel, -tsettel, m. carte, bill of fare. Speisezimmer, -tsimmer, n. dining-room.

Spelt, zhpelt, or Spelz, zhpelts, m. spelt (German wheat).

Spelunke, zhpelunk'ẹ, f. hovel.

Spelze, zhpelt'sẹ, f. chaff. Spelzig, zhpēlt'sich, a. chaffy.

Spende, zhpen'dẹ, f. gift; charity.

spenden, zhpen'den (spendiren), vt. to give, spend, bestow; distribute.

Spender, zhpen'der, m. dispenser, bestower.

Sperber, zhpēr'ber, m. sparrow-hawk.

Spergel, zhpēr'gel, m. spurry.

Sperling, zhpēr'ling, m. sparrow.

Sperre, zhpēr'rẹ, f. shutting; embargo; prohibition; drag, shoe.

sperren, zhpēr'ren, vt. i. to bar, stop, close, to shut or block (up); to trig, lock; to put spaces between the letters, to print in Italics; to refuse, oppose, struggle against, resist.

Sperruthe, zhpēr'rutẹ, f. temple, templet.

Sperrung, zhpēr'rung, f. shutting, embargo.

sperrweit, zhpērr'vēīt, a. wide-open.

Spesen, zhpā'sen, pl. charges.

Specerei, zhpetserēī', f. spicery, spices, grocery-wares. Specerei=hän=del, -handel, m. grocery. Specerei=händler, -hendler, m. grocer. Spe=cereihandlung, -handlung, f. grocery.

Sphäre, sphā'rẹ, f. sphere. Sphä=risch, sfär'ish, a. spheric.

Spiauter, zhpīou'ter, m. spelter, zinc.

spicken, zhpick'en. vt. to lard, interlard. Spicknadel, -nādel, f. larding-pin.

Spiegel, zhpī'gel, m. looking-glass, mirror; stern; -ei, -ēī, n. poached egg. Spiegelfabrik, -fabrik, -hütte, -hüttẹ, f. looking-glass manufactory. Spiegelfechterei, -fechterēī', f. mock-fight; delusion, false trick. Spiegelglas, -gläs, n. pl. -gläser plate-glass, mirror-glass. Spiegel=glatt, -glatt, a. smooth as glass. Spiegelkies, zhpī'kelkīs, m. specular pyrites. Spiegelkobalt, -kōbalt, m. specular cobalt-ore. Spiegelspaun, -zhpan, n. stern frame.

spiegeln, zhpī'geln, vt. i. r. to reflect, to give a lustre; sich an —, to take an example by.

Spiegelspath, zhpī'gelzhpät, m. specular spar. Spiegelstein, -zhtāën, m. specular stone. Spiegelung, -ung, f. reflection, mirage.

Spiel, zhpīl, n. play; performance; game, deck, set. Spielball, -ball, m. ball; football; sport. spielen, zhpī'len, vt. i. to play; to game; to gamble. Spielend, -ent, ar. as in play. Spieler, zhpī'ler, m. player; -ei, -ēī', f. play; trifling; trick, jugglery. Spielgesellschaft, -gesellshaft, f. playing-party. Spielhaus, -hōus, n. pl. -häuser, gambling-house. Spielkarte, -kartẹ, f. card. Spiel=mann, -mann, m. pl. -männer, musician; -leute, -lëütẹ, s. pl. band. Spielraum, zhpīl'raum, m. play. Spieltisch, -tish, m. gaming-table. Spieluhr, -ur, f. musical clock. Spielverderber, -ferderber, m. bad hand; ill-joy. Spielwerk, -verk, n. plaything; -zeug, -tsëüg, n. playthings.

Spier, zhpīr, n. pin's point; a little, a bit.

Spiere, zhpī'rẹ, f. sheer; spar; boom.

Spieß, zhpīss, m. pl. -e, spear, lance; pike; spit; pick; -bürger, -bürger, m. pike-man; townsman, citizen.

spießen, zhpīs'sen, vt. to empale, to spit. Spießgesell, -gesell, m. accomplice, one of the gang. Spieß=glanz, -glants, m. Spießglas, -gläs, n. antimony. Spießruthe, -rutẹ, f. rod, gauntlet; Spießruthen laufen, to run the gauntlet.

Spiker, zhpī'ker, m. spike.

Spille, zhpīl'lẹ, f. capstern.

Spinat, zhpināt', m. spinage, spinach.
Spindel, zhpin'del, f. spindle. **Spindelbank**, zhpin'delbank, f. mandril, flyer.
Spinnbar, zhpinn'bär, a. textile.
Spinne, zhpin'ne, f. spider.
Spinnen, zhpin'nen (fpann, gefponnen), vt. to spin: to purr (of cats).
Spinnenfeind, zhpin'nenfĕent, a. mortally hating; — fein, to be in dead hostility, a bitter enemy.
Spinnwebe, zhpinn'vâbe, **Spinngeweb**, -gevâb, n. cobweb.
Spinner, zhpin'ner, m. spinner; **-in**, -in, f. spinster.
Spinnerei, zhpinnerēī', f. **Spinnhaus**, -hōus, n. **Spinn'mühle**, -mühle, f. spinning; spinhouse: spinning-mill. **Spinn'maschine**, -mashīne, f. spinning-machine; jenny, spinning-jenny. **Spinn'rad**, -rät, n. spinning-wheel. **Spinn'rocken**, -rokken, m. distaff.
Spion, zhpīōn', m. pl. -e, spy. **Spioniren**, -nī'ren, vi. to spy. **Spionir'system**, -systäm, n. system of espionage.
Spiral, zhpīrāl', a. spiral. **Spiral'e**, f. spiral. **Spiral'feder**, -fēder, f. spiral spring.
Spiritus, zhpī'ritys, m. spirit of wine, etc.: breathing (Gram.).
Spirituosen, zhpirityō'sen, pl. liquors, spirits.
Spital, zhpitāl', n. pl. **Spitäler**, auch **Spit'tel**, n. m. hospital, infirmary.
Spitz, Spitzig, zhpit'sich, a. av. pointed, peaked; sharp, acute; touchy; m. wolf-dog.
Spitzbube, zhpits'bybe, m. rogue, knave, scoundrel, rascal: **-rei**, -rēī', f. roguery, knavery, foul dealing. **Spitzbübisch**, -bübish, a. av. knavish, villainous, roguish.
Spitze, zhpit'se, f. top, point, spike, spire, pinnacle, summit; apex; lace. An der Spitze stehen, to be at the head.
Spitzen, zhpit'sen, vt. to point, sharpen, tib: prick up (the ears).
Spitzengrund, zhpit'sengrunt, washblonde, lace. **Spitz'enhändler**, -hendler, m. dealer in lace. **Spitz'enmuster**, -myster, n. pattern of lace.
Spitz, Spitzer, zhpit'ser, m. Pomeranian dog, wolf-dog.

Spitzfindig, zhpits'findich, a. av. subtile **-keit**, -kāet, f. subtility.
Spitzhacke, zhpits'hakke, **Spitz'haue**, -hāu-e, f. pickaxe. **Spitz'hammer**, -hammer, m. pickaxe.
Spitzmaus, zhpits'mōys, f. shrewmouse.
Spitzname, zhpits'nāme, m. nickname.
Spitzsäule, zhpits'sēūle, f. obelisk, pyramid.
Spitzstahl, zhpits'zhtāl, m. pointed chisel.
Spitzwinkel, zhpits'vinkel, m. acuteangle: **-ig**, -ich, a. acute-angular.
Spitzzahn, zhpits'tsān, m. eye-tooth, canine-tooth.
Spleiße, zhplēīss'e, f. splinter, shiver.
Spleißen, zhplēīss'en (spliß, gespliffen), vt. to split, cleave; vi. to crack, split.
Splint, zhplint, m. pl. -e, peg, pin: sap-wood; splinter.
Spliß, Spließ, f. **Spließen**.
Splißen, zhplis'sen, vt. to splice.
Splitter, zhplit'ter, m. splint, splinter, shiver; spark: **-ig**, -ich, a. splintery. **Splittern**, zhplit'tern, vt. i. to splinter, crack, chop. **Split'ternackt**, -nackt, a. quite or stark naked.
Splitterrichten, zhplit'terrichten, vt. to carp at trifles, to cavil. **Splitterer**, zhplit'terer, m. carper, caviller fault-finder.
Sporer, zhpō'rer, m. spurrier.
Sporn, zhporn, m. pl. **Sporen**, spm. stimulus. **Spornen**, zhporn'en, vt. to spur. **Sporn'rädchen**, -rädchen, n. rowel. **Sporn'rätig**, -zhtātich, a. over-spurred, restive by spurring. **Sporn'flich**, -zhtich, m. spurn-gall. **Sporn'streichs**, -zhträechs, av. at full gallop, with full speed.
Sporteln, zhpor'teln, pl. perquisites, fees.
Spott, zhpott, m. scorn, scoff, mockery, derision; — treiben mit, to have one's jest or joke at. **Spötteln**, zhpöt'teln, vi. to quiz a little. **Spotten**, zhpot'ten, vi. to make sport with, to jeer, rally. **Spötter**, zhpöt'ter, m. railer, mocker, banterer; **-ei**, -ēī', f. derision, scoff. **Spott'geld**, -gelt, n. trifling sum; um ein Spottgeld, at a dead bargain, dogcheap. **Spöttisch**, zhpöt'tish, a. scornful, disdainful, mocking, av. -ly **Spott'name**, -nāme, m. nickname.

Spottschrift, -schrift, *f.* lampoon, satire. **Spott'vogel,** -fogel. *m.* mocking-bird; quiz. **Spott'weife,** -vǟse, *av.* in dirision, mockingly. **Spott'wohlfeil,** zhpott'volfǟel, *a.* dirt-cheap.

Sprache, zhpräch'e, *f.* language, speech, tongue. **Sprachfehler,** zhpräch'fäler, *m.* fault. **Sprach'forschung,** -forshụng, *f.* philology. **Sprach'gelehrter,** -gelärter, *m.* philologer, philologist, linguist. **Sprach'gesetz,** -geşets, *n. pl.* -e, rule *or* law in language, grammar. **Sprach'kundig,** -kụndich, *a.* learned in grammar. versed in philology. **Sprach'lehrer,** -lärer, *m.* teacher of a language. **Sprach'los,** -lös, *a.* speechless; **sinfeit,** -içhkǟet, *f.* speechleseness. **Sprach'meister,** -mäezhter, *m.* teacher of languages. **Sprach'recht,** -recht. **Sprach'gerecht,** -gerecht, **Sprach'richtig,** -richtich, *a.* correct, -ly, grammatical, -ly.

Sprachrohr, zhpräch'rör, *n.* speaking-trumpet. **Sprach'schnitzer,** -shnitser, *m.* grammatical blunder. **Sprach'unterricht,** -ụnterricht, *m.* instruction in a language. **Sprach'werkzeug,** -vẹrktseüg, *n.* organ of speech. **Sprach'widrig,** -vidrich, *a.* ungrammatical, incorrect. **Sprach'wissenschaft,** -vissenshaft, *f.* science of language. **Sprach'zimmer,** -tsimmer, *n.* parlor.

Sprechart, zhprech'ärt, *f.* manner of speaking; discourse, language, idiom, dialect. **Sprech'bar,** -bär, *a.* utterable.

Sprechen, zhprech'en (sprach, gesprochen), *vt. i.* to speak, pronounce; — **ein Urtheil.** to pass a sentence; — **zum Herzen.** to appeal to the heart. **Sprecher,** zhprech'er, *m.* speaker; orator.

Spreissel, zhpröiss'el, *m.* **Spreiss'e,** *f.* splinter. **Spreite,** zhprǟi'te, *f.* airing ground. **Spreiten,** zhprǟi'ten, *vt.* to spread, strew.

Spreizen, zhprǟit'sen, *vt.* to stretch, straddle, sprawl out, prop, shore; — **sich gegen,** to struggle against; oppose, refuse; **Spreizen sich mit,** to boast of.

Sprengel, zhpreng'el, *m.* diocese; district; jurisdiction; precinct.

Sprengen, zhpreng'en, *vt. i.* to make to spring; to burst, explode, to blow up; to sprinkle, strew, scatter. **Sprengwedel,** zhpreng'vädel, sprinkling-brush.

Sprenkel, zhprenk'el, *m.* springe. **Sprenkeln,** zhprenk'eln, *vt.* to speckle. **Sprenkelig,** zhprenk'elich, *a.* spotted, speckled, party-colored.

Spreu, zhpreü, *f.* chaff. **Spreustein,** -shtǟen, *m.* scapolite.

Sprichwort, zhprich'vert, *n.* proverb, saying, adage. **Sprich'wörtlich,** -vört-lich, *a.* proverbial.

Spriegel, zhpri'gel, *m.* hoop, tilt. **Spriessen,** zhpri'ssen (spross, gesprossen), *vi.* to sprout, shoot, germinate. **Spriet,** shprīt, *n. pl.* -e, sprit; **Segel,** -sägel, *n.* sprit-sail.

Spring, zhpring, *f. pl.* -e, sheer. **Springanker,** zhpring'anker, *m.* kedge. **Springbrunnen,** zhpring'brụnnen, *m.* fountain.

Springen, zhpring'en (sprang, gesprungen), *vi.* to spring, jump, leap; vault; — **vom Pferd,** to alight.

Springer, zhpring'-er, *m.* springer; knight (chess).

Springfeder, zhpring'fäder, *f.* spring. **Springfluth,** zhpring'flụt, *f.* spring tide.

Springhengst, zhpring'hengst, *m.* stallion.

Springinsfeld, zhpring'insfelt, *m.* romp.

Springkraft, zhpring'kraft, *f.* elasticity. **Springkräftig,** -kreftich, *a.* elastic.

Springluke, zhpring'lụke, *f.* scuttle. **Springstange,** zhpring'shtang-e, *f.* **Stock,** -shteck, *m.* leaping-pole. **Springstropp,** zhpring'shtropp, *m.* stirrup.

Spritze, zhprits'e, *f.* syringe, squirt; fire-engine.

Spritzen, zhprits'en, *vt.* to syringe, squirt. **Spritzenhaus,** -hōys, *n.* engine-house. **Spritzenmann,** -man, *m.* fireman.

Spröde, zhprö'de, *a. av.* brittle, flawy; coy, shy, prudish. **Sprödigkeit,** -dichkǟet, *f.* brittleness; coyness, prudery.

Spross, *m.* **Sprosse,** zhpross'e, *m.* sprout, shoot, scion; offspring.

Sprosse, zhpross'e, *f.* step, round, rundle (of a ladder).

Sprossen, zhpros'sen, vi. to sprout, shoot; descend.
Sprössling, zhpröss'ling, m. sprout; offspring.
Spratte, zhprot'te, f. sprat.
Spruch, zhpruch, m. sentence, decision, award; saying. **Spruchbuch**, -buch, n. book of scriptural passages.
Spruchreich, zhpruch'reich, a. sententious.
Spruchreif, zhpruch'reif, a. ready for trial.
Sprudel, zhpru'del, m. bubbling, spring, fountain.
Sprudeln, zhpru'deln, vi. to bubble, sputter, boil; to gush.
Sprühen, zhprüh'en, vt. i. to sparkle. **Sprühregen**, -rägen, m. drizzling-rain.
Sprung, zhprung, m. pl. **Sprünge**, leap, bound, jump; crack, chink, fissure; shed; auf bem — ſteben, to be about or ready, on the point: in vollem —, at full speed; thun einen —, to take a leap.
Sprungriemen, zhprung'rimen, m. martingale.
Spucken, zhpuck'en, vt. i. to spit. **Spucknapf**, -napf, m. spittoon, spitting-box.
Spuden, zhpu'den, vr. to speed, to make haste, hasten.
Spuk, zhpuk, m. noise, trouble, bustle; apparition, hobgoblin, spectre.
Spuken, zhpu'ken, vi. to haunt, to be haunted; to make a noise; es ſpukt im Hauſe, the house is haunted.
Spule, zhpu'le, f. spool; bobbin; quill. **Spulen**, vt. i. to spool, wind.
Spülen, zhpüh'len, vt. i. to rinse, wash, scour, clean, cleanse.
Spülicht, zhpül'icht, n. dish-water, hog-wash, swill.
Spulrad, zhpul'rät, n. pl. -räder, spool-wheel.
Spülwaſſer, zhpül'vasser, n. dish-water.
Spulwurm, zhpul'vurm, m. belly-worm.
Spund, zhpunt, m. pl. **Spünte**, bung, stopple, stopper. **Spunden, Spünden**, zhpün'den, vt. i. to bung, stop or close with a bung. **Spundhobel**, -hōbel, m. match-planes. **Spundiſch**, -iſch, n. bunghole. **Spundwand**, -vant, f. pile-plauking, sheet-piling.

Spur, zhpur, f. pl. -en, trace, vestige, track, footstep; step. **Spüren**, zhpüh'ren, vt. to track; to perceive, feel. **Spürhund**, -hunt, m. blood-hound, pointer; f. spy. **Spurlos**, -lös, a. trackless.
Sputen, zhpu'ten, f. **Spuden**.
**St. auch Sct. für Sanft, saint.
St! ij. hush! peace!
Staar, zhtär, m. starling; cataract, glaucoma; amaurosis; leucoma; ſtechen ben —, to couch the cataract; f. to undeceive. **Staarblind**, -blint, a. wall-eyed (of horses); with a cataract.
Staat, zhtät, m. pl. -en, state, commonwealth; display, show.
Staatenbund, zhtä'tenbunt, m. confederation. **Staatsangelegenheit**, zhtäts'angelägenhäet, f. public affair. **Staatsbürger**, -bürger, m. sin, f. citizen. **Staatsdame**, -däme, f. maid or lady of honor. **Staatsdegen**, zhtäts'dägen, m. dress-sword. **Staatseinkünfte**, -einkünfte, f. revenues, finances of the state. **Staatsgeschäft**, -geshäft, n. state affair. **Staatsgesetz**, -gesetz, n. state law, constitutional law. **Staatsgewalt**, -gevalt, f. government. **Staatsgrundgesetz**, -grundgesetz, n. fundamental law of the state.
Staatsgut, zhtäts'gut, n. property of the state. **Staatskleid**, -kläet, n. court-dress. **Staatsklug**, -klug, a. politic, -al; -heit, -häet, f. policy, politics, political wisdom. **Staatskunst**, -kunst, f. statesmanship; policy. **Staatsmann**, -mann, m. statesman. **Staatsminiſter**, -miniſter, m. minister of state. **Staatspapiere**, -papire, pl. public funds, stocks, bonds. **Staatsrath**, -rät, m. counsellor of state. **Staatsrecht**, -recht, n. science of states; public law; right of a state. **Staatsſchuld**, -shult, f. debt of a state. **Staatsverbrechen**, -ferbrechen, n. crime against the state. **Staatsverbrecher**, -ferbrecher, m. state criminal. **Staatsverfaſſung**, -ferfassung, f. constitution. **Staatsverwaltung**, -fervaltung, f. administration of the state. **Staatswirthſchaft**, -virthshaft, f. political economy. **Staatswohl**, -vōl, n. common weal.

Stab, zhtäp, m. staff, stick. **Stab'-eisen**, -eisen, n. car-iron.
Stabilität, zhtabilität', f. stability.
Stabsoffizier, zhtäbs'offitsīr, m. field-officer, staff-officer.
Stach, zhtäch, f. Stechen.
Stachel, zhtäch'el, m. sting: prick, prickle, thorn. tongue (of a buckle).
Stachelbeere, zhtäch'elbā-re, f. gooseberry. **Stach'eibeerstrauch**, -zhtröych, m. gooseberry-bush.
Stachelig, zhtäch'elich, a. prickly, thorny; bristly: f. pungent.
Stacheln, zhtäch'eln, vt. to prick; to stimulate, to spur.
Stachelschwein, zhtäch'elshvein, n. pl. -e, porcupine.
Stachelwort, zhtäch'elvort, n. stinging, pungent word, sarcasm.
Staket, zhtakket', n. palisade, railing, stockade.
Stadium, zhtä'dium, n. stadium.
Stadt, zhtadt, f. pl. Städte, city, town. **Städtchen**, zhtét'chen, n. little town; in der Stadt, in town.
Stadtamt, zhtadt'amt, n. municipal office: office in town; district or jurisdiction of the town.
Stadtarzt, zhtadt'ärtst, m. pl. Aerzte, city physician.
Städter, zhtędt'er, m. townsman; pl. town's) people, townsfolk.
Stadtgerede, zhtadt'gerāde, **Stadt'ge-sprach**, -gezhpräch, n. town-talk. **Stadt'gericht**, -gericht, n. city court. **Stadt'graben**, -gräben, m. pl. -gräben, moat, ditch, fosse. **Stadt'haus**, -hōus, n. court-house.
Städtisch, zhtét'tish, a. municipal; -es Wesen, city manners.
Stadtgewerb, zhtadt'geverb, n. town profession. **Stadt'kundig**, -kundich, a. notorious. **Stadt'leben**, -läben, n. city life. **Stadt'mauer**, -mōyer, f. city wall. **Stadt'obrigkeit**, -ōbrichkäet, f. magistracy. **Stadt'rath**, -rät. m. pl. -räthe, city council.
Stadtschreiber, zhtadt'shrēiber, m. city clerk. **Stadt'schreier**, -shrēier, m. town crier. **Stadt'schule**, -shųle, f. school of a city, city school.
Stadtsoldat, zhtadt'soldät, m. home guard. **Stadt'steuer**, -zhtöier, f. city tax. **Stadt'thor**, n. city gate. **Stadt'viertel**, -fīrtel, n. quarter of a city. **Stadt'volk**, -folk, n. townfolk.

Stadtwappen,, zhtadt'vappen, n. city arms, pl.
Staffel, zhtaf'fel, f. stairs; easel.
Staffelei, zhtaffelēī', f. easel.
Staffette, zhtaffet'te, f, estafette, an express.
Staffiren, zhtaffī'ren, vt. to furnish, provide.
Stag, zhtäg, m. stay, rope; großer —, m. mainstay.
Stagsegel, zhtäg'sāgl, n. stay-sail.
Stahl, zhtäl, m. steel; -arbeit, -arbäet, f. steel-work.
Stahlbad, zhtäl'bät, n. chalybeate bath.
Stahlblau, zhtäl'blāu,a. steel-colored.
Stahlblech, zhtäl'blēch, n. steel-plate. **Stahl'draht**, -drät, m. steel-wire.
Stählen, zhtä'len, vt. to steel. **Stäh-lern**, zhtä'lern, a. (made) of steel. **Stahl'feder**, -fāder, f. steel-pen. **Stahl'grün**, zhtäl'grühn,a. steel-green. **Stahl'hütte**, zhtäl'hütte, f. steel-manufactory.
Stahlwaaren, zhtäl'vāren, s. pl. hardware, cutlery (of steel).
Stähr, zhtär, m. ram. **Stähren**, zhtä'-ren, vi. to be in heat. **Stähr'lamm**, -lamm, m. male lamb.
Staket, zhtakęt', n. stake; fence.
Stall, zhtall, m. stable, stall.
Stallen, zhtä'len, vt. to stable, house, stall; vi. to agree; to make water, urinate.
Stallfütterung, zhtall'füttęrųng, f. stall-feeding. **Stall'knecht**, -knęcht, m. groom; hostler. **Stall'meister**, -māeshter, m. master of the horse, eqnerry. **Stallung**, zhtal'lųng, f. stabling.
Stamm, zhtamm, m. stem, stalk, trunk; race, stock, breed : **-baum**, -bahm, m. pedigree, lineage, descent, genealogy.
Stammbuch, zhtamm'buch, n. album; **-sabe**, -zhtäbe, m. radical letter.
Stammeln, zhtam'meln, vi. to stammer.
Stammen, zhtam'men, vi. to descend, come from. **Stamm'erbe**, -erbe, m. lineal heir; heir of a family.
Stammgut, zhtamm'gųt, n. pl. -güter, n. allodium. **Stamm'haft**, -haft, a. **Stämmig**, zhtém'mich, a. solid, sturdy, stout, robust. **Stammhaftigkeit**, zhtamm'haftichkäet, f. stoutness, sturdiness.

Stammhalter, zhtamm'halter, m. sole scion or representative of a house.
Stammler, zhtamm'ler, m. stammerer.
Stammsprache, zhtamm'zhprăche, f. primitive language.
Stammtafel, zhtamm'täfel, f. genealogy.
Stammvater, zhtamm'fäter, m. ancestor.
Stampfe, zhtamp'fe, f. stamp, stamper, stamping. **Stampfen,** zhtamp'fen, vt. to stamp, pound, beat, pitch; peel; to ride hard; — vor Anker, to heave and set. **Stampf'mühle,** -mühle, f. stamp or stamping-mill.
Stampfsee, zhtampf'sä, f. heavy sea ahead, or over the bow.
Stand, zhtant, m. pl. **Stände,** state, position, standing; situation, condition, order, class, rank; station; zu — e bringen. to accomplish, realize, bring to bear, bring about; — halten, to stand, last, make head, a stand, keep ground; zu — kommen, to be realized or effected, achieved; — mit, to bring about, accomplish; succeed; im Stande sein, to be able, enabled: in — setzen. to enable; außer — setzen, to disable, disenable, disqualify.
Standarte, zhtandar'te, f. standard.
Standbild, zhtant'bilt, n. statue.
Ständchen, zhtent'chen, n. serenade. ein — bringen, to serenade.
Ständer, zhten'der, m. something standing upright; housing-frame; post, pillar.
Standesamt, zhten'desäl, m. hall of the diet.
Standesperson, zhan'despërsōn, m. person of rank.
Standgemäß, zhtaut'gemäss, **Stand'mäßig,** -mässich, a. according to one's rank or standing. **Standwidrig,** -vīdrich, a. contrary to one's rank or standing.
Standgeld, zhtant'gĕlt, n. stallage.
Standort, zhtant'ort, m. stand, station.
Standpunkt, zhtant'pŭnkt, m. standpoint, point of view; station.
Standquartier, zhtant'quartīr, n. cantonment; — e beziehen, to canton, to go into cantonments.
Standrecht, zhtant'recht, n. martial law, court-martial; — halten, to hold or call a court martial over —.

Staubrede, zhtaut'rā-de, f. harangue; parentation; funeral oration.
Stange, zhtang'e, f. pole, bar; die — halten, to countenance.
Stangenstein, zhtang'zhtāĕn, m. pl. -e, pycnite.
Stänker, zhten'ker, m. wrangler; -ei, -ĕī', f. stink; ferreting; quarrel, hobbery, squabble, row, wrangle; —en anfangen, to pick quarrels.
Stänkern, zhten'kern, vi. to stink; to ferret; to smell about; to pick a quarrel.
Stanze, zhtant'se, f. stanza.
Stapel, zhta'pel, m. stocks; heap, pile; staple, emporium, warehouse, mart; vom — lassen, to launch.
Stapeln, zhta'peln, vt. to heap, to pile. **Sta'pelplatz,** -plats, m. pl. -plätze, emporium, mart. **Sta'pelwaaren,** -vāren, f. -güter, -gühter, f. staple commodities. **Sta'pelstadt,** -zhtadt, f. pl. -städte, staple town.
Stapfe, zhtap'fe, f. footprint, footstep.
Stark, zhtark, a. strong, robust, stout, sturdy, corpulent.
Stärke, zhter'ke, f. strength, force, power; thickness. stoutness; starch.
Stärken, zhter'ken, vt. to strengthen, corroborate; to starch, stiffen, size.
Stärkemehl, zhterk'emäl, n. cornstarch, starch-meal.
Starkgliederig, zhtark'glīderich, a. strong-limbed. **Stark'leibig,** -lĕībich, a. stout, corpulent; -keit, -kĕĕt, f. corpulence, stoutness.
Stärkung, zhter'kung, f. strengthening, bracing, invigoration; comfort.
Stärkungsmittel, zhter'kungsmittel, n. corroborative, tonic, cordial.
Starr, zhtarr, a. stiff, rigid, numb, benumbed; staring; obstinate, stubborn; — machen, to stiffen: — ansehen, to stare at. **Starr'blind,** -blint, a. stone-blind, stark-blind.
Starren, zhtar'ren, vi. to be or grow stiff, to stiffen; to stare. **Starr'kopf,** -kopf, m. pl -köpfe, stubborn fellow. **Starrköpfig,** -köpfich, a. headstrong, stubborn; -keit, -kĕĕt, f. stubborness, obstinacy. **Starr'krampf,** m. pl. -krämpfe, tetanus.
Starrsinn, -sinn, m. stubbornness, obstinacy; -ig, -ich, a av stubborn. obstinate, -ly.

Starrsucht, zhtarr'sŭcht, *f.* catalepsy.
Starr'süchtig, -süchtich, *a.* cataleptic, afflicted with catalepsy.
Stät, zhtāt, *a.* steady, steadfast, fixed, continuous. **Stätig,** zhtāt'ich, *a.* immovable, constant, firm, continual, assiduous, restive; ‑feit, ‑kĕit, *f.* continuity; perseverance, firmness.
Statik, zhtat'ik, *f.* statics.
Station, zhtatsiōn', *f.* station, stage. **Stationshaus,** ‑hōus, *n. pl.* ‑häuser, station-house.
Statisch, zhtāt'ish, *a.* static, ‑al.
Statisch, zhtĕt'ish, *a.* restiff, restive.
Statistik, zhtatizh'tik, *f.* statistics.
Stativ, zhtatīf', *n. pl.* ‑e, tripod, stand.
Statt, zhtatt, *f.* stead, place, lieu. Von statten gehen, to do well, succeed, prosper; zu ‑en kommen, to serve one's turn; — haben, — finden, to take place, to happen, to be admitted; — finden lassen, to admit, grant, concede; an meiner —, in my stead, instead of me.
Stätte, zhtĕt'te, *f.* place, spot, site; bleibende —, home, resting *or* dwelling-place.
Statthaft, zhtatt'haft, *a.* admissible, being to be admitted, allowable, lawful. **Statt'halter,** ‑halter, *m.* governor (general); viceroy; lord-lieutenant; ‑schaft, ‑shaft, *f.* governorship. **Stattlich,** zhtatt'lich, *a.* stately, magnificent; ‑feit, ‑kĕit, *f.* stateliness, magnificence.
Statue, zhtā'tṳ‑e, *f.* statue.
Statuiren, zhtatṳī'ren, *vt.* to fix; ein Exempel —, to make an example of.
Statur, zhtatṳr', *f. pl.* ‑en, stature, size.
Statut, zhtatṳt', *n. pl.* ‑en, statute, regulation.
Stau(e), zhtāu, *f.* slack water.
Staub, zhtāub. *m.* dust, powder; sich aus dem — machen, to run away; to rat.
Stäubchen, zhtäup'chen, *n.* particle of dust, atom. **Stauben,** zhtāu'ben, *vi.* to be dusty. **Stäuben,** zhtäu'ben, *vi.* to raise *or* throw up dust, to strew powder: to dust, to free from dust, to winnow. **Staubig,** zhtāu'bich, *a.* dusty. **Staub'regen,** ‑rägen, '*m.* mist, mizzle. **Staub'-wolke,** ‑volke, *f.* cloud of dust.

Stauche, zhtŏu'che, *f.* jolting, pushing. **Stauchen,** zhtŏu'chen, *vt. u.* jolt, push, shake; sprain.
Staude, zhtŏu'de, *f.* shrub; bush; herbaceous plant; head (of lettuce). **Staudengewächs,** ‑gevĕks, *n.* shrub. **Staudensalat,** ‑salāt, *m.* head‑l‑ a. tuce, cabbage-lettuce. **Stauden,** *vi.* to grow in stalks, to shoot into stalk, to a head.
Stauen, zhtŏu'en, *vt.* to stow; to dam, swell.
Staunen, zhtŏu'nen, *vi.* to stare, to be amazed, astonished, astounded. **Stau'nenswerth,** ‑vert, *a.* astonishing, amazing.
Stäupen, zhtŏu'pen, *vt.* to flog, whip, scourge.
Stauße, zhtŏu'pe, *f.* (birch) broom. **Stau'peischlag,** ‑shlāk, *m. pl.* ‑schläge, flogging, scourging.
Stauung, zhtāu'ṳng, *f.* stowage.
Stearin, zhtearīn'. *n.* stearine. **Stearin'licht,** ‑licht, *n. pl.* ‑er, stearine-candle. **Stearinsäure,** ‑sĕure, *f.* stearic acid.
Stechapfel, zhtĕch'apfel, *m.* thorn-apple.
Stechen, zhtĕch'en (stach, gestochen), *vt.* to sting, prick, puncture; bite; stick, strike, pink: to plunge. bury, dig, run, pierce: tobt —, zu Tod, to stab dead: in Kupfer —, Stahl, to engrave; aus dem Sattel —, to unhorse; take (in playing); to burn (of the sun): in die See —, to put to sea; to kill (cattle), butcher.
Stecher, zhtĕch'er, *m.* pricker; engraver; proof-stick. **Stech'fliege,** ‑flīge, *f.* stinging-fly. **Stech'palme,** ‑palme, *f.* holly.
Steckbrief, zhtĕck'brīf, *m.* warrant of caption, writ of arrest.
Stecken, zhtĕck'en (steckte und stack, gesteckt), *vi.* to stick (fast); to be in, to be involved; — bleiben, to be at the bottom; to stumble, hesitate, to come to a (dead) stop, to break down, off; — lassen, to abandon, to leave in —, den Schlüssel — lassen, to leave the key in the lock.
Stecken, zhtĕck'en (steckte, gesteckt), *vt.* to stick, put (up), fix, set; —sich in —, to run into; in Brand —, to set on fire.
Stecken, zhtĕck'en, *m.* stick, cane, staff.

Stecknpferd, zhtĕck'enpfĕrt, n. hobby.
Stecknadel, zhtĕck'nādel, f. pin.
Stecknadelbrief, zhtĕck'nādelbrīf, m. a paper of pins.
Steckreis, zhtĕck'rēis, n. pl. -er, cutting, offset, slip, shoot, layer.
Steert, (Sterz) auch Stert, zhtărt, n. tail (Mar.), handle (Agr.).
Steg, zhtāgk, m. (small, narrow) bridge or path, foot-bridge; cross-piece, traverse; saddle; reglet.
Stegreif, zhtāg'rāĕf, m. stirrup: aus dem —e, extempore, suddenly; aus dem — sprechen, to extemporize.
Stehen, zhtā'en (stand, gestanden), vi. to stand, to be —; to become: anit; — für, to answer, vouch, warrant for: — bleiben, to stop, stand still, make a stand.
Stehlen, zhtā'len (stahl, gestohlen), vt. to steal, thieve, pilfer, purloin, rob.
Steif, zhtēīf, a. stiff, rigid; strong, straight, thick, stretched; -heit, -hĕet, f. stiffness, rigidity; stay, constraint, formality.
Steifen, zhtēī'fen, vt. to stiffen.
Steifleinwand, zhtēīf'lāenvand, n. buckram.
Steigbügel, zhtēīk'bühgel, m. stirrup.
Steig, zhtāĕk, m. pl. -e, way, path; road.
Steige, zhtāĕ'ge, f. ladder, stairs.
Steigen, zhtēī'gen (stieg, gestiegen), vi. to mount, ascend, climb (up); — ins Schiff, to embark.
Steiger, zhtāĕ'ger, m. master-miner, surveyor of mines.
Steigern, zhtāĕ'gern, vt. to enhance, raise, increase, improve. Steigerung, -yung, f. enhancing, gradation.
Steigriemen, zhtēīk'rīmen, m. stirrup-leather.
Steigung, zhtēīg'yung, f. pitch.
Steil, zhtēīl, a. steep, precipitous, abrupt; -heit, -hĕet, f. steepness, precipitousness, acclivity, proneness.
Steilhobel, -hōbel, m. jack-plane.
Stein, zhtāīn, m. pl. -e, stone, rock; man (in play); — des Anstoßes, stumbling-block; -adler, -ādler, m. golden eagle. Stein'alt, -ālt, a. as old as Methusalah. Stein'bock, -bock, m. Capricorn (Astr.); ibex, steinbuck. Stein'butter, -butter, f. rock-butter. Stein'bruch, -bruch, m. pl. -brüche, quarry Stein'butte, -but-

te, f. turbot. Stein'druck, -drnck, m. lithography; -er, -er, m. lithographer; -erei, f. lithographic establishment. Stein'eiche, -āĕche, f. evergreen oak, holm. Steinern, zhtāĕ'nern, a. stone, of stone: stony, flinty.
Steinflachs, zhtāĕn'flax, m. asbestos, amianthus.
Steingrube, zhtāĕn'grube, f. stone-pit, quarry.
Steingut, zhtāĕn'gut, f. stone-ware.
Steinhart, zhtāĕn'hart, a. hard as stone.
Steinhauer, zhtāĕn'hāuer, m. stone-cutter.
Steinigen, zhtāĕn'ichen, vt. to stone.
Steinigung, zhtāĕn'ichyung, f. stoning, lapidation.
Steinicht, zhtāĕn'icht, a. resembling stone. Stein'ig, a. of stone, stone.
Steinkohle, zhtāĕn'kōle, f. coal, fossil coal, pit-coal. Stein'kohlenbergwerk, -bĕrgvĕrk, n. coal-mine. Stein'kohlengräber, -grāber, m. collier. Stein'kohlenlager, -lāger, n. layer of coals.
Steinkunde, zhtāĕn'kunde, f. lithology.
Steinmark, zhtāĕn'mark, n. lithomarge.
Steinmetz, zhtāĕn'mĕts, m. stone-cutter.
Steinobst, zhtāĕn'ōpst, n. drupe, stone-fruit.
Steinöl, zhtāĕn'ōhl, n. petroleum, rock-oil.
Steinplatte, zhtāĕn'platte, f. square of stone.
Steinreich, zhtāĕn'rēich, a. abounding or rich in, full of stones; f. extremely, immensely, mighty rich; s. m. mineral kingdom.
Steinsalz, zhtāĕn'salts, n. mineral salt, rock-salt; -säure, -sāūre, f. lithic or uric acid.
Steinschicht, zhtāĕn'shicht, f. layer or stratum of stone.
Steinschleifer, zhtāĕn'shlēīfer. Stein'schneider, -shnēīder, m. lapidary, polisher or cutter of stones. Stein'schneidekunst, -kunst, f. glyptic.
Steinschnitt, zhtāĕn'shnitt, m. lithotomy.
Steinschrift, zhtāĕn'shrift, f. lapidary style or inscription.
Steinsetzer, zhtāĕn'setser, m. paver
Steinsinter, -sinter, m. stalactite.

Steinwand, zhtīn'vant, f. stone-wall.
Steinwurf, zhtīn'vurf, m. stone's throw.
Steiß, zhtīss, m. pl. -e, buttocks, rump: -bein, -bān, n. coccyx.
Stelldichein, zhtell'dichsēn, n. rendezvous, a place of meeting or resort.
Stelle, zhtell'lē, f. place, spot, stead, lien: case; situation, employment; auf ber —, on the spot, immediately; an Ort und —, on the spot: an bessen —, instead of that; an Ihrer —, in your case; Eines — vertreten, to represent one.
Stellen, zhtell'lēn, vt. to place, put, set, station; zufrieden —, to content, satisfy; Netze —, to pitch, spread, set nets; sich —, to appear, present; to stand; to feign, affect, dissemble; auf die Probe —, to try, to test.
Stellmacher, zhtell'macher, m. wheelwright.
Stellschraube, zhtell'shrōubē, f. adjusting or regulating screw, set-screw.
Stellung, zhtell'ung, f. attitude, position, situation.
Stellvertreter, zhtell'fērträter, m. representative; — Christi, Vicar.
Stellsegel, zhtell'sāgel, n. set of sails.
Stelze, zhtelt'sē, f. stilt; auf —n gehen, to go or walk on stilts; f. to ride a high horse. **Stelzenbein**, -bān, n. Stel'zenfuß, -fuss, m. -füße, wooden leg; a man on stumps, a man with a wooden leg, with two wooden legs.
Stemmen, zhtem'men, vt. to prop, lean; to support, to dam (up), stay, stop, bear up, stem; to fell, hew, cut down; sich —, to oppose, resist.
Stempel, zhtem'pel, m. stamp; impress; seal; post-mark; stamper.
Stenge, zhteng'ē, f. topmast; große —, main-topmast.
Stengel, zhteng'el, m. stalk, stem, shank. **Stengeln**, vi. to shoot into stalks; vt. to stake or prop up.
Steppe, zhtěp'pē, f. steppe, desert, heath.
Steppen, zhtěp'pen, vt. to stitch.
Steppseide, zhtěpp'sāide, f. silk for stitching.
Sterbebett, zhtěr'bebett, n. pl. -en, death-bed. **Sterben**, zhtěr'ben (starb, gestorben), vi. to die, to expire, to depart from life.

Sterbenskrank, zhtěr'benskrank, a dangerously ill.
Sterbfall, zhtěrb'fall, m. pl. -fälle, case of death; decease.
Sterbgebet, zhtěrb'gebāt, n. prayer for the dying.
Sterblich, zhtěrb'lich, a. mortal, perishable, transitory; badly, desperately. **Sterblichkeit**, -kāet, f. mortality.
Sterbling, zhtěrb'ling, m. pl. -e, sickly child; dead animal; ephemeral work.
Sterblingswolle, zhtěrb'lingsvollē, f. morling, mortling.
Stereometrie, zhtereometrī', f. stereometry.
Stereotype, zhtereotühp'ē, f. stereotype. **Stereotypie**, -tüpī', f. printing in stereotype. **Stereotypiren**, -tüpī'ren, vt. to stereotype.
Sterling, zhtěr'ling, m. pl. -e, sterling.
Stern, zhtěrn, m. pl. -e, star. **Stern's Bild**, -bilt, m. constellation; — im Auge, pupil; bis in die Sterne erheben, to extol to the stars.
Sternchen, zhtěrn'chen, n. little star; asterisk.
Sterndeuter, zhtěrn'dēuter, m. astrologer; -ei, -āī', f. astrology. **Stern'deutung**, -ung, f. daß.
Sternenbanner, zhtěrn'enbanner, n. star-spangled banner.
Sternförmig, zhtěrn'förmich, a. stelliform.
Sternhell, zhtěrn'hell, a. starlight.
Sternhimmel, zhtěrn'himmel, m. firmament. **Stern'karte**, -kartē, f. chart of constellation.
Sternig, zhtěrn'ich, a. starry.
Sternkunde, zhtěrn'kundē, f. astronomy. **Stern'schnuppe**, shnuppē, f. shooting-star. **Stern'stein**, -zhtāīn, m. pl. -e, asteroid. **Stern'tag**, -tāg, sidereal day. **Stern'warte**, -vartē, f. observatory.
Sterz, zhtěrts, m. pl. -e, plough-tail; tail (of a horse).
Sterzen, zhtěrt'sen, vt. i. to leave, emigrate.
Stethoskop, stāthōscōp', n. stethoscope.
Stets, zhtāts, av. always, continually, ever.
Steuer, zhtēu'er, f. pl. -n, avail, behalf; contribution; tax, duty.
Steuer, zhtēu'er, n. rudder, helm.

Steuerbar, zhtöü'erbär, a. tributary; taxable. **Steu'erbeamter**, -beamter, m. officer in the tax-office. **Steu'ereinnehmer**, -ënnämer, m. tax-gatherer; collector of taxes. **Steu'erfreiheit**, -frēīhäet, f. exemption from taxes.

Steuermann, zhtöü'ermann, m. pl. -leute, steersman, pilot; mate; **-kunst**, -kunst, f. piloting, pilotage. **Steuern**, zhtöü'ern, vt. to steer, pilot; check, control. **Steuerpflichtig**, zhöü'erpflichtich, a. subject to taxation. **Steuerrad**, zhtöü'errād, n. wheel of helm. **Steu'erreep**, -rāp, n. wheel-rope. **Steu'erruder**, -ryder, n. helm, rudder. **Steuerung**, zhtöü'erūng, f. steering, piloting; checking, valve-motion. **Steuerstange**, zhtöü'ershtange, f. whip staff (Mar.). **Stibitzen**, zhtībīt'sen, vt. to pilfer, filch. **Stich**, zhtich, m. pl. -e, stitch, puncture, stab; sting; prick; bite; thrust; cut, engraving; pang; trick; — halten, to stand the test or one's ground, to prove good; im — lassen, to abandon, forsake. **Stichel**, zhtich'el, f. style, graving-tool. **Stichelei**, zhtīchelēī', f. railery; taunt, scoff. **Stich'eln**, vt. to rally; taunt, tease, satirize. **Stich'elrede**, -rā-de, f. **Stich'elwort**, -vort, n. sarcasm, cutting humor or jest, satire. **Stichhaltig**, zhtich'haltich, a. proof, valid, firm. **Sticken**, zhtick'en, vt. i. to embroider. **Stickerei**, zhtickerēī', f. embroidery. **Stickfluss**, zhtick'flyss, m. pl -füsse, suffocating rheum. **Stickgas**, zhtick'gās, n. nitrogen gas. **Stichhusten**, zhtick'hyzhten, n. choking or whooping cough. **Stickluft**, zhtick'lyft, f. nitrogen, azote. **Sticknadel**, zhtick'nādel, f. needle for embroidering. **Stickrahmen**, zhtick'rämen, m. tambour, embroidering frame. **Stickseide**, zhtick'sēīde, f. silk for embroidering. **Stickstoff**, zhtick'zhtoff, m. nitrogen. **Stickwerk**, zhtick'vërk, n. embroidery, fancy-work, needle-work.

Stieben, zhtī'ben (stob, gestoben), vt. i. to dust, to be dusty; to skedaddle, disperse. **Stiefältern**, zhtīf'eltern, pl. step-father and mother. **Stief'bruder**, -bryder, m. pl. -brüder, step-brother, half-brother. **Stiefel**, zhtī'fel, m. pl. **Stiefeln**, boot; (of beer) quart; (of a pump) sucker, embolus; tube. **Stiefelabsatz**, zhtī'felabsats, m. boot-heel. **Stie'felbind**, -block, m. **Stie'felholz**, -holts, n. boot-last, boot-tree. **Stie'felbürste**, bürzhte, f. blacking-brush. **Stie'felhaken**, -häken, m. boot-hook. **Stie'felknecht**, -k(e)nëcht, m. boot-jack. **Stiefelmacher**, zhtī'felmacher, m. bootmaker. **Stiefeln**, zhtī'feln, vt. to boot, furnish with boots; gestiefelter Kater, puss in boots. **Stie'felputzer**, pytser, m. **Stie'felwichser**, -vikser, m. boot-black, shoe-black, shoe-blacker. **Stiefelschaft**, zhtī'felshaft, m. leg of a boot. **Stie'felwichse**, -vikse, f. blacking. **Stiefgeschwister**, zhtīf'geshvīster, f half-brothers and sisters. **Stief'kind**, -kind, n. step-child. **Stief'mutter**, -mytter, f. step-mother. **Stiefmütterchen**, -mütterchen, n. pansy, heart's ease, garden-violet. **Stiefmütterlich**, -lich, a. novercal, like a step-mother. **Stiefschwager**, -shvāger, m. pl. -schwäger, step-brother-in-law. **Stief'schwester**, -shvester, f. half or step-sister. **Stief'sohn**, -sōn, m. pl. -söhne, step-son. **Stief'tochter**, -tochter, f. step-daughter. **Stief'vater**, -fäter, m. step-father.

Stieg, zhtīg, s. Steigen.
Stiege, zhtī'ge, f. stairs, staircase; Mass von zwanzig Ellen, twenty yards; twenty pieces.
Stieglitz, zhtīg'lits, m. goldfinch, thistlefinch.
Stiel, zhtīl, m. haft, stalk, pedicle, stick, handle, helve, post; foot, ligament. **Stielen**, zhtīl'en, vt. to helve, haft, to set in a haft. **Stiellos**, zhtīl'lōs, a. stalkless, stemless, acaulescent.
Stieper, zhtī'per, m. stanchion.
Stier, zhtīr, a. staring, rigid, fixed.
Stier, zhtīr, m. pl. -e, bull; junger — bullock.

Stieren, zhtī'ren, *vi.* to stare, to gaze steadily.
Stieren, zhtī'ren, *vt. i.* (of the cow) to long for the bull; (of the bull) to cover (the cow).
Stiergefecht, zhtīr'gefecht, *n.* bull-fight.
Stieß, zhtīss, f. Stoßen.
Stift, zhtīft, *m. pl. -e,* tack, pin, peg; pencil; (*n. pl. -er*), foundation; covenant; chapter, monastery, cathedral.
Stiften, zhīft'en, *vt.* to found; cause, make, excite, breed.
Stifter, zhtīft'er, *m.* founder, author.
Stiftsdame, zhtīfts'däme, f. **Stifts'fräulein,** -fräulein, *n.* canoness.
Stiftsherr, zhtīfts'hĕrr, *m.* canon, prebendary. **Stifts'hütte,** -hütte, f. tabernacle. **Stifts'kirche,** -kirche, f. cathedral. **Stifts'prediger,** -prädiger, *m.* chaplain of a collegiate church. **Stift'ung,** -ung, f. foundation.
Stigma, zhtīg'mä, *n.* stigma.
Stil, zhtīl, *m.* style.
Stilet, zhtīlett', *n. pl. -e,* stiletto, pocket-dagger.
Stilisiren, zhtīlīsīr'en, *vt.* to pen or write.
Still, zhtīll, *a.* still, silent, quiet, serene, calm: Stilles Meer, Pacific: im Stillen, secretly, privately; still halten, to keep still, stop; — schweigen, to be silent; — zu, to connive at, to take no notice of, to ignore.
Stille, zhtīl'le, f. stillness, calm, quiet: in der —, secretly, quietly, privately. **Stil'len,** *vt.* to still, appease, suppress; silence; stop; to suckle; to quench (one's thirst).
Stillend, zhtīl'lent, *a.* allaying, lenitive. **Stilleben,** zhtīl'läben, *n.* retired life.
Stillschweigen, zhtīll'shvaigen, *n.* silence; -end, -ent. *a. av.* silent, tacitly.
Stillstand, zhtīll'zhant, *m.* stand-still, stand, cessation, stop.
Stimme, zhtīm'me, f. *pl. -n,* voice; sound; vote; judgment; opinion.
Stimmen, zhtīm'men. *vt.* to tune; to dispose, determine, induce; *vi.* to accord, agree: to vote.
Stimmenmehrheit, zhtīm'menmährhäet. f. majority of votes.
Stimmfähig, zhtīmm'fähig, *a.* entitled to vote.
Stimmgabel, zhtīmm'gäbel, f. tuning-fork. **Stimm'hammer,** -hammer, *m.* tuning-hammer, tuning key.
Stimmrecht, stimm'recht, *n.* right of suffrage or voting.
Stimmritze, zhtīmm'ritze, f. glottis.
Stimmung, zhtīmm'ung, f. tuning, tune; disposition, humor; öffentliche —, public mind; — halten, to keep tune.
Stinkbock, zhtīnk'bock, *m. pl. -böcke,* stinking-goat.
Stinken, zhtīn'ken (stank, gestunken), *vi.* to stink. **Stinker,** zhtīnk'er. *m.* stinkard. **Stinkthier,** zhink'tīr, *n.* skunk, pole-cat.
Stipendiat, zhtīpendiät', *m.* foundationer, scholar. **Stipendium,** zhtīpen'dīum, *n.* scholarship, foundation.
Stippen, zhtīp'pen, *vt. i.* to steep, dip; to stick, sting; to dot.
Stirn, zhtīrn, f. *pl. -en.* forehead, brow, front; die — bieten, to cope with, to face, to make head against; -ader, -äder, f. frontal vein.
Stöberig, zhtö'berich. *a.* sleety, showery. **Stöbern,** zhtöh'bern, *vt.* to blow or fly about like dust; to rummage, scour. **Stö'berwetter,** -vĕtter, *n.* showery, sleety weather.
Stochern, zhto'chern, *vt.* to stir, pick, poke.
Stock, zhtock, *m. pl.* Stöcke, stick, cane; stock, stalk; story, floor (Stockwerf); über Stock und Stein, over hedge and ditch: legen in den —, to put or clap into the stocks.
Stockblind, zhtock'blind, *a.* stone-blind. [cane.
Stockdegen, zhtock'dägn, *m.* sword-
Stockdumm, zhtock'dum, *a.* thick-headed.
Stocken, zhtock'en, *vi.* to stop, to stagnate, to cease to flow; to stop short; to be down; to curdle; *vt.* to stock (an anchor), to pall.
Stockfinster, zhtock'finster, *a.* pitchy, dark as pitch.
Stockfisch, zhtock'fish. *m. pl. -fische,* stockfish, codfish; blockhead.
Stockfleck, zhtock'flĕck, *m.* fusty stain.
Stockfremd, zhtock'fremd, *a.* quite unacquainted or strange.
Stockgetriebe, zhtock'getrībe, *n.* trundle, lantern (wheel), wallower.
Stockhaus, zhtock'hŏus, *n. pl. -häuser* jail, prison.

63

Stỏdig, zhtock'ĭch, a. fusty.
Stodmeister, zhtock'mǎ̈ester, m. jailer.
Stockscheere, zhtock'shǎrẹ, f. pl. -n, stock shears.
Stockprügel, zhtock'prügl, pl. cudgeling.
Stockschlag, zhtock'shlǎk. m. pl. -schlä̈ge, stroke or blow with a stick; **Stockstreiche**, -zhtǎěchẹ, pl. flogging, caning.
Stockschnupfen, zhtock'shnupfẹn, m. dry coryza.
Stockung, zhtock'ung, f. stopping, cessation, stagnation.
Stockwerk, zhtock'věrk, n. story, floor.
Stockzahn, ztock'tsän, m. grinder, jaw-tooth, molar-tooth.
Stockzwinge, zhtock'tsvingẹ, f. stick-ferrule.
Stoff, zhtoff. matter, subject; -haltig, -haltich, a. substantial, material.
Stöhnen, zhtöh'nen, vi. to groan.
Stollen, zhtol'len, m. cake, sort of bread; shaft, stulm (min.); -befahrung, -befǎrung, f. visiting of, or getting into a stulm.
Stolpern, zhtol'pẹrn, vi. to stumble, blunder.
Stolz, zhtolts, a. haughty, proud.
Stolz, zhtolts, m. pride, haughtiness.
Stolziren, zhtolsi'ren, vi. to strut, prance, to be proud.
Stopfen, zhtopf'en, vt. to fill, stuff, stop (up), cram; to darn, mend, fine-draw. **Stopfgarn**, zhtopf'garn, n. darning yarn.
Stoppel, zhtop'pl, f. pl. -n, stubble; -acker, äckẹr, m., -feld, -felt, n. pl. -er, stubble-field. **Stoppeln**, zhtop'pẹln, vt. i. to glean.
Stoppelwerk, zhtop'pelvěrk, n. patch-work, cento.
Stoppine, zhtoppĭ'nẹ, f. quick-match.
Stöpsel, zhtöp'sel, m. stopper, stopple, plug; cork.
Stör, zhür, m. pl. -e, sturgeon.
Storax, zhtŏr'ax, m. storax.
Storch, zhtorch, m. pl. **Störche**, stork; crane; pantograph.
Störeisen, zhtör'ĕlsen, n. poker.
Stören, zhtör'en, vt. to disturb, trouble, derange; interrupt; to rummage, poke, stir up.
Störenfried, zhtör'enfrĭd, m. disturber, mischief-maker.
Störrig, zhtör'rich, **Störrisch**, zhtör'-rish, a. refractory; stubborn, dogged, obstinate; -keit, -kǎ̈et, f stubbornness, obstinacy.
Störung, zhtör'ung, f. pl. -en. disturbance.
Stoss, zhtŏss, m. pl. **Stöße**, push, thrust, shock, blow; (bill) stroke; (with the foot) kick; pile, heap; file (of papers); -degen, -dägn, m. rapier.
Stößel, stöhs'sel, m. pestle; rammer.
Stoßen, zhtŏs'sen (stiess, gestoßen), vt. thrust, push; — auf, to meet, to light upon, fall in with; to strike; (with the foot) to kick; — sich (an) —, to hurt one's self; to scruple with: to take offense at.
Stoßfeile, zhtŏs'fĕllẹ, f. paring file.
Stoßgebet, zhtŏs'gẹbǎt, n. ejaculatory prayer.
Stoßnaht, zhtoss'nǎt, f. pl. -nähte. darn.
Stoßseufzer, zhtŏs'sŏüfzẹr, f. ejaculation.
Stoßtalje, zhtoss'talyẹ, f. rolling-tackle.
Stoßwaffe, ztŏss'vaffẹ, f. pl. -waffen, weapon for thrusting.
Stoßweise, zhtŏss'wĕlse, av. by fits or starts.
Stotterer, zhtŏt'terer, m. stutterer, stammerer. **Stottern**, zhtŏt'tẹrn, vi. stammer, stutter.
Stracks, zhtraks, av. straightway.
Strafbar, zhträf'bär, a. guilty; -keit, -kǎ̈et, f. guiltiness.
Strafe, zhträ'fẹ, f. penalty, punishment. **Strafen**, zhträ'fen. vt. to punish, chastise; — mit Worten, rebuke, reprove; um Geld —, to fine; Lügen strafen, to give one the lie.
Straff, zhtraff, a. strait, tight, strained; — machen, to strain, to tighten, straiten, stretch; -heit, -hǎ̈et, f. tightness, straitness.
Sträflich, zhträf'flich, a. culpable.
Strafgericht, zhträf'gericht, n. vengeance.
Sträflich, zhträf'lich, a. guilty, criminal; -keit, -kǎ̈et, f. criminality; -ling, -link, m. pl. -e, convict.
Straflos, zhträf'lōs, a. av. unpunished, with impunity; -igkeit, -ichkǎ̈et, f impunity. **Strafpredigt**, zhträf'prä̈dikt, f. severe lecture, castigatory sermon. **Strafrecht**, zhträf'rěcht, a

penal *or* criminal law. **Strafwür'-
dig**, -vürdich, *a.* guilty, criminal.
Strahl, zhträl, *m. pl.* **Strahlen**, ray,
beam, flash of (lightning *or* water):
frog (of a horse): **•blenbe**, -blende,
f. black-jack. **Strahlen**, zhträ'len,
vt. to radiate, beam; sparkle; shine;
to emit rays *or* beams; *vt.* to beam
(out). **Stahlenbrechen**, *a.* reflecting,
reflexive; **•brechung**, -brěchung, *f.*
refraction of rays; **•voll**, -foll *a.*
beaming, bright. **Strahlig**, zhträ'-
lich. *a.* radiant; radiated.
Strähn, zhträn, *m. pl.* **-e**. hank, skein.
Stramm, zhträm. *a.* = **Straff**.
Strampeln, zhträm'peln, *vt.* to
trample, kick. **Strampfen**, zhträmp'-
fen. *vt. i.* to stamp. trample, kick.
Strand, zhtränd, *m.* strand, beach,
shore. **Stranben**, zhtränd'en, *vt.*
to strand, to run aground, to wreck.
Strandrecht, ztränd'recht, *n.* strand-
law. law respecting stranded goods,
lagan.
Strang, zhträng, *m. pl.* **Stränge**, rope,
cord. string, halter; **zum Strang
verurtheilen**. to condemn to be
hanged. **Strangniren**, zhträngy-
li'ren, *vt.* to strangle.
Strapaje, zhträpä'tse, *f.* toil, hardship. **Strapajiren**, zhträpatsī'ren,
vt. to fatigue, harass, do up.
Straße, zhträ'se, *f.* street; road, highway; straits. **Stra'ßenbeleuchtung**,
-belěuchtung, *f.* lighting of the
streets. **Straßenraub**, -räub, *m.*
highway-robbery; **•räuber**, -räuber,
m. highway-man.
Sträuben, zhträ'u'ben, *vt.* to ruffle.
bristle; **sich —**, to bristle; to strife
or struggle against, oppose.
Straubig, zhtröy'bich, *a.* bristling,
rough, stiff; contrary.
Strauch, zhtröuch, *m. pl.* **Sträuche**,
shrub, bush.
Stranchein, zhtröy'cheln, *vi.* to
stumble, trip.
Strauchwerf, zhtröych'věrk, *n. pl.*
shrubs, bushes.
Strauß, zhträ'ṣs, *m. pl.* **Strauße**,
ostrich.
Strauß, zhtröuss, *m. pl.* **Sträuße**, feud,
quarrel, strife, struggle, combat.
Strauß, zhtröuss, *m. pl.* **Sträuße und
Sträußer**, bouquet, nosegay, bunch.
Sträußchen, Sträußlein, zhtröuss'-
lạen, *n.* little bunch of flowers.

Streben, zhträ'ben, *vi.* to strive, aspire; **— wider**, to struggle against,
to resist.
Strebsam, zhträb'sạm, *a.* aspiring,
assiduous.
Streckbar, zhtreck'bär, *a.* ductile,
malleable; **•keit**, -käět, *f.* malleability, ductility.
Strecke, zhtreck'e, *f.* tract, extent,
distance, stretch, length.
Strecken, zhtreck'en, *vt.* to stretch,
extend.
Streich, zhträch, *m. pl.* **-e**, stroke,
blow; lash; stripe; trick.
Streichblech, zhträch'blěch, *n.* locking
plate.
Streicheln, zhträch'eln, *vt.* to stroke,
caress, cajole.
Streichen, zhträch'en (strich, gestrichen),
vt. to strike; rub, whet; *vi.* to pass,
move, rush, run, fly; reach, extend.
Streichhölzchen, zhträch'hölzchen, *n.*
match.
Streichriemen, zhträch'rīmen, *m.* razor-strap.
Streif, zhträëf, *m. pl.* **-e**, **Streifen**,
zhträëf'en, *n.* stripe; streak; track.
Streifen, zhträë'fen, *vi.* to rove, roam,
ramble; range; to make excur-
sions, incursions, inroads; to scour,
scout; *vt.* to graze, scrape, raze,
wound superficially; to channel,
flute; **Gestreift**, streaked, striated.
Streiferei, zhträëferěï', *f.* ramble, excursion, incursion, inroad. **Streif'-
hieb**, -hīb, *m.* glancing *or* grazing
cut. **Streif'hobel**, -hōbel, *m.* strike-
block. **Streif'ig**, -ich, *a.* striped,
streaky. **Streif'licht**, -licht, *n.* faint
gleam of light. **Streif'parti**, -par-
tī, *f.* flying *or* scouring party. **Streif-
schuß**, zhträëf'shuss, *m.* glancing *or*
grazing shot. **Streif'wunde**, -vun-
de, *f.* scratch. **Streif'zug**, -tsụk, *m.*
excursion, inroad.
Streit, zhträït, *m. pl.* **-e**, quarrel,
struggle, debate, contest, controversy, dispute, fight, combat: **in —
gerathen**, to come to a quarrel; **im
— sein**, to be at variance.
Streitart, zhträït'axt. *f.* battle-ax.
Streitbar, zhträït'bär, *a.* warlike;
•keit, -käět, *f.* warlikeness, fitness for
war.
Streiten, zhträï'ten (stritt, gestritten),
vi. to struggle, quarrel, contend,
dispute, contest, controvert; com-

bat, fight. **Streit'end**, a. military. **Streiter**, zhtrēīt'er, m. warrior, fighter, combatant, champion; disputant. **Streit'frage**, -frāge, f. point at issue (controverted question). **Streit'hammel**, -hammel, m. bully. **Streit'handel**, -handel, m. law-suit, controversy. **Streit'hengst**, -hengst, m. charger, battle-horse. **Streitig**, zhtrēīt'iĉ̣. a. contending, litigating; questionable, disputable; contested, controverted, at issue, contending; — machen, to contest. **Streit'igkeit**, -kāet, f. contention, dispute, controversy. **Streif kolben**, -kolben, m. mace. **Streit'kräfte**, -krefte, f. forces. **Streit punkt**, -pynkt, m. controverted point. **Streit'sache**, -saĉ̣e. f. matter in question. **Streit'schrift**, -shrift, f. controversy. **Streit'sucht**, -syĉ̣t, f. quarrelsome temper or disposition. litigiousness. **Streit'süchtig**, -süĉ̣tig, a. quarrelsome. **Streitwagen**, zhtrēīt'vägen, m. war-chariot.

Streng, zhtreng, a. av. rough, rigid, hard, sharp, severe, strict, intense. **Strenge**, zhtreng'e, f. severity, sharpness, rigidity, strictness.

Strengen, zhtreng'en, vt. to exert.

Streu, zhträü, f. litter, bed of straw. **Streu'büchse**, -büxe, f. sand-box.

Streuen, zhträü'en, vt. to strew, spread, sprinkle, disseminate, scatter. **Streu'sand**, -sand, m. writing sand. **Streu'zucker**, -tsycker, m. powdered sugar.

Strich, zhtriĉ̣. m. stroke; line; touch; region, tract; trip, tour; flight; emigration (of birds of passage); den — halten, to stand the touch. **Strich'punkt**, -pynkt, m. semicolon. **Strich'regen**, -rāgen, m. partial rain, shower. **Strich'zeit**, -tsēīt, f. time of migration: spawning-season.

Strick, zhtrick, m. pl. -e, rope, cord; kleiner —, line, string; halter (to hang malefactors); zum — verurtheilen, to condemn to be hanged.

Stricken, zhtrick'en, vt. i. to knit; vi. to net. **Strick'er**, m. -in, f. knitter. **Strick'garn**, -garn, n. yarn. **Strick's korb**, -korp, m. pl. -körbe, work-basket or box. **Strick'leiter**, -lāēter, f. rope-ladder. **Strick'nadel**, -nādel, f. knitting-needle. **Strick'schule**, -shyle, f. knitting-school. **Strick'zeug**, -tsēük, n. knitting implements **Strick'zwirn**, -tsvirrn, m. knitting thread.

Striegel, zhtrī'gel, m. curry-comb. **Striegeln**, zhtrī'geln, vt. to curry; to censure, cut up.

Strieme, zhtrī'me, f. stripe, streak, scar, weal. **Striemen**, zhtrī'men, vt. to stripe. **Striemig**, zhtrī'miĉ̣, a. striped, streaked, waled.

Strippe, zhtrip'pe, f. strap, band.

Strobel, zhtrō'bel. m. fir-apple; **s kopf**, -kopf, m. pl. -köpfe. bristly head; a person with a bristly head.

Stroh, zhtrō, n. straw: mit — decken, to thatch; leeres — dreschen, to waste one's labor, to work in vain. **Stroh's bett**, -bett, n. straw-bed. **Stroh'dach**, -daĉ̣, n. pl. -bächer, thatch, thatched roof. **Strohern**, zhtrō'ern, a. of straw; dull, insipid. **Stroh'farbe**, -farbe, f. straw-color: **sfarben**, **sfarbig**, zhtrō'farbiĉ̣, a. straw-colored. **Strohgeflecht**, -geflecht. n. straw-plait. **Stroh'gelb**, -ghelp, a. straw-colored. **Stroh'halm**, -halm. m. (blade of) straw, halm. **Stroh'hut**, -hyt, m. straw-hat. **Stroh'hütte**, -hütte, f. thatched hut. **Stroh'junker**, -yunker, m. country-squire. **Stroh's mann**, -mann, man of straw, scarecrow. **Stroh'matratze**, -matratse, f. straw-mattress. **Stroh'matte**, -matte, f. mat plaited of straw. **Stroh'sack**, -sack, m. pl. -säcke, straw-bed. **Stroh's schneider**, zhtrō'shnēīder, m. cutter of straw. **Strohstuhl**, zhtrō'zhtyl, **Stroh'sessel**, -sēssel, m. straw-bottomed chair. **Stroh'waaren**, -vären, f. straw-goods. **Stroh'wisch**, -vish, m. wisp of straw. **Stroh'wittwe**, -vitwe, f. grass-widow.

Strom, zhtrōm, m. pl. **Ströme**, stream, river; current, flood; **sab**, zhtrōmab', a. down the stream or river; **Stromauf**, -ōyf', a. up or against the stream. **Strömen**, zhtröh'men, vi. to stream. **Strom'schnelle**, -shnelle, f. rapids, pl. **Strömung**, zhtröh'myng, f. current; untere —, undercurrent. **Stromweise**, zhtrōm'vēīse, av. in streams.

Strontian, zhtrontsiän', m. strontia, strontian; **sit**, -it', m. strontianite. **Strontium**, zhtron'tsiym, n. strontium.

Strophe, zhtrōf'e, f. strophe.

Stroffe, zhtros'sę, *f.* step.
Stroßen, zhtrots'en, *vi.* to strut, swell, protuberate; to be puffed up; to superabound, teem with. **Strożend**, zhtrots'ent, *a.* exuberant, swelling, tumid.
Strudel, zhtry'del, *m.* whirlpool, eddy. **Stru'delkopf**, -kopf, *m. pl.* -köpfe, hot-brained fellow. **Strudeln**, zhtry'deln, *vi.* to whirl, gush, eddy, spout; to bluster.
Strumpf, zhtrympf, *m. pl.* **Strümpfe**, stocking; *shand*, -bant, *n. pl.* -bänder, garter. **Strumpfhändler**, -hendler, *m.* hosier. **Strumpfweber**, -väber, *m.* stocking-weaver; *rei*, -ēi', *f.* hosiery, manufacture of stocking. **Strumpfwirker**, -virrker, *m.* stocking-weaver; *stuhl*, -zhtyl, *m.* stocking-frame.
Strunf, zhtrynk, *m.* stake, stump; trunk.
Strunze, zhtrynt'sę, *f.* slut.
Strupfen, zhtryp'fen, *vt.* to strip off; *vi.* to shrink, wrinkle.
Struppig, zhtryp'pich, *a.* bristly, shaggy, rough, rugged.
Stübchen, zhtühb'chen, *n.* little room, gallon. **Stube**, zhty'bę, *f.* room, chamber; sitting-room. **Stu'benbursche**, -byrshę. *m.* **Stu'bengenosse**, -genosę, *m.* chum; chamber-fellow. **Stu'bengelehrter**, -gelärter. *m.* bookman. **Stu'benkammer**, -kammer, *f.* chamber-pen to the sitting-room. **Stu'benmädchen**, -mëtchen, *n.* chambermaid. **Stu'benofen**, -ōfen, stove in the room. **Stu'benthür**, -tür, *f.* door of the room. **Stu'benuhr**, -yr, *f.* clock of the room.
Stüber, zhtüh'ber, *m.* stiver.
Stuck, zhtyck, *m.* stucco.
Stück, zhtück, *n. pl.* -e, piece, part, fragment, morsel, bit; point, particular; packet (print.); — für —, a piece, piece by piece, item by item. **Stückchen**, zhtück'chen, *n.* a little bit. **Stück'eln, Stücken**, zhtück'en, *vt.* to cut in pieces. **Stück'faß**, -fass, *n.* butt, large cask. **Stückgießer**, zhtück'gisser, *m.* founder of (large) guns. **Stückgießerei**, -ēi', *f.* gunfoundery.
Stückler, zhtück'ler, *m.* piecer.
Stückweise, zhtück'vēise, *ar.* by pieces, piece by piece. **Stück'werk**, -verk, *n.* fragmentary *or* imperfect work.

Student, zhtydent', *m.* student. **Stu'denten jahre**, -yär-ę. *s. pl.* academic years. **Studentenleben**, -läben, *n.* college life.
Studiren, zhtydīr'en. *vt. i.* to study.
Studirstube, zhydīr'zhtybę, *f.* study.
Studium, zhty'diym, *n. pl.* **Studien**, study.
Stufe, zhty'fę, *f.* step; degree, grade, stage; tuck. **Stu'fenartig**, -ärtich, *a.* gradual. **Stu'fengang**, -gang, *m.* **Stu'fenfolge**, -folgę, *f.* gradation, gradual progress. **Stu'fenleiter**, -läter, *f.* scale, gradation. **Stu'fenweise**, -vēise, *av.* by steps *or* degrees, gradually.
Stuhl, zhtyl, *m. pl.* **Stühle**, chair, stool, seat; (**Kirchen**) —, pew; (weav.) —, loom.
Stuhlgang, zhtyl'gang, *m.* evacuation, stool, discharge.
Stuhllehne, zhtyl'länę, *f.* back of the chair.
Stuhlzwang, zhtyl'tsvang, *m.* tenesmus.
Stuffatur, zhtykkatyr', *f.* stucco, plaster; *arbeiter*, -arbäeter, *m.* plasterer.
Stulpe, zhtyl'pę, **Stülpe**, zhtül'pę, *f.* brim; top. **Stül'pen**, *vt.* to cock.
Stülpnase, zhtülp'näsę, *f.* pug-nose; one having a pug-nose.
Stumm, zhtymm, *a.* dumb, mute; silent. **Stummer**, zhtym'mer, *m.* **Stum'me**, *f.* dumb person.
Stummel, zhtym'mel, *m.* **Stümmel**, zhtüm'mel, *m.* stump; end, bit; short pipe.
Stummheit, zhtymm'hāet, *f.* **Stumm'sein**, -sēen, *n.* dumbness.
Stümper, zhtüm'per, *m.* bungler, smatterer; *ei*, -ēi', *f.* bungle, smatter. **Stüm'perhaft**, -haft, *a.* bungling.
Stümpern, zhtüm'pern, *vt. i.* to bungle.
Stumpf, zhtympf, *m. pl.* **Stümpfe**, stump; trunk; *a.* blunt, dull. obtuse; docked; flat, dead: — machen, stumpfen, to blunt, deaden, dull, weaken, dock, top, crop, curtail; — werben. stumpfen, to get blunt, weakened.
Stumpfnase, zhtympf'näsę, *f.* flat-nose; one having a flat nose.
Stumpfschwanz, zhtympf'shvants, *m.* docked tail, bob-tail (vulg.).

27*

Stumpfsinn, zhtympf'sinn, m. stupidity, dullness; **-ig, -ich,** a. dull, stupid.
Stumpfwinkelig, zhtympf'vinkelich, a. obtusangular, obtuse-angled.
Stunde, zhtun'de, f. hour; lesson.
Stundenglas, zhtun'denglås, n. pl. -gläser, hour-glass.
Stundenlang, zhtun'denlang, av. for one or more hours.
Stundensäule, zhtun'densöule, f. dial; mile-stone.
Stundenweiser, zhtun'denvēlser, m. **Stundenzeiger, -tsäeger,** m. hour-hand.
Stündlich, zhtünt'lich, a. av. hourly, every hour.
Sturm, zhturm, m. pl. **Stürme,** storm, tempest, assault; alarm; — blasen, to beat, sound the alarm or assault; — laufen, to storm, to make an assault.
Sturmbock, zhturm'bock, m. battering-ram.
Sturmdach, zhturm'dach, n. tortoise.
Stürmen, zhtür'men, vt. i. to storm, assail; to rage, war; rush; to ring the alarm-bell.
Sturmgatter, zhturm'gatter, n. portcullis.
Sturmglocke, zhturm'glocke, f. alarm-bell.
Stürmisch, zhtürm'ish, a. stormy, tempestuous; furious, impetuous.
Sturmläufer, zhturm'läufer, m. assailant.
Sturmleiter, zhturm'läeter, f. scaling-ladder.
Sturmvogel, zhturm'fogel, m. (stormy) petrel, storm-finch.
Sturmwind, zhturm'vint, m. squall, hurricane, flaw.
Sturz, zhturts, m. pl. **Stürze,** fall, falling, ruin, rush, bounce; overthrow.
Sturzbad, -bād, n. douche.
Sturzblech, zhturts'blech, n. plate of sheet-iron.
Sturzsee, zhturts'sä. f. pooping sea, breaker, sea washing overboard.
Stürze, zhtürt'se, f. cover, lid.
Stürzel, zhtürt'sel, m. stump.
Stürzen, zhtürt'sen, vi. to rush, fall, squirt, spout, dart, to fling or throw one's self, plunge; vt. to precipitate; to overthrow, ruin, oust, supplant, break; to tilt; hinunter stürzen, to gulp.

Stute, zhtu'te, f. mare. **Stuterei, -reï'.** f. stud. **Stutfüllen, -füllen,** n. filly.
Stutz, zhtuts, m. short rifle.
Stutzbart, zhtuts'bärt, m. mustache, auch pl. mustaches.
Stütze, zhtüt'se, f. support. **Stützen,** zhtüt'sen, sich — auf, to rely upon.
Stutzen, zhtut'sen. vt. to trim off, log off; vi. to hesitate.
Stutzer, zhtut'ser, m. dandy.
Stutzig, zhtuts'ich, a. startled, starting; — machen, to startle.
Stutzschwanz, zhtuts'shvants, m. dock-tail.
Suada, svā'da, **Suade,** f. persuasion, gift of the gab.
Subaltern, sybal'tërner, m. **N.** -en subaltern.
Subjekt, sybyëkt', n. subject, person.
Sublimat, sublimät', n. sublimate.
Sublimiren, sublimī'ren, vt. to sublimate.
Subordination, sybordinatsiōn', f. subordination.
Subscribent, sybscribent', m. subscriber.
Subscribiren, sybscribī'ren, vt. i. to subscribe.
Subscription, sybscriptsiōn', f. subscription.
Subsidien, sybsī'di-en, s. pl. subsidies.
Substantiv, syb'zhtantif, n. substantive.
Substanz, sybzhtants', f. substance.
Substituiren, sybzhtitui'ren, vt. to substitute.
Subtrahiren, subtrāhī'ren, vt. to subtract.
Subtraction, subtraktsiōn', f. subtraction.
Subtil, sybtīl', a. subtile, subtle.
Subtilität, sybtilität', f. subtility.
Suchen, sū'chen, vt. to seek, to search for; to attempt, try, endeavor.
Sucht, sucht, f. passion: distemper, sickness; mania; fallende —, epilepsy.
Sud, syd, m. pl. **Süde, Sude,** brewing
Süd, sūd. **Süden,** sū den, m. south.
Sudelbuch, sy'delbuch, n. pl. -bücher waste-book.
Sudelei, sydeleī', f. dirty work.
Sudeln, su'deln, vt. to soil, sully, dirt, to muddle.

Sud 319 **Syn**

Sudern, su'dern, *vt.* to wet crude iron with muddy water.
Sudler, sud'ler, *m.* scrawler, scribbler.
Südlich, sühd'lich, *a. av.* southern, austral, southerly; südlichst, southernmost, most southerly.
Südwärts, sühd'värts, *a.* southward.
Südpolarkreis, sühd'polärkrëes, *m.* antarctic circle.
Südwest, sühdvëst', *a.* southwest.
Südwind, sühd'vind, *m.* south wind, auster.
Sühnaltar, sühn'altär, *m.* propitiatory altar.
Sühnbar, sühn'bär, *a.* expiable.
Sühne, süh'ne, **Sühnung,** -ung, *f.* expiation, propitiation.
Sühnen, süh'nen, *vt.* to expiate.
Sultan, sul'tän, *m.* sultan, soldan; -in, *f.* sultana, sultaness.
Sulze, sült'se, auch **Sülze,** sylt'se, *f.* jelly, corned meat. **Sulzen,** sylt'sen, *vt.* to salt, corn, pickle, cover with jelly, reduce to jelly.
Sumach, su'mach, *m.* sumach.
Summa, sum'mä, *f.* sum.
Summarisch, summär'ish, *a. av.* summary, -rily, shortly, abridged.
Summe, sum'me, *f.* sum.
Summen, sum'men, *vi. auch* **Sumsen,** sum'sen, to hum, bumble, buzz, sing.
Summiren, summī'ren, **Summen,** sum'men, *vt.* to sum (up), add.
Sumpf, sumpf, *m. pl.* Sümpfe, swamp, bog, marsh, moor.
Sumpferz, sumpf'ärts, *n.* swamp-ore, bog-iron.
Sumpfig, sumpf'ich, *a.* swampy, boggy, marshy.
Sund, sund, *m. pl. -e,* straits; sound.
Sünde, sün'de, *f.* sin, trespass.
Sündenbock, sün'denbock, *m.* scape-goat.
Sünder, sün'der, *m. sin, f.* sinner.
Sündfluth, sünd'flut, *f.* deluge.
Sündhaft, sünd'haft, **Sündig,** -ich, *a. av.* peccable, sinful, -ly; -igkeit, -ichkeit, *f.* sinfulness.
Sündigen, sün'dichen, *vi.* to sin.
Sündlich, sünd'lich, *a.* sinful; -keit, sünd'lichkeit, *f.* sinfulness, criminality.
Superintendent', *m.* superintendent.
Superiorität, superiorität', *f.* superiority.

Superfein, sup'perkluk, *a.* all-sufficient, overwise.
Superlativ, sup'perlatīf, *m.* superlative.
Supernaturalismus, supernaturälis'-mus, *m.* supernaturalism. **Supernaturalist,** -ist', *m. pl. -en,* supernaturalist.
Superrevision, supperrevisiōn', *f.* press proof, press revise.
Suppe, sup'pe, *f.* soup. **Suppenlöffel,** -löffel, *m.* soup-spoon. **Suppenschüssel,** -shüssel, *f.* tureen, soup-dish or bowl. **Suppennapf,** -napf, *m.* the same. **Suppenteller,** -töller, *m.* soup-plate.
Supplement, supplement', *n. pl. -e,* supplement; -band, -bant, *m.* supplementary volume.
Supplicant, supplikant', *m. pl. -en,* supplicant, suppliant (humble), petitioner. **Supplik,** supplik', *f. pl. -en.* petition. **Suppliziren,** supplizī'ren, *vt.* to petition.
Supremat, suprëmät', *n.* supremacy.
Surren, sur'ren, *vi.* to hum, buzz, whizz; ring.
Surrogat, surrogät', *n.* substitute, succedaneum.
Suspendiren, suspendī'ren, *vt.* to suspend. **Suspension,** suspensiōn', *f.* suspension.
Süß, sühss, *a.* sweet; -holz, -holts, *a.* licorice. **Süßigkeit,** -ichkeit, *f.* sweetness. **Süßlich,** -lich, *a. av.* sweetish.
Sylbe, sil'be, *f.* syllable. **Sylbenmaß,** -mäss, *n.* measure, metre, quantity.
Syllabirbuch, sillabīrbuch, *m.* primer.
Syllogismus, sillogis'mus, *m.* syllogism.
Symbol, simbōl', *n.* symbol; -isch, -ish, *a.* symbolical.
Symmetrie, simmetrī', *f.* **Symmetrisch,** simmä'trish, *a.* symmetric, -al, -ally.
Sympathie, simpatī', *f.* sympathy. **Sympathisiren,** simpatisī'ren, *vi.* to sympathize.
Symphonie, simfonī', *f.* symphony.
Symptom, simptōm', *n. pl. -e,* symptom. **Symptomatisch,** -mat'ish, *a. av.* symptomatic, *a.*
Synagoge, sinagōgh'e, *f.* synagogue.
Synedrium, synä'drium, *n.* sanhedrim (better sanhedrin).
Synode, sinō'de, *f.* synod.

Syntar, sin'tax, *f. pl. -en.* syntax.
Synthese, sintā'se, *f.* synthesis.
Synthetisch, sintāt'ish, *a.* synthetic.
Syrup, sī'rŭp, *m.* syrup, molasses.
System, sĭstām', *n. pl. -e,* system.
Systematisch, sistemat'ish, *a. av.* systematic, -ally.

Tabak, tabak', *m.* tobacco; snuff; **-beutel,** -bēŭtẹl, *m.* tobacco-bag, tobacco-pouch. **Tabaksbüchse,** -büxẹ, *f.* tobacco-box. **Tabaksdose,** -dōsẹ, *f.* snuff-box. **Tabaksfabrik,** -fabrik, *f.* tobacco-factory. **Tabakshändler,** -hẹndler, *m.* tobacconist. **Tabakskäuer,** -käŭer, *m.* chewer of tobacco. **Tabakspfeife,** -pfeifẹ, *f.* tobacco-pipe. **Tabaksraucher,** tabak'räŭcher, *m.* smoker.
Tabatiere, tabat'ĭ-ār, *f.* snuff-box.
Tabellarisch, tabellär'ish, *a.* tabular, in tables.
Tabelle, tabẹl'lẹ, *f.* table, synopsis.
Tableau, tablō', *n.* tableau.
Tabulet, tabŭlet', *f.* pedlar's box.
Tabuletkrämer, tabŭlet'krämer, *m.* pedlar.
Takt, takt, *m. pl. -e,* time, measure; tact, feeling; — **schlagen,** to beat time: — **halten,** to keep time; **aus dem — kommen,** to get out of time. **Takt-fest,** -fest, *a.* keeping time. **Takt-mäßig,** takt'mässich, *a.* in time, measured.
Tadel, tā'del, *m.* blemish, fault; blame, censure. **Tadelhaft,** -haft, *a.* blamable, faulty. **Tadellos,** -lōs, *a.* blameless, faultless. **Tadeln,** tā'deln, *vt.* to blame, censure. **Tadelnswerth,** -värt, *a.* blamable.
Tadler, täd'ler, *m.* censurer, faultfinder, carper.
Tafel, tä'fel, *f.* table; plate, tablet, board; cake (of chocolate); **-basalt,** -basalt, *n.* tabular basalt. **Tafelmusik,** -mŭsĭk, *f.* table-music.
Tafeln, tä'feln, *vi.* to feast, to sit or be at table.
Tafelrunde, tä'felrundẹ, *f.* the round-table.
Tafelservice, tä'felsērvĭs, *n.* dinner-set, service for dinner.
Tafeltuch, tä'feltŭch, *n.* table-cloth.
Tafelwerk, tä'felvẹrk, *n.* wainscot.
Taffet, taf'fẹt, *m.* taffeta, taffety.

Taffetband, taf'fẹtbant, *n.* taffeta riband.
Taffetweber, taft'väber, *m.* taffeta-weaver.
Tag, tāk, *m.* day; **bei —,** in the day-time; **heut zu Tage,** now-a-days, in these days; **eines Tages,** once, one day; **Tag für Tag,** day by day; **von Tag zu Tag,** from day to day; **einen Tag um den andern,** every other day; **nächster Tage,** one of these days; **heute über acht Tage,** this day week *or* sennight; **heute über vierzehn Tage,** this day fortnight; **es wird Tag,** it dawns; **es liegt am Tage,** it is clearly evident; **an den Tag bringen,** to bring to light; **gute Tage haben,** to live at one's ease; **an den Tag legen,** to manifest; **in den Tag hinein,** at random, from hand to mouth, thoughtlessly.
Tagearbeit, tä'gearbāët, *f.* day-work.
Tageblatt, tä'geblatt, *n. pl. -blätter,* daily paper, journal, diary.
Tagedieb, tä'gedīb, *m.* idler, sluggard.
Tagelohn, tāg'lōn, *m.* **Tagelöhne,** -löhnẹ, *pl.* wages. **Tage(e)löhner,** -löhner, *m.* day-laborer, workman.
Tagemarsch, tä'gemarsh, *f.* day's march.
Tagen, tä'gen, *vi.* to dawn.
Tag(e)reise, täg'räesẹ, *f.* a day's journey.
Tagesanbruch, tä'gesänbrych, *m.* day-break.
Tag(e)sbefehl, tä'g(e)sbẹfāl, *m.* order of the day.
Tageslänge, tä'geslengẹ, *f.* length of the day.
Tageslicht, tä'geslicht, *n.* daylight.
Tagesordnung, tä'gesordnung, *f.* order of the day.
Tagespresse, tä'gespressẹ, *f.* daily press.
Tageszeit, tä'gestsāīt, *f.* day-time; **zu früher Tageszeit,** early in the day.
Tagewerk, tä'gevẹrk, *n.* day-work.
Täglich, täg'lich, *a. av.* daily, every day, quotidian, diurnal.
Tagreise, täg'räesẹ, *f.* day's journey.
Tag- und Nachtblume, täg und nacht-blumẹ, *f.* heart's ease, pansy.
Taille, tal'yẹ, *f.* waist, figure, shape.
Takel, tak'el, *n.* **Takelwerk,** -verk, *n.* rigging, tackle. **Takler,** tak'ler *m.* rigger.
Takt, *f.* Tact.
Taktik, tak'tĭk, *f.* tactics.

Taf 321 **Tau**

Taktiker, tĕk'tiker, *m.* tactician.
Talar, talär', *m. pl. -e*, robe, gown.
Talent, talẹnt', *n.* talent, endowment.
Talg, talk, *m.* tallow, suet.
Talgen, talg'en, *vi.* to yield tallow.
Talgig, talg'ich, *a.* tallowy.
Talgicht, talk'icht, *a.* resembling tallow, tallowy, tallowish.
Talglicht, talg'licht, *n.* tallow-candle.
Talgsäure, talk'söűre, *f.* stearic acid.
Talgstoff, talg'zhtoff, *m.* stearine.
Talgsaures Salz, talk'sŏŭres salts, *n.* stearate.
Talje, tal'ye, *f.* tackle.
Talk, talk, *m.* talc.
Tamarinde, tamarin'de, *f.* tamarind.
Tambour, tam'bur, *m.* drummer.
Tamburin, tamburẽē(n); *f.* tamburine, tambour. **Tamburiren**, -rī'ren, *vt.* to tambour.
Tand, taut, *m.* prattle, gossip; trifle, vanity.
Tändeln, ten'deln, *vi.* to trifle, dally.
Tangente, tangen'te, *f.* tangent.
Tangentialebene, tangentsiäl'äbene, *f.* tangent plane. **Tangentpunkt**, -pynkt, *m.* point of contact.
Tanne, tan'ne, *f.* fir, auch **Tan'nenbaum**, -bäum, *m.* fir-tree. **Tan'nenhain**, -hain, *m.* fir grove. **Tan'nenharz**, -härts, *n.* resin from fir trees. **Tan'nensäure**, -söŭre, *f.* abietic acid.
Tannzapfen, taun'tsapfen, *m.* cone of a pine.
Tantalit, tantalitt', tantalite, columbite. **Tantalium**, tantä'liųm, *n.* tantalium. **Tantalsäure**, -söŭre, *f.* tantalic acid.
Tante, tan'te, *f.* aunt.
Tanz, tants, *m.* dance, hop. **Tanzbär**, -bär, *m.* dancing-bear. **Tanzboden**, -böden, **Tanzsaal**, -säl, *m.* ball or dancing-room, hall for dancing.
Tanzen, tant'sen, *vi.* to dance.
Tänzer, tent'ser, *m.* sin, *f.* dancer.
Tanzkunst, tauts'kynst, *f.* art of dancing. **Tanzmeister**, -mäester, *m.* dancing-master. **Tanzplatz**, -plats, *m.* dancing-ground. **Tanzschritt**, -shritt, *m.* dancing-step. **Tanzschuh**, -shy, *m.* pump.
Tapet, tapät', *n.* tapis, carpet; auf dem — sein, to be on or upon the tapis or carpet: aufs — bringen, to bring in, introduce, to bring on the carpet.
Tapete tapä'te, *f.* hanging, tapestry, paper-hangings. **Tapeziren**, tapetsī'ren, *vi.* to hang with tapestry to paper. **Tapezirer**, tapetsī'rer, *m* upholsterer.
Tapfer, tap'fer, *a. av.* brave, valiant, gallant; **-keit**, -käet, *f.* bravery, valor.
Tappe, tap'pe, *f.* paw. **Tappen**, tap'pen, *vi.* to feel, fumble or grope about.
Täppish, tẹp'pish, *a.* awkward, clumsy.
Tara, tä'rä, *n.* tare.
Tarantel, täran'tel, *f.* tarantula.
Tariff, tarĭf', *pl. -e.* tariff.
Tariren, tarī'ren, *vt.* to tare, to ascertain or deduct the amount of the tare.
Tarok, tärok', *n.* taroc.
Tartane, tartä'ne, *f.* tartan (Mar.).
Tartsche, tart'she, *f.* target.
Tartüffel, tartüf'fel, *f.* truffle; potato.
Tasche, tash'e, *f.* pocket. pouch. **Taschenausgabe**, tash'enousgäbe, *f.* pocket-edition. **Taschenbuch**, -bych, *n. pl. -bücher*, pocket-book, note-book. **Taschendieb**, -dīb, *m. pl. -biebe*, pickpocket. **Taschengeld**, -gĕlt, *n.* pocket-money. **Taschenmesser**, -mĕsser, *n.* pocket-knife, clasp-knife. **Taschenspiel**, tash'enzhpīl, *n.* juggle, juggling; **-er**, -er, *m.* juggler, conjurer; **-ei**, -ēī, *f.* jugglery. **Taschenspielerstreich**, -zhirkĕch, *m. or -stück*, -zhtück, *n.* juggling trick.
Taschentuch, tash'entych, *n.* pocket-handkerchief.
Taschenuhr, tash'enyr, *f.* watch.
Taschenwörterbuch, tash'envörterbych, *n. pl. -bücher*, pocket-dictionary.
Tasse, tas'se, *f.* cup and saucer, cup.
Tastbar, tazht'bär, *a.* touchable.
Taste, tazhte, *f.* key. **Taster**, tazht'er. *vt. i.* to touch, feel, grope.
Tätscheln, tĕtsheln, *vt.* to stroke, caress.
Tatze, tat'se, *f.* paw, claw; hand; blow or stroke on the hand; Einem Tatzen geben, to strike one on the hand.
Tättowiren, tẹttovī'ren, *vt.* to tattoo.
Tau, täu. *n.* cable, rope, cord.
Taub, täup, *a.* deaf; benumbed; weak, empty; dead.
Täubchen, tẹup'ch *n, n.* little dove or **Taube**, töy be, *f.* pigeon, dove; wilde —, wood-pigeon, stockdove. **Taubenei**, -ēī, *n.* pigeon's-egg. **Tau**

Taub, -falk, **Tau'bengeier**, -eïer, m. goshawk. **Tau'benhaus**, -hôys, n. **Tau'benfchlag**, -shläk. m. dovecot. pigeon-house. **Tau'benzucht**, -tsųχt, f. breeding of pigeons. **Tauber**, tôy'ber, **Täuber**, tëū'ber, **Täu'berih**, -iχ, m. cock-pigeon. **Taubin**, tǟūb'in, f. hen-pigeon.
Taubheit, tǟųp'hāėt, f. deafness.
Tauchen, tôy'χ'n. vi. r. to dive, duck. dip: rt. to d p. immerge, immerse, submerge. **Tauchente**, tôyχ'ėntė, f. plungeon, diver. **Taucher**, tôyχ'er, m. diver. **Tauchergans**, tôy'χ'ėrgans, f. pl. -gänſe. goosander. merganser. **Tauchergloche**, -glocke, f. diving-bell.
Tauf'act, tǟūf'act, m. act of baptizing. **Tauſbecken**, tǟūf'bȧcken, n. font; **Tauf'buch**, -byχ. n. parish-register. **Tauf'name**, -nāmė, m. christian name. **Tauf'pathe**, -pātė. m. godfather. godmother: child (being or to be) baptized or christened, called also **Taufpathe**. **Tauf'ſchein**, -shēn, m. certificate of baptism. **Tauf'ſchmaus**, -shmōųs, m. christening feast. **Tauffein**, -stȯn, m. baptistery, font. **Tauf'zeug**, -tsöǖg, n. christening apparel or dress. **Tauf'zeuge**, -tsöǖge. m. godfather; **ſeuzegin**, tsǟū'gin, f. godmother.
Taugen, tǟū'gen. vi. to fit, to be good for, nicht — ſx —, to be foreign to. **Taugenichts**, tǟū'genichts, m. a good-for-nothing fellow. **Tauglich**, tǟūg'liχ, a. fit, good, able, capable, proper; -feit, -kȧėt, f. fitness, ableness, aptness, propriety, skill, capability.
Taumel, tǟū'mel. m. giddiness, intoxication, passion, ecstacy. **Taumeln**, tǟū'meln, vi. to reel, stagger, tumble. **Tau'melnd**, **Taumelig**, tǟūm'ėliχ, a. giddy, reeling, staggering.
Tauſch, tôysh. m. exchange, bargain. **Tauſchen**, tôysh'en, vt. to exchange, barter, truck.
Täuſchen, tēūsh'en, vt. to delude, to deceive, cheat; ſich —, to be deceived, disappointed, mistaken. **Täuſchung**, tēūsh'ųng, f. delusion, deceit, illusion, disappointment.
Tauſchhandel, tôysh'handl, m. swap, traffic, barter, truck, exchange, trade.
Tauſend, tôy'ṡėnd, a. and s. thousand. **Tauſender**, m. thousand; -lei, -lāė,
a. of thousand different sorts. **Tau'ſendfach**, -fach -fältig, -feltiχ, a thousandfold: -jährig, -yāriχ, a millennial: —es Reich, n. millennium. **Tauſendkünſtler**, tôų'ṡendkünzthler, m. conjurer, juggler, jack of all trades. **Tauſendmal**, -māl, av. a thousand times. **Tauſendſt**, tôų'ṡendst. **Tau'ſendſtel** or **Tauſendstel**, tôų'ṡentstel, n. a thousandth.
Tauwerk, tǟū'verk, n. pl. -e, cordage, tackling.
Taxe, tax'ė, f. pl -n, assize, tax. import, duty. **Taxiren**, taxīr'en, vt. to tax, rate, fix (the price. **Taxirung**, tax'īrųng, f. pl. -en, estimate.

Taxus, tax'ųs (Tar. tax), m. pl. -us, yew-tree. (f. Eibenbaum.)
Technik, teχ'nik. f. pl. technics. **Techniſch**, teχ'nish, a. technic, -al **Technologie**, teχnologī', f. technology.
Teich, tēiχ, m. pl. -e, pond.
Teig, tāėk. m. dough: **maſſe**, -mųldė, f. kneading-trough.
Telegraph, telegrȧf', m. pl. -en, telegraph. **Telegraphiſch**, telegräfish, a. telegraphic; —e Depeſche, f. telegram.
Teleſkop, teleskōp', n. pl. -e, telescope.
Teller, tel'ler, m. plate; -tuch, -tyχ. n. pl. -tücher, napkin.
Tellur, tellųr', **Tellurium**, n. tellurium; **Tellurſäure**, tellu're acd. **Tellurige Säure**, tellurite. **Tellurſaures Salz**, n. tellurate.
Tempel, tem'pl, m. templ— unbedecter Tempel, hypæthral. **Tempelherr**, -härr, m. pl. -herren, templar.
Temperatur, tempęrätųr', f. pl. -en, temperature.
Temperament, tempęrament', n. pl. -e, temper, temperament. **Temperiren**, tempėrī'ren, vt. to temper.
Tempo, tem'pō, n. time.
Tender, ten'der, m. tender.
Tenne, ten'nė, f. pl. -n, thrashing-floor.
Tenor, tenōr'. m. **Tenoriſt**, tenōrizht', m. pl. -en, tenor.
Teppich, tep'piχ, m. pl. -e, carpet; f. cover, covering. **Tep'pichfabrikant**, -fabrīkant: -wirker, -virrker, m. carpet-manufacturer. **Teppichhändler**, tep'piχhȧndler, m. dealer in carpets.
Termin, tėrmīn' m. pl. -e, term.

Terminologie, tèrmīnologhī', f. terminology, technical language.
Terminweise, termīn'vèise, av. by terms.
Terpentin, tèrpentīn', m. turpentine.
Terpentinöl, tèrpentīn'öhl, n. oil of turpentine.
Terrain, terrāēn', n. ground.
Terrasse, terras'sę, f. pl. -n torrace.
Terrine, terrī'ne, f. pl. -n, tureen, terreen.
Territorial, tèrrītoriāl', a. territorial.
Territorium, tèrrītō'rium, n. pl. Territorien, territory.
Tertianfieber, tèrtiān'fīber, n. tertian ague.
Tertie, tèr'tsi-ę, **Terze,** ter'tse, f. pl. -n, third.
Terzerol, tèrtserōl', n. pistolet, pocket-pistol.
Terzett, tertsètt', n. trio.
Testament, tèzhtāment', n. will, last will; testament. **Testamentarisch,** tèzhtāmentā'rish, a. testamentary.
Testator, tèzhtā'ter, m. testator.
Testiren, tèzhtī'ren, vi. to make one's will; to testify.
Tetraeder, tetraā'der, m. tetrahedron.
Teufel, tê'fel, m. devil; twilly-devil.
Teufelei, tà::felēī', f devilish trick, wanton trick. **Teufelsdreck,** tê.'-felsdrèck, m. assafoetida. **Teuflisch,** tēūf'lish, a. devilish.
Text, text, m. text; words: double pica: lecture, reprimand; einem den Text lesen, to read one a lecture.
Textbuch, tèxt'buch, n. pl. -bücher, text-book.
Textur, tèx'tụr, f. texture.
Thal, tāl, n. pl. Thäler, tā'ler, valley, dale.
Thaler, tā'ler, n. dollar.
Thallit, tallit', m, thallite.
That, tāt, f. deed, action, fact, act; achievement.
Thäter, tā'ter, m. doer, perpetrator, culprit; actor.
Thätig, tā'tich, a. active; -keit, -kāēt, f. activity.
Thatkraft, tāt'kraft, f. energy.
Thätlich, tāt'lich, a. av. active, violent, -ly; -keit, -kāēt, f. violence, act of violence.
Thatsache, tāt'sache, f. fact, matter of fact.
Thau, tāū, m. dew. **Thauen,** tāū'en, vi. to thaw. **Thauig,** tāū'ich, a. dewy. **Thautropfen,** tāū'tropfen, pl. dewdrops. **Thauwetter,** -vetter, n. thaw. **Thauwind,** -vind, m. thawing-wind.

Theater, teä'ter, n. theatre, playhouse, stage. **Theatralisch,** teätrā'lish, a. theatrical, pompous. **Theaterzettel,** -tsèttel, m. play-bill.
Thee, tā, m. pl. Thee-e, tea. **Theeblatt,** tā'blatt, n. pl. -blätter, tea-leaf. **Theebrett,** -brèt, n. waiter, tea-tray. **Theebüchse,** -bükse, f. box or can for tea, tea-caddy, tea-canister. **Theekanne,** -kanne, **Theekessel,** -kessel, m. tea-kettle, tea-pot. **Theelöffel,** -löffel, m. tea-spoon. **Theemaschine,** -mashīne, f. tea-urn.
Theer, tār, m. tar. **Theeren,** tār'en, vt. to tar. **Theericht,** tār'icht, **Theerig,** tā'rich, a. tarry.
Theeschale, tā'shāle, **Theetasse,** tā'-tasse, f. tea-cup. **Theezeug,** tā'tsēūk, n. tea-set, tea-things.
Theil, tāēl, m. pl. -e, part, deal, portion; share, lot; tome, volume; party; zum Theil, in part, partly; — haben, to share, to participate in, to be party to; — nehmen, to participate in, partake, join in; to take an interest in; größten Theils, for the most part: ich für mein Theil, I for my part; zu Theil werden, to fall to one's lot or share, to be bestowed on.
Theilen, tāē len, vt. to divide; to share. **Theilhaber,** -hāber, m. partaker, sharer. **Theilhaftig,** -hāftich, partaking, participant. **Theilnahme,** -nāme, f. participation; interest, sympathy. **Theilnamlos,** -nāmlōs, a. uninterested. **Theilnehmer,** -nāmer, m. participant, partaker.
Theils, tāēls, a. partly.
Theilung, tāēl'ụng, f. division, partition; sharing; -zahl, tāēl'ụngetsāl, f. dividend. **Theilungszirkel,** -tsīrkel, m. divider.
Theilweise, tāēl'vēise, av. in part, partially.
Theist, tā-izht', m. pl. -en, deist.
Theismus, tā-īs'mụs, m. deism.
Thema, tā-ma, n. theme, subject.
Theodolit, tā-ōdōlīt', m. theodolite.
Theokratie, teōkratī', f. theocracy.
Theolog, teōlōk', m. theologian, divine. **Theologie,** teōlōgī', f. theology. **Theologisch,** teōlō'gish, a. theological.

Theoretiker, teorĕt'iker, *m.* one who speculates, theorist, theorizer.
Theoretisch, teorĕt'ish, *a.* theoretic.
Theorie, teorī', *f.* theory, speculation.
Theosoph, teŏsōf', *m.* theosophist.
Theosophie, teŏsōphī' *f.* theosophy, theosophism.
Theosophisch, teŏsō'phish, *a.* theosophical.
Thermoelectricität, tĕrmōĕlĕktrītsitāt', *f.* thermo-electricity.
Thermometer, tèrmomä'ter, *m.* thermometer.
Thermoskop, tĕrmŏscōp', *n.* thermoscope.
Theuer, teü'er, *a.* dear. **Theuerung,** teüĕr'ŭng, *f.* dearness, dearth, scarcity.
Thier, tīr, *n. pl.* **Thiere,** animal, beast, brute.
Thierarzt, tīr'artst, *m.* farrier, veterinary surgeon.
Thiergarten, tīr'garten, *m.* menagerie.
Thierheit, tīr'hāet, *f.* animality; beastliness, brutality, bestiality, brutishness. **Thierisch,** tīr'ish, *a.* animal; bestial, brutal. **Thierkreis,** krēis, *m.* zodiac. **Thierreich,** -rēĭch, *n.* animal kingdom.
Thon, tön, *m.* clay. **Thonartig,** tōn'artich, *a.* clayey, like clay. **Thönern,** tŏhn'ern, *a.* clayey, (made of) clay. **Thongrube,** tōn'grŭbe, *f.* clay-pit. **Thonig,** tōn'ich, *a.* clayey. **Thonschiefer,** -shīfer, *m.* clay-slate.
Thor, tōr, *m.* fool.
Thor, tōr, *n. pl.* -*e,* gate, gateway.
Thorheit, tōr'hāet, *f.* folly, foolishness.
Thorhüter, tōr'hühter, *m.* gate-keeper.
Thöricht, töhr'icht, *a.* foolish.
Thörin, töh'rin, *f.* fool, foolish woman.
Thorschluß, tōr'ahlŭss, *m.* shutting of the gate(s).
Thorweit, tōr'vĕīt, *av.* as wide as a town-gate.
Thorweg, tōr'vāg, *m.* gateway.
Thran, trän, *m.* train-oil: **-brenner,** brenner, *m.* boiler of train-oil.
Thräne, trä'ne, *f.* tear. **Thränen,** trän'en, *vi.* to weep, shed tears; to run with tears.
Thränenfistel, trän'enfistel, *f.* lachrymal fistula.
Thränenleer, trän'enlār, **Thrä'nenlos,** -lōs, *a.* tearless, void of tears.

Thranicht, trän'icht, *a.* resembling train-oil. **Thranig,** trän'ig, *a.* containing train-oil.
Thron, trōn, *m.* throne: auf den — setzen, to enthrone; vom — stürzen, to dethrone. **Thronbesteigung,** -leżhtēigung, *f.* accession to the throne. **Thronen,** trōn'en, *rt.* to reign, to sit on the throne. **Thronerbe,** -erbe, *m.* heir to the throne. **Thronfolger,** -folger, *m.* successor to the throne. **Thronhimmel,** -himmel, *m.* canopy.
Thulich, tŭ'lich. **Thunlich,** tun'lich. *a.* feasible, practicable; possible: **-keit,** -kāet, *f.* feasibleness, practicability, possibility.
Thun, tŭn (that, gethan), *vt.* to do, to accomplish; put: thun als ob. to feign *or* pretend to: seine Pflicht —, to do one's duty; leid —, to be sorry; zu wissen —, to inform, send word; gut —, to be of use, to benefit; zu — haben, to be busy, occupied; schön —, to cajole; *n.* action.
Thür, tŭhr, *f.* door; Thür und Thor öffnen, to open the door to ...; vor der Thür sein, to approach, be at hand *or* near; mit der Thür in's Haus fallen, to blunder, be (over) hasty, rash, precipitate headlong.
Thürangel, tŭhr'ang-el, *f.* hinge of the door. **Thürflügel,** -flühgel, *m.* fold of a door. **Thürfutter,** -futter, *n.* jamb-linings. **Thürhüter,** -hühter, **Thürsteher,** -zhtä-er, *m.* door-keeper, porter.
Thurm, tŭrm, *m.* tower, steeple.
Thürmchen, tŭrm'chen, *n.* turret, dungeon, prison. **Thürmen,** tŭr'men, *vi.* to tower. **Thürmer,** tür'mer, *m.* warden of a tower.
Thurmfahne, tŭrm'fā-ne, *f.* vane.
Thurmhoch, tŭrm'hōch, *a.* towering, (as) high as a tower. **Thurmschwalbe,** tŭrm'shvalbe, *f.* black-martin.
Thurmuhr, -ŭr, *f.* church-clock.
Thurmwächter, -vächter, *m.* warder of the steeple. **Thurmzinne,** tŭrm'tsinne, *f.* pinnacle of a tower.
Thürpfosten, tŭhr'pfosten, *f.* door-post.
Thürschloß, tŭhr'shloss, *n.* lock of a door. **Thürschlüssel,** -shlüssel, *m.* key of a door. **Thürschwelle,** tŭhr'shvelle, *f.* threshold, sill. **Thürstock,** -zhtock, *m.* stanchion (of the door).
Thymian, tī'miän, *m.* thyme.

Tia   325   **Tob**

Tiara, tĭă'rä, **Tiare,** tĭă're, f. tiara.
Tid, tick, m. gentle touch, tickling.
Tiden, ticken, vt. to tick (of a watch).
Tidtaden, tick'tacken, vi. to tick.
Tief, tĭf, a. deep, profound, intense. **Tief'blid,** -blick, m. penetration, sharpsightedness. **Tief'denker,** -denker, m. profound thinker. **Tiefe,** tĭ'fe, f. depth, deepness, profoundness, profundity. **Tiefen,** tĭ'fen, vr. — sich, to grow deeper and deeper; vt. to sound, cast the lead. **Tief'sinn,** -sinn, m. sigfeit, -ichkeit, f. profoundness of thinking, thoughtfulness; melancholy; sig, -ich, a. pensive; melancholy.
Tiegel, tĭ'gel, m. crucible, skillet.
Tiger, tĭ'ger, m. tiger. **Tigerthier,** tĭ'gertĭr, n. -in, f. tigress. **Tigertase,** tĭ'gerkatse, f. tiger-cat. **Tigern,** tĭ'gern, vt. to spot, as tigers are.
Tilgbar, tilg'bär, a. extinguishable, redeemable. **Tilgen,** til'gen, vt. to extinguish, annul, blot out, abolish, to sink, discharge, cancel, pay. **Tilg'ung,** -ung, f. extinction, redemption, extermination, blotting out; paying, liquidation, sinking.
Tille, til'le, f. socket.
Tinctur, tinctur', f. tincture.
Tinte, tin'te, f. ink. f. **Dinte.**
Tirade, tirä'de, f. tirade.
Tisch, tish. m. table; -blatt, -blatt, n. pl. -blätter, table-top, a flap, leaf of an extension-table, drop-leaf. **Tisch'decke,** -decke, f. table-cover. **Tischtuch,** tish'tych, table-cloth, n. **Tischfreund,** tish'frăund, m. one who likes or whom we like to dine with us. **Tisch'gebet,** -gebĕt, n. grace. **Tisch'geld,** -gĕld, n. board; board-wages. **Tischgenoss,** tish'genöss, m. messmate, fellow-boarder. **Tisch'gesellschaft,** -gesellshaft, f. company at table, dinner-party. **Tisch'gespräch,** -gespräch, a. table-talk. **Tisch'-kasten,** -kasten, m., **Tisch'lade,** -läde, f. drawer of the table.
Tischler, tish'ler, m. joiner. **Tisch'-lerin,** -in, f. wife of a joiner. **Tisch'-lerei,** -ĕi, **Tisch'lerkunst,** -kunst, f. joinery. **Tisch'lerhandwerk,** -handvĕrk, n. joiner's trade. **Tisch'lergesell,** -gesell, m. journeyman-joiner. **Tisch'lerhobel,** -höbel, m. joiner's plane. **Tisch'lerherberge,** -härberge, f. house of call for joiners.

Tisch'zeug, tish'tseyk, n. table-linen.
Titan, tĭtän', m. titanium. **Titanit.** titänit', m. titanite.
Titansäure, titän'seŭre, f. titanic acid
Titansaures Salz, titän'sayres salts n. titanate.
Titel, tĭt'gel, m. title. **Titelblatt,** tit'elblatt, n. title page.
Titelvignette, tit'elvinyĕtte, n. front ispiece. **Titelsucht,** -sucht, f. mania for titles. **Tituliren,** tit'gliren, vt. to title, name, call.
Toast, tŏst, m. pl. -e, toast.
Toben, to'ben, vi. to bluster, roar, to make a noise, to rave, rage.
Tobsucht, töb'sucht, f. madness, insanity, frenzy, rage.
Tochter, toch'tĕr, pl. **Töchter,** f. daughter, daughter-in-law: -kind, -kĭnd, n. daughter's child, grandchild. **Tochtermann,** -mann, m. pl. -männer, son-in-law. **Töchterschule,** töch'ter-shule, f. female seminary.
Tod, töd, m. death. **Todesangst,** töd'esangst, f. pl. -ängste, agony, pangs of death, anguish, mortal fright or fright of death. **Todesanzeige,** tö'desänt-kege, f. announcement of one's death, obituary notice. **Todesart,** -ärt, f. manner of death. **Todesblässe,** to'desblesse, f. deadly paleness. **Todesfurcht,** to'desfurcht, f. fear of death. **Todesfall,** to'desfall, m. pl. -fälle, case of death, casualty. **Todesgefahr,** -gefär, f. peril of death. **Todeskampf,** -kampf, m. pl. -kämpfe, agony, death-struggle. **Todesmüde,** -müde, a. weary unto death. **Todesschweiss,** -shvĕiss, m. cold sweat of death. **Todesstrafe,** -strafe, f. capital punishment. **Todestag,** -täk, m. death-day. **Todesurtheil,** -urtĕĕl, n. death-warrant, sentence of death. **Todfeind,** töd'fĕind, m. mortal enemy. **Todfeindschaft,** -fĕindshaft, f. deadly enmity. **Todkrank,** -krank, a. sick unto death, dangerously ill. **Todsünde,** -sünde, f. deadly or mortal sin.
Todt, tödt, a. dead. **Todter,** tö'ter, m. dead. **Tödten,** töd'ten, vt. to kill. **Todtenacker,** töt'enacker, m. cemetery, burying-ground. **Todtenbahre,** -bäre, f. bier, hearse. **Todtenbett,** -bet, n. death-bed. **Todtenbeschwörer,** -beshvöhrer, m. necroman-

28

Tod   326   **Ton**

cer. **Todt'enbeschwörung,** -ung, f. necromancy. **Todt'enblaß,** -blass, a. deadly pale. **Todt'enblässe,** -blesse, f. paleness of death. **Todt'enerscheinung,** -ershönung, f. apparition of the dead. **Todt'enfleck,** -fleck, m. death-spot. **Todt'engeripp,** -gėripp, n. skeleton. **Todtenglocke,** tödten'glocke, f. knell, funeral-bell. **Todt'engräber,** -gräber, m. gravedigger. **Todt'engruft,** -gruft, f. vault. **Todt'enkopf,** -kopf, m. skull, death's-head. **Todt'enliste,** f., **-zettel,** -zettel, m. obituary, list of the dead. **Todt'enmarsch,** -marsh, m. dirge, funeral-march. **Todt'enreich,** -reich, n. realm of the dead. **Todt'enschau,** -shāū, f. coroner's inquest. **Todt'enstille,** -stille, f. -silence of death. **Todt'enurne,** -ūrne, f. funeral urn. **Todt'enuhr,** -ur, f. death-watch. **Todt'envögel,** -fögel, m., **-eule,** -ēūle, f. screech-owl. **Todt'geboren,** tödt'gebōren, a. born dead, stillborn. **Tödtlich,** tühdt'lich, a. deadly, fatal, mortal. **Tödt'lichkeit,** -kėīt, f. deadliness. **Todtschlag,** tödt'shläk, m. manslaughter. **Todt'schläger,** -shläger, m. man-slayer, man-killer, homicide. **Tödtung,** töht'ung, f. killing.

Toilette, toălĕtt', f. toilet, dressing table; seine — machen, to dress one's self, to make one's toilet.

Tolerant, tolerănt', a. tolerant, liberal-minded.

Toleranz, tolerants', f. tolerance; toleration.

Toll, toll, a. mad, frantic, furious, rash; — machen, to madden. **Tollbreit,** toll'drēïst, a. overbold. **Tollen,** toll'en, vi. to rage, to have one's fun. **Tollhaus,** toll'haus, n. insane hospital, lunatic asylum, madhouse. **Toll'häusler,** -heüsler, m. madman. **Tollheit,** -hāēt, f. madness, frenzy; rage. **Tollkühn,** toll'-kühn, a. over-bold, rash, mad. **Tollkühnheit,** toll'kühnhāēt, f. rashness.

Tölpel, töl'pel, m. blockhead, fool, clown; churl. **Tölpelhaft,** -haft, a. clumsy, awkward. **Tölpelhaftigkeit,** -kāēt, f. awkwardness. **Tölpisch,** töl'pish, a. awkward, clumsy.

Tombac, tombäck, m. tombac.

Ton, tōn, m. pl. **Töne,** sound, note,

key; accent, stress, den **Ton nicht halten,** to get out of tune, den **Ton angeben,** to lead the fashion, to bear the sway. **Ton'angeber,** -āngaber, m. leader of the fashion. **Ton'art,** -art, f. key-tone, tone. **Tönen,** töhn'en, vi. to sound. **Tonika,** tō'nika, f. tonic, key-note. **Ton'kunst,** -kunst, f. science of music. **Ton'künstler,** -künzhtler, m. musician. **Ton'leiter,** -līēter, f. scale, gamut. **Ton'maß,** -māss, n. measure, bar.

Tonne, ton'ne, f. tun, large cask, barrel, ; ton. **Ton'nengehalt,** -gehalt, m. tonnage. **Ton'nengeld,** -gėlt, n. pl. -er, tonnage. **Ton'nenweise,** -vēīse, an. by tuns, barrels; in tuns, barrels.

Tonsetzer, tōn'setser, m. composer. **Ton'silbe,** -silbe, f. accented syllable. **Ton'zeichen,** -tskēchen, n. accent; den **Ton setzen,** to place the accent, to accentuate. **Ton'stück,** -stück, n. a piece of music.

Tonsur, tonsur', f. pl. -en, tonsure.

Topas, tōpās', m. topaz.

Topf, topf, m. pl. **Töpfe,** pot. **Topf'brett,** -brett, n. shelf for pots or kitchen utensils. **Töpfer,** töpf'er, m. potter. **Töpf'erarbeit,** -arbāet, f. potter's work, potter's ware, crockery, pottery. **Töpf'ererde,** -ērde, f. potter's clay. **Töpf'erwaare,** -vāre, f. crockery, pottery. **Töpf'erscheibe,** -shēībe, f. potter's wheel. **Töpf'erwerkstätte,** -vērkstette, f. pottery. **Töpfern,** töpf'ern, a. earthen, made of clay. **Topfmarkt,** topf'markt, m. earthenware market.

Topp! topp! a. well done! agreed! **Topp,** topp, m. pl. -e, top, summit, head (of a mast); vor **Topp und Tafel treiben,** to take in all sails. **Toppsegel,** topp'sägel, n. topsail.

Torf, torf, m. turf, sward, sod; peat. **Torf'stechen,** -zhtechen, n. to cut turf or peat. **Torf'grube,** -grube, f. turf-pit. **Torf'grund,** -grund, m. turf or peat-ground. **Torf'kohle,** -kōle, f. peat or turf coal.

Torkel, tor'kel, f. wine-press.

Tornist, torn'hēlts, n. raft.

Tornister, tornīs'ter, m. knapsack.

Tort, tort, m. mischief, wrong, injury.

Torte, tor'te, f. tart, cake.

Tortur, tortṳr', f. torture, rack.
Tosen, tö'sen, vi. to rush, to rage; roar, n. roar.
Toß, tost, m. plume, top.
Total, totäl', a. total, whole, entire.
Tour, tṳr, f. tour, journey, travel.
Trab, trab, m. trot.
Trabant, trabant', m. pl. -en, satellite, moon; yeoman of the guard.
Traben, trä'ben, vi. to trot, run, to go in trot. **Traber**, trä'ber, m. trotter.
Träber, trä'ber, m. pl. husks, refuse.
Tracht, tracht, f. reach, span; load, course; litter; dress, fashion, costume; tüchtige — Prügel, sound thrashing.
Trachten (nach), trach'ten, vi. to endeavor, strive or aspire (after), seek, try; nach dem Leben trachten, to attempt one's life.
Trachten, trach'ten, n. endeavor, effort.
Trächtig, trech'tig, a. having one's load, cargo; pregnant, big with, being with; fertile; — werden, to conceive; — machen, (the ground) to fertilize.
Tractament, tractament', n. treat, entertainment.
Tractat, tractät', m. treaty, treat.
Tractiren, tractīr'en vi. to treat.
Tractätchen, tractät'chen, n. tract.
Traf, träf. vt. hit, f. Treffen.
Tragbar, träg'bär, a. portable; fertile.
Trage, trä'ge, f. hand-barrow.
Träge, trä'ge, a. lazy, inert, tardy.
Tragbaum, träg'baûm, m. shaft of a litter.
Tragen, trä'gen (trug, getragen), vt. to bear, to carry; wear; to produce, yield; suffer; Bedenken —, to scruple, hesitate; Sorge —, to take care.
Träger, trä'ger, m. bearer, porter.
Trägerlohn, -lön, m. porter's fee.
Trägheit, träg'hëet, f. laziness, sluggishness.
Tragiker, träg'iker, m. tragic poet, tragedian.
Tragisch, trä'gish, a. tragic, -al, av. -ally.
Tragkorb, träg'korb, m. dorsel, hamper, (large) basket.
Tragödie, trägö'die f. tragedy. **Tragödiendichter**, trägö'diendichter, m. tragic poet. **Tragödienspieler**, -spī'ler, m. tragic actor, tragedian.
Tragpfeiler, träg'pfëller, m. pillar.
Tragsäule, -säûle, f. pillar, supporter. **Tragreff**, -röf, n. carrying frame. **Tragsessel**, -sössel, m., **Tragstuhl**, shtṳl, m. pl. -stühle, sedan (chair).
Train, train, m. train. **Trainiren**, trainī'ren, vt. to draw out, protract
Traiteur, trätöhr', m. landlord of a tavern.
Trillern, trïl'lern, vt. to trill.
Trampeln, tram'peln, vt. to trample.
Trampelthier, tram'peltīr, n. dromedary, camel.
Tranchiren, transhī'ren, vt. to carve, cut up. **Tranchirmesser**, -mosser, n. carving-knife.
Trank, trank, m. pl. **Tränke**, drink, potion. **Tränke**, trenky, f. watering. **Tränken**, tren'ken, vt. to water, give to drink; to soak, steep, saturate; irrigate.
Transcendent, transtsendent' a. transcendent; -al, -philosophie, fīlō'sōfï, f. transcendental philosophy.
Transit, transit', pl. **Transite**, m. transit. **Transithandel**, -handel, m. transit-trade. **Transitzoll**, -tsoll, m. pl. -zölle, transit-duty.
Transparent, transpärent', a. transparent; s. n. transparency.
Transport, transport', m. transportation. **Transportiren**, transportī'ren, vt. to transport. **Transporteur**, transportöhr', m. carrier.
Trapez, trapëts', m. trapezium.
Trappe, trap'pe, f. foot-print.
Trappe, trap'pe, m. bustard.
Trappen, trap'pen, vi. to tread or go noisily.
Trassiren, tras'sīren, vt. i. to draw.
Tratte, trattʼe, f. draft.
Traß, trass, m. tarras, tarrace, trass.
Traube, trów'be, f. grape, cluster, bunch.
Traubensaft, trów'bensaft. m. juice of the grape. **Traubenzucker**, -tsuck'er, m. grape-sugar. **Traubig**, trów'bich, a. clustering.
Trauen, trów'en, a. to trust, confide in, rely on, give faith, vt. to marry, to join or unite in marriage.
Trauer, trów'er, f. mourning. **Trauerbotschaft**, -botshaft: -post, f. mournful, sad news or tidings. **Trauerfall**, -fall, m. case of mourning. **Trauerflor**, -flör, m. crape worn for mourning. **Trauergedicht**, -gedicht, n. elegy, funeral poem

Trau´ergesang, -gesang, m. dirge, funeral hymn. **Trau´ergeläut**, geläut, n. knell. **Trau´erkleid**, kläet, n. mourning dress. **Trau´ermusik**, -musīk, f. funeral music.

Trauern, trou´ern, vi. to mourn; to be dressed in mourning. **Trau´erspiel**, -spīl, n. tragedy. **Trau´erweide**, -veīde, f. weeping willow.

Traufe, träu´fe, f. eaves. **Träufeln**, träu´feln, vt. i. to drip, drop; trickle; to let fall; pour. **Traufen**, träu´fen; **Träufen**, träu´fen, vi. to drop, fall in drops, vt. to drop, pour.

Traufaß, träuf´fass, n. pl. -fässer, water-butt.

Traulich, trou´lich, a. cordial, intimate, familiar; comfortable. **Trau´lichkeit**, -kået, f. cordiality, intimacy.

Traum, troum, m. pl. **Träume**, dream, fancy. **Traumbild**, troum´bilt, n. pl. Traumbilder, vision, dreamlike phantom, fancy. **Traum´deuter**, -deuter, m. interpreter of dreams. **Träumen**, tröom´en, vi. to dream. **Träumer**, tröom´er, m. -in, f. -ei, -ei, f. revery, imagination. **Träum´erisch**, -ish, a. dreaming, dreamlike, imaginary, fanciful.

Traun, troun, int. surely, forsooth, certainly.

Traurig, trou´rig, a. sad, dreary, melancholy, mournful, sorrowful, doleful; fatal, tragical. **Traur´igkeit**, -kået, f. sadness, sorrow.

Trauring, trou´ring, m. wedding-ring. **Trau´schein**, -shein, m. certificate of marriage.

Traut´, trout, a. loving, trusty, true. **Trauung**, trou´ung, f. nuptials, marrying, wedding.

Travestie, travestī´, f. travesty, parody.

Treff, treff, m. hit, blow, finishing-stroke.

Treffen, treff´en (traf, getroffen), vt. to hit, find, meet with; strike; to light upon, fall in with; to guess; to befall, happen: nicht treffen, to miss; s. n. engagement, action, battle.

Treffend, treff´fent, a. appropriate, hitting, striking. **Trefflich**, treff´lich, a. excellent, exquisite, admirable. **Treff´lichkeit**, -kået, f. excellence. [ice.

Treibeis, treīb´eīs, n. drift or floating ice.

Treibeisen, treīb´eīsen, n. stamper. **Treib´auker**, treīb´anker, m. flood-anchor. **Treib´beet**, -bāt, n.pl. -e, hotbed. **Treiben**, treī´ben (trieb, getrieben), vt. to drive, to impel, to move, push, press; to carry on, exercise, practise, pursue, make, perform: to emboss, chase; force; to separate, refine; vi. to drive, drift, float; spring; auf —, to run foul (of a ship); to shoot forth, to spout **Treiber**, treī´ber, m. driver; buster, taskmaster.

Treibfeile, treīb´feīle, f. pinion-file. **Treibhaus**, treīb´hous, n. hot-house. **Treibholz**, treīb´holts, n. drift-wood. **Treibjagd**, treīb´yacht f. battue. **Treibkugel**, treīb´kugl, f. pitch-block. **Treibrad**, treīb´rāt, n. driver (wheel). **Treibscherben**, treīb´sherben, m. test-cupel.

Treibsand, treīb´sant, m. drifting sand, quicksand.

Treil, treīl, n. pl. -e, tow-line, tow-rope. **Treilen**, treī´len, vt. to tow with a rope.

Tremel, trām´el, m. stick, club, cudgel. **Tremulant**, tre´mulant´, m. tremolo. **Trennbar**, tren´bär, a. separable. **Trennbarkeit**, tren´bärkået, f. separability.

Trennen, tren´en, vt. to separate, disjoin, part, divide.

Trennung, tren´ung, f. separation, partition, division.

Trense, tren´se, f. snaffle. **Trensen**, tren´sen, vt. to snaffle.

Trepan, trepan´, m. pl. -e, trepan. **Trepaniren**, trepanī´ren, vt. to trepan.

Treppe, trep´pe, f. stairs, staircase. **Trep´pengeländer**, -gelen´der, n. baluster, banister. **Trep´penflaume**, -klampe, f. step of the gangway. **Trep´penabsatz**, -absats, m. landing. **Trep´penteppich**, -tep´pich, m. stair carpet.

Tresor, tresōr´, m. treasure. **Tresor´schein**, -sheīn, m. treasury-bill, treasury-note.

Trespe, tres´pe, f. cockle. **Tresse**, tres´se, f. galloon, lace. **Tres´senhut**, -hŭt, m. laced hat. **Tres´senkleid**, -klået, n. garment trimmed with lace.

Trester, trester, m. grape-skin, grounds (of beer).

Treten, trä'ten (trat, getreten), *vt. i.* to tread, step; näher —, to approach; zu nahe —, to offend, insult, wrong; daneben oder fehl —, to slip, stumble; an eines Stelle —, to take any one's place; auf die Kanzel —, to ascend the pulpit; unter die Augen —, to appear before; in ein Amt —, to enter an office; einem auf den Fuß —, to tread on one's foot; unter die Füße —, to trample on; die Orgel —, to tread the bellows of an organ; den Takt —, to beat time.
Tretmühle, trĕtt'mühle, *f.* tread-mill.
Tret'rad, -rät, *n.* tread-wheel.
Treu, treü, *a.* true, faithful, strict, exact, tenacious, honest.
Treubruch, treü'bruch, *m.* breach of trust *or* faith. **Treu'brüchig**, -brüch-ich, *a.* faithless.
Treue, treü'e, *f.* faith, fidelity, loyalty.
Treuherzig, treü'hĕrtsich, *a.* confident, true-hearted, open-hearted; -keit, -käet, *f.* true-heartedness, sincerity.
Treulich, treü'lich, *ad.* faithfully, truly, honestly.
Treulos, treü'lōs, *a.* faithless, perfidious; -igkeit,- ichkäet, *f.* faithlessness, perfidy.
Triangel, trī'angl, *m.* triangle.
Triangular, triangulär', *a.* -zahl, -tsäl, *f. pl.* -en, triangular-number.
Tribun, trībyn', *m.* tribune. **Tribunal**, trībynäl', *n.* tribunal. **Tribune**, trībüh'ne, *f.* tribune. **Tribut**, trī'byt', *m.* tribute. **Tributär**, tributär', *a.* tributary.
Trichter, trich'ter, *m.* funnel, crater; -förmig, -förmich, *a.* funnel-shaped. **Trichtern**, trich'tern, *vt.* to pour in, to bottle.
Trieb, trīb, *m.* driving, drift; shoot; spout; pasture; motion; spring; impulse; instinct. **Trieb'feder**, -fäder, *f.* spring; motive, incitement. **Triebkraft**, -kraft, *f.* impellent, impulsive *or* motive power; driving-vegetative force. **Trieb'rad**, -rät, *n.* pinion, lantern (wheel).
Triebrecht, trīp'recht, *n.* right of pasture.
Triebsand, trīp'sand, *m.* quicksand, drifting sand.
Triebwerk, trīp'vĕrk, *n.* machinery, mechanism, moving apparatus.

Triefen, trī'fen (trof, getrieft), *vt.* to drop. **Triefauge**, trīf'äuge, *f.* running *or* blear-eye. **Trief'äugig**, -äügich, *a.* blear-eyed.
Trieler, trī'ler, *m.* bib; pinafore.
Trift, trift, *f.* pasture, pasturage; drove. **Triftig**, trif'tig, *a.* driving. **Trif'tig**, (treffen, to hit), weighty, sufficient; ein triftiger Grund good *or* sufficient reason; hitting, cogent, urgent, valid. **Trif'tigkeit**, -käet, *f.* solidity, validity, cogency.
Trigonometrie, trigonometrī'. *f.* trigonometry. **Trigonome'trisch**, trigonomet'rish. *a.* trigonometrical; —es Netz, triangulation; — Vermessung, trigonometrical survey.
Trillen, trīl'len, *vt.* to turn rapidly. **Triller**, trīl'ler. *m.* trill. **Trillern**, trīl'lern, *vt.* to trill.
Trillion, trillion'. *f.* trillion.
Trinität, trinität', *f.* trinity.
Trinkbar, trink'bär. *a.* drinkable, potable: -keit, -käet, *f.* potableness. **Trinken**, trink'en, (trank, getrunken), *vt.* to drink. **Trinker**, trink'er, *m.* drinker, sot.
Trinkgeld, trink'gĕlt, *n.* drink-money. **Trink'glas**, -gläs, *n.* drinking-glass, tumbler. **Trink'lied**, -līd, *n. pl.* -er, drinking-song.
Trio, trī'ō, *n.* trio. **Triole**, triō'le, *f.* triplet (music).
Tripel, trī'pel. *m.* tripoli.
Trippeln, trip'peln, *vi.* to trip, to take small steps.
Tripper, trip'per, *m.* gonorrhœa.
Tritt, tritt, *m.* step, tread, pace; kick.
Triumph, triymph', *m.* triumph; -gen, -bögen, *m.* triumphal arch. **Triumphiren**, triymfī'ren, *vi.* to triumph. **Triumph'wagen**, -vägen, *m.* triumphal car. **Triumph'zug**, -tsug, *m. pl.* -züge, triumphal procession.
Trivial, triviäl', *a.* trivial, commonplace.
Trocken, trock'en, *a.* dry; -heit, -häet, *f.* dryness. **Trock'enplatz**, -plats, *m.* drying-place. **Trocknen**, trock'nen, *vt. i.* to dry, get dry.
Troddel, trod'del, *f.* tassel.
Trödel, trö'del, *m.* frippery, lumber, old clothes.
Trödelmarkt, trö'delmarkt, *m.* rag-fair.
Trödeln, trö'deln, *vi.* to deal in frippery; to delay, to be slow. **Trö-**

Tro   330   **Tuch**

ler, tröd'ler, *m.* dealer in old things (second hand).
Trog, trōg, *m. pl.* **Tröge**, trough.
Trommel, trom'mel, *f.* drum; **-flöpfel**, -klöppel, *m.* **Trommelſchlägel**, -ſhlägel, *m.* drumstick. **Trommeln**, trom'meln, *v/. i.* to drum, to beat the drum. **Trom'melſchlag**, -ſhläg, *m.* beat of the drum. **Trommler**, *m.* drummer.
Trompete, trompā'te, *f.* trumpet.
Trompeten, trompā'ten, *vi.* to trumpet. **Trompeter**, trompā'ter, *m.* trumpeter.
Tropfe, tro'pe, *f.* tropics: **-nländer**, -lender. *pl.* tropical countries.
Tropf, tropf, *m. pl.* **Tröpfe**, fool, ninny, blockhead, noodle; armer **Tropf**; poor fellow.
Tropfen, trop'fen, *m.* drop.
Tropfbad, tropf'bād, *n. pl.* **-bäder**, shower-bath. **Tropf'bar**, -bär, *a.* liquid, fluid. **Tröpfeln**, tröp'feln, *vt. i.* to drip; trickle, drop. **Tropfen**, trop'fen, *vi.* to drop: **-weiſe**, -vēlse, *a.* by drops. **Tropfnaß**, tropf'-nass, *a.* dripping wet. **Tropfſtein**, -ṣhtīin, *m.* stalactite, stalagmite.
Trophäe, trofä'e, *f.* trophy.
Tropiſch, trop'ish, *a.* tropic. -al.
Troß, tross, *m.* baggage; **-bube**, -by-be, *m.* baggage-boy. **Troß'pferd**, -pfērt, *n.* baggage-horse. **Troßwagen**, -vägen, *m.* baggage-wagon.
Troſt, trōzht, *m.* consolation, comfort.
Tröſten, tröhzh'ten, *vt.* to console, to comfort. **Tröſter**, tröhzh'ter, *m.* consoler, comforter.
Troſtgrund, trōzht'grunt, *m.* consoling argument. **Tröſtlich**, tröhzht'lich, *a.* consolatory. **Troſtlos**, trozht'lōs, *a.* disconsolate; **-igkeit**, -ichkäet, *f.* disconsolateness. **Troſtreich**, -rēich, *a.* consolatory, comforting.
Tröſtung, tröhzht'ung, *f.* consolation, comfort. **Troſtwort**, trozht'vort, *n.* word of consolation.
Trott, trott, *m.* trot. **Trotten**, trot'-ten, *vi.* to trot.
Trotz, trots, *m.* defiance, obstinacy, disdain, spite; — bieten. to defy; to brave; ihm zum —, in spite of him; — ihm. — ſeiner, in spite of him.
Trotzen, trot'sen, *vi.* to defy, to brave. **Trotzig**, trots'ich, *a.* defiant, head-strong. **Trotzkopf**, -kopf, *m. pl.* **-köpfe**, headstrong fellow.

Trübe, trüh'be, *a.* troubled, muddy thick, dull, gloomy, sad.
Trubel, trū'bel, *m.* bustle, trouble.
Trüben, trüh'ben, *vt.* to trouble, to muddy, to disturb.
Trübſal, trühb'säl, *f. pl.* **-e**, affliction, distress, adversity, tribulation.
Trübſelig, trühb'sālich, *a.* sorrowful, afflicted, miserable, pitiful, paltry, gloomy; **-keit**, -käet, *f* sadness, dejection, melancholy.
Trübſinn, trühb'sinn, *m.* melancholy, sadness, gloominess; **-ig**, -ich, *a.* melancholy, sad.
Trüffel, trüf'fel, *f.* truffle.
Trug, trūk, *m.* deceit, fraud, illusion; **-bild**, -bilt, *n. pl.* **-er**, phantom.
Trügen, trüh'gen, *vt. i.* to deceive, to prove fallacious. **Trüg'eriſch**, -er-ish, **Trüg'lich**, -lich, *a.* deceitful, delusive, fallacious.
Trugſchluß, trūk'shluss, *m. pl.* **-ſchlüſſe**, paralogism, sophism, fallacy.
Truhe, trū'e, **Truche**, truch'e, *f.* chest, trunk.
Trümmer, trüm'mer. *gen. pl.* ruins.
Trumpf, trumpf, *m. pl.* **Trümpfe**, trump. **Trumpfen**, trum'pfen, *vt.* to trump.
Trunk, trunk, *m.* drink, draught; drinking: **-en**, *a.* drunken, intoxicated; **-heit**, -häet, *f.* drunkenness, intoxication. **Trunkenbold**, -bolt, *m.* drunkard.
Trupp, trupp. *m.* troop, band, gang.
Truppe, trup'pe, *f.* troop; *pl.* troops.
Truppweiſe, trupp'vēlse, *av.* in troops or flocks.
Truthahn, trūt'hān, *m. pl.* **-bähne**, turkey (cock). **Trut'henne**, -henne, *f.* turkey-hen. **Trut'hühner**, -hühner, *s. pl.* turkeys.
Trutz, truts, *m.* defiance; zu Schutz und —, for defense and for attack; Schutz- und Trutz-Bündniß, alliance offensive and defensive.
Tſchako, tshak'ō. *m.* soldier's cap.
Tuch, tūch. *n. pl.* **Tücher**, cloth, woolen cloth, drap; **-en**, *a.* cloth, of cloth. **Tuchfabrik**, -fabrick, *f.* cloth-manu-factory **Tuchfabrikant**, **-fabrikant**, *m.* manufacturer of cloth. **Tuchhänd-ler**, -hendler, *m.* draper, cloth-mer-chant. **Tuchhandlung**, -handlung, *f.* cloth-store. **Tuchmacher**, -macher, *m.* clothier, maker of cloth. **Tuch'-ſcherer**, -shārer, *m.* cloth-shearer.

Tüchtig, tüch'tich, *a.* qualified, apt, fit, able, solid, strong; large, hearty, sterling; **-keit**, -kāēt, *f.* aptness, fitness, solidity, ability, qualification.

Tuchweber, tuch'vāber, *m.* cloth-weaver.

Tück, tück, *m. pl.* -e, **Tücke**, tück'e, *f. pl.* -en, malice, prank, trick.

Tückisch, tück'ish, *a.* mischievous, malicious, insidious.

Tugend, tü'gent, *f.* virtue; **-haft**, -haft, *a.* virtuous; **-haftigkeit**, -haftichkāēt. *f.* virtuousness. **Tu'gendheld**, -helt, *m. pl.* -en, hero in virtue.

Tugendsam, -sām, *a.* virtuous.

Tüll, tüll, *m.* tulle, blonde, illusion.

Tulpe, tul'pe, *f.* tulip; **-baum**, tul'penbāum, *m. pl.* -bäume, tulip. **Tul'penzwiebel**, -tsvībel, *m.* bulb of a tulip.

Tummeln, tum'meln, *vi. t.* to bustle, haste, work; to break (a horse), to drill, exercise. **Tum'melplatz**, -plats, *m. pl.* -plätze, place of action.

Tummler, tumm'ler, *m.* tumbler.

Tumult, tumult', *m.* tumult, row, riot, uproar. **Tumultuant**, -uant', *m.* rioter. **Tumultuarisch**, -uār'ish. *a.* tumultuous, disorderly. **Tumultuiren**, -uī'ren, *vi.* to make a tumult.

Tünche, tün'che, *f.* whitewash.

Tünchen, tün'chen, *vt.* to whitewash.

Tüncher, tün'cher, *m.* whitewasher.

Tunke, tun'ke, *f.* sauce.

Tunken, tunk'en. *vt. i.* to dip.

Tupf, tupf, *m. pl.* Tüpfe (*dim.* Tüpfelchen), dot, tittle. point.

Tupfen, tup'fen, **Tüpfen**, tüp'fen, *vt. i.* to dot, tip. **Tüpfelein**, tüp'feln, *vt.* to dot.

Tüppel, tüp'pel. *m.* blockhead.

Turban, tur'bān, *m.* turban.

Turbine, turbī'ne, *f.* turbine, tubewheel.

Türkis, tür'kiss, *m.* turkois, turquois.

Turnen, tur'nen, *vi.* to practise gymnastics. **Turner**, tur'ner, *m.* gymnast, turner; **-ei**, -ēī'. *f.* gymnastics. **Turnhalle**, turn'halle, *f.* gymnasium.

Turnier, turnīr', *n.* tournament, tilt; **-en**, *vi.* to tilt, joust. **Turnier'platz**, -plats, *m. pl.* -plätze tilting-yard.

Turnkunst, turn'kunzht, *f.* gymnastics. **Turn'lehrer**, -lārer, **Turn'-**

wart, -vart, *m.* teacher of gymnastics.

Turteltaube, tur'teltōube, *f.* turtle, turtle-dove.

Tusch, tush, *m.* **Tusche**, tush'e, *f.* Indian ink.

Twist, tvizht, *n.* twist, cotton yarn.

Type, tī'pe, *f.* type. **Typograph**, tipo-gräf', *m.* typographer, printer.

Typographie, tipogräfī', *f.* typography.

Tyrann, tīrann', *m.* -en, *pl.* -en, tyrant; **-ei**, -ēī', *f.* tyranny **Tyrannisiren**, -isī'ren, *vt. i.* to tyrannize.

Uebel, üh'bl, *a.* evil, ill, bad, -ly; — auf, ill, indisposed.

Uebel, üh'bl. *n.* evil, ill, injury; **-keit**, -kāēt. *f.* sickness, nausea, qualmishness.

Uebelklang, üh'blklang, *m. pl.* -klänge, dissonance.

Uebelsein, üh'blsāēn, *n.* indisposition.

Uebelstand, üh'blzhtant, *m.* inconvenience.

Uebelthat, üh'bltāt, *f.* misdemeanor, misdeed, wickedness, trespass. **Uebelthäter**, üh'bltāter, *m.* malefactor, trespasser.

Ueben, üh'ben, *vt.* to exercise, practise, do, perform, drill, train; **Rache** —, to take vengeance.

Ueber, üh'ber, *prep.* over, above, upon, on, beyond, besides, more than, past, through, by way of, via, across, about, concerning; — und —, all over; — die Maßen, beyond measure, exceedingly: — acht Tage, in a week; — vierzehn Tage, this day fortnight; über's Jahr, next year, — Nacht, during the night; das Jahr —, throughout the year; den ganzen Tag —, all day; — dem Schreiben, while writing; — hundert, upwards of a hundred.

Ueberackern, ühberack'ern, *vt.* to plough over.

Ueberall, üh'berāll, *av.* everywhere.

Ueberantworten, ühberant'worten, *vt.* to deliver up.

Ueberarbeiten, ühberar'bāēten, *vt.* to revise, to do over again; **sich** —, to overwork.

Ueberaus, üh'beröus, *av.* exceedingly, extremely, excessively.

Ueberbau, üh'berbŏy, m. superstructure. **Ueberbau'en,** -bŏyen, vt. to overbuild.

Ueberbein, üh'berbān, n. wen, ganglion, exostosis.

Ueberbieten, übberbī'ten (-bot, -boten), vt. to outbid.

Ueberbinden, übberbin'den, vt. to tie upon.

Ueberbleibsel, üh'berblëīpsel, n. remainder, remnant, remains.

Ueberblick, üh'berblick, m. pl. -blicke, general view, quick survey; **-blicken,** -blick'en, vt. to look over, survey.

Ueberbreiten, übberbrēi'ten, vt. to spread over.

Ueberbringen, übberbring'en, vt. to deliver. **Ueberbringer,** -bring'er, m. bearer, deliverer.

Ueberbrücken, übberbrück'en, vt. to bridge (over).

Ueberdecken, überdeck'en, vt. to cover over, lay over.

Ueberdem, übberdām', av. besides, moreover.

Ueberdenken, übberdenk'en, vt. to consider, to reflect upon.

Ueberdies, üh'berdīs, av. besides, moreover.

Ueberdruß, üh'berdruss, m. ennui, tedium, disgust.

Ueberdrüssig, üh'berdrüssig, a. weary, tired of, disgusted with.

Ueber(s)ecf, übbereck', av. across: bunt übereck, queer, topsy-turvy.

Ueberellen, übberēl'len, vt. to overtake; ſich —, to hurry, precipitate. **Uebereilt,** -ēilt, a. precipitate, rash, hasty. **Uebereilung,** -ung, f. precipitation.

Ueberein, übberāēn', av. in accordance.

Uebereinander, übbergōnan'der, av. one over another; **-ſetzung,** -setzung, f. superposition, lying over or upon.

Uebereinkommen, übbergōn'kommen, vi. to agree. s. n. agreement, conformity. auch **Uebereinkunft.**

Uebereinstimmen, übbergōn'zhtimmen, vi. to accord, agree. **Uebereinstimmend,** übbergōn'zhtimmend, a. agreeing, accordant, unanimous. **Uebereinstimmung,** -ung, f. agreement, accord, conformity.

Ueberessen, übberēs'sen, vr. ſich —, to overeat, to eat to excess.

Ueberfahren, übberfār'en, vt. (-fuhr, -fahren), to drive over (a child etc.). **Ueberfahren,** vi. to ferry over, to carry across; to overstock. **Ueberfahrt,** -fārt, f. passage, trip across.

Ueberfall, üh'berfall, m. pl. -fälle, sudden attack, surprise.

Ueberfallen, übberfal'len (-fiel, -fallen), vt. to surprise, to attack suddenly, to overtake, to invade.

Ueberfein, üh'berfēīn, a. over-fine, over-refined.

Ueberfirnißen, übberfir'nissen, vt. to varnish over.

Ueberfliegen, übberflī'gen (-flog, -flogen), vt. to fly or soar across, over or above.

Ueberfließen, übberflīs'sen (-floß, -flossen), vi. to flow over, to overflow with.

Ueberflügeln, übberflüh'geln, vt. to outflank, outstrip, surpass.

Ueberfluß, üh'berfluss, m. abundance, plenty; zum —, abundantly; unnecessarily. **Ueberflüſſig,** -flüssig, a. superfluous, ample, plenteous, superabundant.

Ueberfordern, übberfor'dern, vt. to overcharge.

Ueberfracht, üh'berfracht, f. overload, overfreight.

Ueberfressen, übberfrēs'sen (-fraß, -fressen), vr. to overeat.

Ueberfrieren, übberfrīr'en (-fror, -froren), vi. to freeze over.

Ueberfuhr, -üh'berfur, f. transport. **Ueberführen,** üh'berführen, vt. to carry over, convey, transport. **Ueberführen,** übberfüh'ren, vt. to glut, overstock (a market); to convince; to convict. **Ueberführung,** -ung, f. conviction.

Ueberfüllen, übberfül'len, vt. to overfill, cram, gorge. **Ueberfüllen,** vt. to decant.

Ueberfüttern, übberfüt'tern, vt. to overfeed.

Uebergabe, üh'bergābe, f. surrender; delivery.

Uebergang, üh'bergang, m. passage, transition; desertion; shade.

Uebergeben, übbergā'ben (-gab, -geben), vt. to give up, surrender, deliver; ſich —, to surrender; to vomit.

Uebergehen, übbergā'en (-ging, -gangen), vt. to overlook, to omit. **Uebergehen,** üh'bergāen, vi. (zum Fein-

be), to desert, to surrender; (von den Augen), to be suffused with tears.
Uebergewicht, üh'bergevicht, *n.* overweight; preponderancy; ascendency.
Uebergolden, ühbergol'den, *vt.* to gild, to overlay with gold.
Ueberhand, üh'berhant, *f.* upperhand, superiority, pre-eminence; Ueberhand' nehmen, to predominate.
Ueberhang, üh'berhang, *m.* projection; fruit hanging over a fence.
Ueberhangen, üh'berhangen (-hing, -gehangen), *vi.* to hang over, project; -hängen, -heng'en, *vt.* to hang over; to cover with, to deck.
Ueberhäufen, ühberheüf'en, *vt.* to heap up, to load, accumulate, overload, overwhelm; -häufung, -heüf'yng, *f.* accumulation, overwhelming.
Ueberhaupt, ühberhäupt', *av.* generally, in general: at all.
Ueberheben, ühberhä'ben (-hob, -hoben), *vt.* to exempt, spare; sich —, to pride one's self, to glory in.
Ueberhelfen, üh'berhelfen (-half, -geholfen), *vt.* to help over.
Ueberhin, ühberhin', *av.* over, slightly, superficially.
Ueberhören, ühberhöh'ren, *vi.* to overhear; not to hear.
Ueberhüpfen, ühberhüp'fen, *vt.* to over-jump, to pass, to skip over, omit.
Ueberirdisch, üh'berirdish, *a.* supernatural, unearthly.
Ueberkippen, üh'berkippen, *vt.* to tip or tilt over.
Ueberkleben, ühberklä'ben, *vt.* to paste over, to glue over.
Ueberkleiden, ühberkläi'den, *vt.* to clothe.
Ueberklug, üh'berklyk, *a.* over-wise.
Ueberkochen, ühberkoch'en, *vt.* to boil too much. Ue'berkochen, *vi.* to boil over.
Ueberkommen, üh'berkommen (-kam, -gekommen), *vi.* to come over. Ueberkomm'en, *vt.* to obtain, get, receive.
Ueberladen, üh'berläden (-lud, -geladen), *vt.* to carry *or* bring over. Ueberla'den (-lud, -laden), *vt.* to overburden, overload, overcharge.
Ueberladung, ühberläd'yng, *f.* overloading.
Ueberlassen, ühberlas'sen (-ließ, -las-

fen), to yield, to leave to, to abandon, give up. Ue'berlassen (-ließ -gelassen), *vt.* to allow to pass, to give passage.
Ueberlast, üh'berlahzt, *f.* load, burden. Ueberlästig, -lözlitich, *a.* overburdened; troublesome.
Ueberlauf, üh'berläuf. *m.* spar-deck.
Ueberlaufen, üh'berläufen (-lief, -gelaufen), *vi.* to run over. Ueberlauf'en, *vt.* to pester. Ueberläufer, üh'berläufer, *m.* deserter.
Ueberlaut, üh'berlöut, *av.* very loud; too loud.
Ueberleben, ühberlä'ben, *vt. i.* to survive, outlive; -lebender, -lä'bender, *m.* survivor.
Ueberlegen, üh'berlägen, *a.* superior, more eminent: *vt.* to cover, deck: to reflect upon. to consider, deliberate; -heit, -häet, *f.* superiority. Ueberle'gen, üh'berlägen, *vt.* to lay over; das Ruder —, to shift the helm. Ueberlegt, ühberläkt', *a.* premeditated, deliberate. Ueberlegung, -läg'yng *f.* consideration, deliberation, premeditation, reflection.
Ueberlesen, ühberlä'sen (-las, -lesen), *vt.* to read over, to peruse.
Ueberliefern, ühberlif'fern, *vt.* to deliver, surrender, give up, transmit; -ung, -yng, *f.* delivery, surrender, tradition.
Ueberlisten, ühberlizh'ten, *vt.* to outwit, overcome by stratagem; to cheat; -ung, -yng, *f.* outwitting.
Uebermachen, ühbermach'en, *vt.* to transmit, remit.
Uebermacht, üh'bermacht, *f.* predominance, superiority. Ue'bermächtig, *a.* too powerful, overwhelming.
Uebermalen, ühbermäl'en, *vt.* to paint over.
Uebermannen, ühberman'nen, *vt.* to overpower, overcome, overwhelm, to subdue.
Uebermaß, üh'bermäss, *n.* excess.
Uebermäßig, üh'bermäsich, *a.* excessive, immoderate, beyond measure.
Uebermenschlich, üh'bermenshlich, *a.* superhuman.
Uebermessen, ühbermes'sen (übermaß', -mess'en), *vt.* to measure with the eye. Ue'bermessen, *vt.* to measure out from one vessel into another.
Uebermorgen, üh'bermorgen, *av.* the day after to-morrow.

Uebermuth, üh'bermūt, m. haughtiness, wantonness. **Uebermüthig,** -müthig, a. wanton, haughty, supercilious, presumptuous.

Uebernachten, übernach'ten, vi. to pass the night. **Uebernächtig,** -nächtig, a. transient, short-lived; of the day before; flat.

Uebernahme, üh'bernāme, f. acceptation, undertaking, entrance upon.

Uebernatürlich, üh'bernatührlich, a. supernatural.

Uebernehmen, üh'bernāmen (-nahm, -nommen), vt. to accept, receive, undertake, to take charge of. **Uebernehmer,** m. undertaker, manager, contractor.

Ueberordnen, üh'berordnen, vt. to put, place or rank over.

Ueberquellen, üh'berquellen (-quoll, -gequollen), vi. to run over.

Ueberragen, überrā'gen, vt. to tower above, to be prominent.

Ueberraschen, überrash'en, vt. to surprise. **Ueberraschung,** -rash'ung, f. surprise, amazement.

Ueberrechnen, überrech'nen, vt. to count over, to cast up, to calculate.

Ueberreden, überrā'den, vt. to persuade. **Ueberredung,** -ung, f. persuasion. **Ueberredungsgabe,** -rād'ungsgābe, f. power of persuasion.

Ueberreichen, überreich'en, vt. to hand over, deliver. **Ueberreichung,** -reichung, f. delivery.

Ueberreif, üh'berreīf, a. over-ripe.

Ueberreiten, überreit'en (-ritt, -ritten), vt. to ride over.

Ueberreiz, üh'berrēits, m. over-excitement, excess of excitement. **Ueberreizen,** -reit'sen, vt. to exite too much or to excess.

Ueberrennen, überren'nen (-rannte, -rannt), vt. to overrun, to outrun; vi. to fatigue by running.

Ueberrest, üh'berrēsht, m. rest, remnant, remains.

Ueberrock, üh'berrock, m. overcoat, surtout.

Ueberrumpeln, überrum'peln, vt. to surprise, to come on unawares. **Ueberrumpelung,** überrum'pelung, f. surprise.

Uebersalzen, übersalt'sen, vt. to salt too much.

Uebersatt, üh'bersatt, a. surfeited.

Uebersättigen, -ett'igen, vt. to overfeed, surfeit.

Ueberschatten, ühbershat'ten, vt. to overshadow.

Ueberschätzen, ühbershēt'sen, vt. to overestimate, to overrate.

Ueberschauen, ühbershāu'en, vt. to overlook, survey. **Ueberschauung,** -shāūung, survey.

Ueberschicken, ühbershick'en, vt. to send, forward, transmit.

Ueberschießen, ühbershīī'sen (-schoß, -schossen), vt. i. to overshoot.

Ueberschiffen, ühbershiff'en, vt. to sail over. **Ueberschiffen,** vt. to ship.

Ueberschimmern, ühbershim'mern, vt. to outshine.

Ueberschlag, üh'bershlāk, m. pl. -schläge, (of a scale), turn; estimate, calculation; little collar (of a minister); cuff.

Ueberschlagen, ühbershlāg'en (-schlug, -schlagen), vt. to estimate; **Blätter** —, to skip over, vi. to tumble or fall over.

Ueberschleichen, üh'bershleīchen, vt. to creep on, to surprise.

Ueberschmieren, ühbershmī'ren, vt. to smear over, besmear.

Ueberschnappen, üh'bershnappen, vi. to become crazy.

Ueberschneien, ühbershneī'en, vt. to over-snow, cover with snow.

Ueberschreiben, ühbershreī'ben, vt. to superscribe.

Ueberschreien, ühbershreī'en (-schrie, -schrien), vt. to cry down.

Ueberschreiten, ühbershreī'ten (-schritt, schritten), vt. to overstep, transgress, cross. **Ueberschreitung,** -ung, f. crossing, transgression, violation.

Ueberschrift, üh'bershrift, f. superscription.

Ueberschuh, üh'bershȳ, m. over-shoe, galoche.

Ueberschuß, üh'bershuss, m. overplus.

Ueberschütten, ühbershütten, vt. to pour over.

Ueberschwang, üh'bershvang, m. overflow.

Ueberschwänglich, ühbershveng'lich, a. superabundant, extravagant.

Ueberschwemmen, ühbershvem'men, vt. to inundate, deluge, flood. **Ueberschwemmung,** -ung, f. inundation, deluge, flood.

Ueberschwung, üh'bershvung, m.

Ueberſegeln, ühbersä'geln, *vt.* to sail over, navigate, to cross; outsail; **Ue'berſegeln,** (*Pp.* übergeſegelt), *vi.* to sail to.

Ueberſehen, ühberså'en (-ſah. -ſehen), *vt.* to overlook; to pass by indulgently; to slight.

Ueberſein, üh'beraēn, to be over; to be surrendered.

Ueberſenden, ühbersen'den (-ſandte, -ſandt ober -ſendet), *rt.* to send, transmit, forward. **Ue'berſenden** (-ſandte, -geſandt o b e r -geſendet), *vt.* to send over.

Ueberſetzbar, ühbersēts'bär, *a.* translatable. **Ueberſetzen,** übersęt'sen, *vt.* to translate; to overcharge. **Ue'berſetzen** (*Pp.* übergeſetzt, *vt.* to ferry, transport, carry (over); to set on the fire; *vi.* to cross, to bound, leap over. **Ueberſetzer,** -set'ser, *m.* translator. **Ueberſetzung,** -sętsyng, *f.* translation, version.

Ueberſicht, üh'bersiċht, *f.* general view, survey; synopsis. **Ue'berſichtig, -ich,** *a.* purblind, near-sighted. **Ue'berſichtlich, -lich,** *a. av.* synoptic, -ally.

Ueberſilbern, ühbersil'bern, *vt.* to plate with silver, to silver.

Ueberſinnlich, üh'bersinnlich, *a.* supersensual, immaterial, abstract, transcendental.

Ueberſintern, ühbersin'tern, *vt.* to incrust.

Ueberſpannen, überzhpan'nen, *vt.* to stretch over; overstrain.

Ueberſpannt, ühberzhpant', *a.* eccentric, extravagant; **-heit, -hēit,** *f.* eccentricity, extravagance. **Ueberſpannung,** -ung, *f.* overstraining.

Ueberſpinnen, ühbershpin'nen (-ſpann, -ſponnen), *vt.* to spin over.

Ueberſpringen, üh'berzhpringen, *vt.* (-ſprang, -ſprungen), to leap over; *vt.* to overleap; to skip.

Ueberſprudeln, ühberzhprų'deln (*pp.* übergeſprudelt), *vi.* to boil *or* bubble over. **Ueberſprųd'elnd,** -zhprydelnd, *a.* exuberant, luxuriant.

Ueberſtehen, überzhtä'en (überſtand, ſterſtanden), *vt.* to endure, overcome, to get the better of. **Ue'berſtehen** (*Pp.* überſtanden), *vi.* to stand over, to project.

Ueberſteigbar, ühberzhtēik'bär, *a.* surmountable. **Ueberſteigen,** ühberſtāl'gen (haben; -ſtieg, -ſtiegen), *vt.* to surmount, to cross over; — mit Leitern, to scale. **Ue'berſteigen** (-ſtieg, -geſtiegen), *vi.* (mit ſein), to mount over. to cross over.

Ueberſtich, üh'berzhtich, *m.* residue, rest.

Ueberſteuern, üh'berzhtöuern (*Pp.* übergeſteuert), *vt.* to cross *or* steer over. **Ueberſteuern,** ühberzhtöu'ern, *vt.* (*pp.* überſteuert), to overtax.

Ueberſtimmen, ühberzhtim'men, *vt.* to outvote.

Ueberſtrahlen, ühberzhträ'len (*Pp.* -ſtrahlt), to radiate, irradiate; to outshine.

Ueberſtreichen, ühberzhtrēich'en (überſtrich', -ſtrich'en), *vt.* to besmear; — mit Fett. to grease: — mit Pech, to pitch. **Ue'berſtreichen** (-ſtrich. -geſtrichen), *rt.* to smear, to spread something over.

Ueberſtreifen, üh'berzhtrēifen, *vt.* to roll back (the sleeves); to strip off.

Ueberſtrengen, ühberzhtręng'en, *vt.* to overstrain.

Ueberſtreuen, ühberzhträü'en, *vt.* to besprinkle, bestrew, strew. **Ue'berſtreuen** (*Pp.* übergeſtreut), *vt.* to strow, sprinkle, scatter over.

Ueberſtrömen, üh'berzhtröhmen (*Pp.* übergeſtrömt), *vi.* to overflow; to flock (over) to; (*Pp.* überſtrömt), *vt.* to overflow, inundate, deluge, overwhelm.

Ueberſtürzen, ühberzhtür'tsen (*Pp.* überſtürzt), *vt.* to overset, precipitate; ſich —, to precipitate, to act rashly. **Ue'berſtürzen** (*Pp.* übergeſtürzt), *vi.* to overset, to be turned topsy-turvy; *vt.* to put over, to cover with.

Ueberſüß, üh'berslhss, *a.* over-sweet, too sweet.

Uebertäuben, übertäü'ben, *vt.* to deafen, stun.

Uebertheuern, ühbertöü'ern, *vt.* to overprize.

Uebertölpeln, ühbertöl'peln, *vt.* to dupe.

Uebertönen, ühbertöh'nen, *vt.* to drown the sound of.

Uebertrak, üh'bertrāk, *m.* transfer.

Uebertragen, üh'bertrāgen (-trug, -getragen), *vt.* to transfer.

Uebertragen, ühbertrā'gen (-trug, -tragen), *vt.* to charge, to commission with; to confer (an office) upon; to translate. **Uebertrag'ung,** -yng, *f.* transmission, translation; transcription.

Uebertreffen, üh'bertrĕf'fen (übertraf, übertroffen), *vt.* to surpass, excel.

Uebertreiben, üh'bertreïben (-trieb, -getrieben), *vt.* to drive over or across. **Uebertreib'en,** (*Pp.* übertrieben). *vt.* to overdrive, overdo, harass, worry; to exaggerate; to push too far or to excess. **Uebertreib'ung,** -ung, *f.* exaggeration.

Ue'bertreten, üh'bertrēten or -trāten (-trat, -getreten), *vi.* to step over; to go over. **Uebertre'ten,** *vt.* (*Pp.* übertreten), to transgress; den Fuß —, to sprain the ankle. **Uebertret'ung,** -ung, *f.* transgression, trespass, offence.

Uebertrieben, üh'bertrī'ben, *a.* excessive.

Uebertrumpfen, üh'bertrump'fen, *vt.* to trump over, to out-trump.

Uebertünchen, üh'bertün'chen, *vt.* to whitewash, to color; to gloss.

Uebervölkern, überföl'kern, *vt.* to overstock with inhabitants.

Uebervoll, üh'berfoll, *a.* over-full.

Uebervortheilen, üh'berfor'täelen, *vt.* to overreach, to take in. **Uebervortheil'ung,** -for'täelung, *f.* overreaching.

Ueberwachen, üh'bervach'en, *vt.* to watch over, to superintend.

Ueberwachsen, üh'bervaksen (-wuchs, -gewachsen), *vi.* to grow over. **Ueberwach'sen** (*Pp.* -wachsen), to overgrow, outgrow.

Ueberwallen, üh'berwallen (*Pp.* übergewallt), *vt.* to boil over. **Ueberwal'len** (*Pp.* überwallt), *vt.* to overwhelm, overflow.

Ueberwälzen, üh'bervöl'tsen, *vt.* to roll over.

Ueberwältigen, üh'bervel'tichen, *vt.* to overcome, to overpower.

Ueberwehen, üh'bervä'en; *vt.* to blow over.

Ueberweisen, üh'bervěi'sen (-wies, -wiesen), *vt.* to convict, to convince. **Ueberweis'ung,** -ung *f.* conviction, eviction.

Ueberweltlich, üh'bervěltlich, *a.* supermundane.

Ueberwerfen, üh'bervěrfen (-warf, -geworfen), *vt.* to throw over. **Ueberwerf'en** (*Pp.* -worfen), to throw higher than; sich —, to get crazy; — mit, to fall out with.

Ueberwichtig, üh'bervichtich, *a.* overbalancing.

Ueberwiegen, üh'bervī'gen (-wog, -wogen), *vt.* to outweigh, preponderate.

Ueberwinden, üh'bervin'den (-wand -wunden), *vt.* to overcome, vanquish conquer. **Ueberwinder,** -vin'der, *m.* conqueror, victor. **Ueberwind'ung,** -ung, *f.* conquest; self-restraint.

Ueberwintern, üh'bervin'tern, *vt.* to winter, to pass the winter. **Ueberwin'terung,** -ung, *f.* wintering.

Ueberwölben, üh'bervöl'ben, *vt.* to arch, vault, cover with a vault.

Ueberwölken, üh'bervöl'ken, *vt.* to overcloud.

Ueberwurf, üh'bervurf, *m.* coverlet.

Ueberzählen, übertsä'len, *vt.* to count over. **Ueberzäh'lig,** -ich, *a.* supernumerary.

Ueberzeitig, üh'bertseïtich, *a.* overripe.

Ueberzeugen, üh'bertseü'gen, *vt.* to convince. **Ueberzeug'ung,** -ung, *f.* conviction.

Ueberziehen, üh'bertsīen (-zog, -gezogen), *vi.* to migrate, transmigrate, to remove. **Ueberzieh'en** (*Pp.* -zogen), *vt.* to draw over; to coat, cover; mit Krieg —, to wage war against; to invade.

Ueberzug, üh'bertsuk, *m. pl.* Ueberzüge, bed-clothes.

Ueberzuckern, üh'bertsuck'ern, *vt.* to sugar, to sprinkle with sugar.

Ueblich, ühb'lich, *a.* usual, customary, in use; nicht mehr üblich, out of use.

Uebrig, ühb'rich, *a.* remaining, left, over, rest, to spare; superfluous; — bleiben, to be left, to remain over; — haben, to have to spare; — lassen, to leave over.

Uebrigens, üh'brigens, *ar.* for the rest, besides, otherwise; moreover.

Uebung, übb'ung, *f.* exercise, practice, use, drilling. **Ueb'ungsstück,** -zhtück, *n.* exercise.

Ufer, ü'fer, *n.* shore, beach, coast; bank (of a river).

Uhlan, ulän', *m. pl.* -en, ulan.

Uhr, ur, *f.* watch, clock; wie viel — ist es? what o'clock is it? what time is it? **Uhr'band,** -bant, *n. pl.* -bänder, watch-string. **Uhrfeder,** -fader, *f.* watch-spring. **Uhr'gehänge,** -gehenge, *n.* trinkets. **Uhr'gehäuse,** -gehäuse, *n.* watch-case. **Uhr'glas,**

-glās, *n. pl.* -gläser, watch-glass.
Uhr'kette, -kette, *f.* watch-chain.
Uhr'macher, -macher, *m.* watch-maker. Uhrschlüssel, -schlüssel, *m.* watch-key. Uhr'tasche, -tasche, *f.* fob.
Uhr'werk, -wērk, *n.* clock-work.
Uhr'zeiger, -tsäēger, *m.* hand (of the watch).
Uhu, y'hu, *m.* horn-owl.
Ulme, ul'me, *f.* elm, elm-tree. Ulmen, *a.* elm, of elm.
Ultramarin, ultramarīn', *n.* ultramarine.
Um, ym, *prep.* about, around; — und —, round about; — zu, in order to; um Gotteswillen, for God's sake; *av.* past, over.
Umackern, ym'ackern, *vt.* to plough up.
Umändern, ym'ändern, *vt.* to change, alter. Um'änderung, -änderyng, *f.* change, alteration.
Umarbeiten, ym'arbäēten, *vt.* to reform, correct; Land —, to plough up. Um'arbeitung, -yng, *f.* revision; reformation.
Umarmen, ymarm'en, *vt.* to embrace.
Umarm'ung, -yng, *f.* embrace.
Umbehalten, ym'behalten, *vt.* to keep on.
Umbeugen, ym'beügen, Um'biegen, -bīgen (-bog, -gebogen), *vt.* to bend or turn (round *or* up).
Umbilden, ym'bilden, *vt.* to reform, remodel, metamorphose. Um'bildung, -yng, *f.* reformation, transformation.
Umbinden, ym'binden (-band, -gebunden), *vt.* to tie about, to bind; to rebind.
Umblasen, ym'blāsen (-blies, -geblasen), *vt.* to blow down. Umbla'sen, to blow round, — upon all sides.
Umbrechen, ym'brechen (-brach, -gebrochen), *vt.* to break down *or* up; *vi.* to break down; to impose (the pages).
Umbringen, ym'bringen (-bracht, -gebracht), *vt.* to kill, destroy, murder.
Umdecken, ym'decken (*Pp.* umgedeckt), *vt.* to relay, to cover anew. Um'deckung, -yng, *f.* relaying.
Umdrängen, ymdreng'en, *vt.* to crowd around.
Umdrehen, ym'drä-en, *vt.* to turn around, to revolve. Um'drehung, -yng, *f.* revolution.

Umdrucken, ym'drycken, *vt.* to reprint.
Umfahren, ym'fāren (-fuhr, -gefahren), *vt.* to drive out of the way: (*Pp.* umfahren), to drive *or* ride around.
Umfang, ym'fang, *m.* compass, circumference, circuit, extent. size.
Umfangen, ymfang'en (-fing, -fangen), *vt.* to surround. environ. encompass, enclose; mit den Armen —, to embrace.
Umfänglich, ym'fenglich, *a.* ample, comprehensive.
Umfassen, ymfas'sen, *vt.* to clasp, span, grasp, comprehend; to embrace.
Umfassend, ymfas'send, *a.* comprehensive, extensive.
Umfassung, ymfas'syng, *f.* enclosure.
Umflattern, ymflat'tērn, *vt.* to flutter, flit around.
Umfliegen, ymflīg'en (-flog, -flogen), *vt.* to fly around.
Umfließen, ymflīs'sen (-floß, -flossen), *vt.* to flow around.
Umformen, ym'formen, *vt.* to remodel.
Umfrage, ym'frāge, *f.* inquiry. Um'fragen, -frägen (*Pp.* umgefragt), *vt.* to inquire (all around).
Umführen, ym'führen, *vt.* to take one a long way around.
Umfüllen, ym'füllen, *vt.* to decant.
Umgang, ym'gang, *m. pl.* Umgänge, going round, turn round, revolution; intercourse, company, conversation; — nehmen, to avoid; nicht —, not to help.
Umgänglich, ym'genglich, *a.* affable, sociable: -keit, -käet, *f.* affability, sociability.
Umgangssprache, ym'gangszhprache, *f.* conversational language.
Umgeben, ymgā'ben (-gab, -geben), *vt.* to surround. encompass, inclose.
Umgebung, ymgāb'yng, *f.* inclosure, environs, neighborhood; company.
Umgehen, ym'gāen (-ging, -gegangen), *vt. i.* to go round *or* about; to go out of one's way; to have to do *or* deal with; to converse, to have intercourse with; to meditate, design, intend; to handle.
Umgehen, ymgā'en (*Pp.* umgangen), *vt.* to go around; to elude, avoid.
Umgehend, ym'gäent, *a.* prevalent, prevailing, epidemic: mit umgebender Post, by return of mail.
Umgebung, ymgā'yng, *f.* setting aside,

putting away, leaving out, omission.
Umgekehrt, ŭm'gĕkärt, a. av. converse, -ly.
Umgestalten, ŭm'gĕzhtalten, vt. to transform, transmute, alter, reform.
Umgießen, ŭm'gĭssen (-goß, -gegossen), vt. to refound.
Umgränzen, ŭmgrĕnt'sen, vt. to bound, encircle, circumscribe.
Umgreifen, ŭm'grēīfen (-griff, -gegriffen), vt. i. to grasp; to spread.
Umgürten, ŭm'gürten, vt. to gird.
Umhaben, ŭm'häben, vt. to have on.
Umhacken, ŭm'hacken, vt. to hew down; to chop down, hoe down.
Umhalsen, ŭmhal'sen, vt. to embrace, hug. **Umhalsung**, -ŭng, f. close embrace, hug.
Umhang, ŭm'hang, m. pl. Umhänge, curtain.
Umhangen, ŭmhang'en (-hing, -hangen), vi. to hang round or about, to curtain. **Umhängen**, -hengen (-gehängt), vt. to hang round, to clothe, cover.
Umhauen, ŭm'häŭ-en (-hieb, -gehauen), vt. to hew down, to fell.
Umheften, ŭm'heften, vt. to pin on.
Umher, ŭmhâr', av. all around. **Umherblicken**, -här'blicken, vt. to look around.
Umhin, ŭmhīn', av. round, around; nicht — können, not to be able to forbear, forego or help; ich konnte nicht umhin, I could not avoid.
Umhüllen, ŭmhül'len, vt. to envelop.
Umirren, ŭm'irren, vt. to wander round.
Umkehr, ŭm'kâr or ŭm'kâr, f. return, turning round. **Umkehren**, ŭm'kären, ŭm'kären, vt. i. to turn round or back, to return, upset, overset, invert. **Umgekehrt**, ŭm'gĕkärt, a. inverse, reverse.
Umkippen, ŭm'kippen, vt. i. to overset, tip, topple, tilt.
Umklaftern, ŭmklaf'tern, vt. to clasp, embrace.
Umklammern, ŭmklam'mĕrn, vt. to clasp, fasten or shut by clasps; to grasp, embrace.
Umkleiden, ŭm'klāĕden, vt. to change one's clothes or dress.
Umkleiden, ŭmklāĕd'en, vt. to dress out, to hang with...

Umkommen, ŭm'kommen (-kam, -gekommen), vi. to perish, die, fall; to be killed, lost.
Umkränzen, ŭmkrĕn'tsen, vt. to crown; to wreathe with.
Umkreis, ŭm'krĕĭs, m. pl. -e, circuit, circumference, periphery; extent.
Umkreisen, ŭmkrĕē'sen, vt. to revolve around.
Umladen, ŭm'läden, vt. to tranship, transfer.
Umlagern, ŭmlä'gern, vt. to surround, envelop.
Umlauf, ŭm'lăŭf, m. pl. Umläufe, circulation, rotation, revolution; in — bringen, to circulate. **Umlaufschreiben**, -shrēīben, n. circular (letter).
Umlaufen, ŭm'lăŭfen (-lief, -gelaufen), vi. to run round, circulate, revolve; to shift (vom Winde); vt. (Pp. umlaufen.) to run round.
Umlaut, ŭm'lŏŭt, m. one of the (German) sounds ä, ö, ü.
Umlegen, ŭm'lägen, vt. to lay or put round or on; to lay or bend back or down.
Umlenken, ŭm'lenken, vi. to turn round.
Umleuchten, ŭmlŏŭch'ten, vt. to shine around, irradiate.
Umliegend, ŭm'līgent, a. circumjacent, neighboring.
Ummauern, ŭmmŏŭ'ĕrn, vt. to wall (round).
Umnebeln, ŭmnä'beln, vt. to shroud in fog or mist, to dim, darken, cloud.
Umnehmen, ŭm'nämen (-nahm, -genommen), vt. to take round, put on, wrap one's self up in.
Umpacken, ŭm'packen, vt. to repack.
Umpflanzen, ŭm'pflautsen, vt. to transplant. **Umpflanzen**, vt. to plant round.
Umpflügen, ŭm'pflühgen, vt. to plough up. **Umpflügen**, vt. to plough round.
Umprägen, ŭm'prägen, vt. to recoin.
Umranken, ŭmrang'ken, vt. to twine around.
Umreißen, ŭm'rēīssen (-riß, -gerissen), vt. to pull down.
Umreiten, ŭm'rēīten (-ritt, -geritten), vt. to ride out of one's way, to ride down. **Umreiten**, (Pp. umritten), to ride around.
Umrennen, ŭm'rennen (-rann, -gerannt), vt. to run down, overrun.

Umringen, ụmring'en, *vt.* to surround.
Umriß, ụm'riss, *m. pl.* -e, outline, sketch, contour.
Umrollen, ụm'rollen, *vi.* to revolve.
Umrühren, ụm'rühren, *vt.* to stir up.
Umsägen, ụm'sägen, *vt.* to saw down.
Umsatteln, ụm'satteln, *vt.* to change saddles; *vi.* to change one's profession, etc..
Umsatz, ụm'sats, *m.* trade; sale, return.
Umschaffen, ụm'shaffen, *vt.* to transform, remodel.
Umschanzen, ụmshan'tsen, *vt.* to intrench.
Umschatten, ụmshat'ten, *vt.* to shade.
Umschauen, ụm'shâu-en, *vi.* to look around.
Umschießen, ụm'shīssen (-schoß, -schossen), *vt.* to shoot down.
Umschiffen, ụmshiff'en, *vt.* to sail round, double, circumnavigate; (*Pp.* ụmgeschifft), to reship.
Umschlag, ụm'shlăk, *m. pl.* Umschläge, change, turning, reverse; fold, envelop, cover; cataplasm, poultice.
Umschlagen, ụm'shlägen (-schlug, -geschlagen), *vt.* to knock down; overset, overturn, upset; to turn down, up, over; to put on *or* round, to apply; *vi.* to upset, degenerate; turn.
Umschleiern, ụmshlāe'ern, *vt.* to veil.
Umschließen, ụmshlīs'sen (-schloß, -schlossen), *vt.* to inclose, surround.
Umschlingen, ụmshling'en (-schlang, -schlungen), *vt.* to clasp, to twine around, to embrace.
Umschmeißen, ụm'shmēissen (-schmiß, -geschmissen), *vt.* to upset, overturn.
Umschmelzen, ụm'shmeltsen (-schmolz, -geschmolzen), *vt.* to remelt, recast, recoin.
Umschnallen, ụm'shnallen, *vt.* to buckle round, buckle again.
Umschreiben, ụmshrēib'en (-schrieb, -schrieben), *vt.* to circumscribe, periphrase. **Umschreibung**, -ụng, *f.* circumlocution. **Umschrift**, -shrift, *f.* inscription, motto, device; legend (of a coin).
Umschütteln, ụm'shütteln, *vt.* to shake.
Umschütten, ụm'shütten, *vt.* to spill.
Umschweben, ụmshvá'ben, *vt.* to hover *or* float around.
Umschweifen, ụni'shvăē-en, *vi.* to swing around; to wear, veer.

Umschweif, ụm'shvāēf, *m. pl.* -e, ambages, circumlocution, round about — ohne —, freely, bluntly.
Umschwung, ụm'shvụng, *m.* revolution.
Umsegeln, ụmsā'geln, *vt.* to sail around, double, circumnavigate.
Umsehen, ụm'sā-en, *vi.* to look about *or* around.
Umsetzbar, ụm'setsbăr, *a.* convertible.
Umsetzen, ụni'setsen, *vt.* to transplant; to exchange; to sell.
Umsicht, ụm'sicht, *f.* prospect, view; foresight, circumspection. **Umsichtig**, *a.* circumspect, cautious.
Umsinken, ụni'sinken (-sank, -gesunken), *vi.* to sink down.
Umsonst, ụmsonzht', *av.* in vain; gratis, for nothing, gratuitously.
Umspannen, ụm'zhpannen, *vi.* to change horses. **Umspannen**, *vt.* to span around, encircle.
Umspielen, ụmzhpī'len, *vt.* to play around.
Umspinnen, ụnizhpin'nen (-spann, -sponnen), *vt.* to spin around.
Umspringen, ụm'zhringen (-sprang, -gesprungen), *vi.* to proceed with, manage, handle; (of the wind), to chop about, veer.
Umstand, ụni'zhtant, *m. pl.* Umstände, circumstance; affair, fact; ohne Umstände, without ceremony.
Umständlich, ụm'zhtentlich, *a.* circumstantial, detailed; -keit, -kāet, *f.* minuteness; formality.
Umstandswort, ụni'zhtantsvort, *n. pl.* -wörter, *n.* adverb.
Umstehen, ụnizhtā'en (-stand, -standen), *vt.* to stand around, surround.
Umstehender, ụm'zhtā-ender, *m.* bystander.
Umstellen, ụmzhtel'len, *vt.* to beset, surround, close round.
Umstimmen, ụm'zhtimmen, *vt.* to change the tone, to tune; *fig.* to alter, bring round.
Umstoßen, ụm'zhtōssen (-stieß, -gestoßen), *vt.* to upset, push down, overthrow, overturn; to abolish, annul.
Umstricken, ụmzhtrick'en (*Pp.* umstrickt), *vt.* to ensnare.
Umsturz, ụm'zhtụrts, *m.* overthrow.
Umstürzen, ụm'zhtürtsen, *vt.* to overthrow.
Umtaufe, ụm'tāufe, *f.* re-baptism.

Umtaufen, ym'täufen, vt. to rebaptize.

Umtaumeln, ym'täymeln, vi. to stagger and fall.

Umtausch, ym'töysh, m. exchange, barter. **Umtauschen, -en,** vt. to exchange, to barter.

Umthun, ym'tyn (-that, -gethan), vt. to put on; sich —, to look or strive hard for.

Umtreiben, ym'tröiben, vt. to drive or turn round, about; to revolve; to carry on (a trade); to conduct, keep (a public house).

Umtrieb, ym'trīb, m. circulation, revolution; pl. -e, plots, intrigues.

Umtriebsmaschine, ym'trībsmashīne, f. receiver.

Umwachsen, ymvak'sen (-wuchs, -wachsen), vt. to grow round; to cover.

Umwälzen, ym'veltsen, vt. to revolve, to roll (round). **Umwälzung, -yng,** f. revolution.

Umwandeln, ym'vandeln, vt. to change, turn, transform, convert, metamorphose.

Umwechseln, ym'vekseln, vt. i. to change, exchange. **Umwechselung, -yng,** f. alternation.

Umweg, ym'vāk, m. pl. -e, circuitous or roundabout way.

Umwenden, ym'venden (-wantte, -gewandt), vt. to turn (round, about).

Umwerfen, ym'verfen (-warf, -geworfen), vt. i. to overthrow, overset, upset (a judgment), to reverse.

Umwickeln, ymvick'eln, vt. to wrap, roll, pack up.

Umwinden, ymvin'den (-wand, -wunden), vt. to wind about or round.

Umwölken, ymvöl'ken, vt. to cloud, becloud.

Umwühlen, ym'vühlen, vt. to root up.

Umwurf, ym'vyrf, -m. pl. Umwürfe, anything thrown or put on.

Umzäunen, ymtsäůn'en, vt. to fence, inclose. **Umzaunung, -yng,** f. fence, inclosure.

Umziehen, ym'tsī-en (-zog, -gezogen), vt. to move, migrate; to draw or pull down; (Pp umzogen,) vt. to put or draw round, to surround; sich —, to grow overclouded.

Umzingeln, ymtsing'eln, vt. to surround.

Umzug, ym'tsyk, m. pl. Umzüge, move, moving, removal; procession.

Unabänderlich, ynaben'derlich, a. unalterable.

Unabhängig, yn'abhengich, a. independent, av. -ly; -keit, -kāēt, f. independence. **Unabhängigkeitserklärung, -kāētsērklärung,** f. declaration of independence.

Unabläßig, yn'ablässich, a. av. incessant, -ly, unceasing, unremitting.

Unabsehbar, ynabsā'bär, a. interminable, endless, unbounded.

Unabsichtlich, yn'absichtlich, a. av. undesigned, unintended, -ly, unintentional, -ly.

Unabweislich, yn'abvēislich, a. inevitable, imperative, -ly.

Unachtsam, yn'achtsäm, a. inadvertent, -ly, careless; -keit, -kāēt, f. inadvertency, carelessness, negligence.

Unadelig, yn'ādelich, a. not noble, plebeian.

Unähnlich, yn'änlich, a. unlike, dissimilar; -keit, -kāēt, f. unlikeness, dissimilarity.

Unandächtig, yn'andechtich, a. av. undevout, -ly.

Unanfechtbar, yn'anfechtbär, a. indisputable.

Unangebaut, yn'angeböyt, a. uncultivated.

Unangefochten, yn'angefochten, a. undisputed, unmolested.

Unangemessen, yn'angemëssen, a. inadequate, improper.

Unangenehm, yn'angenām, a. av. unpleasant, disagreeable, -bly.

Unangerührt, yn'angerührt, a. untouched, left alone.

Unangesehen, yn'angesē-en, a. av. notwithstanding; disregarded; unseen.

Unannehmbar, yn'annämbär, a. -lich, unacceptable, inconvenient; -ligkeit, -lichkäet, f. inconvenience.

Unansehlich, yn'änsälich, a. insignificant: -keit, -kāēt, f. insignificance.

Unanständig, yn'änzhtendich, a. av. indecent, -ly, improper, unbecoming; -keit, -kāēt, f. indecency, impropriety.

Unanstößig, yn'änzhtöhsich, a. av. inoffensive, -ly.

Unanwendbar, yn'änventbär, a. inapplicable, impracticable, -ably.

Unappetitlich, yn'appetitlich, a. distasteful, loathesome, unpleasant.

Unart, yn'ärt, f. pl. -en, improper behavior, naughtiness, wantonness;

Una   341   **Unb**

Unartig, -ich. a. ill-bred; naughty. wanton; =igkeit, -ichkäet, f. naughtiness, impropriety.

Unaufgefordert, un'oufgefordert. a. uncalled for, on one's own accord.

Unaufhaltbar, un'oufhaltbär, Un'auf=haltsam, -sam, a. unrestrainable, uncontrollable, irresistible; =keit. -käet, f. irresistibility.

Unaufhörlich, un'oufhöhrlich, a. av. incessant, -ly.

Unauflöslich, un'ouflöhslich, a. indissoluble, av. -bly.

Unaufmerksam, un'oufmerksam, a. inattentive; =keit, -käet, f. inattention.

Unaufrichtig, un'oufrichtig, a. insincere; =keit, -käet, f. insincerity.

Unausbleiblich, un'ousbleiblich, a. inevitable, unfailing.

Unausführbar, un'ousführbär, a. av. impracticable, -bly; =keit, -käet, f. impracticability.

Unausgebacken, un'ousgebacken, a. underdone.

Unausgesetzt, un'ousgesetzt, a. continual.

Unauslöschlich, un'ouslöshlich, a. unquenchable; indelible.

Unaussprechlich, un'ousshprech'lich, a. ineffable, unspeakable; =keit, -käet, f. ineffableness, unspeakableness.

Unausstehlich, un'ousshtäh'lich, a. intolerable, unbearable, insupportable, unsufferable; =keit, -käet, f. intolerableness.

Unbändig, un'bendich, a. unmanageable, unruly; indomitable; =keit, -käet, f. unruliness.

Unbarmherzig, un'barmhertsich, a. unmerciful, pitiless, ruthless; =keit, -käet, f. ruthlessness.

Unbartig, un'bärtich. a. beardless.

Unbeachtet, un'be-achtet, a. unnoticed; — lassen, to ignore, disregard.

Unbeantwortet, un'be-antvortet, a. unanswered. Un'beantwortlich, a. unanswerable.

Unbedacht, un'bedacht, a. =sam, -sam, a. inconsiderate; =keit, -käet, f. inconsiderateness, indiscretion.

Unbedeckt, un'bedeckt, a. uncovered.

Unbedenklich, un'bedenklich, a. av. unscrupulous, unhesitating, -ly.

Unbedeutend, un'bedeutend, Un'bedeutsam, -sam, a. insignificant; =keit, -käet, f. insignificance.

Unbedingt, un'bedingt, a. unconditional, unqualified, implicit, -ly.

Unbeeidigt, un'be-ëédicht. a. unsworn.

Unbefangen, un'befangen, a. ingenuous, unbiased; =heit, -häet, f. purity, integrity, ingenuousness.

Unbefleckt, un'befleckt, a. immaculate, pure, unblemished, spotless; =heit, -häet, f. purity, integrity.

Unbefriedigend, un'befridichent, ι. unsatisfactory. Unbefriedigt, un'befridicht, a. unsatisfied.

Unbefugt, un'befukt, a. unauthorized.

Unbegränzt, un'begrentst, a. unbounded.

Unbegreiflich, un'begreiflich, a. incomprehensible; =keit, -käet, f. incomprehensibility.

Unbehaglich, un'behäklich, a. uncomfortable, uneasy; =keit, -käet, f. Unbehagen, un'behägen, n. uneasiness.

Unbehilflich, un'behilflich, a. awkward; =keit, -käet, f. awkwardness.

Unbehutsam, un'behutsam, a. inconsiderate, careless; =keit, -käet, f. carelessness.

Unbekannt, un'bekannt, a. unknown, unacquainted with, ignorant of; =schaft, -shaft, f. unacquaintedness.

Unbekümmert, un'bekümmert, a. heedless, unconcerned.

Unbelesen, un'belässen, a. unlettered.

Unbelohnt, un'belönt. a. unrewarded.

Unbemerkt, un'bemerkt, a. unnoticed.

Unbemittelt, un'bemittelt, a. poor, fortuneless.

Unbenommen, un'benommen, a. free, not forbidden.

Unbequem, un'bequäm, a. =lich, -lich, a. av. inconvenient, av. -ly; =keit, -käet, f. inconvenience.

Unberechtigt, un'berechticht, a. unauthorized.

Unberichtigt, un'berichticht, a. not corrected; not settled, unpaid.

Unberitten, un'beritten, a. dismounted.

Unberühmt, un'berühmt, a. unrenowned.

Unberufen, un'berufen, a. not called for.

Unbeschadet, un'beshädet, a. safe, unhurt. Un'beschädigt, -shädicht, a. uninjured.

Unbeschäftigt, un'beshefticht, a. unoccupied, not busy, unemployed.

29*

Unb 342 **Unb**

Unbeſcheiden, un'beshēlden, a. arrogant, assuming, without modesty; ‑heit, ‑hāət, f. arrogance.
Unbeſcholten, un'beshôlten, a. blameless, unexceptionable; ‑heit, ‑hāət, f. integrity, blamelessness.
Unbeſchränkt, un'beshrĕnkt, a. unlimited, absolute; ‑heit, ‑hāət, f. unlimitedness.
Unbeſchreiblich, un'beshrēlblich, a. indescribable.
Unbeſchrieben, un'beshrīben, a. blank, not written on; undescribed.
Unbeſchuht, un'beshŭt, a. unshod.
Unbeſeelt, un'besālt, a. inanimate.
Unbeſiegbar, un'besīg'bǟr, a. invincible.
Unbeſonnen, un'besonnen, a. thoughtless, rash; ‑heit, ‑hāət, f. rashness, indiscretion.
Unbeſorgt, un'besŏrkt, a. careless, regardless, heedless, fearless, unconcerned; ‑heit, ‑hāət, f. unconcern, carelessness.
Unbeſtand, un'bezhtänt, m. instability, fickleness. Unbeſtändig, un'bezhtĕndich, a. unstable, fickle, unsteady; ‑heit, ‑hāət, f. fickleness, instability, unsteadiness.
Unbeſtechlich, un'bezhtĕchlich, a. incorruptible; ‑heit, ‑hāət, f. incorruptibility.
Unbeſtellbar, un'bezhtellbǟr, a. not deliverable; unbeſtellbarer Brief, dead letter.
Unbeſtimmt, un'bezhtĭmmt, a. indeterminate, uncertain, undefined; indefinite (in Gram.); ‑heit, ‑hāət, f. uncertainty, indefiniteness; vagueness.
Unbeſtochen, un'bezhtŏchen, a. unbribed.
Unbeſtreitbar, un'bezhtrēītbǟr, a. incontestable, incontrovertible, unquestionable. Unbeſtritten, un bezhtritten, a. uncontested.
Unbetheiligt, un'betǟelicht, a. uninterested, unconcerned.
Unbetont, un'betōnt, a. unaccented.
Unbeträchtlich, un'betrĕchtlich, a. inconsiderable.
Unbetreten, un'betrāten, a. unbeaten, untrodden; unembarrassed.
Unbeugſam, un'böüksam, a. inflexible.
Unbevölkert, un'befölkert, a. thinly populated.

Unbewaffnet, un'bevaffnet, a. unarmed.
Unbeweglich, un'bevǟklich, a. immovable, motionless; ‑heit, ‑hāət, f. immobility.
Unbewehrt, un'bevārt, a. unarmed.
Unbeweibt, un'bevēlpt, a. unmarried.
Unbeweint, un'bevēnt, a. unwept.
Unbewohnbar, un'bevōnbǟr, a. uninhabitable; ‑heit, ‑hāət, f. uninhabitableness. Unbewohnt, un'bevōnt, a. uninhabited.
Unbewußt, un'bevusst, a. unconscious.
Unbezahlt, un'betsǟlt, a. unpaid.
Unbezähmbar, un'betsämbǟr, a. untamable, indomitable.
Unbezweifelt, un'betsvēīfelt, a. undoubted.
Unbezwingbar, un'betsvingbǟr, Unbezwinglich, ‑lich, a. invincible, unconquerable; ‑heit, ‑hāət, f. invincibility.
Unbiegſam, un'bīksam, a. inflexible, unbending; ‑heit, ‑hāət, f. inflexibility.
Unbild, un'bilt, n. pl. ‑er, ugly figure.
Unbilde, un'bilde, n. pl. Unbilden, Unbill, un'bill, f. injury, wrong, insult.
Unbillig, un'billich, a. unreasonable, unfair; ‑heit, ‑hāət, f. unreasonableness, unfairness; unfair act.
Unbrauchbar, un'brŏuchbǟr, a. of no use, useless, unsuitable; ‑heit, ‑hāət, f. uselessness, unfitness.
Unbußfertig, un'busfertich, a. impenitent. Unbußfertigkeit, ‑hāət, f. impenitence.
Unchriſtlich, un'krizhtlich, a. unchristian.
Und, unt, Cj. and.
Undank, un'dank, m. ingratitude; ‑bar, ‑bǟr, a. ungrateful; ‑heit, ‑hāət, f. ungratefulness, ingratitude.
Undehnbar, un'dānbǟr, a. not ductile.
Undenkbar, un'denkbǟr. Undenklich, ‑lich, a. inconceivable, unimaginable; immemorial.
Undeutlich, un'dēūtlich, a. indistinct, confused; ‑heit, ‑hāət, f. indistinctness, obscurity.
Undeutſch, un'dēütsh, a. not good German; unintelligible.
Undienlich, un'dīnlich, a. unfit, unsuitable, unserviceable; ‑heit, ‑hāət, f. unfitness.

Und 343 **Une**

Undienſtfertig, ŭn'dīnzhtfẽrtĭch, a. disobliging; ‑feit, -kāĕt, f. disobligingness.

Unding, ŭn'dĭng, n. pl. -e, nonentity, nothing.

Undulation, ŭndȳlātsīŏn', f. undulation.

Unduldſam, ŭn'dŭldsam, a. intolerant, -ly; ‑feit, -kāĕt, f. intolerance, intoleration.

Undurchdringlich, ŭn'dŭrchdrĭnglĭch, a. impenetrable; ‑feit, -kāĕt, f. impenetrability.

Undurchſichtig, ŭn'dŭrchsĭchtĭch, a. opaque, not transparent; ‑feit, -kāĕt, f. opacity.

Uneben, ŭn'ãben, a. uneven, unequal; ‑heit, -hāĕt, f. unevenness, inequality.

Unecht, ŭn'ĕcht, a. not genuine, counterfeit, false.

Unedel, ŭn'ãdel, a. ignoble, illiberal; mean, base.

Unehelich, ŭn'ã-elĭch, a. illegitimate, av. -ly.

Unehrbar, ŭn'ãrbãr, a. dishonorable, unbecoming; ‑feit, -kāĕt, f. dishonesty; indecency. **Unehre,** ŭn'ã-re, f. dishonor, disgrace; — machen, to disgrace. **Un'ehrerbietig, -erbŭtig,** a. disrespectful; irreverent; av. -ly. **Un'ehrlich,** a. dishonest, unfair, infamous; ‑feit, -kāĕt, f. dishonesty.

Uneigennützig, ŭn'ãgennŭt-ĭch, a. disinterested, unselfish; ‑feit, -kāĕt, f. disinterestedness, unselfishness.

Uneigentlich, ŭn'ãgentlĭch, a. improper; figurative (in Gram.).

Uneingedenk, ŭn'ãngedenk, a. unmindful.

Uneinig, ŭn'ãnĭch, **Uneins,** ŭn'ãns, a. av. disunited, discordant, at variance; — ſein, to disagree, differ; — werden, to fall out with. **Un'einig‑feit,** -kāĕt, f. disunion, disagreement.

Unempfänglich, ŭn'empfẽnglĭch, a. unsusceptible; ‑feit, -kāĕt, f. unsusceptibility.

Unempfindbar, ŭn'empfĭndbãr, a. imperceptible, insensible; ‑feit, -kāĕt, f. insensibility.

Unendlich, ŭnentlĭch, a. infinite; ‑feit, -kāĕt, f. infinity, infinitude.

Unentbehrlich, ŭn'entbãrlĭch, a. indispensable; ‑feit, -kāĕt, f. indispensableness, indispensability.

Unentdeckt, ŭn'entdĕckt, a. undiscovered.

Unentgeltlich, ŭn'entgẽltlĭch, a. av. gratuitous, gratis, free of charge.

Unenthaltſam, ŭn'enthaltsam, a. incontinent; ‑feit, -kāĕt, f. incontinence.

Unenträthſelt, ŭn'entrãtselt, a. undeciphered, unexplained.

Unentſchieden, ŭn'entshĭden, a. undecided; ‑heit, -hāĕt, f. indecision, irresolution.

Unentſchloſſen, ŭn'entshlossen, a. irresolute.

Uneractet, f. **Ungeachtet.**

Unerbaulich, ŭn'erbŏulĭch, a. unedifying.

Unerbittlich, ŭn'erbĭttlĭch, a. inexorable. **Un'erbittlichfeit, -kāĕt,** f. inexorableness.

Unerfahren, ŭn'erfãren, a. inexperienced; ‑feit, -kāĕt, f. inexperience.

Unerforſchlich, ŭn'erforshlĭch, a. inscrutable; ‑feit, -kāĕt, f. inscrutableness.

Unerfreulich, ŭn'erfrãulĭch, a. cheerless, sad, unpleasant.

Unergründlich, ŭn'ergrŭntlĭch, a. unfathomable; ‑feit, -kāĕt, f. unfathomableness.

Unerheblich, ŭn'erhãplĭch, a. indifferent; ‑feit, -kāĕt, f. inconsiderableness.

Unerhört, ŭn'erhŏhrt, a. unheard of, unprecedented; not heard or granted.

Unerkannt, ŭn'erkãnnt, a. unrecognized, unknown. **Unerkenntlich,** ŭn'erkenntlĭch, a. unrecognizable; ungrateful; ‑feit, -kāĕt, f. ungratefulness.

Unerklärbar, ŭn'erklãrbãr, a. **Un'erflärlich,** -lĭch, a. inexplicable; ‑feit, -kāĕt, f. inexplicableness.

Unerläßlich, ŭn'erlẽsslĭch, a. indispensable: ‑feit, -kāĕt, f. indispensableness.

Unerlaubt, ŭn'erlãubt, a. illicit, unlawful.

Unermeßlich, ŭn'ermẽsslĭch, a. immense, immeasurable; ‑feit, -kāĕt, f. immensity.

Unermüdet, ŭn'ermŭhdet, a. unwearied, indefatigable. **Un'ermüdlich,** -lĭch, a. ‑feit, -kāĕt, f. indefatigableness.

Unerörtert, un'ērörtĕrt, a. undiscussed, unexplained.
Unerreichbar, un'ĕrrächbär, a. unattainable.
Unersättlich, un'ĕrsęttlich, a. insatiable; ‑feit, ‑käĕt, f. insatiableness, insatiability.
Unerschaffen, un'ĕrshaffen, a. uncreated.
Unerschöpflich, un'ĕrshöpflich, a. inexhaustible.
Unerschrocken, un'ĕrshrocken, a. dauntless, intrepid; ‑heit, ‑häĕt, f. intrepidity.
Unerschütterlich, un'ĕrshütterlich, a. unshaken; ‑feit, ‑käĕt, f. imperturbation.
Unerschwinglich, un'ĕrshvinglich, a. unattainable, unobtainable, what cannot be raised.
Unersetzlich, un'ĕrsęzslich, a. irreparable, irretrievable; ‑feit, ‑käĕt, f. irreparability.
Ersteiglich, un'ĕrzhtāiklich, a. inaccessible, not scalable, unsurmountable.
Unerträglich, un'ĕrträklich, a. unsufferable, intolerable; ‑feit, ‑käĕt, f. intolerableness.
Unerwachsen, un'ĕrvaksen, a. not full grown, not adult, of tender age.
Unerwähnt, un'ĕrvänt, a. unmentioned.
Unerwartet, un'ĕrvartet, a. unexpected, unhoped for; av. unawares.
Unerweislich, un'ĕrvĕislich, a. not demonstrable. **Unerwiesen**, un'ĕrvīsen, a. unproved.
Unerwogen, un'ĕrvögen, a. unconsidered.
Unerwünscht, un'ĕrvünsht, a. unwished for.
Unerzogen, un'ĕrtsögen, a. uneducated.
Unfähig, un'fä'‑ich, a. unfit, unable; incompetent, incapable; — machen, to disable; ‑feit, ‑käĕt, f. inability; incompetence, incapacity, unfitness.
Unfall, un'fall, pl. Unfälle, accident.
Unfaßlich, un'fasslich, a. incomprehensible, unintelligible.
Unfehlbar, un'fälbär, a. infallible; ‑feit, ‑kĭĕt, f. infallibility.
Unfein, un'fęen, f. indelicate.
Unfern, un'fĕrn, av. not far o.I.
Unflath, un'flät, m. dirt, filth. **Unflätter**, un'flätĕr, m. dirty, filthy, lewd, obscene fellow: ‑ei, ‑ēi', f. filthiness, obscenity. **Unflätig**, un'flätich, a. filthy, dirty, nasty, obscene.
Unfleiß, un'flēiss, m. indolence, inapplication; ‑ig, ‑ich, a. indolent, slothful, lazy.
Ungehorsam, un'folksam, a. disobedient; ‑feit, ‑käĕt, f. disobedience.
Unförmlich, un'förmlich, a. misshapen, shapeless, disproportionate; ‑feit, ‑käĕt, f. shapelessness, deformity, auch **Unform**, un'form.
Unfrankirt, un'frankīrt, a. not prepaid.
Unfrei, un'frēi, a. unfree, under restraint; ‑heit, ‑häĕt, f. want of freedom; restraint; bondage; ‑willig, ‑villich, a. involuntary.
Unfreundlich, un'frŏintlich, a. unfriendly, unkind: ‑feit, ‑käĕt, f. unfriendliness, unkindness. **Unfreundschaftlich**, ‑shaftlich, a. unfriendly.
Unfriede, un'frīde, m. discord.
Unfruchtbar, un'iruchtbär, a. barren, sterile; ‑feit, ‑käĕt, f. sterility, barrenness.
Unfug, un'fūk, m. mischief, nuisance; misdemeanor. **Unfügsam**, un'fūksam, a. uncomplying, refractory.
Unfüglich, un'fühklich, a. unfitting, improper, inconvenient.
Unfurchtsam, un'furchtsam, a. intrepid.
Ungangbar, un'gangbär, a. impassable, unsalable, uncurrent; not current; ‑feit, ‑käĕt, f. impassability.
Ungastlich, un'gastlich, **Ungastfreundlich**, un'gastfrŏintlich, a. inhospitable.
Ungeachtet, un'gĕachtĕt, pr. in spite of; Cj. notwithstanding, although.
Ungeaendet, un'gĕ-ĕndĕt, a. unpunished.
Ungebahnt, un'gĕbänt, a. unbeaten.
Ungebärdig, un'gĕbĕrdich, a. unruly, unmannerly.
Ungebeten, un'gĕbĕten, a. unasked, uninvited.
Ungebildet, un'gĕbildĕt, a. uneducated, uncultivated, rude, impolite.
Ungeboren, un'gĕbōren, a. unborn.
Ungebräuchlich, un'gĕbrŏichlich, a. unusual.
Ungebühr, un'gĕbühr, f. impropriety; ‑end, ‑ent, **Ungebührlich**, ‑lich, a

improper, undue, unbecoming; ſkeit, -kået, f. impropriety, indecency, improper action.

Ungebunden, un'gebunden, a. unbound; dissolute, licentious; prosaic; —e Rede. prose; ſheit, -håst, f. licentiousness, wantonness.

Ungebeihlich, un'gedeihlich, a. thriftless.

Ungedruckt, un'gedruckt, a. unprinted.

Ungeduld, un'gedult, f. impatience; -ig, -ich, a. impatient, av. -ly.

Ungefähr, un'gefähr, a. av. approximate, about, almost; von Ungefähr, accidental, -ly; s. n. accident, chance, hap.

Ungefährdet, un'gefärdet, a. safe, unhurt.

Ungefällig, un'gefällich, a. unpleasant, disobliging; ſheit, -kået, f. disobligingness, unpleasantness.

Ungefesselt, un'gefesselt, a. unfettered.

Ungeflissen, un'geflissen, -tlich, -tlich, a. av. unintentional, -ly.

Ungefordert, un'gefordert, a. undemanded.

Ungefragt, un'gefrågt, a. unasked.

Ungegründet, un'gegründet, a. unfounded.

Ungehalten, un'gehalten, a. angry, indignant; — ſein, to be angry with, — at.

Ungeheißen, un'gehäessen, a. unbidden, voluntary; av. voluntarily, on one's own accord.

Ungeheuchelt, un'gehöuchelt, a. unfeigned.

Ungeheuer, un'gehöuer, a. enormous, prodigious, awful, vast; s. n. monster.

Ungehindert, un'gehindert, a. unhindered.

Ungehobelt, un'gehöbelt, a. not planed; unpolished, uncouth.

Ungehörig, un'gehöhrich, a. undue.

Ungehorſam, un'gehorsam, a. disobedient; — ſein, to disobey; s. m. disobedience.

Ungeiſtig, un'gäszhtich, a. not spiritual.

Ungekannt, un'gekannt, a. unknown.

Ungekocht, un'gekocht, a. unboiled, raw.

Ungekünſtelt, un'geklinzhtålt, a. unaffected, natural, artless.

Ungeladen, un'geläden, a. uninvited; unloaded, uncharged.

Ungeläufig, un'geläufich, a. not fluent, not natural; heavy (tongue).

Ungeläutert, un'geläutert, a. unrefined, not clarified.

Ungelegen, un'gelägen, a. av. inopportune, inconvenient, -ly; unreasonable, -bly; ſheit, -håst, f. unreasonableness, inconvenience.

Ungelehrig, un'gelährich, a. indocile, unteachable; ſheit, -kået, f. indocility. Ungelehrt, un'gelårt, a. unlearned, illiterate.

Ungelenk, un'gelenk, a. heavy, clumsy, awkward; ſheit, -håst, f. awkwardness.

Ungelöſcht, un'gelöſht, a. unquenched, unextinguished; —er Kalk, unslaked lime, quicklime.

Ungemach, un'gemäch, n. trouble, inconvenience, hardship.

Ungemächlich, un'gemechlich, a. uncomfortable, uneasy; ſheit, -kået, f. uneasiness, inconvenience.

Ungemäß, un'gemäss, a. inappropriate.

Ungemein, un'gemäen, a. uncommon, wonderful, extraordinary; av. exceedingly, uncommonly, extremely.

Ungemessen, un'gemässen, a. unmeasured, immense.

Ungemüthlich, un'gemühtlich, a. uncomfortable; formal.

Ungemiſcht, un'gemisht, a. unmixed.

Ungenannt, un'genannt, a. unnamed, anonymous.

Ungenau, un'genäu, a. av. inaccurate, inexact, -ly, unprecise; ſigkeit, -ich-kået, f. inaccuracy, inexactness.

Ungeneigt, un'genåekt, a. disinclined.

Ungenießbar, un'genissbår, a. not eatable, distasteful, disgusting; ſheit, -kået, f. distastefulness.

Ungenossen, un'genossen, a. unenjoyed.

Ungenügend, un'genühgent, a. unsatisfactory, insufficient, not sufficient.

Ungenügſam, un'genühksam, a. discontented, unsatisfiable; ſheit, -kået, f. insatiability.

Ungenützt, un'genützt, a. unused.

Ungeordnet, un'ge-ordnet, a. unarranged, disorderly.

Ungepflaſtert, un'gepflazhtårt, a. unpaved.

Ungepflügt, un'gepflühkt, a. unploughed.

Ungeprüft, un'gepruhft, a. unexamined.

Ungeputzt, un'geputzt, a. uncleaned, untrimmed, undressed.

Ungerächt, un'gerächt, a. unavenged.

Ungerade, un'gerā-de, a. uneven, odd.

Ungerathen, un'gerāten, a. unsuccessful, degenerate.

Ungerechnet, un'gerĕchnet, a. uncounted.

Ungerecht, un'gerĕcht, a. unjust, av. -ly; -igfeit, -ichkăet, f. injustice.

Ungereimt, un'gerēmt, a. not rhymed, not in rhyme, absurd, preposterous; -heit, -hăet, f. absurdity.

Ungern, un'gĕrn, av. unwillingly.

Ungerochen, un'gerŏchen, a. unavenged.

Ungesalzen, un'gesaltsen, a. unsalted, unseasoned; insipid.

Ungesättigt, un'gesettigt, a. unsated, unsatisfied.

Ungesäuert, un'geseüert, a. unleavened.

Ungesäumt, un'gesäumt, a. unhemmed.

Ungesäumt, un'gesäumt, a. undelayed, immediate, speedy, prompt; av. immediately.

Ungeschaffen, un'geshaffen, a. uncreated.

Ungeschehen, un'geshā-en, a. undone.

Ungescheut, un'gesheūt, a. unscared; without restraint; foolish, silly.

Ungeschichtet, un'geshichtĕt, a. unstratified.

Ungeschick, un'geshick, n. awkwardness; -lichfeit, -lichkăet, f. clumsiness, awkwardness. **Ungeschickt**, un'geshickt, a. clumsy, awkward; inopportune.

Ungeschlacht, un'geshlacht, a. uncouth, boorish; -heit, -hăet, f. boorishness, rudeness, uncouthness.

Ungeschliffen, un'geshliffen, a. unpolished, unmannerly; -heit, -hăet, f. unpoliteness.

Ungeschmälert, un'geshmălĕrt, a. undiminished, unimpaired.

Ungeschmeidig, un'geshmëdich, a. unpliant; -feit, -kăet, f. unpliantness.

Ungeschminkt, un'geshminkt, a. unpainted; unvarnished, undisguised, plain, simple.

Ungeschoren, un'geshōren, a. unshorn, unshaven, uncut (velvet); alone, unmolested.

Ungeschwächt, un'geshvecht, a. not weakened; undefiled.

Ungeschworen, un'geshvōren, a. unsworn; av. without oath.

Ungesehen, un'gesā-en, a. unseen.

Ungesellig, un'gesellich, a. unsocial, unsociable; -feit, -kăet, f. unsociableness, unsociability.

Ungesetzlich, un'gesetslich, a. illegal; -feit, -kăet, f. illegality, unlawfulness.

Ungesittet, un'gesittet, a. ill-bred, unmannerly, uncivil; -heit, -hăet, f. unmannerliness.

Ungesotten, un'gesotten, a. unboiled.

Ungestalt(et), un'gezhtalt(et), a. misshapen, ill formed; s. f. und -heit, -hăet, f. misshapenness, deformity.

Ungestört, un'gezhtöhrt, a. undisturbed.

Ungestraft, un'gezhträft, a. unpunished; -heit, -hăet, f. impunity.

Ungestüm, un'gezhtüm, a. impetuous, violent, stormy, tempestuous; s. n. impetuosity, fury.

Ungesucht, un'gesucht, a. unsought (for).

Ungesund, un'gesunt, a. unhealthy, unwholesome; -heit, -hăet, f. unhealthiness, insalubrity.

Ungetauft, un'getäuft, a. unbaptized.

Ungethan, un'getän, a. undone.

Ungetheilt, un'getăelt, a. undivided, general.

Ungethier, un'getīr, n. pl. -e, monster.

Ungethüm, un'getüm, n. pl. -e, monster.

Ungetreu, un'getreū, a. faithless, unfaithful, false; -er, -er, m. Un'getreue, f. false, faithless lover.

Ungetröstet, un'getrōzhtĕt, a. unconsoled.

Ungeübt, un'ge-ühpt, a. unexercised.

Ungewarnt, un'gevärnt, a. unwarned.

Ungewaschen, un'gevashen, a. unwashed.

Ungeweiht, un'gevĕlt, a. unconsecrated.

Ungewiß, un'geviss, a. uncertain; -heit, -hăet, f. uncertainty.

Ungewissenhaft, un'gevissenhaft, a. unconscientious; -igfeit, -ichkăet, f. unconscientiousness.

Ungewitter, un'gevitter, n. thunderstorm.

Ungewogenheit, un'gevōgenhăet, f. disaffection.

Ungewöhnlich, un'gevöhnlich, a. uncommon, unusual; -feit, -kăet, f.

singularity, novelty, unusualness, uncommonness. **Ungewohnt,** un'gevönt, a. unused (to), strange, extraordinary, unaccustomed; **-heit,** -häet, f. unwontedness, uncommonness; rareness, rarity.
Ungewürzt, un'gevürtst, a. unseasoned.
Ungezählt, un'getsält, a. uncounted.
Ungezähmt, un'getsämt, a. untamed.
Ungeziefer, un'getsïfer, n. vermin.
Ungeziemend, un'getsïmend, a. unbecoming.
Ungeziert, un'getsïrt, a. unadorned, unaffected.
Ungezogen, un'getsögen, a. ill-bred, unmannered, naughty. **Un'gezogenheit,** -häet, f. ill-breeding, naughtiness.
Ungezügelt, un'getsühgelt, a. unbridled.
Ungezwungen, un'getsvung-en, a. unconstrained, easy, unaffected; **-heit,** -häet, f. ease, easiness, unaffectedness.
Ungiltig, un'giltich, a. invalid; not current; **-keit,** -käet, f. invalidity.
Unglaube, un'glåubø, m. disbelief; irreligion, infidelity, unbelief.
Ungläubig, un'gläubich, a. infidel, unbelieving; **-er,** -er, m. **Un'gläubige,** f. infidel, unbeliever.
Unglaublich, un'gläublich, a. incredible; **-keit,** -käet, f. incredibility.
Ungleich, un'glëich, a. av. unequal, uneven, odd; dissimilar; — besser, by far better; **-artig,** -ärtich, a. heterogeneous, dissimilar; **-keit,** -käet, f. heterogeneity, dissimilarity. **Un'gleichförmig,** -förmich, a. not uniform; **-keit,** -käet, f. want of uniformity. **Ungleichheit,** un'glëichhäet, f. unlikeness, imparity, inequality.
Unglimpf, un'glimpf, m. unkindness, harshness; **-lich,** -lich, a. unkind, harsh.
Unglück, un'glück, n. misfortune, ill luck, bad luck, calamity, adversity; **-lich,** -lich, a. av. unhappy, unlucky, -ily, unfortunate, -ly. **Un'glückselig,** -sälich, a. unhappy; **-keit,** -käet, f. unhappiness. **Un'glücksfall,** -fall, m. pl. **Unglücksfälle,** accident.
Ungnade, un'g(e)nä-de, f. disgrace, loss of favor. **Ungnädig,** un'g(e)nädich, a. ungracious, angry.

Ungöttlich, un'göttlich, a. ungodly, impious; **-keit,** -käet, f. ungodliness, impiety.
Ungrund, un'grunt, m. groundlessness. **Ungründlich,** un'gründlich, a. av. superficial, -ly.
Ungunst, un'gunzht, f. disfavor, disgrace, adversity. **Ungünstig,** un'günzhtich, a. unfavorable, ungracious, inauspicious.
Ungut, un'gut, a. bad, not good or kind. **Ungütig,** un'gühtich, a. av. unkind, -ly; — aufnehmen, to take amiss, unkindly.
Unhaltbar, un'haltbär, a. untenable; **-keit,** -käet, f. indefensibility.
Unheil, un'häel, n. mischief, harm, disaster; **-bar,** -bär, a. incurable; **-keit,** -käet, f. incurability.
Unheilig, un'häelich, a. unholy, profane; **-keit,** -käet, f. unholiness, profanity.
Unheilsam, un'häelsam, a. unwholesome, insalubrious. **Un'heilvoll,** un'häelfoll, a. inauspicious, disastrous.
Unheimlich, un'häemlich, a. dismal, haunted, forbidding; es ist, wird mir unheimlich, I feel uneasy.
Unhöflich, un'höflich, a. impolite, -ly, uncivil, rude, -ly; **-keit,** -käet, f. impoliteness, incivility, rudeness.
Unhold, un'holt, a. graceless; ungracious, unfavorable, unkind; s. m. fiend, devil; **-in,** f. hag, witch, sorceress.
Unhörbar, un'hörbär, a. inaudible.
Uniform, u'niform, f. uniform, regimentals; **-iren,** -ïren, vt. to clothe (in uniforms).
Union, unïön', f. union; confederation. **Uniren,** unï'ren, vt. to unite.
Universal, unïfersäl', a. universal, sovereign; **-erbe,** -erbø, m. **-n,** pl. **-n,** heir general or at law.
Universalist, unïfersälizht', m. **-en,** pl. **-en,** universalist.
Universalmittel, unïfersäl'mittel, n. universal remedy, panacea.
Universell, unïfersëll', a. universal.
Universität, unïfersïtät', f. university.
Universum, unïfer'sum, n. universe.
Unke, ung'ke, f. toad; frog; snake.
Unkenntlich, un'kenntlich, a. irrecognizable; indiscernible. **Un'kenntniss,** -niss, f. ignorance, want of knowledge.

Unkeusch, ŭn′kēŭsh, a. unchaste; **‑heit**, ‑hĕĕt, f. unchastity.
Unkindlich, ŭn′kĭntlĭch, a. unfilial; not childlike.
Unklar, ŭn′klär, a. obscure, confused; entangled; foul (Mar.).
Unklug, ŭn′klŭk, a. av. imprudent, ‑ly; **‑heit**, ‑hĕĕt, f. imprudence.
Unkörperlich, ŭn′körpĕrlĭch, a. incorporeal, immaterial; **‑keit**, ‑kĕĕt, f. incorporeity, immateriality.
Unkosten, ŭn′kŏshten, s. pl. expenses, costs, charges.
Unkräftig, ŭn′kreftĭg, a. inefficacious.
Unkraut, ŭn′krŏŭt, n. pl. Unkräuter, weed.
Unkultivirt, ŭn′kŭltĭfīrt, a. uncultivated.
Unkunde, ŭn′kŭnde, f. ignorance.
Unkundig, ŭn′kŭndĭch, a. ignorant.
Unlängst, ŭn′lengzht, av. of late, the other day, lately, not long ago or since.
Unläugbar, ŭnlŏŭk′bär, a. undeniable, incontestable; **‑keit**, ‑kĕĕt, f. incontestableness.
Unlauter, ŭn′lŏŭter, a. impure; interested; **‑keit**, ‑kĕĕt, f. impurity, uncleanness.
Unleidlich, ŭn′lītlĭch, a. intolerable, unbearable, unsufferable. tedious.
Unlenksam, ŭn′lenksam, a. unmanageable, unruly; **‑keit**, ‑kĕĕt, f. unruliness.
Unlesbar, ŭn′lāsbär, **Unleserlich**, ŭn′lāsĕrlĭch, a. illegible, not decipherable; **‑keit**, ‑kĕĕt, f. illegibility.
Unlieb, ŭn′līb, a. unpleasant; **‑lich**, ‑lĭch, basf.
Unlöblich, ŭn′löhblĭch, a. blamable.
Unlust, ŭn′lŭzht, f. dislike, disinclination, disgust, displeasure; **‑ig**, ‑ĭch, a. ill‑humored, out of humor.
Unmacht, ŭn′macht, f. impotence: swoon. **Unmächtig**, ŭn′mechtĭch, a. impotent, powerless; faint.
Unmanierlich, ŭn′manĭrlĭch, a. unmannerly; **‑keit**, ‑kĕĕt, f. unmannerliness.
Unmannbar, ŭn′mannbär, a. unmarriageable. **Unmännlich**, ŭn′mennlĭch, a. unmanly; **‑keit**, ‑kĕĕt, f. unmanliness.
Unmass, ŭn′mäss, n. excess; **gebend**, ‑gäbent, **Unmassgeblich**, ‑gäblĭch, a. humble, unassuming, under favor or correction, not prescribing.

Unmässig, ŭn′mässĭch, a. av. immoderate, intemperate, excessive, to excess, exceedingly, enormous, ‑ly **‑keit**, ‑kĕĕt, f. intemperance, excess.
Unmensch, ŭn′mensh, 'm ‑en pl. ‑en, savage, monster; **‑lich**, ‑lĭch, a. inhuman; savage, brutal; **‑keit**, ‑kĕĕt, f. inhumanity, savageness.
Unmerklich, ŭn′merklĭch, a. imperceptible, av. ‑ly.
Unmittelbar, ŭn′mittelbär, a. immediate, ‑ly; **‑keit**, ‑kĕĕt, f. immediateness, directness.
Unmöglich, ŭn′möhklĭch, a. impossible; **‑keit**, ‑kĕĕt, f. impossibility.
Unmoralisch, ŭn′mŏrälish, a. immoral.
Unmündig, ŭn′mündĭch, a. minor, under age; **‑keit**, ‑kĕĕt, f. minority, nonage, legal immaturity.
Unmusikalisch, ŭnmŭsĭkälĭsh, a. unmusical.
Unmuth, ŭn′mŭt, m. bad or ill‑humor, peevishness; **‑ig**, ‑ĭch, a. ill‑humored, peevish.
Unmuthsvoll, ŭn′mŭtsfoll, a. basf.
Unnachahmlich, ŭn′nachämlĭch, a. inimitable; **‑keit**, ‑kĕĕt, f. inimitableness.
Unnachtheilig, ŭn′nachtkĕlĭch, a. uninjurious.
Unnahbar, ŭnnā′bär, a. inapproachable.
Unnatürlich, ŭn′natührlĭch, a. unnatural; **‑keit**, ‑kĕĕt, f. unnaturalness.
Unnatur, ŭn′natŭr, f. basf.
Unnennbar, ŭnnenn′bär, a. ineffable, inexpressible.
Unnöthig, ŭn′nöhtĭch, a. unnecessary, ‑ily, needless: **‑keit**, ‑kĕĕt, f. needlessness, auch **Unnust**, ŭn′nŏt.
Unnütz, ŭn′nüts, a. av. useless, ‑ly, unprofitable, to no use or purpose.
Unordentlich, ŭn′ordentlĭch, a. disorderly, irregular; **‑keit**, ‑kĕĕt, f. disorderliness. **Unordnung**, ŭn′ort‑nŭng, f. disorder, confusion.
Unparteiisch, ŭn′partēĭ‑ish, a. av. impartial, ‑ly. **Unparteilichkeit**, ‑lĭch‑kĕĕt, f. impartiality.
Unpassirbar, ŭn′passĭrbär, a. impassable; not current.
Unpass, ŭn′pass, **Unpässlich**, ŭn′pèss‑lĭch, a. av. unwell; **‑keit**, ‑kĕĕt, f. indisposition, illness.
Unpersönlich, ŭn′persöhnlĭch, a. impersonal.

Unpoetisch, ŭn'po-etish, a. unpoetic.
Unpolitisch, ŭn'politish, a. av. impolitic, -ally, unwise, imprudent, imprudently.
Unrath, ŭn'rät, m. rubbish, filth, dirt; — merken, to smell a rat.
Unräthlich, ŭn'rätlich, a. inexpedient, unadvisable; -keit, -käet, f. inexpediency.
Unrecht, ŭn'rĕcht, a. av. not right or just, wrong, false; unjust, -ly, unfair; s. n. wrong, injustice; — haben, to be wrong; — thun, to injure, to wrong; -lich, -lich, a. wrongful, unjust, -ly. **Un'rechtmäßig**, -mässich, a. illegitimate, unlawful, illegal; -keit, -käet, f. illegitimacy, unlawfulness.
Unredlich, ŭn'rätlich, a. dishonest; -keit, -käet, f. dishonesty, unfairness.
Unreif, ŭn'rēif, a. unripe, immature.
Unreife, ŭn'rēife, f. unripeness, immaturity.
Unrein, ŭn'rein, a. av. unclean, impure; -igkeit, -ichkäet, f. uncleanness. **Un'reinlich**, -lich, a. av. not cleanly; unclean.
Unrichtig, ŭn'richtich, a. incorrect, wrong; -keit, -käet, f. incorrectness, fault.
Unruhe, ŭn'ru-e, f. unquietness, unrest, uneasiness; (watchm.) balance; -stifter, -zhtifter, m. agitator.
Unruhig, ŭn'ru-ich, a. unquiet, restless; uneasy; turbulent, -ly.
Unrühmlich, ŭn'rühmlich, a. inglorious, disgraceful; -keit, -käet, f. ingloriousness, disgrace.
Uns, ŭns, pron. us, to us, ourselves, to ourselves.
Unsäglich, ŭnsäk'lich, a. unspeakable, ineffable; immense, av. -ly.
Unsanft, ŭn'sanft, a. not soft, hard, rude, -ly.
Unsauber, ŭn'sŏŭber, a. not clean, unclean, foul, dirty; -keit, -käet, f. uncleanness.
Unschadhaft, ŭn'shädhaft, **Unschädlich**, ŭn'shädlich, a. harmless, innoxious; -keit, -käet, f. harmlessness, innoxiousness.
Unschätzbar, ŭn'shĕtsbär, a. inestimable, invaluable; -keit, -käet, f. inestimableness.
Unscheinbar, ŭn'shaenbär, a. simple, humble, inconspicuous, unassuming,

without show; -keit, -käet, f. humble appearance, unsightliness.
Unschicklich, ŭn'shicklich, a. unbecoming, unseemly, indecent, improper -keit, -käet, f. impropriety, indecency, inconveniency.
Unschiffbar, ŭn'shiffbär, a. unnavigable.
Unschlitt, ŭn'shlitt, n. tallow.
Unschlüssig, ŭn'shlüssich, a. irresolute, undecided; -keit, -käet, f. irresolution.
Unschmackhaft, ŭn'shmackhaft, a. insipid, tasteless, vapid, unsavory; -igkeit, -ichkäet, f. insipidity, unsavoriness.
Unschön, ŭn'shöhn, a. not beautiful, distasteful, unpleasant.
Unschuld, ŭn'shult, f. innocence; guiltlessness; -ig, -ich, a. innocent, guiltless, not guilty.
Unschwer, ŭn'shvär, a. av. easy, easily.
Unsegen, ŭn'sägen, m. want of success or prosperity, bad luck; curse.
Unselbstständig, ŭn'sĕlpzhtzhtĕndich, a. av. not independent, -ly; -keit, -käet, f. lack of independence or of self-reliance.
Unselbstsüchtig, ŭn'selpzhtsüchtich, a. av. unselfish, av. -ly.
Unselig, ŭn'sälich, a. not blessed, unhappy, fatal; -keit, -käet, f. unhappiness, damnation.
Unser, ŭn'ser, -ig, -ich, a. our, ours, of us; die Unfern. Unfrigen, ours, our family; das Unsere, Unsrige, ours, our property, our things; our duty. **Unsertshalben**, ŭn'sĕrt-halben, **Un'sertwegen**, -vägen, **Un'sertwillen**, -villen, av. on our account, in our behalf, for our sake.
Unsicher, ŭn'sicher, a. insecure, unsafe, unsure, uncertain; -heit, -häet, f. insecurity, unsafeness, uncertainty.
Unsinn, ŭn'sinn, m. nonsense; madness; -ig, -ich, a. nonsensical, absurd, insane, mad; -keit, -käet, f. folly, absurdity; madness.
Unsinnlich, ŭn'sinlich, a. not sensual.
Unsitte, ŭn'sitte, f. corrupt manner, bad custom. **Unsittig**, ŭn'-sittich, a. unmannered, ill-bred. **Un'sittlich**, a. immoral; -keit, -käet, f. immorality.
Unstandhaft, ŭn'zhtant-haft, a. inconstant.
Unstät, ŭn'zhtät, a. unsteady, incon-

Unf 350 Unt

stant, fickle, changeable, unsettled, restless; -igfeit, -ichkeit, f. unsteadiness.
Unstatthaft, un'zhtatt-haft, a. inadmissible, illegal: -igfeit, -ichkeit, f. inadmissibility, illegality.
Unsterblich, unzhtėrp'lich, a. immortal; — machen, to immortalize, perpetuate; -feit, -käst, f. immortality.
Unstern, un'zhtėrn, m. ill luck, misfortune, disaster.
Unsträflich, un'zhträf-bär. Unsträflich, un'zhträflich, a. unexceptionable, blameless, unblemished; -feit,-käet, f. unblamableness.
Unstreitig, un'zhträĭtich, a. av. incontestable, incontrovertible, indisputable, -ably.
Unstudirt, un'zhtudirt, a. unlettered, unschooled, illiterate.
Unsündlich, un'süntlich, Unsündhaft, -haft, a. sinless, not sinful; -igfeit, -ichkeit, f. sinlessness.
Untadelhaft, un'tädelhaft, a. av. unexceptionable, blameless, -ly.
Untadelig, un'tädelich, a. basf.
Untauglich, un'täuklich, a. unfit, unable, incompetent; — machen, to disable; -feit, -käst, f. unfitness, inability, unaptness.
Unten, un'ten, av. below, beneath, underneath.
Unter, un'tėr, pr. below, under, beneath, underneath; among, amid, amidst, betwixt; during; unterwegs, on the way; -er, Untere, -s, a. lower, inferior, nether, under.
Unterabtheilung, un'tėraptäĕlung, f. subdivision.
Unterarm, un'tėrar(e)m, m. forearm.
Unterarzt, un'tėrärtst, m. surgeon's assistant.
Unterbalfen, un'terbalken, m. architrave: (print.) winter, cross-piece.
Unterbau, un'terbou, m. substructure.
Unterbauch, un'terbouch, m. hypogastrium, lower part of the belly.
Unterbaum, un'terbäum, m. pl. -bäume, cloth-beam, work-beam, forebeam (of a loom); side-piece (of a wagon).
Unterbefehlshaber, un'terbefäls-häber, m. second in command.
Unterbehörde, un'terbehörde, f. subordinate, lower office.
Unterbeinfleider, un'terbäenkläeder, s. pl. drawers.

Unterbett, un'terbett, n. pl. -en, under-bed.
Unterbibliothefar, un'terbibliŏtekär, m. assistant librarian.
Unterbinden, unterbin'den (-bant, -gebunden), vt. to tie up, underneath. Unterbin'dung, -ung, f. ligature, subligation, tying up.
Unterbleiben, unterbleī'ben (-blieb, -blieben), vi. to cease, discontinue; to be left undone.
Unterbrechen, unterbrėch'en (-brach, -brochen), vt. to interrupt. Unterbrechung, unterbrėch'ung, f. interruption.
Unterbreiten, un'terbräten (Pp. untergebreitet), vt. to spread under.
Unterbreiten, unterbrä'ten (Pp. unterbreitet), vt. to lay before.
Unterbringen, un'terbring-en (-brachte, -gebracht), vt. to provide, to get a place for.
Unterdessen, unterdes'sen, av. in the mean time.
Unterdrucken, un'terdrucken (Pp. untergedruckt), vt. to print under.
Unterdrücken, unterdrück'en (Pp. unterdrückt), vt. to suppress, repress, oppress. Unterdrück'er, m. oppressor. Unterdrück'ung, -ung, f. oppression, suppression, repression, crushing.
Unterfahren, unterfä'ren (-fubr, -fabren), vt. to build a new foundation.
Unterfangen, unterfang'en (-fing, -fangen), vt. to dare, venture, undertake.
Unterfeldherr, un'terfelt-hėrr, m. -n, pl. -n, lieutenant general; second in command.
Unterförster, un'terförshter, m. deputy forester.
Unterfutter, un'terfutter, n. lining.
Untergang, un'tergang, m. setting, sunset, West, Occident; sinking, ruin, destruction, loss.
Untergeben, untergä'ben, vt. to submit, subject; -er, -er, m. Untergebene, f. subject, inferior, subaltern, pupil, clerk.
Untergehen, un'tergä-en (-ging, -gegangen), vi. to go down, to sink, set, perish.
Untergeordnet, un'tėrge-ordnėt, a. subordinate, inferior.
Untergericht, un'tergeright, n. lower, inferior court.

Untergeſtell, un'tergezhtell, *n.* under-carriage.

Untergewehr, un'tergevår, *n.* side-arms.

Untergraben, untergrä'ben (-grub, -graben), *vt.* to undermine.

Unterhalb, un'terhalp, *av. pr.* below, under.

Unterhalt, un'terhalt, *m.* maintenance, sustenance, living, livelihood; alimony.

Unterhalten, unterhal'ten (-hielt, -halten), *vt.* to maintain, sustain, support, keep; to cultivate, carry on, keep up (a correspondence, etc.); to entertain (a company); to keep alive *or* burning, to feed (a fire, etc.); ſich —, to converse with, to talk on. **Unterhalten,** un'terhalten (*Pp.* untergehalten), *vt.* to hold under. **Unterhaltung,** -ung, *f.* conversation; entertainment, amusement; keeping up, maintenance, support.

Unterhandeln, unterhan'deln, *vt. i.* to negotiate, treat, transact.

Unterhändler, un'terhentler, *m.* negotiator; broker, commissioner, agent.

Unterhandlung, unterhant'lung, *f.* negotiation.

Unterhaus, un'terhous, *n.* House of Commons.

Unterhefen, un'terhefen, *pl.* sediment of yeast.

Unterhöhlen, unterhöh'len, *vt.* to sap, undermine.

Unterholz, un'terholts, *n.* underwood, coppice.

Unterhosen, un'terhōsen, *s. pl.* drawers.

Unterirdiſch, un'terirdish, *a.* subterraneous; underground.

Unterjochen, unteryoch'en, *vt.* to subjugate, subdue. **Unterjochung,** -ung, *f.* subjugation.

Unterkinn, un'terkinn, *n.* double chin; -lade, -lāde, *f.* lower jaw-bone.

Unterkleid, un'terklēed, *n. pl.* -er, under-clothes, petticoat.

Unterkommen, un'terkommen (-kam, -gekommen), *vi.* to get shelter, to find employment *or* a situation; *s. n.* place, employment, shelter.

Unterkunft, un'terkunft, *f.* baſf.

Unterlage, un'terlāge, *f.* base, stay, support, bed, substratum; lining, trestle

Unterland, un'terlant, *n.* lowland.

Unterlaß, un'terlass, *m.* intermission; ohne —, continually.

Unterlaſſen, unterlas'sen (-ließ, -laſſen), *vt.* to omit, discontinue, cease from, leave off. **Unterlaſſungsſünde,** -ungssünde, *f.* sin of omission.

Unterlaſt, un'terlazht, *f.* ballast.

Unterlaufen, unterläufen (-lief, -lauſen), *vt. i.* to slip in, under; to suffuse.

Unterleder, un'terlāder, *n.* under leather.

Unterlefze, un'terlēftse, *f.* under-lip.

Unterlegen, un'terlägen (*Pp.* untergelegt *or* unterlegt), *vt.* to underlay, lay under.

Unterlehrer, un'terlārer, *m.* assistant-teacher.

Unterleib, un'terlēip, *m.* abdomen, belly; -krankheit, -krankhāit, *f.* abdominal affection, disorder of the bowels.

Unterliegen, unterli'gen (-lag, -legen), *vi.* to lie under; to succumb, to sink under.

Unterlieutenant, un'terleütnant, *m.* second lieutenant.

Unterlippe, un'terlippe, *f.* under-lip.

Untermauern, untermöy'ern, *vt.* to make a foundation *or* ground-work of masonry.

Untermengen, untermeng'en, *vt.* to intermingle, intermix.

Untermini(e)ren, untermini'ren, *vt.* to sap, to undermine.

Untermiſchen, untermish'en, *vt.* to intermix, intermingle.

Unternehmen, unternä'men (-nahm, -nommen), *vt.* to undertake, attempt; *s. n.* auch **Unternehmung,** -ung, *f.* attempt, enterprise, undertaking. **Unternehmend,** -ent, *a.* enterprising, bold, daring. **Unternehmer,** *m.* undertaker, contractor.

Unteroffizier, un'teroffitsēr, *m.* sergeant.

Unterordnen, un'terordnen, *vt.* to subordinate. **Unterordnetter,** -geordnēter, *m.* subaltern. **Unterordnung,** -ordnung, *f.* subordination.

Unterpfand, un'terpfant, *n. pl.* Unterpfänder, pledge, pawn.

Unterpfarrer, un'terpfarrer, *m.* curate, vicar.

Unterphosphorige Säure, un'terfosförich-e seü're, *f.* hypophosphoric acid.

Unterreden, ŭnterrā'den, vr. ſich —, to converse. **Unterredung**, -ŭng, f. conversation, discourse.
Unterricht, ŭn'terricht, m. instruction; **-en**, -en, vt. to instruct, teach, inform.
Unterrichter, ŭn'terrichter, m. judge of an inferior court.
Unterrock, ŭn'terrock, m. pl. -röcke, petticoat.
Untersagen, untersä'gen, vt. to forbid.
Untersalpeterſäure, ŭn'tersalpätersöü-re, f. hyponitric acid. **Un'terſalpe-terſaures Salz**, -söures salts, n. hyponitrite.
Untersatz, ŭn'tersats, m. stand, stay; stereobate, stylobate; minor (in logic).
Unterschale, ŭn'tershāle, f. saucer.
Unterscheiden, untershāed'en (-schied, -schieben), vt. to distinguish, discriminate. **Unterscheidung**, -ŭng, f. discrimination, distinction.
Unterschenk, ŭn'tershenk, m. -en, pl. -en, under-butler.
Unterschenkel, ŭn'tershenkel, m. lower part of the thigh.
Unterschieben, ŭn'tershīben (-schob, -geschoben), vt. to shove, thrust, put under.
Unterschieben, untershī'ben (Pp. unterschoben), vt. to substitute, to forge.
Unterschied, ŭn'tershīd, m. difference, distinction; **-en**, untershī'den, a. different, diverse, several. **Unter-ſchiedlich**, ŭn'tershīdlich, a. different, several.
Unterschlächtig, ŭn'tershlöchtich, a. undershot.
Unterschlag, ŭn'tershlăk, m. embezzlement, fraud.
Unterschlagen, ŭn'tershlägen (-schlug, -geschlagen), vt. to trip up, supplant.
Unterschlagen, untershlā'gen (Pp. unterschlagen), vt. to intercept, detain (letters); to embezzle, purloin.
Unterschlagung, untershlāg'ŭng, f. embezzlement; interception.
Unterschleif, ŭn'tershlīef, m. pl. -e, embezzlement, fraud.
Unterschoben, untershō'ben, a. suppositious, spurious.
Unterschreiben, untershrēi'ben (unterschrieb, unterschrieben), vt. to underwrite, to subscribe, sign. **Unter-ſchrift**, ŭn'tershrift, f. signature, subscription.

Unterschwefelsaures Salz, ŭn'tershvefelsöures salts, n. - hyposulphate Unterschwefligſaure Verbindung, hyposulphite.
Unterschwelle, ŭn'tershvelle, f. sill.
Unterseeiſch, ŭn'tersēä-ish, a. submarine.
Unterſetzen, ŭn'tersetsen (Pp. untergeſetzt), vt. to put or set under.
Unterſetzen, unterset'sen, vt. to mix (wood).
Unterſetzt, untersetst', a. stout, strong set.
Unterſiegeln, untersī'geln, vt. to put a seal under; to seal. **Unterſiegelung**, untersī'gelŭng, f. sealing.
Unterſinken, ŭn'tersinken (-sank, -geſunken), vi. to sink, to go to the bottom.
Unterſollen, ŭn'tersollen, vt. to have to go or pass under.
Unterſt, ŭn'terzht, a. undermost, lowest, nethermost.
Unterſtaatsſekretär, ŭn'terzhtätssecretār, m. under-secretary of state.
Unterſtatthalter, ŭn'terzhtatt-halter, m. lieutenant-governor.
Unterſtecken, ŭn'terzhtecken, vt. to mix, to blend with, to join to, fasten to; to embody, incorporate.
Unterſtehen, ŭn'terzhtā-en (-ſtand, -geſtanden), vi. to stand under, to shelter one's self.
Unterſtehen, unterzhtā'-en (Pp. unterſtanden), vt. to dare, to be so bold.
Unterſtellen, ŭn'terzhtellen (Pp. untergeſtellt). vt. to place or put under.
Unterſtellen, unterzhtell'en (Pp. unterſtellt), vt. to impute, presuppose.
Unterſtreichen, unterzhtrēī'ch'en (-strich, -strichen), vt. to score, underline.
Unterſtreuen, ŭn'terzhtröü-en (Pp. untergeſtreut), vt. to strew under; to intersperse.
Unterſtützen, unterzhtüt'sen, vt. to prop, support; to countenance, favor. **Unterſtützung**, -ŭng, f. aid, relief, support.
Unterſuchen, untersŭch'en, vt. to inquire, investigate, examine. **Unter-ſuchung**, -sŭch'ŭng, f. inquiry, examination, trial.
Untertaſſe, ŭn'tertasse, f. saucer.
Untertauchen, ŭn'tertöüchen, vt. i. to dive, duck, to submerge.
Unterthan, ŭn'tertān, m. subject.

Unterthänig, ŭn'tertänich, a. submissive, humble; ‑keit, ‑kāet, f. submissiveness, dependence, subjection.
Untertheil, ŭn'tertäel, m. lower part, bottom.
Untertheilen, ŭn'tertäelen, vt. to subdivide.
Unterthor, ŭn'tertōr, n. tail-gate.
Untertreten, ŭn'tertrāten (‑trat, ‑getreten), vt. to tread down, to depress; to stand under, to take shelter.
Untertunken, ŭn'tertŭnken, vt. to dip, submerge; to sop.
Unterwachsen, ŭntervak'sen, a. interlarded, streaked with.
Unterwald, ŭn'tervalt, m. underwood.
Unterwärts, ŭn'terverts, av. downward.
Unterweg(e)s, ŭnterväks', av. on the way; unterwegen lassen, to leave alone, to desist from.
Unterweisen, ŭntervëi'sen (‑wies, ‑wiesen), vt. to instruct, teach. **Unterweisung**, ‑ŭng, f. instruction.
Unterwelt, ŭn'tervëlt, f. nether world, lower regions.
Unterwerfen, ŭntervër'fen (unterwarf, unterworfen), vt. to subject, subdue, subjugate; to submit, refer; sich —, to submit, to undergo. **Unterwerfung**, ‑ŭng, f. subjection, submission, surrender.
Unterworfen, ŭntervorf'en, a. subject.
Unterwinden, ŭntervĭn'den (‑wand, ‑wunden), vt. sich —, to presume, dare.
Unterwuchs, ŭn'tervŭks, m. underwood, coppice.
Unterwühlen, ŭntervüh'len, vt. to root up, undermine.
Unterwürfig, ŭn'tervürfich, a. submissive, subject; ‑keit, ‑kāet, f. submissiveness, subjection.
Unterzahn, ŭn'tertsän, m. pl. ‑zähne, lower tooth.
Unterzeichnen, ŭntertsäch'nen, vt. to sign, subscribe. **Unterzeichner**, m. signer, subscriber. **Unterzeichneter**, ‑neter, m. undersigned. **Unterzeichnung**, ‑nŭng, f. signature, subscription.
Unterziehen, ŭntertsī'en (‑zog, ‑zogen), vt. sich —, to undertake, to bear.
Unterzug, ŭn'tertsŭk, m. summer (Arch.).
Unthat, ŭn'tät, f. misdeed, crime, atrocity. **Unthätchen**, ŭn'tät-chen,

spot, blemish. **Unthätig**, ŭn'tätich, a. inactive, idle, indolent; ‑keit, ‑kāet, f. inactivity, inaction.
Untheilbar, ŭn'tälbär, a. indivisible; ‑keit, ‑kāet, f. indivisibleness.
Untheilnehmend, ŭn'tälnäment, a. unsympathizing.
Unthier, ŭn'tīr, n. monster.
Unthulich, ŭn'tŭlich, a. unfeasible, impracticable; ‑keit, ‑kāet, f. impracticability, infeasibleness.
Untiefe, ŭn'tīfe, f. shallowness; shoal; flat, shallow place.
Untilgbar, ŭntĭlk'bär, a. inextinguishable, indelible.
Untrennbar, ŭntrenn'bär, **Untrennlich**, ‑lich, a. inseparable.
Untreu, ŭn'treü, a. faithless, unfaithful. **Untreue**, ŭn'treü‑e, f. unfaithfulness, faithlessness.
Untröstlich, ŭn'tröhztlich, a. inconsolable, disconsolate; ‑keit, ‑kāet, f. disconsolateness.
Untrüglich, ŭn'trŭhklich, a. infallible, unerring, sure; ‑keit, ‑kāet, f. infallibility.
Untüchtig, ŭn'tŭchtich, a. unable, unfit, inapt, unapt; ‑keit, ‑kāet, f. unaptness, inaptness, unfitness, incapacity, inaptitude.
Untugend, ŭn'tŭgent, f. bad habit, vice; ‑haft, ‑haft, a. ar. vicious, ‑ly.
Unüberlegt, ŭn'ŭhberläkt, a. inconsiderate; ‑heit, ‑häet, f. inconsiderateness, rashness.
Unübersehbar, ŭnŭhbersä'bär, a. immense, unbounded.
Unübersetzbar, ŭn'ŭhbersetsbär, a. untranslatable.
Unübersteigbar, ŭnŭhberzhtäik'bär, a. insurmountable, insuperable; ‑keit, ‑kāet, f. insuperability.
Unübertragbar, ŭn'ŭhberträkbär, a. not transferable.
Unübertrefflich, ŭn'ŭhbertrefflich, a. incomparable, excellent.
Unüberwindlich, ŭn'ŭhbervintlich, a. invincible; ‑keit, ‑kāet, f. invincibility.
Unumgänglich, ŭn'ŭmgenglich, a. indispensable; ‑keit, ‑kāet, f. indispensableness.
Unumschränkt, ŭn'ŭmshrenkt, a. unlimited, absolute, sovereign; ‑heit, ‑häet, f. sovereignty, absoluteness.
Unumstößlich, ŭn'ŭmztöhslich, a. irrefutable, incontestable, incontrover

tible; ‑feit, ‑këet, f. incontrovertibility.
Unumwölft, ųn'ųmvölkt, a. unclouded.
Unumwunden, ųn'ųmvųnden, a. frank, open, plain, ‑ly.
Ununterbrochen, ųn'ųnterbroĸen, a. uninterrupted, ‑ly.
Ununtersucht, ųn'ųntersųĸt, a. uninvestigated.
Ununterwürfig, ųn'ųntervürfiĸ, a. unsubmissive, unsubdued.
Unveränderlich, ųn'ferenderliĸ, a. invariable, unchangeable, unalterable; ‑feit, ‑këet, f. invariableness, unchangeableness. **Unverändert**, ųn'ferendert, a. unchanged, unvaried.
Unverantwortlich, ųn'ferantvortliĸ, a. irresponsible, not answerable; ‑feit, ‑këet, f. irresponsibility.
Unverarbeitet, ųn'ferarbëetet, a. raw, unwrought.
Unveräußerlich, ųn'ferëusserliĸ, a. inalienable.
Unverbesserlich, ųn'ferbesserliĸ, a. incorrigible, irreclaimable; ‑feit, ‑këet, f. incorrigibleness, irreclaimableness.
Unverbindlich, ųn'ferbintliĸ, a. not binding; disobliging, unkind.
Unverblümt, ųn'ferblühmt, a. blunt, open.
Unverborgen, ųn'ferborgen, a. unconcealed.
Unverboten, ųn'ferböten, a. unforbidden.
Unverbrennlich, ųn'ferbrenniĸ, a. incombustible; ‑feit, ‑këet, f. incombustibility.
Unverbrüchlich, ųn'ferbrüĸliĸ, a. inviolable; ‑feit, ‑këet, f. inviolability.
Unverbürgt, ųn'ferbürkt, a. unwarranted, inauthentic.
Unverdächtig, ųn'ferdëĸtiĸ, a. unsuspected, unsuspicious.
Unverdaulich, ųn'ferdëulliĸ, a. indigestible; ‑feit, ‑këet, f. indigestibleness, crudity. **Unverdaut**, ųn'ferdëut, a. indigested, undigested, crude.
Unverderblich, ųn'ferderpliĸ, a. incorruptible. **Unverderbt, Unverdorben**, ųn'ferdorben, a. incorrupt, incorrupted; ‑heit, ‑hëet, f. incorruptness, soundness, incorruption.
Unverdient, ųn'ferdint, a. undeserved.
Unverdrossen, ųn'ferdrossen, a. unwea-

ried, sedulous; ‑heit, ‑hëet, f. indefatigableness, assiduity.
Unverehelicht, ųn'ferë‑eliĸt, a. unmarried.
Unvereinbar, ųn'ferëenbär, a. incompatible; ‑feit, ‑këet, f. incompatibility.
Unverfälscht, ųn'ferfelsht, a. unadulterated.
Unverfänglich, ųn'ferfengliĸ, a. not captious.
Unvergänglich, ųn'fergengliĸ, a. imperishable; ‑feit, ‑këet, f. imperishableness.
Unvergessen, ųn'fergessen, a. unforgotten, memorable.
Unvergleichbar, ųn'ferglëiĸbär, **Unvergleichlich**, ‑liĸ, a. incomparable, unparalleled, matchless, peerless; ‑feit, ‑këet, f. incomparableness.
Unvergolten, ųn'fergolten, a. unrewarded.
Unverhältnißmäßig, ųn'ferheltnissmäsiĸ, a. disproportionate, unproportioned; ‑feit, ‑këet, f. disproportion.
Unverheirathet, ųn'ferhëirätet, a. unmarried.
Unverhofft, ųn'ferhofft, a. unhoped for; unexpected, sudden.
Unverholen, ųn'ferhölen, a. unreserved, frank, open.
Unverjährbar, ųn'feryärbär, a. imprescriptible, inalienable. **Unverjahrt**, ųn'feryärt, a. not alienated.
Unverkennbar, ųn'ferkenbär, a. unmistakable.
Unverletzlich, ųn'ferletsliĸ, a. inviolable; ‑feit, ‑këet, f. inviolability.
Unverletzt, ųn'ferletst, a. unhurt; inviolate.
Unverloren, ųn'ferlören, a. not lost.
Unverlöschlich, ųn'ferlöshliĸ, a. ineffaceable, inextinguishable.
Unvermeidlich, ųn'fermëidliĸ, a. inevitable, unavoidable; ‑feit, ‑këet, f. inevitableness.
Unvermerkt, ųn'fermerkt, a. unperceived, unawares.
Unvermischt, ųn'fermisht, a. unmixed, unmingled.
Unvermögen, ųn'fermöbgen, n. incapacity, inability; impotence. **Unvermögend**, a. incapable, unable; impotent.
Unvermuthet, ųn'fermųtet, a. unexpected, unlooked for, unawares.

Unvernehmlich, ŭn'fērnämlich, a. inaudible, indistinct.
Unvernichtlich, ŭn'fērnĭchtlĭch, a. indestructible.
Unvernunft, ŭn'fērnŭnft, f. want of reason, irrationality.
Unvernünftig, ŭn'fērnŭnftĭg, a. irrational, reasonless; unreasonable, absurd; -keit, -kāèt, f. irrationality; unreasonableness, absurdity.
Unverrichtet, ŭn'fērrĭchtĕt, a. unperformed, unfinished; —er Dinge, without having succeeded, unsuccessfully.
Unverrückt, ŭn'fērrŭckt, a. motionless, unmoved, steadfast, fixed, firm, av. -ly.
Unversagt, ŭn'fērsakt, a. unforbidden; es bleibt ihm unversagt, he is free to; disengaged, not engaged.
Unverschämt, ŭn'fērshämt, a. impudent, -ly, barefaced, insolent, shameless, brazen-faced; -keit, -hāèt, f. impudence, insolence, shamelessness.
Unverschuldet, ŭn'fērshŭldet, a. undeserved, -ly; not indebted.
Unversehen(s), ŭn'fērsā-ĕns, a. av. unexpected, unforeseen, unlooked for, unaware.
Unversehrbar, ŭn'fērsārbăr, a. inviolable; -keit, -kāèt, f. inviolability.
Unversehrt, ŭn'fērsārt, a. unhurt, unharmed, undamaged, safe.
Unversichert, ŭn'fērsĭchĕrt, a. uninsured.
Unversiegbar, ŭn'fērsīkbăr, a. inexhaustible.
Unversiegelt, ŭn'fērsīgĕlt, a. unsealed.
Unversöhnlich, ŭn'fērsöhnlĭch, a. implacable; -keit, -kāèt, f. implacability.
Unversorgt, ŭn'fērsorkt, a. unprovided for.
Unverstand, ŭn'fērzhtant, m. folly, want of judgment or sense, want of understanding.
Unverständig, ŭn'fērshtĕndĭch, a. unwise, imprudent, injudicious; -keit, -kāèt, f. imprudence, injudiciousness, indiscretion. **Unverständlich**, -lĭch, a. unintelligible; -keit, -kāèt, f. unintelligibleness.
Unversucht, ŭn'fērsŭcht, a. untried, unattempted.
Unvertheidigt, ŭn'fērtāèdĭcht, a. undefended, defenceless.

Unvertilgbar, ŭn'fērtĭlkbăr, a. indelible, inextinguishable; -keit, -kāèt, f. indelibleness, indelibility.
Unverträglich, ŭn'fērtrāklĭch, a. incompatible; unsocial; -keit, -kāèt, f. incompatibility; unsociableness.
Unverwahrt, ŭn'fērvärt, a. unguarded, neglected.
Unverwandt, ŭn'fērvant, a. steadfast, av. -ly. without turning.
Unverwehrt, ŭn'fērvārt, a. unforbidden, unprohibited.
Unverweigerlich, ŭn'fērvāègĕrlĭch, a. not to be refused or denied.
Unverwerflich, ŭn'fērvĕrflĭch, a. unexceptionable.
Unverwelklich, ŭn'fērvĕlklĭch, a. unfading, imperishable.
Unverweslich, ŭn'fērvāslĭch, a. incorruptible; -keit, -kāèt, f. incorruptibility, incorruption.
Unverwundbar, ŭn'fērvŭntbăr, a. invulnerable.
Unverwüstlich, ŭn'fērvühzhtlĭch, a. indestructible, never-failing.
Unverzagt, ŭn'fērtsakt, a. intrepid, undaunted, undismayed; -keit, -hāèt, f. intrepidity, undauntedness.
Unverzeihlich, ŭn'fērtsāèlĭch, a. unpardonable, inexcusable, irremissible, av. -ly; -keit, -kāèt, f. inexcusability, irremissibleness.
Unverzüglich, ŭn'fērtsühklĭch, a. av. immediate, -ly.
Unvollendet, ŭn'follĕndĕt, a. unfinished, incomplete.
Unvollkommen, ŭn'follkommen, a. av. imperfect, incomplete, -ly; -keit, -hāèt, f. imperfection.
Unvollständig, ŭn'follzhtĕndĭg, a. incomplete; -keit, -kāèt, f. incompleteness.
Unvollzählig, ŭn'follĭsălĭch, a. incomplete, not having the full number.
Unvorsätzlich, ŭn'fōrsètslĭch, a. av. unintentional, undesigned, unpremeditated, -ly.
Unvorsichtig, ŭn'fōrsĭchtĭch, a. av. incautious, improvident, -ly; -keit, -kāèt, f. improvidence.
Unvortheilhaft, ŭn'fortāèlhāft, a. av. disadvantageous, disadvantageously, improfitable.
Unwählbar, ŭn'vālbăr, a. ineligible.
Unwahr, ŭn'vär, a. av. untrue, false, -ly; -keit, -hāèt, f. falsehood, falsity, untruth.

Unwahrscheinlich, ṇn'vārshạēnlich, a. improbable, unlikely; **-keit, -käet**, f. unlikelihood, improbability.
Unwandelbar, ṇn'vandẹlbār, a. immutable, unchangeable; **-keit, -käet**, f. immutability.
Unwegsam, ṇn'vāksam, a. impassable.
Unweigerlich, ṇn'vāegẹrlich, a. implicit, blind, unhesitating.
Unweise, ṇn'vēīsẹ, a. unwise.
Unweit, ṇn'vēīt, av. not far.
Unwerth, ṇn'vārt, m. unworthiness; worthlessness; a. unworthy.
Unwesen, ṇn'vāsen, n. nuisance, disorder, mischief; **-lich, -tlich**, a. unessential, immaterial, unsubstantial; **-keit, -käet**, f. immateriality; inconsiderableness.
Unwetter, ṇn'vētter, n. bad, rough, stormy weather.
Unwichtig, ṇn'vichtich, a. unimportant, insignificant; **-keit, -käet**, f. insignificance.
Unwiderleglich, ṇn'vidẹrlāklich, a. irrefutable.
Unwiderruflich, ṇn'viderrụflich, a. irrevocable; **-keit, -käet**, f. irrevocableness, irrevocability.
Unwidersprechlich, ṇn'vidẹrzhprēchlich, a. incontestable, indisputable; **-keit, -käet**, f. indisputableness.
Unwiderstehlich, ṇn'vidẹrzhtālich, a. irresistible; **-keit, -käet**, f. irresistibility.
Unwiederbringlich, ṇn'vīdẹrbringlich, a. irreparable, unrecoverable.
Unwille, ṇn'villẹ, m. indignation.
Unwillig, ṇn'villich, a. av. indignant, -ly, angry, angrily; unwilling, -ly; **-keit, -käet**, f. unwillingness.
Unwillkommen, ṇn'villkommen, a. unwelcome.
Unwillkürlich, ṇn'villkührlich, a. av. involuntary, -arily.
Unwirklich, ṇn'virklich, a. av. unreal, -ly; **-keit, -käet**, f. unreality.
Unwirksam, ṇn'virksam, a. inefficacious, inefficient, ineffectual, -ly; **-keit, -käet**, f. inefficacy, inefficaciousness.
Unwirsch, ṇn'virsh, a. av. angry, rough, -ly.
Unwirthbar, ṇn'virtbār. **Unwirthlich**, -lich, a. ar. inhospitable, -ably; **-keit, -käet**, f. inhospitality.
Unwissend, ṇn'vissent, a. ignorant, not informed. **Unwissenheit**, -häet,
f. ignorance. **Unwissentlich**, -lich, a. unknowingly, unconsciously. **Unwissenschaftlich**, -shaftlich, a. ar. unscientific, -ally.
Unwohl, ṇn'vōl, a. ar. unwell, indisposed, ill; **-sein, -sāēn**, n. indisposition.
Unwürdig, ṇn'vürdich, a. unworthy; **-keit, -käet**, f. unworthiness.
Unzaghaft, ṇn'tsākhaft, a. av. intrepid, undaunted, -ly.
Unzahl, ṇn'tsāl, f. infinite number.
Unzahlbar, ṇn'tsālbār, a. not payable.
Unzählbar, ṇn'tsāl'bār, a. innumerable, countless, numberless; **-keit, -käet**, f. innumerability, countlessness.
Unzählig, ṇn'tsālich, a. countless, numberless, innumerable.
Unzähmbar, ṇn'tsām'bār, a. indomitable.
Unzart, ṇn'tsārt, a. indelicate; **-keit, -häet**, f. indelicacy.
Unzärtlich, ṇn'tsārtlich, a. not tender; rough; **-keit, -käet**, f. roughness, want of tenderness.
Unze, ṇn'tsẹ, f. ounce.
Unzeit, ṇn'tsāēt, f. untimeliness; **-ig, -lich**, a. av. untimely, unseasonable, -ably, ill-timed, out of season; unripe; **-keit, -käet**, f. unseasonableness.
Unzerbrechlich, ṇn'tsẹrbrēchlich, a. infrangible.
Unzerreißbar, ṇn'tsẹrrēīsbār, a. not lacerable.
Unzerstörbar, ṇn'tsẹrzhtöhrbār, a. indestructible; **-keit, -käet**, f. indestructibility.
Unzertrennlich, ṇn'tsẹrtrennlich, a. inseparable, indissoluble; **-keit, -käet**, f. indissolubility.
Unziemlich, ṇn'tsīmlich, a. av. unseemly, indecent, unbecoming; **-keit, -käet**, f. unseemliness, indecency.
Unzierlich, ṇn'tsīrlich, a. ar. inelegant, -ly; **-keit, -käet**, f. want of grace, inelegance.
Unzucht, ṇn'tsụcht, f. unchastity, prostitution, lewdness; **Unzucht treiben mit**, to have criminal intercourse with.
Unzüchtig, ṇn'tsüchtich, a. unchaste, lewd, lascivious, obscene; **-keit, -käet**, f. unchastity, lewdness, immodesty.
Unzufrieden, ṇn'tsụfrīden, a. discontent, -ed, dissatisfied, malcontent

-heit, -hăĕt, *f.* discontent, dissatisfaction, malcontentedness.
Unzugänglich, ŭn'tsŭgĕnglĭch, *a.* inaccessible; **-keit**, -kăĕt, *f.* inaccessibility.
Unzulänglich, ŭn'tsŭlĕnglĭch, *a.* insufficient, inadequate, -ly; **-keit**, -kăĕt, *f.* insufficiency.
Unzulässig, ŭn'tsŭlĕssĭch, *a.* inadmissible; **-keit**, -kăĕt, *f.* inadmissibility.
Unzureichend, ŭn'tsŭrīchĕnt, *a.* insufficient, -ly.
Unzuverlässig, ŭn'tsŭfĕrlĕssĭch, *a.* unreliable, precarious, uncertain; **-keit**, -kăĕt, *f.* unreliability, uncertainty.
Unzweckmässig, ŭn'tsvĕckmĕssĭch, *a.* unsuitable, inexpedient, inappropriate; **-keit**, -kăĕt, *f.* inexpediency.
Unzweideutig, ŭn'tsvīdŏĭtĭch, *a.* unequivocal, plain; **-keit**, -kăĕt, *f.* unequivocalness, unambiguity.
Unzweifelhaft, ŭn'tsvīfĕlhaft, *a. av.* doubtless, indubitable, unquestionable, *ar.* -ly.
Üppig, ŭp'pĭch, *a.* luxurious; luxuriant, rank, wanton, exuberant; **-keit**, -kăĕt, *f.* luxury, luxuriousness, wantonness.
Ur, ŭr, *m.*(ure-ox),urus.
Urahn, ŭr'ăn, *m. pl.* -en, great-grandfather, ancestor, forefather; **-lich**, -lĭch, *a.* ancestral.
Uralt, ŭr'alt, *a.* primeval, very old *or* ancient; **vors, -ors, von uralters her**, *ar.* from olden times, from time immemorial.
Urältern, ŭr'ĕltĕrn, *s. pl.* ancestors.
Uran, ŭrăn', *n.* uran, uranium; **-blüthe**, -blühte, *f.* uran-bloom, uranochre. **Uranglimmer**, -glimmer, *m.* uranite. **Urangrün**, -grün, *n.* uran-green. **Uransäure**, -sŏīrĕ, *f.* uranic acid.
Urbar, ŭr'bär, *a.* arable, productive; — **machen**, to clear, break up, cultivate.
Urbedeutung, ŭr'bĕdŏītŭng, *f.* primitive meaning.
Urbewohner, ŭr'bĕvōnĕr, *m.* aboriginal *or* primitive inhabitant, *pl.* aborigines.
Urbild, ŭr'bĭlt, *n. pl.* -er, ideal, archetype, prototype.
Urenkel, ŭr'ĕnkĕl, **-s**, *pl.* **-n**, great-grandson; **-in**, *f.* great-granddaughter *or* child.

Urfehde, ŭr'fādĕ, *f.* cessation of a feud.
Urgebirge, ŭr'gĕbĭrgĕ, *n.* primitive mountains.
Urgrossmutter, ŭr'grōsmŭttĕr, *f.* great-grandmother.
Urgrossvater, ŭr'grōsfātĕr, *m.* great-grandfather.
Urgrund, ŭr'grŭnt, *m.* primitive, first, original cause.
Urheber, ŭr'hābĕr, *m.* **-in**, *f.* author, originator.
Urin, ŭrīn', *m.* urine, water; **-glas**, -gläs, *n.* urinal. **Uriniren**, ŭrĭnī'rĕn, *vi.* to urinate, to make water.
Urkirche, ŭr'kĭrchĕ, *f.* primitive *or* most ancient church.
Urkraft, ŭr'kraft, *f. pl.* Urkräfte, primitive power *or* force.
Urkunde, ŭr'kŭndĕ, *f.* document, deed, title, charter, record; **zu —bessen**, in witness whereof.
Urkunden, ŭr'kŭndĕn, *vt.* to testify, attest, prove. **Ur'kundlich**, -lĭch, *a.* authentic, documentary; in testimony whereof.
Urland, ŭr'lant, *n.* virgin-soil.
Urlaub, ŭr'lăŭb, *m.* furlough, leave of absence.
Urlicht, ŭr'lĭcht, *n.* primitive light.
Urne, ŭr'nĕ, *f.* urn.
Urplötzlich, ŭr'plötzlĭch, *a.* sudden, instantaneous, -ly.
Urquell, ŭr'quĕll, *m.* fountain-head, first source.
Ursache, ŭr'sachĕ, *f.* cause, principle, reason, motive, agency, origin; **-r**, **Ur'sacher**, -sĕchĕr, *m.* author. **Ur'sächlich**, -lĭch, *a.* causal.
Urschrift, ŭr'shrift, *f.* original.
Ursprache, ŭr'zhpräche, *f.* original language.
Ursprung, ŭr'zhprŭng, *m. pl.* Ursprünge, origin, fountain, source.
Ursprünglich, ŭr'zhprünglĭch, *a. ar.* original, primitive, primeval, -ly; **-keit**, -kăĕt, *f.* primitive state.
Urstoff, ŭr'zhtoff, *m.* element, principle, primitive matter.
Urtext, ŭr'tĕxt, *m.* original text.
Urtheil, ŭr'tīl, *n.* judgment, decision, verdict, sentence, opinion; **-en**, -en, *vt.* to judge, decide, to pass sentence. **Ur'theilskraft**, -kraft, *m.* power *or* faculty of judging.
Ururenkel, ŭr'ŭrĕnkĕl, *m.* **-in**, -in, *f.* great-great-grandson *or* daughter.

Urb 358 **Ver**

Urвater, ur'fāter, m. (first) ancestor.
Urwald, ur'valt, m. pl. -wälber, primeval forest.
Urwelt, ur'velt, f. primitive or primeval world; **-lich**, -lich, a. antediluvian.
Urwesen, ur'vāsen, n. first being.
Urzeit, ur'tsēit, f. primitive time.
Us, u'sō, m. usance.
Usurpation, usurpatsiōn', f. usurpation.
Usurpiren, usurpī'ren, vt. to usurp.

Vacant, fakant', a. vacant, void.
Vacanz, fakants', f. vacancy; vacation, holidays.
Vaccination, faktsinatsiōn', f. vaccination. **Vaccine**, fakts'ī'ne, f. vaccina. **Vacciniren**, faktsinī'ren, vt. to vaccinate.
Vagabund, fagabunt', m. -e, pl. -en, vagabond, vagrant.
Vagiren, fagī'ren, vi. to rove about.
Vampyr, fam'pīr, m. vampire.
Vanadin, fanadīn', m. vanadium; **-säure**, -sēŭre, f. vanadic acid.
Vanadinspath, fanadīn'zhpāt, m. vanadinite.
Vanille, fanil'le, f. vanilla.
Variation, fariatsiōn', f. variation; **-rechnung**, -rechnyng, f. calculus of variation.
Varietät, fari-etāt', f. variety.
Variiren, fari-ī'ren, vi. to vary.
Varioliden, fariolī'den, s. pl. varioloids, water-pox.
Vasall, fasall', m. vassal.
Vase, fā'se, f. vase.
Vater, fā'ter, m. pl. Väter, father; **-land**, -lant, n. fatherland, native land. **Vaterländisch**, fä'terlendish, a. native: of one's country; patriotic. **Va'terlandsliebe**, -landslī-be, f. patriotism. **Va'terliebe**, -lī-be, f. paternal love. **Väterlich**, fä'terlich, a. av. paternal, fatherly. **Vaterlos**, fä'terlōs, a. fatherless. **Va'termord**, -mort, m. parricide. **Va'termörder**, -mörder, m. parricide; standing collar; **-lich**, -lish, a. parricidal. **Va'tersbruder**, -bryder, m. uncle. **Va'terschacht**, -shacht, m. main shaft. **Va'terschaft**, -shaft, f. fathership, paternity; authorship. **Va'terschraube**, -shrōybe, f. male-screw. **Va'ter-**

schwester, -shvezhter, f. paternal aunt. **Va'terstadt**, -zhtatt, f. native town. **Va'terstelle**, -zhtelle, f. place of a father; — vertreten, to be as a father. **Va'tertheil**, -tāel, m. patrimony. **Vaterunser**, fāterun'ser, n. Lord's prayer.
Vauquelinit, voklinit', m. vauquelinite.
Vegetabilien, fegetabī'li-en, s. pl. vegetables. **Vegetabilisch**, fegetabī'lish, a. vegetable. **Vegetation**, fegetatsiōn', f. vegetation. **Vegetiren**, fegetī'ren, vi. to vegetate.
Vehikel, fehick'el, n. vehicle.
Veilchen, fēil'chen, n. violet; **-blau**, -blāū, a. violet, violet-blue.
Velinpapier, velin'papīr, n. vellum-paper.
Venerie, fenerī', f. venereal disease.
Venerisch, fenā'rish, a. venereal.
Ventil, fentīl', n. valve; **-sitz**, -atsion', f. ventilation. **Ventilator**, fentilā'tor, m. ventilator. **Ventiliren**, fentilī'ren, vt. to ventilato. **Ventilsitz**, fentīl'sits, m. valve-seat.
Venus, fā'nus, f. Venus; evening-star, morning-star.
Verabfolgen, ferap'folgen, vt. to deliver. **Verab'folgung**, -ung, f. delivery, remittance.
Verabreden, ferap'rāden, vt. r. to agree upon. **Verab'redung**, -ung, f. agreement.
Verabreichen, ferap'rāechen, vt. to deliver.
Verabsäumen, ferap'sōumen, vt. to neglect.
Verabscheuen, ferap'shōu-en, vt. to detest, abhor, abominate. **Verab'scheuung**, -ung, f. abomination, detestation; **-würdig**, -vürdich, a. abominable, detestable.
Verabschieden, ferap'shīden, vt. to discharge, send away, disband: **sich** —, to take leave. **Verab'schiedung**, ferap'shīdung, f. dismissal, discharge.
Veraccisen, ferakts'ī'sen, vt. to pay the excise.
Veraccordiren, feraccordī'ren, vt. to give out on contract.
Verachten, ferach'ten, vt. to contemn, scorn, despise. **Verächter**, ferech'ter m. scorner, despiser. **Verächtlich**, ferecht'lich, a. contemptuous, scornful, av. -ly, despicable, av. -bly **-keit**, -kāet, f. despicableness.

Berachtung, fĕracht'yng, *f.* contempt, scorn.
Berallgemeinern, fĕrall'gemæ̈nĕrn, *vt.* to generalize.
Beralten, fĕral'ten, *vi.* to grow obsolete, stale.
Beränderlich, fĕrĕn'dĕrlich, *a.* changeable, variable, inconstant, fickle, fluctuating; **-keit**, -kǣĕt, *f.* mutability, inconstancy, fickleness.
Berändern, fĕrĕn'dĕrn, *vt.* to change, alter, vary; to shift, turn.
Beränderung, fĕrĕn'dĕryng, *f.* change, alteration, variation.
Berankern, fĕrang'kĕrn, *vt.* to moor.
Beranlassen, fĕrän'lassen, *vt.* to cause, to bring on, to occasion, to give rise to. **Beranlassung**, -yng, *f.* occasion, inducement; — **geben**, to give rise to.
Beranschaulichen, fĕrän'shäulichen, *vt.* to illustrate, to render plain.
Beranstalten, fĕrän'zhtalten, *vt.* to arrange, bring about. **Beranstaltung**, -zhtaltyng, *f.* management, arrangement.
Berantworten, fĕrant'vorten, *vt.* to answer for, to justify, apologize; **sich —**, to defend, vindicate one's self. **Berantwortlich**, -lich, *a.* responsible, answerable, accountable, amenable; **-keit**, -kǣĕt, *f.* responsibility. **Berantwortung**, fĕrant'vortyng, *f.* defence, apology, vindication.
Berarbeiten, fĕrar'bäĕten, *vt.* to work up, manufacture, consume, to convert; to work out, digest. **Berar'beitung**, -yng, *f.* working, consumption, manufacture.
Berargen, fĕrarg'en, *vt.* to take amiss or ill.
Berarmen, fĕrarm'en, *vi.* to become poor, to be impoverished. **Berar'mung**, -yng, *f.* impoverishment.
Berarten, fĕrär'ten, *vi.* to degenerate. **Berart'ung**, -yng, *f.* degeneracy.
Berauktioniren, fĕrŏykťsĭonī'ren, *vt.* sell by auction.
Beräußerlich, fĕrŏĭss'ĕrlich, *a.* alienable. **Beräußern**, fĕrŏĭss'ĕrn, *vt.* to alienate, dispose of.
Berbacken, fĕrback'en, *vt.* to bake.
Berband, fĕrbant', *m. pl.* -bände, bandage; union, society.
Berbannen, fĕrban'nen, *vt.* to banish, exile.

Berbannter, fĕrbann'ter, *m.* exile.
Berbannung, fĕrban'nyng, *f.* banishment, exile.
Berbauen, fĕrbŏŭ'en, *vt.* to build up to spend by building; to obstruct by building. **Berbau'ung**, -yng, *f.* lodgment (Fort).
Berbauern, fĕrbŏŭ'ĕrn, *vt.* to contract boorish manners.
Berbeißen, fĕrbĕĭs'sen (-biß, -bissen), *vt.* to bite to pieces; to gulp down, to suppress, restrain; digest; **sich in etwas —**, to lock one's teeth, to be wedded to a thing.
Berbergen, fĕrbĕr'gen (-barg, -borgen), *vt.* to conceal, hide. **Berber'gung**, -yng, *f.* concealment.
Berbesserer, fĕrbĕs'ĕrer, *m.* improver, reformer, corrector. **Berbes'serlich**, -lich, *a.* corrigible, amendable.
Berbessern, fĕrbĕs'sĕrn, *vt.* to better, improve, amend, correct. **Berbes'serung**, -yng, *f.* amendment, correction.
Berbeugen, fĕrbŏĭ'gen, *vr.* to bow, to make a bow *or* courtesy. **Berbeu'gung**, -yng, *f.* bow, courtesy.
Berbiegen, fĕrbī'gen (-bog, -bogen), *vt.* to bend, crook, twist.
Berbieten, fĕrbī'ten (-bot, -boten), *vt.* to forbid, prohibit.
Berbilden, fĕrbil'den, *vt.* to educate in a wrong way.
Berbinden, fĕrbin'den (-band, -bunden), *vt.* to join, tie, conjoin; to dress (a wound); to bind wrong; to oblige. **Berbind'lich**, -lich, *a.* obliging; obliged; **-keit**, -kǣĕt, *f.* obligation; civility; obliging manner **Berbindung**, -yng, *f.* conjunction, junction, connection; communication; alliance, match, marriage; confederacy.
Berbitten, fĕrbit'ten, *vr.* **sich —**, to deprecate (condolence); to decline; to beg not to be done; to beg to be excused.
Berbittern, fĕrbit'tern, *vt.* to embitter. **Berbit'terung**, -yng, *f.* exasperation, embittering.
Berblasen, fĕrblā'sen, *vi.* to blow over.
Berblassen, fĕrblas'sen, *vi.* to grow pale.
Berbleiben, fĕrblĕĭ'ben (-blieb, -blieben), *vi.* to remain.
Berbleichen, fĕrblĕĭ'chen (-blich, -blichen), *vi.* to grow pale.

Verbleien, ferblēī'en, vt. to lead, fit with lead; alloy with lead.
Verblenden, ferblend'en, vt. to blind, dazzle; infatuate, delude. **Verblend'ung**, -ung, f. blinding, dazzling fascination, infatuation.
Verblieb, Prt. -en, pp. from **Verbleiben**.
Verblüffen, ferblüf'fen, vt. to dumfound, confound, perplex, puzzle, put out of countenance.
Verblühen, ferblüh'en, vi. to fade, decay.
Verblümt, ferblühmt', a. covered, figurative, euphemistic.
Verbluten, ferblu̇'ten, vr. sich —, to bleed to death.
Verborgen, ferbor'gen (Prt. von verbergen), a. hidden, concealed; **-heit**, -heit, f. concealment; retirement; obscurity.
Verbot, ferbōt', n. pl. -e, forbiddance, prohibition, interdiction.
Verbrämen, ferbrä'men, vt. to border, to trim. **Verbräm'ung**, -ung, f. bordering.
Verbrauch, ferbrouch', m. consumption. **Verbrauch'en**, vt. to consume, spend.
Verbrechen, ferbrech'en, vt. to break; to offend, commit; s. n. crime.
Verbrecher, ferbrech'er, m. criminal; **-isch**, -ish, a. av. criminal, -ally.
Verbreiten, ferbrā'ten, vt. to spread, diffuse. **Verbreit'ung**, -ung, f. spreading, diffusion, propagation.
Verbrennbar, ferbrenn'bär, a. combustible; **-keit**, -käet, f. combustibility.
Verbrennen, ferbren'nen (verbrannte, verbrannt), vt. to burn (up, out).
Verbringen, ferbring'en (verbracht, verbracht), vt. to spend.
Verbröckeln, ferbröck'eln, vt. vi. to crumble.
Verbrüdern, ferbrüh'dern, vi. sich —, to fraternize. **Verbrü'derung**, -ung, f. fraternization.
Verbrühen, ferbrüh'en, vt. to scald. **Verbrüh'ung**, -ung, f. scald, scalding.
Verbuhlen, ferbu̇'len, vt. to spend or waste by debauchery, or with bad women.
Verbum, fer'bum, n. pl. Verbe, verb.
Verbunden, ferbun'den, f. **Verbinden**.
Verbünden, ferbün'den, sich —, vt. to ally, associate, confederate, to league form a league. **Verbün'det**, a. allied, associate. **Verbündt'eter**, m. ally, confederate.
Verbürgen, ferbür'gen, vt. to bail, warrant, answer for; sich —, to stand bail, security, to guaranty.
Verbürgung, ferbürg'ung, f. bailing, bail, surety.
Verbüßen, ferbüh'sen, vt. to atone for.
Verbutten, ferbut'ten, vi. to be stunted.
Verdacht, ferdacht', m. suspicion; — haben, to suspect. **Verdächtig**, ferdächtich, a. suspected, suspicious.
Verdäch'tigen, vt. to render suspected. **Verdäch'tigkeit**, -käet, f. suspectedness. **Verdäch'tigung**, -ung, f. rendering suspected. **Verdächtislos**, ferdacht'lōs, a. unsuspicious; unsuspected.
Verdammen, ferdam'men, vt. to condemn, damn. **Verdamm'lich**, -lich, a. damnable; **-keit**, -käet, f. damnableness. **Verdamm'nis**, -niss, f. damnation. **Verdamm'ung**, -ung, f. condemnation.
Verdampfen, ferdampf'en, vt. i. to evaporate.
Verdämpfen, ferdempf'en, vt. to evaporate.
Verdanken, ferdang'ken, vt. to owe, to be indebted for.
Verdauen, ferdau̇'en, vt. to digest.
Verdaulich, ferdäu'lich, a. digestible; **-keit**, -käet, f. digestive quality.
Verdauung, ferdäu'ung, f. digestion. **Verdau'ungsmittel**, -mittel, n. digestive.
Verdeck, ferdeck', s. n. deck; **-en**, -en, vt. to cover.
Verdenken, ferdenk'en (verdachte, verdacht), vt. to blame, to take amiss.
Verderb, ferderp', m. wasting; **-en**, -en (verdarb, verdorben), vt. to spoil, wither, perish.
Verderben, ferderb'en, vt. to spoil, destroy, corrupt, ruin.
Verderben, ferder'ben, s. n. destruction, ruin, corruption.
Verderber, ferderb'er, m. destructor, destroyer, corruptor, spoiler.
Verderblich, ferderb'lich, a. pernicious, destructive, ruinous; **-keit**, -käet, f. corruptibility, corruptibleness.
Verderbnis, -erderb'niss, f. corruption, depravity.

Berberbt, ferderbt', *a.* corrupt, corrupted, depraved; **.heit, -hkeit,** *s.* corruptedness, corruption.

Berbeutichen, ferdeüt'shen, *vt.* to render German.

Berbichten, ferdich'ten, *vt. i.* to condense, condensate, to compress; *f.* condensation.

Berbiden, ferdick'en, *vt.* to thicken, inspissate. **Berbid'ung, -yng,** *f.* thickening, concretion, condensation.

Berbienen, ferdi'nen, *vt.* to earn, gain; deserve, merit.

Berbienft, ferdinst', *m.* earnings, gain; reward, profit; *s. n.* merit; — um, merit in behalf of, in regard to.

Berbienftlich, ferdinst'lich, *a.* meritorious; profitable, lucrative, gainful; **.feit, -kkeit,** *f.* meritoriousness.

Berbienftloß, ferdinst'lös, *a.* undeserving. **Berbienft'boll, -foll,** *a.* well-deserving, full of merit.

Berbient, ferdint', *Pp. a.* merited, meritorious, deserving; **fich — machen um,** to deserve well of.

Berbing, ferding', *m.* contract, letting anything for rent; agreement.

Berbingen, ferding'en (verbung, verbungen), *vt.* to contract for; hire; **fich —,** to enter into service. **Berbing'ung, -yng,** *f.* contract, agreement, bargain.

Berbolmetichen, ferdol'metshen, *vt.* to interpret. **Berbol'metichung, -yng,** *f.* interpretation.

Berboppeln, ferdop'peln, *vt.* to double. **Berbop'pelung, -yng,** *f.* doubling, duplication.

Berborben, ferdor'ben, *a.* spoiled, marred, wasted, corrupted; **.heit, -hkeit,** *f.* corruption, depravity.

Berborren, ferdor'ren, *vi.* to wither, dry up.

Berbrängen, ferdreng'en, *vt.* to crowd out, to oust, displace.

Berbrehen, ferdrä'en, *vt.* to strain, wrench; to distort, pervert; **bie Augen verbrehen,** to roll the eyes. **Berbreh'ung, -yng,** *f.* distortion, perversion, malicious interpretation.

Berbreifachen, ferdrei'fachen, *vt.* to triple.

Berbriegen, ferdrie'sen (.bros, .brossen), *vt.* to vex, grieve, fret, trouble, disgust. **Berbrieß'lich, -lich,** *a.* vexatious, sulky, sad, peevish, angry,

out of humor; **.feit, -kkeit,** *f.* annoyance, trouble; fretfulness, peevishness.

Berbroffen, ferdros'sen, *a. av.* peevish, vexed, fretted, unwilling, slow; **.heit, -hkeit,** *f.* unwillingness, peevishness.

Berbruden, ferdruck'en, *vt.* to misprint.

Berbrüden, ferdrück'en, *vt.* to crush, to press out of shape.

Berbruß, ferdruss', *m.* vexation, trouble, annoyance.

Berbuften, ferduf'ten, *vi.* to evaporate, pass off, vanish; *vt.* to evaporate, exhale, breathe forth.

Berbummen, ferdum'men, *vt.* to make stupid *or* dull, to imbrute; *vi.* to become stupid.

Berbumpfen, ferdump'fen, *vt. i.* to make *or* become dull.

Berbunkeln, ferdun'keln, *vt.* to obscure, darken, dim, cloud; to eclipse. **Berdun'kelung, -kelung,** *f.* obscuration, darkening; eclipse; shading, deepening.

Berbünnen, ferdün'nen, *vt.* to thin, rarefy, dilute. **Berbün'nung, -yng,** *f.* thinning, rarefaction, dilution.

Berbunften, ferdün'zhten, *vi.* to evaporate, to fume away. **Berbünften,** ferdün'zhten, *vt.* to evaporate, fume away. **Berbün'ftung, -yng,** *f.* evaporation, exhalation.

Berburften, ferdurzh'ten, *vi.* to die of thirst, to perish with thirst.

Berburftet, ferdurzh'tet, *a.* parched with thirst, very dry, thirsty.

Berbüftern, ferdüsh'tern, *vt.* to darken, obscure.

Berbuten, ferduts'en, *vt.* to bewilder, disconcert, puzzle, astound.

Berbust, ferdutst', *a.* abashed.

Berebeln, ferä'deln, *vt.* to ennoble, to improve, elevate, ameliorate; to refine, work up. **Bereb'lung, -yng,** *f.* refinement, perfection, improvement.

Berehelichen, ferä(ä)'lichen, *vr.* **fich —** to marry. **Bere'helichung, -yng,** *f.* marrying, marriage.

Berehren, ferä'ren, *vt.* to respect, revere, venerate, adore, worship; to present with.

Berehrer, ferä'rer, *m.* admirer, worshiper.

Berehrlich, ferär'lich, *a.* honorable.

Verehrung, fĕrār'ŭng, f. veneration, adoration, reverence, respect. **Verehrungswürdig**, -würdig, a. venerable, adorable.
Vereiden, fĕrīā'den, vt. to swear (in).
Verein, fĕrąēn', m. pl. -e, association, society; -bar, -bär, a. compatible; -keit, -kāět, f. compatibility.
Vereinbaren, fĕrąēn'bāren, vt. to reconcile; sich —, to agree upon.
Vereinen, fĕrąēn'en, vt. to unite.
Vereinfachen, fĕrąēn'fachen, vt. to simplify. **Vereinfachung**, -ŭng, f. simplification.
Vereinigen, fĕrąēn'ichen, vt. to unite, combine, join, conjoin; reconcile; sich —, to agree. **Vereinigung**, -ŭng, f. union, combination, agreement.
Vereinzeln, fĕrąēn'tseln, vt. to isolate, dismember. **Vereinzelung**, -ŭng, f. isolation.
Vereisen, fĕrēī'sen, vi. to congeal.
Vereiteln, fĕrēī'teln, vt. to disappoint, frustrate, baffle. **Vereitelung**, -ŭng, f. frustration.
Verenden, fĕrĕn'den, vi. to die.
Verengen, fĕrĕng'en, vt. to narrow, contract.
Vererben, fĕrĕr'ben, vt. to transmit, to leave as inheritance.
Verewigen, fĕrā'vichen, vt. to immortalize, perpetuate. **Verewigt**, a. deceased.
Verfahren, fĕrfā'ren (-fuhr, -fahren), vi. to proceed, act, treat; vt. to convey, transport, to cart; s. n. procedure, proceeding. **Verfahrungsart**, -ŭngsärt, f. procedure.
Verfall, fĕrfall', m. decay, decline; expiration, forfeiture: in — gerathen, to decay, to go to ruin. **Verfallen**, fĕrfal'len (-fiel, -fallen), vi. to decay, to go to ruin, to expire; to become due; to be forfeited: — auf, to hit upon. Pp. **Verfallen**, in ruins, decayed, dilapidated; due; forfeited, escheated.
Verfalltag, fĕrfall'tāk, m. pay-day, day of payment.
Verfallzeit, fĕrfall'tsāīt, f. time of payment.
Verfällen, fĕrfĕl'len, vt. in eine Strafe —, to fine.
Verfälschen, fĕrfĕl'shen, vt. to falsify, to interpolate, to forge, counterfeit. **Verfälscher**, m. falsifier, interpolator, forger, counterfeiter. **Verfälschung**, fĕrfĕlsh'ŭng, f. falsification, interpolation; adulteration; forgery.
Verfangen, fĕrfang'en (-fing, -fangen), vr. to be caught, to betray one's self; vt. to work, take effect, operate.
Verfänglich, fĕrfĕng'lich, a. captious; -keit, -kāět, f. captiousness.
Verfärben, fĕrfĕr'ben, vr. sich —, to change color, blush; to fade.
Verfassen, fĕrfas'sen, vt. to compose, write. **Verfasser**, -fas'ser, m. author, composer. **Verfassung**, -ŭng, f. constitution; state, condition; composition; -mäßig, -mässich, a. constitutional. **Verfassungswidrig**, -vidrich, a. unconstitutional.
Verfaulen, fĕrfŏu'len, vi. to rot.
Verfechten, fĕrfĕch'ten, vt. to contend, fight for; to defend, maintain.
Verfechter, fĕrfĕch'ter, m. champion, defender.
Verfehlen, fĕrfāl'en, vt. to miss; vr. to transgress.
Verfeinden, fĕrfąēn'den, vt. to render hostile, offend; sich — mit, to fall out with.
Verfeinen, fĕrfąēn'en, **Verfein'ern**, vt. to refine, improve. **Verfeinerung**, fĕrfąēn'ĕrŭng, f. refinement, improvement.
Verfertigen, fĕrfĕr'tichen, vt. to make, compose, prepare, construct, form, manufacture, fabricate. **Verfertiger**, fĕrfĕr'ticher, m. maker, composer, manufacturer. **Verfertigung**, fĕrfĕr'tichŭng, f. making, composition, manufacturing.
Verfeuern, fĕrfŏǐ'ĕrn, vt. to burn up, to fire away, to consume by burning or firing.
Verfilzen, fĕrfīl'tsen, vt. to entangle, mat.
Verfinstern, fĕrfīn'zhtĕrn, vt. to darken, obscure, eclipse. **Verfinsterung**, -ŭng, f. eclipse.
Verfitzen, fĕrfīt'sen, vt. to entangle, mat.
Verflachen, fĕrflach'en, vi. to render flat, to lower.
Verflechten, fĕrflĕch'ten (-flocht, -flochten), vt. to entwine, interlace, to plait together.
Verfliegen, fĕrflī'gen (-flog, -flogen), vi. to fly away, evaporate, to be volatilized.

Verfließen, fėrflī'sen (verfloß, verflossen), vi. to elapse, to pass, to flow off.

Verfluchen, fėrflü'chen, vt. to curse, execrate. **Verflucht,** fėrflücht', a. cursed, execrable.

Verflüchtigen, fėrflüch'tichen, vt. to volatilize, evaporate.

Verfluß, fėrflüss', m. lapse, expiration.

Verfolg, fėrfolk', m. course, progress. **Verfolgen,** fėrfol'gen, vt. to pursue, persecute; to prosecute; to continue; nicht —, to neglect. **Verfolger,** fėrfol'ger, m. pursuer, persecutor. **Verfolgung,** -ung, f. pursuit, persecution, chase; prosecution.

Verfrachten, fėrfrach'ten, vt. to pay the freight.

Verfremden, fėrfrem'den, vi. to be estranged.

Verfressen, fėrfrēs'sen (-fraß, -fressen), vt. to consume; to corrode.

Verfrieren, fėrfrī'ren (-fror, -froren), vi. to freeze.

Verfrühen, fėrfrüh'en, vt. to do prematurely, to anticipate.

Verfügbar, fėrfühk'bär, a. disposable. **Verfügen,** fėrfüh'gen, vt. to dispose, arrange, provide, enact, order; vr. to go to. **Verfügung,** -ung, f. disposition, order.

Verführen, fėrfüh'ren, vt. to convey, transport; te seduce, corrupt.

Verführer, fėrfüh'rer, m. seducer; -isch, -ish, a. seducing, seductive.

Verführung, fėrführ'ung, f. seduction.

Verfüttern, fėrfüt'tern, vt. to consume or spend as provender or food.

Vergaffen, fėrgaf'fen, vr. sich —, to be dazzled at, to be smitten with; to gape at.

Vergällen, fėrgäl'len, vt. to embitter.

Vergaloppiren, fėrgalopp'iren, vr. sich —, to run too fast.

Vergangen (Vergehen), fėrgang'en, pp. gone, past, last; -heit, -hāet, f. the past, things past. **Vergänglich,** fėrgeng'lich, a. transient, transitory, perishable; -keit, -kāet, f. transientness, transitoriness.

Verganten, fėrgan'ten, vt. to bring any one's goods to the hammer.

Vergeben, fėrgā'ben (-gab, -geben), vt. to forgive, pardon; to misdeal; to poison; sich —, to injure, prejudice. **Vergebens,** vėrgā'bens, av. in vain. **Vergeblich,** -lich, a. fruitless, vain, useless; -keit, -kāet, f. uselessness. **Vergebung,** fėrgāb'ung, f. forgiveness, pardon.

Vergegenwärtigen, fėrgā'genvėrtichen, vt. to represent, recall, to bring home to one's mind.

Vergehen, fėrgā'en (-ging, -gangen), vi. to perish, to pass away, disappear, vanish; sich —, to trespass; s. n. offense, trespass.

Vergeistigen, fėrgāezht'ichen, vt. to spiritualize.

Vergelben, fėrgel'ben, vi. to turn yellow.

Vergelten, fėrgel'ten (-galt, -golten), vt. to recompense, reward, requite, remunerate; to repay, retaliate.

Vergelter, fėrgel'ter, m. rewarder.

Vergeltung, fėrgelt'ung, f. requital, retaliation, return, recompense.

Vergessen, fėrgēs'sen (-gaß, -gessen), vt. to forget; -heit, -hāet, f. oblivion, forgetfulness. **Vergeßlich,** fėrgess'lich, a. forgetful; -keit, -kāet, f. forgetfulness, obliviousness.

Vergeuden, fėrgöu'den, vt. to lavish, spend, squander. **Vergeuder,** m. spendthrift, squanderer. **Vergeudung,** -ung, f. lavishment, dissipation.

Vergewissern, fėrgevis'sern, vt. to ascertain, to assure; to convince.

Vergewisserung, fėrgevis'serung, f. assurance, confirmation.

Vergießen, fėrgī'sen (-goß, -gossen), vt. to shed, pour out; to effuse, to spill; mit Blei —, to seal with lead; mit Kalk —, to spread with mortar; s. n. shedding, effusion.

Vergiften, fėrgif'ten, vt. to poison.

Vergiftung, fėrgift'ung, f. poisoning.

Vergissen, fėrgis'sen, vi. to make mistakes in dead reckoning.

Vergißmeinnicht, fėrgiss'mēnnicht, n. forget-me-not (Bot.).

Vergittern, fėrgit'tern, vt. to grate.

Verglasen, fėrglā'sen, vt. to glaze, vitrify. **Verglasung,** -ung, f. glazing, vitrification.

Vergleich, fėrglāech', m. comparison; settlement, compromise.

Vergleichen, fėrglāech'en (-glich, -glichen), vt. to compare; to make equal; to settle. **Vergleichlich,** -lich, **Ver-**

gleich'bar, -bār, *a.* comparable. **Ver-gleich'ung**, -ŭng, *f.* comparison; **-weise**, -svēise, *av.* comparatively, in comparison.

Verglimmen, fĕrglim'men (-glomm, -glommen), **Verglühen**, fĕrglüh'en, *vi.* to glow on; to cease glowing.

Vergnügen, fĕrg'(e)nüh'gen, *vt.* to gratify, content, to satisfy, divert, rejoice, delight, please; *s. n.* pleasure, sport. **Vergnüglich**, -lich, *a.* pleasant, delightful. **Vergnügt**, *a.* cheerful, pleased, delighted. **Vergnügung**, fĕrg(e)nüh'kŭng, *f.* pleasure, amusement, pastime; **-reise**, -srāese, *f.* pleasure-party.

Vergolden, fĕrgol'den, *vt.* to gild. **Vergolder**, fĕrgol'dĕr, *m.* gilder. **Vergoldung**, -ŭng, *f.* gilding.

Vergönnen, fĕrgön'nen, *vt.* not to grudge, to allow.

Vergöttern, fĕrgöt'tĕrn, *vt.* to idolize, deify. **Vergötterung**, -ŭng, *f.* idolizing, idolatry; deification, apotheosis.

Vergraben, fĕrgrā'ben (-grub, -graben), *vt.* to bury.

Vergreifen, fĕrgrī'fen (-griff, -griffen), *vt.* to mistake (in seizing); to sprain (a hand); to lay hands on; to meddle with; to violate, outrage, profane; sich — (of books), to be sold.

Vergriffen, fĕrgrif'fen, *a.* sold, out of print.

Vergrößern, fĕrgröh'sĕrn, *vt.* to enlarge, increase, aggrandize, amplify, magnify, exaggerate. **Vergrößerung**, -ŭng, *f.* enlargement, amplification, exaggeration, aggrandizement; **-glas**, -glās, *n. pl.* -gläser, microscope, magnifying-glass.

Vergünstigen, fĕrgün'zhtichen, *vt.* to favor. **Vergünstigung**, -ŭng, *f.* favor.

Vergüten, fĕrgüh'ten, *vt.* to make amends for, to requite, to indemnify. **Vergütung**, -ŭng, *f.* amends, indemnification.

Verhack, fĕrhack', *m.* abatis; **sen**, -en, *vt.* to chop up, mince.

Verhaft, fĕrhaft', *m.* arrest; in — nehmen, to imprison; **-en**, -en, *vt.* to arrest, imprison. **Verhaft'ung**, -ŭng, *f.* arrest, imprisonment.

Verhallen, fĕrhal'len, *vi.* to die away.

Verhalt, fĕrhalt', *m.* fact, state; **-en**, -en, *vt.* to hold *or* keep back, to retain; to be; sich gut, schlecht —, to conduct *or* behave well *or* badly; *s. n.* behavior, conduct.

Verhältnis, fĕrhęlt'nĭss, *n.* proportion, ratio, rate; **-mäßig**, -māsich, *a.* proportioned, proportional, special.

Verhältnißwidrig, fĕrhęlt'nisvīdrich, *a.* disproportionate.

Verhaltung, fĕrhalt'ŭng, *f.* conduct, acting; **-sbefehl**, -sbefāl, *m.* instruction, order.

Verhandeln, fĕrhan'dĕln, *vt.* to negotiate, transact, treat; dispose of; sell. **Verhand'lung**, -ŭng, *f.* transaction, proceedings, minutes.

Verhängen, fĕrhęng'en, *vt.* to cover by hanging; to inflict, destine, decree. **Verhängniß**, fĕrhęng'niss, *n.* destiny, fate, lot; **-voll**, -foll, *a.* ominous, fatal; momentous.

Verharren, fĕrhar'ren, *vi.* to remain, continue, persist, hold out. **Verharrung**, -ŭng, *f.* perseverance.

Verharschen, fĕrhar'shen, *vi.* to close, to crust.

Verhärten, fĕrhęr'ten, *vt. i.* to harden, obdurate, indurate. **Verhärtung**, -ŭng, *f.* obduracy, hardening.

Verhaßt, fĕrhasst', *a.* hateful, odious, obnoxious.

Verhätscheln, fĕrhęt'sheln, *vt.* to spoil; to fondle.

Verhau, fĕrhäu', *m. pl.* -e, abatis.

Verhauen, fĕrhäu'en, *vt.* to lop, cut down; to cut wrong.

Verhauchen, fĕrhöu'chen, *vt.* to breathe out.

Verheben, fĕrhā'ben, *vt.* to overstrain one's self by lifting.

Verheeren, fĕrhā'ren, *vt.* to desolate, ravage, lay waste, devastate. **Verheerung**, -ŭng, *f.* devastation, desolation.

Verheften, fĕrhęf'ten, *vt.* to sew, stitch; to sew wrong.

Verhehlen, fĕrhā'len (*Pp.* verhehlt, verhohlen), *vt.* to conceal. **Verhehlung**, -ŭng, *f.* concealment.

Verheimlichen, fĕrhāem'lichen, *vt.* to hide, conceal. **Verheimlichung**, -ŭng, *f.* concealment.

Verheirathen, fĕrhāi'rāten, *vt.* to marry, bestow *or* giv in marriage; sich —, to marry, get married.

Verheißen, fĕrhāes'sen (verhieß, verheißen), *vt.* to promise. **Verheißung**, -ŭng, *f.* promise.

Verhelfen, fĕrhĕl'fen (verhalf, verholfen), vt. to help.
Verhenkert, fĕrhenk'ert, a. devilish; ein verhenkerter Streich, a confounded, devilish trick.
Verherrlichen, fĕrhĕrr'lichen, vt. to glorify. **Verherrlichung,** -ung, f. glorification.
Verhetzen, fĕrhet'sen, vt. to incite, exasperate, to set on.
Verhexen, fĕrhex'en, vt. to bewitch.
Verhinderlich, fĕrhind'erlich, a. preventable. **Verhindern,** vt. to prevent, hinder. **Verhinderung,** -ung, f. hindrance, obstacle, prevention.
Verhoffen, fĕrhŏf'fen, vt. to hope (for).
Verhöhnen, fĕrhöh'nen, vt. to scoff, scorn. **Verhöhnung,** -ung, f. insult, contumely.
Verholen, fĕrhō'len, vt. to tow; haul.
Verhör, fĕrhöhr', n. hearing, trial; **-en,** -en, vt. to try, examine, interrogate; to mishear.
Verhüllen, fĕrhül'len, vt. to cover, veil. **Verhüllung,** -ung, f. disguise, veil.
Verhundertfachen, fĕrhun'dĕrtfachen, vt. to multiply by hundreds.
Verhungern, fĕrhung'ern, vt. to starve or perish with hunger.
Verhunzen, fĕrhunt'sen, vt. to spoil, bungle.
Verhuren, fĕrhu'ren, vt. to whore away, to spend in whoring.
Verhüten, fĕrhü'ten, vt. to prevent.
Verhütung, fĕrhüh'tung, f. prevention.
Verinteressiren, fĕrinteressī'ren, vr. to pay interest.
Verirren, fĕrīr'ren, vt. to stray, wander, to lose one's way. **Verirrung,** -ung, f. wandering; error.
Verjagen, fĕryā'gen, vt. to chase or drive (away), scare, expel.
Verjährbar, fĕryār'bär, a. prescriptible. **Verjähren,** fĕryār'en, vt. to grow out of date, be prescribed, to be rooted in. **Verjährt,** a. prescriptive (right); inveterate (prejudice). **Verjährung,** -ung, f. prescription.
Verjüngen, fĕryüng'en, vt. to make young again. **Verjüngter Maßstab,** reduced or plotting scale, scale of reduction. **Verjüngung,** -ung, f. rejuvenescence; (Arch.) diminution, reduction; —(eines Models), delivery.

Verkalken, fĕrkalk'en, vt. to calcine reduce to lime.
Verkälten, fĕrkel'ten, vt. sich —, to take cold. **Verkältung,** -ung, f. cold.
Verkannt, fĕrkannt', Pp. von Verkennen.
Verkappen, fĕrkap'pen, vt. to mask.
Verkauf, fĕrkäuf, m. pl. **Verkäufe,** sale **Verkaufen,** vt. to sell. **Verkäufer,** fĕrkäu'fer, m. seller. **Verkäuflich,** -lich, a. salable, marketable, venal, corruptible; -keit, -käet, f. salableness. **Verkaufspreis,** fĕrkäufs'preis, m. selling price.
Verkehr, fĕrkā-r', m. intercourse; trade, commerce.
Verkehren, fĕrkā'ren, vi. to trade, carry trade, do business; have intercourse, dealings; vt. to pervert; turn; die Augen —, to roll, twist. **Verkehrt,** fĕrkärt', a. perverted, wrong; **-heit,** -häet, f. perversity, crossness. **Verkehrung,** -kār'ung, f. turning, change; perversion; inversion.
Verkeilen, fĕrkā'len, vt. to wedge; to drive up the quoins (Print.); to sell.
Verkennen, fĕrken'nen (verkannte, verkannt), vt. to mistake, misapprehend, misjudge, misdeem.
Verketten, fĕrket'ten, vt. to chain up, link together, connect with, concatenate. **Verkettung,** -ung, f. concatenation.
Verketzern, fĕrkĕt'sern, vt. to decry; to accuse of. tax with heresy. **Verketzerung,** -ung, f. accusation of heresy.
Verkitten, fĕrkit'ten, vt. to cement.
Verklagen, fĕrklā'gen, vt. to accuse, bring to justice.
Verkläger, fĕrklā'ger, m. plaintiff.
Verklagter, fĕrklāk'ter, m. defendant.
Verklären, fĕrklā'ren, vt. to clear, brighten; transfigure, transform, glorify. **Verklärt,** fĕrklärt', a. bright, beaming with bliss, glorified. **Verklärung,** -ung, f. transfiguration, glorification.
Verkleben, fĕrklā'ben, vt. to plaster over.
Verkleiden, fĕrklā́den, vt. to cover or case with; to wainscot; to disguise. **Verkleidung,** -ung, f. disguise; (Fort.) revetment.
Verkleinern, fĕrklā'nern, vt. to diminish, lessen; to backbite, detract, derogate, disparage. **Verkleinerung,**

-ung, f. diminution; detraction, derogation, disparagement. **Verkleinerungsglas**, -glas, n. diminishing glass. **Verkleinerungswort**, -wort, n. diminutive.
Verkleistern, fĕrklĕī'zhtĕrn, vt. to paste (up), plaster over.
Verklingen, fĕrkling'en (-klang, -klungen). vi. to die away.
Verknallen, fĕrk(e)nal'len, vi. to explode.
Verknüpfen, fĕrknüpf'en, vt. to tie, bind, knit; to unite, conjoin, combine. **Verknüpfung**, -ung, f. connection.
Verkochen, fĕrkoch'en, vt. to boil away; spoil, consume by boiling.
Verkohlen, fĕrkō'len, vt. to char, carbonize, convert into coal; vi. to burn to coal.
Verkommen, fĕrkom'men (verkam, verkommen), vi. to pine away, perish, starve.
Verkorken, fĕrkor'ken, vt. to cork up.
Verkörpern, fĕrkürp'ern. vt. to embody, give a body. **Verkörperung**, -ung, f. embodiment, corporification.
Verköstigen, fĕrközht'igen, vt. to board, feed.
Verkramen, fĕrkrä'men, vt. to mislay.
Verkratzen, fĕrkrät'sen, vt. to scratch out; spoil by scratching.
Verkriechen, fĕrkrī'chen (verkroch, verkrochen), vr. to creep away; to abscond.
Verkrümeln, fĕrkrüh'meln, vt. i. to crumb, crumble, melt away; to waste by little and little.
Verkrüppeln, fĕrkrüp'peln, vt. to cripple.
Verkühlen, fĕrkūh'len, vi. to cool off.
Verkümmern, fĕrküm'mern, vt. to stint in, sequester; embitter; vi. to pine away. **Verkümmerung**, -ung, f. sequestration; embittering; pining away.
Verkünden, fĕrkün'den, **Verkündigen**, -dichen, vt. to announce, proclaim. **Verkündigung**, -ung, f. annunciation, promulgation; proclamation.
Verkünstelt, fĕrkün'shtelt, a. unnatural, studied.
Verkuppeln, fĕrkup'peln, vt. to match; pander.
Verkürzen, fĕrkürt'sen, vt. to shorten, abridge; prejudice; (time) to pass away. **Verkürzung**, -ung, f. abridgment, abbreviation.
Verlachen, fĕrlach'en, vt. to laugh at, deride. **Verlachung**, -ung, f. laughing at, derision.
Verladen, fĕrlä'den, vt. to ship. **Verladung**, -ung, f. shipping, shipment, loading.
Verlag, fĕrläg', m. publication; in — nehmen, to publish; **Verlagsartikel**, -artikel, m. publication. **Verlagsbuchhändler**, -buchhendler, m. publisher. **Verlagsrecht**, -recht, n. copy-right.
Verlahmen, fĕrlä'men, vi. to grow lame.
Verlangen, fĕrlang'en, vt. to desire, long for; s. n. desire, want, request.
Verlängen, fĕrleng'en, **Verlängern**, -ern, vt. to lengthen, prolong, protract. **Verlängerung**, -ung, f. prolongation.
Verlappern, fĕrlĕp'pern, vt. to spend, waste in trifles.
Verlarven, fĕrlar'fen, vt. to mask, disguise; vi. to pass into the chrysalis state.
Verlassen, fĕrlas'sen (verließ, verlassen), vt. to leave, relinquish, forsake, abandon; desert; schaft, -shaft, f. inheritance.
Verlässig, fĕrläss'ich, **Verläßlich**, -lich, a. reliable, trustworthy.
Verlästern, fĕrlezh'tern, vt. to slander. **Verlästerung**, -ung, f. slander, calumniation.
Verlaub, fĕrlaup', m. permission.
Verlauf, fĕrlauf', m. course; lapse; detail, particulars.
Verlaufen, fĕrläuf'en, vt. to subside (of water); pass, elapse; to go astray, to pocket one's own bail.
Verläugnen, fĕrläug'nen, vt. to deny, disown; renounce. **Verläugnung**, fĕrläug'nung, f. denial, abnegation.
Verleben, fĕrlä'ben, vt. to pass, spend. **Verlebt**, fĕrlebt', a. broken down, worn with age.
Verlechzen, fĕrlech'tsen, vt. to languish, perish, die of.
Verlegen, fĕrlä'gen, vt. to lay in another place, dislodge, remove; mislay; to publish.
Verlegen, fĕrlä'gen, a. spoiled by lying; puzzled, embarrassed, distressed; -heit, -hĕĭt, f. embarrassment, perplexity, dilemma, distress

in — fein, to be at a loss; in Verlegenheit 'feyen, to embarrass, perplex.
Verleger, ferlä'ger, m. publisher.
Verleiden, ferlä'den, vt. to give or cause a disgust for.
Verleihen, ferläih'en, vt. to lend (out), to bestow on, to grant, confer. Verleih'ung, -yng, f. grant, bestowal.
Verleiten, ferläi'ten, vt. to mislead; lead, induce, persuade. Verlei'tung, -yng, f. seduceement.
Verlernen, ferler'nen, vt. to unlearn.
Verlesen, ferlä'sen (verlas, verlesen), vt. to pick (wool); to read (out, loud, aloud); recite.
Verletzen, ferlet'sen, vt. to hurt, injure, violate, damage, offend. Verletzlich, Verletz'bar, -bär. a. damageable, violable, vulnerable. Verletz'ung, -yng, f. violation, hurt, wound, injury.
Verleumden, ferleum'den, vt. to slander, calumniate. Verleum'bung, -dyng, f. calumny, slander.
Verlieben, ferli'ben, vr. fich —, to fall in love. Verliebt, ferlibt', a. enamored, in love; — in, fond of; -heit, -häit, f. amorousness.
Verliegen, ferli'gen, vt. to spoil by lying.
Verlieren, ferli'ren (verlor, verloren), vt. to lose; fich —, to disappear, to die away, to fade.
Verließ, ferlis', n. pl. -e, dungeon, keep.
Verloben, ferlö'ben, vt. to betroth, affiance. Verlöbniß, ferlöhb'niss, s. betrothment, espousals. Verlobter, ferlöb'ter, -e, pl. -en, affianced. Verlob'ung, -yng, f. betrothment, affiance, espousals.
Verlocken, ferlock'en, vt. to allure, entice, seduce. Verlock'ung, -yng, f. enticement, allurement, seduction.
Verlohnen, ferlö'nen, vt. to repay, pay.
Verloren, ferlö'ren, f. Verlieren.
Verlöschen, ferlösh'en (verlöschte, verlosch, verlöscht, verloschen), vt. i. to expire, to be extinguished; vt. to extinguish.
Verlosen, ferlö'sen, vt. to allot, to draw lots. Verlos'ung, -yng, f. allotment.
Verlor, ferlör' (Prt. lost, verloren, Pp. and a. of verlieren), lost, for-
lorn; — geben, to be lost; — er Sohn prodigal son.
Verlust, ferlyzht', m. loss; sig, -ich, a. losing, lost; — werden, geben, fich — machen, to lose, forfeit.
Vermachen, fermach'en, vt. to bequeath, leave; to stop, shut, close.
Vermächtniß, fermächt'niss, n. legacy bequest.
Vermählen, fermä'len, vt. r. to marry, give in marriage. Vermäh'lung, -yng, f. marriage, espousals.
Vermahnen, fermän'en, vt. to admonish, warn. Vermah'nung, -nyng, f. admonition.
Vermaledeit, fermaledëit', a. cursed, execrable.
Vermäntelung, fermen'telyng, f. palliation.
Vermauern, fermöy'ern, vt. to mure up.
Vermehren, fermä'ren, vt. to increase, multiply. Vermehr'ung, -yng, f. increase, augmentation.
Vermeiden, fermëi'den, vt. to avoid. Vermeid'ung, -yng, f. avoiding. Vermeid'lich, -lich, a. avoidable.
Vermeinen, fermëin'en, vt. to presume. Vermeint'lich, -lich, a. pretended, presumed.
Vermelden, fermël'den, vt. to announce.
Vermengen, fermëng'en, vt. to mix, mingle; to confound.
Vermenschlichen, fermensh'lichen, vt. to incarnate; to humanize. Vermensch'lichung, -yng, f. incarnation.
Vermerken, fermër'ken, vt. to mark, notice.
Vermessen, fermës'sen (vermaß, vermessen), vt. to measure, survey; to make a mistake in measuring; vr. to dare, presume; to protest, boast; a. av. auch Vermes'sentlich, -lich, a. presumptuous, -ly. Vermes'senheit, -häit, f. presumption. Vermes'sung, -yng, f. survey.
Vermiethen, fermi'ten, vt. to let, lease. Vermieth'er, m. landlord, lessor; conveyancer.
Vermindern, fermin'dërn, vt. to diminish, reduce. Vermin'derung, -yng, f. diminution, reduction.
Vermischen, fermish'en, vt. to mix, mingle. Vermischt, a. mixed; confused. Vermisch'ung, -yng, f. mixture, confusion.

Vermissen, fĕrmĭs'sen, vt. to miss, want.
Vermitteln, fĕrmĭt'tĕln, vt. to mediate; to adjust (by mediation).
Vermittelung, fĕrmĭt'telyng, f. mediation, adjustment, instrumentality.
Vermittler, fĕrmĭtt'lĕr, m. mediator.
Vermittelst, fĕrmĭtt'elst, pr. by means of.
Vermodern, fĕrmō'dĕrn, vi. to moulder, rot.
Vermöge, fĕrmöh'ge, pr. by virtue of.
Vermögen, n. faculty, power, ability; fortune, means; vt. i. (vermocht, vermocht), to be able (to do); einen —, to induce, to prevail upon.
Vermögend, Vermöglich, -lich, a. wealthy, opulent, rich, of means.
Vermummen, fĕrmym'men, vt. to mask, disguise, muffle.
Vermuthen, fĕrmyt'en, vt. to conjecture, guess, presume, suppose.
Vermuthlich, fĕrmyt'lich, a. av. likely, probable, probably. **Vermuthung,** fĕrmyt'yng, f. supposition, conjecture.
Vernachlässigen, fĕrnăch'lässĭchen, vt. to neglect, disregard. **Vernachlässigung,** -yng, f. neglect, inattention, disregard.
Vernageln, fĕrnă'gĕln, vt. to nail up; to spike (a gun).
Vernähen, fĕrnă'-en, vt. to sew up, to use up in sewing; to sew wrong.
Vernarben, fĕrnar'ben, vi. to scar over.
Vernarren, fĕrnar'ren, vr. sich —, to dote on, to become foolishly fond of.
Vernarrt, fĕrnarrt', a. infatuated, doting; -heit, -hĕĭt, f. infatuation.
Vernaschen, fĕrnash'en, vt. to spend in delicacies or dainties.
Vernehmbar, fĕrnăm'băr, **Vernehmlich,** -lich, a. distinct, perceptible, audible; -keit, -kĕĭt, f. audibleness, perceptibility. **Vernehmen,** fĕrnă'-men (-nahm, -nommen), vt. to perceive, hear, to give a hearing.
Verneigen, fĕrnăĭ'gen, vt. to courtesy, bow. **Verneigung,** -yng, f. bow, courtesy, inclination.
Verneinen, fĕrnăĭn'en, vt. to deny, negative. **Verneinend,** a. negative. **Verneinung,** -yng, f. denial, negation.
Vernichten, fĕrnĭch'ten, vt. to annihilate, annul, cancel, destroy. **Ver-**

nichtung, -yng, f. annihilation, destruction.
Vernieten, fĕrnī'ten, vt. to rivet. **Vernietung,** -yng, f. riveting.
Vernunft, fĕrnynft', f. reason.
Vernünfteln, fĕsnünf'tĕln, vi. to reason. **Vernünftig,** -tich, a. rational, av. -ly, reasonable, av. -ably; -keit -kĕĭt, f. rationality, reasonableness.
Vernunftlos, -nynft'lōs, a. irrational; -igkeit, -ĭchkĕĭt, f. irrationality.
Vernunftmäßig, -mässĭch, a. according to reason, rational, reasonable; -keit, -kĕĭt, f. reasonableness, rationality. **Vernunftreligion,** -religiōn, f. natural religion. **Vernunftrecht,** -recht, n. natural law. **Vernunftschluß,** -shlyss, m. syllogism. **Vernunftstaat,** -zhtăt, m. pl. -en, a state rationally constituted. **Vernunftwesen,** -vāsen, n. rational being. **Vernunftwidrig,** -vĭdrĭch, a. irrational; -keit, -kĕĭt, f. irrationality.
Veröden, fĕröh'den, vt. to desolate, lay waste; vi. to become or be desolated, waste. **Verödung,** -yng, f. desolation.
Veronesergrün, fĕrona'sĕrgrühn, n. Verona-green, mountain-green.
Verordnen, fĕrord'nen, vt. to order, decree, command, ordain, prescribe. **Verordnung,** -yng, f. order, decree, command; prescription.
Verpachten, fĕrpach'ten, vt. to farm, lease, rent.
Verpachter, fĕrpach'tĕr, m. lessor, landlord. **Verpachtung,** -yng, f. renting, leasing, farming.
Verpacken, fĕrpack'en, vt. to pack up, to pack away.
Verpallisadiren, fĕrpalisadī'ren, vt. to palisade.
Verpanieren, fĕrpanīĕrn, vt. to mail.
Verpappen, fĕrpap'pen, to paste over.
Verpassen, fĕrpas'sen, vt. to let slip, to lose by delay.
Verpesten, fĕrpĕzh'ten, vt. to infect, poison, envenom.
Verpfänden, fĕrpfen'den, vt. to pledge, pawn. **Verpfändung,** -yng, f. pawning, mortgage.
Verpfeffern, fĕrpfĕf'fern, vt. to pepper too much.
Verpflanzen, fĕrpflan'tsen, vt. to transplant. **Verpflanzung,** -yng, f. transplantation.

Ver 369 **Ver**

Verpflegen, fĕrpflä'gen, *vt.* to tend, nurse, foster. **Verpflegung**, -ŭng, *f.* nursing, tending.
Verpflichten, fĕrpflĭch'ten, *vt.* to oblige, engage. **Verpflicht'et**, *a.* bound, obliged. **Verpflicht'ung**, -ŭng, *f.* obligation.
Verpfuschen, fĕrpfŭsh'en, *vt.* to bungle, spoil, murder.
Verpichen, fĕrpĭch'en, *vt.* to pitch, stop by pitching.
Verpicht, fĕrpĭcht', *a.* bent, intent upon, eager, mad for.
Verplämpern, fĕrplĕm'pĕrn, *vt.* to spend *or* waste foolishly.
Verplaudern, fĕrplŏu'dĕrn, *vt.* to chat *or* blabber away.
Verpönen, fĕrpöh'nen, *vt.* to forbid under a certain penalty.
Verprassen, fĕrpras'sen, *vt.* to waste, squander, lavish.
Verproviantiren, fĕrprofiantī'ren, *vt.* to supply with provisions, to provision.
Verpuppen, fĕrpŭp'pen, *vt.* to change into a chrysalis.
Verqualmen, fĕrqual'men, *vt. i.* to evaporate, to pass off in thick steam *or* smoke.
Verquicken, fĕrquĭck'en, *vt.* to amalgamate.
Verrammeln, fĕrram'meln, *vt.* to ram.
Verrath, fĕrrät', *m.* treason.
Verrathen, fĕrrä'ten (-rieth, -rathen), *vt.* to betray.
Verräther, fĕrrä'tĕr, *m.* traitor; -ei, -ei', *f.* treachery.
Verrätherin, fĕrrä'terin, *f.* traitress. **Verräth'erisch**, -ish, *a.* treacherous.
Verrauchen, fĕrrŏu'chen, *vt.* to go off in smoke.
Verräumen, fĕrrŏu'men, *vt.* to misplace, mislay.
Verrauschen, fĕrrŏu'shen, *vt.* to rush away, die away.
Verrechnen, fĕrrĕch'nen, *vt.* to charge, to book, to place to account; sich —, *vr.* to miscalculate, to misreckon. **Verrech'nung**, -ŭng, *f.* error in reckoning, miscalculation.
Verrecken, fĕrrĕck'en, *vt.* to die (vulg.).
Verreden, fĕrrä'den, *vi.* to make a slip of the tongue.
Verregnen, fĕrrāg'nen, *vt.* to spoil by raining.
Verreiben, fĕrrī'ben (-rieb, -rieben), *vt.* to rub, triturate; to rub out.

Verreibung, fĕrrēīb'ŭng, *f.* trituration.
Verreisen, fĕrrĭë'sen, *vi.* to set out on a journey; *vt.* to spend in travelling.
Verreißen, fĕrrēīs'sen, *vt.* to tear (up).
Verreiten, fĕrrēī'ten (verritt, verritten), *vt.* to spend, expel by riding.
Verrenken, fĕrrenk'en, *vt.* to luxate, dislocate. **Verrenk'ung**, -ŭng, *f.* luxation, dislocation.
Verrichten, fĕrrĭch'ten, *vt.* to do, perform, execute. acquit one's self of; seine Nothdurft —, to ease one's self. **Verricht'ung**, -ŭng, *f.* doing; performance; function.
Verriechen, fĕrrī'chen (verroch, verrochen), *vi.* to pall, lose flavor.
Verriegeln, fĕrrī'geln, *vt.* to bolt.
Verringern, fĕrring'ern, *vt.* to diminish, lessen. **Verring'erung**, -ŭng, *f.* diminution.
Verrinnen, fĕrrĭn'nen (verrann, verronnen), *vi.* to run off *or* away.
Verrücheln, fĕrrŭch'eln, *vi.* to die rattling, in rattles.
Verrollen, fĕrrŏl'len, *vi.* to roll away.
Verrosten, fĕrrŏsh'ten, *vi.* to rust.
Verrotten, fĕrrŏt'ten, *vi.* to rot.
Verrucht, fĕrrŭcht', *a.* profligate, wicked; -heit, -hāēt, *f.* wickedness, profligacy.
Verrücken, fĕrrück'en, *vt.* to displace, derange. **Verrückt**, fĕrrückt', *a.* **Verrückt'er**, *s.* deranged, crazy, lunatic, mad, madman. **Verrückt'heit**, -hāēt, *f.* craziness, lunacy, madness. **Verrückung**, fĕrrück'ŭng, *f.* displacing, derangement.
Verruf, fĕrrŭf', *m.* decrial. **Verrufen**, *vt.* to decry; *a.* decried, infamous.
Vers, fārs, *m. pl.* Verse, verse.
Versagen, fĕrsä'gen, *vt. i.* to engage; to refuse; to miss fire. **Versag'ung**, -ŭng, *f.* denial, refusal.
Versägen, fĕrsä'gen, *vt.* to saw up.
Versalzen, fĕrsal'tsen, *vt.* to oversalt; overcharge; to spoil.
Versammeln, fĕrsam'meln, *vt.* to assemble. **Versamm'lung**, -lŭng, *f.* assembly, meeting, congregation.
Versanden, fĕrsan'den, *vi.* to be covered with sand.
Versatz, fĕrsats', *m.* pledge, pawn; alloy; joggle.
Versauern, fĕrsŏu'ern, *vi.* to turn sour *or* acid.

Verſaufen, fĕrsŏy'fon (verſoff, verſoffen), *vt.* to waste on drink.
Verſäumen, fĕrsŏim'men, *vt.* to neglect, miss, lose. **Verſäum'niß**, -niss, *n. pl. -e.* omission, neglect.
Verſchachern, fĕrshăch'ern, *vt.* to sell unfairly, to hawk, chaffer (away).
Verſchaffen, fĕrshaf'fen, *vt.* to procure.
Verſchallen, fĕrshal'len, *vi.* to die away (of sound).
Verſchämt, fĕrshämt', *a.* bashful, -ly; -heit, -hăĕt, *f.* bashfulness.
Verſchanzen, fĕrshan'tsen, *vt.* to intrench, barricade. **Verſchanz'ung**, -ung, *f.* intrenchment.
Verſchärfen, fĕrshĕr'fen, *vt.* to sharpen, heighten, augment (in violence).
Verſchärfung, fĕrshĕrf'ung, *f.* sharpening.
Verſcharren, fĕrshar'ren, *vt.* to cover with earth.
Verſcheiden, fĕrshī'den (verſchied, verſchieben), *vi.* to expire.
Verſchenken, fĕrshenk'en, *vt.* to give away; to retail, sell.
Verſcherben, fĕrshĕrb'en, *vt.* to scarf.
Verſcherzen, fĕrshĕrts'en, *vt.* to trifle away, spend in joking; to forfeit.
Verſcheuchen, fĕrshăuch'en, *vt.* to scare, frighten away.
Verſchicken, fĕrshick'en, *vt.* to send away or off, forward, transmit; to export, ship off.
Verſchieben, fĕrshī'ben (verſchob, verſchoben), *vt.* to shift, displace, get out of its place; defer, delay.
Verſchied, Verſchieden, fĕrshīd'en, *f.* Verſcheiden.
Verſchieden, fĕrshī'den, *a.* different, diverse; several, divers; -heit, -hăĕt, *f.* diversity, variety, difference. **Verſchiedent'lich**, -lich, *av.* differently, variously.
Verſchieß, fĕrshīss', *m.* degradation (of colors).
Verſchießen, fĕrshīss'en (verſchoß, verſchoſſen), *vt.* to shoot, fire away, spend; *vi.* to fade.
Verſchiffen, fĕrshif'fen, *vt.* to ship. **Verſchiff'ung**, -ung, *f.* shipping, shipment.
Verſchimmeln, fĕrshim'meln, *vi.* to mould, get mouldy.
Verſchlafen, fĕrshlā'fen, *vi.* to oversleep, to sleep too long; *vt.* to lose or neglect by sleeping.

Verſchlag, fĕrshlăg', *m. pl.* -ſchläge partition.
Verſchlagen, fĕrshlā'gen (verſchlug verſchlagen), *vt.* to nail up; to partition (rooms); to disperse; *vi.* to cool; to matter, import; *a.* adrift; driven from the right course; cunning, crafty, sly; -heit, -hăĕt, *f.* cunning, cunningness, craft, craftiness.
Verſchlammen, fĕrshlam'men, *vi.* to get filled with mud.
Verſchlang, fĕrshlang', *Prt.* von Verſchlingen.
Verſchlechtern, fĕrshlĕch'tern, *vt.* to deteriorate. **Verſchlech'terung**, -ung, *f.* deterioration.
Verſchleichen, fĕrshlĕi'chen, *vi.* to creep away.
Verſchleiern, fĕrshlă'ern, *vt.* to veil.
Verſchlemmen, fĕrshlem'men, *vt.* to squander, dissipate, waste in debauchery.
Verſchlendern, fĕrshlen'dern, *vt.* to trifle away.
Verſchleppen, fĕrshlep'pen, *vt.* to embezzle, purloin; protract, draw out.
Verſchleudern, fĕrshlĕü'dern, *vt.* to throw away, squander, waste; to sell at a dead loss.
Verſchließen, fĕrshlī'essen (verſchloß, verſchloſſen), *vt.* to lock, close.
Verſchlimmern, fĕrshlim'mern, *vt.* to make worse; *vr.* to become worse. **Verſchlim'merung**, -ung, *f.* deterioration.
Verſchlingen, fĕrshling'en (verſchlang, verſchlungen), *vt.* to insnare, entangle, entwine; complicate; devour, swallow.
Verſchloß, fĕrshlōs' (*Pp.* verſchloſſen, verſchloſſen), *a.* shut; reserved.
Verſchloſſenheit, fĕrshlōs'senhăĕt, *f.* reserve, reservedness.
Verſchlucken, fĕrshlŭck'en, *vt.* to swallow.
Verſchlummern, fĕrshlŭm'mern, *vt.* to slumber or sleep away or off.
Verſchlungen, fĕrshlŭng'en, *pp.* von Verſchlingen.
Verſchluß, fĕrshlŭss', *m.* custody, confinement; sale; unter — baten, to keep under lock and key.
Verſchmachten, fĕrshmăch'ten, *vi.* to languish, pine away.
Verſchmachtung, fĕrshmacht'ung, *f.* pining away.

Verschmähen, fershmāh'en, vt. to disdain, to scorn. **Verschmäh'ung,** -ung, f. disdain, contempt, scorn.

Verschmauchen, fershmäu'ċhen, vt. to spend, pass in smoking.

Verschmausen, fershmöu'sen, vt. to spend in feasting.

Verschmelzen, fershmelt'sen (-schmelz, -schmolzen), and fershmël'tsen, vi. to melt (up).

Verschmerzen, fershmër'tsen, vt. to get over.

Verschmieren, fershmī'ren, vt. to plaster up; to waste in scribbling.

Verschmitzt, fershmitst', a. av. crafty, cunning, -ly; -heit, -hāit, f. craftiness, shrewdness, cunning.

Verschnappen, fershnap'pen, (vulgar) vr. to blurt, to make a slip of the tongue.

Verschnaufen, fershnöu'fen, vi. r. to respire, recover one's breath.

Verschneiden, fershnī'den (-schnitt, -schnitten), vt. to cut up; to cut wrong; to use up; to mutilate, castrate.

Verschneien, fershnī'en (reg. or verschnie, verschnien), vt. to cover with snow.

Verschnitten, fershnit'ten, a. gelded, castrated; -er, -er, m. eunuch.

Verschnupfen, fershnup'fen, vt. to spend in snuff; to nettle, vex.

Verschollen, fershol'len, a. forgotten, unknown, not heard of.

Verschonen, fershōn'en, vt. to spare, forbear; dispense with, exempt from.

Verschönen, Verschönern, fershöhn'ern, vt. to beautify, embellish, decorate. **Verschön'erung,** -ung, f. embellishment.

Verschränken, fershreng'ken, vt. to cross. **Verschränk'ung,** -ung, f. crossing.

Verschrauben, fershröu'ben (Pp. verschroben), vt. to screw wrong, to distort.

Verschreiben, fershrī'ben (verschrieb, verschrieben), vt. to use up by writing; to order, write for; to assign; to prescribe (medicine); vr. to make a mistake in writing. **Verschreib'ung,** -ung, f. bond, obligation; order; assignment; prescription.

Verschreien, fe'shrēī'en, (verschrie, verschrien), vt. v decry.

Verschroben, fershrō'ben, a. distorted, preposterous, perverse.

Verschrumpfen, fershrum'pfen, vi. to shrink, shrivel.

Verschub, fershÿb', m. delay, postponement.

Verschüchtern, fershüċh'tërn, vt. to frighten, intimidate.

Verschulden, fershul'den, vt. i. to involve in debt; to be guilty of; to do, to commit, to bring upon; s.n. fault. **Verschul'det,** a. Pp. involved in debts, encumbered. **Verschul'dung,** -ung, f. fault, guilt; misconduct.

Verschütten, fershüt'ten, vt. to spill; to fill up, to cover.

Verschwägern, fershvā'gern, vt. r. to ally by marriage. **Verschwä'gerung,** -ung, f. affinity.

Verschwärzen, fershvęrts'en, vt. to dirty, soil; to slander.

Verschwatzen, fershvats'en, vt. to talk away; to slander; to blab out.

Verschweben, fershvā'ben, vi. to float away.

Verschweigen, fershvēï'gen (-schwieg, -schwiegen), vt. to keep secret, to conceal. **Verschweig'ung,** -ung, f. concealment.

Verschweigen, fershvēï'gen, vt. to spend in debauchery, to waste in excess.

Verschwenden, fershven'den, vt. to lavish, squander, waste.

Verschwender, fershven'der, m. sin., f. spendthrift, prodigal. **Verschwen'derisch,** -ish, a. prodigal, profuse, lavish. **Verschwen'dung,** -ung, f. prodigality, profusion.

Verschwiegen, fershvīg', Prt. -en, Pp. kept secret; secret, silent, reserved, discreet; -enheit, -hāit, f. secrecy, keeping secrets, discretion.

Verschwimmen, fershvim'men (verschwamm, verschwommen), vi. to dissolve away.

Verschwinden, fershvin'den (-schwand -schwunden), vi. to vanish, disappear.

Verschwistert, fershvīsh'tërt, a. kindred.

Verschwitzen, fershvits'en, vt. to exude; emit by sweating; to unlearn.

Verschwören, fershvöh'ren (-schwur, -schworen), vt. to forswear, abjure vr. to protest by oaths, conspire.

Verschwörer, fĕrshvöh'rer, **Verschwörner**, fĕrshvör'ner, m. conspirator.
Verschwörung, -ŭng, f. conspiracy.
Versehen, fĕrsä'en (-sah, -sehen), vt. to attend to, to manage, administer; — mit, to supply with; —sich, to overlook, make a mistake, commit an error; s. n. error, mistake, inadvertency.
Versehren, fĕrsä'ren, vt. to hurt, injure.
Versenden, fĕrsen'den (versandte, versandt), vt. to send away, off, transmit, forward; to export; zu Schiff —, to ship. **Versendung**, -ŭng, f. conveyance, transport, transmission; shipment; -geschäft, -geshäft, n. forwarding-business.
Versengen, fĕrseng'en, vt. to singe. **Versengung**, -ŭng, f. singeing.
Versenken, fĕrsenk'en, vt. to sink. **Versenkung**, -ŭng, f. sink, sinking, submersion.
Versessen, fĕrsĕs'sen, a. (eagerly) bent on or intent upon.
Versetzen, fĕrsets'en, vt. to put, place; remove; to transpose; transplant; put out of place, misplace; to pawn; to mix, alloy; vi. to reply. **Versetzung**, -ŭng, f. placing, displacing, removal; translocation, transposition; misplacing; alloy. **Versetzer**, m. shutter (foundry).
Verseufzen, fĕrseüf'tsen, vt. to spend or consume in or pass with sighing.
Versichern, fĕrsich'ern, vt. to assure, affirm; vt. to secure; ascertain; insure. **Versicherung**, -ŭng, f. assurance; security, surety; insurance; -anstalt, -änzhtalt, f. insurance-office.
Versiegeln, fĕrsīg'eln, vt. to seal (up). **Versiegelung**, -ŭng, f. sealing.
Versiegen, fĕrsī'gen, vt. to dry up.
Versilbern, fĕrsil'bern, vt. to silver, plate; to convert into silver or money. **Versilberung**, -ŭng, f. silvering; heiße —, galvanisch, silverplating.
Versingen, fĕrsing'en (-sang, -sungen), vt. to sing away; to spend in singing.
Versinken, fĕrsink'en (versank, versunken), vi. to sink.
Versinnlichen, fĕrsinn'lichen, vt. to illustrate; render conspicuous; sensualize.

Versitzen, fĕrsits'en (versaß, sersessen) vt. to sit away, lose by sitting; vi. to die away in sitting.
Versmacher, färs'macher, m. verseman, poetaster.
Versoffen, fĕrsof'fen (Prt. versoffen, pp. versaufen), a. drunken.
Versöhnen, fĕrsöh'nen, vt. to reconcile, propitiate; expiate, atone for.
Versöhner, fĕrsöh'ner, m. reconciler; mediator. **Versöhnlich**, -lich, a. reconcilable, expiable, placable; -keit, -käĕt, f. placableness, reconcilableness. **Versöhnung**, -ŭng, f. reconciliation.
Versorgen, fĕrsor'gen, vt. to provide, provide for. **Versorger**, m. provider. **Versorgung**, -ŭng, f. providing, provision; maintenance, sustenance; -haus, -hoüs, n. pl. -häuser, hospital.
Versparen, fĕrzhpä'ren, vt. to spare, save; put off, reserve.
Verspäten, fĕrzhpä'ten, vt. to retard, delay; vr. to come or be too late.
Verspeisen, fĕrzhpēi'sen, vt. to eat up, consume.
Versperren, fĕrzhper'ren, vt. to bar, stop, block up.
Verspielen, fĕrzhpī'len, vt. to lose in gaming; to lose, to come off a loser.
Verspiĕfern, fĕrzhpī'kern, vt. to spike, to bolt the timbers of —.
Verspinnen, fĕrzhpin'nen (versponn, versponnen), vt. to spin (up), consume in spinning.
Versplittern, fĕrzhplit'tern, vt. to scatter.
Verspotten, fĕrzhpot'ten, vt. to scoff, deride. **Verspottung**, -ŭng, f. derision, scoffing, mockery.
Versprechen, fĕrzhprech'en (versprach, versprochen), vt. to promise; to make a slip of the tongue; s. n. promise. **Versprechung**, -ŭng, f. promise.
Versprengen, fĕrzhspreng'en, vt. to burst; disperse, scatter.
Verspringen, fĕrzhpring'en (versprang, versprungen), vi. to burst; vt. r. to sprain.
Verspritzen, fĕrzhprit'sen, vt. to squirt away; sein Blut —, to shed one's blood.
Versprochen, fĕrzhproch'en, Pp. ver Versprechen.
Verspünden, fĕrzhpün'den, vt. to bung (up).

Verspüren, fĕrzhpüh'ren, *vt.* to perceive, feel, to be aware of.
Verstählen, fĕrzhtä'len, *vt.* to steel.
Verstand, fĕrzhtant', *m.* understanding, intellect, intelligence, judgment; **-eskräfte, -kräfte,** *s. pl.* intellectual powers *or* faculties. **Verstandesmensch, -mensh,** *m.* **-en,** *pl.* **-en,** cold, calculating man.
Verständig, fĕrzhtĕn'dich, *a. av.* intelligent, -ly; **-en, -en,** *vt.* to make to understand; **sich —,** to come to an agreement. **Verständigkeit, -kāet,** *f.* discretion, sensibleness. **Verständigung, -ung,** *f.* understanding, agreement. **Verständlich, -lich,** *a. av.* intelligible, -bly; clear, perspicuous, -ly; **-keit, -kāet,** *f.* intelligibility, clearness, perspicuity.
Verständlichen, fĕrzhtĕnd'lichen, *vt.* to render intelligible. **Verständniß, -niss,** *n.* understanding, intelligence.
Verstärken, fĕrzhtĕr'ken, *vt.* to strengthen, to corroborate; to reinforce. **Verstärk'ung, -ung,** *f.* reinforcement.
Verstatten, fĕrzhtat'ten, *vt.* to permit, allow, grant. **Verstatt'ung, -ung,** *f.* permission.
Verstäuben, fĕrzhtäüb'en, *vt.* to scatter like dust, sprinkle.
Verstauchen, fĕrzhtäü'chen, *vt.* to crush; to sprain, to wrench. **Verstauch'ung, -ung,** *f.* sprain, crush, strain, wrench.
Versteck, fĕrzhtyck', *m.* ober *n.* hiding-place; **-spiel, -zhpïll,** *n.* play at hide and seek. **Versteck'en,** *vt.* to conceal, hide. **Versteckt',** *a. av.* concealed; close, reserved.
Verstehen, fĕrzhtä'-en (-**stand, -standen**), *vt.* to understand, comprehend, hear; **zu — geben,** to intimate; **sich zu —,** to agree to.
Versteigen, fĕrzhtei'gen (-**stieg, -stiegen**), *vr.* to climb *or* mount too high; to go too far, to attempt too much, soar too high.
Versteigern, fĕrzhtäe'gern, *vt.* to sell by auction. **Verstei'gerung, -ung,** *f.* auction.
Versteinen, Versteinern, fĕrzhtäen'ĕrn, *vi.* to petrify; to become stone; to be struck with terror; *vt.* to petrify, turn to stone, convert into stone *or* stony substance.

Versteinerung, fĕrzhtäen'erung, *f.* petrification.
Verstellen, fĕrzhtĕl'len, *vt.* to displace, disarrange, place wrong; disfigure; disguise; to cloak, cover, dissemble. **Verstellt',** *a.* feigned, false, assumed, hypocritical. **Verstell'ung, -ung,** *f.* dissimulation.
Versteuern, fĕrzhtäü'ern, *vt.* to pay taxes, duty for.
Verstieben, fĕrzhtī'ben (**-stob, -stoben**), *vi.* to scatter, to be dissipated, dispersed (like dust).
Verstiegen, fĕrzhtī'gen, *a.* high-flown; eccentric.
Verstimmen, fĕrzhtim'men, *vt.* to put out of tune, to mistune; to put out of humor or temper. **Verstimmt',** *a.* out of tune *or* humor. **Verstimmung, -ung,** *f.* ill-temper or humor.
Verstocken, fĕrzhtock'en, *vt. i.* to harden, make obdurate. **Verstockt',** *a.* obdurate, unfeeling; **-heit, -hāet,** *f.* obduracy, hardness, obstinacy in wickedness.
Verstohlen, fĕrzhtō'len, *a. av.* stealthily, stealthy, clandestine, unperceived, by stealth.
Verstopfen, fĕrzhtopf'en, *vt.* to stop, obstruct, constipate. **Verstopf'ung, -ung,** *f.* obstruction; costiveness, constipation.
Verstorben, fĕrzhtor'ben, *a.* deceased, dead, defunct.
Verstören, fĕrzhtöh'ren, *vt.* to disturb, startle, confound.
Verstört, fĕrzhtört', *a.* dejected, confused, troubled, agitated.
Verstoß, fĕrzhtōss', *m. pl.* **Verstöße,** fault, mistake, blunder, error; **den — haben,** (of horses) not to feed *or* eat.
Verstoßen, fĕrzhtöss'en (**verstieß, verstoßen**), *vt.* to pound; blunt; wear out; turn out, expel, reject, discard; repudiate; (one's wife) divorce; *vi. rr.* to offend; violate; to mistake, blunder; to miscalculate, miscount. **Verstoß'ung, -ung,** *f.* expulsion, repudiation.
Verstreichen, fĕrzhträï'chen (**-verstrich, verstrichen**), *vt.* to spread over, cover with, besmear; *vi.* to pass away.
Verstreuen, fĕrzhträü'en, *vt.* to scatter, disperse; waste by scattering.

32

Ver 374 **Ver**

Verſtricken, fĕrzhtrĭck′en, *vt.* entangle, insnare.
Verſtrömen, fĕrzhtröh′men, *vt.* to pour out; *vi.* to flow out.
Verſtudiren, fĕrzhtyd′ren, *vt.* to spend, consume in *or* by studying, *or* study.
Verſtümmeln, fĕrzhtüm′meln, *vt.* to mutilate. **Verſtüm′melung**, -yng, *f.* mutilation.
Verſtummen, fĕrzhtym′men, *vi.* to be struck dumb; *vt.* to strike dumb, to silence.
Verſtutzen, fĕrzhtyts′en, *vt.* to' cut short.
Verſuch, fĕrsych′, *m. pl. -e*, attempt, experiment, trial, proof; **—weise**, by way of trial.
Verſuchen, fĕrsych′en, *vt.* to try, attempt, endeavor; to tempt; to taste. **Verſuch′er**, *m.* tempter, seducer, enticer; **-in**, *f.* temptress. **Verſuch′ung**, -yng, *f.* temptation, enticement.
Verſucht, fĕrsycht′, *a.* experienced.
Verſudeln, fĕrsyd′eln, *vt.* to soil.
Verſündigen, fĕrsün′dichen, *vr.* to sin, offend, trespass. **Verſün′digung**, -yng, *f.* sin, trespass.
Verſunken, fĕrsyn′ken (*Pp.* von **Verſinken**); **-heit**, -hĕit, *f.* prostration, depravity, corruption, demoralization.
Verſüßen, fĕrsüh′sen, *vt.* to sweeten.
Vertagen, fĕrtä′gen, *vi.* to adjourn; prorogate. **Vertag′ung**, -yng, *f.* adjournment, prorogation.
Vertändeln, fĕrtĕnd′eln, *vt.* to trifle away.
Vertanzen, fĕrtants′en, *vt.* to dance away, pass, spend, waste in dancing.
Vertauſchen, fĕrtŏy′shen, *vt.* to exchange, change. **Vertauſ′ch′ung**, -yng, *f.* change, exchange.
Verteuen, fĕrtĕü′en, *vt.* to moor.
Verteufelt, fĕrtĕü′felt, *a. av.* devilish, devil of, infernal, cursed.
Vertheidigen, fĕrtǟ′dichen, *vt.* to defend. **Verthei′diger**, *m.* defender. **Verthei′digung**, -yng, *f.* defence, apology; **-ſtand**, -zhtant, *m.* defensive.
Vertheilen, fĕrtǟ′len, *vt.* to divide, distribute. **Verthei′lung**, -yng, *f.* distribution; partition.
Verthenern, fĕrtĕü′ern, *vt.* to raise the price of, make dear. **Verthen′rung**, -yng, *f.* rise, raising.
Verthieren, fĕrtī′ren, *vt.* to bestialize, brutalize.
Verthun, fĕrtyn′ (verthat, verthan), *vt.* to lavish, squander.
Vertikal, fĕrtikǟl′, *a.* vertical; **-kreis**, -kŕeis, *m.* vertical circle.
Vertiefen, fĕrtī′fen, *vt.* to deepen; (Paint) shadow; verteift ſein in, tõ be lost, absorbed in. **Vertief′ung**, -yng, *f.* deepening, depth, hollow; background.
Vertilgen, fĕrtīl′gen, *vt.* to extirpate, exterminate, destroy. **Vertilg′ung**, -yng, *f.* extermination.
Vertrackt, fĕrtrackt′, *a.* distorted, desperate, mischievous, damned.
Vertrag, fĕrträk′, treaty, covenant, contract, compact.
Vertragen, fĕrträ′gen (vertrug, vertragen), *vt.* to wear out; *vr.* to agree, to come to an understanding.
Verträglich, fĕrträk′lich, *a.* peaceable; compatible; **-keit**, -kĕit, *f.* peaceableness, sociableness.
Vertrauen, fĕrtrŏy′en, *vi.* to trust, confide; *vt.* to entrust; *z. u.* confidence, trust, reliance. **Vertrau′lich**, -lich, *a. av.* confidential, -ly, intimate, familiar, -ly; **-keit**, -kĕit, *f.* intimacy, familiarity; liberty.
Verträumen, fĕrtrŏü′men, *vt.* to dream away.
Vertraut, fĕrtrŏyt′, *a. av.* intimate, -ly, familiar; versed in, conversant with; **-er**, *m.* **Vertrau′te**, *f.* confidant, intimate friend. **Vertraut′heit**, -hĕit, *f.* intimacy, familiarity.
Vertreibrief, fĕrtrĕk′brĭf, *m.* letter of departure.
Vertreiben, fĕrtrēib′en (vertrieb, vertrieben), *vt.* to drive away, off, expel, dispel; scare; to banish, exile; remove; to pass away, beguile; to shade (paint.); to cure; to dispose of, sell. **Vertreib′ung**, -yng, *f.* expulsion.
Vertreten, fĕrtrĕt′en, *or* fĕrträ′ten (vertrat, vertreten), *vt.* to tread down; (the foot) to sprain; (the way) obstruct; (one's place) to represent; to appear for, look after. **Vertre′ter**, *m.* representative; deputy; advocate. **Vertre′tung**, -yng, *f.* representation; defence, protection.
Vertrieb, fĕrtrīb′ (*Prt. v.* vertreiben),

s. m. f. sale, market. **Vertrieb'en,** (*Pp. v.* vertreiben), banished, exiled; *s. m.* exile, banished person.
Vertrinken, fĕrtrin'ken (vertrank, vertrunken), *vt.* to drink up (the whole); to spend in drinking.
Vertrocknen, fĕrtrock'nen, *vi. t.* to dry up.
Vertröbeln, fĕrtröh'deln, *vt.* to idle away.
Vertrösten, fĕrtröhzht'en, *vt.* to feed with hope, to put *or* keep off, amuse with promise. **Vertröst'ung,** -ung, *f.* giving hope, fair words.
Vertuschen, fĕrtush'en, *vt.* to hush up, conceal.
Verübeln, fĕrüh'beln, *vt.* to take ill *or* amiss, to blame for.
Verüben, fĕrüh'ben. *vt.* to perpetrate, commit. **Verüb'ung,** -ung, *f.* perpetration.
Verunehren, fĕrun'ären, *vt.* to dishonor, disgrace. **Verun'ehrung,** -ung, *f.* disgracing, aspersion.
Veruneinigen, fĕrun'zeiniĥen, *vt.* to disunite, set at variance; ſich —, to fall out, quarrel. **Verun'einigung,** -ung, *f.* disunion, quarrel.
Verunglimpfen, fĕrun'glimpfen, *vt.* to defame, calumniate, asperse. **Verun'glimpfer,** *m.* defamer, slanderer. **Verun'glimpfung,** -ung, *f.* slander, defamation.
Verunglücken, fĕrun'glücken, *vi.* to fail, have an accident, miscarry, perish, to be lost.
Verunreinigen, fĕrun'raenichen, *vt.* to soil, stain, defile, pollute. **Verun'reinigung,** -ung, *f.* defilement, pollution.
Verunstalten, fĕrun'zhtalten, *vt.* to disfigure, deface, mar. **Verun'staltung,** -ung, *f.* defacement.
Veruntreuen, fĕrun'trŏüen, *vt.* to embezzle, purloin.
Verunzieren, fĕrun'tsīren, *vt.* to mar, disfigure.
Verursachen, fĕrur'sachen, *vt.* to cause.
Verurtheilen, fĕrur'tŏelen, *vt.* to condemn, sentence, doom. **Verur'theilung,** -ung, *f.* condemnation, doom.
Vervielfältigen, fĕrfīl'fĕltichen, *vt.* to multiply. **Vervielfältigung,** *f.* multiplication.
Vervierfachen, fĕrfīr'fachen, *vt.* to quadruplicate, to double twice, make fourfold.

Vervollkommnen, fĕrfoll'kommen, *vt.* to perfect, finish, accomplish, consummate, complete. **Vervoll'kommnung,** -ung, *f.* accomplishment, finish, finishing, perfection.
Vervollständigen, fĕrfoll'zhtendichen, *vt.* to complete. **Vervoll'ständigung,** -ung, *f.* completion.
Verwachen, fĕrvach'en, *vt.* to watch away.
Verwachsen, fĕrvak'sen (verwuchs, verwachsen), *vi.* to grow over, together; *a.* crooked, ill-formed, deformed, misshapen.
Verwahren, fĕrvä'ren, *vt.* to preserve, keep, guard; ſich —, to protest.
Verwahrer, fĕrvär'er, *m.* keeper, preserver.
Verwahrlosen, fĕrvär'lösen, *vt.* to neglect, abandon. **Verwahr'losung,** -ung, *f.* neglect, inattention.
Verwahrsam, fĕrvär'sam, *m.* custody, care. **Verwahrung,** fĕrvär'ung, *f.* keeping, care; protestation (at law).
Verwaisen, fĕrväs'sen, *vi.* to become an orphan; *vt.* to make an orphan. **Verwaist,** *a.* orphaned; bereft of.
Verwalten, fĕrval'ten, *vt.* to manage, conduct, administer. **Verwal'ter,** *m.* administrator, manager, steward. **Verwalt'ung,** -ung, *f.* administration, government, management. **Verwalt'ungszweig,** -tsvĕig, *m.* department.
Verwandeln, fĕrvan'deln, *vt.* to transform, transmute, metamorphose, alter, convert, turn, change. **Verwan'delung,** -ung, *f.* transformation, metamorphosis, change.
Verwandt, fĕrvant'. *a.* related, kindred, cognate, kin, congenial. **Verwandt'er,** *m.* **Verwandt'e,** *f.* relation, kinsman, kinswoman. **Verwandt'schaft,** -shaft, *f.* relation, kindred, parentage; affinity, congenial, -ity, -ness; ſich, -lich, *a.* kindred, cognate, congenial.
Verwarnen, fĕrvar'nen, *vt.* to warn, forewarn, caution. **Verwar'nung,** -ung, *f.* warning.
Verwaschen, fĕrvash'en (verwusch, verwaschen), *vt.* to waste *or* wear out by washing.
Verwässern, fĕrvĕs'sern, *vt.* to soak water too much; to dilute.
Verweben, fĕrvä'ben (verwob, verwo-

ben), *vt.* to interweave, weave in, intermix, intermingle, insert.
Verwechſeln, fĕrvĕk'seln, *vt.* to change; confound, mistake. **Verwech'ſelung**, -yng, *f.* changing, mistaking.
Verwegen, fĕrvā'gen, *a. av.* audacious, bold, daring; rash, desperate: ‑heit, ‑hĕit, *f.* audaciousness, boldness, temerity.
Verwehen, fĕrvā'en, *vt.* to blow away or off; (a ship) to drive from the right course.
Verwehren, fĕrvā'ren, *vt.* to prohibit, prevent, forbid, refuse.
Verweichlichen, fĕrvĕich'lichen, *vt.* to effeminate, enervate, weaken, unman.
Verweigern, fĕrvăī'gern, *vt.* to deny, refuse. **Verwei'gerung**, -yng, *f.* denial, refusal.
Verweilen, fĕrvĕil'len, *vi.* to abide, sojourn, dwell, delay.
Verweinen, fĕrvāē'nen, *vt.* to pass weeping, in tears; verweinte Augen, eyes red with weeping.
Verweis, fĕrvēīs', *m.* rebuke, reproof, reprimand; admonition.
Verweiſen, fĕrvēī'sen (verwies, verwieſen), *vt.* to refer to; to rebuke, reprove, reprimand; to banish, exile. **Verweiſ'ung**, -yng, *f.* reprimand, rebuke; reference; banishment, exile.
Verwelken, fĕrvĕl'ken, *vi.* to wither, fade, pine away, languish, flag.
Verwenden, fĕrvend'en (verwandt, verwandt, verwendet), *vt.* to bestow upon, employ, spend; ſich —, to use one's interest for. **Verwend'ung**, -yng, *f.* employment; mediation, intercession, influence; use.
Verwerfen, fĕrvĕr'fen (verwarf, verworfen), *vt.* to reject, refuse, repudiate, condemn; *vi.* (of young) to cast, miscarry, suffer abortion. **Verwerf'lich**, -lich, *a.* objectionable; ‑heit, ‑hĕit, *f.* exceptionableness, blamableness. **Verwerf'ung**, -yng, *f.* rejection, refusal, reprobation; condemnation.
Verwerthen, fĕrvār'ten, *vt.* to turn to account; convert into money; dispose of, realize.
Verweſen, fĕrvā'sen, *vi.* to rot, corrupt; *vt.* to administer, manage.
Verweſer, fĕrvā'ser, *m.* administrator; manager; substitute.

Verweslich, fĕrvās'lich, *a.* corruptible, subject to decay, to destruction; ‑keit, ‑kĕit, *f.* corruptibleness, corruptibility. **Verweſ'ung**, -yng, *f.* administration; corruption; decay.
Verwetten, fĕrvĕt'ten, *vt.* to lose by betting.
Verwichen, fĕrvĭch'en, *a.* last, past.
Verwickeln, fĕrvĭck'eln, *vt.* to complicate, entangle, involve, perplex. **Verwick'elung**, -yng, *f.* complication, entanglement, intricacy; implication (play); intrigue, knot.
Verwieſen, fĕrvī'sen (*Pp. v.* verweiſen), *s. m. f.* exile, outlaw.
Verwildern, fĕrvĭl'dern, *vi.* to run, grow wild, savage, unruly, unmanageable. **Verwil'derung**, -yng, *f.* growing wild.
Verwilligen, fĕrvĭl'ligen, *vt.* to grant. **Verwil'ligung**, -yng, *f.* grant; allowance, stipend.
Verwinden, fĕrvĭn'den (verwand, verwunden), *vt.* to get over, overcome.
Verwirken, fĕrvĭr'ken, *vt.* to knead up; to forfeit; do a harm; incur. **Verwir'kung**, -yng, *f.* forfeiture.
Verwirklichen, fĕrvĭrk'lichen, *vt.* to realize. **Verwirk'lichung**, -yng, *f.* realization.
Verwirren, fĕrvĭr'ren, *vt.* to entangle, complicate, confound, puzzle, confuse, embroil, disorder. **Verwir'rung**, -yng, *f.* entanglement; confusion: intricacy.
Verwiſchen, fĕrvĭsh'en, *vt.* to wipe out, obliterate, efface.
Verwittern, fĕrwĭt'tern, *vt.* to effloresce, to get weathered, to decay from weathering.
Verwittwen, fĕrvĭtt'ven, *vt. i.* to widow.
Verwogen, fĕrvō'gen, *a.* desperate, daring.
Verwöhnen, fĕrvöh'nen, *vt.* to spoil, pamper. **Verwöhn'ung**, -yng, *f.* spoiling, pampering.
Verworfen, fĕrvor'fen, *a.* reprobate, wicked, profligate; ‑heit, ‑hĕit, *f.* profligacy, wickedness.
Verworren, fĕrvor'ren, *a.* mixed, confused, intricate; ‑heit, ‑hĕit, *f.* confusion, intricacy.
Verwundbar, fĕrvunt'bär, *a.* vulnerable; ‑keit, ‑kĕrkĕit, *f.* vulnerability. **Verwunden**, fĕrvun'den, *vt.* to wound.

Verwundern, fĕrvund'ern, *vt.* to astonish; *vr.* to wonder, to be astonished. **Verwund'erung,** -ŭng, *f.* astonishment, amazement, surprise.
Verwundung, fĕrvund'ŭng, *f.* wound.
Verwünschen, fĕrvünsh'en. *vt.* to curse, execrate, imprecate. **Verwünscht',** *a.* cursed, damned, confounded. **Verwünschung,** fĕrvünsh'ŭng, *f.* curse, execration.
Verwüsten, fĕrvühzht'en, *vt.* to desolate, waste, lay waste. **Verwüster,** *m.* destroyer. **Verwüstung,** -ŭng, *f.* desolation, ruin, havoc.
Verzagen, fĕrtsä'gen, *vi.* to despair, despond. **Verzagt',** fĕrtsägt', *a.* timid, faint-hearted, timorous, cowardly; **-heit,** -hēt, *f.* despondency, faint-heartedness, cowardice.
Verzählen, fĕrtsä'len, *vt.* to miscount.
Verzahnen, fĕrtsä'nen, *vt.* to indent.
Verzapfen, fĕrtsapf'en, *vt.* to retail (liquor). **Verzapf'ung,** -ŭng, *f.* (join.) mortising.
Verzärteln, fĕrtsär'teln, *vt.* to bring up *or* rear too delicately. **Verzär'telung,** -ŭng, *f.* spoiling by delicacy.
Verzaubern, fĕrtsäů'bern, *vt.* to enchant, bewitch.
Verzäunen, fĕrtsaü'nen, *vt.* to fence in, to inclose. **Verzäun'ung,** -ŭng, *f.* fence, inclosure.
Verzehnten, fĕrtsän'ten, *vt.* to tithe.
Verzehren, fĕrtsä'ren, *vt.* to consume, eat up, spend. **Verzehr'ung,** -ŭng, *f.* consumption.
Verzeichnen, fĕrtsäėch'nen, *vt.* to note down, register, write down, specify; to draw *or* trace wrong.
Verzeichniß, fĕrtsäėch'niss, *n.* list, roll, catalogue, register, inventory; specification.
Verzeihen, fĕrtsäi'en (verzieh, verziehen), *vt.* to pardon, forgive; to excuse. **Verzeih'lich,** -lich, *a.* pardonable, excusable, venil. **Verzei'hung,** -ŭng, *f.* pardon, forgiveness.
Verzerren, fĕrtsėr'ren, *vt.* to distort. **Verzerr'ung,** -ŭng, *f.* distortion.
Verzetteln, fĕrtsėt'teln, *vt.* to scatter.
Verzicht, fĕrtsĭcht', *m.* renunciation; — **leisten,** to renounce, give up; **-leistung,** -läėzhtŭng, *f.* renunciation.
Verzieh, fĕrtsĭ', *Prt.* verziehen, *Pp. v.* verzeihen.

Verziehen, fĕrtsĭ'en (verzog, verzogen) *vt.* to distort, spoil; *vi.* to delay, pass away.
Verzieren, fĕrtsĭ'ren, *vt.* to decorate, adorn, deck. **Verzier'ung,** -ŭng, *f.* decoration, ornament.
Verzinken, fĕrtsĭn'ken, *vt.* to zink; to mortise.
Verzinnen, fĕrtsĭn'nen, *vt.* to cover with tin.
Verzinsen, fĕrtsĭn'sen, *vt.* to pay interest for. **Verzins'ung,** -ŭng, *f.* paying interest; interest.
Verzögern, fĕrtsöh'gĕrn, *vt.* to delay, retard, protract. **Verzö'gerung,** -ŭng, *f.* delay, procrastination.
Verzollen, fĕrtsŏl'len, *vt.* to pay tax, duty, toll.
Verzuckern, fĕrtsuck'ĕrn, *vt.* to sugar.
Verzücken, fĕrtsück'en, *vt.* to enrapture, entrance. **Verzückt',** *a.* in ecstacy, entranced. **Verzück'ung,** -ŭng, *f.* ecstacy, trance, rapture.
Verzug, fĕrtsŭk', *m.* delay, stay, stop, procrastination.
Verzweifeln, fĕrtsvēī'fĕln, *vi.* to despair, despond. **Verzweifelt,** *a.* desperate; hopeless.. **Verzweif'lung,** -lŭng, *f.* despair, desperation.
Verzweigen, fĕrtsvēī'gen, *vr.* to branch out.
Verzwickt, fĕrtsvickt', *a.* odd, queer, quaint, troublesome.
Vesper, fezh'pĕr, *f.* vespers; **-brod,** -brōd, *n.* luncheon, afternoon-lunch, afternoon's repast.
Veste, fezh'tĕ, *f.* fortress, fastness.
Veteran, fĕtĕrän', *m.* veteran, old soldier.
Veterinärschule, fĕtĕrĭnär'shŭlĕ, *f.* college for veterinary surgeons.
Vettel, fĕt'tĕl, *f.* wench, strumpet.
Vetter, fĕt'tĕr, *m. pl. -n.* cousin; **-lich,** *a.* cousinly. **Vetterschaft,** fĕt'tĕrshaft, *f.* relationship.
Vexiren, fĕxĭ'rn, *vt.* to vex, trouble, tease.
Vezier, fĕtsĭr', *m.* vizier.
Viaduct, fĭadŭkt', *m.* viaduct.
Vibration, fĭbratsĭōn', *f.* vibration.
Vibriren, fĭbrĭ'ren, *vi.* to vibrate.
Vice, fĭ'tse, *prefix,* vice-; **-könig,** -kühnich, *m.* viceroy.
Victualien, fiktŭä'lĭ-en, *s. p.* victuals, provisions.
Vieh, fĭ, *n. pl. -e. or -er,* beast, cattle brute; **-arzneikunde,** -artsĕnēīkŭn-

Bie 378 **Bif**

de, f. veterinary art. **Bieharzt,** fī'-ārtzt, m. veterinarian, veterinary surgeon. **Bieh'futter,** -futter, n. provender, fodder. **Bieh'handel,** -handel, m. trade in cattle. **Bieh'-händler,** -hendler, m. dealer in cattle, grazier. **Bieh'hirt,** -hirt, m. -en, pl. -en, herdsman. **Bieh'isch,** -ish, a. beastly, brutish, bestial, brutal. **Bieh'magd,** -makt, f. pl. -mägde, dairy-maid. **Bieh'markt,** -markt, m. pl. -märkte, cattle-market. **Bieh'-mast,** -mazht, f. fattening, mast of cattle. **Bieh'mäster,** -mexhter, m. grazier. **Bieh'seuche,** -söiche, f. cattle-disease, murrain. **Bieh'stall,** -shtall, m. pl. -ställe, stable, stall. **Bieh'stand,** -zhtant, m. stock of cattle, live-stock. **Bieh'weide,** -vāide, f. pasturage, pasture. **Bieh'zucht,** -tsuḣt, f. breeding or raising of cattle. **Bieh'züchter,** -tsüḣter, m. grazier, raiser of cattle.

Biel, fīl, a. av. much; pl. many; -ed, -eck, n. polygon. **Biel'erlei,** -erlāe, a. various, multifarious, of many kinds. **Biel'fach,** -faḣ. **Biel'fältig,** -feltiḣ, a. manifold; -keit, -kāet, f. multiplicity, variety. **Biel'farbig,** -farbiḣ, a. many-colored, variegated. **Biel'fraß,** -frās, m. pl. -fraße, glutton. **Biel'fräßig,** -frässiḣ, a. gluttonous; -keit, -kāet, f. gluttony. **Biel'götterei,** -götterēī, f. polytheism. **Biel'heit,** -hāet, f. multitude, great number. **Biel'jährig,** -yäriḣ, a. of many years, many years old. **Bielleicht,** fīllāiḣt', av. perhaps. **Biel'mals,** -māls, av. many times, frequently. **Biel'mehr,** -mār, av. rather, much the more. **Biel'seitig,** -sāitiḣ, a. many-sided, multilateral; extensive, comprehensive. **Biel'silbig,** -silbiḣ, a. polysyllabic. **Biel'weiberei,** -vāiberēī, f. polygamy. **Biel'wisser,** -visser, m. sciolist, smatterer.

Bier, fīr, a. four; -beinig, -bāeniḣ, a. four-legged. **Bier'ed,** -eck, n. quadrilateral, quadrangle; square; -ig, -iḣ, a. quadrilateral, quadrangular. **Bier'erlei,** -erlāe, a. of four kinds or sorts. **Bier'fach,** -faḣ. **Bier'fältig,** -feltiḣ, a. fourfold, quadruple. **Bier'füßig,** -füssiḣ, a. four-footed, four-legged. **Bier'füßler,** -füssler, m. quadruped. **Bier'händig,** -hen-diḣ, a. (music) for four hands. **Bier'hundert,** -hundert, a. four hundred. **Bierhundertst,** -hundertzht, a. four hundredth. **Bier'jährig,** -yäriḣ, a. four years old. **Bier'jährlich,** -yärliḣ, a. quadriennial. **Bier kantpressen,** vt. to square. **Bier'mal,** -māl, av. four times; -ig, -iḣ, a. four times repeated. **Bier-pfündig,** -pfündiḣ, a. four-pound. **Bier'räderig,** -rāderiḣ, a. four wheeled. **Bier'ruder,** -ruder, n. quadrireme. **Bier'saitig,** -sāitiḣ, a. of four strings. **Bier'seitig,** -sāitiḣ, a. quadrilateral. **Bier'silbig,** -silbiḣ, a. of four syllables. **Bier'sitzig,** -sitsiḣ, a. having seats for four. **Bier'spaltig,** -shpaltiḣ, a. quatrifid. **Bier'spann,** -zhpenniḣ, a. four-horse; — fahren, to ride in a coach and four. **Bier'tägig,** -tägiḣ, a. of four days; — fieber, quartan (fever). **Biert,** fīrt, a. fourth. **Biertehalb,** fīr'tehalb, three and a half. **Biertel,** fīr'tel, n. fourth, quarter. **Bierteljahr,** fīr'-teljār, n. three months, quarter. **Bierteljährig,** -yäriḣ, a. quarterly. **Bier'teln,** vt. to quarter. **Bier'telstündig,** -zhtündiḣ, a. of a quarter of an hour. **Bier'telstündlich,** -liḣ, a. every quarter of an hour. **Biertens,** fīr'tens, av. fourthly. **Bier'theilen,** -tāelen, vt. to divide into four parts, to quarter.

Bierzehn, fīr'tsān, a. fourteen. **Bier'zehnt,** -tsānt, a. fourteenth.

Bierzig, fīr'tsiḣ, a. forty. **Bier'zigst,** -tsikzht, a. fortieth.

Bierziger, fīr'tsiger, m. man of forty years.

Bierzinkig, fīr'tsinkiḣ, a. four pronged.

Billa, fīl'lā, n. villa.

Biole, fīō'le, **Biola,** fīō'lā, f. violet; retort.

Bioline, fīōlī'ne, f. violin, fiddle.

Biolinist, fīōlinizht', m. -en, pl. -en, violinist.

Bioslon, fīōlōn', m. bass-viol. **Biolon-cell,** fīōlōntshell', n. violoncello.

Biper, fīp'er, f. viper.

Birtuos, fīrtyōs', m. virtuoso.

Bifir, fīzīr', n. visor, beaver; sight. **Bifir'ebene,** -ābene, f. plane of direction. **Bifiren,** fīzī'ren, vt. to aim to gauge; to put the visa to (a passport).

Visitation, fisitatsiōn', *f.* visitation, examination.
Visitator, fisitā'tor, *m. pl. -en*, exciseman.
Visite, fisīt'e, *f.* visit; — machen, to pay a visit
Visitiren, fisitīr'en, *vt.* to visit, inspect, search.
Vista, vīsh'tā. *f.* sight, view, vista.
Vitriol, fītriōl', *m.* vitriol, sulphate; -öl, -öhl, *n.* oil of vitriol. Vitriol'salz, -salts, *n.* salt of vitriol. Vitriolsäure, -säure, *f.* vitriolic acid.
Vivianit, fīfiānīt', *m.* vivianite.
Vocal, Vokal, fokāl', *m.* vowel; -musik, -muzik, *f.* vocal music.
Vocativ, fok'ātīf, *m.* vocative.
Vogel, fō'gel, *m.* bird, fowl; -bauer, -bōyer, *n.* bird-cage.
Vogelbeere, fō'gibāre, *f.* sorb, service-tree. Vo'gelbeersäure, -säure, *f.* sorbic acid.
Vogeldunst, fō'gldunzht, *m.* small-dust.
Vogelfang, fō'glfang, *m.* fowling, catching birds. Vo'gelfänger, -fenger, *m.* bird-man, fowler, bird-catcher, birder.
Vogelflinte, fō'gifllnte, *f.* fowling-piece.
Vogelfrei, fō'glfrēī, *a.* outlawed, proscribed.
Vogelgarn, fō'glgarn, *n.* birding-net.
Vogelgesang, fō'glgesang, *m.* song of birds.
Vogelhaus, fō'glhōys, *n.* aviary.
Vogelherd, fō'glhārd, *m.* decoy.
Vogelkirsche, fō'glkīrshe, *f.* bird-cherry.
Vogelleim, fō'gllęm, *m.* bird-lime.
Vogelnest, fō'glnest, *n.* bird's nest.
Vogelperspettive, fō'glperzpēktīfe, *f.* bird's-eye perspective.
Vogelpfeife, fō'glpfeife, *f.* bird-call.
Vogelschau, fō'glshāū, *f.* augury; -er, *m.* angur.
Vogelscheuche, fō'glshāūche, *f.* scarecrow.
Vogelschiessen, fō'glshīssen, *n.* shooting at a wooden bird; shooting-match.
Vogelsteller, fō'glzhtęller, *m.* Vogler, fōg'ler, *m.* f. Vogelfänger.
Vöglein, föhg'lęen, *n.* little bird.
Vogt, fogt, *m. pl.* Vögte, bailiff; governor, prefect; steward. Vogtei, fogtēī', *f.* office, jurisdiction, residence of a bailiff, prefecture.

Volk, folk, *n. pl.* Völker, people, nation. Völkchen, fölk'chen, *n.* small nation.
Völkerkunde, föl'kerkunde, *f.* ethnography, ethnology.
Völkerrecht, föl'kerrecht, *n.* international law, law of nations.
Völkerschaft, föl'kershaft, *f.* nation; tribe.
Völkerwanderung, föl'kervanderung, *f.* migration of nations or of tribes, hordes.
Volkreich, folk'reich, *a.* populous.
Volksblatt, folks'blatt, *n. pl. -blätter*, popular paper.
Volkscharakter, folks'karakter, *m.* national character.
Volksfest, folks'fest, *n. pl. -e*, national or public festival.
Volksherrschaft, folks'herrshaft, *f.* democracy, government by the people.
Volkslied, folks'līd, *n. pl. -er*, popular or national song.
Volksmässig, folks'mässich, *a.* popular.
Volksmenge, folks'menge, *f.* multitude, crowd; population.
Volkssage, folks'sāge, *f.* popular tradition.
Volksschule, folks'shule, *f.* public school.
Volkssitte, folks'sitte, *f.* national custom.
Volkssprache, folks'zhprāche, *f.* popular tongue or language.
Volksversammlung, folks'fersamlung *f.* public meeting.
Volksvertreter, folks'fertreter, *m.* representative or deputy of the people.
Volks'vertretung, -ung, *f.* national assembly; representation.
Volkswirthschaft, folks'virtshaft, *f.* national economy.
Volkszählung, folks'tsālung, *f.* census.
Voll, foll, *a.* full, filled, lined with.
Vollauf, follōuf, *a.* plenty, abundant.
Vollblut, foll'blyt, *a.* full-blooded (horse). Voll'blütig, -blühtich, *a.* plethoric; -heit, -kēīt, *f.* plethora, sanguineness.
Vollbringen, follbring'en, *vt.* to accomplish, achieve, perform. Vollbrin'gung, -ung, *f.* accomplishment, achievement.
Vollbrüstig, foll'brüzhtich, *a.* full-breasted.
Vollenden, follend'en, *vt.* to end, finish,

accomplish. **Vollender**, m. accomplisher. **Vollends**, foll'ends, av. quite, wholly, entirely. **Vollen'dung**, -ung, f. accomplishment, consummation, perfection.

Völlerei, föllerei', f. gluttony, debauchery, ebriety.

Vollführen, follfüh'ren, vt. to execute, accomplish.

Vollgenuß, foll'genuss, m. full enjoyment.

Vollgiltig, foll'giltich, a. of full value, fully worth, valid.

Vollheit, foll'hāet, f. fullness.

Völlig, föl'lig, a. av. full, fully, entire, -ly.

Vollkommen, foll'kommen, a. av. perfect, -ly, consummate, complete; -heit, -heit, f. perfection.

Vollmacht, foll'macht, f. pl. -en, full power or authority, warrant.

Vollmond, foll'mōnd, m. full moon.

Vollständig, foll'zhtendich, a. complete; -keit, -kāet, f. completeness.

Vollstimmig, foll'zhtimmich, a. full-toned.

Vollstrecken, follzhtreck'en, vt. to execute. **Vollstrecker**, m. executor. **Vollstreck'ung**, -ung, f. execution.

Vollwichtig, foll'vichtich, a. of full weight; -keit, -kāet, f. full weight.

Vollzählig, foll'tsälich, a. full in number.

Vollziehen, folltsē'en (vollzog, vollzogen), vt. to execute, to perform, carry out, consummate. **Vollzieh'er**, m. executor; -in, f. executrix. **Vollzieh'ung**, -ung, f. execution, consummation, performance.

Voltaisch, vol'tāish, a. voltaic; **Voltaische Säule**, voltaic pile.

Volumen, folu'men, n. volume.

Vom, fohm (for von dem), of the, from the.

Von, fōn, pr. from, of, by.

Vor, fōr, pr. before, in front of; from, against; for.

Vorabend, för'äbent, m. eve.

Vorahnen, för'änen, vt. to have a presentiment. **Vorahn'ung**, -ung, f. presentiment, foreboding.

Voreltern, för'eltern, pl. ancestors, forefathers.

Voran, forän', av. before, in front, ahead, on, onward; — **gehen**, to go or walk before, to take the lead; precede.

Voranstalt, för'anzhtalt, f. pl. -en preparation; **Voranstalt treffen**, to prepare.

Vorarbeit, för'arbāet, f. pl. -en, previous, preparatory work. **Vorarbeiten**, vt. to work before, to prepare work; outwork, surpass in working.

Vorärnte, för'ärnte, f. first harvest.

Voraus, forays', av. before, beforehand, in advance; foremost; -bezahlen, -betsālen, vt. to prepay, to pay in advance. **Voraus'bezahlung**, -ung, f. payment in advance. **Voraus'haben**, -haben, vt. to have (get) the start of, to have in advance. **Voraussagen**, -sägen, vt. to predict, foretell. **Voraus'sehen**, -sā-en, vt. to foresee. **Voraus'setzen**, -setsen, vt. to suppose, presume, presuppose. **Voraus'setzung**, -ung, f. presumption, supposition. **Voraus'sicht**, -sicht, f. foresight; -lich, -lich, a. av. presumable, presumptive, probable.

Vorbauen, för'böyen, vt. to build before; to obviate, prevent; take precaution.

Vorbedacht, för'bedacht, m. forethought, premeditation; mit —, on purpose, purposely, with (in) cold blood.

Vorbedenken, för'bedenken (vorbedachte, vorbedacht), vt. to premeditate, consider beforehand.

Vorbedeuten, för'bedeyten, vt. to portend, foreshow, forebode, presage **Vor'bedeutung**, -ung, f. omen, presage, prognostic, portent.

Vorbehalt, för'behalt, m. pl. -e, **Vor'behaltung**, -ung, f. reservation; proviso.

Vorbehalten, för'behalten (vorbehielt, vorbehalten), vt. to reserve, except; withhold. **Vor'behaltlich**, -haltlich, a. excepting.

Vorbei, forbēī', av. by. over, past, passing; — **gehen**, to pass by; im —, passing; by the way; — **fahren**, to ride by; -**können**, -können, vi. to be able to pass. **Vorbei'lassen**, -lassen, vt. to let pass. **Vorbei'müssen**, -müssen, vi. to be obliged to pass. **Vorbei'sein**, -sāen, vi. to be over; to have past.

Vorbemeldet, för'bemēldet, **Vorbenannt**, -nannt, **Vor berührt**, -rührt, a. aforesaid.

Vorbereiten, för'berāten, *vt.* to prepare. **Vorbereitung,** -ung, *f.* preparation, preparative.
Vorbericht, för'bericht, *m. pl.* -e, preamble, preliminary account.
Vorbescheid, för'beshäet, *m. pl.* -e, summons.
Vorbescheiden, för'beshāden (-schied, -schieden). *vt.* to summon.
Vorbestimmen, för'beshtimmen, *vt.* to appoint beforehand; predestine.
Vorbeten, för'bāten, *vt.* to lead in praying *or* in prayers.
Vorbeugen, för'böügen, *vt. i.* to bend forward; to obviate, prevent.
Vorbild, för'bild, *n. pl.* -er, example, pattern, exemplar, standard. **Vor-bilden,** *vt.* to model, typify, represent.
Vorblasen, för'bläsen (vorblies, vorgeblasen), *vt.* to blow, play to.
Vorbohrer, för'börer, *m.* first bit.
Vorbote, för'bote, *m.* harbinger.
Vorbramraa, för'brāmrā, *n.* foretopgallant yard.
Vorbramsegel, för'brāmsāgel, *s.* foretopsail.
Vorbramstenge, för'brāmshtenge, *f.* foretop-gallant-mast.
Vorbringen, för'bringen (-brachte, -gebracht), *vt.* to bring forward, produce, prefer, proffer.
Vordem, för'dām, *av.* once, formerly, of old.
Vorder, för'der, *a.* fore, anterior; **-ach-se,** -akse, *f.* leading axis. **Vorder-arm,** -arm, *m. pl.* -e, fore-arm. **Vor-derfuß,** -fuse, *m. pl.* -füße, forefoot. **Vordergeschirr,** -geshirr, *n.* leading harness. **Vordergrund,** -grunt, *m.* foreground. **Vorderrad,** -rāt, *n. pl.* -räber, leading wheel. **Vordersatz,** -sats, *m. pl.* -sätze, antecedent, premise. **Vorderst,** *a.* foremost. **Vor-derseite,** -seite, *f.* (of a house) façade, front, frontispiece. **Vordersitz,** -sits, *m. pl.* -e, front seat. **Vorderstube,** -zhtūbe, *f.* front room. **Vorderteil,** -täel, *m.* forepart. **Vordertür,** -tühr, *f.* front door. **Vordertreffen,** -treffen, *n.* van, front. **Vorderzahn,** -tsān, *m. pl.* -zähne, fore-tooth. **Vorderzimmer,** -tsimmer, *n.* front room.
Vordrängen, för'drengen, *vt.* to press, push *or* crowd forward.
Vordringen, för'dringen (vordrang, vorgedrungen), *vi.* to advance, to push on, penetrate.
Vordrucken, för'drucken, *vt.* to print before; to prefix.
Voreilig, för'ēilich, *a. av.* precipitate, rash, hasty; -keit, -kāet, *f.* precipitation, rashness.
Vorempfinden, för'empfind-en (-empfand, -empfunden), *vt.* to anticipate, to have a presentiment of. **Vor-empfindung,** -ung, *f.* presentiment, anticipation.
Vorenthalten, för'enthalten (-enthielt, -enthalten), *vt.* to withhold, keep back *or* from, out of, deforce. **Vor-enthaltung,** -ung, *f.* unjust retention, deforcement.
Vorerinnern, för'erinnern, *vt.* to premonish, fore-warn, premise. **Vor-erinnerung,** -ung, *f.* premonition; preface, preamble.
Vorerst, för'ārsht, *av.* before all, first of all, in the first place.
Vorerwählen, för'ervälen, *vt.* to predestine, elect.
Vorerwähnt, för'ervānt, *a.* aforesaid.
Voressen, för'ēsen, *n.* first course of dishes.
Vorfahr, för'fār, *m. pl.* -en, predecessor; ancestor, forefather.
Vorfahren, för'fāren (-fuhr, -gefahren), *vt.* to drive up to; to beat (in driving); to try to pass.
Vorfall, för'fall, *m. pl.* **Vorfälle,** occurrence, accident, case, event.
Vorfallen, för'fallen (vorfiel, vorgefallen), *vi.* to occur, happen.
Vorfeile, för'fäle, *f.* rough file.
Vorfinden, för'finden (vorfand, vorgefunden), *vt.* to find, meet with.
Vorfordern, för'fordern, *vt.* to summon(s), challenge, cite. **Vorforder-ung,** -ung, *f.* summons, citation.
Vorfrage, för'frāge, *f.* previous question.
Vorführen, för'führen, *vt.* to bring, carry, lead out.
Vorgang, för'gang, *m.* precedence, antecedence; event. **Vorgänger,** för'genger, *m.* predecessor. **Vorgängig,** -ich, *a.* previous.
Vorgeben, för'gāben, *vt.* to give out, pretend; to set *or* impose a task; (in game) to give points; *s. n.* pretense, pretext.
Vorgebirg, för'gebīrg, *n.* promontory, cape.

Vor 362 **Vor**

Vorgefaßt, för'gefasst, a. preconceived.
Vorgefühl, för'gyfühl, n. presentiment.
Vorgehen, för'gāen (vorging, vorgegangen), vi. to go before, to have the precedence, preference; to happen, occur.
Vorgemeldet, för'gemäldet, **Vorgenannt**, -nannt, a. aforementioned, aforenamed, aforesaid.
Vorgeschmack, för'geshmack, m. foretaste.
Vorgesetzter, för'gesetster, m. superior.
Vorgestern, för'gexhtern, a. (the day before yesterday. **Vorgestrig**, -ich, a. (done) the day before yesterday.
Vorgreifen, för'greifen (-griff, -gegriffen), vi. to encroach, forestall, anticipate.
Vorgrund, för'grynd, m. foreground; front.
Vorhaben, för'hāben (vorhatte, vorgehabt), vt. to intend, design; to have before, on, to wear: n. design, intention.
Vorhalt, för'halt, m. remonstrance, expostulation; — machen, to remonstrate.
Vorhalten, för'halten (vorhielt, vorgehalten), vt. to hold forth; to expostulate, remonstrate.
Vorhand, för'hant, f. precedence, option; (at cards) lead, leading hand, precedence.
Vorhanden, forhan'den, a. at hand, present, extant, actual; — sein, to be, exist, to be at hand.
Vorhang, för'hang, n. pl. Vorhänge, curtain.
Vorhangen, för'hangen (vorbing, vorgehangen), vi. to hang or to be hanged before. **Vorhängen**, -hengen. vt. to hang up before.
Vorhängeschloß, förhengeshloss, n. padlock.
Vorhaus, för'hōys, n. vestibule.
Vorhaut, för'hōyt, f. pl. -häute, preputial.
Vorher, för'hār, av. before, beforehand, previously; **bestimmen**, -be-zhtimmen, vt. to predetermine; predestine, foreordain. **Vorherbestimmung**, -yng. f. predestination.
Vorhergehen, forhār'gā-en (-ging, -gegangen), vi. to go before. **Vorhergehend**, a. foregoing, previous, precedent, former.

Vorherrschen, för'hērshen, vi. to prevail, predominate.
Vorhersagen, förhān'sāgen, vt. to predict, foretell. **Vorhersagung**, -yng, f. prediction.
Vorhersehen, forhār'sā-en (-sah, -gesehen), vt. to foresee.
Vorhin, för'hīn, av. before, just before.
Vorhof, för'hōf, m. pl. -höfe, m. vestibule, parvis.
Vorhut, för'hyt, f. van, vanguard.
Vorig, fō'rich, a. former, last, ultimo.
Vorjährig, för'yärich, a. of last year.
Vorkämpfer, för'kempfer, m. champion.
Vorkauen, för'kāu̇en, vt. i. to chew before.
Vorkauf, för'kāuf, m. pl. -läufe, forestalling, forestalment; -**en**, vt. to forestall.
Vorkehren, för'kāren, vt. to turn out or forward; to provide, prepare. take measures, take care. **Vorkehrung**, -yng, f. precaution, preparation, measure.
Vorkenntniß, för'kenntniss, f. gewöhnlich pl. **Vorkenntnisse**, rudiments, first elements (of a science).
Vorkommen, för'kommen (-kam, -gekommen), vi. to occur: to appear: to come before; -**heit**, -hāet, f. occurrence.
Vorkost, för'kozht, f. first course.
Vorladen, för'lāden (-lud, -geladen), vt. to cite, summon.
Vorladung, för'lādyng, f. citation, summons; challenge; wad (Art.).
Vorlage, för'lāge, f. projection, plan, proposition; receiver (Chem.).
Vorlängst, för'lengzht, av. long ago.
Vorlaß, för'lass, m. first running.
Vorlassen, för'lassen (-ließ, -gelassen), vt. to let come out; to give the precedence; to admit.
Vorlastig, för'lazhtich, a. too much by the head.
Vorlauf, för'lāuf, m. first running.
Vorlaufen, för'lāufen (-lief, -gelaufen) vt. to outrun.
Vorläufer, för'lāufer, m. fore-runner, precursor.
Vorläufig, för'lāufich, a. preliminary. provisional, preparatory; prime.
Vorlaut, för'lōyt, a. av. forward, pert, indiscreet, inconsiderate. **Vorlauten**, vt. to sound stronger.

Borlegelöffel, för'lägelöffel, m. soup ladle. **Borlegemesser**, -messer, n. carver.
Borlegen, för'lägen, vt. to put, lay, place before; offer, propose; submit; carve.
Borlegeschloß, för'lägeschloss, n. pl. -schlösser, padlock.
Borleiern, för'leiern, vt. to harp (on the same string) to.
Borleik, för'leik, n. fore-leech of a staysail.
Borlese, för'läse, f. beginning of the gathering of the grapes.
Borlesen, för'läsen (-las, -gelesen), vt. to read to. **Borleser**, m. reader, lecturer. **Borlesung**, -ung, f. lecture; reading.
Borletzt, för'letst, a. last but one, (of syllables) penultimate.
Borleuchten, för'leuchten, vt. to outshine, shine brighter than —; to shine (as) a pattern to.
Borlieb, för'lib', — nehmen mit, to put up with, to take pot-luck.
Borliebe, för'libe, f. predilection.
Borliegen, för'ligen, vi. to lie or be before, in front of, against. **Borliegend**, a. present, (being) in question.
Borlügen, för'lühgen, vt. to tell a story, falsehood, a lie to.
Bormachen, för'machen, vt. to put or place before; to show how to do; to impose upon.
Bormagen, för'mägen, m. antestomach.
Bormalen, för'mälen, vt. to depict; to show how to paint.
Bormalig, för'mälich, a. former, of old. **Bormals**, för'mäls, av. formerly, of old.
Bormann, för'man, m. foreman; (in a boat) strokesman.
Bormars, för'märs, m. foretop; -raa, -rä, f. foretop-yard.
Bormauer, för'mouer, f. bulwark, rampart, safeguard.
Bormessen, för'messen, vt. to measure out to.
Bormittag, för'mittäk, m. forenoon. **Bormittägig**, för'mittägich, a. antemeridian, being before noon.
Bormund, för'mund, m. **Bormünder**, -münder, m. sin, f. guardian. **Bormundschaft**, -schaft, f. guardianship; -lich, -lich, a. tutorial.

Bormüssen, för'müssen, vt. to be obliged to go forth.
Born, förn, av. before, in front; **borverne**, from before; from the beginning, da capo.
Borname, för'näme, m. Christian name.
Bornahm, för'näm, a. of rank; fashionable. **Bornehmst**, a. chief, principal.
Bornehmen, för'nämen (-nahm, -genommen), vt. to undertake, to take in hand; to examine, try; to upbraid with, reprimand; wieder —, to resume; sich —, to resolve, purpose, intend, design; s. n. design, resolution.
Bornehmheit, för'nämhäet, f. rank, distinction; air of superiority.
Bornehmlich, för'nämlich, av. chiefly, principally.
Borplaudern, förplöudern, vt. to chat, talk to.
Borposten, för'pozhten, m. outpost.
Borpredigen, för'prädigen, vt. i. to preach, lecture to.
Borquellen, för'quellen, vi.t. to exude, gush forth.
Borragen, för'rägen, vi. to project.
Borrang, för'rang, m. first, higher, superior rank, precedence.
Borrath, för'rät, m. pl. -räthe, store, stock, provision. **Borräthig**, -rätich, a. ready, at hand, in store.
Borrathshaus, för'rätshöys, n. **Borrathskammer**, -kammer, f. storehouse, magazine.
Borrechnen, för'rechnen, vt. to reckon before or to, to give account of.
Borrecht, för'recht, n. prerogative, privilege.
Borrede, för'räde, f. preface, preamble; — machen, to preface. **Borredner**, m. prefacer.
Borreiten, för'reiten (-ritt, -geritten), vt. to ride before. **Borreiter**, m. outrider.
Borrennen, för'rennen (-rannte, -gerannt), vi. to run before.
Borrichten, för'richten, vt. to prepare. **Borrichtung**, -ung, f. preparation, contrivance, mechanism; apparatus.
Borriss, för'riss, m. sketch, outline.
Borrücken, för'rücken, vt. to move forward; to upbraid or reproach with. vt. i. to advance.

Vorrufen, för'rŭfen (vorrief, vorgerufen), vt. to call forth.
Vorsaal, för'sāl, m. pl. -säle, antechamber, ante-room.
Vorsagen, för'sägen, vt. to say to; to dictate to. **Vorgesagtes, -gesägtes**, n. dictation.
Vorsänger, för'sengėr, m. precentor, chanter.
Vorsatz, för'sats, m. pl. -sätze, purpose, design, intention; rise, gob (Min.); mit —, on purpose, intentionally. **Vorsätzlich**, -setslich, a. av. intentional, -ly, wilfully.
Vorschein, för'shăėn, m. appearance; zum — kommen, to come to light, appear; zum — bringen, to bring to light, produce.
Vorschieben, för'shīben (vorschob, vorgeschoben), vt. to push on or forward; to interpose, to plead.
Vorschießen, för'shīsen (vorschoß, vorgeschossen), vt. to advance; vi. to gush forward, to rush forward; to shoot.
Vorschlag, för'shlāk, m. pl. Vorschläge, proposition, proposal; motion.
Vorschlagen, för'shlägen (vorschlug, vorgeschlagen), vt. to propose, to motion, nominate. **Vorschlaghammer, -hammer**, m. sledge, sledge-hammer.
Vorschmack, för'shmack, m. foretaste; anticipation; antepast.
Vorschmecken, för'shmęcken, vi. to prevail, predominate.
Vorschneiden, för'shnēĭden (vorschnitt, vorgeschnitten), vt. to carve. **Vorschneider**, m. carver.
Vorschnell, för'shnĕll, a. rash, hasty.
Vorschreiben, för'shrēĭben, vt. to set a copy; to prescribe, command, order.
Vorschreiten, för'shrēĭten (vorschritt, vorgeschritten), vi. to step forth, forward, advance.
Vorschrift, för'shrift, f. pl. -en, writing-copy; precept; instruction; order, command; **mäßig, -māsich**, a. av. prescribed; according to prescription, order or direction.
Vorschub, för'shŭb, m. aid, assistance, abetment.
Vorschuhen, för'shŭ-en, vt. to foot, fox.
Vorschuß, för'shuss, m. pl. Vorschüsse, advance (of money).
Vorschütten, för'shütten, vt. to give provender.
Vorschützen, för'shütse·, vt. to pretend.

Vorschwatzen, för'shvatsen, vt. to talk to; pull the wool over one's eyes.
Vorschweben, för'shväben, vi. to be before one's eyes or mind.
Vorsegel, för'sāgl, n. foresail.
Vorsehen, för'sā-en (vorsah, vorgesehen) vt. to foresee; to provide; sich —, to heed, take care. **Vorsehung, -ŭng**, f. providence.
Vorsein, för'sāĕn, vi. to be before or under cognizance or examination; to be foremost or stand out; da sei Gott vor! God forbid!
Vorsetzen, för'setsen, vt. to set, place before; to prefix; vr. to resolve (upon).
Vorsicht, för'sicht, f. foresight, caution, precaution, circumspection, prudence. **Vorsichtig, -ich**, a. prudent, -ly, cautious: **-keit, -kāĕt**, f. cautiousness. **Vorsichtsmaßregel, -maßrägel**, f. precautionary measure.
Vorsingen, för'singen (vorsang, vorgesungen), vt. i. to sing to; to lead (in singing).
Vorsitz, för'sīts, m. chair, presiding; den — haben, to preside, to be chairman or in the chair. **Vorsitzen**, för'sitsen (vorsaß, vorgesessen), vi. to preside, to be in the chair; **-der, -der**, m. chairman, president.
Vorsommer, för'sommer, m. early summer.
Vorsorge, för'sorge, f. foresight, care, precaution. **Vorsorglich, -lich**, a. provident.
Vorspann, för'zhpann m. pl. -e, additional horses; relay; **-en, -en**, vt. to stretch before; to put additional horses to a carriage; to assist or supply with a horse.
Vorspiegeln, för'zhpīgeln, vt. to decoy by a false show. **Vorspieglung, -ŭng**, f. illuding by delusive appearance or show.
Vorspiel, för'zhpīl, n. pl. -e, prelude. **Vorspielen**, vt. i. to prelude; to play before.
Vorsprechen, för'zhprēchen (vorspraсh, vorgesprochen), vt. to pronounce before; to give a call.
Vorspringen, för'zhpringen (-sprang, -gesprungen), vi. to outleap, outrun. **Vorsprung, -zhprŭng**, m. start, advantage, advance; jutty, projection prominence; set-off, offset.

Vorstadt, för'zhtat, *f. pl.* **Vorstädte,** suburb. **Vorstädter,** -zhtętter, *m.* suburban.

Vorstand, för'zhtant, *m. pl.* -ftände, personal appearance (before judge); bail, security; directory, board of directory; director.

Vorstechen, för'zhtĕchen (vorstach, vorgestochen), *vi.* to prick, to pierce; to predominate, to be prominent.

Vorstecken, för'zhtecken, *vt.* to stick before, to prefix. **Vorstecker,** *m.* pin; key, peg.

Vorstehen, för'zhtä-en (vorstand, vorgestanden), *vi.* to stand out, project, jut; to direct.

Vorsteher, för'zhtä-er, *m.* director, chief, manager, principal.

Vorstellen, för'zhtęllen, *vt.* to place before, present; frame; represent; introduce; remonstrate; sich —, to imagine, suppose. **Vorstellung,** -ung, *f.* presentation; representation; introduction; idea, notion, conception.

Vorstęnge, för'zhtęnge, *f.* foretopmast.

Vorstęven, för'zhtäfen, *m.* stem (Mar.).

Vorstrecken, för'zhtrękken, *vt.* to stretch forward, forth; to advance, tend.

Vorströmen, för'zhtröhmen, *vi.* to gush forth.

Vorstürzen, för'zhtürtsen, *vi.* to rush forward.

Vorsündflutlich, för'sündflytlich, *a.* antediluvian.

Vortanzen, för'tantsen, *vi.* to dance before; to lead the dance. **Vortänzer,** -tęntser, *m.* leader of the dance.

Vortheil, för'tkĕl, *m.* advantage, profit, gain; -haft, -haft, *a.* advantageous, profitable, gainful, lucrative; -igkeit, för'tgĕlhaftichkĕĕt, *f.* advantageousness.

Vorthun, för'tyn, *vt.* to put before; to put on; sich —, to distinguish one's self.

Vorthür, för'tühr, *f.* first door of a double door.

Vortrab, för'träp, *m.* van, vanguard, first line.

Vortrag, för'träg, *m. pl.* Vorträge, delivery, diction; report, relation; execution, performance; proposition; lecture.

Vortragen, för'trägen (vortrug, vorgetragen), *vt.* to carry before; to deliver; report, state; bring in.

Vortrefflich, för'trĕfflich. *a.* excellent, choice, exquisite; -keit, -kĕĕt, *f.* excellence.

Vortreten, för'trăten (vortrat, vorgetreten), *vi.* to step forth or forward, before, to advance.

Vortrinken, för'trinken (vortrank, vorgetrunken), *vt.* to drink first or before: to pledge.

Vortritt, för'tritt, *m.* precedence, lead; step before a door.

Vorüben, för'ühben, *vt.* to exercise previously; rehearse.

Vorüber, forüh'ber, *av.* over, past, by. **Vorü'bergehen,** -gä-ĕn, *vi.* to pass, go by. **Vorü'berziehen,** -tsīen, *vi.* to pass by.

Vorübung, för'ühbung, *f.* previous exercise.

Vorurtheil, för'yrtäĕl, *n.* prejudice, prepossession, bias.

Vorwache, för'vache, *f.* outpost, picket.

Vorwägen, för'vägen (vorwog, vorgewogen), *vt.* to weigh before.

Vorwahl, för'väl, *f. pl.* -en, previous election, nomination.

Vorwalten, för'valten, *vi.* to prevail.

Vorwand, för'vant, *m.* pretext, pretence.

Vorwärts, för'värts, *av.* forward, on.

Vorweg, förvĕk', *av.* before, in advance.

Vorwegnehmen, förvĕk'nämen, *vt.* to anticipate; take before.

Vorweis, för'vĕīs, *m.* pass: passport.

Vorweisen, för'vĕīsen (vorwies, vorgewiesen), *vt.* to exhibit, present, produce.

Vorwelt, för'vĕlt, *f.* former or ancient times or ages, antiquity, the ancients.

Vorwenden, för'vęnden (vorwandte, vorgewandt, vorgewendet), *vt.* to pretend.

Vorwerfen, för'vĕrfen (vorwarf, vorgeworfen), *vt.* to throw or cast before; to upbraid, reproach with; to object.

Vorwerk, för'vĕrk, *n. pl.* -e, out-work.

Vorwiegen, för'vīgen (vorwog, vorgewogen), *vt.* to preponderate, exceed in weight.

Vorwimmern, för'vimmern, **Vorwinseln,** -vīnseln, *vt.* to whimper to, in relation to.

Vor 386 **Wach**

Vorwissen, fŏr'vissen. *n.* knowledge, prescience; ohne sein —, unknown to him.
Vorwitz, fŏr'vits, *m.* forwardness, inquisitiveness.
Vorwitzig, fŏr'vitsich, *a. av.* forward, pert, inquisitive.
Vorwort, fŏr'vort, *n.* preface.
Vorwurf, fŏr'vurf, *m. pl.* **Vorwürfe**, bait, lure; subject; objection, reproach.
Vorwurfsvoll, fŏr'vurfsfoll, *a.* reproachful.
Vorzählen, fŏr'tsälen, *vt.* to count to or before, to enumerate.
Vorzeichen, fŏr'tsäichen, *n.* omen, sign, portent, presage.
Vorzeichnen, fŏr'tsäichnen, *vt.* to draw before a copy, to point or trace out.
Vorzeichnung, fŏr'tsäichnung, *f.* tracing, copy.
Vorzeigen, fŏr'tsäigen, *vt.* to exhibit, produce, present.
Vorzeiger, fŏr'tsäiger, *m.* bearer.
Vorzeigung, fŏr'tsäigung, *f.* exhibition, show.
Vorzeit, fŏr'tsäit, *f.* time of old, past ages, former times.
Vorzeitig, fŏr'tsäitich, *a.* precocious, premature, untimely.
Vorziehen, fŏr'tsī-en (vorzog, vorgezogen), *vt.* to prefer.
Vorzimmer, fŏrtsimmer, *n.* ante-room, ante-chamber.
Vorzug, fŏr'tsug, *m. pl.* **Vorzüge**, preference, superiority; accomplishment.
Vorzüglich, fŏr'tsühklich, *a. av.* excellent, exquisite, capital, superior; chiefly, particularly, pre-eminently.
Vorzüglichkeit, fŏr'tsühklichkäit, *f.* excellence, superiority, choiceness, pre-eminence.
Vorzugsweise, fŏr'tsūksväise, *av.* in preference.
Votiren, fotī'ren, *vi.* to vote.
Votivtafel, fotīf'tăfel, *f.* votive tablet.
Votum, fō'tum, *n.* vote.
Vulkan, fulkān', *m. pl. -e*, volcano, vulcano.
Vulkanisch, fulkānish, *a.* volcanic.
Vulkanisiren, fulkanisī'ren, *vt.* to vulcanize.
Vulkanisirt, fulkanisīrt', *a.* vulcanired.

Waare, vä're, *f.* ware, commodity, merchandise.
Waarenhaus, vä'renhŏus, *n. pl. -häuser*, **Waarenlager**, -lăger, *n.* ware-house, magazine.
Waarenpreis, vä'renpräis, *m.* price of goods.
Waarenrechnung, vä'renrechnung, *f.* invoice.
Wabe, vä'be, *f.* honey-comb.
Wach, vach, *a.* awake, alert.
Wachdienst, vach'dīnzht, *m.* duty.
Wache, vach'e, *f.* watch, guard, sentry, sentinel.
Wachen, vach'en, *vi.* to wake, to be or continue awake.
Wacheuer, vach'föier, *n.* watchfire.
Wachhabend, vach häbent, *a.* on duty.
Wachhaus, vach'hŏus, *n. pl. -häuser*, watch-house.
Wachholder, vach'hol'der, *m.* juniper; -holz, -holts, *n.* juniper wood. **Wachholderbaum**, -bŏum, *m. pl. -bäume*, juniper-tree. **Wachholderbeere**, -bäre, *f.* juniper-berry. **Wachholderbranntwein**, -brantväin, *m.* Geneva, gin. **Wachholderstrauch**, -shtrŏuch, *m. pl. -sträucher*, juniper-shrub.
Wachmeister, vach'mäschter, *m.* sergeant.
Wachtparade, vach'parāde, *f.* parade.
Wachs, vax, *n.* wax.
Wachsam, vach'sam, *a.* watchful, vigilant, wakeful; **-keit**, -käit, *f.* watchfulness, vigilance, heed.
Wachsbild, vax'bilt, *n. pl. -er*, waxen image, wax-figure. **Wachsbleiche**, -bläiche, *f.* wax-bleaching.
Wachsen, vax'en (wuchs, gewachsen), *vi.* to grow, wax, increase.
Wachsern, väk'sern, *a.* waxen.
Wachsfarbe, vax'farbe, *f.* wax-color. **Wachsfigur**, vax'figur, *f. pl.* wax-work. **Wachskerze**, -kertse, *f.* wax-candle. **Wachshändler**, -hendler, *m.* wax-chandler. **Wachsleinwand**, -läinvant, *f.* oil-cloth, wax-cloth. **Wachslicht**, -licht, *n.* wax candle. **Wachsmalerei**, -mālöräi, *f.* wax-painting. **Wachsscheibe**, -shäibe, *f.* cake of wax. **Wachsstock**, -shtock, *m. pl. -stöcke*, wax-taper. **Wachstaffet**, -taffet, *m.* oiled silk.
Wachsthum, vax'tum, *n.* growth.
Wachstuch, vax'tuch, *n.* oil-cloth.

Wach   387   **Wah**

Wachszieher, vax'tsīer, m. wax-chandler.
Wacht, f. Wache.
Wachtel, vach'tel, f. quail; **-hund, -hunt,** m. pointer.
Wächter, věch'ter, m. watchman.
Wachtthurm, vach'tųrm, m. pl. **-thürme,** belfry, watch-tower.
Wacke, vack'e, f. wacke; toadstone.
Wackelig, vack'elich, a. shaky, loose, wavering. **Wackeln,** vack'eln, vi. to totter, vacillate, shake.
Wacker, vack'er, a. stout, vigorous; brave, valiant, gallant.
Wade, vā'de, f. calf of the leg.
Wadezeit, vā'deltseït, f. season for felling timber.
Waffel, vaf'fel, f. waffle; **-eisen,** -ei̇sen, n. waffle-iron.
Waffe, vaf'fe, f. weapons, arms; gew. pl. **Waffen.**
Waffenbruder, vaf'fenbrųder, m. brother in arms, comrade.
Waffenlos, vaf'fenlös, a. unarmed.
Waffenrüstung, vaf'fenrüzhtųng, f. armor.
Waffenschmied, vaf'fenshmīd, m. pl. **-e,** armorer.
Waffenstillstand, vaf'fenshtillzhtant, m. armistice, truce.
Waffenthat, vaf'fentät, f. exploit.
Waffenübung, vaf'fenühbųng, f. military exercise.
Waffnen, vaf'nen, vt. to arm.
Wagbar, vāg'bär, a. ponderable; **-keit,** -kěet, f. ponderability.
Wage, vä'ge, f. (pair of) scales, balance: die — halten, to balance, counterbalance, counterpoise.
Wagebalken, vä'gebalken, m. beam.
Wagegeld, vä'gegeld, n. weighage.
Wagehals, vä'gehals, m. pl. **-hälse,** daring fellow.
Wagen, vä'gen, m. wagon, carriage, coach.
Wägen, vä'gen (wag, wägte, gewogen, gewägt), vt. to weigh, balance.
Wagen, vä'gen, vt. to dare, venture, hazard, risk, jeopard(ize).
Wagenachse, vä'genax-e, f. axle-tree.
Wagendeichsel, -dëïksel, f. coachpole, shaft. **Wagengeleise, -geleäse,** n. track. **Wagengestell, -gezhtell,** n. wagon-body, wagon-frame. **Wagenhaus, -höys,** n. coach-house. **Wagenkasten, -kazhten,** m. wagon-body. **Wagenkessel, -kęssęl,** m.

wagon-head, boiler. **Wagenleiter, -lēiter,** m. ladder of the wagon. **Wagenlenker, -lęnker,** m. charioteer. **Wagenmacher, -macher,** m. wheelwright. **Wagenremise,** coach-house. **Wagenschmiere, -shmīre,** f. wagon-grease. **Wagenschuß, -shōs, Wagenschatt, -shett,** m. wainscot. **Wagenschwer, -shēller. Wagenschoppen, -shoppen, Wagenschuppen, -shųp, -peu,** m. coach-house. **Wagenwinde, -vīnde,** f. screw-jack.
Wäger, vä'ger, m. weigher.
Wagerecht, vā'gerecht, a. av. horizontal, level.
Wagestück, vā'gezhtück, n. bold stroke, daring feat. **Waglich,** väk'lich, a. hazardous.
Wagner, väk'ner, m. wheel-wright.
Wagschale, väk'shäle, f. scale, basin.
Wahl, väl, f. choice, option; election, poll. **Wählbar,** väl'bär, a. eligible; **-keit, -käet,** f. eligibility. **Wählen,** vä'len, vt. to elect; to choose, select.
Wähler, vä'ler, m. elector; **-isch,** -ish, a. dainty, nice, fastidious.
Wahlfähig, väl'fä-ich, a. eligible: having a vote; **-keit, -käet,** f. eligibility; elective franchise. **Wahlfreiheit, -häet,** f. elective franchise. **Wahlkasten, -kazhten,** m. ballot-box. **Wahlkugel, -kųgel,** f. ballot.
Wahlmann, -mann, m. pl. **-männer,** elector. **Wahlrecht, -recht,** n. elective franchise, right of voting, of suffrage. **Wahlspruch, -zhprųch,** m. pl. **-sprüche,** motto.
Wahlstatt, väl'zhtatt, f. pl. **-stätte,** field of battle.
Wahlstimme, vęl'zhtimme, f. suffrage, vote. **Wahltag, -täk,** m. pl. **-e,** election-day. **Wahlurne, -ųrne,** f. ballot-box. **Wahlverwandschaft, -fervantshaft,** f. elective affinity.
Wahlzettel, väl'tsęttel, m. (voting) ticket.
Wahn, vän, m. fancy, illusion, false, erroneous opinion or belief.
Wähnen, vä'nen, vt. to fancy, imagine presume (erroneously).
Wahnglaube, vän'gläübe, m. false, erroneous or vain belief, illusive faith.
Wahnsinn, vän'sinn, m. insanity, madness, craziness, franticness, fury, frenzy, rage; **-ig, -ich,** f. insane, mad, frantic, crazy, furious; lunatic

Wah 388 **Wan**

Wahnwitz, wän'vits, *m.* = **Wahnsinn,**
ig, = **Wahnsinnig.**
Wahr, vär, *a.* true, veritable, actual,
real. **Wahres,** vä'res, *n.* truth.
Wahren, vä'ren, *vt.* to preserve, keep,
guard; fich —, to beware of.
Währen, vä'ren, *vi.* to last, continue,
endure. **Wäh'rend,** *pr.* during; *Cj.*
while, whilst, when.
Wahrhaft, vär'haft, *ig,* -ich, *a. av.*
true, actual, real; indeed, truly, really; *-keit,* -käet, *f.* veracity; truthfulness; truth.
Wahrheit, vär'hæt, *f.* truth, verity;
truthfulness.
Wahrlich, vär'lich, *a.* truly, verily.
Wahrnehmen, vär'nämen (-nahm, -genommen), *vt.* to perceive, observe,
see. **Wahr'nehmung,** -yng, *f.* perception, observation.
Wahrsagen, vär'sägen, *vt. i.* to soothsay, divine, foretell, predict, prophesy, to tell fortunes; fich — laßen,
to have one's fortune told. **Wahr's
sager,** -säger, *m.* soothsayer, prophet,
foreteller, fortune-teller. **Wahrsa=
gerei,** -säggerö́i′, **Wahr'sagung,**- yng,
f. soothsaying, divination.
Wahrscheinlich, vär'shäenlich, *av. a.*
likely, probable; *-keit,* -käet, *f.*
likelihood, probability.
Wahrspruch, vär'zhpruch, *m.* verdict.
Währung, vär'yng, *f.* duration; coin,
money, value: valuation, standard.
Wahrzeichen, vär'tsäechen, *n.* presage,
omen, sign, prognostic, token.
Waid, väet, *m.* woad, **Paſtel;** *-küpe,*
-kühpe, *f.* pastel-vat.
Waidmann, väet'mann, *m. pl.* -män=
ner, sportsman, huntsman, woodman. **Waid'werk,** -verk, *n.* chase,
hunting: game.
Waise, vä̀ĕ'se, *f.* orphan; **=haus,**
-hous, *n. pl.* -häuser, orphan-asylum.
Wai'senkind, -kint, *n. pl.* -er, orphan
(child). **Wai'senknabe,** -knäbe, -n,
pl. -n, m. orphan-boy. **Wai'senmäd=
chen,** -mädchen, *n.* orphan-girl.
Wakern, vak'kern, *vt.* to freshen.
Wald, valt, *m. pl.* **Wälber,** wood, forest; **=brand,** -brant, *m. pl.* -bränbe,
burning of a wood. **Wald'bruder,**
-bryder, *m. pl.* -brüder, hermit.
Wäldchen, vĕlt'chen, *n.* grove.
Waldhorn, valt'horn, *n. pl.* -hörner,
bugle, (hunting-)horn. **Wald'igt,**
-icht, *a.* resembling a wood. **Waldig,**
val'dich, *a.* woody, wooded. **Wald=
ſchütze,** -shütse, *m.* -*n, pl.* -*n,* forester,
woodward. **Wald'ſtrom,** -zhtrōm,
m. pl. -ſtröme, torrent (in a forest).
Wald'ung, -yng, *f.* wood, forest,
woodland.
Walfiſch, val'fish, *m.* whale; *-ſang,*
-fang, *m.* whale-fishery.
Walke, val'ke, *f.* fulling. **Wal'ken,**
vt. to full. **Walk'mühle,** -mühle, *f.*
fulling-mill. **Walk'müller,** -müller,
Walker, val'ker, *m.* fuller. **Walk's
erbe,** -ördə, *f.* fuller's earth.
Wall, vall, *m. pl.* **Wälle,** wall, rampart; dam, dike.
Wallach, vallach', *m.* gelding, castrated
animal, *spec.* horse.
Wallen, val'len, *vi.* to go, walk, to go
on a pilgrimage; to rise, bubble,
boil; to wave, undulate.
Wällen, vel'len, *vt.* to make to boil.
Waller, val'ler, *m.* pilgrim, wanderer.
Wallfahren, vall'fären, **Wallfahrten,**
vall'färten, *vi.* to go on a pilgrimage.
Wall'fahrer, **Wall'fahrter,** *m.* *-in,*
f. pilgrim. **Wall'fahrt,** -färt, *f.* pilgrimage.
Wallnuß, vall'nuss, *f. pl.* -nüſſe, walnut; *-baum,* -bayum, *m. pl.* -bäume,
walnut (tree).
Wallung, vall'yng, *f.* boiling, ebullition; in — gerathen, to be agitated.
Walmdach, valm'dach, *n. pl.* -dächer,
hip-roof.
Walrath, val'rät, *m.* sperm, spermaceti.
Walruß, val'ross, *n.* walrus, sea-horse,
morse.
Walten, val'ten, *vi.* to govern, sway,
bear rule.
Walzblech, valts'blĕch, *n.* plate or
rolled metal.
Walze, valt'se, *f.* cylinder, roller, bar
rel. **Walzen,** val'tsen, *vi.* to roll,
to waltz, to dance a waltz.
Wälzen, velt'sen, *vt.* to roll, wallow;
fich —, to wallow, roll.
Walzenförmig, val'tsenförmich, *a.* cylindric(al).
Walzer, val'tser, *m.* waltz.
Wamms, vamms, *n. pl.* **Wämmſer,**
jacket.
Wampe, vam'pe, *f.* belly, dewlap.
Wand, vant, *f. pl.* **Wänbe,** wall, partition; steep side; **=beſleidung,** -bekledung, *f.* (höslerne) wainscot.
Wandel, van'del, *m.* conduct, course

of life; walk: $\mathfrak{H}$andel und $\mathfrak{W}$andel, trade, business, commerce of life: **-bar**, -bär, *a.* inconstant, changeable; **-barfeit**, -käet, *f.* changeableness, inconstancy. $\mathfrak{W}$an'dellos, -lōs, *a.* unchanging. $\mathfrak{W}$andeln, van'deln, *vi.* to wander, walk, live; fich —, to change, turn. $\mathfrak{W}$andelftern, van'delzhtêrn. *m. pl. -e.* planet.

$\mathfrak{W}$anderer, van'dêrer, $\mathfrak{W}$an'dersmann, *m.* traveler, wanderer. $\mathfrak{W}$an'der: jahr, -yâr, *n.* traveling-year. $\mathfrak{W}$an'dern, *vi.* to wander; travel. $\mathfrak{W}$an's derfchaft, -shaft, *f.* travel, traveling. $\mathfrak{W}$an'derung, -yng, *f.* wandering, traveling.

$\mathfrak{W}$andkalender, vant'kalender, *m.* sheet-almanac.

$\mathfrak{W}$andknopf, vant'k(e)nopf, *m. pl.* -fnöpfe, *m.* shroud-knot.

$\mathfrak{W}$anduhr, vant'ur, *f.* clock (in a room).

$\mathfrak{W}$ange, vang'e, *f.* cheek; string-board (of wooden stairs).

$\mathfrak{W}$ankelmuth, vang'kelmyt, *m.* fickleness, inconstancy, unsteadiness.

$\mathfrak{W}$ankelmüthig, vang'kelmühtich, *a.* fickle, changeful, unsteady, capricious; **-feit**, -käet, *f.* fickleness.

$\mathfrak{W}$anken, vang'ken, *vi.* to shake, vacillate, waver, totter, stagger.

$\mathfrak{W}$ann, vann, *av.* when; dann und wann, now and then, sometimes; feit —, since when? how long?

$\mathfrak{W}$annen, van'nen (only with von), von wannen, whence.

$\mathfrak{W}$anne, van'ne, *f.* fan, van, tray; oblong. $\mathfrak{W}$annen, van'nen, *vt.* to winnow.

$\mathfrak{W}$anft, vanzht, *m. pl.* $\mathfrak{W}$änfte. paunch, belly.

$\mathfrak{W}$anze, van'tse, *f.* bed-bug, bug.

$\mathfrak{W}$anzig, van'tsich, *a.* buggy, abounding in bed-bugs.

$\mathfrak{W}$anzeit, vän'tsëlt, *f.* tide and half-tide.

$\mathfrak{W}$appen, vap'pen, *n.* arms, escutcheon. $\mathfrak{W}$ap'penkunde, -kunde, *f.* heraldry.

$\mathfrak{W}$appnen, vap'pnen, *vt.* to arm; fich —, to guard against.

$\mathfrak{W}$arb, vârp, *Prt. v.* $\mathfrak{W}$erben.

$\mathfrak{W}$ardein, vard'ëen, *m.* warden.

$\mathfrak{W}$arm, varm, *a.* warm, hot; **-blütig**, -blühtich, *a.* warm-blooded; irritable, hot-brained, high-spirited.

$\mathfrak{W}$ärmeleiter, ver'melaëter, *m.* conductor (of heat).

$\mathfrak{W}$ärmeelektrizität, verme'elektritsität, *f.* thermo-electricity.

$\mathfrak{W}$ärmemeffer, ver'memesser, *m.* thermometer, calorimeter.

$\mathfrak{W}$ärmen, ver'men, *vt.* to warm.

$\mathfrak{W}$ärmpfanne, verm'flanne, *f.* warming-pan; chafing-dish.

$\mathfrak{W}$arnen, var'nen, *vt.* to warn, caution.

$\mathfrak{W}$ar'nung, -yng, *f.* warning, caution.

$\mathfrak{W}$art, vart, *m.* warder. $\mathfrak{W}$arte, var'te, *f.* watch-tower; observatory.

$\mathfrak{W}$arten, var'ten, *vi.* to wait; — auf, to await, expect, stay for; to attend, nurse; — laffen, to keep waiting.

$\mathfrak{W}$ärter, vêr'ter, *m.* waiter, keeper, nurse; **-in**, *f.* $\mathfrak{W}$artfrau, vart'frâu, *f.* nurse.

$\mathfrak{W}$artgeld, vart'gëlt, *n.* money for nursing *or* attending.

$\mathfrak{W}$artfaal, vart'sâl, *m. pl.* -fäle, waiting-room.

$\mathfrak{W}$artung, vart'yng, *f.* nursing, attendance.

$\mathfrak{W}$arum, varum', *av.* why, wherefore.

$\mathfrak{W}$arze, var'tse, *f.* wart.

$\mathfrak{W}$arzig, varts'ich, *a.* warty, full of warts; verrucous (of plants).

$\mathfrak{W}$as, vâs, *pron.* what, which; that; something.

$\mathfrak{W}$afchbär, vash'bâr, *m. -en, pl. -en,* raccoon. $\mathfrak{W}$afch'becken, -becken, *n.* basin; laver. $\mathfrak{W}$afchbrett, -brét, *n. pl.* -bretter, wash-board. $\mathfrak{W}$afch'bütte, -bütte, *f.* tub. $\mathfrak{W}$afche, vesh'e, *f.* wash, linen; washing.

$\mathfrak{W}$afchen, vash'en (wufch, gewafchen), *vt.* to wash. $\mathfrak{W}$afcher, vash'er, *m.* idle prattler; **-in**, *f.* wash-woman. $\mathfrak{W}$afchgold, vash'gôlt, *n.* gold obtained by washing. $\mathfrak{W}$afch'haus, -hôus, *n. pl.* -häufer, laundry.

$\mathfrak{W}$afchkeffel, vash'kessel, *m.* wash-kettle. $\mathfrak{W}$afch'flammer, -klammer, *f.* $\mathfrak{W}$afch'flämmchen, -klemmchen, *n.* clothes-pin. $\mathfrak{W}$afch'forb, -korp, *m.* buck-basket, clothes-basket.

$\mathfrak{W}$afchlappen, vash'lappen, *m.* dishclout. $\mathfrak{W}$afch'leine, -lëne, *f.* clothesline, auch $\mathfrak{W}$afch'feil, -säel, *n.*

$\mathfrak{W}$afchtrog, vash'trôk, *m. pl.* -tröge, washing trough. $\mathfrak{W}$afch'wanne, -vanne, *f.* wash-tub. $\mathfrak{W}$afch'waffer, -vasser, *n.* water for washing. $\mathfrak{W}$afch'zettel, -tsëttel, *m.* wash-bill.

33*

Waſ 890 **Wei**

Waſchzuber, vash'tsuber, *m.* washing-tub.
Waſen, vä'sen, *m.* vapor; turf.
Waſſer, vas'ser, *n.* water; **-bad, -back**, *n.* manger. **Waſſerbau, -bou**, *m.* water-works, hydraulic engine or machine; **-kunſt, -kunzht**, *f.* hydraulic architecture.
Waſſer-blaſe, vas'serbläse, *f.* bubble; **-blei, -bleï**, *n.* molybdena; **-bord, -bort**, *m.* weather-board; **-bicht, -dicht**, *a.* water-proof; **-eimer, -ē-mer**, *m.* water-bucket; **-fahrt, -färt**, *f.* trip or excursion in a boat; **-fall, -fall**, *m.* waterfall, cascade, cataract; **-farbe, -farbe**, *f.* water-color; **-farbig, -farbich**, *a.* water-colored; **-faß, -fass**, *n. pl.* **-fäſſer**, cask or butt for holding water; **-flut, -flyt**, *f.* deluge, inundation; **-gang, -gang**, *m.* water-way; **-glaß, -gläs**, *n. pl.* **-gläſer**, tumbler; **-hahn, -hän**, *m.* pet-cock (of a steam-cylinder); **-hoſe, -hō-se**, *f.* water-spout; **-huhn, -hyn**. *n. pl.* **-hühner**, water-hen, coot; **-hund, -hunt**, *m.* water-spaniel.
Waſſerig, vës'serich, *a.* watery, aqueous; insipid; **-keit, -kāet**, *f.* wateriness, aqueousness; insipidity.
Waſſer-jungfer, vas'ser-yungfer, *f.* dragon-fly, libellula; **-kopf, -kopf**, *m.* hydrocephalus, dropsy of the head; **-kraft, -kraft**, *f.* water-power; **-kraftlehre**, vas'serkraftläre, *f.* hydraulics; **-kreſſe, -krësse**, *f.* water-cress; **-krug, -kryk**, *m.* water-pitcher; **-leitung, -läetung**, *f.* aqueduct; **-lilie, -lïli-e**, *f.* water-lily; **-linie, -lïni-e**, *f.* water-line; **-los, -lōs**, *a.* waterless; **-mangel, -mang-el**, *m.* scarcity of water; **-mann, -mann**, *m.* aquarius; **-maus, -mōys**, *f. pl.* **-mäuſe, -ratte, -ratte**, *f.* water-rat; **-melone, -melōne**, *f.* water-melon; **-mühle, -mühle**, *f.* water-mill.
Wäſſern, vës'sern, *vt.* to water, irrigate; to wet, to overflow with water; to water (silk).
Waſſer-paß, vas'serpass, *m.* level of the water; **-pflanze, -pflantse**, *f.* water-plant; **-preſſe, -prësse**, *f.* water-press, hydraulic press; **-pumpe, -pumpe**, *f.* pump; **-rad, -räd**, *n. pl.* **-räder**, water-wheel; **-ratte, -ratte**, *f.* water-rat; **-raum, -roum**, *m.* water-hold; **-recht, -rècht**, *a.* level, horizontal; **-reich, -rēich**, *a.*

abounding in water, watery; **-reich, -rēich**, *n.* watery expanse; **-reis, -reïs**, *n. pl.* **-er**, water-shoot; **-rinne, -rinne**, *f.* water-course; **-röhre, -röhre**, *f.* water-pipe, conduit, channel; **-röſte, -röhzhte**, *f.* water-retting, watering; **-ſäbler, -säbler**, *m.* avoset, avosetta; **-ſack, -sack**, *m. pl.* **-ſäcke**. bucket (of a water-wheel); (surg.) cyst, cystis; **-ſäule, -seüle**, *f.* column of water; **-ſchacht, -shacht**, *m.* pit or shaft through which water is raised; **-ſchaden, -shäden**, *m.* damage caused by water or inundation; **-ſcheide, -shäede**, *f.* water-shed; **-ſcheu, -shëü**, *a.* hydrophobic; *s. f.* hydrophobia, canine madness; **-ſchlange, -shlang-e**, *f.* water-snake; (Mar.) water-pipe; **-ſchraube, -shrōybe**, *f.* water-screw; **-ſegel, -sëgel**, *n.* water-sail; **-ſpiegel, -zhpï-gel**, *m.* surface of the water, surface of the sea; **-ſtand, -zhtant**, *m.* water-line, water-mark; **-ſtation, -zhtatsi-ōn**, *f.* water-station, watering-station; **-ſtoff, -zhtoff**, *m.* hydrogen; **-ſtrahl, -zhträl**, *m.* stream of water; **-ſucht, -zycht**, *f.* dropsy; **-ſüchtig, -süchtich**, *a.* dropsical, hydropsical; **-ſuppe, -syppe**, *f.* water-gruel, water-soup; **-träger, -träger**, *m.* water-carrier; **-transport, -transport**, *m.* water-carriage; **-trog, -trōk**, *m. pl.* **-tröge**, water-trough; **-tropfen, -tropfen**, *m.* water-drop; **-trommel, -trommel**, *f.* water-blowing engine or machine; **-uhr, -yr**, *f.* water-clock.
Wäſſerung, vës'serung, *f.* watering; irrigation.
Waſſer-wage, vas'servägę, *f.* water-level; water-poise; gauge; **-wanne, -vanne**, *f.* water-trough; **-zeichen, -tsäechen**, *n.* water-mark; **-zoll, -tsoll**, *m. pl.* **-zölle**. water-inch; toll paid on navigable streams; **-zuber, -tsyber**, *m.* water-tub.
Waten, vä'ten, *vi.* to wade.
Watſcheln, vatsh'eln, *vi.* to twaddle.
Watte, vat'te, *f.* wad, wadding.
Wattiren, vattï'ren, *vi.* to line, wad.
Wau, vau, *av.* dead, becalmed (Mar.)
Wau, vau, *m.* weld, dyer's weed; **-menſel, väü'āmenühl**, *n.* weld-seed oil.
Wauwau, väü'väü, *m.* bugbear.
Webe, vā'be, *f.* web.

Weben, vā'bẹn (wob, gewoben), *vt. i.* to weave; to move.
Weber, vā'bẹr, *m.* weaver. **We'be(r)baum**, -bǎum, *m.* (weaver's) beam. **We'berblatt**, -blatt, *n. pl.* -blätter, weaver's reed. **We'berdistel**, -dizh-tẹl, *f.* fuller's thistle. **Weberei**, -ēī', *f.* weaving. **We'bergeſell**, -gesẹll, *m.* -en, *pl.* -en, journeyman weaver. **We'berſchiff**, -shiff, *n.* **We'berſchütze**, -shütsẹ, *m.* shuttle. **We'be(r)ſtuhl**, -shtỵl, *m. pl.* -stühle, loom. **We'berzange**, -tsang-ẹ, *f.* tweezers, (weaver's) nippers. **We'berzettel**, -tsẹt-tẹl, *m.* warp.
Wechſel, věk'sẹl, *m.* change, alteration, vicissitude, variation, alternation; bill of exchange; -agent, -agent, *m.* -en, *pl.* -en, broker. **Wech'ſelbalg**, -balk, *m. pl.* -bälge, changeling, oaf, urchin. **Wech'ſelbank**, -bank, *f. pl.* -bauten, exchange, bank. **Wech'ſelbrief**, -brīf, *m.* bill of exchange. **Wech'ſelcurs**, -kurs, *m. pl.* -e, course of exchange. **Wech'ſelfieber**, -fīber, *n.* intermittent fever, ague. **Wech'ſelgeſchäft**, -gesheft, *n.* banking business.
Wechſeln, věk'sẹln, *vt. i.* to change, exchange, alternate.
Wechſelordnung, věk'sẹlordnung, *f.* exchange-regulations. **Wech'ſelrechnung**, -rechnung, *f.* banker's account. **Wech'ſelrecht**, -recht, *n.* laws of exchange. **Wech'ſelſeitig**, -sēītich, *a.* mutual, reciprocal; -keit, -kāet, *f.* reciprocity, mutuality. **Wech'ſelsweiſe**, -vēīsẹ, *av.* alternately, mutually.
Wechſler, věk'slẹr, *m.* money-changer, broker, banker.
Weck, věck, *m.* **Wecke**, věck'ẹ *f.* **Weck-en**, věck'ẹn, *m.* roll, white bread (in rolls).
Wecken, věck'ẹn, *vt.* to wake, awaken, to rouse from sleep.
Wecker, věck'ẹr, *m.* rouser, alarm-clock.
Wedel, vā'dl, *m.* fan, brush, duster.
Wedeln, vā'dẹln, *vt. i.* to wag, flirt, to fan.
Weder, vā'der, *Cj.* neither; — noch, neither. — nor.
Weg, věk, *av.* away, hence, off; *Imperatively*, be gone!
Weg, vāg, *m.* way, road, path, walk, passage; course, manner, means.

Wegarbeiten, věk'arbāētẹn, *vt.* to work away, remove (by working).
Wegäzen, věk'ätsẹn, **Wegbeizen**, věg'bāētsẹn, *vt.* to cauterize.
Wegbegeben, věk'begāben, *vr.* ſich —, to absent one's self; to retire, withdraw.
Wegbeißen, věck'bēīssẹn (wegbiß, weggebiſſen), *vt.* to bite away *or* off; supplant, eject.
Wegbekommen, věk'bekemmen (wegbekam, wegbekommen), *vt.* to make out.
Wegblaſen, věk'blāsẹn (wegblies, wegeblaſen), *vt.* to blow away.
Wegbleiben, věk'blēīben (wegblieb, weggeblieben), *vi.* to stay away.
Wegbrennen, věk'brẹnnen (wegbrannte, weggebrannt), *vt.* to cauterize, to burn away.
Wegbringen, věk'bringen (wegbrachte, weggebracht), *vt.* to carry away, to remove.
Wegdürfen, věk'dürfen (wegdurfte, weggedurft *or* wegdürfen), *vt.* to be permitted to withdraw *or* leave *or* go away.
Wegebau, vā'gebōy *s.* making roads.
Wegeilen, věk'ēīlen, *vi.* to hasten away.
Wegelagerer, vā'gelāgerẹr, *m.* waylayer. **Wegelagern**, *vt.* to waylay, to beset in ambush.
Weglos, vāg'lōs, *a.* invious, impassable.
Wegen, vā'gẹn, *pr.* on account *or* because of, about, for.
Wegeſſen, věk'ēssen (wegaß, weggegeſſen). *vt.* to eat away *or* up.
Wegfahren, věk'fāren (wegfuhr, weggefahren), *vt.* to drive *or* ride away. **Wegfahrt**, věck'fārt, *f.* departure.
Wegfangen, věk'fangen (wegfing, weggefangen), *vt.* to catch (away).
Wegfeilen, věk'fēīlen, *vt.* to file off.
Wegfiſchen, věk'fishen, *vt.* to fish; to catch.
Wegfliegen, věk'flīgen (wegflog, weggeflogen), *vi.* to fly away.
Wegfreſſen, věk'frẹssen (wegfraß weggefreſſen), *vt.* to eat *or* gobble up; to consume.
Wegführen, věk'führen, *vt.* to lead *or* carry away.
Weggang, věk'gang, *m.* departure.
Weggeben, věk'gāben (weggab, weggegeben), *vt.* to give away.

Weggehen, vĕk'gä-en (wegging, weggegangen), vi. to go away, off.
Weghaben, vĕk'häbən, vt. to anticipate, to be aware of, to understand.
Weghalten, vĕk'halten (weghielt, weggehalten), vt. to hold or keep away or off.
Weghaschen, vĕk'hashen, vt. to catch.
Weghauen, vĕk'häu-en (weghieb, weggehauen), vt. to cut away or off.
Weghohlen, vĕk'hōlen (vt. to call or take away.
Weghüpfen, vĕk'hüpfen, vi. to hop away.
Wegjagen, vĕk'yägen, vt. to drive away.
Wegkapern, vĕk'kapern, vt. to capture; snatch away.
Wegkehren, vĕk'kären, vt. to avert, to turn off; to sweep away.
Wegkommen, vĕk'kommen (wegkam, weggekommen), vi. to come off, to get away.
Wegkönnen, vĕk'können (wegkonnte, weggekonnt and weggekönnen), vi. to be able to come off, or to go away.
Wegkriechen, vĕk'krĭchen (wegkroch, weggekrochen), vi. to creep away.
Wegkriegen, vĕk'krĭgen, vt. to get away.
Weglassen, vĕk'lassen (wegließ, weggelassen), vt. to let go, to suffer to go; to omit, leave out. **Weglassung**, -ung, f. omission.
Weglaufen, vĕk'läufen (weglief, weggelaufen), vi. to run away, off.
Weglegen, vĕck'lägen, vt. to lay aside, put away.
Wegleihen, vĕk'lĕī-en (-lieh, -geliehen), vt. to lend away.
Weglocken, vĕk'locken, vt. to decoy, entice away.
Wegmachen, vĕck'machen, vt. to remove: sich —, to withdraw, depart.
Wegmögen, vĕk'mögen (-mochte, -gemocht), vt. to want to leave.
Wegmüssen, vĕk'müssen (-mußte, -gemußt or -müßen), vi. to be obliged to leave.
Wegnahme, vĕk'nämę, f. taking away, seizure.
Wegnehmen, vĕk'nämen (-nahm, -genommen), vt. to take away, to capture, seize.
Wegradiren, vĕk'rädīren, vt. to scratch out.

Wegraffen, vĕk'raffen, vt. to snatch away, sweep off.
Wegrauben, vĕk'räuben, vt. to snatch away.
Wegräumen, vĕk'räumen, vt. to remove, to clear away.
Wegreiben, vĕk'rēiben (-rieb, -gerieben), vt. to rub off.
Wegreichen, vĕk'rēichen, vt. to hand away or down.
Wegreisen, vĕk'rēisen, vi. to depart, set off.
Wegreißen, vĕk'rēissen (-riß, -gerissen), vt. to tear away.
Wegreiten, vĕk'rēiten (-ritt, -geritten), vi. to ride off or away.
Wegrollen, vĕk'rollen, vt. i. to roll away.
Wegrücken, vĕk'rücken, vt. to move away, inch off.
Wegrufen, vek'rufen (-rief, -gerufen), vt. to call away or off.
Wegsägen, vĕk'sägen, vt. to saw off.
Wegsam, vĕk'sam, a. passable, pervious.
Wegschaben, vĕk'shäben, vt. to scrape away or off.
Wegschaffen, vĕk'shaffen, vt. to remove. **Wegschaffung**, -ung, f. removal.
Wegschaufeln, vĕk'shōufeln, vt. to shovel away.
Wegscheeren, vĕk'shären, vt. to shear or clip off; sich —, to sheer off, pack off.
Wegscheuchen, vĕk'shäuchen, vt. to scare away.
Wegscheuern, vĕk'shĕü-ern, vt. to scour off.
Wegschicken, vĕk'shicken, vt. to send off or away, to dispatch.
Wegschieben, vĕk'shīben (-schob, -geschoben), vt. to shove off, push away, to remove.
Wegschießen, vĕk'shīssen (-schoß, -geschossen), vt. to shoot away.
Wegschiffen, vĕk'shiffen, vi. to sail away.
Wegschleichen, vĕk'shlēichen (-schlich, -geschlichen), vt. to steal or slip away, slide off.
Wegschleifen, vĕk'shlēifen (-schliff, -geschliffen), vt. to grind off.
Wegschleppen, vĕk'shleppen, vt. to drag away.
Wegschleudern, vĕk'shlēudern, vt. to fling away.

Wegschlüpfen, vĕk'shlüpfen, *vi.* to slip away.
Wegschmeißen, vĕk'shmeissen (-schmiß, -geschmissen), *vt.* to throw away.
Wegschmelzen, vĕk'shmeltsen (-schmolz, -geschmolzen), *vt. i.* to melt away.
Wegschnappen, vĕk'shnappen, *vt.* to snap or snatch away.
Wegschneiden, vĕk'shneiden (-schnitt, -geschnitten), *vt.* to cut off.
Wegschwemmen, vĕk'shvemmen, *vt.* to float away.
Wegschwimmen, vĕk'shvimmen (-schwamm, weggeschwommen), *vi.* to swim away.
Wegsehen, vĕk'sā-en (-sah, -gesehen), *vi.* to look away.
Wegsein, vĕk'-sen (-war, -gewesen), *vi.* to be away or absent.
Wegsenden, vĕk'senden (-sandte, -gesandt), *vt.* to send away, off.
Wegsengen, vĕk'seng-en, *vt.* to singe off.
Wegsetzen, vĕk'setsen, *vt.* to put away; *vi.* to clear, leap over; *vr.* sich — über, to disregard, to be above, to set one's self above.
Wegsinken, vĕk'sinken (-sank, -gesunken), *vi.* to sink away, subside.
Wegsprengen, vĕk'zhpreng-en, *vt.* to blast off.
Wegspringen, vĕk'zhpring-en (-sprang, -gesprungen), *vi.* to run away, to bound or leap away.
Wegspülen, vĕk'zhpühlen, *vt.* to wash away.
Wegstechen, vĕk'zhtĕchen (-stach, -gestochen), *vt.* to cut off, to remove by piercing.
Wegstehlen, vĕk'zhtälen (-stahl, -gestohlen), *vt.* to steal away, purloin; sich —, to steal, slip away, to sneak off, skedaddle.
Wegstellen, vĕk'zhtellen, *vt.* to place or put aside or away.
Wegstoßen, vĕk'zhtössen (-stieß, -gestoßen), *vt.* to push away.
Wegstreichen, vĕk'zhtreichen (-strich, -gestrichen), *vt.* to strike away or out.
Wegthun, vĕk'tyn (-that, -gethan), *vt.* to put away or aside; to hold off; to remove.
Wegtragen, vĕk'trägen (-trug, -getragen), *vt.* to carry off or away.
Wegtreiben, vĕk'treiben (-trieb, -getrieben), *vt.* to drive away.

Wegtreten, vĕk'träten (-trat, -getreten), *vt.* to remove by treading; *vi.* to step aside, stand away.
Wegwälzen, vĕk'veltsen, *vt.* to roll away.
Wegwaschen, vĕk'vashen (-wusch, -gewaschen), *vt.* to wash off.
Wegweisen, vĕk'veisen (-wies, -gewiesen), *vt.* to send away, to turn off, to discard.
Wegweiser, vāg'veiser, *m.* finger-post, guide-post.
Wegwelken, vĕk'völken, *vi.* to pine away.
Wegwenden, vĕk'venden (-wandte, -gewandt), *vt.* to turn away, off or from, to avert.
Wegwerfen, vĕk'vĕrfen (-warf, -geworfen), *vt.* to throw away, to cast off, to reject; sich —, to debase one's self, to degrade or prostitute one's self.
Wegwischen, vĕk'vishen, *vt.* to wipe away.
Wegwollen, vĕk'vollen, *vi.* to want to leave.
Wegwünschen, vĕk'vünshen, *vt.* to wish away.
Wegzaubern, vĕk'tsäübern, *vt.* to charm or conjure away.
Wegzeiger, vāg'tsäĕger, *m.* guide-post.
Wegzerren, vĕk'tserren, *vt.* to tear or drag away.
Wegziehen, vĕk'tsī-en (-zog, -gezogen), *vt.* to pull or draw away.
Wegzug, vĕk'tsuk, *m. pl.* -züge, departure, starting, setting; passage, migration.
Weh, vā, **Wehe,** vā'-e, *n.* woe, pang, anguish, grief; curse: *Interj.* woe.
Wehe, vā'-e, *f.* throe, labor, anguish of travail; -ruf, -ryf, *m.* lamentation, moan, groan.
Wehen, vā'en, *vi.* to blow; to float.
Wehklage, vā'kläge, *f.* lamentation.
Wehklagen, vā'klägen, *vi.* to lament.
Wehmuth, vā'myt, *f.* melancholy, sadness. **Wehmüthig,** vā'mühtich, *a.* melancholy, sad, sorrowful, woful, doleful; -keit, -kāĕt, *f.* wofulness, dolefulness.
Wehmutter, vā'mytter, *f. pl.* -mütter, midwife.
Wehr, vär, **Wehre,** vā're, *f.* defence, resistance; weapon.
Wehr, vär, *n. pl.* -e, wear, weir, dam, dike; bulwark, defence.

Weh 594 **Wei**

Wehren, vā'ren, *vt.* to defend, resist; to hinder, restrain, check, stop, prohibit, prevent.
Wehrgehäng, Wehrgehenk, vār'gehęng, vār'gehęnk, *n.* sword-belt.
Wehrhaft, vār'haft, *a.* capable of bearing arms, able to carry arms; — machen, to arm; ſigkeit, -ichkäet, *f.* capability of bearing arms.
Wehrlos, vār'lōs, *a.* defenceless, unarmed; — machen, to disarm; ſigkeit, -käet, *f.* want of defence, inoffensiveness.
Wehrstand, vār'zhtant, *m.* military (order).
Wehrwolf, vār'volf, *m. pl.* -wölfe, were-wolf.
Wehtage, vā'tāge, *s. pl.* days of sorrow.
Weib, vēīp, *n. pl.* -er, wife; woman.
Weibchen, vēīp'chen, *n.* little woman; little wife; woman; female. **Weiberarbeit,** vēī'berarbäet, *f.* woman's work. **Weiberart,** -art, *f.* manner, custom, habit of, way with women. **Weiberfeind,** -fäent, *m.* misogynist, woman-hater. **Weiberhaft,** -haft, *a.* womanlike, womanish, feminine. **Weiberhemde,** -hęmde, *n.* chemise. **Weiberherrschaft,** -berhērrshaft, *f.* gynarchy, government by a woman, petticoat government. **Weiberlist,** -lizht, *f.* woman's craft or cunning or trick. **Weibername,** -näme, *m.* woman's name. **Weiberstimme,** -zhtimme, *f.* female voice; soprano, treble. **Altweiberſommer,** -sommer, *m.* Indian summer. **Weibertracht,** -tracht, *f.* woman's dress. **Weibertreue,** -trēūe, *f.* woman's fidelity or devotion. **Weiberwolf,** -folk, *n.* women, females.
Weibiſch, vēīb'ish, *a.* effeminate, womanish, unmanly. **Weiblich,** -lich, *a.* female, feminine, delicate; -keit, -käet, *f.* womanhood, womanlike delicacy, softness.
Weibsbild, vēībs'bīlt, *n. pl.* -er, female.
Weibsleute, vēīps'lēūte, *f. pl.* women, females.
Weich, vēīch, *a.* weak, soft, tender.
Weichbild, vēīch'bīlt, *n.* precinct.
Weiche, vēīch'e, *f.* softness, weakness; side, groin.
Weicheisen, vēīch'ēīsen, *n.* wrought iron.

Weichen, vēī'chen (w ch. gewichen), *vi.* to yield, to give way; — von, to abandon, forsake.
Weichheit, vēīch'häet, *f.* softness; weakness.
Weichherzig, vēīch'hērtsich, *a.* soft-hearted, gentle, meek; -keit, -käet, *f.* tender-heartedness.
Weichlich, vēīch'lich, *a.* tender, delicate, effeminate; -keit, -käet, *f.* tenderness, delicateness, effeminacy.
Weichling, vēīch'ling, *m.* effeminate, unmanly fellow.
Weichſchiene, vēīch'shīne, *f.* siding-rail, switch.
Weichenwärter, vēīch'envērter, *m.* switchman, switcher, pointsman.
Weichthier, vēīch'tīr, *n.* mollusk.
Weide, vēī'de, *f.* willow.
Weide, vēī'de, *f.* pasture, pasturage.
Weiden, vēī'den, *vt.* to pasture, feed; to delight; *vi.* to feed, graze, pasture.
Weiden, vēī'den, *a.* of willow or osier; -baum, -bāūm. *m. pl.* -bäume, willow-tree. **Weidenkorb,** -korp, *m. pl.* -körbe, willow-basket. **Weidenruthe,** -rute, *f.* willow-twig.
Weidlich, vēīt'lich, *a. av.* brave, lively, lusty; in a high degree, soundly.
Weife, vēī'fe, *f.* reel. **Weifen,** *vt.* to reel : *s. n.* reeling.
Weigern, vēī'gern, *vt.* to deny, refuse, decline. **Weigerung,** -ung, *f.* refusal, denial.
Weihe, vēī'e, *m. pl.* -en, kite; hen-driver.
Weihe, vēī'e, *f.* consecration, inauguration; ordination.
Weihen, vēī'en, *vt.* to consecrate, inaugurate, ordain; devote; dedicate.
Weiher, vēī'er, *m.* fish-pond.
Weihgeschenk, vēī'geshenk, *n.* offering.
Weihnacht, vēī'nacht, *f.* Christmas.
Weihnachtsabend, vēī'nachtsäbent, *m.* Christmas-eve.
Weihnachtsbaum, vēī'nachtsbāūm, *m. pl.* -bäume, Christmas-tree.
Weihnachtsfest, vēī'nachtsfezht, *n. pl.* -e, Christmas-festival or feast, Christmas-day.
Weihnachtsgabe, vēī'nachtsgābe, *f.* **Weihnachtsgeschenk,** -geshenk, *n.* Christmas-gift.
Weihrauch, vēī'rāūch, *m.* incense, frankincense; -faß, -fass, *n. pl.* -fäſſer, censer.

Weihung, vēī'ŭng, *f.* dedication.
Weihwasser, vēī'vasser, *n.* holy *or* consecrated water.
Weil, vēīl, *Cj.* because: while.
Weiland, vēī'lant, *av.* formerly, of old, once, late, deceased: ex —.
Weile, vēī'le, *f.* while, time; lange —, ennui, tedium, irksomeness: eine —, for a while; gut Ding will Weile haben, nothing good is done in a hurry; Eile mit Weile, slow and sure.
Weilen, vēī'len, *vi.* to tarry; stop, stay.
Weiler, vēī'ler, *m.* hamlet.
Wein, vaēn, *m.* wine; -artig, -artig, *a.* vinous. **Weinbau**, vaēn'boŭ, *m.* cultivation of vine. **Wein'bauer**, -boŭer, *m.* wine-grower. **Wein'beere**, -bā-re, *f.* grape. **Wein'berg**, -berk, *m. pl.* -e. vineyard. **Wein'blatt**, -blatt, *n. pl.* -blätter, vine-leaf.
Weinblüthe, vaēn'blühte, *f.* flower *or* blossom of the vine.
Weinen, vaē'nen, *vi.* to weep. **Weinerlich**, vaēn'erlig, *a.* whining, weeping.
Weinessig, vaēn'essig, *m.* wine-vinegar. **Wein'faß**, -fass, *n. pl.* -fässer, wine-cask, wine-barrel. **Wein'flasche**, -flashe, *f.* wine-bottle. **Wein'garten**, -garten, *m.* vineyard. **Wein'gärtner**, -gērtner, *m.* vine-dresser. **Wein'gegend**, -gāgent, *f.* wine-country, wine-growing country. **Wein'geist**, -gāezht, *m.* spirit of wine, alcohol. **Weingeschäft**, vaēn'gesheft, *n.* wine business. **Wein'glas**, -glās, *n. pl.* -gläser, wine-glass. **Wein'handel**, -handel, *m.* wine-trade. **Wein'händler**, -hendler, *m.* dealer in wine, wine-merchant. **Wein'haus**, -hoŭs, *n. pl.* -häuser, wine-house. **Wein'hefe**, -hefe, *f.* dregs *or* lees of wine. **Weinicht**, vaēn'igt, *a.* winy. **Wei'nig**, *a.* vinous. **Wein'jahr**, -yār, *n.* wine-year. **Wein'keller**, -keller. *m.* (wine) vaults, wine-cellar. **Wein'kelter**, -kelter, *f.* wine-press. **Wein'kenner**, -kenner, *m.* connoisseur *or* judge of wines. **Wein'lager**, -lāger, *n.* stock of wine. **Wein'land**, -lant, *n. pl.* -länder, wine-country. **Wein'laub**, -loŭp, *n.* vine-leaf; foliage of the vine. **Wein'lese**, -lāse, *f.* vintage. **Wein'leser**, *m.* vintager.
Weinlied, vaēn'līd, *n. pl.* -er, drinking-song. **Wein'most**, -mozht, *m.* must **Wein'presse**, -presse, *f.* wine-press. **Wein'ranke**, -ranke, *f.* wine-branch, tendril. **Wein'rausch**, -roŭsh, *m. pl.* -räusche, intoxication from wine. **Wein'rebe**, -rā-be, *f.* vine-(shoot).
Weinsauer, vaēn'soŭr, *a.* sour as wine; winy, vinous. **Wein'säure**, -seŭre, *f.* acidity of wine. **Wein'säufer**, -seŭfer, *m.* wine-bibber. **Wein'schenke**, -shenke, *f.* wine-tavern, wine-house. **Wein'stein**, -zhtaēn, *m.* tartar: -äther, -āter, tartaric ether. **Wein'steingeist**, -gāezht, *m.* spirit of tartar. **Wein'steinsalz**, -salts, *n.* salt of tartar. **Wein'steinsauer**, -soŭer, *a.* tartarous, tartaric. — **Salz**, *n.* tartrate. **Wein'steinsäure**, -seŭre, *f.* tartaric acid. **Wein'stock**, -zhtock, *m.* vine. **Wein'traube**, -troŭbe, *f.* bunch *or* cluster of grapes. **Wein'trester**, -treshter, *s. pl.* husks *or* skins of grapes. **Wein'trinker**, -trinker, *m.* wine-drinker; wine-bibber. **Wein(ver)fälscher**, vaēn'felsher, *m.* adulterator of wine.
Weise, vēī'se, *a. av.* wise, ly, sage.
Weiser, vēī'ser, *m.* wise man.
Weise, vēī'se, *f.* manner, mode, fashion; guise, wise.
Weisen, vēī'sen (wies, gewiesen), *vt.* to point out, show; zu Recht —, to put to rights; to reprimand.
Weiser, vēīs'er, *m.* guide; hand (of a watch, etc.).
Weisel, vēī'sel, *f.* queen-bee.
Weisheit, vēīs'hāēt, *f.* wisdom.
Weislich, vēīs'lig, *av.* wisely.
Weismachen, vēīs'magen, *vt.* to make believe, to impose on, to mislead by a false pretense, delude.
Weiß, vēīs, *a.* white.
Weissagen, vēīs'sāgen, *vt.* to foretell, prophesy, predict. **Weis'sager**, *m.* prophet, foreteller; -in, *f.* prophetess. **Weis'sagung**, -ŭng, *f.* prophecy foretelling, prediction.
Weißbad, vēīs'bād, *n.* white-bath (for dyeing).
Weißbier, vēīs'bīr, *n.* white beer.
Weißblech, vēīs'blēg, white iron, tinplate.
Weißbrod, vēīs'brōt, *n.* wheat bread, white bread.
Weißbuche, vēīs'bŭge, *f.* hornbeam, yoke-elm; -n, *a.* hornbeam, hawthorn.

Weiße, vēl'se, *f.* whiteness. **Weißen**, vēl'sen, *vt.* to whiten, whitewash.
Weißerz, vēls'ärts, *n.* sparry iron-ore; white copper-ore.
Weißfisch, vēls'fish, *m.* white-fish, bleak.
Weißgärber, vēls'gėrbėr, *m.* tawer; -ei, -ēī', *f.* tawery.
Weißgrau, vēls'grāū, *a.* light gray, hoary, whitish gray.
Weißkraut, vēls'krout, *n.* white cabbage.
Weißlich, vēls'lich, *a.* whitish. **Weißling**, -ling, *m.* whiting.
Weißpappel, vēls'pappl, *f.* white poplar.
Weißstein, vēls'zhtaēn, *m.* white-stone.
Weißtanne, vēls'tanne, *f.* white pine.
Weißzeug, vēls'tseūk, *m.* linen.
Weisung, vēls'ẏng, *f.* order, direction.
Weit, vēit, *a. av.* distant, far; wide, widely, broad; von weitem, from afar; bei weitem, by far; weiter, farther, further; weitest, farthest, furthest.
Weite, vēi'te, *f. or n.* width; distance; largeness, amplitude; lichte Weite, span (Arch.).
Weiten, vēi'ten, *vt. i.* to widen, expand, extend.
Weiterung, vēit'ẏrung, *f.* procrastination.
Weithin, vēit'hīn, *av.* to a great distance. **Weitläufig**, vēit'lāūfich, *a.* large, vast; distant; detailed, prolix, at full, at full length; *skeit,* -käet, *f.* vast extent; diffusiveness, prolixity. **Weitschweifig**, -shäēfich, *a.* prolix, diffuse; *skeit,* -käet, *f.* prolixity. **Weitsichtig**, -sichtich, *a.* far-sighted.
Weizen, vāēts'en, *m.* wheat; -brod, -bröt, *n.* wheat bread. **Weizenkorn**, -korn, *n. pl.* -förner, grain of wheat.
Welch, velch, *et, -t, -es, a. pron.* who, which. **Welcherlei**, -erlāē, *a.* of what kind.
Welk, vēlk, *a.* withered, faded, flagging, languid; *sen, vt.* to wither, fade, decay, flag, languish.
Welle, vēl'le, *f.* wave, billow; (Mech.) roller; aufrechte —, spindle; **unförmig**, -förmich, *a.* undulatory, waving, undulating. **Wellenreich,** -rēich, *n.* realm of the sea.
Weller, vēl'ler, *w.* cylinder.

Wellermauer, vēl'lermōu-er, **Wellerwand**, -vant, *f.* loam-wall, mud-wall. **Wellern**, vēl'lern, *vt.* to make mud-walls.
Welt, vēlt, *f.* world, universe; earth; -all, -all, *n.* universe. **Weltalter**, -alter, *n.* age (of the world), period. **Weltbekannt**, -bekannt, *a.* notorious. **Weltberühmt**, -berühmt, *a.* far-famed, renowned. **Weltbürger**, -bürger, *m.* cosmopolite; *slich,* -lich, *a.* cosmopolitical. **Weltbürgersinn**, -sinn, *m.* cosmopolitism. **Weltgebäude**, -gebäūde, *n.* system or fabric of the world. **Weltgegend**, -gägent, *f.* region, quarter of the world.
Weltgeist, vēlt'gāēzht, *m.* spirit of the universe, creative spirit; *licher, m.* secular priest. **Weltgericht**, vēlt'gericht, *n.* last judgment. **Weltgeschichte**, -geshichte, *f.* universal history. **Welthandel**, -handel, *m.* commerce. **Weltheiland**, -hāē-lant, *m.* Saviour. **Weltkenntniß**, -kenntniss, *f.* knowledge of the world. **Weltkind**, -kint, *n. pl. er,* worldling. **Weltklug**, -klūk, *a.* prudent; *sheit,* -hāēt, *f.* worldly wisdom. **Weltkörper**, vēlt'körper, *m.* heavenly body. **Weltkugel**, -kūgel, *f.* globe. **Weltkunde**, -kunde, *f.* cosmology. **Weltkundig**, -kundich, *a.* notorious; skilled in history. **Weltlauf**, -lāūf, *m.* course or way of the world. **Weltlich**, -lich, *a.* worldly, secular; *skeit,* -käet, *f.* worldliness, worldly-mindedness; secularity. **Weltliebe**, -līb̄e, *f.* love of the world. **Weltling**, -ling, *m.* worldling. **Weltmann**, -mann, *m.* man of the world. **Weltmeer**, -mär, *n.* ocean, main (sea). **Weltpriester**, -prīshter, *m.* secular priest. **Weltsinn**, -sinn, *m.* worldly-mindedness, worldliness. **Welttheil**, -tāēl, *n.* part of the world, continent. **Weltweiser**, -vēīser, *m.* philosopher. **Weltweisheit**, -vēīshāēt, *f.* philosophy.
Wendeeisen, ven'de-āēsen, *n.* tap-iron. **Wendekreis**, -krāēs, *m.* tropic.
Wendeltreppe, ven'deltreppe, *f.* winding-stairs.
Wenden, ven'den (wandte, gewandt), *vt.* to turn, direct; sich —, *tr* turn, change; sich — an, to apply to, to address one's self to; durch or gegen

den Wind —, or bei dem Winde —, to tack.
Wendehaufe, ven'dĕhtufe, f. winder.
Wendung, vend'ung, f. turn, turning.
Wenig, vā'nich, a. ar. little, few; ser, a. less, lesser, fewer. **Wenigst,** vā'nikzht. a. least, fewest; wenigstens, zum Wenigsten, at least. **Wenigkeit,** -kǟet, f. smallness, trifle; meine —, my humble self.
Wenn, ven, cj. when; if; — nicht, if not, unless; — auch, although; — je, — immer, whenever.
Wer, vār, pron. who; — auch, whoever.
Werben, vĕr'ben (warb, geworben), vt. to sue for, petition; to court, woo; to recruit. **Werber,** m. recruiting-officer, recruiter; suitor, wooer.
Werbung, vĕrb'ung, f. recruiting, levy, enlistment; wooing, courting.
Werden, vĕr'den (warb, wurde, geworben), to become, grow, turn, get, to be, happen, come to pass; to come into existence.
Werder, vĕr'der, m. small island, holm.
Werfen, vĕr'fen (warf, geworfen), vt. to cast, throw, fling; to bring forth, bear; sich —, to warp (of wood).
Werft, vĕrft, n. wharf.
Werft, vĕrft, m. n. **Werfte,** vĕrf'te, f. warp, weft.
Werg, vĕrk, n. tow, hards; sleinwand, -laenvant, f. tow-linen.
Werk, vĕrk, n. work, deed, production; zu — geben mit, to deal with; seltag, -eltǟk, n. working-day.
Werkmeister, vĕrk'mǟzhter, m. foreman, superintendent. **Werkfat,** -satz, m. skeleton (Carpent.).
Werkstatt, vĕrk'zhtatt, f. pl. -stätte. **Werkstätte,** -zhtette, f. workshop. **Werkstein,** -zhtēn, m. **Werkstück,** -zhtück, n. square-stone. **Werktag,** -tǟk, m. working day. **Werkzeug,** vĕrk'tsěük, n. pl. -e, tool, instrument.
Wermuth, vǟr'mut, m. wormwood.
Werptrosse, vĕrp'trosse, n. warp, warping hawser (Mar.).
Werth, vǟrt, a. worth, valuable; dear, precious; -los, a. worthless.
Werthschätzen, vĕrt'shĕtsen, vt. to esteem highly, to regard. **Werthschätzung,** -ung, f. estimation, esteem.

Wesen, vā'sen, n. being, existence, substance, essence, nature.
Wesenlos, vā'senlōs, a. unsubstantial.
Wesentlich, vā'sentlich, a. essential, substantial, real; -keit, -kǟet, f. essentiality, essence, substance.
Wespe, vĕs'pe, f. wasp; -nest, vĕs'pennest, n. wasp's nest.
Wespenstich, vĕs'penzhtich, m. wasp-bite.
Wessen, ves'sen, **Wes,** vess, pn. whose, of whom, of which; -halb, -halp, **Weswegen,** -vāgen, av. wherefore, why, on what account.
West, vĕzht, **Westen,** m. west; west wind.
Weste, vĕzh'te, f. vest, waistcoat; -ntasche, -tashe, f. vest-pocket.
Westgegend, vĕzht'gāgent, f. **Westland,** -lant, n. pl. -länder, western country. **Westlich,** -lich, a. western, westerly; **Westnordwest,** west-north-west; **Westsüdwest,** west-southwest; **Westsüdwestwind,** west-south-west wind, west-southwester. **Westwärts,** vĕst'vĕrts, av. westward, westwardly. **Westwind,** vĕst'vint, m. west wind.
Wett, vet, a. av. even, equal; — machen, to quit scores.
Wette, vet'te, f. bet, wager; um die — thun, to vie in.
Wetteifer, vett'ēifer, m. emulation; -n, vt. to emulate, vie, contend.
Wetten, vet'ten, vt. to bet, to lay a bet or wager.
Wetter, vĕt'ter, n. weather; thunderstorm, tempest; air, current of air; -ableiter, -ablĕster, m. lightning-rod, conductor. **Wetterbeobachtung,** -bĕōbachtung, f. meteorological observation. **Wetterdach,** -dach. n. pl. -dächer, penthouse. **Wetterfahne,** -fǟne, f. **Wetterhahn,** -hän, m. pl. -hähne, vane, weather-vane, weather-cock. **Wetterglas,** -glǟs, n. pl. -gläser, weather-glass, barometer, thermometer. **Wetterlaunisch,** launish, a. peevish, capricious. **Wetterleuchten,** -lěüchten, n. heat-lightning. **Wetterlösung,** -lösung, f. ventilation. **Wettern,** vĕt'tĕrn, vi. to thunder. **Wetterprophet,** -profāt, m. weather-spy. **Wetterrad,** -rät, n. pl. -räder, ventilating-fanner. **Wetterstrahl,** -shtrǟl, m. -es, pl. -en, flash of lightning. **Wetterwendisch,**

-vendish, *a.* changeable, fickle, inconstant, peevish. **Wetterwolke**, -wolke, *f.* thunder-cloud.

Wettrennen, vett'rennen, *n.* race: — zu Fuß, foot-race: — zu Pferd, horse-race; — in Booten, boat-race.

Wettrenner, *m.* racer; race-horse.

Wettstreit, -zhtrīt, *m.* emulation, contention, contest, rivalry.

Wetzen, vets'en, *vt.* to whet. **Wetzschiefer**, -shīfer, *m.* whetslate. **Wetzstein**, -zhtēn, *m.* whetstone.

Wichse, vix'e, *f.* blacking; waxing. **Wichsen**, vix'en, *vt.* to blacken; to wax.

Wicht, vicht, *m.* wight, fellow.

Wichtig, vich'tig, *a.* weighty, important; **-keit**, -kāēt, *f.* importance.

Wicke, vick'e, *f.* vetch.

Wickel, vick'el, *m.* roller.

Wickelmaschine, vick'elmashīne, *f.* winding machine, 'lap machine; spreader.

Wickelkind, vickl'kīnt, *n. pl.* **-er**, child in swaddling-cloth.

Wickeln, vick'eln, *vt.* to roll, wind up.

Wickelwalze, vick'elvaltse, *f.* roller.

Widder, vid'der, *m.* ram; aries; hydraulischer —, hydraulic ram.

Wider, vī'der, *pr.* against, contrary or in opposition to: **-bellen**, -bellen, *vt.* to contradict. **Widerbeller**, vī'derbeller, *m.* wrangler.

Widerchrist, vī'derkrizht, *m.* antichrist: **-lich**, -lich, *a.* antichristian.

Widerdruck, vī'derdruck, *m.* second form; reiteration; reaction; **-bogen**, -bōgen, *m.* tympan-sheet.

Widerfahren, viderfā'ren (widerfuhr, widerfahren), *vt.* to happen, befall, occur.

Widerhaken, vī'derhāken, *m.* barb, beard.

Widerhalt, vī'derhalt, *m.* hold, support, resistance.

Widerhalten, vī'derhalten (widerhielt, widergehalten), *vt.* to hold out, resist.

Widerlage, vī'derlāge, *f.* counterfort, buttress.

Widerlager, vī'derlāger, *n.* springing-stone.

Widerlegbar, viderlāg'bār, **Widerleglich**, -lich, *a.* confutable, refutable, disprovable.

Widerlegen, vīde·lā'gen, *vt.* to disprove, confute refute. **Widerlegung**, -ung, *f.* confutation, refutation.

Widerlich, vī'derlich, *a.* disgusting, offensive; **-keit**, -kāēt, *f.* offensiveness.

Widern, vī'dern, *vt.* to disgust.

Widernatürlich, vī'dernatürlich, *a.* unnatural, preternatural, contrary to nature.

Widerpart, vī'derpart, *m.* opponent; opposition.

Widerraten, viderrāt'en (-rieth, -rathen), *vt.* to dissuade, tc represent as unfit.

Widerrechtlich, vī'derrěchtlich, *a.* illegal, unlawful; **-keit**, -kāēt, *f.* unlawfulness, illegality.

Widerrede, vī'derrāde, *f.* contradiction, opposition.

Widerreissen, vī'derrizht, *m.* withers.

Widerruf, vī'derruf, *m. pl.* **-e**, recall, repeal, recantation, retraction.

Widerrufen, viderru'fen, *vt.* to recall, retract, unsay, repeal. **Widerruflich**, -lich, *a.* repealable, reversible, revocable.

Widersacher, vī'dersacher, *m.* **-in**, *f.* adversary.

Widerschein, vī'dershēin, *m.* reflexion, reverberation of light.

Widersetzen, vidersets'en, *vr.* sich —, to oppose, resist.

Widersetzlich, vidersets'lich, *a.* refractory; **-keit**, -kāēt, *f.* refractoriness. **Widersetzung**, -ung, *f.* resistance, opposition.

Widersinnig, vī'dersinnich, *a.* nonsensical, absurd; **-keit**, -kāēt, *f.* non sensicalness, absurdity.

Widerspenstig, vī'derzhpenstich, *a.* resistive, refractory; **-keit**, -kāēt, *f.* restiveness, refractoriness.

Widerspiel, vī'derzhpīl, *n.* contrary, reverse.

Widersprechen, viderzhprěch'en (widersprach, widersprochen), *vt.* to contradict, gainsay; **-d**, *a.* contradictory.

Widerspruch, vī'derzhpruch, *m. pl.* Widersprüche, contradiction, inconsistency.

Widerstand, vī'derzhtant, *m.* resistance, opposition.

Widerstehen, viderzhtā'en (widerstand, widerstanden), *vt.* to resist, oppose, withstand.

Widerstreben, viderzhtrā'ben, *vt.* tc strive or struggle against, repugn

resist; *s. n.* repugnancy, resistance.
Widerstreit, vī'derzhtrīt, *m.* conflict; antagonism, contradiction; **-en,** vīderzhtrī'ten, *vt.* to conflict, contend. **Widerstreitend,** *a.* conflicting; contradictory.
Widerstrom, vī'derzhtrōm, *m.* counter-current.
Widerwärtig, vī'dervertig, *a.* disgusting, adverse, loathsome, disagreeable; **-keit, -kket,** *f.* adversity, reverse; unpleasantness.
Widerwille, vī'derville, *m.* aversion, disgust, antipathy, reluctance.
Widerwillig, vī'dervillich, *a.* reluctant, unwilling, backward.
Widmen, vid'men, *vt.* to devote; dedicate, consecrate. **Widmung, -ung,** *f.* devotion; dedication.
Widrig, vid'rich, *a.* averse, contrary; nauseous, disgusting; **-keit, -kket,** *f.* adversity.
Widrigenfalls, vī'drigenfalls, *a.* else, otherwise, in the other case.
Wie, vī, *pr.* how, as, when.
Wiede, vī'de, *f.* willow, osier, withy.
Wiedehopf, vī'dehopf, *m. pl.* **-e,** lapwing, pewit, green plover, hoopoo.
Wieder, vī'der, *av.* back, again, anew, afresh.
Wiederabdruck, viderap'druck, *m. pl.* **-abdrücke,** re-impression.
Wiederanstellen, vī'deranzhtellen, *vt.* to re-appoint.
Wiederaufbauen, viderkūf'bōyen, *vt.* to rebuild.
Wiederbekommen, vī'derbekommen (-bekam, -bekommen), *vt.* to recover, get again.
Wiederbeleben, vī'derbelēben, *vt.* to revive, revivify. **Wiederbelebung, -ung,** *f.* revivification.
Wiederbringen, vī'derbringen (-wiederbringen, wiedergebracht), *vt.* to bring back, restore, retrieve.
Wiederbringlich, vī'derbring'lich, *a.* retrievable. **Wiederbringung, -ung,** *f.* restoration.
Wiedereinsetzen, videržen'setsen, *vt.* to reinstate, replace, restore, re-establish.
Wiedererlangen, vī'dererlangen, *vt.* to recover. **Wiedererlangung, -ung,** *f.* recovery.
Wiedererobern, vī'dererōbern, *vt.* to reconquer.

Wiedererstatten, vī'derērzhtatten, *vt.* to restore, return, reimburse, repay. **Wiedererstattung, -ung,** *f.* return, restitution, repayment.
Wiederfinden, vī'derfinden, *vt.* to find again.
Wiedergeben, vī'dergäben (-gab, -gegeben), *vt.* to return, give back, render.
Wiedergeboren, vī'dergebören, *a.* regenerate(d). **Wiedergeburt, -burt,** *f.* regeneration.
Wiedergenesung, vī'dergenäsung, *f.* recovery.
Wiederhall, vī'derhall, *m.* echo; **-en,** *vi.* to re-echo.
Wiederherstellen, viderhār'zhtellen, *vt.* to restore, recover; redintegrate, re-establish. **Wiederherstellung, -ung,** *f.* restoration, restitution; recovery.
Wiederholen, viderhō'len, *vt.* to repeat, reiterate. **Wiederholung, -ung,** *f.* repetition, reiteration.
Wiederkäuen, vī'derkäuen *vt.* to ruminate.
Wiederkauf, vī'derkūf, *m. pl.* **-käufe,** redemption, repurchase; **-en,** *vi.* to repurchase, redeem. **Wiederkäuflich, -käuflich,** *a.* redeemable.
Wiederkehr, vī'derkār, *f.* return, recurrence; **-en,** *vi.* to return, come back.
Wiederklang, vī'derklang, *m.* echo.
Wiederklingen, vī'derklingen, *vi.* to re-echo.
Wiederkommen, vī'derkommen (-kam, -gekommen), *vi.* to come again, return. **Wiederkunft, -kunft,** *f.* return.
Wiederöffnen, vīderöff'nen, *vt.* to re-open.
Wiederschein, vī'dershaēn, *m.* reflex, reflected light.
Wiedersehen, vī'dersäen (-sah, -gesehen), *vt.* to see *or* meet again; *s. n.* seeing, meeting again.
Wiedertäufe, vī'dertäufe, *f.* rebaptism, rebaptization; **-en,** *vt.* to rebaptize. **Wiedertäufer, -täufer,** *m.* rebaptizer; anabaptist.
Wiedertönen, vī'dertōnen, *vt. i.* to resound.
Wiederum, vī'derum, *av.* again, once more, repeatedly.
Wiedervergelten, vī'derfergelten, *vt.* to requite, retaliate, remunerate recompense, reward, repay.

Wiederbergeltung, vī'derfĕrgĕltŭng, f. requital, retaliation, retribution, recompense, reward.
Wiederverkaufen, vī'derfĕrkäūfen, vt. to resell, retail.
Wiederversöhnen, vī'derfĕrsöhnen, vt. to reconcile, conciliate; propitiate.
Wiege, vī'ge, f. cradle.
Wiegemesser, vī'gemĕsser, n. chopping knife.
Wiegen, vī'gen, vt. to rock, cradle; fich —, to lull one's self with.
Wiegen, vī'gen (wog, gewogen), vi. t. to weigh; vt. wiegte, gewiegt.
Wiegenkind, vī'genkint, n. baby.
Wiegenlied, vī'genlīd, n. pl. -er, lullaby.
Wiehern, vī'hern, vi. to neigh, whinny; wieherndes Gelächter, horselaugh.
Wief, vīk. n. pl. -e, inlet, bay.
Wiefe, vī'ke, f. lint.
Wiese, vīs'e, f. meadow.
Wiesel, vī'sel, n. weasel.
Wiesenbau, vī'senbōw, m. cultivation of meadows. **Wiesengrund,** -grŭnt, m. pl. -gründe. **Wiesenland,** -lant, n. pl. -länder, meadow.
Wiesewachs, vī'sewaks, **Wieswachs,** -vŭks, m. meadows.
Wieviel, vī'fīlzht, **Wievielt,** a. what or which number.
Wiewohl, vivöl'. Cj. although, though.
Wild, vilt, a. wild, savage; s. n. game, venison; -brät, -brēt, n. deer, game, venison. **Wildbraten,** -brāten, m. roast venison. **Wildbieb,** -dīb, m. poacher. **Wilber,** m. savage. **Wild's fang,** -faŋg, m. pl. -fänge. mad cap. **Wildfremd,** -frĕmt, a. quite strange. **Wildgeschmack,** -geshmack, m. flavor of game. **Wildheit,** -hēit, f. wildness, savageness. **Wildnis,** vilt'nis, f. wilderness, savageness. **Wildpret,** -prēt, = Wildbrät.
Wildschütz, vilt'shüts, m. pl. Wildschützen, poacher.
Willemit, villemīt', m. Willemite.
Wille(n), vil'len, m. will; um — willen, for the sake of, on account of; um meinetwillen, for my sake; um Gotteswillen, for God's sake; Willens sein, to intend, purpose, to have a mind. **Willenlos,** vil'lenlös, a. having no will of one's own.
Willfahren, villfār'en, vi. to comply with. **Willfährig,** vill'fārig, a. com-

pliant, compliable; -keit, -kāēt, f. compliance, readiness. **Willfahrung,** -ŭng, f. compliance.
Willig, vil'lich, a. willing; -en, vi. to agree or consent to. **Willigkeit,** -kāēt, f. willingness.
Willkomm, vill'komm, n. -en, m. welcome, salutation.
Willkommen, villkom'men, a. welcome.
Willkür, vill'kühr, f. arbitrariness, discretion; -lich, -lich, a. arbitrary, discretional; -keit, -kāēt, f. arbitrariness.
Wimmeln, vim'meln, vi. to swarm, teem, crowd.
Wimmern, vim'mern, vi. to whimper, moan, whine, groan.
Wimpel, vim'pel, f. or m. pennon, pendant.
Wimper, vim'per, f. eye-lash. **Wimpern,** vi. to wink, blink, twinkle.
Wind, vint, m. pl. -e, wind, breeze, air; scent, hint; flatulence, windiness; — bekommen, to get scent of; — machen, to vapor, brag, boast; stehender —, settled wind; knapper, schiefer —, scant, sharp wind; starker —, high wind; offener —, fair wind; halber —, large wind; -anker, m. lower anchor. **Windbeutel,** -bēūtel, m. braggart, humbug; -ei, -ēī', f. humbug, boasting. **Windbüchse,** -büxe, f. air-gun, windgun.
Winde, vin'de, f. windlass, pulley.
Winde, vin'de, f. bindweed; morning glory.
Windei, vind'āē, n. pl. -er, wind-egg.
Windel, vin'del, f. swaddling clothes; -kind, -kīnt, n. pl. -er, child in swaddling clothes.
Winden, vin'den (wand, gewunden), vt. to wind, wring, wrest, twist.
Windfahne, vint'fāne, f. vane, weather-cock. **Windfang,** -faŋg, m. ventilator. **Windhund,** -hŭnt, m. greyhound.
Windig, vind'ich, a. windy.
Windklappe, vint'klappe, f. valve.
Windlicht, vint'licht, n. torch.
Windmesser, vint'mĕsser, m. windgange, anemometer.
Windmühle, vint'mühle, f. wind-mill.
Windofen, vint'ōfen, m. wind-furnace.
Windpocken, vint'pocken, s. pl. chicken-pox.

Windbrad, vint'răt, *n. pl.* -räber, ventilator.
Windrose, vint'rōse, *f.* (compass-)card; anemone (Bot.).
Windruthe, vint'ryte, *f.* whip; windarm.
Windsbraut, vints'brŏyt, *f. pl.* -bräute, hurricane, whirlwind, squall; tornado.
Windschaden, vint'shäden, *m.* damage done by the wind.
Windschief, vint'shīf, *a.* warped.
Windsegel, vint'sāgl, *n.* wind-sail.
Windseite, vint'sëite, *f.* weather-side.
Windspiel, vint'zhpīl, *n.* greyhound.
Windstill, vint'zhtīll, *a.* calm; -e, *f.* calm. **Windstoß**, -zhtoss, *m. pl.* -stöße, blast, gust, puff of wind.
Windstrich, vint'zhtrich, *m.* rhumb point, current of the wind.
Windung, vin'dyng, *f.* winding, turning; worm, spire, thread (of a screw).
Windwehe, vint'vä-e, *f.* drift of snow.
Windweiser, vint'vēiser, **Windzeiger**, vint'tsāger, *m.* anemo-scope, vane, fane.
Windwirbel, vint'vīrbl, *m.* whirlwind.
Windzug, vint'tsyg, *m. pl.* **Windzüge**, draught or current of air; ventiduct.
Wink, vink, *m.* wink; nod, hint.
Winkel, vīnk'l, *m.* angle; corner; nook.
Winkeladvokat, vīnkl'advokät, *m.* -en, *pl.* -en, pettifogger.
Winkelehe, vīnkl'ä-e, *f.* clandestine or hedge-marriage.
Winkeleisen, vīnkl'ēisen, *n.* iron rule, square.
Winkelhaken, vīnkl'häken, *m.* iron rule, (Print.) stick.
Winkelig, vin'kelig, *a.* angular, cornered.
Winkelmaß, vīnkl'mäs, *n.* square.
Winkelmesser, vīnkl'messer, *m.* protractor.
Winkelrecht, vīnkl'recht, *a.* rectangular, right-angled, perpendicular.
Winkelzug, vīnkl'tsyg, *m. pl.* -züge, trick, evasion, shift.
Winken, vink'en, *vi.* to wink, beckon.
Winseln, vin'seln, *vi.* to moan, whimper, whine.
Winter, vīn'ter, *m.* winter.
Winterammer, vīn'terammer, *f.* snow-bird. **Winterbeule**, -bölle, *f.* chilblain. **Winterdrossel**, -drossel, *f.* red-wing. **Wintergegend**, -gāgent, *f.* wintery region. **Winterhaft**, *a.* **Winterig**, vin'terich, **Winterlich**, -lich, *a.* wintery, as it winter, winter-hyemal. **Wintern**, vīn'tērn, *vi.* to grow winter; *vt.* to winter, to feed during the winter; *vi.* to winter, pass the winter. **Winterquartier**, -kvārrtīr, *n.* winterquarters. **Winterjaat**, -sāt, *f. pl.* -en, winter-crop. **Winterjeite**, -sēite, *f.* north side. **Winterung**, -yng, *f.* wintering. **Winterzeit**, -tsēit, *f.* winter-time, winter-season.
Winzer, vint'ser, *m.* -in, *f.* vintager; vine-dresser.
Winzig, vin'tsich, *a.* petty, little, diminutive.
Wipfel, vip'fel, *m.* top.
Wippe, vip'pe, *f.* swape, sweep, seesaw. **Wippen**, *vt.* to swing, to balance; to tip. **Wipper**, vip'per, *m.* clipper.
Wir, vīr, *pn.* we.
Wirbel, vīr'bl, *m.* whirl, twirl, top; crown; eddy, vortex; whirlpool; whirlwind; giddiness; roll, beat of drum.
Wirbelig, vīr'belich, *a.* whirled, whirling, vertical. **Wirbeln**, vīr'beln, *vi.* to whirl. **Wirbelwind**, -vīnt, *m.* whirl-wind.
Wirkeisen, virk'ēisen, *n.* (tawer's) paring-knife (farr.); searcher.
Wirken, vīr'ken, *vt.* to work, operate; effect, tell; to knead; pare.
Wirklich, vīrk'lich, *a.* actual, real, true; -keit, -kāet, *f.* reality, actuality; truth. **Wirksam**, -sam, *a.* efficacious, efficient, effective, powerful; active; -keit, -kāet, *f.* efficiency, efficaciousness, efficacy, activity.
Wirkstuhl, virk'zhtyl, *m. pl.* -ſtühle, loom.
Wirkung, vīrk'yng, *f.* working, effect, action; impression; kneading.
Wirkungskreis, vīr'kyngskräes, *m. pl.* -e, sphere of action or of activity.
Wirr, virr, *a.* confused, confuse, harebrained. **Wirren**, vīr'ren, *vt.* to entangle, confuse. **Wirrgarn**, -garn, *n.* entangled yarn. **Wirrtopf**, virr'kopf, *m. pl.* -köpfe, confused head. **Wirrseide**, vīr'sēide, *f.* refuse of silk. **Wirrstroh**, -zhtrō, *n.* short straw. **Wirrung**, -yng, *f.* confu-

sion, trouble. **Wirrwarr,** vĭrr′vărr, *m.* confusion, disturbance, trouble.
Wirtel, vĭr′tel, *m.* whirl.
Wirth, vĭrrt, *m. pl. -e,* husbandman; economist; host; landlord, innkeeper; ≈in, *f.* lady of the house; housekeeper; landlady, hostess.
Wirthbar, vĭrrt′bār, *a.* habitable; ≈keit, -kāĕt, *f.* hospitality.
Wirthlich, vĭrrt′lĭch, *a.* hospitable; frugal; ≈keit, -kāĕt, *f.* hospitality, frugality.
Wirthschaft, vĭrrt′shăft, *f.* house-keeping, economy, husbandry; household; public house, inn.
Wirthschaften, vĭrrt′shăften, *vt.* to manage, administer, economize; to keep house, to husband.
Wirthschafter, vĭrrt′shăfter, *m.* manager, steward; ≈in, *f.* housekeeper.
Wirthschaftlich, vĭrrt′shăftlĭch, *a. av.* economical, -cally; ≈keit, -kāĕt, *f.* economy, frugality, frugal management.
Wirthshaus, vĭrrts′hŏŭs, *n. pl.* -häuser, inn, tavern, public house.
Wirthsleute, vĭrrts′lāŭte, *s. pl.* hosts, landlord and landlady.
Wirthstisch, vĭrrts′tĭsh, *m.* **Wirthstafel,** vĭrrts′tāfl, *f.* ordinary *or* table d'hote.
Wisch, vĭsh, *m. pl. -e,* whisk, wisp; clout; trash, scrawl.
Wischen, vĭsh′en, *vt.* to wipe, rub; *vi.* to slip. **Wischer,** *m.* wiper; sponge; reprimand. **Wischkolben,** -kŏlben, *m.* sponge-head. **Wischlappen,** -lăppen, *m.* dish-cloth, dish-rag, duster.
Wismuth, vĭs′mŭt, *m.* bismuth.
Wispern, vĭzh′pern, *vt.* to whisper.
Wisbegier, vĭss′begīr, ≈de, -de, *f.* curiosity, inquisitiveness, desire of knowledge, wish to learn.
Wissen, vĭs′sen (wußte, gewußt. gevust) *et.* to know; zu wissen thun. *or* wissen lassen, to acquaint with; to send word, to inform; Dank —, to be thankful.
Wissenschaft, vĭs′senshaft, *f.* science; ≈lich, -lĭch, *a.* scientific.
Wissenswerth, vĭs′sensvărt, **Wissenswürdig,** -vürdĭch, *a.* worth knowing, remarkable.
Wissentlich, vĭs′sentlĭch, *a. av.* knowing; wilful, voluntary; knowingly, wittingly, by design.
Witherit, vĭt′erĭt, *n.* witherite.

Wittern, vĭt′tern, *vt. i.* to thunder; of to scent, smell.
Witterung, vĭt′terŭng, *f.* weather, scent.
Wittthum, vĭt′tŭm, *n.* jointure.
Wittwe, vĭt′ve, **Wittfrau,** -frāŭ, *f. pl.* -en, widow. **Wittwenjahr,** -yār, *n.* widow's year. **Wittwenstand,** vĭt venzhtant, *m.* widowhood.
Wittwer, vĭt′ver, **Wittmann,** -mann, *m. pl.* -männer, widower.
Witz, vĭts, *m.* sense; intellect, understanding, wit; seinen — verlieren, to lose one's wits; wittiness.
Witzbold, vĭts′bolt, *m.* wit; witty fellow. **Witzelei,** vĭtselēi′, *f.* witticism.
Witzeln, vĭts′eln, *vi. i.* to be vastly witty; to affect wittiness. **Witzig,** vĭts′ĭch, *a.* witty. **Witzigen,** vĭts′īgen, *vt.* to make wiser, to teach wit.
Witzling, vĭts′lĭng, *m.* witling, pretender to wit, punster, low wit.
Wo, vō, *pn.* where; somewhere, anywhere; if, when, in case.
Wobei, vobēi′, *av.* whereby, whereat, where.
Woche, vŏch′e, *f.* week, sennight; in die Wochen kommen, to be delivered; to be brought to bed; in den Wochen liegen, to lie in bed, to be confined.
Wochenbett, vŏch′enbet, *n.* confinement; childbed.
Wochenblatt, vŏch′enblat, *n. pl.* -blätter, weekly.
Wochenkind, vŏch′enkĭnt, *n. pl.* -er, new-born child.
Wochenlang, vŏch′enlang, *av.* for weeks.
Wochenlohn, vŏch′enlōn, *m.* weekly pay, week's wages.
Wochenmarkt, vŏch′enmarkt, *n.* weekly market (day).
Wochentag, vŏch′entāg, *m. pl. -e,* weekday.
Wöchentlich, vŏch′entlĭch, *a. av.* weekly, by the week, hebdomadal, -dary.
Wochenweise, vŏch′envēise, *av.* by the week.
Wöchnerin, vŏch′nerin, *f.* woman lying-in.
Wocken, vŏk′en, *m.* distaff, rock.
Wodurch, vodŭrch′, *av.* whereby, by what.
Wofern, vofērn′, *Cj.* if; wofern nicht, unless, if not.
Wofür, vofūhr′, *av.* wherefore, for what.

Woge, vō'ge, *f.* billow, wave, surge.
Wogegen, vogā'gen, *av.* against what *or* which, for *or* to what, which.
Wogen, vō'gen, *vi. i.* to wave, billow, surge, fluctuate.
Wogig, vō'gig, *a.* wavy, surgy.
Woher, vohār', *a.* whence, wherefrom.
Wohin, vohin', *a.* whither, where, what way.
Wohl, vōl, *a. av.* well, certainly, indeed; perhaps, may be; Wohl Dir! happy for thee! happy you! er ist wohl, he is well, in good health; *s. n.* welfare, weal, well-being, good, benefit, interest.
Wohlan, vōlän', *av.* well, come on!
Wohlanständig, vōl'anzhtendig, *a.* decent, -ly, (well-)becoming; -keit, -käet, *f.* decency.
Wohlauf, vōlōuf', *ij.* well! cheer up! — fein, to be well, *or* in good health.
Wohlbedacht, vōl'bedacht, *a. av.* well considered. Wohl bedachtig, -bedächtig, Wohl bedächtlich, -lich, *a. av.* deliberate, -ly, considerate.
Wohlbefinden, vōl'befinden, *n.* good health.
Wohlbehagen, vōl'behägn, *n.* ease, comfortableness, comfort. Wohlbehaglich, -lich, *a. av.* comfortable, -ly, at ease.
Wohlbehalten, vōl'behalten, *a. av.* safe.
Wohlbekannt, vōl'bekannt, *a.* well known, fully known.
Wohlbeleibt, vōl'beleibt, *a.* corpulent, fleshy, bulky, stout, fat; -heit, -häet, *f.* corpulence, fatness.
Wohlbeschaffen, vōl'beshaffen, *a.* in good condition.
Wohlbewußt, vōl'bevusst, *a.* conscious; well-remembered.
Wohlergehen, vōl'ergä-en, *n.* well-being, prosperity.
Wohlerzogen, vōl'ertsōgn, *a.* well-bred.
Wohlfahrt, vōl'fārt, *f.* welfare, prosperity.
Wohlfahrtsausschuß, vōl'fārtsōyshuss, *m.* committee of public safety.
Wohlfeil, vōl'fäel, *a. av.* cheap, -ly; -heit, -häet, *f.* cheapness.
Wohlgeartet, vōl'geärtet, *a.* well natured, well mannered.
Wohlgebildet, vōl'gebildet, Wohlgebaut, -gebōyt, *a.* well-shaped, well-made, well-formed.
Wohlgeboren, vōl'gebören, *a.* noble-born. Sir (address).

Wohlgefallen, vōl'gefallen, *n.* pleasure, satisfaction; *vi.* wohlgefiel, wohlgefallen, to please, satisfy.
Wohlgefällig, vōl'gefellig, *z. av.* pleasant, pleasing, agreeable.
Wohlgelaunt, vōl'gelaunt, *a.* in good humor.
Wohlgelitten, vōl'gelitten, *a.* favored, well-wished.
Wohlgemeint, vōl'gemaent, *a.* well-intended, benevolent, sincere.
Wohlgemuth, vōl'gemut, *a. av.* cheerful, -ly.
Wohlgenährt, vōl'genärt, *a.* well-fed.
Wohlgeneigt, vōl'geneigt, *a.* kind.
Wohlgerathen, vōl'geräten. *a.* successful; successfully educated.
Wohlgeruch, vōl'keruch, *m. pl.* -gerüche, fragrancy, pleasing *or* sweet scent, grateful odor, perfume.
Wohlgeschmack, vōl'geshmack, *m.* relish, good flavor, pleasing taste.
Wohlgesinnt, vōl'gesinnt, *a.* well-disposed; loyal.
Wohlgestalt, vōl'gezhtalt, *f.* fine shape; -et, *a.* well-formed, shapely.
Wohlgezogen, vōl'getsōgen, *a.* well-educated.
Wohlhabend, vōl'hābent, *a.* opulent, wealthy, easy, (being) well off; -heit, -häet, *f.* opulency.
Wohlklang, vōl'klang, *f.* agreeable, easy sound, euphony.
Wohlklingend, vōl'kling-ent, *a.* well sounding, pleasing to the ear, euphonic.
Wohllaut, vōl'lōut, *m.* euphony, easy sound; -end, -ent, *a.* euphonic, well sounding.
Wohlleben, vōl'lāben, *n.* good cheer, high life, luxury.
Wohllöblich, vōl'löhblich, *a.* highly esteemed.
Wohlmeinend, vōl'maenent, *a.* well-meaning.
Wohlriechend, vōl'rīchent, *a.* fragrant, odorous, sweet-scented; balmy, aromatic.
Wohlschmeckend, vōl'shmeckent, *a.* savory, flavory, delicious.
Wohlsein, vōl'saen, *n.* health, comfort, prosperity.
Wohlstand, vōl'zhtant, *m.* good condition, prosperity, welfare; propriety, decency.
Wohlthat, vōl'tät, *f. pl. -en*, benefit, kindness, service, favor.

Wohlthäter, vōl'täter, *m.* benefactor; **‑in,** *f.* benefactress. **Wohlthätig, ‑thätich.** *a.* beneficial, beneficient, charitable; wholesome, salutary; salubrious; ‑keit, ‑kät, *f.* beneficence, charity.

Wohlthun, vōl'tun, *vi.* to do well *or* good; to benefit, to be beneficial; *es thut ihm wohl,* he likes, is pleased, delighted.

Wohltönend, *f.* **Wohllautend.**

Wohlverdient, vōl'ferdīnt, *a.* well deserved.

Wohlverhalten, vōl'ferhalten, *n.* good conduct *or* behavior.

Wohlverstanden, vōl'ferzhtanden, *a.* understood.

Wohlweislich, vōl'vīslich, *av.* very wisely, prudently.

Wohlwollen, vōl'vollen, *vi.* Einem ‑, to wish the good of; *s. n.* benevolence, good will, goodness; *ab, a. av.* benevolent, ‑ly, kind.

Wohnen, vō'nen, *vi.* to dwell, live, lodge, reside.

Wohnhaft, vōn'haft, *a.* residing; ‑sein, to reside in, to be an inhabitant of.

Wohnhaus, vōn'hǒus, *n. pl.* ‑häuser, **Wohn'gebäude,** ‑gebäude, *n.* dwelling-house.

Wohnlich, vōn'lich, *a.* comfortable.

Wohnort, vōn'ort, *m. pl.* ‑örter. **Wohnplatz,** vōn'plats, *m. pl.* **Wohnplätze. Wohnstatt,** vōn'zhtatt, *f.* dwelling-place, residence. **Wohnsitz,** ‑sits, *m. pl.* ‑e. domicile. **Wohnstube,** ‑zhtube, *f.* **Wohnzimmer,** ‑tsimmer, *n.* sitting-room.

Wohnung, vōn'ung, *f.* residence; lodging, abode, habitation.

Woid, Woit, voit, *f.* jigger (*Mar.*).

Wölben, völ'ben, *rt.* to vault, arch.

Wölbung, völb'ung, *f.* vault, arch.

Wolf, volf, *m. pl.* **Wölfe,** wolf; (wool) devil, deviling *or* opening machine; wool-mill.

Wolfen, volf'en, *s. n.* willowing.

Wölfin, völ'fīn, she-wolf. **Wölfisch,** ‑ish. *a.* wolfish.

Wolfram, volf'ram, *m.* wolfram.

Wolframsäure, volf'ramsöure, *f.* tungstic acid, wolframine.

Wolfshunger, volfs'hung-er, *m.* canine *or* ravenous appetite.

Wolke, vol'ke, *f.* cloud. **Wölkchen,** völk'chen, *n.* little cloud.

Wolken, vōl'ken, *vi.* to cloud.

Wolkenbruch, vōl'kenbruch, *m. pl.* ‑brüche, heavy shower, waterspout.

Wolkig, vōl'kig, *a.* cloudy.

Wollarbeit, voll'arbāet, *f.* work in wool; ‑er, *m.* worker in wool.

Wolle, vol'le, *f.* wool.

Wollen, vol'len, *a.* woolen, worsted.

Wollen, vol'len, *vi.* to will, to be willing, to wish, to warrant: lieber ‑, to like rather, to prefer; *s. n.* volition, will.

Wollenfabrik, vol'lenfabrik, *f.* woolen cloth manufactory, factory of woolen goods. **Wol'lenfabrikant,** ‑fabrikant, *m.* manufacturer of woolen goods.

Wollengarn, vol'lengarn, *n.* woolen yarn, worsted. **Wol'lenweber,** ‑vāber, *m.* woolen-weaver.

Wollhandel, voll'handel, *m.* wool-trade. **Wollhändler,** ‑hendler, *m.* dealer in wool, wool-merchant.

Wollicht, vol'licht, **Wollig,** vol'lig, *a.* woolly, resembling wool.

Wollkamm, voll'kamm. *m. pl.* ‑kämme, wool-comb. **Wollkämmer,** ‑kemmer, *m.* wool-comber.

Wollmarkt, vol'märkt, *m. pl.* ‑märkte, wool-market, wool-staple.

Wollsack, voll'sack, *m. pl.* ‑säcke, woolsack, wool-pack.

Wollschur, vol'shur, *f.* clip, sheep-shearing.

Wollspinner, vol'zhpinner. *m.* wool-spinner; ‑in, *f.* wool-spinster.

Wollspinnerei, valzhpinnerēī', *f.* wool-spinning.

Wollzeug, vol'tsěüg, *n. pl.* ‑e, woolen stuff.

Wollust, vol'luxht, *f. pl.* ‑lüste, delight; lust, luxury; voluptuousness.

Wollüstig, vol'lüzhtich, *a.* voluptuous, sensual; ‑keit, ‑kāet, *f.* voluptuousness, sensuality, lust. **Wollüstling,** vol'lüzhtling, *m.* voluptuary.

Womit, vomit', *av.* wherewith, with which *or* what.

Wonach, vonāch', *av.* after which, at, to which *or* what.

Woneben, vōnā'ben, *av.* near to wi‑h.

Wonne, von'ne, *f.* delight.

Wonnig, von'nich, *a. av.* delightful, delightfully.

Woran, vörān', *av.* whereon, whereat, whereto, to which *or* what.

Worauf, vōrǎuf', *av.* whereon, whereupon, on which.

Woraus, vöröys', *av.* wherefrom, whence, out of which.
Worein, vörȧen', *av.* whereinto, into what *or* which.
Worf, *f.* Wurf.
Worin, vörin', *av.* wherein, in which, in what.
Wornach, *f.* Wonach.
Wort, vort, *n. pl. -e*, **Wörter**, vör'ter, *f.* word; term; Wort für Wort, word for word; literally; mit einem Worte, in a word; sein Wort halten, to keep one's word.
Wortart, vort'ȧrt, *f.* part of speech.
Wortbruch, vort'bryʤ, *m.* breach of promise. **Wortbrüchig**, -brüʤig, *a.* faithless, -ly.
Wörtchen, vört'ʤen, *n.* little word.
Wörterbuch, vör'terbyʤ, *n. pl. -bücher*, vocabulary, dictionary.
Wortforschung, vort'forshyng, *f.* etymology, philology.
Wortfügung, vort'fühgyng, *f.* syntax.
Wortführer, vort'führer, *m.* spokesman; foreman (of a jury).
Wortgepränge, vort'geprenge, *n.* bombast, fustian, swelling style.
Wortkarg, vort'karg, *a.* sparing of words.
Wörtlich, vört'liʤ, *a.* literal, verbal, word for word.
Wortreich, vort'rēiʤ, *a.* verbose, rich in words.
Wortschwall, vort'shval, *m.* bombast, fustian.
Wortspiel, vort'zhpīl, *n.* pun, quibble.
Wortstreit, vort'zhtreīt, *m.* logomachy, war of words.
Wortwechsel, vort'vexl, *m.* altercation, dispute.
Worüber, vorüh'br, *av.* whereupon, whereon, whereat, at, about, upon *or* of, which *or* what.
Worunter, vorụn'ter, *av.* under *or* among which.
Wovon, vofọn', *av.* of which, whereof.
Wovor, vofōr', *av.* before, for *or* from which, wherefrom.
Wozu, votsụy', *av.* whereat, whereto, for what.
Wrack, vrak, *n.* wreck, wrack.
Wricken, vrik'ken, *vt.* to wriggle.
Wucher, vụ'ʤer, *m.* usury. **Wucherer**, vụ'ʤerer, *m.* usurer. **Wucherisch**, -ish, *a.* usurious. **Wuchern**, vụ'ʤern, *vt.* to practice usury; to grow exuberantly.

Wuchs, vụks, *m.* growth, height.
Wucht, vụʤt, *f.* weight, heavy burden bulk.
Wühlen, vüh'len, *vi.* to root (up), stir.
Wulen, vụ'len, *vi.* to woold. **Wulfling**, **Wulling**, vụ'ling, *a.* woolding, gammoning of the bowsprit.
Wulst, vụlzht, *m. pl.* Wülste, pad, cushion; (Arch.) ovolo.
Wulstig, vül'zhtiʤ, *a.* puffy, turgid, bombastic.
Wund, vụnt, *a.* sore, galled, wounded.
Wundarzt, vụnt'ȧrtst, *m. pl. -ärzte*, surgeon. **Wundärztlich**, -ȧrtstliʤ, *a.* surgical.
Wunde, vụn'de, *f.* wound.
Wunder, vụn'der, *n.* wonder, miracle. **Wunderbar**, -bȧr, *a.* wonderful, miraculous: -liʤ, -liʤ, *av.* miraculously. **Wunderding**, -ding, *n.* wondrous thing. **Wundergroß**, -gros, *a.* prodigious. **Wunderkind**, -kint, *n. pl. -er*, prodigy of a child. **Wunderkraft**, -kraft, *f. pl. -kräfte*, miraculous power. **Wunderlich**, -liʤ, *a. av.* strange, odd; capricious; -keit, -kȧet, *f.* capriciousness.
Wundern, vụn'dern, *vt. r.* to wonder, to be astonished: es wundert mich, I am surprised, astonished, I wonder. **Wundersam**, -sam, *a.* wonderful. **Wunderschön**, -shöhn, *a.* exceedingly beautiful *or* fine; of a wonderful beauty. **Wunderselten**, -selten, *a. av.* extraordinarily rare, -ly. **Wunderthat**, -tȧt, *f.* wonderful deed, miracle, prodigy. **Wunderthäter**, -tȧter, *m.* worker of miracles. **Wunderthätig**, -tȧtiʤ, *a.* wonder-working, miraculous. **Wunderthier**, -tīr, *n.* wonderful animal, prodigy, monster. **Wundervoll**, -foll, *a.* wonderful, miraculous, marvelous; admirable. **Wunderwerk**, -verk, *n.* wonder, miracle.
Wundfieber, vụnt'fīber, *n.* fever from wounds.
Wundkraut, vụnt'krọut, *n.* woundroot.
Wundwasser, vụnt'vasser, *n.* vulnerary water, arquebusade, vulnerary.
Wunsch, vụnsh, *m. pl.* Wünsche, wish, desire.
Wünschelruthe, vün'shelrụte, *f.* (magic) wand.
Wünschen, vün'shen, *vt.* to wish; Glück —, to congratulate; -swerth, -vȧrt, *a.* desirable.

Weiße, vēl'ʐe, *f.* whiteness. **Weißen**, vēl'sen, *vt.* to whiten, whitewash.
Weißerz, vēls'ārts, *n.* sparry iron-ore; white copper-ore.
Weißfisch, vēls'fish, *m.* white-fish, bleak.
Weißgärber, vēls'gĕrbẹr, *m.* tawer; -*ei*, -ēī', *f.* tawery.
Weißgrau, vēls'grāu, *a.* light gray, hoary, whitish gray.
Weißkraut, vēls'krout, *n.* white cabbage.
Weißlich, vēls'lich, *a.* whitish. **Weißling**, -ling, *m.* whiting.
Weißpappel, vēls'pappl, *f.* white poplar.
Weißstein, vēls'zhtẹn, *m.* white-stone. **Weißtanne**, vēls'tannẹ, *f.* white pine.
Weißzeug, vēls'tseūk, *m.* linen.
Weisung, vēls'ụng, *f.* order, direction.
Weit, vēlt, *a. av.* distant, far; wide, widely, broad; **von weitem**, from afar; **bei weitem**, by far; **weiter**, farther, further; **weitest**, farthest, furthest.
Weite, vēl'tẹ, *f. or n.* width; distance; largeness, amplitude; **lichte Weite**, span (Arch.).
Weiten, vēl'tẹn, *vt. i.* to widen, expand, extend.
Weiterung, vēl'ẹrụng, *f.* procrastination.
Weithin, vēlt'hīn, *av.* to a great distance. **Weitläufig**, vēlt'lāūfich, *a.* large, vast; distant; detailed, prolix, at full, at full length; -*keit*, -kāet, *f.* vast extent; diffusiveness, prolixity. **Weitschweifig**, -shāēfich, *a.* prolix, diffuse; -*keit*, -kāet, *f.* prolixity. **Weitsichtig**, -sichtig, *a.* far-sighted.
Weizen, vāets'ẹn, *m.* wheat; -*brod*, -brōt, *n.* wheat bread. **Weizenkorn**, -korn, *n. pl.* -körner, grain of wheat.
Welch, velch, **er**, **e**, **es**, *a. pron.* who, which. **Welcherlei**, -ẹrlāē, *a.* of what kind.
Welk, velk, *a.* withered, faded, flagging, languid; -*en*, *vi.* to wither, fade, decay, flag, languish.
Welle, vēl'lẹ, *f.* wave, billow; (Mech.) roller; **aufrechte** —, spindle; **unförmig**, -fürmich, *a.* undulatory, waving, nudulating. **Wellenreich**, -rāēch, *n.* realm of the sea.
Weller, vēl'lẹr, *n.* cylinder.

Wellermauer, vẹl'lermoūẹr, **Weller**-**wand**, -vant, *f.* loam-wall, mud-wall. **Wellern**, vēl'lẹrn, *vt.* to make mud-walls.
Welt, vēlt, *f.* world, universe; earth; -*all*, -all, *n.* universe. **Weltalter**, -alter, *n.* age (of the world), period.
Weltbekannt, -bekannt, *a.* notorious. **Weltberühmt**, -berühmt, *a.* far-famed, renowned. **Weltbürger**, -bürger, *m.* cosmopolite: -*lich*, -lich, *a.* cosmopolitical. **Weltbürgersinn**, -sinn, *m.* cosmopolitism. **Weltgebäude**, -gẹbāūdẹ, *n.* system or fabric of the world. **Weltgegend**, -gāgẹnt, *f.* region, quarter of the world.
Weltgeist, vēlt'gāēzht, *m.* spirit of the universe, creative spirit; -*licher*, -licher, *m.* secular priest. **Weltgericht**, vēlt'gẹricht, *n.* last judgment. **Weltgeschichte**, -gẹshichtẹ, *f.* universal history. **Welthandel**, -handel, *m.* commerce. **Weltheiland**, -hāēlant, *m.* Saviour. **Weltkenntniß**, -kenntnisẹ, *f.* knowledge of the world. **Weltkind**, -kint, *n. pl.* -*er*, worldling. **Weltklug**, -klụk, *a.* prudent; -*heit*, -hāēt, *f.* worldly wisdom. **Weltkörper**, vēlt'körpẹr, *m.* heavenly body. **Weltkugel**, -kụgel, *f.* globe. **Weltkunde**, -kụndẹ, *f.* cosmology. **Weltkundig**, -kụndich, *a.* notorious; skilled in history. **Weltlauf**, -lāūf, *m.* course *or* way of the world. **Weltlich**, -lich, *a.* worldly, secular; -*keit*, -kāēt, *f.* worldliness, worldly-mindedness; secularity. **Weltliebe**, -lībẹ, *f.* love of the world. **Weltling**, -ling, *m.* worldling. **Weltmann**, -mann, *m.* man of the world. **Weltmeer**, -mār, *n.* ocean, main (sea). **Weltpriester**, -prīzhter, *m.* secular priest. **Weltsinn**, -sinn, *m.* worldly-mindedness, worldliness. **Welttheil**, -tāēl, *n.* part of the world, continent. **Weltweiser**, -vāēsẹr, *m.* philosopher. **Weltweisheit**, -vāēshāēt, *f.* philosophy.
Wendeeisen, vẹn'dẹ-āēsẹn, *n.* tap-iron. **Wendekreis**, -krāēs, *m.* tropic.
Wendeltreppe, vẹn'dẹltrẹppẹ, *f.* winding-stairs.
Wenden, vẹn'dẹn (wandte, gewandt), *vt.* to turn, direct; **sich** —, *tr.* turn, change; **sich** — **an**, to apply to, to address one's self to; **durch** *or* **gegen**

Wen   397   **Wet**

den Wind —, or bei dem Winde —, to tack.
Wendeſtufe, vęn'dẹzhtụfẹ, *f.* winder.
Wendung, vęnd'ụng, *f.* turn, turning.
Wenig, vā'nich, *a. av.* little, few; ſer, *a.* less, lesser, fewer. **Wenigſt**, vā'-nikzht. *a.* least, fewest; **wenigſtens**, ʒum Wenigſten, at least. **We'nig-keit**, -kāet, *f.* smallness, trifle; meine —, my humble self.
Wenn, vęn, *Cj.* when; if; — nicht, if not, unless; — auch, although; — je, — immer, whenever.
Wer, vār, *pron.* who; — auch, whoever.
Werben, věr'bęn (warb, geworben), *vt.* to sue for, petition; to court, woo; to recruit. **Wer'ber**, *m.* recruiting-officer, recruiter; suitor, wooer.
Werbung, věrb'ụng, *f.* recruiting, levy, enlistment; wooing, courting.
Werden, věr'den (warb, wurde, geworben), to become, grow, turn, get, to be, happen, come to pass; to come into existence.
Werder, věr'dęr, *m.* small island, holm.
Werfen, věr'fęn (warf, geworfen), *vt.* to cast, throw, fling; to bring forth, bear; ſich —, to warp (of wood).
Werft, věrft, *n.* wharf.
Werft, věrft, *m. n.* **Werfte**, věrf'tẹ, *f.* warp, weft.
Werg, věrk, *n.* tow, hards; **-leinwand**, -laēnvant, *f.* tow-linen.
Werk, věrk, *n.* work, deed, production; ʒu — geben mit, to deal with; **-tag**, -tāk, *n.* working-day.
Werkmeiſter, věrk'māezhtęr, *m.* foreman, superintendent. **Werk'jach**, -sach, *m.* skeleton (Carpent.).
Werkſtatt, věrk'zhtatt, *f. pl.* **-ſtätte**, **Werkſtätte**, -zhtettẹ, *f.* workshop. **Werkſtein**, -zhtaēn, *m.* **Werk'ſtück**, -zhtück, *n.* square-stone. **Werktag**, -tāk, *m.* working day. **Werk'ʒeug**, věrk'tseūk, *n. pl.* -ẹ, tool, instrument.
Wermuth, věr'mụt, *m.* wormwood.
Werptroß, věrp'tross, *n.* warp, warping hawser (Mar.).
Werth, věrt, *a.* worth, valuable; dear, precious; **-loß**, -lōs, *a.* worthless.
Werthſchätzen, věrt'shētsęn, *vt.* to esteem highly, to regard. **Werth'-ſchätzung**, -ụng, *f.* estimation, esteem.

Weſen, vā'sęn, *n.* being, existence, substance, essence, nature.
Weſenloß, vā'senlōs, *a.* unsubstantial.
Weſentlich, vā'sentlich, *a.* essential, substantial, real; **-keit**, -kāet, *f.* essentiality, essence, substance.
Weſpe, věs'pẹ, *f.* wasp; **-neſt**, věs'-pennest, *n.* wasp's nest.
Weſpenſtich, věs'penzhtich, *m.* wasp-bite.
Weſſen, vẹs'sen, **Weß**, vęss, *pn.* whose, of whom, of which; **-halb**, -halp, **Weß'wegen**, -vāgęn, *av.* wherefore, why, on what account.
Weſt, věxht, **Weſt'en**, *m.* west; west wind.
Weſte, věxh'tẹ, *f.* vest, waistcoat; **-ntaſche**, -tashẹ, *f.* vest-pocket.
Weſtgegend, věxht'gāgent, *f.* **Weſt'-land**, -lant, *n. pl.* **-länder**, western country. **Weſt'lich**, -lich, *a.* western, westerly; **Weſtnordweſt**, west-northwest; **Weſtſüdweſt**, west-southwest; **Weſtſübweſtwind**, west-south-west wind, west-southwester. **Weſtwärts**, věst'věrts, *av.* westward, westwardly. **Weſtwind**, věst'vint, *m.* west wind.
Wett, vęt, *a. av.* even, equal; — machen, to quit scores.
Wette, vęt'tẹ, *f.* bet, wager; um bie — thun, to vie in.
Wetteifer, vętt'ēlfęr, *m.* emulation; **-n**, *vt.* to emulate, vie, contend.
Wetten, vęt'ten, *vt.* to bet, to lay a bet *or* wager.
Wetter, vět'ter, *n.* weather; thunderstorm, tempest; air, current of air; **-ableiter**, -ablāeter, *m.* lightning-rod, conductor. **Wet'terbeobachtung**, -beōbachtụng, *f.* meteorological observation. **Wet'terdach**, -dach, *n. pl.* **-bächer**, penthouse. **Wet'terfahne**, -fānẹ, *f.* **Wet'terhahn**, -hān, *m. pl.* **-hähne**, vane, weather-vane, weather-cock. **Wet'terglas**, -glās, *n. pl.* **-gläſer**, weather-glass, barometer, thermometer. **Wet'terlaunisch**, laụ-nish, *a.* peevish, capricious. **Wet'-terleuchten**, -leūchten, *n.* heat-lightning. **Wet'terloſung**, -lōsụng, *f.* ventilation. **Wettern**, vět'těrn, *vt.* to thunder. **Wet'terprophet**, -prōfāt, *m.* weather-spy. **Wet'terrab**, -rāt, *n. pl.* **-räber**, ventilating-fanner. **Wet'-terſtrahl**, -zhtrāl, *m.* **-es**, *pl.* **-en**, flash of lightning. **Wet'terwendisch**,

34

-vendish, a. changeable, fickle, inconstant, peevish. **Wet′terwolke**, -volke, f. thunder-cloud.
Wettrennen, vett′rĕnnen, n. race; — zu Fuß, foot-race: — zu Pferd, horse-race; — in Booten, boat-race.
Wett′renner, m. racer; race-horse.
Wett′streit, -zhtrīt, m. emulation, contention, contest, rivalry.
Wetzen, vĕts′en, vt. to whet. **Wetz′schiefer**, -shīfer, m. whetslate. **Wetz′stein**, -zhtīēn, m. whetstone.
Wichse, vix′e, f. blacking; waxing.
Wichsen, vix′en, vt. to blacken; to wax.
Wicht, viçt, m. wight, fellow.
Wichtig, viç′tig, a. weighty, important; **-keit**, -kāēt, f. importance.
Wicke, vick′e, f. vetch.
Wickel, vick′el, m. roller.
Wickelmaschine, vick′elmashīne, f. winding machine, lap machine; spreader.
Wickelkind, vickl′kĭnt, n. pl. -er, child in swaddling-cloth.
Wickeln, vick′eln, vt. to roll, wind up.
Wickelwalze, vick′elvaltse, f. roller.
Widder, vid′der, m. ram; aries; **hydraulischer —**, hydraulic ram.
Wider, vī′der, pr. against, contrary or in opposition to; **-bellen**, -bellen, vt. to contradict. **Widerbeller**, vī′derbeller, m. wrangler.
Widerchrist, vī′derkrizht, m. antichrist; **-lich**, -liç, a. antichristian.
Widerdruck, vī′derdrŭck, m. second form; reiteration; reaction; **-bogen**, -bōgen, m. tympan-sheet.
Widerfahren, viderfā′ren (widerfuhr, widerfahren), vi. to happen, befall, occur.
Widerhaken, vī′derhāken, m. barb, beard.
Widerhalt, vī′derhalt, m. hold, support, resistance.
Widerhalten, vī′derhalten (widerhielt, widergehalten), vi. to hold out, resist.
Widerlage, vī′derlāge, f. counterfort, buttress.
Widerlager, vī′derlāger, n. springing-stone.
Widerlegbar, viderlāg′bār, **Widerleglich**, -liç, confutable, refutable, disprovable.
Widerlegen, vīde-lā′gen, vt. to disprove, confute, refute. **Widerlegung**, -ŭng, f. confutation, refutation.

Widerlich, vī′derliç, a. disgusting, offensive; **-keit**, -kāēt, f. offensiveness.
Widern, vī′dern, vi. to disgust.
Widernatürlich, vī′dernatürliç, a. unnatural, preternatural, contrary to nature.
Widerpart, vī′derpart, m. opponent; opposition.
Widerraten, vīderrāt′en (-rieth, -raten), vt. to dissuade, to represent as unfit.
Widerrechtlich, vī′derreçtliç, a. illegal, unlawful; **-keit**, -kāēt, f. unlawfulness, illegality.
Widerrede, vī′derrāde, f. contradiction, opposition.
Widerrist, vī′derrizht, m. withers.
Widerruf, vī′derrŭf, m. pl. -e, recall, repeal, recantation, retraction.
Widerrufen, vīderrŭ′fen, vt. to recall, retract, unsay, repeal. **Widerruflich**, -liç, a. repealable, reversible, revocable.
Widersacher, vī′dersacher, m. -in, f. adversary.
Widerschein, vī′dershāēn, m. reflexion, reverberation of light.
Widersetzen, vīdersets′en, vr. sich —, to oppose, resist.
Widersetzlich, vīdersets′liç, a. refractory; **-keit**, -kāēt, f. refractoriness.
Widersetzung, -ŭng, f. resistance, opposition.
Widersinnig, vī′dersinniç, a. nonsensical, absurd; **-keit**, -kāēt, f. nonsensicalness, absurdity.
Widerspänstig, vī′derzhpenstiç, a. resistive, refractory; **-keit**, -kāēt, f. restiveness, refractoriness.
Widerspiel, vī′derzhpīl, n. contrary, reverse.
Widersprechen, vīderzhpreç′en (widersprach, widersprochen), vt. to contradict, gainsay; **-d**, a. contradictory.
Widerspruch, vī′derzhprŭç, m. pl. **Widersprüche**, contradiction, inconsistency.
Widerstand, vī′derzhtant, m. resistance, opposition.
Widerstehen, vīderzhtā′en (widerstand, widerstanden), vi. to resist, oppose, withstand.
Widerstreben, vīderzhtrā′ben, vi. to strive or struggle against, repugn

resist; *s. n.* repugnancy, resistance.

Widerstreit, vī'derzhtrīt, *m.* conflict; antagonism, contradiction; **en,** vīderzhtrēi'ten, *vt.* to conflict, contend. **Widerstreitend,** *a.* conflicting; contradictory.

Widerstrom, vī'derzhtröm, *m.* countercurrent.

Widerwärtig, vī'dervärtig, *a.* disgusting, adverse, loathsome, disagreeable; **keit, -kāet,** *f.* adversity, reverse; unpleasantness.

Widerwille, vī'dervillę, *m.* aversion, disgust, antipathy, reluctance.

Widerwillig, vī'dervillich, *a.* reluctant, unwilling, backward.

Widmen, vĭd'men, *vt.* to devote; dedicate, consecrate. **Wid'mung, -ung,** *f.* devotion; dedication.

Widrig, vĭd'rich, *a.* averse, contrary; nauseous, disgusting; **keit, -kāet,** *f.* adversity.

Widrigenfalls, vī'drigenfalls, *a.* else, otherwise, in the other case.

Wie, vī, *pr.* how, as, when.

Wiede, vī'dę, *f.* willow, osier, withy.

Wiedehopf, vī'dehopf, *m. pl.* **-e,** lapwing, pewit, green plover, hoopoo.

Wieder, vī'der, *av.* back, again, anew, afresh.

Wiederabdruck, vīderap'druck, *m. pl.* **-abdrücke,** re-impression.

Wiederanstellen, vī'deranzhtęllen, *vt.* to re-appoint.

Wiederaufbauen, vīderāūf'bǫyen, *vt.* to rebuild.

Wiederbekommen, vī'derbekommen (**-kam, -bekommen**), *vt.* to recover, get again.

Wiederbeleben, vī'derbelāben, *vt.* to revive, revivify. **Wiederbelebung, -ung,** *f.* revivification.

Wiederbringen, vī'derbringen (**-wiederbringen, wiedergebracht**), *vt.* to bring back, restore, retrieve.

Wiederbringlich, vīderbring'lich, *a.* retrievable. **Wiederbring'ung, -ung,** *f.* restoration.

Wiedereinsetzen, vīderęīn'setzen, *vt.* to reinstate, replace, restore, re-establish.

Wiedererlangen, vī'dererlangen, *vt.* to recover. **Wiedererlangung, -ung,** *f.* recovery.

Wiedererobern, vī'dererōbĕrn, *vt.* to reconquer

Wiedererstatten, vī'derĕrzhtatten, *vt.* to restore, return, reimburse, repay. **Wiedererstattung, -ung,** *f.* return, restitution, repayment.

Wiederfinden, vī'derfinden, *vt.* to find again.

Wiedergeben, vī'dergāben (**-gab, -gegeben**), *vt.* to return, give back, render.

Wiedergeboren, vī'dergebōren, *a.* regenerate(d). **Wiedergeburt, -burt,** *f.* regeneration.

Wiedergenesung, vī'dergęnāsung, *f.* recovery.

Wiederhall, vī'derhall, *m.* echo; **en,** *vt.* to re-echo.

Wiederherstellen, vīderhĕr'zhtęllen, *vt.* to restore, recover; redintegrate, re-establish. **Wiederherstellung, -ung,** *f.* restoration, restitution; recovery.

Wiederholen, vīderhō'len, *vt.* to repeat, reiterate. **Wiederhol'ung, -ung,** *f.* repetition, reiteration.

Wiederkäuen, vī'derkāuen *vt.* to ruminate.

Wiederkauf, vī'derkāuf, *m. pl.* **-käufe,** redemption, repurchase; **en,** *vt.* to repurchase, redeem. **Wiederkäuflich, -käuflich,** *a.* redeemable.

Wiederkehr, vī'derkār, *f.* return, recurrence; **en,** *vt.* to return, come back.

Wiederklang, vī'derklang, *m.* echo.

Wiederklingen, vī'derklingen, *vi.* to re-echo.

Wiederkommen, vī'derkommen (**-kam, -gekommen**), *vi.* to come again, return. **Wiederkunft, -kunft,** *f.* return.

Wiederöffnen, vīderöff'nen, *vt.* to re-open.

Wiederschein, vī'derzhęīn, *m.* reflex, reflected light.

Wiedersehen, vī'dersāen (**-sah, -gesehen**), *vt.* to see *or* meet again; *s. n.* seeing, meeting again.

Wiedertaufe, vī'dertāufe, *f.* rebaptism, rebaptization; **en,** *vt.* to rebaptize. **Wiedertäufer, -täufer,** *m.* rebaptizer; anabaptist.

Wiedertönen, vī'dertöhnen, *vt. i.* to resound.

Wiederum, vī'derum, *av.* again, once more, repeatedly.

Wiedervergelten, vī'derfĕrgälten, *vt* to requite, retaliate, remunerate recompense, reward, repay.

Wiederbergeltung, vī'derförgěltŭng, *f.* requital, retaliation, retribution, recompense, reward.
Wiederverkaufen, vī'derfĕrkäufen, *vt.* to resell, retail.
Wiederversöhnen, vī'derfĕrsöhnen, *vt.* to reconcile, conciliate; propitiate.
Wiege, vī'gĕ, *f.* cradle.
Wiegemesser, vī'gĕměsser, *n.* chopping knife.
Wiegen, vī'gen, *vt.* to rock, cradle; **sich —,** to lull one's self with.
Wiegen, vī'gen (wog, gewogen), *vi. t.* to weigh; *vt.* wiegte, gewiegt.
Wiegenkind, vī'genkĭnt, *n.* baby.
Wiegenlied, vī'genlīd, *n. pl.* -er, lullaby.
Wiehern, vī'hĕrn, *vi.* to neigh, whinny; **wieherndes Gelächter,** horse-laugh.
Wiek, vīk. *n. pl.* -e, inlet, bay.
Wieke, vī'kĕ, *f.* lint.
Wiese, vīs'ĕ, *f.* meadow.
Wiesel, vī'sel, *n.* weasel.
Wiesenbau, vī'senbŏu, *m.* cultivation of meadows. **Wiesengrund,** -grŭnt, *m. pl.* -gründe, **Wiesenland,** -lant, *n. pl.* -länder. meadow.
Wiesewachs, vī'sĕvaks, **Wiesewuchs,** -vŭks, *m.* meadows.
Wievielst, vī'fīlzht, **Wievielt,** *a.* what or which number.
Wiewohl, vivōl', *cj.* although, though.
Wild, vĭlt, *a.* wild, savage; *s. n.* game, venison; **-brät,** -brĕt, *n.* deer, game, venison. **Wildbraten,** -brāten, *m.* roast venison. **Wilddieb,** -dīb, *m.* poacher. **Wilder, wildsavage. Wild's fang,** -fang, *m. pl.* -fänge. mad cap.
Wildfremd, -frĕmt, *a.* quite strange.
Wildgeschmack, -geshmack, *m.* flavor of game. **Wildheit,** -hāet, *f.* wildness, savageness. **Wildniß,** vĭlt'nĭss, *f.* wilderness, savageness.
Wildpret, -prĕt, = **Wildbrät.**
Wildschütz, vĭlt'shüts, *m. pl.* **Wildschützen,** poacher.
Willemit, vĭllemit', *m.* Willemite.
Willen(n), vĭl'len, *m.* will; **um — willen,** for the sake of, on account of; **um meinetwillen,** for my sake; **um Gotteswillen,** for God's sake; **Willens sein,** to intend, purpose, to have a mind. **Willenlos,** vĭl'lenlōs, *a.* having no will of one's own.
Willfahren, vĭllfär'en, *vi.* to comply with. **Willfährig,** vĭll'färĭch, *a.* compliant, compliable; **-keit,** -kāet, *f.* compliance, readiness. **Willfahrung,** -ŭng, *f.* compliance.
Willig, vĭl'lĭch, *a.* willing; **-en,** *vi.* n. agree or consent to. **Willigkeit,** -kāet, *f.* willingness.
Willkomm, vĭll'kŏmm, *n.* -en, *m.* welcome, salutation.
Willkommen, vĭllkŏm'men, *a.* welcome.
Willkür, vĭll'kühr, *f.* arbitrariness, discretion; **-lich,** -lĭch, *a.* arbitrary, discretional; **-keit,** -kāet, *f.* arbitrariness.
Wimmeln, vĭm'meln, *vi.* to swarm, teem, crowd.
Wimmern, vĭm'mĕrn, *vi.* to whimper, moan, whine, groan.
Wimpel, vĭm'pel, *f. or m.* pennon, pendant.
Wimper, vĭm'pĕr, *f.* eye-lash. **Wimpern,** *vi.* to wink, blink, twinkle.
Wind, vĭnt, *m. pl.* -e, wind, breeze, air; scent, hint; flatulence, windiness; **— bekommen,** to get scent of; **— machen,** to vapor, brag, boast; **stehender —,** settled wind; **kurzer, schiefer —,** scant, sharp wind; **starker —,** high wind; **offener —,** fair wind; **halber —,** large wind; **-anker,** -anker, *m.* lower anchor. **Windbeutel,** -bëŭtel, *m.* braggart, humbug; **-ei,** -ēī', *f.* humbug, boasting. **Windbüchse,** -büxĕ, *f.* air-gun, wind-gun.
Winde, vĭn'dĕ, *f.* windlass, pulley.
Winde, vĭn'dĕ, *f.* bindweed; morning glory.
Windei, vĭnd'ĕē, *n. pl.* -er, wind-egg.
Windel, vĭn'del, *f.* swaddling clothes; **-kind,** -kĭnt, *n. pl.* -er, child in swaddling clothes.
Winden, vĭn'den (wand, gewunden), *vt.* to wind, wring, wrest, twist.
Windfahne, vĭnt'fäne, *f.* vane, weather-cock. **Windfang,** -fang, *m.* ventilator. **Windhund,** -hŭnt, *m.* greyhound.
Windig, vĭnd'ĭch, *a.* windy.
Windklappe, vĭnt'klappe, *f.* valve.
Windlicht, vĭnt'lĭcht, *n.* torch.
Windmesser, vĭnt'mĕsser, *m.* windgauge, anemometer.
Windmühle, vĭnt'mühle, *f.* wind-mill.
Windofen, vĭnt'ōfen, *m.* wind-furnace.
Windpocken, vĭnt'pocken, *s. pl.* chicken-pox.

Windbrad, vint'răt, *n. pl.* -räder, ventilator.
Windrose, vint'röse, *f.* (compass-)card; anemone (Bot.).
Windruthe, vint'ruṭe, *f.* whip; windarm.
Windsbraut, vints'brŏut, *f. pl.* -bräute, hurricane, whirlwind, squall; tornado.
Windschaden, vint'shăden, *m.* damage done by the wind.
Windschief, vint'shīf, *a.* warped.
Windsegel, vint'sägl, *n.* wind-sail.
Windseite, vint'sĕite, *f.* weather-side.
Windspiel, vint'zbpīl, *n.* greyhound.
Windstill, vint'zhtill, *a.* calm; -e, *f.* calm. **Windstoss,** -zhtoss, *m. pl.* -stösse, blast, gust, puff of wind.
Windstrich, vint'zhtrich, *m.* rhumb point, current of the wind.
Windung, vin'dŭng, *f.* winding, turning; worm, spire, thread (of a screw).
Windwehe, vint'vă-e, *f.* drift of snow.
Windweiser, vint'vĕīser, **Windzeiger,** vint'tsäěger, *m.* anemo-scope, vane, fane.
Windwirbel, vint'vīrbl, *m.* whirlwind.
Windzug, vint'tsŭg, *m. pl.* **Windzüge,** draught *or* current of air; ventiduct.
Wink, vink, *m.* wink; nod, hint.
Winkel, vīnk'l, *m.* angle; corner; nook.
Winkeladvokat, vīnkl'ădfokăt, *m.* -en, *pl.* -en, pettifogger.
Winkelehe, vīnkl'ā-e, *f.* clandestine *or* hedge-marriage.
Winkeleisen, vīnkl'ĕisen, *n.* iron rule, square.
Winkelhaken, vīnkl'häken, *m.* iron rule. (Print.) stick.
Winkelig, vīn'kelich, *a.* angular, cornered.
Winkelmass, vīnkl'măs, *n.* square.
Winkelmesser, vīnkl'měsser, *m.* protractor.
Winkelrecht, vīnkl'recht, *a.* rectangular, right-angled, perpendicular.
Winkelzug, vīnkl'tsŭg, *m. pl.* -züge, trick, evasion, shift.
Winken, vink'en, *vi.* to wink, beckon.
Winseln, vin'seln, *vi.* to moan, whimper, whine.
Winter, vin'ter, *m.* winter.
Winterammer, vin'terammer, *f.* snowbird. **Winterbeule,** -bĕule, *f.* chilblain. **Winterdrossel,** -drossel, *f.* red-wing. **Wintergegend,** -gĕgent, *f.* wintery region. **Winterhaft,** -haft, *a.* **Winterig,** vin'terich, **Winterlich,** -lich, *a.* wintery. as it winter, winter-hyemal. **Wintern,** vin'tern, *vi.* to grow winter; *rt.* to winter, to feed during the winter; *vi.* to winter, pass the winter. **Winterquartier,** -kvarrtĭr, *n.* winterquarters. **Wintersaat,** -săt, *f. pl.* -en, winter-crop. **Winterseite,** -sĕite, *f.* north side. **Winterung,** -ŭng, *f.* wintering. **Winterzeit,** -tsĕit, *f.* winter-time, winter-season.
Winzer, vint'ser, *m.* -in, *f.* vintager; vine-dresser.
Winzig, vin'tsich, *a.* petty, little, diminutive.
Wipfel, vip'fel, *m.* top.
Wippe, vip'pe, *f.* swape, sweep, seesaw. **Wippen,** *rt.* to swing, to balance; to tip. **Wipper,** vip'per, *m.* clipper.
Wir, vīr, *pn.* we.
Wirbel, vīr'bl, *m.* whirl, twirl, top; crown; eddy, vortex; whirlpool; whirlwind; giddiness; roll, beat of drum.
Wirbelig, vīr'belich, *a.* whirled, whirling, vortical. **Wirbeln,** vīr'beln, *rt. i.* to whirl. **Wirbelwind,** -vīnt, *m.* whirl-wind.
Wirteisen, vīrk'ĕīsen, *n.* (tawer's) paring-knife (farr.); searcher.
Wirken, vīr'ken, *vt.* to work, operate; effect, tell; to knead; pare.
Wirklich, vīrk'lich, *a.* actual, real, true; -keit, -kĕet, *f.* reality, actuality, truth. **Wirksam,** -sam, *a.* efficacious, efficient, effective, powerful; active; -keit, -kĕet, *f.* efficiency, efficaciousness, efficacy, activity.
Wirkstuhl, vīrk'zhtŭl, *m. pl.* -stühle, loom.
Wirkung, vīrk'ŭng, *f.* working, effect, action; impression; kneading.
Wirkungskreis, vīr'kungskräes, *m. pl.* -e, sphere of action *or* of activity.
Wirr, virr, *a.* confused, confuse, hare-brained. **Wirren,** vīr'ren, *vt.* to entangle, confuse. **Wirrgarn,** -garn, *n.* entangled yarn. **Wirrkopf,** vīrr'kopf, *m. pl.* -köpfe, confused head. **Wirrseide,** vīr'sĕide, *f.* refuse of silk. **Wirrstroh,** -zhtrō, *n.* short straw. **Wirrung,** -ŭng, *f.* confu-

Weiße, wēi'sẹ, *f.* whiteness. **Weißen,** wēi'sen, *vt.* to whiten, whitewash.
Weißerz, wēis'ärts, *n.* sparry iron-ore; white copper-ore.
Weißfisch, wēis'fish, *m.* white-fish, bleak.
Weißgerber, wēis'gĕrbẹr, *m.* tawer; -rei, -ēi', *f.* tawery.
Weißgrau, wēis'grāu, *a.* light gray, hoary, whitish gray.
Weißkraut, wēis'krōut, *n.* white cabbage.
Weißlich, wēis'lich, *a.* whitish. **Weißling,** -ling, *m.* whitling.
Weißpappel, wēis'pappl, *f.* white poplar.
Weißstein, wēis'zhtēn, *m.* white-stone. **Weißtanne,** wēis'tannẹ, *f.* white pine.
Weißzeug, wēis'tsēūk, *m.* linen.
Weisung, wēis'ung, *f.* order, direction.
Weit, vēit, *a. ar.* distant, far; wide, widely, broad; **von weitem,** from afar; **bei weitem,** by far; **weiter,** farther, further; **weitest,** farthest, furthest.
Weite, vēi'tẹ, *f. or n.* width; distance; largeness, amplitude; **lichte Weite,** span (Arch.).
Weiten, vēi'ten, *vt. i.* to widen, expand, extend.
Weiterung, vēit'ẹrung, *f.* procrastination.
Weithin, vēit'hīn. *av.* to a great distance. **Weitläufig,** vēit'lāūfich, *a.* large, vast; distant; detailed, prolix, at full, at full length; **-keit,** -kāet, *f.* vast extent; diffusiveness, prolixity. **Weitschweifig,** -shwēfich, *a.* prolix, diffuse: **-keit,** -kāet, *f.* prolixity. **Weitsichtig,** -sichtich, *a.* far-sighted.
Weizen, vāets'en, *m.* wheat; **-brod,** -brōt, *n.* wheat bread. **Wei'zenkorn,** -korn, *n. pl.* **-körner,** grain of wheat.
Welch, velch, **-er, -e, -es,** *a. pron.* who, which. **Welcherlei,** -erlāē, *a.* of what kind.
Welk, velk, *a.* withered, faded, flagging, languid; **-en,** *vi.* to wither, fade, decay, flag, languish.
Welle, vel'lẹ, *f.* wave, billow; (Mech.) roller; **aufrechte —** spindle; **-nförmig,** -förmich, *a.* undulatory, waving, uudulating. **Wel'lenreich,** -rēich, *n.* realm of the sea.
Weller, vel'lẹr, *w* cylinder.

Wellermauer, vel'lermōu̇-ẹr, **Wel'lermand,** -vant, *f.* loam-wall, mudwall. **Wellern,** vel'lẹrn, *vt.* to make mud-walls.
Welt, velt, *f.* world, universe: earth; **all,** -all, *n.* universe. **Welt'alter,** -alter, *n.* age (of the world), period.
Welt'bekannt, -bekannt, *a.* notorious. **Welt'berühmt,** -berühmt, *a.* far-famed, renowned. **Welt'bürger,** -bürger, *m.* cosmopolite: **-lich,** -lich, *a.* cosmopolitical. **Welt'bürgersinn,** -sinn, *m.* cosmopolitism. **Welt'gebäude,** -gebäude. *n.* system *or* fabric of the world. **Welt'gegend,** -gägent, *f.* region, quarter of the world.
Weltgeist, velt'gāezht, *m.* spirit of the universe, creative spirit; **-licher,** -licher, *m.* secular priest. **Welt'gericht,** velt'gericht, *n.* last judgment. **Welt'geschichte,** -geshichte, *f.* universal history. **Welt'handel,** -handel, *m.* commerce. **Welt'heiland,** -hēlant, *m.* Saviour. **Welt'kenntniß,** -kenntnis, *f.* knowledge of the world. **Welt'kind,** -kint, *n. pl.* **-er,** worldling. **Welt'klug,** -klūk, *a.* prudent; **-heit,** -hāet, *f.* worldly wisdom. **Welt'körper,** velt'körper, *m.* heavenly body. **Welt'kugel,** -kugel, *f.* globe. **Welt'kunde,** -kundẹ, *f.* cosmology. **Welt'kundig,** -kundich, *a.* notorious; skilled in history.
Welt'lauf, -lāūf, *m.* course *or* way of the world. **Welt'lich,** -lich, *a.* worldly, secular; **-keit,** -kāet, *f.* worldliness, worldly-mindedness; secularity. **Welt'liebe,** -lībẹ, *f.* love of the world. **Welt'ling,** -ling, *m.* worldling. **Welt'mann,** -mann, *m.* man of the world. **Welt'meer,** -mār, *n.* ocean, main (sea). **Welt'priester,** -prīzhter, *m.* secular priest. **Welt'sinn,** -sinn, *m.* worldly-mindedness, worldliness. **Welt'theil,** -tāel, *n.* part of the world, continent. **Welt'weiser,** -vēiser, *m.* philosopher. **Welt'weisheit,** -vēishāet, *f.* philosophy.
Wenbeeisen, ven'dẹ-ēisẹn. *n.* tap-iron. **Wen'dekreis,** -krāes, *m.* tropic.
Wendeltreppe, ven'deltreppẹ, *f.* winding-stairs.
Wenden, ven'den (wandte, gewandt), *vt.* to turn, direct; **sich —,** *v* turn, change; **sich — an,** to apply to, to address one's self to; **durch** *or* **gegen**

Wen 897 **Wet**

ben Wind —, *or* bei bem Winbe —, to tack.
Wendeſtufe, vęn'dęzhtųfę, *f.* winder.
Wendung, vęnd'ųng, *f.* turn, turning.
Wenig, vā'nich, *a. ar.* little, few; **er**, *a.* less, lesser, fewer. **Wenigſt**, vā'-nikzht. *a.* least, fewest; **wenigſtens**, ųm Wenigſten, at least. **Wenigkeit**, -kāet, *f.* smallness, trifle; mei-ne —, my humble self.
Wenn, vęn, *Cj.* when; if; — nicht, if not, unless; — auch, although; — je, — immer, whenever.
Wer, vār, *pron.* who; — auch, whoever.
Werben, věr'bęn (warb, geworben), *vt.* to sue for, petition; to court, woo; to recruit. **Werber**, *m.* recruiting-officer, recruiter; suitor, wooer.
Werbung, věrb'ųng, *f.* recruiting, levy, enlistment; wooing, courting.
Werden, věr'den (warb, wurbe, geworben),to become, grow, turn, get, to be, happen, come to pass; to come into existence.
Werder, věr'dęr, *m.* small island, holm.
Werfen, věr'fęn (warf, geworfen), *vt.* to cast, throw, fling; to bring forth, bear; ſich —, to warp (of wood).
Werft, věrft, *n.* wharf.
Werſt, věrft, *m. n.* **Werſte**, věrf'tę, *f.* warp, weft.
Werg, věrk, *n.* tow, hards; **·leinwand**, -lǝenvant, *f.* tow-linen.
Werk, věrk, *n.* work, deed, production; ṣu — gehen mit, to deal with; **·eltag**, -ęltāk, *n.* working-day.
Werkmeiſter, věrk'mǣzhtęr, *m.* foreman, superintendent. **Werkſat**, -sat·, *m.* skeleton (Carpent.).
Werkſtatt, věrk'zhtatt, *f. pl.* **-ſtätte**. **Werkſtätte**, -zhtęttę, *f.* workshop. **Werkſtein**, -zhtǟęn, *m.* **Werkſtück**, -zhtück, *n.* square-stone. **Werktag**, -tāk, *m.* working day. **Werkzeug**, věrk'tsěůk, *n. pl.* **-e**, tool, instrument.
Wermuth, vǟr'mųt, *m.* wormwood.
Werptroſs, věrp'tross, *n.* warp, warping hawser (Mar.).
Werth, vǟrt, *a.* worth, valuable; dear, precious; **·loſs**, -lōs, *a.* worthless.
Werthſchäzen, vērt'shētzęn, *vt.* to esteem highly, to regard. **Werth-ſchäzung**, -ųng, *f.* estimation, esteem.

Weſen, vā'sęn, *n.* being, existence, substance, essence, nature.
Weſenlos, vā'sęnlōs, *a.* unsubstantia.
Weſentlich, vā'sęntlich, *a.* essential, substantial, real; **·keit**, -kǟet, *f.* essentiality, essence, substance.
Weſpe, věs'pę, *f.* wasp; **·neſt**, věs'-pęnnęst, *n.* wasp's nest.
Weſpenſtich, věs'pęnzhtich, *m.* wasp-bite.
Weſſen, vęs'sęn, **Weſs**, vęss, *pn.* whose, of whom, of which; **·halb**, -halp, **Wesswegen**, -vāgęn, *av.* wherefore, why, on what account.
Weſt, věst, **Weſten**, *m.* west; west wind.
Weſte, vězh'tę, *f.* vest, waistcoat; **·ntaſche**, -tashę, *f.* vest-pocket.
Weſtgegend, věsht'gägęnt, *f.* **Weſt-land**, -lant, *n. pl.* **·länder**, western country. **Weſtlich**, -lich, *a.* western, westerly; **Weſtnordweſt**, west-northwest; **Weſtſüdweſt**, west-southwest; **Weſtſüdweſtwind**, west-south-west wind, west-southwester. **Weſtwärts**, věst'věrts, *av.* westward, westwardly. **Weſtwind**, věst'vint, *m.* west wind.
Wett, vęt, *a. av.* even, equal; — machen, to quit scores.
Wette, vęt'tę, *f.* bet, wager; um bie — thun, to vie in.
Wetteifer, vętt'ǟifer, *m.* emulation; **·n**, *vt.* to emulate, vie, contend.
Wetten, vęt'ten, *vt.* to bet, to lay a bet *or* wager.
Wetter, vět'ter, *n.* weather; thunderstorm, tempest; air, current of air; **·ableiter**, -ablǟter, *m.* lightning-rod, conductor. **Wetterbeobachtung**, -bęōbachtųng, *f.* meteorological observation. **Wetterdach**, -dach. *n. pl.* **-dächer**, penthouse. **Wetterfahne**, -fānę, *f.* **Wetterhahn**, -hān, *m. pl.* **-hähne**, vane, weather-vane, weather-cock. **Wetterglas**, -glǟs, *n. pl.* **-gläſer**, weather-glass, barometer, thermometer. **Wetterlaunisch**, launish, *a.* peevish, capricious. **Wet-terleuchten**, -lěůchtęn, *n.* heat-lightning. **Wetterlöſung**, -lōsųng, *f.* ventilation. **Wettern**, vět'těrn, *vt.* to thunder. **Wetterprophet**, -profǟt. *m.* weather-spy. **Wetterrab**, -rāt, *n. pl.* **-räder**, ventilating-fanner. **Wet-terſtrahl**, -zhtrāl, *m.* **-es**, *pl.* **-en**, flash of lightning. **Wetterwendiſch**,

34

-wendish, a. changeable, fickle, inconstant, peevish. **Wetterwolke,** -wolke, f. thunder-cloud.

Wettrennen, vett'rennen, n. race; — zu Fuß, foot-race: — zu Pferd, horse-race; — in Booten, boat-race.

Wettrenner, m. racer; race-horse. **Wettstreit,** -shtrīt, m. emulation, contention, contest, rivalry.

Wetzen, vets'en, vt. to whet. **Wetzschiefer,** -shīfer, m. whetslate. **Wetzstein,** -shtīn, m. whetstone.

Wichse, vix'e, f. blacking; waxing. **Wichsen,** vix'en, vt. to blacken; to wax.

Wicht, vicht, m. wight, fellow.

Wichtig, vich'tig, a. weighty, important; -keit, -kīt, f. importance.

Wicke, vick'e, f. vetch.

Wickel, vick'el, m. roller.

Wickelmaschine, vick'elmashīne, f. winding machine, lap machine; spreader.

Wickelkind, vickl'kint, n. pl. -er, child in swaddling-cloth.

Wickeln, vick'eln, vt. to roll, wind up.

Wickelwalze, vick'elvaltse, f. roller.

Widder, vid'der, m. ram; aries; hydraulischer —, hydraulic ram.

Wider, vī'der, pr. against, contrary or in opposition to; -bellen, -bellen, vt. to contradict. **Widerbeller,** vī'derbeller, m. wrangler.

Widerchrist, vī'derkrisht, m. antichrist; -lich, -lich, a. antichristian.

Widerdruck, vī'derdruck, m. second form; reiteration; reaction; -bogen, -bōgen, m. tympan-sheet.

Widerfahren, viderfā'ren (widerfuhr, widerfahren), vi. to happen, befall, occur.

Widerhaken, vī'derhāken, m. barb, beard.

Widerhalt, vī'derhalt, m. hold, support, resistance.

Widerhalten, vī'derhalten (widerhielt, widergehalten), vi. to hold out, resist.

Widerlage, vī'derlāge, f. counterfort, buttress.

Widerlager, vī'derlāger, n. springing-stone.

Widerlegbar, vīderlāg'bār, **Widerleglich,** -lich, a. confutable, refutable, disprovable.

Widerlegen, vide-lā'gen, vt. to disprove, confute refute. **Widerlegung,** -ung, f. confutation, refutation.

Widerlich, vī'derlich, a. disgusting offensive; -keit, -kīt, f. offensiveness.

Widern, vī'dern, vi. to disgust.

Widernatürlich, vī'dernatürlich, a. unnatural, preternatural, contrary to nature.

Widerpart, vī'derpart, m. opponent; opposition.

Widerrathen, vīderrāt'en (-rieth, -rathen), vt. to dissuade, to represent as unfit.

Widerrechtlich, vī'derrechtlich, a. illegal, unlawful; -keit, -kīt, f. unlawfulness, illegality.

Widerrede, vī'derrāde, f. contradiction, opposition.

Widerriß, vī'derrizht, m. withers.

Widerruf, vī'derruf, m. pl. -e, recall, repeal, recantation, retraction.

Widerrufen, viderru'fen, vt. to recall, retract, unsay, repeal. **Widerruflich,** -lich, a. repealable, reversible, revocable.

Widersacher, vī'dersacher, m. -in, f. adversary.

Widerschein, vī'dershēn, m. reflexion, reverberation of light.

Widersetzen, vidersets'en, vr. sich —, to oppose, resist.

Widersetzlich, vidersets'lich, a. refractory; -keit, -kīt, f. refractoriness.

Widersetzung, -ung, f. resistance, opposition.

Widersinnig, vī'dersinnich, a. nonsensical, absurd; -keit, -kīt, f. nonsensicalness, absurdity.

Widerspänstig, vī'derzhpenstich, a. resistive, refractory; -keit, -kīt, f. restiveness, refractoriness.

Widerspiel, vī'derzhpīl, n. contrary, reverse.

Widersprechen, viderzhprech'en (widersprach, widersprochen), vt. to contradict, gainsay; -b, a. contradictory.

Widerspruch, vī'derzhpruch, m. pl. **Widersprüche,** contradiction, inconsistency.

Widerstand, vī'derzhtant, m. resistance, opposition.

Widerstehen, viderzhtā'en (widerstand, widerstanden), vt. to resist, oppose, withstand.

Widerstreben, viderzhtrā'ben, vi. to strive or struggle against, repugn

resist; *s. n.* repugnancy, resistance.
Widerstreit, vī'dershtrīt, *m.* conflict; antagonism, contradiction; **-en,** vīderzhtrēī'ten, *vt.* to conflict, contend. **Widerstreitend,** *a.* conflicting; contradictory.
Widerstrom, vī'dershtrōm, *m.* countercurrent.
Widerwärtig, vī'dervertig, *a.* disgusting, adverse, loathsome, disagreeable; **-keit, -käet,** *f.* adversity, reverse; unpleasantness.
Widerwille, vī'dervillë, *m.* aversion, disgust, antipathy, reluctance.
Widerwillig, vī'dervillich, *a.* reluctant, unwilling, backward.
Widmen, vīd'men, *vt.* to devote; dedicate, consecrate. **Widmung, -ung,** *f.* devotion; dedication.
Widrig, vīd'rich, *a.* averse, contrary; nauseous, disgusting; **-keit, -käet,** *f.* adversity.
Widrigenfalls, vī'drigenfalls, *a.* else, otherwise, in the other case.
Wie, vī, *pr.* how, as, when.
Wiede, vī'dë, *f.* willow, osier, withy.
Wiedehopf, vī'dehopf, *m. pl.* **-e,** lapwing, pewit, green plover, hoopoo.
Wieder, vī'der, *av.* back, again, anew, afresh.
Wiederabdruck, vīderap'druck, *m. pl.* **-abdrücke,** re-impression.
Wiederanstellen, vī'deranshtellen, *vt.* to re-appoint.
Wiederaufbauen, vīderäūf'bōyen, *vt.* to rebuild.
Wiederbekommen, vī'derbekommen (**-bekam, -bekommen**), *vt.* to recover, get again.
Wiederbeleben, vī'derbelāben, *vt.* to revive, revivify. **Wiederbelebung, -ung,** *f.* revivification.
Wiederbringen, vī'derbringen (**-wiederbringen, wiedergebracht**), *vt.* to bring back, restore, retrieve.
Wiederbringlich, vīderbring'lich, *a.* retrievable. **Wiederbringung, -ung,** *f.* restoration.
Wiedereinsetzen, vīderaën'setsen, *vt.* to reinstate, replace, restore, re-establish.
Wiedererlangen, vī'dererlangen, *vt.* to recover. **Wiedererlangung, -ung,** *f.* recovery.
Wiedererobern, vī'dererōbërn, *vt.* to reconquer

Wiedererstatten, vī'derërzhtatten, *vt* to restore, return, reimburse, repay. **Wiedererstattung, -ung,** *f.* return, restitution, repayment.
Wiederfinden, vī'derfinden, *vt.* to find again.
Wiedergeben, vī'dergāben (**-gab, -gegeben**), *vt.* to return, give back, render.
Wiedergeboren, vī'dergebōren, *a.* regenerate(d). **Wiedergeburt, -burt,** *f.* regeneration.
Wiedergenesung, vī'dergenäsung, *f.* recovery.
Wiederhall, vī'derhall, *m.* echo; **-en,** *vi.* to re-echo.
Wiederherstellen, vīderhär'zhtellen, *vt.* to restore, recover; redintegrate, re-establish. **Wiederherstellung, -ung,** *f.* restoration, restitution; recovery.
Wiederholen, vīderhō'len, *vt.* to repeat, reiterate. **Wiederholung, -ung,** *f.* repetition, reiteration.
Wiederkäuen, vī'derkäüen *vt.* to ruminate.
Wiederkauf, vī'derkäuf, *m. pl.* **-käufe,** redemption, repurchase; **-en,** *vt.* to repurchase, redeem. **Wiederkäuflich, -käuflich,** *a.* redeemable.
Wiederkehr, vī'derkär, *f.* return, recurrence; **-en,** *vi.* to return, come back.
Wiederklang, vī'derklang, *m.* echo.
Wiederklingen, vī'derklingen, *vi.* to re-echo.
Wiederkommen, vī'derkommen (**-kam, -gekommen**), *vi.* to come again, return. **Wiederkunft, -kunft,** *f.* return.
Wiederöffnen, vīderöff'nen, *vt.* to re-open.
Wiederschein, vī'dershaën, *m.* reflex, reflected light.
Wiedersehen, vī'dersäen (**-sah, -gesehen**), *vt.* to see *or* meet again; *s. n.* seeing, meeting again.
Wiedertaufe, vī'dertäufe, *f.* rebaptism, rebaptization; **-n,** *vt.* to rebaptize. **Wiedertäufer, -täufer,** *m.* rebaptizer; anabaptist.
Wiedertönen, vī'dertöhnen, *vt. i.* to resound.
Wiederum, vī'derum, *av.* again, once more, repeatedly.
Wiedervergelten, vī'derfërgëlten, *vt* to requite, retaliate, remunerate, recompense, reward, repay.

Wie 400 **Win**

Wiederbergeltung, vi'derfergëltung, *f.* requital, retaliation, retribution, recompense, reward.

Wiederverkaufen, vi'derfērkäufen, *vt.* to resell, retail.

Wiederversöhnen, vi'derfērsöhnen, *vt.* to reconcile, conciliate; propitiate.

Wiege, vi'ge, *f.* cradle.

Wiegemesser, vi'gemësser, *n.* chopping knife.

Wiegen, vi'gen, *vt.* to rock, cradle; sich —, to lull one's self with.

Wiegen, vi'gen (wog, gewogen), *vi. t.* to weigh; *vt.* wiegte, gewiegt.

Wiegenkind, vi'genkïnt, *n.* baby.

Wiegenlied, vi'genlid, *n. pl.* -er, lullaby.

Wiehern, vi'hern, *vi.* to neigh, whinny; wieherndes Gelächter, horselaugh.

Wiek, vik. *n. pl.* -e, inlet, bay.

Wieke, vi'ke, *f.* lint.

Wiese, vis'e, *f.* meadow.

Wiesel, vi'sel, *n.* weasel.

Wiesenbau, vi'senböy, *m.* cultivation of meadows. **Wiesengrund,** -grŭnt, *m. pl.* -gründe, **Wieseuland,** -lant, *n. pl.* -länder, meadow.

Wiesewachs, vi'sevaks, **Wiesewuchs,** -vŭks, *m.* meadows.

Wievielst, vi'filzht, **Wievielt,** *a.* what or which number.

Wiewohl, vivōl', *Cj.* although, though.

Wild, vilt, *a.* wild, savage; *s. n.* game, venison; Bröt, -brēt, *n.* deer, game, venison. **Wildbraten,** -bräten, *m.* roast venison. **Wilddieb,** -dīb, *m.* poacher. **Wilder,** *m.* savage. **Wild'fang,** -faug, *m. pl.* -fänge, mad cap. **Wildfremd,** -fremt, *a.* quite strange. **Wildgeschmack,** -geshmack, *m.* flavor of game. **Wildheit,** -häet, *f.* wildness, savageness. **Wildniss,** vilt'niss, *f.* wilderness, savageness. **Wildpret,** -prêt, = **Wildbrät.**

Wildschütz, vilt'shüts, *m. pl.* **Wildschützen,** poacher.

Willemit, villemit', *m.* Willemite.

Wille(n), vil'len, *m.* will; um — willen, for the sake of, on account of; um meinetwillen, for my sake; um Gotteswillen, for God's sake; Willens sein, to intend, purpose, to have a mind. **Willenlos,** vil'lenlōs, *a.* having no will of one's own.

Willfahren, villfär'en, *vi.* to comply with. **Willfährig,** vill'fārĭcḣ, *a.* compliant, compliable; -keit, -kāet, *f.* compliance, readiness. **Willfahrung,** -ung, *f.* compliance.

Willig, vil'licḣ, *a.* willing; -en, *vi.* to agree or consent to. **Willigkeit,** -kāet, *f.* willingness.

Willkomm, vill'komm, *n.* -en, *m.* welcome, salutation.

Willkommen, villkom'men, *a.* welcome.

Willkür, vill'kühr, *f.* arbitrariness, discretion; -lich, -licḣ, *a.* arbitrary, discretional; -keit, -kāet, *f.* arbitrariness.

Wimmeln, vim'meln, *vi.* to swarm, teem, crowd.

Wimmern, vim'mern, *vi.* to whimper, moan, whine, groan.

Wimpel, vim'pel, *f.* or *m.* pennon, pendant.

Wimper, vim'per, *f.* eye-lash. **Wimpern,** *vi.* to wink, blink, twinkle.

Wind, vint, *m. pl.* -e, wind, breeze, air; scent, hint; flatulence, windiness; — bekommen, to get scent of; — machen, to vapor, brag, boast; stehender —, settled wind; knapper, schiefer —, scant, sharp wind; starker —, high wind; offener —, fair wind; halber —, large wind; -anker, *m.* lower anchor. **Windbeutel,** -bëŭtel, *m.* braggart, humbug; -ei, -ēi', *f.* humbug, boasting. **Windbüchse,** -büxe, *f.* air-gun, wind-gun.

Winde, vin'de, *f.* windlass, pulley.

Winde, vin'de, *f.* bindweed; morning glory.

Windei, vind'ǟē, *n. pl.* -er, wind-egg.

Windel, vin'del, *f.* swaddling clothes; -kind, -kint, *n. pl.* -er, child in swaddling clothes.

Winden, vin'den (wand, gewunden), *vt.* to wind, wring, wrest, twist.

Windfahne, vint'fāne, *f.* vane, weather-cock. **Windfang,** -fang, *m.* ventilator. **Windhund,** -hunt, *m.* greyhound.

Windig, vind'icḣ, *a.* windy.

Windklappe, vint'klappe, *f.* valve.

Windlicht, vint'licht, *n.* torch.

Windmesser, vint'nësser, *m.* windgauge, anemometer.

Windmühle, vint'mühle, *f.* wind-mill.

Windofen, vint'ōfen, *m.* wind-furnace.

Windpocken, vint'pocken, *s. pl.* chicken-pox.

Windrad, vint'rāt, n. pl. -räder, ventilator.
Windrose, vint'rōse, f. (compass-)card; anemone (Bot.).
Windruthe, vint'ryte, f. whip; wind-arm.
Windsbraut, vints'brout, f. pl. -bräute, hurricane, whirlwind, squall; tornado.
Windschaden, vint'shāden, m. damage done by the wind.
Windschief, vint'shīf, a. warped.
Windsegel, vint'sāgl, n. wind-sail.
Windseite, vint'sēite, f. weather-side.
Windspiel, vint'zhpīl, n. greyhound.
Windstill, vint'zhtīll, a. calm; -e, f. calm. **Windstoß**, -zhtoss, m. pl. -stöße, blast, gust, puff of wind.
Windstrich, vint'zhtrich, m. rhumb point, current of the wind.
Windung, vin'dyng, f. winding, turning; worm, spire, thread (of a screw).
Windwehe, vint'vā-e, f. drift of snow.
Windweiser, vint'vēiser, **Windzeiger**, vint'tsāiger, m. anemo-scope, vane, fane.
Windwirbel, vint'vīrbl, m. whirlwind.
Windzug, vint'tsyg, m. pl. **Windzüge**, draught or current of air; ventiduct.
Wink, vink, m. wink; nod, hint.
Winkel, vīnk'l, m. angle; corner; nook.
Winkeladvokat, vīnkl'advokāt, m. -en, pl. -en, pettifogger.
Winkelehe, vīnkl'ā-e, f. clandestine or hedge-marriage.
Winkeleisen, vīnkl'ēisen, n. iron rule, square.
Winkelhaken, vīnkl'hāken, m. iron rule. (Print.) stick.
Winkelig, vīn'kelich, a. angular, cornered.
Winkelmaß, vīnkl'mās, n. square.
Winkelmesser, vīnkl'messer, m. protractor.
Winkelrecht, vīnkl'recht, a. rectangular, right-angled, perpendicular.
Winkelzug, vīnkl'tsyg, m. pl. -züge, trick, evasion, shift.
Winken, vink'en, vt. to wink, beckon.
Winseln, vin'seln, vi. to moan, whimper, whine.
Winter, vīn'ter, m. winter.
Winterammer, vīn'terammer, f. snow-bird. **Wir terbeule**, -bēüle, f. chil-blain. **Winterdrossel**, -drossel, f. red-wing. **Wintergegend**, -gāgent, f. wintery region. **Winterhaft**, -haft, a. winterig, vin'terich, **Win'terlich**, -lich, a. wintery, as it winter, winter-hyemal. **Wintern**, vīn'tern, vi. to grow winter; vt. to winter, to feed during the winter; vi. to winter, pass the winter. **Winterquartier**, -kvartīr, n. winter-quarters. **Winterfaat**, -sāt, f. pl. -en, winter-crop. **Winterseite**, -sēite, f. north side. **Winterung**, -ung, f. wintering. **Winterzeit**, -tsēit, f. winter-time, winter-season.
Winzer, vint'ser, m. sin, f. vintager; vine-dresser.
Winzig, vīn'tsich, a. petty, little, diminutive.
Wipfel, vīp'fel, m. top.
Wippe, vīp'pe, f. swape, sweep, see-saw. **Wippen**, vt. to swing, to balance; to tip. **Wipper**, vīp'per, m. clipper.
Wir, vīr, pn. we.
Wirbel, vīr'bl, m. whirl, twirl, top; crown; eddy, vortex; whirlpool; whirlwind; giddiness; roll, beat of drum.
Wirbelig, vīr'belich, a. whirled, whirling, vortical. **Wirbeln**, vīr'beln, vt i. to whirl. **Wirbelwind**, -vīnt, m. whirl-wind.
Wirkeisen, vīrk'ēisen, n. (tawer's) paring-knife (farr.); searcher.
Wirken, vīr'ken, vt. to work, operate; effect, tell: to knead; pare.
Wirklich, vīrk'lich, a. actual, real, true; -keit, -kāet, f. reality, actuality; truth. **Wirksam**, -sam, a. efficacious, efficient, effective, powerful; active; -keit, -kāet, f. efficiency, efficaciousness, efficacy, activity.
Wirkstuhl, vīrk'zhtyl, m. pl. -stühle, loom.
Wirkung, vīrk'ung, f. working, effect, action; impression; kneading.
Wirkungskreis, vīr'kyngskrāes, m. pl. -e, sphere of action or of activity.
Wirr, vīrr, a. confused, confuse, hare-brained. **Wirren**, vīr'ren, vt. to entangle, confuse. **Wirrgarn**, -garn, n. entangled yarn. **Wirrkopf**, vīrr'kopf, m. pl. -köpfe, confused head. **Wirrscheibe**, vīr'sēibe, f. refuse of silk. **Wirrstroh**, -zhtrō, n. short straw. **Wirrung**, -ung, f. confu-

Wei 396 **Wen**

Weiße, vīl'sĕ, *f.* whiteness. **Weißen**, vīl'sen, *vl.* to whiten, whitewash.

Weißerz, vīs'ārts, *n.* sparry iron-ore; white copper-ore.

Weißfisch, vīs'fish, *m.* white-fish, bleak.

Weißgärber, vīs'gĕrbĕr, *m.* tawer; -rei, -ĕī', *f.* tawery.

Weißgrau, vīs'grāū, *a.* light gray, hoary, whitish gray.

Weißkraut, vīs'kroŭt, *n.* white cabbage.

Weißlich, vīs'lich, *a.* whitish. **Weißling**, -ling, *m.* whiting.

Weißpappel, vīs'pappl, *f.* white poplar.

Weißstein, vīs'zhtĕn, *m.* white-stone. **Weißtanne**, vīs'tannĕ, *f.* white pine.

Weißzeug, vīs'tsĕŭk, *m.* linen.

Weisung, vīs'ŭng, *f.* order, direction.

Weit, vīt, *a. av.* distant, far; wide, widely, broad; von weitem, from afar; bei weitem, by far; weiter, farther, further; weitest, farthest, furthest.

Weite, vī'tĕ, *f. or n.* width; distance; largeness, amplitude; lichte Weite, span (Arch.).

Weiten, vī'tĕn, *vt. i.* to widen, expand, extend.

Weiterung, vīt'ĕrŭng, *f.* procrastination.

Weithin, vīt'hīn. *av.* to a great distance. **Weitläufig**, vīt'lāŭfich, *a.* large, vast; distant; detailed, prolix, at full, at full length; weit, -keit, *f.* vast extent; diffusiveness, prolixity. **Weitschweifig**, -shāēfich, *a.* prolix, diffuse; -keit, -keit, *f.* prolixity. **Weitsichtig**, -sichtich, *a.* far-sighted.

Weizen, vīts'ĕn, *m.* wheat; -brod, -brōt, *n.* wheat bread. **Weizenkorn**, -korn, *n. pl.* -körner, grain of wheat.

Welch, velch, *ser, se, ses, a. pron.* who, which. **Welcherlei**, -erlāē, *a.* of what kind.

Welk, vĕlk, *a.* withered, faded, flagging, languid; -en, *vi.* to wither, fade, decay, flag, languish.

Welle, vĕl'lĕ, *f.* wave, billow; (Mech.) roller; aufrechte —, spindle; unförmig, -fūrmich, *a.* undulatory, waving, nudulating. **Wellenreich**, -rēich, *n.* realm of the sea.

Weller, vĕl'lĕr, *r* cylinder.

Wellermauer, vĕl'lermoŭ-er, **Wellerwand**, -vant, *f.* loam-wall, mud-wall. **Wellern**, vĕl'lern, *vt.* to make mud-walls.

Welt, vĕlt, *f.* world, universe; earth; -all, -all, *n.* universe. **Weltalter**, -alter, *n.* age (of the world), period. **Weltbekannt**, -bekannt, *a.* notorious. **Weltberühmt**, -berühmt, *a.* far-famed, renowned. **Weltbürger**, -bürger, *m.* cosmopolite; -lich, -lich, *a.* cosmopolitical. **Weltbürgersinn**, -sinn, *m.* cosmopolitism. **Weltgebäude**, -gebāŭdĕ. *n.* system *or* fabric of the world. **Weltgegend**, -gägent, *f.* region, quarter of the world.

Weltgeist, vĕlt'gāēzht, *m.* spirit of the universe, creative spirit; -licher, -licher, *m.* secular priest. **Weltgericht**, vĕlt'gericht, *n.* last judgment. **Weltgeschichte**, -geshichtĕ, *f.* universal history. **Welthandel**, -handel, *m.* commerce. **Weltheiland**, -hāē-lant, *m.* Saviour. **Weltkenntniß**, -kenntniss, *f.* knowledge of the world. **Weltkind**, -kint, *n. pl.* -er, worldling. **Weltklug**, -klŭk, *a.* prudent; -heit, -hāēt, *f.* worldly wisdom. **Weltkörper**, vĕlt'körper, *m.* heavenly body. **Weltkugel**, -kŭgel, *f.* globe. **Weltkunde**, -kŭndĕ, *f.* cosmology. **Weltkundig**, -kŭndich, *a.* notorious; skilled in history. **Weltlauf**, -lāŭf, *m.* course *or* way of the world. **Weltlich**, -lich, *a.* worldly, secular; -keit, -kāēt, *f.* worldliness, worldly-mindedness, secularity. **Weltliebe**, -lībe, *f.* love of the world. **Weltling**, -ling, *m.* worldling. **Weltmann**, -mann, *m.* man of the world. **Weltmeer**, -mār, *n.* ocean, main (sea). **Weltpriester**, -prīshtĕr, *m.* secular priest. **Weltsinn**, -sinn, *m.* worldly-mindedness, worldliness. **Welttheil**, -thāēl, *n.* part of the world, continent. **Weltweiser**, -vāēser, *m.* philosopher. **Weltweisheit**, -vāēshāēt, *f.* philosophy.

Wendeisen, ven'dĕ-āēsĕn. *n.* tap-iron. **Wendekreis**, -krāēs, *m.* tropic.

Wendeltreppe, ven'deltreppĕ, *f.* winding-stairs.

Wenden, ven'dĕn (wandte, gewandt), *vt.* to turn, direct; sich —, *v.* turn, change; sich — an, to apply to, to address one's self to; durch or gegen

den Wind —, *or* bei dem Winde —, to tack.
Wendestufe, ven'dęzhtŭfę, *f.* winder.
Wendung, vend'ŭng, *f.* turn, turning.
Wenig, vā'nĭch, *a. av.* little, few; wer, *a.* less, lesser, fewer. **Wenigst**, vā'nĭkzht. *a.* least, fewest; wenigstens, zum Wenigsten, at least. **Wenigkeit**, -kĕet, *f.* smallness, trifle; meine —, my humble self.
Wenn, ven, *Cj.* when; if; — nicht, if not, unless; — auch, although; — je, — immer, whenever.
Wer, vār, *pron.* who; — auch, whoever.
Werben, vĕr'bęn (warb, geworben), *vt.* to sue for, petition; to court, woo; to recruit. **Werber**, *m.* recruiting-officer, recruiter; suitor, wooer.
Werbung, vĕrb'ŭng, *f.* recruiting, levy, enlistment; wooing, courting.
Werden, vĕr'den (warb, wurde, geworben), to become, grow, turn, get, to be, happen, come to pass; to come into existence.
Werder, vĕr'dęr, *m.* small island, holm.
Werfen, vĕr'fęn (warf, geworfen), *vt.* to cast, throw, fling; to bring forth, bear; sich —, to warp (of wood).
Werft, vĕrft, *n.* wharf.
Werft, vĕrft, *m. n.* **Werste**, vĕrf'tę, *f.* warp, weft.
Werg, vĕrk, *n.* tow, hards; -leinwand, -lānvant, *f.* tow-linen.
Werk, vĕrk, *n.* work, deed, production; zu — gehen mit, to deal with; -eltag, -ęltāk, *n.* working-day.
Werkmeister, vĕrk'mĕezhtęr, *m.* foreman, superintendent. **Werksatz**, -satz, *m.* skeleton (Carpent.).
Werkstatt, vĕrk'zhtatt, *f. pl.* -stätte, **Werkstätte**, -zhtętte, *f.* workshop. **Werkstein**, -zhtzĕn, *m.* **Werkstück**, -zhtück, *n.* square-stone. **Werktag**, -tāk, *m.* working day. **Werkzeug**, vĕrk'tsĕŭk, *n. pl.* -e, tool, instrument.
Wermuth, vār'mŭt, *m.* wormwood.
Werptross, vĕrp'tross, *n.* warp, warping hawser (Mar.).
Werth, vārt, *a.* worth, valuable; dear, precious; -loss, -lōs, *a.* worthless.
Werthschätzen, vĕrt'shĕtzęn, *vt.* to esteem highly, to regard. **Werthschätzung**, -ŭng, *f.* estimation, esteem.

Wesen, vā'sen, *n.* being, existence, substance, essence, nature.
Wesenlos, vā'senlōs, *a.* unsubstantial.
Wesentlich, vā'sentlĭch, *a.* essential, substantial, real; -keit, -kĕet, *f.* essentiality, essence, substance.
Wespe, vĕs'pę, *f.* wasp; -nest, vĕs'pennest, *n.* wasp's nest.
Wespenstich, vĕs'penzhtĭch, *m.* wasp-bite.
Wessen, vęs'sen, **Wes**, vęss, *pn.* whose, of whom, of which; -halb, -halp, **Wesswegen**, -vāgęn, *av.* wherefore, why, on what account.
West, vĕzht, **Westen**, *m.* west; west wind.
Weste, vĕzh'tę, *f.* vest, waistcoat; -tasche, -tashę, *f.* vest-pocket.
Westgegend, vĕzht'gāgęnd, *f.* western land, -lant, *n. pl.* -länder, western country. **Westlich**, -lĭch, *a.* western, westerly: **Westnortwest**, west-north-west; **Westsüdwest**, west-southwest; **Westsüdwestwind**, west-south-west wind, west-southwester. **Westwärts**, vĕst'vĕrts, *av.* westward, westwardly. **Westwind**, vĕst'vĭnt, *m.* west wind.
Wett, vet, *a. av.* even, equal; — machen, to quit scores.
Wette, vęt'tę, *f.* bet, wager; um die — thun, to vie in.
Wetteifer, vętt'ĕĭfęr, *m.* emulation; -n, *vt.* to emulate, vie, contend.
Wetten, vęt'ten, *vt.* to bet, to lay a bet or wager.
Wetter, vĕt'ter, *n.* weather; thunderstorm, tempest; air, current of air; -ableiter, -ablĕeter, *m.* lightning-rod, conductor. **Wetterbeobachtung**, -bęōbachtŭng, *f.* meteorological observation. **Wetterdach**, -dach, *n. pl.* -dächer, penthouse. **Wetterfahne**, -fānę, *f.* **Wetterhahn**, -hān, *m. pl.* -hähne, vane, weather-vane, weather-cock. **Wetterglas**, -glās, *n. pl.* -gläser, weather-glass, barometer, thermometer. **Wetterlaunisch**, lą̄nĭsh, *a.* peevish, capricious. **Wetterleuchten**, -lĕŭchten, *n.* heat-lightning. **Wetterlösung**, -lōsŭng, *f.* ventilation. **Wettern**, vĕt'tĕrn, *vt.* to thunder. **Wetterprophet**, -profāt, *m.* weather-spy. **Wetterrath**, -rāt, *n. pl.* -räder, ventilating-fanner. **Wetterstrahl**, -zhtrāl, *m.* -es, *pl.* -en, flash of lightning. **Wetterwendisch**,

34

-vendish, a. changeable, fickle, inconstant, peevish. **Wetterwolfe,** -volke, f. thunder-cloud.
Wettrennen, vett'rĕnnen, n. race; — zu Fuß, foot-race: — zu Pferd, horse-race: — in Booten, boat-race.
Wett'renner, m. racer; race-horse.
Wett'streit, -shtrīt, m. emulation, contention, contest, rivalry.
Wetzen, vĕts'en, vt. to whet. **Wetz'schiefer,** -shīfer, m. whetslate. **Wetzstein,** -shtīĕn, m. whetstone.
Wichse, vix'e, f. blacking; waxing.
Wichsen, vix'en, vt. to blacken; to wax.
Wicht, vicht, m. wight, fellow.
Wichtig, vich'tig, a. weighty, important; -keit, -kīĕt, f. importance.
Wicke, vick'e, f. vetch.
Wickel, vick'el, m. roller.
Wickelmaschine, vick'elmashīne, f. winding machine, lap machine; spreader.
Wickelkind, vickl'kint, n. pl. -er, child in swaddling-cloth.
Wickeln, vick'eln, vt. to roll, wind up.
Wickelwalze, vick'elvaltse, f. roller.
Widder, vid'der, m. ram; aries; hydraulischer —, hydraulic ram.
Wider, vī'der, pr. against, contrary or in opposition to; **bellen, -bellen,** vt. to contradict. **Widerbeller,** vī'derbĕller, m. wrangler.
Widerchrist, vī'derkrizht, m. antichrist; -lich, -lich, a. antichristian.
Widerdruck, vī'derdruck, m. second form; reiteration; reaction; -bogen, -bōgen, m. tympan-sheet.
Widerfahren, vīderfā'ren (widerfuhr, widerfahren), vi. to happen, befall, occur.
Widerhaken, vī'derhāken, m. barb, beard.
Widerhalt, vī'derhalt, m. hold, support, resistance.
Widerhalten, vī'derhalten (widerhielt, widergehalten), vi. to hold out, resist.
Widerlage, vī'derlāge, f. counterfort, buttress.
Widerlager, vī'derlāger, n. springing-stone.
Widerlegbar, vīderlāg'bār, **Widerleglich,** -lich, coufutable, refutable, disprovable.
Widerlegen, vīderlā'gen, vt. to disprove, confute refute. **Widerlegung,** -ung, f. confutation, refutation.
Widerlich, vī'derlich, a. disgusting, offensive; -keit, -kīĕt, f. offensiveness.
Widern, vī'dern, vi. to disgust.
Widernatürlich, vī'dernatürlich, a. unnatural, preternatural, contrary to nature.
Widerpart, vī'derpart, m. opponent; opposition.
Widerrathen, vīderrāt'en (-rieth, -rathen), vt. to dissuade, to represent as unfit.
Widerrechtlich, vī'derrĕchtlich, a. illegal, unlawful; -keit, -kīĕt, f. unlawfulness, illegality.
Widerrede, vī'derrāde, f. contradiction, opposition.
Widerrist, vī'derrizht, m. withers.
Widerruf, vī'derruf, m. pl. -e, recall, repeal, recantation, retraction.
Widerrufen, vīderry'fen, vt. to recall, retract, unsay, repeal. **Widerruflich,** -lich, a. repealable, reversible, revocable.
Widersacher, vī'dersacher, m. -in, f. adversary.
Widerschein, vī'dershĕin, m. reflexion, reverberation of light.
Widersetzen, vīderset'en, vr. sich —, to oppose, resist.
Widersetzlich, vīdersets'lich, a. refractory; -keit, -kīĕt, f. refractoriness.
Widersetzung, -ung, f. resistance, opposition.
Widersinnig, vī'dersinnich, a. nonsensical, absurd; -keit, -kīĕt, f. nonsensicalness, absurdity.
Widerspänstig, vī'derzhpenstich, a. resistive, refractory; -keit, -kīĕt, f. restiveness, refractoriness.
Widerspiel, vī'derzhpīl, n. contrary, reverse.
Widersprechen, vīderzhprĕch'en (widersprach, widersprochen), vt. to contradict, gainsay; -d, a. contradictory.
Widerspruch, vī'derzhpruch, m. pl. Widersprüche, contradiction, inconsistency.
Widerstand, vī'derzhtant, m. resistance, opposition.
Widerstehen, vīderzhtā'en (widerstand, widerstanden), vt. to resist, oppose, withstand.
Widerstreben, vīderzhtrā'ben, vi. to strive or struggle against, repugn

resist; *s. n.* repugnancy, resistance.
Widerstreit, vī'derzhtrīt, *m.* conflict; antagonism, contradiction; **en**, vī'derzhtrī'ten, *vt.* to conflict, contend. **Widerstrei'tend**, *a.* conflicting; contradictory.
Widerstrom, vī'derzhtröm, *m.* countercurrent.
Widerwärtig, vī'dervĕrtig, *a.* disgusting, adverse, loathsome, disagreeable; **keit**, -kǟet, *f.* adversity, reverse; unpleasantness.
Widerwille, vī'dervillẹ, *m.* aversion, disgust, antipathy, reluctance.
Widerwillig, vī'dervillich, *a.* reluctant, unwilling, backward.
Widmen, vīd'men, *vt.* to devote; dedicate, consecrate. **Wid'mung**, -ung, *f.* devotion; dedication.
Widrig, vīd'rich, *a.* averse, contrary; nauseous, disgusting; **keit**, -kǟet, *f.* adversity.
Widrigenfalls, vī'drigenfalls, *a.* else, otherwise, in the other case.
Wie, vī, *pr.* how, as, when.
Wiede, vī'dẹ, *f.* willow, osier, withy.
Wiedehopf, vī'dehopf, *m. pl.* -e, lapwing, pewit, green plover, hoopoo.
Wieder, vī'der, *av.* back, again, anew, afresh.
Wiederabdruck, vīderap'drụck, *m. pl.* -abdrücke, re-impression.
Wiederanstellen, vī'deranzhtẹllen, *vt.* to re-appoint.
Wiederaufbauen, vīderäuf'bōyen, *vt.* to rebuild.
Wiederbekommen, vī'derbekommen (-bekam, -bekommen), *vt.* to recover, get again.
Wiederbeleben, vī'derbelāben, *vt.* to revive, revivify. **Wie'derbelebung**, -ung, *f.* revivification.
Wiederbringen, vī'derbringen (-wiederbringen, wiedergebracht), *vt.* to bring back, restore, retrieve.
Wiederbringlich, vīderbring'lich, *a.* retrievable. **Wiederbring'ung**, -ung, *f.* restoration.
Wiedereinsetzen, vīderẹin'setzen, *vt.* to reinstate, replace, restore, re-establish.
Wiedererlangen, vī'dererlangen, *vt.* to recover. **Wie'dererlangung**, -ung, *f.* recovery.
Wiedererobern, vī'dererōbĕrn, *vt.* to reconquer

Wiedererstatten, vī'derẹrzhtatten, *vt.* to restore, return, reimburse, repay. **Wie'dererstattung**, -ung, *f.* return, restitution, repayment.
Wiederfinden, vī'derfinden, *vt.* to find again.
Wiedergeben, vī'dergāben (-gab, -gegeben), *vt.* to return, give back, render.
Wiedergebären, vī'dergebören, *a.* regenerate(d). **Wie'dergeburt**, -burt, *f.* regeneration.
Wiedergenesung, vī'dergenāsung, *f.* recovery.
Wiederhall, vī'derhall, *m.* echo; **en**, *vi.* to re-echo.
Wiederherstellen, vīderhăr'zhtẹllen, *vt.* to restore, recover; redintegrate, re-establish. **Wiederher'stellung**, -ung, *f.* restoration, restitution; recovery.
Wiederholen, vīderhō'len, *vt.* to repeat, reiterate. **Wiederhol'ung**, -ung, *f.* repetition, reiteration.
Wiederkäuen, vī'derkäuen *vt.* to ruminate.
Wiederkauf, vī'derkäuf, *m. pl.* -läufe, redemption, repurchase; **en**, *vt.* to repurchase, redeem. **Wie'derkäuflich**, -käuflich, *a.* redeemable.
Wiederkehr, vī'derkār, *f.* return, recurrence; **en**, *vi.* to return, come back.
Wiederklang, vī'derklang, *m.* echo.
Wiederklingen, vī'derklingen, *vi.* to re-echo.
Wiederkommen, vī'derkommen (-kam, -gekommen), *vi.* to come again, return. **Wie'derkunft**, -kunft, *f.* return.
Wiederöffnen, vīderöff'nen, *vt.* to re-open.
Wiederschein, vī'dershẹin, *m.* reflex, reflected light.
Wiedersehen, vī'dersāen (-sah, -gesehen), *vt.* to see or meet again; *s. n.* seeing, meeting again.
Wiedertaufe, vī'dertäufẹ, *f.* rebaptism, rebaptization; **en**, *vt.* to rebaptize. **Wie'dertäufer**, -täufer, *m.* rebaptizer; anabaptist.
Wiedertönen, vī'dertöhnen, *vt. i.* to resound.
Wiederum, vī'derụm, *av.* again, once more, repeatedly.
Wiedervergelten, vī'derfẹrgĕlten, *vt.* to requite, retaliate, remunerate recompense, reward, repay.

Wiederbergeltung, vī'derfērgëltung, *f.* requital, retaliation, retribution, recompense, reward.
Wiederverkaufen, vī'derfērkäufen, *vt.* to resell, retail.
Wiederversöhnen, vī'derfērsöhnen, *vt.* to reconcile, conciliate; propitiate.
Wiege, vī'ge, *f.* cradle.
Wiegemesser, vī'gemësser, *n.* chopping knife.
Wiegen, vī'gen, *vt.* to rock, cradle; fich —, to lull one's self with.
Wiegen, vī'gen (wog, gewogen), *vt.* to weigh; *vt.* wiegte, gewiegt.
Wiegenkind, vī'genkīnd, *n.* baby.
Wiegenlied, vī'genlīd, *n. pl.* -er, lullaby.
Wiehern, vī'hern, *vi.* to neigh, whinny; wiehernes Gelächter, horse-laugh.
Wiek, vīk, *n. pl.* -e, inlet, bay.
Wieke, vī'ke, *f.* lint.
Wiese, vīs'e, *f.* meadow.
Wiesel, vī'sel, *n.* weasel.
Wiesenbau, vī'senbow, *m.* cultivation of meadows. **Wiesengrund**, -grunt, *m. pl.* -gründe, **Wiesenland**, -lant, *n. pl.* -länder, meadow.
Wiesewachs, vī'sevaks, **Wiesewuchs**, -vyks, *m.* meadows.
Wievielst, vī'fīlzht, **Wievielt**, *a.* what *or* which number.
Wiewohl, vivōl', *Cj.* although, though.
Wild, vilt, *a.* wild, savage; *s. n.* game, venison; -brät, -brēt, *n.* deer, game, venison. **Wildbraten**, -brāten, *m.* roast venison. **Wildbieb**, -dīb, *m.* poacher. **Wilber**, *m.* savage. **Wilds-fang**, -faug, *m. pl.* -fänge, mad cap. **Wildfremd**, -fremt, *a.* quite strange. **Wildgeschmack**, -geshmack, *m.* flavor of game. **Wildheit**, -hāet, *f.* wildness, savageness. **Wildnis**, vilt'niss, *f.* wilderness, savageness.
Wildpret, -prēt, = **Wildbrät**.
Wildschütz, vilt'shüts, *m. pl.* **Wildschützen**, poacher.
Willemit, villemīt', *m.* Willemite.
Willen, vil'len, *m.* will; um — willen, for the sake of, on account of; um meinetwillen, for my sake: um Gotteswillen, for God's sake; Willens sein, to intend, purpose, to have a mind. **Willenlos**, vil'lenlōs, *a.* having no will of one's own.
Willfahren, villfār'en, *vi.* to comply with. **Willfährig**, vill'fārich, *a.* compliant, compliable; -keit, -kāet, *f.* compliance, readiness. **Willfah-rung**, -ung, *f.* compliance.
Willig, vill'lich, *a.* willing; -en, *vi.* n agree *or* consent to. **Willigkeit**, -kāet, *f.* willingness.
Willkomm, vill'komm, *n. sen, m.* welcome, salutation.
Willkommen, villkom'men, *a.* welcome.
Willkür, vill'kühr, *f.* arbitrariness, discretion; -lich, -lich, *a.* arbitrary, discretional; -keit, -kāet, *f.* arbitrariness.
Wimmeln, vim'meln, *vi.* to swarm, teem, crowd.
Wimmern, vim'mern, *vi.* to whimper, moan, whine, groan.
Wimpel, vim'pel, *f. or m.* pennon, pendant.
Wimper, vim'per, *f.* eye-lash. **Wimpern**, *vi.* to wink, blink, twinkle.
Wind, vint, *m. pl.* -e, wind, breeze; air; scent, hint; flatulence, windiness; — bekommen, to get scent of; — machen, to vapor, brag, boast; stehender —, settled wind; knapper, schiefer —, scant, sharp wind; starker —, high wind; offener —, fair wind; halber —, large wind; -anker, *m.* lower anchor. **Windbeutel**, -böitel, *m.* braggart, humbug; -ei, -ēī', *f.* humbug, boasting.
Windbüchse, -büxe, *f.* air-gun, windgun.
Winde, vin'de, *f.* windlass, pulley.
Winde, vin'de, *f.* bindweed; morning glory.
Windei, vind'āē, *n. pl.* -er, wind-egg.
Windel, vin'del, *f.* swaddling clothes; -kind, -kīnt, *n. pl.* -er, child in swaddling clothes.
Winden, vin'den (wand, gewunden), *vt.* to wind, wring, wrest, twist.
Windfahne, vint'fāne, *f.* vane, weather-cock. **Windfang**, -faug, *m.* ventilator. **Windhund**, -hunt, *m.* greyhound.
Windig, vind'ich, *a.* windy.
Windklappe, vint'klappe, *f.* valve.
Windlicht, vint'licht, *n.* torch.
Windmesser, vint'mësser, *m.* windgange, anemometer.
Windmühle, vint'mühle, *f.* wind-mill **Windofen**, vint'ōfen, *m.* wind-furnace.
Windpocken, vint'pocken, *s. pl.* chicken-pox.

Windbraut, vint'rāt, *n. pl.* -räber, ventilator.

Windrose, vint'röse, *f.* (compass-)card; anemone (Bot.).

Windruthe, vint'ruthe, *f.* whip; wind-arm.

Windsbraut, vints'brout, *f. pl.* -bräute, hurricane, whirlwind, squall; tornado.

Windschaden, vint'shāden, *m.* damage done by the wind.

Windschief, vint'shīf, *a.* warped.

Windsegel, vint'sägl, *n.* wind-sail.

Windseite, vint'sīte, *f.* weather-side.

Windspiel, vint'shpīl, *n.* greyhound.

Windstill, vint'zhtill, *a.* calm; -e, *f.* calm. **Windstoß**, -zhtoss, *m. pl.* -stöße, blast, gust, puff of wind.

Windstrich, vint'zhtrich, *m.* rhumb point, current of the wind.

Windung, vin'dụng, *f.* winding, turning; worm, spire, thread (of a screw).

Windwehr, vint'vǟr-e, *f.* drift of snow.

Windweiser, vint'vēiser, **Windzeiger**, vint'tsǟger, *m.* anemo-scope, vane, fane.

Windwirbel, vint'virbl, *m.* whirlwind.

Windzug, vint'tsụg, *m. pl.* **Windzüge**, draught *or* current of air; ventiduct.

Wink, vink, *m.* wink; nod, hint.

Winkel, vink'l, *m.* angle; corner; nook.

Winkeladvokat, vinkl'advokāt, *m.* -en, *pl.* -en, pettifogger.

Winkelehe, vinkl'ā-e, *f.* clandestine *or* hedge-marriage.

Winkeleisen, vinkl'ēisen, *n.* iron rule, square.

Winkelhaken, vinkl'hāken, *m.* iron rule. (Print.) stick.

Winkelig, vin'kelich, *a.* angular, cornered.

Winkelmaß, vinkl'mās, *n.* square.

Winkelmesser, vinkl'messer, *m.* protractor.

Winkelrecht, vinkl'recht, *a.* rectangular, right-angled, perpendicular.

Winkelzug, vinkl'tsụg, *m. pl.* -züge, trick, evasion, shift.

Winken, vink'en, *vt.* to wink, beckon.

Winseln, vin'seln, *vi.* to moan, whimper, whine.

Winter, vin'ter, *m.* winter.

Winterammer, vin'terammer, *f.* snowbird. **Win'terbeule**, -bēule, *f.* chil-

blain. **Win'terdrossel**, -drossel, *f.* red-wing. **Win'tergegend**, -gägent, *f.* wintery region. **Win'terhaft**, -haft, *a.* **Winterig**, vin'terich, **Win'terlich**, -lich, *a.* wintery. as it winter, winter-hyemal. **Wintern**, vin'tern, *vi.* to grow winter; *vt.* to winter, to feed during the winter; *vi.* to winter, pass the winter. **Win'terquartier**, -kvarrtīr, *n.* winter-quarters. **Win'tersaat**, -sāt, *f. pl.* -en, winter-crop. **Win'terseite**, -sēite, *f.* north side. **Win'terung**, -ung, *f.* wintering. **Win'terzeit**, -tsēit, *f.* winter-time, winter-season.

Winzer, vint'ser, *m.* -in, *f.* vintager; vine-dresser.

Winzig, vin'tsich, *a.* petty, little, diminutive.

Wipfel, vip'fel, *m.* top.

Wippe, vip'pe, *f.* swape, sweep, see-saw. **Wip'pen**, *vt.* to swing, to balance; to tip. **Wipper**, vip'per, *m.* clipper.

Wir, vīr, *pn.* we.

Wirbel, vīr'bl, *m.* whirl, twirl, top; crown; eddy, vortex; whirlpool; whirlwind; giddiness; roll, beat of drum.

Wirbelig, vīr'belich, *a.* whirled, whirling, vertical. **Wirbeln**, vīr'beln, *vt. i.* to whirl. **Wir'belwind**, -vint, *m.* whirl-wind.

Wirkeisen, virk'ēisen, *n.* (tawer's) paring-knife (farr.); searcher.

Wirken, vīr'ken, *vt.* to work, operate; effect, tell; to knead; pare.

Wirklich, virk'lich, *a.* actual, real, true; -keit, -kāet, *f.* reality, actuality; truth. **Wirk'sam**, -sam, *a.* efficacious, efficient, effective, powerful; active; -keit, -kāet, *f.* efficiency, efficaciousness, efficacy, activity.

Wirkstuhl, virk'zhtul, *m. pl.* -stühle, loom.

Wirkung, virk'ung, *f.* working, effect, action; impression; kneading.

Wirkungskreis, vir'kụngskrǟes, *m. pl.* -e, sphere of action *or* of activity.

Wirr, virr, *a.* confused, confuse, hare-brained. **Wirren**, vir'ren, *vt.* to entangle, confuse. **Wirr'garn**, -garn, *n.* entangled yarn. **Wirrkopf**, virr'kopf, *m. pl.* -köpfe, confused head. **Wirrseide**, vir'sēide, *f.* refuse of silk. **Wirrstroh**, -zhtrō, *n.* short straw. **Wirr'ung**, -ụng, *f.* confu-

Weiße, wēī'sę, *f.* whiteness. **Weißen**, wēī'sen, *vt.* to whiten, whitewash.
Weißerz, wēīs'ārts, *n.* sparry iron-ore; white copper-ore.
Weißfisch, wēīs'fish, *m.* white-fish, bleak.
Weißgärber, wēīs'gėrber, *m.* tawer; -ei, -ēī', *f.* tawery.
Weißgrau, wēīs'grāu, *a.* light gray, hoary, whitish gray.
Weißkraut, wēīs'krout, *n.* white cabbage.
Weißlich, wēīs'lich, *a.* whitish. **Weißling**, -ling, *m.* whiting.
Weißpappel, wēīs'pappl, *f.* white poplar.
Weißstein, wēīs'zhtaēn, *m.* white-stone. **Weißtanne**, wēīs'tanne, *f.* white pine.
Weißzeug, wēīs'tsěūk, *m.* linen.
Weisung, wēīs'ŭng, *f.* order, direction.
Weit, wēīt, *a. ar.* distant, far; wide, widely, broad; von weitem, from afar; bei weitem, by far; weiter, farther, further; weitest, farthest, furthest.
Weite, wēī'tę, *f. or n.* width; distance; largeness, amplitude; lichte Weite, span (Arch.).
Weiten, wēī'ten, *vt. i.* to widen, expand, extend.
Weiterung, wēīt'ęrŭng, *f.* procrastination.
Weithin, wēīt'hīn. *av.* to a great distance. **Weitläufig**, wēīt'lāūfich, *a.* large, vast; distant; detailed, prolix, at full, at full length; -keit, -kāēt, *f.* vast extent; diffusiveness, prolixity. **Weitschweifig**, -shāēfich, *a.* prolix, diffuse; -keit, -kāēt, *f.* prolixity. **Weitsichtig**, -sichtich, *a.* far-sighted.
Weizen, wāēts'ęn, *m.* wheat; -brod, -brōt, *n.* wheat bread. **Weizenkorn**, -korn, *n. pl.* -körner, grain of wheat.
Welch, welch, -er, -e, -es, *a. pron.* who, which. **Welcherlei**, -erlāē, *a.* of what kind.
Welk, velk, *a.* withered, faded, flagging, languid; -en, *vi.* to wither, fade, decay, flag, languish.
Welle, vēl'lę, *f.* wave, billow; (Mech.) roller; aufrechte —, spindle; -nförmig, -förmich, *a.* undulatory, waving, undulating. **Wellenreich**, -rēīch, *n.* realm of the sea.
Weller, vēl'ler, *m.* cylinder.

Wellermauer, vēl'lermōu-er, **Wellerwand**, -vant, *f.* loam-wall, mud-wall. **Wellern**, vēl'lern, *vt.* to make mud-walls.
Welt, vēlt, *f.* world, universe; earth; -all, -all, *n.* universe. **Weltalter**, -alter, *n.* age (of the world), period.
Weltbekannt, -bekannt, *a.* notorious. **Weltberühmt**, -berühmt, *a.* far-famed, renowned. **Weltbürger**, -bürger, *m.* cosmopolite; -lich, -lich, *a.* cosmopolitical. **Weltbürgersinn**, -sinn, *m.* cosmopolitism. **Weltgebäude**, -gebäūde. *n.* system *or* fabric of the world. **Weltgegend**, -gāgent, *f.* region, quarter of the world.
Weltgeist, vēlt'gāēzht, *m.* spirit of the universe, creative spirit; -licher, -licher, *m.* secular priest. **Weltgericht**, vēlt'gericht, *n.* last judgment. **Weltgeschichte**, -geshichtę, *f.* universal history. **Welthandel**, -handęl, *m.* commerce. **Weltheiland**, -hāē-lant, *m.* Saviour. **Weltkenntniß**, -kenntnīss, *f.* knowledge of the world. **Weltkind**, -kint, *n. pl.* -er, worldling. **Weltklug**, -klŭk, *a.* prudent; -heit, -hāēt, *f.* worldly wisdom. **Weltkörper**, vēlt'körper, *m.* heavenly body. **Weltkugel**, -kŭgel, *f.* globe. **Weltkunde**, -kŭnde, *f.* cosmology. **Weltkundig**, -kŭndich, *a.* notorious; skilled in history. **Weltlauf**, -lāūf, *m.* course *or* way of the world. **Weltlich**, -lich, *a.* worldly, secular; -keit, -kāēt, *f.* worldliness, worldly-mindedness; secularity. **Weltliebe**, -lībę, *f.* love of the world. **Weltling**, -ling, *m.* worldling. **Weltmann**, -mann, *m.* man of the world. **Weltmeer**, -mār, *n.* ocean, main (sea). **Weltpriester**, -prīzhter, *m.* secular priest. **Weltsinn**, -sinn, *m.* worldly-mindedness, worldliness. **Welttheil**, -tāēl, *n.* part of the world, continent. **Weltweiser**, -vēīzer, *m.* philosopher. **Weltweisheit**, -vēīshāēt, *f.* philosophy.
Wendeeisen, ven'dę-ēīsęn, *n.* tap-iron. **Wendekreis**, -krēīs, *m.* tropic.
Wendeltreppe, ven'deltreppę, *f.* winding-stairs.
Wenden, ven'den (wandte, gewandt), *vt.* to turn, direct; sich —, *v.* turn, change; sich — an, to apply to, to address one's self to; durch *or* gegen

Wen 897 **Wet**

den Wind —, *or* bei dem Winde —, to tack.
Wendestufe, ven'dęhtufę, *f.* winder.
Wendung, vęnd'yng, *f.* turn, turning.
Wenig, vā'nich, *a. ar.* little, few; **er**, *a.* less, lesser, fewer. **Wenigst**, vā'nikzht. *a.* least, fewest; **wenigstens**, zum Wenigsten, at least. **We'nigkeit**, -kāet, *f.* smallness, trifle; meine —, my humble self.
Wenn, vęn, *Cj.* when; if; — nicht, if not, unless; — auch, although; — je, — immer, whenever.
Wer, vār, *pron.* who; — auch, whoever.
Werben, vēr'bęn (warb, geworben), *vt.* to sue for, petition; to court, woo; to recruit. **Wer'ber**, *m.* recruiting-officer, recruiter; suitor, wooer.
Werbung, vērb'yng, *f.* recruiting, levy, enlistment; wooing, courting.
Werden, vēr'den (warb, wurde, geworben), to become, grow, turn, get, to be, happen, come to pass; to come into existence.
Werder, vēr'dęr, *m.* small island, holm.
Werfen, vēr'fęn (warf, geworfen), *vt.* to cast, throw, fling; to bring forth, bear; sich —, to warp (of wood).
Werft, vērft, *n.* wharf.
Werft, vērft, *m. n.* **Werfte**, vērf'tę, *f.* warp, weft.
Werg, vērk, *n.* tow, hards; **-leinwand**, -lāenvant, *f.* tow-linen.
Werk, vērk, *n.* work, deed, production; zu — gehen mit, to deal with; **-tag**, -tāk, *n.* working-day.
Werkmeister, vērk'māezhtęr, *m.* foreman, superintendent. **Werk'sat**, -sats, *m.* skeleton (Carpent.).
Werkstatt, vērk'zhtatt, *f. pl.* **-stätte**. **Werk'stätte**, -zhtęttę, *f.* workshop. **Werk'stein**, -zhtāen, *m.* **Werk'stück**, -zhtück, *n.* square-stone. **Werk'tag**, -tāk, *m.* working day. **Werk'zeug**, vērk'tsöük, *n. pl.* -e, tool, instrument.
Wermuth, vēr'mųt, *m.* wormwood.
Werptross, vērp'tross, *n.* warp, warping hawser (Mar.).
Werth, vārt, *a.* worth. valuable; dear, precious; **-los**, -lōs, *a.* worthless.
Werthschätzen, vērt'shētsęn, *vt.* to esteem highly, to regard. **Werth'schätzung**, -yng, *f.* estimation, esteem.

Wesen, vā'sęn, *n.* being, existence, substance, essence, nature.
Wesenlos, vā'senlōs, *a.* unsubstantial.
Wesentlich, vā'sentlich, *a.* essential, substantial, real; **-keit**, -kāet, *f.* essentiality, essence, substance.
Wespe, vēs'pę, *f.* wasp; **nest**, vēs'pęnnest, *n.* wasp's nest.
Wespenstich, vēs'penzhtich, *m.* wasp-bite.
Wessen, vęs'sen, **Wes**, vęss, *pn.* whose, of whom, of which; **-halb**, -halp, **Wes'wegen**, -vāgęn, *av.* wherefore, why, on what account.
West, vęzht, **West'en**, *m.* west; west wind.
Weste, vēzh'tę, *f.* vest, waistcoat; **-ntasche**, -tashę, *f.* vest-pocket.
Westgegend, vęzht'gägent, *f.* **West'land**, -lant, *n. pl.* **-länder**, western country. **West'lich**, -lich, *a.* western, westerly; **Westnordwest**, west-north-west; **Westsüdwest**, west-south-west; **Westsüdwestwind**, west-south-west wind, west-south-wester. **Westwärts**, vēst'vērts, *av.* westward, westwardly. **Westwind**, vēst'vint, *m.* west wind.
Wett, vęt, *a. av.* even, equal; — machen, to quit scores.
Wette, vęt'tę, *f.* bet, wager; um die — thun, to vie in.
Wetteifer, vętt'ēifęr, *m.* emulation; **n**, *vt.* to emulate, vie, contend.
Wetten, vęt'ten, *vt.* to bet, to lay a bet or wager.
Wetter, vēt'ter, *n.* weather; thunderstorm, tempest; air, current of air; **ableiter**, -ablāeter, *m.* lightning-rod, conductor. **Wet'terbeobachtung**, -beöbachtyng, *f.* meteorological observation. **Wet'terdach**, -dach. *n. pl.* -bächer, penthouse. **Wet'terfahne**, -fānę, *f.* **Wet'terhahn**, -hān, *m. pl.* -hähne, vane, weather-vane, weather-cock. **Wet'terglas**, -glās, *n. pl.* -gläser, weather-glass, barometer, thermometer. **Wet'terlaunisch**, launish, *a.* peevish, capricious. **Wet'terleuchten**, -lēüchten, *n.* heat-lightning. **Wet'terlösung**, -lōsyng, *f.* ventilation. **Wettern**, vēt'tęrn, *rt.* to thunder. **Wet'terprophet**, -profāt, *m.* weather-spy. **Wet'terrabe**, -rāt, *n. pl.* -räber, ventilating-fanner. **Wet'terstrahl**, -zhtrāl, *m.* **-es**, *pl.* **-en**, flash of lightning. **Wet'terwendisch**,

34

-vendish, *a.* changeable, fickle, inconstant, peevish. **Wetterwolke,** -volke, *f.* thunder-cloud.

Wettrennen, vett'rennen, *n.* race; — zu Fuß, foot-race; — zu Pferd, horse-race; — in Booten, boat-race. **Wett'renner,** *m.* racer; race-horse. **Wett'streit,** -shtrīt, *m.* emulation, contention, contest, rivalry.

Wetzen, vets'en, *vt.* to whet. **Wetzschiefer,** -shīfer, *m.* whetslate. **Wetzstein,** -shtīn, *m.* whetstone.

Wichse, vix'e, *f.* blacking; waxing. **Wichsen,** vix'en, *vt.* to blacken; to wax.

Wicht, vicht, *m.* wight, fellow.

Wichtig, vich'tig, *a.* weighty, important; -keit, -kīt, *f.* importance.

Wicke, vick'e, *f.* vetch.

Wickel, vick'el, *m.* roller.

Wickelmaschine, vick'elmashīne, *f.* winding machine, lap machine; spreader.

Wickelkind, vickl'kīnt, *n. pl.* -er, child in swaddling-cloth.

Wickeln, vick'eln, *vi.* to roll, wind up.

Wickelwalze, vick'elvaltse, *f.* roller.

Widder, vid'der, *m.* ram; aries; hydraulischer —, hydraulic ram.

Wider, vī'der, *pr.* against, contrary or in opposition to; -bellen, -bellen, *vt.* to contradict. **Widerbeller,** vī'derbeller, *m.* wrangler.

Widerchrist, vī'derkrīsht, *m.* antichrist; -lich, -lich, *a.* antichristian.

Widerdruck, vī'derdruck, *m.* second form; reiteration; reaction; -bogen, -bōgen, *m.* tympan-sheet.

Widerfahren, vīderfā'ren (widerfuhr, widerfahren), *vi.* to happen, befall, occur.

Widerhaken, vī'derhāken, *m.* barb, beard.

Widerhalt, vī'derhalt, *m.* hold, support, resistance.

Widerhalten, vī'derhalten (widerhielt, widergehalten), *vi.* to hold out, resist.

Widerlage, vī'derlāge, *f.* counterfort, buttress.

Widerlager, vī'derlāger, *n.* springingstone.

Widerlegbar, vīderlāg'bār, **Widerleglich,** -lich, confutable, refutable, disprovable.

Widerlegen, vīde·lā'gen, *vt.* to disprove, confute refute. **Widerlegung,** -ung, *f.* confutation, refutation.

Widerlich, vī'derlich, *a.* disgusting offensive; -keit, -kīt, *f.* offensiveness.

Widern, vī'dern, *vi.* to disgust.

Widernatürlich, vī'dernatürlich, *a.* unnatural, preternatural, contrary to nature.

Widerpart, vī'derpart, *m.* opponent; opposition.

Widerrathen, vīderrāt'en (-rieth, -rathen), *vt.* to dissuade, to represent as unfit.

Widerrechtlich, vī'derrechtlich, *a.* illegal, unlawful; -keit, -kīt, *f.* unlawfulness, illegality.

Widerrede, vī'derrāde, *f.* contradiction, opposition.

Widerrist, vī'derrizht, *m.* withers.

Widerruf, vī'derruf, *m. pl.* -e, recall, repeal, recantation, retraction.

Widerrufen, vīderru'fen, *vt.* to recall, retract, unsay, repeal. **Widerruflich,** -lich, *a.* repealable, reversible, revocable.

Widersacher, vī'dersacher, *m.* -in, *f.* adversary.

Widerschein, vī'dershīn, *m.* reflexion, reverberation of light.

Widersetzen, vīdersets'en, *vr.* sich —, to oppose, resist.

Widersetzlich, vīdersets'lich, *a.* refractory; -keit, -kīt, *f.* refractoriness. **Widersetzung,** -ung, *f.* resistance, opposition.

Widersinnig, vī'dersinnich, *a.* nonsensical, absurd; -keit, -kīt, *f.* nonsensicalness, absurdity.

Widerspänstig, vī'derzhpenstich, *a.* resistive, refractory; -keit, -kīt, *f.* restiveness, refractoriness.

Widerspiel, vī'derzhpīl, *n.* contrary, reverse.

Widersprechen, vīderzhprech'en (widersprach, widersprochen), *vt.* to contradict, gainsay; -d, *a.* contradictory.

Widerspruch, vī'derzhpruch, *m. pl.* Widersprüche, contradiction, inconsistency.

Widerstand, vī'derzhtant, *m.* resistance, opposition.

Widerstehen, vīderzhtā'en (widerstand, widerstanden), *vt.* to resist, oppose, withstand.

Widerstreben, vīderzhtrā'ben, *vi.* to strive *or* struggle against, repugn

resist; *s. n.* repugnancy, resistance.
Widerſtreit, vī'dĕrzhtrēīt, *m.* conflict; antagonism, contradiction; **-en**, vīderzhtrēī'tĕn, *vt.* to conflict, contend. **Widerſtrei'tend**, *a.* conflicting: contradictory.
Widerſtrom, vī'dĕrzhtröm, *m.* counter-current.
Widerwärtig, vī'dĕrvĕrtig, *a.* disgusting, adverse, loathsome, disagreeable; **-keit**, -kāĕt, *f.* adversity, reverse: unpleasantness.
Widerwille, vī'dĕrvillĕ, *m.* aversion, disgust, antipathy, reluctance.
Widerwillig, vī'dĕrvillich, *a.* reluctant, unwilling, backward.
Widmen, vĭd'mĕn, *vt.* to devote; dedicate, consecrate. **Wid'mung**, -ŭng, *f.* devotion; dedication.
Widrig, vĭd'rich, *a.* averse, contrary; nauseous, disgusting; **-keit**, -kāĕt, *f.* adversity.
Widrigenfalls, vī'drigĕnfalls, *a.* else, otherwise, in the other case.
Wie, vī, *pr.* how, as, when.
Wiede, vī'dĕ, *f.* willow, osier, withy.
Wiedehopf, vī'dĕhopf, *m. pl.* **-e**, lapwing, pewit, green plover, hoopoo.
Wieder, vī'dĕr, *av.* back, again, anew, afresh.
Wiederabdruck, vīdĕrap'drŭck, *m. pl.* **-abdrücke**. re-impression.
Wiederanstellen, vī'dĕranzhtĕllĕn, *vt.* to re-appoint.
Wiederaufbauen, vīdĕrāŭf'bŏŭĕn, *vt.* to rebuild.
Wiederbekommen, vī'dĕrbekommĕn (-bekam, -bekommen), *vt.* to recover, get again.
Wiederbeleben, vī'dĕrbelābĕn, *vt.* to revive, revivify. **Wie'derbelebung**, -ŭng, *f.* revivification.
Wiederbringen, vī'dĕrbringĕn (-wiederbringen, wiedergebracht), *vt.* to bring back, restore, retrieve.
Wiederbringlich, vīdĕrbring'lich, *a.* retrievable. **Wiederbring'ung**, -ŭng, *f.* restoration.
Wiedereinsetzen, vīdĕrēĭn'setzĕn, *vt.* to reinstate, replace, restore, re-establish.
Wiedererlangen, vī'dĕrerlangĕn, *vt.* to recover. **Wie'dererlangung**, -ŭng, *f.* recovery.
Wiedererobern, vī'dĕrerŏbĕrn, *vt.* to reconquer

Wiedererstatten, vī'dĕrĕrzhtattĕn, *vt.* to restore, return, reimburse, repay. **Wie'dererstattung**, -ŭng, *f.* return, restitution, repayment.
Wiederfinden, vī'dĕrfindĕn, *vt.* to find again.
Wiedergeben, vī'dĕrgābĕn (-gab, -gegeben), *vt.* to return, give back, render.
Wiedergebären, vī'dĕrgebŏrĕn, *a.* regenerate(d). **Wie'dergeburt**, -bŭrt, *f.* regeneration.
Wiedergenesung, vī'dĕrgenāsŭng, *f.* recovery.
Wiederhall, vī'dĕrhall, *m.* echo; **-en**, *vi.* to re-echo.
Wiederherstellen, vīdĕrhār'zhtĕllĕn, *vt.* to restore, recover; redintegrate, re-establish. **Wiederher'stellung**, -ŭng, *f.* restoration, restitution; recovery.
Wiederholen, vīdĕrhō'lĕn, *vt.* to repeat, reiterate. **Wiederhol'ung**, -ŭng, *f.* repetition, reiteration.
Wiederkäuen, vī'dĕrkāŭĕn *vt.* to ruminate.
Wiederkauf, vī'dĕrkāŭf, *m. pl.* **-käufe**, redemption, repurchase; **-en**, *vt.* to repurchase, redeem. **Wie'derkäuflich**, -kāŭflich, *a.* redeemable.
Wiederkehr, vī'dĕrkār, *f.* return, recurrence; **-en**, *vt.* to return, come back.
Wiederklang, vī'dĕrklang, *m.* echo.
Wiederklingen, vī'dĕrklingĕn, *vi.* to re-echo.
Wiederkommen, vī'dĕrkommĕn (-kam, -gekommen), *vi.* to come again, return. **Wie'derkunft**, -kŭnft, *f.* return.
Wiederöffnen, vīdĕrŏff'nĕn, *vt.* to re-open.
Wiederschein, vī'dĕrshāĕn, *m.* reflex, reflected light.
Wiedersehen, vī'dĕrsāĕn (-sah, -gesehen), *vt.* to see or meet again; *s. n.* seeing, meeting again.
Wiedertaufe, vī'dĕrtāŭfĕ, *f.* rebaptism, rebaptization; **-n**, *vt.* to rebaptize. **Wie'dertäufer**, -tāŭfĕr, *m.* rebaptizer; anabaptist.
Wiedertönen, vī'dĕrtöhnĕn, *vt. i.* to resound.
Wiederum, vī'dĕrŭm, *av.* again, once more, repeatedly.
Wiedervergelten, vī'dĕrfĕrgĕltĕn, *vt.* to requite, retaliate, remunerate recompense, reward, repay.

Wiederbergeltung, vī'derfērgĕltŭng, *f.* requital, retaliation, retribution, recompense, reward.
Wiederverkaufen, vī'derfērkäŭfen, *vt.* to resell, retail.
Wiederversöhnen, vī'derfērsöhnen, *vt.* to reconcile, conciliate; propitiate.
Wiege, vī'gĕ, *f.* cradle.
Wiegemesser, vī'gĕmĕssĕr, *n.* chopping knife.
Wiegen, vī'gen, *vt.* to rock, cradle; **sich —,** to lull one's self with.
Wiegen, vī'gen (wog, gewogen), *vi. t.* to weigh; *vt.* wiegte, gewiegt.
Wiegenkind, vī'genkĭnt, *n.* baby.
Wiegenlied, vī'genlīd, *n. pl.* -er, lullaby.
Wiehern, vī'hĕrn, *vi.* to neigh, whinny; **wieherndes Gelächter,** horse-laugh.
Wiek, vīk. *n. pl.* -e, inlet, bay.
Wieke, vī'kĕ, *f.* lint.
Wiese, vīs'ĕ, *f.* meadow.
Wiesel, vī'sĕl, *n.* weasel.
Wiesenbau, vī'sĕnbŏŭ, *m.* cultivation of meadows. **Wiesengrund,** -grŭnt, *m. pl.* -gründe, **Wieseuland,** -lant, *n. pl.* -länder. meadow.
Wiesewachs, vī'sĕvaks, **Wiesewuchs,** -vŭks, *m.* meadows.
Wievielst, vī'fīlxht, **Wievielt,** *a.* what or which number.
Wiewohl, vivōl'. *Cj.* although, though.
Wild, vilt, *a.* wild, savage; *s. n.* game, venison; **-brät,** -brĕt, *n.* deer, game, venison. **Wildbraten,** -brāten, *m.* roast venison. **Wildbieb,** -dīb, *m.* poacher. **Wilber, w. savage. Wild's-fang,** -fang, *m. pl.* -fänge. mad cap. **Wildfremd,** -fremt, *a.* quite strange. **Wildgeschmack,** -geshmack, *m.* flavor of game. **Wildheit,** -hāĕt, *f.* wildness, savageness. **Wildniß,** viltˈnĭss, *f.* wilderness, savageness. **Wildpret,** -prĕt, = **Wildbrät.**
Wildschütz, vilt'shüts, *m. pl.* **Wildschützen,** poacher.
Willemit, villĕmĭt', *m.* Willemite.
Willen(n), vill'ĕn, *m.* will; **um — willen,** for the sake of, on account of; **um meinetwillen,** for my sake: **um Gotteswillen,** for God's sake; **Willens sein,** to intend, purpose, to have a mind. **Willenlos,** vil'lenlōs, *a.* having no will of one's own.
Willfahren, villfăr'en, *vi.* to comply with. **Willfährig,** vill'färĭg, *a.* compliant, compliable; **-keit,** -kāĕt, *f.* compliance, readiness. **Willfährung,** -ŭng, *f.* compliance.
Willig, vĭl'lĭg, *a.* willing; **-en,** *vi. n.* agree *or* consent to. **Willigkeit,** -kāĕt, *f.* willingness.
Willkomm, vill'kŏmm, *n.* -en, *m.* welcome, salutation.
Willkommen, villkŏm'men, *a.* welcome.
Willkür, vill'kühr, *f.* arbitrariness, discretion; **-lich,** -lĭch, *a.* arbitrary, discretional; **-keit,** -kāĕt, *f.* arbitrariness.
Wimmeln, vim'meln, *vi.* to swarm, teem, crowd.
Wimmern, vim'mĕrn, *vi.* to whimper, moan, whine, groan.
Wimpel, vim'pel, *f.* or *m.* pennon, pendant.
Wimper, vim'pĕr, *f.* eye-lash. **Wimpern,** *vi.* to wink, blink, twinkle.
Wind, vint, *m. pl.* -e, wind, breeze, air; scent, hint; flatulence, windiness; **— bekommen,** to get scent of; **— machen,** to vapor, brag, boast; **stehender —,** settled wind; **knapper, schiefer —,** scant, sharp wind; **starker —,** high wind; **offener —,** fair wind; **halber —,** large wind; **-anker,** *m.* lower anchor. **Windbeutel,** -bēŭtĕl, *m.* braggart, humbug; **-ei,** -ĕī', *f.* humbug, boasting. **Windbüchse,** -bŭxĕ, *f.* air-gun, windgun.
Winde, vin'dĕ, *f.* windlass, pulley.
Winde, vin'dĕ, *f.* bindweed; morning glory.
Windei, vind'ĕi, *n. pl.* -er, wind-egg.
Windel, vin'dĕl, *f.* swaddling clothes; **-kind,** -kĭnt, *n. pl.* -er, child in swaddling clothes.
Winden, vin'den (wand, gewunden), *vt.* to wind, wring, wrest, twist.
Windfahne, vint'fānĕ, *f.* vane, weather-cock. **Windfang,** -fang, *m.* ventilator. **Windhund,** -hŭnt, *m.* greyhound.
Windig, vind'ĭch, *a.* windy.
Windklappe, vint'klappĕ, *f.* valve.
Windlicht, vint'lĭcht, *n.* torch.
Windmesser, vint'mĕssĕr, *m.* windgauge, anemometer.
Windmühle, vint'mühlĕ, *f.* wind-mill
Windofen, vint'ōfen, *m.* wind-furnace.
Windpocken, vint'pŏcken, *s. pl.* chicken-pox.

Windrad, vint'rǎt, *n. pl.* -räder, ventilator.

Windrose, vint'rōsę, *f.* (compass-)card; anemone (Bot.).

Windruthe, vint'rutę, *f.* whip; windarm.

Windsbraut, vints'brōut, *f. pl.* -bräute, hurricane, whirlwind, squall; tornado.

Windschaden, vint'shāden, *m.* damage done by the wind.

Windschief, vint'shīf, *a.* warped.

Windsegel, vint'sāgl, *n.* wind-sail.

Windseite, vint'seīte, *f.* weather-side.

Windspiel, vint'shpīl, *n.* greyhound.

Windstill, vint'zhtĭll, *a.* calm; **-e,** *f.* calm. **Windstoß,** -zhtoss, *m. pl.* -stöße, blast, gust, puff of wind.

Windstrich, vint'zhtrich, *m.* rhumb point, current of the wind.

Windung, vin'dȳng, *f.* winding, turning; worm, spire, thread (of a screw).

Windwehe, vint'vā-ę, *f.* drift of snow.

Windweiser, vint'vēīser, **Windzeiger**, vint'tsāēger, *m.* anemo-scope, vane, fane.

Windwirbel, vint'vīrbl, *m.* whirlwind.

Windzug, vint'tsȳg, *m. pl.* **Windzüge**, draught *or* current of air; ventiduct.

Wink, vink, *m.* wink; nod, hint.

Winkel, vĭnk'l, *m.* angle; corner; nook.

Winkeladvokat, vĭnkl'adfokāt, *m.* -en, *pl.* -en, pettifogger.

Winkelehe, vĭnkl'ā-ę, *f.* clandestine *or* hedge-marriage.

Winkeleisen, vĭnkl'ēīsen, *n.* iron rule, square.

Winkelhaken, vĭnkl'hāken, *m.* iron rule, (Print.) stick.

Winkelig, vin'kęlich, *a.* angular, cornered.

Winkelmaß, vĭnkl'mǎs, *n.* square.

Winkelmesser, vĭnkl'měsser, *m.* protractor.

Winkelrecht, vĭnkl'rě*ch*t, *a.* rectangular, right-angled, perpendicular.

Winkelzug, vĭnkl'tsȳg, *m. pl.* -züge, trick, evasion, shift.

Winken, vink'en, *vi.* to wink, beckon.

Winseln, vin'seln, *vi.* to moan, whimper, whine.

Winter, vĭn'ter, *m.* winter.

Winterammer, vĭn'terammer, *f.* snowbird. **Winterbeule**, -beūlę, *f.* chilblain. **Winterdrossel**, -drossel, *f.* red-wing. **Wintergegend**, -gāgęnt, *f.* wintery region. **Winterhaft,** -haft, *a.* **Winterig,** vin'terich, **Winterlich,** -lich, *a.* wintery, as it winter, winter-hyemal. **Wintern,** vĭn'tern, *vi.* to grow winter; *vt.* to winter, to feed during the winter; *vi.* to winter, pass the winter. **Winterquartier,** -kvarrtīr, *n.* winter-quarters. **Winterjaat,** -sāt, *f. pl.* -en, winter-crop. **Winterseite,** -seīte, *f.* north side. **Winterung,** -ȳng, *f.* wintering. **Winterzeit,** -tseīt, *f.* winter-time, winter-season.

Winzer, vĭn'tser, *m.* **-in,** *f.* vintager; vine-dresser.

Winzig, vin'tsich, *a.* petty, little, diminutive.

Wipfel, vĭp'fel, *m.* top.

Wippe, vĭp'pę, *f.* swape, sweep, seesaw. **Wippen**, *vt.* to swing, to balance; to tip. **Wipper,** vĭp'per, *m.* clipper.

Wir, vīr, *pn.* we.

Wirbel, vīr'bl, *m.* whirl, twirl, top; crown; eddy, vortex; whirlpool; whirlwind; giddiness; roll, beat of drum.

Wirbelig, vīr'belich, *a.* whirled, whirling, vortical. **Wirbeln,** vīr'beln, *vt. i.* to whirl. **Wirbelwind,** -vĭnt, *m.* whirl-wind.

Wirkeisen, virk'ēīsen, *n.* (tawer's) paring-knife (farr.); searcher.

Wirken, vīr'ken, *vt.* to work, operate; effect, tell: to knead; pare.

Wirklich, vĭrk'lich, *a.* actual, real, true; **-keit,** -kēīt, *f.* reality, actuality; truth. **Wirksam,** -sam, *a.* efficacious, efficient, effective, powerful; active; **-keit,** -kēīt, *f.* efficiency, efficaciousness, efficacy, activity.

Wirkstuhl, virk'zhtyl, *m. pl.* -stühle, loom.

Wirkung, vĭrk'ȳng, *f.* working, effect, action; impression; kneading.

Wirkungskreis, vĭr'kȳngskrāēs, *m. pl.* -e, sphere of action *or* of activity.

Wirr, virr, *a.* confused, confuse, harebrained. **Wirren,** vĭr'ren, *vt.* to entangle, confuse. **Wirrgarn,** -garn, *n.* entangled yarn. **Wirrkopf,** virr'-kopf, *m. pl.* -köpfe, confused head. **Wirrseide,** vīr'sēīdę, *f.* refuse of silk. **Wirrstroh,** -zhtrō, *n.* short straw. **Wirrung,** -ȳng, *f.* confu-

sion, trouble. **Wirrwarr**, vĭrr'varr, m. confusion, disturbance, trouble.
Wirtel, vĭr'tel, m. whirl.
Wirth, vĭrrt, m. pl. -e. husbandman; economist; host; landlord, innkeeper; *in, f.* lady of the house; housekeeper; landlady, hostess.
Wirthbar, vĭrrt'bär, a. habitable; *keit, -käet, f.* hospitality.
Wirthlich, vĭrrt'lich, a. hospitable; frugal; *keit, -käet, f.* hospitality; frugality.
Wirthschaft, vĭrrt'shaft, f. house-keeping, economy, husbandry; household; public house, inn.
Wirthschaften, vĭrrt'shaften, vt. to manage, administer, economize; to keep house, to husband.
Wirthschafter, vĭrrt'shafter, m. manager, steward; *in, f.* housekeeper.
Wirthschaftlich, vĭrrt'shaftlich, a. av. economical, -cally; *keit, -käet, f.* economy, frugality, frugal management.
Wirthshaus, vĭrrts'hŏŭs, n. pl. -häuser, inn, tavern, public house.
Wirthsleute, vĭrrts'läŭte, s. pl. hosts, landlord and landlady.
Wirthstisch, vĭrrts'tish, m. **Wirthstafel**, vĭrrts'täfl, f. ordinary or table d'hote.
Wisch, vish, m. pl. -e, whisk, wisp; clout; trash, scrawl.
Wischen, vish'en, vt. to wipe, rub; vi. to slip. **Wischer**, m. wiper; sponge; reprimand. **Wischfahnen**, -kolben, m. sponge-head. **Wischlappen**, -lappen, m. dish-cloth, dish-rag, duster.
Wismuth, vis'mŭt, m. bismuth.
Wispern, vizh'pern, vt. to whisper.
Wißbegier, viss'begĭr, *de, -de, f.* curiosity, inquisitiveness, desire of knowledge, wish to learn.
Wißen, vis'sen (wußte, gewußt. gevußt) vt. to know; ju wißen thun. or wißen laßen, to acquaint with; to send word, to inform; Dank —, to be thankful.
Wißenschaft, vis'senshaft, f. science; *lich, -lich, a.* scientific.
Wißenswerth, vis'sensvärt, **Wißenswürdig**, -vürdich, a. worth knowing, remarkable.
Wißentlich, vis'sentlich, a. av. knowing; wilful, voluntary; knowingly, wittingly, by design.
Witherit, vĭt'erit, n. witherite.

Wittern, vĭt'tern, vt. i. to thunder; to scent, smell.
Witterung, vit'terŭng, f. weather, scent.
Witthum, vit'tŭm, n. jointure.
Wittwe, vit've, **Wittfrau**, -fräu, f. pl. -en, widow. **Wittwenjahr**, -yär, n. widow's year. **Wittwenstand**, vit'venztant, m. widowhood.
Wittwer, vit'ver, **Wittmann**, -mann, m. pl. -männer, widower.
Witz, vits, m. sense; intellect, understanding, wit; seinen — verlieren, to lose one's wits; wittiness.
Witzbold, vits'bolt, m. wit; witty fellow. **Witzelei**, vitselēi', f. witticism.
Witzeln, vits'eln, vi. i. to be vastly witty; to affect wittiness. **Witzig**, vits'ich, a. witty. **Witzigen**, vits'igen, vt. to make wiser, to teach wit.
Witzling, vits'ling, m. witling, pretender to wit, punster, low wit.
Wo, vō, pn. where; somewhere, anywhere; if, when, in case.
Wobei, vōbēi', av. whereby, whereat, where.
Woche, voch'e, f. week, sennight; in die Wochen kommen, to be delivered; to be brought to bed; in den Wochen liegen, to lie in bed, to be confined.
Wochenbett, voch'enbet, n. confinement; childbed.
Wochenblatt, voch'enblat, n. pl. -blätter, weekly.
Wochenkind, voch'enkĭnt, n. pl. -er, new-born child.
Wochenlang, voch'enlang, av. for weeks.
Wochenlohn, voch'enlōn, m. weekly pay, week's wages.
Wochenmarkt, voch'enmarkt, n. weekly market (day).
Wochentag, voch'entäg, m. pl. -e, week-day.
Wöchentlich, vöch'entlich, a. av. weekly, by the week, hebdomadal, -dary.
Wochenweise, voch'envēse, av. by the week.
Wöchnerin, vöch'nerĭn, f. woman lying-in.
Wocken, vok'en, m. distaff, rock.
Wodurch, vodurch', av. whereby, by what.
Wofern, vofērn', cj. if; wofern nicht, unless, if not.
Wofür, vofŭhr', av. wherefore, for what.

Wage, vō'gĕ, f. billow, wave, surge.
Wagegen, vegä'gen, av. against what or which. for or to what, which.
Wagen, vō'gen, vt. i. to wave, billow, surge, fluctuate.
Wayig, vō'gig, a. wavy, surgy.
Waher, vohär', a. whence, wherefrom.
Wahin, vohīn', a. whither, where, what way.
Wahl, vōl, a. av. well, certainly, indeed; perhaps, may be; **Wohl Dir!** happy for thee! happy you! er ist wohl, he is well, in good health; s. n. welfare, weal, well-being, good, benefit, interest.
Wohlan, völän', av. well, come on!
Wohlanständig, völ'anzhtendich, a. decent, -ly. (well-)becoming; **-keit,** -kāet, f. decency.
Wohlauf, vōlöuf', ij. well! cheer up! — fein, to be well, or in good health.
Wohlbedacht, völ'bedacht, a. av. well considered. **Wohl bedächtig,** -bedechtig, **Wohl bedächtlich,** -lich, a. av. deliberate, -ly, considerate.
Wohlbefinden, völ'befinden, n. good health.
Wohlbehagen, völ'behägn, n. ease, comfortableness, comfort. **Wohlbehaglich,** -lich, a. av. comfortable, -ly, at ease.
Wohlbehalten, völ'behalten, a. av. safe.
Wohlbekannt, völ'bekannt, a. well known, fully known.
Wohlbeleibt, völ'beleïbt, a. corpulent, fleshy, bulky, stout, fat; **-heit,** -hāet, f. corpulence, fatness.
Wohlbeschaffen, völ'beshaffen, a. in good condition.
Wohlbewußt, völ'bevusst, a. conscious; well-remembered.
Wohlergehen, völ'ẽrgä-en, n. well-being, prosperity.
Wohlerzogen, völ'ertsōgn, a. well-bred.
Wohlfahrt, völ'färt, f. welfare, prosperity.
Wohlfahrtsausschuß, völ'färtsöusshuss, m. committee of public safety.
Wohlfeil, völ'feil, a. av. cheap, -ly; **-heit,** -hāet, f. cheapness.
Wohlgeartet, völ'geärtet, a. well natured, well mannered.
Wohlgebildet, völ'gebildet, **Wohl gebaut,** -geböut, a. well-shaped, well-made, well-formed.
Wohlgeboren, völ'gebōren, a. noble-born. Sir (address).

Wohlgefallen, völ'gefallen, n. pleasure satisfaction; vt. wohlgefiel, wohlgefallen, to please, satisfy.
Wohlgefällig, völ'gefellich, a. av. pleasant, pleasing, agreeable.
Wohlgelaunt, völ'gelåunt, a. in good humor.
Wohlgelitten, völ'gelitten, a. favored, well-wished.
Wohlgemeint, völ'gemēnt, a. well-intended, benevolent, sincere.
Wohlgemuth, völ'gemȗt, a. av. cheerful, -ly.
Wohlgenährt, völ'genärt, a. well-fed.
Wohlgeneigt, völ'geneïkt, a. kind.
Wohlgerathen, völ'geräten, a. successful; successfully educated.
Wohlgeruch, völ'geruch, m. pl. -gerüche, fragrancy, pleasing or sweet scent, grateful odor, perfume.
Wohlgeschmack, völ'geshmack, m. relish, good flavor, pleasing taste.
Wohlgesinnt, völ'gesinnt, a. well-disposed; loyal.
Wohlgestalt, völ'gezhtalt, f. fine shape; **-et,** a. well-formed, shapely.
Wohlgezogen, völ'getsōgen, a. well-educated.
Wohlhabend, völ'häbent, a. opulent, wealthy, easy, (being) well of; **-heit,** -hāet, f. opulency.
Wohlklang, völ'klang, f. agreeable, easy sound, euphony.
Wohlklingend, völ'kling-ent, a. well sounding, pleasing to the ear, euphonic.
Wohllaut, völ'löut, m. euphony, easy sound; **-end,** -ent, a. euphonic, well sounding.
Wohlleben, völ'lāben, n. good cheer, high life, luxury.
Wohllöblich, völ'lōblich, a. highly esteemed.
Wohlmeinend, völ'mēnent, a. well-meaning.
Wohlriechend, völ'rīchent, a. fragrant, odorous, sweet-scented; balmy, aromatic.
Wohlschmeckend, völ'shmeckent, a. savory, flavory, delicious.
Wohlsein, völ'sēn, n. health, comfort, prosperity.
Wohlstand, völ'zhtant, m. good condition, prosperity, welfare; propriety, decency.
Wohlthat, völ'tät, f. pl. -en, benefit, kindness, service, favor.

Weiße, vīs'ẹ, *f.* whiteness. **Weißen,** vīs'sen, *vt.* to whiten, whitewash.
Weißerz, vīs'ārts, *n.* sparry iron-ore; white copper-ore.
Weißfisch, vīs'fish, *m.* white-fish, bleak.
Weißgärber, vīs'gėrbẹr, *m.* tawer; *-ei, -ēi', f.* tawery.
Weißgrau, vīs'grāū, *a.* light gray, hoary, whitish gray.
Weißkraut, vīs'krōut, *n.* white cabbage.
Weißlich, vīs'lich, *a.* whitish. **Weißling,** -ling, *m.* whiting.
Weißpappel, vīs'pappl, *f.* white poplar.
Weißstein, vīs'zhtīn, *m.* white-stone.
Weißtanne, vīs'tannẹ, *f.* white pine.
Weißzeug, vīs'tsēūk, *m.* linen.
Weisung, vīs'ŭng, *f.* order, direction.
Weit, vīt, *a. av.* distant, far; wide, widely, broad; von weitem, from afar; bei weitem, by far; weiter, farther, further; weiteſt, farthest, furthest.
Weite, vī'tẹ, *f. or n.* width; distance; largeness, amplitude; lichte Weite, span (Arch.).
Weiten, vī'tẹn, *vt. i.* to widen, expand, extend.
Weiterung, vīt'ẹrŭng, *f.* procrastination.
Weithin, vīt'hīn, *av.* to a great distance. **Weitläufig,** vīt'lāūfich, *a.* large, vast; distant; detailed, prolix, at full, at full length; *-keit, -kāēt, f.* vast extent; diffusiveness, prolixity. **Weit'ſchweifig, -shīēfich,** *a.* prolix, diffuse; *-keit, -kāēt, f.* prolixity. **Weit'ſichtig, -sichtich,** *a.* far-sighted.
Weizen, vīēts'ẹn, *m.* wheat; *-brod, -brōt, n.* wheat bread. **Wei'zenkorn,** *-kẹrn, n. pl. -kērner,* grain of wheat.
Welch, vẹlch, *-er, -e, -es, a. pron.* who, which. **Welch'erlei,** *-ẹrlāē, a.* of what kind.
Welk, vẹlk, *a.* withered, faded, flagging, languid; *-en, vi.* to wither, fade, decay, flag, languish.
Welle, vẹl'lẹ, *f.* wave, billow; (Mech.) roller; aufrechte —, spindle; *-förmig, -fürmich, a.* undulatory, waving, undulating. **Wel'lenreich, -rēich,** *n.* realm of the sea.
Weller, vẹl'lẹr, *n.* cylinder.

Wellermauer, vẹl'lẹrmōu̇-ẹr, **Wel'lerwand,** *-vant, f.* loam-wall, mud-wall. **Wellern,** vẹl'lẹrn, *vt.* to make mud-walls.
Welt, vẹlt, *f.* world, universe; earth; *-all, -all, n.* universe. **Welt'alter,** *-altẹr, n.* age (of the world), period. **Welt'bekannt,** *-bekannt, a.* notorious. **Welt'berühmt,** *-berühmt, a.* far-famed, renowned. **Welt'bürger,** *-bürgẹr, m.* cosmopolite; *-lich, -lich, a.* cosmopolitical. **Welt'bürgersinn,** *-sinn, m.* cosmopolitism. **Welt'gebäude, -gebāūdẹ. n.* system or fabric of the world. **Welt'gegend,** *-gāgẹnd, f.* region, quarter of the world.
Weltgeist, vẹlt'gīēzht, *m.* spirit of the universe, creative spirit; *-licher, -lichẹr, m.* secular priest. **Welt'gericht,** vẹlt'gericht, *n.* last judgment. **Welt'geschichte,** *-geshichtẹ, f.* universal history. **Welt'handel,** *-handẹl, m.* commerce. **Welt'heiland,** *-hāē-lant, m.* Saviour. **Welt'kenntniß,** *-kẹnntnīss, f.* knowledge of the world. **Welt'kind,** *-kint, n. pl. -er,* worldling. **Welt'klug,** *-klŭk, a.* prudent; *-heit, -hāēt, f.* worldly wisdom. **Welt'körper,** vẹlt'kẹrpẹr, *m.* heavenly body. **Welt'kugel,** *-kŭgẹl, f.* globe. **Welt'kunde,** *-kŭndẹ, f.* cosmology. **Welt'kundig,** *-kŭndich, a.* notorious; skilled in history. **Welt'lauf,** *-lāūf, m.* course or way of the world. **Welt'lich,** *-lich, a.* worldly, secular; *-keit, -kāēt, f.* worldliness, worldly-mindedness; secularity. **Welt'liebe,** *-līēbẹ, f.* love of the world. **Welt'ling,** *-ling, m.* worldling. **Welt'mann,** *-mann, m.* man of the world. **Welt'meer,** *-mār, n.* ocean, main (sea). **Welt'priester,** *-prīzhtẹr, m.* secular priest. **Welt'sinn,** *-sinn, m.* worldly-mindedness, worldliness. **Welt'theil,** *-tāēl, n.* part of the world, continent. **Welt'weiser,** *-vīsẹr, m.* philosopher. **Welt'weisheit,** *-vīshāēt, f.* philosophy.
Wendeisen, vẹn'dẹ-īsẹn, *n.* tap-iron. **Wen'dekreis,** *-krāēs, m.* tropic.
Wendeltreppe, vẹn'dẹltrẹppẹ, *f.* winding-stairs.
Wenden, vẹn'dẹn (wandte, gewandt), *vt.* to turn, direct; ſich —, *tr* turn, change; ſich — an, to apply to, to address one's self to; durch or gegen

Wen   897   **Wet**

den Wind —, *or* bei dem Winde —, to tack.

Wendestufe, vĕn'dĕzhtŭfe̱, *f.* winder.

Wendung, vĕnd'ŭng, *f.* turn, turning.

Wenig, vā'nĭch, *a. av.* little, few; ſer, *a.* leſs. lesser, fewer. **Wenigſt**, vā'nĭkzht, *a.* least, fewest; wenigſtens, zum Wenigſten, at least. **Wenigkeit**, -kāet, *f.* smallness, trifle; meine —, my humble self.

Wenn, vĕn, *Cj.* when; if; — nicht, if not, unless; — auch, although; — je, — immer, whenever.

Wer, vār, *pron.* who; — auch, whoever.

Werben, vĕr'bĕn (warb, geworben), *vt.* to sue for, petition; to court, woo; to recruit. **Werber**, *m.* recruiting-officer, recruiter; suitor, wooer.

Werbung, vĕrb'ŭng, *f.* recruiting, levy, enlistment; wooing, courting.

Werden, vĕr'dĕn (ward, wurde, geworden), to become, grow, turn, get, to be, happen, come to pass; to come into existence.

Werder, vĕr'dĕr, *m.* small island, holm.

Werfen, vĕr'fĕn (warf, geworfen), *vt.* to cast, throw, fling; to bring forth, bear; ſich —, to warp (of wood).

Werft, vĕrft, *n.* wharf.

Werft, vĕrft, *m. n.* **Werfte**, vĕrf'te, *f.* warp, weft.

Werg, vĕrk, *n.* tow, hards; -leinwand, -laenvant, *f.* tow-linen.

Werk, vĕrk, *n.* work, deed, production; zu — gehen mit, to deal with; -tag, -tāk, *n.* working-day.

Werkmeister, vĕrk'māezhtĕr, *m.* foreman, superintendent. **Werkſatz**, -satz, *m.* skeleton (Carpent.).

Werkſtatt, vĕrk'zhtatt, *f. pl.* -ſtätte. **Werkſtätte**, -zhtĕtte, *f.* workshop. **Werkſtein**, -zhtāen, *m.* **Werkſtück**, -zhtück, *n.* square-stone. **Werktag**, -tāk, *m.* working day. **Werkzeug**, vĕrk'tsēūk, *n. pl.* -e, tool, instrument.

Wermuth, vār'mŭt, *m.* wormwood.

Werptroſs, vĕrp'tross, *n.* warp, warping hawser (Mar.).

Werth, vārt, *a.* worth. valuable; dear, precious; -los, -lōs, *a.* worthless.

Werthſchätzen, vĕrt'shĕtzĕn, *vt.* to esteem highly, to regard. **Werth-ſchätzung**, -ŭng, *f.* estimation, esteem.

Weſen, vā'sĕn, *n.* being, existence, substance, essence, nature.

Weſenlos, vā'sĕnlōs, *a.* unsubstantial.

Weſentlich, vā'sĕntlĭch, *a.* essential, substantial, real; -keit, -kāet, *f.* essentiality, essence, substance.

Wespe, vēs'pe, *f.* wasp; -nest, vĕs'pennest, *n.* wasp's nest.

Wespenſtich, vēs'penzhtĭch, *m.* wasp-bite.

Weſſen, vĕs'sĕn, **Weſs**, vĕss, *pn.* whose, of whom, of which; -halb, -halp, **Weſswegen**, -vāgen, *av.* wherefore, why, on what account.

Weſt, vĕzht, **Weſten**, *m.* west; west wind.

Weſte, vĕzh'te, *f.* vest, waistcoat; -ntaſche, -tashe, *f.* vest-pocket.

Weſtgegend, vĕzht'gāgent, *f.* **Weſtländer**, -lant, *n. pl.* -länder, western country. **Weſtlich**, -lĭch, *a.* western, westerly: **Weſtnordweſt**, west-north-west; **Weſtſüdweſt**, west-south-west; **Weſtſüdweſtwind**, west-south-west wind, west-south-wester. **Weſtwärts**, vĕst'vĕrts, *av.* westward, westwardly. **Weſtwind**, vĕst'vĭnt, *m.* west wind.

Wett, vĕt, *a. av.* even, equal; — machen, to quit scores.

Wette, vĕt'te, *f.* bet, wager; um die — thun, to vie in.

Wetteifer, vĕtt'ēifer, *m.* emulation; -n, *vt.* to emulate, vie, contend.

Wetten, vĕt'ten, *vt.* to bet, to lay a bet or wager.

Wetter, vĕt'ter, *n.* weather; thunderstorm, tempest; air, current of air; -ableiter, -ablāeter, *m.* lightning-rod, conductor. **Wetterbeobachtung**, -beōbachtung, *f.* meteorological observation. **Wetterdach**, -dach, *n. pl.* -dächer, penthouse. **Wetterfahne**, -fāne, *f.* **Wetterhahn**, -hān, *m. pl.* -hähne, vane, weather-vane, weather-cock. **Wetterglas**, -gläs, *n. pl.* -gläſer, weather-glass, barometer, thermometer. **Wetterlaunisch**, launish, *a.* peevish, capricious. **Wetterleuchten**, -lēŭchten, *n.* heat-lightning. **Wetterlöſung**, -lōsŭng, *f.* ventilation. **Wettern**, vĕt'tĕrn, *vt.* to thunder. **Wetterprophet**, -profāt, *m.* weather-spy. **Wetterrad**, -rāt, *n. pl.* -räder, ventilating-fanner. **Wetterſtrahl**, -zhtrāl, *m.* -es, *pl.* -en, flash of lightning. **Wetterwendiſch**,

34

-vendish, *a.* changeable, fickle, inconstant, peevish. **Wetterwolke,** -volke, *f.* thunder-cloud.

Wettrennen, vett'rennen, *n.* race; — zu Fuß, foot-race; — zu Pferd, horse-race; — in Booten, boat-race. **Wett'renner,** *m.* racer; race-horse. **Wett'streit,** -ztreït, *m.* emulation, contention, contest, rivalry.

Wetzen, vetz'en, *vt.* to whet. **Wetz'schiefer,** -shīfer, *m.* whetslate. **Wetz'stein,** -shtäen, *m.* whetstone.

Wichse, vix'e, *f.* blacking; waxing. **Wichsen,** vix'en, *vt.* to blacken; to wax.

Wicht, viçt, *m.* wight, fellow.

Wichtig, viç'tig, *a.* weighty, important; -keit, -kāet, *f.* importance.

Wicke, vick'e, *f.* vetch.

Wickel, vick'el, *m.* roller.

Wickelmaschine, vick'elmashīne, *f.* winding machine, lap machine; spreader.

Wickelkind, vickl'kīnt, *n. pl.* -er, child in swaddling-cloth.

Wickeln, vick'eln, *vt.* to roll, wind up.

Wickelwalze, vick'elvaltse, *f.* roller.

Widder, vid'der, *m.* ram; aries; hydraulischer —, hydraulic ram.

Wider, vī'der, *pr.* against, contrary or in opposition to: -bellen, -bellen, *vt.* to contradict. **Widerbeller,** vī'derbeller, *m.* wrangler.

Widerchrist, vī'derkrīzht, *m.* antichrist; -lich, -liç, *a.* antichristian.

Widerdruck, vī'derdruck, *m.* second form; reiteration; reaction; -bogen, -bōgen, *m.* tympan-sheet.

Widerfahren, vīderfā'ren (widerfuhr, widerfahren), *vi.* to happen, befall, occur.

Widerhaken, vī'derhāken, *m.* barb, beard.

Widerhalt, vī'derhalt, *m.* hold, support, resistance.

Widerhalten, vī'derhalten (widerhielt, widergehalten), *vi.* to hold out, resist.

Widerlage, vī'derlāge, *f.* counterfort, buttress.

Widerlager, vī'derlāger, *n.* springingstone.

Widerlegbar, viderlāg'bār, **Widerleglich,** -liç, confutable, refutable, disprovable.

Widerlegen, vīde·lā'gen, *vt.* to disprove, confute, refute. **Wi'derlegung,** -ŭng, *f.* confutation, refutation.

Widerlich, vī'derliç, *a.* disgusting offensive; -keit, -kāet, *f.* offensiveness.

Widern, vī'dern, *vi.* to disgust.

Widernatürlich, vī'dernatürliç, *a.* unnatural, preternatural, contrary to nature.

Widerpart, vī'derpart, *m.* opponent; opposition.

Widerrathen, viderrāt'en (-rieth, -rathen), *vt.* to dissuade, to represent as unfit.

Widerrechtlich, vī'derreçtliç, *a.* illegal, unlawful; -keit, -kāet, *f.* unlawfulness, illegality.

Widerrede, vī'derrāde, *f.* contradiction, opposition.

Widerrist, vī'derrizht, *m.* withers.

Widerruf, vī'derrŭf, *m. pl.* -e, recall, repeal, recantation, retraction.

Widerrufen, viderrŭ'fen, *vt.* to recall, retract, unsay, repeal. **Widerruf'lich,** -liç, *a.* repealable, reversible, revocable.

Widersacher, vī'dersacher, *m.* sin, *f.* adversary.

Widerschein, vī'dershāen, *m.* reflexion, reverberation of light.

Widersetzen, vīdersetz'en, *vr.* sich —, to oppose, resist.

Widersetzlich, vīdersetz'liç, *a.* refractory; -keit, -kāet, *f.* refractoriness. **Widersetz'ung,** -ŭng, *f.* resistance, opposition.

Widersinnig, vī'dersinniç, *a.* nonsensical, absurd; -keit, -kāet, *f.* non sensicalness, absurdity.

Widerspänstig, vī'derzhpenstiç, *a.* resistive, refractory; -keit, -kāet, *f.* restiveness, refractoriness.

Widerspiel, vī'derzhpīl, *n.* contrary, reverse.

Widersprechen, vīderzhpreç'en (widersprach, widersprochen), *vt.* to contradict, gainsay; -d, *a.* contradictory.

Widerspruch, vī'derzhpruç, *m. pl.* **Widersprüche,** contradiction, inconsistency.

Widerstand, vī'derzhtant, *m.* resistance, opposition.

Widerstehen, viderzhtā'en (widerstand, widerstanden), *vi.* to resist, oppose, withstand.

Widerstreben, viderzhtrā'ben, *vi.* to strive or struggle against, repugn

resist; *s. n.* repugnancy, resistance.

Widerstreit, vī'derzhtrēīt, *m.* conflict; antagonism, contradiction: **-en,** vī'derzhtrēī'ten, *vt.* to conflict, contend. **Widerstreitend,** *a.* conflicting: contradictory.

Widerstrom, vī'derzhtröm, *m.* countercurrent.

Widerwärtig, vī'dervērtig, *a.* disgusting, adverse, loathsome, disagreeable; **-keit, -kāēt,** *f.* adversity, reverse: unpleasantness.

Widerwille, vī'dervillę, *m.* aversion, disgust, antipathy, reluctance.

Widerwillig, vī'dervillich, *a.* reluctant, unwilling, backward.

Widmen, vīd'men, *vt.* to devote; dedicate, consecrate. **Wid'mung, -ung,** *f.* devotion; dedication.

Widrig, vīd'rich, *a.* averse, contrary; nauseous, disgusting; **-keit, -kāēt,** *f.* adversity.

Widrigenfalls, vī'drigenfalls, *a.* else, otherwise, in the other case.

Wie, vī, *pr.* how, as, when.

Wiede, vī'dę, *f.* willow, osier, withy.

Wiedehopf, vī'dehopf, *m. pl.* **-e,** lapwing, pewit, green plover, hoopoo.

Wieder, vī'der, *av.* back, again, anew, afresh.

Wiederabdruck, vīderap'drųck, *m. pl.* **-abdrücke,** re-impression.

Wiederanstellen, vī'deranzhtęllen, *vt.* to re-appoint.

Wiederaufbauen, vīderāūf'bōyen, *vt.* to rebuild.

Wiederbekommen, vī'derbekommen (-bekam, -bekommen), *vt.* to recover, get again.

Wiederbeleben, vī'derbelāben, *vt.* to revive, revivify. **Wie'derbelebung, -ung,** *f.* revivification.

Wiederbringen, vī'derbringen (-wiederbringen, wiedergebracht), *vt.* to bring back, restore, retrieve.

Wiederbringlich, vī'derbring'lich, *a.* retrievable. **Wiederbring'ung, -ung,** *f.* restoration.

Wiedereinsetzen, vīderaēn'setsen, *vt.* to reinstate, replace, restore, re-establish.

Wiedererlangen, vī'dererlangen, *vt.* to recover. **Wie'dererlangung, -ung,** *f.* recovery.

Wiedererobern, vī'dereröbern, *vt.* to reconquer

Wiedererstatten, vī'derērzhtatten, *vt.* to restore, return, reimburse, repay. **Wie'dererstattung, -ung,** *f.* return, restitution, repayment.

Wiederfinden, vī'derfinden, *vt.* to find again.

Wiedergeben, vī'dergāben (-gab, -gegeben), *vt.* to return, give back, render.

Wiedergeboren, vī'dergebōren, *a.* regenerate(d). **Wie'dergeburt, -byrt,** *f.* regeneration.

Wiedergenesung, vī'dergenāsųng, *f.* recovery.

Wiederhall, vī'derhall, *m.* echo; **-en,** *vi.* to re-echo.

Wiederherstellen, vīderhār'zhtęllen, *vt.* to restore, recover; redintegrate, re-establish. **Wiederher'stellung, -ung,** *f.* restoration, restitution; recovery.

Wiederholen, vīderhō'len, *vt.* to repeat, reiterate. **Wiederhol'ung, -ung,** *f.* repetition, reiteration.

Wiederkäuen, vī'derkāūen *vt.* to ruminate.

Wiederkauf, vī'derkāūf, *m. pl.* **-käufe,** redemption, repurchase: **-en,** *vt.* to repurchase, redeem. **Wie'derkäuflich, -kāūflich,** *a.* redeemable.

Wiederkehr, vī'derkār, *f.* return, recurrence; **-en,** *vi.* to return, come back.

Wiederklang, vī'derklang, *m.* echo.

Wiederklingen, vī'derklingen, *vi.* to re-echo.

Wiederkommen, vī'derkommen (-kam, -gekommen), *vi.* to come again, return. **Wie'derkunft, -kunft,** *f.* return.

Wiederöffnen, vīderöff'nen, *vt.* to re-open.

Wiederschein, vī'dershaēn, *m.* reflex, reflected light.

Wiedersehen, vī'dersāen (-sah, -gesehen), *vt.* to see or meet again; *s. n.* seeing, meeting again.

Wiedertaufe, vī'dertāūfę, *f.* rebaptism, rebaptization; **-n,** *vt.* to rebaptize. **Wie'dertäufer, -tāūfer, m.** rebaptizer; anabaptist.

Wiedertönen, vī'dertöhnen, *vt. i.* to resound.

Wiederum, vī'derųm, *av.* again, once more, repeatedly.

Wiedervergelten, vī'derfergōlten, *vt.* to requite, retaliate, remunerate recompense, reward, repay.

Wiederbergeltung, vī'dĕrfĕrgĕltung, *f.* requital, retaliation, retribution, recompense, reward.
Wiederverkaufen, vī'dĕrfĕrkäufĕn, *vt.* to resell, retail.
Wiederversöhnen, vī'dĕrfĕrsöhnen, *vt.* to reconcile, conciliate; propitiate.
Wiege, vī'gĕ, *f.* cradle.
Wiegemesser, vī'gĕmĕssĕr, *n.* chopping knife.
Wiegen, vī'gĕn, *vt.* to rock, cradle; fich —, to lull one's self with.
Wiegen, vī'gĕn (wog, gewogen), *vi. t.* to weigh; *vt.* wiegte, gewiegt.
Wiegenkind, vī'gĕnkĭnt, *n.* baby.
Wiegenlied, vī'gĕnlĭd, *n. pl.* -er, lullaby.
Wiehern, vī'hĕrn, *vi.* to neigh, whinny; wiehernbes Gelächter, horse-laugh.
Wiek, vīk, *n. pl.* -e, inlet, bay.
Wieke, vī'kĕ, *f.* lint.
Wiese, vīs'ĕ, *f.* meadow.
Wiesel, vī'sel, *n.* weasel.
Wiesenbau, vī'sĕnböṷ, *m.* cultivation of meadows. **Wiesengrund,** -grunt, *m. pl.* -gründe, **Wieseuland,** -lant, *n. pl.* -länder, meadow.
Wiesewachs, vī'sĕvaks, **Wiesewuchs,** -vuks, *m.* meadows.
Wievielst, vī'fīlxht, **Wievielt,** *a.* what or which number.
Wiewohl, vivöl', *Cj.* although, though.
Wild, vilt, *a.* wild, savage; *s. n.* game, venison; -brät, -brĕt, *n.* deer, game, venison. **Wildbraten,** -brätĕn, *m.* roast venison. **Wilddieb,** -dīb, *m.* poacher. **Wilder,** *m.* savage. **Wildsfang,** -fang, *m. pl.* -fänge, mad cap. **Wildfremd,** -frĕmt, *a.* quite strange. **Wildgeschmack,** -geshmack, *m.* flavor of game. **Wildheit,** -hăĕt, *f.* wildness, savageness. **Wildniß,** vilt'niss, *f.* wilderness, savageness. **Wildpret,** -prĕt, = Wildbrät.
Wildschütz, vilt'shüts, *m. pl.* Wildschützen, poacher.
Willemit, villĕmit', *m.* Willemite.
Wille(n), vil'lĕn, *m.* will; um — willen, for the sake of, on account of; um meinetwillen, for my sake: um Gotteswillen, for God's sake; Willens sein, to intend, purpose, to have a mind. **Willenlos,** vil'lĕnlōs, *a.* having no will of one's own.
Willfahren, villfār'en, *vi.* to comply with. **Willfährig,** vill'färiḵ, *a.* compliant, compliable; -keit, -kăĕt, *f.* compliance, readiness. **Willfahrung,** -ung, *f.* compliance.
Willig, vil'liḵ, *a.* willing; -en, *vi. t.* agree *or* consent to. **Willigkeit,** -kăĕt, *f.* willingness.
Willkomm, vill'kŏmm, *n.* -en, *m.* welcome, salutation.
Willkommen, villkŏm'men, *a.* welcome.
Willkür, vill'kühr, *f.* arbitrariness, discretion; -lich, -liḵ, *a.* arbitrary, discretional; -keit, -kăĕt, *f.* arbitrariness.
Wimmeln, vim'mĕln, *vi.* to swarm, teem, crowd.
Wimmern, vim'mĕrn, *vi.* to whimper, moan, whine, groan.
Wimpel, vim'pel, *f. or m.* pennon, pendant.
Wimper, vim'pĕr, *f.* eye-lash. **Wimpern,** *vi.* to wink, blink, twinkle.
Wind, vint, *m. pl.* -e, wind, breeze, air; scent, hint; flatulence, windiness; — bekommen, to get scent of; — machen, to vapor, brag, boast; stehender —, settled wind; knapper, schiefer —, scant, sharp wind; starker —, high wind; offener —, fair wind; halber —, large wind; -anker, *m.* lower anchor. **Windsbeutel,** -beütel, *m.* braggart, humbug; -ei, -ēī', *f.* humbug, boasting. **Windbüchse,** -büxĕ, *f.* air-gun, wind-gun.
Winde, vin'dĕ, *f.* windlass, pulley.
Winde, vin'dĕ, *f.* bindweed; morning glory.
Windei, vind'āĕ, *n. pl.* -er, wind-egg.
Windel, vin'dĕl, *f.* swaddling clothes; -kind, -kĭnt, *n. pl.* -er, child in swaddling clothes.
Winden, vin'den (wand, gewunden), *vt.* to wind, wring, wrest, twist.
Windfahne, vint'fānĕ, *f.* vane, weather-cock. **Windfang,** -fang, *m.* ventilator. **Windhund,** -hunt, *m.* greyhound.
Windig, vind'iḵ, *a.* windy.
Windklappe, vint'klappĕ, *f.* valve.
Windlicht, vint'lĭcht, *n.* torch.
Windmesser, vint'mĕssĕr, *m.* windgauge, anemometer.
Windmühle, vint'mühlĕ, *f.* wind-mill.
Windofen, vint'ōfen, *m.* wind-furnace.
Windpocken, vint'pŏcken, *s. pl.* chicken-pox.

Windbrad, vint'rāt, *n. pl.* -räder, ventilator.
Windrose, vint'rōse, *f.* (compass-)card; anemone (Bot.).
Windruthe, vint'ruṭe, *f.* whip; windarm.
Windsbraut, vints'broṳt, *f. pl.* -bräute, hurricane, whirlwind, squall; tornado.
Windschaden, vint'shäden, *m.* damage done by the wind.
Windschief, vint'shīf, *a.* warped.
Windsegel, vint'sāgl, *n.* wind-sail.
Windseite, vint'sēīte, *f.* weather-side.
Windspiel, vint'shpīl, *n.* greyhound.
Windstill, vint'zhtill, *a.* calm; -e, *f.* calm. **Windstoss,** -zhtoss, *m. pl.* -stösse, blast, gust, puff of wind.
Windstrich, vint'zhtrich, *m.* rhumb point, current of the wind.
Windung, vīn'dṳng, *f.* winding, turning; worm, spire, thread (of a screw).
Windwehe, vint'vā-e, *f.* drift of snow.
Windweiser, vint'vēīser, **Windzeiger,** vint'tsāēger, *m.* anemo-scope, vane, fane.
Windwirbel, vint'vīrbl, *m.* whirlwind.
Windzug, vint'tsṳg, *m. pl.* **Windzüge,** draught *or* current of air; ventiduct.
Wink, vink, *m.* wink; nod, hint.
Winkel, vinkʹl, *m.* angle; corner; nook.
Winkeladvokat, vinkl'ädfokät, *m.* -en, *pl.* -en, pettifogger.
Winkelehe, vinkl'ä-e, *f.* clandestine *or* hedge-marriage.
Winkeleisen, vinkl'ēīsen, *n.* iron rule, square.
Winkelhaken, vinkl'häken, *m.* iron rule, (Print.) stick.
Winkelig, vin'kelich, *a.* angular, cornered.
Winkelmass, vinkl'mäs, *n.* square.
Winkelmesser, vinkl'messer, *m.* protractor.
Winkelrecht, vinkl'recht, *a.* rectangular, right-angled, perpendicular.
Winkelzug, vinkl'tsṳg, *m. pl.* -züge, trick, evasion, shift.
Winken, vink'en, *vt.* to wink, beckon.
Winseln, vin'seln, *vi.* to moan, whimper, whine.
Winter, vin'ter, *m.* winter.
Winterammer, vīn'terammer, *f.* snowbird. **Winterbeule,** -bēūle, *f.* chilblain. **Winterdrossel,** -drossel, *f.* red-wing. **Wintergegend,** -gāgent, *f.* wintery region. **Winterhaft,** -haft, *a.* wintering, vin'terich, **Winterlich,** -lich, *a.* wintery, as in winter, winter-hyemal. **Wintern,** vin'tern, *vi.* to grow winter; *vt.* to winter, to feed during the winter; *vi.* to winter, pass the winter. **Winterquartier,** -kvarrtīr, *n.* winter-quarters. **Wintersaat,** -sät, *f. pl.* -en, winter-crop. **Winterseite,** -sēīte, *f.* north side. **Winterung,** -ṳng, *f.* wintering. **Winterzeit,** -tsēīt, *f.* winter-time, winter-season.
Winzer, vint'ser, *m.* -in, *f.* vintager; vine-dresser.
Winzig, vin'tsich, *a.* petty, little, diminutive.
Wipfel, vipf'el, *m.* top.
Wippe, vip'pe, *f.* swape, sweep, see-saw. **Wippen,** *vt.* to swing, to balance; to tip. **Wipper,** vip'per, *m.* clipper.
Wir, vīr, *pm.* we.
Wirbel, vīr'bl, *m.* whirl, twirl, top; crown; eddy, vortex; whirlpool; whirlwind; giddiness; roll, beat of drum.
Wirbelig, vīr'belich, *a.* whirled, whirling, vortical. **Wirbeln,** vīr'beln, *vt. i.* to whirl. **Wirbelwind,** -vint, *m.* whirl-wind.
Wirfeisen, virk'ēīsen, *n.* (tawer's) paring-knife (farr.); searcher.
Wirken, vīr'ken, *vt.* to work, operate; effect, tell: to knead; pare.
Wirklich, vīrk'lich, *a.* actual, real, true; -keit, -kāēt, *f.* reality, actuality; truth. **Wirksam,** -sam, *a.* efficacious, efficient, effective, powerful; active; -keit, -kāēt, *f.* efficiency, efficaciousness, efficacy, activity.
Wirkstuhl, vīrk'zhtṳl, *m. pl.* -stühle, loom.
Wirkung, vīrk'ṳng, *f.* working, effect, action; impression; kneading. **Wirkungskreis,** vīr'kṳngskrāēs, *m. pl.* -e, sphere of action *or* of activity.
Wirr, virr, *a.* confused, confuse, harebrained. **Wirren,** vīr'ren, *vt.* to entangle, confuse. **Wirrgarn,** -garn, *n.* entangled yarn. **Wirrkopf,** virr'kopf, *m. pl.* -köpfe, confused head. **Wirrseide,** vīr'sēīde, *f.* refuse of silk. **Wirrstroh,** -zhtrō, *n.* short straw. **Wirrung,** -ṳng, *f.* confu-

Wir   402   **Wof**

sion, trouble. **Wirrwarr,** vĭrr'varr, *m.* confusion, disturbance, trouble.
Wirtel, vĭr'tel, *m.* whirl.
Wirth, vĭrrt, *m. pl.* -e, husbandman; economist; host; landlord, innkeeper; -in, *f.* lady of the house; housekeeper; landlady, hostess.
Wirthbar, vĭrrt'bär, *a.* habitable; -keit, -keit, *f.* hospitality.
Wirthlich, vĭrrt'lich, *a.* hospitable; frugal; -keit, -keit, *f.* hospitality; frugality.
Wirthschaft, vĭrrt'shaft, *f.* house-keeping, economy, husbandry; household; public house, inn.
Wirthschaften, vĭrrt'shaften, *vt.* to manage, administer, economize; to keep house, to husband.
Wirthschafter, vĭrrt'shafter, *m.* manager, steward; -in, *f.* housekeeper.
Wirthschaftlich, vĭrrt'shaftlich, *a. av.* economical, -cally; -keit, -keit, *f.* economy, frugality, frugal management.
Wirthshaus, vĭrrts'hŏys, *n. pl.* -häuser, inn, tavern, public house.
Wirthsleute, vĭrrts'lŏyte, *s. pl.* hosts, landlord and landlady.
Wirthstisch, vĭrrts'tish, *m.* **Wirthstafel,** vĭrrts'tăfl, *f.* ordinary *or* table d'hote.
Wisch, vish, *m. pl.* -e, whisk, wisp; clout; trash, scrawl.
Wischen, vish'en, *vt.* to wipe, rub; *vi.* to slip. **Wischer,** *m.* wiper; sponge; reprimand. **Wischkolben,** -kolben, *m.* sponge-head. **Wischlappen,** -lappen, *m.* dish-cloth, dish-rag, duster.
Bismuth, vis'mŭt, *m.* bismuth.
Wispern, vizh'pern, *vt.* to whisper.
Wißbegier, viss'begĭr, -de, -de, *f.* curiosity, inquisitiveness, desire of knowledge, wish to learn.
Wissen, viss'en (mußte, gewußt, gevußt)*vt.* to know; zu wissen thun. *or* wissen lassen, to acquaint with; to send word, to inform; Dank —, to be thankful.
Wissenschaft, vis'senshaft, *f.* science; -lich, -lich, *a.* scientific.
Wissenswerth, vis'sensvärt, **Wissenswürdig,** -vürdich, *a.* worth knowing, remarkable.
Wissentlich, vis'sentlich, *a. av.* knowing; wilful, voluntary; knowingly, wittingly, by design.
Witterit, vĭt'erit, *n.* witherite.

Wittern, vĭt'tern, *vt. i.* to thunder; vt to scent, smell.
Witterung, vĭt'terŭng, *f.* weather, scent.
Witthum, vĭt'tŭm, *n.* jointure.
Wittwe, vĭt've, **Wittfrau,** -fräu, *f. pl.* -en, widow. **Wittmenjahr,** -yăr, *n.* widow's year. **Wittwenstand,** vit venzhtant, *m.* widowhood.
Wittwer, vĭt'ver, **Wittmann,** -mann, *m. pl.* -männer, widower.
Witz, vits, *m.* sense; intellect, understanding, wit; seinen — verlieren, to lose one's wits; wittiness.
Witzbold, vits'bolt, *m.* wit; witty fellow. **Witzelei,** vitsele'ī', *f.* witticism. **Witzeln,** vits'eln, *vt. i.* to be vastly witty; to affect wittiness. **Witzig,** vits'ich, *a.* witty. **Witzigen,** vits'īgen, *vt.* to make wiser, to teach wit.
Witzling, vits'ling, *m.* witling, pretender to wit, punster, low wit.
Wo, vŏ, *pn.* where; somewhere, anywhere; if, when, in case.
Wobei, vobeī', *av.* whereby, whereat, where.
Woche, voch'e, *f.* week, sennight; in die Wochen kommen, to be delivered; to be brought to bed; in den Wochen liegen, to lie in bed, to be confined.
Wochenbett, voch'enbet, *n.* confinement; childbed.
Wochenblatt, voch'enblat, *n. pl.* -blätter, weekly.
Wochenkind, voch'enkĭnt, *n. pl.* -er, new-born child.
Wochenlang, voch'enlang, *av.* for weeks.
Wochenlohn, voch'enlōn, *m.* weekly pay, week's wages.
Wochenmarkt, voch'enmarkt, *n.* weekly market (day).
Wochentag, voch'entäg, *m. pl.* -e, weekday.
Wöchentlich, vöch'entlich. *a. av.* weekly, by the week, hebdomadal, -dary.
Wochenweise, voch'envēïse, *av.* by the week.
Wöchnerin, vöch'nerin, *f.* woman lying-in.
Wocken, vok'en, *m.* distaff, rock.
Wodurch, vodurch', *av.* whereby, by what.
Wofern, vofërn', *Cj.* if; wofern nicht, unless, if not.
Wofür, voführ', *av.* wherefore, for what.

Wog 403 **Woh**

Woge, vō'gĕ, *f.* billow, wave, surge.
Wogegen, vṓgā'gen, *av.* against what or which, for *or* to what, which.
Wogen, vō'gen, *vi. i.* to wave, billow, surge, fluctuate.
Wogig, vō'gig, *a.* wavy, surgy.
Woher, vohār', *a.* whence, wherefrom.
Wohin, vohīn', *a.* whither, where, what way.
Wohl, vōl, *a. av.* well, certainly, indeed; perhaps, may be; **Wohl Dir!** happy for thee! happy you! er ist wohl, he is well, in good health; *s. n.* welfare, weal, well-being, good, benefit, interest.
Wohlan, vōlän', *av.* well, come on!
Wohlanständig, vōl'anzhtendig, *a.* decent, -ly, (well-)becoming; *-keit,* -käet, *f.* decency.
Wohlauf, vōlōuf', *ij.* well! cheer up! — fein, to be well, *or* in good health.
Wohlbedacht, vōl'bedacht, *a. av.* well considered. **Wohl bedächtig,** -bedächtig, **Wohl bedächtlich,** -lich, *a. av.* deliberate, -ly, considerate.
Wohlbefinden, vōl'befinden, *n.* good health.
Wohlbehagen, vōl'behägn, *n.* ease, comfortableness, comfort. **Wohl behaglich,** -lich, *a. av.* comfortable, -ly, at ease.
Wohlbehalten, vōl'behalten, *a. av.* safe.
Wohlbekannt, vōl'bekannt, *a.* well known, fully known.
Wohlbeleibt, vōl'belēibt, *a.* corpulent, fleshy, bulky, stout, fat; *-heit,* -häet, *f.* corpulence, fatness.
Wohlbeschaffen, vōl'beshaffen, *a.* in good condition.
Wohlbewußt, vōl'bevusst, *a.* conscious; well-remembered.
Wohlergehen, vōl'ergā-en, *n.* well-being, prosperity.
Wohlerzogen, vōl'ertsōgn, *a.* well-bred.
Wohlfahrt, vōl'färt, *f.* welfare, prosperity.
Wohlfahrtsausschuß, vōl'färtsōusshuss, *m.* committee of public safety.
Wohlfeil, vōl'fīel, *a. av.* cheap, -ly; *-heit,* -häet, *f.* cheapness.
Wohlgeartet, vōl'geärtet, *a.* well natured, well mannered.
Wohlgebildet, vōl'gebildet, **Wohl gebaut,** -gebōut, *a.* well-shaped, well-made, well-formed.
Wohlgeboren, vōl'gebōren, *a.* noble-born. Sir (address).

Wohlgefallen, vōl'gefallen, *n.* pleasure satisfaction; *vi.* wohlgefiel, wohlgefallen, to please, satisfy.
Wohlgefällig, vōl'gefellig, *a. av.* pleasant, pleasing, agreeable.
Wohlgelaunt, vōl'gelāunt, *a.* in good humor.
Wohlgelitten, vōl'gelitten, *a.* favored, well-wished.
Wohlgemeint, vōl'gemēent, *a.* well-intended, benevolent, sincere.
Wohlgemuth, vōl'gemūt, *a. av.* cheerful, -ly.
Wohlgenährt, vōl'genärt, *a.* well-fed.
Wohlgeneigt, vōl'genēekt, *a.* kind.
Wohlgerathen, vōl'geräten, *a.* successful; successfully educated.
Wohlgeruch, vōl'geruch, *m. pl. -gerüche,* fragrancy, pleasing *or* sweet scent, grateful odor, perfume.
Wohlgeschmack, vōl'geshmack, *m.* relish, good flavor, pleasing taste.
Wohlgesinnt, vōl'gesinnt, *a.* well-disposed; loyal.
Wohlgestalt, vōl'gezhtalt, *f.* fine shape; *-et, a.* well-formed, shapely.
Wohlgezogen, vōl'getsōgen, *a.* well-educated.
Wohlhabend, vōl'häbent, *a.* opulent, wealthy, easy, (being) well of; *-heit,* -häet, *f.* opulency.
Wohlklang, vōl'klang, *f.* agreeable, easy sound, euphony.
Wohlklingend, vōl'kling-ent, *a.* well sounding, pleasing to the ear, euphonic.
Wohllaut, vōl'lōut, *m.* euphony, easy sound; *-end, -ent, a.* euphonic, well sounding.
Wohlleben, vōl'lāben, *n.* good cheer, high life, luxury.
Wohllöblich, vōl'löhblich, *a.* highly esteemed.
Wohlmeinend, vōl'mēenent, *a.* well-meaning.
Wohlriechend, vōl'rīchent, *a.* fragrant, odorous, sweet-scented; balmy, aromatic.
Wohlschmeckend, vōl'shmeckent, *a.* savory, flavory, delicious.
Wohlsein, vōl'sēen, *n.* health, comfort, prosperity.
Wohlstand, vōl'zhtant, *m.* good condition, prosperity, welfare; propriety, decency.
Wohlthat, vōl'tät, *f. pl. -en,* benefit, kindness, service, favor.

Wohlthäter, vōl'tāter, m. benefactor; ‑in, f. benefactress. **Wohlthätig**, ‑tātiġ, a. beneficial, beneficient, charitable; wholesome, salutary; salubrious; ‑keit, ‑kĕet, f. beneficence, charity.

Wohlthun, vōl'tųn, vi. to do well or good; to benefit, to be beneficial; es thut ihm wohl, he likes, is pleased, delighted.

Wohltönend, f. **Wohllautend**.

Wohlverdient, vōl'ferdīnt, a. well deserved.

Wohlverhalten, vōl'ferhalten, n. good conduct or behavior.

Wohlverstanden, vōl'fershtanden, a. understood.

Wohlweislich, vōl'vēīsliġ, av. very wisely, prudently.

Wohlwollen, vōl'vollen, vi. Einem —, to wish the good of; s. n. benevolence, good will, goodness; ‑b, a. av. benevolent, ‑ly, kind.

Wohnen, vō'nen, vi. to dwell, live, lodge, reside.

Wohnhaft, vōn'haft, a. residing: — sein, to reside in, to be an inhabitant of.

Wohnhaus, vōn'hōųs, n. pl. ‑häuser. **Wohngebäude**, ‑gebēüde, n. dwelling‑house.

Wohnlich, vōn'liġ, a. comfortable.

Wohnort, vōn'ort, m. pl. ‑örter. **Wohnplatz**, vōn'plats, m. pl. **Wohnplätze**. **Wohnstatt**, vōn'zhtatt, f. dwelling‑place, residence. **Wohnsitz**, ‑sits, m. pl. ‑e. domicile. **Wohnstube**, ‑zhtųbe, f. **Wohnzimmer**, ‑tsimmer, n. sitting‑room.

Wohnung, vōn'ųng, f. residence; lodging, abode, habitation.

Woid, **Woit**, voit, f. jigger (Mxr.).

Wölben, völ'ben, vi. to vault, arch.

Wölbung, völb'ųng, f. vault, arch.

Wolf, volf, m. pl. **Wölfe**. wolf; (wool) devil, deviling or opening machine; wool‑mill.

Wolfen, volf'en, s. n. willowing.

Wölfin, völ'fin, she‑wolf. **Wölfisch**, ‑ish, a. wolfish.

Wolfram, volfram, m. wolfram.

Wolframsäure, volf'ramsēüre, f. tungstic acid, wolframine.

Wolfshunger, volfs'hųng‑er, m. canine or ravenous appetite.

Wolke, vol'ke, f. cloud. **Wölkchen**, völk'ċhen, n. little cloud.

Wolken, vōl'ken, vi. to cloud.

Wolkenbruch, vol'kenbrųċh, m. pl. ‑brüċhe, heavy shower, waterspout.

Wolkig, vel'kig, a. cloudy.

Wollarbeit, voll'arbāet, f. work in wool; ‑er, m. worker in wool.

Wolle, vol'le, f. wool.

Wollen, vol'len, a. woolen, worsted.

Wollen, vol'len, vi. to will, to be willing, to wish, to warrant; lieber —, to like rather, to prefer; s. n. volition, will.

Wollenfabrik, vol'lenfabrīk, f. woolen cloth manufactory, factory of woolen goods. **Wollenfabrikant**, ‑fabrikant, m. manufacturer of woolen goods.

Wollengarn, vol'lengarn, n. woolen yarn, worsted. **Wollenweber**, ‑vāber, m. woolen‑weaver.

Wollhandel, voll'handel, m. wool‑trade. **Wollhändler**, ‑hendler, m. dealer in wool, wool‑merchant.

Wollicht, vol'liċht, **Wollig**, vol'lig, a. woolly, resembling wool.

Wollkamm, voll'kamm. m. pl. ‑kämme, wool‑comb. **Wollkämmer**, ‑kemmer, m. wool‑comber.

Wollmarkt, vol'markt, m. pl. ‑märkte, wool‑market, wool‑staple.

Wollsack, voll'sack, m. pl. ‑säċke, wool‑sack, wool‑pack.

Wollschur, vol'shųr, f. clip, sheep‑shearing.

Wollspinner, vol'zhpinner, m. wool‑spinner; ‑in, f. wool‑spinster.

Wollspinnerei, valzhpinnerēī', f. wool‑spinning.

Wollzeug, vol'tsēüg, n. pl. ‑e, woolen stuff.

Wollust, vol'lųzht, f. pl. ‑lüste, delight; lust, luxury; voluptuousness.

Wollüstig, vol'lüzhtiġ, a. voluptuous, sensual; ‑keit, ‑kēet, f. voluptuousness, sensuality, lust. **Wollüstling**, vol'lüzhtling, m. voluptuary.

Womit, vomit', av. wherewith, with which or what.

Wonach, vonāċh', av. after which, at, to which or what.

Woneben, vōnā'ben, av. near to which.

Wonne, von'ne, f. delight.

Wonnig, von'niġ, a. av. delightful, delightfully.

Woran, vōran', av. whereon, whereat, whereto, to which or what.

Worauf, vōrāuf', av. whereon, whereupon, on which.

Woraus, vŏrŏys', *av.* wherefrom, whence, out of which.
Worein, vŏrşēn', *av.* whereinto, into what *or* which.
Worf, *f.* Wurf.
Worin, vŏrin', *av.* wherein, in which, in what.
Wornach, *f.* Wonach.
Wort, vort, *n. pl. -e*, **Wörter**, vŏr'ter, *f.* word; term; Wort für Wort, word for word; literally; mit einem Worte, in a word; fein Wort halten, to keep one's word.
Wortart, vort'ärt, *f.* part of speech.
Wortbruch, vort'brŭch, *m.* breach of promise. **Wort'brüchig**, -brüchig, *a.* faithless, -ly.
Wörtchen, vŏrt'chen, *n.* little word.
Wörterbuch, vŏr'terbuch, *n. pl. -bücher*, vocabulary, dictionary.
Wortforschung, vort'forshung, *f.* etymology, philology.
Wortfügung, vort'fügung, *f.* syntax.
Wortführer, vort'führer, *m.* spokesman; foreman (of a jury).
Wortgepränge, vort'geprenge, *n.* bombast, fustian, swelling style.
Wortkarg, vort'karg, *a.* sparing of words.
Wörtlich, vŏrt'lich, *a.* literal, verbal, word for word.
Wortreich, vort'reich, *a.* verbose, rich in words.
Wortschwall, vort'shval, *m.* bombast, fustian.
Wortspiel, vort'zhpīl, *n.* pun, quibble.
Wortstreit, vort'zhtrēīt, *m.* logomachy, war of words.
Wortwechsel, vort'vexl, *m.* altercation, dispute.
Worüber, vorüh'br, *av.* whereupon, whereon, whereat, at, about, upon *or* of, which *or* what.
Worunter, vorun'ter, *av.* under *or* among which.
Wovon, vofōn', *av.* of which, whereof.
Wovor, vofŏr', *av.* before, for *or* from which, wherefrom.
Wozu, votsy', *av.* whereat, whereto, for what.
Wrack, vrak, *n.* wreck. wrack.
Wricken, vrik'ken, *vt.* to wriggle.
Wucher, vy'cher, *m.* usury. **Wucherer**, vy'cherer, *m.* usurer. **Wucherisch**, -ish, *a.* usurious. **Wuchern**, vy'chern, *vt.* to practice usury; to grow exuberantly.

Wuchs, vyks, *m.* growth, height.
Wucht, vycht, *f.* weight, heavy burden bulk.
Wühlen, vüh'len, *vt.* to root (up), stir.
Wuhlen, vy'len, *vi.* to woold. **Wuhling**, **Wuling**, vy'ling, *a.* woolding, gammoning of the bowsprit.
Wulst, vylzht, *m. pl.* Wülste, pad, cushion; (Arch.) ovolo.
Wulstig, vül'zhtich, *a.* puffy, turgid, bombastic.
Wund, vunt, *a.* sore, galled, wounded.
Wundarzt, vunt'ärtst, *m. pl. -ärzte*, surgeon. **Wund'arztlich**, -ärtstlich, *a.* surgical.
Wunde, vyn'de, *f.* wound.
Wunder, vyn'der, *n.* wonder, miracle. **Wun'derbar**, -bār, *a.* wonderful, miraculous: **-lich**, -lich, *av.* miraculously. **Wun'derding**, -ding, *n.* wondrous thing. **Wun'dergroß**, -gross, *a.* prodigious. **Wun'derkind**, -kint, *n. pl. -er*, prodigy of a child. **Wun'derkraft**, -kraft, *f. pl. -kräfte*, miraculous power. **Wun'derlich**, -lich, *a. av.* strange, odd; capricious; **-keit**, -kāet, *f.* capriciousness.
Wundern, vyn'dern, *vt. r.* to wonder, to be astonished; es wundert mich, I am surprised, astonished, I wonder. **Wun'dersam**, -sam, *a.* wonderful. **Wun'derschön**, -shöhn, *a.* exceedingly beautiful *or* fine; of a wonderful beauty. **Wun'derselten**, -selten, *a. av.* extraordinarily rare, -ly. **Wun'derthat**, -tät, *f.* wonderful deed, miracle, prodigy. **Wun'derthäter**, -täter, *m.* worker of miracles. **Wun'derthätig**, -tätich, *a.* wonderworking, miraculous. **Wun'derthier**, -tīr, *n.* wonderful animal, prodigy, monster. **Wun'dervoll**, -foll, *a.* wonderful, miraculous, marvelous; admirable. **Wun'derwerk**, -vērk, *n.* wonder, miracle.
Wundfieber, vunt'fīber, *n.* fever from wounds.
Wundkraut, vunt'krŏut, *n.* woundroot.
Wundwasser, vunt'vasser, *n.* vulnerary water, arquebusade, vulnerary.
Wunsch, vynsh, *m. pl.* Wünsche, wish, desire.
Wünschelruthe, vün'shelrute, *f.* (magic) wand.
Wünschen, vün'shen, *vt.* to wish; Glück —, to congratulate; **-swerth**, -vārt, *a.* desirable.

Würbe, vür'dg, *f.* dignity, worth, honor; -träger, -träger, *m.* dignitary. **Würdvoll,** -toll, *a. av.* dignified, stately, grave.

Würdig, vür'dig, *a. av.* worthy, -ily, deserving, meritorious. -ly.

Würdigen, vür'dichen, *vt.* to appreciate, deign, to vouchsafe, to honor with. **Würdigkeit,** -kāēt, *f.* worthiness, worth, merit meritoriousness. **Würdigung,** -ung, *f.* appreciation, just valuation.

Wurf, vųrf. *m. pl.* **Würfe,** cast, throw; a thing thrown; litter; -anker, -anker, *m.* (größerer) stream-anchor; (kleiner) kedge.

Würfel, vür'fel, *m.* die, cube; (of a column) die, dado, cubic base; hexahedron; -becher, -becher, *m.* dicebox. **Würfelicht,** -icht, *a.* resembling a die. **Würfelig,** -ig, *a.* cubiform, cubic.

Würfeln, vür'feln, *vi.* to play at dice; *vt.* to checker, tesselate; to form or cut into squares. **Würfelspiel,** -zhpīl, *n.* game at dice; -er, -er, *m.* player at dice.

Wurfen, vųrf'en, *vt.* to fan, winnow.

Wurfschaufel, vųrf'shōufel, *f.* fan.

Wurfscheibe, vųrf'shōibe, *f.* discus, quoit. **Wurfspieß,** -zhpīs, *m.* javelin, dart. **Wurfweite,** -vāīte, *f.* range.

Würgen, vür'gen, *vt.* to choke, throttle, suffocate; to destroy, murder.

Würgengel, vürg'eng-el, *m.* destroying angel. **Würger,** *m.* destroyer, murderer.

Wurm, vųrm. *m. pl.* **Würmer,** worm, vermin, reptile; (of horses) farcin, farcy; -arzt, -artst, *m. pl.* -ärzte, worm-doctor.

Würmen, vür'men, *vt. i.* Einen *or* Einem —, to fret, irritate, vex, make angry.

Wurmförmig, vųrm'förmich, *a.* vermiform, vermicular. **Wurmfraß,** -frās, *m.* food for worms; wormeatenness; worm holṣ. **Wurmfräßig,** -frässig, *a.* worm-eaten. **Wurmig,** vųrm'ich, *a.* worm-eaten; wormy. **Wurmloch,** -loch, *n. pl.* -löcher worm-hole.

Wurmmittel, vųrm'mittel, *n.* anthelmintic, remedy for worms, vermifuge. **Wurmpulver,** vųrm'pulfer, *n.* worm-powder. **Wurmstichig,** vųrm'shtichig, *a.* worm-eaten.

Wurst, vųrzht, *f. pl.* **Würste** sausage pudding; **Wurst** wider **Wurst,** trick for trick, tit for tat.

Würze, vür'tse, *f.* spice, seasoning. **Wurzel,** vųr'tsel, *f.* root; -größe, -größag, *f.* radical quantity.

Wurzeln, vųr'tseln, *vi.* to root, to fix the root; to take root.

Wurzelwerk, vųr'tselverk, *n.* roots. **Würzen,** vür'tsen, *vt.* to spice, season; aromatize.

Wurzgarten, vųrts'garten (für **Würzelgarten,** besser als **Würzgarten,)** *m.* garden for pot herbs.

Würzhaft, vürts'haft, **Würzig,** -ig, *a.* spicy, aromatic.

Würzladen, vürts'lāden, **Würzkram,** -krām, *m.* grocery.

Würzhändler, vürts'hendler, **Würzkrämer,** -krämer, *m.* grocer.

Würznelken, vürtsnelken, **Würznägel,** -nägl (from their form of nails), *f.* clove.

Wuseln, vū'seln, *vi.* to wiggle.

Wust, vųzht, *m.* chaos, confused mass, rubbish, trash.

Wüst, vüsht, **Wüste,** *a. av.* waste, desolate, uncultivated, wild, deserted.

Wüste, vüzh'te. **Wüstenei,** -eī', *f.* wilderness, desert.

Wüstling, vüzht'ling, *m.* debauchee, rake.

Wuth, vųt, *f.* rage, fury, madness. **Wüthen,** vüh'ten, *vi.* to rage, to be mad, furious with anger, to rave, prevail.

Wüthend, vüht'ent, **Wüthig,** -ich, *a.* furious, mad, frenzy, enraged. **Wütherich,** vüh'terich, **Wüthrich,** *m. pl.* -e, tyrant.

Xanthin, xanthï', *n.* xanthine. **Xanthinsaures Salz,** xanthï'sāgres salts, *n.* xanthate. **Xanthinsäure,** xanthïn'sōïre, *f.* xanthic acid.

Xanthogen, xantegän', *n.* xanthogen. **Xenotim,** xēnotīm', *n.* xenotime, phosphate of yttria.

Xereswein, kā'res-vāēn, *m.* sherry. **Xylit,** xillit', *n.* xylite. **Xylograph,** xillegraf', *m.* xylographer. **Xylographie,** xillegrafī', *f.* xylography, wood-engraving.

Yacht, yacht, *f.* yacht.
Yard, yärt, *f.* yard.
Yttererde, yt'terērde, *f.* yttria.
Yttrium, it'trium, *n.* yttrium.
Yttrocerit, ittrōtserit', *m.* yttrocerite.

Zacke, tsĕck'e, *f.* tick.
Zacken, tsacken, *m.* point, spike, tooth, prong, twig. **Zackig**, tsack'ich, *a. av.* pointed, pronged, toothed, notched; branched.
Zaffer, tsaf'fer, *m.* zaffar, zaffa, zaffre.
Zagen, tsä'gen, *vi.* to delay from fear, to hesitate, to be dismayed.
Zaghaft, tsäk'haft, *a.* timid, fainthearted, cowardly; **-igkeit, -ichkeit**, *f.* timorousness, timidity, cowardice.
Zähe, tsä'e, *a.* tough, viscid, viscous, clammy, gluey, clingy, sticky, tenacious. **Zäheit, Zähigkeit**, tsä'ichkĕit, *f.* toughness, tenacity, ductility; obstinacy.
Zahl, tsäl, *f.* number, figure, cipher.
Zahlamt, tsäl'amt, *n.* pay-office, treasury.
Zahlbar, tsäl'bär, *a.* payable.
Zählbar, tsäl'bär, *a.* numerable.
Zahlen, tsä'len, *vt.* to number.
Zählen, tsä'len, *vt.* to pay.
Zähler, tsä'ler, *m.* numerator, teller, counter.
Zahler, tsäl'er, *m.* payer.
Zahllos, tsäl'lōs, *a.* numberless.
Zahlpfennig, tsäl'pfennich, *m.* counter.
Zahlreich, tsäl'rĕich, *a.* numerous, frequent, *av.* -ly.
Zahlung, tsäl'ung, *f.* payment.
Zählung, tsä'lung, *f.* counting, numeration; census, poll.
Zahlungsfrist, tsäl'ungsfrizht, *f.* term or respite of payment.
Zahlungsunfähig, tsäl'ungsunfä-ich, *a.* insolvent, incapable of paying.
Zahlungsvermögen, tsäl'ungsfermöhgen, *n.* solvency.
Zahlwoche, tsäl'vŏche, *f.* pay-week.
Zahm, tsäm, *a.* tame, domestic, *av.* tamely.
Zähmbar, tsäm'bär, *a.* tamable.
Zähmen, tsä'men, *vt.* to tame, domesticate, break in; to subdue, restrain, bridle, curb; sich —, to contain.
Zähmer, tsä'mer, *m.* tamer.

Zahmheit, tsäm'hĕit, *f.* tameness.
Zahn, tsän, *m. pl.* Zähne, tooth, dent, incision, notch; spoke, tooth, cog, Zähne bekommen, to cut one's teeth, to teeth; die Zähne bieten, to show one's teeth; auf den Zahn fühlen, to feel one's pulse, to sound one.
Zahnarzt, tsän'ärtst, *m.* dentist.
Zahnbuchstabe, tsän'buchzhtäbe, *m.* dental (letter).
Zahnbürste, tsän'bürzhte, *f.* toothbrush.
Zähneln, tsä'neln, *vt.* to tooth, to notch.
Zahnen, tsä'nen, *vi.* to teeth, to cut one's teeth; *vt.* to tooth, indent; to rough-hew (sculpt.); das Eisen —, to form into bars.
Zahnfistel, tsän'fizhtel, *f.* fistula in the gums.
Zahnfieber, tsän'fīber, *n.* fever in teething.
Zahnfleisch, tsän'flĕish, *n.* gums.
Zahnfletschend, tsän'flĕtshend, *a.* showing the teeth.
Zahngeschwür, tsän'geshvühr, *n.* ulcer on the gums.
Zahnhobel, tsän'hōbel, *m.* toothing-plane.
Zahnhöhle, tsän'höhle, *f.* socket of a tooth, alveolus.
Zahnig, tsän'ich, **Zähnig**, tsän'ich, *a.* toothed, notched, denticulated.
Zähnklappern, tsän'klappern, *n.* gnashing of the teeth.
Zahnlos, tsän'lōs, *a.* toothless.
Zahnlücke, tsän'lücke, *f.* gap (of a tooth).
Zahnpulver, tsän'pulfer, *n.* tooth-powder.
Zahnschmerz, tsän'shmĕrts, *m.* Zahnweh, -vä, *n.* tooth-ache.
Zahnstocher, tsän'zhtocher, *m.* toothpick.
Zähre, tsä're, *f.* tear.
Zain, tsĕin, *m.* ingot, wedge, bar.
Zampelstuhl, tsäm'pelshtyl, *m.* simple, symbolt.
Zamten, tsam'ten, *vt.* to fix the yarn upon the looms.
Zange, tsang'e, *f.* tongs, pincers, nippers, plyers.
Zank, tsank, *m.* quarrel, altercation.
Zankapfel, tsank'apfel, *m.* bone (or apple) of contention.

Zan   408   **Zeh**

Zanken, tsank'en, *vi.* to quarrel, dispute, wrangle.
Zanker, tsænk'er, *m.* quarreler, wrangler, scold. **Zänkerei,** -ěī', *f.* quarrel, altercation, brawl. **Zänkisch,** -ish, *a.* quarrelsome.
Zanksucht, tsank'sŭcht, *f.* quarrelsomeness. **Zanksüchtig,** -süchtig, *a.* quarrelsome; *-keit,* -kāet, *f.* litigiousness.
Zapfen, tsap'fen, *m.* peg, pin, plug, tenon. **Zäpfchen,** tsĕpf'chen, **Zäpflein,** -lāen. *n.* little peg, plug; uvula.
Zapfen, tsap'fen, *vt.* to tap, draw, to sell by retail.
Zapfenbohrer, tsap'fenbörer, *m.* auger.
Zapfenfeile, tsap'fenfēile, *f.* pivot-drill.
Zapfenstreich, tsap'fenzhtrāch, *m.* tattoo, retreat.
Zappeln, tsap'peln, *vi.* to sprawl, struggle, kick; to move convulsively.
Zarge, tsarge, *f.* brim, edge; cramp, hold-fast (Joiner.); — eines Fensters, window-frame; — einer Thüre, door-case; — eines Fasses, rim; — eines Mühlsteines, drum, box.
Zart, t-ärt, *a.* tender, fine, delicate, slender, *av.* -ly.
Zartheit, tsärt'hāet, *f.* tenderness, softness. fineness, subtility, delicacy.
Zartgefühl, t-ärt'gefühl, *n.* tenderness of feeling, fine feeling.
Zärtlich, tsärt'lich, *a.* delicate, tender, soft, weak, *av.* -ly; *-keit,* -kāet, *f.* tenderness, softness **Zärtling,** -ling, *m.* tenderling, fondling.
Zartsinn, tsärt'sinn, *m.* refinement, delicacy.
Zaser, tsā'ser, *f.* fibre, string; *-ig,* -ich, *a.* fibrous. **Za'sern,** *vt.* to untwine, unravel, fenze.
Zauber, tsāū'ber, *m.* enchantment, incantation, spell, charm. **Zauberei,** -ěī', *f.* magic, witchcraft, sorcery. **Zauberer,** *m.* sorcerer, magician. **Zauberin,** tsāū'berin *f.* sorceress.
Zauberisch, tsāū'berish, **Zauberhaft,** -haft, *a.* magic, enchanting, bewitching. **Zauberkraft,** -kraft, *f.* magic power. **Zauberkunst,** -kŭnzht, *f.* magic art, witchcraft. **Zauberlaterne,** -laterne, *f.* magic lantern.

Zaubern, tsāū'bern, *vi.* to practice magic *or* witchcraft; *vt.* to enchant, bewitch.
Zaudern, tsōy'dern, *vi.* to delay, loiter linger, dally, trifle, to be dilatory.
Zauderer, tsōy'derer, *m.* loiterer, delayer, lingerer.
Zauderhaft, tsōy'derhaft, *a.* dilatory tardy, slow; *-igkeit,* -ichkāet, *f.* dilatoriness.
Zaum, tsaŭm, *m.* bridle; im — halten to bridle, check, restrain, curb, control. **Zäumen,** tsaü'men, *vt.* to bridle, rein, curb, restrain.
Zaumlos, tsaŭm'lōs, *a.* unbridled.
Zaun, tsaŭn, *m. pl.* Zäune, fence, hedge. **Zäunen,** tsāū'nen, *vt.* to fence, hedge.
Zaunkönig, tsaŭn'köhnich, *m.* wren.
Zaunpfahl, tsaŭn'pfāl, *m.* fence-stake.
Zausen, tsōy'sen, *vt.* to touse, tug, pull.
Zeche, tsěch'e, *f.* mining-company, mine; reckoning, bill: die — bezahlen, to pay the piper; die — ohne den Wirth machen, to count without one's host.
Zecher, tsěch'er, *m.* carouser, toper.
Zechfrei, tsěch'frēī, *a.* scot-free.
Zecke, tsěck'e, *f.* tick, acarus.
Zehe, tsā'e, *f.* toe; clove.
Zehn, tsān, *a.* ten; *s. n.* ten.
Zehnt, tsänt, *a.* tenth.
Zehnerlei, tsän'erlāī, *a.* of ten sorts, kinds, species **Zehner,** tsěhn'er, **Zehner,** tsāner, *m.* ten, half a score; decemvir; a coin (ten kreutzers). **Zehnfach,** -fach, *a.* tenfold. **Zehnjährig,** -yärich, *a.* ten years old. **Zehnmal,** -māl, *av.* ten times; *-ig,* -ich, *a.* repeated ten times. **Zehnpfünder,** -pfünder, *m.* ten-pounder. **Zehnpfündig,** -ig, *a.* of ten pounds. **Zehnmonatig,** -mōnātich, *a.* of ten months. **Zehnmonatlich,** -mōn'atlich, *a. av.* taking place every ten months. **Zehnstündig,** -zhtündich, *a.* of ten hours **Zehnstündlich,** -zhtündlich, *a.* every ten hours. **Zehntägig,** -tāgich, *a.* ten days of age. **Zehntäglich,** *a.* every ten days.
Zehnt, tsänt. *a.* tenth. **Zehntel,** tsän'tel, *n.* tenth. **Zehnten,** *v.* to tithe, to take a tenth.
Zehntens, tsān'tens, *av.* tenthly, in the tenth place.
Zehren, tsā'ren, *vi.* to consume; at

(vom Wein) to grow less; — von, to live, feed upon.

Zehrfieber, tsār'fīber, n. hectic fever.

Zehrpfennig, tsār'pfẹnnig, m. viaticum, something to live on (in a journey).

Zehrung, -ụng, f. shot, viaticum; living.

Zeichen, tsāē'chen, n. sign, token; mark, signal.

Zeichenbuch, tsāē'chenbụch, n. drawing-book.

Zeichendeuter, tsāē'chendöüter, m. soothsayer, astrologer. Zeichendeuterei, -ēī', f. interpretation of signs, omens.

Zeichenkunst, tsāē'chenkụnst, Zeich'nungskunst, -nungskụnst, f. drawing, art of drawing.

Zeichenmeister, tsāē'chenmöster, m. drawing-master.

Zeichenpapier, tsāē'chenpapīr, n. drawing-paper.

Zeichensprache, tsāē'chensbräche, f. language or expression of thoughts or ideas by signs.

Zeichenstift, tsāē'chenztift, m. drawing-pencil.

Zeichnen, tsāēch'nen, vt. i. to draw, design, delineate; to mark; sign; — nach dem Leben, to draw from life; — nach der Natur, to draw from nature.

Zeichner, tsāēch'ner, m. drawer; designer.

Zeichnung, tsāēch'nụng, f. drawing.

Zeideln, tsāī'deln, vt. i. to cut honeycombs.

Zeidler, tsāīd'ler, m. bee-master.

Zeigefinger, tsāī'gefing-er, m. forefinger or pointing-finger; index.

Zeigen, tsāī'gen, vt. to show.

Zeiger, tsāī'ger, m. hand; pointer.

Zeihen, tsāī'en (pr. zieh, pp. geziehen), vt. to charge or tax with.

Zeile, tsāī'le, f. line; row. Zei'lenlänge, -lẹnge, f. justification (Print.). Zei'lenweise, -vēīse, av. by lines; by rows.

Zeisig, tsāī'sig, m. pl. -e, aberdevine, siskin; nice chicken, fine fellow.

Zeit, tsāīt, f. pl. -en, time; season; (Mar.) tide; von — zu — from time to time; zu rechter —, in time, in right time; eine neue —, a new era; in — von, in space of; zur —, at present, just now; bei Zeiten, early; Zeit n eines Lebens, in all my life, all my life long; zu Zeiten, some times now and then; zu seiner Zeit, seasonably, in due time.

Zeitalter, tsāīt'alter, n. age, generation; goldenes —, golden age.

Zeitbuch, tsāīt'bụch, n. pl. -bücher chronicle.

Zeitfolge, tsāīt'folg-e, f. succession of time.

Zeitform, tsāīt'form, f. tense.

Zeitgeist, tsāīt'gāēst, m. genius or spirit of the age or century.

Zeitgemäß, tsāīt'gemās, a. av. suited to circumstances.

Zeitgenoß, tsāīt'genose, m. contemporary.

Zeither, tsāīt'hār, av. hitherto, since; -ig, -ich, a. previous, up to this time.

Zeitig, tsāīt'tich, a. actual, temporary, for the time being; early; timely; ripe; -en, vt. i. to ripen, to mature. Zei'tigung, -ụng, f. ripening; — eines Geschwüres, maturation.

Zeitkunde, tsāīt'kụnde, f. chronology.

Zeitlauf, tsāīt'lāūf, m. pl. Zeitläufe, course of time; juncture, conjuncture.

Zeitlebens, tsāīt'lābens, av. in all my, his, etc., life; as long as I live, lived, etc.

Zeitlich, tsāīt'lich, a. temporal, wordly, secular, earthly; das Zeitliche, temporal concerns or things; -keit, -kāēt, f. mortal state.

Zeitlose, tsāīt'lōse, f. meadow-saffron.

Zeitmaß, tsāīt'mās, s. n. pl. -e, measure of time. Zeit'messer, -messer, m. chronometer. Zeit'ordnung, -ordnụng, f. order of time. Zeit'punkt, -pụnkt, m. pl. -e, point of time, conjuncture, epoch. Zeit'raum, -rāūm, m. pl. -räume, space of time.

Zeitrechnung, tsāīt'rẹchnụng, f. chronology.

Zeitschrift, tsāīt'shrift, f. journal, periodical.

Zeitumstände, tsāīt'ụmzhtẹnde, pl. circumstances, times.

Zeitung, tsāīt'ụng, f. newspaper, paper, gazette; -blatt, -blatt, n. pl. -blätter, newspaper. Zei'tungsexpedition, -ẹxpeditsīōn, f. newspaper office. Zei'tungsnachricht, -nāchricht, f. news, newspaper-report, newspaper-intelligence. Zei'tungsträger, -träger, m. newsboy, news-carrier.

Zei   410   **Zer**

Zeitverderb, tsēlt'ferdĕrp, *m.* waste of time. **Zeitverlust**, -ferlųzht, *m.* loss of time. **Zeitvertreib**, -fertrīp, *m.* pastime.

Zeitwort, tsēlt'vort, *n.* verb.

Zelle, tsĕl'lẹ, *f.* cell. **Zellenförmig**, -fŭrmiç, *a.* cellular. **Zellengewebe**, -gẹvābẹ, *n.* cellular texture.

Zelot, tsẹlōt', *Ci.* -ẹn, *pl.* -n, zealot.

Zelt, tsĕlt, *n. pl.* -e, tent, pavilion; -dach, -dach, *n. pl.* -dächer, tent-cover.

Zelter, tsĕl'tẹr, *m.* ambler, palfrey.

Zeltpfahl, tsĕlt'pfāl, *m. pl.* -pfähle, tent-pole. **Zeltschneider**, -shnēldẹr, *m.* tent-maker. **Zeltwagen**, -vägen, *m.* baggage-wagon.

Zenith, tsẹnitt', *m.* zenith.

Zentner, tsẹnt'ner, *m.* quintal, hundred-weight. **Zentnerlast**, -last, *f.* **Zentnerschwere**, -shvārẹ, *f.* heavy weight. **Zentnerschwer**, -shvār, *a.* very heavy.

Zephyr, tsā'fīr, *m.* zephyr.

Zepter, tsĕp'ter, *n.* sceptre; **-träger**, *m.* ruler, prince.

Zerbeißen, tsĕrbēī'sen, *vt.* to bite to pieces.

Zerbersten, tsĕrbĕr'zhten (*pr.* -borst, *pp.* -borsten), *vi.* to burst asunder.

Zerbläuen, tsĕrblāū'en, *vt.* to beat (black and blue).

Zerbrechen, tsĕrbrĕch'en, *vt. i.* to break (to pieces), to fracture. **Zerbrechlich**, -lich, *a.* fragile, brittle; **-keit**, *f.* fragility, brittleness.

Zerbröckeln, tsĕrbrōk'keln, *vt. i.* to crumble.

Zerdrücken, tsĕrdrük'ken, *vt.* to crush.

Zerfahren, tsĕrfā'ren (*zerfuhr, zerfahren*), *vi.* to fly *or* burst asunder; *vt.* to crush by driving.

Zerfall, tsĕrfall', *m.* decay.

Zerfallen, tsĕrfal'len (*zerfiel, zerfallen*), *vi.* to fall to pieces *or* ruins; to decay; — mit, to fall out with.

Zerfetzen, tsĕrfĕt'sen, *vt.* to slash (to pieces), to tatter.

Zerfleischen, tsĕrflāīsh'ehen, *vt.* to tear (to pieces), dilaniate, lacerate.

Zerfließen, tsĕrflī'sen, *vi.* to melt, to liquify; deliquesce.

Zerfressen, tsĕrfrĕs'sen, *vt.* to corrode, to gnaw to pieces, eat away.

Zergehen, tsĕrgā'en, *vi.* to melt, to dissolve.

Zergliedern, tsĕrglī'dẹrn, *vt.* to dismember, dislimb, dissect, anatomize; analyze. **Zergliederung**, -ung, *f.* dissection, dismemberment, anatomy; analysis; **-messer**, -mĕsser, *n.* scalpel.

Zerhacken, tsĕrhak'ken, *vt.* to hack *or* cut to pieces.

Zerhauen, tsĕrhāū'en, *vt.* to chop *or* cut asunder *or* into pieces.

Zerklopfen, tsĕrklop'fen, *vt.* to beat to pieces, to break; to pound; to beat soundly.

Zerknacken, tsĕrk(e)nak'ken, *vt.* to crack *or* break.

Zerknicken, tsĕrk(e)nik'ken, *vt.* to break, to crush.

Zerknirschen, tsĕrk(e)nīr'shen, *vt.* to bruise, crush, crash, squash.

Zerknirscht, tsĕrkniršht', *a.* contrite. **Zerknirschung**, -ung, *f.* contrition.

Zerknittern, tsĕrknit'tern, *vt.* to rumple, crumble, ruffle.

Zerkratzen, tsĕrkrats'en, *vt.* to scratch, disfigure by scratching.

Zerkrümeln, tsĕrkrüm'ẹln, *vt.* to crumble.

Zerlassen, tsĕrlas'sen (*zerließ, zerlassen*), *vt.* to melt, liquefy, dissolve.

Zerlegen, tsĕrlā'gẹn, *vt.* to disjoin, cut up, carve.

Zerlumpt, tsĕrlųmpt', *a.* ragged, tattered.

Zermahlen, tsĕrmā'len, *vt.* to grind. **Zermalmen**, tsĕr'mal'mẹn, *vt.* to crush, pound, triturate, grind.

Zernagen, tsĕrnā'gẹn, *vt.* to corrode, to gnaw to pieces.

Zernichten, tsĕrnich'ten, *vt.* to annihilate, destroy. **Zernichtung**, -ung, *f.* annihilation, destruction.

Zerpflücken, tsĕrpflük'en, *vt.* to pluck to pieces.

Zerplatzen, tsĕrplats'ẹn, *vi.* to burst asunder, to blow to pieces.

Zerquetschen, tsĕrquĕt'shen, *vt.* to squash, crush, bruise.

Zerraufen, tsĕrrāū'fen, *vt.* to pull out (one's hair).

Zerrbild, tsĕrr'bilt, *n.* caricature.

Zerreiben, tsĕrrēī'ben (-rieb, -rieben), *vt.* to rub, grind, pound, triturate; zu Pulver —, to pulverize.

Zerreiblich, tsĕrrēīb'lich, *a.* friable; **-keit**, -kāēt, *f.* friability. **Zerreibung**, -ung, *f.* trituration.

Zerreißbar, tsĕrrēīs'bār, *a.* lacerable.

Zerreißen, tsĕrrēīs'en (-riß, -rißen),

Zer 411 **Zeu**

vt. to rend, to tear to pieces; to dismember, force asunder; dilacerate.
Zerreiß'ung, -ung, *f.* rending, dismemberment, dilaceration.
Zerren, tṡer'ren, *vt.* to pull, tug, tear.
Zerrgesicht, tṡerr'gesicht, *n.* grimace.
Zerrinnen, tsḕrrin'nen (zerrann, zerronnen), *vi.* to melt, liquefy, dissolve; to waste away, decay; wie gewonnen, so zerronnen, lightly come, lightly gone.
Zerritzen, tsērrits'en, *vt.* to scratch.
Zerrühren, tsērrüh'ren, *vt.* to stir; beat up, to mash.
Zerrütten, tsērrüt'ten, *vt.* to derange, disorder, shake, ruin. **Zerrüttung,** -ung, *f.* disorder, confusion.
Zersägen, tsērsä'gen, *vt.* to saw up or in two.
Zerscheitern, tsērshẽl'tern, *vi.* to be wrecked.
Zerschellen, tsērshēl'len, *vt. i.* to dash (to pieces), to crash, fracture, break.
Zerschlagen, tsērshlä'gen (zerschlug, zerschlagen), *vt.* to dash or beat to pieces, to crush, break; sich —, to be broken up; — an. to break on or against.
Zerschmelzen, tsērshmel'tsen (-schmolz, -schmolzen), *vt. i.* to melt away, liquefy.
Zerschmettern, tsērshmöt'tern, *vt.* to dash, smash to pieces; to break, shatter, shiver.
Zerschneiden, tsērshnēi'den (-schnitt, -schnitten) *vt.* to cut to pieces.
Zersetzen, tsērsets'en, *vt.* to decompose; (Min.) to break to pieces.
Zersetzung, tsērsets'ung, *f.* decomposition, analysis, solution.
Zerspalten, tsērzhpal'ten, *vt. i.* to cleave, split, break.
Zersplittern, tsērzhplit'tern, *vt. i.* to split, shiver, scatter. **Zersplitterung,** -ung, *f.* shivering, breaking up.
Zersprengen, tsērzhpreng-en, *vt.* to burst, to blow up or to pieces.
Zerspringen, tsērzhpring'en (-sprang, -sprungen), *vi.* to burst, to fly asunder or to pieces.
Zerstampfen, tsērzhtam'pfen, *vt.* to stamp down or to pieces.
Zerstauben, tsērzhtäu'ben, *vi.* to fall to dust. **Zerstäuben,** tsērzhtäu'ben, *vt.* to reduce to dust, to disperse.

Zerstieben, tsērzhtī'ben (-stob, -stoben) *vi.* to fly away (as dust); to vanish.
Zerstören, tsērzhtöh'ren, *vt.* to destroy. **Zerstörer,** *m.* destroyer. **Zerstö'rung,** -ung, *f.* destruction.
Zerstoßen, tsērzhtō'sen (-stieß, -stoßen) *vt.* to pound, crush, triturate, break.
Zerstreuen, tsērzhträu'en, *vt.* to strew about, to scatter, disperse, dissipate.
Zerstreu'ung, -ung, *f.* dispersion, scattering, dissemination; diversion; distraction, absent-mindedness.
Zerstückeln, tsērzhtück'eln, *vt.* to dismember, to parcel out, to cut up. **Zerstück'elung,** -ung, *f.* dismemberment.
Zerstücken, tsērzhtücken, *vt.* to cut to pieces.
Zertheilen, tsērtkēl'en, *vt.* to divide, dissever, distribute, dissolve, parcel out. **Zertheil'ung,** -ung, *f.* division, resolution, dissolution.
Zertrennbar, tsērtrenn'bär, *a.* separable, divisible: -keit, -käet, *f.* separability, dissolubility.
Zertrennen, tsērtren'nen, *vt.* to separate; to unsew, to rip up.
Zertreten, tsērträ'ten (-trat, -treten), *vt.* to tread down, trample down, to crush.
Zertrümmern, tsērtrüm'mern, *vt.* to lay in ruins, to upset, destroy.
Zertrümmerung, tsērtrüm'merung, *f.* destruction, overthrow.
Zerwerfen, tsērvērf'en (-warf, -worfen), *vt.* to break to pieces, smash; to set at enmity with.
Zerwühlen, tsērvüh'len, *vt.* to root up.
Zerzausen, tsērtsōy'sen, *vt.* to touse, worry, dishevel.
Zeter, tsēt'ter, *m.* outcry, clamor, cry of distress.
Zettel, tsēt'tel, *m.* billet, ticket.
Zettel, tsēt'tel, *m.* warp.
Zeug, tsēūk, *m.* stuff, matter, material, cloth; ordnance; *s. n.* trash, trifle, rubbish.
Zeuge, tsēū'ge, *m.* witness deponent.
Zeugen, tsēū'gen, *vi.* to testify, witness, depose, to give evidence, to bear witness.
Zeugen, tsēū'gen, *vt.* to generate, beget, procreate, breed.
Zeugen, tsēū'gen, *vt.* to rig (a ship).
Zeugenaussage, tsēū'genöussäge, *f.* deposition. **Zeu'genverhör,** -fērhöhr

Zeu 412 **Zim**

n. hearing *or* examination of witnesses.

Zeugfabrik, tsŏŭk'fabrik, *f.* manufactory of woolen (*or* other) stuffs. **Zeughaus**, -hŏŭs, arsenal, armory. **Zeugmacher**, -macher, *m.* manufacturer of stuffs.

Zeugniß, tsŏŭk'nĭss, *n.* testimony, evidence.

Zeugschmied, tsŏŭk'shmīd, *m.* armorer.

Zeugsichter, tsŏŭk'sichter, *m.* pulp-strainer.

Zeugung, tsŏŭg'ŭng, *f.* generation, procreation, begetting; **-sgeschäft**, -gesheft, **Zeugungswerk**, -verk, *n.* coition, copulation. **Zeugungskraft**, -kraft, *f.* generative power. **Zeugungstheile**, -thely, *s. pl.* genitals.

Zibethkatze, tsib'etkatse, *f.* civet-cat.

Zicklein, tsick'ĕln, *vi.* to kid.

Zickzack, tsick'tsack, *n. or av.* zigzag.

Zieche, tsī'che, **Züche**, tsü'che, *f.* (bed-) tick.

Ziege, tsī'ge, *f.* goat, she-goat.

Ziegel, tsī'gl, *m.* tile; **-brenner**, -bren-ner, *m.* brick-maker.

Ziegelei, tsīgelī', *f.* brick-kiln.

Ziegeldach, tsī'geldach, *n. pl.* -dächer, tiling. **Ziegeldecker**, -dekker, *m.* tiler. **Ziegelerde**, -erde, *f.* brick-earth. **Ziegelerz**, -ärts, *n.* tile-ore. **Ziegelfarben**, -farben, *a.* brick-colored. **Ziegelmehl**, -mēl, *n.* tile-dust. **Ziegelofen**, -ofen, *m.* brick-kiln. **Ziegelscheune**, -shŏŭne, *f.* **Ziegelhütte**, -hütte, *f.* brick-kiln. **Ziegelstein**, -shtāen, *m.* brick. **Ziegelzeug**, -zŏŭk, *n.* something foolish.

Ziegenbart, tsī'genbärt, *m. pl.* -bärte, goat's beard. **Ziegenbock**, -bock, *m.* he-goat. **Ziegenhaar**, -här, *n.* goat's-hair. **Ziegenhirt**, -hirt, *m.* -en, *pl.* -en, goat's-herd. **Ziegenkäse**, -käse, *m.* goat-cheese. **Ziegenmilch**, -milch, *f.* goat's-milk.

Ziehband, tsī'bant, *n. pl.* -bänder, string, yoke-hoop, gripe, tire-clip. **Ziehbar**, -bär, *a.* drawable, ductile. **Ziehbrunnen**, -brŭnnen, *m.* draw-well.

Ziehen, tsī'en (zog, gezogen), *vt.* to draw, pull, drag, tug; einen Stein —, move; in die Höhe —, to raise; in sich —, to draw *or* soak in; auf sich —, to a tract; in die Länge —, to protract; in Erwägung. Betracht

—, to take into consideration; auf Flaschen —, to bottle; (Saft) ziehen aus, to extract; den Hut —, to take off (the hat); Lichter —, to make, mould, dip candles; die Worte — to drawl; einen Graben —, to dig, throw up (a ditch); ein Rohr —, to rifle; zu Rathe —, to consult, to ask advice of; in Zweifel —, to doubt; = Erziehen, to educate, breed, cultivate; *vi.* to go, march, move; sich —, to stretch, extend; to warp.

Ziehung, tsī'ŭng, *f.* drawing, casting; conscription, enrolment.

Ziel, tsīl, *n. pl.* -e, butt, scope, mark; term, limit, end; aim.

Zielen, tsī'len, *vi.* to aim, to take one's aim; to point *or* drive, level at; to allude *or* tend to.

Zielscheibe, tsīl'shāibe, *f.* target, mark; — des Witzes, butt, laughing-stock.

Zielschießen, tsīl'shīssen, *n.* target practice.

Ziemen, tsī'men, *vi.* to become.

Ziemlich, tsīm'lich, *a. av.* pretty, tolerable, -bly.

Ziemer, tsī'mer, *m.* saddle (of venison).

Zier, **Zierde**, tsīr'de, *f.* ornament, grace, honor, decoration; finery.

Zierath, tsī'rät, *m.* basf.

Zieren, tsī'ren, *vt.* to adorn, decorate, embellish, trim up; sich —, to coy, to behave with reserve, to be affected. **Ziererei**, tsīrerī', *f.* affectation, prudness, airs. **Zierlich**, -lich, *a. av.* elegant, nice, neat; steif, -käst, *f.* elegance, neatness, nicety. **Zierling**, -ling, **Zierbengel**, -ben-gel, *m.* dandy, coxcomb, fop, popin-jay, fancy-man.

Ziffer, tsif'fer, *f.* cipher, figure, number; **-blatt**, -blatt, *n. pl.* -blätter, dial-plate.

Ziffern, tsif'fern, *vt.* to cipher.

Zigeuner, tsigŏŭ'ner, *m.* -inn, *f.* gipsey.

Zimmer, tsim'mer, *n.* room, apartment; chamber; **-arbeit**, -arbait, *f.* carpenter's work. **Zimmerart**, -axt, *f. pl.* -äxte, carpenter's axe. **Zimmerbrief**, -brīf, *m. pl.* -e, contract for building a ship. **Zimmerdecke**, -decke, *f.* ceiling. **Zimmermeister**, *m.* carpenter. **Zimmergesell**, -gesel, *m.* journeyman carpenter. **Zimmerhandwerk**, -hantverk, *n.* car-

Zim 413 **Zög**

ter's trade. **Zim'merhof**, -hōf, m. pl. -höfe, carpenter's yard. **Zim'mer-holz**, -holts, n. timber. **Zim'mer-kunst**, -kynzht, f. carpentry. **Zim's mermann**, -mann, m. pl. -leute, carpenter. **Zim'mermeister**, -mäster, m. master carpenter. **Zim'mern**, vt. to work, frame, square, cut, shape, fabricate; to make, prepare. **Zim's merplatz**, -plats, m. pl. -plätze, timber-yard. **Zim'merreihe**, -rā-e, f. suit of apartments. **Zim'merwerk**, -vërk, n. carpenter's work.

Zimmet, tsim'met, **Zimmt**, m. cinnamon; **-baum**, -bōum, m. cinnamon-tree. **Zimmt'blüthe**, -blühte, f. cinnamon flower. **Zimmt'öl**, -öhl, n. oil of cinnamon. **Zimmt'rinde**, -rīnde, f. bark of the cinnamon-tree.

Zimperlich, tsim'perlich, a. coy, prim, mincing; **-keit**, -käet, f. primness, affectedness. **Zimpern**, tsim'pern, vi. to coy.

Zink, tsink, f. cinque (in dice).

Zink, tsink, n. zinc, spelter.

Zinke, tsink'e, f. tooth, prong, tine; summit (of a mountain); spike (of a pitchfork); troching (of an antler); clove (of garlic); cornet.

Zinkenist, tsinkenist', m. corneter, cornist; town-musician.

Zinkenit, tsinkenit', m. zinkenite.

Zinn, tsinn, n. tin; **-asche**, -ashe, f. putty of tin. **Zinn'bergwerk**, -bërkvërk, n. **Zinn'grube**, -grybe, f. tin-mine.

Zinne, tsin'ne, f. battlement, pinnacle.

Zinnern, tsin'nern, a. tin, pewter.

Zinnerz, tsinn'ërts, n. tin-ore. **Zinn's gießer**, -gīser, m. worker in tin.

Zinngraupe, tsinn'groupe, pl. crystal of tin. **Zinn'haltig**, -haltich, a. containing tin. **Zinn'kalk**, -kalk, m. calcined tin, tin-putty. **Zinn'loth**, -lōt, n. tin-solder, soft solder.

Zinnober, tsinnō'ber, m. cinnabar; vermilion.

Zins, tsins, pl. **Zinfe** and **Zinfen**, rent, tribute, use, interest; **-bar**, -bār, a. tributary. **Zins'buch**, -byḥ, n. pl. -bücher, rental, rent-roll.

Zinfen, tsin'sen, vt. i. to pay rent; to yield rent.

Zinsfrei, tsins'frēī, a. allodial. **Zins-pflichtig**, tsins'pflichtig, a. tributary; subject to rent or tithe.

Zipf, tsipf, m. pip.

Zipfel, tsip'fel, m. tip, corner; **-mütze**, -mütse, f. night-cap.

Zipperlein, tsip'perlaen, n. gout.

Zirbeldrüse, tsir'beldrühse, f. pineal gland.

Zirkel, tsir'kl, m. circle; compasses, a pair of compasses; **-abschnitt**, -apshnit, m. segment. **Zir'kelausschnitt**, -öysshnit, m. sector. **Zir'kelbogen**, -bōgen, m. (circular) arch. **Zir'kelförmig**, -förmich, a. circular. **Zir's kelform**, -form, f. circular form.

Zirkeln, tsir'keln, vt. i. to measure with compasses. **Zirkelrunde**, tsir'kelrynde, f. circular form, circularity. **Zir'kelsäge**, -sä-ge, f. circular-saw.

Zirkon, tsir'cōn, m. circon; **-erbe**, -érde, f. zirconia.

Zirkonit, tsircōnit', m. zirconite.

Zirkonium, tsircō'nium, n. zirconium.

Zirpen, tsir'pn, vi. to chirp.

Zischeln, tsish'eln, vt. i. to whisper.

Zischen, tsish'en, vi. to hiss, whiz.

Zischlaut, tsish'lōyt, m. sibilant.

Zither, **Zitter**, tsit'ter. f. cittern; guitar.

Zitrone, **Citrone**, tsitrō'ne, f. lemon; **-baum**, -baŭm, m. lemon, lemon-tree. **Zitronenholz**, -hölts, n. Jamaica rose-wood.

Zitteraal, tsitt'ëräl, m. pl. -äle, cramp-fish; electric ray, torpedo.

Zitterer, tsitt'erer, m. trembler; quaker.

Zittern, tsitt'ern, vi. to tremble, shake, quake.

Zitwer, tsit'ver, m. zedoary; worm-seed.

Zitz, tsits, m. calico (in England chintz).

Zitze, tsits'e, f. teat, nipple, dug; pap.

Zobel, tsō'bl, m. sable; **-pelz**, -pelts, m. sable.

Zodiakallicht, tsōdiakäl'licht, n. zodiacal light.

Zofe, tsō'fe, f. waiting or chambermaid, lady's maid.

Zog, tsōg, Prt. v. ziehen.

Zögel, tsöh'gel, m. pig (of iron, etc.).

Zögerer, tsöh'gerer, m. loiterer, lingerer.

Zögern, tsöh'gern, vi. to tarry, linger, delay. **Zö'gerung**, -yng, f. delay tarrying.

35*

Zög 414 **Zuc**

Zögling, tsöhk'ling, *m.* pupil.
Zoll, tsoll, *m. pl.* **Zolle,** inch.
Zoll, tsoll, *m. pl.* **Zölle,** toll, duty, custom; tribute; **-amt,** -amt, *n. pl.* **-ämter,** custom-office. **Zoll'anschlag,** -anshläk, *m.* tariff. **Zoll'bar,** -bär, *a.* paying duty *or* custom. **Zoll'beamter,** -beämter, *m.* custom n-house-officer. **Zoll'einnahme,** -einnämẹ, *f.* revenue of customs.
Zollen, tsoll'en, *vt.* to pay duty *or* custom; to give, to pay. **Zoll'frei,** -freï, *a.* free of duty. **Zoll'haus,** -hôus, *n. pl.* **-häuser,** custom-house.
Zöllner, tsöll'ner, *m.* toller, toll-gatherer; publican.
Zollstab, tsoll'zhtäp, *m. pl.* **-stäbe,** **Zoll'stock,** -zhtock, *m. pl.* **-stöcke,** rule.
Zolltarif, tsoll'tariff, *m. pl.* **-e,** tariff.
Zollverein, tsoll'ferein, *m.* custom's union, zollverein.
Zone, tsō'ne, *f.* zone.
Zoograph, tsōōgräf', *m.* zoographer.
Zoolog, tsōōlōg', *m.* zoologist.
Zoophyt, tsōōfit', *m. pl.* **-en,** zoophyte.
Zopf, tsopf, *m. pl.* **Zöpfe,** braid; (of men) cue, pigtail; **-ende,** -endẹ, *n.* top-end.
Zorn, tsorn, *m.* anger, wrath, passion, rage; **-ig,** -iḉ, *a.* angry, hot, wrathful, passionate.
Zote, tsō'tẹ, *f.* obscenity, ribaldry; **Zoten reißen,** to utter obscene things; **-nreißer,** -reïsser, *m.* obscene talker; **-ei,** -ēī', *f.* obscene talking, bawdry. **Zotig,** tsō'tig, *a.* obscene, bawdy.
Zotte, tsot'tẹ, *f.* tuft, lock. **Zottel,** tsot'tl, *f.* tuft, lock. **Zottelbär,** -bär, *m.* shaggy bear. **Zottig,** tsot'tich, *a.* tufty, shaggy, hairy.
Zu, tsụ, *pr.* to; at; **zu Deutsch,** in German; **zu Fuß,** on foot; **zu Hause,** at home; **zu guter Letzt,** to finish (well *or* with); **zu Wasser,** at sea; **zu Wasser und zu Land,** by sea and by land; **zu Zeiten,** at *or* by times; **zum Glück,** fortunately, luckily; **zur Hälfte,** by half; **zur Noth,** at the worst, if need be; **zur Zeit,** for the time, at present.
Zu, tsụ, *av.* (one end to the other), **zugehen,** to shut; to close; **zusein,** to be closed *or* shut; **zuthun,** to close; add (properly in addition to what is just *or* right) to.

Zubauen, tsụ'bôyen, *vt.* to close by building, to obstruct.
Zubehör, tsụ'behöhr, *n.* appurtenance.
Zuber, tsụ'ber, *m.* tub.
Zubereiten, tsụ'beräeten, *vt.* to prepare, fit, adjust. **Zu'bereitung,** -ụng, *f.* preparation.
Zubinden, tsụ'binden, *vt.* to tie *or* bind up; **die Augen** —, to blindfold.
Zublasen, tsụ'blāsen, *vi.* to blow on; *vt.* to blow to; to close by blowing; to prompt.
Zubringen, tsụ'bringen, *vt.* to bring to; to report; **seine Zeit** —, to spend one's time.
Zubrocken, tsụ'brocken, *vt.* to spend of one's own; **zuzubrocken haben,** to be well off.
Zubuße, tsụ'buse, *f.* increase; contribution. **Zubüßen,** tsụ'büssen, *vt.* to contribute, to supply, to spend, to lose.
Zucht, tsụcht, *f. pl.* **Züchte,** breeding; breed; culture; education; modesty; discipline; **-haus,** -hôus, *n.* penitentiary, house of correction.
Züchtig, tsüch'tig, *a.* chaste, pure; **-en,** -n, *vt.* to chastise, to punish. **Züchtigkeit,** tsüch'tigkẹèt, *f.* chastity. **Züchtigung,** -ụng, *f.* chastisement.
Züchtling, -ling, *m.* convict; prisoner.
Zuchtlos, tsụcht'lōs, *a.* unruly, disorderly, licentious; **-igkeit,** -ichkẹèt, *f.* licentiousness. **Zuchtmeister,** -mëezhter, *m.* task-master, disciplinarian. **Zuchtruthe,** tsụcht'rụtẹ, *f.* scourge. **Zuchtvieh,** -fī, *n.* cattle for breeding.
Zuck, tsụck, *m.* start, twitch. **Zucken,** tsụck'en, *vi.* to quiver, twitch, start, palpitate; to move convulsively; — **vom Licht,** to flash.
Zücken, tsück'en, *vt.* to twitch; shock, to pull; **das Schwert** —, to draw the sword; **die Achseln** —, to shrug the shoulders.
Zucker, tsụck'er, *m.* sugar; **-ahorn,** -āhorn, *m.* sugar-maple, sugar-tree.
Zuckeralaun, tsụck'erälặụn, *m.* alum-sugar. **Zuckerbäcker,** -becker, *m.* confectioner. **Zuckerbau,** -bôụ, *m.* cultivation of sugar-cane. **Zuckerbrod,** -brōt, *n.* small cake. **Zuckerbüchse,** -büxe, **Zuckerdose,** -dōse, *f.* sugar-box. **Zuckerhut,** -hụt, *m. pl.*

Zuc   415   **Zug**

-büte, sugar-loaf. **Zuckermühle**, -mühle, *f.* sugar-mill. **Zuckerig**, tsuck'ėrich, *a.* sugary. **Zuckern**, tsuck'ėrn, *a.* sugar, of sugar, saccharine.
Zuckern, tsuck'ėrn, *vt.* to sugar.
Zuckerzange, tsuck'ertsange, *f.* sugar-tongs.
Zuckung, tsuck'ung, *f.* convulsion.
Zudecken, tsu'dekken, *vt.* to cover up.
Zudem, tsudäm', *m.* moreover.
Zudenken, tsu'denken, *vt.* to intend to add, give, to imagine shut up.
Zudrängen, tsu'drengen, *vr.* sich —, to intrude *or* obtrude one's self.
Zudrang, tsu'drang, *m.* thronging to.
Zudringlich, tsu'dringlich, *a.* obtrusive; importunate; -keit, -käet, *f.* importunity.
Zudrucken, tsu'drucken, *vt.* to go on printing.
Zudrücken, tsu'drücken, *vt.* to shut by pressure: ein Auge — bei, to connive *or* wink at, overlook.
Zueignen, tsu'ägnen, *vt.* to appropriate; to dedicate. **Zu'eignung**, -nung, *f.* appropriation; dedication.
Zueilen, tsu'ėilen, *vi.* to hasten *or* run to, up to.
Zuerkennen, tsu'ėrkennen, *vt.* to award, adjudge, adjudicate. **Zu'erkennung**, -nung, *f.* award, adjudication.
Zuerst, tsuärzht', *av.* first, at first, firstly.
Zufahren, tsu'fären, *vt.* to drive on; to rush upon; to act rashly, *or* hastily; *vt.* to carry to.
Zufall, tsu'fall, *m.* chance, accident.
Zufallen, tsu'fallen, *vi.* to fall to one's share; to devolve on; to shut of itself.
Zufällig, tsu'fellich, *a.* accidental, casual; -keit, -käet, *f.* contingency, casualty, accidentalness.
Zufertigen, tsu'fertichen, *vt.* to dispatch *or* send to.
Zuflicken, tsu'flicken, *vt.* to patch up.
Zufließen, tsu'fliesen, *vi.* to flow *or* come to; — lassen, to bestow upon.
Zuflucht, tsu'flucht, *f.* refuge; recourse, shelter; — nehmen, to take refuge, to resort to; -ort, -ort, *m.* asylum, sanctuary, place of refuge.
Zufluß, tsu'fluss, *m. pl.* -flüsse, afflux, supply.

Zuflüstern, tsu'flüzhtern, *vt.* to whisper to.
Zufolge, tsufol'ge, *av.* according to.
Zufördern, tsu'fördern, *vt.* to forward to.
Zuförderst, tsufōr'derzht, *av.* in the first place, first of all, before all.
Zufrieden, tsufrid'en, *a.* content, -ed, satisfied; -heit, -häet, *f.* content, contentment, contentedness.
Zufrieren, tsu'friren, *vi.* to freeze up.
Zufügen, tsu'fühgen, *vt.* to add; to cause, to inflict.
Zufuhr, tsu'fur, *f.* supply, import.
Zuführen, tsu'führen, *vt.* to carry, convey to; to supply with; (somebody) to take *or* introduce to.
Zuführwalze, tsu'führvaltse, *f.* licker-in.
Zufüllen, tsu'füllen, *vt.* to fill up.
Zug, tsug, *m.* draught, pull, haul, tug; move; procession; expedition; feature, lineament: trait; flight (of birds); team (of horses), yoke (of oxen).
Zugabe, tsu'gäbe, *f.* addition.
Zugang, tsu'gang, *m. pl.* -gänge, access, approach. **Zu'gänglich**, -genglich, *a.* accessible, affable; -keit, tsu'genglichkäet, *f.* accessibility, affability.
Zugbrücke, tsug'brücke, *f.* drawbridge.
Zugeben, tsu'gäben, *vt.* to add; to give into the bargain; to follow suit; to allow, grant, concede, permit.
Zugegen, tsugä'gen, *a.* present.
Zugehen, tsu'gä-en, *vi.* to go on, proceed; spitzig zugehen, to end in a point; to close.
Zugehör, tsu'gehöhr, *n.* appurtenance; -en, *vi.* to appertain *or* belong to.
Zugehörig, tsu'gehöhrig, *a.* appertaining, belonging, proper to.
Zügel, tsüh'gel, *m.* bridle, rein, curb; im — halten, to bridle, rein, check.
Zügellos, tsüh'gellös, *a. av.* unbridled, unrestrained, licentious; -keit, -ichkäet, *f.* licentiousness.
Zügeln, tsüh'geln, *vt.* to bridle, curb, check. restrain.
Zugemüse, tsu'gemühse, *n.* green, herbs, vegetables.
Zugenannt, tsu'genannt, *a.* surnamed.
Zugesellen, tsu'gesellen, *vt. i.* to associate.

Zug 416 **Zum**

Zugestehen, tsu'gĕshtä-en, *vt.* to grant, concede.
Zugethan, tsu'gĕtän, *a.* attached, devoted.
Zuggarn, tsuk'garn, *-netz,* -nets, *n.* drag-net.
Zugießen, tsu'gīsen, *vt.* to pour to, on.
Zugleich, tsuglīch', *av.* at once, together, at the same time; **-sein,** -säen, *n.* simultaneousness.
Zugloch, tsuk'loch, *n.* vent, air-hole.
Zugluft, tsuk'luft, *f.* draught of air.
Zugochs, tsuk'oks, *m.* draft-ox.
Zugofen, tsuk'ōfen, *m.* wind-furnace.
Zugpflaster, tsuk'pflazhter, *n.* blister, vesicatory.
Zugpferd, tsuk'pfĕrt, *n.* draft-horse.
Zugreifen, tsu'grīfen (-griff, -gegriffen), *vi.* to take hold of, to seize.
Zugseil, tsuk'sĕēl, *n.* hawser, halser.
Zugvieh, tsuk'fī, *n.* cattle for draught.
Zugvogel, tsuk'fōgl, *m.* bird of passage.
Zugweise, tsuk'vīse, *av.* by troops, in flocks.
Zugwind, tsuk'vīnt, *m.* draught of air.
Zuhaben, tsu'häben, *vi.* to have *or* keep shut.
Zuhalten, tsu'halten, *vt.* to keep shut *or* closed. **Zuhaltung,** tsu'haltung, *f.* tumbler of a French doorlock.
Zuhängen, tsu'hengen, *vt.* to cover with curtains.
Zuhauen, tsu'hauen (-hieb, -gehauen), *vi.* to strike; to keep cutting; to rough-hew, to dress, form, shape by cutting.
Zuheften, tsu'heften, *vt.* to pin.
Zuheilen, tsu'hēlen, *vt.* to close, to heal up.
Zuhorchen, tsu'horchen, *vi.* to listen, hearken.
Zuhören, tsu'hōhren, *vi.* to hear, to listen; to give ear to; to attend.
Zuhörer, tsu'hōhrer, *m.* hearer, auditor; **-schaft,** -shaft, *f.* audience, auditory.
Zujauchzen, tsu'youchtsen, *vi.* to shout to, to hail, huzza.
Zukehren, tsu'kāren, *vt.* to turn to; den Rücken —, to turn one's back to *or* upon.
Zuklappen, tsu'klappen, *vt. i.* to clap to shut suddenly.

Zuklatschen, tsu'klatshen, *vi.* to clap to applaud.
Zukleiden, tsu'klēden, *vt.* to serve (Mar.).
Zuklinken, tsu'klinken, *vt.* to latch.
Zuknöpfen, tsu'knöpfen, *vt.* to button up.
Zuknüpfen, tsu'knüpfen, *vt.* to tie up.
Zukommen, tsu'kommen (-kam, -gekommen), *vi.* to come up to, to approach; to belong; to be suitable — lassen, to let have, to communicate, accommodate with.
Zukönnen, tsu'können, *vi.* to be able to reach *or* get near.
Zukorken, tsu'korken, *vt.* to cork.
Zukost, tsu'kosht, *f.* additional dish, vegetables.
Zukunft, tsu'kunft, *f.* future, futurity, time to come. **Zukünftig,** -künftich, *a. av.* future; —e Zeit, (Gram.) future (tense).
Zulächeln, tsu'lĕcheln, *vi.* to smile on.
Zulage, tsu'lāge, *f.* increase (of salary); addition.
Zulangen, tsu'langen, *vt. i.* to help one's self, to fall to; to suffice, to be sufficient.
Zulänglich, tsu'lenglich, *a.* sufficient, competent, *av.* -ly; **-keit,** -kāet, *f.* competence, sufficiency.
Zulassen, tsu'lassen (-ließ, -gelassen), *vt.* to admit, allow, permit, grant; die Thür ꝛc. —, to leave shut.
Zulässig, tsu'lässich, tsu'lessich. *a.* admissible; **-keit,** -kāet, *f.* admissibility. **Zulassung,** -lassung, *f.* admission, admittance.
Zulauf, tsu'lāuf, *m. pl.* Zuläufe, concourse, confluence, run, crowd; **-en,** -en (-lief, -gelaufen), *vi.* to run up to, to flock.
Zulegen, tsu'lāgen, *vt.* to add, superadd, to increase by.
Zulehnen, tsu'lānen, *vt.* to shut partly, to leave on the latch.
Zuletzt, tsuletst', *av.* at last, lastly, last, finally.
Zulispeln, tsu'lispeln, *vt. i.* to whisper to; to put a flea in one's ear.
Zulp, tsulp, *m. pl.* Zülpe, sucking-bag.
Zumachen, tsu'machen, *vt.* to shut, close, stop up; den Rock —, to button up the coat; to fold (a letter).
Zumal, tsumāl', *av.* at once, all at once, together; chiefly, especially, particularly.

Zum 417 **Zur**

Zumauern, tsŭ'mŏŭ-ẽrn, *vt.* to wall or brick up.

Zumeist, tsŭmāẽzht', *av.* mostly, for the most part.

Zumessen, tsŭ'mĕssen, *vt.* to measure out.

Zümperlich, tsŭm'perlich, *a.* affected, prudish.

Zumuthen, tsŭ'mŭten, *vt.* to demand, desire, exact, expect; to request from, pretend to, charge with, to impute. **Zumuthung**, -ŭng, *f.* demand, expectation, pretension, request.

Zunächst, tsŭnĕxt, *av.* next *or* nearest to: first of all.

Zunageln, tsŭ'nāgeln, *vt.* to nail up.

Zunähen, tsŭ'nā-en, *vt.* to sew up.

Zunahme, tsŭ'nāme, *f.* increase.

Zuname, tsŭ'nāme, *m.* surname.

Zündbar, tsŭnt'bār, *a.* inflammable.

Zünden, tsŭn'den, *vt.* to kindle; *vi.* to catch fire, to take fire.

Zunder, tsŭn'der, *m.* tinder.

Zünder, tsŭn'der, *m.* one who lights; linstock, fuse, smift.

Zunderbüchse, tsŭn'derbŭxe, *f.* tinderbox.

Zündhölzchen, tsŭnt'hŏltschen, match.

Zündkorn, tsŭnt'korn, **Zündkraut**, -krŏut, *n.* **Zündpulver**, -pŭlfer, *n.* priming. **Zündloch**, -loch, *n. pl.* -löcher, touch-hole, vent. **Zündnadelgewehr**, -nādelgevār, *n.* needlegun. **Zündpfanne**, -pfanne, *f.* pan, touch-pan. **Zündschnur**, -shnŭr, *f.* quick-match. **Zündwurst**, -vŭrsht, *f. pl.* -würste, saucisse, saucisson.

Zunehmen, tsŭ'nāmen (-nohm. -genommen), *vi.* to increase, to grow, prosper, thrive.

Zuneigen, tsŭ'nāēgen, *vt.* to bend, incline, turn to. **Zuneigung**, -ŭng, *f.* inclination, affection.

Zunft, tsŭnft, *f.* guild, body, corporation, society, tribe.

Zünftig, tsŭnf'tich, *a.* incorporated, corporate.

Zunge, tsŭng'e, *f.* tongue; language.

Züngelchen, tsŭng'elchen, *n.* little tongue; point (Typ.); languet.

Züngeln, tsŭng'eln, *vi.* to wag one's tongue, to lick.

Zungenbuchstabe, tsŭng'enbuchshtābe, *m.* lingual (letter). **Zungendrescher**, -drēsher, *m.* wrangler, pettifogger. **Zungenförmig**, -förmich, *a.* linguiform, tongue-shaped. **Zungenspitze**, -shpitse, *f.* tip of the tongue.

Zunichte, tsŭnicht'e (*properly* zu Nichte, to nothing), undone, ruined; — machen, to destroy, ruin, waste, annihilate.

Zunicken, tsŭ'nicken, *vi.* to nod to.

Zuordnen, tsŭ'ordnen, *vt.* to join to, to associate, adjoin.

Zupfen, tsŭp'fen, *vt.* to pull, pluck; to unravel.

Zupflastern, tsŭ'pflazhtern, *vt.* to plaster over; to pave up.

Zupfropfen, tsŭ'pfropfen, *vt.* to cork.

Zupichen, tsŭ'pichen, *vt.* to pitch.

Zuplatzen, tsŭ'platsen, *vi.* to blurt, blunder out.

Zurathen, tsŭ'rāten (-rieth, -gerathen), *vi.* to advise to do.

Zurathehalten, tsŭrā'tehalten (zu Rathe halten), *vt.* to husband, economize. **Zurathehaltung**, -ŭng, *f.* husbanding.

Zuraunen, tsŭ'rŏunen, *vt.* to whisper (into one's ear).

Zurechnen, tsŭ'rechnen, *vt.* to impute, ascribe, attribute to; to put to one's account. **Zurechnung**, -nŭng, *f.* imputation; -fähig, -fā-ich, *a.* to whom something can be imputed, responsible, accountable.

Zurecht, tsŭrecht' (zu Recht), *av.* aright; — bringen, to put in order, to right; — machen, to prepare; — weisen, to direct, to show the right way. **Zurechtweisung**, -vēīsŭng, *f.* reprimand, correction.

Zureden, tsŭ'rāden, *vi.* to encourage, exhort.

Zureichen, tsŭ'rāēchen, *vi.* to suffice, to be enough *or* sufficient; *vt.* to hand *or* reach.

Zureissen, tsŭ'rēīssen (-riss, -gerissen), *vt.* to close by jerking.

Zureiten, tsŭ'rēīten (-ritt, -geritten), *vt.* to break (a horse); *vi.* to ride on.

Zurichtebogen, tsŭ'richtebōgen, *m.* register sheet.

Zurichten, tsŭ'richten, *vt.* to prepare, dress; to turn to; to cook; to cut (a stone); übel —, to treat ill, badly roughly. **Zurichtspan**, -shpān, *m.* reglet. **Zurichtung**, -ŭng, *f.* preparing, dressing, cooking.

Zuriegeln, tsŭ'rīgeln, *vt.* to bolt.

33

Zur 418 **Zur**

Zurlit, tsuṛlit', m. zurlite.
Zürnen, tsür'nen, vi. to be angry.
Zurollen, tsy'rollen, vt. to roll to, towards.
Zurück, tsurück', av. back, backwards.
Zurückbeben, tsurück'bāben, vi. to shrink from.
Zurückbegeben, tsurück'begāben, vr. sich —, to betake one's self back.
Zurückberufen, tsurück'berufen, vt. to call back.
Zurückbezahlen, tsurück'betsālen, vt. to pay back, repay.
Zurückbleiben, tsurück'blēiben (-blieb, -geblieben), vi. to remain, stay behind.
Zurückblicken, tsurück'blicken, vi. to look back.
Zurückbringen, tsurück'bringen (zurückbrachte, zurückgebracht), vt. to bring back, to return.
Zurückdenken, tsurück'denken (-dachte, -gedacht), vi. to think one's self back: to reflect.
Zurückdrängen, tsurück'drengen, vt. to drive back, crowd back, repel.
Zurückfahren, tsurück'fāren (-fuhr, -gefahren), vi. to recoil, to start or fall back. Zurückfahrt, -fart, f. drive or ride back, return.
Zurückfallen, tsurück'fallen (-fiel, -gefallen), vi. to fall back.
Zurückfließen, tsurück'flīsen (-floß, -geflossen), vi. to flow back.
Zurückfordern, tsurück'fordern, vt. to demand back.
Zurückführen, tsurück'führen, vt. to lead or bring back, to reduce. Zurückführung, -ung, f. reduction.
Zurückgabe, tsurück'gābe, f. restitution, returning, rendition.
Zurückgeben, tsurück'gāben (-gab, -gegeben), vt. to give back, restore, return.
Zurückgehen, tsurück'gā-en (-ging, -gegangen), vi. to go back, to return.
Zurückgezogen, tsurück'getsōgen (zurückzieben), a. retired; -heit, -hāet, f. retirement.
Zurückhaben, tsurück'hāben, vt. to get or have got back.
Zurückhalten, tsurück'halten (-hielt, -gehalten), vt. to hold back, restrain, detain, prevent; sb. p. reserved, distant, cautious. Zurückhaltung,

-ung, f. reserve; holding back, retention.
Zurückkehren, tsurück'kāren, vi. to turn or bend back ; vi. to return.
Zurückkommen, tsurück'kommen (zurückkam, zurückgekommen), vi. to come back, to return.
Zurückkönnen, tsurück'können, vi. t. be able to return, recant, recall, unsay or undo.
Zurückkunft, tsurück'kunft, f. return.
Zurücklassen, tsurück'lassen (-ließ, -gelassen), vt. to leave (behind), to abandon. Zurücklassung, -ung, f. abandonment.
Zurücklegen, tsurück'lāgen, vt. to lay apart or aside; to clear, travel over; to lay or put by, to spare.
Zurücknehmen, tsurück'nāmen (zurücknahm, zurückgenommen), vt. to take back, withdraw, recall.
Zurückprallen, tsurück'prallen, vi. to rebound, recoil, reverberate.
Zurückrufen, tsurück'rufen (-rief, -gerufen), vt. to call back, recall.
Zurückschaudern, tsurück'shoudern, vi. to shudder, shrink or start back, to recoil.
Zurückschauen, tsurück'shauen, vi. to look back.
Zurückschieben, tsurück'shīben (-schob, -geschoben), vt. to push back, defer.
Zurückscheuchen, tsurück'shäuchen, vt. to scare back.
Zurückschlagen, tsurück'shlāgen (zurückschlug, zurückgeschlagen), vt. i. to beat or strike back, to repulse; to recoil.
Zurücksehen, tsurück'sā-en (-sah, -gesehen), vi. to look back.
Zurücksetzen, tsurück'setsen, vt. to set back, put back; to replace; to slight, disregard; to reduce. Zurücksetzung, -ung, f. slight, neglect, disregard.
Zurückspringen, tsurück'zhpringen (-sprang, -gesprungen), vi. to bound back, rebound, recoil.
Zurückstehen, tsurück'zhtā-en (-stand, -gestanden), vi. to stand back.
Zurückstoßen, tsurück'zhtōsen (-stieß, -gestoßen), vt. to push or thrust back, to repel.
Zurückstrahlen, tsurück'shtrālen, vi. to reflect.
Zurückstürzen, tsurück'zhtürtsen, vt. i. to throw back, to rush or fall back.

Zur 419 **Zuf**

Zurücktreiben, tsyrü̆k'trēibən (-trieb, -getrieben), *vt*. to drive back, to repel.

Zurücktreten, tsyrück'trätən (-trat, -getreten), *vi*. to step back, withdraw.

Zurückweichen, tsyrück'vēīḫən (-wich, -gewichen), *vi*. to recede, give way, retire, withdraw.

Zurückweisen, tsyrück'vēīsən (-wies, -gewiesen), *vt*. to order back, repel; refuse. **Zurückweisung**, -ŭng, *f*. refuse.

Zurückwerfen, tsyrück'vērfən (-warf, -geworfen), *vt*. to cast back, throw back; to reflect.

Zurückzahlen, tsyrück'tsälen, *vt*. to pay back, repay.

Zurückziehen, tsyrück'tsī-ən (-zog, -gezogen), *vt. r.* to withdraw, retreat, retire.

Zuruf, tsy'rŭf, *m.* acclamation.

Zurufen, tsy'rŭfen (-rief, -gerufen), *vt. i.* to call to; to cry out.

Zurüsten, tsy'rü̆hten, *vt*. to prepare. **Zurüstung**, -ŭng, *f.* preparation, equipping, fitting out.

Zusage, tsy'sägə, *f.* promise.

Zusagen, tsy'sägən, *vi*. to consent; to agree, suit.

Zusammen, tsysam'mən, *av*. together.

Zusammenballen, tsysam'mənballən, *vt.* to ball together, to conglomerate.

Zusammenblatten, tsysam'mənblatten, *vt*. to scarf.

Zusammenbrechen, tsysam'mənbrĕḫen (-brach, -gebrochen), *vi*. to break down.

Zusammenbringen, tsysam'mənbringən (-brachte, -gebracht), *vt*. to bring together, to collect, gather.

Zusammendrehen, tsysam'məndrä-ən, *vt*. to twist together.

Zusammendrängen, tsysam'məndrengən, *vt*. to crowd together; to compress.

Zusammendrücken, tsysam'məndrücken, *vt*. to press together, compress, squeeze. **Zusammendrückung**, -ŭng, *f.* compression.

Zusammendürfen, tsysam'məndürfen (-durfte, -gedurft), *vi*. to be allowed to meet.

Zusammenfahren, tsy'sam'mənfären (-fuhr, -gefahren), *vi*. to ride together; to shrink; to curdle, coagulate.

Zusammenfallen, tsysam'mənfallen (-fiel, -gefallen), *vi*. to collapse, to go to ruins.

Zusammenfassen, tsysam'mənfassen, *vt*. to comprehend; to concentrate, abridge.

Zusammenfließen, tsysam'mənflīsən (-floß, -geflossen), *vi*. to flow together. **Zusammenfluß**, -flŭss, *m.* conflux, confluence, concourse.

Zusammenfügen, tsysam'mənfügen, *vt*. to join.

Zusammengehen, tsysam'məngā-en (-ging, -gegangen), *vi*. to shrink, coagulate; to come together.

Zusammengesetzt, tsysam'məngesetzt, *a*. compound, composite.

Zusammenhalt, tsysam'mənhalt, *m.* consistence, cohesion; tie; concord; *-en, vt. i.* to hold or keep together; to compel, confront, to stick together.

Zusammenhang, tsysam'mənhang, *m.* connection.

Zusammenhangen, tsysam'mənhangen (-hing, -gehangen), *vi*. to cohere, to be connected.

Zusammenklang, tsysam'mənklang, *m.* unison, concord, agreement.

Zusammenkommen, tsysam'mənkommen (-kam, -gekommen), *vi*. to come together, convene, meet, assemble. **Zusammenkunft**, -kunft, *f.* meeting, assembly, convention.

Zusammenlegen, tsysam'mənlägen, *vt*. to lay together, to contribute, to club together.

Zusammennehmen, tsysam'mənnämen (-nahm, -genommen), *vt*. to take together; sich —, to guard one's self.

Zusammenrechnen, tsysam'mənrĕḫnen, *vt*. to count up, cast up.

Zusammenrufen, tsysam'mənrŭfen (-rief, -gerufen), *vt*. to call together, convoke.

Zusammenschrauben, tsysam'mənshrŏŭben, *vt*. to screw together.

Zusammenschweißen, tsysam'mənshväsen, *vt*. to weld.

Zusammensetzen, tsysam'mənsetsen, *vt*. to compound, compose, put together. **Zusammensetzung**, -ŭng, *f.* composition.

Zusammenstellen, tsysam'mənshtellen, *vt*. to place together, to compare.

Zusammenstimmen, tsysam'mənshtimmen, *vi.* to agree, accord, harmonize.

Zusam'menstimmung, -ung, *f.* agreement, harmony.

Zusammenstoppeln, tsusam'menshtoppeln, *vt.* to compile.

Zusammenstoß, tsusam'menshtoss, *m. pl.* -stöße, collision, conflict.

Zusammenstoßen, tsusam'menshtossen (-stieß, -gestoßen), *vi.* to strike together, conflict, collide.

Zusammenstürzen, tsusam'menshtürtsen, *vi.* to fall together *or* to the ground, to collapse.

Zusammentreffen, tsusam'mentreffen (-traf, -getroffen), *vi.* meet, fall in; coincide, concur.

Zusammentreten, tsusam'menträten (-trat, -getreten), *vi.* to assemble, meet.

Zusammentritt, tsusam'mentritt, *m.* congress, meeting.

Zusammenziehen, tsusam'mentsi-en (-zog, -gezogen), *vt.* to draw together, to contract. **Zusam'menziehung, -ung,** *f.* contraction.

Zusatz, tsu'sats, *m. pl.* Zusätze, addition.

Zuschanzen, tsu'shantsen, *vt.* to provide, supply with, procure.

Zuscharren, tsu'sharren, *vt.* to cover by scraping over.

Zuschauen, tsu'shäu-en, *vi.* to look on, to be a spectator. **Zuschauer,** *m.* spectator.

Zuschicken, tsu'shicken, *vt.* to send to.

Zuschieben, tsu'shiben (-schob, -geschoben), *vt.* to shove to, to close; to offer.

Zuschießen, tsu'shīsen (-schoß, -geschossen), *vt.* to add, advance; *vi.* to rush upon; to shoot, to go on shooting.

Zuschlag, tsu'shläk, *m.* knocking down; addition.

Zuschlagen, tsu'shlägen (-schlug, -geschlagen), *vt.* to strike to; to knock down; to add; to slam (door), to shut with violence.

Zuschleudern, tsu'shlöüdern, *vt.* to fling toward.

Zuschließen, tsu'shlīsen (-schloß, -geschlossen), *vt.* to lock, to close fast.

Zuschmeißen, tsu'shmeīsen (zuschmiß, zugeschmissen), *vt.* to fling to; to shut with vehemence.

Zuschnallen, tsu'shnallen, *vt.* to buckle.

Zuschneiden, tsu'shneīden (zuschnitt, zugeschnitten), *vt.* to cut out.

Zuschneien, tsu'shnei-en, *vt.* to cover with snow.

Zuschnitt, tsu'shnitt, *m.* cut, pattern; style.

Zuschnüren, tsu'shnüren, *vt.* to tie up, to lace, strangle.

Zuschrauben, tsu'shröüben, *vt.* to screw up.

Zuschreiben, tsu'shrēiben (zuschrieb, zugeschrieben), *vt.* to ascribe, attribute; to lay *or* put, pass to account of; to dedicate.

Zuschreien, tsu'shrēien (zuschrie, zugeschrien), *vt.* to cry (out) *or* shout to.

Zuschrift, tsu'shrift, *f.* letter, epistle; dedication.

Zuschuß, tsu'shuss, *m.* supply; additional sum; contribution; (Print.) waste.

Zuschütten, tsu'shütten, *vt.* to fill up; to pour to.

Zuschwören, tsu'shvöhren, *vt.* to swear to.

Zusehen, tsu'sē-en, *vi.* to look at; to wait; to connive at; -*ds,* *av.* sensibly, visibly.

Zusein, tsu'sīen, *vi.* to be shut, closed, locked.

Zusetzen, tsu'setsen, *vt.* to add; to put *or* set to, on (the fire); Segel —, to set sail; einem —, to press close or hard; (money) to spend, lose.

Zusichern, tsu'sichern, *vt.* to assure, secure, promise. **Zu'sicherung, -ung,** *f.* assurance, promise.

Zusiegeln, tsu'sīgeln, *vt.* to seal.

Zuspitzen, tsu'shpitsen, *vt.* to point; to taper.

Zusprechen, tsu'shprechen (zusprach, zugesprochen), *vt. i.* to talk to; to exhort, cheer; comfort; adjudge; — bei, to call in, upon.

Zuspruch, tsu'shpruch, *m.* call, visit; customers; comfort; exhortation.

Zuspunden, tsu'shpunden, *vt.* to bung.

Zustand, tsu'shtant, *m. pl.* Zustände, state, condition, disposition.

Zuständig, tsu'shtendig, *a.* belonging to; -keit, -keit, *f.* appurtenance property.

Zustatten kommen, prop. zu Statten —, to be useful *or* of use, to serve one's turn.

Zustechen, tsu'shtechen (zustach, zugestochen), *vt.* to stitch up.

Zustecken, tsu'shtecken, *vt.* to pin up to give *or* the sly.

Zuſtehen, tsu'shtā-en and tsushtä'-en (zuſtand, zugeſtanden), vi. to behoove, to be fit, meet for.
Zuſtellen, tsu'zhtellen, vt. to deliver, or hand.
Zuſtimmen, tsu'zhtimmen, vi. to agree, consent. Zuſtimmung, -ṇg; f. agreement, consent.
Zuſtopfen, tsu'shtopfen, vt. to stop (up); to darn, mend; (Mar.) to calk.
Zuſtöpſeln, tsu'zhtöpseln, vt. to cork.
Zuſtoßen, tsu'zhtōsen, vi. to push or thrust on; to befall; vt. to kick the door, to shut by a kick.
Zuſtrömen, tsu'shtröhmen, vi. to flow or stream to, pour in.
Zuſtürmen, tsu'shtürmen, vi. to rush on, upon.
Zuſtürzen, tsu'zhtürtsen, vi. to rush, precipitate one's self upon.
Zuſtutzen, tsu'zhtutsen, vt. to drill, train (into).
Zutappen, tsu'tappen, vi. to tumble or grope clumsily.
Zutäppiſch, tsu'täppish, a. awkward, clumsy.
Zutat, tsu'tāt, f. ingredient; material.
Zuthätig, tsu'tätig, Zuthulich, tsu'tulich, a. insinuating; ſeit, -kāĕt, f. insinuation.
Zuthun, tsu'tun, vt. to add; to close, shut; ſich —, to insinuate; to interfere; s. interference, interfering, agency.
Zutheilen, tsu'tĕlen, vt. to allot, assign, parcel out.
Zutragen, tsu'trägn, vt. to carry to; to report; vr. ſich —, to come to pass, to happen, occur.
Zuträger, tsu'trägr, m. tell-tale; ſei, -eī', f. tell-tale, babbling.
Zuträglich, tsu'träklich, a. useful, conducive, profitable; ſeit, -kāĕt, f. usefulness, conduciveness.
Zutrauen, tsu'trŏuen, vt. to confide.
Zutraulich, tsu'trŏulich, a. confidential, -ly; ſeit, -kāĕt, f. confidence, intimacy.
Zutreffen, tsu'treffen, vi. to turn out or prove right.
Zutrinken, tsu'trinken (zutrank, zugetrunken), vt. to drink to, to pledge.
Zutritt, tsu'tritt, m. access, entrance.
Zuverläſſig, tsu'ferlässig, a. trusty, reliable, sure; certain; ſeit, -kāĕt, f. certainty.

Zuverſicht, tsu'fersicht, f. trust, confidence; ſich, -lich, a. confident; ſeit, -kāĕt, f. confidence, positiveness.
Zuvor, tsufōr', av. before, once, formerly.
Zuvörderſt, tsuför'derzht, av. first of all, in the first place.
Zuvörderſt, tsufor'derzht, av. foremost.
Zuvorkommen, tsufōr'kemmen, ri. to anticipate, prevent; -d, a. obliging.
Zuvorthun, tsufōr'tun (-that, -gethan), vt. to outdo, surpass.
Zuwachs, tsu'vaks, m. increase.
Zuwachſen, tsu'waksen (-wuchs, -gewachſen), vi. to accrue; to close; to be overgrown.
Zuwägen, tsu'vägn, vt. to weigh to.
Zuwege, tsuvā'ge, prop. zu Wege bringen, vi. to bring about, to effect, realize.
Zuweilen, tsuvēl'len, av. sometimes.
Zuweiſen, tsu'vēlsen (zuwies, zugewieſen), vt. to address to.
Zuwenden, tsu'venden, vt. to turn to.
Zuwerfen, tsu'verfen, vt. to throw towards.
Zuwider, tsuvī'der, av. contrary to, repuguant; — handeln, contravene; — ſein, to offend.
Zuwinken, tsu'vinken, vt. i. to nod to.
Zuwölken, tsu'völken, vt. to overcloud.
Zuzählen, tsu'tsälen, vt. to add; count to.
Zuziehen, tsu'tsīen (-zog, -gezogen), vt. to draw (to); to contract; vr. incur or involve (one's self) in, to bring upon; consult; catch (a disease).
Zwacken, tsvak'ken, vt. to pinch; tease.
Zwang, tsväng, Prt. of Zwingen.
Zwang, tsvang, m. compulsion, constraint, force.
Zwängen, tsveng'en, vt. to force or press.
Zwanglos, tsvangl'ōs, a. unconstrained at indefinite periods.
Zwangsjacke, tsvangs'yacke, f. strait jacket or waist-coat.
Zwangsmittel, tsvangsmittel, n. coercive measure.
Zwangsweiſe, tsvangs'vāise, av. by force or compulsion.
Zwanzig, tsvan'tsig, a. twenty; -ſt, a. twentieth. Zwan'zigſtel, -zhtyl, n. twentieth.

Zwa 422 **Zwi**

Zwar, tsvär, *av.* indeed, certainly.
Zweck, tsvĕck, *m.* aim, design, end, object.
Zweck, tsvĕck, *f.* tack; (of a shuttle) spit.
Zwecken, tsvĕck'ĕn, *vt.* to tack; aim.
Zweckmäßig, tsvĕck'mäsĭch, *a. av.* appropriate; -keit, -kāĕt, *f.* appropriateness, fitness.
Zweckwidrig, tsvĕckvĭd'rĭg, *a.* inappropriate, unsuitable; -keit, -kāĕt, *f.* unsuitableness.
Zwei, tsvāĕ, *a.* two.
Zweidecker, tsvāĕ'decker, *m.* two-decker.
Zweideutig, tsvāĕ'doŭtig, *a.* ambiguous, equivocal; -keit, -kāĕt, *f.* ambiguity.
Zweierlei, tsvāĕ'erläĕ, *a.* of two (different) kinds *or* sorts.
Zweifach, tsvāĕ'fach, *a.* twofold; double; also **Zweifaltig,** tsvāĕ'faltig, **Zwei'fältig,** -feltig, *a.*
Zweifalter, tsvāĕl'falter, *m.* butterfly.
Zweifel, tsvāĕl'fl, *m.* doubt, scruple; -haft, -haft, *a. av.* doubtful, dubious; -haftigkeit, -ĭchkāĕt, *f.* doubtfulness.
Zweifeln, tsvāĕl'feln, *vi.* to doubt.
Zweifelsohne, tsvāĕl'felsōne, *av.* no doubt, without any doubt, undoubtedly.
Zweifelsmann, tsvāĕl'felsinn, *m.* **Zweif'selsucht,** -sucht, *f.* skepticism.
Zweifler, tsvāĕl'fler, *m.* doubter, scrupler, skeptic.
Zweifüßig, tsvāĕ'füsĭch, *a.* two-footed, two-legged, biped.
Zweig, tsvāĕk, *m.* twig, bough, branch.
Zweihändig, tsvāĕ'hendĭg, *a.* two-handed.
Zweiheit, tsvāĕ'hāĕt, *f.* duality.
Zweijährig, tsvāĕ'yärig, *a.* two years old; continuing two years.
Zweijährlich, tsvāĕl'yärlĭch, *a.* biennial, every two years.
Zweikampf, tsvāĕ'kampf, *m. pl.* **Zweikämpfe,** duel.
Zweiköpfig, tsvāĕ'köpfig, *a.* two-headed, bicipital.
Zweimal, tsvāĕ'māl, *av.* twice; -ig, -ĭg, *a.* done twice.
Zweimännisch, tsvāĕ'mennish, *a.* for two men, double.
Zweimaster, tsvāĕ'mazhter, *m.* brig, two-masted vessel.

Zweipfünder, tsvāĕ'pfŭnder, *m.* two pounder.
Zweipfündig, tsvāĕ'pfŭndĭg. *a.* of two pounds.
Zweischläferig, tsvāĕ'shläferig, *a.* for two persons, double (bedstead).
Zweischneidig, tsvāĕ'shnāĕldig, *a.* two-edged.
Zweiseitig, tsvāĕ'sāĕtig, *a.* bilateral, two-sided.
Zweisilber, tsvāĕ'silber, *m.* dissyllable.
Zweisilbig, tsvāĕ'sĭlbig, *a.* dissyllabic.
Zweisitzig, tsvāĕ'sitsĭg, *a.* having seats for two persons.
Zweispänner, tsvāĕ'zhpenner, *m.* carriage and pair.
Zweispännig, tsvāĕ'zhpennig, *a.* drawn by two horses.
Zweistündig, tsvāĕ'zhtŭndĭg, *a.* lasting two hours, of two hours.
Zweit, tsvāĕt, *a.* second.
Zweitbest, tsvāĕt'best, *a.* second-best.
Zweitens, tsvāĕt'ens, *av.* secondly, in the second place.
Zweiweiberei, tsvāĕvāĕbĕrāĕ', *f.* bigamy.
Zwerchs, tsvāĕ'vŭks, *m.* rickets, rachitis.
Zwerchsüchtig, tsvāĕ'vŭksĭg, *a.* rickety.
Zweizackig, tsvāĕ'tsackĭg, *a.* forked.
Zweizüngig, tsvāĕ'tsŭngĭg, *a.* double-tongued, deceitful.
Zweizüngler, tsvāĕ'tsŭngler, *m.* double-dealer.
Zwerch, tsvĕrch, *av.* athwart, across
Zwerchfell, tsvĕrch'fĕll, *n.* diaphragm.
Zwerchsack, tsvĕrch'sack, *m.* knapsack, mallet.
Zwerg, tsvĕrk, *m.* dwarf.
Zwergbaum, tsvĕrk'bäŭm, *m.* dwarf-tree.
Zwetsche, tsvĕt'she, **Zwetschke,** tsvĕtsh'ke, *f.* prune, plum, damson.
Zwickel, tsvick'ĕl, *m.* gusset (of a stocking).
Zwickelbart, tsvick'ĕlbārt, *m.* whiskers.
Zwicken, tsvick'en, *vt.* to pinch, nip.
Zwickmühle, tsvick'mühle, = **Sichmühle,** *f.* double-mill (morris).
Zwieback, tsvī'back, *m.* biscuit.
Zwiebel, tsvī'bĕl, *m.* onion; bulb.
Zwiebelfisch, tsvī'belfish, *m.* pie (printing); **Zwiebelfische auflesen,** to pick up pie.
Zwiebelgewächs, tsvī'belgevēx, *n.* bulbous plant.

Zwielicht, tsvī'licht, *n.* twilight.
Zwier, tsvīr, *av.* twice.
Zwiespalt, tsvī'zhpalt, *m.* dissent, dissension, discord.
Zwietracht, tsvī'tracht, *f.* discord.
Zwieträchtig, tsvī'trechtig, *a.* discordant, at variance.
Zwillich, tsvil'lich, *m.* ticking.
Zwilling, tsvil'ling, *m.* twin.
Zwilling(s)bruder, tsvil'lingsbruder, *m.* twin-brother.
Zwillingspaar, tsvil'lingspär, *n.* pair of twins.
Zwillingsschwester, tsvil'lingsshvezhter, *f.* twin-sister.
Zwingen, tsving'en (zwang, gezwungen), *vt.* to compel, constrain, force, necessitate, oblige.
Zwinger, tsving'er, *m.* false-bray, enceinte, rampart; prison, dungeon.
Zwingherr, tsving'herr, *m.* -n, *pl.* -en, despot, tyrant.
Zwingherrschaft, tsving'herrshaft, *f.* despotism, tyranny.
Zwirn, tsvīrn, *m.* (linen) doubled yarn *or* twine, thread.
Zwirnband, tsvīrn'bant, *n. pl.* -bänder, tape.
Zwirnen, tsvīr'nen, *vt.* to twist *or* twine together.
Zwirnstrumpf, tsvīrn'zhtrumpf, *m. pl.* -strümpfe, thread-stocking.
Zwischen, tsvish'en, *pr.* between, betwixt; among, amongst.
Zwischendeck, tsvish'endeck, *n.* steerage, deck between.
Zwischengericht, tsvish'engericht, *n.* side-dish.
Zwischengeschoss, tsvish'engeshös, *n. pl.* -e, mezzanine.
Zwischenlinie, tsvish'enlīnīe, *f.* line between two others.
Zwischenlinig, tsvish'enlīnig, *a.* interlinear, -ary.
Zwischenmahl, tsvish'enmāl, *n. pl.* -e, lunch; — halten, to lunch.

Zwischenraum, tsvish'enraum, *m. pl.* -räume, interval.
Zwischensatz, tsvish'ensats, *m. pl.* -sätze, clause interposed *or* inserted.
Zwischenspiel, tsvish'enzhpīl, *n. pl.* -e, interlude.
Zwischenstation, tsvish'enshtatsiōn, *f.* intermediate station.
Zwischenträger, tsvish'enträger, *m.* tell-tale, mischief-maker; -ei, -eī', *f.* babbling, tell-tale.
Zwischenwand, tsvish'envant, *f. pl.* -wände, party-wall.
Zwischenzeit, tsvish'entseit, *f. pl.* -en, interval.
Zwischgold, tsvish'gold, *n.* party-gold.
Zwist, tsvist, *m. pl.* -e, difference, discord, dissension, quarrel, strife; -igkeit, -igkäēt, *f.* difference; in —, at variance.
Zwitschern, tsvit'shern, *vi.* to chirp, warble.
Zwitter, tsvit'ter, *m.* hermaphrodite, bastard, mongrel, hybrid; -artig, -ärtig, **Zwitterhaft,** -haft, *a.* androgynal, androgynous.
Zwölf, tsvölf, *a.* twelve.
Zwölfeck, tsvölf'eck, *n. pl.* -e, dodecagon.
Zwölfer, tsvölf'er, *m.* figure of twelve; -lei, -lāē, *a.* of twelve (different) kinds *or* sorts.
Zwölffach, tsvölf'fach, *a.* twelve-fold.
Zwölfjährig, tsvölf'yārig, *a.* twelve years old.
Zwölfjährlich, tsvölf'yārlich, *av.* every twelve years repeated *or* done.
Zwölfpfünder, tsvölf'pfünder, *m.* twelve-pounder. **Zwölfpfündig,** -dig, *a.* of twelve pounds.
Zwölfstündig, tsvölf'zhtündig, *a.* of twelve hours.
Zwölft, tsvölft, *a.* twelfth.
Zwölftel, tsvölf'tel, *n.* twelfth part.
Zwölftens, tsvölf'tens, *a.* in the twelfth place.

PROPER NAMES.

Aachen, ä'ċen, *n.* Aix-la-Chapelle.
Aar, är, *f.* Aar.
Aargau, är'gäu, *n.* Aargau.
Aaron, ä'ron, *m.* Aaron.
Abraham, äb'raham, *m.* Abraham.
Adelbert, ä'dlbĕrt, *m.* Ethelbert.
Adelheid, ä'dlhäed, *f.* Adelaide, Adelina.
Adeline, ädelīn'e, *f.* Adelina, Adeline.
Adolph, ä'dolph, *m.* Adolph, Adolphus.
Adrian, ä'drikn, *m.* Adrian.
Adrianopel, ädrianōp'l, *n.* Adrianople.
Adriatisch, adrīat'ish, *a.* Adriatic.
Aegeisch, ägä'ish, *a.* Aegean.
Aethiopien, ätiop'ien, *n.* Ethiopia.
  Aethiop'ier, -ier, *m.* Ethiop, Ethiopian. **Aethiop'isch,** -ish, *a.* Ethiopic.
Afrika, af'rikä, *n.* Africa. **Afrikaner,** afrikän'er, *m.* -in, *f.* African. **Afrikan'isch,** -ish, *a.* African.
Agathe, agä'te, *f.* Agatha.
Agnes, agn'es, *f.* Agnes.
Alabama, alabä'ma, *n.* Alabama.
Alarich, ä'larich, *m.* Alaric.
Albert, al'bĕrt, *m.* Albert.
Alexander, alexan'der, *m.* Alexander.
Alfred, al'fräd, *m.* Alfred.
Algerien, algär'ien, *s.* Algeria.
Algier, algīr', *n.* Algiers.
Alpen, al'pen, *f. pl.* Alps. **Al'pisch,** -ish, *a.* Alpine.
Amalie, amä'lie, *f.* Amelia.
Ambrosius, ambrō'sius, *m.* Ambrose.
Amerika, amä'rikä, *n.* America. **Amerikaner,** amārikä'ner, *m.* -in, -in, *f.* American. **Amerika'nisch,** -nish, *a.* American.
Amiens, amian', *n.* Amiens.
Andreas, andrä'as, *m.* Andrew.
Anna, an'nä, *f.* Ann, Anne, Anna; Annette.
Anjou, an'zhu, *n.* Anjou.
Antillen, antill'en, *f. pl.* Antilles.
Antiochien, antioch'ien, *n.* Antioch.
Anton, ant'on, *m.* Anthony. **Antonie,** antō'nie, *f.* Antonia.
Antwerpen, antvĕr'pen, *n.* Antwerp.
Apenninen, apennī'nen, *pl.* Apennines.

Araber, ä'raber, *m.* Arab, Arabian. **Arabien,** arä'bien, *n.* Arabia. **Ara'bisch,** -bish, *a.* Arabian.
Aranjuez, arän'ċuez, *n.* Aranjuez.
Archangel, arċh'angl, *n.* Archangel.
Arkansas, arkan'sas, *also* är'kansä, *n.* Arkansas.
Armenien, armä'nien, *n.* Armenia. **Armenier,** armän'yer, *m.* -in, -in, *f.* Armenian. **Armen'isch,** -ish, *a.* Armenian.
Arnold, ar'nold, *m.* Arnold.
Artois, art'wa, *n.* Artois.
Asien, ä'sien, *n.* Asia. **Asiat,** asyat', **Asiat'isch,** -ish, *a.* Asiatic.
Athen, ätän', *n.* Athens. **Athener,** ätä'ner, *m.* Athenian. **Athen'isch,** -ish, *a.* Athenian.
Augsburg, äuks'byrk, *n.* Augsburg.
August, äu'gust, *m.* Augustus.
Auguste, äugyzh'te, *f.* Augusta.
Augustin, äu'gushtīn, *m.* Augustin(e), Austin.
Babel, bäb'el, **Babylon,** bä'bīlōn, *n.* Babel, Babylon.
Baiern, bäe'ern, *n.* Bavaria. **Baier,** *m.* -in, -in, *f.* Bavarian. **Bai'risch,** -ish, *a.* Bavarian.
Balduin, bal'duīn, *m.* Baldwin.
Baltasar, bal'tasar, *m.* Balthasar.
Baltisch, bal'tish, *n.* -es **Meer,** Baltic (sea).
Barbara, barb'arä, *f.* Barbara.
Barbarei, barbarēī', *f.* Barbary.
Barthel, bar'tl, **Bartholomäus,** bartolomä'us, *m.* Bartholomew.
Bartolph, bar'tolf, *m.* Bartolph.
Basel, bä'sl, *n.* Bale, Basle.
Batavia, batä'fyä, *n.* Batavia.
Bayonne, bayonn', *n.* Bayonne.
Beatrix, beä'trix, *f.* Beatrice.
Belgien, bel'ghien, *n.* Belgium. **Belgier,** bel'ghier, *m.* Belgian. **Belgisch,** -ish, *a.* Belgian, Belgic.
Benedikt, ben'edict, *m.* Benedict.
Bengalen, bengä'len, *n.* Bengal.
Benjamin, ben'yamin, *m.* Benjamin (*dim.*) Ben, Benny.

424

PROPER NAMES.

Berlin, bĕrlīn', n. Berlin.
Bernhard, bĕrn'hart, n. Bernard.
Bertha, bĕr'tă, f. Bertha.
Bessarabien, bĕssarä'bien, n. Bessarabia.
Blanka, blan'kă, f. Blanch, Blanche.
Blasius, blă'sius, m. Blase.
Böhmen, böh'men, m. Bohemia. **Böhme,** böh'me, m. Bohemian. **Böhmisch,** böh'mish, a. Bohemian.
Bokhara, bockä'rä, n. Bokhara.
Bologna, bolon'yä, n. Bologne.
Bonifacius, bonifă'tsius, m. Boniface.
Brasilien, bräsī'lyen, n. Brazil.
Braunschweig, bräun'shvēig, n. Brunswick.
Breisgau, brēis'gäu, n. Brisgau.
Bremen, brä'men, n. Bremen.
Brescia, brēsh'a, n. Brescia.
Breslau, brēs'läu, n. Breslau, Breslaw.
Bretagne, bretän', n. Brittany.
Brigitte, brīghitt'e, f. Bridget, Brigit; (dim.) Biddy.
Britannien, britan'nien, n. Britain. **Britte,** brit'te, m. Briton. **Britisch,** brit'ish, a. British.
Brüssel, brüs'sl, n. Brussels.
Buenos Ayres, buä'nos aērēs, Buenos Ayres.
Bulgar, bulgăr', m. Bulgarian. **Bulgarien,** bulgä'rien, n. Bulgary.
Burgund, burgunt', n. Burgundy. **Burgunder,** burgun'der, m. Burgundian.

Cabrera, căbrä'rä, n. Cabrera.
Cacilie, tsätsī'lie, f. Cecilia, Cecily.
Cadix, că'dix, n. Cadiz.
Cagliari, calyä'rī, n. Cagliari.
Cairo, căē'rō, n. Cairo.
Calabrien, calä'brien, n. Calabria.
Calcutta, calcut'tă, n. Calcutta.
Cambridge, kăm'bridzh, n. Cambridge.
Canada, can'adä, n. Canada. **Canadier,** canä'dier, m. Canadian.
Canarische Inseln, canä'rishe in'seln, f. Canary Islands, Canaries.
Carl, carl, m. Charles. **Carlchen,** carl'chen, n. Charley.
Caroline, carolī'ne, n. Caroline.
Carrara, carrä'rä, n. Carrara.
Carthago, cartä'gō, n. Carthage.
Cäsar, tsä'sar, m. Cæsar.
Caspar, cazh'par, m. Jasper.
Caspisches Meer, cas'hp'ishes mär, n. Caspian sea

Catharine, catar'īne, f. Catharine, Catherine.
Caucasus, cou'casus, m. Caucasus.
Ceylon, tseī'lon, f. Ceylon.
Chaldäa, caldä'a, n. Chaldea. **Chaldäer,** caldä'er, m. Chaldean, Chaldee.
Champagne, shampan', Champagne.
Charlotte, sharlot'te, f. Charlotte.
China, chī'nă, n. China. **Chinese,** chīnä'se, m. Chinese. **Chinesisch,** -ish, a. Chinese.
Christian, crizht'yan, m. Christian.
Christine, crizhtī'ne, n. Christina.
Christianchen, crizht'yanchen, n. Christie.
Christoph, crizh'toph, m. Christopher.
Christus, krizh'tus, m. Christ.
Cincinnati, sinsinnä'tī, n. Cincinnati.
Clara, clä'rä, f. Clara, Clarice.
Clemens, clä'mens, m. Clement.
Coblenz, cō'blents, n. Coblentz.
Cöln, köln, n. Cologne.
Columbus, cōlom'bus, m. Colombo, Columbo.
Conrad, con'rad, m. Conrad.
Constantin, con'zhtantīn, m. Constantine.
Constantinopel, conzhtantīnop'el, n. Constantinople.
Constanz, con'zhtants, n. Constance.
Cordilleren, cordillä'ren, n. Cordilleras.
Cracau, crac'äu, n. Cracow.
Cupido, cupī'dō, m. Cupid.
Cypern, tsīp'ern, n. Cyprus.
Dalmatien, dalmä'tsien, n. Dalmatia.
Däne, dä'ne, m. Dane. **Dänisch,** dä'nish, a. Danish.
Dänemark, dä'nemark, n. Denmark.
Daniel, dä'nīäl, m. Daniel.
Dardanellen, dardanëll'en, pl. Dardanelles.
David, dä'fīd, m. David.
Deutsch, deūtsh, a. German. **Deutscher,** deūt'sher, German. **Deutschland,** -lant, m. Germany.
Dietrich, dī'trich, m. Derrick.
Dionysius, dīonī'sius, m. Dionysius, Denis, Dennis.
Dominicus, domīnī'cus, m. Dominic.
Donau, dōn'äu, f. Danube.
Dornick, dor'nick, n. Tournay.
Dorothea, dōrotä'a, f. Dorothy, Dorothea.
Dublin, dublīn', n. Dublin

Dünkirchen, dühn'kirchen, n. Dunkirk.
Eberhard, ā'berhart, m. Everard.
Ebro, ā'bro, m. Ebro.
Eduard, ā'duart, m. Edward.
Egypten, āghip'ten, n. Egypt. **Egypter,** āghip'ter, m. Egyptian. **Egyptisch,** -tish, a. Egyptian.
Elbe, ĕl'be, f. Elbe.
Eleonore, eleŏnō're, f. Eleanor, Elinor.
Elias, eli'as, m. Elias, Elijah.
Elise, eli'ĕa, f. Eliza.
Elsass, el'säss, n. Alsace.
Emil, ā'mīl, m. Emile.
Emilie, āmīl'ye, f. Emily.
Emma, em'mä, f. Emma, Emmy.
Emmerich, em'merich, m. Emeric.
England, eng'laut, n. England. **Engländer,** eng'lender, m. Englishman. **Engländerin,** -lenderin, f. Englishwoman. **Englisch,** eng'lish, a. English.
Ernst, ĕrnst, m. Ernest, Ernestus.
Esaias, esaī'as, m. (Esaius) Isaiah, Jesaiah.
Ethiopien, f. Aethiopien.
Etsch, etsh, f. Adige.
Eugen, ŏu'ghän, m. Eugene.
Eugenie, ŏugā'nīe, f. Eugenia.
Euphrat, ŏu'frat, m. Euphrates.
Europa, ŏurō'pä, n. Europe. **Europäer,** ŏurōpä'ĕr, m. -in, -in, f. European. **Europäisch,** -pä'ish, a. European.
Eustachius, ŏustä'chius, m. Eustace.
Eva, ā'fä, f. Eve.
Fabian, fä'bian, m. Fabian.
Fanny, fan'ny, f. Fanny.
Ferdinand, fĕr'dinant, m. Ferdinand.
Flamand, fläm'ant, gewöhnlich **Flandern,** flan'dern, n. Flanders. **Flamänder, Flamländer,** fläm'lender, **Flaminger,** flä'minger, oder **Flandrier,** flan'drier, m. Fleming. **Flämisch,** flä'mish, **Flandrisch,** flan'drish, a. Flemish, s. Flemish language.
Flandern, f. Flamand.
Flora, flō'rä, f. Flora.
Florenz, flōrents', n. Florence. **Florenzer** or **Florentiner,** florentī'ner, m. Florentine. **Florentinisch,** -tīn'ish, a. Florentine.
Francisca, frantsis'ka, f. Frances.
Franken, fran'ken, n. **Frankenland,** -lant, n. Franconia.

Frankfurt, frank'furt, n. Frankfort.
Frankreich, frank'rëich, n. France.
Franzose, frantsō'ze, m. Frenchman. **Französin,** frantsöh'sin, f. French woman. **Französisch,** frantsöh'sish, a. French.
Franz, frants, m. Francis, Frank.
Fränzchen, frents'chen, n. (Franky) Frank.
Friederich, frī'derich, m. Frederick.
Fritz, Fritzchen, frits'chen, m. Fred.
Galicien, galits'ien, n. Galicia. **Galicier,** galits'ier, m. Galician.
Gallien, gal'lien, n. Gaul. **Gallier,** gal'lier, m. Gaul.
Geldern, gĕl'dern, n. Guelderland, Guelders.
Genf, ghenf, n. Geneva. **Genfer,** m. Genevan.
Gent, ghent, n. Ghent, Gand.
Genua, ghän'uä, n. Genoa. **Genueser,** ghĕnuä'ser, m. **Genuesisch,** ghenuä'sish, a. Genoese.
Georg, ghĕorg', m. George.
Georgien, ghĕor'ghien, n. Georgia.
Gerhard, ghär'hart, m. Gerard, Gerald.
Gertrud, ghĕr'trud, f. Gertrude.
Gibraltar, ghibral'tar, n. Gibraltar.
Gironde, zhīrond', n. Gironde.
Glarus, glä'rus, n. Glarus.
Glauchau, glaüch'äū, n. Glauchau.
Glogan, glōg'äü, n. Glogan, Glogaw.
Gloucester, glōs'ter, n. Gloucester.
Gnesen, gnä'sen, n. Gnesna.
Gotha, gō'tä, n. Gotha.
Gothland, gōt'lant, n. Gothia.
Gottfried, gott'frīd, m. Godfrey.
Gotthard, gott'hart, m. Goddard.
Gotthelf, gott'helf, a. Gotthelf (God help).
Göttingen, gött'ing-en. n. Göttingen.
Gottlieb, gott'lip, m. Theophilus.
Gottlob, gott'lōp, m. Gottlob.
Granada, granä'dä, n. Grenada.
Graubünden, graūbünd'en, Grisons. **Graubündner,** -bünd'ner, m. Grison.
Greenwich, grīn'nidzh, n. Greenwich.
Gregor, grĕgōr', m. Gregory.
Grenoble, grenō'bl, n. Grenoble.
Grete, grä'te, f. Margaret, Margery, Margary.
Gretchen, grät'chen, f. Gritty, Mag, Madge, Maggy, Margie, Meg, Meggy, Meta, Peg, Peggy.
Grieche, grīch'e, m. -in, f. Greek, Grecian.

PROPER NAMES. 427

Griechisch, grīch'ish. *a.* Grecian, Greek; *s. n.* the Greek language. **Griechenland**, -enlant, *n.* Greece.
Grönland, gröhn'lant, *n.* Greenland.
Großbritannien, gröss'britannien, *n.* Great Britain.
Guido, guī'dō, *m.* Guido, Guy.
Guienne, ghienn', *n.* Guienne.
Guinea, ghinā'ä, *n.* Guinea.
Gustav, guzh'äf, *m.* Gustavus.
Haag, häk, *das*, the Hague.
Halifax, hä'lĭfax, *n.* Halifax.
Halle, hal'le, *n.* Halle.
Hamburg, ham'burgh, *m.* Hamburg.
Hameln, hä'meln, *n.* Hameln.
Hanau, hän'äu, *n.* Hanau.
Hanne, han'ne, *f.* Jane; *s. n.* Johanna. **Hannchen**, hann'chen, *f.* Jennet, Janet, Jenny.
Hannover, hannō'ver, *n.* Hannover: **-aner**, -än'er, *m.* **Hannoveranerin**, -än'erin, *f.* Hannoverian. **Hannoveranisch**, -än'ish, *a.* Hannoverian.
Hans, hans, *m.* John, Jack. **Hänschen**, hens'chen, *m.* Jackey, Johnny.
Harz, härts, *m.* Hartz.
Hebräer, hebrä'er, *m. -in, f.* Hebrew. **Hebräisch**, -ish, *a.* Hebrew; *s. das*, Hebrew language.
Hedwig, hed'wĭk, *f.* Hedwig.
Heilbronn, haēlbroun', *n.* Heilbronn.
Heinrich, hāen'rich, *m.* Henry, Harry. **Heinricke**, hāen'ricke, *f.* Henrietta, Harriet, Harriot; *gew.* **Henriette**, henriēt'te, *dim.* Etta, Hetty.
Helene, helän'e, *f.* Helen, Helena, Ellen.
Hennegau, hen'negäu, *n.* Hainault.
Hermann, her'maun, *m.* Herman, Arminius.
Herzogenbusch, hertsōgenbysh', *n.* Hertsogenbush.
Hessen, hes'sen, *n.* Hesse. **Hesse**, hes'se, *m.* Hessian. **Hessisch**, hes'sish, *a.* Hessian.
Hieronymus, hierōn'īmus, *m.* Jerome.
Hilarius, hilär'ius, *m.* Hilary.
Hiob, hī'ob, *m.* Job.
Holland, hol'lant, *n.* Holland. **Holländer**, hol'lender, *m.* Dutchman; *-in, f.* Dutch woman. **Holländisch**, hol'lendish, *a.* Dutch.
Homer, homär', *m.* Homer.
Horaz, horäts', *m.* Horace, Horatio.
Hottentotte, hottentot'te, *m. -in, f.* Hottentot.

Hugo, hu'gō. *m.* Hugh, Hugo.
Ida, ī'dä, *f.* Ida.
Immanuel, imma'nuäl, *m.* Immanuel, Emanuel.
Indianer, Indlä'ner, *m. -in, f.* Indian.
Indien, In'dien, *n.* India, Indies.
Irland, Ir'lant, *n.* Ireland. **Irländer**, ir'lender, *m.* Irishman; *-in, -in, f.* Irish woman.
Isaak, ī'sac, *m.* Isaac.
Isabella, Isabël'le, *f.* Isabel, Isabella.
Isar, ī'zar, *f.* Isar.
Ischia, is'klä, *m.* Ischia.
Island, is'lant, *n.* Iceland. **Isländer**, is'lender, *m. -in, f.* Icelander. **Isländisch**, is'lendish, *a.* Icelandish.
Italien, Itä'lien, *n.* Italy. **Italiener**, -än'er, *m. -in, f.* Italian. **Italienisch**, -nish, *a.* Italian.

Jakob, ya'kob, *m.* Jacob, James. **Jäkobchen**, ya'köbchen, *m.* Jem, Jemmy. **Jakobine**, yakobi'ne, *f.* Jacobine.
Jamaica, yämä'ica, *n.* Jamaica.
Japan, yä'pän, *n.* Japan. **Japaner**, yapän'er, *m.* **Japanese**, yapanä'se, *m.* Japanese.
Java, yä'fa, *n.* Java.
Jena, yā'na, *n.* Jena.
Jeremias, yeremī'as, *m.* Jeremiah, Jeremy.
Johann, yō'han, **Johannes**, yōhan'nes, *m.* John, Jack.
Johanna, yōhan'nä, *f.* Jane, Jean, Jeanne, Joan, Joanna, Johanna.
Jonathan, yō'nätän, *m.* Jonathan.
Joseph, yō'sef, *m.* Joseph. **Josephchen**, yō'sefchen, *m.* Joe, Josey.
Josua, yō'sua, *m.* Joshua, *dim.* Josh.
Judäa, yudä'ä, *n.* Judea.
Julian, yu'liän, *m.* Julian. **Julianne**, *f.* Julian.
Julie, yu'lie, **Julia**, yu'liä, **Julchen**, yul'chen, *f.* Juliet.
Julich, yü'lich, *n.* Juliers.
Jürge, yür'ge, *m.* George.
Just, yuxht, *m.* Justus.
Justine, yushti'ne, *f.* Justina.
Kaffer, kaf'fer, *m.* Caffre. **Kafferland**, -lant, *n.* Caffraria.
Kalmuck, kalmyck', *m.* Kalmouk.
Kärnthen, kern'ten, *n.* Carinthia.
Katharine, *f.* Catharine. **Käthe**, kä'te, **Kätchen**, kät'chen, *f.* Kate, *dim. of* Katharine.
Kentucky, kentuck'y, *n.* Kentucky.
Kroatien, krōä'tsien, *n.* Croatia.

PROPER NAMES.

Kunz, kunts, m. Conrad.
Lappe, lap'pe. **Lappländer**, lap'lender, m. Laplander. **Lappland**, lap'lant, n. Lapland.
Lätitia, lătits'lă, n. Letitia, Lettice.
Laurentius, löyren'tsĭus, **Lorenz**, lō'rents, m. Lawrence.
Lausanne, lōzann', n. Lausanne.
Lausitz, löy'sits, n. Lusatia. **Lausitzer**, m. ·in, f. **Lausitzisch**, -ish, a. Lusatian.
Lazarus, lä'tsarus, m.: fig. Lazar.
Leipzig, lēĭp'tsik, n. Leipsic.
Lene, lä'ne, f. **Lenchen**, län'chen, n. f. Magdalene.
Leonhard, lā'ōnhard, m. Leonard.
Levante, levan'te, f. Levant.
Liefland, lĭf'lant, n. Livonia. **Liefländer**, -lender, m. ·in, f. Livonian. **Liefländisch**, -lendish, a. Livonian.
Lieschen, lĭs'chen, n. Betsy, Betty, Bess.
Lille, lĭl, n. Lille.
Lissabon, lis'sabon, n. Lisbon.
Lithauen, lĭt'täyen, n. Lithuania.
Lithauer, lĭt'äuer, m. Lithuanian.
Livadien, lĭfäd'ĭen, n. Livadia.
Livorno, livor'nō, n. Leghorn.
Lombardei, lombardēĭ', f. Lombardy.
Lothringen, lōt'ringen, n. Lorraine.
Lotte, lot'te, f. Charlotte. **Lottchen**, lott'chen, n. Lottie.
Loire, lŏär', n. Loire.
St. Louis, sänt lŭ'ī, n. St. Louis.
Louis, lŭ'ī, m. Lewis. **Louise**, lŭī'se, f. Louis-, Louisa.
Louisiana, lŭīsian'a, n. Louisiana.
Löwen, löh'ven, n. Louvain.
Lucie, lŭ'tsĭe, f. Lucy.
Ludwig, lŭd'wik, = **Louis**, m. Ludovic, Lewis. **Ludowike**, ludovī'ke, f. Louisa.
Lukas, lŭ'kas, m. Luke.
Lüttich, lüt'tich, n. Liege.
Luzern, lutsērn', n. Lucerne.
Lyon, lĭōn', n. Lyons.
Maas, mäs, f. Meuse: Maese.
Madera, madă'rä, n. Madeira.
Magdalene, magdalä'ne, f. Magdalene, Madeline, Maud, Maudlin.
Magenta, madzhen'tä, n. Magenta.
Mähren, mä'ren, n. Moravia.
Mainz, maints, n. Mentz, Mainz.
Margarethe, margärä'te, f. Margaret, f. **Gretchen**.
Mariane, marĭä'ne, f. Marianne.

Marie, marī'e, f. Maria, Mary. **Mariechen**, marī'chen, f. Moll, Molly Pol, Polly, Malkin, May.
Martha, mar'tä, f. Martha. **Märtchen**, mart'chen. n. Mat, Matty.
Mathilde, mathil'de, f. Mastilda. **Mathildchen**, matild'chen. n. Mat, Matty, Maud, Patty.
Matthäus, mattä'us, m. Matthew.
Matthias, mattī'as, m. Matthias.
Maximilian, maximĭl'ĭän, m. Max, max, m. Maximilian.
Meissen, mēĭs'sen, s. Meissen, Misnia.
Melitta, melit'tä, s. Melitta, Melissa.
Merkur, mèrkur', s. Mercury.
Michael, mich'aēl, s. Michael.
Moldau, mol'däu, f. Moldavia.
Monroe, monrō', n. Monroe.
Moritz, mō'rits, s. Maurice.
Mosel, mō'zel, f. Moselle.
Moses, mō'sēs, m. Moses.
Moskau, mos'käu, n. Moscow.
München, mün'chen, n. Munich.
Münster, mün'zhter, n. Munster.
Nannette, nannett'e, **Nanny**, nan'nī, f. Nancy, Nan, Nina.
Neapel, nek'pel. n. Naples. **Neapolitaner**, neäpolitän'er, m. **Neapolita's nisch**, -nish, a. Neapolitan.
Neptun, nēptŭn', m. Neptune.
Nikolaus, nīkolä'us, .m. Nicholas, Nicolas.
Niederlande, nī'derlande, pl. Netherlands, Low-countries. **Niederländer**, nī'derlender, m. ·in, f. Netherlander. **Niederländisch**, -dish, a. Netherlandish.
Nil, nīl, **Nilstrom**, nīl'zhtrōm, m. Nile
Nizza, nĭt'sä, n. Nice.
Nordamerika, nord'amärica, n. North-America.
Normandie, normandī', f. Normandy. **Normanne**, norman'ne, m. Norman (Northman).
Norwegen, nor'wägen, n. Norway.
Norweger, nor'wäger, m. ·in, f. **Norwegisch**, nor'wägish, a. Norwegian.
Norwich, nor'ĭtsh, n. Norwich.
Nova Scotia, nō'vä scō'tsiä, n. Nova Scotia.
Nürnberg, nührn'bergh, n. Nuremberg.
Oceanien, otseän'ĭen, n. Oceania.
Oder, ō'der, f. Oder.
Ofen, ō'fen. n. Ofen. Buda.
Oliver, ō'lĭfer, m. Oliver

PROPER NAMES.

Olivia, ŏlī'fĭa. *f.* Olive, Olivia.
Oranien, ŏrā'nĭen, *n.* Orange.
Oskar, ŏs'kar, *m.* Oscar.
Osmane, ŏsman'e, *m.* Ottoman.
Osmanisch, osman'ish, *a.* (Reich) Ottoman empire, Turkey.
Ostende, ostęn de, *n.* Ostend.
Ostindien, ozhtin'dĭen, *n.* East-India. Ostindisch, -dish, *a.* East-Indian.
Oestreich, özht'reīch, *n.* Austria. Oesterreicher, -reīcher, *m.* -in, *f.* Oesterreichisch, -ish, *a.* Austrian.
Ostsee, ozht'sā, *f.* Baltic.
Ottilie, ottĭ'lĭe. *f.* Odelia, Delia.
Otto, ot'tō, *m.* Otto, Otho.
Paderborn, päderborn', *n.* Paderborn.
Padua, Pä'dŭa, *n.* Padua.
Palestina, palezhtī'na. *n.* Palestine.
Paris, paris', *n.* Paris. Pariser, *m.* -in, *f.* Parisisch, paris'ish, *a.* Parisian.
Patricius, patrī'tsĭus, *m.* Patrick.
Paul, päul. *m.* Paul, Paulus. Pauline, päulī'ne, *f.* Paulina.
Pavia, pavī'ä, *n.* Pavia.
Peru, pā'ru, *n.* Peru. Peruaner, pärua'ner, Peruvianer, -fiäu'er, *m.* Peruvian.
Persien, pêr'sĭen, *n.* Persia. Perser, *m.* Persian.
Perugia, perud'shä, *n.* Perugia.
Peter, pā'tęr, *m.* Peter.
Petersburg, pä'tęrsburgh, *n.* Petersburgh.
Pfalz, pfalts, *f.* Palatinate. Pfälzer, pfel'tser. *m.* -in, *f.* Pfälzisch, -ish, *a.* Palatine.
Philadelphia, filadel'fĭä, *n.* Philadelphia.
Philipp, fĭl'ĭp. *m.* Philip. Philippine, filippī'ne. *f.* Philippa.
Philippinen, filippī'nen, *pl.* Philippines.
Piemont, pī'emont, *n.* Piedmont.
Pole, pō'le. Polak, pōlak', *m.* Pole.
Polen, pō'len. *n* Poland. Polnisch, pol'nish, *a.* Polish.
Pommern, pom'mern, *n.* Pomerania. Pommer, pom'mer, *m.* Pommerisch, -ish. *a.* Pomeranian.
Pompejus, pompā'yus, *m.* Pompey.
Portugal, por'tygal. *n.* Portugal.
Portugiese, portugī'se, *m.* -in, *f.* Portugiesisch, -ish, *a.* Portuguese.
Prag, prägh, *n.* Prague.
Preußen, preŭ'ssen, *n.* Prussia.
Preuße, preŭs'se, *m.* Preuß'in, *f.* Preußisch, -ish, *a.* Prussian.
Provence, prov-ans', *f.* Provence.
Pyrenäen, pĭrenä'en, *pl.* Pyrenees.
Quebek, kwebek', *n.* Quebec.
Quintilian, kwintĭlĭän', *m.* Quintilian.
Rahel, rä'hel, *f.* Rachel.
Raimund, rā'imunt, *m.* Raymond.
Regensburg, rā'gensburgh, *n.* Regensburg.
Regine, rä'gĭne, *f.* Regina.
Reinhold, rĭen'holt, *m.* Reinold.
Rhein, reen, *m.* Rhine. Rheinisch, -ish. *a.* Rhenish. Rheinwein, -vien, *m.* Rhenish.
Rhodus, rhō'dus, *f. and n.* Rhodes.
Robert, rō'bert, *m.* Robert. Ruprecht, ru'precht, *m.* Rupert.
Rom, röm, *n.* Rome. Römisch, rōh'mish, *a.* Roman; Romish. Römer, röh'mer, *m.* -in, *f.* Roman.
Rosa, rō'sä, *f.* Rose. Röschen, röhs'chen, *n.* Rosetta.
Rosalie, rösä'lĭē, *f.* Rosalia.
Rosamunde, rozamun'de, *f.* Rosamond.
Rudolph, ru'dolf, *m.* Rodolph, Rudolphus. Rudolph.
Rumelien, rumā'lĭen, *n.* Rumelia.
Russe, rus'se, *m.* -in, *f.* Russisch, rus'sish, *a.* Russian, Russ. Rußland, russ'lant, *n.* Russia.
Sabine, säbī'ne, *f.* Sabina.
Sachse, sak'se, *m.* Sächsin, zek'sin, *f.* Saxon.
Sachsen, sax'en. *n.* Saxony. Sächsisch, sek'sish. *a.* Saxon.
Sahara, zahä'rä, *f.* Sahara.
Salomo, zä'omō, *m.* Solomon.
Samuel, zä'muęl, *m.* Samuel. Sa'muelchen, -chen, *n.* Sam, Sammy.
Sanct Paul, sanct päul, *n.* St. Paul.
Sandwich, sand'vĭch, *n.* Sandwich.
San, zŏn, *n.* Save.
Savoyen, sawŏĭ'en, Savoy. Savoyer, Savoyard, savŏyart', *m.* Savoyard.
Scandinavien, scandĭnä'fĭen, *n.* Scandinavia. Scandinavier, scandĭnä'fĭer, *m.* Scandinavisch, -ish, *a.* Scandinavian.
Schlesien, shlā'sĭen, *n.* Silesia. Schlesier, shlā'sĭer. *m.* -in, *f.* Schlesisch, shlā'sish. *a.* Silesian.
Schonen, shō'nen, *n.* Scania.
Schotte, shot'te, *m.* Scotchman.

430 PROPER NAMES.

Schottin, shət'tin. *f.* Scotchwoman.
Schottisch, shət'tish, *a.* Scotch, Scottish. **Schottland,** shət'lant, *n.* Scotland. **Schottländer,** -lənder, *m.* = Schotte.
Schwabe, shnä'bə, *m.* **Schwäbin,** shuäbin, *f.* **Schwäbisch,** -ish, *a.* Suabian. **Schwaben, Schwabenland,** shuä'benlant, *n.* Suavia.
Schwarzwald, shvartsvalt, *m.* Black Forest.
Schwede, shvä'də, *m.* **Schwedin,** shvä'din, *f.* Swede. **Schwedisch,** shvä'dish, *a.* Swedish. **Schweden,** shvä'dən, *n.* Sweden.
Schweiz, shve̱'ts. *f.* Switzerland.
Schweizer, shvei'tser, *m.* **Schweizerin,** *f.* **Schweizerisch,** -ish, *a.* Swiss.
Siebenbürgen, sibenbür'gen, *n.* Transylvania.
Sibirien, sibī'riən, *n.* Siberia.
Sicilien, sitsī'liən, *n.* Sicily.
Sigmund, sig'munt, *m.* Sigismund.
Simon, sim'ōn, *m.* Simon.
Simson, sim'sən, *m.* Samson.
Slave, slā'fə, *m.* Slavonian. **Slavisch,** slä'ish, *a.* Slavonic, Slavonian. **Slavonien,** släfōn'iən, *n.* Slavonia, Sclavonia.
Solothurn, so'lotyrn, *n.* Soleure.
Sophie, sofī'ə. *f.* Sophia.
Spanien, zhpän'iən, *n.* Spain. **Spanier,** zhpän'ier, *m.* Spaniard. **Spanisch,** zhpän'ish, *a.* Spanish.
Speier, zhpeī'er, *n.* Spire.
Sporaden, zhperä'den, *f. pl.* Sporades.
Steiermark, zhtēi'ermark, *n.* Styria. **Steiermärker,** -märker, *m.* Styrian.
Stephan, zhtēi'an, *m.* Stephen. **Stephanie,** zhtefän'ye, *f.* Stephana.
Steuben, zhtēü'ben, *m.* Steuben.
Stockholm, zhtock'holm, *n.* Stockholm.
Strassburg, zhtrāss'burg, *n.* Strasburg.
Stuttgart, zhtytt'gart, *n.* Stuttgard.
Sudeten, sudā'ten, *m. pl.* Sudetes.
Sulz, sults, *n.* Sulz.
Sulzbach, sults'bach. *n.* Sulzbach.
Südamerika, süd'amarikä, *n.* South America.
Sund, sunt, *n.* Sound.
Susanna, susan'nä, *f.* Susan, Susanna. **Suschen,** sus'chen, *n.* Sue, Suke, Suky, Susy.
Syrakus, sīrakys', *n.* Syracuse.

Syrien, sī'riən, *n.* Syria. **Syrier,** **Syrisch,** -rish, *a.* Syrian.
Tajo, tä'yō, *m.* Tagus.
Tatarei, tätärēī', *f.* Tartary. **Tatar,** tätär', *m.* Tartar, Tatar. **Tatarisch,** tatär'ish, *a.* Ta(r)tarian.
Teheran, tä'heran, *n.* Teheran.
Themse, tem'se, *f.* Thames.
Theobald, tä'obalt, *m.* Theobald.
Theodor, tä'odōr, *m.* Theodore.
Therese, tärä'se, *f.* Theresa.
Thessalien, tessä'liən, *n.* Thessaly.
Thomas, tō'mas, *m.* Thomas. **Thomaschen,** tōm'aschen, Tom, Tommy.
Thüringen, tüh'ringen, *n.* Thuringia.
Timotheus, timət'eys, *m.* Timothy.
Tirol, tirōl', *n.* Tirol, *also* Tyrol. **Tiroler,** tirō'ler, *m.* **Tirolerisch,** -ish, *a.* Tirolian.
Tobias, tōbī'as, *m.* Tobiah, Tobias; *dim.* Toby.
Tokay, to'käō *and* tokäō', *n.* Tokay.
Toscana, toscä'na, *n.* Tuscany.
Troja, trō'ya, *n.* Troy. **Trojaner,** troyän'er, *m.* **-in,** *f.* **Trojanisch,** trəyä'nish, *a.* Trojan.
Tscherkassien, tshërkas'siən, *n.* Circassia.
Tullius, tyll'īus, *m.* Tully, Cicero.
Türke, tür'ke, *m.* **Türkin,** *f.* Turk. **Türkei,** türkēī', *f.* Turkey. **Türkisch,** türk'ish, *a.* Turkish.
Turkomanne, turkəman'nə, *pl.* Turcoman.

Ukraine, ykräē'nə, *f.* Ukraine.
Ulm, ulm, *n.* Ulm.
Ulrich, ul'rich, *m.* Ulric. **Ulrike,** ulrī'ke, *f.* Ulrica.
Ulysses, ulis'sēs, *m.* Ulysses.
Ungarn, un'garn, *n.* Hungary. **Ungar,** un'gar, *m.* **-in,** *f.* **Ungarisch,** ung'arish, *a.* Hungarian.
Urban, ur'bän, *m.* Urban.
Ursula, ur'sulä, *f.* Ursula.
Utah, y'täh, *n.* Utah.

Valentin, fal'entīn. *m.* Valentine.
Valois, va'loä, *n.* Valois.
Valparaiso, valpärāī'sō, *n.* Valparaiso.
Veit, fēit, *m.* Vitus (Guido, Guy).
Venedig, fenä'dic, *n.* Venice. **Venetianer,** fenätsiä'ner, *m.* **-in,** *f.* **Venetianisch,** -nish, *a.* Venetian.
Venus, fä'nys, *f.* Venus.
Vesuv, fesyf', *m.* Vesuvius.
Victor, fic'tor *m.* Victor.

Vincenz, fin'tsents, *m.* Vincent.
Vierwaldstädter See, fīrvalt'zhtetter sä, *m.* Lake of Lucerne.
Virginien, fīrgī'nien, *n.* Virginia.
Vivian, fī'fiän, *m.* Vivian.
Vließingen, fli'singen, *n.* Flushing.
Vogesen, fogä'sen, *m. pl.* Vosges.
Vaudt, vät, *n.* Vaud.
Waiblingen, väeb'ling-en, *n.* Waiblingen.
Wales, väls, *n.* Wales.
Wallachei, vallachī', *f.* Wallachia.
Wälsch. Welsch, vėlsh, *a.* (properly foreign) Italian, French. **Wälsch-land,** vėlsh'lant, *n.* Italy (France).
Waltham, väl'tam, *n.* Waltham.
Walther, val'ter, *m.* Walter.
Warschau, var'shäū, *n.* Warsaw.
Washington, väsh'ington, *m. also n.* Washington.
Waterloo, vä'terlō, *n.* Waterloo.
Weichsel, vēīk'sel, *f.* Vistula.
Wenzel, ven'tsel, *m.* Venceslaus.
Wesel, vä'sel, *f.* Wesel.
Weser, vä'ser, *f.* Weser.
Westindien, vēahtīn'dien, *n.* West-Indies

Westphalen, vėstfä'len, *n.* Westphalia. **Westphale,** vėstphä'le, **Westphalinger,** vėstphä'linger, *m.* **Westphälisch,** -lish, *a.* Westphalian.
Wien, vīn, *n.* Vienna.
Wilhelm, vil'hėlm, *m.* William.
Wilhelmine, vilhėlmī'ne, *f.* Wilhelmina.
Winfried, vin'frīd; *m.* Winfred.
Wolga, vol'ga, *f.* Volga. Wolga.
Woolwich, vul'idzh, *n.* Woolwich.
Worcester, vus'ter, *n.* Worcester.
Würtemberg, vür'temberg, *n.* Wurtemberg.
Würzburg, vürts'burgh, *n.* Würzburg.
Xeres, chär'ēs, *n.* Xeres.
Yorf, york, *n.* York.
Ypern, ī'pern, **Ypres,** ī'per, *n.* Ypres.
Yssel, īs'sel, ēī'sel, *n.* Yssel.
Zacharias, tsächarī'as. *m.* Zachariah.
Zürich, tsüh'rich, *n.* Zürich.
Zuyder See, seü'dersä, *m.* Zuider Zee.
Zweibrücken, twäe'brükken, *n.* Deux-Ponts.

STRONG AND IRREGULAR VERBS.

INFINITIVE.	PRESENT.	IMPERATIVE.	PRETERIT INDICATIVE	IMPERFECT SUBJUNCTIVE	PAST PARTICIPLE.
Backen	(Ich) backe, bu bäckſt, er bäckt	backe	ich buk, backte	ich büke, backte	gebacken
Bedingen	ich bedinge	bedinge	bedung, bedingte	bedünge, bedingte	bedungen, bedingt
Befehlen	ich befehle, bu befiehlſt, er-befiehlt, wir befehlen	befiehl	befahl	beföhle	befohlen
Befleißen	ich befleiße ꝛc.	befleiß(e)	befliß	ich befliße	beflißen
Beginnen	ich beginne ꝛc.	beginne	ich begann	begönne, begänne	begonnen
Beißen	ich beiße ꝛc.	beiße	ich biß	ich biße	gebißen
Bergen	ich berge, bu birg(e)ſt, er birgt, wir bergen ꝛc.	birg	ich barg	ich bärge, bürge	geborgen
Berſten	ich berſte, bu birſteſt, berſteſt, er birſt, berſtet	birſt, berſte	ich borſt (barſt)	bärſte, börſte, berſtete	geborſten
Beſinnen	ich beſinne ꝛc.	beſinn(e)	beſann, beſonn	beſänne, beſönne	beſonnen
Beſitzen	ich beſitze ꝛc.	beſitze	beſaß	beſäße	beſeßen
Betrügen	ich betrüge ꝛc.	betrüg(e)	betrog	betröge	betrogen
Bewegen	ich bewege ꝛc.	beweg(e)	bewog	bewöge	bewogen
Biegen	ich biege (beuge), bu biegſt, er biegt, bieg(e)	bieg(e)	bog, beugte	böge, beugete	gebogen
Beugen	bu beugſt, er beugt				
Bieten	ich biete, bu bieteſt, beutſt, er bietet, beut	biet(e)	ich bot	ich böte	geboten
Binden	ich binde ꝛc.	binde	ich band	ich bände	gebunden
Bitten	ich bitte ꝛc.	bitt(e)	ich bat	ich bäte	gebeten
Blaſen	ich blaſe, bu bläſ(e)ſt, er bläſt	blaſe	ich blies	ich blieſe	geblaſen
Bleiben	ich bleibe ꝛc.	bleib(e)	ich blieb	ich bliebe	geblieben
Bleichen	ich bleiche ꝛc.	bleiche	ich blich	ich bliche	gebleicht, geblichen
Braten	ich brate, bu brätſt, brateſt, er brät, bratet	briet, brate	ich bratete, briet	ich briete, bratete	gebraten
Brechen	ich breche, bu brichſt, er bricht, wir brechen ꝛc.	brich	ich brach	ich bräche	gebrochen
Brennen	ich brenne ꝛc.	brenn(e)	ich brannte	ich brennete	gebrannt
Bringen	ich bringe ꝛc.	bring(e)	ich brachte	ich brächte	gebracht

INFINITIVE.	PRESENT.	IMPERATIVE.	PRETERIT INDICATIVE	IMPERFECT SUBJUNCTIVE	PAST PARTICIPLE.
Denken	ich denke ꝛc.	denk(e)	ich dachte	ich dächte	gedacht
Dingen	ich dinge ꝛc.	dinge	ich dung, dingte	ich dünge, dingete	gedungen, geding
Dreschen	ich dresche, du drischest, er drischet, drischt ꝛc.	drisch, dresche	ich drasch, drosch	ich drösche, drüsche	gedroschen
Dringen	ich dringe ꝛc.	dring(e)	drang	ich dränge	gedrungen
Dürfen	ich darf, du darfst, er darf, wir dürfen		ich durfte	ich dürfte	gedurft, (dürfen)
Empfangen	ich empfange, du empfängst, er empfängt	empfang(e)	ich empfing	ich empfinge	empfangen
Empfehlen	ich empfehle, du empfiehlst, er empfiehlt	empfiehl, empfehle	ich empfahl	ich empfähle, empföhle	empfohlen
Empfinden	ich empfinde ꝛc.	empfinde	ich empfand	ich empfände	empfunden
Entrinnen	ich entrinne ꝛc.	entrinne	ich entrann	ich entränne	entronnen
Entsprechen	ich entspreche, du entsprichst, er entspricht	entsprich	entsprach	ich entspräche	entsprochen
Erbleichen	ich erbleiche ꝛc.	erbleiche	ich erblich, erbleichte	ich erbliche, erbleichete	erbleicht, erblichen
Erfrieren	ich erfriere ꝛc.	erfriere	ich erfror	ich erfröre	erfroren
Erlöschen	ich erlösche, du erlöschest, er erlischt	erlisch, erlösche	ich erlosch	ich erlösche	erloschen
Ersaufen	ich ersaufe, du ersäufst, er ersäuft	ersaufe	ich ersoff	ich ersöffe	ersoffen
Erschallen	ich erschalle ꝛc.	erschalle	ich erscholl, erschallte	erschölle, erschall(e)te	erschollen
Erscheinen	ich erscheine ꝛc.	erscheine	ich erschien	ich erschiene	erschienen
Erschrecken	ich erschrecke, du erschrickst, er erschrickt	erschrick	ich erschrak	ich erschräke	erschrocken
Ertrinken	ich ertrinke ꝛc.	ertrink(e)	ich ertrank	ich ertränke	ertrunken
Erwägen	ich erwäge ꝛc.	erwäge	ich erwog	ich erwöge	erwogen
Essen	ich esse, du issest, ißt	iß	ich aß	ich äße	gegessen
Fahren	ich fahre, du fährst, er fährt	fahr(e)	ich fuhr	ich führe	gefahren
Fallen	ich falle, du fällst, er fällt	falle	ich fiel	ich fiele	gefallen
Fangen	ich fange, du fängst, er fängt	fange	ich fing	ich finge	gefangen
Fechten	ich fechte, du fichst, fechtest er ficht, fechtet	ficht, (fechte)	ich focht	ich föchte	gefochten

INFINITIVE.	PRESENT.	IMPERATIVE.	PRETERIT INDICATIVE	IMPERFECT SUBJUNCTIVE	PAST PARTICIPLE
Finden	ich finde ꝛc.	finde	ich fand	ich fände	gefunden
Flechten	ich flechte, du flichst, er flicht	flicht	ich flocht	ich flöchte	geflochten
Fliegen	ich fliege, bu fliegſt, fleugſt, er fliegt, fleugt	fliege, fleug	ich flog	ich flöge	geflogen
Fliehen	ich fliehe, bu flieh(e)ſt, fleuchſt, er fliebt, fleucht	fliehe, fleuch	ich floh	ich flöhe	geflohen
Fließen	ich fließe, bu fließeſt, (fleußſt), er fließt, fleußt	fließe, fleuß	ich floß	ich flöße	geflossen
Fragen	ich frage, bu fragſt, frägſt, er fragt, frägt	frage	ich fragte, frug	ich fragte, früge	gefragt
Fressen	ich fresse, bu frisseſt, er frißt	friß	ich fraß	ich fräße	gefressen
Frieren	ich friere ꝛc.	friere	ich fror	ich fröre	gefroren
Gähren	ich gähre, bu gährſt, giersſt, gährt, giert	gähre	ich gohr, gährte	ich göhre, gährte	gegohren, gegähret
Gebären	ich gebäre, du gebierſt, gebärſt, sie gebiert, gebärt	gebier, gebäre	ich gebar	ich geböre, gebäre	geboren
Geben	ich gebe, bu gibſt, er gibt	gieb	ich gab	ich gäbe	gegeben
Gebieten	ich gebiete, bu gebieteſt, gebeutſt, er gebietet, gebeut	gebiete	ich gebot	ich geböte	geboten
Gedeihen	ich gedeihe ꝛc.	gedeihe	ich gedieh	ich gediehe	gediehen
Gefallen	ich gefalle, bu gefällſt, er gefällt	gefalle	ich gefiel	ich gefiele	gefallen
Gehen	ich gehe ꝛc.	geh	ich ging	ich ginge	gegangen
Gelingen	es gelingt	gelinge	es gelang	es gelänge	gelungen
Gelten	ich gelte, bu giltſt, er gilt	gilt	ich galt	ich gälte	gegolten
Genesen	ich genese ꝛc.	genese	ich genas	ich genäse	genesen
Genießen	ich genieße, bu genießeſt, geneußſt, er genießt, geneußt	genieße, geneuß	ich genoß	ich genöße	genossen
Gerathen	ich gerathe, bu gerätſt, er geräth	gerathe	ich gerieth	ich geriethe	gerathen
Geschehen	es geschieht, sie geschehen	geschehe	es geschah	es geschähe	geschehen
Gewinnen	ich gewinne	gewinne	ich gewann	ich gewänne, gewönne	gewonnen
Gießen	ich gieße, bu gießeſt, geußeſt, er gießt, geußt	gieße, geuß	ich goß	ich göße	gegossen
Gleichen	ich gleiche ꝛc.	gleich(e)	ich glich	ich gliche	geglichen
Gleiten	ich gleite, bu gleiteſt, er gleitet	gleite	ich glitt	ich glitte	geglitten

INFINITIVE.	PRESENT.	IMPERATIVE.	PRETERIT INDICATIVE	IMPERFECT SUBJUNCTIVE	PAST PARTICIPLE.
Glimmen	ich glimme ꝛc.	glimme	ich glomm, glimmte	ich glömme	geglommen
Graben	ich grabe, du gräbst, er gräbt	grabe	ich grub	ich grübe	gegraben
Greifen	ich greife ꝛc.	greife	ich griff	ich griffe	gegriffen
Haben	ich habe, du hast, er hat	habe	ich hatte	ich hätte	gehabt
Halten	ich halte, du hältst, er hält	halt(e)	ich hielt	ich hielte	gehalten
Hangen	ich hange, du hängst, er hängt	hange	ich hieng	ich hienge	gehangen
Hauen	ich haue ꝛc.	haue	ich hieb	ich hiebe	gehauen
Heben	ich hebe ꝛc.	hebe	ich hob	ich höbe, hübe	gehoben
Heißen	ich heiße ꝛc.	heiß(e)	ich hieß	ich hieße	geheißen
Helfen	ich helfe, du hilfst, er hilft	hilf	ich half	ich hülfe, hälfe	geholfen
Keifen	ich keife ꝛc.	keife	ich kiff	ich kiffe	gekiffen
Kennen	ich kenne ꝛc.	kenne	ich kannte	ich kennete	gekannt
Klieben	ich kliebe ꝛc.	kliebe	ich klob	ich klöbe	gekloben
Klimmen	ich klimme ꝛc.	klimme	ich klomm	ich klömme	geklommen
Klingen	ich klinge ꝛc.	klinge	ich klang	ich klänge	geklungen
Kneifen	ich kneife ꝛc.	kneife	ich kniff	ich kniffe	gekniffen
Kneipen	ich kneipe ꝛc.	kneipe	ich knipp, kneipte	ich knippe, kneipte	geknippen, gekneipt
Kommen	ich komme, du kommst, kömmst, er kommt, kömmt	komm(e)	ich kam	ich käme	gekommen
Können	ich kann, du kannst, er kann, wir können		ich konnte	ich könnte	gekonnt, (können)
Kriechen	ich krieche, du kriechst, kreuchst, er kriecht, kreucht	krieche, kreuch	ich kroch	ich kröche	gekrochen
Küren	ich küre ꝛc.	küre	ich kor	ich köre	gekoren
Laden	ich lade, du ladest, lädst, er ladet, lädt	lade	ich lud	ich lüde, lüde	geladen
Lassen	ich lasse, du läff(e)st, er lässet, läßt	laß, lasse	ich ließ	ich ließe	gelassen
Laufen	ich laufe, du läufst, er läuft	lauf	ich lief	ich liefe	gelaufen
Leiden	ich leide ꝛc.	leide	ich litt	ich litte	gelitten
Leihen	ich leihe ꝛc.	leih(e)	ich lieh	ich liehe	geliehen
Lesen	ich lese, du liesest, liest, er lieset, liest	lies	ich las	ich läse	gelesen
Liegen	ich liege ꝛc.	liege	ich lag	ich läge	gelegen
Lügen	ich lüge, du lügst, (leugst), er lügt, (leugt)	lüge, leug	ich log	ich löge	gelogen

INFINITIVE.	PRESENT.	IMPERATIVE.	PRETERIT INDICATIVE	IMPERFECT SUBJUNCTIVE	PAST PARTICIPLE.
Mahlen	ich mahle, du mahlst, (mählst), er mahlt (mahlt)	mahle	mahlte, (muhl)	ich mahl(e)te	gemahlen
Meiden	ich meide ꝛc.	meide	ich mied	ich miede	gemieden
Melken	ich melke, du melkest, milkst, er melkt, milkt	melke, milk	ich molk, ich melkte	ich mölke, melkte	gemolken gemelkt
Messen	ich messe, du missest, er misst	miss	ich maß	ich mäße	gemessen
Mißfallen	ich mißfalle, du mißfällst, er mißfällt	mißfalle	ich mißfiel	ich mißfiele	mißfallen
Mögen	ich mag, du magst, er mag, wir mögen ꝛc.		ich mochte	ich möchte	gemocht, (mögen)
Müssen	ich muß, du mußt, er muß		ich mußte	ich müßte	gemußt, (müssen)
Nehmen	ich nehme, du nimmst, er nimmt	nimm	ich nahm	ich nähme	genommen
Nennen	ich nenne ꝛc.	nenn(e)	ich nannte	ich nennete	genannt
Pfeifen	ich pfeife ꝛc.	pfeif(e)	ich pfiff	ich pfiffe	gepfiffen
Pflegen	ich pflege, du pflegest, (pflichst, pflegst,) er pflegt, pflicht, pflegt	pflege	ich pflegte, (pflag, pflog)	ich pflöge, pflegete	gepflogen gepflegt
Preisen	ich preise, ꝛc.	preise	ich pries, preiste	ich priese, preisete	gepriesen gepreiset
Quellen	ich quelle, du quillst, er quillt, quillet	quill	ich quoll	ich quölle	gequollen
Rächen	ich räche ꝛc.	räche	ich rächte, (roch)	ich rächete, (röche)	gerächt, gerochen
Rathen	ich rathe, du räthst, rathest, er räth rathet	rathe	ich rieth	ich riethe	gerathen
Reiben	ich reibe ꝛc.	reibe	ich rieb	ich riebe	gerieben
Reißen	ich reiße ꝛc.	reiß	ich riß	ich riße	gerissen
Reiten	ich reite ꝛc.	reite	ich ritt	ich ritte	geritten
Rennen	ich renne ꝛc.	renn(e)	ich rannte	ich rennete	gerannt
Riechen	ich rieche, du riechst (reuchst), er riecht, (reucht)	rieche, reuch	ich roch	ich röche	gerochen
Ringen	ich ringe ꝛc.	ring(e)	ich rang	ich ränge	gerungen
Rinnen	ich rinne ꝛc.	rinne	ich rann	ich ränne, rönne	geronnen
Rufen	ich rufe ꝛc.	ruf(e)	ich rief, rufte	ich riefe, rufete	gerufen
Salzen	ich salze ꝛc.	salze	ich salzte	ich salzete	gesalzen
Saufen	ich saufe, du säufst, saufest, er säuft, sauft	saufe	ich soff	ich söffe	gesoffen
Saugen	ich sauge ꝛc.	saug(e)	ich sog	ich söge	gesogen
Schaffen	ich schaffe ꝛc.	schaff(e).	ich schuf	ich schüfe	geschaffen

INFINITIVE.	PRESENT.	IMPERATIVE.	PRETERIT INDICATIVE	IMPERFECT SUBJUNCTIVE	PAST PARTICIPLE.
Scheiden	ich scheide ꝛc.	scheide	ich schied	ich schiede	geschieden
Scheinen	ich scheine ꝛc.	scheine	ich schien	ich schiene	geschienen
Scheißen	ich scheiße ꝛc.	scheiße	ich schiß	ich schiße	geschißen
Schelten	ich schelte, du schiltst, er schilt	schilt	ich schalt, scholt	ich schälte, schölte	gescholten
Scheren (Scheeren)	ich schere, du schierst, er schiert, (scheert)	scher (scheere)	ich schor	ich schöre	geschoren
Schieben	ich schiebe, du schiebst (scheubst), er schiebt (scheubt)	schiebe, (scheub)	ich schob	ich schöbe	geschoben
Schießen	ich schieße ꝛc.	schieß(e)	ich schoß	ich schöße	geschoßen
Schinden	ich schinde ꝛc.	schinde	ich schund	ich schünde	geschunden
Schlafen	ich schlafe, du schläfst, er schläft	schlaf, schlafe	ich schlief	ich schliefe	geschlafen
Schlagen	ich schlage, du schlägst, er schlägt	schlag	ich schlug	ich schlüge	geschlagen
Schleichen	ich schleiche ꝛc.	schleiche	ich schlich	ich schliche	geschlichen
Schleifen	ich schleife ꝛc.	schleife	ich schliff	ich schliffe	geschliffen
Schleißen	ich schleiße ꝛc.	schleiß	ich schliß, schloß	ich schliße	geschlißen
Schließen	ich schließe, du schließest, schleußest, er schließt, schleußt	schließ(e) schleuß	ich schloß	ich schlöße	geschloßen
Schlingen	ich schlinge ꝛc.	schling(e)	ich schlang	ich schlänge	geschlungen
Schmeißen	ich schmeiße ꝛc.	schmeiße	ich schmiß	ich schmiße	geschmißen
Schmelzen	ich schmelze, du schmilzest (schmelzest) er schmilzt	schmilz	ich schmolz	ich schmölze,	geschmolzen,
Schneiden	ich schneide ꝛc.	schneide	ich schnitt	ich schnitte	geschnitten
Schnieben	ich schniebe ꝛc.	schniebe	ich schnob	ich schnöbe	geschnoben
Schreiben	ich schreibe ꝛc.	schreibe	ich schrieb	ich schriebe	geschrieben
Schreien	ich schreie ꝛc.	schrei(e)	ich schrie	ich schriee	geschrieen
Schreiten	ich schreite ꝛc.	schreite	ich schritt	ich schritte	geschritten
Schwären	ich schwäre ꝛc.	schwäre	ich schwor	ich schwöre	geschworen
Schweigen	ich schweige ꝛc.	schweige	ich schwieg	ich schwiege	geschwiegen
Schwellen	ich schwelle, du schwillst er schwillt	schwill	ich schwoll,	ich schwölle,	geschwollen

INFINITIVE.	PRESENT.	IMPERATIVE.	PRETERIT INDICATIVE	IMPERFECT SUBJUNCTIVE	PAST PARTICIPLE.
Schwimmen	ich schwimme ꝛc.	schwimm(e)	ich schwamm	ich schwämme	geschwommen
Schwinden	ich schwinde ꝛc.	schwinde	ich schwand	ich schwände	geschwunden
Schwingen	ich schwinge ꝛc.	schwinge	ich schwang	ich schwänge	geschwungen
Schwören	ich schwöre ꝛc.	schwör(e)	ich schwor, (schwur)	ich schwüre, schwöre	geschworen
Sehen	ich sehe, du siehst, er sieht	sieh(e)	ich sah	ich sähe	gesehen
Sein	ich bin, du bist, er ist, wir sind, ihr seid, sie sind	sei	ich war	ich wäre	gewesen
Senden	ich sende ꝛc.	sende	ich sandte, sendete	ich sendete	gesandt, gesendet
Sieden	ich siede ꝛc.	siede	ich sott	ich sötte	gesotten
Singen	ich singe ꝛc.	sing(e)	ich sang	ich sänge	gesungen
Sinken	ich sinke ꝛc.	sinke	ich sank	ich sänke	gesunken
Sinnen	ich sinne ꝛc.	sinne	ich sann	ich sänne, (sönne)	gesonnen
Sitzen	ich sitze ꝛc.	sitz(e)	ich saß	ich säße	gesessen
Sollen	ich soll, du sollst, er soll		ich sollte	ich sollte	gesollt, (sollen)
Spalten	ich spalte ꝛc.	spalt(e)	ich spaltete, (spielt)	ich spaltete	gespalten, gespaltet
Speien	ich speie ꝛc.	spei(e)	ich spie	ich spiee	gespieen
Spinnen	ich spinne ꝛc.	spinne	ich spann	ich spänne, spönne	gesponnen
Spleißen	ich schleiße ꝛc.	spleiß	ich spliß	ich spließe	gespliffen
Sprechen	ich spreche, du sprichst, er spricht	sprich	ich sprach	ich spräche	gesprochen
Sprießen	ich sprieße, du sprießest ꝛc.	sprieß, (preuß)	ich sproß	ich sprösse	gesprossen
Springen	ich springe ꝛc.	springe	ich sprang	ich spränge	gesprungen
Stechen	ich steche, du stichst, er sticht, wir stechen.	stich	ich stach	ich stäche	gestochen
Stecken	ich stecke ꝛc.	stecke	ich stak, steckte	ich stäke, steckte	gesteckt
Stehen	ich stehe ꝛc.	steh(e)	ich stand, (stund)	ich stände, stünde	gestanden
Stehlen	ich stehle, du stiehlst, er stiehlt	stiehl	ich stahl, (stohl)	ich stähle, (stöhle)	gestohlen
Steigen	ich steige ꝛc.	steig(e)	ich stieg	ich stiege	gestiegen
Sterben	ich sterbe, du stirbst, er stirbt	stirb	ich starb	ich stürbe, stärbe	gestorben
Stieben	ich stiebe ꝛc.	stiebe	ich stob	ich stöbe	gestoben
Stinken	ich stinke ꝛc.	stinke	ich stank	ich stänke	gestunken
Stoßen	ich stoße, du stößest, stoßest, er stößt, stößt	stoße	ich stieß	ich stieße	gestoßen

INFINITIVE.	PRESENT.	IMPERATIVE.	PRETERIT INDICATIVE	IMPERFECT SUBJUNCTIVE	PAST PARTICIPLE.
Streichen	ich streiche ꝛc.	streich	ich strich	ich striche	gestrichen
Streiten	ich streite ꝛc.	streit(e)	ich stritt	ich stritte	gestritten
Thun	ich thue, du thust, er thut	thu, thue	ich that	ich thäte	gethan
Tragen	ich trage, du trägst, er trägt	trag(e)	ich trug	ich trüge	getragen
Treffen	ich treffe, du triffst, er trifft	triff	ich traf	ich träfe	getroffen
Treiben	ich treibe ꝛc.	treib(e)	ich trieb	ich triebe	getrieben
Treten	ich trete, du trittst, er tritt	tritt	ich trat	ich träte	getreten
Triefen	ich triefe, du triefest (treufst), er trieft (treuft)	triefe, (treuf)	ich triefte, troff	ich tröfe triefte	getrieft, getroffen
Trinken	ich trinke ꝛc.	trink	ich trank	ich tränke	getrunken
Trügen, Triegen	ich trüge, triege, du trügest, treugst, er trügt, treugt	trüge, triege	ich trog	ich tröge, trügte	getrogen
Verbergen	ich verberge, du verbirgst, er verbirgt	verbirg	ich verbarg	verbärge, verbörge	verborgen
Verbieten	ich verbiete, du verbietest, verbeutst, er verbietet, verbeut	verbiete	ich verbot	ich verböte	verboten
Verbleiben	ich verbleibe ꝛc.	verbleibe	ich verblieb	ich verbliebe	verblieben
Verbleichen	ich verbleiche ꝛc.	verbleiche	ich verblich	ich verbliche	verblichen, verbl. cht
Verderben	ich verderbe, du verbirbst, er verdirbt	verdirb	ich verdarb	ich verdärbe, verdürbe	verdorben,
Verdrießen	es verdrießt, verdreußt		es verdroß	es verdrösse	verdrossen
Vergessen	ich vergesse, du vergissest, er vergißt	vergiß	ich vergaß	ich vergäße	vergessen
Verlieren	ich verliere ꝛc.	verliere	ich verlor	ich verlöre	verloren
Verlöschen	ich verlösche, du verlöschest, er verlöscht, verlischt	verlisch, verlösche	ich verlosch, verlöschte	ich verlösche, verlöschete	verloschen, verlöscht
Verwirren	ich verwirre ꝛc.	verwirre	ich verwirrte	ich verwirrte	verwirrt, verworren
Verzeihen	ich verzeihe ꝛc.	verzeih	ich verzieh	ich verziehe	verziehen
Wachsen	ich wachse, du wächsest, wächst, er wächst	wachse	ich wuchs	ich wüchse	gewachsen
Waschen	ich wasche, du wäschest, er wäscht.	wasche	ich wusch	ich wüsche	gewaschen
Weben	ich webe ꝛc.	webe	ich wob	ich wöbe, webete	gewoben, gewebt
Weichen	ich weiche ꝛc.	weiche	ich wich	ich wiche	gewichen

INFINITIVE.	PRESENT.	IMPERATIVE.	PRETERIT INDICATIVE	IMPERFECT SUBJUNCTIVE	PAST PARTICIPLE.
Weisen	ich weise ꝛc.	weise	ich wies	ich wiese	gewiesen
Wenden	ich wende ꝛc.	wende	ich wandte, wendete	ich wändte, wendete	gewandt, gewendet
Werben	ich werbe, du wirbst, er wirbt	wirb	ich warb	ich würbe, wärbe	geworben
Werden	ich werbe, du wirst, er wird, wir werden ꝛc.	werde	ich warb, wurde, du warbst, du wurdest, er ward, wurde, wir wurden ꝛc.	ich würde	geworden worden
Werfen	ich werfe, du wirfst, er wirft	wirf	ich warf	ich würfe, wärfe	geworfen
Wiegen	ich wiege ꝛc.	wiege	ich wog	ich wöge	gewogen
Winden	ich winde ꝛc.	winde	ich wand	ich wände	gewunden
Wissen	ich weiß, du weißt, er weiß, wir wissen ꝛc.	wisse	ich wußte	ich wüßte	gewußt
Wollen	ich will, du willst, er will, wir wollen ꝛc.	wolle	ich wollte	ich wollte	gewollt, (wollen)
Zeihen	ich zeihe ꝛc.	zeihe	ich zieh, zeihte	ich ziehe, zeihte	geziehen, (gezeiht)
Ziehen	ich ziehe, du ziehest, zeuchst, er zieht, zeucht	zieh, ziehe, zeuch	ich zog	ich zöge	gezogen
Zwingen	ich zwinge ꝛc.	zwinge	ich zwang	ich zwänge	gezwunge.

Verlag von Jg. Kohler,
911 Arch Str., Philadelphia.

Bibeln.

Die Bibel, für Kirche, Schule und Haus. Groß Quart-Format, mit großem Druck.

Volks-Bilder-Bibel, kleine. Mit 100 in den Text eingedruckten Abbildungen.

Büchner, Gottfried W. Biblische Real- und Verbal-Hand-Concordanz.

Erbauungsbücher.

Arndt, J. Sechs Bücher vom wahren Christenthum.

Goßner, Johannes. Schatzkästchen.

Habermann, Dr. J. Christl. Morgen- u. Abendgebete.

Habermann, Dr. J. Morning and Evening Prayers.

Hofacker, M. Ludw. Predigten für alle Sonn-, Fest- und Feiertage.

Hübner. Biblische Historien aus dem Alten und Neuen Testamente.

Huebner Biblical Stories from the Old and New Testaments.

Ingraham. Das Leben Jesu. Der Fürst aus David's Hause.

Liturgie und Agende der Pennsylvanischen Synode der evangelisch-lutherischen Kirche.

Luther, Dr. Martin. Hauspostille.

—— Kleiner Katechismus, erklärt in Fragen und Antworten, zum Gebrauch in Kirche, Schule und Haus, von Dr. W. J. Mann und G. F. Krotel.

—— Der kleine Katechismus, nebst beigefügter unveränderter Augsburger Confession.

Neues Testament unseres Herrn und Heilandes, mit 30 Bildern und großem Druck.

Sänger am Grabe, Der.

Schaff, Dr. Philpp. Kleiner Heidelberger Katechismus.
—— Jubel-Ausgabe des Heidelberger Katechismus.
—— Christlicher Katechismus, kleine Ausgabe.
—— Große Ausgabe.
Schmolke, Benj. Himmlisches Vergnügen in Gott.
Stark, Joh. Friedrich. Tägliches Handbuch.
Stark, John Frederick Daily Handbook
Witschel, Joh. Heinr. Wilh. Morgen u. Abendopfer.
Zschokke, Heinrich. Stunden der Andacht, zur Beförderung des wahren Christenthums und häuslicher Gottesverehrung.

Choral- und Gesangbücher.

John Endlich. Choralbuch mit Liturgie und Chor-Gesängen.
Landenberger, G. F. Kirchenchöre, I. und II Theil.
—— Choralbuch für die Orgel.
—— Trauer Gesänge für den gemischten Chor.
Schaff, Dr. Philipp. Deutsches Gesangbuch. Neue verbesserte und vermehrte Auflage.
—— Gesang- und Choralbuch.
Sonntagsschul-Gesangbuch der reformirten Kirche in den Vereinigten Staaten.
Kirchenbuch für evangelisch-lutherische Gemeinden
Sonntagsschulbuch für die Sonntagsschulen der ev.-luth. Kirche.
Gesangbuch für die evang.-luth. Kirche in den V. St.

Classische und Unterhaltungs-Literatur.

Schiller's Sämmtliche Werke. Imperial-Ausgabe in zwei Bänden, auf schönem weißen Papier, mit 58 großen Illustrationen.
—— In zwölf Bänden, klein Octav, auf feinem Tonpapier, schöne große Schrift.
—— Gedichte. Klein Octav. Auf feinem Tonpapier, mit Illustrationen.

Scherr, Johannes. Schiller und seine Zeit. Mit zahlreichen Illustrationen.
Schiller's Complete Works, in English. In two volumes, Imperial 8vo; large, clear and legible type; 1282 pages With 56 full-page illustrations.
—— Poems. Published both in German and English (the two languages on opposite pages)
—— —— In English only, on tinted paper, illust.
Schiller and his Times. By Dr. Johannes Scherr. Translated from the German by Elizabeth McClellan.
Baskerville. The Poetry of Germany.
Bechstein, Ludw. Märchenbuch. Mit Illustrationen.
Eia Popeia. Deutsche Kinderheimath in Wort, Sang und Bild.
Frost. Interessante Abenteuer unter den Indianern.
Hey, W. 50 Fabeln für Kinder.
Franklin, Benjamin. Sein Leben. Von ihm selbst beschrieben.
Horn, W. O. v. Erzählungen. Vollständig in 14 Bbn.
—— Des alten Schmied-Jakob's Geschichten.
Hoffmann, Franz Erzählungen von No. 1 bis 52. Mit je einem Holzschnitt.
Robinson Crusoe Von Daniel De Foe.
Struwelpeter. Enthaltend lustige Geschichten und drollige Bilder.
Wollenweber. L. A., (der Alte vom Berge). Treu bis in den Tod. Die Berg-Maria, oder Wer nur den lieben Gott läßt walten. Geschichtliche Erzählung aus Pennsylvania. Mit Illustrationen von F. Schlitte.
—— Zwei treue Kameraden. Die beiden ersten deutschen Ansiedler in Pennsylvania. Historische Erzählung aus der ersten Epoche der deutschen Einwanderung in Pennsylvania. Mit Illustr. von F. Schlitte.
Die „Gute alte Zeit" in Pennsylvania.
64 Sonntagsschul-Karten, Denksprüche.
Sunday-School Album, containing sixty-four from Holy Scripture.

Wörterbücher, Grammatiken, Schulbücher ꝛc.

Appleton, John L. Neue praktische Methode, die englische Sprache in kurzer Zeit zu lernen.
Dolmetscher, der große amerikanische.
Grieb, Chr. Fr. Dictionary of the English and German Languages
Kunst, P J. Amerikanisches Wörterbuch der englischen und deutschen Sprache.
Tafel, Dr. J. F. Leonh. und L. H., A. B. Neues vollständiges Englisch-Deutsches und Deutsch-Englisches Taschen-Wörterbuch.
Rupp, Prof. J. Daniel Chronologisch geordnete Sammlung von mehr als 30,000 Namen von Einwanderern in Pennsylvania aus Deutschland ꝛc.
Vereinigte Staaten Briefsteller, deutsch-englischer
— Deutscher.
Deutsches Lesebuch. Erste Stufe. Von J B. Herzog.
— Erste Stufe. Für Sonntagsschulen.
Zweites Lesebuch. Von J. C. Oehlschläger. Neue Ausgabe. 280 Seiten.

Classenbuch für Sonntagsschullehrer.
Das Herz des Menschen.
Heart of Man.
Leib, Isaac. Wohlerfahrener Pferdearzt.
Davidis, Frau Henriette. Praktisches Kochbuch für die Deutschen in Amerika.
Türke, Carl. Der Kindergarten. 250 Declamirstücke.
Luther's Portrait.
Christus-Bildniß
Taufscheine, deutsche oder englische. Hübsch colorirt.
Traufscheine, schwarz.
Confirmationsscheine.
Album für Sonntagsschüler, mit Illustrationen.
Tickets für Sonntagsschulen.
Des Christen Weihnachtslichter für's ganze Jahr.
Bilder aus dem Leben Jesu. Mit Bibeltext.

www.ingramcontent.com/pod-product-compliance
Lightning Source LLC
LaVergne TN
LVHW020423271025
824339LV00008B/141